Psychotropedia

A Guide to Publications on the Periphery

Russ Kick

Critical Vision
An imprint of Headpress

A Critical Vision Book
Published in 1998
by Headpress

Critical Vision
PO Box 26
Manchester
M26 1PQ
Great Britain
Fax: +44 (0)161 796 1935
email: david.headpress@zen.co.uk

Psychotropedia: A Guide to Publications on the Periphery
Text copyright © Russ Kick
This volume copyright © 1998 Headpress
All photographs & illustrations copyright © respective owners, reproduced for the purpose of review.
Layout & design: David Kerekes & Walt Meaties
World Rights Reserved

Psychotropic / *n.* (of a drug) acting on the mind.
Encyclopedia / *n.* a book giving information on many subjects or on many aspects of the same subject, usu. arranged alphabetically.

Caveat In a nutshell, *Psychotropedia* is a book about other books. Some of these you might find in your local high street bookseller. Many you won't. Some are published by major publishing houses, the majority aren't. *Psychotropedia* is an attempt to chronicle these 'publications on the periphery', a subcontinent of 'alternative thought' that covers everything from the frivolous through the intriguing to the inflammatory. *Psychotropedia is not an endorsement of the subject matter of any book or organisation that comes under discussion.* In presenting this information, neither the author nor the publisher are giving you — the reader — legal, financial, medical, or any other type of advice. They are not saying you should do these things. Your life is your own.

Given that inconsistencies exist between the spelling of certain words in Britain and the United States, and in order to maintain a uniformity of text, the publisher has adopted the British standard throughout this book. Therefore, words which might have been spelled "traveling" and "gray" in the original manuscript, now read "travelling" and "grey". These changes include direct quotes taken from reviewed material, but do not include actual titles and contact information.

British Library Cataloguing in Publication Data
A catalogue record for this book is available from the British Library.

ISBN 1 900486 03 2

Contents

Acknowledgements As always, the big thanks go to my
parents for their non-stop support in all kinds of ways. Thanks also to my friends, who,
whether they realise it or not, help me stay sane — Billy, Gretchen, Terry, Nan Darrell, Susanna,
David, my sis, and all the members of my extended families. Every visit, call, email, letter,
and card helps keep me going.

Of course, many thanks go to David Kerekes of Headpress for publishing this monster
unabridged and uncensored. I owe a debt of gratitude to Michael Butterworth of Savoy for
alerting David that Psychotropedia was looking for a publisher.

Also, I want to pass on thanks to the many others who helped in some way with this
book, supported my first book, and/or have generally been all-around wonderful people:
Ramsey Kanaan and the rest of the AK crew; Killjoy; Seth Friedman; Bill Brent; Tristan
Taormino; Barry Hoffman; Judith Schoolman, Jen Angel, Erik Davis, Pat Hartman, and eve-
ryone else who told the world about Outposts; Lucy Gwin and the other Mouth-ers,
Loompanics, Atomic Books, Essential Media, and everyone else who carried Outposts; the
wonderful people of Breitenbush; Danny, Ronnie, and the rest of the gang at the Post Office;
the staff at the Mail Box and UPS; Amazon.com, Yahoo!, Alta Vista, and all the other Websites
I use mercilessly; the Acquisitions Department at the library for letting me use the Books in
Print CD-ROM; Simon Whitechapel for proofing; and all the readers who have sent me comments and suggestions.

Once again, I want to extend sincere thanks to the writers, editors, and publishers who
create the material I review. (And extra-special thanks go to the publishers who send me
their books and other publications.) Keep up the good work!

Looking over this list, I realise that I must be forgetting quite a few people. A book this big
doesn't get written without a lot of help. I apologise to anyone who accidentally got bumped…
rest assured that I deeply appreciate your assistance.

To all my loved ones who passed on while this book was being written.

Why This Book?

Because more and more of the world's media — including book publishers — are in the hands of fewer and fewer gigantic corporations. Because bookstore megachains now have a direct say in whether or not some books get published. Because independent publishers have a hard time getting their books reviewed. Because anyone foolhardy enough to become a writer needs all the exposure they can get for their books. Because Salman Rushdie has a price on his head. Because a leading French intellectual was recently put on trial and fined $40,000 for questioning the orthodox view of history. Because one of the most courageous publishers of all time, Lyle Stuart, was sued out of business and into personal bankruptcy over a book he published. Because the US's largest bookseller is facing multiple felony charges because of some of the books it carries. Because Paladin Press and its owner are the targets of a multimillion dollar lawsuit over the actions of someone they never knew. Because the World Health Organisation suppressed a scientific report showing that marijuana is less harmful than tobacco or alcohol. Because reporters are still being murdered and dissidents are still disappearing all over the world. Because information wants to be free. Because censorship never sleeps. Because the forces of oppression are so goddamn arrogant. Because I love books. Because the middle of the road leads nowhere. Because you can't make informed decisions unless you know what's going on. Because we have to follow the evidence no matter where it leads. Because <u>Psychotropedia</u> was snuffed by its original publisher. Because, like a schoolboy who never grew up, I want to know what I'm not supposed to; the more you forbid, the harder I try. Because I am human, and therefore, nothing human is alien to me. Because we should listen to those who are seeking the truth and doubt those who have found it. Because it's interesting. Because in a world where "alternative" has become a meaningless marketing word, it's nice to know that some things will never be co-opted by the Spectacle. Because even in nonconformist circles, there are still topics and ideas that are strictly taboo. Because censorship leads to more violent forms of expression. Because every fact, opinion, and idea deserves to be heard and judged on its own merits. Because wondering what new things I'll learn gets me out of bed every day.

—Russ Kick

Credit where credit is due: "I am a human…" is a quote from the Roman playwright Terence. "Listen to those who are seeking…" is a quote from Andre Gide. "Censorship leads to more violent…" is taken from a work of graffito. The format of "Why? Because…" was, as far as I know, originally used by Supermasochist performance artist Bob Flanagan.

Using This Book

Most of the material reviewed in <u>Psychotropedia</u> is in book form. At the end of each review, you'll first find the book's publisher, which can be looked up in **Appendix B: Publishers' Ordering Information**. (If the publisher's name is followed by a second name in parentheses, it means the first publisher is actually a division, subsidiary, or imprint of the second one. It is this second one that you should look up in Appendix B.) You'll also find the price, which is typically in US dollars unless otherwise marked.

The next line starts with the year the book was originally published. If the book is a new edition, the first year indicates when the book originally came out and the second year indicates when the newer edition was released. A second year in parentheses indicates that the book is a republication of a book that was published several years or decades ago. Next, the book's format is listed. If it's a hardcover, you might want to check to see if a softcover version is available before buying it.

On the third line, you'll see "illus" if the book is illustrated. "Heavily illus" means that there is generally at least one graphic per spread. Finally, the ISBN (International Standard Book Number) is a nine-digit number that uniquely identifies the book and can be very helpful in tracking it down.

Ordering information for all periodicals immediately follows each review. Unless otherwise noted, checks and money orders should be made out to the first line of the address, which is often but not always the name of the periodical. If you're only buying a single issue, consider sending cash.

Out-of-Print Books

Unfortunately, almost all of the books in <u>Psychotropedia</u> will eventually go out of print, though some may take longer than others. (Actually, there is a new system being implemented in the publishing world that assures that some books will stay in print indefinitely. **Lightning Print, Inc.**, (**www.lightningprint.com**) is making arrangements with many publishers to provide on-demand printing of books, in runs as low as a <u>single copy</u>, for customers who order a title through a bookseller that uses **Ingram**, the US's largest book distributor. Right now this system is being used primarily by the corporate publishers, but some independents and university presses are signing up.) The best way to find out-of-print books is on the Web. **Amazon.com** will track down books and report back to you within a week, but I don't think they actually stock any used books. The famous **Moe's Books** (**www.moesbooks.com**) stocks new and used books. Most helpful of all, some Websites contain searchable databases of inventory from hundreds of used bookstores around the world. Among the best are:

Advanced Book Exchange (www.abebooks.com)
Bibliocity (www.bibliocity.com)
Bibliofind (www.bibliofind.com)
Interloc (www.interloc.com)

Bleedin' Yank You may notice that in many ways this book is US-centric. I became highly aware of this after I signed up with a British publisher. To my credit — as with <u>Outposts</u> — I have always attempted to give ordering info for people who live outside the US, although publishers don't always supply this information. In my reviews, I've tried not to simply say "this country" or "here" when referring to the US, although a few instances probably slipped through. I've probably used some US slang and cultural references that will go over the heads of anyone outside the United States. To partially make up for being an Ugly American, I'm including a handy conversion table below, so hopefully non-Americans — particularly Britons — will understand what I'm talking about. God save the Queen!

$1 = £1.65 (this is very approximate, as currency exchange rates fluctuate daily)
Celsius temperature = (Fahrenheit - 32) x 5/9
An inch = 2.54 cm
A foot = 30.48 cm or .3048 m
A yard = 0.9144 m
A mile = 1.6093 km
An ounce = 28.35 g
A pound (weight) = 0.4536 kg
A US ton (2000 pounds) = 1016 kg or 1.016 t
A fluid ounce = 29.574 ml
A gallon = 3.7854 l

My Website If you just can't get enough, come by my Website, **Mind Pollen (www.mindpollen.com)** for more reviews of the latest, greatest books (and a few zines, movies, etc.). You'll also find interviews, excerpts from books, original material from myself and others, important but overlooked news, and more things to delight you. A section of the site will be devoted to keeping <u>Psychotropedia</u> up-to-date, with notes of books that have gone out of print, addresses that have changed, and new ordering information. Check it out at **www.mindpollen.com/psy**.

FREEDOM

FIRST AMENDMENT
Freedom of
Expression

CENSORSHIP
(The Ready Reference Series)

Dawn P. Dawson, editor in chief

Before I tell you about this incredible, wonderful, incomparable resource, I have to give you some bad news. Its intended audience is libraries, so it carries a steep price tag. Hopefully, a library near you will purchase it. If you own a business, get it and write it off your taxes.

OK, now that I can't be accused of setting you up for heartbreak, let me tell you about the towering greatness of this 3-volume encyclopaedia on censorship. Employing 997 entries, almost 300 contributors, over 275 illustrations, and 905 pages, *Censorship* covers its subject with a breadth and depth that can easily be described as epic. People, issues, specific works, laws, court cases, organisations... anything that relates to the suppression of expression is here.

Naturally, you'll find all the usual suspects: Robert Mapplethorpe, Salman Rushdie, Edwin Meese, flag burning, the Pentagon Papers, *Tom Sawyer*, *I Know Why the Caged Bird Sings*, *Ulysses*, *Playboy*, *Deep Throat*, the neo-Nazi march at Skokie, the Communications Decency Act, book burning, Lenny Bruce, 2 Live Crew, the American Civil Liberties Union, and so on. But to come up with almost 1000 entries, you know this publication is going to delve into *every* issue and aspect that relates to its subject, not just the most famous.

There are essays that overview general topics: libel, obscenity, picketing, loyalty oaths, prior restraint, symbolic speech, hate laws, blasphemy, and many more. Others look at genres that are routinely targeted for censorship, including comic books, pornography, children's literature, advertisements, and video games. Some entries are uniquely informative because they draw together examples of how certain taboo subjects — such as adultery, alcohol, interracial relationships, and suicide — are suppressed in books, movies, and other media. A few of these general entries don't directly relate to free speech but do address other freedoms that involve school dress codes, school prayer, and nude dancing.

AP photo of an extremely controversial form of protest in Seattle. *Censorship*.

The subjects span all of history, from Socrates and the Library of Alexandria — which was destroyed in one of the most devastating acts of cultural censorship ever committed — to *Beavis and Butthead*, Howard Stern, and Jello Biafra. Along the way, you'll find out that:

☞ "Hard-core pornographic films were produced virtually from the invention of the motion picture camera."

☞ Walt Whitman "apparently lost his job in the US Department of the Interior for publishing *Leaves of Grass*."

☞ In 1994 a Federal Court ruled that a driver's First Amendment rights had been violated when the Virginia Department of Motor Vehicles revoked his licence plates which read, "GOVT SUX".

☞ While at Columbia University, Allen Ginsberg had "been suspended for writing graffiti critical of Columbia's president on a dormitory window"

☞ "Henry [VIII] was the first English monarch to use censorship of printed books to shape religious and political opinion."

☞ The *Erznoznik v. Jacksonville* Supreme Court decision, "holding unconstitutional an ordinance prohibiting drive-in theatres with screens visible from public areas from showing films containing nudity, denied that government could shield citizens from all exposure to nudity in film".

☞ A fascinating article on scientific censorship reveals that: "In 1988 when the Environmental Protection Agency had to determine safe levels for several chemicals, including the nerve gas phosgene, its agency report included data originating from Nazi experiments on French prisoners. The EPA administrator expunged the data at the request of twenty-two EPA scientists."

With yet other articles, you'll be able to answer such nagging questions as, Why are Émile Zola's writings so controversial? (His novels "focused on the characters from the lower strata of society, describing every aspect of their often sordid lives with vivid and colourful detail.") And, What the heck is *I Am Curious (Yellow)* about anyway? (It's an "Exploration of the intimate relationship of a young Swedish couple", which contains only ten minutes of sex scenes).

The focus is mainly on the US, but there are many entries dealing with other countries, including the *Spycatcher* episode in Britain and Australia, the suppression of information regarding the Basque independence movement, and the official denial of the genocide committed against Armenians by Turkey, plus articles on Denmark, Israel, India, Pakistan, and 30 other countries.

Further entries cover Sally Mann, Louis Farrakhan, Joseph Stalin, John Steinbeck, Anthony Comstock, Judy Blume, Supreme Court Justice Hugo Black, photographic film processing, the Internet, Three Mile Island, the My Lai Massacre, airline safety news, male pseudonyms, Mormonism, draft-card burning, *Amos 'n' Andy*, "Cop Killer", *Doonesbury*, *Who's Afraid of Virginia Woolf?*, *Uncle Tom's Cabin*, dictionaries, Son of Sam laws, Morality in the Media, Alabama, African newspapers, obituaries, bumperstickers, TASS, and political correctness.

Added bonuses include a film censorship timeline, a chronological guide to significant court cases, a glossary, an extensive bibliography (many entries also have their own small bibliographies), a listing of all entries broken down by category, and a resource guide that lists groups that are for and against censorship. The extensive index will help you pin down exactly what you want to know, which is quite helpful because some information isn't in the expected locations. (Olympia Press doesn't have its own entry, but its founder, Maurice Girodias, does. Likewise, *In the Spirit of Crazy Horse* — which sparked the longest legal battle in American publishing history — wasn't given a separate entry but is discussed under "Native Americans".)

It goes without saying that this is *the* towering work on the suppression of thought, speech, information, and the written word (strangely, the visual arts, except for film, are practically ignored). If you're interested in the subject, you must find a way to get your mitts on it, even if it means driving to a distant library.

Salem Press; $280
1997; oversized hardcovers; 3 volumes, 905 pp
illus; 0-89356-445-1, -446-X, -444-3

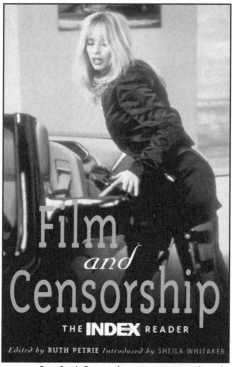

From Crash, Rosanna Arquette gets autoerotic on the cover of this look at freedom of celluloid expression. *Film and Censorship.*

FILM AND CENSORSHIP
The *Index* Reader
edited by Ruth Petrie

For twenty-five years, *Index on Censorship* has covered world-wide instances of oppression, primarily the quashing of free expression. The best of its writing on movie censorship has been brought together in this collection of 31 essays. In keeping with *Index*'s international scope, there are articles and essays about occurrences in Africa, Brazil, Britain, Chile, China, Eastern Europe, France, Iran, Latin America, the Soviet Union, Turkey, and the US.

In "Screening Disaster", Karen Rosenberg looks at the honest and dishonest approaches of several Soviet documentaries about the Chernobyl nuclear disaster. The film *Threshold* interviewed citizens of Chernobyl who have been hospitalised. "The diagnoses on their medical charts indicate that they are suffering from the most ordinary ailments, not radiation-related concerns. From this description, it is clear that *Threshold* concerns more than Chernobyl; it documents the continuation of old methods of hiding and doctoring data."

Reza Allamehzadeh reveals the horrifying extent of film censorship that occurred when the Islamic fundamentalists were taking over Iran. "Cinema burning reached its climax in September 1978, when the Rex Cinema in Abadan in the south of Iran was set on fire by religious fundamentalist supporters of the Imam Khomeini, who had locked all the exits of the cinema which contained an audience of over 400 people. Three hundred and seventy-seven men, women and children, who had come to watch an Iranian film were burned alive."

"No Ecstasy, Please, We're British" is a short piece on the banning of the eighteen-minute film *Visions of Ecstasy*, about St. Teresa of Avila, who had ecstatic visions. "It includes sequences in which St Teresa is shown erotically caressing the body of Christ, and sexually embracing a female who is said by videomakers to represent her alter ego."

"Britain: Out of Fear and Ignorance" gives a history of film censorship in Britain from 1909 through 1981, paying particular attention to a few films including *Life of Brian*, *Salò*, and *Caligula*. Likewise, "China: A Hundred Flowers or Poisonous Weeds?" chronicles the ups and downs of cinema freedom in China from the 1940s through 1980. In his rant, filmmaker Pedro Almodóvar rails against the US ratings system, which slapped an X on his movie *Atame* because of its sole sex scene. "Politics and Porn" focuses primarily on France's banning of "pornographic" films during the 1970s.

Because it reprints articles as they appeared at the time without updating them, *Film and Censorship* often feels dated. However, viewed as a historical document and not as an up-to-the-minute report, it's an important collection of information on censorship that is otherwise hard to find.

Cassell; $21.95
1997; softcover; 193 pp
illus; 0-304-33937-7

FORBIDDEN PASSAGES
Writings Banned in Canada
edited by Cleis Press

This anthology is almost entirely made up of fiction and nonfiction dealing with sex, particularly of the gay and lesbian variety. I have not listed it in the Sex chapter, though, because this is definitely one case where the sexual is the political. What all of these selections have in common is that they caused the books and magazines in which they originally appeared to be seized by Canadian Customs (for more information, see *Restricted Entry*, below). The Canadian Thought Police have a long and disgraceful history of seizing (stealing) and destroying gay, lesbian, SM, and other non-vanilla material being shipped into Canada, particularly if it's headed for gay and lesbian bookstores. This collection brings together sixteen essays, short stories, and excerpts, one comic, and some art that Customs officials decided their citizens had no right to read or view. Among them: "Mama" by Dorothy Allison, "Spiral" by David Wojnarowicz, "Egg Sex" by Susie Bright, "Numb" by Dennis Cooper, "Daddy's Little Girl" by Ann Wertheim, as well as excerpts from *Macho Sluts* by Pat Califia, *My Biggest O*, *The Man Sitting in the Corridor* by Marguerite Duras, *Hothead Paisan* by Diane DiMassa, and *Tom of Finland: A Retrospective*. Two lengthy introductions are supplied by sex radical Pat Califia and Janine Fuller, manager of Little Sister's Book & Art Emporium, a gay and lesbian bookstore in Canada that has fought Canadian Customs in court. Sales of this book go towards paying their massive legal bills. If you want to contribute directly (in addition to buying this great book, of course), their address is 1221 Thurlow St/Vancouver, BC V6E 1X4/Canada.

Cleis Press; $14.95
1995; softcover; 176 pp
illus; 1-57344-019-1

FREEDOM OF SPEECH, PRESS, ASSEMBLY
by Darien A. McWhirter

If you want an accessible yet thorough overview of the issues surrounding the First Amendment's speech, press, and assembly clauses, this reader-friendly textbook fits the bill perfectly. Despite the fact that it's intended for use in college classrooms, it is written in a readable style, not like the obtuse academic mush you may have encountered. The main focus is on Supreme Court decisions and how they've affected three of our First Amendment rights.

Each chapter contains a discussion of relevant cases (over 115 in all) regarding the many different issues — from fighting words to publishing the names of rape victims — that have arisen through the years. The second main part of each chapter has sizeable excerpts from the most important Supreme Court rulings, as well as some dissenting opinions. Finally, there are the dreaded discussion questions, but you'll probably want to skip those.

The opening chapter tackles the intriguing question of what speech is. "Or, more specifically, what kinds of communicative activities are protected by the right of free speech?" In 1931 a counsellor at a California summer camp was convicted of raising a red flag, a symbol of communism and revolution. The Court ruled that raising a flag is symbolic speech and is therefore protected. The right not to speak, even when ordered to by the government, was established in 1940, when eight of the Justices declared that it was impermissible to force schoolchildren to recite the Pledge of Allegiance. In 1943, six Justices voted in a similar case — which involved saluting the flag — to uphold the right not to symbolically speak.

Other speech issues that are covered include leaflet distribution on public property, airports as public forums, membership in political parties that advocate revolution, criminal syndicalism, movies, obscenity, adult entertainment and zoning laws, boycotts, commercial speech, and more. The chapter on freedom of the press tackles criticism of public officials, libel, public figures and private citizens, gag orders, and press attendance at trials. Lastly, the chapter on the right to assemble and petition the government deals with picket lines, parades, civil rights demonstrations, parade fees, and anti-abortion protests.

The last parts of the book look at our freedoms today and offer a glossary of legal terms, further reading, the US Constitution, and a listing of the Justices of the Supreme Court. Since it's a textbook, it's kind of pricey, but the large chunks of Supreme Court rulings make it extra valuable.

Oryx Press; $29.95
1994; hardcover; 191 pp
0-89774-853-0

PORNOGRAPHY AND THE JUSTICES
The Supreme Court and the Intractable Obscenity Problem
by Richard F. Hixson

For just over 100 years, the US Supreme Court has wrestled with the concept of obscenity. In 1896 the Court was called upon to review two lower-court rulings. In the first, it upheld the conviction of a publisher who mailed "indecent" pictures, which violated the notorious Comstock Act. In the second, it overturned the conviction of a newspaper publisher who used sexual language to assassinate the character of an unnamed individual. Since then, the Court has gone on a century-long rollercoaster ride trying to define and handle obscene materials (in 1965 alone, three obscenity cases produced fourteen separate opinions). The author examines these ups and downs by focusing mainly on the individual Justices who have had the most influence on the matter. "William J. Brennan said obscenity was 'utterly without redeeming social importance.' [Justice John Marshall] Harlan said it had to be 'fundamentally offensive', 'prurient', and 'inherently sexually indecent.' Potter Stewart always looked for 'hard-core' pornography before he decided what was obscene and unprotected by the Constitution. Admitting his inability to formulate a coherent test for obscenity, Stewart claimed 'I know it when I see it.' Thurgood Marshall, who rejected the notion that watching obscene materials in the privacy of one's home might lead to criminal conduct, compared such illogic to the prohibition of chemistry books on the grounds that they may lead to the making of home-made spirits."

Pornography and the Justices is detailed enough to satisfy students and scholars of free speech (particularly sexual free speech), but it's written in language that is comprehensible to us non-law types. Each chapter examines a different Justice and the particular spin he put on the question of obscenity: "Isolated Passages", "Dominant Theme", "Community Standards", "Variable Obscenity", "Politics and Pandering", "Social Importance", "Consenting Exposure", "Content Restriction", "Expressive Activity", "Syndicated Sex", and "Viewpoint Discrimination". As the book progresses, it covers such disparate topics as hardcore pornography, kiddie porn, peepshows, George Carlin, *Fanny Hill*, and *Ulysses* by James Joyce.

In the end, the author attempts a summary and synthesis of the Court's viewpoints. "From the judge, the justices, and the scholars, we could say that it will behove the Court in future obscenity rulings to give less time to *defining* obscenity — the problem Justice Stewart spotted — and even less time limiting speech protection on the basis of possible *effects*." He indicates that it would be best to follow Justice Brennan's philosophy: "let the government protect minors and unconsenting adults; the rest is up to the individual."

Southern Illinois University Press; $29.95
1996; hardcover; 273 pp
0-8093-2057-6

RESTRICTED ENTRY
Censorship on Trial

(Second Edition)
by Janine Fuller & Stuart Blackley

Unless you keep track of freedom of speech issues, you might not know what an arrogant, fascist, pig-headed asshole the Canadian government is. Books and magazines dealing with gay, lesbian, SM, and other not-hetero, non-vanilla forms of sex are routinely seized and destroyed when being imported. (Extreme political material and "sacrilegious" writing sometimes meet the same fate.) Customs officials often target material headed to gay and lesbian bookstores, whose financial positions are usually not rock solid in the first place. Among the most persecuted of these stores is Little Sister's in Vancouver. Tired of dealing with the Canadian Thought Police, they counterattacked, launching a lawsuit against Customs to change the tyrannical law. The core forty days of that trial are the focus of this book. A parade of artists, writers, booksellers, civil libertarians, vice cops, bureaucrats, and control freaks duked it out in the courtroom.

After two and a half months, 200 hours of testimony, and over 1000 pages of court transcripts, the trial ended in late December 1994. Unfortunately, the court takes a long time to rule on constitutional matters, and when the first edition of *Restricted Entry* went to press, no verdict had been returned. This edition, however, contains the news of the verdict, delivered thirteen months later. "Simply stated, the Supreme Court of British Columbia ruled that Canada Customs was constitutionally entitled to its powers of prior restraint, and that Customs legislations didn't, in theory, discriminate against gays and lesbians. But the judge also found that Customs' actions had violated both the equality and freedom of speech of gays and lesbians. As significantly, he discussed queer sexual materials in a manner that was refreshingly positive." In other words, the judge had ruled that the despicable laws that allow the detainment, seizure, and destruction of material coming into Canada were just fine, but the Customs officials had been discriminatory in applying their censorious powers. Talk about a partial victory. A little later, the judge also awarded money to Little Sister's to pay for their legal expenses, plus some extra cash as a rebuke to the government. The bookstore decided that although they had achieved a lot, they wouldn't rest till Canada's anti-free speech laws have been struck down. They are currently appealing the decision. (For more on Canadian censorship, see *Forbidden Passages*, above.)

Press Gang Publishers; $16.95, $18.95 Cdn
1996; softcover; 245 pp
illus; 0-88974-066-6

THE SEPARATION OF CHURCH AND STATE
by Darien A. McWhirter

The two clauses in the First Amendment dealing with religion are comprised of a mere sixteen words, yet they have triggered some of the most furious, emotional debates of any part of the Constitution. They read: "Congress shall make no law respecting an establishment of religion, or prohibiting the free exercise thereof..." The first clause is known as the Establishment Clause, and the second as the Free Exercise Clause. In this volume of the readable and lucid *Understanding the Constitution* series of college textbooks, the author guides us through over 50 Supreme Court cases that have ruled on crucial aspects of these rights. The first part of each chapter discusses the cases, and the second part reproduces large parts of the Court's rulings.

Three chapters deal with the Establishment Clause. One looks at Sunday closing laws, registering religions as charities, prayer in legislatures, nativity displays, and religious oaths in public office. In 1961 a case came before the Court that dealt with Maryland's law requiring people to swear that they believe in God before they could hold public office. A man who wanted to be a notary public refused to take the oath and was denied the office. "A unanimous Court ruled that this practice did violate the Establishment Clause. The Court thought that by requiring people to who wished to hold public office to take such an oath, the State of Maryland was supporting a particular group of religions — those that believe in the existence of one supreme god." Another chapter examines religious practices in public schools — official prayer, Bible readings, teaching evolution, posting the Ten Commandments, a moment of silence, prayer at graduation, and equal treatment for the Christian story of creation. The last of the Establishment chapters tackles the question of government support for religious schools.

The other three chapters are concerned with the Free Expression Clause. Chapter Seven looks at what happens when religious practices break laws. Members of the Santería religion wanted to build a temple in Florida, and, in an effort to stop them, the city outlawed the "ritual sacrifice" of animals, which is one of that Caribbean religion's practices. "Rather than outlawing the killing of animals in general, the law made the killing of animals a crime only if it was performed for a 'religious' purpose." The Court ruled unanimously that this law violated exercise of religion. Also covered in this chapter are polygamy, miraculous claims and fraud, school attendance, and peyote use. The other two chapters look at the Pledge of Allegiance, solicitation of money for religious purposes, licence fees, child labour laws, conscientious objectors, the right to receive an education, and the special case of the exemption from compulsory schooling for the Amish.

The last sections of the book concern the wall of separation today and offer a glossary of legal terms, further reading, the US Constitution, and a listing of the Justices of the Supreme Court. Reading *The Separation of Church and State* will provide you with a greater understanding of the thorny issues surrounding the government's inability to interfere with religion.

Oryx Press; $29.95
1994; hardcover; 189 pp
0-89774-852-2

SEVERING THE TIES THAT BIND
Government Repression of Indigenous Religious Ceremonies on the Prairies
by Katherine Pettipas

In 1885 Canada outlawed the practising of many Native American customs — including ritual piercings and give-away customs, such as potlatches — because the government and Christian missionaries felt these "heathenish" customs were interfering with the Indians' religious conversions and their integration into the rest of society. Even practices not specifically outlawed, such as Sun Dances, were undermined in indirect ways. This book traces the history of this religious persecution from the mid-1800s to 1951, when these regulations were removed from the Canadian Indian Act. It also reveals the ways in which the Native Americans resisted these authoritarian laws and the effects they still have today.

University of Manitoba Press; $18.95
1994; softcover; 320 pp
illus; 0-88755-638-8

SILENCING THE OPPOSITION
Government Strategies of Suppression of Freedom of Expression
edited by Craig R. Smith

This collection contains seven academic essays that examine various times in US history when the Federal government has sought to restrict freedom of expression, including freedom of speech, of assembly, and of religion. Each instance of silencing governmental opponents occurred either during time of war, threat of war, or threat of civil violence. Besides looking at the ways in which the government restricts freedoms, the authors examine three more specific theses. "First, that government suppression of opponents is an inevitable cycle in times of crisis. Second, that government methods of suppression have become more and sophisticated as old methods are exposed and new technologies are developed. Third, that the wider the gulf between the oppressed and the oppressors the more militant and extralegal the forms of suppression become."

Specifically, the essays look at the Alien and Sedition Acts, Lincoln's suspension of Habeas Corpus during the Civil War (which allowed people to be arrested with no cause and detained indefinitely), the Radical Republicans' persecution of the South, the holocaust against Native Americans, the Presidential war against unions in the late-1800s, Joseph McCarthy's hunt for communists, and the tactics used by Nixon and Johnson to silence opposition to the Vietnam War.

State University of New York Press; $21.95
1996; softcover; 289 pp
0-7914-3086-3

SLAPPs
Getting Sued for Speaking Out
by George W. Pring & Penelope Canan

It may seem impossible, but American citizens are being regularly sued for participating in the political process. Residents of West Covina, California, protested to the government about the practices of a large landfill operation. The landfill slammed a federal suit against a citizen's group, twelve private individuals, and various city officials. After hearing reports of unsafe school buses, some Pennsylvania parents expressed their concerns at a school board meeting. The bus company sued them for $680,000. A county government in Iowa sued anyone who protested its fiscal budget. A bar owner sued for $8,000,000 when "Baltimore neighbours protested a liquor licence renewal for a controversial tavern." Other people have been targeted for writing a letter to the President, testifying before Congress, reporting official misconduct, reporting law violations to the authorities, lobbying for legislation, collecting signatures for a petition, and other activities that are necessary to the functioning of an allegedly free and democratic society. These types of lawsuits are now occurring in other countries, including Britain and Canada.

The professors who wrote this book are the ones who coined the name for this nauseating form of litigation: Strategic Lawsuits Against Public Participation (SLAPPs). Such actions started appearing in the late 1970s and have become more and more common. Although such lawsuits usually don't succeed, they do have the effect of ruining people's lives and destroying citizens' groups with the financial and psychological damage of extended litigation. Plus, SLAPPs have a chilling effect on other people who might want to speak out.

Just how does a business or government entity get away with such a gross violation of the rights to free speech and petition for redress of grievances? Specifically, the lawsuits often use libel, defamation, slander, contractual interference, business interference, and prima facie tort — as well as conspiracy to commit any of the preceding acts — as excuses to silence critics. The authors examine specific cases involving several areas: real estate SLAPPs, SLAPPs launched by public servants, environmental SLAPPs, "Not In My Backyard" SLAPPs, consumer SLAPPs, employment SLAPPs, and women's rights SLAPPs.

After you become thoroughly disheartened and pissed off by the actions of corporate and governmental bullies, the authors give three chapters of hope. They discuss what to do if you become the target of a SLAPP, how to file a countersuit (known as a SLAPPback), and the attempts to pass anti-SLAPP legislation at federal and state levels.

Temple University Press; $24.95
1996; softcover; 285 pp
1-56639-369-8

TELLING IT ALL
A Legal Guide to the Exercise of Free Speech
by Harold W. Fuson, Jr

If you're an activist, an investigative reporter, or any other kind of rabble-rouser, you open yourself up for all kinds of lawsuits. Media attorney Harold Fuson will help you avoid legal pitfalls placed by people and companies who want to shut you up. He offers practical, street-level advice written in plain English.

When telling it like it is, you're most likely to get sued for alleged libel. Accordingly, over one-third of this book deals with avoiding this problem. Like so many legal issues, this one is not cut and dried. In theory, libel occurs when you write something that is false and damaging about a person

or business. In reality, it just ain't that easy. Was the contested statement actually published? Does a private memo count as "being published"? Was the plaintiff specifically identified or was he/she part of a group that was named? How small is the group? Is the statement defamatory? Is the statement true? Can you prove it? Was the statement presented as fact, opinion, or fair comment? Did it show malice or negligence? You get the idea. The author sorts through these grey areas, and shows you how you can cover your ass before the fact and defend yourself afterwards.

Another way to get into trouble is by "publicly presenting private facts", even if those facts are true. While trying to gather information, you have to be careful about trespassing, intrusion, crossing police lines, eavesdropping, working undercover, and violating prior restraints on speech. You also should know about accessing information through court records and proceedings, government meeting and records, public places, and the private sector.

At some point, you may be called to court to divulge your sources of information. Chapter 6 discusses testifying and protecting your sources. The next chapter involves the touchy issue of copyright and how not to violate it. Finally, there are chapters on finding a good lawyer and keeping speech free. A resources section points to organisations, books, and court cases that can benefit you.

Telling It All is a good and unfortunately necessary companion for people who fight the power.

Andrews and McMeel; $8.95
1995; softcover; 118 pp
0-8362-7025-8

SECOND AMENDMENT
The Right to Bear Arms

THE ARMED CITIZEN SOLUTION TO CRIME IN THE STREETS
So Many Criminals, So Few Bullets
by Mack Tanner

Mack Tanner doesn't want to hear excuses about why there's so much crime — inequality, poverty, drugs, liberalism, no prayer in school, etc., etc., etc. No matter what the roots of the problem may be, what it comes down to in every instance of murder, rape, robbery, or assault is that some asshole who doesn't give a damn about you thinks that he can harm you with impunity. "You are responsible because you have given up the most valuable right you ever had. You were born with it: the right to defend yourself against anyone who would use force to end your life or take what you own."

The answer is to arm yourself and know how to kick ass and take names if the situation calls for it. Tanner discusses arming yourself legally, keeping guns at home, taking guns with you in public, avoiding trouble, confronting criminals, running away, taking prisoners, shooting to kill ("and keep shooting until he drops"), hostage situations, preserving evidence, alternatives to firearms, and much more. My biggest complaint about the book is that there is no specific information on which types of guns are available and which ones are best for personal protection, depending on your situation.

The next step from there, should you be interested, is forming an informal alliance with other people in your neighbourhood. You and like-minded neighbours simply agree to help each other out. When someone wants to walk a dog or go to an Automatic Teller Machine at night or do any other activity that might be dangerous in your neck of the woods, he or she will always be accompanied by an armed neighbour.

For areas that are practically run by criminals — such as inner cities — Tanner suggests forming a local militia. This is not a militia in the sense the word has been used lately — a group of people preparing to fight the New World Order — but simply a self-defence committee of armed citizens trying to make the streets safe. "The purpose is to stop crime from happening by legally occupying the streets in sufficient strength that a criminal will not be able to find and attack his victim without serious risk to his own life and freedom." He gives tips on dealing with gangs, taking back public playgrounds, stopping serial rapists, and handling other problems. As always, the emphasis is on using only necessary force, working with police, and not becoming a vigilante who metes out .32-caliber justice.

If you're tired of living in fear of violence, the answer is simple. Get rid of the victim/prey mentality and use your right to hurt or kill anyone who is trying to do the same to you.

Paladin Press; $15
1995; softcover; 189 pp
0-87364-806-4

THE FIREARMS SENTINEL

This tabloid is published by Jews for the Preservation of Firearms Ownership. Upon first hearing the name of this group, it might strike you as an odd combination. What do Jews have to do with gun ownership? Plenty. The JFPO believes that if the European Jews — and other targets of Nazi aggression — had been armed, there would not have been a Holocaust. As one of the group's slogans states: "Political prisoners and Death Camps can't exist without 'Gun Control'."

That theory also applies to other mass killings. Seven major genocides of the twentieth century were all preceded by laws that disarmed the population (more about that in *Lethal Laws*, below). Now we're seeing efforts to completely or partly disarm US citizens. As history shows, this is an open invitation to tyranny. Whether or not you think that there is actually a plot underway by the federal government to turn America into a police state doesn't matter. The fact is that with a disarmed population, a government take-over is very easy. The Founders of the US certainly knew this. That's why they created the Second Amendment. If you study the issues and debates surrounding the creation of this Amendment, you'll see that it had nothing to do with hunting, collecting, target shooting, or even self-defence. As Thomas Jefferson said: "The strongest reason for the people to retain the right to keep and bear arms is, as a last resort, to protect themselves from tyranny in government" (quoted in issue 2, page 17).

The JFPO stands foursquare against any kind of restriction on firearms and ammo, including bans, waiting periods, and registration. (The reason for being against registration is simple: it lets the government know exactly who has what guns. The next step, confiscating the guns, becomes much easier.) *The Firearms Sentinel* discusses gun laws, combats gun control, examines how out of control the federal government has become, and prints "consumer reports"-style tests on firearms.

The first issue of the *Sentinel* contains a lengthy article on a perfect example of hidden history — the Battle of Athens. In 1946, upon returning from W.W.II, GIs who lived in McMinn County, Tennessee, found that the government of State Senator Paul Cantrell and Sheriff Pat Mansfield was hopelessly corrupt. Pay-offs to politicians and misuse of government funds were the order of the day. The elections were transparently rigged, with both parties stuffing ballot boxes, buying votes, and counting the returns in an unsupervised area.

The GIs decided to oppose Cantrell, Mansfield, and the rest of the Democrats in the 1946 election. They ran as Republicans, promising to clean up the government and restore the will of the people. Above all, they promised a fair election in which there would be no tampering and the ballots would be counted in public, where every interested voter could watch. This is actually a requirement under Tennessee State law. They contacted state and federal authorities for assistance in supervising the election. They received no help.

Unfortunately, the County administration was determined to corrupt the process, as usual. Mansfield brought in 200 armed "deputies", who harassed and intimidated voters throughout the county. They even shot an African American who was trying to vote and beat one of the GIs who was watching for voter fraud.

After the polls closed, Mansfield and his thugs took the ballot boxes to the County jail, where they were to be counted in private. The general population was held at bay across the street from the jail by the deputies, who promised to kill anyone who crossed the street.

Around 8:00 that night, over 100 GIs and local men gathered all the firearms they could find and surrounded the jail. Someone in the jail fired, and the battle began. After midnight, those in the jail surrendered and the ballot boxes were rescued. The Secretary of the McMinn County Election Commission certified that the GI/Republicans had won by a wide margin. The new government immediately made good on its promise of restoring a fair and lawful government. The JFPO feels that this uprising shows "when and how aggrieved Americans can and should use armed force for a lawful purpose, and why their access to arms should be unimpaired....The Battle of Athens shows that the civil right to be armed is, in fact, the ultimate guarantor of all other civil rights."

Another article in the same issue demolishes the alleged firearms violations of the Branch Davidians that were used to justify the raid. Further articles examine the state of firearms ownership in Canada, the pro-gun control stance of the Anti-Defamation League, and the use of the military against the civilian population.

Jews for the Preservation of Firearms Ownership/2872 S Wentworth Ave/Milwaukee WI 53207
WWW: www.mcs.net/~lpyleprn/jpfo.html
one year sub (4 issues): included in membership dues of $20 per year

FROM MY COLD DEAD FINGERS
Why America Needs Guns!
by Richard I. Mack & Timothy Robert Walters

Richard Mack is an Arizona sheriff who filed suit in Federal Court to fight the Brady Bill, which imposes a five-day waiting period for a background check if you want to legally buy a handgun. So far, the suit and others like it have been winning partial victories in the courts. In this book, Mack and Timothy Robert Walters explain why it is important for citizens to own weapons and what some people are doing to take away that right.

They argue that it was the Founders' intent that everyone should be armed to prevent the government from becoming a tyranny. "Some confusion has existed regarding the reference in the Second Amendment to a 'well regulated militia.' Militia was defined by the Founding Fathers as every able-bodied male, and had absolutely nothing to do with the army or a national guard. The Second Amendment right to keep and bear arms is the right of an individual to possess and carry firearms."

While more than 20,000 gun control laws have been put into effect in the US, crime has done nothing but go up. The authors blame a court system that drags its feet, the failure of rehabilitation, and unbelievably short prison sentences. "The average sentence given a murderer is 11 years; actual time served is less than seven."

Gun control groups, lobbyists, and sympathetic legislators have drawn up plans to virtually disarm the population. According to the authors, a bill created by Handgun Control, Inc., and New York Congressman Charles Schumer is a case in point. "The concept is to levy enormous fees, taxes and liability insurance requirements on all lawful firearms ownership, to require new licensing and registration schemes (enabling easier gun confiscation in the future), to implement gun ownership rationing, to impose such restrictions on licenced

It was the Founders' intent that everyone should be armed to prevent the government from becoming a tyranny.
From My Cold Dead Fingers.

dealers so as to put them out of business (another whack at free enterprise), to institute bans on handguns, long guns, and ammunition, and to require fingerprinting, photographing and permanent waiting periods on handgun ownership (all designed to make confiscation quick and simple in the future)."

The authors use statistics to poke holes in anti-gun arguments. For example, they contend that guns result in significantly fewer accidental deaths of children per year than motor vehicles, drowning, burns, or suffocation. According to the National Safety Council, in 1991 2226 kids between five and fourteen were killed by motor vehicles, while 95 in the same age group were killed by guns.

From My Cold Dead Fingers also covers Bernard Goetz, Ruby Ridge, Waco, the attack on "assault weapons", emotional manipulation tactics, using guns for self-defence, and taking action to preserve the Second Amendment.

Rawhide Western Publishing; $12.95
1994; softcover; 221 pp
0-9641935-1-5

"GUN CONTROL"
Gateway to Tyranny
by Jay Simkin & Aaron Zelman

When the Nazis came to power in 1933, they inherited lists of registered gun owners from the Weimar Republic, whose 1928 Law on Firearms and Ammunition made registration mandatory. The Nazis began seizing guns from Jews and other groups who were not considered "reliable". Five years later, Hitler's government enacted its own gun control law. The Nazi Weapons Law prevented Jews — and anyone else except Nazi party members and other "reliables" — from owning firearms or any other weapons, including knives and clubs. This helped make possible the massacre of six million Jews and seven million Gypsies, disabled people, gays and lesbians, and other victims of the Holocaust.

But the main focus of *"Gun Control"* is not the Nazi Weapons Law... it's the modern-day incarnation of that law: the American Gun Control Act of 1968 and its subsequent amendments. The book's authors go beyond saying that the GCA '68 is a Naziesque law — they claim that it is explicitly and purposely based on the Nazis' gun control law. They reprint the Nazi Weapon Law (both in the original German and in English) in full. Then, in the most revealing part of the book, they print the Nazi law and the American law side by side, to demonstrate the incredible parallels. Both laws exempt government organisations and officials from restrictions placed on law-abiding citizens. Both laws turn gun ownership into a privilege and give government bureaucrats the right to decide which types of firearms may be owned by private individuals. The GCA '68 allows the government to ban firearms that are not for "sporting purpose". Unfortunately, the term "sporting purpose" is never defined by the law, leaving it open for the Secretary of Treasury to interpret however he or she wants to. Also, the BATF Form 4473 (Firearms Transaction Record) and the Nazi Firearm Acquisition Permit are shown to be strikingly similar. They both "require almost identical information about the purchaser and the firearm purchased."

An additional article in the back of the book shows that this might not be coincidence — GCA '68 may have been intentionally based on the Nazi Weapons Law. The late Senator Thomas J. Dodd (D-CT) was the chief architect of the gun control law. A letter to Dodd from a law librarian at the Library of Congress, which is reprinted in this book, shows that Dodd had German and English versions of the Nazi laws at least four months before his bill was enacted.

The authors also show that some state and local laws have added more Nazi-like restrictions on gun owners. For example, gun owners in Massachusetts, Illinois, and New Jersey are required to get "Firearm Owner Identity Cards", a process that involves being photographed and finger-printed. During the last week of 1991, Los Angeles banned the sale of ammunition (allegedly so New Year's Eve partiers wouldn't fire their guns into the air).

The final section of *"Gun Control"* contains interesting documents not directly related to the rest of the book. "Dial 911 and Die!" is a particularly disturbing report that shows, through court rulings and actual incidents, that the police have no legal duty to protect you from danger. Other documents cover the Armenian genocide and a Jewish concentration camp inmate who used guns to fight the Nazis.

Jews for the Preservation of Firearms Ownership; $22.90 postpaid
1993; oversized softcover with plastic comb binding; 139 pp illus; 0-9642304-1-0

LETHAL LAWS
"Gun Control" Is the Key to Genocide
by Jay Simkin, Aaron Zelman, & Alan M. Rice

If you take guns away from people, they become easy pickings for a government-sponsored genocide. You don't have to believe this... all you have to do is look at history. Seven major genocides of the twentieth century were all preceded by laws that disarmed the civilian population.

First of all, I'm sure the fact that there have been seven genocides this century will surprise a lot of people. Most people only know about the Nazi holocaust against the Jews, and maybe a few know about one other, such as the Turkish or Russian holocausts. But there have been at least seven, as of the early 1980s. If you include more recent events not covered in this book, such as those in Rwanda and the former Yugoslavia, the tally is even higher.

Anyway, the crux of *Lethal Laws* is an examination of the gun control laws of seven countries and the horrible mass slaughters that followed. The authors present the case that almost 56 million people have died this century because they couldn't fight back against a government bent on exterminating them. The seven genocides are:

1) Ottoman Turkey, from 1915 to 1917, killed 1 to 1.5 million Armenians.

2) The Soviet Union, from 1929 to 1953, killed 20 million political opponents.

3) Nazi Germany, from 1933 to 1945, killed 13 million Jews, Gypsies, disabled people, gays and lesbians, political subversives, and others.

4) China, from 1949 to 1952 and then from the mid-1960s to the mid-1970s, killed 20 million political opponents.

5) Guatemala, for two decades starting in 1960, killed 100,000 Mayan Indians.

6) Uganda, during the 1970s, killed 300,000 Christians and political rivals.

7) Cambodia, from 1975-1979, killed one million educated people (i.e., the "cultural elite").

Each chapter explains the various forces and events that led up to the genocide, as well as describing the genocide itself. The various gun-banning laws of each country are reprinted in their original language and English translation.

Of course, there are those who say that genocide could never happen in the US of A. Why not? Well, er, because — um, because, this is America dammit! It just couldn't. If history shows us anything, it shows us that governments exist simply to increase their power. America is no different. Don't forget, the US was created through the genocide of Native Americans and the forced labour of African slaves and poor white "indentured servants". The authors point out that there was almost a genocide in the United States during W.W.II. Around 100,000 citizens, who happened to be of Japanese descent, were rounded up and put into detention camps. Although the purpose was to detain but not murder the inmates, the book states that if the Japanese had taken Midway, which they almost did, they could have easily invaded the US. "The Japanese-American internees might then have met with the same fate as Jews in Hitler's Europe: extermination."

Unfortunately, the type of firearm that is most effective in warding off genocide is the one under heaviest attack in the US. So-called assault rifles, or military-style guns, are in hot water these days. The authors cite statistics showing that these types of guns are almost never used by criminals, even though crime is used as the excuse to ban them. For example, according to the Chicago Police Department's own Murder Analysis Report: "Between 1965 and end-1992 — 28 years — 21,204 persons were murdered in Chicago. Of these murders, 387 — 1.8% of the total — involved abuse of a rifle... No more than 9 of these 21,204 murders (0.04244%, four-hundredths of one percent) involved rifles that — by bullet size — could have been military type rifles."

Lethal Laws also looks at the non-lethality of military-style ammo compared to hunting ammo, why Japan should not be used as a case for gun control, how the media promotes gun control, and more topics.

Jews for the Preservation of Firearms Ownership; $28.95 postpaid
1994; oversized softcover with plastic-comb binding; 347 pp
0-9642304-0-2

THE FOURTH AMENDMENT

Freedom from unwarranted Search and Seizure

F.E.A.R. CHRONICLES

F.E.A.R. is an acronym for Forfeiture Endangers American Rights. If you don't know about the travesty of property forfeiture, read the review of *Forfeiting Our Property Rights* [below] to familiarise yourself with this government-run form of theft. *F.E.A.R. Chronicles* is a newsletter that keeps you apprised of property seizures and the battle against them. Be prepared to see red.

Case in point: In February 1986, a small plane crashed a mile outside a 4000-acre family ranch in Florida. Because of this, the feds seized the ranch, valued at $6 million. The government claimed that, while no drugs were found in the plane's wreckage, they did recover grommets that "were similar to those of duffel bags used by dealers to pack drugs." Therefore, in a telepathic piece of detective work, they concluded that the plane was carrying drugs and that it was headed to the ranch when it crashed. The ranch's owners and employees were never charged with any crimes. In May of 1994 the ranch was finally returned to its owners, but the family will not be reimbursed for the $700,000 they've spent on legal fees.

But all is not lost, because there are occasional indications that the tide is turning. The best news is that the Ninth Circuit Court has ruled that forfeiting a person's property because of a crime and then convicting that person for the same crime constitutes double jeopardy. In 1984, the Supreme Court had ruled the opposite way, but in 1994 the court implied that forfeiture and conviction for the same crime is unconstitutional. In 1995 the Circuit Court made this fact explicit. Some inmates who had their property taken from them have already been released from jail.

F.E.A.R. Chronicles is an important resource in the fight against a police-state tactic that has become commonplace in the United States.

F.E.A.R./PO Box 1542/Washington DC 20003
WWW: www.fear.org/
Four issue sub: part of $35 annual membership dues

FORFEITING OUR PROPERTY RIGHTS
Is *Your* Property Safe from Seizure?
by Representative Henry Hyde

Believe it or not, federal, state, and local law enforcement officials can take your property away from you on a whim. You don't have to be guilty of a crime — you don't even have to be charged with a crime. The officers just have to say that they have probable cause to believe that your cars, house, boat, money, business, or other possessions were used in or resulted from an illegal action, usually (but not always) of a drug-related nature. Once your property has been stripped from you on the spot without even the illusion of due process, the ones who end up with your property are the officials who took it. If you want it back, you must initiate legal proceedings in which the burden is for you to prove that you're not guilty. What makes these legal actions even harder is that without transportation, a house, or a bank account, it's kind of tough to wage a legal battle. Plus, you cannot get a court-appointed attorney, you only have ten or twenty days to file a claim for a federal seizure, and you must post a cash bond worth 10% of the seized property.

This sickening state of affairs is caused by civil forfeiture law. It blatantly deprives people of due process, trial by jury, the presumption of innocence, protection against warrantless search and seizure, the right to private property, and other basic Constitutional and human rights. This book reveals the whole sorry affair. It's written by Representative Henry Hyde (R-IL), who — as the Chair of the House Judiciary Committee — is actually in a position to do something about it.

He rails against the injustices that occur in the name of these laws. Asset forfeiture targets minorities, especially African Americans and Hispanics, to a much higher degree. The "probable cause" needed to permanently take your property from you is the same flimsy probable cause that is needed simply to get a search warrant. "Often 'probable cause' is mere rumour, gossip, a police hunch, or self-serving statements from anonymous paid police informants, from criminals co-operating in order to obtain a lighter sentence on pending charges, or from incarcerated convicts trying to shorten an existing jail term." There is usually no crime involved. "In more than *80 percent* of asset forfeiture cases the property owner is *not even charged with a crime*, yet the government officials can and usually do keep the seized property" (emphasis mine). Since the department that does the seizing gets to keep the property, this has resulted in wholesale greed as officials use the laws as an excuse to fill their coffers.

How widespread is this forfeiture? Here are some stats. Cash value of forfeitures made by the Justice Department between 1985 and 1993: over $3.2 billion. Total for 1993 alone: $556 million. Number of forfeited properties the Justice Dept owned in 1993: 27,000. Estimated value: $2.9 billion. On top of that, a figure in the billions of dollars' worth of goods taken by other federal departments and state and local officials.

Hyde presents a cataloguing of outrageous actions that our government has performed:

- Hotels have been seized because gang members used some of the rooms for drug transactions.
- Interstate 95, Volusia County, FL: The Sheriff's Department stops any motorist who fits a "drug courier profile". If the motorist is carrying over $100 in cash, the excess money is taken on the spot.
- Washington, DC: Police seize the cars of men accused of soliciting prostitutes.
- Boston, MA, 1988: An investigation reveals that members of the Drug Control Unit "routinely fabricated the existence of informants and lied to obtain warrants from judges".
- Jacksonville, FL, 1989: The Customs Service storms a new $24,000 sailboat looking for drugs (they didn't find any). "In the seven-hour rampage, the boat was damaged beyond repair. Using axes, power drills, and crowbars, agents dismantled the engine, ruptured the fuel tank, and drilled more than 30 holes in the hull, half of them below the waterline." Do you think they compensated the owner?
- Malibu, CA, 1992: 30 local, state, and federal agents burst into a millionaire's home. When he tries to defend his wife with a handgun, he is killed. The drug allegations against him are found to be false. Evidence is uncovered that officials were quite interested in seizing his 200-acre estate.

Hyde shows how we got into this mess. The laws are based on a quaint notion that property can have innocence or guilt, which began in the Old Testament, then passed through Medieval law, and into our hysterical War on Some Drugs. He shows how forfeiture has been used to line pockets not only of government and police departments, but also of individuals.

In the last two chapters — which you may have trouble reading because by this time you'll be so mad you won't be able to see straight — Hyde discusses what must be done and what is being done to tame civil asset forfeiture laws and try to patch up a shredded Constitution. His ideas consist of shifting the burden of proof, toughening probable cause, strengthening the "innocent-owner" defence, restricting how seized property is used, easing the process of fighting forfeiture, and more. Hyde doesn't propose getting rid of forfeiture altogether. He wants it to return to its original mission of relieving drug kingpins of their ill-gotten booty.

Consider this one of the essential books in this chapter.

Cato Institute; $8.95

1995; softcover; 100 pp

1-882577-19-1

SEARCH, SEIZURE, AND PRIVACY

by Darien A. McWhirter

Search, Seizure, and Privacy is part of the *Exploring the Constitution* series of college textbooks [see *Freedom of Speech, Press, and Assembly* above], and, as such, it is imminently readable and understandable. This volume covers the Fourth Amendment — both the search and seizure that it specifically limits and the privacy that it seems to imply. It's a tough and tangled lesson. "In no other area of constitutional law has the Court been faced with such terrible decisions: enforce the Fourth Amendment and a murderer goes free; don't enforce it and the Bill of Rights becomes meaningless." The Supreme Court has issued confusing, vague, and contradictory decisions in these matters.

Like the other books in the series, each chapter examines Supreme Court cases on a variety of related issues, and then reprints large portions of significant rulings. Among the search and seizure topics covered: open fields, curtilage (area immediately surrounding a house), garbage, homes, businesses, cars, baggage in cars, arrest warrants and searches, arrest in a public place, hot pursuit, stop and frisk, searches in schools, warrantless arrests, probable cause, exceptions to the warrant requirement, and the exclusionary rule (which says that unconstitutionally-seized evidence is inadmissible). Privacy issues that don't directly involve search and seizure are covered much less fully. Basically, wiretaps, abortions, and the general expectation of privacy are the only subjects discussed. The back of the book contains a glossary of legal terms, further reading, the US Constitution, and a listing of the Justices of the Supreme Court.

What shocked me about this book is how it ignores the rampant property seizure that is occurring today. After reading it, you still wouldn't know that law enforcement agents from all levels of government are taking billions of dollars' worth of property away from people without a trial and, in many cases, without ever filing charges. I know that this textbook series is objective, so I don't expect the author to raise a hue and cry, but I can't understand how he could not cover such a crucial topic, especially in the chapter "The Fourth Amendment Today". This is a serious drawback to an otherwise worthwhile book.

Oryx Press; $29.95

1994; hardcover; 190 pp
0-89774-854-9

SURVIVING THE SECOND CIVIL WAR
The Land Rights Battle... and How to Win It
by Timothy Robert Walters

Lately, a battle that once was waged quietly has become more widespread and worrisome. People who own their own property have been involved in an escalating war with the government and other entities that want to dictate how they can and cannot use their property. In his foreword, Arizona Governor Fife Symington makes clear the importance of property. "To say that property is the cornerstone of liberty comes up short. I would say that property *is* liberty. I believe that with all my heart and soul. You start fooling around with private property rights and you are on the road to slavery."

Who are the ones fooling around with people's right to do what they want with their own land? "The assault on property rights is coming from many fronts — politicians, federal agencies, regulation-obsessed bureaucrats, elite and well-funded preservationist groups, independent agencies with government approval, the federal government itself. Legislators are enacting hundreds of new laws based on the agendas of well-financed special interest groups, powerful bureaucrats and noetic idealists." All kinds of people are affected by this trend. "Farmers cannot work their own land. Ranchers are being regulated out of business. Miners can no longer explore the earth for minerals and metals. Entire towns are dying because of lost timber sales." On top of that, regular homeowners are being kicked out of their houses because adjacent national parks want to expand. In some areas, people are not allowed to build add-on rooms for their own houses.

Ruby Henderson is an 80-year-old widow who still works her farm near Bixby, Oklahoma. In 1989 she was notified that the Soil Conservation Service Field Office located in Tulsa had decided that six acres of her farm were wetlands and that if she tampered with them in any way, she would lose all Federal farm programme benefits, including loans, crop insurance, and disaster payments. Henderson protested that for 30 years those acres had been workable, grazeable land, but two years ago a bunch of beavers (who had been introduced to the area by another government agency) had dammed up a drainage ditch, causing the land to flood. She battled with the bureaucrats for two years without a lawyer, and — as of this book's publication — is no nearer a resolution than she ever was.

The author relates many other horror stories, taking care to show who's behind them and why they occurred. Sometimes the reasons are greed-based, which is often why government agencies take people's land; sometimes they're egotistical, as with many bureaucrats who think they have a licence to ride roughshod over people's rights; and sometimes they're well-intentioned, as in the case of conservationists who believe that nature is sacred and must be completely protected in every case no matter what the cost.

Among the other campaigns the author covers are the efforts to eject everyone from federally-controlled lands, to kick people off of government-managed lands, to expel everyone from Western rangelands, to take all forest area out of private hands by whatever means necessary, and to create a centralised international government. The book ends with a look at what is being done to fight the assault on property rights and some signs that there is hope.

Rawhide Western Publishing; $12.95
1994; softcover; 190 pp
0-9641935-0-7

TAXATION

HOW TO BEAT THE IRS AT ITS OWN GAME
Strategies to Avoid — and Survive — an Audit
by Amir D. Aczel, PhD

Dr. Amir Aczel is a mathematician and statistician who was subjected to a lengthy and decidedly uncivilised tax audit. Aczel found out that the IRS uses statistics to decide which of the almost one million taxpayers it will audit annually. This formula is one of the most closely-guarded secrets in all of government. Aczel cracked it.

By contacting associates, CPAs, accounting organisations, and others, he got his hands on 1289 tax returns, almost half of which had triggered an audit. He analysed the returns using an artificial-intelligence algorithm on a Cray-2 supercomputer, a method that is about fifteen years more advanced than what the IRS uses. After easily cracking the code, Aczel tested his formula on other tax returns and found that he could predict with over 90% accuracy which ones would and would not get audited. In this book, he reveals what the formula is and how to apply it to your situation.

One of the general pieces of advice Aczel gives is to file your return late. If you file the correct form with the IRS, you will automatically receive an extension till August 15. You can even get a second extension, to October 15, but this must be accompanied by a reason and approved by an IRS official. Your taxes will still be due April 15, so you must send in a cheque of your estimated amount, but you'll have several months to file the return itself. Of the 73 late returns that Aczel examined, twelve of them were likely to trigger an audit, yet none of them did.

The more specific variables that affect your likelihood of getting called on the carpet are all ratios. For example, the ratio of your Adjusted Gross Income to your Total Itemised Deductions will be scrutinised. If your deductions total 44% or more of your gross income, the IRS computer will definitely tag you for an audit. (All returns that are tagged by the computer will be looked at by a human classifier who makes the final decision to audit or not.) If your ratio is between 35% and 43%, you're still rolling the dice. If it's less than 35%, you're pretty safe.

Should you get audited, this book will also come in handy. Aczel spends a lot of time giving unfettered, knee-to-the-groin advice on how to handle one of life's most unpleasant situations. You can psych out auditors, delay as long as possible, not grant them extensions, refuse to cut deals, appeal their decision, and much more.

At last, there is a book that levels the playing field by telling us what the Taxman looks for when he tries to burn us. There isn't a single taxpayer who wouldn't benefit greatly from reading this book.

Four Walls Eight Windows; $10.95
1994; small softcover; 144 pp
illus; 1-56858-048-7

IRS HUMBUG
by Frank Kowalik

Like *Vulture in Eagle's Clothing* [below] and *The Federal Mafia* [*Outposts* p 12], *IRS Humbug* states that most people in the United States technically do not have to pay income tax. "You are controlled by false belief when you believe you are a 'taxpayer' under the Internal Revenue Code. You are also controlled by false belief when you believe that the IRS employees have authority to control you and your income. Their authority extends only to the return of the US Government income in the possession of persons who are effectively connected with it."

The book's position is that basically everything you (and your accountant and your tax preparer) know about federal income tax is wrong. The true legal definitions of "taxpayer", "income", "withholding", "individual", "return", etc. have all been universally misinterpreted. Frank Kowalik attempts to set the record straight. He does so in a very detailed, deliberate manner. Needless to say, it's a pretty heavy course of study.

The whole crux of the matter is that income tax only applies to employees of the federal government. A federal employee's employment agreement declares that all income that emanates from the US Treasury is taxable. Therefore, any money that comes from employment in the private sector, from interest earned on savings accounts, or from a huge variety of other sources cannot be taxed by the federal government.

One of the big problems is that the Internal Revenue Code contains one unconstitutionally vague law after another. "The entire I.R. Code could be classified as vague based upon reports that IRS employees arrive at different conclusions when presented with the same set of facts and figures… When vague standards exist, and one does not understand his rights under the laws of the United States of America, his freedom of choice can be controlled by Federal Government employees."

Kowalik goes on to explain these and other principles in sections such as "Federal Income Tax Is a False Belief; It Is a Kickback", "US Judges, The Original Tax Protesters", "Sales Tax on Necessities Is Prohibited", "IRS Forms Are Voluntary", "Private Sector Employees Are Not Part of I.R. Code", "'Individual' Is Defined As a Federal Government Employee", "False Charges and Malicious Prosecutions Establish Fear of IRS", and many others. Like many people who refuse to pay taxes, Kowalik has landed in jail. He gives the full story in several chapters.

Kowalik also offers an eight-cassette tape recording of his seminar, in which he gives much more detailed information about the true nature of income tax. It comes with a thick comb-bound companion book that offers hundreds of pages of Internal Revenue Codes, IRS documents, United States Codes, court decisions, and more documentation backing up Kowalik's assertions. Write for details.

Frank Kowalik; $29.95
1991; hardcover; 356 pp
0-9626552-0-1

VULTURES IN EAGLE'S CLOTHING
by Lynne Meredith

This book is one of the foremost of its kind. It tells you how to legally (allegedly) stop paying federal income tax. Entering into this kind of action is a very risky business. It's like walking in a mine field — one false move and you're done for. If you decide to go for it, you must learn as much as you can and be prepared for the possibility of a lengthy battle that you may lose.

Vulture in Eagle's Clothing is based on the idea that paying income tax is voluntary for most people. You see, there's an obscure clause in the tax code that says some items are exempt from taxation and may be excluded from gross income. Among these items is any income which, under the Constitution, is not taxable by the federal government. The Supreme Court has ruled that all compensation (i.e., money) received by a citizen of the 50 states who is "exercising his or her fundamental Right to Labour in a common, lawful occupation" is not taxable income.

Interestingly, the IRS codes themselves never define income. The Supreme Court has defined income, however, in several still-standing decisions. Income "is only **gains and profits** severed from capital." Salary, wages, tips, etc. are equivalent compensation for labour and thus are not income in the taxable sense.

I'm trying to simplify this as best I can, but as you can imagine, it gets pretty complicated. Since all legalities are nothing but made-up abstractions, things become quite arcane very fast. *Vulture* is filled with talk of non-resident aliens, sovereign citizens, the Federal Reserve, the monetary system, Codes of Federal Regulation, and much more.

The author offers plenty of Supreme Court decisions, federal statutes, and IRS code to support the claims being made. Throughout the book there are many reproductions of letters sent to the IRS by citizens carefully stating why they are not obligated to pay taxes. Amazingly, there are also reproductions of letters from the IRS informing these people that "we agree that you aren't legally required to file a tax return for the above tax period(s)." In the back of the book, the author includes eleven forms exempting you from withholding, declaring your sovereign citizenship, etc.

The IRS is really a mouse that roars. It intimidates people into obeying, when it truly doesn't have a leg to stand on (although it does have a damn big gun). As former IRS Officer Jack W. Wade has said: "The Tax Code represents the genius of legal fiction... The IRS has never really known why people pay income taxes... The IRS encourages voluntary compliance through fear."

We the People; $39.95
1994; oversized softcover; 260 pp
0-9645192-6-7

PRIVACY

ASSET PROTECTION SECRETS
The Ultimate Guide to Total Financial Security
by Arnold S. Goldstein, LLM, PhD

In this huge book, attorney and professor Arnold Goldstein reveals over 230 ways to legally hide and/or shield your assets — home, money, business, vehicles, etc. — from creditors, divorces, lawsuits, and other ways you could lose your shirt. There are all kinds of tricks for automatically shielding assets, doing asset transfers that can't be contested, using a corporation to protect wealth, gaining total financial security through a limited partnership, using asset protection trusts, building wealth invisibly, using bankruptcy to keep your assets and ditch your debts, keeping the IRS away from assets, stopping foreclosures and repossessions, making your business untouchable, and much more.

Secret #40 reveals that there are laws that exempt part of your income from creditors. "Under the federal wage exemption established by the Consumer Credit Protection Act (CCPA), a creditor may not garnish more than the lesser of: (1) 25 percent of your disposable income, per week, or (2) the amount by which the disposable income earnings for the week exceeds 30 times the federal minimum hourly wage then in effect." Florida and Texas have completely outlawed all wage garnishment. However, because of federal law, limitations of garnishment do not apply in cases of child support or alimony.

The book's final sections contain a glossary, assets exempt from seizure under bankruptcy (federal and state guidelines), and a resources section.

Garrett Publishing; $29.95
1993; oversized softcover; 332 pp
1-880539-004

THE ELECTRONIC PRIVACY PAPERS
Documents on the Battle for Privacy in the Age of Surveillance
by Bruce Schneier & David Banisar

Privacy experts/advocates Bruce Schneier, who upset the National Security Agency (NSA) by writing the DIY manual *Applied Cryptography* [*Outposts* p 20], and David Banisar, an attorney for the Electronic Privacy Information Centre (EPIC), have assembled this humongous collection of documents regarding recent issues in electronic privacy. Government reports, public laws, press statements, Executive Orders, speeches, memos, email, editorials, letters, and — best of all — previously-classified government documents all paint a picture of the US government's battle to seriously erode the privacy of citizens. Specifically, these 100 reprints cover the interrelated areas of digital telephony, wiretapping, the Clipper chip, and cryptography.

Since the telephone system has started moving from analogue to digital, the FBI and other agencies have become concerned about their ability to tap phones. They drafted legislation that requires the phone companies, when creating their new systems, to build in automatic wiretapping capabilities. The government will pay them $500 million for this inconvenience, because the FBI wants the capability to simultaneously tap one in every ten people. According to a report from the Administrative Office of the US Courts (reproduced in this book), the combined number of federal and state wiretaps in one year has never exceeded one thousand. Yet the Feds want to spend half a billion so they can be able to tap 25,000 people at same time. Some of the documents that deal with this issue are the text of the law itself (Communications Assistance for Law Enforcement Act of 1994), the House Judiciary Committee's Conference Report on the law, FBI Director Louis Freeh's "apocalyptic" speech before the American Law Institute, the FBI's cost-benefit analysis, a memo from Brent Scowcroft, a letter from the National Security Agency (NSA) to a freelance writer, and an editorial from the *New York Times*.

Similarly, the government has also tried to get people to use phones that powerfully encrypt communication, with one catch... there's a "key" to each phone that easily allows tapping. President Clinton has tried to push this technology — dubbed the Clipper chip — on manufacturers, who would then push it on the public. The "key" to each Clipper chip would be held in escrow by the government, natch. When this tactic was torpedoed, the next suggestion was that the keys be held by private entities. That failed, too, but the government apparently isn't ready to give up its efforts to have everybody in the US (and even the rest of the world) use a form of compromised encryption that provides the government with an automatic backdoor. Among the documents presented are the White House's "Announcement of the Clipper Adoption, Statement of the Press Secretary", the Justice Department report *Authorization Procedures for Release of Encryption Key Components in Conjunction with Intercepts Pursuant to Title III*, a technical factsheet for the Clipper chip, Clinton's Presidential Decision Directive 5 (which ordered adoption of the Clipper while the Prez was telling the public it was only being considered), a letter to the Attorney General from the Vice Admiral of the NSA, several National Security Council memos, the American Civil Liberty

Union's response to Clipper, and William Safire's column "Sink the Clipper Chip".

Digital telephony and the Clipper chip are just two parts of a wider war for control of cryptography. Several other parts of the book look at other issues, including export controls on strong cryptography and plans to require "key escrow" back-door entry into any form of communication that is encrypted, including video and software (such as email programmes, Pretty Good Privacy (PGP), etc.). Documents include Schneier's article "Electronic Speech — for Domestic Use Only", a CIA memo titled "Selected Foreign Trends in Tel-ecommunications Technology", "Letter to President Clinton on Export Controls" from the House of Representative Com-mittee on Foreign Affairs, "Options to Address Encryption Effects on Law Enforcement [censored]" from the NSA, and the text of the Anti-Electronic Racketeering Act of 1995, which wasn't passed.

Several documents provide some basic, general expla-nations of cryptography and the issues around it, including the editors' own excellent contribution, "The Field of Battle: An Overview". They also give background for every repro-duced document, explaining where it fits within this compli-cated puzzle.

While overall this book is too detailed, technical, and pricey to be considered by people who just want a popular-ised treatment of the subject, it is an absolutely essential collection of documents for anyone who wants to delve deep into current issues in privacy and cryptography. It will be re-ferred to for a long time to come.

John Wiley & Sons; $59.99
1997; hardcover; 750 pp
0-471-12297-1

ENCYCLOPEDIA OF CRYPTOLOGY
by David E. Newton

Cryptography — writing messages in code so that they aren't readily readable — has ancient origins, but it is more widely discussed now than ever, as the rise of the Internet and other information/communication technologies make it imperative that we have better ways to shield our privacy. As the ability to encrypt and decrypt moves out of the world of spooks and into the world at large, the publication of the *Encyclopedia of Cryptology* provides a welcome load of information about the subject.

Everything having to do with cryptography is covered, from the technical (the ADFGVX cipher, Diffie-Hellman key exchange, Freemasons' cipher, musical cryptography, RSA algorithm) to the political (National Security Agency, black chambers, information warfare, ULTRA) to the historical (Bat-tle of Midway, the Election of 1886, "The Gold Bug" by Edgar Allan Poe, the Rosetta Stone, Shakespeare ciphers) to im-portant personalities (Francis Bacon, Cypherpunks, French codebreaker Étienne Bazeries, theoretical cryptologist Lester Hill). Current real-world uses of cryptography are also ex-amined in entries on the Universal Product Code, electronic mail, personal identification numbers (PINs), and smart cards. Naturally, hot topics such as the Clipper chip and Pretty Good Privacy software are covered.

Amazingly, even the most technical cryptographic and mathematical subjects are made fairly understandable. For each entry on a particular type of code or cipher — polyalphabetic substitution, puncture cipher, Vigenere Square, etc. — the author not only lucidly explains how it works but also gives at least one example.

As with every reference work on a specific subject, there are some holes (not listing the exposé *The Puzzle Palace* in the "further reading" section of the National Security Agency entry is like discussing famous paintings of smiling women without mentioning the *Mona Lisa*), but I won't quibble. The *Encyclopedia of Cryptology* has gathered too much valu-able information in one place to be damaged by inevitable oversights.

ABC-CLIO; $60
1997; hardcover; 333 pp
illus; 0-87436-772-7

MIND YOUR OWN BUSINESS
The Battle for Personal Privacy
by Gini Graham Scott

The vast majority of people will never have to wage a battle to say what they want to say or to get a fair trial. However, the issue of privacy affects everyone in the world. Many things make the effort to maintain one's privacy one of the central personal struggles of the present day. Because of "new information-age technologies, threats of crime and un-checked immigration in a society experiencing an uncertain transforming economy, computerised marketing and sophis-ticated polling methods to a target market, concerns about threatening diseases, family members trying to evade re-sponsibilities, an increasingly intrusive media racing to re-veal secrets about celebrities and soon-to-be celebrities," and other developments, your right to be left alone is being attacked on numerous fronts.

Gini Graham Scott traces the battle for privacy from the 1850s, when America became urbanised and the modern printed news media came into being. She believes that the first major battle over privacy was fought in the early 1960s to get access to contraceptives and contraception informa-tion. The Supreme Court ruled that the many state laws ban-ning such access were unconstitutional. "The Court deci-sion was an extremely important one in establishing a fun-damental right to make these kinds of personal choices re-garding private areas of one's life."

Today, the battle has reached insane proportions. Your employer gives you psychological tests, watches you with video cameras, reads your email on company computers, and demands the right to examine your urine. On top of that, "new computer software programmes, such as PC-Sentry, Direct Access, and Peek and Spy monitor every word and keystroke command that crosses the computer screen, not-ing the time and date when different activities occur. They not only record how long a computer was used, what files were accessed, and typing speed, but even the length of the user's bathroom breaks."

On other fronts, roadblocks require every driver to be examined by police. Your garbage can legally be taken and examined by anyone. If authorities accidentally mention the name of a rape victim, newspapers can print it. If you're gay or lesbian, the media is basically free to publicise your sexuality. All kinds of individuals and organisations have access to your financial records.

Scott discusses all of the issues and more, including searches of homes, sexual harassment, wiretaps and bugs, parody, naming people who have AIDS, national ID cards, cameras in the courtroom, students' rights, gossip, caller ID, nude photos of ex-spouses, and keeping assets private. For each one, she discusses laws, court cases, and/or specific occurrences that document the often ambiguous or contradictory status of privacy. *Mind Your Own Business* is so comprehensive and fact-filled that it's hard to think of an appropriate area or subject that it doesn't cover.

Insight Books (Plenum Publishing Corporation); $26.95
1995; hardcover; 394 pp
0-306-44944-7

PGP
Pretty Good Privacy
by Simson Garfinkel

The programme Pretty Good Privacy (more often called PGP) brought encryption to the masses. And not just any encryption — messages encoded with PGP cannot be broken even by governments. Needless to say, the government is not at all happy with this software. Also needless to say, you need to get it if you have electronic files that you want protected. PGP will not only guarantee that your information is not read by anyone who isn't supposed to read it, it also makes sure that no one can tamper with your information, and it provides verification of the sender of a document.

PGP was created by Phil Zimmermann, a computer scientist who has become a privacy hero and outlaw. Because of Zimmerman's anti-government stance, he believes that everybody should have access to unbreakable cryptography. By 1991 he had developed PGP, which used an encryption algorithm called RSA that was patented by another party. A battle ensued, and sparing you the many details offered in this book, it was eventually ended to everyone's mutual satisfaction. Zimmerman had PGP almost ready for release when the US Senate was considering Anti-Crime Bill S.266, a section of which called for the outlawing of unbreakable cryptography. Knowing that the government might make PGP illegal, Zimmermann hastily released PGP as freeware. He gave it to a friend, who posted it to the Internet. It wasn't long before people all over the world had copies, which has created large headaches for the program's creator. US law forbids the export of anything but pitifully weak encryption software. The feds have accused Zimmerman of exporting PGP and have been working hard to bust him in a battle that was still going on when this book was published. (In early 1996, the government suddenly dropped all charges against Zimmerman with no comment.)

PGP uses a system known as public-key cryptography. When someone wants to send you something that's encoded, she'll get your public key from you and attach it to the file. That file can only be opened by your private key (guard it with your life), which will recognise your unique public key and unscramble the information.

This book gives you all the knowledge you need to successfully use PGP. For background, there are chapters on the basics of cryptography, the history of cryptography and PGP, and current privacy issues. The rest of the book discusses getting PGP (commercial and freeware versions), installing it, protecting files and email, using digital signatures, configuring PGP, and creating, managing, distributing, and disabling keys.

Even if your files and email don't contain information that could cause the collapse of the free world, it's still a good idea to use PGP. After all, you use envelopes to send even non-crucial letters. Why let anything you write be as naked and vulnerable as a postcard? This book is dated in many ways, but unfortunately, no other guides to using PGP have been published since 1995.

O'Reilly & Associates; $24.95
1995; softcover; 426 pp
1-56592-098-8

PRIVACY NEWSLETTER

Privacy Newsletter offers practical information for people wanting to protect their personal information and activities from the prying eyes of the government, bankers, telemarketers, hackers, the IRS, and other snoops. Their Sample Issue offers a smattering of short tips and longer articles on decoding your Social Security Number, gambling at casinos, playing lotteries and sweepstakes, not revealing your religion at job interviews, finding unknown phone numbers, dealing with caller ID, the benefits of mail drops, and more.

One article lays down the Ten Commandments of Privacy. The Second Commandment is, "Thou shall pay in cash whenever possible." Cash is the most private form of payment, money orders are next, followed by cheques, and lastly, credit cards. "The Bank Secrecy Act of 1970 requires banks to microfilm both sides of all your cheques, and this information is at the disposal of the Internal Revenue Service (IRS) and other governmental agencies..." Commandment Four advises: "Thou shalt use a paper shredder in thy daily life". The courts have decided that people don't have a reasonable expectation of privacy when it comes to their trash, so anyone can legally take whatever they want from your garbage.

With its accent less on privacy news and more on actual things you can do to cover yourself, the *Privacy Newsletter* is an important asset.

Privacy Newsletter/PO Box 8206/Philadelphia PA 19101-8206
Twelve issue sub (one year): $99. Non-US: $149.
Voice: 215-533-7373
Email: privacy@interramp.com
Payment: cash, ck, Visa, MC

PROTECT YOUR PRIVACY ON THE INTERNET
Privacy Defense Tools and Techniques You Can Use Right Now

by Bryan Pfaffenberger

Although it seems that you are anonymous while using the Internet, the fact is that every time you log on, you are leaving all kinds of electronic trails on your own computer, on your service provider's computer, and on the Webservers hosting the sites you visit. Posting to the Usenet, sending email, and creating a Webpage can also cause privacy problems. To top it all off, even if you're not on the Net — even if you don't own a computer — some of your personal information is probably listed in databases that are searchable on the Web.

Protecting Your Privacy on the Internet provides loads of clear information on the specific ways in which info about you can be and is being gathered from your Net surfing, then explains relatively simple things you can do to combat these problems. There are no ways to become completely anonymous and private in every aspect of Internet usage, and the author makes clear what his techniques will and won't do. Included with this book is a CD-ROM of Windows freeware and shareware to help you out.

One crucial area to investigate is the privacy policy of your Internet service provider (ISP), the company that you call in order to tie into the Net. Some ISPs actually keep track of the Websites you visit and the parties you email. They then create marketing analyses of their customers and sell these to third parties. Other ISPs keep copies of email you've received, even after you've retrieved it. Find out what your ISP's policies are. And if you log on from your system at work, the author flatly states: "You have no privacy at all."

Another chapter deals with cookies, which are small files that are written to your hard drive, almost always without your permission. When you visit a Website that uses cookies, the host computer puts this little file into your computer, enabling the site to track exactly which pages within the site you look at and, often, identifying you as a returning visitor when you come back. If you've done any Websurfing at all, I guarantee that you have cookies on your hard drive. The author explains how cookies work, why they're used, the benefits they provide, the ways they invade privacy, and what you can do to fight them (which is definitely an uphill battle).

Your own computer is also a big threat to your privacy. Co-workers, family members, roommates, significant others, and — in some situations — law enforcement officials all have the potential to find out things about you that you may not want them to know. Many of the chapters that relate to securing your computer contain great advice that applies to everything on your computer, not just Net-related stuff. The author explains how to use the programmes on the CD-ROM to password protect some or all of your files and applications, encrypt files and directories, and make sure that files you delete are completely gone. (It's not a widely known fact that when you simply delete a file from your hard drive, it isn't really erased and can still be retrieved by knowledgeable people.) You'll also find steps for cleaning up the info your Internet browser keeps on you, such as the URL of every single Webpage you've ever visited, every word(s) you've entered in the search engines, credit card numbers you've uploaded to online merchants, the name of every

Usenet group you've visited along with information identifying each specific message you read, and lots more.

Other chapters cover the creation of "bulletproof" passwords, filling out online forms, creating homepages, the dangers of Web application languages (Java, JavaScript, and ActiveX), removing your personal info from Web-based databases, safeguarding children's Net surfing, using a cookieless browser (included on the CD-ROM), posting and emailing anonymously, and encrypting email.

There are few points, large and small, that the author fails to make. For example, he doesn't mention the Internet function known as "fingering". Using a simple programme (several of which are freely available on the Net) or a Web-based utility, you can finger someone (no giggling please) with just their email address and, often times, find out their full name, when they last logged on to the Net, if they have new email, and when they last checked their email. Some ISPs won't accept finger requests, some allow you to decide what will be shown during a finger request, and others simply narc on you. It's worth checking to see how your ISP handles this.

Despite oversights such as this one, *Protect Your Privacy* does a remarkable job of lucidly explaining threats to your privacy and security and how to counter them. If you spend any time on the Net, especially the Web, you need this book.

John Wiley and Sons; $29.99
1997; oversized softcover and CD-ROM; 326 pp
illus; 0-471-18143-9

OVERVIEWS OF OUR VANISHING RIGHTS

THE LIBERTY CRISIS

by Bruce G. Siminoff

The Liberty Crisis presents a wide range of absurdities and atrocities regarding the government's hunger for power. Well over half the book is devoted to regulations that repress businesses, farmers, emergency medical, economic growth, etc., while the rest of the material examines the erosion of our individual rights. An example of the government's surrealistic over-regulation is the Agriculture Department's Nectarine Administrative Committee (N.A.C.). "The N.A.C. developed a colour matching system consisting of fourteen shades. In order for a grower to sell a nectarine legally, he must match it to a U.S.D.A. colour card. The colour match is unrelated to the nectarine's taste, desirability, or marketability. Further, and more importantly, it has no relation to consumer health or safety." Because it couldn't ship nectarines until they had been colour-matched, one company lost a fortune after its peaches became overripe. Also, because this company makes a strain of peach that isn't as yellow as most peaches, it was forced to throw away almost a million peaches in 1990.

Fear of open-ended liability that lasts for decades has brought innovations in light, single-engine aircraft to an almost complete standstill. Potential developers and manufacturers are simply too terrified of never-ending lawsuits to bring anything to the market.

The Superfund that Congress established to clean up toxic sites all over the country has turned into a nightmare. For one thing, if a bank lends money to a business that illegally pollutes, the bank can be held liable for cleanup costs. Likewise, many small businesses are being financially destroyed because of actions they had nothing to do with. For example, the Gilbert Spruance Company made paints and coatings for decades. It had a contract to have its waste removed by a waste disposal company. Unknown to the GS Company, this disposal company illegally dumped the waste during the 1960s and 1970s. Under Superfund, the EPA demanded that the GS Company had to pay for the cleanup, at a cost of $175,000 to $1,000,000 for each of the eleven sites where the disposal people had dumped its waste. The owners of GS Company fought in court but had to sell their business cheap because of legal costs.

On the free speech front, the author notes that John Gotti's lawyer was found guilty of contempt of court by a federal judge, a ruling that could land him in jail for six months and give him a fine of $5000. His "crime" was talking to reporters about the case before the trial began.

The book's "Liberty Index" uses charts to rate how well our rights are doing on a ten-point scale. The First Amendment rates an eight, the Second a six, and the Ninth ("rights retained by the people") is virtually dead, earning a two.

The Liberty Crisis is similar to *Lost Rights* [*Outposts* p 26], but it is not as detailed or wide-ranging as that book. Its focus definitely favours economic repression rather than personal repression.

Glenbridge Publishing; $24.95
1995; hardcover; 275 pp
0-944435-27-0

THE RAPE OF THE AMERICAN CONSTITUTION

by Chuck Shiver

In *The Rape of the American Constitution*, attorney Chuck Shiver angrily charges: "Our Constitution, the result of so many hard lessons in tyranny learned by Founders such as Madison, Hamilton, and Washington, has been weakened to a point where our liberties are more threatened now than they were in 1775 when the American Revolution broke out. In the 220 years since independence, our liberty has been almost completely stolen from us by our own government. It may already be too late to avert the Orwellian nightmare."

After giving a 50-page lesson on the origins of the Con-

Chronicling 220 years of violation.
The Rape of the American Constitution.

stitution and the plain-English meaning of the Bill of Rights, Shiver delves into 21 cases where the judicial, legislative, and/or executive branches of the government have violated our rights. The first disgraceful action to be covered is the Alien and Sedition Acts of 1798. In a tactic still being used over two centuries later, Congress invoked national security as the reason for passing flagrantly unconstitutional laws. The four laws were passed by the Federalist Party mainly as a way to destroy support for the Democratic-Republican Party. The worst of them was the Sedition Act, which "barred American citizens and others from saying, writing, or publishing any false, scandalous, or malicious statements against the US government, congress, or the president." Violation resulted in two years in jail and a $2000 fine. As if that weren't bad enough, "This law was never ruled unconstitutional by the courts, and never repealed." To make matters even worse, this law wasn't an isolated occurrence... many more laws have been passed that are based on the Sedition Act.

President Andrew Jackson's removal of Native Americans from east of the Mississippi was a decade-long campaign of shameful proportions. "Twelve major Indian nations were moved west. Countless numbers were murdered. The Cherokee Nation did not go without a fight. It was not the vicious head-scalping, savage massacre that the American media has always portrayed; it was a legal battle."

As you might guess from the book's title, Shiver is not pretending to be detached — he's a civil libertarian to the core. In the chapter on the great flag-burning flap of 1989-90, he counters the argument that the flag should be protected as a symbol of everyone who died to defend it by pointing out that in every war since the War of 1812, the US got involved because of paranoia over communism, the need to protect capitalist trading partners, and other less-than-noble reasons. "It must also be pointed out that it is the Constitution, not the flag, that is and should be the symbol of this nation. Presidents and soldiers take an oath, swearing allegiance to the Constitution, not the flag. The Constitution has given us our liberties and allowed this country to achieve greatness. It is much more important than a piece of cloth."

The other atrocities against freedom that the author covers include the treatment of the Confederacy ("secession is and always has been a legal right of an American state"), the politically-motivated impeachment of President Andrew Johnson, Japanese-American internment in 1942, McCarthyism, gun control, "the War on Drugs", roadblocks, the terror tactics of the IRS, music censorship, intrusive federal regulations, and more. *The Rape…* is an excellent book for those who want specific facts about how our rights have been flushed down the toilet for the past two centuries.

Loompanics Unlimited; $18.95
1995; softcover; 371 pp
illus; 1-55950-127-8

SHAKEDOWN
How the Government Screws You from A to Z
by James Bovard

When I reviewed *Lost Rights: The Destruction of American Liberty* by James Bovard in *Outposts* [p 26], I said that it was one of the most important books to come out in a long time. Filled with hundreds of cases of American governmental tyranny and fuelled by the author's righteous anger, it is a book that must be read. *Shakedown*, the sequel to *Lost Rights*, uses a different format, but is no less crucial.

This book is made up of short anecdotes covering the kinds of injustices that were first brought up in *Lost Rights*. Think of *Shakedown* as a companion piece to Bovard's first book. The chapters include "Asset Forfeiture: Hundreds of Thousands of Government Robbery Victims", "Deadheads: The DEA's War on Music Fans", "Entrapment: Destroying Lives for Cash Bonuses", "Medical Device Madness: Suffering for Bureaucrats' Convenience", "Police Brutality: A License to Maul", and "Zoning: The New American Dictatorship".

Bovard's anger and his ability to cut right to the bone are in full display. In the chapter on the amazing medicinal properties of marijuana, he writes: "Are you suffering from cancer, AIDS, multiple sclerosis, or epilepsy? Uncle Sam has an important message for you: Suffer." He goes on to relate the horror stories of people who used a harmless plant to ease their pain, such as Jimmie Montgomery of Oklahoma. Montgomery has severe scoliosis (a misalignment of the spine) and muscle spasms and has been paralysed for 23 years. He used marijuana to cope with the pain of these conditions, as well as his 27 operations. His home was raided, the cops found two ounces of pot and two pistols, and he was sentenced to life in prison.

Bovard also rails at governmental regulations and restrictions that put a chokehold on productivity and people's lives. He says that because of the northern spotted owl, the government shut down most of Washington, Oregon, and Northern California, forcing 100,000 people out of work, and doubling the cost of timber (which added an average of $5000 to the cost of a new home). The Food and Drug Administration's foot-dragging kills people who might otherwise have been saved: "One hundred fifty thousand heart attack victims may have lost their lives as a result of the FDA's delays in approving the emergency blood-clotting drug TPA."

The Americans with Disabilities Act is allowing almost anybody to sue on the grounds that they're disabled. Case in point: A police clerk was fired after missing too many workdays. She claimed the she was agoraphobic (afraid of public/social situations) and that "the police department was obliged to accommodate her fear of dealing with people."

In the chapter on handgun grabbing, Bovard relates that in 1992, BATF agents responded to bogus allegations by raiding the home of an Ohio couple. One of the agents slammed the pregnant wife, who was posing no threat, up against a wall, causing her to miscarry. A federal judge threw out all of the trumped-up allegations. The couple is suing the BATF.

Shakedown will piss you off to no end. Even if you haven't read *Lost Rights*, this slim book will convince you on its own that our government has gone totally and completely out of control.

Penguin; $7.95
1995; softcover; 132 pp
0140258191

HUMAN RIGHTS

BRITAIN'S SECRET SLAVES
An Investigation into the Plight of Overseas Domestic Workers
by Bridget Anderson

Founded in 1839, Anti-Slavery International is the world's oldest human rights organisation. Its main focus is exposing and eliminating all forms of slavery. The organisation estimates that there are currently 200 million slaves world-wide.

That includes the several thousand foreign domestic servants in Britain, who are really little more than slaves. Almost 92% report psychological abuse, over 33% physical abuse, and over 6% sexual abuse. Around 60% do not eat regularly, and somewhere over half don't have a bedroom or a bed. About 80% aren't paid regularly and/or as promised in their contracts. They work an average of over 17 hours a day, but fewer than 5% get any time off.

British laws actually help perpetuate this situation. Although "employers" are allowed to swap and sell their maids, the "employees" themselves cannot change employers. Their passports are valid only as long as they are working for the rich bastards whose name is on their paperwork. If they try to quit, they will be deported back to the extreme poverty of their home country, which is usually India, Sri Lanka, Nigeria, Morocco, the Philippines, or Sierra Leone.

Domestic slaves are usually lured into their jobs by false promises from agencies. These agencies sell them to well-to-do Britons or foreign dignitaries who visit Britain, bringing the help with them. Two Kuwaiti princesses, for example, lived in London for half the year. The way they treated their servants is not unusual: "They subjected these women to extreme cruelty, both physical and mental beatings, whether with a broomstick, a knotted electric flex or a horsewhip, were routine; [their servant] Laxmi's eyes were damaged when they threw a bunch of keys at her face; they yanked out two gold teeth. They told her that one of her four children had been killed in a motorcycle accident, and beat her when she broke down and cried. It was only years later that she discovered they had been lying."

The book also looks at the larger issue of domestic slavery in the European Community and examines how Hong Kong and Canada have handled similar problems.

Anti-Slavery International; £5.50
1993; softcover; 125 pp
illus; 0-900918-29-2

"DISAPPEARANCES" AND POLITICAL KILLINGS
Human Rights Crisis of the 1990s — A Manual for Action
by Amnesty International

The human rights group Amnesty International estimates that over the last twenty-five years more than one million people have been victims of "disappearances" and extrajudicial executions. An untold number of other people have been killed by groups that oppose a country's government. "A '**disappearance**' occurs whenever there is reason to believe that a person has been taken into custody by agents of the state, and the authorities deny that the victim is in custody, thus concealing his or her whereabouts and fate. **Extrajudicial executions** are unlawful and deliberate killings, carried out by order of a government or with its acquiescence. **Political killings** include both extrajudicial executions and **deliberate and arbitrary killings by armed opposition groups**." Victims may be a single individual or an entire segment of the population. They may be targeted for their political or religious beliefs, their ethnicity, their profession, or other reasons.

This book acts partly as a report on the problem and partly as a manual for action. The first six chapters each investigate killings and kidnappings in a country — Iraq, Sri Lanka, Colombia, Zimbabwe, Turkey, and Morocco. In Colombia paramilitary "death squads" — operating with the government's blessing — not only kill suspected members and sympathisers of guerrilla groups but also union leaders, teachers, lawyers, journalists, Indian leaders, and anyone

else who opposes the government in any way or who investigates human rights violations. "In the cities people branded as 'social undesirables', including homosexuals, prostitutes, minor drug peddlers and addicts, vagrants, 'street children', and the mentally retarded have also been killed."

The next two chapters look at how these various atrocities happen and how they violate accepted standards of international human rights. Then four chapters give specific steps for preventing atrocities, investigating them when they occur, and bringing the perpetrators to justice through criminal courts, civil courts, or the United Nations. Chapter Thirteen looks at the problem of killings by opposition groups, and the final chapter shows how groups, governments, and families of the dead and missing are trying to effect change. Nine appendices reproduce such documents as "Universal Declaration of Human Rights", "Geneva Conventions and Other Protocols", "Code of Conduct for Law Enforcement Officials", and "Amnesty International 14-Point Program for the Prevention of 'Disappearances'".

Amnesty International; $16.95
1994; softcover; 300 pp
0-939994-91-7

EDUCATION

DESCHOOLING OUR LIVES
edited by Matt Hern

An essential collection of classic and new material that condemns the contemporary school system and offers alternative visions of ways to foster intellectual growth, such as homeschooling, community learning networks, and democratic/free schools. Essays include "On Education" by Leo Tolstoy, "Instead of Education" by John Holt, "Sweet Land of Liberty" by Grace Llewellyn, "The Public School Nightmare: Why Fix a System Designed to Destroy Individual Thought?" by John Taylor Gatto, "Learning? Yes, Of Course. Education? No, Thanks.", "Homeschooling As a Single Parent", "Learning As a Lifestyle", and "A History of Albany Free School and Community". Ends with a list of books, periodicals, and organisations devoted to deschooling.

New Society Publishers; $14.95
1996; softcover; 156 pp
illus; 0-86571-342-1

DUMBING US DOWN
by John Taylor Gatto

John Gatto was a school teacher in New York City for twenty-six years, and during that time he taught everyone from the children of the elite to the children of the extremely poor. In 1991 he was named New York State Teacher of the Year. Ever since his acceptance speech, he's used his

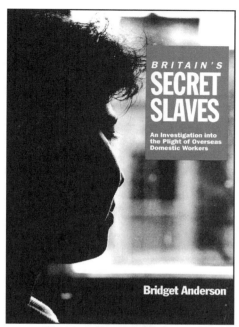

"Wage slavery" is not hyperbole for most of Britain's foreign maids. *Britain's Secret Slaves*.

new-found visibility to tell the ugly truth about the educational system (actually, Gatto refers to it as the schooling system, since the word "education" is a misnomer).

Gatto began noticing that even the most unlikely kids displayed flashes of genius, creativity, and wisdom in the classroom. This caused him to question his own role: "Was it possible I had been hired not to enlarge children's power, but to diminish it? That seemed crazy on the face of it, but slowly I began to realise that the bells and the confinement, the crazy sequences, the age-segregation, the lack of privacy, the constant surveillance, and all the rest of the national curriculum of schooling were designed exactly as if someone had set out to prevent children from learning how to think and act, to coax them into addiction and dependent behaviour." After this realisation he adopted a new philosophy towards teaching. He saw himself not as the all-knowing teacher who must stuff children's heads full of facts, but as someone who must break down the barriers that block children's natural intelligence and learning abilities. Naturally, his efforts ran into the brick wall of bureaucracy, and he quit public schools to practice his "unique guerrilla curriculum" at the Albany Free School.

Just before he resigned, he was named as NY's Teacher of the Year. His rebellious acceptance speech is one of the essays reprinted in *Dumbing Us Down*. I can just imagine the jaws hitting the floor as Gatto listed for his audience the seven universal lessons that are taught by all teachers:

1) Confusion. Teachers teach too many facts and not enough connections. They don't show the larger picture or how things work together.

2) Class position. Children are grouped into classes based on "intelligence" — special needs, average, or gifted — and that's where they stay.

3) Indifference. Teachers demand that students get highly involved in a lesson for fifty minutes, and when the bell rings, forget about it and go to the next class. "Indeed, the lesson of the bells is that no work is worth finishing, so why care too deeply about anything."

4) Emotional dependency. Teachers and higher authorities decide everything for students, from what they are allowed to say to who may use the bathroom.

5) Intellectual dependency. Teachers decide what will be taught and when and how it will be taught. "It is the most important lesson, that we must wait for other people, better trained than ourselves, to make the meanings of our lives."

6) Provisional self-esteem. Students are constantly judged and evaluated. Their feelings of self-worth depend on how an outsider rates them.

7) One can't hide. Students have no private time or private space. They are encouraged to snitch on each other. "I teach students that they are always watched, that each is under constant surveillance by myself and my colleagues."

Ingraining these seven lessons in children is the main reason that schools keep children in their clutches from ages five or six until seventeen or eighteen. According to Gatto, it only takes around 100 hours to teach the fundamentals of reading, writing, and arithmetic to people who are eager to learn. Textbooks from the 1850s were written at what we would consider college level. There's no legitimate excuse for keeping kids for twelve years.

Gatto sees many ways to radically restructure the schooling system so it becomes a truly educational system. First of all, he wants a return to the system that existed until the Civil War. "Some free market system in public schooling is the likeliest place to look for answers, a free market where family schools, and small entrepreneurial schools, and religious schools and craft schools and farm schools exist in profusion to compete with government education." Also, the kids have to experience self-education. Learning should take the form of students being left alone with a problem to solve. Another thing that must happen is for parents to get involved with their children's learning.

Gatto's message is loud and clear, and at times it even becomes somewhat shrill, but it's obvious that he is an insider telling the harsh truth about what is wrong with the system and what must be done quickly to save it.

New Society Publishers; $9.95
1992; softcover; 104 pp
0-86571-231-X

GENIUS TRIBE

Genius Tribe is a resource centre started by Grace Llewellyn for homeschoolers/unschoolers [see *The Teenage Liberation Handbook* below]. This catalogue contains 170 books and other items — mainly geared for older children/teenagers and adults — covering the arts, philosophy/religion, math, science, social sciences, writing and reading, myths, foreign language, travel, activism, work opportunities, children's liberation, John Holt's writings, breaking your own limits (e.g., *Jump Start Your Brain*, *Radical Honesty*), and much more. Most of the books aren't simply boring homeschool versions of schoolbooks, but interesting stuff like *A People's History of the United States* in the history section and *There Are No Electrons: Electronics for Earthlings* in the science section.

Genius Tribe/PO Box 1014/Eugene OR 97440-1014

Catalogue: free

GROWING WITHOUT SCHOOLING

A magazine for parents of homeschooled children. It covers all aspects of the subject, including legal issues, helping kids learn and grow, resources for homeschool families, and more.

Growing Without Schooling/2269 Massachusetts Ave/
Cambridge MA 02140
WWW: www.holtgws.com
Single issue: $6
Six issue sub (one year): $25. Non-US Surface Mail: $29. Non-US Airmail: $40

HOME EDUCATION MAGAZINE

Home Education Magazine covers a wide range of topics, such as what's wrong with the educational system, overcoming legal and financial obstacles, socialising kids, preparing them for life, giving homeschooling a positive image, starting to homeschool, homeschooling chronically ill or disabled children, helping children write and get published, teaching various subjects, and using PBS, the Internet, and other media resources.

Each issue has a lengthy "News Watch" section that talks about struggles, triumphs, setbacks, and other news concerning homeschooling. In-depth software, book, movie, and video reviews help parents find good and appropriate material. There's also an extensive list of groups and organisations and plenty of ads offering all kinds of helpful products and services.

Home Education offers a free catalogue that describes all their back issues, booklets, and seventeen books. It also includes a resource directory and two question and answer sections.

Home Education Press/PO Box 1587/Palmer AK 99645
Voice: 1-800-236-3278 (Visa, MC, Disc)
Email: HEM@home-ed-press.com
WWW: www.home-ed-press.com
Sample issue: $4.50
Six issue sub (one year): $24 ($20 for homeschoolers). Canada: add $15. Elsewhere Surface Mail: add $18

THE HOMESCHOOLING HANDBOOK

by Mary Griffith

If you have the time and other necessary resources, homeschooling is definitely the way to go. Don't let your kids enter the soul-deadening, ineffective, good-little-citizen factories known as public schools. Certain private schools can be better, but unless you know you're dealing with a radically different school that gets results, I wouldn't risk it.

A large and growing number of people agree. Homeschooling is on the rise. A lot of homeschooling is being done by Christians upset by secular humanism, sex ed, etc., and thus the movement as a whole is often seen as a Christian thing. This, however, is not the case. Many parents' decisions to teach at home are not based on strictly religious principles. Many simply want their kids to learn how to think and become knowledgeable human beings. Others don't want their kids exposed to whitewashed versions of history and social studies. Still other are afraid of school violence.

Whatever the reasons you've yanked your kids out of the system, *The Homeschooling Handbook* will definitely help you. This recent addition to the literature covers every aspect of the topic, from deciding if homeschooling is right for your family all the way to options once homeschooling is completed. Mary Griffith's two children have always been homeschooled and she is on the board of the Homeschool Association of California. She uses her own experiences, plus those of many other parents and children who are extensively quoted, to provide a non-romanticised view of homeschooling reality. "No matter how supportive your family and community, there will be days things don't go right, days when you think you were crazy to have even attempted homeschooling. Or sometimes you'll worry that things are actually going too well, too smoothly, so that you start to think there must be something you've missed, something important that you're not dealing with." Many parts of the book deal these and related problems by discussing local support groups, state and national organisations, conferences, newsletters, Internet support sources, "parental panic attacks", burnout, sibling wars, and kids changing their minds and wanting to go to school.

That kind of real world advice is likewise suffused throughout the rest of the book. The initial chapters examine the history of homeschooling, research showing how well it works, and deciding if you should take the plunge. Should you decide to go for it, you'll find out about the legalities of homeschooling, with sections on the states with the most stringent laws, and information on getting legal help, if a situation arises.

Griffith discusses the general ways to structure your teaching — with input from the theories of Jean Piaget, John Holt, Maria Montessori, and others — including school-at-home, unit studies, and unschooling (letting children lead the general direction of their education). Separate chapters look at specific issues involving children in their primary years, middle years, and teen years.

Further chapters involve finding learning resources ranging from textbooks to trips to local court, keeping records and evaluating your children's progress, dealing with sceptical family members, money matters, learning and physical disabilities, single parent homeschooling, college and other post-homeschool options, and more. The book is rounded out by extensive appendices with an annotated resources section, homeschool organisations in all 50 states, and suppliers of learning material.

Prima Publishing; $14
1997; softcover; 306 pp
0-7615-0192-4

REAL LIVES
Eleven Teenagers Who Don't Go To School
edited by Grace Llewellyn

OK, so you've taken Grace Llewellyn's advice in *The Teenage Liberation Handbook* [below] and have freed yourself from the intellectually and emotionally lethal confines of school. Now what? In *Real Lives*, Llewellyn presents essays by eleven kids — aged twelve to seventeen — who have dropped out and are getting a real education. They discuss what they do, why they do it, how they make friends, and how they are learning from their experiences.

Jeremiah Gingold is a sixteen-year-old who teaches himself English, math, science, social studies, and auto repair. He and his sister — an "unschooled" thirteen-year-old — publish the newsletter *Homeschoolers for Peace*. Belonging to the Boy Scouts (temporarily) fulfilled several of Gingold's needs, including an unexpected one. "Besides the obvious benefits of providing friends and a means of recognition, it gave me something to rebel against... I found that I actually enjoyed having something concrete and immediate to rebel against, after years of rebelling against 'the system' by homeschooling, protesting war, etc."

Amanda Bergson-Shilcock — another sixteen-year-old — works ten to twelve hours a week at the local library and is a senior member of the Devon Festival Ballet Company and a member of a violin quintet that has played at the White House. She also writes and is being mentored through the mail by the editor of *Growing Without Schooling*. In her essay, she refutes several myths of homeschooling, including the most common one — that homeschoolers never become socialised. She points out that, unlike kids who are stuck in school all day with other kids their own age, she has adult friends and younger friends, as well as friends around her age.

Other contributors to *Real Lives* go biking in South America, work at homeless shelters, tend honeybees, answer the phone at a crisis line, assist midwives during births, play sports, and much more. By their examples, they prove that there is plenty to do, study, and learn in the biggest classroom of all — the real world.

Lowry House Publishers; $14.95
1993; softcover; 318 pp
illus; 0-9629591-3-8

THE TEENAGE LIBERATION HANDBOOK
How to Quit School and Get a Real Life and Education
by Grace Llewellyn

OK, it's pretty well established that school is a boring, stifling waste of your life. But what can you do about it? According to former middle school teacher Grace Llewellyn, the first step is simple: quit. That's right... get out of that mental/physical/spiritual prison and start learning and living in a whole new free, dynamic way. "Did your guidance counsellor ever tell you to consider quitting school?... That legally you can find a way out of school, that once you're out you'll learn and grow better, faster, and more naturally than you ever did in school, that there are zillions of alternatives, that you can quit school and still go to A Good College and even have a Real Life in the Suburbs if you so desire? Just in case your counsellor never told you these things, I'm going to."

The *Handbook* is not about homeschooling in the sense of Mom and Dad teaching their teen in a structured, pseudo-academic setting. It's about what Llewellyn calls "unschooling" — letting kids get involved in real-world, open-ended activities that provide important life experiences. "This book wants you to quit school and do what you love."

Throughout the first six chapters, Llewellyn mercilessly trashes schools, telling in no uncertain terms what they really do and don't do, how they are the antithesis of freedom, and how they crush the wonderfully vibrant nature of adolescence. She doesn't drub on teachers too hard, knowing that they are basically unwitting accomplices in the choking of young people's love of life and learning. However, she flatly states: "Teachers sit in the teachers' lounge and laugh about you behind your backs."

Once you've decided to quit, you can use the advice on telling your parents, dealing with legal issues, having a social life, buying unschool supplies, and seeing adults as friends and equals. Part Three has lots of detailed information on learning "school subjects" — hard science, social science, math, English, foreign languages, and the arts — without school. You'll learn how to put libraries, museums, school resources, travel, and the outdoors to good use. An important chapter discusses getting into college without a diploma, and it's a lot more common and accepted than you might think.

Work is a very important part of self-education and, sooner or later, will become desirable or necessary to almost every teenager. Llewellyn discusses apprenticeships, internships, volunteering, entrepreneurship, farm work, and finding jobs that you love, like the unschooler who got a job at an exotic animal breeding compound.

The final section of the book examines the lives of several unschoolers, showing what real kids do with their lives when not constrained by the educational system. One chapter lists the many famous people who escaped most or all teenage schooling, among them: Jack London, Abraham Lincoln, Beatrix Potter, Ansel Adams, Keith Richards, and Whoopi Goldberg. Several appendices list books, magazines, organisations, and suppliers that can assist you in unschooling yourself.

In its ability to affect lives and bring about massive change for the better, *The Teenage Liberation Handbook* is one of the most important books reviewed in *Psychotropedia*. If you know a teenager who is depressed, angry, or bored, give this book to him or her. It could make the difference between being a self-actualised person and being just another cog in the machine.

Lowry House Publishers; $14.95
1991; oversized softcover; 402 pp
illus; 0-9629591-0-3

KIDS

AS SOON AS YOU'RE BORN THEY MAKE YOU FEEL SMALL
Self-Determination for Children
by anonymous

First published in England in 1986, this thin book has become a classic in the field of children's liberation. It's a strictly samizdat affair, with newspaper clippings, original text, and photos cut and pasted by hand and then xeroxed.

Under the section "Authority and Control", the author laments, "So it is that the parent-child relationshi[p [sic] is one of the few, if only, areas where authority is still considered to be 'natural' and not contractual. To give life to a new human being also confers considerable legal power over them. This is confirmed, both legally and socially, as being just and proper. Children are effectively their parents' possessions until they reach the majority." In the same section, we read: "Obedience is what is expected from children. In no other inter-human relationship is this assumption so uncontested. The 'good' child means the compliant and obliging one. Thus, virtue for children is linked to obedience rather than active qualities such as initiative or compassion."

As Soon As You're Born also rails against child abuse, corporal punishment, gender stereotypes, discriminatory language (i.e., "childish"), lack of money, state intervention, exclusion from work, harmful toys, school, and more. The final page reprints a couple of manifestos — "School Students Charter" and "Youth Liberation Program".

> available from AK Press; $2.50
> 1986; oversized softcover; 36 pp
> heavily illus; no ISBN

ESCAPE FROM CHILDHOOD
The Needs and Rights of Children
by John Holt

The name John Holt is virtually synonymous with alternative forms of education, particularly unschooling. This unorthodox educator wrote ten highly influential books (translated into 14 languages) and founded a magazine (*Growing Without Schooling*) covering how children learn, why the educational system is basically worthless, and how children should be taught. Because he is so influential and respected, it is somewhat surprising that he also penned the most radical, well-reasoned manifesto of children's liberation that I have ever read. This topic is extraordinarily controversial, but Holt jumps right in and takes no prisoners.

"… I have come to feel that the act of being a 'child,' of being wholly subservient and dependent, of being seen by older people as a mixture of expensive nuisance, slave, and super-pet, does most young people more harm than good. I propose instead that the rights, privileges, duties, responsibilities of adult citizens be made *available* to any young person, of whatever age, who wants to make use of them." Holt

believes that children of every age should be given the "right to do, in general, what any adult may legally do." This includes the rights to vote, to drive, to work for money, to direct their own education, to travel, to live away from home, to choose their guardians, to have sex, to take any drugs that are legal for adults, to be financially independent ("i.e., the right to own, buy, and sell property, to borrow money, establish credit, sign contracts, etc."), and to receive equal treatment under the law.

These proposals — besides being bone-jarringly revolutionary — may seem irresponsible at first glance, but Holt backs them up with level-headed ideas. For example, he thinks that a minor of any age should be allowed to drive, but only if he or she can pass driver's tests and continue to demonstrate the ability to drive responsibly. He's not suggesting handing an untrained eight-year-old the keys to the family car and saying, "Have at it!" Furthermore, he states that the requirements for *all* people to be allowed to drive should be significantly toughened. "My own belief is that tests for a driver's licence should be made harder, that people should have to take them more often, and that people should much more easily than now, and for a wider range of driving offences, lose their licences."

Holt also talks about issues relating to the family structure. "At its very best, the family can be what many people say it is, an island of acceptance and love in the midst of a harsh world. But too often within the family people take out on each other all the pain and frustrations of their lives that they don't dare take out on anyone else. Instead of a ready-made source of friends, it is too often a ready-made source of victims and enemies, the place where not the kindest but the cruellest words are spoken." But Holt is not for the eradication of the nuclear family; instead, he's for its expansion. The nuclear family is a historically recent development. He urges a return to the extended family, where children are in constant contact with young and old non-relatives and relatives who aren't part of the immediate family. He thinks that children should have adult friends, who don't necessarily have to be friends of the parents.

Some chapters covering other topics include "The Institution to Childhood", "On the Loss of Authority of the Old", "The Burden of Having Children", "How Children Exploit Cuteness", and "Love May Not Cure Everything". This is an extremely important book. If the kids of today don't get raised in a better way, how will this screwed-up world ever get any better?

> Holt Associates; $9.95
> 1974 (1995); paperback; 227 pp
> 0-913677-04

FREE THE KIDS!

This children's liberation newsletter has a narrower focus than *Kids Lib News* (below). It is entirely concerned with stopping physical, verbal, and emotional punishment/assaults on children. "No adult is legally required to accept being struck, slapped, confined or verbally humiliated by another. Yet we accept and even applaud these things being done to children — who, since they are small and cannot defend themselves, should be granted every legal and humanitarian protection against such treatment."

They offer plenty of letters and articles ranting against any form of negativity towards kids and proposing other ways of dealing with problems, including constructive praise, redirection, showing respect, and avoiding vague commands and requests. Adults write about how their parents' methods of child rearing affected them and how they are raising their own children. "It's the responsibility of all adults to stop the sacrifice of children's physical and psychological well-being to adult frustration, negativity and abusive conditioning. **There is no excuse for hitting a child.**"

Free the Kids!/PO Box 942/Rochester VT 05767-0942
Sample issue: $2
2 issue sub (one year): $10 or more donation. Also gets you on their list for other mailings and info.
Will be sent free to low-income or unemployed families.

KIDS LIB NEWS

This long-running, chaotically designed zine is dedicated to children's liberation and conscious/holistic parenting. There are many, many facets to their ideas for raising children in a free, loving, safe, and sane environment. Among the things they strive for:

- A drugless, healthy pregnancy
- Home delivery, natural childbirth, waterbirthing
- No Caesarian-sections, no premature cord-cutting
- No circumcision
- Breast-feeding
- Indoor and outdoor nudity for children
- No junk food, including sugar and meat
- Lots of time outdoors for kids
- No hyper-cleanliness
- No kiddie drugs, only natural cures
- No war toys or competitive games
- No threats, punishments, bribes, shame, or guilt
- The right for kids to express emotions, including crying and tantrums
- Total freedom of expression, through speech, art, etc.
- The right for kids to have privacy
- No stifling of bodily functions
- Lots of hugging, cuddling, and touching
- Natural sexploration
- Homeschooling
- Children's spiritual growth
- Teaching kids environmental responsibility
- Promoting peace and disarmament
- Kids attending births and deaths
- Living with an extended or communal family

Quite a tall order, but they believe that it will result in happier, well-adjusted kids, who should turn into happy, well-adjusted adults. I think it just might work. After all, it's pretty amazing when you realise how much your family life as a child has affected you. Who you are is almost completely based on your family life. No other factor even comes close. So, if we could just get parents to stop screwing up

their kids, we might have a better world.

The issue of *Kids Lib News* I saw had articles on Geo-toys, parent-child co-dependency, Rudolph Dreikurs' Individual Psychology, raising peaceful children, home schooling, achieving parent/child equality, why babies cry, play therapy, baby talk, babies sleeping in their parents' bed, reviews of books, and more. The drawback of this zine is that it is designed so manically, that sometimes I can't tell what's going on. And, unless I'm mistaken, some of the articles chop off before being finished.

Oness Press/PO Box 176/Kilawea HI 96754
Single issue: $4
One year sub (4 issues): $12

LICENSING PARENTS
Can We Prevent Child Abuse and Neglect?

by Jack C. Westman

The government requires licences for some of the most important aspects of our lives — driving, marriage, running a business. Yet there is absolutely no licence, training, or test of any kind required for the biggest responsibility of all — having a child. Just about anybody at anytime can pop out a kid, and — as you've probably noticed — just about anybody does. I've known parents who I wouldn't trust to care for my plants, yet they are in the position of raising another human being.

What can be done? Psychiatrist Jack Westman, who has worked with abused and neglected children for 30 years, has an idea. Require a licence for people to become parents. This would recognise children as full human beings, who have human and civil rights, including "the right to competent parenting." Such a plan would also benefit society. Westman discusses the public cost of bad parenting, including welfare dependency, homeless children, public health problems, a decline in national productivity, the costs of child protective agencies, and an overall erosion of quality of life in the US.

The author feels that just because you performed an act of sexual intercourse, you don't have the inalienable right to force a child to come into this world, treat him like shit, ruin his life, set him up for failure in adulthood, and clog the world with yet another maladjusted jerk. "The traditional mystique of biological parenthood needs to be placed in perspective, so that parenthood can be seen accurately, not as a state determined by conception and birth but as a relationship based on a parent-child affectionate bond with reciprocal obligations between parents and children. As adoptive parents well know, parenthood really is a relationship and is not simply a status awarded by conceiving or giving birth to a child." Once we accept this view, the idea of licensing parents make more sense. "It would designate parenthood as a privilege for which one is qualified rather than as a right that accompanies the event of childbirth."

In the chapter "A National Parenting Policy", Westman explains how his plan would work. People would need to apply for licences when they get married, when they decide to adopt, when unmarried people decide to have a child, during pregnancy, or at the birth of the child. To receive a licence, a person would have to meet three basic criteria — be at least eighteen years old, certify "that he or she agrees to care for and nurture the child and to refrain from abusing or neglecting the child", and complete a course in parenting. For people under eighteen, their parents must agree to assume parenting responsibilities. If parents violate the terms of the licence, the government might terminate parental rights. Or the parents might be put on a probationary period during which they would receive training while their child lives with foster parents. Should the parents be unwilling or unable to improve, their child will be taken from them. Similarly, an unlicenced woman who gives birth may be put on a probationary period, or she may just have her child taken from her for adoption.

Westlake realises there are many arguments against his plan, so he presents and rebuts all of them — the imposition of majority standards, violating the sacred parent-child relationship, fostering the blaming of parents, restricting the rights of adults to freedom of action, enforcing conformity in child rearing, objectionable prior restraint, the unfeasibility of administration, and several more.

Despite these intriguing arguments, this concept gives me the heebie jeebies. Children need to be helped, but letting anyone — especially that monstrosity known as the government — decide who can and who can't reproduce is fascist to the core. Still, when I see how all these losers treat their kids, the idea crosses my mind...

Insight Books (Plenum Publishing); $27.95
1994; hardcover; 347 pp
0-306-44766-5

HOBOES

Hoboes don't need a utopian community or a temporary autonomous zone to be free. They simply own what they can carry and ride freight trains all over North America and Mexico. In a way, they have the ultimate life — no mortgage, no spouse and kids, no crummy job, no insurance premiums to pay... Yeah, you say, but also no food, no shelter, no security. But to the true hobo that doesn't matter. To them, living a day-to-day existence is a small price to pay for being truly free.

Most hobos these days, however, do have homes, marriages, and children. They manage to ride the rails on a part-time basis, getting the best of both worlds.

AROUND THE JUNGLE FIRE
A Collection of Original
Hobo Poetry
edited by Oats

Hoboes, as a whole, express themselves primarily through poetry. *Around the Jungle Fire* collects 27 poems from as many hoboes, ranging from old timers who rode the rails during the Depression to the newest generation of train-hoppers. In "Wanderlust", Jungle Jene writes: "Hear the wind? The road is callin'./I gotta go and I won't be back./It ain't so bad, so just be glad/That we met along life's tracks."

Iowa Blackie describes the challenge of riding in a "Rumbling Boxcar": "I slip and slide from side to side/And even bouncing off the wall/Positions many I have tried/Including backward crabby sprawl". In "Love Those Hobo Men", Minneapolis Jewel sings the praises of her male counterparts: "I ain't got no man in my life/That's OK, 'cuz they cause too much strife./But I'll tell you what, I really do know/That I love those hobo men/'Cuz they come — then they go!"

The Hobo Press; $3
1994; staple-bound booklet; 44 pp
illus; no ISBN

HOBO TIMES
America's Journal of Wanderlust

Hobo Times is a glossy, full-colour magazine devoted to the hobo life and the love of railroads and trains. Most of the articles are written by actual 'Boes (see how fast I pick up on this subcultural slang?). They interview other 'Boes or reminisce about their own adventures, most of which seem to have taken place during the glory days of 'Boing, the 1930s.

Arvel "Sunshine" Pearson recalls skinny-dipping in a water tower when the Kansas wind blew his pants across a wheatfield. "Hearin' the train whistle a blowin' and the drivers a hummin', I took off a runnin'... my feet was bare, no clothes, not a stitch; through that fence and then stumbled in a ditch. Every time I would get close enough to grab my pants, the wind would do the St. Vitus' dance." Eventually Sunshine was able to grab his clothes and hop the train in the buff. (Volume 9 #3).

A news section of the magazine reports on line closings and openings, new crew change points, and the future of railroad companies. Another section features poetry by hoboes, and the events calendar is the only way to keep track of the surprisingly numerous 'Bo gatherings, conventions, and "hootenannies".

The National Hobo Association/PO Box 706/Nisswa MN 56468
Email: hobousa@uslink.net
WWW: www.hobo.org
one year sub (6 issues): included in membership dues of $21 for a year

HOPPING FREIGHT TRAINS
IN AMERICA
by Duffy Littlejohn

Whether you want to live the permanently transient life of a full-time hobo or you just want to get away from the rat race for a while, *Hopping Freight Trains in America* will show you how to ride the rails. The book's author, Duffy Littlejohn, is a lawyer with wanderlust who's hopped trains all over the US, Canada, Mexico, and France. After logging hundreds of thousands of miles, he's sharing his knowledge and wisdom with us. With the numerous details and advice Littlejohn offers, you'll be as prepared as possible to sneak aboard any train.

"Riding the rails is the last pure red-blooded adventure in North America." It's dangerous, it's illegal, and it lets you "beat the system in every way." Most importantly, it's fun. Littlejohn divides the book into chapters that each deal with an essential aspect of train-hopping. Among the questions that are answered at length:

☞ What should I bring?
☞ What's the best time to catch a freight train?
☞ Where do I go to catch a freight train?
☞ Who is working on the railroad?
☞ How do I keep from getting nailed in freight yards?
☞ How do railroads run freight trains?
☞ How do I catch a freight train over the road?
☞ How do I get off a freight train?

Expect to find lots of hard-edged advice. Littlejohn discusses the pros and cons of riding in several types of cars, including boxcars, closed hopper cars, gondolas, refrigeration cars, flatcars, and auto racks. Discussing gondolas (rail cars with open tops), Littlejohn reveals that they are the best cars for dodging security guards but terrible when it comes to viewing scenery. "Gonodolas are easy to get into. Climb up the stirrup and ladder, go over the wall or 'top sill' and jump down onto the floor. The problem is getting back out."

The concept of safety is repeatedly stressed throughout the book. In 1988, 598 railroad "trespassers" were killed and 920 were injured (and that includes being permanently maimed). Besides getting clobbered by trains and their cargo, you have to watch out for railroad security guards, called bulls. This shouldn't be too much problem, though, because bulls fail to stop 90% of all illegal activity. "The reason he's not there to stop anything is his unparalleled sloth and laziness… He can pretty much do what he wants — which very often is sleep."

Littlejohn's love for the rails is obvious and his enthusiasm is infectious. You'll be ready and eager to go on a hobo adventure once you're through reading this book.

Sand River Press; $13.95
1993; softcover; 360 pp
illus; 0-944627-34-X

DISABILITIES

DEAF PRESIDENT NOW!
The 1988 Revolution at Gallaudet University
by John B. Christiansen & Sharon M. Barnartt

Gallaudet University in Washington DC is the nation's only liberal arts university for the hearing impaired, but for the first 124 years of its existence it never had a deaf president. In August 1987, Gallaudet's president announced his resignation. In March of the next year, the board of trustees — contrary to many people's expectations — appointed yet another hearing person, Elisabeth Zinser, to the office of president.

Dismay soon led to outrage, and the students took over the campus. On the morning of Monday, March 7, they parked their cars in front of all the gates into the school, let the air out of their tires, and padlocked the gates. Hundreds of students gathered on the sealed campus to protest against the decision, talk with the media, and draw up a position paper. The students ended up making four demands: get rid of Zinser; elect a deaf president; make the board of trustees composed of at least 51% deaf people; and take no reprisals against anyone involved in the campus revolution. In a turn of events that should bring a tear of joy to the eye of any rabble-rouser, three of the students' conditions were met within a week.

Zinser resigned after just two days in office. Jane Basset Spilman, the Chair of the board, also quit her post. The board appointed I. Jordan King, who is hearing-impaired, as president. It was agreed that no one would be punished for participating in the uprising. The demand for a majority of deaf trustees was not explicitly met. However, the board agreed to set up a task force to determine how to acquire more deaf trustees.

This book presents a detailed, revelatory picture of what happened on the campus from August 1987 to the end of the take-over, which has become known as Deaf President Now (DPN). The story we got at the time from the media was misleading. They presented the students' actions as being spontaneous, but in *Deaf President Now!* we find out for the first time that a group of six alumni known as "the Ducks" orchestrated the events. At first they stirred up discontent and helped launch the demand for a deaf president. When the board didn't respond, they and some student leaders ignited the take-over.

The authors got the inside story by conducting extensive interviews with over 50 participants, including the Ducks, student leaders, former Chair Spilman, president-for-two-days Zinser, and current prez Jordan. They end their book by analysing why this student action succeeded when so many others fail and what the ramifications of the revolution are. "DPN seems to have produced a willingness to protest among some members of the deaf community, and it has produced tactics widely seen as successful and which are being emulated. In addition, perhaps most important, DPN, as a revolutionary event in the history of the deaf community in America, has given deaf people renewed hope that they can indeed control their own destiny."

Gallaudet University Press; $24.95
1995; hardcover; 254 pp
illus; 1-56368-035-1

THE RAGGED EDGE
An uncompromising disability rights zine that refuses to be nice and quiet. The cover story on the March/April 1996 is-

At a rally, a student burns Gallaudet University's president in effigy. *Deaf President Now!*

sue (when it was known as *The Disability Rag and Resource*) shouts: "Damn Straight We're a <u>Real</u> Political Movement!" Inside, we find "No Way to Die", "Paratransit Paranoia", "An American Wheelchair in London", "Will Mass. Pass a 'Potty Bill'?", "A Disability Outing" (which "outs" Ronald Reagan), "The Darker Moments in Crippin' History", reviews, poetry, and more. Articles from issues starting when *The Rag* became *The Ragged Edge* at the beginning of 1997 include "Kevorkian Blues", "Living Like a Cripple", "FDR: Rolling in His Grave???", and "*Chicken Soup* is Pabulum Say Disabled People".

The Advocado Press/PO Box 145/Louisville KY 40201
Email: editor@ragged-edge-mag.com
WWW: www.ragged-edge-mag.com
Six issue sub: $15

PIECES OF PURGATORY
Mental Retardation In and Out of Institutions
by J. David Smith

Mentally retarded people are among the most disenfranchised people in society. No one knows this fact more that John Lovelace, the subject of *Pieces of Purgatory*. This book follows Lovelace from his birth to his early sixties. It "is about the struggle of a socially imperfect person to connect with the society into which he was born but that has been reluctant to allow him to participate… In his lonely existence he has rarely been touched, has often been ignored, and has regularly been avoided."

David Smith is a college professor who met Lovelace at a Jaycee's weekend camp for retarded people. Smith was troubled by a medical document that had been included in Lovelace's paperwork for the camp. It read, in part: "Not a surgical candidate… No code… Do not resuscitate in the event of a cardiac arrest." Lovelace had no degenerative condition and did not suffer from chronic pain. He was simply retarded, poor, and alone. In other words, expendable. Smith decided to chronicle the life of a man that no one deeply cares about.

Lovelace's mother was one of the victims of the mandatory sterilisation laws of the 1930s. Before the government forcibly tied her tubes because of her "feeblemindedness", she had Lovelace out of wedlock. He lived with a foster family until he was eighteen, when he was institutionalised. Less than a year later, he was sterilised. Smith traces Lovelace's yo-yo activities into and out of institutions over the next 40 or so years. At the same time, Smith weaves in his struggles to assist Lovelace, and he tells of a totally unexpected consequence… he and Lovelace have become good friends.

Pieces of Purgatory tells a personal story, but also one that represents a large number of people. They live at the fringes of society, and this book represents a chance to hear their largely untold story.

Brooks/Cole Publishing Co; $13.50
1995; softcover; 144 pp
illus; 0-534-25206-0

THE RIGHTS OF PEOPLE WITH MENTAL DISABILITIES
by Robert M. Levy & Leonard S. Rubenstein

Having a mental disability — whether it's mental retardation or a "mental illness" such as schizophrenia, bipolar disorder, or depression — can easily lead to situations where you are denied rights that you may not even know you have or may not know how to defend. In this thick guide from the American Civil Liberties Union, mentally disabled people and others can learn exactly what rights they have with regard to involuntary commitment to institutions, informal and voluntary admission, release and transfer, refusal of treatment (including drugs and electroshock therapy), discrimination in employment, housing, public accommodation, the right to receive treatments and services, the rights of people in institutions, confidentiality of records, access to records, and more. One appendix reprints the rights of institutionalised people as set forth in the case *Wyatt v Stickney*, and another appendix lists contact information for appropriate federal agencies and national and state organisations.

(This book is part of a series put out by the ACLU covering the rights of all kinds of people. There are separate volumes for aliens and refugees, crime victims, Indians and tribes, lesbians and gay men, older people, patients, prisoners, public employees, racial minorities, single people, students, young people, and others. Contact a bookseller or the publisher for more information.)

Southern Illinois University Press; $13.95
1996; paperback; 370 pp
0-8093-1990-X

WHEN BILLY BROKE HIS HEAD
And Other Tales of Wonder

About eight years ago, Billy Golfus was on a scooter when a car hit him from behind. He went flying 67 feet and ended up with brain damage and restricted use of his left arm and leg. Although at first he couldn't even count change, he has gone on to get a master's degree and make this multiple award-winning documentary. But he warns us up front: "This ain't exactly your inspirational cripple story."

Actually, though, in many ways, it is. How can you not admire someone who fought for eight friggin' years just for the right to take a driver's test? Golfus rides in a van with Robin, who is in a wheelchair, has facial spasms, and has a right arm which is always perpendicular to her body. She says she failed her first test because the examiner was scared, but she passed the second one with no problem and has only had one minor traffic ticket and no accidents in nine years.

However, the reason Robin is so inspiring is not because she "overcame" her disability but because she overcame the System. As Golfus points out, disabilities aren't the problem — people's attitudes are. This is a lesson he's learned first-hand. While he was able-bodied and even for years after his accident, he didn't know many other disabled people. His first awakening came when he drove up to Chicago to film a civil disobedience. Disabled people were protesting at the lack of access to the State of Illinois Building by physically barricading it. In voice-over, Golfus says: "Like everyone else, I thought disabled folks were supposed to act tragically brave — or else cute and inspirational." Instead he saw fed-up people refusing to let anyone into the building. A man tried to break through the line, but a person in a wheelchair knocked him off balance, he fell backwards, and the person boosted himself out of his chair and landed on top of the guy.

Using perfect editing and a strong, forward narration, Golfus shows us what's going on in his life, such as getting his already poverty-level benefits slashed by two-thirds as he's trying to get this documentary made. He also introduces us to around ten disabled people. Barb had to fight through four levels of appeal to get the government to buy her a wheelchair so she could work and get out of the System. Joy uses her wheelchair to dance gracefully with two able-bodied dancers. "Special" Ed — the granddaddy of the independent living movement in Berkeley — is completely paralysed from the neck down and sleeps in an iron lung. In the 1960s, when he approached the State Department of Rehabilitation Services about getting a job, he was told it was "infeasible". He ended up as Director of that agency.

When Billy Broke His Head is an amazing piece of work. It's got grit, humour, and moxie… and not one bit of pity. You'd never realise it was made over a period of years on a very uncertain shoestring budget. It's so engaging (and enraging) and it draws you in with such a fascinating and likeable cast of characters, I daresay that everyone — not just the disabled — will love it.

available from Mouth; $29.95
1995; videocassette; 54 min

ANTI-PSYCHIATRY

CALL ME CRAZY
Stories from the Mad Movement
by Irit Shimrat

Irit Shimrat "went crazy" three times in her life. The first two times, she went to psychiatric facilities, which didn't do her any good and actually proved counterproductive. Several years after she got out, she became the editor of the magazine *Phoenix Rising: The Voice of the Psychiatrized*. While at a conference on women and mental health, Shimrat once again had a schizophrenic break. "By 7 a.m. I was staggering around one of the sumptuous lobbies of the Banff Springs Hotel, going up to mental health professionals and saying, 'Hi, I'm having a psychotic episode. Can you help me?' Fortunately, they all ignored me." Shimrat was attending the conference with a friend who had been through the mental health system too and was also working at *Phoenix Rising*. She calmed Shimrat, held her, and talked her through it. "I thought it was interesting that the first and second times I went mad, I got professional help — hospitalisation and drugs — and stayed crazy for months, and the third time I got help from a friend who wasn't scared because she'd been there herself — and it was over in a few hours."

Call Me Crazy is partly an autobiography of Shimrat. It is partly a history of the anti-psychiatry movement (also called the mental patients' liberation movement) — particularly in Canada — and an overview of its philosophy. Fifteen people contribute essays describing what's wrong with the mental health industry and what can be done about it. Many of them were at one point mental patients and later became activists in the movement. Lanny Beckman, founder of the Mental Patients Association in Vancouver, writes: "I believe that there's no such thing as mental illness. But there's something wrong with some people. What's wrong with them is that they experience great amounts of pain and suffering. They may or may not be weird. If they're not weird, they're called 'neurotic.' If they're weird, they're called 'psychotic.'"

Lastly, *Call Me Crazy* is part resource for anyone who wants alternatives to psychiatry. Some of the suggestions are large-scale changes that need to be implemented in society as a whole, but others — including the sections "When Things Are Bad", "If You're Locked Up", and "Helping Someone Else" — can be of immediate practical use to individuals.

Press Gang Publishers; $14.95, $18.95Cdn
1997; softcover; 181 pp
0-88974-070-4

A LEXICON OF LUNACY
Metaphoric Malady, Moral
Responsibility, and Psychiatry
by Thomas Szasz

Psychiatrist Thomas Szasz is one of the leading lights of the anti-psychiatry movement. With dozens of books and hundreds of articles to his credit, he's probably done more than any other single person to shake the very foundations of the mental health field (except perhaps RD Laing). His thesis is basically that there is no such thing as mental "illness". Sure some people act strangely and perceive reality differently than most of us, but to slap labels on them and couch their differences in the terms of medicine and disease is nonsensical. Szasz writes that "psychiatry is, among other things, the institutionalised denial of the reality of free will and of the tragic nature of life; individuals who seek impersonal explanations of horrifying human action and reject the inevitability of personal responsibility can thus medicalise life and entrust its management to health professionals."

This book is divided into two main parts. The first section takes a critical look at the language and terms used to describe mental illness. "… I regard our psychiatric vocabulary as a type of pseudo-scientific slang." Szasz discusses madness in *Hamlet*, the *Diagnostic and Statistical Manual of Mental Disorders* (the Bible of the mental health profession), the creation and dissolution of mental diagnoses, and more. He includes a double-column, thirty-page listing of synonyms for mental illness, including *abnormal*, *ape-shit*, *bananas*, *daffy*, *does not have both oars in the water*, *fruitloops*, *impulsive personality*, *listless*, *schizophrenic*, *wigged out*. Note how Szasz mixes supposedly "legitimate" phrases like *schizophrenic* with slang. There's also a page of synonyms for mental hospitals and — because alcoholism is now considered a "disease" — thirteen pages of synonyms for being drunk, pickled, tanked, shit-faced, etc.

The second part of the book "is a collection of previously published papers that illustrate our propensity to use the language of mental illness to influence social relationships — in particular, to reduce or annul personal responsibility by shifting it from self to others or to the fiction of mental illness." Chapter titles such as "The Religion Called 'Psychiatry'", "The Illusion of Mental Patients' Rights", "The Illusion of Drug Abuse Treatment", and "The Case Against Suicide Prevention" should give you a pretty good idea of Szasz's views. Take a look at the opening sentence of that last essay: "My aim in this essay is to rebut the contemporary view that suicide is a mental health problem, that psychiatric practitioners and institutions have a professional duty to try to prevent it, and that it is a legitimate function of the state to empower such professional and institutions — especially psychiatrists and mental health hospitals — to impose coercive interventions on persons diagnosed as posing a suicidal risk."

Transaction Publishers; $34.95
1993; hardcover; 202 pp
1-56000-065-1

LUNATIC FRINGE
Journal of the Psychiatric Inmates' Liberation Movement

Morgan Firestar worked on the famous *Madness Network News* until it folded in 1985 and now puts out this one-person zine. Volume 3 #1 contains a reprint of "Declaration of Principles from the Tenth International Conference on Human Rights and Psychiatric Oppression", which also serves as the principles of the Psychiatric Inmates' Liberation Movement. The first declaration reads: "We oppose involuntary psychiatric intervention including civil commitment and the administration of psychiatric procedures ('treatments') by force or coercion or without informed consent." Principle 9: "We oppose the psychiatric system because it punishes individuals who have had or claim to have had spiritual experiences and invalidates those experiences by defining them as 'symptoms' of 'mental illness'." The issue also has excerpts from *Madness, Heresy, and the Rumor of Angels* [below] and reprints about the war against immigrants from *National NOW Times* and *The Revolutionary Worker*. A short essay considers society's attitude towards the homeless, and song lyrics by Firestar mourn the deaths caused by the Holocaust.

The next issue has excerpts from *Tyranny of Kindness* concerning the welfare system, an essay on condoms and sex education, a review of a book on homelessness, Firestar's song "Shrinks", and a list of demands from a 1976 Boston anti-psychiatry conference. As with every issue, there's a recipe on the back.

Lunatic Fringe doesn't focus as much on psychiatric oppression as it does on concerns that are related to the poor people who are involved with the mental health system — homelessness, welfare, and unwanted pregnancy.

Lunatic Fringe/PO Box 7652/Santa Cruz CA 95061
Single issue: $2
Five issue sub: $10
Free to inmates of psychiatric institutions and prisoners.

MADNESS, HERESY, AND THE RUMOR OF ANGELS
The Revolt Against the Mental Health System
by Seth Farber

Dr. Seth Farber believes that there is something inherently spiritual about insanity, that it may provide a glimpse into other realities. "In their time of madness the subjects interviewed here became aware of the 'spiritual' dimension of human existence; they experienced their oneness with all beings."

Farber also thinks the psychiatric system is inhuman, degrading, and wrongheaded. It takes people who are not literally "ill", and imprisons, drugs, and shocks them. He tells the story of seven individuals who submitted to the mental health system, realised that it was doing more harm than good, and broke free. Though all of them have been diagnosed with severe mental disorders, including schizophrenia and manic-depression, they've managed to rebuild their lives on their own terms and live independently.

One such person in Cheryl. As with all the people profiled, Farber tells her story with lots of direct quotes. Cheryl's father was diagnosed as manic-depressive and had numerous nervous breakdowns. He was in and out of mental institutions during Cheryl's entire life. Around the time she was seventeen or eighteen, Cheryl experienced severe depression, and, when she came out of it, she suddenly became energetic and vivacious. Her family was alarmed at this sudden change from being mousy to being outgoing. Cheryl got involved in a minor car accident and was told she had a slight concussion. Her brother convinced her to have a second opinion, but he tricked her by actually taking her to a mental hospital where she was committed. She was told that she was "genetically destined" to be manic-depressive for the rest of her life, and she was put on Lithium. "If I wanted to have my say, I was punished by extra sedatives. If I wanted to visit another patient and a staff member wanted me to go into my room and I didn't do what I was told, I would be threatened with more medication."

She escaped the institution and hid out at a friend's house. Again she was tricked into seeing a psychiatrist who committed her against her will. They doped her up with Thorazine, which destroyed her eyesight and her mind. When she didn't recognise her brother, who had come to visit, he took her away. But, yet again, he tricked her into seeing a therapist who had her forcibly committed. She tried to tell him she was all right, but, "If your sanity is being questioned, then there is nothing you can do to prove you're sane. You can't talk your way out of it." This time she played the part of good little patient and was released in three weeks.

After getting out, she attempted suicide but survived. With the support of her husband, she got off Lithium permanently. She started seeing a therapist who, for the first time ever, helped Cheryl get at the root of her problems instead of just filling her full of drugs. She conquered her depression. She is now happily married, has a child, and is active in the nuclear disarmament movement.

The rest of the book contains interviews with mental health revolutionaries, some of whom are survivors of the psychiatric system. Professor James Mancuso bluntly says: "Mental illness is a concept used to characterise behaviour that is unwanted. It exists in the mind of the person who uses the concept to categorise others." Former mental health inmate Leonard Frank gives a long interview about his own institutionalisation and his subsequent fight against the establishment. Dr. Ron Leifer discusses psychiatry as social control and how to get off psychiatric drugs.

Open Court Publishing; $17.95
1993; softcover; 284 pp
0-8126-9200-4

MEMORY AND ABUSE
Remembering and Healing the Effects of Trauma
by Charles L. Whitfield, MD

In *Memory and Abuse*, psychotherapist Charles L. Whitfield explains how memories of childhood abuse — particularly sexual abuse — can be repressed and can later be retrieved. In doing so, he often directly attacks the theories of the False Memory Syndrome Foundation, Dr. Elizabeth Loftus [author of *The Myth of Repressed Memory*, reviewed below], and others who believe that recovered memories are fictional.

This book is aimed mainly at mental health professionals, although Whitfield is careful to avoid becoming too technical. So while it is more demanding than a strictly popular treatment of the subject, it shouldn't be over the heads of most interested laypeople. Whitfield provides an explanation of how memory works in general and proceeds to show how traumatic memory in particular can be buried in the subconscious. He repeatedly stresses that memories of abuse are different from ordinary memories in many important ways. "Ordinary memory tends to be more conscious, voluntary and flexible, while traumatic memory is usually more involuntary and unconscious, and it is often rigid. Ordinary memory tends to be more oriented in time, whereas traumatic memory is usually frozen outside of time in a kind of space that has been described as 'primary process' or coming from our unconscious mind."

Whitfield admits that details of decades-old abuse can become clouded or even completely inaccurate in the victim's mind. Sceptics point to this as evidence that the entire memory is bogus, but Whitfield maintains that the basic "core memory" is almost always correct, even if the specifics aren't. At the beginning of chapter five, he asks, "Do you remember how many 1's and One's are printed on a dollar bill? If you cannot, does it prove that you have never seen, handled or spent one?"

Other arguments against the existence of delayed memories are also rebutted. Sceptics argue that repressed memories of abuse have ever been corroborated. "Independent corroborations are too numerous and diverse to count," Whitfield responds. Apparently, several hundred people who recovered memories of abuse later recanted, saying their memories were false. Whitfield believes that the retractors may be re-repressing their memories or lying in order to avoid facing the shame and pain of confronting their abusers, who are usually family members.

So, is there such a thing as a false traumatic memory? Have some people recovered memories of abuse that never actually happened? "Based on my knowledge of the literature and nearly 20 years of front-line clinical experience, my answer is 'Yes, rarely.'" Whitfield estimates that there are 50 to 80 million sexual abuse survivors in the United States, and — of these — perhaps 3000 to 6000 have false memories.

But Whitfield does more than just answer critics in his book. Operating under the assumption that almost all recovered traumatic memories are real, he tells therapists and abused individuals how to retrieve these memories, how to cope with them, and how to get external and internal corroboration. He also covers lawsuits based on repressed memories, the phenomenon of abusers who repress memories of the abuse they inflicted, the problem of incompetent therapists, and more. A large resources section has addresses of 40 groups involved in the area of child abuse and adults who were abused as children. Most of these organisations believe in the reality of recovered memories, but, in the interest of fairness, Whitfield has also listed the two most prominent sceptical groups — the False Memory Syndrome Foundation and Victims of Child Abuse Laws.

Health Communications; $12.95
1995; softcover
1558743200

THE MYTH OF PSYCHOLOGY

by Fred Newman

Dr. Fred Newman is a lay therapist who founded the practice of social therapy. This type of therapy flies in the face of standard psychology/psychotherapy — which it denounces as Eurocentric and ineffective — and attempts to apply Marxist ideas to personal, rather than social, issues. Social therapy views individuals as revolutionary, that is, capable of changing themselves and the world. Mainstream psychology is obsessed with adaptation. "There's no question that we can adapt to societal norms — sometimes all too easily. But to presume adaptiveness to be the essence of a human being yields a therapeutic approach which is totally, qualitatively different from what you get if you presume that a person is fundamentally a revolutionary."

If you help someone adapt to a society that is "reactionary, racist, sexist, homophobic, backward, alienated, classist", then what real good have you accomplished? Social therapy seeks to help the individual by addressing the root of psychological problems — society itself. Newman writes, "I think revolution needs to be the substitute of psychology."

The problem isn't that people who come for psychological help have denied reality… it's that they have finally seen reality and it scared the hell out of them. They want traditional psychology to help them once again put on their blinders and become oblivious to the real world. Capitalist society automatically alienates people because everything we buy, eat, and entertain ourselves with was made by some faceless company. Everything, including ourselves, has become commodified. Social therapy attempts to reintegrate people, to help them feel part of a community again.

Newman examines how his ideas apply to depression, anxiety, panic, addiction, and other such states of mind. He claims that social therapy has helped thousands of people in ways that traditional psychology never did. People who have gone through 15 to 20 years of ineffective orthodox treatment report feeling better. This book claims that when Horizon House — which treats addiction, among other things — started using social therapy as its primary modality, its success rate skyrocketed. Eighty-five percent of the people who went through the programme remain drug- and alcohol-free, compared to the national average of 7% (or less).

Naturally, this sort of therapy has its critics. Some people have accused it of being cult-like, of brainwashing vulnerable people into becoming radicals. Newman addresses such concerns head-on. As always, I invite you to make up your own mind.

Castillo International; $12.95
1991; softcover; 265 pp
0-9628621-2-6

THE MYTH OF REPRESSED MEMORY
False Memories and Allegations of Sexual Abuse

by Dr. Elizabeth Loftus & Katherine Ketcham

Dr. Elizabeth Loftus is a cognitive psychologist who specialises in the study of memory. As she watched the growing occurrence of adults who were "recovering" repressed memories of childhood sexual abuse, she became extremely suspicious. In experiments she performed, she had repeatedly been able to use suggestion to implant memories of nonexistent events in her subjects' minds. When she looked at how memories of abuse were being recovered, she recognised a similar pattern. It appears that many therapists and self-help books are unintentionally planting these suggestions into people who were never abused.

Loftus repeatedly emphasises that she believes that incest and other types of sexual abuse are widespread problems. She also does not intend to cast aspersions on people whose memories of childhood abuse have been with them since the incident(s) occurred. She is, however, extremely sceptical of "memories that did not exist until someone went looking for them".

Loftus shows that therapists and popular books on incest/sex abuse recovery are often quick to tell women that they were sexually abused and that this is responsible for their depression, low self-esteem, nightmares, etc. When these supposed memories resurface, many women accuse their parents and/or break off all contact with their families, without ever seeking any kind of verification that the events really happened. Using actual cases based on "recovered memories", Loftus shows how families have been shattered and parents have gone to jail based on nothing more than someone who claims to have suddenly remembered something decades after the fact. No corroborating testimony, no physical evidence, just a resurfaced memory.

The problem, Loftus asserts, is in how most of us think of memory. We want to feel secure knowing that our minds are like camcorders, flawlessly recording and retrieving everything that has happened to us. But she "defies the oft-heard explanation that memories reside in a certain part of the brain, like coded computer disks or crisp manila folders carefully placed in a file drawer for safekeeping. Memories don't sit in one place, waiting to be retrieved; they drift through the mind, more like clouds or vapour than something we can put our hands around." Later, she reinforces the point: "[M]emory must be recognised and appreciated as a creative mechanism in which fact and fiction are inextricably woven."

Throughout her examinations of clinical cases, popular books, psychological experiments, and the leaders of the recovery movement, Loftus shows herself to be devoted to scientific fairness. She is willing to consider the possibility that true memories can be buried for long periods and then resurface in an accurate form. However, as she sees it, the current evidence simply does not support this phenomenon. As she explains in a conversation with Ellen Bass, author of the incest recovery bible, *The Courage to Heal*: "'All I ask for is proof that repression is a common phenomenon and that the brain routinely responds to trauma in this way… That's all I'm asking for — proof.'"

St. Martin's Press; $13.95
1994; softcover
0312141238

THE SLAMMER

CAGES OF STEEL
The Politics of Imprisonment in the United States
edited by Ward Churchill & JJ Vander Wall

Cages of Steel asserts that, contrary to the official line, US prisons house a number of political prisoners. These prisoners are there strictly because of their radical leftist political beliefs and activities. Some of them were framed for crimes, while others committed relatively minor crimes but have mysteriously stayed in jail for decades after a non-radical who committed the same crime would've been released. The editors have collected forty articles, essays, and interviews about or by these political prisoners, showing that they have been persecuted because of their beliefs and are subjected to physical and psychological torture, as well as murder.

Leonard Peltier, member of the American Indian Movement, is perhaps the most famous political prisoner in the country [*Outposts* p 19]. In 1975 two plain clothes FBI agents were killed during a shoot-out on the Pine Ridge Sioux Reservation in South Dakota. Peltier remains in jail for the murders even though "... it has subsequently been shown through the FBI's own documents that incomplete and inaccurate ballistics evidence was deliberately presented at trial in order to 'establish Peltier's guilt.'... Prosecutor Lynn Crooks has since admitted the government 'has no idea' who killed the agents, and the Eighth Circuit Court of Appeals has formally acknowledged that the original case against Peltier no longer exists." Yet he still can't get a new trial.

Similarly, Geronimo ji Jaga Pratt — head of the Black Panther Party's LA chapter in the late 1960s — was convicted of killing a white school teacher in Santa Monica. His defence was that at the time she was murdered, he was at a major Panther gathering in Oakland (350 miles away). He said that the FBI had bugged the event, and therefore their logs would establish his alibi. "At trial, FBI representatives lied under oath, denying that any such bugging would occur. They also denied that they had infiltrated the defence team when, in fact, they had." Years later, with revelations about the FBI's COINTELPRO activities, it was shown that the Bureau had bugged the Oakland conference. When Pratt's attorneys demanded the logs, the FBI claimed that they had lost them. In the early 1980s two private investigators came forward saying that while working on a different case, they had scrutinised the FBI's surveillance logs of the Oakland meeting, which show that Pratt was there. Yet he still can't get a new trial. (Update: In June 1997, a Superior Court Judge ruled that Pratt hadn't received a fair trial and overturned his murder conviction. After spending 27 years in prison, Pratt was freed on $25,000 bail.)

Even when these activists do commit crimes, they are slapped with outrageous sentences. Susan Rosenberg and Tim Blunk are anti-imperialists who apparently aren't affiliated with any group. In 1984 they were convicted of possessing dynamite, which had not been fashioned into bombs. They each received 58 years in federal prison, "far and away the heaviest [terms] for any possessory offence in the history of federal law." By way of comparison, a man who was convicted of actually bombing abortion clinics across the nation received seven years and was released in four.

Cages of Steel contains writings from members of the Puerto Rican Independence movement, the Black Panthers, and the Black Liberation Army, as well as Leonard Peltier, Susan Rosenberg, Tim Blunk, and others. George Jackson, Geronimo Pratt, and another Panther — Dhoruba al-Mujahid Bin Wahad — are interviewed. Articles examine the prison in Marion, Illinois, the Lexington High Security Unit for Women, control unit prisons, Mumia Abu-Jamal, using the RICO Act against political targets, abuse of prisoners with AIDS, women and imprisonment, "preventative detention", and more. Listings in the back of the book give contact info for political prisoners and organisations that are trying to help them.

Maisonneuve Press; $16.95
1992; softcover; 435 pp
illus; 0-944624-17-0

LIVE FROM DEATH ROW
by Mumia Abu-Jamal

The case of Mumia Abu-Jamal has become a *cause célèbre* for people and groups concerned with human rights and social justice. Abu-Jamal is an award-winning journalist who has never been too popular with the authorities. As a teenager he belonged to the Black Panthers, and later he became the only reporter in Philadelphia to give a fair hearing to MOVE, the radical African American group whose headquarters were burned to the ground by the government in a case that's so much like Waco, it's hard to believe [see *20 Years on the MOVE*, in the No Compromises chapter].

In 1982 Abu-Jamal was found guilty and later sentenced to death for the murder of a Philadelphia police officer. The incident in question took place on December 9, 1981, when Abu-Jamal was driving a taxi at night. He saw his brother being beaten by a cop who had pulled him over. What happened next is hotly disputed, and Abu-Jamal's life hangs in the balance. Somehow, the officer was shot to death, and Abu-Jamal was critically wounded by the cop's gun.

The trial was a travesty. Abu-Jamal invoked his right to represent himself and was given three weeks to prepare for his murder trial. Midway through jury interviews, the judge somehow denied Abu-Jamal the right to represent himself and the right to choose who would assist him at the counsel table. Instead, an unprepared public attorney was assigned to the case and given the insulting sum of $150 with which to conduct a pre-trial investigation. The jury was heavily biased against Abu-Jamal, who was not even allowed to be present during most of the prosecution's phase of the trial. The witnesses — some of whom had criminal records and were offered deals for testifying against the defendant — gave absurdly conflicting police statements and trial testimony. Some of them reported that the man who shot the officer bore no resemblance to Abu-Jamal. Much of the prosecution's case rested on the defendant's political beliefs, which were distorted when presented to the jury. Despite these and many more irregularities, Abu-Jamal was convicted by the nearly all-white jury. In September 1995, about a week before he was to be killed, Abu-Jamal received a stay of execution while his case is re-examined.

During his time on death row, Abu-Jamal has been busy writing essays on racism and injustice in the judicial system and the horror of prisons. This anthology collects over 40 of these essays, including the ones that Abu-Jamal was supposed to read on National Public Radio before NPR chickened out and cancelled his appearances.

"Descent Into Hell" relates the story of an inmate under psychiatric treatment who had been put into "the hole" (solitary disciplinary confinement). He set himself on fire. After smelling burning hair, the prisoners alerted guards, who put out the fire. "Moments later, a naked man walked down the tier, his front darkened like wheat toast, an acrid stench rising like an infernal sacrifice. He walked slowly, deliberately, as if lost in thought, as if involved in a languid, aimless stroll on the beach. Twelve hours later he was pronounced dead, with over 70 percent of his body burned."

In "The Visit", Abu-Jamal recalls his then-seven-year-old daughter's first visit. "She burst into the tiny visiting room, her brown eyes aglitter with happiness; stopped, stunned, staring at the glassy barrier between us; and burst into tears at this arrogant attempt at state separation. In milliseconds, sadness and shock shifted into fury as her petite fingers curled into tight fists, which banged and pummelled the Plexiglas barrier, which shuddered and shimmied but didn't shatter. 'Break it! Break it!' she screamed."

Other essays are more political than personal. In "Slavery Daze II" Abu-Jamal attacks the drug crack, which is destroying poverty-stricken black communities. "Harvested in Latin America's Peruvian highlands, treated in jungle labs, 'cured' in a chemical bath of ether and kerosene, carried into the USA by government-hired pilots as a way to pay the fledgling contras' bills, cocaine comes to Chocolate City, USA, and, transformed into crystalline crack, wreaks havoc on poor black life." Abu-Jamal stops short of saying that the influx of crack is a government conspiracy against African Americas, but he does feel that, whatever the reason for crack's appearance, the government is more than happy to let it destroy black communities.

Other writings concern Clinton's racism, Rodney King, Waco, Huey Newton, Malcolm X, and, of course, more on prisons and death row. Abu-Jamal's attorney contributes the afterward, which examines his client's infuriating trial in detail.

It should be noted that this book ignited furious reactions from police organisations and conservatives. Luckily, unlike NPR, Addison-Wesley didn't cave in, instead standing up to the pressure, which included a boycott of their books.

Addison-Wesley; $20
1994; small hardcover; 250 pp
0-201-48319-X

YOU ARE GOING TO PRISON
by Jim Hogshire

With more and more laws constantly being passed to criminalise more and more activities, it become all the more likely that any one of us may eventually do some time. This is especially true if you live in states, such as Texas, that get off on imprisoning people. The Lone Star State has the highest per capita amount of prisoners... but I digress. Jim Hogshire has written a book to give you some idea of what you can really expect should you wind up in the pokey. *You Are Going to Prison* is a rough and tumble look at an unnerving subject.

"To the simple question 'Am I going to get buttfucked?' the simple answer is 'yes.' Sorry, the odds are not with you Mr. Fish." Most prison rapes are perpetrated sneakily, by "wolves" who trick new prisoners into "owing them" for pot, cigarettes, soap, etc. Though they're not as common as usually believed, gang rapes do occur, especially in crowded rooms with three-level bunk beds. These are pushed into an approximate square and draped in sheets, forming a "covered wagon". "Guys beaten and dragged into the covered wagon are set upon by dozens of men. They have all their teeth knocked out, they are forced to perform fellatio for hours and hours while being savagely fucked up the ass until their assholes literally gush blood."

Don't expect guards to help you. They know exactly what's going on, but they will not interfere with the laws of the prison jungle. In fact, they are often accomplices.

The key to surviving in prison is to stand up for yourself. Don't disrespect people or act like a badass, but don't take any shit either. Otherwise, you'll be perceived as a weakling and your troubles will escalate out of control. "If you must, don't hesitate to fight, or even more so, to kill. If you have to live in prison any length of time you may as well do it on your terms and not as somebody's fuck boy/slave."

Race relations in prisons are horrible. Some joints are in a constant state of race war, but don't expect "sensitivity training courses" for prisoners any time soon. Officials purposely use a divide and conquer strategy. "Prisons rely on fomenting intense and violent hatred between the races in order to more easily rule the prisoners."

The author gives advice on illegal ways of making money inside the big house. Smuggling drugs such as pot, hard drugs, Sudafed, Dramamine, and inhalants for huffing is one way. You can even make "prison wine" using the instructions given. Tattooing, selling food, and running gambling pools are other lucrative operations.

Other topics covered include dealing with cops when you're being arrested, getting interrogated, jumping bail, the trial, solitary confinement, filing lawsuits from prison, living on death row, and various forms of execution. A 30-page resource section has addresses for every conceivable organisation or publication that could be useful to prisoners.

Loompanics Unlimited; $14.95
1994; softcover; 181 pp
1-55950-119-7

SELF-SUFFICIENCY

HOW TO BUY LAND CHEAP
(Fifth Edition)
by Edward Preston

In this revised and expanded fifth edition of Edward Preston's classic 1977 book, he explains *exactly* how you can still buy land — sometimes with a house on it — from all levels of government in the US (county, city, state and federal) for insanely cheap prices, generally from $10 to $1000. A short chapter looks at grabbing land for peanuts in Canada.

Loompanics Unlimited; $14.95
1996; softcover; 127 pp
illus; 1-55950-145-6

HOW TO LIVE WITHOUT ELECTRICITY — AND LIKE IT
by Anita Evangelista

Prolific self-sufficiency expert Anita Evangelista — author of *How to Develop A Low-Cost Family Food-Storage System* — now shows us how to unhook our houses from the utility company. Despite the book's title, not every technique discussed shuns electricity. Some use it, but it's generated from alternative sources, such as solar cells, gas-powered generators, and standard batteries.

The chapters are divided up based on different needs:

☞ light: battery, oil and kerosene, propane, flashlights, candles (including how to make melted wax back into candles)

☞ water: rainwater, groundwater, wells, filters

☞ cooking: wood, gas, butane stoves, solar cookers

☞ heat: wood stoves, gas stoves, solar heating

☞ keeping cool: wind, shade, "cooling from the earth"

☞ refrigeration and freezing: ice-boxes, holes in the ground, cold shafts, fridges that run on alternate energy sources

☞ communication: radios, short wave radios, CBs, the Internet

The book ends with a chapter on general sources of alternative power and books, magazines, and catalogues dealing with self-sufficiency and getting back to the land.

Loompanics Unlimited; $13.95
1997; softcover; 158 pp
illus; 1-55950-162-6

SELF-SUFFICIENCY GARDENING
Financial, Physical and Emotional Security from Your Own Backyard
by Martin P. Waterman

Martin Waterman has written over 500 articles and columns in *The Old Farmer's Almanac, Harrowsmith, Plant and Garden*, and other magazines. In this book, he tells beginners how to raise a small-scale garden and maybe even make some money.

Waterman teaches organic gardening, that is, growing crops without pesticides, herbicides, and fungicides. He gives many solutions for controlling pesky critters naturally. Fences, dogs, scarecrows, and cayenne peppers can keep away small animals. Slugs will not cross lime, and grubs and caterpillars can be killed with a bowl of beer, which they fall into and drown.

Further chapters give specific instructions for raising vegetables (asparagus, beans, carrots, corn, lettuce, etc.), fruit (grapes, apples, etc.), nuts, herbs and medicinal plants, and non-food crops (such as ivy for baskets). One chapter is devoted to decorating with these crops, thereby creating an "edible landscape".

If you want to extend your growing season, Waterman provides chapters on greenhouse gardening and hydroponic gardening, which doesn't use soil. Hydroponic systems are coming down in price, and it's not too difficult to make your own. This way you can grow year round, and increase your efficiency. One hydroponic farm claims that it can yield as much produce in 10,000 square feet as in ten acres of greenhouse space or 100 acres of farmland.

The author is also a computer consultant and writer, and he takes gardening into the modern age with a chapter on gardening software and using the Internet to find valuable information. Next, he discusses how to propagate seeds and cuttings so you don't have to keep buying them. Finally, you'll get a quick course in storing and preserving your bounty, and a chapter on earning income from your efforts.

A handy resource guide lists addresses for gardening book publishers, used gardening books, newsletters, magazines, seed companies, and organisations.

Loompanics Unlimited; $13.95
1995; oversized softcover; 120 pp
illus; 1-55950-135-9

TRAVEL-TRAILER HOMESTEADING UNDER $5,000
by Brian Kelling

Would you like to live in a beautiful part of the country for only $5000? And that's including the land and shelter. It's possible. Brian Kelling has done it, and now he's going to teach us.

What it boils down to is getting a relatively small tract of land and putting a travel-trailer or Recreational Vehicle [RV] on it. While land in urban areas is expensive, it's still fairly cheap in many of the more sparsely-populated areas of the US. A few years ago, the author bought five acres in beautiful San Luis Valley of southern Colorado for $2195. There are still tracts available for $2500. Taxes on the author's property are $52 a year!

He lives in a 21-foot travel-trailer. They're still inexpensive, and you can buy a broken down RV for even less. Water can be had by digging a well, tapping into hot springs, having a stream on your property, or, most likely, by hauling water. Your septic system will only cost around $100, and a wood stove will give you plenty of cheap heat. Electricity can be had from a small portable generator, solar power, or wind power. Finally, propane refrigerators will take care of your cold storage needs.

Kelling makes this option seem awfully tempting. It's not exactly the high life, but owning your own sliver of the American dream for under five grand is hard to beat. His instructions and many diagrams seem reasonably detailed, but I'm sure anyone actually doing this — especially non-handy people like me — would need extra guidance.

Loompanics Unlimited; $8
1995; softcover; 77 pp
heavily illus; 1-55950-132-4

THE WILD AND FREE COOKBOOK
by Tom Squier

Tom Squier — military survival specialist, gourmet cook, self-acknowledged earth steward, and "Road Kill King" — has written a massive book that divulges instructions and hundreds of recipes for dishes made from plants you pick and game you kill. Covers wild greens, dandelions, strawberries, blueberries, cherries, plums, prickly pear cactus, mushrooms, cheese, jelly, groundhog, rabbit, snake, alligator, catfish, buffalo, racoon, dove, oysters, natural spices, tea, road kill, and much, much more.

Loompanics Unlimited; $19.95
1996; oversized softcover; 300 pp
heavily illus; 1-55950-128-6

INTENTIONAL COMMUNITIES

AMERICA'S COMMUNAL UTOPIAS
edited by Donald E. Pitzer

Representing the cutting-edge of the upsurge of scholarly activity surrounding historical intentional communities, this book looks at over 20 such communities that were founded before 1965. Some of them are famous: the Shakers, the Harmony Society, the Mormon communitarians, the Oneida Perfectionists, the Icariens, and the Hutterites. Others are not nearly as well known, such as the Janssonists, Jewish agricultural communities, The Society of the Woman in the Wilderness, Llano del Rio, Koreshan Unity, and the Theosophical communities. Several essays cover the more general subjects of Roman Catholic monasticism, communities in Colonial America, and California's socialist utopias. Besides examining all these experimental communities, the authors employ the new perspective of "developmental communalism", which takes into account the outside forces that led to a community's founding and eventual end (if it no longer exists). A 42-page index contains the most comprehensive list of pre-1965 intentional communities ever published, and

A "family portrait" of the Oneida community.
America's Communal Utopias.

the "Bibliographical Essay" provides many more leads for the serious researcher.

The University of North Carolina Press; $24.95
1997; softcover; 550 pp
illus; 0-8078-4609-0

COMMUNITIES
Journal of Cooperative Living

Put out by the Fellowship for Intentional Community, creators of the *Communities Directory* [below], this carefully crafted magazine deals with issues important to people living in cooperative settings. Past issues of *Communities* have focused on building, art, leadership, growing up, women, earning a living, and love, romance, and sex. Issue 88 focuses on communities and "cults". The magazine's position is that "cult" is a meaningless word. Guest editor Tim Miller writes: "For [American society] 'cult' simply means a group we don't like… When the word 'cult' enters the typical American conversation, the jury has already returned. From that point on, we're discussing the sentence, not the verdict." In another article, Miller deconstructs the list of traits that supposedly identify a group as a cult, showing that such traits also apply to other groups — including the Catholic Church — that are generally not regarded as cults.

Other articles examine the tribulations of several communities labelled as cults. In 1984 the Messianic community of Island Pond was raided by 90 state troopers and 50 social workers, who scooped up the 112 children living there and took them away. Thanks to anti-cult groups, publicity-hungry politicians, and the gullible media, the accusations of an upset ex-member resulted in this overreaction. The trial went well for the group, though. "When the state could produce no evidence of abuse, the judge observed the children, then ordered all of them returned to their parents at Island Pond. He later commented that Vermont had committed 'the worst state-sanctioned violation of children since Herod.'"

Obviously, no community, cultic or otherwise, is perfect. Steven J. Gelberg explains why he left the Krishna movement after 17 years. It wasn't because of brainwashing or child abuse — he simply saw the hypocrisy that is so common in religions applied to his organisation as well. He accuses the Hare Krishnas of ethical shortcomings, uncaring attitudes, disrespect for women, spiritual depersonalisation, and a unrealistically militant attitude toward celibacy.

Other articles examine the Love Israel Family, Jesus People USA, what really happened at Waco, handling actual abuse, a Bill of Rights for communities, practical information for obtaining land, and more. Sections in the back update the group's Directory by providing listings of new communities, groups that have folded, and groups with openings for new members.

Communities/138-W Twin Oaks Road/Louisa, VA 23093
Voice: 540-894-5798 [Visa, MC, Disc]
Email: communities@ic.org
WWW: http://www.ic.org
Single issue: $6. Non-US: $7
Four issue sub (one year): $18. Non-US: $22

COMMUNITIES DIRECTORY
A Guide to Cooperative Living
(Second Edition)
by the Fellowship for Intentional Community

According to one of the 32 articles in this book: "An 'intentional community' is a group of people who have chosen to live together with a common purpose, working cooperatively to create a lifestyle that reflects their core values. The people may live together on a piece of rural land, in a suburban home, or in an urban neighbourhood, and they may share a single residence or live in a cluster of dwellings. This definition spans a wide variety of groups, including (but not limited to) communes, student cooperatives, land co-ops, cohousing groups, monasteries and ashrams, and farming collectives." Other articles deal with the many issues surrounding such communities, including group dynamics, raising children, disabilities, bioregionalism, legal concerns, finding a community that's right for you, and more.

The crux of the directory, though, is its listings of over 500 communities in North America and over 50 in other parts of the world. Each listing includes a fairly detailed summary of the group's structure and philosophy (written by the group itself) and usually some contact information. The groups are a diverse lot to say the least. The Black Cat Collective is a group of seven adults and one child living in a house in San Francisco. They describe themselves as a "housing collective with two bases of unity — Feminist Witchcraft (or compatible spiritual focus: we have an engaged Buddhist, etc.) and Direct Action Politics." The Christ of the Hills Monastery is a Texas community based on Russian Orthodoxy. The 19 adults and three teenagers "are celibate, share all income and nearly all meals."

Other groups are more ambitious. "At Dancing Rabbit, our vision is this: a town organised around the principles of radical ecological sustainability. Affordable, non-intrusive eco-houses such as 'Earthships' for both nuclear families and communal homes, using a grey/black water system to cycle the water back to the land and extract energy and nutrients from the waste." Utopiaggia is a 250-acre community in Italy comprised of thirty-five people.

A couple of groups are actually squatters. Christiania is a city — housing 1000 to 2000 people — set up without permission on an abandoned military base in Denmark. Perhaps the most unusual listing is for The Dolphin Tribe, located in Costa Rica: "We are organising an interspecies community of dolphins and people, for the purpose of communicating and having cultural contact with dolphins and whales. We are planning to buy a ship and build an undersea village, to be called Atlantis."

Another section contains listings of over 250 resources of interest to communitarians, including organisations and periodicals covering agriculture, earth-centred spirituality, conflict resolution, environmental and social issues, nonmonogamy, homeschooling, etc. The index lists groups and resources according to focus, philosophy, activity, and other criteria.

Communities Directory is a towering achievement. People looking for a community or trying to start one of their own won't want to leave home without it.

Communities; $31 ppd. Non-US: $30 ppd
1995; oversize softcover; 440 pp
illus; 0-9602714-3-0

LES ICARIENS
The Utopian Dream in Europe
and America
by Robert P. Sutton

This is the first complete account of the Icariens, a group of mainly French artisans who came to America and founded some of the most successful and longest-lived utopian communities ever created. Basing their ideology on no private property, no money, and the Golden Rule, the Icariens set up six communal societies in Illinois, Iowa, and California from 1848 to 1898. This book examines in detail the group's genesis, its founder, its activities in France, and its relatively long history in America.

University of Illinois Press; $26.95
1994; hardcover; 199 pp
illus; 0-252-02067-7

JANUARY THAW
People at Blue Mt. Ranch Write About
Living Together in the Mountains
by the Blue Mountain Ranch collective

The Blue Mountain Ranch is the pseudonym of one of the more famous "hippie communes" started in the 1960s. Located deep in the mountains somewhere in the Northwest, this collective decided to disguise the ranch's name and location for privacy purposes. In this book, around 50 of the members contribute their thoughts about living on the ranch through essays, poems, journal entries, drawings, and photos.

The commune was started in September 1968 by 25 "women, men, and children/revolutionary-anarchists" in the middle of the mountains. "Large towns are at least 2 ½ hours away, and the two nearest villages, each supporting only one store, school and post office, take an hour and a half to drive to." Their lighting is supplied by kerosene lamps and propane gas, and they get hot water by piping it through the stove. They have large gardens and raise goats for dairy products and hogs for meat.

If you have some sort of starry-eyed vision of a hard-working but utopian life on a commune, this book will put an end to that. Living together with a bunch of people in a non-hierarchic system is a constant struggle to grow and adapt. Take for instance, this notice put on the bulletin board after the group raised and slaughtered hogs for the first time: "I questioned then what seemed to be a bad feeding arrangement [before the slaughter, the author was the only one who fed the pigs] and suggested that people try it for a few days and see if they came away with as much excitement as they had while standing around the stove in the main house talking to the air about breeding pigs. Pig care, as I saw it, was shit work… "

A lot of the writing concerns sexualove relationships among the group. Besides traditionally married couples, there were also triads and groups of four. Many of the group came out of the closet after they moved to Blue Mountain. Others experimented with voluntary celibacy. Myeba, a woman, writes: "Becoming a person who's not involved in sexual tension with men takes time. Sometimes it made me uncomfortable and confused, but I liked it. I found I felt whole and complete, not missing and fragmented."

January Thaw is a very valuable document for its down in the trenches view of life in a rural commune. Although the world has changed a lot since the late 1960s/early 1970s, you should still read it before you go traipsing off to take part in any back-to-the-land intentional communities.

Times Change Press; $7.50
1974; softcover; 157 pp
illus; 0-87810-030-X

WORK

THE ABOLITION OF WORK
by Bob Black

Bob Black is one of the most controversial characters on the anti-authoritarian scene, and he's become quite hated since he narked on fellow controversial writer Jim Hogshire. This long essay, *The Abolition of Work*, has achieved classic status. It is one of the touchstones in any overview of the anti-work ethic.

Black wastes no time in getting to the point. His essay opens: "No one should ever work. Work is the source of nearly all the misery in the world. Almost any evil you'd care to name comes from working or living in a world designed for work. In order to stop suffering, we have to stop working." He goes on to emphasise his position: "Liberals say we should end employment discrimination. I say we should end employment. Conservatives support right-to-work laws. Following Karl Marx's wayward son-in-law Paul Lafargue I support the right to be lazy. Leftists favour full employment. Like

the surrealists—except that I'm not kidding—I favour full unemployment. Trotskyists agitate for permanent revolution. I agitate for permanent revelry."

Black rails against the totalitarian, dehumanising, dangerous, boring, soul-sapping, life-wasting nature of work. He then presents a plan for eliminating work. Well—not so much eliminating work as transforming it. "The secret of turning work into play… is to arrange useful activities to take advantage of whatever it is that various people at various times in fact enjoy doing."

In a shorter essay, "No Future for the Workplace", Black covers basically the same territory. The importance of this essay is that it was actually published in the *Wall Street Journal* (although they "edited" it to the point of bowdlerisation). It's funny to think of all those Fortune 500 executives scratching their heads while reading lines like: "Work devalues life by appropriating something so priceless it cannot be bought back no matter how high the GNP is."

Additional material includes a history of Black's anti-work writings, snippets of interviews with him, an article on him, and a list of suggested reading.

"Workers of the world… relax!"
Feh! Press; $2
1985, 1995; stapled-bound booklet; 26 pp
illus; no ISBN

BEST OF *TEMP SLAVE!*
edited by Jeff Kelly

The life of a temporary worker is beyond thankless. The temp agency you signed up with sends you out to do a job for another business. While you work there for (usually) anywhere from a day to a month, the business is paying the temp agency approximately $10 an hour, of which you get $6. Jeff Kelley sums up temp work as a "never ending treadmill of low pay, no benefits, no security and no respect." You're a disposable body being used by a corporation in a situation that's as close to slavery as the law allows.

Kelly knows about the situation first-hand. He's worked many temp jobs, including one in a mailroom at a large insurance company. He had worked there for a year, quite a long time for a temp. When he started he was promised an eventual full-time job, but in late December 1994, he was given his two-week notice. He used his remaining time on the job to create the first issue of *Temp Slave!* From there, it blossomed into one of the most popular zines around, gaining thousands of subscribers and loads of mainstream media attention. This anthology collects the best material from this chronicle of the economy's underbelly.

Many of the contributors describe their experiences temping. Kelly Winters went to work for a company that tries to collect from people who are late paying back their student loans. On her first day, she couldn't get in because she didn't have a security card, so she slid in through the back entrance, following a guy delivering Coke. "When the Suits find me cooling my heels in the lobby, waiting for my temp assignment to begin, the witch hunt begins before they even say hello: 'Who let you in?' 'I don't know. I just walked in.' 'Someone had to let you in. What did they look like? Was it

MERRY CHRISTMAS FROM THE TEMP INDUSTRY!

SANTA, IT'S DECEMBER 25TH. YOU'RE FIRED!

"The indentured servants of the modern plantation" speak out. *Best of Temp Slave!*

male or female?' 'I don't know.' My stupid act convinces them that I'll be a good worker, and they issue me a security card and show me to my cubicle."

Other pieces have a more serious tone. In "African-American Temp Workers" Sam Smucker writes: "Much like offshore money laundering operations or shell corporations used by the rich to avoid taxes, temporary companies are a legal shenanigans which allow the bosses to get around laws for which many workers fought and died." Malcolm Riviera aptly refers to temps as "the indentured servants of the modern plantation."

Sabotage and other acts of defiance are a common part of the contributors' experiences. In "10 Tenets of Temping", Temp X advises workers to work slowly, come in a little late, look busy while not doing anything, pilfer, make personal long-distance calls, commit sabotage, and, "Deny knowledge

of any job skills other than the basics; advanced abilities lead to more difficult work assignments at no extra pay." Brenden P. Bartholmew worked at Sega's customer help line. He tells of masturbating on company time, antagonising customers, stealing confidential memos, and harassing obnoxious customers ("I've often had access to my customer's phone numbers, addresses and credit card numbers. If someone was nasty to me, I would record said info with the intention of tormenting them until they die.").

Temp Slave! is filled with comix and graphix that make stinging commentaries on temping, as well as corporate greed and working in general. In one, a worker does numerous dangerous jobs, including hauling toxic chemicals and putting fuses in bombs, while repeatedly consoling himself, "This job's just temporary." A set of *Temp Slave!* "trading cards" features "The stoned co-worker", "Worker run amok!", and "Plastics Make Me Brain Feel Funny".

> Garrett County Press; $10
> 1997; softcover; 168 pp
> heavily illus; 1-891053-42-6

SABOTAGE IN THE AMERICAN WORKPLACE
Anecdotes of Dissatisfaction, Mischief and Revenge
edited by Martin Sprouse

The editor of *Sabotage in the American Workplace*, Martin Sprouse, worked in the mailroom of a corporation where his department (and all the others) performed some form of sabotage. He doesn't issue a call to the workers of the world to monkeywrench the machine, but he isn't against it either. When he appeared on a radio talk show, "the interviewer asked what I thought could be done to solve the problem of sabotage. I told him I didn't see sabotage as a problem, but as a necessary and valid reaction to dissatisfaction caused by work."

Divided into sections based on type of occupation, these 133 anecdotes — ranging from a couple of paragraphs to over a page — are told by the workers in their own words. They have engaged in slowdowns, pilfering, destruction, and creative pranks for reasons including "low pay, harassment, bad company ethics, poor working conditions, and boredom."

Ramiro is a corpsman who had access to important military records, which he would flush down the toilet. "I found the executive officer's health record and threw the whole thing away. He had to be re-immunised because he had no record. He was pissed."

Video-dating sales manager Nancy says that she and the other employees aren't allowed to date clients of the service but they do anyway. "Several of our consultants have gotten married to clients. We have first pick. If our boss caught us, he would fire us, but we all see it as a perk."

Owen is a cashier in a record store chain whose owners don't know music and won't stock artists who aren't white hit-makers. He and the other employees stole money from the register and lifted records. "We also let shoplifters come in and steal from the place... If we saw that someone had refined taste we would encourage them and recommend

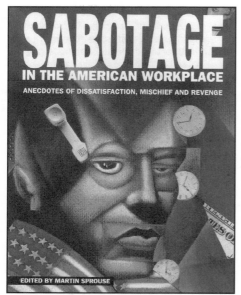

"Even if just one can lid was put in upside down, the entire system would jam." *Sabotage in the American Workplace.*

other albums."

One of the most damaging acts was committed by Lazlo, a programmer who had to fix Bank of America's crummy payroll programme. He couldn't get the monumental job done in the short amount of time he was given, and his so-called superiors stopped paying him. To strike back, he planted a logic bomb in the system, which wiped out the payroll programme and eventually corrupted the entire system. He happily notes, "On payday, nobody got paid in Northern California's PayNet system."

Other people who tell of their revenge include a cab driver, fish canner, teacher, telephone surveyor, cemetery groundskeeper, stripper, casino poker dealer, toy store floor manager, waitress, bank teller, and bodyguard. In the margins of this well-designed book are hundreds of quotes from various sources relating to the horrors of work and the pleasures of sabotage.

Sabotage in the American Workplace does three things. 1) It provides entertainment by regaling us with often humorous tales of mischief. 2) It gives insight into the reasons why people sabotage and how they justify their actions. 3) It might just give you a few ideas…

Pressure Drop Press and AK Press; $12
1992; oversized softcover; 175 pp
heavily illus; 0-9627091-3-1

STRIKE!
(Revised and Updated Edition)
by Jeremy Brecher

Strike! is the classic history of workers' revolts in the United States. It first appeared in 1972 and has recently been republished in an expanded version that takes into account the tumultuous 25 years that have passed since its original publication. Reading this book is something of a revelation because it clearly demonstrates the bias that exists in the version of history we're taught.

I don't remember hearing anything in history classes about the Great Upheaval of 1877. In September 1873, America's largest bank declared bankruptcy, and by the end of that month the stock market had literally shut down. "In 1873 alone, 5,183 businesses worth over $200 million failed." The US entered its worst depression in its history, lasting even longer than the "Great Depression" of the early 1930s. Over one million labourers were out of work, and wages for those lucky enough to have jobs were cut 25 percent. These intolerable conditions led to the Great Upheaval, "the first great American mass strike, a movement that was viewed at the time as a violent rebellion. Strikers seized and closed the nation's most important industry, the railroads, and crowds defeated or won over first the police, then the state militias, and in some cases even the federal troops. General strikes brought work to a standstill in a dozen major cities and strikers took over authority in communities across the nation." Over 100 strikers and sympathisers were killed by the government. In the end, the Upheaval was put down, but in many cases it resulted in higher wages and, more importantly for the long term, it showed the power that workers could wield when they organised.

From there, the author covers the strike wave of 1886, the Pullman strike, the mass strike of 1919, labour revolts during the Great Depression, the movement during 1946 that was "the closest thing to a national general strike of industry in the twentieth century", the often overlooked massive strikes during the Vietnam War Era, the Hormel strike of 1985, the UPS strike of 1997, and other key instances of organised labour resistance.

South End Press; $22
1972, 1997; softcover; 421 pp
illus; 0-89608-569-4

MISCELLANEOUS

THE ABUSE EXCUSE
And Other Cop-Outs, Sob Stories, and Evasions of Responsibility
by Alan M. Dershowitz

I love this book because it so perfectly crystallises one of my biggest pet peeves. Namely, we've become a society of crybabies. No one is responsible for their actions anymore. Go ahead, commit a crime, even murder. Then say that you couldn't help it… your childhood, PMS, Prozac, voices in your head, nicotine withdrawal, or TV shows made you do it. There's a good chance you'll be found not guilty or at least

The <u>M/V Fury</u> pirate radio ship.
Access to the Airwaves.

convicted of a lesser offence.

Famed defence attorney Alan Dershowitz critically examines this sorry state of affairs. In the introduction, he writes, "... the abuse excuse is a symptom of a general abdication of responsibility by individuals, families, groups, and even nations. Its widespread acceptance is dangerous to the very tenets of democracy, which presuppose personal accountability for choices and actions. It also endangers our collective safety by legitimating a sense of vigilantism that reflects our frustration over the apparent inability of law enforcement to reduce the rampant violence that engulfs us."

Dershowitz presents dozens of distressing instances of excuse-making. In 1989, a man broke into a married couple's house and slashed them to death while they were sleeping. The murder was unsolved until he admitted at an Alcoholics Anonymous meeting that he did it. He has offered several creative justifications for his heinous crime, but the one that takes the cake is his excuse for getting caught — namely, that AA *made* him confess. He says he confessed because "he was 'obligated' to follow the rules of AA in order to recover." What's worse is that many experts are agreeing with him. They feel that confessions made at an AA meeting should be treated like confessions made to a priest or psychiatrist — that is, not admissible in court.

Some of these types of defence enjoy wide support among Americans. Many people have sympathy for abused wives who kill their husbands and then invoke battered woman syndrome. Dershowitz, however, considers this another excuse. His reasoning is that if a woman kills her husband because she is in immediate jeopardy of being injured or killed (or reasonably believes that she is), then that is completely justifiable as simple self defence, without needing to use any type of psychological condition as rationalisation. "The battered woman syndrome purports to explain not why the abused woman killed her batterer, but rather why she did not — and indeed could not — leave her batterer." Thus, this syndrome excuses homicide in cases where the danger was not immediate and much less drastic action (leaving) could have been employed.

Besides examining adopted child syndrome, urban survival excuse, "I read a book" excuse, and many others, Dershowitz also looks hard at the unending excuses used by people in power — Caspar Weinberger, President Clinton,

the former senior trustee of Yale, an openly anti-Semitic judge, police who perjure, and others. The final section of the book examines censorship and lawsuits brought about by the "political correctness excuse". Dershowitz is sure to ruffle feathers as he blows the whistle on false reports of rape, the unreported epidemic of same-sex rape (mostly in prisons), and the fact that women are the defendants in over 40% of spousal murders.

The Abuse Excuse is harsh medicine for a country full of people who don't want to take responsibility for their own actions.

Little, Brown and Company; $12.95
1994; softcover; 341 pp
0-316-18102-1

ACCESS TO THE AIRWAVES
My Fight for Free Radio
by Allan H. Weiner as told to Anita Louise McCormick

Allan H. Weiner is the legendary figure behind some of the most well-known pirate radio stations ever to broadcast in North America, including Radio New York International. In this autobiography, he tells of his battle to use the airwaves, the technical and legal obstacles (including arrests and the destruction of his equipment by the FCC) he's overcome, and his general philosophy (which is best summed up in the line, "I hold radio communications as sacred as the printed word.").

Loompanics Unlimited; $17.95
1997; softcover; 254 pp
illus; 1-55950-163-4

BLOODY SUNDAY IN DERRY
What Really Happened
by Eamonn McCann

Eamonn McCann was one of the key organisers of the civil rights march that took place in Derry, Ireland, on October 5, 1968. The unarmed marchers were viciously beaten by the Royal Ulster Constabulary, an event that is widely seen as ushering in the modern era of Troubles in Northern Ireland. McCann was also at the peaceful march on January 30, 1972, that turned into a bloodbath. This book focuses solely on that Bloody Sunday and its aftermath.

Ten thousand people had assembled in Derry to protest against Unionist rule and its practice of jailing and torturing opponents. The unarmed protesters came to a barricade erected by the British Army. They demanded to be let through, to be able to march in their own town. When they weren't allowed through, they threw stones and bottles. The soldiers answered with rubber bullets. When the protesters tried to get through with makeshift shields, they were tear-gassed. Suddenly the British began firing into the unarmed crowd, shooting people in the back as they ran away. Thirteen marchers — almost half of them seventeen-years-old — were killed and twelve others were wounded.

Besides explaining what happened on that fateful day, McCann looks at the whitewash that followed. He dissects the bogus Widgery Report, the government's official investigation of the massacre. Not surprisingly, the report vindicated the British Army, saying that the decision to contain the march was "fully justified by events and successfully carried out." McCann says that the "inconsistency and illogicality" of the report "is not based on incompetence or carelessness but on politically motivated dishonesty…"

Throughout the book friends and family offer remembrance of those who were killed. Jim Wray's sister writes: "I am rearing children of my own now. I try to explain to them how my brother was killed and I tell them not to be bitter, but sometimes even when I'm saying it I can feel bitterness inside myself. They shot him the first time and then, as he was lying on his stomach on the ground, they shot him again in the back. What damage could he have done them, lying there wounded? How could they have had such fear of him then as to put more bullets into his back?"

Brandon Book Publishers; $11.95

1992; softcover; 254 pp

illus; 0-86322-139-4

BOYCOTT QUARTERLY

One way of attempting to influence corporations is to withhold your dollars from them and convince other people to do the same. Boycotts are a time-tested way to get the attention of the Goliaths. With the huge number of corporations and all they ways in which they can act unethically, boycotting has become a popular activity. So popular in fact, that *Boycott Quarterly* was created to keep people informed of all the boycotts currently underway in the US.

Each issue discusses several new boycotts and looks at the progress of some continuing boycotts. The boycotts are usually organised because of what are typically considered "leftist concerns" (the environment, animal rights, labour issues, etc.), although there are notices of boycotts by conservative religious groups. Among the boycotts *BQ* has covered include PeTA's boycott of Alaska Airlines and other businesses that support the Iditarod dogsled race, which always results in dead dogs; the League of United Latin American Citizens boycotting the sponsors of Howard Stern's radio show because of comments Stern made after the death of Selena; the Atlanta chapter of Queer Nation reinstating the boycott on Cracker Barrel restaurants because of the company's alleged discrimination against gay and lesbian employees and patrons; the American Family Association's boycott of Disney because of that company's enlightened attitude towards gays and lesbians; a boycott of the Make-a-Wish foundation because it granted a dying seventeen-year-old's wish to hunt a Kodiak bear in Alaska; and a boycott of Texaco for racist and anti-Semitic remarks made by high-ranking executives during a meeting in which they discussed destroying evidence in a racial-discrimination lawsuit against them.

The section "On-Going Boycotts" in each issue gives capsule descriptions of all known boycotts. The winter 1997 issue lists over 100 boycotts, which is a typical amount. Among those being targeted are Adidas, Carnegie Mellon University, farm-raised fish, Holiday Inn, McDonald's, Puerto Rico, Starbucks bottled coffee drinks, and Wal Mart.

But that's not all *Boycott Quarterly* reports on. It also

Boycotting TexaKo and other Korporate Kreeps.
Boycott Quarterly.

keeps track of activist groups who are being denied their rights to free speech and protest by corporations who sue them for organising boycotts. The Ontario Divisional Court declared that a boycott organised against a paper company is illegal because it might financially harm the company. Of course, hitting a company in the pocketbook is the whole point of every single boycott that's ever been organised, but Canadian judges apparently don't want to be bothered by facts, common sense, and the right to protest.

A large number of feature articles don't address boycotts directly but look at environmental, animal, social, and other concerns usually — but not always — from an economic angle. Past issue have covered bogus environmental fronts for corporations, police abuse in Philadelphia, the car-bombing of two of Earth First!'s organisers, the censorship of *ANSWER Me!* #4 in Washington State, the possibility of Mad Cow disease in the US, clear-cutting and logging, how to organise boycotts, and labour disputes at Detroit newspapers.

Centre for Economic Democracy/PO Box 30727/Seattle WA 98103-0727

Email: boycottguy@aol.com

Single issue: $5

Four issue sub (one year): $20. Can/Mex: $27. Others: $40

THE COMPLETE GUIDE TO OFFSHORE MONEY HAVENS
(Revised and Updated)

by Jerome Schneider

By following the advice of offshore banking and investing expert Jerome Schneider, "your money will be safely protected and working for you in offshore havens that offer handsome profits, genuine tax protection, and an unparalleled level of financial privacy." Making money and covering your heinie by investing in offshore money havens has the reputation of being an option only available to big corporations and very wealthy individuals, but Schneider shows how most upper-income individuals in the US and Canada can profit from doing business away from North America. He gives instructions for opening an offshore bank account, investing in offshore funds, creating an offshore corporation, setting up an offshore living trust, and even establishing your own offshore bank. He looks at the ways to maximise your privacy, minimise your taxes, and protect your assets from lawsuits, creditors, and ex-spouses. A separate chapter looks at the pros and cons of several locations for doing offshore finances, including Aruba, Barbados, Bermuda, the Cook Islands, Liechtenstein, and Switzerland. An appendix lists contact information for dozens of banks in these and other locations.

Prima Publishing; $30
1997; hardcover; 361 pp
0-7615-0996-8

DEFENDING THE UNDEFENDABLE
by Walter Block

Psychotropedia tries to present the radical aspects of as many areas of human knowledge and endeavour as possible. This includes finding the unorthodox side of what is widely regarded as the most arcane and boring field of study — economics, "the dismal science". In this entertaining book libertarian economics professor Walter Block dares to propose that every profession is necessary and somehow contributes to the working of the free market economy.

In the chapter on pimps, Block admits that some of them use threats and violence against their "girls", but he says that we can't condemn a whole profession because of the actions of a few of its members. Overall, pimping is a beneficial transaction for all three parties. The prostitute gets a customer she might not have otherwise had, and she gets protection. The john is spared the time and effort of finding a prostitute himself, and he "has the security of knowing that the prostitute comes recommended." Of course, the pimp makes some money from the transaction. "The prostitute is no more exploited by the pimp than is the manufacturer exploited by the salesman who drums up business for him, or the actress who pays an agent a percentage of her earnings to find new roles for her."

In another rollicking good chapter, Block defends police officers who take money from criminals to "look the other way". Because he is a libertarian, Block's belief is that all consensual transactions should be allowed to occur, including gambling, prostitution, and the selling and buying of drugs. Thus, when a cop takes a bribe, he is allowing legitimate (though technically illegal) business to be conducted. There are times when turning a blind eye is a bad thing... such as when crimes of violence are occurring. Then a cop is morally obligated to stop the injuring or killing of another person. But when the "crime" is a mutually agreeable transaction among adults, cops who accept money for allowing it are "acting quite properly."

Among the other "economic scapegoats" whom Block defends are prostitutes, drug pushers, blackmailers, ticket scalpers, counterfeiters, slumlords, litterers, stripminers, and businesses that use child labour. *Defending the Undefendable* has the power to change the way you view economics and the roles of people engaged in activities considered illegal and/or immoral. You may not always agree, but it is great food for thought.

Fox & Wilkes; $12.95
1976; softcover; 232 pp
illus; 0-930073-05-3

DID BIG BROTHER GIVE YOU PERMISSION TO GO WEE-WEE?
by Thomas Metzger

In this book iconoclast Thomas Metzger is out to break down your preconceived notions about government and freedom. His main point is that individuals and businesses have become overloaded with thousands upon thousands of restrictive, ineffective, petty laws and regulations that attempt to control every aspect of our lives and our society.

Metzger asks you to imagine what would happen if suddenly there were no laws. "Did you think that there would be wholesale murder, rape, and violence in your neighbourhood? Will people go into banks and steal money? Will people hold you up and take your valuables?" Probably none of these things would occur, because "95 percent or more of the people are honest, hardworking people who don't need laws to be good people. Most people would only accidentally do something to cause harm to another person, and that will happen if we have ten times the laws we have today." In other words, laws don't keep criminals from breaking the law, because they're going to do what they want anyway. And laws don't affect all the other people because they wouldn't be engaging in such activities even if they were legal.

Metzger challenges you to make a list of ten things that aren't controlled through laws, taxes, or some other form of regulation. Someone once replied that he can go to the bathroom anytime he wants to. "If one goes out in the open and one gets caught one will get cited. If you go at home and you're on a city sewer system, you must get permission from big brother to hook up to the sewer line. If you have a septic system, you must get permission to put it in and hook up to it. You can't have an outhouse, it's against the law... Did Big Brother give you permission to go wee-wee?"

To make the point that we are being over-regulated, Metzger publishes two pictures side by side. One shows two hands holding a book of medium thickness. That book is the entire California Penal Code from 1871. The other picture shows a large bookcase filled with books. Specifically, 160 books totalling 240,000 pages. That is the California Penal Code for the 1990s. Granted things are more complex now than in 1871, but have they really become that bad? "Now ask yourself, how complicated was government in 1871 and how complicated is government today? For whose benefit has it become so convoluted and perplexing?"

Metzger's book is filled with solid, libertarian-style defence of free markets and free minds and attacks on "social-ist knuckleheads". Occasionally Metzger's social conserva-tism becomes apparent, but otherwise he constantly blasts away at any type of restrictions on freedom.

Blue Dolphin Publishing; $12.95
1994; softcover; 136 pp
illus; 0-931892-98-8

DOING PUBLIC JOURNALISM

by Arthur Charity

Doing Public Journalism looks at a small but growing trend in which the media — especially newspapers — take a more social activist role. This kind of journalism aims to help peo-ple truly understand the issues and choices that confront them and then help them make their voices heard and effect change. Sections include "Techniques for Hearing Citizens", "The Twin Roles of Experts and Ordinary People", "The Newspaper and Community Forums", "How Do You Spot — and Spotlight — an Evolving Public Consensus?", and "Why Public Journalism Makes Economic Sense". A final resource section lists newspapers, magazines, and other media out-lets and groups involved in the movement.

The Guilford Press; $16.95
1995; softcover; 188 pp
1-57230-030-2

EXPAT WORLD

Expat World is a magazine designed to give hard-to-find in-formation to expatriates, international travellers, financial privacy seekers, vagabonds, pirates, and rakehells. There are a lot of loopholes and secrets around the world that will give you freedom and power. *Expat World* is dedicated to finding them and letting you know. In each issue, they report on at least one new product or service they offer for sale. For example, they'll enter you in the Irish lottery for a small fee. The beautiful thing about this lottery is that whenever you buy a £5 ticket, it stays in the lottery week after week indefinitely. You never need to buy another ticket, unless you want to increase your chances of winning.

There are also many articles and snippets that aren't trying to sell anything. They vary widely in their usefulness… some are quite practical, others are interesting to know but not directly useful, and others are just more like "New of the Weird" (i.e., not much use at all). Articles in the first category cover how to get a European Community driver's licence even if you failed the test in your home country, the newest scams being perpetrated, quickie college degrees by mail, fake degrees and certificates, untraceable voice mail boxes, tricks casinos use to make you gamble more, and moving money quietly. Articles in the second category cover the cou-ple who was arrested for possessing psychedelic toads, the fiendish computer programme SATAN, and the Dutch pro-posal to legalise hard drugs. In the third category you'll find a collection of lawyer jokes, the weirdest sights in America, etc.

Even though all the info in *Expat World* isn't hard-edged, it does have enough worthwhile tips to justify a subscription if you really plan on doing some of these things. It's too ex-pensive for curiosity seekers.

Expat World/Box 1341/Raffles City/Singapore 9117
Email: eugenevl@singnet.com.sg
WWW: ultimate.org/expat/
Single issues not available
A three-issue trial subscription to EXPAT WORLD, a 30-page catalogue of products/services, a SECURELINE(tm) phonecard, and a 60-page report (Passports By Mail): $50US
Payment: cash, ck, mo, Visa, MC

EXPAT WORLD'S CATALOGUE OF PRODUCTS AND SERVICES

If you're interested in the information in *Expat World* [above], then you'll probably want their catalogue, too. Inside you will find loopholes, well-kept secrets, and other ways to get around pesky governments. You want a second passport? It's yours for $20,500. Or how about a diplomatic passport? With it, you'll have full diplomatic immunity around the world. It'll cost you 37 grand. If your company or product could use some prestige, you can receive a royal warrant from several princes or a reigning monarch. It's kind of like having a ce-lebrity endorsement, except it's from a royal house. If that's not enough for you, and you'd actually like to *become* a member of the royalty, that can be arranged. You can legiti-mately become a royal title holder in the British Isles. For just $2000 your title could be the Baron-Marshal of Middleton or the Baroness-Chancellor of Willmount. If you're willing to shell out more, you can become a duchess or a prince.

Secret Swiss bank accounts were abolished in 1991, but there is still a way to have a bank account that is abso-lutely untraceable. An Austrian Sparbuch account is the only 100% secret type of bank account left in the world. To get one, you don't have to show any ID or references — you don't even have to give them your name or address! Natu-rally, you won't receive any statements, but that's a small drawback compared to the absolute financial privacy you'll have.

Expat World works with the (in)famous Universal Life Church in California to grant you tax exemption, if not eter-nal salvation. For a $40 fee, you will become a legally or-dained minister and have the right to open a legitimate, tax-exempt church. The only catch is that you must put Uni-versal Life in front of your church's name and pay the central church a $2 a month filing fee. Other than that, you have no obligations. You can name your church the Universal Life Church of Free Love and Good Pot, if you wish.

OK, here's a doozy. Screw the divorce lawyers, you can get your hellish, dead-end marriage annulled by an Eastern Orthodox Church founded in the sixth century CE. For $1000 they will dissolve your marriage. Poof! It's like it never hap-pened. For an extra grand, they'll include a clause that says that there will be no alimony, child support, property settle-ment, etc. Also, you can be granted full custody of your chil-dren, for a thou per child. If you're thinking that this is too good to be true, it is for us Americans. However, these an-nulments have been recognised in Mexico, Spain, Hungary, Argentina, the Dominican Republic, a few African and Asian countries, and others.

You can also get your hands on an international driver's licence recognised in 160 countries, mail order brides, a camouflage passport, and other great stuff. Expat World can help you set up a tax exempt company in Panama, obtain a green card, and get a mail forwarding service.

What more could a modern-day pirate want?

Expat World/Box 1341/Raffles City/Singapore 9117
Catalogue: $5

THE FIJActivist

There is an aspect of the justice system that judges, prosecutors, and many other powerful people don't want you to know about. Namely, that as a juror, you have the right to judge not just the defendant but the law itself. If you think a law is bad, unjust, or being applied unfairly, you can vote not guilty, even if the accused technically did break the law. (You also have the power to find defendants guilty of lesser offences.) Judges will often state that this is not true and will even threaten defence attorneys with contempt of court if they mention it. In many cases, potential jurors are asked if they are aware of their right of juror nullification. If they know, they are not chosen to sit on the jury.

Obviously, the powers-that-be are scared to death of putting this kind of power in the hands of the people, but it's too late. The power is already there... the challenge is to let people know. This is where the Fully Informed Jury Association (FIJA) comes in. FIJA has spread the word far and wide that juries are allowed — indeed, are supposed to — judge the law. They also push for legislation that would require judges to stop lying to juries and instead fully inform them as to their powers and duties.

If jury veto power sounds like a fantasy, think again. In colonial times and during the early days of the US, judges did fully inform juries. The Founders believed in it, and US courts — including the Supreme Court — have constantly upheld it. In 1972 the DC Circuit Court of Appeals opined that a jury has an "... unreviewable and irreversible power... to acquit in disregard of the instruction on the law given by the trial judge. The pages of history shine upon instances of the jury's exercise of its prerogative to disregard instructions of the judge; for examples, acquittals under fugitive slave law."

Juror nullification also undermined early laws against "seditious libel" (which meant criticising the government) and preaching forbidden religious doctrines. More recently, juries have vetoed convictions of people for drug possession, gun ownership, and tax protest. Many high profile cases — Randy Weaver, the Branch Davidians, and Jack Kevorkian — may have been affected by FIJA letting prospective jurors know their powers.

FIJActivist is FIJA's 40-page quarterly tabloid that keeps members apprised of the struggle. Issue 17 brings word that FIJA activists have been charged with jury tampering for distributing literature outside courtrooms! It's amazing that it's come to this — people who try to tell us of our rights are being persecuted as criminals. Issue 18 has an article on the most serious harassment of a *FIJActivist* yet. Yvonne Regas, a 51-year-old florist, has been charged with "con-spiracy to commit offences against the United States". Her horrendous crime? You guessed it — putting FIJA leaflets under the windshield wipers of cars near a courthouse where her son and ex-husband were on trial on drug charges.

On the plus side, Rodger Sless — whose business had been raided by armed FDA agents because he sold vitamins — was acquitted of all but four minor counts in a fifteen-count indictment. Several of the jurors directly credit FIJA for letting them know they had the right to nullify ridiculous anti-vitamin laws. Also, FIJA handed out their leaflets to potential jurors in the Heidi Fleiss "Hollywood Madam" case, which might help undermine invasive laws that forbid exchanging sex for money.

Besides such news, FIJActivist offers articles on the history of juror nullification and looks at bogus contemporary trials, such as the one against the surviving Branch Davidians. You can also order a slew of buttons, bumper stickers, banners, videos, literature, etc.

Call the number below to hear a recorded message and receive a free information kit in the form of an eight-page flier. Or just go ahead and join, so you can help people learn the immense power against government tyranny that they wield.

FIJA/PO Box 59/Helmville MT 59843
WWW: www.fija.org
Message: 1-800-TEL-JURY
One year sub (4 issues): included in membership fee of $25 (student and low income: $20)

THE FIRST HONEST BOOK ABOUT LIES

by Jonni Kincher

What a great idea for a book. Jonni Kincher exposes all the ways in which we are misled and bamboozled — through bogus historical facts, manipulated statistics, advertising and PR, lying to ourselves, and even how our senses can deceive us. *The First Honest Book About Lies* was written for teenagers, but it will also be useful to people of all ages who want a primer on how they are being manipulated.

Using lots of sidebars, exercises, short sections, and snappy illustrations, Kincher aims to make readers more savvy and rob liars of their power. "As you learn about truth and lies, you become a living 'lie detector,' sensing when the truth is being twisted to influence your feelings and behaviours... The power source for your inner lie detector is knowledge. The more you know about everything — especially about the many methods used to influence you — the more you can see and hear the truth."

The chapter on how your senses can mislead you contains some valuable insights into how we automatically organise information. We want to make sense of the multitude of sensations that flood our brains, and in order to so, we unknowingly make certain assumptions. A good example of this is how people answer the age-old question, "Is a zebra black with white stripes or vice versa?" "People from countries of mostly dark-skinned people tend to see a black animal with white stripes. But those from countries of mostly light-skinned people tend to see a white animal with black stripes."

"The larger the group, the stricter the control."
The Heart of Progress.

"Social Lies" is an especially important chapter for teens. It discusses lies of convenience, protective lies, changing the rules, getting approval, peer pressure, and conforming. "There are so many groups with so many rules that you may wonder how you can possibly win everybody's approval. The answer is: you can't, so don't even try."

The "Myth-Matics" chapter is a short lesson, packed with examples, that shows the problems with correlations, averages, polls, scientific studies, charts and graphs, predictions, and other statistical sleights of hand. "Adver-Lies" shows how to decode label language, weasel words, and "green" advertising, among other things. The final chapter gives some practical advice on "how to live in a world of lies".

Because *The First Honest Book* is aimed at adolescents, it tends to be somewhat superficial in its treatment of truth vs. lies, as if the world is truly that black and white. At one point, the author recommends the *Skeptical Inquirer*, a magazine "dedicated to fighting nonsense". It's written by scientists who do everything they can to debunk any kind of paranormal phenomenon. There's no mention of the fact that materialism and scepticism are not bastions of absolute truth, but are instead just two more examples of belief systems whose adherents often ignore or ridicule facts that don't fit into their worldview. I guess such complex arguments are beyond the scope of this book.

Despite this drawback, Kincher has done an admirable job in introducing impressionable minds to the many forms of deception.

Free Spirit Publishing; $12.95
1992; oversized softcover; 170 pp
heavily illus; 0-915793-43-1

THE HEART OF PROGRESS
An Illustrated Guide
by Paul Klem

Professional engraver Paul Klem delivers sixty blunt etchings, accompanied by prose poems, that form a polemic against the ills of capitalism, racism, sexism, classism, consumerism, the media, environmental destruction, and conformity. "In the name of the divine White Buga/Buga, the golden, the pure as snow.../Class, gender, poverty, race, illiteracy/A crime, a punishable offence."

Black Crow Books; $11
1996; softcover; 60 pp
heavily illus; 0-9681535-0-X

INFLUENCING MINDS
A Reader in Quotations
by Leonard Roy Frank

In *Influencing Minds*, anti-psychiatry activist Leonard Roy Frank has assembled 1500 quotations relating to the shaping of the human mind, for better or for worse, through a variety of means. The quotes are divided into 32 categories, including truth, education, public speech, books and reading, journalists and the media, advertising, propaganda, brainwashing, creativity, and dreams. Each aphorism is given an exact reference, if known.

Here are a few representative examples, minus their bibliographic references:

☞ "Advertising is a means of convincing people to buy things they don't need at prices they can't afford. ANONYMOUS"

☞ "We are not at war with Egypt. We are in a state of armed conflict. ANTHONY EDEN (British prime minster), while Egypt was under attack by British, French and Israeli forces during the Suez Crisis, House of Commons speech, 4 November 1956."

☞ "Sometimes a scream is better than a thesis. [Ralph Waldo Emerson]"

☞ "My own education operated under a succession of eye-openers each involving the repudiation of some previously held belief. GEORGE BERNARD SHAW"

☞ "More and more, what doesn't show up on the [television] screen doesn't exist, and what shows up badly is doomed. STANLEY HOFFMAN"

☞ "Propaganda, n. Their lies. Public information, n. Our lies. EDWARD S. HERMAN"

☞ "Never do anything without conscience, even if the state demands it. ALBERT EINSTEIN"

☞ "I went to America to convert the Indians; but oh! who shall convert me? JOHN WESLEY (English founder of the Methodist Church)"

☞ "A really efficient totalitarian state would be one in which the all-powerful executive of political bosses and their army of managers control a population of slaves who do not have to be coerced, because they love their servitude. To make them love it is the task assigned, in present-day totalitarian states, to ministries of propaganda, newspaper editors and schoolteachers. ALDOUS HUXLEY"

Influencing Minds contains lots of nutritious food for

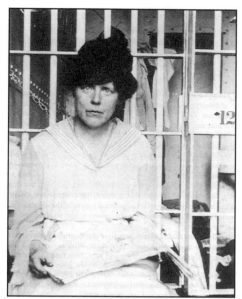

Lucy Burns in jail for demanding the right to vote.
Jailed for Freedom.

thought and plenty of material for nonconformists to sprinkle in their essays, zines, books, T-shirts, etc.

Feral House; $12.95

1995; softcover; 247 pp

0-922915-25-3

JAILED FOR FREEDOM
American Women Win the Vote

by Doris Stevens, edited by Carol O'Hare

One of the things that never ceases to amaze me about the United States is that until 1920 a little over half the population was not allowed to vote. The conditions were simple: if you had a penis, you could vote. If you had a vagina, you couldn't. This idiotic suppression of basic rights in "the land of freedom" was finally stopped by a group of women who wouldn't back down. In an age when women were never supposed to speak up, the suffragists marched, protested, got in President Wilson's face, were beaten, went to prison, went on hunger strikes, and eventually got what they were after.

Jailed for Freedom, originally published in 1920, was written by one of the militant suffragists who was always in the thick of the action. In this edition, Carol O'Hare has edited out much of the "minute detail" and "verbiage" that would make the original version unappealing to modern readers. By cutting out the rambling, she has made created a readable, even suspenseful narrative.

For around six years, the suffragists held President Wilson's feet to the fire. Despite constantly being arrested, they wouldn't shut up and go away. Like all politicians, Wilson talked a good game but would never back it up. He promised to pass an Amendment to give women the right to vote,

but he didn't try very hard. In early 1918, with just fifteen days left in the session, Congress voted on the Nineteenth Amendment. The House of Representatives passed the legislation by a single vote. The Senate, however, was one vote shy of the two-thirds needed. Many of the holdouts were Democrats. As a Democrat, the Prez should have been able to twist one of their arms enough to get a vote, but he didn't. A new amendment was drawn up, with slightly different wording, and one Democratic Senator declared he would vote for it. However, the Republicans blocked the vote, and the session ended.

In the November elections of the previous year, Republicans had won the majority of Congress. The suffragists found that they now had enough votes in the House but were still one short in the Senate. When the last session of the Democratic congress ended disappointingly, the suffragists put pressure on the President to win the one Senatorial vote and to convene a special session of Congress to pass the Amendment, so twenty-five of them protested outside the Metropolitan Opera House where Wilson was speaking one night. As they approached the building, 200 policemen attacked them with billy clubs, and — even more despicable — a crowd of soldiers and sailors who had recently returned from fighting W.W.I joined the cops. The women were beaten bloody. Stevens recalls: "Margaretta Schuyler, a fragile young girl, was holding a silken American flag which she had carried at the head of the procession when a uniformed soldier jumped upon her, twisted her arms until she cried in pain, cursed, struggled until he had torn her flag from its pole, and then broke the pole across her head. When I appealed to the policeman, who at that moment was pounding me on the back, to intercept the cruel attack, his only reply was, 'Oh, he's helping me.'"

I hate to ruin the book for you, but I think we all know how this one ends. One of the new Democratic Senators said that he would vote for the Amendment. Wilson called a special Congressional session, and on May 19, 1919, the legislators passed the Nineteenth Amendment. On August 18, 1920, Tennessee ratified the amendment, giving it the necessary three-fourths majority of states needed to add it to the Constitution. Women could finally vote.

O'Hare provides concluding information on what became of seven of the leading suffragists, as well as suffrage in the Western states, the Equal Rights Amendment, and other related topics.

NewSage Press; $12.95

1995; softcover; 220 pp

illus; 0-939165-25-2

LIVING FREE

Want to be as free as possible while still living in the US? Jim Stumm's bi-monthly libertarian-oriented newsletter will certainly help. The original articles, reprints, and letters it contains discuss a wide range of issues, from food caching to which states are the most free. Issue 89 gives a recipe for a refreshing drink made from the weed sumac, discusses the concept of Federal Zones, and compares snakebite treatments. An essential article in issue 90 lists the best and worst states for freedom-lovers to live in. Taking into account each state's incarceration rate, wrongful convictions, types of taxes, tolerance of diversity, and other factors, the best states to live in are Montana, New Hampshire, and Oregon. Among the worst are Alabama, Florida, Louisiana, and Texas.

Occasionally, there are articles about other countries where you can live free. Issue #90 has two such guides: "Thai: Land of the Free" and "Estonia: The World's Greatest Government" (although Thailand doesn't sound that great to me).

Debate is openly encouraged. One letter claims that homesteading is a good way to become self-reliant but it simply entangles you with the government: "You automatically get in every govt record book, on every tax roll, subject to multitudinous environmental inspectors and regulations." A letter in issue 90 takes Stumm to task for writing that claiming state citizenship doesn't work when avoiding federal income tax.

Jim Stumm/Box 29, Hiler Branch/Buffalo NY 14223

Single issue: $2; outside US/Can/Mex: $3

6 issue sub (approximately one year): $12; outside US/Can/Mex: $15

MARKETING MADNESS
(A Survival Guide for a Consumer Society)

by Michael F. Jacobson & Laurie Ann Mazur

If you have any doubts that the US is a nation of consumers instead of citizens, or that marketers have managed to invade every aspect of our lives, this book will lay those doubts to rest. *Marketing Madness* offers a detailed, comprehensive look at the ingeniously insidious ways in which corporations violate our psyches.

Ralph Nader gives an overview of the book in his foreword: "In area after area that was generally off limits to commercialism, the mercantile juggernaut has moved in or swarmed over — into our schools and colleges, our public media, our amateur sports, our holidays and rituals, our arts, our children, our privacy and private sensibilities, our religious institutions, our environment, our language, and our politics." *Marketing Madness* covers all of these topics and more.

The first two chapters deal with the corporate targeting of children. Kids represent an extremely lucrative market... it's been estimated that children aged 4-12 spend $9 billion, teenagers spend $93 billion, and kids directly influence $130 billion of family spending. Moreover, marketers try to reach kids so they'll build life-long brand loyalty. As Mike Searles, the president of Kids "R" Us, candidly said, "If you own this child at an early age, you can own this child for years to come."

Kids are inculcated with detrimental ideas through marketing. Mall Madness, a game from Milton Bradley, teaches young girls to be compulsive, credit-card wielding shoppers. The acne cream commercials convince kids that they are nasty, freakish laughingstocks if they have as few as one or two pimples.

Movies, which are supposed to be an art form, have

You can't run from corporate influence.
Marketing Madness.

become little more than merchandising schemes in the hands of the major studios. Just try to find one "blockbuster" that doesn't have some kind of merchandising tie-in with fast food joints, toys, soundtracks, etc. Of course, we are also seeing commercials being played in theatres before the movie we just paid $7 to see. Advertisers love having a "captive audience". Even more sneaky is the booming business of product placement. Corporations pay big bucks to have their products written into movie scripts. To give an example, "Disney solicited product placements for a film called *Mr. Destiny* according to a hierarchy of prominence: $20,000 to appear on screen, $40,000 for a verbal mention, and $60,000 if the product was actually used by an actor or actress."

The line between news and advertising has blurred to the point of being indistinguishable. Corporations provide local and even national news reports with video news releases, which are pre-packaged "stories" produced and distributed by the companies themselves. *USA Today* runs ads in the upper part of the front page of each interior section, a spot where actual news headers are also placed. *The New Yorker* ran two cartoons by Robert Weber, one an ad for Diet Coke in the same issue.

There is nothing that marketers will hold sacred. Politics: In 1993 Anheuser-Busch, an alcohol company, placed a horse-drawn Budweiser wagon in the middle of President Clinton's inaugural parade. Art: "The Los Angeles County Museum of Art held an exhibit called 'Salvatore Ferragamo: The Art of the Shoe, 1896-1960,' paid for by — you guessed it — Ferragamo, a high-priced Italian shoe company. After the gala opening preview, a reception was held at a Ferragamo store, and a Ferragamo boutique was installed in the museum's lobby." The Olympics: Reebok sponsored the 1992 US Olympic team with the stipulation that all medalists wear Reebok outfits on the winner's stand.

Marketing Madness also covers home shopping, the corporate take-over of PBS, infomercials, sexism in advertising, sex as a commodity, using social issues for profit, telemarketing, direct mail campaigns, privacy issues, billboards, misleading and lying ads, the advertising practices of alcohol and tobacco companies, the commercialisation of Christmas, and more. Chapter nine looks at the effects that this corporate carpet bombing is having on us as individuals and a society. The last chapter — as well as sidebars at the end of each of the other chapters — gives concrete actions you can take to "reclaim your mental environment" (to use a phrase from *Adbusters* magazine).

Marketing Madness is profusely illustrated. Each page contains one to five visuals, most of which are examples of ads, infomercials, product placements, ambush advertising, etc. I think it's safe to say that this book is absolutely essential if you want understand the mediascape we live in. No matter how savvy you think you are, this book will teach you new tricks that are being used on you.

Westview Press, $23
1995; softcover; 260 pp
heavily illus; 0-8133-1981-1

NAFTA, GATT & THE WORLD TRADE ORGANIZATION
The Emerging New World Order
by Kristin Dawkins with Jeremy Brecher

The North American Free Trade Agreement (NAFTA) and the General Agreement on Tariffs and Trade (GATT) sparked some resistance in the US, but not enough to stop their passage. These two insidious agreements have taken away a lot of sovereignty and decision-making power from the US and many other nations. In Kristin Dawkins' essay for this pamphlet, she writes that GATT has created the World Trade Organization, "a brand new institution designed to manage a world order based on corporate control of the planet's productive and reproductive rights... Under the World Trade Organization, each member country 'shall ensure the conformity of its law, regulations and administrative procedures with its obligations as provided' in the new rules of the GATT."

NAFTA is no better. It "establishes new international laws that can neutralise or override a given country's democratically enacted policies." Dawkins foresees these two agreements leading to higher deficits and unemployment and environmental devastation. She discusses some of the reasons why these things will happen, the role of the military, what happens when NAFTA and GATT clash, and what can be done to counter their negative effects.

In his shorter essay, "Global Village or Global Pillage?", Jeremy Brecher looks at the consequences of globalisation — global stagnation, polarisation of haves and have-nots, loss of democratic control, unaccountable global institutions, and more. He also offers some general ways to resist these effects.

Open Magazine Pamphlet Series; $4
1994; long thin pamphlet; 21 pp
1-884519-04-0

NONVIOLENCE IN AMERICA
A Documentary History
(Revised Edition)
edited by Staughton Lynd & Alice Lynd

This massive compilation of writings presents source documents concerning America's rich tradition of civil disobedience and other non-violent stands against authority. The first three of the 56 documents are from Quakers, who resisted British authority in the Colonies. John Woolman, for example, was opposed to slavery, the terrible treatment of Native Americans, and paying taxes, which support wars.

Among the documents from the abolitionists is Henry David Thoreau's classic "Civil Disobedience", an extremely radical document that is still relevant today. "I heartily accept the motto, — 'The government is best which governs least'; and I should like to see it acted up to more rapidly and systematically. Carried out, it finally amounts to this, which I also believe, — 'That government is best which governs not at all'; and when men are prepared for it, that is the government which they will have."

Although the anarchists of the late-nineteenth and early twentieth centuries are not noted for their non-violence, there were some who called for peaceful solutions. In her later years, Emma Goldman reversed her attitude towards violence and expounded the theory of direct (non-violent) action. In "Anarchism: What It Really Stands For", she writes, "The political superstition is still holding sway over the hearts and minds of the masses, but the true lovers of liberty will have no more to do with it. Instead, they believe with Stirner that man has as much liberty as he is willing to take. Anarchism therefore stands for direct action, the open defiance of, and resistance to, all laws and restrictions, economic, social, and moral."

Naturally, war protesters and draft resisters figure prominently into this collection. A subsection on the Vietnam War chapter reveals the active duty soldiers who conscientiously objected, went AWOL, or resisted in other ways. In one essay, a soldier who went AWOL rather than go to Vietnam ended up in the Presidio stockade with other resisters. "On Monday morning, about a hundred prisoners were in the yard in formation. At the planned moment, at a certain point in the roll call, twenty-seven of us walked to a corner, sat down, and began singing 'We Shall Overcome.' The guards shit bricks."

Other selections relate the words of suffragists, trade unionists, radical Catholics, Martin Luther King, anti-imperialists, members of the peace and environmental movements, W.W.I and W.W.II protesters, and others. (Because this book is published by a Catholic press, non-violent abortion protesters are included.) These are essential and moving writings from people who have resisted coercion for the last 200 years.

Orbis Books; $25
1966, 1995; oversized softcover; 576 pp
1-57075-010-6

NONVIOLENT ACTIVIST

A bimonthly magazine from the War Resisters' League, a group of uncompromising pacifists who oppose war using every possible non-violent means (including civil disobedience actions, withholding taxes, and paying taxes under protest). Each issue brings opinions, activist news, reviews, upcoming events, and more.

War Resisters League/339 Lafayette St/New York 10012
WWW: www.nonviolence.org/wrl
Cover price: $1.50
Six issue sub: $15

ON NEW ECONOMIC PARTNERSHIP
Free Enterprise Socialism and the Rise and Fall of the Cold War — Letters and Essays, 1979-1992
by Thomas Kuna-Jacob

Bound in a ring binder, these writings by Thomas Kuna-Jacob of the Association for World Peace present his unique vision for a just, peaceful world. His philosophy is a surprising blend of Christianity (particularly Catholicism), Judaism, Islam, socialism, capitalism, environmentalism, pro-gay and pro-drug attitudes, and other seemingly contradictory strains of thought.

Part One contains two chapters on the creation of a new economic model, called free enterprise socialism. One of the main features of this type of system is that three groups — investors, workers, and consumers — will each have an equal say in how medium to large enterprises and holding companies are run. Each group will elect a third of the Board of Directors. The second major feature of this new economy will be the gradual redistribution of income and the sharing of jobs. Third, all investors whose income is more than the average worker or farmer must donate or reinvest all their excess income.

The single chapter in part two of the book is titled "Listen, Leftist!: The Christo-Judean Faith and the Philosophy of Classless Society". It postulates that "Christianity and Communism are natural allies both in practice and in theory." If these two worldviews would co-operate, they could bring about a classless, equitable society.

The final part of the book is devoted to political and cultural reform. Kuna-Jacob calls for the legalisation and regulation of all drugs. He not only objects to the discriminatory nature of the War on Drugs, but also to the moral wrongness of outlawing "the simple enjoyment of God's green plants and herbs".

He is against abortion (except in cases of rape or when the mother's life is in danger), because it goes against the Biblical sanctity of life. However, he also feels that recent discoveries are leading to the conclusion that a tendency towards homosexuality is genetic. If in the future parents are able to tell if their unborn child will be gay or lesbian, they may choose to abort it, which could lead to genocide.

Kuna-Jacob speaks further of sexual matters in his introductory material. He foresees a radical new restructuring of relationships. "[W]e posit that bi-sexual group marriage in externally exclusive groups of from 3 to 33 is to become the typical way in which human consciousness, both personal and social, seeks to fulfil itself without being enslaved to suppressed libidinal drives, and that hetero-sexual monogamous union is only for those people whos [sic] mutual consciousnesses achieve an extraordinary degree of monogamous romantic love, on the model of God the Father's marriage with Jerusalem (and He is not to her a monogamous spouse [Ez. 16:61]) and God the Son's marriage to the Catholic, Christian Church."

Other chapters include "Peace Process in the Holy Land, World Peace and the Future Architecture of the Universe", "The Objective Necessity to Indict, Arrest and Try Saddam Hussein for Crimes Against the Humanity of One or More Peoples", and "On New Economic Citizenship", as well as notes and sketches for many future essays.

Association for World Peace; $39
1992; ring binder; 356 pp
878030-00-0

PASSPORT TO FREEDOM
Introduction to state Citizenship, Volume 1
by Herb Crawford

The idea behind becoming a state Citizen is to declare that you are a citizen of the state in which you live, not a citizen of the construct known as the United States. The US federal government was created as a co-operative effort among the various states to regulate state-to-state matters and matters that affect all states (e.g., national defence). It was not meant to be a dominant force that has absolute control over every person living in each state.

Passport to Freedom is a basic guide to the concept of state Citizenship. It spends a lot of time explaining what's wrong with the current situation in America — an abusive federal government, an avalanche of laws and regulations, plans for national ID cards, etc. According to the author, we have reversed the natural flow of rights. The hierarchy — from the top down — should be "our Creator, the sovereign people, the state constitution, state government, US Constitution, the US government." Instead, it has become "the ruling elite, the US federal government, state government, US citizen subjects, our Creator."

Next, the author examines how we ended up in this mess. The troubles began with Lincoln. In 1862 he declared war on the Confederacy, issued money to pay for the war, introduced the first income tax, suspended habeas corpus, and introduced the first draft law. He did not have the power to do any of these things. Over the years, several laws and amendments further eroded our rights. The final blow came when Congress set up income tax in 1939. It knew that it had no jurisdiction to tax any citizens of any state, so the next year it passed the Buck Act, which set up all states as Federal Areas. In other words, it placed an overlay on top of all the states, declaring that they are extensions of the federal government located in Washington, DC. Congress has the right to pass laws and govern the people of Washington, DC, but not any of the states. However, with the Buck Act, it created a fictitious legal entity wherein the entire US is an extension of the District of Columbia. Now they can do whatever they want.

The final section of the book gives a general description of how and why you should stop being a federal citizen and assert your rights as a state Citizen. There are many ways in which you unknowingly enter into contracts with the federal government, thus giving it dominion over you. If you have a Social Security number, motor vehicle registration, birth certificate, marriage licence, or voter registration card, then you are consenting to the rule of the Federal Areas. Once you become a state Citizen, you no longer pay income tax or are required to have a driver's licence or have to do a number of other things. Naturally, going through the steps to break free of the federal government and become a citizen of your state is tricky and can be dangerous. If you stop paying your income tax, especially, you can expect to be harassed.

This book is only intended to familiarise you with the basic principles involved. If you're interested in actually trying it, there are several groups and individuals who offer to guide you through the process. The author of *Passport to Freedom* has put together a mail course for state Citizenship that is much cheaper than most others. Write for details.

Herb Crawford; $19.95
1994; staple-bound oversized softcover; 76 pp
illus; no ISBN

A PENNY A COPY
Readings from the Catholic Worker
by Thomas C. Cornell

An eight-page monthly tabloid published since 1933, *The Catholic Worker* represents one of the most radical aspects of Christianity — Jesus as the rabble-rousing champion of the poor, the oppressed, and the workers of the world. Mixing Christianity with radical leftist (and even anarchist) philosophy, anti-war stances, and non-violent direct action, the 100 articles in *A Penny a Copy* cover over 60 years of agitation.

Orbis Books; $16.50
1995; softcover; 365 pp
1-57075-012-2

THE RADICALISM HANDBOOK
Radical Activists, Groups and
Movements of the Twentieth Century
by John Button

Environmental activist and author John Button has created an impressive guide to twentieth century individuals, groups, and movements of a politically radical bent. All of the entries represent a leftist/liberal/progressive outlook. Almost all of them try to change the system from within, and some may engage in civil disobedience. Don't expect to find any groups that are widely considered terrorist, although some of the groups covered, such as the Black Panther Party and Earth First!, have been known to take drastic action to achieve their ends.

The scope is truly global. Although the Western world is the focus, there are plenty of entries from Brazil, China, India, Japan, Nigeria, Tibet, Turkey, Vietnam, and elsewhere around the world. Individuals include anarchists, anti-Apartheid campaigners, artists, civil rights campaigners, economists, environmentalists, essayists, feminists, indigenous people's rights campaigners, journalists, labour organisers, musicians, novelists, pacifists, poets, politicians, priests, social reformers, suffragists, and utopianists.

After a lengthy essay on the history of twentieth century radicalism, *The Handbook* opens with entries for 38 pre-1900 radicals, including anarchist Mikhail Bakunin, poet and artist William Blake, Karl Marx, John Stuart Mill's unacknowledged writing partner Harriet Taylor, and abolitionist and feminist

The original group of senior hellraisers.
The Raging Grannies Songbook.

Sojourner Truth. Next comes the meat of the book, with entries on more than 350 radicals of the twentieth century: Chilean Marxist Salvador Allende, socialist-feminist writer Simone de Beauvoir, South African martyr Steve Biko, sexologist Havelock Ellis, radical feminist Andrea Dworkin, pomo philosopher Michel Foucault, Mahatma Gandhi, anarchist Emma Goldman, Abbie Hoffman, Mother Jones, Japanese environmental campaigner Kuroda Joichi, Nelson and Winnie Mandela, humanist psychologist Abraham Maslow, German antifascist activist Ulrike Meinhof, educator Maria Montessori, Brazilian native rights leader Paulinho Paiakan, radical psychoanalyst and scientist Wilhelm Reich, peace activist and philosopher Betrand Russell, Islamic liberationist Ali Shari'ati, feminist Wiccan activist and writer Starhawk, Leon Trotsky, Polish unionist Lech Walesa, and Malcolm X.

The 84 organisations and loose-knit movements covered in the next section include AIDS Coalition to Unleash Power (ACT UP), the American Civil Liberties Union, the American Indian Movement, Amnesty International, the Beat Generation, the Congress of Racial Equality, Daughters of Bilitis ("the world's first politically-oriented lesbian organisation"), the Filipino women's rights group GABRIELA, the German Green party, the youth protest movements of May 1968, the Mexican trade union September 19th National Union of Garment Workers, the Stonewall riots, War Resisters International, and the Yippies.

Each entry is just the right length (usually about a page) to give a good rundown of each individual's life or organisation's history, the impacts they made, and a short bibliography of major works by or about them. Appendices and a long index help assure that *The Radicalism Handbook* is a much-needed reference work as well as a good read.

ABC-CLIO; $49.50
1995; hardcover; 476 pp
0-87436-838-3

THE RAGING GRANNIES SONGBOOK
edited by Jean McLaren & Heide Brown

The Raging Grannies are a loose-knit coalition of old women who use protest songs to agitate for peace, environmentalism, and various other causes. They have found that using humour and irony in their songs and skits helps get messages across. "The audience swallows the pill, and gets exposed to a different point of view quite painlessly. To many people this is a welcome change from political rhetoric." The Grannies have found out something else important. Cops and other authorities are not overly anxious to bust the heads of little old ladies. Young women, no problem. But women who look like their grandmothers? That's a little harder. Plus, when the Grannies are peacefully arrested, they always gain lots of public sympathy.

The Grannies use this to their advantage. They regularly get access to forbidden areas, such as nuclear testing facilities and secret NAFTA meetings. During the Gulf War they invaded recruiting stations, demanding they be enlisted in order to "spare our children and grandchildren from having to fight the Gulf War." Because recruiters are not allowed to ask age, they were forced to go through all the formal paperwork with the Grannies.

The Grannies are a decentralised organisation, and anyone can start a group. One chapter of this book tells how to do just that. The key to being an RG is clothing. The Grannies dress in outrageously stereotypical little old lady clothes, such as frumpy dresses, aprons, shawls, and flowery hats with price tags hanging off (the twist is that the tags say, "Hell raiser"). It also helps to wear peace buttons and pink running shoes ("which, besides being comfy, are good for a fast getaway!"). Just get together with some friends, write songs or use the ones in this book, and have fun causing havoc.

The 102 song lyrics presented here are all sung to the tune of familiar ditties, making them easier to write and learn besides automatically striking a responsive cord within listeners. "Song to Introduce Us" is sung to the tune of "Daisy, Daisy". It displays the Grannies' self-deprecating humour: "We try to sing out loudly/And say the words out proudly/Tho' we have stiff backs/And our voices might crack/We hope you will bear with us." "Corporation Green" (to the tune of "Wearing of the Green") mocks multinationals who put on an environmentally correct face: "Let's start with Dow, remember how/They used to make napalm?/And 2-4-D, in case a tree/Still stood in Vietnam".

The Grannies cause a commotion whenever they sing "Safe Sex" ("It's Off to Work We Go"): "Hey ho! Hey ho! As off to bed we go/We grannies smile because we know/Safe sex is quite the best". Can you picture your grandmother singing that one? One of many anti-war songs, "Clementine's Lament" ("Oh My Darling, Clementine"), goes a little something like this: "On our waters, in our harbour/US ships do come and go/Many of them carry warheads/But you're not supposed to know."

The Grannies take on George Bush in "Mr. President" ("Mr. Sandman"): "Mr. President, give us a dream/Show us you're not quite as dumb as you seem/Don't choose more Ollies, Poindexters or Caseys/ — That bunch of out-to-lunch White House crazies." Other songs include "Cycle of Abuse", "Polychlorinated Biphenols", "Take Me Out to the Clearcut", "Santa Doesn't Like War Toys", and "Biggest Lot of Liars in

Black block at the anti-Reagan demonstration, June 12, 1987. *The Subversion of Politics.*

the World".

I really hope I get to see these women in action one day. Rage on, Grannies!

New Society Publishers; $14.95
1993; spiral-bound softcover; 134 pp
illus; 0-86571-255-7

REBELS & DEVILS
The Psychology of Liberation
edited by Christopher S Hyatt, PhD

Rebels & Devils contains writings from 40 iconoclasts and troublemakers, ranging from the little-known to the famous. These essays (plus a few poems and a comic) can be enlightening, humorous, dense, cryptic, lucid, meandering, but almost all of them deal with the issue of breaking free from society's rules and following your own path.

I have to admit that I've never paid much attention to Aleister Crowley, but the selection of his writings included here has intrigued me. He rails against religion and other forms of hypocrisy and calls for unfettered freedom with regard to sex, drugs, and every other aspect of life. "Each star is unique and each orbit apart; indeed, that is the cornerstone of my teaching, to have no standard goals or standard ways, no orthodoxies and no codes." He speaks of the path to true freedom: "The Aspirant must well understand that it is no paradox to say that the Annihilation of the Ego in the Abyss is the condition of emancipating the true Self, and exalting it to unimaginable heights. So long as one remains 'one's self,' one is overwhelmed by the Universe; destroy the sense of self, and every event is equally an expression of one's Will, since its occurrence is the resultant of the concourse of the forces which one recognises as one's own." His belief regarding drugs is equally as radical: "If you are really free, you can take cocaine as simply as salt-water taffy. There is no better rough test of a soul than its attitude to drugs. If a man is simple, fearless, eager, he is all right; he will not become a slave. If he is afraid, he is already a slave. Let the whole world take opium, hashish, and the rest; those who are liable to abuse them were better off dead."

Another surprise was the contribution from Osho Rajneesh, the late spiritual teacher and "cult leader". In "Rebellion Is the Biggest 'Yes' Yet", Rajneesh writes:

You say that in history all the rebellions were based on 'no.' Those were not rebellions; change the word. All the revolutions were based on 'no.' They were negative, they were against something, they were destructive, they were revengeful and violent.

Certainly, my rebellion is based on 'yes' — yes to existence, yes to nature, yes to yourself. Whatever the religions may be saying and whatever the ancient traditions may be saying, they are all saying no to yourself, no to nature, no to existence; they are all life-negative.

My rebellion is life-affirmative. I want you to dance and sing and love and live as intensely as possible and as totally as possible. In this total affirmation of life, in this absolute 'yes' to nature we can bring a totally new earth and a totally new humanity into being.

This book is filled with great quotes that will inspire you to shake off the chains that bind you. "The Fourteen Steps" by Daniel Suders contains this gem: "It is a well-known fact that we do not see those we meet — we only see little faces of ourselves in their eyes and evaluate ourselves by the way we perceive ourselves in their perceptions of us." Later, he suggests this: "Write letters to your most beloved folks and let them know they no longer have any power over your emotions and if they try to control you any longer that you will kill them in a rage so uncontrollable that they will have to shoot you up with Thorazine for about ten years." Rocket scientist and renowned occultist Jack Parsons also has some advice: "What is the person you most desire to be — (I mean, freely and honestly, not morally)? Imitate that person, and what began as imitation will end as perfection." Phil Hine, a practitioner of Chaos magick, offers up a radical notion: "It is more in my interest to support and propagate diversity of belief, rather than attempt mass conversion."

Other writings in *Rebels & Devils* include "Paradise Mislaid" by William S. Burroughs, an interview with Francis Israel Regardie, "Eternity Is Good for You" by Dave Lee, "The Attainment of Bliss" by John Payne, "Devil Be My God" by Lon Milo DuQuette, "How Brain Software Programs Brain Hardware" by Robert Anton Wilson, "Twenty-two Alternatives to Involuntary Death" by Timothy Leary and Eric Gullichsen, "Thee Splinter Test" by Genesis P-Orridge, and "Caressing the Body of Liberty" by Edwin Drummond.

New Falcon Publications; $17.95
1996; softcover; 384 pp
illus; 1-56184-121-8

THE SUBVERSION OF POLITICS
European Autonomous Social Movements and the Decolonization of Everyday Life
by George Katsiaficas

The author offers a rare look at the autonomous social movements of Europe — particularly Germany and Italy — from 1968 to 1996. These leftist/anarchist movements often resulted in the formation of intentional communities that squatted houses and used direct action to agitate for feminism, disarmament, and labour and against fascism and racism.

Humanities Press International; $19.95
1997; softcover; 300 pp
illus; 0-391-04045-6

THE THIRTY YEARS' WARS
Dispatches and Diversion of a Radical Journalist
by Andrew Kopkind

The Thirty Years' Wars contains over 100 articles written by the late Andrew Kopkind, whom Alexander Cockburn calls "the greatest radical journalist of his time". Kopkind saw history being made, and these are his dispatches from the front. He issues his reports from Prague, Moscow, Hanoi, Woodstock, and other landmark spots of modern history. Although a lifelong liberal, Kopkind wasn't afraid to look at the shortcomings and failures of the left. He covers the civil rights movement, the Black Panthers, Students for a Democratic Society, peace demonstrations, race riots, the Dominican Republic, the House Un-American Activities Committee, Martin Luther King's assassination, sabotage of industrial and military targets in the US, government oppression, the Chicago 7, Janis Joplin, Nashville, gays in the military (way back in 1975), gay liberation, disco, cocaine, Jamaica, John Lennon's funeral, prayer in public schools, Bernard Goetz, Jim Bakker, Jesse Jackson, the Persian Gulf War, Ross Perot, Bill Clinton, and more.

Verso; $20.00
1995; softcover; 546 pp
1-85984-096-5

TROUBLEMAKER
One Man's Crusade Against China's Cruelty
by Harry Wu with George Vecsy

Chinese-born American citizen Harry Wu — branded as the Number One Troublemaker by the brutal old men who run China — is one of the bravest political dissidents of our time. After spending nineteen years in his home country's inhuman prison system because of his political views, Wu was released in 1979. He moved to the US, but instead of railing against China from afar, he returned incognito four times to document human rights violations. During his 1995 mission, the government finally managed to capture their most hated enemy. Tremendous political pressure was brought against the Chinese government, and Wu was expelled from the country after a show trial.

Proudly wearing the label the Chinese government has given him, Wu concentrates in *Troublemaker* on his efforts to draw world attention to the *laogai*, China's system of prison labour camps populated with many people who committed no crimes (the equivalent of Russia's *gulag* system). He also explains how he originally got into trouble with the communists and tells a little bit about life in the slave camps. Interwoven with this, we also get a picture of Wu as a person through tales of his early life and his relationship with his wife.

Wu was born in Shanghai in 1937 into a rich, extremely strict household. He gradually learned to question authority and stand up for his beliefs, but when he went to college in Beijing, he had no plans to become a political agitator. Chairman Mao was telling the people that dissent and competing ideas were welcome in his country, so Wu made his dislike of Chinese policies known during discussions at the university. He was immediately put on Mao's shitlist. Along with three other students, he hatched a plan to escape China, but — unbeknownst to him — one of them forged his name to withdraw some needed money. It was the opportunity the communists were waiting for.

In April 1960 Wu was arrested and entered the *laogai*, "where they send our misfits, our outlaws, our dissidents, our class enemies, our thinkers, our questioners, our doubters, our dreamers, our scholars, our optimists, and our pessimists — anybody who thinks or feels — millions of us." He relates a little of what life in this hell is like, including following rats to their lairs in order to steal back the food the rodents have been hoarding. For more detail, check out another of Wu's books, *Bitter Winds: A Memoir of My Years in China's Gulag*.

In this book, Wu goes into detail about his excursions back into China. On one of his trips he revealed a primary reason China has become an international economic power — it uses its prison population as slave labourers. The resulting products are then sold to the US, Europe, the UK, and elsewhere. Even more disturbing is China's organ harvesting, which Wu helped to expose. Prisoners are executed so their corneas, kidneys, and other body parts can be transplanted into important Chinese or wealthy foreigners (including Americans) who fly into the country for the operations. Sometimes the doctors will remove vital organs *before* the prisoner has been executed. Wu goes into the most detail about his fourth trip back, including the arrest and trial which resulted from it. He and the rest of the world wondered whether he would go back to the *laogai*, be executed, or be allowed to physically deteriorate. A kangaroo court found him guilty of being a spy and sentenced him to fifteen years in the *laogai* and expulsion from China. Probably due to international pressure, the second part of the sentence, expulsion, was carried out first, and Wu was kicked out of China.

Wu plans to keep fighting for an end to the Chinese slave camps. He estimates that there are currently six to eight million prisoners in the system, and perhaps ten percent of them are being held because of their political or religious beliefs. "Each one has a name, a face, a soul, a family. Some of them were my friends. How can I neglect them now that I have freedom? This is my cry. This is my mission."

Times Books (Random House); $25
1996; hardcover
0812963741

THE WAY THINGS AREN'T
Rush Limbaugh's Reign of Error
by Steven Rendall, Jim Naureckas, Jeff Cohen

In June 1994 — when Rush Limbaugh actually mattered — the leftist media watchdog group Fairness and Accuracy in Reporting (FAIR) released a report entitled "Rush Limbaugh's Reign of Error", which exposed distortions, contradictions, and outright lies from the man they call "The Lyin' King". This book is an expanded version of that very telling report.

If you need any proof that Limbaugh is some kind of demagogue/propagandist, the authors offer Limbaugh's words to his fans when he signs off on Fridays: "I will devote my weekend to keeping track of relevant events so you don't have to…" On top of that, he "regularly tells his listeners not to read newspapers because 'I will do all your reading, and I will tell you what to think about it.'" And people called David Koresh a cult leader?

Limbaugh likes to pretend that he's "just an entertainer". He has even claimed, "I have no cause, no political agenda," and likes to portray himself as a political outsider. Then how, I wonder, do you explain the following: "On the day before the November '94 election, Limbaugh used his TV show to issue a call to action, urging his troops to 'be ready at dawn tomorrow, dawn Tuesday' to work hard to 'gain Republican control of Congress.'" Or this: "On a daily basis, conservative lawmakers brief Limbaugh by phone or fax on issues around which they want him to mobilise pressure on Congress." Speaker of the House Newt Gingrich "faxes Limbaugh regular briefings for the Republican leadership…" When "political outsider" Limbaugh's TV show went on the air in September 1992, its executive producer was Roger Ailes, who had been communication director for Bush's 1988 campaign, and was then a high level adviser in Bush's 1992 campaign. At the same time, Limbaugh was being briefed by the campaign's political director, Mary Matalin.

The Way Things Aren't also exposes the man behind the BS. It turns out that Limbaugh's protestations that he has middle class roots and that no one handed him his career are deceptive, as are his cagey explanations about how he managed not to get drafted for Vietnam. The authors sum up Limbaugh this way: "He was a strong supporter of the Vietnam war, which he neatly avoided. He's a great patriot who didn't register to vote until he was 35 years old — after a columnist exposed his lack of civic duty… He decries the high divorce rate — which he blames on liberals or the 1960s — while he's working on his third marriage. He is a crusader for God and religion, but does not attend church."

Some of the quotes in the book show Limbaugh's Christian sensitivity and love of fellow humans. "I don't give a hoot that [Columbus] gave some Indians a disease that they didn't have immunity against" (from *The Way Things Ought to Be*). "Those of you who want to take off the Clinton/Gore bumper stickers, just go get a handicapped parking sticker instead, and people will know why you voted that way" (radio show, 7/23/93). According to *Newsday*, Limbaugh once told a black caller: "Take that bone out of your nose and call me back."

The majority of the book is made up of quotes from Limbaugh that are compared side-by-side with reality. The quotes are taken from Limbaugh's two books, his newsletter, transcripts from ten months of his TV show, and his radio show. On his TV show (5/4/94) Limbaugh said that "she [Anita Hill] wanted to continue to date him [Clarence Thomas]" and that no other women came forth after Anita Hill to accuse Thomas of harassment. The reality is that both Hill and Thomas admitted that they never dated, so it's hard for

Hill to keep wanting to. Also, two women did come forth and accuse Thomas of sexual misconduct right after Hill did.

On his radio show (6/19/92), Limbaugh claimed that, "Even if the polar ice caps melted, there would be no rise in ocean levels." While that may be true if only the North Pole melted, most of the world's ice is on land in Antarctica. Therefore, if the South Pole melted, the world's oceans would rise 200 feet, wiping out many smaller islands and covering coastal cities on the continents.

On January 19, 1994, Limbaugh flatly stated on his TV show that the investigation of the Iran-Contra affair by Lawrence Walsh resulted in "not one indictment. There is not one charge." This is an outright lie only a Limbecile could believe. Walsh actually got fourteen indictments, and eleven resulted in convictions or guilty pleas (some of which were for felony charges).

When speaking of Whitewater on his TV show (2/17/94), Limbaugh said, "I don't think the New York Times has run a story on this yet. I mean, we haven't done a thorough search, but I — there has not been a big one, front-page story, about this one that we can recall." Apparently Limbaugh and his crack research staff missed the fact that the Times is the paper that "broke the Whitewater story on March 8, 1992, in a front-page, 1700-word report by Jeff Gerth. The Times published more than a half-dozen additional front-page Whitewater stories in the two months immediately prior to Limbaugh's utterance."

In the section "Limbaugh vs. Limbaugh", the authors show Limbaugh contradicting himself. In April and May of 1994 he frequently supported Paula Jones, who has accused Clinton of sexual harassment. However, in USA Weekend (1/26/92), "He boasted of a sign on his office door: 'Sexual harassment at this work station will not be reported. However. . . it will be graded!'" In The Way Things Ought to Be, Limbaugh blasted CNN's Bernard Shaw for saying that journalists "can't take sides" during the Persian Gulf War: "Can't take sides — ! These were American journalists and they can't take sides? That attitude illustrates the haughty arrogance of people in the news business." Then, a mere two pages later, he writes, "The job of a journalist is to chronicle events, not stand up and cheer for one side or the other."

Other sections in the book look at Limbaugh's anti-communism, his attacks on other people's physical appearances, his claims of being a victim of censorship, his ridiculous response to FAIR's initial report, and what can be done about the Limbaugh menace. I've got one suggestion: Start thinking for yourselves, dittoheads, because you've been had. You can begin by getting this damning book. It's the best single antidote to a lunatic whose ravings are actually being taken seriously by millions of people, although a lot of those people have come to their senses, since Limbaugh no longer has the clout he once had.

The New Press; $6.95
1995; softcover; 128 pp
heavily illus; 1-56584-260-X

WE THE JURY...
The Impact of Jurors on Our Basic

Freedoms
by Godfrey D Lehman

If you are unfamiliar with the concept of jury nullification, please read the review of FIJActivist above. Basically, this tenet says that jurors have the right and the obligation not just to judge the accused but to judge the law itself. If a law is unjust or discriminatory, they can find the accused not guilty. Jury nullification is an established part of Anglo-American jurisprudence, yet it is often squelched by the legal system. We the Jury... sets the record straight by examining a dozen cases from the US and Europe in which the jurors stood up to the powers that be, sometimes risking imprisonment and torture, to declare a bad law null and void.

The earliest trial took place in London in 1760. William Penn and William Mead were being tried for preaching Quakerism, a violation of a law that established the Church of England as the only legal form of worship. On the jury for this ridiculous trial was shipping magnate Edward Bushell, known as an independent thinker. The author cannot praise Bushell enough: "He, together with eleven colleagues, laid down the boundary lines. Together they set the limits to tyranny. The limits they set exist today, safeguarded by other groups of twelve." He also writes of Bushell: "If he had not done so, there might never have been a Declaration of Independence or a United States Constitution."

After a patently unfair trial, which is recounted in detail, the jury was ordered to deliberate and return with a guilty verdict. To make sure that the court received the verdict it wanted, it denied the jury food, drink, or the ability to relieve themselves from the time the trial began in the morning until they returned with a verdict. At the end of an hour and a half of deliberation — an incredibly long time in those days — the jury delivered its verdict. Penn was "guilty of speaking on Gracechurch Street." "The ploy which the jurors had adopted was to return a special verdict of 'guilty,' having been directed to do so, but applied to a harmless act. They had hoped that this would satisfy the directive while making it impossible for the court to declare Penn guilty of any real offence in a general verdict, since to speak on the street was no crime." However, this ruling displeased the court to say the least. The judge commanded the jurors to deliberate again — without food, drink, or bathroom privileges — until they delivered their "proper verdict".

After two days of being inhumanly imprisoned, the jurors became even more uncompromising, declaring Penn and Mead not guilty of all charges. At this point the judge fined each juror the outrageous amount of forty marks because of their insolence. They were locked away in the hellhole known as Newgate until they paid the fines. Eight of the jurors quickly were released when friends and supporters came up with the money, but Bushell and three others refused to pay the fines, even though Bushell was rich enough to pay for all the jurors. Sir Richard Newdigate — a former Chief Justice of King's Bench and a friend of Bushell's — took the case to the oldest court in the land, the Court of Common Pleas. In a ruling entitled "Bushell's Case", the Court freed the remaining jurors and, in their written opinion, gave a ringing defence of the right of juries to independently rule as they see fit and not to be influenced by the judge. This document is considered one of the six precursors — along with the Magna Charta — to the Declaration of Independence and Constitution of the US.

In other cases covered in this book, juries nullified laws against "witchcraft" in Salem, laws against criticising public officials in Colonial America, the repugnant Alien and Sedition Acts, laws upholding slavery in the US, laws forbidding African Americans to buy homes in certain areas, the law against women's suffrage, and other tyrannical laws in the US and elsewhere.

Prometheus Books; $26.95
1997; hardcover; 369 pp
0-57392-144-0

THE WRONG WAY HOME
Uncovering the Patterns of Cult Behavior in American Society
by Arthur J. Deikman, MD

The prevailing view of so-called "cults" is that only people who are somehow "different" join them... only weak-willed saps could get involved with something like that. Psychiatrist Arthur Deikman reveals that none of us should feel so smug — we all engage in cult-like behaviour to some degree. These behaviours include complying with a group, depending on a leader, demonising outsiders, and avoiding dissent. To some extent, this sheep-like attitude of followers is "present in the familiar and legitimate activities of our established religions, large corporations, government, the media, and the professions."

The main problem is that people don't want to think for themselves and are scared of the consequences (and responsibilities) of being truly free. According to Deikman, the most obvious manifestation of this evasion is joining a new religion that exerts totalistic control over its members' lives. But most people do other things that, while usually less extreme, amount to basically the same thing. What about the people who lick the bosses' boots? "Achieving a strong corporate culture that managers really care about requires a process of indoctrination to convert a recruit to the corporation's point of view." Similarly: "Making the welfare of the corporation more important than anything else, believing in its overriding importance, is the qualitative equivalent to a cult's belief in its divine mission."

Of course, "cults" aren't the only groups who think they have a divine mission. Many sects of mainstream religions believe they too are carrying on the work of the supreme being(s). In the monotheistic religions especially, God is seen as a strict, all-powerful father, and the followers are bad little children who need to do what daddy says. Even in the more mystical polytheistic religions, there has arisen a class of priests or others who claim to be closer to the divine than everybody else and who expect to be treated reverentially. "Thus, as in any authoritarian system, the basic perspective of most religious groups is one of superior/inferior relationships; as obedience is the prime virtue in all authoritarian systems, so obedience to God's commandments is a prime virtue in theistic religions."

Deikman also looks at groupthink and arrogance among presidential advisory staffs, activist groups, governments, and the medical community. Regarding the treatment of people who propose ideas that contradict the orthodoxy, he offers the nineteenth-century Hungarian physician IP Semmelweis as an example. Semmelweis, concerned about the high rate of puerperal fever among new mothers, dared to suggest that maybe physicians should wash their hands when they come from the autopsy room to the delivery room. "His theory and his recommendation that physicians wash was received with such ridicule and followed by such professional persecution that he eventually went mad."

The author's main theory about why we have this need to follow a leader blindly and conform to a group is that we are set up for this mode of thinking in our childhood. We are helpless and completely dependent on our parents (and perhaps other family members) for everything. This sets up a life-long need to be led around by the nose and an aversion to thinking for ourselves or asserting our individuality. Deikman ends the book with suggestions on how we can recognise our own cult-like behaviours and how we can change these behaviours throughout society by fostering autonomy and encouraging dissent.

Beacon Press; $12.95
1990; softcover; 195 pp
0-8070-2915-7

CONSPIRACIES COVER-UPS & HIDDEN AGENDAS

JFK

ASSIGNMENT: OSWALD

by James P. Hosty, Jr, with Thomas Hosty

James Hosty was a career counter-intelligence agent with the FBI who was assigned to investigate Lee Harvey Oswald a month before the assassination. After JFK was killed, Hosty headed the FBI's post-assassination investigation. Naturally, by having such a prominent governmental role, Hosty has figured into many conspiracy theories. In this book, for the first time, he speaks for himself.

Hosty believes that Oswald was the sole gunman. However, he also thinks that some Cuban and Soviet parties knew about his plan. According to Hosty, Oswald actually told officials at the Cuban Embassy in Mexico City that he was going to kill Kennedy. Shortly after that, in late September 1963, Oswald had meetings at the Soviet embassy with various officials, including a KGB agent who handled terrorism and assassinations in the Western Hemisphere. Still, the author is unsure of how strong a role the Cubans and Soviets had in the plot. "This involvement could range from active involvement to tacit encouragement."

Since he was in Dallas on the day of the killing, Hosty has lots of insight to offer. For one thing, he was present for part of Oswald's initial interrogation, and he presents a transcript based on the notes he took at the time. He claims that during the questioning, Oswald was cool, snide, and smart alecky... until he was asked about his trips to Mexico City. Just as he started to lose his composure, he was taken away to a police line-up. Hosty was not allowed to participate in the rest of the interrogation.

Hosty alleges that he was set up as a scapegoat to take heat for the FBI's failure to prevent the assassination. The Bureau secretly changed some of Hosty's responses about how he handled the case to make it appear that he had acted incompetently. FBI director J. Edgar Hoover came down hard on him, but subsequent directors have cleared Hosty of any negligence.

Hosty covers a lot of other enlightening topics: the Warren Commission's wiretap on Marina Oswald's home, why

The infamous three "tramps".
Coup d'Etat in America.

the FBI suspected Marina of being a deep cover Soviet agent, how Jack Ruby was able to kill Oswald, why the US government left certain trails unexplored because of their fear of starting World War III, how FBI agents and superiors kept information from Hoover, how intergovernmental rivalries and turf wars have irreversibly crippled the search for truth, and more. The book also includes 62 pages of important documents, many of which were only recently released.

Arcade Publishing; $13.95
1996; softcover; 328 pp
illus; 1-55970-366-0

COUP D'ETAT IN AMERICA
The CIA and the Assassination of John F. Kennedy

by Alan J. Weberman & Michael Canfield

This book focuses mainly on the mysterious "three tramps" who were at the site of Kennedy's assassination. Right after the shots rang out, police and government agents spread out over the area. The railroad yard was searched three times by hundreds of cops, and it was only after all this activity that three men were found in a boxcar. These characters are generally described as tramps or hoboes, despite the fact that they are clean shaven, their shoes are shined, and their clothes are not shabby. Two of them look as though they've recently had haircuts.

The "tramps" were taken into custody, but, amazingly, were quickly released. Their names were not taken, and there is no official documentation of their having been questioned. Pretty unbelievable, especially when you consider that their descriptions are very close to eyewitness descriptions of unidentified men seen both in the windows of the book depository before the shots and running from the depository after the shots.

The authors of this book think they've discovered the tramps' identities. Two of the tramps are said to be CIA agents and Watergate figures E. Howard Hunt and Frank Sturgis. The third tramp is supposedly an unknown CIA agent who used the pseudonym Daniel Carswell. As evidence, the book contains several photographs of the tramps, along with photos of Hunt, Sturgis, and "Carswell". There are also close-ups of the tramps with acetate overlays of their alleged real identities. The visual evidence that the short, old tramp is Hunt is pretty convincing. The clues that Sturgis is the tall tramp are only slightly less convincing. The match between the third tramp and "Carswell" is the weakest, but that may be because there are only two extant photos of the anonymous spook.

Other subjects tackled by the book include Lee Harvey Oswald as a CIA deep agent, Oswald's double, Hunt and Sturgis's long working relationship, Hunt's lawsuit against the authors, and more. There's also an exclusive interview with Sturgis, in which he admits that the CIA has a squad for carrying out foreign and domestic assassinations.

Quick American Archives (Quick Trading Company); $14.95
1975, 1992; softcover; 405 pp
illus; 0-932551-10-6

FINAL JUDGEMENT
The Missing Link in the JFK Assassination Conspiracy
(Third Edition)
by Michael Collins Piper

Final Judgement is a JFK conspiracy book that you will probably never see mentioned, even by other assassination researchers. Michael Piper's thesis is that Israel — specifically, its intelligence agency, the Mossad — orchestrated Kennedy's assassination.

Piper is a long-time employee of the Liberty Lobby, a very conservative, populist organisation which publishes the weekly newspaper The Spotlight. Its critics say that Liberty Lobby is anti-Semitic, but it says that it is simply highly critical of Israel. I mention this as background information, not to take sides on the issue. You can decide for yourself.

Anyway, the book's basic argument comes down to this: "The state of Israel had integral links with all of the major power groups that wanted John F. Kennedy removed from the American presidency. Israel's global network had the power to orchestrate not only the assassination of Kennedy, but also the subsequent cover-up. Israel was indeed a key player in the JFK assassination conspiracy and, the evidence suggests, the primary instigator of the crime."

Although it's not widely known, relations between Kennedy and Israel's Prime Minister David Ben-Gurion were severely strained. Because of Kennedy's outreach to Arab countries and resistance to Israel's building of nuclear bombs, Ben-Gurion considered Kennedy a threat to Israel's existence. On other fronts, Kennedy was giving Meyer Lansky — the ruler of an international crime syndicate — a very hard time. He was also threatening to withdraw troops from Vietnam, consolidate all intelligence agencies into one group under Robert Kennedy's direction, and drop Lyndon Johnson from the ticket during his re-election bid. All of the interlocking enemies he made with these stances joined forces and — with the Mossad in the forefront — knocked off the President.

End material takes a look at George Bush's possible role in the assassination, Lee Harvey Oswald's links to undercover intelligence operatives in neo-Nazi groups, the continuing cover-up of a conspiracy, and reactions to the previous editions of Final Judgement.

Wolfe Press (Liberty Library); $20
1995; softcover; 408 pp
0-935036-49-0

OSWALD TALKED
The New Evidence in the JFK Assassination
by Ray & Mary La Fontaine

Ray and Mary La Fontaine are investigative journalists who have written for the Houston Post and the Washington Post and have produced shows for PBS. They claim that they are not out to prove any theory but simply to follow the evidence concerning Kennedy's murder wherever it leads. Much of the evidence they examine is newly released. When public pressure helped bring about the opening of many previously closed files on the JFK assassination, it seemed that almost everybody was quick to pronounce that they contained "very little" new information. The La Fontaines beg to differ — they have found many new leads and avenues of inquiry. On top of that, they have re-examined older evidence that has been ignored or misinterpreted.

One crucial document — reproduced in the book — is a Department of Defence card that shows that Oswald was employed by the government in some manner after he was discharged from the Marines in 1959. This was the same kind of card that was carried by Gary Powers, the CIA agent whose U2 spy plane was shot down over the Soviet Union. The authors contend that Oswald was an FBI informant who warned the Bureau one week ahead of time that a "Cuban faction" was going to take the President down.

This is why the FBI and other government factions worked so hard to sell Oswald down the river. They could never let it be known that they were warned of the assassination but did not stop it. "Recently released audiotapes of conversations between new president Lyndon Johnson and Bureau director J. Edgar Hoover, held some twenty-four hours after the assassination, show that even then it was Hoover's contention that the case was already solved — that the man Dallas police were holding on the fifth floor of the downtown city jail, Lee Harvey Oswald, had shot Kennedy as a lone-nut assassin. Johnson concurred, and a curtain was drawn shutting out all other investigative directions. It remained only for the Commission, which LBJ would appoint, headed by US Supreme Court Justice Earl Warren, to formalise Hoover's forgone conclusion."

The authors also reveal previously unpublished records of a burglary of a military armoury that occurred just one week before the assassination. Jack Ruby's associates were implicated in the theft. Some of the weapons were never recovered by the authorities.

The three tramps arrested at the assassination site have always been one of the most enigmatic aspects of the case. The La Fontaines use arrest records to identify these allegedly anonymous men, who really were just innocent bystanders. The whole brouhaha over these hoboes was engineered by the authorities to distract attention from two other people who were arrested that day — both of whom were locked in a cell with Oswald for several hours right after the assassination. "During this interval — documented with a full arsenal of telephone logs and other records — the men overheard Oswald 'talk.' Oswald talked about Jack Ruby, about a secret motel-room meeting where money and guns changed hands, and about another prisoner already held in the Dallas jail (and whom Oswald identified to unknown authorities in the corridor outside the cell, most likely the FBI, as having been present at the motel meeting)."

The La Fontaines, needless to say, cover much, much more ground in their investigation and back up their allegations with hard evidence — telephone logs, arrest records, agents' reports, suppressed Congressional testimony, military documents, and more. *Oswald Talked* is one of the most important new JFK books in quite a while.

Pelican Publishing Company; $25
1996; hardcover; 454 pp
illus; 1-56554-029-8

ZR RIFLE
The Plot to Kill Kennedy and Castro
by Claudia Furiati

This investigation into JFK's assassination is the first to make extensive use of newly-opened intelligence files from the Cuban State Security Department. Based on this information, it looks as though the part of the CIA that was involved in anti-Cuban operations was the architect of the three-fold plan to kill Kennedy, kill Castro, and take over Cuba. Upset over Kennedy's handling of the Cuban Missile Crisis and the Bay of Pigs, they enlisted the help of the Mafia, who hated Castro because he nixed their plans to turn Cuba into a casino resort haven. Of course, they weren't fond of the Kennedy brothers either, because of their pursuit of organised crime. The CIA faction also found allies in the anti-Communist paramilitary groups in the US. In this scenario, Oswald really was a patsy, set to take the fall for Kennedy's death.

ZR Rifle also contains a transcript of the first interview ever conducted with General Fabián Escalante, Cuba's chief of counterintelligence, who was in charge of infiltrating CIA-led anti-Castro groups in the US. He claims that the assassination was plotted by CIA chief Richard Helms, CIA

Lee Harvey Oswald's elusive Department of Defence card, which may identify him as a CIA contract agent. *Oswald Talked.*

officer Howard Hunt, David Phillips, Santos Trafficante, Sam Giancana, John Roselli, General Charles Cabell, and others, using the office of Guy Banister, a former FBI agent who ran weapons for the Mafia.

This book doesn't claim to have produced a final, airtight solution to the mystery, but it does bring some previously unknown pieces to the puzzle.

Ocean Press; $14.95 US, $22.95 Australian
1994; softcover; 183 pp
illus; 1-875284-85-0

INTELLIGENCE AGENCIES

CHE GUEVARA AND THE FBI
The U.S. Political Police Dossier on the Latin American Revolutionary
edited by Michael Ratner & Michael Steven Smith

Ernesto "Che" Guevara was an Argentinian doctor who became best-known as a revolutionary who, along with Fidel Castro, organised and led the overthrow of Cuba's dictatorship in the late 1950s. He helped to lead the new Cuban government until 1965, when he "disappeared". Although many believed he was dead, we now know that he spent several months helping fight a guerrilla war in the Congo, then went to Bolivia to participate in the revolution against that country's US-sponsored right-wing dictatorship. "Wounded and captured by US-trained and supervised Bolivian counter-insurgency groups on October 8, 1967, he was murdered the following day." Since then, this photogenic, anti-imperialist man of action has become an icon of armed revolution.

This book presents 109 previously classified FBI documents that have been wrested away from the Bureau through the Freedom of Information Act by two human rights lawyers. These documents demonstrate the FBI's intense interest in and surveillance of Guevara from the time they first noticed him, when he entered Miami in 1952, to the year after his murder. His every movement is noted, speeches are reproduced (especially the parts critical of the US), his political affiliations are debated, and, when he disappears, his whereabouts are speculated on. One document, which was actually created by the CIA and put in FBI files, has this to say: "His political views are those of a very emotional 'Latino' nationalist... He has the emotional hostility of the nationalist inhabitant of a small and backward and weak country towards the big and rich and strong country... In sum, [deleted] 'Che's' attitude toward the US is dictated more by somewhat childish emotionalism and jealousy and resentment than by a cold, reasoned, intellectual decision... Che is fairly intellectual for a 'Latino.'" A physical description noted by the CIA says, "He has rather clownish features. By ordinary middle class standards, 'Che' has bad teeth, but by the standards of his companions in the mountains his teeth are perhaps better than average... The remaining noticeable physical trait of 'Che' is his filth. He hates to wash and will never do so."

Other documents include apparently inaccurate transcripts of Guevara's speeches, an informant's claim that Castro and Guevara were suspicious of each other, memos from Kennedy aide Richard Goodwin to JFK, a report on rumours of Guevara's whereabouts in May 1965 ("Another rumour stated that Guevara was presently in Moscow undergoing treatment for a cancerous throat"), premature reports of Guevara's death, and a description of his bloody execution. None of these documents points to US intelligence's direct role in Guevara's murder, but that evidence must exist somewhere, because this publisher has announced a forthcoming book titled *CIA Hunt for Che: Mission Bolivia — How the CIA Captured and Assassinated Che Guevara*. For those unfamiliar with Guevara, there is a well-done short bio, an extensive chronology of his life, and several pages of photographs.

> Ocean Press; $18.95
> 1997; oversized softcover; 221 pp
> illus; 1-875284-76-1

CIA TARGETS FIDEL
The Secret Assassination Report

A reprint of the secret CIA report — written in 1967 and declassified in 1994 — that details eight of the Agency's plots to assassinate Cuban leader Fidel Castro. Includes commentary by the former Cuban spy chief whose role was to protect Castro.

> Ocean Press; $11.95
> 1996; softcover; 122 pp
> 1-875284-90-7

FBI SECRETS
An Agent's Exposé
by M. Wesley Swearingen

Che Guevara: revolutionary icon.
Che Guevara and the FBI.

M. Wesley Swearingen was an FBI agent from 1951 to 1977. During those particularly volatile 26 years of American history, he was involved in the FBI's dirtiest deeds against US political dissidents, including burglaries, disinformation campaigns, and other unethical activities. On top of that, he has insider knowledge of even more extreme FBI tactics, including assassination. After quitting the agency in disgust and spending a year of mental anguish, Swearingen became a whistleblower, documenting the FBI's terrifying domestic policies.

When he arrived as a rookie agent in Chicago, Swearingen had visions of doing battle with Mobsters. Instead, he was assigned to do surveillance on the wives of two leaders of the Communist Party of the United States. Soon after that, he was participating in black bag jobs, in which he illegally and unconstitutionally broke into people's homes. He estimates that the FBI performed 23,800 such break-ins over thirty-five years, and he personally participated in hundreds of them.

The author's accusations get even stronger: "... I learned how the FBI had arranged to assassinate members of the Black Panther Party by using hit men in the United Slaves organisation, a black cultural nationalist organisation based in southern California, who were FBI informers. I learned how the FBI had neutralised the charismatic leader of the Los Angeles Black Panther Party, Elmer 'Geronimo' Pratt, by framing him for murder." The feds also set up Stokely Carmichael to make it appear that he was a CIA informant. The ploy worked and Carmichael had to flee to Africa when another Panther tried to kill him. A colleague of Swearingen's admitted to him that the FBI had orchestrated the murders of Chicago Panthers Fred Hampton and Mark Clark.

Elsewhere, Swearingen claims that the FBI lied to the General Accounting Office during its audit of Bureau files and that top FBI brass committed perjury before Congress. He also reveals internal problems within the FBI — authorised cheating on FBI training exams, attitudes of extreme racism and sexism, anally retentive neatness rules, thievery and laziness, and the apparently random dismissals of agents.

The last part of *FBI Secrets* details the author's involvement in bringing the agency's misdeeds to light. One of the appendices gives no-nonsense instructions for performing a black bag job, FBI-style.

If Swearingen's accusations are correct, then he has presented us with a searing and damaging insider's account of how the FBI treats American citizens. It is the first such book to appear in twenty years.

South End Press; $13
1995; softcover; 197 pp
0-89608-501-5

THE INFORMANT FILES
The FBI's Most Valuable Snitch
by Robert James

The disappearance of Jimmy Hoffa — the controversial president of the International Brotherhood of Teamsters — in 1975 is one of the great modern mysteries. It has always been assumed that he was murdered and his body was hidden, but no one has been able to provide answers. In *The Informant Files*, Robert James unravels what he thinks happened. It's a complicated tale involving the Mob, the Teamsters, the FBI, Bobby Kennedy, several Presidents, Watergate, hit men, money laundering, and other elements of intrigue. James reveals who financed the hit, what happened to Hoffa's body, the identity of Watergate's infamous Deep Throat, and more.

EMP, Inc; $19.95
1994; hardcover; 429 pp
illus; 0-916067-06-8

INSIDE CIA'S PRIVATE WORLD
Declassified Articles from the
Agency's Internal Journal, 1955-1992
edited by H. Bradford Westerfield

Studies in Intelligence is the in-house journal published by the Central Intelligence Agency for forty years. Up until recently, this classified publication was intended for CIA eyes only, but researcher H. Bradford Westerfield was granted access as part of the CIA's new image of openness. He was suspicious that the Agency would only release cream-puff articles, but he was pleasantly surprised that they let him reprint some material that sheds new light on CIA operations, methods, and philosophy. Overall, Westerfield selected 64 articles for this book, the CIA approved 47 of them, and he ended up using 32.

The article that Westerfield most wanted to use was — unbelievably — cleared by the spooks. "Clandestiny and Current Intelligence", by 28-year CIA veteran William R. Johnson, presents the controversial viewpoint that the CIA is fundamentally flawed. It is expected to gather large amounts of information, yet it is supposed to use espionage techniques to do this — an incompatible situation. Johnson feels that "the techniques employed by journalists and the journals to gather and report information have been appro-

priated by our clandestine service and have seriously degraded our emphasis on the real technique of espionage." On the matter of espionage, he writes: "Because its planning and execution require foresight and phased preparation, it cannot produce volume without degenerating into the mere purchase of easily acquirable information at low risk, i.e., without competing with the overt collectors at the expense of its own discipline."

"Defence Against Communist Interrogation Organisations" is a steely-eyed article about resisting the interrogation techniques of commies. Of course, reading between the lines, it also gives instructions on how to "extract" information from unwilling enemy agents. The techniques that are revealed, however, stop short of physical violence. A prisoner may be made to confess by being "almost executed" by a firing squad, treated kindly after periods of cruelty, imprisoned with diseased people, told that his captors know what crimes he committed but are giving him a chance to justify himself, and so on. "A particularly devastating trick is to compel the prisoner to tell his cover story or legend backwards." The techniques for resisting interrogation are just as sneaky. "With a little practice, however, some persons can vomit at will, and it could be effective if the prisoner did so upon the interrogator or in his presence. No interrogator enjoys close and continued contact with a prisoner who has lost control of his bowel movements."

Another eye-opener is "Techniques of Domestic Intelligence Collection", published in 1959. It details many of the methods the CIA used (uses) to get information on foreign countries from businesspeople, academics, and aliens in the US. Other revealing articles deal with imagery intelligence (e.g., photographs), using language interpreters as agents, the psychology of treason, squabbling between the State Department and the CIA, the bureaucratic politics of intelligence analysis, the case of Soviet defector Yuriy Nosenko, and the memoirs of a double agent. The articles are enhanced by Westerfield's short introductions, which put them in perspective.

Yale University Press; $18
1995; softcover; 511 pp
illus; 0-300-07264-3

THE SECRET WAR
CIA Covert Operations Against Cuba, 1959-1962
by Fabián Escalante

General Fabián Escalante has been a member of Cuban State Security Forces, the chief of the Cuban State Security Department (G-2), and head of the Political Office of the Interior Ministry. In this book he reveals the CIA's early efforts to overthrow/eliminate Castro, which he claims was done with the help of the Mafia and anti-Castro Cubans. He calls these operations "the largest-ever covert action launched against another nation." While they were being put into action, Escalante was the head of a counterintelligence unit whose mission was to infiltrate the CIA-run anti-Castro Cuban groups in the US.

In early 1960, President Eisenhower signed a National

Security Council directive initiating Operation 40, and in so doing, "the White House gave the green light to its armies of mercenaries, political schemers, plunderers and assassins for hire to topple the Cuban revolution." The CIA's plan was to send in a bunch of unsavoury characters who would take control of and unify the clandestine groups in Cuba working to overthrow Castro. Only 85 men were selected and trained for this action. Just 35 of them managed to infiltrate, and, of these, 20 were captured.

Other aspects of Operation 40 include the much-laughed-about plans to undermine Castro's credibility in strange ways. He was to be given LSD before one of his TV broadcasts. Similarly, his tobacco was to be coated in a chemical that would cause dementia. In an even more bizarre vein, Castro would be exposed to thallium salts, which would make his beard fall out. This was supposed to strike a blow to his charisma and machismo.

Escalante says that these operations — and the many others that he details — have violated "international law, treaty commitments signed by the United States, the principles and stipulations of the Charter of the United Nations or the regional Organisation of American States." Obviously, he has an extreme pro-Cuba bias, but in many ways the record does speak for itself.

Ocean Press; $15.95 US, $23.95 Australian
1995; softcover; 199 pp
1-875284-86-9

UNLOCKING THE FILES OF THE FBI
A Guide to Its Records and
Classification System
by Gerald K. Haines & David A. Langbart

If you're a researcher who wants to use the Freedom of Information Act to get your hands on FBI documents, you'll find that you have entered a thick, almost impenetrable jungle without even a compass. But fear not, for this one-of-a-kind book will act as your faithful guide.

The bulk of *Unlocking the Files* consists of detailed information concerning 258 of the FBI's 278 file classifications. These classifications run the gamut from Interstate Transportation of Gambling Devices (#143), Destruction of Energy Facilities (#254), and Police Killings (#184) to Illegal Use of Railroad Pass (#142), Motor Vehicle Seat Belt Act (#171, now obsolete), and Gold Hoarding (#81, now obsolete).

For each classification, the authors relate the following: 1) A general history of the classification, including what kind of cases fall under its scope. 2) Volume. The number of existing cases as of 1980. 3) Dates the classification was used. 4) Location. Where the files are located. As of the book's publication in 1993, only a small number of files had been turned over to the National Archives, although many more are scheduled to be housed there. 5) National Archives disposition recommendations. Which kinds of files, if any, are to be destroyed. 6) Access. Describes how to get access to the files. In almost every single classification, the "Access" section reads: "To gain access to the records in this classification a researcher must file a Freedom of Information Act

request with the FBI." 7) Related files. This section reveals other federal, state, or local government files that cover the same or similar subjects.

Another section of the book contains information on the almost 100 indexes the FBI is either keeping or has kept in the past. "In the strict sense, many of these indexes would not normally be considered indexes — that is, finding aids to particular data collections. Many are instead simply lists, photograph albums, collections of wanted circulars or posters, or administrative files." Among these indexes are the Agitator Index (now obsolete), Bank Robbery Nickname Index, Con Man Index, Extremist Photo Albums (now obsolete), Known Gambler Index, Prostitute Photo Albums, and Rabble-Rouser Index (apparently still being used). The Administrative Index has "descriptive data on individuals the Bureau has designated for intensive investigation in times of national emergency." The Mail Cover Index lists the groups and individuals who are the target of a mail cover. That is, the return address of any mail sent to them is duly noted.

A section on "Special Files" discusses J. Edgar Hoover's infamous "Official and Confidential Files", electronic surveillance files, FBI budget records, and others. Several appendixes list FBI abbreviations and symbols, FBI records released under the FOIA, how to use the FOIA, Justice Department classifications, and more.

Unlocking the Files of the FBI is undoubtedly one of the most important books ever published on penetrating the veil of government secrecy. Professional and amateur researchers should get it immediately.

Scholarly Resources; $60
1993; hardcover; 348 pp
0-8420-2338-0

SECRET SOCIETIES AND THE HIDDEN GLOBAL ELITE

SECRET SOCIETIES AND
PSYCHOLOGICAL WARFARE
by Michael A. Hoffman II

This book takes the fundamentalist Christian view that the Freemasons are trying to enslave humanity, primarily by waging subliminal psychological warfare against us through symbols, numbers, ceremonies, etc. that are all around us.

The author exposes a wide range of this secret symbolism. It often is promulgated by the establishment, which claims to be against it. "The mechanism of prissy, six o'clock TV news show put-downs and 'exposes' of the very Satanic sex and violence which are lustily celebrated on the same channel on their ten o'clock movie is sheer hypocrisy of the most blatant and perverse form."

Hoffman believes that the Jack the Ripper murders were bloody Masonic rituals. The Ripper was Sir William Gull, Queen Victoria's physician, and he had the co-operation of the highest levels of British government. Another serial killer, David Berkowitz, convicted as the Son of Sam murderer, was actually just part of the Son of Sam cult, which "leads to highest levels of U.S. officialdom." The death of John Kennedy, the "King of Camelot", was yet another Masonic murder.

The assassination attempt on Ronald Reagan is tied to a crappy ABC series, according to Hoffman. Two weeks before Hinkley shot Reagan, *The Greatest American Hero* aired. What was the name of this "hero"? Hinkley. An ad for the show "mentions the government and hired killers. We are informed that Hinkley has the ability to become invisible, disappear and be in 'the wrong places.'"

As further proof of conspiracy, the book contains two photos of public figures — Marion Barry and Mario Cuomo — making the "devil's hand" gesture. (This gesture is also sign language for "I love you".) There's also a reproduction of the infamous castle from *The Little Mermaid*, in which one of the golden towers is a penis. A ring offered in a police supply catalogue bears a Cross of Lorraine, which supposedly represents the "Beast system".

Hoffman believes that "life in our modern era is little more than life in an open-air mind control laboratory…" The evidence is all around us, if we just know how to see it.

Independent History and Research; $12.95
1992; softcover; 115 pp
illus

THE "SKULL AND BONES" CONSPIRACY AND THE LINK BETWEEN THE WACO MASSACRE AND THE YUGOSLAV CIVIL WAR

by Thomas Kuna-Jacob, BSFS, MA

In this cut-and-pasted photocopied essay, Thomas Kuna-Jacob advances the theory that the Yale secret society, the Skull and Bones, has been responsible for many wars, assassinations, and other atrocities since the 1850s. The Skull and Bones, which counts many of the most powerful men in America (including George Bush) as its members, is trying to destroy the governments of the world so that it can build a society based on its own vision.

The report explains why the Skull and Bones was behind the Vietnam War, John Kennedy's assassination, the Branch Davidian massacre, the Civil War in Yugoslavia, and Somalia. Kuna-Jacob offers some radical advice for stopping the conspiracy and creating a more peaceful America. He advises legalising drugs, outlawing abortion except in the case of rape or threat to the mother's life, and passing a Constitutional Amendment "'outlawing speech, press, assem-

bly and religion which promote the denial of dignity and human rights to any person or persons on account of race, gender, ethnic or national origin, gender preference [see Ezekiel 16:55-63], age, handicap, or life-affirming religion'…"

Association for World Peace; $4
1993; stapled report; 9 pp
no ISBN

WARNING!
How the FBI's Criminal-Espionage Investigations of the CFR Was Foiled

Formed in 1922, the Council of Foreign Relations (CFR) is a secretive group made up of "the most elite names in the world of government, labour, business, finance, communication, the foundations, and the academies". Because its members are the most powerful people in the US — in fact, almost every important position in every administration since FDR has been filled by a member — this unaccountable, invitation-only group has an undue influence on US policy. Apparently it has no consistent ideology (i.e., communism, democracy, etc.) except for its overriding goal to create a world government.

The FBI has investigated this body many times in the past, but, unsurprisingly, these inquiries are always blocked. Currently, the FBI denies that it ever investigated the CFR, but the 336 pages of Bureau documents the author obtained through the Freedom of Information Act demolish this lie. *Warning!* examines the four major investigations of the CFR and the continuing cover-up of FBI interest in the group.

From 1941 to 1950 the FBI investigated the CFR's suspected Nazi and communist ties. From 1954 to 1970 the FBI monitored the CFR in response to concerns raised by legislators and citizens. In 1972 a teletype sent from the FBI's New York office to J. Edgar Hoover indicated that the CFR was in possession of stolen classified documents. Apparently around this time Hoover launched a major probe of the Council, and a few weeks later he died. Hoover's successor tried to continue the investigation but in less than a year he resigned his post under intense pressure (the book doesn't specify what the pressure was about, though). Since then, the FBI has denied that it has ever been interested in the CFR.

Warning! contains reprints of over 20 FBI documents, as well as other material, supporting its conclusions.

Sunset Research Group; $5 (three copies for $10)
1994; staple-bound oversized softcover; 30 pp
no ISBN

MEDIA MANIPULATION

CENSORED
The News That Didn't Make the News — and Why (The 1995 Project Censored Yearbook)

by Carl Jensen & Project Censored

Every year the media watchdogs at Project Censored release their list of important news stories that were ignored, spiked, or underreported by the news media. In the yearly book that results from this list, Carl Jensen and his colleagues review the top twenty-five stories that they picked. In the 1995 edition, the most important story to get the cold shoulder was "The Deadly Secrets of the Occupational Safety Agency". In the early 1980s the National Institute for Occupational Safety and Health (NIOSH) performed 69 studies that revealed that almost 250,000 American workers were being exposed at work to hazardous materials that dramatically increase the risk of getting cancer and other major diseases. NIOSH and the Centres for Disease Control determined that the government had an ethical obligation to alert the workers to their dangerous situations. The Reagan administration, however, blocked funding for the project and killed legislation that would have required notification. As of 1994, only 30% of workers have been notified that their jobs are exposing them to asbestos, uranium, and other deadly materials.

Other stories the Project covers involve the Council for National Policy, a super-secret, agenda-setting group that contains every important right-winger in the country; the Pentagon's secret plan to subsidise defence contract mergers; censorship of human radiation experiments; the dumping of 60 billion pounds of fish annually; the mysterious HAARP project; the Treasury Department's refusal to try to track the billions lost from the Savings and Loan debacle; the failure of the Nuclear Regulatory Commission to report the shoddy state of nuclear reactors; the fallibility of the AIDS test; pharmacists taking kickbacks from drug companies; the epidemic of unnecessary caesarean sections; deaths caused by over-the-counter diet pills; and many more. The original articles that "broke" the top ten stories are reprinted in their entirety.

On top of that, *Censored* contains reviews of twenty important books that were virtually ignored, the year in censorship, a 55-page annotated chronology of censorship from 605 BCE to 1994, a resource guide, an essay titled "Mediasaurus" by Michael Crichton, and a writer's market guide for investigative reporters. The "Déjà Vu" section reports on the dozens of Project Censored stories of past years that the mainstream media are finally getting around to reporting. For example, the *New York Times* reported in July

1994 that a test for the Star Wars defence system had been rigged in 1984. Project Censored revealed that information in *1985*.

If you want to find out what's really going on and stay a decade ahead of the mainstream media numbskulls, make *Censored* a yearly purchase. Don't wait till 2009 to find out what's happening today!

Four Walls Eight Windows; $14.95
1995; softcover; 332 pp
illus; 1-56858-030-4

CENSORED
The News That Didn't Make the News — and Why (The 1996 Project Censored Yearbook)

by Carl Jensen & Project Censored

As usual, the latest *Project Censored Yearbook* contains an enormous amount of news that was underreported or completely unreported by the mainstream news media. The top twenty-five neglected stories this time around deal with telecommunication deregulation ("Closing Up America's 'Marketplace of Ideas'"), child labour, the privatisation of the Internet, medical fraud, Russia's disposal of nuclear waste, NAFTA, Gulf War Syndrome, *E. Coli*, needle exchange programmes, disease cures from rain forest plants, the 180,000 patients who die annually from treatment in hospitals, and more. Also included are the regular yearly features: "junk food" news, reviews of censored books, a chronology of censorship, an "Alternative Writer's Market", reprints of the complete articles featuring the top ten censored stories, *This Modern World* comix, etc.

Seven Stories Press; $14.95
1996; softcover; 352 pp
illus; 1-888363-01-0

CENSORED 1997
The News That Didn't Make the News — The Year's Top 25 Censored News Stories

by Peter Phillips & Project Censored

Regular as clockwork, the members of Project Censored have created another guide to the important news stories of the past year that most of us probably never heard. In the 1997 edition, the most important story to get the cold shoulder was NASA's plan to send up the Cassini probe, loaded with 72.3 pounds of plutonium. If the probe blew up during launch (or if it malfunctions when it comes back into the earth's orbit in 1999), it could've strewn radioactivity all over the earth. This story actually garnered some mainstream media attention, but only in the days immediately preceding the launch on October 15, 1997, when it was way too late to get the public involved in a debate. The alternative press had been trying to sound the alarm since May 1996.

The number two story involves Shell Oil. "In the wake of Nigeria's execution of nine environmental activists, including Nobel prize winner and leader of the Movement for the Survival of Ogoni People (MOSOP), Ken Saro-Wiwa, evidence has indicated that Shell has fomented civil unrest in

Nigeria, contributed to unfair trials, and failed to use its leverage to prevent the unjustified executions." Any guesses who the activists had been protesting against? Yep, Royal Dutch/Shell Group.

Some of the 23 other stories cover cushy incentives for multinational corporations hidden within the so-called "minimum wage bill" of 1996; the smearing of activists by large PR firms working for corporations; the Justice Department's ignoring of white collar crime, which "costs America 10 to 50 times more money than street crime"; how "pawn shops, cheque-cashing outlets, rent-to-own stores, finance companies, and high-interest mortgage lenders" are screwing the poor; new high-tech surveillance equipment being used on ordinary American and British citizens; predictions of an upcoming world-wide food shortage; the possible danger of cow's milk; the patently anti-free speech "food disparagement laws", which allow food manufacturers to sue anyone who claims that a certain food is unhealthy, even if they don't mention any specific brands; the statistics that show there is no "drug crisis" among teens; the horrible conditions inside Immigration and Naturalisation Service (INS) detention centres; and the damaging effects of the chemicals in our environment.

Each of the stories is neatly summarised, and reporters in the alternative press who covered the stories are given a chance to comment on the treatment the stories have received by the mainstream media. The original articles that broke the top five stories are reprinted in full.

"Censored Déjà Vu" looks at how the top ten censored stories of last year have fared in the media, and the section on "junk food news stories" examines all the unimportant, worthless stories that gobbled up vast amounts of media resources while meaningful stories were ignored (1996 junk stories include celebrity pregnancies, the Macarena, and the Kennedy's auction and wedding). *Censored 1997* also contains reviews of a dozen books; several *This Modern World* comic strips; diagrams showing the many tentacles of corporate media giants General Electric, Time Warner, Disney/ Cap Cities, and Westinghouse; a guide to hundreds of alternative media outlets; a writer's market guide to the alternative press; and several articles, including "Censorship within Modern, Democratic Societies", "Free the Media", and "Less Access to Less Information by and about the US Government".

Essential as ever.

Seven Stories Press; $16.95
1997; softcover; 382 pp
illus; 1-888363-41-X

GROSSED-OUT SURGEON VOMITS INSIDE PATIENT!
An Insider's Look at Supermarket Tabloids
by Jim Hogshire

Jim Hogshire — the persecuted author of several books on outpost topics — used to write for the weekly tabloids *The Globe* and *The Sun*. Based on what he saw — plus his painstaking research into the other rags, such as the *National*

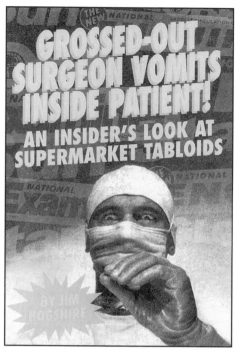

More than just worthless tripe.
Grossed-Out Surgeon Vomits Inside Patient!

Enquirer — he has created a portrait of these publications as more than just worthless tripe for maroons standing in checkout lines. There are secret agendas and hidden connections galore.

Hogshire maintains that tabloids are an especially brazen example of media as propaganda. He examines specific examples of the many kinds of stories that are "designed to reinforce values that foster social control. In the tabloid world, hard work and honesty pay off and those who attempt to cheat their way through life will eventually be caught and punished… Other stories stress the dangers of straying outside the limits of one's gender, class, or even race."

Tabloids often contain subtle and blatant racist messages. "*The Examiner* called Arabs 'camel jockeys' in one of its pre-Gulf War headlines. *The Sun* ran photos of hanged Arabs, supposedly executed for drinking alcohol (even though the signs in Arabic around their necks accused them of spying — a minor detail). The same issue ran a story about Chinese people with the headline 'No Tickee, No Shirtee' written in chopstick-type strokes."

But Hogshire also points out that tabloids aren't as pathetic as they are generally thought to be. While the mainstream media consider the tabloids beneath contempt, the two are more alike than different. "For all its pretensions, the establishment press is dependent on the same tools for investigating, writing and marketing its product. In 1972 the *New York Times* devoted editorial space to decry the *National Enquirer*'s digging through Henry Kissinger's trash to find clues as to what the powerful 'statesman' was up to. This opinion was printed just one year after the *Times* had printed the now-famous Pentagon Papers, documents admittedly stolen from the State Department." When it comes to credibility, let's not forget that it was tabloids that broke the stories concerning Dick Morris, Gennifer Flowers, and many aspects of the OJ Simpson case, while it was the *Washington Post* that ran the Pulitzer Prize-winning story about an eight-year-old junkie who didn't exist.

The tabloids' ties to government and religious leaders, the intelligence community, and the Mafia are also examined. Perhaps the most obvious connection has to do with the *National Enquirer*. "The *Enquirer*'s founder and long-time publisher, Generoso Pope, worked as a CIA officer and was intimately connected with Mafia figures like Frank Costello, who in turn was closely tied to anti-Castro Cubans, the CIA and Israeli intelligence services. The CIA, Sophia Loren and the Mafia were the three topics said to be forbidden at the *National Enquirer* during Pope's reign."

A tantalising appendix makes you wonder why back issues of tabloids are so hard to find. *The Enquirer* claims that even it doesn't own any issues from before 1967, a statement that Hogshire says is patently false. The New York Public Library has perhaps the largest collection of tabloids, but access is severely restricted. Some of the librarians claim there is no such collection at all. What the hell is going on??

Other parts of *Grossed-Out Surgeon* cover the people who read tabloids, lawsuits against the tabloids (in reality, they hardly ever get sued and when they do, they rarely lose), a history of tabloids, the design and layout of the tabloids, reprints of memos from tabloid offices, and more. This is an entertaining and fascinating look at a topic that is much deeper than its shallow appearance would indicate.

> Feral House; $12.95
> 1997; softcover; 147 pp
> illus; 0-922915-42-3

HOW YOU CAN MANIPULATE THE MEDIA
Guerrilla Methods to Get Your Story Covered by TV, Radio, and Newspapers
by David Alexander

Why should greedy corporations and posturing politicians be the only ones who use the media to their advantage? You can get in on the action too, but you have to know how. The key to getting your position, story, viewpoint, cause, etc. aired is knowing how and to whom you should pitch it. David Alexander has spent his adult life in radio, TV, and newspaper newsrooms, so he knows the ins and outs.

He explains how each of the three types of newsroom works (including local and national TV news) and who is in charge of what. He also shows how interrelated the three are. For example, if you get coverage in the *New York Times*, *Washington Post*, or *Wall Street Journal*, you have a good chance of being approached by reporters from network news.

To get a media outlet interested in your story, it must have a peg, also known as a "spin" or a "hook". Among the

pegs that are discussed are impact, timeliness, conflict, novelty, curiosity, self-help, and celebrities. Methods you can use to get coverage are piggybacking on other events, picketing, hanging highway signs, making fake newspapers, being an "expert", becoming a candidate for federal office, developing local commercials that gain national attention, and doing really wild stunts, like the anti-nuke protester who rushed the stage and smashed a glass award being given to Ronald Reagan. Starting to get the idea?

Alexander gives details on preparing a press release, using a satellite feed, and handling interviews. The final chapter relates fifteen beautiful real-life examples of media manipulation, ranging from creative events (such as kiss-ins) to taking advantage of reporters' lust for the "big scoop" to outright lying like a dog.

This book comes through by providing lots of solid, practical advice for anybody, anywhere who wants media coverage for any reason. It's easier than you think.

> Paladin Press; $12
> 1993; softcover; 110 pp
> 0-87364-729-7

MEDIA CONTROL
The Spectacular Achievements of Propaganda
by Noam Chomsky

Noam Chomsky briefly discusses how the government, the media, the public relations industry, and others manufactured consent, engineered opinion, and otherwise fooled the US population into blindly accepting involvement in W.W.I and the Persian Gulf War, the overthrow of the democratic government of Guatemala, and other such actions.

> Seven Stories Press; $4.95
> 1991 (1997); paperback; 58 pp
> 1-888363-49-5

SIGN WARS
The Cluttered Landscape of Advertising
by Robert Goldman & Stephen Papson

Two sociology professors analyse and decipher TV and print ads from the past few years to discover how they are getting their messages across, what they try to tell you about yourself, how they commodify culture, and more. Makes a lot of use of postmodernism, semiotics, and concepts like "reflexivity" and "intertextuality" but still manages to stay fairly understandable and insightful. Covers ads from Levis, Pepsi, Benetton, Nike, Reebok, GE, Diesel, Miller, American Express, Taco Bell, McDonald's, and dozens of other companies.

> Guilford Press; $19.95
> 1996; oversized softcover; 327 pp
> heavily illus; 1-57230-034-5

THE SPONSORED LIFE
Ads, TV, and American Culture
by Leslie Savan

Leslie Savan writes a column in the *Village Voice* in which she critiques TV commercials and — to a lesser extent, print ads — showing how they manipulate us and what they say about us. In the more than 100 columns collected in this book, she skewers the hucksters mercilessly. Her piece on Nestlé's practice of marketing infant formula to the Third World is titled, "Forget the Dead Babies". In a cynical look at Dow Chemical's attempt to soften its image, Savan writes, "Like Napalm and Agent Orange victims, Dow says it got burned during Vietnam and claims to have high-tailed it away from the weapons business…"

Savan savagely deconstructs the advertisements that assaulted our brains from 1985 to 1993. In 1991 she had fun with the well-known resemblance of Joe Camel to a guy's equipment. "Marlboro may be macho, but Camel has *cojones* — it's as plain as the nose on its face." Another column slams the health and nutritional claims in several commercials. "When the Florida Department of Citrus promotes orange juice as 'cholesterol-free,' it's depending on and fostering a thudding dullness of mind. This is like saying, 'Fly Eastern — it's dandruff-free!'"

A lot of columns look at the meanings behind many of the trends that occur at certain times — from a proliferation of rabbit imagery to invoking religion and spirituality. "So we don't hate ourselves (or them [the advertisers]) too much for being greedy monsters of excess, marketers must sow a higher meaning into the cars and refrigerators they push."

Corporate image ads take a beating, too. Savan makes us look at the transparent, self-serving intentions behind DuPont's spot with an amputee playing basketball and the many ads that celebrate the fall of communism. "As McDonald's, PepsiCo, Coca-Cola, GE, and other giant advertisers make us feel good about ourselves, they are balkanising Eastern Europe; the commie bloc replaced by the corp blocs." And she has no patience for hypocritical "green" advertising either. "You can almost bet on an inverse relationship between reality and ad: The worse a company's environmental transgressions, the more glorious its 'celebration of the planet.'"

The Sponsored Life is a terrific antidote to the mind-cluttering tripe that we often swallow because it's done so cleverly. Savan deftly and humorously cuts to the bone.

Temple University Press; $16.95
1994; softcover; 354 pp
illus; 1-56639-245-4

STUDIES SHOW
A Popular Guide to Understanding Scientific Studies
by John H. Fennick

Every day we are hit with the results of some new study drawing conclusions about heart disease, breast cancer, AIDS, the health risks of certain substances, illegal drug use, teen pregnancy, and all kinds of other topics related to our personal and societal well-being. But how are those studies performed and what do their results really mean? After reading this book, you'll realise they don't mean a whole lot. John H. Fennick — who used to run computer simulations and statistical studies for Bell Telephone Laboratories — uses a style that ranges from tongue-in-cheek to downright cynical in order to convey the inherent weaknesses of scientific studies, specifically those that deal with health issues. When you get through, you'll realise that when you hear about "the latest study showing…", you don't anything more about the study's subject than you did before.

Prometheus Books; $17.95
1997; softcover; 240 pp
illus; 1-57392-136-X

THROUGH THE MEDIA LOOKING GLASS
Decoding Bias and Blather in the News
by Jeff Cohen & Norman Solomon

This collection of 65 columns by Jeff Cohen and Norman Solomon will help you see how the media have fallen down on the job by failing to inform the public. The authors are unabashed leftists… wait a second! Two liberals slamming the so-called "liberal media"?! How can this possibly be? The media are just so gosh-darned left-wing. How come they're being attacked by two of their own? The answer is simple — the media aren't liberal. With stunning regularity, the media kiss up to corporations, shaft labour, shy away from scandals, portray immigrants in a bad light, ignore human rights violations, and let a bunch of white pundits offer their oh-so-important opinions. Who could forget the way the media slobbered all over themselves to heap adulation on that late dirtbag, Richard Nixon? "While media reports have noted that Watergate brought words like 'cover-up' and 'stonewalling' into the lexicon, they didn't mention that Nixon's effort to subvert Chilean democracy introduced another word into the language: 'destabilisation.'"

The media sometimes expose human rights violations in one country, but will totally ignore atrocities in another. "A big factor is that the U.S. media outlets usually don't set their own foreign news agenda; they let the White House lead. And American administrations are anything but 'objective' — their PR goal is to highlight brutal enemies, while turning the spotlight away from brutal friends." Even that supposed bastion of liberalism, PBS, refuses to fund or distribute *Rights & Wrongs*, a weekly show that exposes human rights violations, some of which are approved by Washington.

The book ends with the "P.U.-litzer Prizes" for 1993 and 1994. The Media Hypocrite of the Year for 1994 was Rupert Murdoch, who has pontificated on the power of new media to go beyond state-sponsored television and bring important information to people in closed societies. Strange, then, that he kissed the Chinese leaders' butts by dropping the BBC from his broadcasts into China because of the BBC's reportage of that country's human rights abuses.

Common Courage Press; $13.95
1995; softcover; 275 pp
illus; 1-56751-048-5

TOXIC SLUDGE IS GOOD FOR YOU!
Lies, Damn Lies and the Public Relations Industry

by John Stauber & Sheldon Rampton

Until you read this book, you may not realise to what extent the media landscape — and thus the "facts" and opinions we're exposed to — is dominated by the public relations industry. PR, also called "free media", is the flipside of advertising. It's the art and science of getting a message to the public in such a sly way that we never realise that we're being manipulated. The industry's unwritten slogan is, "The best PR is never noticed."

The modern PR industry is usually thought to have been launched in 1929 when the American Tobacco Company secretly paid for a contingent of women to march during the New York Easter parade brazenly smoking cigarettes. It was billed by its stealth organisers as a blow for liberty and female emancipation, when actually it was a stunt to open up the tobacco market to the female half of the population. It worked like a charm. Since then, "PR has become a communications medium in its own right, an industry designed to alter perception, reshape reality and manufacture consent." The industry now has a giant arsenal of weapons, including creating phoney "grassroots" movements, planting stories in the media, using false science, creating third party advocacy, orchestrating censorship, infiltrating civic and political groups, and committing industrial espionage.

PR firms have helped to destroy books that are critical of their clients. The DuPont family hired a flack to call the Book of the Month Club and tell them that his clients found the highly-critical book *DuPont* to be objectionable. Although BMOC had already contracted with Prentice-Hall to feature the book as a selection, they reneged on the deal. As a result, "the publisher reduced the book's press run from 15,000 to 10,000 copies, and cut its advertising budget from $15,000 to $5,500, even though the book was getting favourable reviews in major publications."

In one of the most extreme PR moves of all time, a surgical products company hired a firm to use two agents provocateurs to discredit the animal rights movement. The two agents twisted the arm of a somewhat unbalanced animal rights protester into attempting to kill the president of the company. One of the agents drove the protester, and two pipe bombs, from New York to Connecticut, where she (the protester) was arrested by police who had been alerted. Amazingly, law enforcement chose not to arrest the protester at her New York home that contained the bombs (bought with money from the provocateurs). Instead, they let the two drive the explosives across the interstate. "The arrest seemed staged for maximum publicity value, with public safety a secondary concern." The whole set-up was exposed during the trial, but the company still continued to refer to the arranged incident as an act of terrorism.

Toxic Sludge Is Good for You! also documents the machinations used to get the public to accept and even relish nuclear power, smoking, toxic waste, chlorine, bovine growth hormones, the Persian Gulf War, the Colombian government's constant political murders, "environmentally-responsible" corporations, and more. It will help you cast a jaundiced eye on an ethically-challenged industry whose flacks would accuse their own mothers of murder if someone paid them enough.

If you still wonder how pervasive PR is, reflect on this rare moment of candour from a senior VP of Gray & Company, an industry giant: "Most of what you see on TV is, in effect, a canned PR product. Most of what you read in the paper and see on television is not news."

Common Courage Press; $16.95
1995; softcover; 236 pp
illus; 1-56751-060-4

WIZARDS OF MEDIA OZ
Behind the Curtain of Mainstream News

by Norman Solomon & Jeff Cohen

In this follow-up to *Through the Media Looking Glass* [above], over 60 columns by Norman Solomon and Jeff Cohen, published during 1995-6, once again demonstrate in detail how full of shit the mainstream media are. Just look at the goods the authors spill on the "liberal" Sam Donaldson: "A multimillionaire who has pocketed up to $30,000 per speech to corporate gatherings, Donaldson holds down the 'left wing' of the Brinkley show [*This Week*]. He has also pocketed $97,000 in federal wool and mohair subsidies in the last two years for owning a ranch in New Mexico." Of *20/20*'s openly pro-industry, anti-regulation reporter John Stossel, they say: "Here's a reporter who makes money from (and shares podiums with) political interests on one side of the regulation debate — then takes their message to Congress." Using other examples, they show that the so-called liberal media is in reality dominated by conservatives and that the pundits labelled as liberal are actually middle-of-the-road, at best.

Many of the columns reveal exactly how the media distort and lie, as the authors deflate the Promise Keepers (an anti-gay, theocratic, male supremacist Christian group), William Bennett, the Public Broadcasting System, Ted Koppel, Bill Gates, Bob Dole, Columbus Day, Egypt, Russian elections, the Internet, the nuking of Japan, and Colin Powell. The uniformly glowing press that Powell, the former Chairman of the Joint Chiefs of Staff, receives never mentions his dark side. "In December 1968, as an Army major assigned to the Americal Division headquarters in Vietnam, Powell received orders to investigate a letter from a soldier claiming that U.S. troops were shooting Vietnamese civilians 'indiscriminately' and torturing prisoners. Without contacting the letter-writer, Powell submitted a dismissive memo asserting that 'relations between Americal soldiers and the Vietnamese people are excellent.' Actually, by then the Americal Division had been responsible for some of the most heinous atrocities of the war, including My Lai."

Further chapters examine how the media dropped the ball in handling the CIA-cocaine connection, HMOs, affirmative action, the Oklahoma City bombing, unionisation, AIDS, human rights, and other issues and stories. The authors also cover ABC capitulating to tobacco corporations, Robert Parry's struggles to get his investigative reporting published, Newt Gingrich blaming the Susan Smith child-murders on the Democratic Party, and the reduction of sound bites to "sound nibbles". "During the 1968 presidential race, when

Nixon squared off against Hubert Humphrey, the average length of one of their soundbites on network TV news was 43 seconds. By 1988, when George Bush and Michael Dukakis ran for president, the average length had dropped to nine seconds… Which should raise a key question: What, of substance, can be said in nine seconds?"

Common Courage Press; $15.95
1997; softcover; 294 pp
illus; 1-56751-118-X

20 YEARS OF CENSORED NEWS
by Carl Jensen & Project Censored

For two decades, the media watchdog program Project Censored has released its yearly report of supremely important news stories that the mainstream media somehow missed. *20 Years* gathers together complete listings, summaries, and updates of the top ten stories from 1976 through 1995, making it a textbook for the true recent history of the United States. The number one story of the Project's premiere year was newly-elected President Jimmy Carter's membership in the Trilateral Commission, a supersecret organisation of the world's most powerful people. The establishment press ignored this, instead focusing on his *Playboy* interview, in which he admitted he had lusted in his heart, and on his daughter Amy's lemonade stand. Twenty years later, the scary implications of the Commission are still a non-issue in the mainstream and are seen as the providence of ultraconservatives.

The number seven story of 1978 noted that the sperm count among humans was drastically less than it was in the 1950s and that chemical pollution looked like an important factor. It wasn't until 1996 that the media finally decided to make note of the problem.

Among the 198 other stories, some of which have become well-known and some of which haven't: the US's selling of banned pesticides and drugs to the Third World, where they poison 500,000 people yearly (1976); the US government's inability to account for the whereabouts of 11,000 pounds of weapons-grade plutonium (1976); the mass slaughter by the Khmer Rouge (1977); the worst nuclear spill in US history, which was all but ignored (1979); the existence of the National Security Agency, which monitors communications everywhere in the world and automatically records every phone call from or to the US (1980); the death every two seconds of a starving child somewhere in the world (1981); Israel's active support of brutal regimes in Central America (1983); Ronald Reagan's attacks on civil liberties (1984); several stories on mergers and acquisitions that put control of the world's media into the hands of a few megacorporations; the dangers of food irradiation (1988); US support for the holocaust in Mozambique, where over one million men, women, and children have been killed and many more have been brutalised (1989); bias and censorship in the Gulf War coverage (1990, 1991); the defanging of the Freedom of Information Act (1991); the quiet resumption of chemical warfare testing by the US Army (1993); the Pentagon's use of taxpayer money to subsidise defence contractors (1994); the wasting of 60 billion pounds of fish annually by large-scale fishing methods (1994).

Just as the Censored yearbook is a required annual purchase, *20 Years* is an even more absolutely essential book to have. Since most of Project Censored's reports are out of print or were never published in book form, this is the only way to find out what they've uncovered.

Seven Stories Press; $16.95
1997; softcover; 336 pp
illus; 1-888363-52-5

CLINTON SHENANIGANS

CIRCLE OF DEATH
Clinton's Climb to the Presidency
by Richard Odom

Allegations surrounding the "Clinton body count" have been swirling around for several years now. I've seen articles in zines, postings on the Net, and even a pamphlet about it, but *Circle of Death* is the first book I've seen that gives detailed accounts of "the deaths of a startling number of people who either possessed personal information, or had the misfortune of having befriended those possessing information, about drug smuggling, gun running, money laundering, and murder in Arkansas in the 1980s." (Of course, it's published by a conservative Christian publisher. Doesn't anybody but the religious right think there's something deeply fishy about Clinton?). Because it came out in 1995, this book doesn't take into account the more recent violent deaths of people who may have known too much, including Labor Secretary Ron Brown and a female White House intern who was mysteriously gunned down with two other workers at a Starbuck's coffeeshop in Washington DC in July 1997 (the killer didn't steal any money, and he has never been captured).

Huntington House Publishers; $10.99
1995; softcover; 213 pp
1-56384-089-8

THE CLINTON CHRONICLES

This video has become an instant underground classic, and with good reason. It presents many allegations of serious wrongdoing by Bill and Hillary Clinton from their Arkansas days. Much of the video centres around the statements of Larry Nichols, the former director of marketing for the Arkansas Development Financial Authority (ADFA). ADFA was created by Governor Clinton to supposedly make loans to colleges, churches, businesses, etc. When Bill appointed his friend Nichols to work there, Nichols asked ADFA's president Wooten Epes, "What's the criteria for loans?" Epes' response was, "Whoever Bill wants to get a loan." The video claims that ADFA's true purpose was to funnel millions of dollars to Clinton's campaigns, his inner circle of friends, and Rose Law Firm, where Hillary practised.

The legislation creating ADFA was drawn up and paid for by Webster Hubbell, a senior partner at the Rose Law Firm. By sheer coincidence, ADFA was set up so that everyone applying for a loan had to go through the Rose Law Firm, paying them a handsome $50,000 fee. Also by sheer coincidence, the video claims that the first loan made by ADFA was $2.75 million to Park-O-Meter, a business owned by Hubbell's brother-in-law.

Nichols claims that ADFA was also used to launder the drug money being brought in by the cocaine-running operation based in Mena, Arkansas. ADFA sent money to banks in Florida and Georgia, to a bank in Chicago partly owned by Dan Rostenkowski (Chair of the House Ways and Means Committee), and overseas. According to Nichols, Bill and all his cronies knew exactly what was going on. In fact, Bill personally signed off on every single loan made by the ADFA.

In August 1987 two teenaged boys went out after midnight, possibly to poke around a small airstrip near their Arkansas home (this airstrip is suspected of being used in the Mena operations). They were found the next morning run over by a train. The state medical examiner ruled that both boys had fallen asleep on the tracks and had not heard the train bearing down on them. The family suspected a cover-up, so they demanded to be given all the samples and evidence used by the examiner. He refused to turn them over, even when ordered to by the courts. After a long battle, it was eventually proven that one of the boys had been stabbed in the back and the other's skull had been crushed before they were put on the tracks.

The examiner stood by his original findings, and Bill stood by his medical examiner, who had often made controversial rulings that benefited the Clintons. The epitome of his baseless conclusions is the case in which he ruled that a decapitated man had died of "natural causes". On a related note, six people who had told friends and family that they knew about the boys' murders ended up dying violent deaths.

The video also looks at one of Bill's best friends, Dan Lasater, who ended up doing time for cocaine distribution (along with Bill's brother Roger). It is alleged that Lasater helped to launder the money at ADFA and seduced teenage girls with coke. He was given a full pardon by Bill after serving less than a year at a minimum security prison. And speaking of cocaine, the video briefly touches on allegations that Bill himself was a user while he was governor.

When Bill first became President, he and Hillary made a lot of noise about how their health care plan would attack the pharmaceutical companies. Not surprisingly, these companies' stocks went down. Hillary and her law firm partner Vince Foster snatched up the stocks. Then Bill announced at a gathering of governors that he wasn't going to go after the drug companies after all, and the stocks went back up.

Bill is also said to have used ADFA funds to visit his many sexual partners, who number over 100. Five Arkansas State Troopers have come forward saying that they procured women for Bill, guarded him during sex, and lied to Hillary about his whereabouts. Many of these women received career boosts. The troopers were all smeared by the Clintons' spin doctors, whose stories were parroted by the media. During Bill's Presidential campaign, *60 Minutes* aired an interview with him in which he denied his trysts with Gennifer Flowers. In one of the most amazing parts of this video, the executive producer of *60 Minutes* admits on camera that the interview was aired specifically to save Bill's campaign. (Any remaining faith I may have had in this "bastion of investigative journalism" has been utterly destroyed.)

The video also reveals the smear campaign against Nichols, Bill's relationship with food tycoon Don Tyson, Paula Jones' accusations, Bill's anti-war activities as a student, Whitewater, Vince Foster's death, and more. An epilogue gives a rundown of many more people who have had the goods on Bill and who have died violent deaths, most of which were labelled suicides. Interestingly, one of Bill's last acts as governor was to pass a law that an autopsy does not have to performed on anyone whose death is ruled a suicide, even if there is evidence of foul play.

Citizens for Honest Government; $19.95
VHS videocassette

THE CLINTON CHRONICLES BOOK
edited by Patrick Matrisciana

Designed as a companion to the *Clinton Chronicles* video, this book backs up the video's allegations with documentation and adds some new information. The first chapter looks at how the media did a hatchet job on the video without even bothering to talk to the people whom it featured or checking to see how many of the accusations carried weight.

Former Arkansas Senator and Arkansas Supreme Court Justice Jim Johnson contributes a chapter in which he elaborates on his statements in the video. Larry Nichols — who provided much of the testimony in the documentary — also writes a chapter in which he offers more detail on his allegations against Bill, which involve cocaine, sexual escapades, ADFA, and much more.

The video devotes just a short amount of time to the fate of Jerry Parks, who was head of security for Bill's Presidential 1992 campaign. Parks had managed to develop an extensive file — which included photographs — pertaining to Bill's alleged non-stop extramarital activities. His home was broken into and only those files were stolen. Eleven days later Parks was gunned down on his way home. In this book, Parks' son, Gary, writes a whole chapter about what his father had discovered and what happened to him as a result.

Other chapters cover Vince Foster, the boys who were run over by a train, Bill's anti-war/anti-US activities, his reneging on his promise to bring POWs home, his incompetence in handling military operations, his globalist philosophy, his promotion of the "gay agenda" (yes, conservatives are behind this book and video), and more.

An appendix recaps the video section by section and provides hundreds of references to newspaper and magazine articles, reports from federal agencies, government memoranda, interviews, etc. Another appendix reproduces over 30 pertinent documents, including DEA reports, FBI reports, Arkansas State Police records, and more.

Jeremiah Books (Citizens for Honest Government); $12.95
1994; softcover; 312 pp
1-878993-63-1

THE DEATH OF VINCE FOSTER
What Really Happened?

This video absolutely pulverises the official version of how Deputy White House Counsel Vince Foster died. On July 20, 1993, Foster was found in Fort Marcy Park, just outside Washington, DC, dead of a gunshot wound to the mouth. Almost before his body was cold, the media and the President were declaring it was a suicide. Even though 1) Foster was the highest government official to die under murky circumstances since John Kennedy and 2) his death fell under the FBI's jurisdiction, Clinton and Janet Reno made sure that the investigation was headed by the Park Police, instead of the infinitely more experienced and equipped FBI. Not only is this idiotic, it's also illegal.

The video exposes a dozen inconsistencies and impossibilities involving Foster's body and where it was found. Among them:

☞ There was very little blood at the scene. When people shoot themselves in the head, it results in a disgusting mess of blood and brains. Yet emergency medical workers and police officers who were among the first on the scene say they were astounded by the lack of blood and tissue.

☞ Despite the fact that a coroner's report shows a gaping one inch exit wound in the back of Foster's skull, no skull fragments or brain tissue was found during a meticulous sweep of the area.

☞ No one has found the bullet that killed Foster. After sweeping the area with a metal detector, the authorities found 70 metal objects — including twelve modern bullets and artefacts dating back to the Civil War — but none of them is the bullet from Foster's gun.

☞ Foster's wife and children deny that the gun found at the scene was Foster's. It is a Colt .38 pistol from 1913 and is therefore untraceable.

☞ Even though Foster supposedly walked hundreds of yards through the Park, he had no traces of soil on his shoes, according to the FBI's own report.

☞ The FBI's report also admits that they did not find Foster's fingerprints on the gun. The single print that was found did not belong to Foster. No effort was made to find out whose it was.

The Park Police at first said that they didn't have any photos of the crime scene, which led to rumours that none were taken. However, the Police said that pictures had been taken, but that they were underexposed and useless. They also said they took some extremely close-up Polaroids of Foster's body. The one photo that was released shows Foster's hand and the gun amidst foliage, which contradicts the official story that Foster's body was found in an area of dirt.

X-rays of Foster have proven even more elusive. The medical examiner who performed the autopsy indicated on the autopsy report that X-rays had been taken. Park Police said that the examiner had discussed the X-rays with them. However, when the government's official report came out (the Fiske Report), it revealed that the examiner was claiming that he did *not* take X-rays because the machine was broken. When contacted, the technician who installed the X-ray equipment said that it was only a month old when Foster was killed and that the first maintenance call they got about it — for a minor adjustment — was in October (remember, Foster died in July). Also, it might interest you to know that the examiner has had two of his suicide rulings overturned (i.e., relabelled as homicides) because he somehow overlooked key pieces of evidence.

The very night that Foster was found dead, the White House incomprehensibly demanded that the Park Police turn over to them scads of crucial evidence, which they did. The Police immediately ordered Foster's office to be sealed, but several members of Bill and Hillary's staff ransacked the office and took documents, which is a felony. Two days later, White House staffers again raided the sealed office and forced federal agents to wait outside. Margeret William — Hillary's Chief of Staff — was one of the people who took papers. In a press conference, Hillary denied Williams had taken documents out of Foster's office. Under sworn Congressional testimony involving Whitewater, however, Williams testified that she gave those documents to Hillary.

When asked about his last conversation with Foster, Bill Clinton has given four completely different answers. At first, he said he couldn't remember why or when he last talked to his lifelong friend. Suddenly his memory cleared, and he claimed he talked to Foster on July 18 to invite him to a movie. When asked again, he said that he had talked to him on July 19 to invite him to a movie. When the White House started claiming that Foster had been "depressed", Bill came up with a fourth story, saying he had talked to Foster on July 19 to "cheer him up".

This video also covers Foster's so-called "suicide note", all the people close to Foster who at first said that he seemed normal and was not depressed, the shredding of Foster's documents by the Rose Law Firm, the gunpowder on Foster's hands and clothing, and lots more. It may not convince you that Foster was murdered, but you'll have a hard time saying that there isn't more than enough reason to reopen the investigation.

Citizens for Honest Government; $20
1995; VHS videocassette; 60 min

SECRET
FBI Documents Link Bill and Hillary Clinton to Marxist-Terrorist Network
by David Mark Price

The Institute for Policy Studies (IPS) is a Marxist think-tank headquartered in Washington, DC. Former Naval Intelligence officer David Price says that the "IPS is a violence-prone group of extremists" and that Bill and Hillary Clinton are deeply connected to them.

"The FBI has compiled some 2705 pages of information which document how IPS is a violent and subversive organisation." Among the charges Price presents: a member of the USSR's original Communist Party supplied most of the money to start the IPS; a cofounder of IPS aided Nicaraguan and North Vietnamese communist dictators; the other cofounder of IPS helped the KGB assassinate American and British intelligence agents; an IPS leader aided Fidel Castro; and members or benefactors of the IPS "have been implicated in a number of politically motivated criminal activities; including conspiracy to kidnap the U.S. Secretary of State, treason, bombings, espionage, and murder." These accusations are often backed up with FBI documents or quotes from the involved parties.

Besides demonstrating the IPS's ideas and actions, Price shows the many ways in which the Clintons are connected to this group. Bill heavily identifies with a think-tank called the Progressive Policy Institute, which Price says is an IPS front organisation. Bill appointed an old friend, Derek Shearer, as his top economic advisor. Shearer has long been an active member of IPS and advocates the dismantling of capitalism and turning the US into a communist country. But he's not the only IPS-related person Bill has appointed to power. Secretary of Defence Les Aspin and Former Chief of Staff Leon Panetta raised funds for the IPS in 1983. Panetta co-signed a letter to the Speaker of the House written by an IPS leader. National Security Advisor Anthony Lake has been an IPS instructor. Also scrutinised for their IPS connections are Undersecretary of State Timothy Wirth, Congresswoman Pat Schroeder, Secretary of Labour Robert Reich, Ambassador to Japan Walter Mondale, and Goodwill Ambassador to the United Nations Population Fund Jane Fonda.

During 1987-1988, Hillary served as Director and Chair of the Board of Directors of the New World Foundation. In that position, Hillary "praised and gave away significant sums of money to several far left organisations", including the IPS, the Committee in Support of the People of El Salvador (CISPES), the National Lawyers Guild, William Kunstler's Centre for Constitutional Studies, and the Christic Institute. The CISPES is said to support the communist Salvadoran guerrillas, who plant Soviet mines disguised as toys that kill and maim children.

It's obvious that *Secret*'s politics are quite conservative, but nevertheless, the evidence of wrongdoing it uncovers indicates that it is not a trumped-up attack piece. (In fact, the publisher offers this challenge: "$1000.00 Reward to the First Person to Provide Sunset Research Group With Valid Evidence of Any Quotation Cited in This Booklet Being Materially False.") The discomforting facts it brings up deserve wide attention. Any President and First Lady who have such strong ties to any authoritarian ideology should be regarded warily.

Sunset Research Group; $10 (three copies for $20)
1994; staple-bound oversized softcover; 52 pp
illus; no ISBN

PESKY REPUBLICANS

FIREWALL
The Iran-Contra Conspiracy and Cover-Up
by Lawrence E. Walsh

In *Firewall*, Lawrence Walsh — the independent counsel who led the investigation of the Iran-Contra affair — pulls no punches. In telling the detailed story of his investigation and prosecutions, he claims that President Reagan, Vice-President Bush, CIA Director William Casey, Secretary of State George Schultz, Attorney General Edwin Meese, and other officials of the highest rank were actively involved in the arms-for-hostages and funding-the-Nicaraguan-Contra deals, and that they actively sought to cover up these crimes and thwart Walsh's investigation.

WW Norton and Company; $29.95
1997; hardcover; 548 pp
illus; 0-393-04034-8

LIBERTY UNDER SIEGE
by Walter Karp

Republicans like to propagandise about "getting government off the people's backs." A very worthwhile endeavour, certainly, if only they'd really do it. In this book Walter Karp, political essayist for *Harper's, American Heritage*, and other magazines, lays bare what Ronald Reagan really did during his two terms in office. Far from shackling the government, Reagan trashed civil liberties and democracy.

For some reason, Karp spends almost 100 pages (over one-third of the book) discussing Jimmy Carter's crummy presidency, which set the stage for Reagan's reign. The next twenty-five or so pages chronicle Carter's final months in office and the campaign for the 1980 election. Although Karp is a Democrat, he does give a thrashing to wash-out Carter and Ted Kennedy, who challenged Carter for the Democratic nomination. "Kennedy is no leader, no rebel, no honest champion of anything he champions, just Oligarchy's dupe…"

In February 1981, the new President unveiled his financial plan. There must be fiscal restraint! We must cut a whopping $48.6 billion from the fiscal 1982 budget! However, what Reagan really did was *add* $49 billion to the Pentagon's budget. "The huge spending totals and percentages are entirely arbitrary, plucked out of thin air one day at a meeting between Stockman and Defence Secretary Caspar Weinberger. The whole wanton wasteful enterprise, says Richard Stubbins, Stockman's deputy chief of national security, 'had nothing to do with a strategy, nothing to do with a program of what we needed for defence.'"

Reagan brought government secrecy to new highs (or lows) of murkiness and unaccountability. His administration hamstrung the Freedom of Information Act and the Administrative Procedure Act, both designed to let the people know what their government is doing. "New regulations are issued as mere 'guidelines' so that the public need not be notified. Existing regulations are altered by secret internal memoranda, not without danger of public exposure… In early April [1991] the White House proposes a 'National Recipient Information System' to keep files on 20 million Americans who receive a government benefit of some kind; and, some weeks later, an FBI 'Interstate Identification Index' of 40 million Americans with an arrest record — this from a President who two years before had warned against 'Big Brother government' keeping 'a tab' on the American people."

Karp also discusses Reagan's Executive Order 12291, which says "the President's agents in the Office of Management and Budget can veto — in secret — any regulation needed to implement a law if in their private opinion its 'potential costs' outweigh its 'potential benefits'…" And Reagan's Executive Order that allowed 16 million documents a year to be classified as "Confidential", and therefore untouchable, even though they are mostly either trivia or evidence of waste and corruption. And National Security Decision Directive 84, which authorises the FBI to use polygraph tests to trace the source of government "leaks", even when no crime is suspected. The FBI used its power to ask a woman, "Have you ever put your mouth to another woman's sexual parts?"

Karp pretty much says it all with this observation: "The candidate who promised to 'get government off the people's back' is determined, as President, to get the American people off the government's back."

Franklin Square Press; $14.95
1988; softcover; 261 pp
1-879957-11-6

SENATOR FOR SALE
An Unauthorized Biography of Senator Bob Dole
by Stanley G. Hilton

What *Senator Pothole* [*Outposts* p 53] was to Al D'Amato, *Senator for Sale* is to Bob Dole — a shattering exposé that strips away the posturing, the lies, and the spin doctoring to show what politics is really about. Stanley Hilton — a teacher and attorney — worked as Dole's counsel and aide in 1979 and 1980. He has continued to follow Dole's career, and the picture he paints is an unflattering one, to put it mildly. The former Senator is described as "largely a special interest slot machine, a human pendulum dancing to the tune of the highest bidders."

Hilton says that he likes Dole as a person, that he is intelligent and has a great sense of humour. He claims that he and Dole parted on good terms, and he even shows a glowing reference letter Dole wrote for him. But that's where the rosiness ends. "I was repeatedly struck by the banality and superficiality of his character and personality… He had little interest in details. He didn't like to read. His only real concern seemed to be raising money. He had contempt for common voters. And he believed in nothing."

The Republicans had a field day trashing Clinton be-

cause of his waffling, but as anyone who watches politics with open eyes knows, constantly reversing oneself is a widespread practice. Dole has earned the nickname "Senator Flip-Flop" for his two-sided stands on issues. In the early 1980s Dole blasted supply-side economics, then announced that he was a supply-sider after all. He has repeatedly proclaimed himself to be an enemy of higher taxes, yet he has supported massive tax hikes and even "single-handedly crafted a bill in 1982 (his $98 billion TEFRA bill) that resulted in the largest single tax hike in U.S. history." He helped Saddam Hussein by supporting "open vein" loans and wheat sales to Iraq just before the Persian Gulf War, but just after it, he referred to Hussein as "the Butcher of Baghdad". "Condemning Public Action Committees as corrupt in 1982, and saying they wanted 'something in return other than good government,' Dole has led filibusters against any form of campaign finance reform ever since."

Dole discourages critical stories of him in the press in an ingenious way. If a reporter writes something bad about him, Dole "freezes out" the reporter by refusing to grant interviews. Media outlets can't afford to have a reporter on the Capitol beat who can't get access to the Senate's leader, so they replace him or her with someone who will write flattering stories.

Through his various organisations, including Campaign America, Dole raises an obscene amount of money. In 1995 Campaign America alone raked in $500,000 every week. Why are so many special-interest groups willing to pour major bucks into Dole's coffers? Hilton devotes several chapters to showing what contributors get for their money. Commodity traders, mainly based in Chicago, used to have a tricky way of doing business. Because of a tax loophole, they were legally able to roll over their gains for years on end, indefinitely. This meant they never had to pay taxes on their gains, which totalled hundreds of millions. In 1981 Congress outlawed this practice, but the wording was ambiguous as to whether the law was retroactive. The traders said it wasn't, so they didn't have to pay taxes on pre-1982 roll-overs. The IRS said the law was retroactive, so the traders had to pay up. At first, Dole agreed with the IRS. He blasted the traders for receiving "corporate welfare" and for getting out of paying taxes. He personally wrote to the IRS urging it to go after the back taxes. Tellingly, he attacked the commodity traders on the Senate floor for donating to Democrats.

By 1984 the IRS had a glut of cases in progress against the traders. During 1983 and 1984, the traders gave over $70,000 to Dole's Campaign America. Miraculously, Dole backed a provision in the 1984 Tax Reform Act — which was passed — that gave amnesty to traders for roll-overs before 1982. This move cost the government $300 million in uncollected taxes. Also interesting is that the provision "specified that losses for pre-1982 straddles were deductible only by professional commodity traders, and not by ordinary citizens who straddled."

During 1987 and 1988 Dole's presidential campaign violated so many federal election laws that it triggered a record five year investigation that resulted in a record $100,000 fine being levied. Dole's campaign violated maximum expenditures per state, accepted contributions from corporate entities (which has been illegal since 1907), did not reimburse corporations in advance for use of corporate jets, accepted illegally high contributions from individuals and PACs, and committed other illegal acts. Did the Senator do the honourable thing and apologise? "Dole remained unrepentant, arrogant, and bitter."

Besides violating the law with contributions it gets, Dole's political machine also gives money in excess of the law, according to Hilton. During the 1992 elections for the Kansas legislature, "Nine Republican state house and senate candidates received illegal campaign contributions from the Dole for Senate '92 Campaign Committee. These contributions ranged from $1,000 to $5,000, and violated the Kansas Campaign Finance Act."

Hilton examines all of Dole's runs for President (except for the final one, which hadn't occurred yet), his relationship with his hero Richard Nixon, his fondness for obstructionism (he once told the media, "Gridlock is good."), his blocking of campaign reform, his position(s) on Israel, his leadership of the Senate, his wife, his early days, and much more. Although Dole appears to be out of elected office for good, get this book to discover why this is a very good thing.

St. Martin's Press; $6.99
1995; paperback; 308 pp
0-312-95925-7

"SHUT UP, FAG!"
Quotations from the Files of Congressman Bob Dornan
edited and compiled by Nathan Callahan & William Payton

Bob Dornan, a former Republican Representative from California, is one of the big powers of the Religious Right, although you don't hear about him as much as Pat Buchanan or Pat Robertson. Dornan is often on *Crossfire*, sometimes substitutes for Rush Limbaugh, and was on several important committees, including the House Armed Services Committee and the House Permanent Select Committee on Intelligence. He served in the House of Representatives until 1996, when he was barely defeated by Loretta Sanchez, a Hispanic woman.

It is hard to imagine, until you read this book, how extreme, hysterical, and hate-filled an elected national-level official can be. As the authors write: "Welcome to the world of Congressman Bob Dornan; where exaggeration and fixation flourish; where those holding an opposing view are demonised; and where hysterical, self-righteous speeches are the order of the day." They also claim, "Over the course of 16 years in the House of Representatives, he has personally and publicly insulted more Americans than any other elected official."

The provocative title of the book comes from an incident in 1988. Dornan was speaking at a town forum in Orange County, California, and Jeff LeTourneau, a gay activist, was challenging the Congressman on his homophobic beliefs. Suddenly, Dornan's wife Sallie yells at LeTourneau: "Shut up, fag!" Realising she had screwed up big time, Sallie immediately explained to the stunned audience that her gay

Dornan holding up the model of a fetus he always keeps in his pocket. *"Shut Up, Fag!"*

brother was dying of AIDS. Somehow the emotional agony she was going through caused her to lose control and make her hateful remark. Trouble is, when the media got in touch with Sallie's brother the next day, he denied he was gay, said he was HIV-negative, and even threatened to sue his estranged sister.

How could Dornan handle this one? Assuming spin doctor mode, he told the media that his wife was so concerned and scared about AIDS that she had somehow *imagined* that her brother had the disease. "'She'd been worrying,' Bob Dornan told reporters,' and it came out as a reality instead of a fear — that's the only mistake Sallie made.'"

But it's not only Sallie that has made hateful remarks. In 1978, Dornan called his Democratic opponent for the House "a sick, pompous little ass." In 1984 he called his opponent "a sneaky little dirtbag." The next year — on the floor of the House — Dornan referred to TV commentator Vladmir Posner as a "disloyal, betraying little Jew." "Dornan later had the statement erased from the *Congressional Record*. The Congressman claimed that he meant no harm by his remark and explained it as 'inelegant phrasing.'"

Inelegance popped up again in 1985, when Dornan roughed up a fellow Representative. In a speech, he called Representative Tom Downey a "liar" and a "draft-dodger". Downey confronted Dornan as they were leaving the House chamber a few days later, asking him if he had really said those things. Dornan said, "Yeah, so what?" Then he actually grabbed Downey's necktie and started jerking him around. "'Don't let me catch you off the Floor, where you're protected by a sergeant at arms,' Dornan yelled. Then, to punctuate his outburst, Dornan yanked Downey close — eye to eye — and screamed, 'Stay out of my face, now and forever!'"

The seething, hateful quote that takes the cake, however, occurred in 1992. Dornan was facing stiff opposition in the primary from a female opponent. In a televised interview, Dornan said, "Every lesbian spear-chucker in America is hoping I get defeated."

The rest of the book is filled with more quotes that, while not always as full of hatred and violence, still express some very scary and strange opinions on sex, drugs, abortion,

Madonna, the arts, the B-1 bomber, and "the year of the penis" (to use Dornan's own phrase). The authors also reveal Dornan's skimpy legislative record and military career.

"Shut Up, Fag!" is a very disturbing document. Luckily, Dornan's been voted out of office, but the word on the street is that he will try to regain his seat in the House of Reps and that he may run for President again in 2000.

Mainstreet Media; $8.95

1994; softcover; 120 pp

illus; 0-9641241-0-6

WHITE HOUSE E-MAIL
The Top Secret Computer Messages the Reagan/Bush White House Tried to Destroy
edited by Tom Blanton

It's not everyday you get to read a book filled with material that three US Presidents have actively tried to conceal, but with *White House E-Mail* that's exactly what you get to do. Starting in late 1982, the White House used a prototype email system, and by April 1985, the National Security Council Staff was using it. Oliver North and John Poindexter were the two heaviest users, because they considered email to be a truly private line of communication that avoided the White House bureaucracy.

Because all the email users thought that these messages would never see the light of day, they were very open. "The authors were not writing for a public audience or even 'for the file,' the way so many government documents are created. As a result, there's an urgency, an immediacy, and a level of candour very rarely displayed in public records."

The book's suspenseful introduction tells how the National Security Archives — a public interest group that uses the Freedom of Information Act to get government records — rescued these enlightening electronic documents from the brink of destruction. First, Ronald Reagan ordered the email messages erased during his last week in office. The Archives found out and were able to get a restraining order enacted with less than 24 hours until the mass deletions were to take place. This was the first round in a five-year legal battle, during which time the government spent large amounts of taxpayer dollars to make sure the public could never see these documents.

Two Presidents weren't above using even dirtier tricks. "George Bush signed a secret deal with the Archivist of the United States just before midnight on his last day in office, in January 1993 — an attempt to put the White House e-mail under seal and take it with him to Texas. Bill Clinton reversed forty years of legal precedent in March 1994 by defining the National Security Council out of existence as an 'agency' of the U.S. government, in an attempt to put the White House e-mail beyond the reach of the Freedom of Information Act."

Fortunately, the Archives were able to wrest 4000 messages away from the government. Of those, 500 are reprinted in this book and the computer disk that comes with it. They range from major foreign policy revelations to flirtation and petty office politics. One exchange between Oliver North and his boss, National Security Advisor John Poindexter, is quite telling. In the summer of 1986 the criminal activities of Panama's leader Manuel Noriega were being trumpeted all over the press, so he turned to the White House for help. North writes to Poindexter: "In exchange for a promise from us to 'help clean up his (Noriega's) image' and a commitment to lift our ban on FMS sales [foreign military sales] to the Panamanian Defence [Force, he would] undertake to 'take care of' the Sandanista leadership for us."

In his response written two hours later, Poindexter writes: "If he really has assets inside, it could be very helpful, but we can not (repeat not) be involved in any conspiracy on assination [sic]. More sabotage would be another story. I have nothing against him other than his illegal activities."

A November 12, 1986, message from NSC staffer William Cockell to Poindexter's deputy warns of revealing too much information about US aid to Iraq. "I question whether we want to inject what we have been doing to aid the Iraqis into the discussion at this point... Additionally, while we have cast our help to Iran in defensive terms, when we say we helped the Iraqis target [censored] positions, it is difficult to characterise this as defensive assistance. It also raises a new issue which the press could use to keep the story alive for several more days and could lead to press probing which would reveal some of the more sensitive aspects of our assistance to Iraq."

Another particularly eye-opening round of email shows how the NSC tried to get clemency for Honduran General Bueso, who had been a CIA asset and who also conspired to assassinate Hondura's president in a scheme funded by smuggling $10 million of cocaine into the US. Writes North: "Gorman, Clarridge, Revell, Trott and Abrams will cabal quietly in the morning to look at options: pardon, clemency, deportation, reduced sentence. Objective is to keep Bueso from feeling like he was lied to in legal process and start spilling the beans."

In early 1986, the President and Congress were wrangling over a bill to sell arms to Saudi Arabia and the Gulf States. In a message to NSC staffer Jock Covey, Poindexter writes: "I AM PRETTY SURE THAT DOLE IS DELIBERATELY PUTTING OUT DISINFORMATION BUT WE SHOULD DO NOTHING TO EXPOSE HIM."

White House E-Mail incorporates illuminating blow-by-blow commentary, exact reproductions of the email as it was printed, and lots of pictures of the major players into a snazzy design. The ASCII text files on the PC disk (no Mac version) contain further email reproductions and commentary. Nobody who wants to know what really happened during the 1980s can afford to miss this book.

The New Press; $14.95

1995; softcover with PC disk; 254 pp

heavily illus; 1-56584-276-6

WACO

THE ASHES OF WACO
An Investigation
by Dick J. Reavis

Of all the books on Waco that have been published, I was most concerned to see what this one had to say. Since it was put out by one of the giant corporate publishing houses — Simon & Schuster — it is likely to be the most widely-read book on Waco. Given this, I was hoping it wouldn't do what every other mainstream account had done — uncritically rehash the government's lies. But, I thought to myself, why should this book be any different? Luckily, it is different.

Writer and reporter Dick J. Reavis slams the government, the press, and the anti-"cult" attitude that permeates America. He reveals that the Bureau of Alcohol, Tobacco and Firearms's affidavit, used to get the search warrant for Mt. Carmel, was "flawed and perhaps insufficient". It listed only perfectly legal guns and gun parts that the Davidians owned. If used together in certain ways, these items could result in guns that are illegal to own without proper registration. However, not only didn't the feds have anything illegal on the Davidians, Reavis flatly states: "The affidavit did not show intent, a requirement of the law."

He also punctures the idea that the children in Mt. Carmel were abused, sexually or otherwise. Many psychiatrists and social workers who spent time with the children are quoted saying things similar to Dr. Bruce Perry — the chief psychiatrist at the Texas Children's Hospital — who told the Associated Press that the children "are in good condition and show no signs of abuse." In a later interview, he again says, "We have no evidence that the children released from the compound were sexually abused."

Exactly how the final fire got started, Reavis refuses to say. Instead, he presents the differing theories and the evidence for and against them. Amazingly, he doesn't even mention the footage (available to the public in *Waco II*, below) that apparently shows flame-throwing tanks torching the complex. Even if the author doesn't think that this footage reveals what it seems to reveal, it's odd that he didn't at least cover it in his discussion of the various theories. He does demonstrate, however, that the Davidians and the authorities were both concerned about the possibility of a fiery end to the stand-off.

Reavis goes into much-needed detail about the history of the Branch Davidians, David Koresh's life, his leadership at Mt. Carmel, his theological beliefs, and his sexual practices. *The Ashes of Waco* is filled with facts that I haven't heard anywhere else. Some of them are important, some aren't. "When Texas Rangers in 1993 sifted through the ashes of what had been Mt. Carmel's cafeteria, they unearthed a large sign whose inscription they couldn't believe. The sign read: 'This is not a restaurant. If you don't like the food, f.u.'"

Because this book achieved such good publicity and distribution from its publisher, it has undoubtedly helped a lot of people who had only heard the government/media's side of the story come closer to understanding the travesty at Mt. Carmel. [*The Ashes of Waco* will be republished in softcover by Syracuse University Press in 1998, ISBN 0815605021.]

Simon & Schuster; $24
1995; hardcover; 320 pp
0-684-81132-4

WACO II
The Big Lie Continues
by the American Justice Federation

This sequel to the video *Waco: The Big Lie* [*Outposts* p 56] contains even more revelations and accusations regarding the government's actions against the Branch Davidians. Among the things you'll see:

- ☞ A photo that apparently shows a child standing outside the front of the Branch Davidian complex as the ATF starts its assault.
- ☞ Agents holding what may be a small body as they run towards an ambulance.
- ☞ ATF's public relations flak bemoaning the "fact" that the poor little ATF was "outgunned" by the Branch Davidians. "They had bigger firearms than we had," she claims. Later footage shows raiding agents armed with submachine guns.
- ☞ The Treasury Department's report on the Waco affair says that the Davidians started firing on the agents through the front door, causing the door to bow outward. A photo taken by a reporter during the raid shows that not only isn't the door bowed outward, it's actually open inward slightly.
- ☞ The Treasury report says that the Davidians started firing from almost every window. Photos and footage show otherwise.
- ☞ The audio on the footage of the three agents entering a second-story window and then being fired upon by a fourth agent may have been doctored. Although there are at least six different guns firing in that scene, they all sound exactly alike. The background noise fades in and out.
- ☞ Footage from a cameraman who was beaten by ATF agents for trying to film what was going on.
- ☞ Footage of a very bizarre piece of equipment being used against the Branch Davidians at night. No one is certain what it's for.
- ☞ Despite the fact that the government says no military equipment or personnel were used against the Davidians (which would violate federal law), there is plenty of footage of soldiers using tanks and helicopters.
- ☞ Footage that possibly shows agents using portable flame-throwers on the complex.
- ☞ One of the most famous parts of *Waco* showed what appeared to be a flame-thrower tank with fire coming out of its barrel toasting the complex. That footage is shown again, along with a digitally

enhanced version on which it appears that the flames were just a reflection of light. There is also additional footage of several other tanks with fire apparently coming out of their barrels.

Besides seeing this visual evidence, you'll learn the following:

☞ The government says the helicopters used in the raid were unarmed. During David Koresh's 911 call he refers to the copters shooting at the complex. When asked to draw what happened, a surviving Davidian child drew a picture of the complex with the roof riddled with holes.

☞ Janet Reno announced that Koresh was refusing to supply evidence that the children were all right. However, the Treasury report states that Koresh did release a video showing the children and that the negotiators were concerned that Koresh might get some sympathy if this tape were released to the media.

☞ Secretary of the Treasury Lloyd Bentsen is in charge of the ATF, yet he was the one who chose the "independent investigators" to look into Waco. His three choices were all men who had been involved with the government's firebombing of MOVE headquarters in Philadelphia [see *20 Years on the MOVE* in the No Compromises chapter].

☞ The very first Associated Press reports about the initial raid talk only of the ATF launching an assault on the complex. They say nothing about the Branch Davidians firing on the agents.

☞ All the footage of the raid was heavily edited by a local Waco TV station before being released to the world. The station refuses to release the uncut version and won't explain why cuts were made.

☞ Three of the four agents who died in the initial raid worked as President Clinton's bodyguards during the 1992 campaign.

☞ An autopsy report says that bullet fragments consistent with those from an AK 7.62 were removed from one of the dead agents. The Army helicopters that *Waco II* claims were firing on the complex use this type of ammunition.

☞ The Davidians may have been acting legally when they finally did fight back. Under Texas law, a person is allowed to use force to resist an arrest or search if that person believes that the officer is using or plans to use excessive force.

☞ The "independent investigator" who looked into the final fire had an office in the ATF building for ten years, had a card that identified him as an "ATF Fire Investigator", and attended the funeral of one of the ATF agents. His wife is a secretary for the ATF.

☞ While we were being told the Davidians wouldn't come out, they were being told they couldn't come out. The Justice Department's report admits that agents threw concussion grenades at people who came out of the complex.

While some of the points that *Waco II* makes are hard to understand or hard to see on-screen, it still packs an awesome punch.

American Justice Federation; $19.95
1994; VHS videocassette; 90 min

THE WACO WHITEWASH
by Jack DeVault

Retired Air Force Major Jack DeVault personally witnessed the entire trial of eleven surviving Branch Davidians on a variety of counts, the most serious being murder of a federal officer. This trial turned out to be as much of a sham as the whole sorry affair at Waco that triggered it. DeVault's narrative — which includes large chunks of verbatim testimony — touches on two areas. First, it shows that the trial was conducted in a patently unjust manner. Second, it brings to light facts regarding the events at Mt. Carmel that were not previously known and have not been widely disseminated since they were revealed.

DeVault exposes the way in which the jury was selected. Normally, defence attorneys and prosecutors are allowed to question potential jurors in an open session in order to make their selections for the jury. However, Judge Walter Smith sent 300 potential jurors a questionnaire. Federal law says that any such form "shall contain words clearly informing the person that the furnishing of any information with respect to his religion, national origin, or economic status is not a prerequisite for qualification for jury service, that such information need not be furnished if the person finds it objectionable to do so (Title 28, US Code, Section 1869)." However, Smith wrote on his questionnaire: "This is not a voluntary endeavour, as you are required by federal law to answer the following questions." One of the questions asked respondents, "What is your religious affiliation of preference?" Further questions ask how often you attend services and how important religion is in your life. Later on, another question asks: "Have you, your spouse, or any member of your immediate family ever been involved in a non-traditional or unorthodox religious group?" Another question requires you to indicate your annual household income by range.

Furthermore, other questions ask if you own firearms, if you've been to a gun show, if you belong to the NRA, whether you've watched the video *Waco: The Big Lie*, and if you "belong to any organisation that advocates jury nullification or advocates that members of the jury ignore the law given to you by the Judge?" This last question is obviously aimed at members of the Fully Informed Jury Association, which lets people know about their rights as jurors [see *FIJActivist* in the Freedom chapter].

Judge Smith then reviewed the 269 questionnaires that got returned and decided — by himself — which 84 people would be called in for examination. "He was beyond examination and challenge. He was able to select anyone who failed his own private test and no one would ever know!" DeVault believes that Smith stacked the deck. "One media representative who was selected to observe in the courtroom said that most of the 84 jurors who were selected from the 300 believed that only police should have guns."

Of course, that was only the beginning of the irregularities. "[The judge] allowed portraits of the four ATF agents who had died to be kept in the jury's view throughout most of the trial, but when the defence attorneys tried to present pictures of the dead children he found them unacceptable or inappropriate." He allowed a small mountain of the Davidians' guns to be assembled for the jury, even though all of the guns were legal. There's no law against having a lot of guns.

Of the many interesting things revealed at the trial, one of the most crucial is that there was no way the initial raid by the ATF could have ended peacefully, due to the attack plan. The defence questioned Special Agent Kenneth King, who led one of the two teams that climbed the roof of the complex and attempted to storm the second level. Their plan was to break out the window, throw in concussion grenades ("flash bangs"), and enter the room, shooting anyone with a weapon. An attorney asked King, "if David Koresh had welcomed the front door team, that wouldn't have changed anything about your mission and tactics? You still would have thrown in the flash-bang grenade and completed your dynamic entry?" King responded: "That is correct."

DeVault provides many more eye-opening claims. Among them: none of the government's 120 witnesses could prove the Davidians fired first; some of the agents were wounded by other agents, and one or two of them may have been killed by friendly fire; a ATF agent shot and killed Davidian Michael Schroeder in a field outside Mt. Carmel, but there has been no murder investigation; during the gas attack, the Davidians were herded into the centre of the building, where they couldn't escape the fire; fire investigators appeared only to be interested in proving the Davidians started the fire; the jury never heard any evidence regarding the use of CS gas; the supposedly independent Texas Rangers, who were in charge of the investigation, were sworn in as federal agents and were not allowed to examine the site until two days after the fire.

In the end, the defendants were cleared of the most serious charges — conspiracy to murder and aiding and abetting murder. They were found guilty of other counts, including Count Three — "using or carrying" a weapon in order to conspire to commit murder. But since there had been no conspiracy, the judge ruled that Count Three was impossible. Later, the judge reversed himself and declared that the Davidians were guilty of Count Three. In a letter sent to the judge before sentencing, the jury forewoman explained that the jury had been very confused on several matters involving the charges and begged for lenient jail terms. She said that the jury thought it was only convicting the Davidians of minor charges. Nevertheless, the judge gave five of them 40 years in jail, fines in the thousands, and $1,200,000 restitution each. The three others were given five, fifteen, and twenty years, thousands of dollars in fines, and the same amount of restitution.

In Part Three of the book DeVault reprints 120 pages of documents, including a list of witnesses subpoenaed by the government, the grand jury indictment, the jury questionnaire, the court's instructions to the jury, sentencing findings and opinions, excerpts from the Justice Department's report,

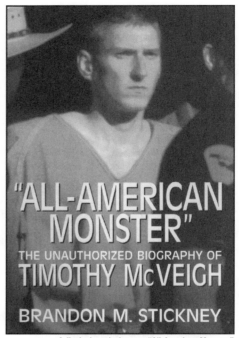

A fleshed-out look at an *"All-American Monster"*.

addresses of the Branch Davidian prisoners, and a transcript of the 911 emergency call that Davidian Wayne Martin made during the ATF's initial raid. DeVault notes that when this document was given to the jury, Judge Smith edited out the two times when Martin says that the feds started shooting first.

Rescue Press; $16.95
1994; softcover; 340 pp
no ISBN

OKLAHOMA CITY BOMBING

"ALL-AMERICAN MONSTER"
The Unauthorized Biography of
Tim McVeigh
by Brandon M. Stickney

Brandon Stickney, a reporter who lives ten minutes away from the home of Tim McVeigh's father, presents the only biography of the man convicted of the Oklahoma City Federal Building bombing. Using "interviews and stories from family, friends, classmates, teachers, military buddies, political insiders, crime witnesses, and government employees", he has pieced together McVeigh's life story, presenting him in human terms, instead of the easy caricature of evil incarnate. The book's narrative ends in April 1996, well before McVeigh's trial.

Prometheus Books; $23.95

1996; hardcover; 336 pp

illus; 1-57392-088-6

INDICTMENT
Inside the Oklahoma City Grand Jury — The Hoppy Heidelberg Story

This video tells the upsetting story behind the grand jury that indicted Timothy McVeigh and Terry Nichols for the Oklahoma City Bombing. The purpose of a grand jury in America is supposedly to look at the evidence against the accused and decide if there is enough reason to proceed with a trial. This jury does not decide guilt or innocence, just whether or not the evidence is sufficient to try the accused. In practice, as *Indictment* demonstrates, grand juries almost always act as rubber-stamps, giving an air of due process while allowing the prosecution to go after their targets. As Hoppy Heidelberg says, these juries are simply a "tool of the prosecution".

Heidelberg knows this through experience. He was on the grand jury for the bombing of the Murrah Federal Building, but he refused to play according to the rigged rules. When he first sat on the jury, he was given a handbook that spelled out his duties and rights. When he tried to exercise his rights as a grand juror to uncover facts instead of swallowing the government's iffy version of events, he was rebuffed at every turn.

The prosecution didn't call in a single explosives expert, seismologist, engineer, or architect to discuss the damage to the building and whether the truck-bomb could have caused it. Heidelberg asked for expert witnesses to be brought in, but the government at first said that they "didn't have the money" to pay for these witnesses. When Heidelberg said he knew people who would testify *pro bono*, the government then changed their tune, saying that he couldn't call in witnesses himself. A majority of the jury would have to vote for such a move. According to the official booklet Heidelberg had originally been given, this is not so. *Any single juror may call witnesses.*

Heidelberg also asked for certain crucial documents to be subpoenaed, which is also his right as a grand juror. Again, the government denied him this right. He also declared that he wanted to question witnesses directly, yet another power of a grand juror. The government at first said no, but then compromised by allowing him to ask only one question of each witness and only after it had been approved.

These and the other travesties that Heidelberg relates on this tape so incensed him that he finally wrote a letter to the judge spelling out his concerns and calling for an investigation of the way the grand jury had been handled. The judge dismissed Heidelberg.

Several other contrarians are interviewed on this tape. Pat Carter is a freelance reporter and photojournalist who

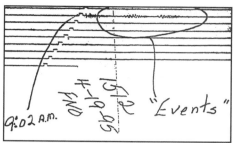

A seismograph from Oklahoma shows two distinct disturbances (explosions?). *OKBOMB!*

often covers Air Force One for AP and other news agencies. He arrived on the scene soon after the bombing and saw many unusual things. He took a photo of an ATF agent in the damaged building. The agent had put a sign in the window saying "ATF trapped ninth floor." Strangely, the agent is standing at an open window, apparently about to drop a safe deposit box to someone below.

Glen and Kathy Wilburn are also interviewed. They are the parents of Eyde Smith, the woman who became something of a celebrity after she lost two young children in the explosion. The Wilburns are heading their own investigation into the bombing, a move they believe has led the FBI to harass them. The feds told them that Glen's fourteen-year-old son from another marriage was under suspicion as being John Doe #2! The Wilburns have talked to twenty witnesses who saw McVeigh the morning of the bombing, and none of them saw McVeigh by himself (which conflicts with the government's scenario). These witnesses were interviewed by the FBI and the US Attorney's Office, yet not one of them was called to testify in the indictment. Ms. Wilburn dryly notes that the government called in witnesses who saw McVeigh in passing at gun shows several years ago, but they didn't want anything to do with people who saw McVeigh right before the bombing.

The video also covers the history and present state of grand juries in general, some facts about the incident that don't add up (the two subsequent bomb scares, the damage to the building, etc.), and the suspicious deaths of eight people involved in some way with the bombing. Police Chief Terry Yeakey, "the hero of the bombing", has been found dead in a field near the prison where McVeigh was held. He apparently slit both his wrists then shot himself in the head. One of the first doctors on the scene of the bombing, who was going to talk to a public official about a possible cover-up, died when his private plane crashed.

Indictment is a professional video that not only tell us about the sneaky things that happened on the Oklahoma City grand jury but also provides a startling look at the whole grand jury system. It's probably not what you want to get if you need a basic introduction to the alternative research on the OK bombing, but it's very worthwhile if you're digging deeper into the situation.

M.Ed Marketing; $19.95

1996; VHS videocassette; 90 minutes

NO AMATEUR DID THIS
What Is the Truth About the Oklahoma City Bombing?

by Ken Armstrong

Perhaps the most diligently researched of the Oklahoma Bombing City books I have seen so far, *No Amateur Did This* scrutinises hundreds of articles, reports, TV news stories, military documents, witness statements, and other sources to wring out the pattern of inconsistencies surrounding this event. The minutest details are sifted out, examined, and compared. This methods sheds a lot of new light on the bombing, but instead of giving us a clearer picture, we are left more confused than ever. But that is the whole point. Despite the fact that the government is presenting this as an open-and-shut case, there are so many contradictions, loose ends, and outright impossibilities that we can easily see how murky the whole thing is.

The witness timeline for April 19, 1995, draws together the statements of all people known to have seen McVeigh, the Ryder truck, and other elements of the puzzle just before the explosion. The statements don't often match each other, but many of them mention a second man, who matches the description of John Doe #2, and is described as olive-skinned, Native American, Hispanic, or Middle Eastern. At 8:55 AM "Dana Bradley was in the Social Security office located in the Murrah Building when she observed John Doe 2. He was described as short and muscular. He got out of the Ryder truck wearing a 'heavy ski parka and ball cap.' He exited the Ryder truck and walked 10-12 feet from the witness. The man walked to the back of the truck. Then went east up Fifth Street toward the Northeast side of the Murrah Building." For its part, the FBI now says that there was no John Doe #2 at the scene.

Soon after the explosion, McVeigh was pulled over for not having a license plate on his car. An article in a California newspaper discusses the plate that belonged on the car. "McVeigh's missing Arizona license plate appears on a mystery vehicle in a videotape taken just before the... bombing... The videotape from a security camera shows another vehicle with the plate — not the Mercury — and also shows the Ryder truck." If McVeigh was the sole bomber at the scene, why is a vehicle other than his displaying his tag?

It's no secret that the most important piece of physical evidence in the case — the federal building itself — was demolished just over a month after the bombing, preventing any meaningful examinations. What is less known is that another crucial piece of evidence was ruined even sooner. The crater that the truck-bomb made was filled in almost immediately after the blast, ostensibly to allow rescue workers better access to the building. "Unless, at some time in the future, it is found that the crater was accurately measured and analysed it can never be verified as to whether or not a 4,800 pound ANFO bomb could have produced the crater."

No Amateur covers dozens upon dozens of other topics, including McVeigh's whereabouts on the day of the bombing, the arrest affidavits McVeigh and Terry Nichols, McVeigh's behaviour after his arrest, items found at Nichols'

home, the Middle Eastern connection, eyewitness and seismic evidence for two explosions, the explosive power of ANFO, explosives illegally stored in the federal building, damage to other buildings, the pattern of damage to the federal building, lots of evidence that there was official foreknowledge of the bombing, the tenuous case against Michael Fortier, the indictments of McVeigh and Nichols, the accusations of grand juror Hoppy Heidelberg, connections to the Christian Identity community known as Elohim, the mysterious leg found in the rubble, Lori Fortier, and the media's propagandistic reportage of the issue. A bibliography, long endnotes section, index, and appendixes showing the pattern of damage to the building and seismographic read-outs make this detailed book even more valuable.

Tom Davis Books; $19.95
1996; oversized softcover; 188 pp
illus; 0-9657155-0-7

OKBOMB!
Conspiracy and Cover-up

by Jim Keith

OKBOMB! is an extensive look at the facts and theories surrounding the Oklahoma City bombing that clash with the government/media's version of events.

Were there additional explosives inside the building? CNN reported live the evacuation of emergency workers from the building because authorities believed there was another bomb. Around 11:30 that morning, a KFOR-TV reporter on CNN said: "The FBI has confirmed there is another bomb in the federal building. It's in the east side of the building... We're not sure what floor, what level, but there is definitely danger of a second major explosion." The general manager of another Oklahoma TV station interviewed the assistant Oklahoma City Fire Chief, "who told him 'that they had found two undetonated bombs in the building as well as one rocket launcher in the building.'"

And what are we to make of the fact that the FBI suspended the rescue of victims just ten hours after the explosion? For twelve hours, the rescue was put on hold while agents carried boxes of documents out of the ATF and DEA offices. The last victim was rescued forty-eight hours after the explosion, so you have to wonder how many people died while the FBI "rescued" the precious files.

Was there foreknowledge of the event? The *Portland Oregonian* reports that Judge Wayne Alley, "who has an office across the street from the Oklahoma City federal building, was warned several days before the blast by 'security specialists' to take 'special precautions.'" Judge Alley is now scheduled to preside over the trial of Timothy McVeigh and Terry Nichols. Many witnesses report hearing ATF agents say that they were told that coming into work on April 19 was optional because of a bomb threat the previous day.

Many eyewitnesses saw things before the explosion that contradict the official story. Mike Moroz, who works at a tire store, says that McVeigh and a man resembling John Doe #2 pulled up in a Ryder truck, and McVeigh asked him for directions to Fifth and Harvey (the location of the federal building). Gary Lewis, a press operator at the *Oklahoma*

Journal Record — which is located near the federal building — was outside just before the bombing. He is reported to have seen a yellow Mercury speed past him. McVeigh was driving, and a man who looked like John Doe #2 was in the passenger's seat. Just as these and other witnesses were coming forward, the FBI was backing off its story about John Doe #2, saying that there hadn't been a collaborator physically with McVeigh that morning. The media had been reporting that the FBI had videotape of two people getting out of the truck in front of the federal building, but the FBI reversed itself, saying it didn't have any such footage.

OKBOMB! also delves into McVeigh's beliefs and actions that contradict normal militia stances, around a dozen other suspects who were taken into custody and released, evidence that the ATF was keeping an arsenal room in the federal building, grand juror Hoppy Heidelberg, seismographic recordings of two explosions, demolitions experts who refute the truck-bomb theory, allegations of evidence tampering, the theory that Japan did the bombing in retaliation for the CIA's sarin gas attack on Tokyo subways, the Middle East connection, the McVeigh lookalike(s), McVeigh's possible connections to military intelligence, and much more. This book may not contain revelations about what did happen, but it forcefully reminds us that there are many, many questions that have yet to be answered.

IllumiNet Press; $14.95
1996; softcover; 237 pp
illus; 1-881-532-08-9

OKLAHOMA CITY BOMBING
The Suppressed Truth
by Jon Rappoport

In a conversational — and at times sarcastic — tone, Jon Rappoport examines some of the holes in the official story surrounding the Oklahoma City bombing. First, he points out how the accepted version of events paints the alleged perpetrators as total idiots. They rent a truck that's easily traceable and make explosives from fertiliser that's easily traceable. Then the alleged perpetrator, Tim McVeigh, rides around in a car with no license plate, begging to get caught. When a policeman pulls him over and notices a bulge under McVeigh's jacket, he admits that he's carrying a 9mm Glock pistol and a five-inch knife but makes no attempt to use them. If he really had just killed over 150 people — including many federal employees — would he have hesitated for one second to waste a cop in order to get away?

Then there's the impossibilities of the explosion scenario. The explosives were mixed in twenty separate plastic containers. This type of explosive — made from ammonium nitrate and fuel oil — has to be detonated at the exact same moment to have a powerful blast. In order to get all twenty containers to ignite at once would take a demolitions expert using very exact techniques. Probably not someone who flees the scene in a car with no plate.

Rappoport also says that the damage done to the building is inconsistent with the truck-bomb theory. A quarter of the building collapsed in upon itself, indicating an implosion. Buildings on the other side of the street did not sustain the kind of damage that they should have if the truck had caused the sole explosion.

Retired Brigadier General USAF Ben Partin says that the damage to the building is identical from the ground floor to the roof, contraindicating an outside explosion. Moreover, when looking at the pattern of damage, it can be seen that "some of the columns collapsed that should not have collapsed or some of the columns are still standing that should have collapsed and did not."

Roy Brown — a geophysicist at the University of Oklahoma — and Charles Mankin — the head of the Geological Survey at the university — say that the seismographic data show that there were two big shockwaves associated with the event, with the second one slightly stronger than the first. They don't believe the second shockwave is an echo of the first one. It possibly represents a second explosion.

Rappoport thinks it's a strong possibility that the deed was done by an intelligence/military faction of the government or perhaps former members of such a group who now do freelance work. The purposes were to discredit the Patriot/militia movement, pass the repressive anti-terrorism legislation that was around before the bombing, and — in general — use it as an excuse to trash our rights in the name of protecting us.

This book displays sympathy for some Patriot ideas, which will turn some people off, but it nonetheless serves a very important role by questioning an inconsistent and improbable story that is being presented as gospel. Other angles it covers include the unwillingness of the press to even consider alternatives to the government's version of events, witnesses who saw McVeigh hanging around with an Iraqi in Oklahoma City a few days before the explosion, witnesses who heard two explosions, the tow missile that was allegedly found in the building's ruins, and more.

Although this was the first book to sceptically view the bombing, it is also the least thorough.

Blue Press; $12
1995; softcover; 112 pp
no ISBN

ALEX CONSTANTINE

BLOOD, CARNAGE AND THE AGENT PROVOCATEUR
The Truth About the Los Angeles Riots and the Secret War Against L.A.'s Minorities
by Alex Constantine

PSYCHIC DICTATORSHIP IN THE U.S.A.

ALEX CONSTANTINE

How the government monkeys with our minds and bodies.
Psychic Dictatorship in the U.S.A.

Alex Constantine presents evidence suggesting that government-sponsored provocateurs set many of the fires during the LA riots and that higher-ups in the LA Police Department purposely delayed action. A national guardsmen and his companion were pulled over in an unmarked car during the riots. They had with them "two gas cans, rags, and bottles — the raw ingredients for Molotov cocktails." A former police dog trainer claimed that the LAPD hired him and his accomplices to set fire to Korean stores. Many residents of the area say that they saw fires set by people who were obviously not locals.

The highly-publicised lack of police action during the crucial early hours of the riots is also examined. Police actually *pulled out* of areas where violence was brewing — including the intersection where Reginald Denny was savagely beaten — and were not brought back until the mayhem was in full swing. Hundreds of the LAPD captains happened to be attending a training seminar during those important hours, and Chief Daryl Gates was at a political fund-raiser. "Some 200 officers, ordered to do nothing, were appalled. They stood around waiting for orders while the carnage escalated." The *New York Times* reported that police "did not follow standard procedures to contain rioting once it began."

Somehow — nobody's quite sure why — seventeen hours passed between the call for National Guard units and their arrival. When they did manage to arrive, "Guard units were deployed at a trickle by Daryl Gates."

Constantine also reports on extreme irregularities in the King and Denny beating trials, the politically-stacked and corrupt Christopher and Webster Commissions — which investigated the riot, and the evidence that the Watts riots were also incited by the government.

The Constantine Report; $3.50
1993; softcover; 80 pp
heavily illus; 0-938331-04-3

THE FLORIDA/HOLLYWOOD MOB CONNECTION, THE CIA AND O.J. SIMPSON
by Alex Constantine

In this booklet in the *Constantine Report* series, Alex Constantine spins a sordid web involving the Mafia, its connection to the CIA, and the travails of one of its alleged friends, OJ Simpson. As usual, the surprising connections, hidden facts, and allegations fly so fast and furiously, you may need to make a flowchart to keep up.

It would be impossible to summarise this rollercoaster report, but the gist is that the Mob and the whole Simpson/Brown/Goldman affair intersect at many odd angles. "Since the start of the Simpson trial, Denise Brown has been the smiling paramour of Tony 'the Animal' Fiato, a marmoset-eyed mob enforcer and FBI informant in a probe of the murder of Hollywood's Frank Cristi, another actor with a Godfather credit." Also, it is claimed that AC Cowlings was the chauffeur and bodyguard for Joey Ippolito, a powerful second-generation Mafioso. Ippolito was using Cowlings to get to Simpson, who gave him inside info on the football industry.

As for who actually committed the murders, Constantine offers different theories. The most far-out is that Simpson was a programmed assassin, as some people claim Sirhan Sirhan and others have been. A caller to a radio show said that he heard some cocaine-smuggling white supremacists he used to be involved with planning to kill Nicole Brown. Or it could have been the work of a particular Mob enforcer who is known to be fond of knives, torture, and beheadings. As for why the murders happened, Constantine mainly relies on a rumour that the three main parties involved couldn't pay their drug debts to the Mob.

Among other spooky and underreported facts, Brett Cantor — who owned a Hollywood night-club where Nicole Brown and Ron Goldman were regulars — was viciously stabbed to death on March 19, 1995 — in almost exactly the same way that Goldman had been killed. Also, in February 1995, a stripper named Tracey Hill was arrested in Northern California with 40 lbs of cocaine. "Police also found a vial of pills in her purse prescribed to Al Cowlings. Donald Re, his attorney (a former law partner of Howard Weitzman) denied any connection to Ms. Hill, but the *Contra Costa Times* reported that Hill's computerised address book listed the telephone numbers of both Cowlings and Simpson (AP, 3-25-95)."

If you think any of this sounds crazy, reserve your judgement until you actually read the whole report. Like many other publications in the Conspiracies chapter, the theories presented may not be totally airtight, but, then again, neither are the official explanations. Enough facts and impossible coincidences are presented to make you realise that something fishy is going on behind the curtain.

The Constantine Report; $3.95
1995; softcover; 40 pp
no ISBN

PSYCHIC DICTATORSHIP IN THE U.S.A.

by Alex Constantine

In this eagerly-awaited (by me) tome, conspiracy researcher Alex Constantine exposes the various ways in which the government is monkeying with our minds and bodies. It's been officially documented that the US government experimented with mind control techniques on citizens in its MK-ULTRA and MK-SEARCH programmes, which lasted from the early 1950s to the early 1970s. And we now know that during that time period the government was also exposing civilians to radiation and spraying cities with mild germ warfare agents. All of these programmes have officially ended, and there are still a lot of people who actually believe that our government has given up its wicked ways in this regard. Constantine demonstrates that this research is being continued today and has reached new levels of horror. (After all, if the government once found this sort of research fruitful, why in the world would it stop doing it and let all its enemies get a potential advantage?)

One area in which this research is proceeding is with the so-called "non-lethal weapons", which are being touted by the authorities as humane methods of crowd control and hostage rescue. They point to acoustic bullets and immobilising foam as prime examples. When they mention electromagnetic weapons, they always point out how they can induce nausea and disorientation in many people at once. What isn't mentioned is that these weapons can also kill people. As investigative columnist Jack Anderson wrote in 1985: "Can the human mind be short-circuited or even destroyed by extremely-low frequency radio waves? Preposterous as such an idea may seem, scientists on both sides of the Iron Curtain have been conducting secret tests." Constantine chronicles the history of this type of technology from the 1940s to today. Not only can it kill, but it can erase memory, implant thoughts, and turn people — such as Sirhan Sirhan — into killers.

Half the book is devoted to the CIA's use of so-called cults as implementers of gun running, money laundering, and mind control experiments. The Sovereign Order of the Solar Temple, the Symbionese Liberation Army (which kidnapped Patricia Hearst), Jonestown, and the Rajneesh movement are some of the better-known examples of puppet organisations, according to Constantine. He shows the intricate, overlapping web that links sect founders and mind control psychiatrists to the Agency. To summarise his findings here would be impossible, but let's say that it's more than a little disturbing.

Constantine spends a lot of time showing that sects really do engage in widespread abuse of children, but they don't do it for fun or sacrifice or because that's what God wants. It's part of mind control conditioning that's being or-

chestrated by the CIA. Physical, sexual, and emotional abuse of children forces them to dissociate, becoming blank slates for experimenters to fill in with their own instructions (namely: kill kill kill). This abuse also causes a related condition known as Multiple Personality Syndrome, which also comes in handy, since one personality can be a killer but the others can be peaceful as lambs.

Adults often claim to uncover long-buried memories of ritual child abuse. In the past few years, a backlash to these claims has appeared. Sceptics say that these memories are untrue, and this line of thinking has been gaining wider acceptance. Constantine says that this is a government-orchestrated front to discredit victims of abuse/ mind control and give the public a false sense of security. To back up his assertions, he makes some intriguing revelations, showing that the False Memory Syndrome Foundation's founder said during an interview with a journal on paedophilia "that it was 'God's Will' adults engage in sex with children." Also, during the 1970s in Los Angeles, two of the foremost researchers who now debunk the idea of ritual abuse published *Finger*, which Constantine characterises as "an underground tabloid for paedophiles".

The McMartin Preschool case — in which the family that ran a day-care centre was accused of sexual abuse — was another instance of CIA experimentation, according to the author. The news media, several books, and a made-for-HBO movie (*Indictment*) produced by Oliver Stone have presented the case as a witch hunt run by the gullible and the incompetent. There was, however, a lot of evidence to the contrary. Of the 389 children examined for the trial, "80 percent had physical symptoms, including blunt force trauma of sexual areas, scarring, rectal bleeding and sexual diseases." During the trial, the children's reports of secret tunnels under the preschool were used as a primary example of their overactive imaginations. Here is where Constantine drops a bombshell: despite complete silence about this fact in the news media, a team of archaeologists, geologists, an excavator, and others *did* find a network of tunnels, exactly where the children said it was.

The book's third section is a smattering of chapters about other CIA chicanery, not all of which has to do with mind control. "The GOP's [Great Old Party, i.e., the Republicans] Pink Triangle and the CIA" is billed as: "The true story of gay Republican power-brokers and the CIA's Neil Livingstone, an influential covert operator who inhabits a grim netherworld of GOP pimps, kidnappers, cocaine, arms smuggling, blackmail, pedophile rings, and Nazi collaborators." Another chapter looks at alleged connections between the CIA, the S&L crisis, cocaine smuggling, John DeLorean, and Johnny Carson. NutraSweet takes a beating in another chapter, in which Constantine claims that aspartame is so harmful that "[t]he Pentagon once listed it in an inventory of prospective biochemical warfare weapons submitted to Congress."

Psychic Dictatorship in the U.S.A. presents an amazing amount of facts and theories to set your head a-spinning. The information ranges from things that are undoubtedly true to things that put a massive strain on credibility. To his credit, Constantine does reference the majority of his material.

Feral House; $12.95
1995; softcover; 235 pp
illus; 0-922915-28-8

VIRTUAL GOVERNMENT
CIA Mind Control Operations
in America
by Alex Constantine

This second collection of Alex Constantine's research presents more claims of the US government's advanced mind control operations. When you read Constantine, you get the distinct feeling that everything you've ever learned is a lie. Luckily for your sanity, not all of his claims are well-supported, but there is still more than enough evidence to make sure that you will sleep fitfully. For example, New Orleans psychologist Valerie Wolf has given sworn testimony about experimentation on children. "'Most of these patients responded to certain sounds,' Wolf reported in testimony to the President's Advisory Committee on Radiation Experiments on March 15, 1995, 'clickers, metronomes or just clicking the tongue or hand clapping. Patients would vacillate from calm to robotically asking, "Who do you want me to *kill*?"'" Chapters such as "The Search for the Manchurian Preschooler", "McMartin Preschool Revisited", and "Acclaimed 1991-92 San Diego Grand Jury Child Abuse Report Demonstrated to Be Fraudulent by Subsequent Grand Jury" delve into the subject of brainwashing kids.

Further scariness can be found in "On the Road to the Fourth Reich". While this title sounds as though it belongs to a chapter about the rise of neo-Nazism, it is actually about something that, in many ways, is much more disturbing: high-ranking members of the US government have been embracing Nazism since its inception. The most viciously anti-Communist politicians are the ones with the closest ties to the Nazis. Before World War II, Senator Robert Rice Reynolds "travelled to Germany and returned chanting his praises for Hitler. He called for the formation of a Nationalist Party back home, and wrote in the *Congressional Record*: 'The dictators are doing what is best for their people. I say it is high time we found out how they are doing it.'"

The second chief investigator for the infamous House Unamerican Activities Committee, Dr. JB Matthews, "Predicted in his autobiography that America's answer to communism would be fascism or 'something so closely akin to it that the difference will not greatly matter.' His autobiography was published by John Cecil, a veteran anti-Semite, and his writings were reprinted by *Contra-Komintern*, the official house organ of the Nazi Foreign Office." Furthermore, HUAC's chief investigator co-edited "a Nazi hate sheet" and ran "an openly fascistic Ukrainian group." Congressmen Burton K. Wheeler, Howard Buffett, and Hamilton Fish (the Republican party leader) made up the recruiting arm of For America, a group founded in 1954. "The stated aim of For America was support of political candidates sympathetic to the Nazi cause." (Among the group's other movers and shakers were the publisher of the *Chicago Tribune*, the former Dean of Law at Notre Dame University, and the CEO of Sears, Roebuck.)

It is no longer a secret that the CIA infiltrated newspapers and magazines by planting reporters and correspondents who were (and undoubtedly still are) actually on the Agency's payroll. Constantine shows us that this is only the tip of the iceberg. The CIA quietly funds the entire publication of newspapers and magazines throughout the world. They also produce a television show, run a world-wide radio network, distribute movies made by private American studios, and bankroll numerous books that are published in the US.

Other unnerving chapters include "Bleak House: A Case of Nazi-Style Experimental Psychiatry in Canada", "The Hollywood/Florida Mob Connection, the CIA, and O.J. Simpson" (originally printed as a separate book, above), "The Good Soldier: The Rise of Timothy McVeigh from 'Robotic' Soldier to Mad Bomber", "CIA Mind Control and the U.S. Postal Service", and the book's centrepiece, "Virtual Government: 'Alien' Abductions, 'Psychic' Warfare and Cult Programming — Military-Corporate, Academic and Quasi-Religious Fronts for Mind Control Operations in America". Sweet dreams.

Feral House; $14.95
1997; softcover; 304 pp
illus; 0-922915-45-8

MISCELLANEOUS

60 GREATEST CONSPIRACIES
OF ALL TIME
by Jonathon Vankin & John Whalen

Co-authored by Jonathon Vankin, author of the essential *Conspiracies, Crimes, and Cover-ups* [below], this book should be considered a primer on conspiracies. If you're a novice in the field, I can't think of a better place to start your education. If you're an advanced conspirologist, this book will be of less help to you, but I bet you'll still learn a lot.

One chapter investigates the CIA's infamous MK-ULTRA mind control experiments, in particular their testing of LSD as a way of reprogramming humans. "Their idea was not to open 'the doors of perception' but to convert otherwise free human beings into automatons." The spooks also investigated the uses of other drugs, electroshock, microwaves, electrical implants, and other techniques. Today the documents from these experiments are few and far between, since most of them were destroyed by then-CIA director Richard Helms to deal with "a burgeoning paper problem." Despite the "official" ending of MK-ULTRA (1954-1963) and its successor MK-SEARCH (1964-1973), the research still goes on under the monikers of "psy-ops" (psychological operations) and "non-lethal weapons".

In "Microfilm at 11", the authors document the CIA's use of journalists, particularly within CBS and the *New York*

Times. Hundreds of reporters have recruited foreign spies, acted as Agency messengers abroad, gathered info for the Agency, and spread propaganda abroad and in the US. In an incident that has become fairly well-known in nonconformist circles, the CIA claims that CL Sulzberger, nephew of the *New York Times'* publisher, once put his name on a CIA briefing paper and had it published verbatim as one of his articles. Also, many CIA agents get jobs as reporters in prestigious news organisations. As a high level CIA official told Carl Bernstein: "One journalist is worth twenty agents."

"Who Slew the Walrus?" deals with the assassination of John Lennon. This is one of the chapters with the fewest facts and the most speculation, but it is still tantalising. The authors show that Lennon's killing could have been politically motivated. The authorities — including Richard Nixon, Attorney General John Mitchell, Senator Strom Thurmond, and J. Edgar Hoover — considered the Thoughtful Beatle to be an extremely dangerous subversive who, with his unlimited media access, could mobilise the younger generation into dangerous action. In fact, Lennon's FBI file notes that he was kept under "constant surveillance." Based on some of his comments and actions, Mark David Chapman may have been programmed through mind control to pull the plug on Lennon.

While Lennon was a reluctant spiritual guide for some people, Pope John Paul I was a spiritual leader for 800 million Catholics. The circumstances surrounding his death are murky at best, and the authors present a good case that he was murdered. Why murder the Pope? Because John Paul was on the record as saying that he wanted to do away with one of the world's sleaziest financial operations, the Vatican Bank, which has strong ties to the Mafia and the fascist terrorist organisation P2. The Pope had no bodyguards and minimal security, making him easy pickings. The night he died, he did manage to press a distress button that set off a flashing light in a guard station. Unfortunately the single guard on duty was in bed asleep. The Pope's light stayed on all night, even though he was known to always hit the sack at 9:30, but no one bothered to check on him. The death was ruled a heart attack, even though no autopsy was performed. "The Vatican tried to pacify the protesting press, falsely stating that church law prohibited autopsies on popes (there was never any such edict)." The head of the Vatican Bank, Bishop Paul Marcinkus, was found walking through the Vatican village at 6 AM on the morning the Pope was found dead. He never went on such walks before, and his presence was never explained.

Other subjects that are covered include assassination attempts against Castro (including a plan to wire a conch shell to explode at Castro's favourite diving spot), the despicable mandatory sterilisation laws of the early twentieth century, the Federal Emergency Management Agency (FEMA) and its plan to declare martial law during a "national emergency", the history of US biological warfare, the travesty known as the Persian Gulf War, the Waco massacre, the theory that the Moon landings were faked, the Nazis' alleged development of UFOs, the strange death and possible continuing life of Jim Morrison, investigative journalist Danny

Casolaro's suspicious "suicide", the Christic Institute's unified conspiracy theory, the alien autopsy footage, the Japanese subway gas attack, Vince Foster, the Oklahoma City bombing, the Unabomber, HAARP [see review *Angels don't play this HAARP*, below], Votescam, Watergate, Jonestown, Pan Am 103, KAL 007, AIDS, fluoridation, Jack the Ripper, the Son of Sam killings, and much more. Of course, the authors look at the possible shenanigans behind the deaths of JFK, RFK, Abraham Lincoln, Martin Luther King, and Marilyn Monroe.

Being an introductory guidebook, *60 Conspiracies* often gives a barebones summary, leaving you frustrated and wanting to know more. But then again, that's the whole point. [The excellent Website listed below contains some chapters from the book (including unpublished chapters), plus the authors' continuing coverage of conspiracies and other strange going-ons.]

Citadel; $18.95

1995, 1996; softcover; 393 pp

0-8065-1833-2

WWW: www.conspire.com

ABOVE THE LAW
Secret Deals, Political Fixes, and Other Misadventures of the U.S. Department of Justice
by David Burnham

The Department of Justice functions as the law enforcer, prosecutor, and jailer of America's citizens. Encompassing the FBI, the Drug Enforcement Administration, the Immigration and Naturalisation Service, the US Marshals, the Bureau of Prisons, and more, the DOJ employs over 100,000 people and has vast powers concerning everything from drugs to pollution to forgery. Investigative reporter David Burnham has utilised inside sources and government documents to present this massive exposure of the incompetence, corruption, and arrogance of what he terms "a chaotic, slipshod, almost medieval institution".

A surprising number of Attorneys General were appointed because they were the President's personal lawyer, the national chair of the President's political party, the President's campaign manager, or a candidate for higher elective office. As it turns out, throughout the DOJ's entire history "most U.S. attorneys and attorneys general have either been young lawyers who see these attention-gathering jobs as the perfect springboard to higher political office, or older men who are buddies of the president... When it comes to the challenging job of running the Justice Department, professional competence has seldom been a concern of either party."

The chapter "Keeping Track of the American People" looks at the scary tactics being used or proposed by the FBI and others — wiretaps built into the new phone networks, the Clipper chip, the battle against personal encryption, powerful databases containing personal information, and the use of pen registers. "Pens", as they're called, secretly log the numbers called by any phones they are attached to. The warrant needed to set up a pen on someone's phone is much easier to get than a warrant for a tap. "One difference is that any attorney in the government can apply for a pen register order. A second difference is that the attorney, instead of being required to establish probable cause, only has to certify that the information sought by the government is 'relevant to an ongoing investigation.'"

Elsewhere in the book — among many other tales of wrongdoing — Burnham shows that Attorneys General have used their powers for political reasons; the FBI has manipulated crime statistics to make things seem worse than they are; and the DOJ has rarely investigated associates of the President, chose to ignore civil and criminal tax code violations by President and Mrs. Reagan, harassed black politicians and helped white ones, blocked prosecutions of corporations, and has used "national security" as an excuse to persecute people with radical political beliefs.

Scribner (Simon & Schuster); $27.50

1996; hardcover; 444 pp

0-684-80699-1

AMERICA UNDER SIEGE
by the American Justice Federation

This video by Linda Thompson's American Justice Federation, creators of *Waco II: The Big Lie Continues* [above], documents the signs that the New World Order is upon us. There is plenty of footage and photos of unmarked black helicopters and vans and their black-clad drivers. The Federation claims that it has been buzzed repeatedly by the strange copters, and they show the video that proves it.

Quite a bit of time is spent on the story of Mike and Carol Benn of Dallas, who claim to have collected 17 million signatures from people calling for the impeachment of President Clinton. In the early morning in 1994 a copter buzzed the Benns' house, and fifteen minutes later their neighbour's house was in flames. Shady inspectors — dressed in suits and sunglasses — claimed that the fire was caused by the water heater, but as the footage clearly shows, there is no damage to the room housing the heater. However, there are large burnt holes in the roof, as if the house had been bombed with incendiary devices. Also suspicious are the shots of the rafters showing that all the burning took place on the *upper* part of the rafters. There is no damage to the underside. Mike Benn thinks the helicopter accidentally torched his neighbour's house.

In Puerto Rico, New York, Chicago, and Boston there have been gun sweeps of public housing projects. If a gun is found, the adults are arrested and their kids are taken. In a crime briefing on February 8, 1994, Attorney General Janet Reno and Vice President Al Gore said the raids were test runs for larger actions.

"Somehow fascism as a model for good behaviour has become commonplace," the narrator matter-of-factly states. She is referring to juvenile bootcamps that brainwash delinquents into becoming cannon fodder for the armed forces. In some of these camps, the kids are taught combat techniques, Air Force history, how to salute, and other strictly military things.

Another portion of the tape offers extensive film of a train repair complex that's been turned into a veritable fortress.

No matter what the underlying truths might be, two things are for sure: Area 51 is there, and it's spooky as hell. *Area 51.*

The Federation thinks that it will be used as a concentration camp for Americans during the coming crackdown. Although a few of the buildings are used to fix trains, most of the complex is empty. Despite this, hundreds of thousands of dollars have been appropriated to the facility. Entrances to empty buildings have been fitted with heavy-duty gated turnstiles. There are several layers of fencing with barbed wire on top tilted inward, which prevents people from getting out more than getting in. There are also windsocks and ground markers for helicopters, lots of radio antennae, and a crane clearly marked "United States Army". Heat furnaces are being installed in buildings that have been unheated for over 20 years.

Across the US, the backs of many road signs have small, solid-coloured stickers on them. The hypothesis is that these are troop transport markers that will help guide UN troops when they take over. If you follow the blue stickers in Utah, you will end up at missile storage sights.

The video also reveals that foreign troops have been practising in the US, a fact backed up by stories in many local newspapers. UN troops have been trained in forcible house-to-house searches in Louisiana, Arkansas, Indiana, Colorado, New Jersey, and other states. Ferocious Nepalese Gurkha assassins trained for three years in Washington state. Plus, there are frequent sightings of foreign war equipment in the States. At a remote sight in Mississippi, a private company has 750 Soviet armoured trucks under lock and key, yet signs on the fences declare it is a US Customs facility. The company claims the trucks are going to converted to foodmobiles for Third World countries, but for months they've remained untouched, complete with attachments for spraying nerve gas.

The Federation also gives a brief introduction to some of the scary government organisations in operation: the Federal Emergency Management Agency (FEMA), which can institute martial law; the Multi-Jurisdictional Task Force (MJTF), a federal police agency that can pull military personnel for law enforcement purposes; and the Financial Crime Enforcement Network (FinCEN), a databank located in Vienna, Virginia, that stores the property, tax, medical, and criminal records of every citizen.

America Under Siege offers some intriguing clues that

something rotten is going on. Even if you don't believe everything it claims, it's impossible not to come away just a little edgy and shaken.

American Justice Federation; $24.95

1994; VHS videocassette

AMERICAN GROUND ZERO
The Secret Nuclear War
by Carole Gallagher

Working for around a decade, documentarian Carole Gallagher recorded in photographs and words "the undecorated casualties of an undeclared war." For twelve years — starting in 1951 — the US government detonated 126 atomic bombs above the ground at the Nevada Test Site. Each explosion released the same amount of radiation into the atmosphere as the near-total meltdown at Chernobyl. It contaminated vast areas of the United States and neighbouring countries. Humans, animals, crops, water, and soil were irradiated nation-wide. Worst off were the people who lived in Nevada, Arizona, and Utah and, of course, those involved with the testing.

Gallagher presents black and white photos, background information, and testimony of these unknowing guinea pigs — soldiers and workers at the test site and people who lived in the surrounding area (or, in many cases, their next of kin). She documents the cancer, birth defects, hideous tumours, disgusting disfigurations, chronic vomiting, and physical agony they experienced (with a few exceptions, the pictures aren't graphic, but the text spares no details), as well as the government's responses (denial, cover-ups, etc.) and the effect of the nuclear bombs on the environment.

Random House; $30

1993; oversized softcover; 391 pp

heavily illus; 0-679-75432-6

...AND THE TRUTH SHALL SET
YOU FREE
by David Icke

In this thick volume, David Icke continues with the line of thinking he started in The Robots' Rebellion [below]. He takes a detailed look at the ways we are being manipulated, who is doing the manipulating, and what their ultimate goals are. He provides lots of scary specifics about shadowy groups who have way too much power, including the Trilateral Commission, the Bilderberg Group, the Orange Order, the House of Rothschild, the Skull and Bones Society, and the P2 Lodge, not to mention the UN and some multinational corporations.

Bridge of Love (Truth Seeker Publications); $21.95

1995; softcover; 525 pp

illus; 0-9526147-1-5

ANGELS DON'T PLAY THIS HAARP
Advances in Tesla Technology
by Dr. Nick Begich & Jeane Manning

The US government is rapidly developing a new super-advanced weapons system called High-frequency Active Auroral Research Program (HAARP). Currently being tested in Alaska, this giant "zapper" uses modulated ra-

dio frequencies to manipulate the ionosphere, inducing all kinds of effects. One of its uses is to track missiles and aircrafts, determine if they are carrying nuclear warheads, disorient them, and possibly destroy them. HAARP can also disrupt land, sea, and air communications, manipulate the weather, and alter ecosystems, for better or worse. Like other "nonlethal weapons" using radio waves, it will be able to affect people's moods and mental functioning and even cause damage to tissue.

The authors explore the history of this technology, who is controlling it now, how it works, what it can conceivably do, the movement to oppose it, and why we need to have more research and some public debates before it is fully unleashed. They make it clear — through quotes from official HAARP documents and military reports — that the government is fully aware of all the uses of HAARP, including its power to incapacitate and kill.

Besides the extremely obvious potential for abuse that such power inherently has, we should also be worried about the possible side effects of HAARP even if it's used ethically. Although the military-industrial complex is quick to reassure us that this technology is totally safe, they really have no idea what's going to happen when they start monkeying around with the atmosphere. There could be a huge number of consequences that could have domino effects. For example, the radio waves could confuse insects, which would then die in large numbers. Animals that depend on insects for food would start dying, and the whole ecosystem would be trashed. So even if you naively believe that HAARP would not or could not be used for evil, it still presents a global problem.

Also, if you think that HAARP is a delusion of paranoid minds, guess again. Congress has appropriated millions for the project, and Popular Science has done a cover story on it. This was the first book to break the silence by giving us the undoctored facts and theories concerning this very disturbing technology.

Earthpulse Press; $14.95 ppd in US, $21.95 ppd elsewhere

1995; softcover; 233 pp

illus; 0-9648812-0-9

AREA 51
The Dreamland Chronicles —
The Legend of America's Most Secret
Military Base
by David Darlington

In this sorely needed book, David Darlington examines the supersecret government facility Area 51 (aka Dreamland, Groom Lake, etc.) without approaching it from a conspiracy standpoint or a debunker's standpoint. He simply delves into what is known about the mysterious base, as well as what is conjectured about it.

The US government officially denies that Area 51 even exists, despite the fact that you can drive way out into the lonely Nevada desert and see it for yourself from a distance. (In case you can't make the trip, the book reproduces one photo, a map, and two satellite images of the area.) It consumes over fifty square miles and contains dozens of structures — "clusters of hangars, radar facilities, satellite dishes, a control tower, four water tanks on an east-facing hillside, a fuel-tank farm at the southern end. There were lots of other, less imposing buildings, but towering over everything was an enormous yellow hangar." Signs warn that deadly force has been authorised for use against trespassers.

Area 51 draws its funds from the infamous $30 billion "black budget", which is secret money used for unreported military and intelligence purposes. Despite this massive level of secrecy and security, some facts have dribbled out over the years, and Darlington has finally gathered together those shards of information.

Area 51 was built in the mid-1950s under the CIA's direction. It has served as a test site for the U-2 spy plane, the F-117 Stealth fighter, and other secretly funded aircraft. Its portion of the black budget continues to grow, as does the amount of real estate it consumes. Approximately 1000 to 2000 people work at the facility. They have all signed security oaths that slap them with ten years in jail and a $10,000 fine if they even *mention* the facility. Nobody's quite sure which part of the government is running Area 51. Some lawsuits have recently been launched because of alleged environmental crimes or abuse of employees (who have been exposed to dangerous chemicals with classified names), but they never get anywhere because Dreamland is unaccountable to anyone, shielded by Presidential decrees.

In the absence of official information, rumours regarding Area 51's activities have flourished. Some people believe that it houses alien bodies and spacecraft from Roswell or some other crash. Others say that grey aliens are working with humans to develop technology at the site. Still others forward the idea that the government is genetically creating creatures that will be presented as malicious aliens, giving the government the excuse it needs for a complete fascist crackdown. As far as who runs the show, candidates include the "shadow government" created by President Truman or a secret cabal of Illuminati types, who may or may not be assisted by aliens.

Darlington heads to Nevada and elsewhere to submerge himself in the subculture of investigators, concerned citizens, thrillseekers, charlatans, and alleged whistleblowers, including the notorious Bob Lazar, who have sprung up around Area 51. He lets all the conspirologists speak for themselves, and relates his own adventures on the land that immediately surrounds Area 51.

In the end, he doesn't draw any conclusions, which is only fitting since there is scant information to base any conclusions on. Instead he paints a portrait of the roles that Area 51 plays in government, law, culture, ufology, and fringe political thinking. No matter what the underlying truths might be, two things are for sure: Area 51 is there, and it's spooky as hell.

Henry Holt and Company; $25
1997; hardcover; 283 pp
illus; 0-8050-4777-8

ASSASSINATION AT ST. HELENA REVISITED

by Ben Weider & Sten Forshufvud

After his defeat at Waterloo, the French Emperor and conqueror Napoleon Bonaparte was exiled to the island of St. Helena. History books tells us that he died there in 1821 of stomach cancer. However, almost from the beginning, there have been rumours that he was poisoned. The authors — two Napoleonic scholars — have assembled massive forensic and eyewitness evidence that Napoleon was given small doses of arsenic over a period of years and was finally killed off by mercury cyanide. His killer was a close associate, a member of his entourage named Charles-Tristan, Count de Montholon. The Count stood to inherit a great deal from Napoleon, and — the authors believe — he was acting on the wishes of the Bourbon government, who feared Napoleon might try to reclaim the imperial throne.

John Wiley & Sons; $30
1995; hardcover; 555 pp
illus; 0471126772

BHOPAL
The Inside Story — Carbide Workers Speak Out on the World's Worst Industrial Disaster

by TR Chouhan and others

During the night of December 3, 1984, around 45 tons of methyl isocyanate (MIC) leaked from Union Carbide's factory in Bhopal, India. It's been estimated that as many as 10,000 people died immediately and 5,000 more have died since then of gas-related causes. "Union Carbide claimed right after the disaster that methyl isocyanate (MIC) was only a minor irritant! And this claim was made despite the fact that Carbide's own safety manual emphasises that it is deadly even in very small doses."

In 1988, Carbide officially presented its theory of what happened. A disgruntled employee, they said, attached a water hose to the tank holding the MIC. This proved to be too much for the workers, and they responded by writing this book. Principal author TR Chouhan, a worker at the plant, presents all kinds of evidence — including testimony from other workers — as to the horrible safety conditions at the plant. To give just one example, during the leak, four of the five major safety systems did not work, because of shoddy maintenance.

In fact, Carbide had almost been forced to relocate away from the city, but luckily, zoning authorities labelled their production "non-noxious". Safety audits of the plant pointed out that there were no plans to evacuate Bhopal in case of a disaster. Management said that coming up with such plans would publicise the dangers of the plant, something they wanted to avoid. Something else extremely interesting was also noted: "Long before the disaster these audits pointed out major safety concerns and explicitly warned of the possibility of a runaway reaction in the MIC storage tanks."

Chouhan tells what it was like to work at the plant since 1975. He relates several accidents that occurred, including leaks of dangerous chemicals and a fire that broke out while the plant's fire truck was disabled. Using Carbide's own manuals and reports, he presents a strong case for the theory

A Black Cobra gunship — one of many types of black helicopter. *Black Helicopters Over America.*

that the MIC escaped because of an improperly-conducted water-washing exercise, which was intended to clear blocked pipes. Of course, this was the immediate cause. Chouhan backs up and reveals the long-term problems with plant design, operating procedures, and personnel training that made conditions ripe for the disaster. He also shows the shaky premises for Carbide's sabotage theory.

The rest of the book contains 25 pages of testimony from other workers, a year-by-year account of how the gassing victims have coped, and an essay on the Indian legal system's failure to bring the culprits to justice

Apex Press; $15
1994; softcover; 212 pp
0-945257-22-8

BLACK HELICOPTERS OVER AMERICA
Strikeforce for the New World Order
by Jim Keith

This book covers many of the same topics as *America Under Siege* [above] and other militia/patriot material — black helicopters, UN troops, detention centres, FEMA, etc. The first chapter offers a 36-page chronology of sightings of black helicopters from 1971 to 1994. Sometimes the copters are in the vicinity of a cattle mutilation. In other reports, the copters and their occupants are confronted by police, hunters, or other people. One report states that black helicopters landed on a beach in Long Island, New York, in 1974. "Men in black uniforms carrying M-16 rifles threatened a local police officer who confronted them and demanded to know what was going on."

The next chapter contains reports of foreign/UN troops and war equipment in the US, plus officially-recognised operations aimed at creating a world-wide police force. Next comes evidence of concentration camps in America, which were created to fulfil Ronald Reagan's Operation Rex 84. There is an 80-acre fenced-in site near Topeka, Kansas, that is marked as a "Zoo Annex". However, locals have found out that it's run by the Department of Corrections. Also reported: "An area of the National Forest is fenced in 'to control animal movement' by high chain link fence with barbed wire on top. Towers are in place outside the fenced area."

"National Emergency by Whose Definition?" is a valuable chapter because it lists a dozen Executive Orders that are on the books. These EOs — which are unarguably known to exist — are Presidential directives that have the force of law even though they are not reviewed by the people or

Congress. They give the executive branch dictatorial powers during a "national emergency", a term that has purposely been left vague and undefined. EO 10999 "authorises the control or confiscation of the nation's transportation sources, public and private." EO 11004 "gives government the mandate to relocate populations from one area to another."

Chapter 6 examines efforts to create a national police force that would be trained in putting down "insurrections" during martial law. Operation Cable Splicer is part of a larger effort to train police, military, and military reserves to become just such a force. "During one Cable Splicer conference, the Deputy Attorney General of California commented that any individual who goes against the policies of the State, even in verbal fashion, is an enemy to the people."

The following chapter supplies quotes from elite policymakers showing that they favour a nationless, one-world system of government. Throughout the book are several photographs of black helicopters in action and US maps of concentration camps, UN bases, etc.

The problem with *Black Helicopters* is that most of the incidents described are not backed up with any references. Some of the references that are given are from bulletins put out by militias, which may not carry a lot of credibility with most people. Still, this book does serve as a good primer on the beliefs and concerns of the anti-New World Order faction.

IllumiNet Press; $12.95
1994; softcover; 155 pp
illus; 1-881532-05-4

BLACK HELICOPTERS II
The Endgame Strategy
by Jim Keith

In this sequel to *Black Helicopters Over America*, Jim Keith updates us on the presence and purpose of mysterious, unmarked black helicopters, but he also does much more. In fact, this book's title is something of a misnomer, since over half the material doesn't deal with black helicopters. Instead, it focuses on signs of an impending fascist crackdown in America, during which martial law will be declared, large segments of the population will be detained in concentration camps, the Federal Emergency Management Agency (FEMA) will run the country, and the US/UN military will supply the muscle. All of this is typically labelled as (far) right-wing paranoia, but it shouldn't be dismissed so smugly.

FEMA really is allowed by several Executive Orders to assume dictatorial powers during a "national emergency", whatever that is. This was covered in the first book, but, like many topics, Keith covers it again and adds new material. He also looks at efforts to increase and centralise surveillance of US citizens. Probably almost no one realises that the Illegal Immigration Reform and Immigrant Responsibility Act, signed into law in 1996, has authorised the creation of a national ID card.

As evidence in the chapter on the formation of a one-world government, Keith cites, among many other things, State Department Publication 7277. "This document clearly explains foreign troops are being billeted within the United

States, while at the same time there is a dispersion of our own forces into myriad foreign hotspots, and a convergence and joint training of our troops with foreign troops world-wide. 7277 also explains why American soldiers are now being commanded by United Nations officers, and why large amounts of Russian military equipment is being imported into the United States."

A military press release trumpeting an exercise involving troops from several countries at Fort Polk, Louisiana, quotes a Marine General as saying, "It is through services such as this that truly we can create a New World Order in which the militaries of the world can work in co-ordination and co-operation to build a better peace." President Clinton, meanwhile, has given one-fifth of America's weapons-grade plutonium to the UN.

I've heard rumblings from New World Order watchers that the strange, coloured stickers that are on the backs of many road signs are actually coded driving directions for troops imposing martial law to follow. This has always struck me as an unusually bizarre theory, and I'm still unconvinced, but Keith reprints a report that gives the topic the fullest, most detailed treatment I've ever seen. Photos of the stickers on many signs are included, and the author gives the keys to their meanings.

As far as the black copters go, they continue to appear with regularity. They are being sighted in areas that are later found to be coated in strange toxins, and they still are seen in the same areas that mutilated cattle are discovered. Keith also points out that black helicopters are "often seen in the vicinity prior to UFO abductions — or what the victims believed were UFO abductions" and later tail people who claim to be abductees. "Among well-known abductees reportedly harassed by black helicopters were Betty Andreasson-Luca, Beth Collins, Leah Haley, Kathy Mitchell, Anna Jamerson, Debbie Jordan, Casey Turner, and Whitley Streiber."

Keith also covers the IRS's new all-encompassing database (part of a programme with the creepy name "Compliance 2000"), Gorbachev's role as a New Agey promoter of a one-world government, further reports of detention centres in the US, the Biological Diversity Treaty, which rides roughshod over national sovereignty, and many other juicy topics. Many new photos of black, unmarked helicopters — the kind the government says doesn't exist — are featured.

IllumiNet Press; $14.95
1997; softcover; 205 pp
illus; 1-881532-14-3

BLAZING TATTLES

A monthly sixteen-page newsletter that examines the negative impacts that pollution has on our health, the weather, and the environment... often in ways that are denied by the establishment. The January 1996 is the Gulf War Issue, with articles on new revelations concerning the cause of Gulf War Syndrome, two newly-released major reports on GWS, the global ramifications of the smoke from the oil well fires in Kuwait, the vast amount of Kuwaiti oil (equal to 600 Exxon Valdezes) that was spilled onto the desert, the devastating after-effects of Depleted Uranium armour piercing shells used

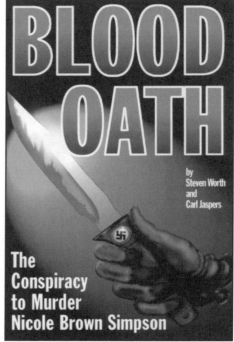

Presenting the theory that Nicole Brown Simpson was snuffed by white supremacists trying to trigger a race war. *Blood Oath.*

by US forces, and more. Other articles cover global warming, sustainability, the Bioregional Association, and the threat that pesticides pose to insects used for food.

Since then, *Blazing Tattles* has repeatedly covered various aspects of GWS, Chronic Fatigue Syndrome, and Environmental Sensitivity Illness. They have also featured articles on cosmetics safety, dangerous air fresheners, intensive agriculture, oyster hazards, postage stamp glue, mad cows and mad elks, and a Native American tribe that is threatening to commit mass suicide to protest at oil exploration.

Blazing Tattles/PO Box 1073/Half Moon Bay CA 94109
Email: blazing@igc.apc.org
WWW: www.concentric.net/~Blazingt
Single issue: $5. Can/Mex: $5.50. Elsewhere: $6
Twelve issues: US/Can/Mex: $25. Retired, students, disabled, underemployed: $18. Other countries: $45

BLOOD OATH
The Conspiracy to Murder
Nicole Brown Simpson
by Steven Worth & Carl Jaspers

I have to admit that the media frenzy that surrounded the whole OJ Simpson affair — especially the criminal trial — made me so ill that I refused to pay attention to the story on general principle. I usually caught the evening wrap-up on the news, but even then I was only half-listening. From what I knew, it certainly appeared that Simpson was guilty as hell.

But then I started reading things on the Net and talking to people who said that the matter wasn't as cut and dried as the media would have us believe. The first publication I saw that offered an alternate take on events was *The Florida/Hollywood Mob Connection, the CIA and O.J. Simpson* [above]. *Blood Oath* is the second.

There are two main thrusts to *Blood Oath*. On the one hand, it pokes holes in the theory that Simpson committed the murders of his ex-wife Nicole Brown Simpson and her friend Ron Goldman. On the other, it provides a theory about who did it.

As far as who did commit the murders, *Blood Oath* offers a startling proposition: Brown and Goldman were killed by members of CAUSE, a supersecret white supremacy group. Brown had been targeted because she was considered a "race traitor" for marrying an African American and having children with him. The CAUSE believed that by killing her and framing Simpson for the murder, they could incite a race war in the US. It is thought by many supremacists that if there is an all-out race war, the whites will win and turn the country into a racially pure, Christian nation.

The main source of this scenario is known only as "Skinner", a man who claims to be a member of CAUSE. He contacted one of the authors of the book in order to get the story told, because, he claims, he lost faith in the movement after seeing the loss of innocent lives that resulted from the Oklahoma City bombing. At first, the authors were sceptical though intrigued, but after checking out as much of Skinner's story as possible, they came to believe him.

Skinner says that the date of the assassinations was picked to coincide with the ten-year anniversary of the supremacy movement's greatest achievement, the killing of Jewish radio talk show host Alan Berg by members of The Order. The CAUSE had tried to blow up the First African Methodist Episcopal (AME) Church of Los Angeles but had failed. Stinging from this setback, they came up with a new plan. In unnerving detail, Skinner and the authors describe the months of surveillance and planning that went into the hit. As the book approaches its climax, we get a minute-by-minute account of the hours before the murders, the bloody assassinations themselves, the planting of the evidence (such as the gloves, stolen from Simpson's residence), and the getaway. (As for the presence of Simpson's blood, Skinner claims that a CAUSE member working in an LA medical facility was able to procure blood that Simpson was having stored in case he needed a transfusion someday.)

Appendixes provide a timeline of the CAUSE theory of the murders, a *Family Circus*-style map showing the path the prosecution alleges that Simpson took into his home when returning from the murders, photos of key locations, an ad for the kind of knife used in the killings, and more.

Obviously *Blood Oath* won't be the final word on the Brown-Goldman murders. The authors have done a nice job showing the contradictions and impossibilities of the prosecution's version of events, the ways in which Judge Ito appeared biased towards the prosecution, Mark Fuhrman's squirrelly testimony, and other problems with the official version of events. However, it's easier to disprove a certain

An earlier car built by the Beetle's <u>true</u> inventor.
Car Wars.

theory than it is to prove another. The CAUSE scenario contains all the pieces of the puzzle and the level of detail is impressive, but, in the end, it remains yet another theory of what really happened on June 12, 1994.

Rainbow Books; $14.95
1996; softcover; 330 pp
illus; 1-56825-058-4

CAR WARS
Fifty Years of Greed, Treachery, and Skullduggery in the Global Marketplace
by Jonathan Mantle

The largest industry in the world is the automobile industry, and with stakes that run into the hundreds of billions, you can bet that is has seen more than its share of deviousness and underhanded manoeuvres. All of this dirty laundry has been hung out to dry in *Car Wars*, a history of the auto biz from the 1940s to the 1990s.

The book looks briefly at the point at which the Age of the Auto began. "In 1938 Los Angeles was still a city of clean Pacific Ocean air. It had the largest electric rail system in the world. The 'Big Red Cars' of Pacific Electric serviced the San Fernando Valley; more than one thousand trains left the downtown area each day. General Motors, joining with Standard Oil of California (Socal) and Firestone, the tire manufacturer, bought up the transit company and closed it down. Los Angeles grew around the roads and not the railroads." GM teamed up with other oil companies in cities all over the US to close electrical mass transit systems and force people to turn to cars.

The auto industry's behaviour during World War II was disgraceful. GM and Ford had plants in operation in Japan, Germany, and other areas held by the Axis powers, but they did not shut down operations when the second war to end all wars broke out. "GM's Opel plant at Brandenberg in Nazi Germany built, with Daimler-Benz, the Blitz truck. The Blitz was the workhorse of the Wehrmacht in their slaughter of American GIs in the Battle of the Bulge and the rearguard action on the road to Berlin. GM's Opel plants at Russelsheim manufactured 50 percent of the propulsion systems for the Junkers 88, the bomber used in the Luftwaffe's mass air raids on civilians." To make matters worse, the US government gave GM $33 million in tax exemptions for the damage done to its plants by Allied bombers! Of course, Henry Ford's and Adolph Hitler's mutual admiration for each other is fairly well-known and is covered here in-depth (including Ford sending Hitler a $50,000 check on the Führer's fiftieth birthday, and Hitler hanging up a life-size portrait of Ford in Nazi headquarters in Munich).

Car Wars goes on to cover the real creator of the Volkswagen Beetle (it is *not* Dr. Ferdinand Porsche, as widely believed), the US Army bailing out the faltering Japanese auto industry in 1953, "the biggest industrial espionage scandal in history" that occurred when GM's wonderboy José Lopez was accused of handing over major secrets to Volkswagen, the targeting of FIAT by the left wing terrorist group the Red Brigades, the aborted merger of Renault and Volvo, the US industry's disastrous loss of eight billion dollars in 1991, Mercedes-Benz's plans to build a Swatchcar, and the smuggling of Western cars into Eastern Europe and the Far East.

Arcade Publishing; $13.95
1995; softcover; 256 pp
illus; 1-55970-400-4

CONSPIRACIES, COVER-UPS & CRIMES
From Dallas to Waco
Jonathon Vankin

Before he co-wrote *The 60 Greatest Conspiracies of All Time* [above], Jonathon Vankin did an amazing thing — he wrote a book on conspiracies that came from the viewpoint of neither an uncritical true-believer nor a nonbeliever determined to demonstrate that we live in a nice, safe world where nothing shadowy occurs. Vankin is *sceptical*, yes, but he is not a sceptic. He simply wants to go where the facts — as best they can be determined — lead him. In some cases, this means that a certain theory comes off looking ridiculous, and Vankin doesn't mind applying his cynical sense of humour to those who promote such theories. Then there are other cases where it does look like something suspicious is going on. Vankin is unafraid to say so and, once again, launch some stingers against the people who lie to our faces.

A good example of Vankin's even-handedness is in his chapter on Lyndon LaRouche, the mysterious burr in the saddle of politics-as-usual. Although Vankin apparently doesn't see a whole lot of merit to LaRouche's conspiratorial worldview — which involves the British government, Nancy Reagan, Henry Kissinger, the Grateful Dead, Satanism, and Thomas Hobbes — he does believe that the US government is "out to get" LaRouche.

In the chapter on JFK's assassination, Vankin discusses resistance to conspiracy theories, especially as they apply to assassinations. Critics of these theories say that they give people comfort by positing that there is a small number of people responsible for the world's problems. Vankin replies that maybe the mainstream doesn't want to believe in conspiracies because it would violate too many comfortable assumptions. "The 'lone nut' doctrine is dogma, and assassination conspiracy theories heresy, because homicidal kooks have no political motives. When film director Oliver Stone, armed with Newman's research, proposed in his 1991 *JFK*

that escalation of the [Vietnam] war and the assassination of President Kennedy may have been more than coincidence, reaction in the national media was ridicule. Yet the suggestion, though not necessarily verifiable, is wholly plausible. But even to acknowledge the link is to give assassination political meaning. It suggests not only a motive for and therefore the possibility of a high-level assassination conspiracy, but it also makes plain a truth even more troubling for America in the long run: violence *can* change the American system."

In other chapters, Vankin casts his eye on Lee Harvey Oswald's Marine buddy Kerry Thornley, William Bramley's theory that the human race was created as slave labour for aliens, the John Birch Society, John Stormer's *None Dare Call It Treason*, Mae Brussell, Jim Garrison, mind-controlled assassins, US government drug-running, the CIA's various misdeeds, George Bush, the Council on Foreign Relations, Freemasonry, and more. This edition of the book contains a new introduction in which the author looks at the popularisation of conspiracy theories; examines the murky circumstances around more recent events, such as Waco, Vince Foster, and Oklahoma City; and looks at new developments surrounding JFK and the October Surprise theory.

If you only get two books from this chapter, make sure they are both Vankin's — this one and *The Sixty Greatest Conspiracies of All Time*.

IllumiNet Press; $16.95
1992, 1996; softcover; 404 pp
1-881532-09-7

CONSPIRACY NATION

Each issue of Brian Redman's monthly newsletter consists of an extensive interview with a conspiracy researcher of some sort. One interview is with Debra von Trapp, a computer/technical consultant, who has dirt on some high-tech shenanigans. She claims that all of the hardware and software that was sold to the Clinton White House had been bugged by American front companies working for the Japanese government. Thus, all of the White House's files and communications are compromised.

She also says that Japan is running a data storage company in Southern California where Hughes Aircraft, MCA Universal, and other huge corporations have stored their most sensitive documents. Japanese intelligence have "got their run of anything they want to read at any time of day or night."

Von Trapp goes on to say that the poison gas attack on the Japanese subway system was the work of an American military team. It was done as retaliation for the compromising of the White House's computers. The Japanese government got even, exactly one month later, by having the federal building in Oklahoma City blown up. Does Clinton know about all this? "The President has direct knowledge!"

The interviewees are almost never hesitant about naming the names of people and companies involved in these murky doings, and *Conspiracy Nation* isn't afraid to run these accusations. It's a great source of unfiltered thought about the hidden political landscape.

Brian Redman/310 S Prarie St #202/Champaign IL 61820

Email: bigred@shoutnet
WWW: www.shout.net/~bigred/cn.html
Twelve issue sub (one year): $20; Canada: $25; Others: $30
Payment: ck or mo to Brian Redman

CONSPIRATORS' HIERARCHY
The Story of the Committee of 300
by John Coleman

The Committee of 300 is probably deserving of the title, "The mother of all conspiracy theories". Dr. John Coleman — a former member of the British intelligence agency MI6 — believes that a supersecret group of 300 people completely control the world. They pull the strings behind every world event and control "every aspect of politics, religion, commerce, industry, banking, insurance, mining and even the **drug trade!**" "Their final objective is the overthrow of the U.S. Constitution and the merging of this country, chosen by God as HIS country, with a godless One World-New World Order Government which will return the world to conditions far worse than existed in the Dark Ages." Besides listing every supposed past and present member of the Committee (George Bush, Winston Churchill, Queen Elizabeth II, Henry Kissinger, Ted Turner), he also reveals by name the institutions, foundations, banks, accountants, legal associations, and corporations that do the Committee's bidding.

America West Publishers; $16.95
1992; softcover; 288 pp
0-922356-57-2

DEATH & TAXES

What happened to Kansas farmer Gordon Kahl is often cited by ultra-conservatives as one of the three most reprehensible examples of the government's murder of its citizens (Waco and Ruby Ridge being the other two). Of the three, Kahl's case has received by far the least attention. I was not familiar with any of the details before I saw this extremely professional video documentary, which is sympathetic towards Kahl. Unfortunately, although I now know quite a bit more, there were many holes left by the narrative.

Kahl served honourably in the Air Force during World War II. Around 1967 or 1968 he stopped paying his income tax and refused to have his social security withheld. Being an extremely fundamentalist Christian, he believed that income tax is unconstitutional and "of Satan". Like other tax protesters, he felt that the government simply has no right to take away a person's earnings.

Kahl eventually served a year in jail for his activities and refused to pay taxes when he was released. Here's where *Death & Taxes* gets a little murky. US Marshals had a warrant to arrest Kahl on a misdemeanour, but we're not told what the specific charge was. Local police and the Marshals followed Kahl, his wife, their adult son, and others from a meeting they had attended. Eventually everyone came to a stop in the middle of the street, and a firefight broke out. Two Marshals were killed, three others were wounded, Kahl's son Yorie was wounded, and Kahl escaped. Naturally, both sides have conflicting stories about who shot first, whether the Marshals identified themselves, etc. Parts of the video inti-

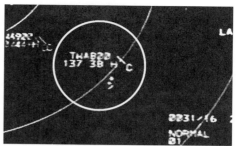

Official radar image shows TWA Flight 800 and an unidentified projectile. *The Downing of TWA Flight 800.*

mate that Kahl killed the Marshals after they shot his son, but this is never given concrete treatment.

Yorie and a friend were convicted of second degree murder in a trial that apparently had some irregularities. Namely, the judge had worked closely with one of the dead Marshals, and one of the jurors and the prosecutor had known each other for most of their lives.

Kahl fled the state and hid out in the home of an Arkansas couple. The authorities eventually found him and surrounded the house. The sheriff went in, gunshots were heard, and the police and agents outside the house opened fire with automatic weapons. They tear-gassed the place and — guess what? — it somehow caught fire. Some media accounts said that — guess what? — the tear gas had somehow ignited. A police officer who was at the scene admits during his on-camera interview that he and some others poured diesel fuel into the house from on top of the roof, and then they each dropped four or five grenades into the house.

The autopsy revealed that Kahl had been shot in the rear right portion of his skull, and the sheriff had been shot in the upper left arm. The official conclusion was that they had shot each other simultaneously. The physical impossibility of this scenario has led some to speculate that Kahl's death was like an execution. Also, Kahl's hands and feet were apparently chopped off at some point, but — despite the fact that they were found unattached to his body — the medical examiner denies that he was mutilated.

There is also rampant speculation that the wrong man was killed, because the body was burned beyond recognition. The corpse has even been exhumed, but the examination has not been able to draw conclusions. Frustratingly, the video doesn't give any explanation about who the dead man might have been, if it was not Kahl. It also doesn't explain how the sheriff managed to kill Kahl execution style if both men were armed or why the law enforcement personnel unleashed a hail of gunfire on the house when the sheriff was still inside. Even though it's impossible to give definitive answers, I would have at least liked to have heard some opinions.

With deft editing, *Death & Taxes* weaves together news footage, re-enactments, police radio transmissions, and interviews with many of the principal players — Kahl's wife, Yorie, attorneys, jurors, police officers, and government agents. While it certainly is informative, it leaves some crucial avenues totally unexplored. I watched the version that was shown at film festivals, but there is also a director's cut, which is 23 minutes longer, available for the same price. Perhaps it has more information.

Country People Productions; $29.95

1993; VHS video; 90 min

THE DOWNING OF TWA FLIGHT 800
The Shocking Truth Behind the Worst Airplane Disaster in U.S. History

by James Sanders

This the first book I've seen that questions the official version of events surrounding TWA Flight 800, which somehow exploded shortly after take-off on July 17, 1996. James Sanders explores the evidence that the US Navy accidentally blew the plane out of the sky while testing its newly upgraded anti-aircraft/antimissile system. He looks at the 34 witnesses who saw a projectile heading towards the plane just before it exploded, the clean entry and exit holes left behind, the residue from missile fuel that was on passenger seats, the radar images that show an object near the plane, the government documents that prove the Navy was testing in the area at the time of the disaster, and more. Images in the book include the radar image of the plane and a projectile, a photograph taken by a bystander that accidentally captures a missile in flight, and colour reproductions of seat padding covered in reddish missile fuel.

Zebra Books (Kensington Publishing Corporation); $6.99

1997; paperback; 240 pp

illus; 0-8217-5829-2

EAST TIMOR
Genocide in Paradise

by Matthew Jardine

The tiny nation of East Timor, just off the southern tip of Indonesia, has been the site of some of the most brutal oppression of this century. Noam Chomsky, in his introduction, says the percentage of the population that has been killed is equal to that of the Holocaust.

East Timor had been a Portuguese colony since the 1500s. In 1974 a coup overthrew Portugal's fascist government, and the next year East Timor declared itself independent. Less than two weeks later, Indonesia launched a full-scale invasion. Within two months, 60,000 East Timorese, including women and children, had been slaughtered. Of course, Indonesian soldiers also engaged in your typical military-style torture, rape, and plunder.

What makes it even worse is that many Western countries knew of the invasion beforehand, but either did nothing to stop it or actually aided Indonesia. One of the worst offenders was the US, because Indonesia supplies the US with lots of raw materials and provides a big market for American goods (including weapons that were used in the invasion). In the two days before the invasion, President Ford and Secretary of State Kissinger were in Indonesia. "Kissinger told reporters in Jakarta that 'the US understands Indonesia's position on the question' of East Timor, and Ford said that, given a choice between East Timor and Indone-

US Marshal's surveillance photo of the late Vicki Weaver, one hour before the shoot-out. *Every Knee Shall Bow.*

sia, the US 'had to be on the side of Indonesia.'" In early 1976, as the slaughter continued, an official at the US State Department said, "In terms of bilateral relations between the US and Indonesia, we are more or less condoning the incursion into East Timor." Canada, Australia, Britain, Japan, and other countries also supported Indonesia.

That support continues to this day, even though the death toll is now over 200,000. During his first Presidential campaign, Clinton called the US's policy towards East Timor "unconscionable", yet he has done very little about it. He has cut some of the money and weapons going to Indonesia, but not much. When Clinton was in Indonesia for a trade conference in November 1994, 29 East Timorese demonstrators risked imprisonment and death by camping out in the US Embassy's parking lot, calling for the President "to voice support for East Timorese self-determination and for the withdrawal of Indonesian troops from their country." He didn't.

There is a growing resistance movement within East Timor, and many countries have solidarity groups, so there is still hope. A section at the end of the book tells how you can get involved.

Odonian Press; $6

1995; paperback; 95 pp

1-878825-20-8

THE ELVIS FILES
Was His Death Faked?

by Gail Brewer-Giorgio

In this sequel to *Is Elvis Alive?*, the author presents more contradictions and clues pointing to the theory that the King faked his death (plus related topics, such as people who might really be Elvis, and Elvis's possible role as an undercover agent for the Drug Enforcement Administration). Why did one of Elvis' best friends refer to him in the present tense in a 1990 TV interview? Why does the death certificate say Elvis weighed 170 lbs when he was known to have weighed 250 at time of his death? Why have so many people commented that the body in the coffin had a pug nose instead of Elvis' strong, classic nose?

S.P.I. Books (Shapolsky Publishers); $4.99

1990; softcover; 275 pp
illus; 1-56171-376-7

EVERY KNEE SHALL BOW
The Truth and Tragedy of Ruby Ridge and the Randy Weaver Family
by Jess Walter

The story of what happened to Randy Weaver and his family — like that of Waco — has become one of the most well-known examples of the government's abusive and homicidal nature. Jess Walter writes: "More even than the deaths at Waco, the Weaver stand-off brings paranoia into the mainstream. For how can you convince people that their government isn't trying to kill its own citizens, when, on Ruby Ridge, the FBI gave itself permission to do just that? How can you tell people to trust their government when it continues to cover up details of the case? There is little wonder it has become a symbol for government tyranny."

The Weaver family lived in a cabin in Ruby Ridge, Idaho. They were Christian Patriots — ultra-fundamentalists who believed that the US is being run by the ZOG (Zionist Occupation Government), which is preparing to institute a totalitarian one-world government. They further believed that the races should be separated and that the Apocalypse is imminent.

An ATF undercover informant tried to convince Randy to sell him two sawn-off shotguns. Randy refused for a while, but after being goaded by the informant — who also instructed him on how to saw the guns' barrels — he relented in October 1989. Eight months later, the ATF used the threat of a conviction to force Randy to infiltrate and report on neo-Nazi groups, but Randy would not go along with their plan. About six months after that, in January 1991, Randy and his wife Vicki were ambushed by federal agents, who took them in for arraignment.

The Weavers went back to their cabin and isolated themselves, refusing to have anything to do with the courts or any other aspect of the government. Randy was given the wrong date for his hearing — he was told it was one month later than it actually was — so naturally he didn't show up. (It should be noted that he didn't appear on the date he had been given, either.) For sixteen months the feds plotted how they would get this man that they had labelled as incredibly dangerous and volatile, even though he had no criminal record, owned no illegal guns, and was a devoted family man.

On August 21, 1992, members of the US Marshals Service Special Operations Group went into action. They were in the woods around the Weaver's cabin, when Randy, his son Sammy (14), his daughters Sara (16) and Rachel (10), and Sammy's friend Kevin Harris, were outside with their guns. The Weaver's dog Striker became aware of the deputies and went into the woods. Sammy and Kevin followed. What happened next is the subject of much dispute, but somehow Sammy was fatally shot in the back, Marshal Billy Degan was fatally shot in the chest, and Striker was killed. The only thing the sides agree on is that the Marshals shot the dog. Walter details the conflicting stories told by both parties.

Whatever happened, what cannot be denied are the next day's events. During the night of the firefight, the Weavers had taken Sammy's body to a shed. The next day, Randy went to the shed to view his dead son. FBI sniper Lon Horiuchi — considered one of the very best — fired at Randy (he thought he was shooting at Harris). Randy, Sara, and Harris all ran as fast as they could to the cabin. Vicki was behind the opened front door, holding 10-month-old Elisheba in her arms. As the three rushed into the cabin, another shot rang out. It blew part of Vicki's head off. As she and the baby fell, the bullet hit Harris in the arm.

During the ten-day stand-off that followed, the hundreds of feds from several agencies who had arrived on the scene called over loudspeakers to Vicki, asking her what she was making for breakfast, among other things. They claimed they didn't know she was dead. Finally, controversial patriot figure Bo Gritz — said to be the real-life model for Rambo — negotiated a peaceful surrender with the surviving Weavers and Harris.

But the story doesn't end there. Walter gives a gripping, witness-by-witness account of the murder trial of Randy and Harris and an enlightening look at the jury's deliberations. Famed defence lawyer Gerry Spence and other attorneys hammered on the government's weak and inconsistent arguments until, in the end, the jury acquitted Harris of all charges and acquitted Randy of all but the least serious charges: failing to appear in court and committing crimes during his pre-trial release. The book ends by looking at what the Weavers did after the trial and what the FBI did to the agents involved (i.e., wrist slaps).

HarperCollins; $6.99
1995; paperback; 375 pp
illus; 0-06-101131-2

FLATLAND

Jim Martin runs Flatland Books [see Appendix A], a source for books and magazines on a variety of outpost topics. *Flatland* is the six-monthly magazine Martin puts out to offer further information on conspiracies, cover-ups, UFOs, suppressed science (with a heavy emphasis on Wilhelm Reich), and more. The theme of issue 11 is mind control. In "The Microchip Injection", the author looks at how microchips are presently being used for tracking and identification and how they might be used to keeps tabs on each one of us in the future. "The Associated Press reports that Dr. Daniel Man, a plastic surgeon in Miami, Fla., holds a patent for an implantable chip that could locate lost children, or find Alzheimer's victims who wander away. Man said that private industry and government agencies have expressed interest in producing it." In an interview, John Taylor Gatto — author of *Dumbing Us Down* [see the Freedom chapter] — examines the origins of another type of mind control: compulsory schooling. Other articles cover hypnosis, psychiatry as mind control, electromagnetic fields, federal government tyranny, the brainwashing of political assassins, and more.

The next issue is devoted to radical psychiatrist, scientist, and healer Wilhelm Reich. It contains two rare interviews with Reich's daughter, Eva. The first was published in an obscure journal in 1977 and appears here for the first time in English. The second interview was conducted by Martin himself. He also interviews Harvey Matusow, who has two claims to fame: he was a McCarthy informant who falsely accused Army personnel of being commies, and when he went to jail for it, he was put in the cell next to Wilhelm Reich's until Reich's death. "Operation Weather Control" demonstrates that Reich was involved in weather modification experiments being run by the University of Arizona. (If you think that sounds far-fetched, you should realise that in 1953 Congress and President Eisenhower passed the Weather Control Act, to study how to influence the weather.) Other pieces cover privacy, problems with the Internet, and Orson Bean — comedian, game show regular, and Reichian.

Issue 13 has the articles "Militia Nation", "Human Sacrifice", "How to Use the Freedom of Information Act", "Lindbergh and Lenin", and others. The latest issue (14) contains an interview with ufologist Jacques Valle, "Slick's Gold, Hot Monks & Rockefeller's Wet-nurses", "Mad Cows and Mad Scientists", and more.

Besides these informative, well-done articles and interviews, each issue also contains listings of around 100 publications available from Flatland Books.

Flatland/PO Box 2420/Fort Bragg CA 95437
Voice: 707-964-8326
Email: flatland@mcn.org
WWW: www.flatlandbooks.com
Single issue: $6
Four issue sub (two years): $16. Non-US Surface: $25. Non-US Air: $30
Payment: cash, ck, mo, Visa, MC

FOUR DEAD IN OHIO
Was There a Conspiracy at Kent State?
by William A. Gordon

On May 4, 1970, following several days of demonstrations, National Guardsmen opened fire on unarmed students at Kent State University in Ohio, killing four and wounding nine. That much we know for certain. But there is a much murkier, complex story beneath the surface. The "official version" of events is that the massacre was unplanned... somebody started shooting and then others joined in spontaneously. There is much evidence, though, that raises doubts. Was there an order to fire on the students? Was President Nixon directly involved? Was there a cover-up? Why did so many of those responsible for the bloodbath escape justice?

William Gordon has spent nineteen years trying to find the answers to these questions. During that time, he's interviewed over 200 people, including students, guardsmen, officers, Kent State officials, and many other key players. He's combed archives, court transcripts, and even federal grand jury proceedings.

Gordon's overall conclusion is that there was no conspiracy among the soldiers, and it doesn't appear that the White House gave orders to kill the students. However, there are strong indications that at least one of the officers gave an order to fire on the students. Because the noise level

National Guardsmen begin to murder unarmed students at Kent State. *Four Dead in Ohio*.

was so high at the time, the order was probably not verbal. "Under the circumstances, it seems much more likely that there was a hand signal to fire." (On the other hand, four of the soldiers did tell their superior officers that they heard an order to fire.) Gordon feels that the officers most likely to have given a hand signal were Major Harry Jones and Sergeant Myron Pryor, although there is no incontrovertible proof that either one did.

During a federal grand jury investigation, Major Jones was questioned by the Justice Department. "The prosecutors showed Jones John Darnell's photograph showing Pryor in front of the firing line, and asked Jones if that photograph seemed to depict Pryor giving 'a hand and arm signal to fire.' Jones answered: 'It would, yes.' However, when Jones was subsequently asked the same question at the 1975 civil trial, he changed his answer..." The plaintiff's attorney pressed Jones and he finally back-pedalled: "'It could be interpreted as a hand signal to fire. There is a possibility, according to the interpretation of the individual.'"

There is overwhelming eyewitness testimony that the Guardsmen turned in unison just before firing, indicating they were acting on an order. Fifty-five witnesses declared to the FBI, the court, or the media that this uniform movement occurred. Among those offering this testimony were *New York Times* reporter John Kifner, Private James McGee, and Sergeant Pryor himself.

One of the ways the Guardsmen justified their murderous actions was by saying that they were endangered by the unarmed students. Still photographs and an 8mm home movie of the event show that there were very few students near the soldiers at the time. Nor were the military men surrounded by students — a previously unpublished picture in this book shows that they "had a clear path of retreat."

Gordon reveals all of the lying and perjury that took place after the incident. He shows that FBI head J. Edgar Hoover flat-out lied at one point by denying that the Bureau had anything to do with Terry Norman, who was in reality an FBI informant. Also, attempts were made to influence witnesses' statements, police statements mysteriously disappeared, damaging allegations were suppressed, crucial witnesses were never called to testify, and Nixon and Hoover attempted to have news reports spiked.

Four Dead in Ohio contains around a dozen photos — some of which are published here for the first time — of the scene immediately before, during, and after the massacre.

Gordon has done an excellent job of showing us that one of the most shameful episodes in American history is even darker than we have been led to believe.

North Ridge Books; $13.95
1990, 1995; softcover; 301 pp
illus; 0-937813-05-2

GASSED IN THE GULF
The Inside Story of the Pentagon-CIA Cover-up of the Gulf War Syndrome
by Patrick G Eddington

After the lop-sided victory of the Gulf War, Americans were busy patting themselves on the back when reports started to surface that something was wrong with many of the soldiers who had fought in the war. They were suffering from chronic illnesses, damaged immune systems, joint and muscle pain, severe headaches, memory loss, and other problems. The spouses of many soldiers have contracted the same disorders, and a frighteningly high number of Gulf War vets' children have been born with major, usually rare, birth defects. At first the Pentagon tried to maintain that Gulf War Syndrome, as it came to be known, was all a coincidence or that the problems were psychosomatic or imagined. Slowly, the walls have begun to crumble, with the Pentagon admitting that perhaps a few soldiers might have been exposed to some chemical or biological weapons at one point. *Gassed in the Gulf* will hopefully help the walls fall right down.

Patrick G. Eddington worked for the Central Intelligence Agency for nine years. He received numerous awards and commendations for his work as an analyst in the CIA's National Photographic Interpretation Centre. In 1993 his wife Robin — also an analyst for the CIA — alerted him to reports that American troops had been exposed to chemical agents during the war. Shortly afterwards, Patrick gathered together all the evidence he could find, including classified and declassified eye-witness accounts, reports, memoranda, and surveillance photos. He reached the inescapable conclusion that tens of thousands of soldiers had been exposed to low levels of chemical weapons and that the Department of Defence had done its best to cover up this fact. Norman Schwarzkopf, he charges, directly took steps to hush up the exposures. Former CIA Director John Deutch attempted to illegally reclassify information about Iraqi chemical munitions in order to conceal the scope of the exposures.

Eddington and his colleagues at the Photographic Interpretation Centre had seen reports of chemical attacks against Coalition forces during Desert Storm but were told by their superiors that all such reports were false. Equipment used by US, UK, French, and Czech forces repeatedly detected chemical weapons during and after the war, yet the Pentagon insists all the results were in error. Caches of Iraqi chemical munitions were often destroyed close to troops, yet this is officially seen as an insignificant fact. Other important points that the author brings up concern 1) the numerous squelched reports that Coalition forces found chemical munitions with US markings being used by Iraq (despite assurances from the government that it has never sold such weapons to Iraq) and 2) the use of 700,000 American military personnel as

guinea pigs for a dangerous, untested pill that was supposed to counter the effects of biological warfare.

But *Gassed in the Gulf* is more than just a presentation of evidence that troops were exposed to chemical agents… it's also the story of what happened to the Eddingtons when they tried to get their employer to look into the situation. The CIA had taken the word of the Department of Defence that nothing had happened. When Patrick and Robin presented their superiors with the evidence they had accumulated, they were treated as the enemy. Eventually the couple quit their jobs at the CIA, disgusted with the way they had been treated and with the way the Agency had handled the Gulf War Syndrome investigation. Since then they have been speaking out publicly about what they know and, of course, Patrick has written this book. His struggles with his former employer aren't over, though. Because of the security agreement he signed as a CIA employee, the Agency had to review his book before it was published. It required that several deletions be made. I'm sure the CIA was especially upset by the appendix that details 55 known chemical incidents during the war, not to mention the maps pinpointing some of these occurrences. Thankfully, Patrick fought them in federal court and managed to get some of the information reinstated, but other passages are still the subject of litigation.

Although it's still not known if low-level chemical weapons are the cause of Gulf War Syndrome, it's very important to know that troops *were* exposed to these toxic chemicals and that they very well could be the cause. *Gassed in the Gulf* succeeds admirably on that count.

Insignia Publishing; $23.95
1997; hardcover; 369 pp
illus; 0-9652400-3-7

IF YOU POISON US
Uranium and Native Americans
by Peter H. Eichstaedt

Towards the end of W.W.II and throughout the Cold War, the US's security hinged on uranium for atom bombs. Some of the largest supplies of this radioactive element are located on the Navajo Reservation and the lands of the Laguna Pueblo on the Colorado Plateau. When the government approached the tribes about mining this material, they were happy to provide for US defence and bring in some sorely needed jobs. Until 1980 approximately 15,000 people — one quarter of them Native American — worked in thousands of mines on Indian lands. They constantly breathed uranium dust and ate and drank uranium-tainted food.

Even before the first atom bombs were built, there were suspicions that uranium was harmful, and government studies on the Colorado Plateau miners confirmed it. "Yet, the Atomic Energy Commission, for years the sole purchaser of uranium, consistently maintained that it had no responsibility for conditions in the mines, and mining companies refused to take the most elementary safety measures. Nor did the Secretary of the Interior take any effective action to protect them. Then, when death started to come to the miners, slowly and painfully, years later, mining companies and federal and state agencies argued over who would compensate the victims and their families — or even if any compensation was due."

The Navajos turned to the courts and spent almost a decade in litigation before ultimately losing their case. The government claimed that it could not be held liable for wrongdoing when it performed certain functions. However, the Native Americans had amassed mountains of evidence showing the government's homicidal negligence, and — responding to their appeals — Congress passed a law requiring compensation for the miners or their next of kin. Unfortunately they put the Justice Department, who had fought the Navajos every step of the way, in charge of administering the programme. Because of the Department's incredibly narrow interpretation of this law, relatively few miners have qualified.

The mines also have caused serious environmental damage and health problems for non-miners on the reservations. "When the boom was over and the mining companies pulled out, they left behind enormous piles of radioactive mine waste from milling operations and more than a thousand open mines on Indian lands. There has been no federal effort to clean up these mines, many of which leak deadly gases and spread radioactive dust — poison that is no less deadly than the small-pox-infected blankets that the government issued to thousands of Mandan Indians in the nineteenth century."

If You Poison Us gives a blow-by-blow account of the cover-up of uranium's effects, the Native American's fight for justice, and the results they achieved. There are also transcripts of interviews with several miners and reprints of government reports, Congressional testimony, and the Radiation Exposure Compensation Act.

Red Crane Books; $20
1994; hardcover; 271 pp
illus; 1-878610-40-6

JOURNEY TO CHERNOBYL
Encounters in a Radioactive Zone
by Glenn Alan Cheney

Immediately after the fall of the Soviet Union, Glenn Cheney headed to the Ukraine to hear the stories of people who were finally allowed to talk about the Chernobyl nuclear disaster. He presents his conversations with scientists, engineers, government officials, doctors, families with sick members, and people who live close to the Chernobyl power station. They tell of panicked evacuations, governmental destruction of data, "Chernobyl AIDS" (the nickname given to a syndrome that's swept the Ukraine in which people's immune systems are wiped out), and more dark secrets.

Academy Chicago Publishers; $20
1995; hardcover; 191 pp
illus; 0-89733-418-3

KAL FLIGHT 007
The Hidden Story
by Oliver Clubb

On September 1, 1983, Korean Airlines Flight 007 — a commercial airliner headed for Seoul — flew far into Soviet airspace and was shot down, killing all 269 people aboard. That event had a devastating effect on the already strained US-USSR relationship and helped the public warm to Reagan's call for increased military spending. But from the beginning, the event has appeared highly suspicious — a civilian passenger plane just happens to fly hundreds of miles off course, coincidentally flying over Kamchatka and Sakhalin, which are filled with sensitive military installations. Oliver Clubb answers some important questions about this event: "What caused KAL 007's pilot to fly his Boeing 747 jetliner hundreds of miles off course? How did he manage to evade Soviet air defences when his plane first penetrated Soviet strategic airspace over Kamchatka? Why did he persist on this course, ignoring Soviet jet fighters and despite the obvious dangers to his plane and its passengers? How could the airplane's huge digression from its normal flight path, overflying Soviet strategic territories, not have been noticed by U.S. and Japanese radar tracking facilities? Why were U.S. and Japanese authorities unable to warn the airliner — or why did they choose not to do so?"

In answering these questions, Clubb shows that the actions of the highly-regarded KAL pilot and the non-actions of all the tracking facilities that knew the jet was far off course all add up to the inescapable conclusion that something fishy was going on. Specifically, that KAL 007 was on an intelligence mission for the National Security Agency (NSA), gathering information about, among other things, the Soviets' air defences.

One of the most enlightening aspects of the book is that it describes an almost identical — but much lesser known incident — that took place five years earlier. In April 1978 another KAL passenger plane, Flight 902, was flown deep into another highly-restricted area of the Soviet Union. Incredibly, the seasoned pilot, who had flown the route to Seoul for five years, had been heading north-west for five hours, when he turned his plane almost completely around, and went south-east. He ignored Soviet interceptors until they shot holes in the plane. By the time he landed, the plane had penetrated 300 miles into top secret territory. *Quelle coincidence!*

Rarely does the official version of a suspicious incident have as many holes as this one does. *KAL Flight 007* makes quite a convincing case.

The Permanent Press; $22
1985; hardcover; 174 pp
0-932966-59-4

THE LAUNDRYMEN
Inside Money Laundering, the World's Third-Largest Business
by Jeffrey Robinson

"Laundering" money is the process of making ill-gotten gain look legitimate. An estimated $200 billion to $500 billion is "cleaned" every year around the globe, making it the third largest industry in the world, behind foreign exchange and oil. Jeffrey Robinson explains exactly how this works and who's in on it, from the drug traffickers, terrorists, and arms dealers who make the money to the accountants, lawyers, and shell companies who wash it to the banks and governments who look the other way. Sometimes money is laundered by corporations engaged in sneaky or downright illegal practices. "The Lockheed Corporation laundered $25.5 million through a Liechtenstein trust to pay off Italian politicians. Lockheed also subscribed to the laundry facilities of Deak-Perera, then an important American foreign-exchange dealer, to bribe Japanese politicians. At Lockheed's behest, Deak put $8.3 million into the washing cycle, then brought it out as fifteen untraceable payments to a Spanish priest in Hong Kong, who hand-carried the cash in flight bags and orange crates to Lockheed customers in Tokyo."

Money laundering has three basic steps: immersion, which involves the use of "bank accounts, postal orders, traveller's cheques, and other negotiable instruments to funnel cash into the world's financial system"; layering, "where the laundryman disassociates the money from its illicit source" by shuffling the money through a large number of accounts set up for dummy companies; and repatriation, during which "washed funds are brought back into circulation, now in the form of clean, often taxable, income."

Robinson describes the money laundering operations of Saddam Hussein, Manuel Noriega, Richard Nixon, Robert Maxwell, Jean-Claude "Baby Doc" Duvalier, the Nugan Hand Bank, BCCI, and a host of lesser-known individuals and institutions. Some chapters look specifically at the roles of shell corporations, the Caribbean, Switzerland, Africa, and organised crime in the laundering racket. The author also sheds light on some fascinating related topics, such as smuggling cash, running scams, and trafficking drugs. "The narco-economy has made drug traffickers the most influential special-interest group in the world. The money generated and controlled by traffickers has reached such monstrous proportions that dozens of Third World countries could not possibly underwrite their own existence were it not for drug money. It has become an unofficial form of U.S. foreign aid. Without an income from drug trafficking, Colombia, Bolivia, Ecuador, and Peru could not remain afloat... The sums involved are way beyond anything easily comprehensible. A few years ago, the late Colombian cocaine cartel boss Pablo Escobar had to write off $40 million in cash because it had literally rotted in a California basement. He wasn't able to get it into the washing cycle fast enough."

If you'd like to get an idea of how the world's economy *really* works, this book will give you a glimpse of what's going on beneath the textbook explanations of GNPs, stock markets, and supply and demand.

Arcade Publishing; $13.95
1996; softcover; 358 pp
1-55970-385-7

LEASING THE IVORY TOWER
The Corporate Takeover of Academia
by Lawrence C. Soley

The invasion of American universities by Political Correctness is now widely-known. Horror stories — such as the female professor who had a poster of a classic nude painting removed from a classroom because it constituted sexual harassment — exist on practically every campus. But there

is another major threat to the "marketplace of ideas", as academia is known, and it has received scant attention. "The real story is about university physics and electrical engineering departments being seduced by Pentagon contracts; molecular biology, biochemistry, and medicine departments being wooed by drug companies and biotech firms; and university computer science departments being in bed with Big Blue and a few high-tech chip makers. The story about universities in the 1980s and 1990s is that they will turn a trick for anybody with money to invest; and the only ones with money are corporations, millionaires, and foundations."

These three well-funded special interests have been able to rearrange universities' priorities, influence research and publications, and generally degrade education. Professors find that to receive tenure and for their departments to receive money, they must move away from the pesky business of teaching students and instead do the research required by the sugar daddies. Some corporations hire professors as consultants or even bankroll professorships.

It gets worse. The College of Hotel Administration arranged for the Japanese-owned slot machine manufacturer ACE Denken to "donate" $2 million to the University of Nevada at Las Vegas. "For the gift, university administrators promised to publish an annual monograph named for ACE on 'issues facing the casino and gaming industry,' to sponsor an annual seminar for ACE management and their friends on a topic picked by ACE, and to present ACE with an annual report on developments in gambling technology."

The Massachusetts Institute of Technology (MIT) has arranged an interesting, cosy relationship by establishing the Industrial Liaison Program. Three hundred corporations pay $10,000 to $50,000 annually to gain access to MIT research reports, symposia, seminars, and the faculty itself. Professors are induced to participate by a point system. They get points by talking to corporate suits on the phone, visiting the corporation's site, etc. These points can be redeemed for neato prizes like office furniture and computer equipment. Even more blatant is the New Products Program, in which a company pays MIT $500,000, and three faculty members and four graduate students create a product for the company within two years.

Corporations also get good publicity out of their kind-hearted donations. "Philip Morris's Miller Brewing Company, for example, donates $150,000 annually to the Thurgood Marshall Scholarship Fund, which provides scholarships to African-American students. But Miller also spends more than $300,000 a year to advertise the programme and its contributions, and these advertisements carry the Miller logo."

Leasing the Ivory Tower is a devastating document showing how and why our bastions of education have become corporate whores.

South End Press; $13
1995; softcover; 204 pp
0-89608-503-1

LOBSTER
Lobster is not widely known in America — even among con-

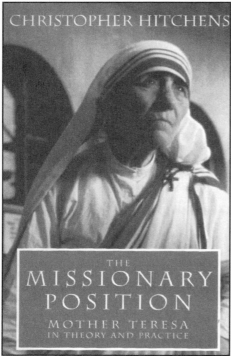

The seamy side of Mother Teresa.
The Missionary Position.

Labour Movement, and much more.

The writing in *Lobster* can be fairly dense, and sometimes the reader is expected to know a good bit about British conspiracy research. Still, it does offer rigorous journalistic standards and material not covered in the US, so it is worth the low price.

Lobster/Robin Ramsay/214 Westbourne Ave/Hull HU5 3JB/UK

WWW: www.knowledge.co.uk/xxx/lobster/

Email: robin@lobster.karoo.co.uk

Single issue: UK: £2.75, Europe: £3.50, US/Canada/Australasia: £4

Two issue sub (one year): UK: £5; Europe: £7; US/Canada/Australasia: £8

Payment: US cash, UK cash, UK ck, international mo

THE MISSIONARY POSITION
Mother Teresa in Theory and Practice
by Christopher Hitchens

A book exposing the seamy side of Mother Teresa?!? How could this possibly be? Well, investigative journalist and polemist Christopher Hitchens simply decided that nothing (and nobody) is above being questioned. He has turned the glare of full light onto the woman whose name is synonymous with charity, devotion, and selfless service and found that not everything is as rosy as most would like to believe.

One of the bones Hitchens has to pick with the Albanian nun is that not only didn't she denounce the world's most ruthless dictators, she actually kissed up to them. In 1981 Mother Teresa visited the Western Hemisphere's poorest nation, Haiti. As the author notes: "This island has been the property of an especially callous and greedy predatory class, which has employed pitiless force in order to keep the poor and the dispossessed in their place." Despite this, Teresa visited Michèle Duvalier and said this about the despot: "Madame President is someone who feels, who knows, who wishes to demonstrate her love not only with words but also with concrete and tangible actions."

For someone who was supposedly a literal saint and so "above this world", Teresa was quite political. She wasn't very focused on alleviating the inequities that cause poverty, but she was heavily into fighting abortion and contraception, something that makes little practical sense in overcrowded Third World countries. She showed even more of her reactionary side when "she told an interviewer that, if faced with a choice between Galileo and the authority of the Inquisition, she would have sided with the Church authorities."

As far as Teresa's actual work caring for the sick, Hitchens again shatters illusions. Even though her large series of health clinics for the destitute receive oodles of money and supplies, they are abysmal places to get medical care. Such testimony comes from — among other people — the editor of Britain's leading medical journal, *The Lancet*, who noticed that there were no strong painkillers and no methods for making a diagnosis! He wrote: "Such systematic approaches are alien to the ethos of the home. Mother Teresa prefers providence to planning; her rules are designed to prevent any drift towards materialism." A former volunteer in Cal-

spiracy researchers — but it is perhaps Britain's most prominent and well-researched magazine of political intrigue. They not only disrespect apologists who support the "there's no such thing as a conspiracy" status quo, they also slam conspirologists who make fanciful, unsubstantiated, and sometimes self-contradictory claims that work to undermine legitimate inquiry. Most of the articles concern the UK, but there are some on the US and other countries.

The lead article in issue 28 concerns Britain's unnerving nuclear policy: "... Britain has long deployed nuclear weapons outside the NATO area and specifically in three conflicts involving non-nuclear powers, an indication of the presumed usability of nuclear systems in a military confrontation falling far short of global war." The article looks specifically at the way Britain was eager to break out the nukes during the Falklands War and the Gulf War.

Other articles examine problems with Terry Reed's *Compromised* [*Outposts* p 47] and Gerald Posner's *Case Closed* [*Outposts* p 33], more on mind control technology, British intelligence agency MI5's search for new enemies, MI5 agent Harry Newton, the inexplicable shortcomings of the anti-fascist magazine *Searchlight*, theories behind the murder of Hilda Murrell, and over a dozen book, magazine, and software reviews.

Articles in subsequent issues have covered the 1953 coup in Iran, neural manipulation by radar, the CIA-Mafia connection, remote viewing, the Shayler affair, the British cutta tells of no antibiotics, needles being reused without being sterilised, and the staff's refusal to take a fifteen-year-old boy to a hospital for an operation.

Missionary Position also points out Teresa's lack of modesty, the tenuousness of her alleged "miracle", her cosy relationships with the contras and Charles Keating, and the veritable cult that has arisen around her. To sum up, Hitchens characterises Mother Teresa as "a religious fundamentalist, a political operative, a primitive sermoniser and an accomplice of worldly, secular powers."

When Hitchens made a British TV documentary about this icon of piety — titled *Hell's Angel* — he was subjected to blistering attacks from various quarters. Many of his critics made personal attacks, one going so far as to make fun of his appearance. I'm sure this book has triggered similar reactions.

Verso; $12.00
1995; softcover; 98 pp
illus; 1-85984-054-X

NASA MOONED AMERICA!
by René

There's a widely-known but seemingly little-believed theory that says that humans have never gone to the Moon, that all the landings were faked in studios. I've always considered this to be one of the more far-fetched conspiracy theories, but I'll be damned if René's book didn't at least plant seeds of doubt in my mind. I'm not saying that this book will convince you that the Moon landings were hoaxes, but you will probably come away from it just a little less positive.

René, however, doesn't stop with just the idea that the Moon remains unvisited. "In a prosecutorial mode therefore I hereby accuse NASA, the CIA and whatever super secret group that controls the shadow government of these United States of fraud on the grandest scale imaginable, of murder by arson, and of larceny of 40 billion plus in conjunction with the Apollo programme that allegedly landed men on the Moon. I also accuse them of violating a federal law against lobbying by government funded entities and of serial murder of low level NASA employees, witnesses and other citizens who happened to be in the wrong place at the wrong time."

The author spends a lot of time pointing out the flaws in the photos and videos said to have been taken during the Moon missions. Why, given the Moon's airless atmosphere, are there never any stars visible in the black sky? Why do the massive landing capsules never disturb the lunar dust around them? In one shot — reproduced in colour — from the Apollo XVI mission, the astronaut and the Rover cast shadows in different directions from the rocks behind them. The largest rock in the photo clearly has the letter C written on it.

Another of the several pictures that receives special attention is one taken during the Apollo XII mission — allegedly a shot of Al Bean taken by Pete Conrad. "Yet — as reflected in Bean's face-plate under magnification, Conrad is carrying no camera. Conrad has his left arm straight down and his right elbow is down with his hand near his navel."

Among the other anomalies: "On the upper left edge are two structural pieces that slant toward the ground and seem to be holding a spotlight. The ground between that spotlight and Bean is unevenly lit, but the brightest area is around him. This is consistent with a spotlight." And: "There is a second shadow that extends from Conrad forward and to his right. It is almost 180 degrees away from his regular shadow. NASA never told us that our solar system has two suns."

The chapter "Mass Murder or Utter Stupidity" looks at the circumstances surrounding the deaths of American astronauts. In 1967 alone eight astronauts died. Most of them died in plane crashes, and "Grissom, Chaffee, & White were cremated in an Apollo capsule test on the launching pad during a completely and suspiciously unnecessary test."

Other subjects that are covered include NASA's space navigation process ("something of a sham"), the contradictions and impossibilities mentioned in the writings of the Moon astronauts, the fatal doses of solar radiation the astronauts should have been exposed to, the impossibilities inherent in the astronauts' suits, NASA's politics, and the physical problems that should have been encountered by the Lunar Landing Modules ("This pile of tin was so fragile that it couldn't support itself here on Earth, and exploded whenever tested in our atmosphere. In fact, it had a perfect record of disaster until it was used on the Moon. Then eight times in a row, it worked perfectly every time by landing safely on the Moon's sunny surface.").

R. René; $25
1992; oversized softcover; 187 pp
illus; no ISBN

NEWSPEAK KATAZZZINE
The Fringe Guide to
Conspiracy, Sex, Weirdness

Even though *Newspeak* covers more than just conspiracies and cover-ups, those subjects make up most of the material, so I'm putting it in this chapter. *Newspeak* is a catazine ("katazzzine") — also known as a magalog — which combines articles and reviews with a catalogue for books and videos. The editorial content makes up over three-quarters of each issue, meaning that you get a lot of reading for the buck. Co-editor Joan d'Arc (who also co-edits *Paranoia*, see *Outposts* p 51) turns in a thoughtful essay on the way in which ideas about UFOs, abductions, and government cover-ups have changed through time and vary among different subcultures and factions. She maintains that anything is possible, managing to balance cynicism and belief. One of the most interesting points she makes is that many New Agers who strongly believe in UFOs, ESP, and channelled entities don't realise that they have a marginal belief system. At one New Age conference "when I handed *Newspeak* 'fringe guide to weirdness' to one woman, she said, 'Thanks, but I'm not into the fringe'. Why are you here, I wondered?"

In "The Case for Citizen Militias", John White does something practically unheard of — he asks us to rationally consider the real viewpoint of militia groups. "Their perspective is: we are patriots acting in the spirit of '76 who respect the values, traditions and institutions which built America and made it the greatest nation in history. Our enemy is not the government per se, but abusive government, government run amok, arrogantly distanced from the people it is supposed to serve."

Other articles zero in on the possibility of a one-world government, multi-dimensional hyperspace experiences, fully informed juries, disinformation about UFOs, the Disneyfication of world culture, artificially-induced visionary experiences, Jewish radicalism, and more. Every issue has excerpts from radical books, and seven pages of reviews cover over 20 books and three videos.

The catalogue section of *Newspeak* has 16 pages of short, four-column listings for hundreds of books on alternative health, conspiracy, George Bush, JFK, hidden history, secret societies, free energy, unorthodox science, UFOs, drugs, the unexplained, magick, occult, New Age, anarchism, mischief, the media, hacking, pop culture, fiction, erotica, fetish magazines, and more. A lot of the stuff you read about in *Outposts* and *Psychotropedia* is in here. Get it immediately.

Newspeak Small Press Guild/5 Steeple St/Providence RI 02903
Single issue: $4. Can/Mex: $5. Others: $6
Four issue sub (one year): $16. Can/Mex: $20. Others: $24

THE OCTOPUS
Secret Government and the Death of Danny Casolaro
by Kenn Thomas & Jim Keith

In the early 1990s, the death of Danny Casolaro was a *cause célèbre* in conspiracy circles. Although interest has waned as new occurrences take centre stage, it remains an intriguing case in which something rotten was almost certainly afoot. Casolaro wrote short stories, a novel, and many non-fiction articles of an investigative nature. He was on the trail of what he called "the Octopus", a many-tentacled conspiracy involving members of the intelligence community, which would form the basis of his next political thriller.

By August 1991 Casolaro was receiving graphic death threats. Early that month he went to Martinsburg, West Virginia, to meet with his main informant, who he believed would supply the final, missing pieces of the Octopus puzzle. Before he left for what would be his last rendezvous, Casolaro told his brother, "If anything happens to me, don't believe it's an accident." These turned out to be prophetic words, because on August 10 a housekeeper at the Sheraton found Casolaro's body in the bathtub. His wrists had been cut, and the authorities immediately declared it a suicide, despite the fact that the cuts were too deep to be self-inflicted. Despite an unconvincing suicide note. Despite the housekeeper's claim that when she entered the bathroom, 1) the floor was smeared with blood as if someone had attempted to wipe it up, and 2) two blood-soaked towels were in a heap under the sink. Despite the fact that Casolaro's voluminous notes and documents on the case — which he carried with him in a large accordion file everywhere he went — were not found and, in fact, are still missing. Adding further suspicion to the issue, Casolaro's body was quickly embalmed without the

permission of his family, and the hotel room and bathroom were almost immediately "cleaned", thus ruining any chance to find clues. Even more bizarre: "At Casolaro's funeral, two unknown figures appear. One of them places a medal on Casolaro's casket and saluted, although Casolaro never served in the military."

Luckily, Casolaro didn't take every bit of documentation and early parts of his manuscript with him. The authors have reviewed all of this material, interviewed some of Casolaro's informants, and otherwise probed into the waters that Casolaro had been in. They give us the first book-length investigation into this shady story. Casolaro had been investigating a series of interconnected crimes. "It included Contra War chemical and biowarfare weapons developed on the tribal lands of the Cabazon Indians of Indio, California, weapons possibly used in the October 23, 1983 blast at a compound in Beirut that left over 300 American and French military personnel dead. His research also looked at bizarre murders among the Cabazon Indians involving administrators of the tribal land; the privatisation of CIA dirty tricks through the notorious Wackenhut security firm, the policemen for both the Cabazons and the mysterious Area 51, home of secret spy planes and rumoured UFOs; Vietnam MIAs; corruption at Hughes aircraft; the human genome project; even the Illuminati secret societies of the 18th century. The list was quite long."

This list also includes the October Surprise, the BCCI scandal, Whitewater, and the case of PROMIS software. PROMIS is a programme that is able to track the cases of individuals being investigated and prosecuted by the Justice Department without having to reprogram existing databases. The Inslaw company received a ten million dollar government grant to develop this software, but when this source of funding stopped, the company went private. It requested that it be given sole rights to any further upgrades of PROMIS, and a Justice lawyer agreed, "verifying that Inslaw had the rights to any privately-funded enhancements added to the public domain version of PROMIS." However, Justice refused to pay Inslaw for new software, triggering a ten-year legal battle. "In September 1987 [federal bankruptcy] Judge Bason ruled on *Inslaw vs. The United States of America*, finding the government guilty of 'trickery, deceit, and fraud,' and ruling that the US Department of Justice had stolen the PROMIS software." He ordered Justice to pay $6.8 million in licensing fees and reimburse Inslaw for approximate $1 million in legal fees. This ruling withstood an appeal but was thrown out on a technicality on a second appeal. Meanwhile, Judge Bason was denied reappointment by a committee headed by a judge who used to work for the Justice Department. (Only three other federal bankruptcy judges out of 136 had been denied reappointment in the preceding four years.) He was replaced on the bench by "a Department of Justice lawyer who had represented the IRS in its audits of Inslaw and had recommended liquidation of the company."

All of this nasty business and more coalesced into a Unified Conspiracy Theory through Casolaro's probing. Whether or not the Octopus is real or as powerful as alleged, this book provides a paranoia-inducing glimpse of what Casolaro was working on when he met his extraordinarily suspicious death.

Feral House; $19.95

1996; softcover; 184 pp

illus; 0-922915-39-3

OJ
101 Theories, Conspiracies & Alibis
by Peter Roberts

This intriguing book offers up plenty of conjecture regarding the murders of Nicole Brown and Ron Goldman. The author isn't trying to promote a single viewpoint, but, conversely, to offer up as many viewpoints as possible to see if the truth might be found in an unexpected place. His ideas range from the plausible to the all-but-impossible.

OJ opens up with a look at the chronologies of the murders as set forth by the prosecution and by the defence. Then there is a run-down of the prosecution's evidence of Simpson's guilt and the defence's evidence of his innocence, which is very helpful if you didn't pay close attention to the trial. Unfortunately, it isn't comprehensive because the book was completed in the middle of the criminal trial.

The author proposes 23 different theories as to how the murders occurred. After presenting each scenario, he offers arguments against that scenario. Ten of the theories assume Simpson is guilty of the murder: OJ planned to murder only his ex-wife, OJ planned to murder only Goldman, OJ was double-crossed by a hitman he hired, OJ made it look like he was framed. The other theories propose that Simpson was innocent: a rapist or robber attacked Brown outside her condo, Brown was killed because of her unpaid debts, Brown was mistaken for Faye Resnik, a gang followed Goldman to the condo after an altercation, Simpson was framed and may not know who did it.

This leads to the next chapter, which quickly outlines a dozen possible conspiracies to let Simpson take the fall for the murders. Among the possibilities: Simpson was framed by a crime ring, a business partner, a jealous ex-girlfriend, an ex-boyfriend of Nicole's, a racist group, or the LA Police Department.

The book's final and longest chapter, "Alibis", presents 66 possible pieces of evidence that would point towards Simpson's innocence. As with the theories, the author offers an argument for and against each alibi. Some of the possible exculpatory evidence: Simpson's abuse of Brown was exaggerated, someone other than Simpson was stalking Brown, Simpson appeared happy at his daughter's dance recital just hours before the murders, one person couldn't have killed both victims, the murderer's glove was planted at Simpson's place, Simpson cut his hand on his Bronco's cellular phone, Simpson cut his hand during a scuffle with the real killers, someone else used Simpson's Bronco to commit the murders, three people reported seeing or hearing suspicious men around Brown's condo that night, Simpson was taking a shower when the limousine driver buzzed for him, Simpson was calm on his flight to Chicago the night of the murders.

Each conspiracy, theory, and alibi is around one to two pages long. They don't present reams of evidence and highly detailed scenarios, but they do at least raise all kinds of alternative possibilities in this unusual case.

Goldtree Press; $9.95

1995; softcover; 155 pp

0-9641565-9-8

PAN AM 103
The Lockerbie Cover-Up
by William C. Chasey

After a bomb went off on Pan Am Flight 103, blowing it out of the sky over Lockerbie, Scotland in 1988, lobbyist and foreign agent William Chasey was sent to Libya to normalise relations between that country and the US. Libya — and two Libyan terrorists, specifically — is generally assumed to have used two of its agents to carry out the bombing. However, Chasey is convinced that the blame actually lies with Syria and Iran, who paid Islamic terrorist groups to carry out the bombing. What makes it so bad is that, according to this scenario, a rogue CIA unit was protecting a drug-running operation in Europe, allowing certain baggage to pass through uninspected. The terrorists duped one of the protected drug runners into smuggling the explosives aboard Flight 103. What's more, Chasey claims that CIA headquarters was aware of the plan but did nothing to stop it.

Bridger House Publishers; $17.95

1995; softcover; 380 pp

illus; 0-9640104-1-0

PARANOID WOMEN COLLECT THEIR THOUGHTS
edited by Joan D'Arc

This is the first annual anthology from the conspiracy research magazine Paranoia [Outposts p 51]. The theme this time is articles from female researchers. Other than that, anything goes — mind control, "nonlethal weapons", UFOs, intelligence agencies, and much more. Articles include "The Travelling Torture Chamber: Microwave Harassment", "E.T. Encounters or Mind Control Hoax?", "Nuclear Hazards: Crime Against Humanity", "The Microchip Injection: Orwellian Implications", "Unveiling the Virgin: Vatican Conspiracy Exposed", "The Vivisection Fraud: Your Child or Your Dog", "TIIIIMMMMMBERRRRR!: The Railroading of Earth First!", "Why Was Patty Hearst Kidnapped?: The CIA's SLA", and "Conspiracy and Kwanzaa: Black Pride and COINTELPRO".

Paranoia; $9.50

1996; oversized softcover; 152 pp

illus; no ISBN

PERCEPTIONS
Broader Concepts for Better Solutions

It's not easy deciding where to put Perceptions, a magazine that combines conspiracy theory, alternative health, and New Age thinking. It could probably fit into any of those three categories, but I put it under Conspiracies because all the material is devoted to uncovering hidden information. It brings together an odd mix of ideas and information. Some articles are much more outlandish than others, but the magazine always contains several great pieces and lots of promising ads.

Perceptions Magazine/c/o 10734 Jefferson Blvd, Suite 502/ Culver City California/Postal Zone 90230
Sample issue: $5
Six issue sub (one year): $25
WWW: http://Smartworld.com/perceptions/perceptions.html

POPULAR ALIENATION
A Steamshovel Press Reader
edited by Kenn Thomas

Popular Alienation contains nine complete issues of *Steamshovel Press* [*Outposts* p 54], one of the most important conspiracy research magazines. This big, hefty book with a wonderful full-colour collage cover is an embarrassment of riches. Between the book's more than 80 main articles, dozens of short articles in the "Things are Gonna Slide" sections, and numerous book reviews, I hardly know where to begin.

Not surprisingly, the JFK assassination is examined from many angles with at least one article per issue. "The Role of Richard Nixon and George Bush in the Assassination of President Kennedy" looks at the link between Nixon and Bush and the roles they might have played in Kennedy's death. It is quite interesting to note that Bush admits that he was in Texas during the assassination but can't remember exactly where he was. Nixon was not only in Texas, but was actually in Dallas during the assassination, even though he originally told the FBI he couldn't recall his whereabouts at the time. To paraphrase a comedian (I can't remember which one), this makes Bush and Nixon the only two members of their generation who can't remember where they were when Kennedy was shot.

Each issue also has at least one interview. In issue 9, 1960s anti-war activist Dave Dellinger talks about why Martin Luther King was pressured into not speaking out against the Vietnam War sooner. He also examines the possibility that 1960s radical Abbie Hoffman did not commit suicide but was murdered, a theory that Hoffman's eldest son wholeheartedly believes. "He tells me that when he saw his father's body, lying there dead, that he had bruises on his face and that he had fists clenched as if he had been resisting somebody." The coroner told Hoffman's family that he had died of a heart attack — not violence, alcohol, or drugs. Against his son's wishes, Hoffman's body was immediately cremated. "And after the body was disposed of, then the coroner switched his story and said that he'd been taking phenobarbital and alcohol."

"Sagan Sees a Moonbase" is a shockeroo. The late astronomer and noted UFO debunker Carl Sagan, early in his career, opined that there is a good chance that extraterrestrials exist and that they've been here. In an article reprinted from *Stars and Stripes*, November 26, 1962 (entitled "Prof Says Beings From Outer Space Visited Earth"), the 28-year-old Sagan lectured members of the American Rocket Society on his theories. Based on the probable number of planets capable of supporting life, at least one million stars

in the Milky Way have planets with highly advanced technological civilisations. Sagan said: "There's a strong probability, then, that they have visited the earth every few thousand years. It is not out of the question that artefacts of these visits still exist or even that some kind of base is maintained, possible automatically, within the solar system, to provide continuity for successive expeditions."

"Hotel Kalifornia" looks at who is profiting from the extremely lucrative, multibillion dollar business of imprisoning people in California. In "Wilhelm Reich Died for Einstein's Sins", Jim Martin writes that the real reason radical psychoanalyst and scientist Wilhelm Reich was imprisoned by the government is because he discovered unpleasant facts about nuclear radiation. "Presidency-as-Theater" presents the intriguing scenario that Ronald Reagan's assassination attempt was faked. The reprinted article "KKK, GOP, and CIA" provides an explanation for why David Duke seems to get out of tight situations, including being drafted: he might be a CIA agent. Other articles and interviews cover the Turin Shroud, the Vatican, Lenny Bruce, President Clinton, cattle mutilation and the FBI, US military occupation of the Amazon Basin, the Men in Black, and lots of information on UFOs.

As a bonus, *Popular Alienation* contains *Steamshovel Press* #13, a "virtual issue" available nowhere else except this book. Because of *Steamshovel*'s massive scope and its influence in conspiracy circles, *Popular Alienation* is a required purchase.

IllumiNet Press; $19.95
1995; oversized softcover; 343 pp
illus; 1-881532-07-0

PREVAILING WINDS
Since 1990, Prevailing Winds Research has offered a catalogue containing a wide variety of material on conspiracies and cover-ups. In 1995 they launched a full-scale magazine devoted to the same topics. It's crammed with revealing articles written with an anti-authoritarian attitude.

An article in the first issue examines the hot topic of non-lethal weapons, such as isotropic radiators that can produce blinding flashes, infrasound that can cause disorientation and vomiting, aqueous foams that can trap people, slippery gels that can make stairs and roads unusable, microwave weapons that can disrupt (or destroy) bodily functions, and Liquid Metal Embrittlement, a method of severely weakening metals. Such weapons can be used to avoid killing while ending hostage situations, prison riots, terrorist situations, and, of course, any situation that the government doesn't like. If you think such technologies are bogeymen made up by paranoid conspiracy theorists, think again. The author of this article was the only journalist at the first conference on non-lethal weapons, held at Johns Hopkins in 1993. The attendees were "sporting name tags identifying them as CIA, DIA, DOE, National Security Council, Secret Service, Martin Marietta, Lockheed, Grumman, and many more." Speakers at the conference included a Pentagon official, a former Military Adviser to President Bush, Dr. Edward Teller, who helped develop the H-bomb, and Attorney General Janet Reno, whose speech was read by an aide because she cancelled at the last minute.

Two articles demolish Gerald Posner and his book *Case Closed*, which argues that Lee Harvey Oswald really was just a lone nut. Allegedly, Posner twisted testimony and lied about interviewing key players. In one instance, Posner said that he interviewed James Tague, a bystander who was nicked by one of Oswald's shots, making him the third person to be injured in the gunfire. Tague has always stated that the first shot absolutely did not hit him, which has proved problematic for people who believe the official version of events. However, Posner claimed to have interviewed Tague, who now admits that the first shot could have hit him. Two researchers who are double-checking Posner's research contacted Tague to ask him why he changed his story. "The answer was clear and shocking: James Tague never spoke to Gerald Posner at all! And Tague stands by his oft-repeated story that the first shot most assuredly did not hit him."

Other articles look at the toxic coating on Stealth aircraft, who Carlos the Jackal is really working for, what Pat Robertson does with his money, how NutraSweet got approved, what may have happened at Roswell, the 1992 massacre outside CIA headquarters, and more. The next issue contains articles on hemp, Robert Kennedy's assassination, Oklahoma City, the real reasons for war, the connections between drug trafficking and US intelligence agencies, and the scapegoating of the Aum sect for the sarin gas attack on Tokyo's subways.

Issue 3 looks at the V-chip, the Dreyfus affair, the World Trade Centre bombing, NAFTA's effect on Canada, Martin Luther King's assassination, mind control, and the connections among the CIA, the Drug Enforcement Agency, the National Security Council, Middle East covert operations, and drug running. The fourth and most recent issue offers up more on the CIA's involvement with drugs, the use of military force in the siege at Wounded Knee, the Zapatistas, OJ Simpson, covert operations in Iraq, interviews with American Indian Movement activists Leonard Peltier and Ward Churchill, and the ties between the Internet, the Pentagon, and Bellcore.

Thirty pages of the 96-page magazine act as PW's catalogue, giving detailed descriptions of hundreds of article reprints, audio tapes, videos, books, and other research material.

Prevailing Winds Research/PO Box 23511/Santa Barbara CA 93121
WWW: www.prevailingwinds.org
Single issue: $7
Four issue sub: $20. Can/Mex: $25. Elsewhere: $32

REVERSE SPEECH
Voices from the Unconscious
by David John Oates

Whenever I start to wonder if there are any unusual theories or ideas that I haven't been exposed to, I trip across something that makes me think of a great line from "It's All Too Much" by the Beatles: "The more I learn, the less I know." In this case, the concept that renewed my faith in the mysteriousness of this world is called reverse speech™. David John

Oates believes that normal human speech contains backwards messages. That is, whenever we speak, we are not only saying things forward, but we are also saying things in reverse. Every five to ten seconds, our speech contains a word, phrase, and sometimes a whole sentence that can only be consciously heard when our speech is recorded and played backwards.

Admittedly, this sounds kooky, but the proof is in the pudding. Included with this book is a tape of instances of reverse speech. First, part of a conversation is played normally. Then it is played in reverse. Lo and behold, most of the backward speech *does* contain segments that sound like forward speech. When speaking of the US plane that was shot down by Cuba in 1996, President Clinton says in reverse, "Denounce this evil."

Oftentimes, reverse speech will tell a completely different story than the forward speech. OJ Simpson says all kinds of incriminating stuff backwards. When speaking of having his arguments with Nicole taped, he says in reverse, "I skinned them all." Another time he talked about how understanding he had been of Nicole's other relationships. Played in reverse, he can be heard to say, "Damn your lust. Never see others."

Oates discovered that children begin reverse speech before they begin talking normally. The tape contains a baby making gurgling noises. Played backwards it is clearly saying, "I love you."

Not every instance is particularly clear, though. Sometime you either have to use your imagination or you may not hear anything intelligible at all. But a high number of them are *amazingly* clear and related to the subject at hand.

Don't take my word for it, though. Listen for yourself. Not only can you get the tape with this book, Oates sells many other tapes filled with examples of reverse speech. You can also go to his Website [www.reversespeech.com] and download WAV files or listen to streaming Real Audio files with the latest reverse speech from newsmakers. Should that not be enough, you can buy equipment and instructional material for recording your own examples of this phenomenon.

The book features hundreds of examples that aren't on the tape. Some of them come from songs, but they are not examples of the "backward masking" first done by the Beatles (in the song "Rain") where something is recorded forwards but then edited into the music backwards. These are examples of singers reverse speaking. A well-known Gospel artist that Oates doesn't name sings the following when played backwards: "I serve you Satan. He's the Lord that I've seen. Serve you Satan, everywhere I've been." In her song "Love Sick Blues", Patsy Cline can be heard to say in reverse, "Lucifer fuck off," "It was the Lord who saved me," and "Jesus, he's the one."

Most of the occurrences, though, come from non-famous people who were recorded by Oates and his fellow researchers. While being interviewed by a woman, an aggressive businessman's reversed speech was full of sex talk: "Lick me," "I want a fuck", and "I like slipping it in without the rubber."

Besides relating all of these examples, Oates discusses patterns, verb tenses, metaphors, images, and other matters as they relate to reverse speech. He also looks at how these backwards messages might be formed in the brain and examines evidence that we hear people's reverse speech at a subconscious level.

This is a fascinating theory, and, if correct, it obviously has huge ramifications. For one thing, there'll be no more lying.

Reverse Speech Enterprises; $19.95 book; $27.95 book and tape 1996; softcover and cassette tape; 278 pp illus; 1-57901-000-8

THE ROBOTS' REBELLION
The Spiritual Renaissance
by David Icke

In this book, which has gained a fair bit of notoriety, David Icke states his case that we are constantly being manipulated by those in power. "We are a race of robots. By that, I mean that most people do not have a thought in their heads that has not been put there by someone or something else. We have become a race of programmed minds which can be persuaded to believe and do almost anything as long as the drip, drip, drip of lies and misinformation continues to bombard us through our political systems, the media, religion, schools, universities, and by infiltration of our consciousness by other universal sources which want to turn Planet Earth into a zombies' prison."

It's pretty hard to argue that we're not manipulated by large institutions every day of our lives, but Icke takes this idea even further. We are not being treated like cattle simply because the nature of those in power is to keep their power by misinforming us. No, he believes that there is a wilful, close-knit conspiracy of global power elites who "are preparing to enter the final phase of their plan to take over the planet and the human race." This conspiracy has erased our memories of our true natures and our true purposes on earth. In this book, he aims to remind us. "The manipulators do not want us to know that we are eternal beings of light and love with limitless potential; nor that we can change the world by changing the way we think. And certainly not that we are all One, all equal parts of the same whole, on a journey of evolution through experience."

The Robots' Rebellion is actually nothing less than the history of the world. Starting with the creation of Earth and moving up to the present day, Icke presents what he believes has really happened. Basically, everything started out fine, with a proper balance between positive and negative energies. But then Lucifer — I'm not able to determine if Icke believes this an actual entity or the name of a force — decided to rebel against the laws of Creation, causing an imbalance. Extraterrestrials came to earth and used their genetic knowledge to affect the human race's evolution. Some good aliens wanted to restore the balance, but bad aliens attempted to keep humans in the dark about their true spiritual nature.

Along the way, a group known as the Brotherhood was formed. On the surface, it promises initiates that they will

Page that Sirhan Sirhan wrote under hypnosis in prison.
Shadow Play.

learn the secrets of the universe. However, the upper levels of the Brotherhood have been using this knowledge to enslave the planet for thousands of years, including the present day. "The Brotherhood elite which includes the Rothschild and Rockefeller empires now have six main front organisations for their covert activities. They are the Council on Foreign Relations, the Trilateral Commission, the Club of Rome, the Bilderberg Group, the Royal Institute of International Affairs, and the United Nations."

Although this sounds a lot like right wing Christian conspiracy theories, Icke is not in that boat. In fact, he feels that organised religion is one of the tools that has been used to mislead and misinform people. He feels that "the belief that anyone has a monopoly on truth and wisdom is probably the most destructive and stupid belief it is possible to have."

Icke thinks that the Brotherhood is going to attempt overt domination of the planet within our lifetimes. At the same time, however, he says that many people all over the world are waking up to their true spiritual natures and to the machinations of the secret societies. The human race is now at a pivotal moment that will determine whether we become completely enslaved or completely free. "If we are going to return freedom to the Earth, we have seriously to harass the system into realising that the robots are not co-operating anymore. We will not be lied to and manipulated. There are billions of us and only a relative handful who operate the secret world government. They cannot impose their will on us unless we allow them to. Are you going to be a robot or a rebel? That is your choice for there will be no in-betweens."

Truth Seeker Publications; $19.95
1994; softcover; 347 pp
1-85860-022-7

SHADOW PLAY
The Murder of Robert F. Kennedy, the Trial of Sirhan Sirhan, and the Failure of American Justice
by William Klaber & Philip H. Melanson

After interviewing dozens of witnesses and examining thousands of Los Angeles Police Department documents that were finally unsealed in 1988, the authors of *Shadow Play* contend that not only is the official version of events regarding Robert Kennedy's assassination wrong, the trial of Sirhan Sirhan was also hopelessly unjust due to incompetence and outright corruption. They expose an ill-prepared defence team primarily concerned with advancing their careers (and getting a book deal) and a police investigation team that bullied witnesses into changing their stories and incinerated crucial evidence. Among the revelations: a former FBI investigator says that two guns had to have been firing; the coroner who performed the autopsy on Kennedy states that the wounds couldn't have been caused by Sirhan; and officials retrieved twelve bullets from the scene, even though Sirhan's gun only holds eight.

St. Martin's Press; $24.95
1997; hardcover; 365 pp
illus; 0-312-15398-8

SHOOTING AT THE MOON
The Story of America's Clandestine War in Laos
by Roger Warner

Using the narrative style of a novel, Roger Warner tells the true story of the US's secret, illegal war that occurred in Laos concurrent with the conflict in Vietnam. "Though Operation Momentum began with a different motive, to help defend Laos, America ended up sacrificing the tribals and the lowland Laotians for U.S. goals in Vietnam. These allies, or proxies, were abandoned once the war was over, and the results were a permanent stain on America's reputation."

Steerforth Press; $18
1996; softcover; 440 pp
illus; 1-883642-36-1

SUBVERSION AS FOREIGN POLICY
The Secret Eisenhower and Dulles Debacle in Indonesia
by Audrey R. Kahin & George McT. Kahin

Despite the fact that it is one of the most blatant and important abuses of power in recent times, the US's destabilisation of Indonesia in the 1950s is not widely known. Using still-secret documents and interviews with many participants, the authors shows how President Truman and Secretary of State John Foster Dulles — without the knowledge of Congress or the public — orchestrated and abetted the overthrow of Indonesia's government. Using parts of the CIA, Navy, and Air Force, the highest levels of the US government secretly started the Indonesian civil war, which resulted in thousands of lives lost (including massive civilian fatalities) and utterly failed in its objectives.

The New Press; $25

1995; hardcover; 318 pp
1-56584-244-8

UNDERGROUND BASES AND TUNNELS
What Is the Government Trying to Hide?
by Richard Sauder, PhD

The US government/military has constructed around twelve large underground facilities that are known, and, according to Richard Sauder, there are many more that remain rumoured. Among the most famous of those that are admitted to exist are the NORAD facility in Colorado, which keeps track of air traffic and missiles, and Mount Weather in Virginia, which will house the key personnel of the federal government in case of nuclear attack or some other severe crisis. "The mountain contains what amounts to a small town. The infrastructure includes: a small lake; a pair of 250,000 gallon water tanks, capable of supplying water for 200 people for over a month; a number of ponds 10 ft. deep and 200 ft. across, blasted out of solid rock; a sewage plant capable of treating 90,000 gallons per day; a hospital; a cafeteria; streets and sidewalks; a diesel powered electrical generating plant; private living quarters and dormitories able to accommodate hundreds of residents; a sophisticated, internal communication system using closed-circuit colour TV consoles; a radio and TV studio; massive super-computing facilities; a 'situation room' equipped with communication links to the White House and 'Site R' [an underground military nerve centre] in southern Pennsylvania; and a transit system of electric cars that transport personnel around the complex."

Other underground facilities discussed by the author include a command post for the Strategic Air Command in Omaha, Nebraska; the NORAD centre in Ontario; a monitoring station for the Federal Reserve at Mount Pony in Virginia; a mini-town for 800 people beneath the swanky Greenbriar Hotel in West Virginia; the National Security Agency's Maryland eavesdropping centre, which contains ten acres of supercomputers; the network of tunnels created by the Department of Energy under Nevada; three facilities built by Northrop, Lockheed, and McDonnell Douglas in California's Antelope Valley; and the military's plans for a missile system consisting of 400 miles of tunnels built 2400 to 8000 feet underground. There is also evidence of elaborate structures underneath the White House, the Pentagon, and the Presidential retreat at Camp David, Maryland.

Some of Sauder's sources seem less than definitive — he bases some info on the claims of a single person — but in other cases, he has some serious sources to back him up. For example, "A 1981 *Wall Street Journal* article says that, 'Nine of the 12 Federal Reserve Banks have underground emergency headquarters, where records are updated daily.'" In "Physics at the Proposed National Underground Science Facility" published in the *Proceedings of the XIV International Symposium on Particle Dynamics, Granlibakken, Lake Tahoe, California, 22-27 June 1983*, the speaker for the Los Alamos National Laboratory proposed a

"National Underground Science Facility" to be built 3500 to 6000 feet below the surface of southern Nevada. In a similarly weighty conference in 1987, the Deputy Director of Engineering and Construction for the US Army Corps of Engineers discussed NORAD's Colorado facility and said: "As stated earlier, there are other projects of similar scope, which I cannot identify, but which include multiple chambers up to 50 feet wide and 100 feet high using the same excavation procedures mentioned for the NORAD facility."

Another chapter looks at the technologies that are (or might be) used to create these tunnels. Three chapters completely ditch the book's theme of underground facilities and, instead, looks at evidence that the government is behind so-called alien abductions, cattle mutilations, and implants. A centre section contains 50 pages of illustrations, photos, and maps related to subterranean facilities.

Adventures Unlimited Press; $15.95
1995; softcover; 142 pp
illus; 0-932813-37-2

WARHOGS
A History of War Profits in America
by Stuart D. Brandes

Every time there is a war, many people pay with their lives and a few people become extremely rich. Warhogs is the first book to look at war profiteering in the US for almost its entire history — from the Revolution to World War II. Specifically, the author examines how America mobilises for war, how people have profited from it, how the government has tried to control this activity, and the public's reactions to profiteering. The four main mobilisations in US history — the Revolutionary War, the Civil War, and both World Wars — receive most of the attention, with the colonial wars, the Indian campaigns, the War of 1812, the Mexican War, and the Spanish-American War getting lesser coverage. The conflicts in Korea, Vietnam, and the Persian Gulf are not discussed.

The main form of war profiteering has been price gouging, which occurs when suppliers of matériel jack up prices to take advantage of the government's desperate need. Some suppliers have provided goods that were of an unnecessarily poor quality, including inferior weapons. Other means include building unnecessary fortifications, plundering the enemy, selling to the enemy, and outright fraud. It's been estimated that during the first year of the Civil War, one-quarter of the money spent by the governments became pure profit based on unethical practices. In the twentieth century, new types of profiteering have taken shape, including "large corporate salaries, commodity speculation, excessive construction costs for military posts, black market trading, evasion of price controls, and gains from post-war re-conversion."

The Colt's Patent Fire Arms Company of Hartford, Connecticut, founded by Samuel Colt, supplied guns to Northerners and Southerners throughout the 1850s. After the South seceded, Colt contacted the Confederate army, hoping to sell them sidearms. "Three days after the Confederate attack on Fort Sumter in 1861, Colt shipped his last or-

der of five hundred guns to Richmond in boxes marked 'hardware.'" After that, Colt dealt strictly with the Union, but his practices were decried as price gouging. For years before the war, he charged the military $25 per revolver, but only charged civilians $14.50, and he sold them to the potentially dangerous British government for $12.50 apiece. In 1860, he cut the military price to $20, still much above the $4 to $9 it's been estimated that each gun cost to produce. During the Civil War, Colt's earnings went from $237,000 per year to over a million.

Although written as an objective survey and not a screed, Warhogs still provides a disheartening look at an understudied aspect of capitalistic greed.

The University press of Kentucky; $34.95
1997; hardcover; 371 pp
illus; 0-8131-2020-9

WASHINGTON BABYLON
by Alexander Cockburn & Ken Silverstein

In the tradition of the classic sleazefest Hollywood Babylon by Kenneth Anger, Washington Babylon gleefully plays in the dirt and slime caked all over the US Capitol. The muckraking editors of Counterpunch have put together the most embarrassing and disgraceful facts concerning Senators, Representatives, lobbyists, reporters, pundits, Cabinet members, Bill and Hillary Clinton, Al and Tipper Gore, and other power players, such as Attorney General Janet Reno and Federal Reserve Chairman Alan Greenspan. In an age where faux objectivity is supposed to be the goal of journalists, the authors take off their gloves. There's no attempt to paint a balanced portrait… they dish up the sleaze using uncompromising language. This a wonderful move, since it provides a counterpoint to the banal, repackaged press releases that usually pass for news. Plus, everybody gets taken to task, Democrats and Republicans, liberals, moderates, and conservatives.

A caption beneath Tom Foley's picture reads, "Former Speaker, his name will endure whenever grizzlies and salmon die or where radioactivity enhances nature's temple." Former Secretary of State and current "respected statesman" Henry Kissinger is described as "arguably the most amoral and criminal public official of the post-war era". The authors write of Senator Phil Gramm: "Gramm is a nasty fellow with a pharaonic belief in his own importance. Whether he's beating up on welfare moms, calling for the death penalty for shoplifting, or exiling federal employees to Alaska for challenging his duckshoots in eastern Maryland, Gramm really is the vicious brute people once considered Bob Dole to be." Senator Larry Pressler is described as "a man long and widely derided in Washington as an imbecile of fantastic proportions."

One of the many great things about this book is that it covers both personal scandal and political scandal. Not only do we hear about the sex and sin, but also the influence peddling, compromised interests, and complete lack of humanity.

On the personal side, we read that, "Strom 'Sperm' Thurmond, South Carolina's senior senator, married a 22-

year-old beauty queen at the age of 66, and sired his first child three years later. He claims to have a permanent erection, and says he keeps a baseball bat in his office so the undertaker can beat down his member in order to close his coffin lid." According to his own diaries, Senator Bob Packwood told one of the staffers he was boffing that, "I was doing my Christian duty by making love to you." And speaking of "family values", look at the shining example of House Speaker Newt Gingrich: "Back in the early Eighties he abandoned his wife, then showed up at her hospital bed where she was recovering from a cancer operation and flourished a legal pad, dictating stinted terms of divorce."

On the political side, there's Alaskan Senator Frank Murkowski, who owns $50,000 of stock in Louisiana-Pacific, owner of the Ketchikan Pulp Company, "which holds an exclusive 50-year contract for timber from south-east Alaska's Tongass National Forest. Over the past 10 years, Murkowski has intervened numerous times to keep timber flowing into the Ketchikan pulp mill despite evidence of severe environmental problems on the Tongass, the largest national forest in the US and the last intact temperate rainforest in North America." You may remember that at one point Vice-Prez Al Gore was gushing over plans to have the government construct the "National Information Infrastructure". After corporations went ballistic, Gore backed off and announced that his utopian infrastructure would be built by the private sector. The Democratic party's coffers were shortly flooded with over half a million dollars from phone and computer companies.

Much to my delight, *Washington Babylon* also prints the most unflattering photos of its subjects that it could find. Al Gore looks drugged, Ted Kennedy has something caked in his teeth, and Newt Gingrich and Janet Reno look more horrifying than usual. You'll also see the infamous pictures of Henry Kissinger picking his nose and apparently eating his boogers while at a conference in Brazil. In the past Kissinger's lawyer has threatened legal action over the publication of these embarrassing images.

To get a brutally honest look at what's really happening in America's halls of power, take a trip to *Washington Babylon*.

Verso; $15
1996; softcover; 316 pp
illus; 1-85984-092-2

WHO KILLED MARTIN LUTHER KING?

by Philip Melanson

Political science prof and assassination researcher Philip Melanson gives a concise overview of the problems with the official version of Martin Luther King's murder. The evidence used to convict James Earl Ray, he says, is "largely circumstantial and seriously flawed." The eyewitness testimony was shaky, experts called before Congress came up with completely opposite findings regarding Ray's fingerprints, ballistics tests were hopelessly inconclusive, and Ray's polygraph tests were conducted poorly.

The 1977 House Select Committee on Assassinations concluded that Ray had probably killed King at the behest of a conspiracy of right-wing racists. Melanson demonstrates why he thinks this theory falls flat and why other conspiracies are much more likely. The Committee also decided that no government agencies at any level had been involved, but there are enough strange circumstances to warrant further investigation. For instance, why were the Memphis Police's tactical units unexpectedly pulled back five blocks away from the assassination on the morning it occurred? Other circumstances indicate the FBI and CIA may have had a role.

Melanson is calling for a new investigation, and to that end, he supplies a list of fifteen new and overlooked leads that must be investigated if we're ever going to uncover the truth.

Odonian Press; $5
1993; paperback; 94 pp
illus; 1-878825-11-9

THE WRONG STUFF
The Space Program's Nuclear Threat to Our Planet

by Karl Grossman

In October 1997, NASA launched the Cassini space probe, which is carrying 72.3 pounds of plutonium. Luckily, the launch went off without incident. This is fortunate considering the probe was piggybacked on a Titan IV rocket, the same kind that exploded during launch in 1993. Had that occurred again, Florida would have been coated in radioactive material. But we're not out of the woods yet, because Cassini is coming back. NASA is going to employ a "slingshot manoeuvre" to loop the probe around the earth's gravitational field, and use this extra momentum to send it sailing to Saturn, its final destination. In August 1999, Cassini is going to hurtle just 312 miles overhead at 42,300 miles per hour. "But after many millions of miles in space, if there is a miscalculation on the 1999 Earth 'flyby,' the probe could make what NASA, in its *Final Environmental Impact Statement on the Cassini Mission*, calls an 'inadvertent re-entry' and fall into the 75-mile high Earth atmosphere, disintegrating and releasing plutonium. If this occurs, NASA says 'approximately 5 billion of the estimated 7 to 8 billion world population at this time... could receive 99 percent or more of the radiation exposure.'"

This isn't the first time that spacecraft have carried plutonium, though. Should Cassini plummet to earth, it also wouldn't be the first time that the plutonium has hit the fan. In April 1964, a US navigational satellite never made it into orbit, falling back to earth and releasing 2.1 pounds of plutonium in the process. When the Apollo 13 lunar module plummeted into the ocean in 1970, it took 8.3 pounds of plutonium with it. On its very next mission, the ill-fated *Challenger* space shuttle was to have been carrying the Ulysses space probe, loaded with 24.2 pounds of plutonium.

The author paints a scary picture based on past incidents. He also warns that more spacecraft carrying radioactive material are scheduled for launch and that NASA has been looking into other ways to bring nuclear power into space. Unfortunately, it has been determinedly ignoring alternative energy sources. 'A combination of solar power and long-lived fuel cells could easily provide all the electricity that Cassini would require,' says Dr. Kaku [professor of nuclear physics at CUNY]. 'NASA is putting ideology ahead of the laws of physics because the amount of energy that you could generate from solar cells is clearly sufficient to energise Cassini.'"

Common Courage Press; $22.95
1997; hardcover; 270 pp
1-56751-125-2

WASHINGTON MONEY-GO-ROUND
by Jack Anderson

For fifty years, Jack Anderson has been digging up political dirt and, for much of that time, reporting it in his nationally-syndicated column. In *Washington Money-Go-Round*, his latest book, he does what he does best — shows you exactly what the federal government is doing with the people's money, and needless to say, it ain't a pretty picture.

Of course, Anderson reveals a shameful list of disgraceful "pork": $5000 for a mahogany planter that went into the new offices of some Justice Department lawyers; $25,000 for a study of where to build a gym for Congressional staffers; $800,000 for Congress to print calendars to give away to constituents; $1.2 million per year to fund the Office of Smallpox Eradication, which continues to exist even though smallpox has been eradicated; millions of dollars per year to broadcast anti-Castro propaganda to Cuba, even though none of it ever gets through because Castro jams the signal; $32 million for research that created the anti-cancer drug Taxol, which is now marketed exclusively by a pharmaceutical corporation that charges $986 for a three-week supply.

He also examines other ways in which the government is its own worst enemy. It's recently come to light that there are staggering amounts of counterfeit $100 bills in circulation outside the US. They're so convincing that not even experts can always tell the difference, and they're threatening to destroy the worth of US currency. (This is the main reason why the design for C-notes was recently changed.) How did these remarkably authentic bills come into existence? Iran is cranking them out on US Mint printing presses that the US gave to that country shortly before the Shah was ousted and the Islamic fundamentalists took over. "The Shah wanted to print pretty money. President Richard Nixon and his major domo, Henry Kissinger, catered to the Shah's every whim because he was controlling oil prices for them and their friends in the oil business."

Another chapter discusses a topic you won't hear about very often — the colossal waste and mismanagement at the United Nations. In December of 1984, the massive starvation in Ethiopia was receiving world-wide attention. The UN literally took up a collection for famine relief by asking its employees and visiting diplomats for donations, while — on the very same day — the General Assembly appropriated $73.5 million to build a conference centre in Ethiopia. In 1994 someone broke into the UN's office in Somalia and walked away with *$3.9 million* in $100 bills from the US. Since Somalia doesn't have any banks, the peacekeeping operation kept all its funds in cash. "The money was not locked in a strongbox but stacked in an old carton that once held water bottles. The carton was not kept in a safe but in a filing cabinet drawer. The filing cabinet was not shut in a vault but stored in a storage room. It could be entered through a door that could be jimmied with a credit card."

Anderson also exposes Pentagon waste, George Washington's pork, corporate welfare, the "King of Pork" (Senator Robert Byrd of West Virginia), the pork spent on Appalachia, the "War on Poverty" (we lost), Social Security, Medicare, and ideas for fighting all this colossal misspending. Anderson thinks that something serious can be done about the deeply ingrained, runaway waste in the government, but considering that he's been exposing fundamentally the same infuriating stories for five decades, it seems hard to believe.

Elliot & James Publishing; $28.95
1997; hardcover; 278 pp
illus; 0-9637899-3-7

NO COMPROMISES

ANARCHISM

AFRICAN ANARCHISM
The History of a Movement
by Sam Mbah & IE Igariwey

With this unprecedented book, two Nigerian political activists provide the first detailed look at the role of anarchism in African life and politics. As leading members of Africa's largest anarchist organisation, the Awareness League, Sam Mbah and IE Igariwey are in a unique position to examine this topic. They start with a thoughtful introduction to the concept of anarchism, which makes a great primer for anyone who thinks that "anarchy" is a synonym for "chaos". Following that is a brief, spotty chapter on the general history of anarchism.

Next comes the meat of the book, "Anarchistic Precedents in Africa", which examines the elements of anarchism that have existed in African societies, particularly in the precolonial period. Although there isn't a systematic body of thought concerning anarchism as a philosophy in Africa, applied anarchism can be seen in traditional societies, which organised themselves in a communal manner. "Among the most important features of African communalism are the absence of classes, that is, social stratification; the absence of exploitive or antagonistic social relations; the existence of equal access to land and other elements of production; equality at the level of distribution of social produce; and the fact that strong family and kinship ties form(ed) the basis of social life in African communal societies. Within this framework, each household was able to meet its own basic needs. Under communalism, by virtue of being a member of a family or community, every African was (is) assured of sufficient land to meet his or her own needs." After examining some of the more pronounced examples of anarchistic societies, the chapter leads us into the period of colonialism and capitalism, which changed things considerably. However, the authors do point out: "Despite the indigenous development of feudalism and the later imposition of capitalism, communal features exist to this day — sometimes pervasively — in the majority of African societies that lie outside the big cities and townships."

The next two chapters don't focus on pure anarchism, but instead examine the effects of socialism and the labour movement on various African countries — particular Tanzania, Guinea, and Ghana — that are fighting the ravaging effects of colonialism. The authors conclude that trying to change the system from within through socialism has been a failure. They look to anarchism as the best hope for their continent. Although there are many obstacles to overcome, Africa has a better-than-average chance of employing anar-

Legendary anarchist and soldier of fortune, Michael Bakunin. *Arnarchist Portraits.*

chism. "The process of anarchist transformation in Africa might prove comparatively easy, given that Africa lacks a strong capitalist foundation, well-developed class formations and relations of production, and a stable, entrenched state system. What is required for now is a long-term programme of class consciousness building, relevant education, and increased individual participation in social struggles."

See Sharp Press; $8.95
1997; softcover; 124 pp
1-884365-05-1

ANARCHIST PORTRAITS
by Paul Avrich

Dr. Paul Avrich, a distinguished professor of history at CUNY, is one of the foremost authorities on the anarchist movement. He has published several books on the subject, travelled to archives and libraries all over the world, and interviewed numerous anarchists, including many of the most famous. What's really amazing is that, despite being an academic, he actually appears sympathetic towards anarchism. This might hurt his standing in academia, but it just makes him that much more respected at the outposts.

This book takes a biographical approach to the subject, portraying the human side of anarchists, complete with their strengths, visions, warts, and failures. In the introduction,

Avrich notes, "Examining the careers of these anarchists, both well known and obscure, one is struck above all by their passionate hatred of injustice, of tyranny in all its forms, and by the perceptiveness of their warnings against the dangers of concentrated power, economic and political alike. They were among the earliest and most consistent opponents of totalitarianism, both of the left and of the right, marked by the growth of a police state, the subjugation of the individual, the dehumanisation of labour, and the debasement of language and culture..."

Anarchist Portraits presents relatively short, readable chapters on a number of anarchists and anarchist groups from around the world. The focus is primarily on the heyday of the movement, the 1800s and early 1900s, when it was a force to be reckoned with. Several chapters are devoted to Michael Bakunin, the tireless man of action who spent little time theorising and most of his time hopping around the globe, stirring up rebellions, leading insurrections, and manning the barricades. He is truly the type of romantic hero that legends are made of. As he once said, "No theory, no ready-made system, no book that has ever been written will save the world. I cleave to no system. I am a true seeker."

Bakunin placed his hope for revolution in unskilled workers, peasants, the poor. He felt that through the unorchestrated release of their fury, true revolution would occur. Bakunin didn't believe in waiting around for revolutions to build up, as Marx did. He wanted action and he wanted it now. "Gradualism and reformism were futile, palliatives and compromises of no use. Bakunin's was a dream of immediate and universal destruction, the levelling of all existing values and institutions, and the creation of a libertarian society on their ashes." He once wrote: "I do not believe in constitutions and laws. The best constitution in the world would not be able to satisfy me. We need something different: inspiration, life, a new lawless and therefore free world."

After taking part in revolts in Paris, Austria, and Germany, Bakunin was arrested in Dresden in 1849. He was locked up for eight years, spending six of them in the Tsar's dungeon, where he went toothless from scurvy and developed other serious health problems. He was sentenced to permanent exile in Siberia, but, incredibly, managed to escape to Japan and then San Francisco. He only stayed in the US two months before travelling all over the world again, stirring up trouble.

In complete contrast with Bakunin is one of the other most famous anarchists of all time, Peter Kropotkin. Both men were born into aristocracy but turned their backs on their birthrights. Both escaped from imprisonment by the Tsars. Kropotkin, however, was more of a theorist than a fighting man. He had, in fact, been a distinguished academic who made discoveries that changed the cartography of eastern Asia. But around this time (he was not yet thirty) he went through a profound awakening in which he lost all faith in government and came to sympathise completely with the oppressed people of the world.

Kropotkin came across two examples of communal living that would form the basis of his ideas. While in Siberia he visited many small autonomous communities that, though cut off from larger society, were actually flourishing. A few years later, he was exposed to the Swiss watchmaking communities in the mountains of Jura. In these communities there was no distinction between labour and management, leaders and subordinates. As a direct result of seeing these two types of autonomous zones, Kropotkin wrote, "I was an anarchist."

Kropotkin based his influential theories of ideal social structure on an unorthodox reading of Darwin's theory of natural selection. While many Darwinists were harping about the world being a "savage jungle, red in tooth and claw", Krop took a different approach. He believed that "in the process of natural selection, spontaneous co-operation among animals was more important than ferocious competition, and that 'those animals which acquire habits of mutual aid are undoubtedly the fittest' to survive."

Mutual aid and co-operation have played fundamental roles in history, and the rise of centralised states has corrupted this process. Kropotkin advanced the concept of anarchist communism, in which all thing belong to all people. "Its underlying theme is that both the instrument and the fruits of production, now unjustly appropriated by the few, are the collective achievement of humanity as a whole." The answer then, is to abolish private property and income and create free distribution of goods and services.

Another chapter is devoted to the case of Sacco and Vanzetti, whose trial for murder is one of the most infamous and important court battles of this century. Nicola Sacco, a shoemaker, and Bartolomeo Vanzetti, a fish peddler, were accused of killing a paymaster and his guard during a robbery of a shoe factory. Both of the accused were Italians, anarchists, atheists, and armed. This made for a very hostile atmosphere, especially since the Red Scare and xenophobia were at an all-time high around 1920.

The trial was extremely unfair. The district attorney was guilty of "coaching and badgering witnesses, withholding exculpatory evidence from the defence, and perhaps even tampering with physical evidence." He used every trick he could to play on the jurors' fears and prejudices. Even the judge was openly hostile to the defendants. During the trial and appeals, he would make comments outside the courtroom such as, "Did you see what I did with those anarchist bastards the other day? I guess that will hold them for a while."

S&V were found guilty and sentenced to die. During the appeals process, evidence accumulated that pointed towards innocence. "Key prosecution testimony was retracted and new evidence was produced that was favourable to the defendants. Herbert Ehrmann, a junior defence attorney, built a strong case against the Morelli gang of Providence, which specialised in stealing shipments from shoe manufacturers." The authorities, however, didn't care and wouldn't listen. A large number of observers who had no sympathy at all for anarchism believed that S&V had been railroaded. "On August 23, 1927, the men were electrocuted, in defiance of world-wide protest and appeals. By then, millions were convinced of their innocence, and millions more were convinced that, guilty or innocent, they had not received impartial justice."

Other chapters weave interesting tales about Nestor Makhno, Benjamin Tucker, Mollie Steimer, JW Fleming, the Paris Commune, Brazilian anarchism, and Jewish anarchism in the US. I want to close this review with a well-known quote that Avrich reprints from *The General Idea of the Revolution in the Nineteenth Century* by the French anarchist Pierre-Joseph Proudhon. It's quite long, but it hits the nail on the head so perfectly, that it deserves to be reprinted as often as possible. "To be governed is to be kept in sight, inspected, spied upon, directed, law-driven, numbered, enrolled, indoctrinated, preached at, controlled, estimated, valued, censured, commanded, by creatures who have neither the right, nor the wisdom, nor the virtue to do so. To be governed is to be, at every operation, every transaction, noted, registered, enrolled, taxed, stamped, measured, numbered, assessed, licensed, authorised, admonished, forbidden, reformed, corrected, punished. It is, under pretext of public utility, and in the name of the general interest, to be placed under contribution, trained, ransacked, exploited, monopolised, extorted, squeezed, mystified, robbed; then, at the slightest resistance, the first word of complaint, to be repressed, fined, despised, harassed, tracked, abused, clubbed, disarmed, choked, imprisoned, judged, condemned, shot, deported, sacrificed, sold, betrayed; and, to crown all, mocked, ridiculed, outraged, dishonoured. That is government; that is its justice; that is its morality."

Princeton University Press; $18.95
1988; softcover; 316 pp
illus; 0-691-00609-1

ANARCHIST VOICES
An Oral History of Anarchism in America
by Paul Avrich

In *Anarchist Voices*, the foremost American historian of anarchism lets members of the movement speak for themselves. Interviewed between 1963 and 1991, almost all of these anarchists were active in America during the glory days of the 1880s through the 1930s. Several of the 180 interviews are not with anarchists but rather with relatives, friends, and acquaintances of the anarchists, such as Emma Goldman's attorney, Peter Kropotkin's daughter, and two witnesses in the Sacco and Vanzetti case.

The interviews are arranged around six aspects of the movement — "Pioneers", "Emma Goldman", "Sacco and Vanzetti", "Schools and Colonies", "Ethnic Anarchists", "The 1920s and After". By letting the people with first-hand knowledge tell what they know, this book brings up fascinating, little-known aspects about the human side of anarchists and anarchism that don't make it into official histories. Oriole Tucker Riché discusses home life with her father, the individualist anarchist Benjamin Tucker. "Father, incidentally, believed in contracts. We had written contractual agreements around the house. When I was eighteen, he wrote a whole contract about my paying a share of what I made from giving piano lessons. That might seems cold and calculating,

"We're not just going to sit around and produce petitions against what you're doing." *Anarchy in the UK.*

but it made everything clear and simple." She also notes that he never changed his views on religion, even in the end. "In his last months he called in the French housekeeper. 'I want her,' he said, 'to be witness that on my deathbed I'm not recanting. I do not believe in God!'"

The interviews in the "Schools and Colonies" section give great insights into what it was like to actually participate in anarchist social experiments. Macie Pop lived at Home Colony near Tacoma, Washington. She tells an anecdote about James Morton, who taught high school at the colony. "He was a learned man and a good teacher, quite strict. He didn't have much patience. Once when a boy gave the wrong answer Morton said, 'Billy, are you an idiot?' The boy snapped back, 'No, are you?'"

In a short interview, Cuban anarchist Gustavo López talks about what went wrong in his homeland. "The Cuban Revolution started out as a libertarian revolution, as in Russia. Castro's own father was an anarchist, and there were many anarchists in his movement, some of whom took part in the famous assault on the fortress. Castro himself was a rebel and in close touch with the anarchists. But when he took power he didn't know what to do with it."

Anarchist Voices provides many details of the anarchist movement that flesh it out, making it vibrant and human. Highly recommended.

Princeton University Press; $17.95
1995; softcover; 577 pp
illus; 0-691-03412-5

ANARCHY IN THE UK
The Angry Brigade
by Tom Vague

As he did with the Red Army Faction in *Televisionaries* [*Outposts* p 133], anarcho-punk Tom Vague gives a fast-paced history of an extreme left wing/anarchist direct-action group — the Angry Brigade. Expanding on his two-part article that originally appeared in the magazine *Vague*, Vague recounts the origins and exploits of the group that terrorised Britain in the early 1970s. The birth of the Brigade can be traced to late February 1970, when two of its founders attended an anarchist meeting at the headquarters of Freedom Press. "You take some English disillusionment, add some French Situationism, and explosives, then some Spanish Anarchism, and BANG! You've got Anarchy in the UK. (There's also some American influence of course from the Weathermen and the Black Panthers.)"

The second half of the year saw the start of violence by the Angry Brigade. In a documentary on the Brigade, members sum up their philosophy on the use of violence: "It's a message passed on to the ruling class. OK your conspiracy will continue and the bombs won't make that much difference to the way it operates. But it's going to be just a little bit more difficult for you. We're not just going to sit around and produce petitions against what you're doing. The bombings are not going to be the be-all and end-all of the situation. They're an announcement of a certain situation where we're no longer going to accept the confines of legality set by the state."

The group first came to mass attention on January 12, 1971, when it bombed the house of Employment Minister Robert Carr. Soon after, six Conservative Party offices were bombed. Arrests were soon made, including the nabbing of some important members. The campaign of violence continued, however, until August 15, with the bombing of an army recruiting office in Holloway, which marked the last official act of the Brigade. Five days later, six members were arrested, and more were soon pinched. Of the twelve who were eventually tried for conspiracy to cause explosions, five went to jail, five were acquitted, and the charges on the other two were dropped before trial.

Anarchy in the UK provides a unique perspective on the events, because instead of relying on news reports from the "bourgeois media", it extensively quotes the Brigade's own communiqués, publications, and other underground press reportage. The book finishes off with a look at King Mob — another pro-situ group who were around at the same time as the Brigade — and a brief examination of relevant events 1977-1990, including the fleeting appearance of the Angry Brigade II.

AK Press; £ 6.95, $14.95
1997; softcover; 162 pp
heavily illus; 1-873176-98-8

bolo'bolo
by P.M.

bolo'bolo is one of the most important and interesting anarchist books written in recent times. The author, P.M., theorises that the generally dismal state of the human race and the planet earth is due to the Planetary Work Machine, which must be destroyed. The Machine is P.M.'s term for the overarching, interlocking politico-economic structure that encompasses the entire world and everyone on it. It thrives on its inner contradictions — workers vs. capital, war vs. peace, men vs. women — and its guiding principle is the economy. "This is the mechanism of the Work machine: split

Founding members of the Situationist International. *Guy Debord.*

society into isolated individuals, blackmail them separately with wages or violence, use their working time according to its plan."

P.M. elaborates on the structure of the Machine, examining its functions, components, and "deals". One of these deals, for example, is the consumer society deal, which offers us lots of material goods but steals our lives through work. The Machine controls every aspect of our lives. Therefore, there is no hope for reform from within.

But P.M. does envision a solution, a radical restructuring of the world into an arrangement he calls *bolo'bolo*. To bring it about, first the Machine must be destroyed by people coming together *en masse* and practising dysinformation, dysproduction, and dysruption. In place of the current planetary structure, there will be a multitude of *bolos* — small, largely self-sufficient communities of 300 to 500 *ibus* (P.M.'s word for people). "The *bolo* replaces the old 'agreement' called money. In and around the *bolo* the *ibus* can get their daily 2000 calories, a living space, medical care, the basics of survival, and indeed much more." *bolo'bolo*, therefore, "is not a system, but a patchwork of micro-systems."

From there, P.M. launches into a detailed explanation of *bolo'bolo* based on 30 invented terms, such as *taku*, a small metal box that holds all of an *ibu*'s personal possessions; *kana*, a subdivision of a *bolo*; *kodu*, agriculture; and *nugo*, a suicide capsule given to every *ibu*.

When *bolo'bolo* was originally published in 1983, P.M. laid out a provisional schedule that called for the establishment of *bolo'bolo* by 1988. In the long introduction (called an "apology") to this edition, P.M. admits that he was way off the mark. "Not only hasn't the Planetary Work Machine (or economy — state, private or mixed — as some prefer to call it) not dissolved, it's kicking and alive, killing to the left and to the right, imposing still lower levels of misery. We are further away from any conceivable Utopia than ever."

Autonomedia; $8
1983, 1995; paperback; 192 pp
0-936756-08-X

GUY DEBORD
Revolutionary
by Len Bracken

This is the first biography in any language of Guy Debord, the avant garde theorist, strategist, writer, cinematographer, and revolutionary. Among other achievements, Debord cofounded the Situationist International, wrote the modern radical classic *Society of the Spectacle*, and played a direct role in the May 1968 uprising in Paris. This book helps flesh out an important chapter in the modern history of radicalism. Contains over 80 photos, many of them rare.

Feral House; $14.95

1997; softcover; 270 pp

illus; 0-922915-44-X

LOVE AND RAGE
A Revolutionary Anarchist Newspaper

According to this tabloid's political statement: "*Love and Rage* is a bimonthly anarchist newspaper intended to foster revolutionary anti-authoritarian activism in North America and build a more effective and better organised anarchist movement... Anarchism is a living body of theory and practice connected directly to the lived experiences of oppressed people fighting for their own liberation."

The November/December 1997 issue offers an anarchist look at the UPS strike of that year and why it occurred. "Working for United Parcel Service is no joke, especially for the 60% of the workforce that labour part-time in warehouses loading, unloading, and sorting packages. Under UPS's management-by-stress, workers are expected to move packages that can weigh up to 150 pounds at a pace of 1,200 per hour. Not surprisingly, UPS has the highest injury rate in the industry; over a third of all employees were hurt in 1996 according to company reports. The turn-over rate for these highly physical jobs is 400%, and those who stick it out average less than half the hourly wage of UPS full-timers; most bring home less than $200 a week. The starting wage at UPS has been frozen since 1982 when the company successfully pushed through this two-tier system. Many workers have even taken on two UPS part-time jobs to make ends meet: full-time work under the same part-time pay."

The same issue reports that 400-500 anti-fascists showed up to protest against a KKK/neo-Nazi rally in Hamilton, Ohio, in September. After the rally, 400 police officers charged the protesters and proceeded to mace and break heads. "Alice Massey, 50, was in downtown Hamilton not to protest, but to shop. She made the mistake of walking in the path of a mounted police officer. When he ordered her to move, and she was unable to do so quick enough for his taste, the cop lunged his horse. The horse struck her head, cracked it open and caused her to fall. Three of her relatives, one a minor, were maced and arrested when they came to her aid."

Love and Rage gives you passionate coverage and analysis of labour issues, police brutality, anti-racist/-sexist/-homophobic actions, prison issues, the Zapatistas, Puerto Rican struggles, political prisoners, and other topics that are ignored by the larger media.

Love and Rage/PO Box 853, Peter Stuyvesant Station/New York NY 10009

WWW: emma.unm.edu/lnr/index.html

Single issue: $2

Six issue sub (one year): $9 for slow delivery, $13 for fast. Free to GIs, PWAs, and prisoners

NATIVE AMERICAN ANARCHISM
by Eunice Minette Schuster

Originally published in 1932, this book is often considered the best history of American anarchism ever written. Despite the phrase "Native American" in the title, this is not about Native Americans as we use the term now. It is about anarchist individuals and groups from the US.

The first part of the book surveys radical individualism in Colonial times. As strange as it may sound, the most prominent freedom-lovers of this time were Christian anarchists. They had a radical vision that the individual, who is an expression of God, is sovereign and that earthly laws, which are made by mortals, are bogus and should not be obeyed. Antinomianism — the most radical of such movements in America — stuck in the craw of the blue-bloods of Boston, who banished two of its leaders, John Wheelwright and Anne Hutchinson. Quakerism was the other main movement of the time, but it was more radical in principle than it was in practice.

The next section covers the Romantic period (1812-1860), during which the radical movements of abolitionism and women's rights contained anarchist tendencies. That beloved American, Henry David Thoreau, "was not only an anarchist in thought, but also in action." He was a tax protester who went to jail rather than pay taxes. He boldly defended the actions of John Brown, the militant abolitionist who led a deadly attack on a pro-slavery encampment in Kansas and later captured a federal arsenal in Harper's Ferry. Perfectionism and Non-Resistance were two other religious philosophies that espoused a spiritual anarchism.

The third and longest section looks at anarchism during the next 40 or so years. The philosophy took many different tracks during this time, including individual anarchism, scientific anarchism, and utopian communities, which incorporated the ideas of Pierre-Joseph Proudhon, Josiah Warren, Benjamin Tucker, Lysander Spooner, and other notables.

"The Great Disillusion" — the book's final section — focuses on anarchist communism and one of its greatest adherents, Emma Goldman. "The overthrow of the Capitalist system, as we know it today, was their ultimate objective." This was a time of much violence... the Chicago Haymarket riots, the assassination of President McKinley, and the "Sacco and Vanzetti murder" were all pinned on anarchists, even though there are many questions about who perpetrated these acts. There was also a backlash against anarchists during this time, which included deportations, lynchings, and the trashing of many civil liberties.

Because of its unique American perspective, *Native American Anarchism* occupies an important niche among the histories of anti-authoritarian thought.

Loompanics Unlimited; $12

1932, 1983; softcover; 202 pp

0-915179-94-6

PIRATE UTOPIAS
Moorish Corsairs and European Renegadoes
by Peter Lamborn Wilson

European Renegadoes enjoying themselves.
Pirate Utopias.

completely by voluntary co-operation without any form of coercion sounds wonderful, it is quite safe to say that it's unworkable. Bouchier isn't completely without hope about some form of societal change for the better, but he bursts a lot of bubbles with his well-reasoned and utterly unromanticised look at the things that stand in the way of a consensual anarchist utopia, such as the problem of modernity. "Short of nuclear catastrophe, hundreds of millions of people are not going to vanish. Nor are the great metropolises they live in, nor are the technologies and productive facilities they depend on. The communal, agrarian society which Jefferson dreamed of has vanished from the realm of possibility." The divisiveness and combativeness of human nature is another major stumbling block. "It is hardly convincing... when social anarchists claim (as they sometimes do) that people are *really* co-operative 'by nature' — and cite evidence from a few remote and long-dead primitive tribes — when so much everyday experience seems to prove the contrary."

Other essays include "Questions and Answers About Anarchism", "The 'Necessity' of the State" by Kirkpatrick Sale, "Let Our Mothers Show the Way", "Anarchomusicology and Participation", "The Abolition of Work" by Bob Black, "Anarchist Perspective on Film", and "The Habit of Direct Action".

AK Press; $19.95
1996; softcover; 389 pp
1-873176-88-0

This is a fascinating account of a little-known aspect of history that teaches important lessons about freedom and government. The general subject is the Muslim corsairs of the Barbary coast, who ransacked European ships from the sixteenth through nineteenth centuries. Most of the book focuses on the Republic of Salé, a group of three cities in what is now Morocco) that throughout most of the 1600s was governed by and for the corsairs. (A corsair is a privateer who attacks ships of other countries in order to bring the booty back to the corsair's "sponsoring" country, in this case Salé. Pirates, by contrast, attack ships in order to keep all the booty for themselves.) The last chapter briefly examines four pirate utopias, which were basically anarchic freezones based partly on individualism and partly on co-operation.

Autonomedia; $8
1996; paperback; 208 pp
illus; 1-57027-024-4

REINVENTING ANARCHY, AGAIN
edited by Howard J. Ehrlich

Reinventing Anarchy, Again is a follow-up to the successful and influential *Reinventing Anarchy*. These 34 essays were all written by living, practising anarchists and address current issues and problems, rather than focusing on the past. They are divided into sections on social organisation, work, art, anarchafeminism, self-liberation, tactics, and more.

These essays aren't afraid to dream big, critique intensely, and question the anarchist status quo. David Bouchier gives a particularly good showing with "Hard Questions for Social Anarchists". While the notion of a society run

WHAT IS SITUATIONISM? A READER
edited by Stewart Home

These eleven essays offer facts, thoughts, and criticism regarding the avant-garde "intellectual terrorist" movement Situationism. Includes "The Realization and Suppression of Situationism", "The Situationist International: A Case of Spectacular Neglect", "Orgone Addicts: Wilhelm Reich versus the Situationists", and "The Situationist Legacy".

AK Press; $14.95, £9.95
1996; softcover; 203 pp
illus; 1-873176-13-9

1936
The Spanish Revolution
by The Ex

This snappy little hardcover is a visual record of one of the most important moments in the history of the struggle for freedom — the Spanish Revolution. In 1936, extreme right-wing elements in Spain — led by Francisco Franco and backed by the military — ignited a civil war by trying to grab power from the left-wing government. While this war was raging, a revolution took place within the country. Millions of workers, farmers, and peasants put anarchist principles into action to a degree that is unequalled in the twentieth century. They collectively ran factories, farms, villages, and even whole cities. The movement was crushed by 1939, and the Fascists seized the country, but this brief, shining moment is looked upon as proof that anarchism's voluntary collectivism can work on a large scale.

Well over 100 photographs from this tumultuous time

show everything from the workers barricading the streets in Barcelona and getting into armed confrontation with the military on July 19, 1936, to the bitter end in early 1939 — farmers fleeing advancing Fascists, bodies in morgues, and Spanish refugees in French concentration camps. In between these points, we see workers in the various factories and farms, day-to-day life on the street and in the countryside, destruction of churches (the Catholic church was seen as an enemy of the people and, in fact, the Pope openly supported the Fascist take-over), seized cars being converted to armoured vehicles, male and female members of the anarchist militias fighting on the front, and the releasing of all prisoners from jails. Bilingual (Spanish and English) captions and introductions to chapters shed further light on this important period.

Packaged with *1936* are two 3-inch CDs by the Ex, "everyone's favourite anarchist-art-agitators". Each CD contains an original Ex composition ("They Shall Not Pass" and "People Again") and a performance of a Spanish anarchist song ("El Tren Blindado" and "Ay Carmela").

AK Press and Allied Recordings; $25
1997; small hardcover, two 3" CDs; 140 pp
heavily illus; 1-873176-01-5

HAKIM BEY

IMMEDIATISM

by Hakim Bey

When I reviewed Hakim Bey's first book, *T.A.Z.*, in *Outposts* [p 30], I'm afraid I didn't make it very clear how important and inspiring it is. That collection of essays contains some of the most stirring writings on freedom and personal liberation to be published in a long time. If you don't own *T.A.Z.*, I suggest you immediately shell out seven bucks and get it from the publisher, Autonomedia, or from AK Distribution, Loompanics, or Autoneme (see Appendix A).

You should especially get *T.A.Z.* if you haven't yet read any of Bey's writings, because reading *Immediatism* first won't convey to you the surging power of his ideas. I guess *Immediatism* could be considered as another example of the dreaded sophomore slump. It's not that it isn't a great book that's very worth having, it just doesn't live up to its predecessor. While reading *T.A.Z.* I cop an incredible buzz that just isn't there with *Immediatism*. [Note: *Immediatism* was previously published as *Radio Sermonettes*.]

Immediatism, as explained in the title essay of the book, is the name Bey has given to a new "movement". "Immediatism is not a movement in the sense of an aesthetic programme. It depends on situation, not style or content, message or School." The main concern of Immediatism is that, "All experience is mediated — by the mechanisms of

Manning the barricades in Barcelona. *1936*.

sense perception, mentation, language, etc. — & certainly all art consists of some further mediation of experience." However, some experiences are more mediated than others. TV is more mediated than reading, which is more mediated than sex. The more directly you are involved in an experience, the less mediated it is.

Bey proposes Immediatism as a way in which to overcome as much as possible the alienation brought on by the media and the arts. "It may take the form of any kind of creative play which can be performed by two or more people, by & for themselves, face-to-face & together." At an Immediatist event, "All spectators must also be performers. All expenses are to be shared, & all products which may result from the play are also to be shared by the participants only (who may keep them or bestow them as gifts, but should not sell them). The best games will make little or no use of obvious forms of mediation such as photography, recording, printing, etc., but will tend toward immediate techniques involving physical presence, direct communication, & the senses." Throughout the rest of the essay and the book, Bey gives concrete ideas for Immediatist happenings.

He also mourns the death of art. "Everything delicate & beautiful, from Surrealism to Break-dancing, ends up as fodder for McDeath's ads; 15 minutes later all the magic has been sucked out, & the art itself is dead as a dried locust." But the media isn't just killing art, it's killing us. "'They' speak, you listen — & therefore turn in upon yourself in a spiral of loneliness, distraction, depression, & spiritual death."

Hopefully, if we put the ideas in *Immediatism* into practice, we can stop this malaise of our individual and collective souls. But Bey cautions that his book is intended as fodder for your own experiments, not some sort of rigid blueprint/ manifesto. "Above all, it does not pretend to know 'what must be done' — the delusion of would-be commissars and gurus. It wants no disciples — it would prefer to be burned — immolation not emulation! In fact it has no interest in 'dialogue' at all, and would prefer rather to attract co-conspirators than readers."

AK Press; $7
1992, 1994; softcover; 59 pp
illus; 1-873176-42-2

MILLENNIUM
by Hakim Bey

The newest book from Hakim Bey contains four essays and an interview. In his interview, Bey discusses the new outlook he has reached since writing the essays that formed his first two books: "… in TAZ and the Radio Sermonettes I was really proposing a third position, a position that was neither capitalism nor Communism. This is basically, you could say, something that all anarchist philosophy does. In this period I was telling it in my own way. It's a neither/nor position. It's a third position. Now, however, when you come to think about it, there are not two worlds any more or two possibilities or two contending opposing forces. There is in fact only one world, and that's the world of global capital. The world order, the world market, too-late capitalism, whatever you wanna call it, is now alone and triumphant. It's determinedly triumphant. It knows it's the winner although really it's only the winner by default, I think. And it tends to transform the world in its image. And that image, of course, is a monoculture based on Hollywood, on Disney, on commodities, on the destruction of the environment in every sense, from trees to imaginations, and the turning of all that into commodity, the turning of all that into money and the turning of money itself into a gnostic phantom-like experience which exists outside the world somewhere in a mysterious sphere of its own where money circulates, never descends, never reaches you and me. So what we're looking at is one single world. Obviously this one single world is not going to go without its revolution, it's not going to go without its opposition. And in fact it's around the word revolution that my thoughts are circulating now, because it seems to me that anarchists and anti-authoritarians in general can no longer occupy this third position; because how can you occupy a third position when there is no longer a second position?"

In the longest essay, "Millennium", Bey elaborates on this idea, paying particular attention to the phenomenon of money and the control it has over the world. Perhaps the most succinct expression of Bey's new thoughts appears on page thirty-six: "The global machinery will never fall ripely into the hands of the insurgent masses, nor will its single Eye pass to the people (as if to one of the three blind Fates); there will be no transition, smooth or bumpy, between Capitalism & some economic utopia, some miraculous salvation for the unified consciousness of post-Enlightenment rationalism & universal culture (with cosy corners for eccentric survivals & touristic bliss) — no Social Democracy taking over the controls in the name of the people. The 'money-power' (as the old agrarians called it) is not in the power of an elite (whether conspiratorial or sociological) — rather the elite is in the power of money, like the hired human lackeys of some sci-fi AI entity in cyberspace. Money-power is the global machinery — it can only be dismantled, not inherited."

The other essays continue in more or less the same direction, critiquing money/Capital/State and imagining how a revolution might take place. This time around, Bey is focusing less on liberation of the self (a practice that has drawn criticism) and more on societal rebellion. "In the present we

"To the Earth warrior, a redwood is more sacred than a religious icon, a species of bird or butterfly is of more value than the crown jewels of a nation…" *Earthforce!*

are faced with the monumental task of constructing an anti-Capitalist resistance movement out of the shattered remnants of radicalism, some glue, some tissue paper, & some hot rhetoric. We can no longer afford the luxury of ignoring politics… I'd like to believe that revolution could be a non-violent 'war for peace' — but like a good scout, one should be prepared."

Autonomedia; $7
1996; paperback; 102 pp
1-57027-045-7

T.A.Z. CD
by Hakim Bey

In this spoken word recording, Hakim Bey reads six of his essays — four from *T.A.Z.* and two from *Immediatism* — over a musical background. The album starts with one of my favourites, "Chaos". Accompanied by Asian percussion, floating wind instruments, and indigenous chanting, Bey informs us: "Avatars of chaos act as spies, saboteurs, criminals of amour fou, neither selfless nor selfish, accessible as children, mannered as barbarians, chafed with obsessions, unemployed, sensually deranged, wolfangels, mirrors for contemplation, eyes like flowers, pirates of all sign & meanings."

Light, spacey keyboards play a happy tune while Bey reads "Amour Fou" (which literally translates as "intoxicated by forbidden love"). "AF is always illegal, whether it's disguised as a marriage or a boyscout troop — always drunk, whether on the wine of its own secretions or the smoke of its own polymorphous virtues. It is not the derangement of the senses but rather their apotheosis — not the result of freedom but rather its precondition."

The final cut is Bey's most specifically socio-political. In "Boycott Cop Culture" he rails against the invasion of pop culture by police. In the days of Buster Keaton and Charlie Chaplin, at least the stories focused on the little guy, the everyman who managed to outwit the "ludicrous minions of a despised & irrelevant Order". Now, it has become *de rigeur* that cops are the heros of every movie and TV show that features them. "Thus the Cop Show has only three characters — victim, criminal, and policeperson — but the first two fail to be fully human — only the pig is real." During Bey's fulminations, sirens fade in and out. Besides being appropriate to the subject matter, they keep the listener tense and on edge, as if you're about to be pulled over and searched. Which is exactly the point.

The three other readings contained on *T.A.Z.* are the underground classic "Poetic Terrorism", "Immediatism", and "The Tong" (about a form of secret society).

Axiom (Island Records); CD: $16.97, tape: $10.98
1994; 53 min

RADICAL ENVIRONMENTALISM & ANIMAL LIBERATION

EARTHFORCE!
An Earth Warrior's Guide to Strategy
by Captain Paul Watson

Ecodefense: A Field Guide to Monkeywrenching [*Outposts* p 147] has become infamous for its detailed instructions and diagrams for protecting the earth in a variety of illegal ways: spiking trees, tearing down powerlines, destroying bulldozers, etc. *Earthforce* — though less well-known than *Ecodefense* — could be considered a companion volume. Written by Captain Paul Watson of the Sea Shepherd Conservation Society, it doesn't give hands-on instructions for sabotage, but instead presents philosophies and basic tactics that Earth Warriors need to adopt.

Watson's ideas are a combination of *The Art of War*, *The Book of Five Rings*, Machiavelli, Marshall McLuhan, and his own personal experiences. At first he lays down a basic philosophical foundation with an Eastern flavour: "Bend like the willow. Flow like the water. Be clear, be pure, and cherish your achievements. Build upon your strengths and be creative. Be focused but do not lose sight of what is around you." He then discusses the six basic roles that Earth warriors may choose — healer, communicator, artist, infiltrator, catalyst, and shaman.

The last two-thirds of the book delves into strategies for those who risk all in their activities. Although Watson is concerned with Earth warriors, his rules apply equally to any individuals and groups engaged in illegal activities for a higher purpose. "If a confrontation lasts too long, your strength will be diminished... Wear down the enemy with hit and run tactics if you find that victory cannot be swift and decisive."

Watson illustrates many of the points he makes with examples of his own daring adventures. For example, when discussing bluffing, he relates how he kept a Canadian sealing fleet from departing by claiming he would ram the first ship to leave the harbour. Another time, Watson and two crew members were in a small boat on the Siberian coast, when two Soviet soldiers aimed rifles at them. On Watson's orders, the crew waved and smiled at the soldiers, confusing them so much that they didn't shoot. This is an example of being unpredictable.

Picking the people with whom you engage in stealthy activity is very important. Never work with someone you haven't known for at least seven years. Never work with a spouse or lover, because if the relationship sours, you're wide open for getting shafted.

If you get caught, there are some rules to remember: don't talk, don't sign anything, and don't admit anything. "If arrested, remember this advice: the authorities are not your friends. They are out to screw you, to put you away, to mess you up."

Watson also has some hard-edged, practical advice for using the media to your advantage. "Without visuals, there is no story on television." "Always talk in sound bites. Keep it simple. Do not clarify. Never overestimate the intelligence of the viewer, the listener or the reader." "Ignore the question put to you if it does not serve your purpose."

Here are some more words of wisdom from the Cap'n:

☞ "To the Earth warrior, a redwood is more sacred than a religious icon, a species of bird or butterfly is of more value than the crown jewels of a nation, and the survival of a species of cacti is more important than the survival of monuments to human conceit like the pyramids."

☞ "Monkey-wrench a bulldozer and they call you a vandal. Spike a tree and they will call you a terrorist. Liberate a coyote from a trap and they will call you a thief. Yet if a human destroys the wonders of creation, the beauty of the natural world, the anthropocentric society calls such people loggers, miners, developers, engineers, and businessmen."

☞ "You must be morally superior to your enemy... If you have and can hold the moral high ground, your followers will follow and your allies will support you, regardless of the risks, undaunted by danger."

☞ "Startled wild animals are the best sign of an approaching opposition."

☞ "The knowledge of the inevitability of your death coupled with your acceptance of death will allow you the freedom to proceed and to fight without fear."

Capt. Paul Watson; $13
1993; softcover; 118 pp
0-9616019-5-7

LIVE WILD OR DIE!

A no-bullshit, rage-filled tabloid promoting Luddism, environmental monkeywrenching, animal liberation, and other radical philosophies and activities. Put together in a hodgepodge style, *Live Wild or Die!* contains new and reprinted articles. One section in issue 5 has newspaper clippings about animals attacking humans (which the staff of *LWoD!* supports), and another section has articles on the misery of work. One of the more controversial pieces is called "Eco-Fuckers Hit List". Complete with bulletholes at the top of the page and an illustration of someone being knifed, it lists the addresses and phone numbers of around twenty corporations — such as Chevron, Exxon, and GM — and the home addresses and phone numbers of the CEOs/presidents of a dozen more corporations. Elsewhere, there's a picture of Clinton with the phrase, "He's no JFK…". Below that is an autopsy shot of Kennedy's body next to the phrase, "… but there's still time."

LWOD/PO Box 15032/Berkeley CA 94701

Single issue: $2

RESIST MUCH, OBEY LITTLE
Remembering Ed Abbey
edited by James R Hepworth & Gregory McNamee

As this anthology makes clear, "desert anarchist" Edward Abbey was a complex man. He cared deeply about the Southwest and was outraged by the political, corporate, and cultural forces that were destroying the land, yet he defied easy labels like environmentalist or left-winger. Some of his ideas and beliefs are generally considered "liberal" (such as his anger over the destruction of public lands). Others are generally considered "conservative" (such as closing the Mexican border to immigrants). Still others are considered radical or even terrorist (his novel *The Monkey Wrench Gang* inspired groups such as Earth First! to destroy bulldozers, tear down powerlines, and commit other illegal acts to save the land). But no matter what, Abbey spoke his mind.

This complexity and honesty is captured in *Resist Much, Obey Little* (the title is a Walt Whitman line which became Abbey's personal credo). Thirty-five people offer remembrances and interpretations of Abbey. Some, such as Wendell Berry, try to give a balanced overview of the man and his work, while others, such as Sam Hamill, serve up meditations on Abbey, and still others remember specific times with Abbey, such as when he and Barbara Kingsolver judged a fiction contest. In the end we see that "Cactus Ed" was filled with concerns, contradictions, and a zest for life. As Hammill puts it: "While every pseudo-eco-freak in the

Taking no prisoners. *Live Wild or Die!*

country is toasting tofu, he's off with a beer pissing vinegar into the fuel tank of a D-8 Cat. He cuts a singular trail, teetering on the brink of hypocrisy. He commits a good-natured heresy."

Sierra Club Books; $14
1996; softcover; 258 pp
0-87156-879-9

SEA SHEPHERD LOG

The Sea Shepherd Conservation Society was formed in 1977 by Captain Paul Watson, author of *Earthforce!* [above]. Its principal activity is not direct-mail fund-raising, petition-signing, or lobbying. No, the Sea Shepherds don't waste their time pushing paper — they go out on the high seas and forcibly stop the slaughter of whales, dolphins, seals, and other sea life. They occasionally will work to save wolves too.

In almost twenty years the Shepherds have sunk eight illegal whaling ships and a sealing ship, destroyed a whale processing plant, rammed Japanese and Taiwanese driftnetters, shut down dolphin hunts, and taken other direct action against killers of marine life. Their slick, partly colour magazine gives thrilling accounts of their daring feats and profiles the people in the Society.

The issue for the second and third quarters, 1994, documents in words and pictures one of the Shepherds' most important conflicts — their confrontation with the Norwegian Navy in neutral international waters. The Norwegians rammed the *Whales Forever*, fired upon it even though it's unarmed, and otherwise tried to arrest or kill the crew, whichever was easier. Luckily, the Shepherds escaped with no arrests, no injuries, and reparable damage to their ship. In a blatant Star Chamber proceeding, Norway tried Watson and a crew member *in absentia* (they weren't even notified of the trial!) and sentenced all of them to four months in prison. The Fall/Winter 1996 issue brings word, however, that Norway has dropped all charges against them.

This same issue has an article on efforts over the years to stop the killing of dolphins in order to catch tuna. As usual, the Shepherd's pull no punches, telling you exactly who has fought for the dolphins and who likes to pretend they have. The House and Senate introduced bills that would lift the embargo against tuna from Latin American fleets who switched to methods that kill less dolphins but still result in thousands of deaths. Furthermore, the bills would redefine the terms "dolphin safe", allowing tuna companies to label tuna from Latin America with that term. "Support for the passage of these two bills came from five of the six mainstream environmental organisations that had attended the meeting where the Panama Declaration was drafted. Greenpeace, the World Wildlife Fund, the Centre for Marine Conservation, the National Wildlife Federation and the Environmental Defence Fund decided to compromise with the tuna industry and with the Clinton administration to accept some dolphin mortality in return for a promise by the industry to be more sensitive to dolphin conservation. These groups, along with the Clinton/Gore Administration, insisted that this bill was needed to 'reward' Latin American countries for reducing dolphin mortality. Passage of this legislation was meant to reward those who kill dolphins and punish those companies in these nations that have taken measures to protect them. Not one of the groups bothered to consult their membership prior to making this decision." In 1996, the House bill passed, but luckily it was voted down in the Senate.

If you want to support the defence of marine wildlife by an uncompromising group that is willing to risk imprisonment and even death for its cause, contribute to the Sea Shepherds.

Sea Shepherd Conservation Society/PO Box 628/Venice CA 90294

WWW: www.seashepherd.org

4 issue sub (one year): included in contribution of $25 or more

LUDDISM

REBELS AGAINST THE FUTURE
The Luddites and Their War on the Industrial Revolution — Lessons for the Computer Age
by Kirkpatrick Sale

Rebels Against the Future is very similar to *Progress Without People*. They both examine the original Luddite uprising, look at the current state of neo-Luddism, and express support for anti-technological stances. However, Kirkpatrick Sales' retelling of the Luddites' brief machine-smashing history is longer and more detailed than in *Progress*.

He brings the debate into the information age by noting:

Norwegian warship rams the Sea Shepherd's unarmed ship in international waters. *Sea Shepherd Log*.

"The simple, overarching fact is that technology always has consequences, far-reaching consequences, usually more so than anyone can predict at the beginning, and this truth is exactly what lies at the heart of Luddism — and is the reason why in fact the name and idea lasted beyond its brief fifteen-month course… [T]here have been throughout these last two centuries, and there are today as perhaps never before, any number of serious minds that have come to see the point of the Luddite challenge, to ask questions about progress and its values, to wonder where the victory of unimpeded technology-for-profit has gotten us."

Sale is uneasy about the way information technology, biotechnology, molecular science, and other world-transforming technologies are being unquestioningly accepted by the majority of scientists and the general population. He offers stinging critiques of technology's alienating effects, its destruction of nature, its role as handmaiden of the government/military, its effect on labour, and the unpredictability of its future ramifications. After examining the words and deeds of neo-Luddites in the 1980s and 1990s, he closes with lessons that we can learn from the Luddites, such as "Technologies are never neutral, and some are harmful," and, "The nation-state, synergistically intertwined with industrialism, will always come to its aid and defence, making revolt futile and reform ineffectual."

Addison-Wesley; $13
1995; softcover; 320 pp
0-201-40718-3

S.E.T. FREE
The Newsletter Against Television
The Society for the Eradication of Television hates the boob tube for a number of reasons. Let me count the ways: 1) It is a colossal waste of time. 2) It desensitises viewers to violence. 3) It promotes illiteracy. 4) It turns people into glassy-eyed zombies who can't communicate well or think for themselves. 5) It turns people into overweight, out-of-shape couch potatoes with bad hearts. 6) It's a propaganda machine for the government, corporations, and other manipulators. 7) TV technology is used for violent purposes, such as "smart bombs". 8) The technology is also used for invasion of privacy through surveillance. 9) It is harmful to the environment. For example, roughly one million birds die

each year from crashing into TV towers. I'm sure there are other reasons SET hates TV, but these appear to be the major ones.

Their view is that TV is unredeemable. PBS, the Discovery Channel, nature shows, and other "positive programming" are just the "sugar coating on a poison pill". Despite the word "eradication" in their name, SET apparently is not in favour of forcibly destroying television as a whole (although some individual members apparently do take that radical stance). They will not smash anyone else's TV. "But we do encourage people to smash their own," says Charles Frink, the New England representative of SET. Members of the group do not watch or own televisions, and they educate people about the benefits of chucking their idiot boxes.

S.E.T. Free is the group's irregularly-published, four page newsletter. It contains articles and essays by members, reprints of articles about SET, and relevant statistics, quotes, and studies regarding TV's harmfulness. Membership in the Society — which includes a card and some information — is free. The newsletter is sent to people who make contributions, so send in a few bucks. Or give them the $40 or more per month you used to spend on cable.

Society for the Eradication of Television/PO Box 10491/Oakland CA 94610

THE UNABOMBER MANIFESTO
Industrial Society and Its Future
by FC

FC ("Freedom Club") claims to be a group of individuals. The authorities, on the other hand, claim that FC is actually one person, whom they call the Unabomber. Since the authorities had been unable for eighteen years to capture this person or persons and only arrested a suspect (Theodore Kaczynski) because his brother turned him in, I am not going to take their word for anything about this case. As *Psychotropedia* goes to press, Kaczynski is being tried, and — from what the media have said — it certainly looks like he'll be found guilty. A few people though, are questioning whether Kaczynski acted alone. Therefore, until we know more (if we ever do), I will be using the term FC and the pronoun "them" when referring to this situation.

FC's bombing campaign began in May 1978, when a bomb in a parcel at Northwestern Technological Institute exploded, injuring a university police officer. Since then, they have sent more than fifteen other mail bombs that have killed three people and wounded many more. Targets have included United Airlines President Percy Wood, computer science professors, the fabrication division of the Boeing Company, a psychology professor, a geneticist, an advertising executive, and a timber industry lobbyist. In letters sent to newspapers, FC claims to be a group of anarchists.

1995 proved to the Year of the Unabomber, as FC made various mail-bomb attacks and threats. It turns out that the group had written a long essay laying out their philosophy. They claimed that if it were published by a major media outlet, the killing would stop. After much hand-wringing, debating, and further demands and conditions by FC, the whole thing was published by the *Washington Post* on September 15, 1995. Other papers followed suit.

Supposedly, the whole bombing campaign had simply been a way to force people to listen to what FC had to say. In this way, it could be considered the most extreme publicity stunt ever devised. When it worked and the manifesto was released, it left thousands of other writers wondering, "Who do I have to blow (up) to get my manuscript published?"

This book is a reprinting of the entire essay in a corrected edition that patches up the omissions and mistakes found in the newspaper and Internet versions. What it all boils down to is that FC are actually extreme Luddites. Their complaint is that technology is destroying the human race. Their answer is to eliminate technology and the institutions that support it.

The Manifesto is fairly well-written. I was expecting a disjointed rant, but it is actually a competent — though not brilliant — piece of work. The problem is that its relentless critique of technology, while holding some degree of truth, is certainly nothing new. In paragraph 117 (all the paragraphs are numbered), FC writes: "In any technologically advanced society the individual's fate MUST depend on decisions that he personally cannot influence to any great extent. A technological society cannot be broken down into small, autonomous communities, because production depends on the co-operation of very large numbers of people and machines. Such a society MUST be highly organised and decisions HAVE TO be made that affect very large numbers of people. When a decision affects, say, a million people, then each of the affected individuals has, on the average, only a one-millionth share in making the decision." Paragraph 125 starts: "It is not possible to make a LASTING compromise between technology and freedom, because technology is by far the more powerful social force and continually encroaches on freedom through REPEATED compromises."

Not much separates this book from other neo-Luddite tracts, until you get to the proposals for changing things. FC calls for all-out revolution: "This is not to be a POLITICAL revolution. Its object will be to overthrow not governments but the economic and technological basis of the present society." Paragraph 166 gets specific: "Therefore two tasks confront those who hate the servitude to which the industrial system is reducing the human race. First, we must work to heighten the social stresses within the system so as to increase the likelihood that it will break down or be weakened sufficiently so that a revolution against it becomes possible. Second, it is necessary to develop and propagate an ideology that opposes technology and the industrial society if and when the system becomes sufficiently weakened. And such an ideology will help assure that, if and when industrial society breaks down, its remnants will be smashed beyond repair, so that the system cannot be reconstituted. The factories should be destroyed, technical books burned, etc."

The corrected, "preferred" version of the Manifesto is also available on the Web at http://www.paranoia.com/coe/resources/fc/unabe2.html. I'm sure FC just *love* that.

Jolly Roger Press; $9.95
1995; softcover; 90 pp
0-9634205-2-6

THE MILITIA/ PATRIOT MOVEMENT

CARL KLANG'S MUSIC

Carl Klang provides the soundtrack for the militia/patriot movement. With a pleasing voice and acoustic accompaniment, he sings the concerns and viewpoints of people, particularly fundamentalist Christians, who distrust the federal government.

His first cassette, *Warning: It's Dangerous to Be Right When the Government Is Wrong* ($12), was released in 1993. The title track opens with ominous piano chords and changes into a bouncy, quasi-rockabilly number. Klang sings about the illegality of the income tax and the persecution of people who refuse to pay it. In the chorus, he warns: "It's dangerous to be right when the government is wrong/They'll trample down your rights as they break into your home". The lyrics of the song shift when Klang states that eventually the people are going to realise that income tax is fraudulent and will "rout you vipers out by God". The chorus becomes: "Then it's gonna be dangerous 'cause we're right and the government is wrong/We'll trample down their rights as we break into their homes". Among the other five songs are "Wheresoever Eagles Gather (The Ballad of Randy Weaver)", "Jesus The Way and The Truth and The Life", and "Paper Money".

Watch Out for Martial Law (1994, $12) contains nine tracks. "Stars and Stripes (Upside-Down)" is an update of the national anthem. "O say can you see the stars and stripes upside down?/It means the people are asleep as foreign powers take control." "Leave Our Guns Alone" uses hard-edged bass, drums, and vocals to deliver a warning to those who want to ban guns. "So if they ever try to legislate/Send the troops to confiscate/Before the dirty deed gets done/Somebody's blood on down the street might run/If they ever try to come and take my gun". Other cuts include "The Federal Reserve Isn't Federal At All", "Why the Bankers Keep Us Dumb", and "Seventeen Little Children".

The next year, *America, America* ($12) was released. In "Evil, Filthy, Rotten Conspiracy", Klang sings in semi-hushed tones: "Now have you seen the flying saucers/Or some of them black helicopters/Flying low down over my back yard recently/See them foreign troops in ninja suits/Leavin' imprints of their combat boots". "US Citizen" is a humorous take-off on the 1960s song "Secret Agent Man". "There's a man who leads a life of bondage/To the federal government he pays his homage/Seems the more he tries to make, the more they tax and take/Odds are he won't live to pay his mortgage".

"Seventeen Little Children" (1993, $8) is a cassingle containing Klang's piano and strings ballad to the children who died at Waco. "In a church they call the Waco compound/back in April '93/Seventeen little children/All so helpless and small/Died a senseless death of gas and flames". Richard Palmquist, the general manager of a California radio station, provides an unofficial version of events at Waco on side two. The American Justice Federation sells a video of "Seventeen Little Children" called *Forgive Us, We Didn't Know* ($19.95) [see Appendix B for their address].

Carl Klang; see text for prices
1993-5; cassette tapes

CENTER FOR ACTION NEWSLETTER

Colonel Bo Gritz is America's most decorated Green Beret and the real-life model for Rambo. But he's not as well-liked by the government as you might imagine. He lost a few friends when he claimed that he has first-hand knowledge that American intelligence is engaged in drug smuggling in Southeast Asia and that the US knowingly deserted Vietnam POWs, some of whom may still be alive.

Gritz is now one of the movers and shakers in the patriot movement. He has set up three communities — Almost Heaven, Shenandoah, and Woodland Acres — in Idaho, where people who foresee a New World Order tyranny and Armageddon can gather together for mutual protection and support. The *Center for Action Newsletter* contains eleven pages of news and views from the Colonel on a range of topics, such as state citizenship, land patents, income tax, precious metals, abortion, and more.

Nine pages of the newsletter form a catalogue for Gritz's training programme known as S.P.I.K.E. — Specially Prepared Individuals for Key Events. The purpose is to teach people how to be totally self-sufficient and handle any cataclysmic situation, whether natural disaster, nuclear attack, or government crackdown. S.P.I.K.E. is taught either by Gritz in person or through videos. The overall course is taught in ten phases, and by the time you finish, Gritz claims you will be as knowledgeable as a Delta Force member. Among the specific subjects that are taught: self-defence, emergency medicine, lock-picking, marksmanship, homeopathic medicine, hostage situations, child birthing, caching, hunting and trapping, greenhouse gardening, and more.

For each phase, you can also purchase items that are specifically geared towards what you're learning. Items include hair brush dagger, gas mask, compass, lock-pick set, gun scopes, homeopathic items, survival kits, herbs, midwifery kit, and night vision goggles.

Center for Action - Idaho/c/o HC 11 Box 307/Kamiah Idaho PZ 83536
WWW: www.bogritz.com
Twelve issue sub (one year): $30; Overseas: $48; Others: $36

MILITIA OF MONTANA CATALOGUE

The Militia of Montana (MOM) is one of the most important and influential of the militia organisations. Their catalogue contains a large number of hard-to-find videos, books, and audiotapes put out by MOM and others. Videos include *In-*

vasion & Betrayal, The Bomb in Oklahoma, The Death of Vince Foster, Equipping for the New World Order, Militia of Montana: What Is It?, Ruby Creek Massacre: The Randy Weaver Story, Janet (Butch) Reno, Waco Incident, and Reclaiming Our Public Lands Conference. Books include Weather Control (Modification), Blue Print for Survival, Big Sister Is Watching You, and material on survival and military tactics. They also offer chemical suits, gas masks, MOM tee shirts, and more. Pretty indispensable if you're into militias for whatever reasons.

MOM/c/o PO Box 1486/Noxon MT 59853
WWW: www.logoplex.com/resources/mom/
Catalogue: send a dollar or two in cash

OPERATION VAMPIRE KILLER 2000
American Police Action Plan for Stopping World Government Rule
by Police Against the New World Order

The police who wrote this book believe that the overthrow of the United States and the creation of a one-world government are imminent, and they are calling on their colleagues to help stop it by "using every lawful means available". Since the police have sworn to protect the people and the republic, it is their duty to fight against the internationalists' plan to turn US citizens into world citizens. "VERY SOON, IF WE DO NOT STOP THESE WORLD GOVERNMENT PROPONENTS, AND INSTALL IN PLACES OF LEADERSHIP HONOURABLE MEN AND WOMEN, ALL MILITARY, NATIONAL GUARDSMEN AND OFFICERS OF THE LAW WILL BE USED AS THE 'ENFORCEMENT ARM' TO GUARANTEE A FULL COMPLEMENT OF 'VOLUNTEERS' FOR THESE IMPERIALISTS' 'PEACEFUL' SOCIALIST GLOBAL SOCIETY."

Operation explores the plan of globalists, bankers, communists, United Nations bigwigs, Satanists, psychiatrists, and others as they themselves have expressed it. "GEORGE BUSH, New York 1991, 'My vision of a NEW WORLD ORDER foresees a United Nations with a revitalised peacekeeping function.' And one more classic quote from our traitor President: 'It is the SACRED principles enshrined in the UN Charter to which we will henceforth pledge our allegiance.' — UN Building, February 1, 1992."

There are three scenarios that the globalists may use to frighten the people of the US and the rest of the world into accepting martial law — a race war, the bogus threat of ecological collapse, or the bogus threat of an invasion of aliens from space. Police and military personnel will be ordered to disarm the civilian population. They may feel obligated to comply because they are enforcers of law. "As many officers know, that has been the lame excuse offered by the People's 'Protectors' in all the Marxist nations of the world during the last 75 years of totalitarian rule. Fine, dedicated, HIGHLY PATRIOTIC (and brainwashed) police officers by the millions UPHELD THE 'LAW' in these and other countries, and went on to round up and execute 170 million of their own countrymen because they were told by their leaders that 'to save their nation' they must do these things."

Operation Vampire Killer 2000 urges cops to spread the word about the coming take-over and actively resist it. Police Against the New World Order also puts out a sixteen-page newsletter, AID & ABET, which offers further information about the UN, militias, etc. (Single issue: $3. Six issue sub: $20, Can/Mex: $25, Others: $30.) Operation is anti-copyrighted and available at several places on the Web, including www.hevanet.com/nitehawk/nwo48.html.

PATNWO; $7
1992; stapled-bound oversized softcover; 76 pp
heavily illus; no ISBN

NAZISM AND THE HOLOCAUST

ASSASSINS OF MEMORY
Essays on the Denial of the Holocaust
by Pierre Vidal-Naquet

Five essays that refute the charges of Holocaust revisionism, try to explain why this revisionism has occurred, and examine some revisionists. The author, a French classicist, also looks at larger themes, such as the struggle to keep history from being falsified and the tendency of the guardians of orthodox history to become so ideological that revisionism develops as a backlash.

Columbia University Press; $17
1994; softcover; 222 pp
0-231-07459-X

BEST WITNESS
The Mel Mermelstein Affair and the Triumph of Historical Revisionism
by Michael Collins Piper

Published by the leading torchbearer of Holocaust revisionism (the theory that the Holocaust wasn't nearly as destructive as is generally believed), Best Witness tells the story of two trials concerning the Institute for Historical Review (IHR) and Mel Mermelstein, a Holocaust survivor who has written and lectured widely on his experiences. According to the book, this is what happened: The IHR offered a $50,000 reward to anyone who could produce evidence that Jews had been gassed at Auschwitz. Mermelstein claimed that his own experiences constituted that proof. Before the IHR could rule on his claims, Mermelstein sued them for $1 million. The IHR settled out of court, paying him $90,000 and apologising for upsetting him.

During a subsequent radio interview, Mermelstein called the settlement a "judgement" and claimed that the IHR had admitted (as part of the settlement/judgement) that he was right. The IHR sued him for libel but dropped their case be-

A German cuts off a Jew's beard in Warsaw in 1939, while others look on laughing. *Hitler's Willing Executioners.*

fore it went to court. Mermelstein sued back, claiming that the IHR's suit against him was a groundless one meant simply to harass him and that the IHR had defamed him in their newsletter. He was asking for $11 million in damages. After a heated trial, the Jewish judge ruled that the IHR had had reasonable grounds for their libel suit, so Mermelstein's countersuit claiming malicious prosecution was thrown out. Then Mermelstein's lawyers dropped the second main part of the suit — the claim of libel — and the case was closed. Mermelstein appealed the judge's ruling, but it was upheld by the California Court of Appeals.

Center for Historical Review (Liberty Library); $10
1994; softcover; 256 pp
0-935036-48-2

HITLER AND THE OCCULT
by Ken Anderson

Many tales concerning dark occult forces surround Adolf Hitler and the Nazis. In this book, Ken Anderson takes a hard look at them and finds that they are — for the most part — very lacking in evidence. He spends a lot of time on the theory that Hitler drew his power from the Holy Lance (see *The Spear of Destiny* in the Unexplained chapter), concluding that it is very improbable. However, Anderson does admit that the mysterious Thule Society did play some role in Hitler's rise to power, "although exactly how much of a role remains open to debate." Also covered are the origins of the swastika, the degree of Hitler's belief in astrology, the Nazis' propagandistic use of Nostradamus, Hitler's "inner voice" that he claimed guided him, and more.

Prometheus Books; $26.95
1995; hardcover; 244 pp
illus; 0-87975-973-9

HITLER'S WILLING EXECUTIONERS
Ordinary Germans and the Holocaust
by Daniel Jonah Goldhagen

Just how could the Nazi regime have orchestrated the deaths of six million Jews? It would take quite an extensive operation to engage in such wholesale slaughter, yet many historians contend that it was carried out by Hitler, the Nazi Party elite, and the SS, without the knowledge of the German population. Harvard professor Daniel Goldhagen completely rejects this notion, claiming that most Germans knew about the Holocaust and that as many as half a million "ordinary" Germans (i.e., regular citizens not involved in the Nazi Party apparatus) helped carry out the genocide. Not only that, but they did it willingly and gladly.

He counters the arguments that even if some ordinary German citizens helped with the Holocaust, they did it out of fear of their own well-being. Goldhagen believes that Germans had been inculcated with hatred of Jews for centuries. Starting in the 1800s, there arose in Germany a philosophy of "eliminationist anti-Semitism", which argued that the Jews must be destroyed. By the time the Nazis assumed power in 1933, this idea was such a part of the German psyche, that the country was ready to gleefully participate in the butchering of Jewish people.

Among Goldhagen's evidence is the extreme viciousness that tormentors displayed towards their victims. Before the Jews were killed, they were often brutalised and degraded. This would be unnecessary if the goal was simply to get rid of Jews. Germans, the author argues, also wanted to see them suffer. Using graphic details and grim pictures, he shows us how vicious and inhumane this treatment was. It also made very little sense. Even when it was apparent that the war had been lost, many German guards forced Jews to go on death marches. During these long treks, the prisoners were starved, savagely beaten, and usually killed. Rather than try to escape the encroaching Allied forces, the Germans stuck around to torture and kill these Jews. At one point, orders came down from Himmler himself expressly forbidding the killing of any more Jews, yet the slaughter didn't stop. The guards ignored direct orders, self-preservation, and, of course, human decency, just so they could torment their victims a while longer.

Naturally, *Hitler's Willing Executioners* has stirred up a good amount of controversy. The media reported that some people were calling Goldhagen's theory "racist" towards Germans, which I found hard to understand since I didn't think that people born in Germany constituted a separate race. Some fellow historians opined that his explanations are too simplistic and that he failed to fully explore anti-Semitism in other European countries and the Nazis' execution of seven million non-Jews, including Gypsies, the disabled, and gays and lesbians. Goldhagen touched such a nerve that a book, *Hyping The Holocaust: Scholars from 5 Nations Answer Goldhagen's Hitler's Willing Executioners* edited by Franklin H. Littell (Merion Westfield Press International, 1997), was published in response.

Whether it's completely right or not, this book has definitely helped to add another angle to the debate over the

Holocaust.

Vintage Books (Random House); $16
1996; softcover; 634 pp
illus; 0-679-77268-5

THE MEN WITH THE PINK TRIANGLE
The True, Life-and-Death Story of Homosexuals in the Nazi Death Camps
by Heinz Heger

Most of the time when the Holocaust is discussed, we hear about the six million Jewish people who were killed. What is seldom mentioned is that Hitler and his group also orchestrated the deaths of seven million other people, including Gypsies, the disabled, petty criminals, political subversives, and gays and lesbians. The generally-acknowledged estimate is that ten to fifteen thousand gay men were imprisoned in concentration camps on the basis of their sexuality. Far fewer lesbians were consciously imprisoned. Women were often nabbed for prostitution, promiscuity, or some other half-baked reason.

To differentiate among the inmates at the camps, the Nazis made gay men wear pink triangles. Of course, this symbol has been appropriated by the gay and lesbian movement, which has turned it into a symbol of pride.

Heinz Heger was a gay prisoner of the Nazis, and he is one of the very few to speak out about such persecution. Gays often received the harshest treatment at the camps, being given the hardest work and used first for medical experiments. They were segregated from the other prisoners and were looked down upon and even brutalised by the rest of the inmates. "We were to remain isolated as the damnedest of the damned, the camp's 'shitty queers,' condemned to liquidation and helpless prey to all the torments inflicted by the SS and the Capos."

Heger shows the hypocrisy of attitudes towards gays throughout the book. When he first went to a regular prison, prior to being sent to a camp, he was locked in a cell with two crooks. They were married men, and constantly called Heger a filthy queer, said that he was subhuman, etc. Yet these two men propositioned Heger and had sex with each other. "But in their view — the view of 'normal' people — this was only an emergency outlet, with nothing queer about it."

From 1939 to 1945, Heger lived in the camps. His stories of the atrocities and brutality perpetrated by the Germans is almost unreadable. But read it anyway, so you can vicariously experience the depths to which the human race can sink.

Alyson Publications; $9.95
1980; softcover; 120 pp
1-55583-006-4

SALON
A Journal of Aesthetics #22

Holocaust revisionism is the name given to a cluster of theories contending that what is generally assumed to be the truth about the Holocaust is wrong. A tiny number of revisionists say that the Holocaust didn't happen at all, but most of them say that, yes, some terrible things did happen, but 1) there was no master plan to eliminate the Jews and 2) the number of deaths has been grossly exaggerated. Pat Hartman, editor of Salon [see the main review in the Grab Bag chapter] became intrigued by Holocaust revisionism when she learned that she was not supposed to be intrigued by it. "The Holocaust is the sacred cow with which even the hardiest iconoclasts don't want to have an eyeball to eyeball confrontation. The reverential hands-off attitude has made the issue, in the words of Michael R. Marrus, 'held not subject to the wide-ranging investigation, discussion, and debate carried on with other aspects of the recent past,' and 'unapproachable for ordinary analysts of the human record.'"

Hartman spent the better part of a year immersing herself in material about the Holocaust, written from both orthodox and revisionist viewpoints. The vast majority of the 148 pages of this issue of Salon are devoted to what she found, making this a veritable book on the subject. She approached it with a curious mind not guided by any ideology, determined to hear what everyone has to say. Her essays provide a thoughtful overview of all aspects of Holocaust revisionism.

As far as I could glean from this sizeable amount of material, Hartman's end analysis is still that the Holocaust did happen, although she concedes that the revisionists may be right about "some details" (although she doesn't specifically name them). She believes that the revisionists are mostly hatemongers, but opines that there probably are some truth-seekers among them. Overall, Hartman notes, "Holocaust revisionism attracts anti-Semites the way shit attracts flies." However, she is not afraid to point out inconsistencies and arrogance in the Holocaust orthodoxy.

Right after World War II, it was claimed that 22 concentration camps had gas chambers. Mainstream, "establishment" historians now concur that only six camps had chambers. Yet this is not considered revisionism. "Right after the war, signs were put up at Dachau claiming that 238,000 people had been gassed and cremated there. Some time later the signs were removed, and today the official, mainstream version of history is that 32,000 died there over a 13-year span. Does that make the director of the Dachau camp museum a 'revisionist?'"

Hartman is upset over the forces that are out to quash revisionism by whatever means necessary. In France, Austria, Germany, and Israel it's outright illegal to question Holocaust orthodoxy. Many other countries — including Canada and Australia — have severe restrictions on this line of thought. Even in the US, revisionists are constantly threatened, harassed, and assaulted.

Other topics Hartman covers include who the revisionists are, what's in it for them, evidence of the Holocaust, the most "inventive" revisionist arguments, trying to determine statistics, the gas chambers debate, Anne Frank's diary, Holocaust eyewitnesses and survivors, the wildly divergent groups who don't like the Holocaust Museum, Nazi apologists, and much, much more. Several contributors — including a Jewish revisionist — also give their input.

For anyone who would like to get a large, sweeping view of Holocaust revisionism and what its various proponents and opponents believe should get this issue of *Salon*.

Pat Hartman/305 W Magnolia, Ste 386/Fort Collins CO 80521
Single issue: $5

MISCELLANEOUS

20 YEARS ON THE MOVE
by MOVE

During the early 1970s in Philadelphia, an African American man named John Africa started an organisation called MOVE. This booklet tells the story, in words and photographs, of this unusual group of people, who have met with brutal repression and attempted extermination. Their plight bears many eerie parallels to that of the Branch Davidians in Waco. Keep in mind that *20 Years on the MOVE* was written by MOVE members, so it is very sympathetic. Nonetheless, it does give a side of the story that is conspicuously absent from mainstream accounts (with the exception of jailed reporter Mumia Abu-Jamal. See *Live from Death Row* in the Freedom chapter).

Most members of this predominantly — but not completely — African American group change their last names to "Africa", wear dreadlocks, and adopt an extreme philosophy of living in harmony with nature. MOVE fiercely opposes the exploitation and destruction of the environment, people, and animals. They are vegetarians who recycle their garbage and compost their human waste. It's been claimed that they don't bathe or wash their clothes, but they deny these charges. "After adopting MOVE's way of natural living, many individuals overcame past problems of drug addiction, physical disabilities, infertility and alcoholism." MOVE also performed lots of charitable deeds and preached the right to be left alone. They are often labelled as a "cult", which is usually just society's name for any group of people who have the same beliefs and live together.

MOVE took loud political stands against the oppressive, racist government of Philly and earned the wrath of the city's officials and the police. One of their tactics was to use profanity during speeches, which endeared them to the authorities even less. Neighbours complained about the smell from MOVE's garbage and waste and the political rants they broadcast over loudspeakers. Clashes between cops and MOVE became commonplace and brutal. In May 1985, MOVE was having a loud celebration at the big Victorian house that served as its headquarters. Neighbours got annoyed, and the cops raided the place. They started busting heads and in the process killed a three-week-old baby, Life Africa.

After this, MOVE became much more militant. They armed themselves and declared that force from the authorities would be met with equal force. It wasn't illegal for the

Unarmed MOVE member surrenders peacefully, as cops proceed to beat him unconscious. *20 Years on the MOVE.*

group to own guns, so the city managed to dig up some charges to arrest members. Not wanting to make a raid, the police waited for MOVErs to come out, but very few did. According to Pennsylvania law, an arrest warrant must be acted upon in 180 days or else a request for an extension must be filed within the same period. The District Attorney's office filed the request late, which made it void. Amazingly, the court clerks accepted it and a judge approved the technically nullified extension.

To put the squeeze on MOVE, mayor Frank Rizzo — an ex-police chief with racist and authoritarian beliefs — ordered the house to be blockaded. Water was shut off and no food was allowed in to the men, women (some of them pregnant), children, and animals. After two months, MOVE negotiated an agreement. Naturally, the government broke the agreement in numerous ways.

Finally, after MOVE members failed to appear in court over alleged housing code violations, Rizzo ordered an all-out military assault of the MOVE house. The house was flooded and tear-gassed, while 20 officers raided it. Someone fired a shot and the police opened fire. (According to several witnesses, including KYW reporter Paul Bennet, who is now the editor of the *Philadelphia Tribune*, the shot came from across the street from the MOVE house.) One officer, James Ramp, was killed. The MOVE members came out peaceably. Delbert Africa surrendered unarmed with his hands up. Four policemen attacked him and savagely beat him into unconsciousness. Like the Rodney King beating, this act of brutality was captured on video (this time by a news crew). Despite this, a judge acquitted all the officers. *20 Years* contains three pictures of the cops — one of them smiling gleefully — bludgeoning, kicking, and stomping the shit out of Africa.

In a familiar turn of events, the authorities immediately bulldozed the MOVE house, preventing any evidence from being collected. Although Officer Ramp had been shot one time, a judge found *nine* MOVE members guilty of the murder. MOVE denies that they fired a single shot during the siege.

Over the next few years, relations between the city/police and MOVE were as bad as they ever were. Finally, on May 13, 1985, another raid on the group's headquarters was launched, with the police employing automatic weapons and explosives. When that didn't work, someone ordered a bomb to be dropped on the house, making Philadelphia the only American city to be bombed from the air. The highly flammable gel in the bomb caused a fire, which was allowed to rage for 30 minutes before an attempt was made to stop it. (Although it's not reported in this booklet, a *Newsweek* article notes that officials originally said that they kept the fire fighters back out of concern for their safety. But later they actually admitted that they allowed the fire to continue so they would have a hole through which they could pour teargas.)

The resulting fire destroyed two city blocks — a total of 60 houses — and left 250 people homeless. Eleven MOVE members died in the flames, including four children. One adult and one child survived. Grand juries failed to hand down any indictments against the city for its handling of the raid.

At the time this booklet was written (sometime in late 1991), thirteen MOVE members remained in prison, and efforts to have their cases reviewed were going nowhere slowly. In the summer of 1991 the group moved into another large house in West Philadelphia. "The media has tried to give the impression of vehement neighbourhood opposition to MOVE with speculation on the possibility of another catastrophe. MOVE points out that in their over 20-year-history, destruction, violence and death have always been the work of the police, so inquiries as to the future likelihood of such occurrences should be directed to City officials. MOVE has never dropped a bomb, burned down a neighbourhood or killed anyone, they have only demanded the release of innocent members."

no publisher listed (available from AK Press); $6
no date; softcover staple-bound booklet; 59 pp
heavily illus; no ISBN

ALCATRAZ! ALCATRAZ!
The Indian Occupation of 1969-1971
by Adam Fortunate Eagle

For 18 months Native Americans occupied the tiny island of Alcatraz, which had been home to the United States' most infamous prison until 1963. This episode is a classic piece of insurrection, and it's a good thing that one its leaders, Adam Fortunate Eagle, a Chippewa, has recorded it for posterity in this book (although, as Vine Deloria Jr. points out in his preface, "he has omitted all the incriminating incidents that might have gotten him — and a good many others — a permanent residence in Alcatraz or another federal institu-

tion.").

It all began in 1964 when around 40 people, mainly Sioux and some reporters, landed on Alcatraz and claimed it as their own. They did this in accordance with "a 100-year-old treaty permitting non-reservation Indians to claim land the government had once taken for forts and other uses and had later abandoned." The acting warden showed up and threatened everyone with dire consequences if they didn't stop their "trespass" on federal property. With US Marshals on their way to the island, everybody left a mere four hours after the incident started. But the point had been made. The event received lots of media attention in California and made Alcatraz something of a Holy Grail for many Native Americans, who wanted to seize it more permanently. That was what happened four years later.

The United Council was a pan-tribal Indian group located in the Bay area. For more than a year in the late 1960s they had been discussing plans to transfer ownership of Alcatraz from the government to the Indian people. Suddenly they learned that Lamar Hunt of the Texas billionaire Hunt family was making serious progress in his plans to buy Alcatraz and turn it into some sort of amusement park and residential area. Then in October of 1969, the San Francisco Indian Center burned down due to unknown causes. The United Council knew that it was time to move in on Alcatraz, not only for the political statement it would make, but also to head off Hunt and provide a new meeting place.

The first attempt, on November 9, 1969, didn't go off as planned, because the boats that had been chartered to take the activists to Alcatraz chickened out. By nightfall, the group had found another boat to take them. But by this time there were no reporters, no curiosity seekers, and only twenty-five Native Americans instead of 200. Still, with almost no supplies, they "invaded" Alcatraz.

The media, the government, and the Indian community went into an uproar. "A small armada — federal marshals, newspaper reporters, radio and television crews, representatives from the General Services Administration (GSA) which controlled Alcatraz, Coast Guard Officials — arrived at the dock of Alcatraz and looked around for some Indians." The occupiers quickly left the island after the government officials gave an iffy promise to negotiate. Of course, nothing much was done and the Native Americans got the runaround. Another invasion was planned. "This time, we were going to hold on to Alcatraz and force to government to negotiate."

On November 20, around 90 people, including many women, children, and married couples, occupied Alcatraz. This time it would last a year and a half, gaining national support and international press coverage. The Coast Guard immediately set up a blockade, but supporters and sympathisers brought more Native Americans and supplies to the island. The government offered to negotiate if the Indians left the island, but this time they didn't fall for it. Then the government said it would set up Alcatraz as a Native American cultural centre, but the occupiers refused to budge. Next, the island's water supply and electricity was cut off. Another fire of unknown origin devastated part of the island. Yet the

Occupying Alcatraz Island.
Alcatraz! Alcatraz!

occupiers stood firm, using their ingenuity and the help of many allies, including Credence Clearwater Revival, who donated a motorboat to the cause.

By June of 1971, life on the island had become dull and unenjoyable. Vietnam and other civil rights movements were going on, and the public's attention had turned elsewhere. On the 11th, all but fifteen of the Alcatraz residents went into San Francisco to visit families, get supplies, etc. A contingent of 30 federal marshals and agents with automatic weapons used the opportunity to round up the few occupiers and seize the island.

The Alcatraz incident inspired at least a dozen other attempts by Indians to take back their land. Two of these occupations proved successful, and the land was formally given over to Native Americans.

Alcatraz! Alcatraz! is a moving and entertaining account of an extremely important act of resistance. It contains dozens of pictures from before, during, and after the occupation.

Heyday Books; $9.95
1992; softcover; 155 pp
illus; 0-930588-51-7

AMERICA FIRST!
Its History, Culture, and Politics
by Bill Kauffman

America First is the name given to the nationalist movement in the United States. People who subscribe to this philosophy believe that America should not get involved in any wars unless it is being attacked and — more generally — instead of giving billions of dollars in foreign aid, the US should spend that money on food, health care, education, etc. for its own people.

Bill Kauffman is a cynical political observer, and he is obviously sympathetic towards US nativism. However, he is definitely unsympathetic — even caustic — towards the right and the left, Republicans and Democrats. He brazenly slams the political establishment at every turn. While claiming that the real reason Gore Vidal is hated is not his homosexuality, he says that "anyone who has spent any amount of time in Washington, D.C., can attest to this — the grant-grazing conservative herd is rife with closeted gay men who sing the

praises of Republican 'family values' by day and cruise for boy prostitutes by night."

The labels of "populist" and "isolationist" — often applied to America Firsters — have an ugly, racist-conservative ring to them, but Kauffman shows how this perception came about. It might surprise you to know that America Firstism has been embraced by many people who are far from right wing — Gore Vidal, Sinclair Lewis, Jack Kerouac, and "desert anarchist" Edward Abbey, the original radical environmentalist. The author covers these and other nativists in depth. Vidal summed up his position boldly and concisely when he said, "I don't give a God damn what other countries do." Kauffman phrases the America First philosophy another way when he asks: "Do we want to live in an America in which the flickering image of a starving Rwandan on CNN is more immediate to us than the plaintive cries of the hungry girl down the road; a world in which young Americans don helmets and travel halfway around the globe to enforce the resolutions of the United Nations, while in small towns across America volunteer fire departments are undermanned?"

This opinionated book also examines the history of the movement from its nineteenth century predecessor — the Populist Party — to its current status, as represented by Patrick Buchanan and Ross Perot. During the 1992 Presidential campaign, "[t]he journalistic herd mooed on about how Perot was not addressing 'the issues,' when in fact he was an informed and courageous opponent of the Gulf War, an advocate of education reform of the sort enacted under his leadership in Texas — notably a toughening of eligibility requirements for high school athletes — and he broached the topic of entitlement cuts, a hitherto off-limits topic."

America First! is a cage-rattling examination of an oft-derided stream of political thought. Even if it doesn't convince you to join the movement, it shows that there is more to it than xenophobia and intolerance.

Prometheus Books; $25.95
1995; hardcover; 296 pp
0-87975-956-9

THE BLACK PANTHERS SPEAK
edited by Philip S. Foner

You can't hope to understand what any group or individual stands for until you take a look at what they actually say. Of course, this by itself doesn't give you understanding… you also have to look at their actions, what various people think of them, etc. in order to form a more complete opinion. But it's crucial that you read what controversial groups have said, not what the media or our history books tell us they said.

This book will present you with a large, unfiltered selection of writings from a much-mythologised group, the Black Panthers. The Panthers were formed in 1966 by Huey Newton and Bobby Seale. Their name was chosen, according to the introduction, "because the panther is reputed never to make an unprovoked attack but to defend itself ferociously whenever it is attacked." The Panthers were a militant group who believed that African Americans must take up arms in self-defence against the violence of the authorities. They formed armed patrols in Oakland that followed police cars to

DEFEND THE GHETTO

Standing up in the bowels of fascist America.
The Black Panthers Speak.

make sure that no blacks were brutalised by cops. They also set up free breakfast programmes, community centres, and clinics for the poor. This armed black nationalism was too much for the establishment, which used every trick in the book, including murder, to destroy the Panthers. By the time this book was first published in 1970, their leadership had been decimated and the group was on the decline. However, they never completely died. There is still a Black Panther organisation in existence.

Of course, this book contains the Panthers' platform and rules. Among the things they call for in their platform are the "power to determine the destiny of our Black community" and "an immediate end to POLICE BRUTALITY and MURDER of Black people." They also "want all Black men to be exempt from military service. We believe that Black people should not be forced to fight in the military service to defend a racist government that does not protect us."

Most of the selections are articles, essays, and poems taken from the pages of the group's official newspaper, *The Black Panther*. In one article, Landon Williams writes about how "our courageous Minister of Defence, Huey P. Newton, the baddest brother ever to step into history, stood up in the bowels of fascist Amerikkka with a shotgun in his hands and told those murderous mad dogs who occupy our community like a foreign army: 'My name is Huey P. Newton, Minister of Defence of the Black Panther Party. I'm standing on my constitutional right to bear arms to defend my people. If you shoot at me pig, I'm shooting back.'" (By the way, although "pig" was originally applied only to the police, it grew in usage to mean anyone who is part of the power structure — i.e., the Man.)

In an interview, Newton explains his feeling about white revolutionaries. Unlike some black militants, Newton feels that not every white person is the enemy… some white people really are against the system and for the oppressed. "As far as our party is concerned, the Black Panther Party is an all black party, because we feel as Malcolm X felt that there can be no black-white unity until there is first black unity."

Panther Bobby Seale was one of the Chicago 8, that group of radicals who were charged with inciting a riot at the 1968 Democratic Convention in Chicago. Seale refused to be silent during the court proceedings, and eventually the judge had him gagged and bound whenever he (Seale) was in the courtroom. The piece "Bobby Seale vs. Judge Hoffman" is a transcript of the court proceeding prior to this shameful act.

> *Mr. Seale:* What about my constitutional right to defend myself and have my lawyer?
> *The Court:* Your constitutional rights —
> *Mr. Seale:* You are denying them. You have been denying them. Every other word you say is denied, denied, denied, denied, and you begin to oink in the faces of the masses of the people of this country. That is what you begin to represent, the corruptness of this rotten government, for four hundred years.
> *The Marshal:* Mr. Seale, will you sit down.
> *Mr. Seale:* Why don't you knock me in the mouth? Try that.

Other selections include writings by all the most well-known Panthers, including the Panther women, and fliers and comics. Also included is a facsimile reproduction of the entire first issue of *The Black Panther*.

Da Capo Press; $13.95
1970, 1995; softcover; 281 pp
illus; 0-306-80627-4

CHE GUEVARA READER
Writings on Guerrilla Strategy, Politics & Revolution

by Che Guevara, edited by David Deutschmann

With 45 selections, this book is the most complete collection of Ernesto "Che" Guevara's articles, speeches, and letters ever published. (For more on this Latin American revolutionary, see *Che Guevara and the FBI* in the Conspiracies chapter.) Contains his writings from during the Cuban Revolution (which he and Fidel Castro led) and his years helping rule Cuba, his thoughts on international issues, and letters to colleagues, friends, and family. Additional material includes eighteen photos, a 19-page bibliography of Guevara's writings, and a long glossary of people, places, and events.

Ocean Press; $21.95
1997; softcover; 400 pp
illus; 1-875284-93-1

ECOFASCISM
Lessons from the German Experience

by Janet Biehl & Peter Staudenmaier

These two essays show how environmentalist concerns can be twisted and used to promote fascistic, racist, and ultranationalistic political beliefs. This was done by the Nazis and their forerunners and is again happening in Germany's ultra right wing. The authors are particularly concerned that some of these strains of thought are evident in the mainstream environmental movement today. The supremacy of the Earth

Hezbollah fighter on the edge of the security zone in South Lebanon. *Hezbollah.*

over people, mystical and anti-rational "worship" of nature, and scary, Malthusian ideas about population control are all fodder for fascist thought.

AK Press; $7
1995; softcover; 73 pp
1-873176-73-2

EXTREMISM IN AMERICA
A Reader
edited by Lyman Tower Sargent

Although there are lots of books about extremists, it is often very hard to get your hands on writings *by* extremists. This book provides a unique and valuable service by reprinting over 80 essays, articles, and rants from 53 organisations and individuals usually characterised as extremist, including Father Charles E. Coughlin, the John Birch Society, the American Nazi Party, Aryan Nations, The National Association for the Advancement of White People, the Eagle Forum, the American Militia Organisation, the Communist Party of America, Students for a Democratic Society, the Left Green Network, the African People's Party, the Lavender Left, Individualists for a Rational Society, and Call Off Your Old Tired Ethics (COYOTE, a prostitutes' rights group). (I'm not sure if every one of these groups, particularly COYOTE, should be considered extremist — especially when compared to some of the other names on the list. Perhaps "radical" would be a more all-encompassing label.) Overall, the right is more heavily represented than the left.

"Beliefs and Principles of the John Birch Society" explains the guiding philosophy behind the most famous anti-Communist organisation in the US. Item number two reads, in part: "We believe that the Communists seek to drive their slaves and themselves along exactly the opposite and downward direction, to the Satanic debasement of both man and his universe. We believe that communism is as utterly incompatible with all religion as it is contemptuous of all morality and destructive of all freedom. It is intrinsically evil."

The first point of the "African People's Party Ten Point Program" says: "We want self-determination and independent nationhood. We believe African captives in America will not have freedom until they have land of their own and a government; a nation that we govern and run and control. We demand the states of Mississippi, Georgia, South Carolina, Alabama and Louisiana as partial repayment for injus-

tices done to us for over 400 years." The APP goes on to demand the government pay African Americans $400 billion dollars and release "all Black people held in federal, state, county, and city prisons and jails."

Other selections include "American Nazi Party Official Stormtrooper's Manual", "Adolph Hitler Was Elijah", "New Education: The Radicals Are After Your Children", "A Manifesto of Men's Liberation", "Must You Pay Income Tax?", "Industrial Democracy — Complete Democracy", "Government Is Women's Enemy", and "If Washington, Jefferson, Madison, Hancock and Mason Were Alive Today Here Is How the Bill of Rights Would Look".

Extremism in America is an indispensable compendium of source documents from the furthest fringes of American political thought.

New York University Press; $17.95
1995; softcover; 385 pp
0-8147-8011-3

HEZBOLLAH
Born with a Vengeance
by Hala Jaber

To Westerners, the name Hezbollah has become synonymous with Islamic terrorism. Headquartered in Lebanon, this militant organisation instantly became famous in late 1983 when one of its members drove a carload of explosives into the US Marine base in Beirut, killing 241 Marines in "the single largest non-nuclear explosion since the Second World War". Since then, it has engaged in a virtual jihad against Western, Israeli, and other forces that it sees as obstacles to Islamic revolution.

Reporter Hala Jaber, who covers the Middle East extensively, was given unprecedented, exclusive access to the members of Hezbollah. Because of this, she has written the first account from inside this group, revealing its tactics, philosophy, and culture. In the first chapter, Jaber gives a clear history of Hezbollah (whose name means "Party of God") and the treatment of Shiite Muslims that preceded its formation. The Shiites in Lebanon lived mainly in the south, which is where the Palestine Liberation Organisation staged most of its raids into northern Israel. In June 1982, Israel invaded and occupied southern Lebanon in order to drive out the PLO. After this had been accomplished, though, the Israelis didn't leave and it became apparent that they weren't going to any time soon. Resistance to Israeli occupiers grew among the Shiites, eventually turning violent. An underground resistance movement, backed by the new Islamic theocracy in Iran, grew into Hezbollah.

The group blames the United States for everything that is wrong in the Middle East. Its manifesto says, "the leader Imam Khomeini emphasised on many occasions that America is the cause of all our calamities and that she is the mother of all malice. If we fight her we will in effect only be exercising our just rights in defending our Islam and the honour of our nation." Israel is seen as part of a conspiracy to implant Westernism in the Middle East. The manifesto refers to Israel as "America's spearhead in our Islamic world."

The proto-Hezbollah group Lebanese National Resistance created the concept of suicide car bombers "when a young man drove a white Mercedes, filled with explosives, into Israel's military headquarters in Tyre. The blast destroyed the eight-storey building and killed 141 people." In one of the moments that looks at the personal side of Hezbollah, Jaber writes: "Every evening, four-year-old Mohammed watches the same video. He puts the cassette on by himself and calls his baby sister to join him. It is a short film, primitively made, which lasts no more than five minutes. There is a row of buildings in a bleak landscape and then, suddenly, an explosion. 'There's my daddy,' says Mohammed. Mohammed's father, Salah Ghandour, rammed a car packed with 450 kilograms of explosives into an Israeli convoy, in South Lebanon, on 25 May 1995. He blew himself to pieces and killed twelve Israeli soldiers." Ghandour's widow and mother of their three children says, "I knew that this was the only way for him. Even if I had tried to stop him I would not have succeeded. It was the end. Salah had been dreaming of this for a long time. He had been thinking about it and hoping to be allowed to carry out something like this for ages and he finally had the chance and opportunity; there was nothing more to say. He only had one goal at the end and that was to kill the largest number of the enemy."

Further chapters explore Hezbollah's taking of hostages (Jaber interviews some of the kidnappers), US and Israeli actions against Hezbollah, the group's method of organisation, its sources of funding, and its non-terrorist activities (opening hospitals, schools, and supermarkets, providing welfare, and otherwise helping the people of South Lebanon). Consider this an essential book on terrorism and militant revolution.

Columbia University Press; $29.95
1997; hardcover; 260 pp
illus; 0-231-10834-6

LASAGNA
The Man Behind the Mask
by Ronald Cross & Hélène Sévigny

The 500-year war against the native peoples of North America is still going on. This book looks at one of the most recent open battles — the Mohawk defence of Oka village in Quebec. In 1990 the council at Oka gave the go-ahead to expand the existing golf course into sacred Mohawk burial grounds. When this course had originally been proposed in 1961, the Mohawks fought it with legal tactics but lost. This time, they were not going to give up. "In order to protect their land and the graves of their ancestors, the Mohawks erected a barricade to make the Whites understand that they intended to protect this land against all invaders." A Superior Court ordered that the barricade be taken down. Around 40 Mohawks refused to yield and decided to defend the land, beginning a three-month stand-off. (Because of the dense cover the Mohawks had, the authorities thought there were from 400 to 600 of them.)

The defenders were armed, but again, not as heavily as the authorities believed. During the stand-off, the army fired into the blockaded areas, placing women and children at risk. A Canadian SWAT team attacked the encampment with

A soldier and a Mohawk warrior — possibly Lasagna himself — stare each other down. *Lasagna*.

live ammo and concussion grenades, and a Corporal was killed. When the Royal 22nd Regiment began to close in on the barricades on September 1, the Mohawks destroyed their weapons and escaped into the dense woods. Several of them were captured, including Ronald "Lasagna" Cross, one of the most active Warriors (and the most hated by authorities). Not surprisingly, he was thoroughly beaten after being taken into custody. He has spent a total of eleven months in jail and is currently free on bail pending an appeal of his case.

This book chronicles Cross's life and the Oka confrontation through the narrative framework created by Hélène Sévigny, with large sections told by Cross himself. It turns out that Cross was not a lifelong agitator but just an "average guy" who worked at blue collar jobs in New York (where he was born) and all over Canada. He was having a personal crisis in 1990 and decided to go back to Oka, his grandfather's homeland, in order to get himself together. It was at that time that the council decided to expand the golf course. Cross and the others took a stand, and the rest is history.

Lasagna also serves as a stunning indictment of the news media. A full chapter is devoted to showing how the Canadian and American media regurgitated the lies and propaganda of the Canadian government. The defenders of the sacred ground, naturally, were referred to as "terrorists". They were said to have Mafia backing and were plotting to turn control of Indian reservations over to the Mob. When the infamous Lasagna was unmasked and shown to be a man with no criminal record and no ties to the Mafia or any criminal organisations, some of the truth began to poke through the tissue of lies. This book helps even more of the truth shine through.

Talonbooks; US$14.95, Can$17.95
1994; softcover; 254 pp
illus; 0-88922-348-3

MOTHER JONES SPEAKS
Speeches and Writings of a
Working-Class Fighter
edited by Philip S. Foner

Once called "the most dangerous woman in America", Mary

Creation Books; $13.95
1996; softcover; 147 pp
illus; 1-871592-62-3

COLD-BLOODED
The Saga of Charles Schmid, the Notorious "Pied Piper of Tucson"
by John Gilmore

Gritty true-crime author John Gilmore — author of *Severed* and *The Garbage People* [both below] — tells the story of Charles Schmid, a charismatic psychotic who was convicted of killing three teenage girls in Tucson, Arizona, in the mid-1960s. Gilmore met Schmid early in his trial and continued contact with him for over a year. Much of the insight into Schmid's behaviour and thoughts comes from his diaries and letters and from Gilmore's repeated interviews with him.

Feral House; $12.95
1996; oversized softcover; 117 pp
illus; 0-922915-31-8

THE GARBAGE PEOPLE
The Trip to Helter Skelter and Beyond With Charlie Manson and the Family
by John Gilmore & Ron Kenner

John Gilmore's insightful and long out-of-print story of Charles Manson and his Family has finally been reprinted, with updated information and a new photo section. Gilmore got much of his information by interviewing several of the main players — Manson himself, starting shortly after he was arrested in connection with the Tate-LaBianca murders; Bobby Beausoleil, who says that he had his own band of followers who worked with the Family; Family member Lynette "Squeaky" Fromme, who tried to assassinate President Ford; and Family member Sandra Good, who has become the high priestess of the current "Manson Movement".

The book's title comes from Manson's own name for himself and people like him — those who had been cast aside by society. "Where does the garbage go, as we have tin cans and garbage alongside the road, and oil slicks in the water, so you have people, and I am one of your garbage people."

Garbage People traces Manson's childhood and teenage years in and out of foster homes, juvenile centres, reformatories, and jails; his hobnobbing with stars, such as Dennis Wilson of the Beach Boys; his eventual failure to "make it" as a music star; his emergence as leader of a small group composed mainly of women; the gruesome Tate-LaBianca murders; and their aftermath. As for what Manson's goal was, Gilmore says he simply wanted to cause havoc on a society that had screwed him over. "For a person beaten, tormented, raped, warped and abused throughout life, it was simply time to swing back a little of the medicine. There was nothing in our 'society' (as we call it and know it), for Charlie — a dog whipped and chained, learning only the whip and chain."

A centre section contains rarely-seen photos of the Family at Spahn Ranch, Manson at thirteen, and Sharon Tate early on the day of her murder. In *Helter Skelter* — probably the most famous book on Manson — there are photographs

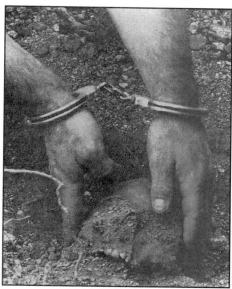

Charles Schmid, manacled, unearthing the skull of Aileen Rowe. *Cold-Blooded.*

of the murder scenes, but the mutilated bodies have been cut out to protect our sensibilities. In *Garbage People*, you get the uncensored goods — Sharon Tate, Abigail Folger, Jay Sebring, Leno LaBianca, and others as they were discovered and at the morgue.

Amok Books; $14.95
1971, 1995; softcover; 190 pp
illus; 0-878923-07-2

GODS OF DEATH
by Yaron Svoray with Thomas Hughes

The existence of snuff films is a hotly debated issue. These home-made movies — in which a person (usually a woman or girl) is brutally raped and killed on-camera — certainly *could* exist. There are surely enough twisted bastards out there who would be willing to do such a thing. The problem is that whenever anyone investigates the matter, they meet dead ends. It's always the acquaintance of an acquaintance who's seen one. But this time it's different. Investigative journalist Yaron Svoray — a former paratrooper and policeman in Israel — may just be the only person to claim in print that he has personally watched snuff films. Not only that, but he claims that he and a famous American actor viewed a snuff film together.

It all started when Svoray went undercover into the German neo-Nazi movement, a disturbing experience that he writes about in his first book, *In Hitler's Shadow*. As part of their training, he and the neo-Nazis watched a movie that showed some of Hitler's speeches and five masked men raping, torturing, and killing a girl who looked eight to ten years old. He explains: "Watching those films is for them a methodical affirmation of their goal, which is absolute power. The slaughter of the girl is tangible evidence of power over human life, and their watching it is their participation in the exercising of that power..."

Haunted by the terrified face of the girl and by the existence of such films in general, Svoray decided to find out who is making them. He hoped to be able to get one and offer it as solid proof to the world that something horrible is happening. Rather than simply talk to law enforcement officials, whose standard line is that a legitimate snuff film has never been found, he actually headed into the seamy underground posing as a buyer of such movies. Although it's a cliché to say this, his adventures really do read like a suspense novel. As he hops from country to country, Svoray follows a string of leads that force him to deal with small-time hustlers, underground pornographers, traffickers in prostitutes, Russian mobsters, neo-Nazis, former gang members, the president of a Connecticut bank, and other assorted characters.

Although he hit many dead ends, he did get to see more snuff films. One was at a viewing in a posh neighbourhood in Connecticut. Svoray's banker acquaintance took him to a house where they and nine other men — who looked like doctors, lawyers, and other professionals ranging in age from their 30s to 50s — paid $1500 each to watch a snuff film brought in by a Mafioso. In another instance — and this is where things get weird beyond your wildest imagination — Robert De Niro got in touch with Svoray for help in writing a movie script involving snuff. Svoray claims that he set up a meeting in Paris at which he, De Niro, one of the actor's friends, and some dealers viewed a snuff film. In order to do this, they had to pretend that they were interested in buying the flick, then declare that it was a piece of garbage that they would never buy, and storm out. Everything went according to plan, and De Niro and his friend agreed that the movie had been real. Svoray was hoping that De Niro would publicly talk about what he had seen and help blow the whistle on the snuff industry. For whatever reasons, this obviously never happened.

Although Svoray was able to watch these movies, he was never able to buy one. In those rare instances when he found himself able to purchase snuff, the cost was so high (around $250,000) that he couldn't afford it. He did manage to steal a couple of tapes along the way, only to find out that they weren't snuff films. Finally, he ended up in Bosnia meeting a man who wanted to become the king of porn in his area of the world. Svoray told him that by selling just a few snuff flicks, they could raise enough money to fund a big-time legitimate porn operation. The man brought out a tape and played it for Svoray. It was a compilation of atrocities filmed by soldiers during the Bosnia-Croatia-Serbia hostilities. "Soldiers with machine guns firing on crowds of men, young and old, rapid-fire bursts echoing soundless laughter. Girls tied up together, young, young, two at a time pushed into bare rooms, naked, struggling, screaming, faces like frightened animals, sense gone, humanity gone — raped, murdered, burned, stabbed. Throats slit like cattle, taken by men with guns at their heads."

[Warning: if you read on from here, you'll find out how the book ends.] The Bosnian pornographer gave Svoray the

A rare photo of the Manson family at Spahn Ranch.
The Garbage People.

tape as a gesture of good will regarding their "partnership". As Svoray tried to leave the country, though, he was arrested and half-heartedly detained. He managed to escape, but his belongings, including the tape, had been taken from him.

So, in the end, Svoray returned from his dangerous and seedy mission empty-handed. This is a disappointment for anyone who would like to see some concrete evidence, and it doesn't solve the mystery of snuff films. However, it isn't a total loss. With Svoray, we finally have someone who is willing to say in writing that he has witnessed numerous films that undoubtedly show people being raped, tortured, and killed. The fact that he has previously penetrated a murky and violent underworld (neo-Nazism) helps bolster his claim. Also — if Svoray can be believed — we now know of another person who has witnessed a snuff film, and he happens to be one of the most famous actors in the world. (I have a hard time believing that Svoray fabricated the story about De Niro, since it would leave his publisher, Simon & Schuster, open to a lawsuit of monumental proportions.)

We still don't have definitive proof that snuff films exist, but at least we have some strong clues that point in that direction. Anybody out there know Robert De Niro?

Simon & Schuster; $24
1997; hardcover; 306 pp
0-684-81445-5

HIT MAN
A Technical Manual for Independent Contractors
by Rex Feral

This book has become the target of legal action that — at the risk of sounding like an alarmist — has the potential to seriously jeopardise freedom of speech. *Hit Man* contains detailed instructions for killing people for money — creating a false identity, using a disposable silencer, making the kill, getting away, etc. In 1993 James Perry killed two women and the child of one of the women, a crime that has earned him a spot on death row. Prosecutors say that in 1992, Perry purchased *Hit Man*, then followed twenty-seven of the book's instructions while killing the women. The victims' families pressed charges against Paladin and its president, trying to prove that they somehow aided and abetted the murders simply by publishing the book. In the summer of 1996, a Federal District Court threw out all the charges and issued a sharp declaration upholding free speech. However, in the fall of the next year, a Federal Appeals Court overturned the lower court's ruling, saying that Paladin *can* be held liable for the actions of someone who read one of their books. This clears the way for a massive civil suit against the publisher. They intend to take the case to the Supreme Court. (You can keep abreast of developments at Paladin's Website, www.paladin-press.com.)

If this new ruling is not overturned, it could very well mean that all publishers — and perhaps others, such as writers — will be legally responsible for the actions of strangers. In essence, it would be saying that books — non-fiction and fiction, as well as music and art — can make people commit crimes. Mystery novel publishers, gangsta rap record labels, studios that release action movies, the producers of *Murder She Wrote*, and countless other businesses and people will have to pray that no murderer is exposed to their products before committing a crime, or they may end up in court, too.

Of course, condolences go out to the victims' families. However, the person who committed the crime is on his way to the chair, and the person who hired him is in jail for life with no parole, so justice has been fully served. There's no need to trash the First Amendment, while at the same time creating a whole new field for product liability lawyers to use as a money trough.

Paladin Press; $10
1983; softcover; 144 pp
illus; 0-87364-276-7

JACK THE RIPPER
"Light-hearted Friend"
by Richard Wallace

In the more than 100 years that have passed since the Whitechapel murders, dozens of suggestions have been made about the true identity of Jack the Ripper. Of all of them, though, none is more unexpected or, on the surface, more outrageous than the one proposed by Richard Wallace. He believes that the Ripper was none other than Reverend Charles Dodgson, better known to history as Lewis Carroll, author of *Alice's Adventures in Wonderland*, *Through the Looking Glass*, and other works of children's literature.

This may seem preposterous, but Wallace is completely serious. In his first book, *The Agony of Lewis Carroll* [reviewed in the Fiction chapter], he presents evidence that Carroll had been endlessly raped in the boys' boarding schools he attended. Not only did this warp Carroll — even

When a badge is treated as a licence to kill.
Killer Cops.

inducing a psychotic break from which he never fully recovered — but it filled him with rage towards his parents, particularly his smothering mother, who were unable or unwilling to help him. Wallace believes that Carroll wrote of his rage and hatred in his books, cleverly hiding his feelings in symbols, illustrations, and anagrams. (Anagrams occur when the letters in a word, sentence, or even a whole paragraph are rearranged to form different words, sentences, and paragraphs.)

After publishing *The Agony of Lewis Carroll*, Wallace carried his theory even further. "Going now beyond my original thinking, whatever Dodgson endured there [at school], he became a psychopath who focused first on secretive antisocial acts and eventually on multiple homicides and mutilations. His emotional life stopped growing; the seeds of rage already laid blossomed forth, and he set himself on a path of childlike revenge against his family and society. Life became obsessed with getting even, filled with spite, a constant search for retribution. The primary target of his rage was his mother, whose favourite he had been and whose task in the family it was to guide and protect him. After her death when he was nineteen, his targets became the symbols-of-mother."

After giving an excellent account of the serial killings, Wallace examines the various clues that support his theory. Many of the clues are, once again, hidden in Carroll's writings, although only the ones that were written after the murders are examined. Carroll began writing *The Nursery "Alice"* — a simpler version of *Alice's Adventures in Wonderland* for

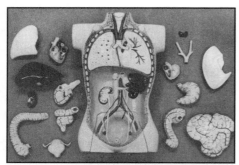

Mr Brown based his anatomical models on
real-life research. *Lustmord.*

children aged five and below — at the tail end of 1888, the
year that saw all of the murders that are generally accepted
as the work of the Ripper. Wallace pays special attention to
a paragraph that appears in *The Nursery "Alice"* but is not
contained in any form in the original *Alice*. In the scene, three
gardeners — the Three, Five, and Seven of Spades — are
painting five white roses red before the Queen of Hearts
arrives. The paragraph in question begins: "You see there
were *five* large white roses on the tree — such a job to get
them all painted red." Wallace believes this entire paragraph
is an anagram which, when rearranged, reads: "Dodgson
and Bayne seethe, tune, hone a weird way — any way — to
laud my father's holy work and let the hate vent. We plot
how to kill dirty women, knife to throat. You see, to them it is
such a large job to get five street whores all painted red.

"If I find one street whore, you know what will happen!
'Twill be 'Off with her head!'

"Work away! Hurry, hurry! Or the Queen's little men will
be coming before he's done."

In this scenario, the roses are the prostitutes who were
"painted" red with their own blood. "Bayne" refers to Thomas Vere Bayne, Carroll's best friend who may have aided
him in some way. The "Queen's little men" are, of course,
the police.

Wallace goes on to uncover clues in the text and illustrations elsewhere in *The Nursery "Alice"*, *Sylvie and Bruno*,
and Carroll's diaries. He also examines the tantalising clues
regarding handwriting analysis, geography, the Ripper's letters and poems, and the dates, names, and numbers having to do with the crimes. Other paths that Wallace follows
include whether Carroll was trying to frame the Masons for
the murders, Carroll's stance on vivisection, and the extent
of Carroll's medical knowledge.

Wallace makes a fascinating case that seems to be supported by many clues. However, he never definitively shows
Carroll to have been the Ripper, but, then again, *no one* has
been able perform that feat with even the most likely suspects after over a century of trying. The case will surely never
be solved, but Wallace has provided yet another piece of
the puzzle. A *strange* piece, but a piece nonetheless.

Gemini Press; $13
1996; softcover; 293 pp
illus; 0-9627195-6-0

KILLER COPS
An Encyclopedia of Lawless Lawmen
by Michael Newton

Michael Newton — our foremost cataloguer of homicidal
maniacs (see *Hunting Humans: The Encyclopedia of Serial
Killers* [*Outposts* p 145] and *Bad Girls Do It: An Encyclopedia of Female Murderers* [*Outposts* p 144]) — is back on the
job. This time around, he provides an impressively in-depth
look at over 60 law officers — sheriffs from the Wild West,
state troopers, campus cops, FBI agents, and others — who
have gone off the deep end, killing people for revenge,
money, or just for fun. With a cast of colourful characters
from nineteenth and twentieth century America, *Killer Cops*
shows what happens when a badge is treated as a licence
to kill.

Newton doesn't include cops who shoot a "menacing"
suspect who turns out to be unarmed, though. Rather than
deal with such grey areas, he sticks to the black and white
material. Such as the case of Guillermo Delacruz, a Los
Angeles policeman who shot and killed his girlfriend and her
male friend — both of them cops in a San Diego suburb —
and then blew his own head off. Or Texas Ranger captain
JM Fox, who, with eight other Rangers and four civilians,
slaughtered fifteen Mexicans because they were wearing
the types of shoes that had recently been stolen from a store
by bandits. Or New Orleans officer Antoinette Frank and an
accomplice, who wasted an off-duty cop and two young
adults who worked at a Vietnamese restaurant, then robbed
the place. Then there's James Miller, also known as "Killin'
Jim", "a trigger-happy backshooter who boasted of 40 or 50
homicides, at least some of them carried out while Miller
was a Texas peace officer." Newton gives detailed accounts
of the lives of Wild Bill Hickok, Wyatt Earp (whose exploits
weren't quite as gallant as traditional history would have us
believe), and notorious *Killer Fiction* author GJ Schaefer. (See
the Fiction chapter for a review of Schaefer's book.)

Michael Newton has done it again. Followers and fans
of sociopathic behaviour now have another definitive book
for their shelves.

Loompanics Unlimited; $14.95
1997; softcover; 221 pp
illus; 1-55950-171-5

LUSTMORD
The Writings and Artifacts of
Murderers
edited by Brian King

Lustmord had been in the works for at least five years, and
1996 finally saw the release of this unprecedented "compilation of essays, short stories, memoirs, confessions, letters,
manifestos, poetry, drawings, photographs and other works
created by serial killers, mass murderers, cannibals,
necrophiles, sexual sadists, psychopaths and assassins." If
you want to glimpse into the violently criminal mind, there is
no better way to do it than with this book. Reading about
crimes and listening to psychologists theorising won't give
you the same insights — not to mention the frissons — that
you'll receive from reading what the killers themselves had

to say.

John George Haigh — dubbed the "Acid Bath Killer" by the London media — wrote his memoirs while in prison. Four-and-a-half pages' worth are excerpted in *Lustmord*:

> "Once acquired, the taste [for blood] obsessed me, and the recollection of it, with certain intervals, pursued me down the years...
>
> "But none of these experiences crystallised into a frantic uncontrollable urge until after a motor accident at Three Bridges, Sussex, during Easter of 1944.
>
> "My car collided with a lorry, and turned over... Blood poured from my head down my face and into my mouth. This revived in me the taste, and that night I experienced another awful dream.
>
> "I saw before me a forest of crucifixes, which gradually turned into trees. At first there appeared to be dew, or rain, dripping from the branches, but as I approached I realised it was blood.
>
> "Suddenly the whole forest began to writhe and the trees, stark and erect, to ooze blood... A man went to each tree catching the blood... When the cup was full he approached me... 'Drink,' he said, but I was unable to move. The dream faded..."

The book's youngest contributor is Mary Bell, an eleven-year-old British girl who murdered a three- and four-year-old in 1968. The day after the murder, police found four notes she had written. One said: "You ArE micey y BECUASE WE murdered Martain GO Brown you BettEr Look out THErE are MurdErs aBout By Fanny AnD and auld Faggot you Srcews". A poem Bell wrote to her mother from jail, two years after the murders, contained these lines: "Please mam put my tiny mind at ease/tell Judge and Jury on your knees/they will Listen to your cries of PLEAS/THE GUILTY ONE IS you not me".

Most of the pieces in *Lustmord* are text, but there is also some art. A middle-aged biology teacher, known only as Mr. Brown, killed his wife and children in 1966. His artwork — including a realistic model of the human torso with removable organs, a painting of a demonic being disembowelling a person, and a sculpture of an E.T.-lookalike staring at a woman whose innards have been ripped out — is reproduced. You'll also get to see three photographs Harvey Glatman took of his bound female victims before he raped and murdered them, self-portraits of serial killer Patrick Mackay, GJ Schaefer's drawings of hanged women, the Zodiac killer's cryptograms, and drawings by "natural born killer" Charles Starkweather.

Other fascinating documents include the book's preface by serial killer Herbert Mullin, two short stories from "Freeway Killer" William Bonin, excerpts from the diary of the matricidal Pauline Parker (the subject of the excellent, can't-recommend-it-highly-enough film *Heavenly Creatures*), the complete autobiography of prolific murderer and rapist Carl Panzram, a fictionalised account of the crime of Japanese murderer/necrophile/cannibal Issei Sagawa, letters, poems, and other writings by President Garfield's assassin, the po-

Danny Rolling's artwork.
The Making of a Serial Killer.

etry of sadistic murderer Joseph Kallinger, a poem from the Yorkshire Ripper, excerpts from *Cry for War* by hippie killers Michael and Suzan Carson, and letters written by David "Son of Sam" Berkowitz, "Boston Strangler" Albert DeSalvo, and Albert Fish. Editor Brian King provides concise background information that puts all the pieces in perspective.

True crime fans, collectors of art and literature *brut*, and students of the most extreme aspects of the human condition will consider this collection a treasure. All of this creative output from the most sociopathic minds of recent times makes for a fierce and unique reading experience. Most highly recommended.

Bloat; $14.95

1996; softcover; 320 pp

illus; 0-9650324-0-X

THE MAKING OF A SERIAL KILLER
The Real Story of the Gainesville Murders in the Killer's Own Words

by Danny Rolling & Sondra London

Danny Rolling is currently doing time for killing one male and four female college students in Gainesville, Florida, in 1990. In this book, Rolling himself talks about his life and crimes, allowing us — as with *Lustmord* [above] — to hear the thoughts of someone who has repeatedly taken human lives. Rolling was aided in his confessions by Sondra London, who dated cop-turned-killer GJ Schaefer before he committed his crimes. As Rolling and London got to know each other, they fell in love and are now engaged.

Rolling writes about growing up with a domineering father, drifting, committing armed robberies, doing time in jails, and eventually committing murders, sometimes combined with mutilation and rape before or after the killing. The murders are described in minute, second-by-second detail, with Rolling writing in the third person and making references to "Gemini", his name for the cruel, homicidal aspect of himself. "The blade sunk to the hilt as Sonja tried to scream, but the hand and tape pressed over her mouth only allowed a muffled cry to escape from her lips. Her eyes bulged in shock! She tried to struggle and kick at her attacker, but this only brought a frenzy of stabbings — blade and bone — blood spurting and splashing on the two embracing in the Dance of Death. It lasted only seconds, but just before she found blissful unconsciousness, Gemini whispered close to her ear, 'I'll come back for you after you're dead.'"

During his testimonials, Rolling makes it clear that he is a devout Christian. "Lord only knows, I'm a pitiful example of a Child of God. Nonetheless, a Christian I am, and a Christian I remain... I've had numerous supernatural experiences. Some so haunting, they were actual visits from demons. Still, most have been beautiful moments with my Saviour Jesus Christ. He is the author and finisher of my soul. He will not leave my soul to the demons that have haunted me all my life."

In the final chapter, Rolling speaks of his intense love for London. "They have plucked the living rose from my hand, and now I am a prisoner indeed. We were so close, only an inch thick glass separated us. So close... and yet so far away. The one thing I long for in this life is to be with my love. Now she is adrift on that forever blue sea and I am marooned on this deserted island, alone — Captain Castaway without his queen."

Illustrated with dozens of Rolling's drawings and written almost entirely by him, *The Making of a Serial Killer* is a book that many people feel should never have been published. But, leaving aside that fact that even the most heinous criminals have the right to be heard, I wonder how we can ever hope to understand ourselves if we don't acknowledge and study every aspect of human existence. This book is yet another piece in the puzzle of that universal human endeavour, murder.

Feral House; $12.95
1996; oversized softcover; 201 pp
illus; 0-922915-40-7

MANSON SPEAKS
by Charles Manson

A spoken-word double CD by Charles Manson. On the first disk, Manson recites some of his poems, tells a story about a dog at the Family's ranch, and offers some philosophical musings. Talking about the "universal mind", he says, "Those in the mind who think they have a mind are not in the mind 'cause the mind has no time." The other disk has more topical comments about the prison system, Daryl Gates, religion, power, prejudice, environmentalism, books and movies about the Family, and lots more. "We need to stop them damn automobiles and do a lot more walkin'. Get back to bicycles. Quit usin' paper. Quit wipin' your ass with the trees. Quit wastin' all the fuckin' paper, man. Take the best of tech-

The body of Elizabeth Short (the Black Dahlia) as it was found. *Severed*.

nology and use that technology to help the nature and help life get back to itself, y'dig? Rather than tryin' to put a man on the moon, let's try to put a man down on earth."

White Devil Records; $24.98
1995; 2 compact disks

SEVERED
The True Story of the Black Dahlia Murder
by John Gilmore

On January 15, 1947, the naked body of Elizabeth Short was found in a small field in Los Angeles. Her corpse had been slashed, cut in half, and drained of blood. The savage killing of "Black Dahlia" (she earned the nickname, a play on the movie title *The Blue Dahlia*, because of her raven hair) would become one of the most famous unsolved murders of modern times. Strangely, no true crime book had ever been written about it until now.

Crime researcher John Gilmore believes that the Black Dahlia case is only unsolved in the most technical sense... it is almost certain that the killer was discovered. Gilmore gives a gripping chronological narrative of Short's entire life, the discovery of her body, the autopsy, the frantic efforts of over 750 investigators, and the media hubbub. After everyone had reached only dead ends, an informant came forward who claimed to know a man who knew Short's killer. He gave a detailed account of the crime and aspects of Short that proved he had real knowledge of the murder. Soon, the police realised that the man the informant knew — "Arnold Smith" — was undoubtedly the murderer himself. This man, whose real name was Jack Anderson Wilson, may also have been involved in the infamous murder of oil heiress Georgette Eilise Bauerdorf. He apparently committed suicide, so the Black Dahlia case remains officially unsolved. However, based on the evidence related in *Severed* — including the informant's gruesome recounting of the torture-killing — it appears as though Wilson was the man.

Gilmore's narrative is compulsively readable. A photo section contains pictures of the story's main players — suspects, investigators, and Short, when she was alive and as she was found at the scene. A worthy acquisition for any fan of true crime books.

Zanja Press; $10.95
1994; softcover; 237 pp
illus; 0-938331-03-5

SQUEAKY
The Life and Times of
Lynette Alice Fromme
by Jess Bravin

Researched for three and a half years, this is a thorough biographical and psychological study of Lynette Alice "Squeaky" Fromme, who went from being a typical suburban girl in 1950s Southern California to one of the most famous members of Charles Manson's "Family" and the attempted assassin of President Gerald Ford. Contains 32 photos, including a topless shot of Fromme and Sandra Good.

Buzz Books (St. Martin's Press); $25.95
1997; hardcover; 432 pp
illus; 0-312-15663-4

GUNS & AMMO

A DO-IT-YOURSELF SUBMACHINE GUN
by Gérard Métral

The Swiss Army reserve Captain who wrote this book isn't kidding around — with these detailed plans you can make your own 9mm, blowback, selective-fire submachine gun from scratch. It will be as powerful as an Uzi but lighter and easier to handle. Of course, it will also never be on an import-ban list and will always be available, even in dire times. In order to make this hot little number, you'll need some equipment — a lathe, a drill press, a heavy vice, a welding set, a grinding wheel, and basic hand tools and materials — mainly steel tubes, bars, and sheets. It's recommended that you buy the barrel, main spring, and magazine ready-made, because they're tough to do yourself.

The author breaks the gun down into sections and guides you through the creation of each: receiver, bolt, trigger mechanism housing, trigger mechanism, pistol grip, sights, folding stock, and handguard and front grip. Besides written instructions, there are eight detailed diagrams and 70 full-page machinist's drawings. For the finishing touch, follow the instructions in making a silencer for your new plaything.

Submachine Gun also tells you how to handle and test the finished gun, how to produce them clandestinely on a large scale, how to make the gun parts out of epoxy resin and glass fabric, and more.

Paladin Press; $20
1995; oversized softcover; 123 pp
heavily illus; 0-87364-840-4

Some assembly required.
A Do-It-Yourself Submachine Gun.

HOMEMADE AMMO
How to Make It, How To Reload It,
How to Cache It
by Duncan Long

Guns aren't much use unless you've also got ammunition. Should future events necessitate making your own ammo, this book teaches you how to make pistol, rifle, and submachine gun bullets from scratch and reload them. The best way to make your own bullets is to buy kits with moulds. You can use lead, plastic, brass, or copper (these last two will create armour-piercing bullets) with these kits. In a fix, bolts and screws can even be modified to form projectiles. You'll need to lubricate the bullets with either ready-made lube or your own mixture of lamb fat and beeswax.

Once you've got bullets, you'll need to house them in brass cartridges. The best thing to do is keep your previously-fired empties or scrounge for them. The author gives instructions for cleaning cartridges for re-use. Since cartridges expand slightly during firing, you'll also need to have a way of compressing them. There are many ways to reload bullets into cartridges meant for other types of bullets, and the author covers them well.

Another crucial ingredient is smokeless powder. The best thing to do is load up on it while you can, but if you need to make it, you can do so out of potassium nitrate, potassium chlorate, black powder, brown powder, nitro-cellulose, or ammonpulver (derived from ammonium nitrate fertiliser). Should getting any of these materials prove to be a problem, the author provides ways to create them. He also covers proper safety and storage techniques.

The final piece of the puzzle is primer, the stuff in the cartridge that is hit by the firing pin and causes a small blast that ignites the powder in the bullet. Again, the best thing to do is load up on primer while it's still legal and plentiful. If you need to make it, though, you can use potassium chlorate, mercury fulminate, or the heads of strike-anywhere matches. Once you've got primer, you'll need to reload it into your cartridges, a tricky process that the author describes in detail.

Finally, a chapter is devoted to caching your ammo and guns. The key things to watch out for are moisture and heat ruining your firepower and making sure you stow the goods where they can't accidentally be found.

Paladin Press; $14
1995; softcover; 92 pp
illus; 0-87364-816-1

MACHINE GUN NEWS
The Magazine for Full Auto
Enthusiasts

As far as I'm aware, this is the only slick, professional magazine devoted to fully-automatic guns — Uzis, Thompsons, Brownings, Berettas, M-16s, and other such firearms. *MGN* also covers semi-automatics (sometimes called "assault rifles"), a topic that many of the larger gun magazines virtually ignore. None of the information is "mischievous" — there are no instructions for converting semi-auto to full-auto, for example — but this kind of stuff still makes the government sweat bullets, so I felt it belonged in this chapter and section.

Besides a technical question and answers column, a look at gunsmithing basics, a calendar of upcoming events, and a column on legalities, each issue offers a few articles on guns, accessories, ammo, shooting events, and gunsmithing. Some of the beauties that have been covered include Quantum 2000 Suppressed Rifles, Saco's M2 QCB, slick-coated bullets, the MB94A1 machine gun mount, the .22 Calibre Maxim Model 1910 Silencer, and the MK19 Mod3 40MM Grenade Machine Gun, which can fire as many as 375 grenades per minute up to 2500 meters.

The advertisements in *MGN* will probably leave you gaping in wonder as you realise all the weaponry that's available through mail order. You'll find ads for machine guns, short-barrelled rifles, 30-round magazines, sound suppressers (also called "silencers"), sniper scopes, destructive devices (such as mortars), flashbang grenades, and more. Some of the businesses only sell to law enforcement, the military, or certain dealers, but a surprisingly large amount of this stuff is available to individuals.

MGN/PO Box 459/Lake Hamilton AR 71951

Voice: 501-525-7514

Fax: 501-525-7519

12 issue sub (one year): $29.95. Can: $44.95. Other countries in the Western Hemisphere: $59.95. Eastern Hemisphere: $69.95. Payment: ck or mo payable to Machine Gun News, Visa, MC, Amex

THE TRUTH ABOUT HANDGUNS
Exploding the Myths, Hype, and
Misinformation
by Duane Thomas

Duane Thomas has been shooting, writing about, and "reviewing" guns for years, and in that time he's discovered that a lot of myths and utter BS are accepted as facts in the gun world. In this book, he aims to set the record straight.

One chapter looks at the baloney surrounding the Colt .45, also called the 1911 auto. To the common belief that, "The ruggedness and reliability of the 1911 auto are unsurpassed," Thomas replies, "Nope. The 1911 auto is in many ways a fairly fragile handgun and small parts breakage is common. The most delicate areas include the plunger tube (prone to snapping off), the barrel bushing (which can fracture), and the extractor (prone to losing its tension, resulting in failures to extract or fully eject). I have had all of these things occur to me in new guns of top quality, featuring either the stock factory parts or primo aftermarket equivalents." He goes on to discuss how supposedly easy it is to learn to use the 1911, how hard it is to shoot, the addition of the firing pin lock, whether it's "better" than a 9mm, and other topics.

Thomas also defends the double-action auto pistol against detractors, gives the full story behind Corporal Alvin York's killing of six charging enemy soldiers with a handgun, boldly claims that the much vaunted "stopping power" of various bullets is relatively unimportant, wades in on the debate over high capacity auto pistols, wonders whether revolvers are obsolete as defensive weapons, deflates the hype surrounding .40 Smith & Wesson cartridges, looks at some silly attitudes towards handguns, and presents a gun trivia quiz. This book is obviously meant for people who are already very familiar with handguns and want to see the conventional wisdom regarding them shot down.

Paladin Press; $14
1997; softcover; 131 pp
illus; 0-87364-953-2

VEST BUSTERS
How to Make Your Own
Body-Armor-Piercing Bullets
by Uncle Fester

At first glance, a book on making bullets that can go through body armour may seem unjustifiable, especially given their nickname "cop-killer bullets". But just remember — anyone can get Kevlar bullet-proof vests. Their sale and use in the US is not regulated in any way. Just pick up your favourite gun or mercenary magazine anywhere magazines are sold, and chances are you'll see ads for them. It would be a minimal investment for a burglar to make in his well-being. Then there's always the chance that a rogue cop or Fed is determined to fuck your world up. Whatever the case, armour-piercing bullets once again level the playing field.

In this concise manual, Uncle Fester tells you what you need to know to coat bullets with Teflon in the comfort of your own home. He reveals which commercially-available ammo is best suited for the job, and then gives step-by-step instructions. It's not very complicated, and it involves chemicals that are easily obtained without raising suspicion. Uncle Fester even gives the phone number of companies that sell Teflon resin emulsion and then tells you exactly what to ask for. What a guy!

Loompanics Unlimited; $12
1996; softcover; 59 pp
illus; 1-55950-150-2

MISCELLANEOUS

ADVANCED DRAGON'S TOUCH
20 Anatomical Targets and
Techniques for Taking Them Out
by Master Hei Long

There are an awful lot of self-defence books on the market. This is one of the minority that teaches you how to mess up someone quickly and permanently. Because these techniques can badly damage your foe or even kill him, they should only be used when the stakes are extremely high, not when somebody spills beer on you at a party… OK, stud? Your manly ego will heal, but crushed vertebrae won't.

Advanced Dragon's Touch focuses on 20 anatomical targets — called "pressure points" — that are most susceptible to unarmed attack. If you hit one of these areas the right way, your opponent won't be getting up anytime soon.

The book opens with a lesson in anatomical weapons. Obviously, besides knowing which body areas to strike, you also need to know which body parts to strike with. The back of your wrist, your palm, the side of your hand, and your elbow are some of the weapons always at your disposal.

The rest of the book covers the twenty pressure points, which include the temple, the eyes, the anterior neck region, the heart, the solar plexus, the coccyx, and the elbow. After locating each point on a diagram and discussing the damage that can be done to it, Master Hei Long presents at least two "practical applications", demonstrating how to deliver a blow to the point during an actual fight situation. There are a total of 52 such techniques, and each one is illustrated by line drawings of two men mixing it up.

Paladin Press; $22
1995; softcover; 269 pp
heavily illus; 0-87364-852-8

ALTERNATIVE INPHORMATION
CONSUMER SURVIVAL CATALOGUE

This catalogue is short, but it packs more hardcore subversive information into every square inch than just about any other catalogue. Its areas of expertise are phone phreaking and hacking mechanical devices. Computer hacking and viruses are covered, but to a lesser extent. There are also reports on unusual money-making ventures and other rare but not scary info.

Here are some of the subjects covered in Alternative Inphormation's publications:

- making red, blue, black, gold, silver, and other colour boxes for phone phreaking
- creating tones that will give you control over phone company operations such as coin return on pay phones, free long distance, ringback, and becoming an operator
- descrambling satellite TV
- tapping the phone of someone who has call

waiting simply by using your own phone
- making fake ID
- jamming police radar
- stopping, slowing down, and reversing utility meters
- beating lie detectors and urine tests
- mailing first class letters for 2¢ each
- *The Black Pages*: a listing of almost unobtainable numbers, such as the immediate offices of the President and the Pentagon, computers of universities and banks, free phone sex, strange recordings, and more
- Postal Service secrets
- making firecrackers up to M-1000
- listening in on cellular phones
- making your own UPC bar codes
- hacking ATMs, vending machines, photocopy machines, voice mail, answering machines, and gas pumps
- writing viruses
- scamming free magazine subscriptions
- making money by being a phoney psychic
- cloning magnetic stripes on the backs of credit cards, ATM cards, etc.
- transmitting pirate radio and pirate TV

AI also carries all 105 back issues of the notorious *TAP*, a magazine full of phreaking and mechanical hacking info started by the Yippies. They also have the entire short run of *TEL*, which dealt only with phreaking. In the 1970s Pacific Bell successfully sued *TEL* and demanded that all issues be destroyed, but, obviously, some survived. Finally, Alt Inpho carries software for breaking copy protection on commercial software and hacking valid credit card numbers.

This catalogue wins *Psychotropedia*'s award of Most Likely to Be the Target of an FBI Mail Cover.

Alternative Inphormation/PO Box 4/Carthage TX 75633-0004
Catalogue: $2

THE ANARCHIST COOKBOOK
by William Powell

Originally published in 1971, *The Anarchist Cookbook* is probably the most famous and undoubtedly the best-selling manual on committing mayhem. It has reportedly sold over one million copies and is still going strong, with classified ads running continuously for years on end in more magazines than I can count.

In the foreword, the author says that the book was not written for fringe political groups, who already know how to do these things, but rather "for the people of the United States of America." "If the real people of America, the silent majority, are going to survive, they must educate themselves. That is the purpose of this book." Nice sentiments, but it makes you wonder what the section on making and using drugs has to do with survival. Two pages later, in the introduction, the author changes his tune: "This book is for anarchists…" Whatever.

The four sections of the book are "Drugs", "Electronics, Sabotage, and Surveillance", "Natural, Nonlethal, and Le-

The footbreaker can come in handy.
Boxing's Dirty Tricks and Outlaw Killer Punches.

tion, but you should be especially alert with *The Anarchist Cookbook*. It is said that some of the drug and explosives recipes are flawed and extremely dangerous. The essay "Recipes for Nonsurvival" in *Secret and Suppressed* [*Outposts* p 52] looks at some of the specific problems with the instructions, drawing heavily on an exposé published in *The Library Journal*, March 15, 1971. The recipe for TNT, to cite just one example, is "quite dangerous and incomplete. In step 1, mixing sulphuric acid and nitric acid will likely result in fulmination and red toxic fumes. Also the crude method he describes does not cover the removal of the Ortho Dinitro groups. If this were not done, the TNT would be extremely unstable." The author wonders if the book might be CIA disinformation, designed to backfire on subversives.

Of course, this is not going to make a difference to most people. I would guess that at least 99% of the people who get *The Anarchist Handbook* aren't going to try any of the recipes. They simply want to own the most notorious subversive manual ever published.

Barricade Books; $25
1971; oversized softcover; 160 pp
heavily illus; 0-9623032-0-8

BOXING'S DIRTY TRICKS AND OUTLAW KILLER PUNCHES
by Champ Thomas

Jay "Champ" Thomas fought in the bloody, brutal amateur boxing circuit of Arizona, California, and Mexico starting in 1923. After fighting in over 10,000 matches and training numerous students, he put together this book, which shows you exactly how to secretly employ such outlaw moves as eye-gouging, elbow-throwing, groin-punching, foot-breaking, arm-breaking, choking, and permanent blinding, plus how to throw a host of punches that can maim and even kill your opponent. Champ says that he never used these moves first, but once he ran into a dirty opponent — and there were plenty of them — he'd give them double what they gave him.

Loompanics Unlimited; $15
1997; softcover; 179 pp
heavily illus; 1-55950-147-2

THE BUG BOOK
Wireless Microphones and Surveillance Transmitters (Second Edition)
by M.L. Shannon

The Bug Book presents nitty-gritty information about eavesdropping devices from defensive (detecting bugs) and offensive (bugging) viewpoints. Although some exotic types are covered, the emphasis is on the practical. "This publication is about, mainly, the types of transmitters that are available to everyone; FM variable frequency and crystal controlled types." Variable frequency transmitters use a tuned circuit (a coil of wire and a capacitor) to broadcast on the FM frequencies, so they can be received with a standard radio. Crystal controlled transmitters use a quartz crystal to broadcast on a frequency that can only be detected with a scan-

thal Weapons", and "Explosives and Booby Traps". The first section covers pot, hash, LSD, peyote, DMT, speed, nutmeg, and others. Powell tells you how to make or grow most of them (he even includes pot and hash recipes), but just talks briefly about others, such as heroin and coke.

Most of the information in the second section is outdated. Phones, bugs, and hidden microphones have changed an awful lot during the past twenty-five years. But some methods of sabotage, such as putting sugar in a car's gas tank, are still viable after all these years.

The section on weapons gives brief instructions for hand-to-hand combat, knives, garrottes, clubs, guns, homemade silencers, and home-made tear gas. Powell always put emphasis on inflicting maximum damage (i.e., paralysis and death) on your opponents. Along those lines, the explosives section has recipes for nitro-glycerine, mercury fulminate, TNT, black powder, various detonators, an incendiary time bomb, an alarm clock time bomb, Molotov cocktails, home-made grenades, a door handle trap, car trap, and many others. Powell also gives storage and handling precautions, basic demolition formulas, and tips for placing the charges.

Naturally, any book with information of this type presents a danger to any nimrod who actually tries to put it into ac-

THE HELD-OUT CARD IS
PALMED IN THE RIGHT
HAND AND GOES OVER
THE TOP AND BEHIND THE
LEFT HAND

Diagram 9

The fine art of mucking.
Cheating at Blackjack Squared.

ner or communication receiver.

The author explains how the various bugs compare regarding frequency coverage and range of transmittal, and he teaches us about different types of antennae, receivers, and batteries. Then it's on to what we've been waiting for — instructions for installing surveillance transmitters and phone taps.

On the other side of the coin, there is information on electronically and physically detecting bugs that others have planted to spy on you and what you should do if you find one. Like other parts of the book, it contains practical, real-world tips. When you do an electronic search, for example, you should use headphones with the detector. "If you don't use headphones, if you use the speaker instead, the detector will start oscillating, making feedback, when it is close to the transmitter. A listening spy will hear this feedback, and you will have tipped him off that you found the bug. Bad move."

There is also a question and answer chapter, a look at legalities, field test results of several bug models, a list of recommended products and books, sources for equipment, and a large glossary. Whether you want to tap somebody or find out if you're a target, *The Bug Book* provides critical information. Remember the author's warning: "Surveillance happens."

Lysias Press; $19.95
1993; oversized softcover; 122 pp
illus; 1-884451-00-4

CHEAP PSYCHOLOGICAL TRICKS
What to Do When Hard Work,
Honesty, and Perseverance Fail
by Perry W. Buffington, PhD

In this somewhat tongue-in-cheek book, psychologist Perry W. Buffington gives advice on how to get ahead in life. These 62 short chapters don't offer the hardcore, "beat the system" subversion of a title from Loompanics, for example, but they may come in handy for day-to-day living. There's advice on getting out of a speeding ticket by reducing the *officer's* anxi-

ety, adjusting to daylight savings time by resetting the time a day early, guessing the right answer on multiple-choice tests, improving your immune system and feeling better simply by speaking your emotional pain out loud (by yourself), falling asleep by trying to stay awake, eating less by changing the kind of plates you use, approaching people at the time of day they are most likely to be positive, using physical clues to determine if people are lying to you, breaking into a line near the front so as not to upset anyone, handling hecklers during a speech by doing nothing, and much more.

While some of the tricks and tips offered seem unbelievably obvious or a little lame, the majority of them appear to be valid and workable. They probably won't give you the knowledge to achieve everything you want in life, but they may be able to turn a few situations to your advantage.

Peachtree Publishers; $9.95
1996; softcover; 182 pp
illus; 1-56145-130-4

CHEATING AT BLACKJACK SQUARED
The Dark Side of Gambling
by Dustin D. Marks

In this sequel to *Cheating (and Advantage Play) at Blackjack* [*Outposts* p 146], former high-stakes cheater "Dustin Marks" tells and shows (through diagrams and illustrations) exactly how to perform over 30 underhanded, illegal moves to win your hand at blackjack. The weakness of Marks' first book was that almost all the ploys required that the dealer be in on the scam. With a lot of the techniques in this book, though, you don't need to be in cahoots with the dealer... you make these moves strictly on your own. A few do require a crooked dealer, though, and some others require an accomplice.

One of the ways to cheat is "chopping" — that is, stealing a card from the table. There are lots of techniques for chopping at various times during play. The time to pull a "top palm" (i.e., steal the top card) is when the cheater cuts the deck. One way to do this is known as the "one hand top card palm". "A very deep cut is made. As the right hand is carrying the cards to the right of the remaining cards, the top card is palmed by pressing the little finger into the corner of the top card. This makes the top card move slightly upward and to the right of the rest of the cards. By pressing downward with the little finger, the top card springs off from the rear of the deck and into the palm of the right hand."

Mucking is the art of bringing a card that you chopped back into play. When you are dealt your first two cards, you see if replacing one of them with your third card would result in a better hand. If so, you pull the old switcheroo. Mucking is tough because not only do you have to bring in the card you swiped, you have to get rid of the card you don't want. The author presents two ways of performing the first action and eight ways to accomplish the second.

Another trick is to secretly add to your bet after you've seen your cards. This is tricky because casinos have an anti-cheating rule that requires chips being bet to be stacked with the largest denomination on the bottom. Still, with one of the five techniques that Marks presents, you can do it.

For all you dishonest dealers out there, chapter six advises you on how to stack the deck. Instructions are also given for the Steer Game, a major scam involving at least three people, including the dealer. A short chapter examines the possibilities of jamming a casino's electronics with a HERF gun and other methods of high-tech cheating. Marks also offers thoughts on counting cards (a legal form of advantage play), wearing disguises, not giving yourself away, casinos that cheat, and more. Finally, there is a glossary and a list of books, periodicals, videos, and other resources to help you win at blackjack by whatever means necessary.

Index Publishing Group; $24.95
1996; softcover; 201 pp
heavily illus; 1-56866-073-1

CONFESSIONS OF A YAKUZA
A Life in Japan's Underworld
by Junichi Saga

Junichi Saga is a doctor in a country town in Tokyo. One day he was visited by a new patient — Ijichi Eiji, an old, retired man whose back was covered with a tattoo of a dragon, a woman, and a peony. Eventually, the old man invited the doctor to his shack for a visit. It turns out that the man was one of the last old-time "godfathers" of the Yakuza, the Japanese version of the Mafia. He had moved to the country to spend his last years quietly. Saga taped his tales of the glory days and preserved them in this book.

Ijichi tells about his younger years working menial jobs, visiting prostitutes, catching syphilis, and living on skid row. His first job on the wrong side of the law was working on a "midnight boat". Most of these boats housed criminals, stolen goods, and anything else that needed to stay hidden from the police, but this one specialised in ferrying gamblers to and from the shady, illegal joints where they played. Eventually he met a Yakuza boss who took an immediate liking to him and made him an apprentice. "Yakuza nowadays are mixed up in all kinds of things — in the construction business, drugs, real estate, loan-sharking, you name it — but it wasn't like that in the old days. The Yakuza's real trade was gambling, and nothing else. In my day, if a Yakuza made money some other way, people would look down on him."

Eventually, after years full of entertaining and harrowing incidents that read like a work of fiction — being tortured by police the first time he was arrested, serving as a soldier in Korea (which in 1924 was a Japanese possession), and doing stints behind bars — Ijichi inherited the gambling joint when his boss died from chronic morphine use. Later, he became the head of the entire area. Unfortunately, he died before he could finish telling the doctor about his life.

Confessions makes an interesting read on several levels. It contains lots of great anecdotes, first-hand information on how the "old school" Yakuza did things, and a good bit of human interest. Ijichi was quite the ladies' man. Like a Yakuza Van Gogh, he cut off two of his fingers to impress a woman he loved.

Kodansha America; $10
1991; paperback; 253 pp
illus; 4-7700-1948-3

CREDIT POWER!
Rebuild Your Credit in 90 Days or Less!
By John Q. Newman

Having bad credit can be a serious pain, whether your credit is crummy because of non-payments, incorrect information on your credit reports, lack of a credit history, or some other reason. *Credit Power!* offers ways to get your credit on the right track.

Besides examining credit grantors and credit bureaus (and the ways they shaft you), this book provides some concrete steps you can take. The information on what to do if you have no credit is skimpy. Basically it tells you how to get a secured bank card, which will be very helpful, but some other methods would be appreciated.

The chapter on handling negative credit information is more informative. Did you realise that you are allowed to insert a short statement into your credit reports telling your side of the story? There are also instructions on how to dispute false information with credit bureaus and how to manage overdue debts by dealing directly with the creditors, rather than a collection agency. You can often pay only 60% of the amount you owe *and* get the damaging information taken out of your credit reports.

Moving into the shadier areas, *Credit Power!* tells you how to alter your personal data so that you don't show up in the credit bureaus' records, instead triggering the creation of a brand new, unsullied report. Some of the methods described are technically legal, but they all seem squirrelly. Furthermore, there are ways that by "using a little inventiveness" you can become more attractive to potential creditors.

Other tips cover getting pre-approved credit card offers in the mail, qualifying for student cards, not triggering warnings at credit bureaus, the problem with debt consolidation loans, dealing with cheque authorisation services (which are similar in many ways to credit bureaus), avoiding "credit repair agencies", using Massachusetts' strong consumer laws to help you, and more tips and tricks. Several helpful appendices provide further credit secrets, as well as sample reports (and how to decode them) from the big three credit bureaus.

INDEX Publishing Group; $19.95
1997; oversized softcover; 198 pp
illus; 1-56866-131-2

DAVID'S TOOL KIT
A Citizens' Guide to Taking Out Big Brother's Heavy Weapons
by Ragnar Benson

When Big Brother breaks out the big guns, what can you do? The famous footage of an unarmed Chinese student standing in front of a column of rolling tanks in Tiananmen Square is one of the most moving images of resistance to authoritarianism the world has ever seen, but it would have been better for the health of the students if they had been able to take the bastards out. With *David's Tool Kit*, modern day small fries can learn exactly how to destroy governmental Goliaths.

Ragnar Benson — author of *Ragnar's Guide to Home and Recreational Use of High Explosives* and *Breath of the Dragon: Homebuilt Flamethrowers* — brings together many of his, um, unusual interests and combines them into one book that tells you how you can destroy tanks, helicopters, jets, armoured personnel carriers, trucks, jeeps, and mortars and other heavy weapons. No need to purchase expensive weaponry — such as stingers — under the table from a government. This book will teach you how to make C-4 (an explosive), thermite grenades, Molotov cocktails, sniper scopes, camouflage, smoke grenades, and more. Unfortunately, sometimes this material is not covered in detail, as when Benson refers us to other books in the sections on flame-throwers and claymore mines. However, the bulk of the book — which covers actually employing these home-made destructive devices (as well as small arms) — is much more detailed. Describing techniques that have been used around the world in do-or-die situations, the author offers a large number of often creative ways to destroy your enemy. Dozens of photos and illustrations provide a visual guide to the targets and their weaknesses.

Loompanics Unlimited; $16.95
1996; softcover; 217 pp
illus; 155950143X

DECEPTION DETECTION
Winning the Polygraph Game
by Charles Clifton

Each year, anywhere from one million to four million people are hooked up to lie detectors. Employees of banks, drug companies, departments stores, fast-food chains, and the government are among the most likely to take polygraph tests. These tests (and the people who administer them) are notoriously unreliable, and the use of test results as evidence in court is still a hotly-debated topic. The author warns, "If you think that you have nothing to worry about by taking a polygraph exam because you have never done anything criminal in nature, then you are sadly mistaken." According to a literature review by the US Office of Technological Assessment, a polygraph's ability to detect if a person is lying is as low as 50.6%. Its ability to detect if a person is telling the truth ranges from 94.1% to 12.5%! Polygraphers are fond of claiming that their machines are right 90% to 95% of the time. Even if we take this demonstrably false statement at face value, it's still scary. "Imagine a situation in which 1,000 suspects are rounded up, but only 50 of them are actually guilty of a crime (which they all deny). If we assume that the polygraph validity rate is 90 percent for both guilty and innocent individuals, then 45 members of the group will be correctly identified, and five will beat the test. Of the 950, innocent suspects, however, 95 will be misidentified as guilty!"

But there is hope. You can outfox the machines. To demystify the process, the author explains how polygraph machines work and how the people running them operate. (All it takes to become an examiner is a high school diploma, six weeks of training, and a nine-month apprenticeship.) You'll learn what kind of questions to expect — "relevant", "irrelevant", "control", and "guilty knowledge" — and the verbal traps often used by polygraphers.

Then it's on to the actual countermeasures you can put into practice. Physical techniques involve breathing, muscle tension, tongue biting, and more. Cognitive techniques include hypnosis, biofeedback, and thought control. A final method is to take tranquillisers before the test, but this is a dicey proposition, as the author explains.

The chapter "The Day of the Test" is the most important part of the book. It tells you what you need to do before you leave for the exam, when you arrive at the exam location, when you meet the examiner, and during all phases of the test — the pre-test interview, the "stim test", the polygraph test, and the post-test interrogation.

Since the use of lie detectors was severely restricted by the Polygraph Protection Act, several other techniques with basically the same goal have become popular — kinesiology (interpreting body movements and speech patterns), psychological stress evaluators, integrity tests, graphology, and brain wave analysis. The author briefly explains how they work and how you can fool them.

Don't let some electronic gizmo have the godlike power to dictate what is the truth and what is a lie. Level the playing field with this book.

Paladin Press; $15
1991; softcover; 145 pp
0-87364-621-5

DOCUMENT FRAUD AND OTHER CRIMES OF DECEPTION
by Jesse M. Greenwald

The author of this book says that he made lots of money for twenty-three years by creating phoney documents. He's also done jail time, including his current stretch in Arizona. He claims that in *Document Fraud* he reveals all of his secrets. "By the time you have finished reading this book, you will be as informed on the subject of creating and passing false documents as anyone in the business."

The first few chapters show how it is relatively easy to get the hardware, software, paper, and notary stamp you will need in your new career. Most of the other chapters give instructions for creating specific documents — cheques, stock certificates, trust deeds, vehicle titles, and fake ID. Making bogus credit cards is also surprisingly easy, since all you need besides your regular equipment is an embosser and maybe some hologram stickers. The author advises against trying to counterfeit money, though. Not only is it extremely difficult, it's a federal offence, while cheque fraud is usually a state offence. The other chapters, as well as parts of chapters, discuss various scams for turning your hot-off-the-press documents into cash.

Along the way, the author also gives general tips on developing a shrewd criminal attitude. "The forger mustn't be naive enough to believe that people can be trusted. Partners are to help spend the forger's money and them rat him off. If the forger keeps this scam to himself he can make all of the money he wants without creating liabilities he cannot control."

Loompanics Unlimited; $15

1997; softcover; 148 pp
illus; 1-55950-155-3

FMX
The Revised Black Book — A Guide to Field Manufactured Explosives
by William Wallace

A review of *Outposts* in *The Bloomsbury Review* mentioned that a library director had heard a colleague actually call for the burning of books that give instructions for making explosives. I thought this was interesting, since first of all, *Outposts* didn't review any bomb books (hey, I can't cover everything). It also made me realise just how controversial such information is. If a librarian — a supposed guardian of knowledge — wants to go Nazi on these books, then this is some hot information. And touchy subjects are what *Outposts* and *Psychotropedia* are all about. Therefore, I knew *Psychotropedia* had to include an example of this distinct, large subgenre of books covering explosive mayhem.

FMX gives the exact ingredients and procedures for preparing 46 explosives, including ANFO, black powder, mercury fulminate, nitro-glycerine, semtex, tetrazene, and TNT. Each recipe also gives the following information: detonation rate, deflagration temperature, impact sensitivity, friction sensitivity, means of initiation (e.g., blasting caps), and more. The author provides further information on over 50 component materials, a glossary, and safety rules.

Let me just say that if you actually try creating any of these explosives, you are a crazy mook who deserves whatever happens to you. I don't mean to impugn the author or publisher, but I am simply not going to risk my arms, sight, and/or life on a few pages of instructions from a $20 book I got through the mail. Caveat emptor in extremis!

Paladin Press; $20
1995; softcover; 145 pp
0-87364-853-6

HANDBOOK FOR VOLUNTEERS OF THE IRISH REPUBLICAN ARMY
Notes on Guerrilla Warfare
by the IRA

This small booklet, issued in 1956 by the General Headquarters of the Irish Republican Army, lays down the basics of sneaky, hit-and-run guerrilla warfare. "The guerrilla attempts to do three things: 1) Drain the enemy's manpower and resources. 2) Lead the resistance of the people to enemy occupation. 3) Break down the enemy's administration." To that end, the *Handbook* offers general advice on strategy and techniques along with specific instructions for sabotaging and attacking the enemy. Some of the topics that are covered include a history of Irish guerrilla warfare, strategy, tactics, deception, organisation, arms, guerrilla bases, attacks, ambushes, withdrawals, defence, the enemy's tactics, explosives, intelligence, and co-operating with the local population.

Paladin Press; $8
1956 (1985); small booklet; 41 pp
0-87364-075-8

Making an unauthorised deposit at a cash machine.
How To Hide Things In Public Places.

HOW TO HIDE THINGS IN PUBLIC PLACES
by Dennis Fiery

We won't go into any details, but there may come a time in your life when — for whatever reasons — you need to hide something. Concealing something in your house often isn't a secure option because of possible discovery by family, roommates, a significant other, a nosy landlord, or cops who raid your place. Hiding something in your vehicle is similarly vulnerable. Safety deposit boxes are easily traceable to you and can be opened with a warrant. Sometimes your best bet is to hide something in a public or semi-public place.

This book goes into an impressive level of detail about doing just that. Not only will you learn about hiding things so that you can retrieve them later, you'll also learn how to do "drops" — leaving something so that a second party can pick it up. Among the buildings and other areas that are covered are parking garages, parked vehicles, construction sites, department stores, restaurants, libraries, storage rooms, and rest rooms. Specific hiding places include stairwells, fluorescent lighting fixtures, ivy-covered fences, rock walls, fence posts (just unscrew the top), hollow columns and railing, potted plants, newspaper boxes, traffic cones, utility boxes, pay phones, and much more.

The instructions are often specific and practical, although some of the techniques will only work if you want to hide something for a few hours to a couple of days at most. One section gives insider information about the locks — called Simplex locks — that are used to secure drop boxes for UPS and FedEx. Typically, only 130 combinations are in use, and there seems to be a single "default" combination that works for many UPS boxes. This technique will only keep your stuff hidden till the next pickup, so you'd better know the schedule.

How to Hide Things in Public Places is one of Loompanics' more concretely useful "how-to" titles.

Loompanics Unlimited; $15
1996; softcover; 216 pp
heavily illus; 1-55950-148-0

THE INFORMATION CENTER CATALOGUE

The Information Center sells over 190 reports (all of which are under $10) revealing how to tap phones, run scams, get utilities for free, "jackpot" pay phones, make disappearing ink and exploding paint, find unlisted phone numbers, make free long distance calls, detect bugs, cook up laughing gas (nitrous oxide), sabotage a car, or hack email, vending machines, answering machines, and ATMs. I've just got to get the report on making cheques that will disintegrate without a trace...

> The Information Center/PO Box 876/Hurst TX 76053
> WWW: www.theinformationcenter.com
> catalogue: $1. Non-US: $6

INFORMATION WARFARE
Chaos on the Electronic Superhighway (Second Edition)
> by Winn Schwartau

At this moment, sabotage of electronic communications and data systems is wreaking havoc on our society and has the potential to practically shut it down. "With over 125 million computers inextricably tying us all together through a complex land- and satellite-based communications systems, a major portion of our domestic $6 trillion economy depends on their consistent and reliable operation. Information warfare is an electronic conflict in which information is a strategic asset worthy of conquest or destruction. Computers and other communications and information systems become attractive first-strike targets."

These attacks are already costing the US $100 billion to $300 billion per year. They come in numerous forms but basically fall into three categories, all of which are covered in detail. Personal information warfare has to do with the vast amounts of data about each of us that's stored in databases... medical, financial, criminal, academic, insurance, and loads of other types of information are all over the place. And they're not very secure from disclosure, modification, or deletion. Corporate information warfare jeopardises trade secrets, crucial information (such as customer records), and day-to-day operations. Global information warfare threatens entire governments.

The author, who publishes an information security newsletter, discusses the threats posed by viruses, hacking/cracking, coloured boxes for phone phreaking, voicemail hacking, cellular phone monitoring, stealing cell phone codes, satellite jamming, electromagnetic eavesdropping (reading computer monitors from a remote location), the Clipper chip, HERF guns (which use radio frequencies to jam electronics), rigged computer chips that fail or malfunction according to a preset plan, etc. He relates numerous instances of purposeful and accidental major power outages, phone systems going down, and corporations being held hostage by hackers. Thirty-five reprinted articles from other writers explore many facets of the situation in greater detail.

Towards the end of the book, the author offers ideas for a protective national information policy and looks at the future of information warfare. There's a great resources sec-

BRITISH INTELLIGENCE AGENT 007 M127...$29.95 — SOVIET KGB M128...$29.95 — MOSSAD ISRAELI INTELLIGENCE M129...$29.95 — MILITARY INTELLIGENCE M130...$29.95 — TEXAS RANGERS (Actual size) M131...$19.95 — ROYAL CANADIAN MOUNTED POLICE M132...$29.95 — SECURITY SPECIAL OFFICER M133...$19.95 — SECURITY ENFORCEMENT M134...$19.95 — EMERGENCY MEDICAL TECH. M135...$19.95

May I see your badge, Officer?
NIC Catalogue.

tion that lists credit reporting agencies, security organisations, security and privacy publications, hacker conventions, government resources, Usenet groups, electronic mailing lists, and lots more. "Who's Who in Information Warfare" lists contact info for 100 people involved in the field.

> Thunder's Mouth Press; $18.95
> 1994, 1996; softcover; 768 pp
> 1-56025-132-8

NIC, INC, LAW ENFORCEMENT SUPPLY CATALOGUE

Most of the items in this catalogue are designed to make you look like someone very official. Naturally, if you are an official, such as a police officer, this stuff will come in handy. If you're not... well, let's just say that everything is sold only for "novelty purposes". You can get some very realistic patches, including those from the Texas Rangers, Interpol, United Nations Security, the CIA, and the Military Police K-9 Corps. Perhaps even scarier is the line of very realistic badges offered. Flash one of these babies and most people are likely to think you really are with the New York State Police, Mossad Israeli Intelligence, the Royal Canadian Mounted Police, the Los Angeles Police, California Highway Patrol, Disney World Security, or dozens of other organisations. You can also get official-looking warning signs, government folders, certificates, and embossers with the seals of all fifty states.

NIC apparently does a brisk business in impressive credentials, which may or may not really apply to you. Each ID card has areas for you to paste in a picture and supply pertinent information (name, address, etc.). The Special Weapons Permit, for example, has space for you to fill in which type of weapon you're allowed to carry (the card in the catalogue says "Automatic"). There's a *faux* official crest on the card and a number that looks like it was hand-stamped. Other cards identify you as a registered mercenary, security guard, pilot, bounty hunter, private investigator, fashion and glamour photographer (great for scoring with chicks), ordained minister (not so great for scoring with chicks), notary public, Marine Sniper, intelligence officer, ranger, reporter, etc.

For $200 you can get a completely legal second passport from another country, such as the British Honduras. You can also buy 30-round magazines, subsonic ammo, a brush with a hidden knife, dissolving spy paper, and a clock that looks like an ultra-realistic time bomb, plus lots of books and videos on performing merry mischief.

NIC, Inc. Law Enforcement Supply/500 Flournoy Lucas Road,
Bldg 3/PO Box 5950/Shreveport LA 71135-5950
WWW: www.nic-inc.com
Catalogue: $4

THE NO-NONSENSE COMPUTER VIRUS AND HACKING RESOURCE BOOK

This little catalogue offers a nice selection of books, magazine issues, and software related to viruses, hacking, and encryption. Be warned, this isn't the pussyfooting stuff you'll find at bookstores or in computer magazines. This is hardcore.

Probably the hottest piece of merchandise on offer is a CD-ROM called *The Collection: Outlaws from America's Wild West*. It contains around 3700 live, executable viruses from 574 families (a total of 37 megabytes in all)! Included are the infamous Internet Worm and the Christmas virus. You also get mutation engines, virus creation kits, Trojan horse programmes, twelve megabytes of source code and disassemblies of viruses, 76 megs of virus-related electronic newsletters, ten megs of text files and databases, eight megs of shareware/freeware anti-virus programmes, and more. Pretty damn scary, eh? If you want this one, you better grab it before it's outlawed.

An available floppy disk contains PGP, the celebrated communications encryption programme, and KOH, which will automatically encrypt all information on your hard drive and floppies. Books that you can purchase include *The Virus Creation Labs*, *Computer Viruses*, *Artificial Life and Evolution*, *Secrets of a Super Hacker*, *Applied Cryptography*, *Digital Privacy*, and *The Big Black Book of Computer Viruses*. These techno outlaws also offer back issues of *Computer Virus Developments Quarterly* and a subscription to its newest incarnation, *The Underground Technology Review*.

American Eagle Publications/PO Box 1507/Show Low AZ 85901
Catalogue: $1

POLITICS AND DIRTY TRICKS
A Guide to Screwing Up the System
by VR Farb

If you've had it up to here with lying, thieving, grandstanding hypocritical politicians and have lost faith in the voting system, which only replaces one liar with another, you have an option. Retaliate against the politicians by using devious, non-violent tricks that make their lives miserable. Most of the insidious methods in this book were devised by professionals who are paid by one politician to shaft an opponent. The author claims that they revealed their secrets to him and now the average schmuck can put them to use.

The first chapter, "Little Things Mean a Lot", covers some of the ways to cause minor inconveniences and embarrassments… not enough to destroy a political career, just enough to cause headaches. Pretending to be on a politician's staff and switching around or cancelling speeches and appearances is effective. "Change airplane reservations so the guy misses flights on do-or-die tickets, move coffees and motel rooms up, and schedule flights to places to which it is senseless to travel… Carefully plan so that no one turns up for scheduled meetings and that motels, tickets, and cars are reserved substantially before the group arrives." (These tactics were reportedly used incessantly against Michael Dukakis.)

A much riskier but potentially more damaging move is to bug the politician's headquarters and tap the phones. A less extreme measure is simply dumpster-diving for credit card carbons, telephone logs, memos, and other important information. You can use the media to your advantage by sending out phoney press releases or giving radio stations bogus sound bites.

To trash a candidate's finances, you can spend lots of money or make pledges to charities while claiming to be on the campaign staff. One hard-hitting tactic is to file fake tax forms with the IRS, making it look like the candidate owes much more than he or she really does. You can also interrupt the flow of incoming money by scaring off individual donators and political action committees (PACs).

Other monkeywrenching techniques include making the candidate look like an idiot, creating chaos at press conferences, tying up the candidate's phone lines, and sabotaging the candidate's vehicle. Who says that a single concerned citizen can't make a difference?

Paladin Press; $14
1995; softcover; 93 pp
illus; 0-87364-821-8

PREEMPLOYMENT INTEGRITY TESTING
How to Ace the Test and Land the Job
by Charles Clifton

If you want to become a wageslave, very often you'll have to go through the intrusive, disturbing procedure of taking an integrity test. These written tests are supposed to magically determine how honest you are and, very often, your tendencies towards: "Substance abuse, insubordination, absenteeism, excessive grievances, willingness to participate in a strike, bogus worker compensation claims, temper tantrums", and any other behaviour that's counterproductive or otherwise gets the Man's panties in a wad.

It's estimated that in 1991 15 million of these tests were administered by 5,000 to 6,000 firms. For some reason, people tend to open up on such tests, admitting to their potential employers such things as drug use and shoplifting.

After discussing the questionable theoretical foundations of integrity tests, the author gets down into the meat of the book — how to answer the questions to make yourself appealing to the company. Tests are divided into two categories: covert tests try to subtly trick you into revealing information about yourself, while overt tests just come out and ask you point-blank questions about your honesty and other traits. An example of a covert test is the Hogan Employee Reliability Index. It tries to uncover malcontents by focusing on four basic themes: "hostility to rules, thrill-seeking impulsiveness, social insensitivity, and alienation." Questions related to thrill-seeking ask if you like crowds, if you'll try anything once, etc. "Those passing the test are usually seen as conscientious, attentive to details, modest, and self-confident… You will fail the test if your responses make you look aggressive, hostile, self-indulgent, impulsive, suspicious, and tense."

The same goes for almost all other tests. It's impossible to keep up with specific tests because new ones are constantly being developed and companies are very secretive about their tests. However, learning about the tests in this book will help you discover the general rules. Basically, you should make yourself fairly appealing, as the above test indicates. Don't go overboard, though. Most tests have questions that are supposed to detect someone who's lying to impress. If you indicate that you have never lied to your parents or that you never curse, it will be counted as a lie.

One of the overt tests that is discussed is the Reid Report. This test mixes attitude questions, biographical questions, and blunt "have you ever…" questions. Among the tips the author gives: "One question will ask you to estimate the percentage of people who steal from their employers. People who pass the test choose low estimates — 10 percent or less. People who fail make estimates in the 30-35 percent (or higher) range."

The end of the book contains a sample, generic integrity test with instructions on how to score yourself. An appendix of do's and don'ts offers plenty of good advice, such as, "**Do** finish the test quickly", and, "**Don't EVER** admit anything of consequence."

Paladin Press; $12
1993; softcover; 102 pp
0-87364-725-4

SPECTRE PRESS PUBLICATIONS

Spectre Press sells disks containing files — taken primarily from the Internet and BBSs — that give lessons on committing illegal acts.

Nuclear Bomb Manual. The two files on the disk *Nuclear Bomb Manual* amount to a mere 78.5 K, just over 9000 words. If you think you can build a nuke from 9000 words of instruction or less (and parts of the documents just give background info on atomic bombs), then you'll be in for a surprise. These two articles tell you more or less what you need to do, but they don't give you step-by-step details on how you'd actually do it. This isn't a bad primer on what makes nuclear bombs tick, so to speak, and it'll give you a general idea of what you need (at least 110 pounds of Uranium-235

or 35.2 pounds of Plutonium, a detonating head made from DuPont blasting caps, an air pressure detonator, etc.), but don't show up with it at your next terrorist meeting unless you want to get drummed out. [$15]

Credit Cards & Magnetic Stripes. The 41 text files (amounting to 508 K) on this disk offer info on finding credit card numbers, ordering stuff with someone else's card, information embedded in the magnetic stripes, meanings of the card number, and so on. Most of the information is repetitious and fairly obvious (get numbers by dumpster-diving for carbons behind businesses that accept credit cards). Here and there is some specific, "insider" info. One file lists Citibank Service Addresses, although I have no idea what they mean, and another tells you how to check whether or not a card is still valid and what its credit limit is. One promising article reveals a supposedly 100% guaranteed system for making up valid American Express numbers. Several GIFs on the disk present a diagram for a magnetic stripe copier, and 13 programmes will generate bogus card numbers that appear legit. [$20]

Stopping Power Meters. The one text file on this disk (11 K) seems detailed enough to actually follow in a real-world situation, allowing you to slow down and even stop or reverse a power meter. It is accompanied by six handdrawn GIFs showing parts of the meter and tools of the trade. [$15]

Electronic Warfare Bible. Over 450 documents (2.5+ megs' worth) give lots of juicy details on listening in on communications, jamming signals, and doing pirate communications. You get frequencies for cordless phones, pagers, bugging and other surveillance devices, world-wide airlines, Andrews Air Force Base, the Goodyear blimp, Boeing, NASCAR, Disney World, the Drug Enforcement Agency, the FBI, and many, many others; instructions for transmitting on all frequencies, making and using numerous antennas, setting up pirate radio and TV stations, jamming TV signals; sources for equipment; and more. [$21]

Cellular Hackers Bible. On this two disk set, hundreds of megabytes' worth of files tell you *exactly* how to monkey with cellular phones. You'll see how to reprogram phones from Alpine, AT&T, Cellquest, Diamontel, Fujitsu, GE, Hitachi, Mitsubishi, Nokia, Panasonic, Radio Shack, Sony, and lots of other manufacturers. Other files cover cloning phones, making unbillable calls, intercepting calls, and other mischief. There are also lists of frequencies and identifying info for several cell phone companies and programmes for gathering info about intercepted calls. As far as I can tell, though, almost all of the instructions were written in 1993, at the latest. Many of them indicate that they were last modified in 1990 or 1991. I have to wonder how much of this technical information still applies. [$21]

A lot of the files on Spectre Press's disks are available on the Net. In fact both the documents on *Nuclear Bomb Manual* are posted in various places on the Web. Check online for newer information before buying any of these titles.

Spectre Press
1996; 3.5" disks for PCs

U.S. MILITARY PRACTICE GRENADES Now available in all three types of casings — pineapple (MK II), egg (M-30) & baseball (M-33) with ALL the mechanical parts IN THE FUSE ASSEMBLY!!! — NO EXPLOSIVES. We did our best to come up with these complete sets of NEW (not reconditioned fired parts) directly from the military contractor, for these most interesting units. Each grenade comes with brand new, never fired, fuse casing, striker arm, spring, pivot pin, handle, pull pin, safety clip, and detonator casing. All the hardware WITHOUT the explosives. Definitely not the usual type 2 or 3 piece surplus grenade available at your local Army-Navy store or from other mail order companies. This is really an outstanding offer that we have never seen approached before. A must for the military collector.
MILITARY OLIVE DRAB GRENADES.............$19.95
#233 Pineapple (MKII)   #234 Egg (M-30)   #235 Baseball (M-33)

For the mercenary who has everything.
Phoenix Systems Catalogue.

PHOENIX SYSTEMS CATALOGUE

If you want to get your hands on more than just books for committing mischief — if you want to get the actual tools to do the job — this is your catalogue. In it you'll find stuff that you won't believe is legal. Take the ammunition, for instance. You want armour-piercing ammo? They've got the only kind that's legally available in the US, the .223 SS-109 Penetrator. You can also buy Glaser bullets, which fragment when they hit tissue, causing massive damage. This ammo "consistently delivers 3½ times greater stopping power than the best hollow point and causes instant and total incapacitation." If that doesn't suit your needs, Phoenix sells subsonic ammo and tracer ammo that burns bright orange-red.

Other weapons you can get include pepper gas, 150,000-volt stunners, brass knuckles, a sleeve knife, a sword umbrella, tactical batons, saps and blackjacks, and more. Can't find a gift for the mercenary who has everything? How about tire shredders, razor tape, smoke grenades, cannon fuses, flares, an easily portable blowtorch, rubber bullets, gun holsters, survival kits, radiation sickness medicine, snowshoes, and all kinds of books and videos? You budding locksmiths <cough, cough> can practice your trade with lock pick sets, pick guns, and a set of super slimjims ("This kit will open almost any car on the road today — foreign or domestic.").

Surveillance/countersurveillance equipment includes bug detectors, phone scramblers, phone recorders, twelve-hour tape recorders, and a microphone disguised as a pen. One nifty device, called The "X" Phone, works like a normal phone. However, it is also a microphone that will pick up all sound in the room it's in, even when it's on the cradle. What's even cooler is that when activated, it will constantly monitor the room, and when it hears a noise, it will call you at whatever number you programme. When you answer the phone, you'll be listening in on the room! Modern technology is amazing.

Phoenix Systems, Inc./PO Box 3339/Evergreen CO 80439
Catalogue: $3

PIRATE RADIO OPERATIONS
by Andrew Yodler & Earl T Gray
If you want to "take back the airwaves" by operating your own unauthorised, low-power radio station, this book will tell you *exactly* how to do it. The costs of starting a sanctioned station are prohibitive. "As a result, you cannot even think about owning a licensed AM or FM station in the US unless you have at least $150,000 in liquid assets. If you want a short-wave station, where the FCC has imposed a 50,000-watt minimum power, you must have at least $1,000,000." In many countries, radio stations are heavily censored and cannot even be owned by non-governmental entities. Pirate radio is a way to break through these blockades. Your station won't have a lot of power, but you'll be able to say and play whatever your little heart desires.

The authors tell you the equipment you need and how to get it cheap. By buying from yard sales and flea markets and by using equipment they owned prior to starting a station, the creators of WBBQ outfitted their studio for $300. A whole chapter is devoted to transmitters, the crucial piece of equipment that turns your studio into a station. Depending on your needs and whether you buy used or new, this can set you back anywhere from $20 to $3,000. Another chapter is devoted to the tricky subject of antennas.

Once you have your hardware set up, it'll be time to move on to the other topics covered: studio techniques and production, publicity, broadcasting, determining times and frequencies, being unobtrusive, safety issues, and dealing (or, even better, not dealing) with the Federal Communications Commission. At the end of the book are a large bibliography and resources section, a glossary, and addresses for over 200 pirate stations in North America and Europe.

Loompanics Unlimited; $19.95
1997; softcover; 364 pp
illus; 1-55950-151-0

THE REVENGE ENCYCLOPEDIA
by anonymous
Revenge books are a particularly popular subgenre of merry mischief material. There are about a jillion such books out there. This one contains a higher than average number of ideas, but presents fewer details on how to carry them out than most other books. The techniques are divided into at least 200 categories, based on who you're going to screw over or how you're going to do it — answering machines, Christmas trees, funerals, jocks, landlords, locks, telephone solicitors, televangelists, and vending machines. Some of these ideas are dumber than hell, some would be almost impossible to pull off, others could ruin the victim's life permanently, and others are ingenious. To wit:

☞ When ordering pay-per-view specials, some cable companies only require a phone number. Punch in your victim's number.

☞ "If your mark is a prude, arrange the fruit and vegetables in her refrigerator to resemble anatomical parts. Kiwi fruit and bananas make a nice showing."

☞ Have different lenses put in your victim's glasses at a one-hour vision store.

☞ If someone at work eats your lunch from the community refrigerator, lace it with laxatives.

☞ "Order a turd sent to your victim through the mail." (Does anyone know of a mail-order place that sells shit?)

Take back the airwaves.
Pirate Radio Operations.

are filled with very specific observations and tips. Some of them involve timing, such as the best/worst times of day, days of the week, and seasons for lifting. There are also tips regarding specific retailers, such as bookstores, clothing stores, food stores, and department stores.

A long chapter provides ideas for over 40 approaches you can take, involving receipts, refunds, tag switching, falling down, creating a diversion, grabbing and running, using emergency exits, creating a false pocket, washroom packing, paying for a cover item, and dressing as an employee. One lifter even got a job as a Santa Claus. "I had this big !@#$ing red suit on, with the bag on my shoulders and as I was merrily distributing candies to the !@#$ing kiddies, I robbed them !@#$ers blind."

The next chapter deals with the security devices designed to thwart lifters. Lots of stores now attach some form of magnetic tag or strip to their merchandise. If this gizmo passes through the electronic "gates" at the exit doors, an alarm rings. Wrapping the tags in aluminium foil will render them useless. With practice, some people can get the tags off quickly, and some professional lifters have lifted the tools that are used to remove the tags at the checkout counter. Be aware that some stores have bogus security systems that look like real magnetic tags and gates, but are just for show. Other stores with real systems sometimes put a tag or strip in an obvious place and hide another one inside a product, where it's less likely to be removed. Another idea to consider is just walking through the gates and letting the alarm sound. For many reasons, some stores may not be able or willing to apprehend someone who has just walked out with merchandise.

Other chapters go into further detail about what to wear for lifting, how to conceal things on your body, handling store employees and security guards, laws regarding shoplifting, what to expect if you're caught, and more.

Lots of manuals on committing illegal activities are filled with obvious, common-sense ploys, but *S(h)elf Help Guide* give lots of meaty, practical advice that has been gained through actual practice. Buy it, and it may be the last purchase you have to make!

TriX Publishing; $24.95CAN, $17.95US
1996; softcover; 273 pp
0-9680761-0-6

☞ If your victim still has a record player, take out the needle and put in a nail.

☞ "Substitute fresh roadkill for the turkey at your mark's next Thanksgiving dinner."

☞ Phone in false charges of child abuse.

☞ Plant cocaine in your victim's car and call the cops.

☞ Throw this book away and learn how to get along with people. (Just kidding — that idea isn't really listed.)

Paladin Press; $15
1995; oversized softcover; 103 pp
0-87364-851-X

S(H)ELF HELP GUIDE
The Smart Lifter's Handbook
by Gabriel Caime & Gabriel Ghone

"When I want something, man, I don't wanna pay for it," said Jane's Addiction. If this is your philosophy too, then *S(h)elf Help Guide* will help you get the infamous five-finger discount. The authors claim that they have never taken stuff without paying, but they have personally interviewed dozens of shoplifters and have read publications written by security firms, so they have the real-life, inside scoop on how to rip off stores.

A lot of the book — especially the first part — gets into the morals and motives of shoplifters, retailers, and the authors themselves. They say that the stores' wails about losses from shoplifting are basically hot air. Such practices account for a 0.7% loss of revenue.

The extensive chapters on actually stealing the goods

STEAL THIS BOOK
(Twenty-Fifth Anniversary Facsimile Edition)
by Abbie Hoffman

Steal This Book — written by Abbie Hoffman, one of the most famous 1960s radicals — is a first tier classic of subversive literature. This edition is an exact reproduction of the book as it was originally published by Pirate Editions in 1971. Hoffman presents hundreds of ingenious and often illegal methods for getting stuff for free, creating mischief, and beating the system.

The first part of the book, "Liberate!", tells you how to get food, clothing, transportation, housing, education, medical care, entertainment, and more without paying. A lot of times, this means simply knowing about freebies. "Fisherman always have hundreds of pounds of fish that they have to throw out. You can have as much as you can cart away, generally for the asking." Other techniques, though, involve scamming or outright stealing. "If you have access to a few addresses, you can get all kinds of records and books from clubs and introductory offers. Since the cards you mail back are not signed there is no legal way you can be held for the bill. You get all sorts of threatening mail, which, by the way, also comes free."

The section on dope has advice on selling it, giving it away ("A group in Los Angeles placed over 2,000 joints in library books and then advised kids to smoke a book during National Library Week."), growing pot, and buying with confidence. "If you buy cocaine, bring along a black light. Only the impurities glow under its fluorescence, thus giving you an idea of the quality of the coke." This chapter also has one of the most controversial lines from the book: "Avoid all needle drugs — the only dope worth shooting is Richard Nixon."

The second section is titled "Fight!" It tells you how to put out an underground newspaper, do pirate radio and TV, not get killed at a demonstration, fight in the streets, make several types of bombs and explosives, perform first aid, avoid the draft, receive political asylum, arm yourself, and pull pranks on the Man. Hoffman gives instructions for shorting out part of the phone system from the comfort of your own home. He also lists the private phone numbers of Nixon, Agnew, Kissinger, and others. This may not do any good now, but it's still pretty funny.

Occasionally Ab gets a little ridiculous. "If you are around a military base, you will find it relatively easy to get your hands on an M-79 grenade launcher, which is like a giant shotgun and is probably the best self-defence weapon of all time. Just inquire discreetly among some long-haired soldiers." Sure, man.

The final section, "Liberate!", gives specific info for getting all kinds of free stuff in New York, Chicago, LA, and San Francisco. In New York, the Hare Krishnas serve a free breakfast at 7 AM, accompanied by chanting and dancing.

Obviously, since the information in this book is now a quarter-century old, an awful lot of it is obsolete. For example, supermarkets use bar codes instead of price stickers, so it's not as easy to pull a switch. Because payphones now charge 25¢ and only have one slot, some of Hoffman's tricks won't work anymore. I'd be surprised if more than a handful of the hundreds of addresses and phone numbers in this book are still the same. One of the most dated tips is under the section on free housing in New York: "On the West Side, there's a poet named Delworth at 125 Sullivan St. that houses kids if he's got room."

However, you can still pick up some useful things from *Steal This Book*. The comix by Skip Williamson and Gilbert Sheldon and the photos with humorous captions also add value. But the real reason to get it is simply to own a piece of outlaw history.

Four Walls Eight Windows; $7.95 (or free, if you steal it)
1971 (1995); paperback; 315 pp
heavily illus; 1-56858-053-3

TORTURE
(Expanded Edition)
by Edward Peters

This new edition of a classic work looks at the history of torture, which is basically defined as state-sponsored brutality inflicted on an individual for a political purpose. The author covers torture from its appearance in Western society in ancient Greece and Rome, its long-lived popularity in Europe through the end of the 1700s, its technical abolition during the Enlightenment, its eventual reappearance, and its widespread practice in the second half of the twentieth century. For the most part, the author doesn't dwell on the specific modes of torture, preferring to look at how the practice was justified and the reasons it was used. That is, until the final chapter, which takes an excruciating, clinical look at torture methods being employed today.

Torture includes a long appendix reproducing fourteen documents, ranging from 437 BCE to 1989, that are crucial in the history of torture. "The Jurisprudence of Torture", published in 1612, pitifully attempts to set up rules and regulations regarding the brutalising of criminal suspects. "Torture cannot be repeated more than three times on the same subject, and then only for justifying reasons and with respect had to the persons and the crimes involved. Confession of guilt works no damage to the party confessing until the confession has been reaffirmed without torture." An excerpt from the Khmer Rouge's Interrogator's Manual elaborates on the reasons for torment. "The purpose of torture is to get their responses. It's not something we do for fun. We must hurt them so they respond quickly. Another purpose is to break them and make them lose their will. It's not something that's done out of individual anger, or for self-satisfaction… Don't be so bloodthirsty that you cause their death quickly. You won't get the needed information."

University of Pennsylvania Press; $16.95
1985, 1996; softcover; 295 pp
0-8122-1599-0

THE ULTIMATE SCANNER
by Bill Cheek

In his latest book, scanning guru Bill Cheek tells you, among other things, how to merge your scanner with your computer to create one awesome machine. Your new souped-up, state-of-the-art scanner will be modified in ways the manufacturer never considered, with expanded memory, almost unlimited coverage, subsidiary carrier authorisation, and all kinds of bells and whistles.

In a conversational manner, Cheek at first raps with you about the best kinds of scanners and related equipment to buy. He gives some general advice about tools and techniques ("Dental plaque scrapers make great circuit trace cutters as well as scorers for raw printed circuit board.") and provides a few basic hacks and tweaks to perform on you scanner.

The section on interfacing your scanner with a PC will allow you to have control and power like you've never dreamed. The computer will auto-programme 400 memory channels in eight minutes, log info from the scanner's display into a text file, automatically reject undesirable frequencies, perform virtually any process normally done by hand, and more.

A lot of the modifications in the book, though, don't require a computer. Most people aren't aware of it, but there is a hidden aspect of FM broadcasting called subsidiary carrier authorisation (SCA). This type of broadcasting is intended only to be received by subscribers, and it carries such things as audio novels for the blind, sports and weather, Muzak, and other "premium" services. It is illegal to receive any SCA without prior permission from the broadcaster, but Cheek shows you how to do it anyway.

Along similar lines, you'll find instructions for the most popular modification of all — allowing your scanner to intercept cellular phone calls. You can also hack your scanner to pick up walkie-talkies, cordless telephones, and other such signals at close range.

On a less subversive note, there are ways to increase your programmable and storable memory and get your scanner to bypass worthless signals. The final chapter, strangely titled "Fun Stuff", contains some serious math lessons on logarithms, decibels, geodetic bearings and distance, diffraction loss, spreadsheets, and more.

Index Publishing Group; $29.95
1995; oversized softcover; 242 pp
heavily illus; 1-56866-058-8

THE WHOLE SPY CATALOGUE
A Resource Encyclopedia for Researchers, PIs, Spies, and Generally Nosy People
by Lee Lapin

Lee Lapin's books — which include *How to Get Anything on Anybody*, volumes 1 and 2 [*Outposts* p 21] — are so thorough in their instructions for sensitive information gathering that intelligence agencies use them as training manuals. *The Whole Spy Catalogue* is a huge compendium of ways that we amateurs can do what the big dogs do. With it, you'll be able to locate individuals, tap phones, bug rooms, track assets, surveil people, break and enter, go to spy school, become a private investigator, and more.

The chapter "How to Locate and Investigate Anyone" gives the low-down on all kinds of information sources, including city and county sources, state sources, credit reporting bureaus, and lots of private companies that will do the searching for you. One company, Tracer's Worldwide Services, can get you a person's address, phone number, bankruptcy records, college degree, credit report, criminal convictions, traffic tickets, place of employment, marriage records, death records, driving records, and other info that should be nobody else's damn business. If you know someone's license plate number, you can find out her name and address. If you know someone's name, address, and date of birth, you can get his driver's license number.

Lapin describes important databases and BBSs for snoops. A special chapter gives step-by-step instructions using the online service Dialog for finding individuals.

Even more high-tech is the ability to use satellite and aerial photography in your pursuits. One company offers black and white, colour, or infrared photos of just about any 20-square-mile area of land you would want. Another place sells enhanced satellite photos that have incredible resolution. According to company literature, their products are being used to solve crimes. For any crime committed between 1964 and the present, you just tell them where and when it happened. "Our technicians will search in excess of 60 databases world-wide to ascertain whether there was a satellite image, aerial, or space photograph taken within your date-time window at your specific location. If there was, through re-sampling data and imaging technology we can provide you with a photograph of the crime scene area as seen from above with clear resolution to two meters."

Much of *The Whole Spy Catalogue*, as the name suggests, is made up of reviews of books and periodicals that will help you in specific areas. Some titles include *Online and CD-ROM Database Searching*, *Inside the CIA*, *The Financial Privacy Report*, *Monitoring Times*, *Hands-on Electronic Surveillance*, *Obtaining Your Private Investigator's License*, *Confidential Information Sources*, *Searching Magazine*, and *County Court Records*. Lapin also provides information on obtaining lock-picking tools, nightvision equipment, listening devices, and cellular phone interception units (that last item is technically available only to law enforcement personnel).

The Whole Spy Catalogue is an important resource for any amateur or professional info-gatherer. If it's good enough for the CIA, the KGB, and the Mossad, it's good enough for us.

Intelligence Incorporated; $44.95
1995; oversized softcover; 436 pp
heavily illus; 1-880231-10-7

DRUGS

PSYCHEDELICS/ ENTHEOGENS

THE AGE OF ENTHEOGENS & THE ANGELS' DICTIONARY
by Jonathan Ott

This most recent of psychonaut Jonathan Ott's publications presents two works under one cover. "The Age of Entheogens" is a relatively short essay (the main body is 26 pages) on the stamping out of ecstatic religions in Western civilisation. At least 50,000 years ago, humans were using sacramental plants ("the flesh of the gods") to bring about visions and personally experience the divine. This long Age of Entheogens was brought to a crashing close somewhere around 400 CE [Common Era], when the new kid on the block brutally suppressed it. Christianity was a recently developed religion which promoted an impersonal God that could not be experienced directly. In place of sacred inebriants, it offered the placebo of the wine and wafer. "The Pharmacratic Inquisition was the answer of the Catholic Church to the embarrassing fact that it had taken all the religion out of religion, leaving an empty and hollow shell with no intrinsic value or attraction to humankind, which could only be maintained by hectoring, guilt-mongering and plain brute force."

But there is hope. Ott says that we are in the beginnings of the Enteogenic Reformation, a time when people are once again starting to directly experience spiritual ecstasy through the use of visionary substances. When Albert Hofmann synthesised LSD and R. Gordon Wasson told the masses about sacred mushrooms around the middle of the century, they helped trigger a raising of collective consciousness. This will lead — according to Ott — to a more enlightened, less materialistic society. The essay is followed by 16 pages of detailed endnotes — which elaborate on many of the points in the body of the text — a poem, and a six-page bibliography.

"The Angel's Dictionary" is a response to Wasson's call for "a vocabulary to describe all the modalities of a Divine Inebriant". Set up in lexicon format, this important work offers definitions for 318 words having to do with sacramental inebriants and the states they induce. The entries are not only defined but are buttressed by well over 400 quotations from drug literature and general literature. "Ecstasy" is defined as, "Literally: the withdrawal of the soul from the body; mystical or prophetic exaltation or Rapture characteristic of shamanism and visionary states, originally and naturally catalysed by entheogenic plants; also, such states artificially induced by breath control, fasting, meditation, drumming and other shamanic and yogic practices." One of the supporting quotes is from Ludlow's *The Hasheesh Eater*: "My ecstasy became so great that I seemed to cast off all shackles of flesh."

An *icaro* is a "magical chant or melody with presumed healing properties; learned from 'Plant-Teachers' by Amazonian Shamans under the influence of Ayahuasca and other entheogenic Potions…" The accompanying quote from the *Journal of Ethnopharmacology* lists *icaros* for many purposes — curing diseases, calling defenders, attracting love, summoning spirits, etc. Other words that are defined include "addiction," "communion," "Holy Grail," "Mysteriarch," "opium," "psilocybine," "Uniao do Vegetal," and "yajé".

This book is probably the best of Ott's books to get if you're fairly new to the subject or if you want a nice, compact summation of his ideas. "The Age of Entheogens" is a good overview of the history of ecstatic religions, and "The Angels' Dictionary" is a major step towards creating a language capable of dealing with psychedelics.

Jonathon Ott Books/Natural Products Co; $18
1995; softcover; 160 pp
0-9614234-7-1

AYAHUASCA ANALOGUES
Pangean Entheogens
by Jonathan Ott

Ayahuasca is the name given to a hallucinogenic potion used widely by indigenous people across South America. Its primary ingredient is the *Banisteriopsis caapi* plant, with some DMT-containing plants thrown in for good measure. Psychonaut Jonathan Ott writes in detail about the history and nature of ayahuasca and related potions (such as yagé). He also gives fascinating accounts of the twenty-three times he ingested the visionary brew, as well as reports from colleagues. In an extremely important chapter, Ott lists over sixty-five plants from around the world that contain the same properties as *B. caapi* and over sixty plants that contain entheogenic tryptamines like DMT. This means that there are theoretically over 4000 combinations that can yield ayahuasca-type potions. Some of these plants are legal, which is good news for law-abiding psychedelic adventurers.

Jonathan Ott Books/Natural Products Co; $15
1994; softcover; 127 pp
illus; 0-9614234-5-5

THE ESSENTIAL PSYCHEDELIC GUIDE
by DM Turner

The Essential Psychedelic Guide is one of the most useful drug books ever published. It gives the scoop on using six psychedelics — LSD, mushrooms, cactus, DMT, harmala alkaloids, ketamine — and two quasi-psychedelic empathogens — ecstasy and 2-CB. If the pseudonymous author (initials: D.M.T.) is to believed — and I see no reason not to — he is sharing extensive first-hand knowledge that has been earned from 18 years of ingesting psychedelics.

Each substance is given its own chapter, in which its intensity is rated on a ten-point scale. LSD earns a 3 to 7, Ecstasy a 2 to 4, DMT a 9 to 10, and ketamine blows the lid off with a rating of 10 to infinity. In each chapter, you'll learn where the drug comes from, its history, how to prepare and ingest it, safety considerations, what the high is like, and how to combine it with other drugs. Turner writes of DMT (an alkaloid that occurs in Amazonian plants and the human body): "What one will experience on DMT is impossible to predict. It can range from heaven to hell, cyberspace to jewelled palaces, fear or personified evil, visions of jungle animals, contacts with extraterrestrials, links with ancient spirits, or adventures with fairies and elves. The DMT user should be prepared for anything."

A separate chapter is devoted to multiple combinations. Turner is a fearless psychonaut who piles one drug on top of another in search of synergistic effects. He describes seven combos, the most elaborate of which is mushrooms, Syrian rue, DMT, nitrous oxide (laughing gas), and ketamine. Taking LSD with the anti-depressant Ludiomil and nitrous oxide caused a distinct transformation: "I can only describe it as totally hilarious, melting through the bottom of the universe as it all came swirling down into me."

Safety is taken quite seriously. Besides the information presented with each substance, there is also a ten-page chapter on physical and mental safety. Additional chapters provide a history of psychedelics, a look at the connection between DMT and water energies, and thoughts on CydelikSpace, the author's name for the level of reality people visit while using hallucinogens.

Turner comes across as a remarkably brave and self-confident explorer, who is eager to discover his own mind. While reading his book, you tend to forget that taking these substances is illegal. To Turner they are the necessary and exciting tools to aid in self-discovery. Highly recommended.

Panther Press; $12.95
1994; softcover; 111 pp
illus; 0-9642636-1-0

GATEWAY TO INNER SPACE
Sacred Plants, Mysticism and
Psychotherapy
edited by Christian Ratsch

This book, published in honour of Albert Hofmann — who first synthesised LSD — contains twelve essays on the connections between psychedelics and consciousness. Psychologist Tom Pinkson, who specialises in grief counselling, contributes the essay, "Purification, Death and Rebirth: The Clinical Use of Entheogens Within a Shamanic Context". In the first half of this essay, Pinkson relates his powerful experiences while consuming psychedelics and engaging in other ceremonies with a Huichol Indian shaman in Mexico. One night while going through an all-night ritual involving drumming, chanting, praying, and ingesting "grandfather peyote", he had a vision. "It was of Christ, being crucified on the Cross.

I saw that each time a negative judgement was made about ourselves or someone else, a spike was driven into Christ's body and he screamed in pain. When a negative judgement was stopped, not repressed or denied, but acknowledged and then released, a spike was removed. A beautiful smile burst from Christ's face lighting all in his presence as he thanked us for our kindness." He goes on to describe a retreat he later led, in which participants used psychedelics and other shamanic rituals to confront their fears, discover new talents, and change their lives.

George Greer is a psychiatrist who has used MDMA (ecstasy) in therapy sessions. In his brief essay, "Using Altered States to Experience Choice", he explains why he thinks MDMA (and ketamine) can help people improve themselves. "The drug changes the brain chemistry, which changes the way the nerve cells communicate with each other. Habitual patterns do not work as well, and (if we are not sedated) our brain asks us which way to go a lot more often. Again and again we are confronted with the question of what our purpose is." Hopefully we will be able to bring this new knowledge back with us: "… the things we learn and the new patterns we consciously arrange in our minds can still be operational once the drug is out of our system."

The other essays — including those written by Terence McKenna and Stanislav Grof — cover the similarities between psychedelic trips and meditation, the neurochemistry of altered states, the newly discovered sacred plant of Egypt, the use of ayahuasca in different settings, the current state of psychedelic research, and how psychedelics relate to shamanism, alchemy, and yoga. [As we go to press, this book is unavailable but is expected to be reprinted soon. Check with the Mind Books folks (below) to find out when it gets released.]

Prism Press; £6.95, $10.95
1989; softcover; 258 pp
illus; 1-85327-037-7

HIGH PRIEST
by Timothy Leary

Out of print for over 25 years, High Priest chronicles 16 psychedelic trips taken by Timothy Leary back in the glorious days when you were allowed to put mushrooms and LSD into your own body. The unifying concept of the book is a little unclear. Each of the trips is said to have a guide, a "high priest" — Allen Ginsberg, Ram Dass, Aldous Huxley, and others. The only catch is, sometimes that person really partakes in the trip and sometimes he (it's always a he) has nothing to do with it. In the second trip Leary describes, "God Reveals Himself in Mysterious Forms", the guide is famed ethnomycologist R. Gordon Wasson, the first outsider to ingest sacred mushrooms in Mexico. Leary and five friends eat the 'shrooms in Cuernavaca, Mexico, but Wasson is not among them. Oh well. Anyway, the trip is very important, because from it Leary realises that his life's work is to explore the hidden aspects of the mind. During this particular journey, he travels back to the creation of the universe. "I am lying unicelled looking up up up through the spiral unfolding of two billion years, seeing it all ahead of me, ovum, seg-

Cactus of the gods.
Peyote.

mentation, differentiation of organs, plant, fish, mammal, monkey, baby, grammar school, college, Harvard, Mexico, Cuernavaca."

In another mushroom trip with a group, Leary didn't partake. Another participant became upset that the others had started without him and furiously demanded that Leary give him some 'shrooms, or else. Uncle Tim refused and learned something valuable and disturbing. "There seemed to be equal amounts of God and Devil (or whatever you want to call them) within the nervous system... We are the architects of the celestial and hellish stages we act upon. I began to get a sinking feeling. Psychedelic drugs didn't solve any problems. They just magnified, mythified, clarified to jewel-like sharpness the basic problem of life and evolution."

Trip 15, "Your Faith Will Perform Miracles", is a recounting of the well-known "Good Friday Experiment" that Leary and a colleague conducted. They assembled a small group of divinity students along with some experienced psychonauts as guides. Half the students and guides swallowed pills with ground up mushrooms in them and half swallowed placebos. Since it was a double-blind experiment, no one knew till it was over who had taken the real stuff. It turns out that every person who took the 'shrooms had a mystical religious experience, but no one who took the placebo did. "There was proof — scientific, experimental, statistical, objective. The sacred mushrooms, administered in a religious setting to people who were religiously motivated, did produce that rare, deep experience which men have sought for thousands of years through sacraments, through flagellation, prayer, renunciation."

High Priest also includes a new introduction by Leary, a

new foreword by Allen Ginsberg, trippy art, and dozens of psychedelic documents reprinted in the margins alongside the main text. It provides a bold, nuanced look at what psychedelic substances have to offer the human race.

Ronin Publishing; $19.95
1968, 1995; softcover; 347 pp
illus; 0-914171-80-1

MIND BOOKS CATALOGUE

Mind Books does a fantastic job carrying just about every in-print book having to do in any way with entheogens/psychedelics (including all of the books in this section). They're currently offering in the neighbourhood of 300 books, plus issues of magazines and journals. Every aspect of the subject is covered, including technical, ethnobotanical, cultural, spiritual, personal, and how to make/grow your own. They keep their Website scrupulously up-to-date, alerting you to upcoming and newly released books. This is an absolute must, even if they were charging for their catalogue... but they're not, so you have no excuse!

Mind Books/321 S. Main St. #544/Sebastopol, CA 95472
Email: books@promind.com
WWW: www.promind.com
catalogue: free

PEYOTE
The Divine Cactus (Second Edition)
by Edward F Anderson

Originally published in 1980, *Peyote* has been greatly expanded and updated to cover just about every aspect of the famed psychoactive cactus: religious, historical, psychotropic, legal, medicinal, botanical, chemical, and pharmacological.

There is evidence that peyote was known to some inhabitants of North America as early as 5000 BCE [Before Common Era]. It has definitely been used for 2000 years, at the very least. The indigenous people of Mexico were the ones who introduced peyote use to Native North Americans in the second half of the 1700s. Use of the cactus in the US was fairly isolated, however, until a century later, when it spread like wildfire through North America, creating a pantribal religious movement called peyotism. The author discusses the origins, rise, and Christian suppression of peyotism, as well as the suppression of the original form of peyote use in Mexico. A separate chapter and appendix provide a detailed look at the legal status of peyote today.

The chapter "The Peyote User's Experience" examines the cactus's effects on the mind as reported by many users, including such famous people as Aldous Huxley and psychologist/sexologist Havelock Ellis. *Chicago Sun-Times* reporter William Braden wrote about his experience of tripping while listening to Beethoven on headphones: "A majestic Beethoven chord exploded inside my brain, and I instantly disappeared. My body no longer existed, and neither did the world... There was only the music, and then bright colours that turned out to be musical notes. The notes danced along a silver staff of music that stretched from one eternity to another, beyond the planets and stars and space itself." A German physician who took mescaline (the primary active ingredient in peyote) describes his experience: "I saw endless passages with beautiful pointed arches, delightfully coloured arabesques, grotesque decorations, divine, sublime, and enchanting in their fantastic splendour. These visions changed in waves and billows, were built, destroyed, appeared again in endless variations first on one plane and then in three dimensions, at last disappearing in infinity."

Although the healing uses of marijuana are fairly well-known, it's unexpected to see a chapter on the medicinal benefits of peyote, which has been referred to as the "Medicine of God" by Native Americans. I thought this referred to the plant's spiritually healing effects, but it apparently can help the body and mind too. It has been used to combat snakebites, rheumatism, and spasms, reduce pain and fever, help nursing mothers to make more milk, and treat many diseases and disorders. Some psychiatrists have experimented with mescaline in therapeutic settings, with some apparent success.

Other topics that are covered include the Native American Church, peyote ceremonies, peyote music, physiological effects, toxicity, adverse reactions, mescaline and other peyote alkaloids, cultivation, biogeography, and the American Indian Religious Freedom Act of 1978.

If there's anything you want to know about this prickly wonder, it's probably here.

University of Arizona Press; $19.95
1996; softcover; 272 pp
illus; 0-8165-1654-5

PEYOTE AND OTHER PSYCHOACTIVE CACTI

by Adam Gottlieb

Although it briefly discusses legality, methods of ingestion, and mental and physical experiences, this book's main purpose is to tell you how to find, grow (from seeds or cuttings), and graft peyote, plus several other psychoactive cacti from central Mexico and the San Pedro cactus (which grows in the Andes Mountains). Other sections discuss how to increase the potency of your plants and how to extract pure mescaline or alkaloid mixtures from them.

Ronin Publishing; $9.95
1997; softcover; 86 pp
illus; 0-914171-95-X

PHARMACOTHEON

by Jonathan Ott

Pharmacotheon is a colossal, towering survey of natural psychedelics (aka entheogens) and their artificial cousins. Pioneering psychonaut Jonathan Ott has put twenty tears of research and two years of writing into this sweeping account of shamanic substances. His multi-disciplinary approach combines pharmacological and botanical facts with his own experiences and those of others, plus his speculations on what these substances mean for the human race.

The first part of the book presents a long, well-reasoned diatribe against the criminalisation of drugs. Ott presents scientific, practical/legal, moral, and economic reasons why outlawing substances is wrong and unworkable. In the sec-

tion "Why Can't We Cope with Ecstasy and Euphoria?", Ott writes: "Even though myriad justifications for the modern laws against entheogens have been offered up, the problem modern societies have with these drugs is fundamentally the same problem the Inquisition had with them, the same problem the early Christians had with the Eleusinian Mysteries — religious rivalry. Since these drugs tend to open up people's eyes and hearts to an experience of the holiness of the universe... yes, enable people to have personal religious experiences without the intercession of a priesthood or the preconditioning of a liturgy, some psychonauts of epoptes will perceive the emptiness and shallowness of the Judaeo-Christian religious tradition; even begin to see through the secular governments which use religious symbols to manipulate people; begin to see that by so ruthlessly subduing the earth we are killing the planet and destroying ourselves."

The main sections of the book cover beta-phenethylamines — mescaline, péyotl, San Pedro, and artificial compounds; indole derivatives — DMT, LSD, ayahuasca potions, psilocybine, and many others; and isoxazole derivatives — ibotenic acid/muscimol. Ott provides mounds of fascinating information on these forbidden molecules. He drops a bombshell by claiming that mescaline is the biggest drug hoax of all time. Millions of doses of alleged mescaline were sold in the 1960s and 1970s. It was second only to LSD in the entheogen market. However, "It is highly unlikely that more than a few tens of thousands of people have ever ingested authentic mescaline in pure form. Everyone else has been 'ripped off' as the saying goes." So what were all those people taking? Lab analyses of various samples show that less than 10% of mescaline tablets and capsules are actually mescaline. The rest are LSD, PCP, LSD with speed, etc. So if you think you have ingested mesc in pill form, the odds are very great that you haven't. Surprise!

Later, Ott describes the sledgehammer effects of smoked DMT: "After inhalation of a full dose of DMT [in] a single breath, the effects will be experienced in ten to fifteen seconds, usually before exhalation of the smoke. The initial 'rush' sensation is similar to the feeling of rapid acceleration and may be accompanied by vertigo. Users often describe high-pitched sounds, which may be perceived as being insect noises. The peak effect occurs within two to three minutes, during which most users are stunned and speechless..."

One of the book's appendices offers short sections on eight more visionary compounds, including asarones, ibcgaine, nicotine, cannabis, and thujones. Ott also offers short descriptions of around 130 plants that may have entheogenic properties but need to be studied more. Further appendices offer condensed technical data on the 50 most important entheogens, and a botanical index. The awe-inspiring bibliography lists 2440 sources, which is three times as many as any previous book on the subject.

Clearly, this is one of the elite group of books that is absolutely required for any collection of drug literature.

Jonathan Ott Books/Natural Products Co; $40
1993; softcover; 639 pp
0-9614234-3-9

There's a psychoactive fungus among us.
Psilocybin Mushrooms of the World.

PRACTICAL LSD MANUFACTURE
by Uncle Fester

Dear Uncle Fester is concerned. According to the DEA, there are only 100 LSD manufacturing labs in the US, and they're almost all in Northern California. This small concentration of labs means not only that the LSD supply of the country is always in jeopardy, but also that we are forced to ingest "mediocre swill comparable to the beer spewed out by the major breweries." To remedy this situation, Fester is putting the power of knowledge into the hands of the people. His book is the first one to present the manufacture of LSD from natural substances in a way that can easily be understood by someone with a good foundation in chemistry.

You will need a fair amount of skill, as Fester says making acid is about twice as hard as making speed, which itself is no walk in the park, judging by Fester's book *Secrets of Methamphetamine Manufacture (fourth edition)*. You'll also need at least $5000 worth of real lab equipment, not the make-do items found in most basement labs.

The process starts by cultivating one of three natural substances: ergot-infested rye, morning glory seeds, or Hawaiian baby woodrose seeds. Fes spends a good deal of time describing how to produce the ergot (and he offers additional sources of info), but he says almost nothing about raising the seeds. Such seeds are available legally from companies specialising in exotic botanicals [see *Outposts* p 63]. However, you'll probably want to get just a few seeds and plant these to produce more, because buying a truckload of seeds will send a signal that something fishy is going on.

All three of these sources yield alkaloids containing lysergic acid amides, the precursors of lysergic acid. Fester gives instructions for extracting and isolating these substances. Once you've done this, you can use several methods to get LSD. Two methods are based on the work of Albert Hofmann, the person who first synthesised acid. These methods are useful because they create your desired end product directly from the amides, instead of having to first create lysergic acid. The drawback is that these procedures involve anhydrous hydrazine, a very carefully watched substance. There are instructions for making your own, but do it wrong, and you'll have a nice explosion on your hands.

For the other five methods, you'll need to create lysergic acid from the amides, a process that Unca Fester nicely explains. Subsequent chapters teach you how to create Lucy by combining lysergic acid with any one of four chemicals.

Other chapters discuss solvent management and staying out of trouble. As a bonus, you also get detailed information on creating the mescaline-like psychedelic TMA-2 from the wild-growing calamus root. Finally, several appendices provide still more helpful information.

Loompanics Unlimited; $15
1995; softcover; 115 pp
illus; 1-55950-123-5

PSILOCYBIN MUSHROOMS OF THE WORLD
An Identification Guide
by Paul Stamets

So you want to pluck some mushrooms containing the psychoactive chemical psilocybin, but you're not sure exactly what they look like? Then refer to this book, which is the most complete, detailed guidebook to magic mushrooms ever published. The focal point of this tome is the 130 pages that describe in words and pictures a dozen species from the genus *Panaeolus*, 63 species from the genus *Psilocybe*, and twelve species from the "minor genera" (plus one genus and one species of mushroom that look like psilocybin mushrooms but are extremely poisonous). The exact physical description of each species of 'shroom in presented in minute detail. This includes separate sections on the cap, gills, stem, microscopic features, habit, habitat, distribution, and additional comments. To help further, each one is shown in a clear colour photograph.

Other material in the book provides helpful information on psilocybin mushrooms in general. A section on their geographical distribution offers some surprising facts. Most such magic 'shrooms — especially the most powerful ones — hardly grow in deep forests and other undisturbed natural areas. Instead, they grow on dead plant material, which can most often be found in more developed areas where civilisation and nature have clashed. "Today, many Psilocybes are concentrated wherever people congregate — around parks, housing developments, schools, churches, golf courses, industrial complexes, nurseries, gardens, city parks, freeway rest areas, and government buildings — including county and state courthouses and jails!" They grow throughout the world, especially in North, Central, and South

America, but they also appear in parts of Europe, Asia, New Zealand, Australia, and Africa.

Further sections give such practical advice as which particular habitats to look for (grasslands, dung deposits, disturbed habitats, etc.), how to identify psilocybin mushrooms (through spore printing, the bluing reactions, and other ways), and the best methods to collect, preserve, and prepare them. Oftentimes, a book such as this one would tell you how to identify and collect trippy mushrooms but then pretend that you only want them as conversation pieces. This book, though, cuts through the malarkey and tells you what you need to know in order to have a great trip, including dosage, rituals, mindset, and physical environment.

On top of all that, you also get historical background on 'shrooms, a warning on the dangers of misidentification, a large glossary and resource section, and diagrams of various mushroom caps, gills, and general morphology.

I think it's safe to say that if your intention is to hunt the magic mushroom, *Psilocybin Mushrooms of the World* is the one book you must own.

Ten Speed Press; $24.95
1996; oversized softcover; 245 pp
heavily illus; 0-89815-839-7

PSILOCYBIN PRODUCTION
Producing Organic Psilocybin in a Small Room
by Adam Gottlieb

Rather than growing full mushrooms, complete with caps and stems, the easiest way to harvest the psychedelic substance psilocybin is to grow the mycelium, "the fibrous underground network of the mushroom." This slim manual will tell you how. "Complete descriptions are given for locating the mushrooms; developing stock cultures for inoculation; cultivating, harvesting, and drying the mycelium; extracting the active alkaloids; and using existing cultures to seed new cultures in order to maintain an ongoing psilocybin farm which can yield a regular crop of the hallucinogenic mycelium." Should you want amounts beyond those for personal use, you'll find out how to expand the procedures to create a large-scale production operation (thousand of hits per week) in a room approximately 10' x 15'. There are also instructions for "fruiting" the mushrooms, that is, growing them fully so that the caps and stems appear.

To further help you on your way, the back of the book lists ten suppliers who will outfit you with mushroom kits, spore prints, and other cultivation supplies. Finally, Richard Glen Boire — an attorney specialising in laws affecting psychedelics — provides a look at the legal standing of psilocybin and magic mushrooms in the US.

Ronin Publishing; $9.95
1997; softcover; 82 pp
illus; 0-914171-92-5

PSYCHEDELIC PRAYERS AND OTHER MEDITATIONS
by Timothy Leary

In the early 1960s Timothy Leary reworked the famous reli-

"I feel that no person, no matter how experienced with other psychedelics or altered states of mind, can be prepared for the intensity of a full-strength salvinorin A journey." *Salvinorin*.

gious text *The Tibetan Book of Dying* within a psychedelic framework. Physically dying and having an hallucinogenic trip are remarkably similar experiences in that you undergo a profound transformation of consciousness and a death of your ego. By reinterpreting the Buddhist instruction manual for people who are crossing over, Leary created a valuable guide for psychonauts.

Later in the decade, Leary rewrote another religious classic in psychedelic terms. This time the text he chose was Lao Tse's *Tao Te Ching*, which forms the basis of Taoism. Calling his version *Psychedelic Prayers*, Leary recast the short poetic meditations in a way that merged the insights of a drug-induced trip with timeless Eastern philosophy. The results are gentle, life-affirming reflections on the worlds inside us and outside us. They are designed to be read to someone who is actually having a psychedelic experience, but you'll probably enjoy them even while grounded.

The book is divided into six parts, each one addressing a different stage or aspect of a trip. The first six meditations deal with preparing for the journey. During the first phase of the actual journey, we encounter the elemental energy which flows through all things but cannot be seen or heard. "Reaching, we do not grasp it/We call it intangible/But here… we spin through it/Electric, silent, subtle". Next we experience "the seed-cell energy" of our own bodies, housed in our DNA, which Leary calls the "ancient serpentine coil".

Each of the five poems in part four is devoted to the neural energy we experience through our physical senses.

The fifth section addresses the energy points of the body known as chakras. For some reason, Leary only addresses five of the seven chakras, completely ignoring the third and the sixth. The final — and largest — section deals with the trick of bringing back what you learned on your voyage and applying it to day-to-day life. This is the wisest part of the book, with some good advice for living peacefully and enjoying life:

"Choose beauty, so you define ugly
Select good, so you define evil
As you choose your joy, so you design your sorrow
The coin you are now imprinting has two sides
Better to return in the flow of the Tao"

This edition of the book also contains five additional psychedelic/Taoist poems that Leary and his then-wife Rosemary wrote two years later, as well as a longer poem that pays tribute to Lao Tse. On top of that, you also get the original foreword by Leary, a new intro by his supporter Ralph Metzner, a new preface by Rosemary Leary, several photos, and a bibliographical history of *Psychedelic Prayers* with reproductions of the covers of various editions, including one by famed Swiss biomechanical artist HR Giger.

Ronin Publishing; $12.95
1966, 1997; softcover; 142 pp
illus; 0-914171-84-4

PSYCHEDELIC RESOURCE LIST
by Jon Hanna

This listing contains names, addresses, phone numbers, and moderately- to well-detailed descriptions of hundreds of organisations relating to psychedelics. Categories include book sellers and publishers, periodicals, cacti and mushroom suppliers, cultural resources, mail order ethnobotanicals, gardening and lighting supplies, hemp-related, information resources, the law, merchandise and gadgets (CDs, T-shirts, smoking accessories), religious and research organisations, posters, radio, tapes, video, seeds, and legal stuff to smoke.

Quarterly updates supply additional entries, plus several book reviews and revised information (new addresses, rip-offs, etc.). These updates are $15 (non-US: $21) for a four-issue subscription

With so much happening on the psychedelic scene, it's hard to keep up. *The List* and its updates are a vital resource. (Soma Graphics also offers reports on making ayahuasca and Yuba gold and growing peyote.)

Soma Graphics; $19.95
1996; oversized softcover; 120 pp
illus; 0-9654383-0-9

PSYCHEDELIC SOURCEBOOK
by Will Beifuss

The *Psychedelic Sourcebook* is basically the same concept as the *Psychedelic Resource List* [above]. The *Sourcebook* has less entries, but they are, on the whole, more detailed. Companies that offer books, tapes, seeds, or plants very often have some of their merchandise listed along with prices.

Categories include spores and kits, spore germination, book catalogues, audio and video tapes, mail order ethnobotanicals, seeds, periodicals, organisations, World Wide Web sites, FTP sites, and newsgroups. There's also a measurement conversion table, a dosage table for various psychedelics, a botanical index, and a suggested reading list.

Rosetta; $13 ppd
1996; softcover; 72 pp
heavily illus; 0-9647946-2-4

SALVINORIN
The Psychedelic Essence of *Salvia Divinorum*
by DM Turner

Salvia divinorum is a rare member of the sage family found in Oaxaca, Mexico. The Mazatec Indians of that region have been enjoying its psychedelic properties for centuries, and it was introduced to the rest of the world by R. Gordon Watson, the pioneering ethnobotanist who also made psilocybin-containing mushrooms famous. It wasn't until the middle of 1993 that someone isolated the principle active compound of the plant — dubbed salvinorin A — and smoked it. As it so happens, salvinorin A is the most powerful natural psychedelic yet discovered, and it acts in ways — on the mind and the body — that no other substance does. Even some experienced psychonauts have come away from the drug completely overwhelmed. "The intensity of a salvinorin A journey is often experienced as being an order of magnitude more potent than smoked DMT, in much the same way that DMT seems an order of magnitude more potent than a typical LSD journey. A large percentage of salvinorin A users also report that the fear-factor is much greater than with DMT, which is saying a lot. I feel that no person, no matter how experienced with other psychedelics or altered states of mind, can be prepared for the intensity of a full-strength salvinorin A journey."

Should you feel up to the challenge, the author includes a section on how to administer salvinorin A — which is usually smoked or inhaled after the crystalline powder has been vaporised — plus sections on the good and bad things you're most likely to experience. More than half the book is given over to descriptions of sixteen trips on salvinorin A or *Salvia divinorum*. While already on the psychedelic/empathogen 2-CB, the author smoked some salvinorin A "and was immediately transported into a dimension where I shared the consciousness of the Salvia entity. My awareness was spread throughout the labyrinthian maze of her roots, stems, and leaves, in connection with many other plant forms… Soon I found myself in a realm that was filled with fairie and elfin creatures. I enjoyed playing with these critters which had a highly distinctive visual appearance. These elves were quite different from those I've frequently encountered while on DMT. They were composed of numerous different elements, were quite abstract, and each was uniquely intricate. The DMT elves tend to form intricate patterns if viewed as a group, being composed of a smaller amount of body-part shapes which are usually replicated in each elf. The salvinorin elves were dressed differently than the DMT elves and acted more goofy and playful."

By bringing to light the usage and effects of a relatively "new" psychedelic, *Salvinorin* — the first book on its subject — has earned a place among the canon of drug books.

Panther Press; $9.95
1996; softcover; 57 pp
illus; 0-9642636-2-9

SCHEDULE-ONE ART

To put LSD into consumable form, a hit is placed on a tiny square of paper, called blotter. Hundreds of these perforated squares are on a single sheet of paper. These sheets of blotter paper have always been an underground artistic medium... each square may contain a repeating piece of art, or several squares — up to the whole sheet — may make up one large work of art. Every imaginable kind of image has been used, from pop culture to fine art. Mickey Mouse, Felix the Cat, Alice in Wonderland, Jesus, fractals, UFOs, flowers, the FBI's emblem, Albert Hofmann, and Mikhail Gorbachev are some of the motifs to make an appearance.

Lately, blotter art has become more widely-recognised as an art form. People are collecting and framing it... a few museums have even put on exhibits. Now you too can own a piece of art and drug history. Thomas Lyttle, the editor and publisher of the *Psychedelic Monographs and Essays* series [*Outposts* p 61], has been collecting acid art for years and is now offering pieces for sale. He removes the LSD from the sheet and gets a psychedelic luminary — such as Timothy Leary, Ken Kesey, Alexander Shulgin, or John Lilly — to autograph it. The price, right now, is $250 per piece. Write for further info and a listing of available works.

Thomas Lyttle Associates/157 B Bristol Ln/Naples FL 33962

THANATOS TO EROS
35 Years of Psychedelic Exploration
by Myron J. Stolaroff

In 1961 Myron Stolaroff, an electrical engineer by trade, founded the International Foundation for Advanced Study in Menlo Park, California. The Foundation studied the psychological and spiritual insights that could be gained from the use of LSD and mescaline. It was instrumental in the creation of the transpersonal psychology movement, which explores personal growth, peak experiences, and enlightenment.

In this autobiographical book, Stolaroff tells how "one neurotic, self-absorbed, occluded individual" ditched his hang-ups and problems and managed to tap into the beautiful, joyful light and energy of life. "This book is the story of how I overcame thanatos, the drive for death, to elicit eros, the drive for life." The main catalyst for this transformation — this opening up to the "Divine Presence" — was psychedelics.

"From my very first [psychedelic] experience in April, 1956, I concluded that LSD is the most profound learning tool available to man." During that session, Storloff relived his birth. He realised that he had been in physical pain during the birth process and that his mother had been in pain

throughout the pregnancy. Causing her so much pain had infused him with guilt he had been carrying around his whole life. After the trip, he also came away knowing that God is real and that we are all interconnected.

Over the next decades, Storloff, his wife, and their friends and acquaintances have also experimented with ecstasy, 2-CB, MEM, BOD, 2C-T-2, 2C-E, and many other entheogenic creations. The book contains dozens upon dozens of detailed descriptions of experiences. Most are wonderful, but Storloff readily admits that the drugs can trigger miserable experiences, and he devotes a chapter to them. But even uncomfortable, scary experiences can be valuable, as Storloff shows.

One of the biggest problems with using psychedelics to achieve understanding is incorporating what you've learned into your everyday life. The trips themselves can be unbelievably beautiful and can leave you walking on air for several days afterwards. But eventually you'll probably return to your "old stinking self", as Aldous Huxley described it. One of the author's biggest accomplishments was learning how to bring back what he learned and constantly experience the beauty of life, even when not under the influence of any substance.

Storloff believes that psychedelics help people come to peace with themselves in two ways. "The first is through their wondrous ability to dissolve defences and resistances for the earnest explorer, so that access to powerful unconscious material is permitted. More important, they allow access to the Celestial level and the discovery of the Divine Love and Grace which permeate the universe... One is willingly led, if need be, through the dungeons of human agony and the distortions of one's own personal creations to achieve freedom, understanding, and a more profound level of love."

Thanatos to Eros is one of the best books on psychedelics I've read, as well as one of the best self-discovery books using any technique, period. If there are any among you who still subscribe to the "drugs are just plain bad" school of thought, do yourself a huge favour and get this book. You'll see that you've been closing your mind to an array of tools that just might help you find yourself and achieve true happiness.

Thaneros Press; $22.95
1994; hardcover; 192 pp

TIKHAL
The Continuation
by Alexander Shulgin & Ann Shulgin

In 1992, psychopharmacological chemist Alexander "Sasha" Shulgin and his wife Ann, a writer and therapist, published the extraordinary book, *PIHKAL* (Phenethylamines I Have Known And Loved) [*Outposts* p 59], a look at the creation and ingestion of many types of psychedelic compounds. With much of the material discussing the couple's romantic relationship and their own drug experiences, *PIHKAL* is a personal book. With loads of instructions for making various drugs, it is also a technical book. The massive and complex *PIHKAL* has become a classic in the field of drug writings.

At long last, the Shulgins are back. This time they are

discussing the tryptamines they have known and loved, but they are still using the same approach. The personal, the technical, and now the political have been brewed together into a massive book that once again adds immeasurably to our understanding of the mind and the substances that expand it.

As before, the book is divided into two parts. Book I: "The Story Continues" offers a melange of personal experiences and fact-based articles written by the Shulgins' alter-egos: Shura and Alice. The opening story, "Invasion", explains why publishing TIHKAL was an even braver act than publishing its predecessor. Soon after PIHKAL was published, the Drug Enforcement Administration pulled a not totally pleasant inspection of the Shulgins' home/lab, which resulted in the revoking of Sasha's license to work with prohibited drugs. "Alice" and "Shura" each recount this disheartening event in minute detail.

In one of the most important chapters in the book, "Places in the Mind", Alice pools the results of her trips (over 1000!), plus those of her husband and others, to create a guide to some of the experiences you are likely to undergo when you alter your consciousness. She covers the Void, certainty and knowing, paranoia, self-hatred, the oceanic experience, synaesthesia (experiencing sights as sounds and so on), laughter, "the Beth state", Kali, flooding, time distortion, out of body experiences, hallucinations, euphoria. She describes a state she calls "inflation", brought on by 2C-T-8: "I sat quietly, radiating light and energy, noticing that, although my mind was suffused with something you'd have to call intense pleasure, each thought was distinct and clear; there was no confusion anywhere in my head, just as there was no illness or weakness within my body. *Oh, my everlovin' God! This is what's meant by a bliss state. I'm a body of energy; my mind is like crystal; there's no question in the universe that I can't find the answer to. All I need in the world is myself, living in this serene rhythm, filled with livingness and knowledge.*"

Another chapter that deserves extra-special recognition is "DMT Is Everywhere", in which Shura reveals the diverse life forms that contain the mind-expanding chemical DMT. You'll find this wondrous substance in certain sea sponges, mushrooms, frogs, grasses (including bamboo and reeds), trees, plants, not to mention the human brain. Shura gives the Latin names of the genuses, families, and species, so you'll know exactly which organisms he's talking about. This is extremely important information that guarantees that access to DMT can never be suppressed.

Other chapters in Book I cover Alice's amazing experience at Lourdes, experiments with marijuana, one of Alice's 'shroom trips, a dream Shura had after ingesting PanSoph-2, Alice's memorable dreams, the truth about flashbacks, therapy sessions involving ecstasy, hoasca vs. Ayahuasca, morning glory seeds, designer drugs, barriers to drug research, and a look at who's actually profiting from the so-called War on Drugs.

Book II: "The Chemistry Continues", much like its PIHKAL counterpart, is a couple hundred pages of recipes for 55 psychedelics that fall into the tryptamine category. The most famous member of this family is undoubtedly LSD, although DMT, harmaline, ibogaine, and even melatonin are members, too. About half of these syntheses have been published (some by Sasha) in obscure technical journals, and the other half have never before appeared in print. The majority of them are Sasha's creations (his most famous children are 2-CB, DOM a/k/a STP a/k/a "Serenity, Tranquility, and Peace", and ecstasy, which he resynthesised after it had fallen into total obscurity).

The production of each chemical is explained in terms that only a scientist would understand, and the effects of ingesting some of them are noted. For example, taking 40 mg of EIPT orally: "Within a half hour, I have sparkling and a very unsure tummy. This is, on one hand, strangely not erotic, and yet I am completely functional sexually. Remarkable orgasm. But still not erotic. No visuals, no sound enhancement, no fantasy…" After taking 250 mg of DPT orally: "I was seeing the Light real strongly. The Light sort of looked like bright bursts of Light but also like a kind of Spiritual Tunnel, and it seemed at one point, along with that, I saw a Human form, but the vision seemed like I was sort of inside the Being and outside, and the Human was inside me and appeared to be outside, but I didn't see the being's face or clearly see the various limbs because the Being seemed to be the tunnel of Light that I was inside in the Vision, and seemed much larger than me."

Let's all be very grateful that the State's intimidation tactics didn't work. Once again, the Shulgins have given us a treasure-trove of previously hidden knowledge.

Transform Press; $24.50
1997; softcover; 824 pp
illus; 0-9630096-9-9

TRIPLEPOINT
LSD in Group Therapy —
A Life Transformed
by Trevor Trueheart

In 1959 Trevor Trueheart (a pseudonym) started what would become twelve years of LSD psychotherapy. Some of the therapy was done one-on-one with Dr. Carole Govren, a clinical psychotherapist, but most of it was done with a group calling itself the Tribe. Every so often, this collection of two dozen individuals would come together to take acid (and other drugs, such as speed and Morning Glory seeds), under the guidance of Dr. Govren. About twenty years after he left the Tribe, Trueheart has sifted through his eleven-inch stack of session notes and 100 hours of tape-recorded individual LSD therapy sessions. What emerges is an insightful story of how one man came to terms with himself.

The school of psychotherapy which Govren subscribed to holds that the patient must remember traumatic events from the past and come to grips with them. LSD allows users to actually relive painful and forgotten episodes in their lives. During LSD therapy, members of the Tribe would experience these devastating events again, but this time they were able to completely express the emotions that they previously withheld. "The context of the Tribe has provided you with a safe space to do this. You are sheltered, supported, encouraged — and sometimes commanded — to encoun-

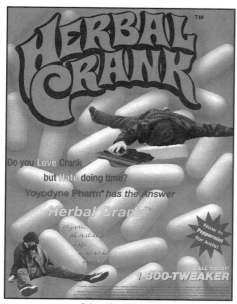

A drug zine not afraid to cast a sometimes jaundiced eye on drug culture. *TRP*.

ter something that has secretly (or otherwise) terrified you for years. Only by engaging and accepting your fear, as it comes into your consciousness, may you free yourself from continuing to carry this psychic load."

During one group session, the members ingested LSD and took turns inhaling carbogen, a mixture of oxygen and carbon dioxide. While breathing this gas, people get enough oxygen to stay fully conscious, but the carbon dioxide makes it feel as though they're suffocating. "Everybody I have known to inhale carbogen experienced extreme fear and seemed to confront all the demons stored in his or her subconscious. This is the stuff of nightmares." Upon breathing it, Trueheart felt as though he were dying and automatically wished someone else were dying in his place. After realising what he had done, he took some more. "I had been trying to do the dying but could not. When I released myself to it, the experience happened to me and not because of me... Feeling weak and totally drained of energy as I regained consciousness, I asked Carole, 'Did I die?' She smiled and said, affectionately, 'Yes, you died.'"

One of Trueheart's most surprising admissions is that he experienced telepathy with several members of the group. During one session, the author had regressed to the age of four and was unable to communicate what was happening to him. One of the other men in the Tribe described exactly what Trueheart was experiencing — mainly, being molested by a doctor who had just extracted a pussywillow that had gotten jammed up the young boy's nose. Trueheart was even more amazed when he asked his mother about this episode and she confirmed that his grandmother had rushed him to an unfamiliar doctor when he had gotten a pussywillow stuck in his nose. Later, Trueheart would "channel" buried memo-

ries from two other Tribe members.

This LSD group psychotherapy also allowed Trueheart to perceive people in their past life forms, learn how to avoid a bad trip, discover the meaning of his "irrational" feelings, interpret his dreams, and get his teeth drilled with no anaesthesia.

Triplepoint contains a lot of New Age and psychoanalytic thought. There's talk about "neurosis" and "narcissism" and references to the ideas of Carl Jung, John Lily, L. Ron Hubbard, and many others. Trueheart can lay on these psychospiritual lines of thought pretty heavily at times. If you keep in mind that they are only one possible explanation for his experiences, you will get a lot more out of the book.

Green Fir Publishing; $19.95
1992; softcover; 215 pp
0-9633979-0-7

TRP
The Resonance Project

The purpose of *TRP* is to expand knowledge regarding consciousness-altering substances, with an eye towards using the visionary effects of these substances to enhance the mind and spirit. The issue known as "Version 2.15" is explicitly devoted to these forms of "metaprogramming". One article offers an intriguing idea regarding genetic engineering. Instead of just using DNA technology to make physical changes in ourselves, why not also use it to elevate our consciousness? Specifically, the author proposes allowing our bodies to constantly create a higher level of tryptamines (we create these substances anyway, but the levels become extremely low after puberty). By producing a higher level of these substances, we could constantly experience their effects, which include profound awareness of our higher nature and our interconnectedness with other humans and with nature.

An article on "netripping" suggests setting up a time at which you and twenty to thirty other people will all trip, each person instantly relating what he or she is experiencing through the use of a private email list. Elsewhere, Robert W describes an experience with Psilocybe mushrooms, and, John Hanna, editor of the *Psychedelic Resource List*, exposes the truth about the shady psychoactive substance Borametz. Some other articles cover metaprogramming and energy healing with ketamine, the geographic dispersion of psychoactive mushrooms, neuronal networks, three recipes for ayahuasca brews, interviews with Howard Rheingold and Dennis McKenna, reviews, and what you can learn about your rights from watching *COPS*.

A highly informative news section reveals many interesting stories and statistics. In July 1997, packets containing almost six tons of pure cocaine (with a street value of $500 million) washed up on the shores of Morocco. In September of that year, 70 percent of Swiss voters rejected a proposal that would have ended their country's progressive drug laws, including the governmental distribution of heroin to addicts.

TRP is a relatively new publication, and I'm looking forward to seeing more of its informative and intelligent coverage of drug/consciousness issues.

Resonant Media/323 Broadway Ave E #318/Seattle WA 98102
Email: trp@resproject.com
WWW: www.resproject.com
Single issue: $6.50
Five issue sub: $25. Canada: $40. Overseas: $45.

50 YEARS OF SUNSHINE

Released in 1993, this 2-CD set is a musical celebration of LSD's golden anniversary. The disks — titled *100 Micrograms* and *250 Micrograms* — each contain eleven tracks that represent "what it might be like to be tripping or on psychedelics" or are simply paeans to the magical molecule. A lot of the tracks are very mellow — often swirling or floating — synthesised music that lets you peacefully ride the ethers. Tracks of this type include "Bliss" by Closedown, "Kykeon" by Love Spirals Downward, "Beetle Crawls Across My Back" by Nurse With Wound, and "Space Dust" by Hawkwind.

Others are more upbeat. Drome's "Bipolar Trip" starts out with manic bass and drums being played at impossible speeds. Suddenly, the song shifts into a more mellow groove (although, anything would be mellow after the first half). "Disillusion" by 68000 will set your toes a-tappin', and "On LSD" by Steel Porn Rhino will make you want to shake your booty.

The Pelican Daughters' "The Bicycle Ride" is a recreation of what LSD's discoverer, Albert Hofmann, may have experienced when he rode his bike home while tripping on his new discovery. In "Thee Spirit Ov Thee Molecule" by XKP and Mr. L, a thumping dancebeat backs up samples of Timothy Leary saying things like, "As Mr. LSD I'm very happy", "Good for you, Albert", and "The spirit of the lysergic acid molecule." Phauss's "Radiator (For Amanita Muscaria & Mark McCloud)" is composed of a slow, rolling sound like thunder accompanied by a noise that resembles paper being ripped. On "InSERGEncy" by Elliot Sharp, a sampled vocal of Hofmann saying "LSD has been discovered" is manipulated by computer until it is completely unrecognisable. In fact, it sounds like a chorus of aliens performing a Gregorian chant in an unknown language.

50 Years of Sunshine is a fitting tribute to one of the most important substances ever synthesised.

Silent Records; $19.95
1993; 2 CDs; 138 min

ECSTASY

THE COMPLETE BOOK OF ECSTASY
(Second Edition)
by UP Yourspigs

This manual contains detailed instructions for making the empathogenic drug MDMA, also called ecstasy, Adam, XTC, and X. It starts with around 20 pages of basic information

Safety card from the Haight-Ashbury Free Clinic. *Ecstasy.*

about chemistry and laboratory processes. Chapter three reveals how to make several necessary chemicals, some of which are illegal or closely watched by the authorities. The next chapter demonstrates the creation of alkyl halides, which are used in the synthesis of safrole and are intermediates in the formation of amines.

In chapter five, we are shown several methods for creating safrole, piperonal, and isosafrole — the precursors of ecstasy. Making amines — necessary to the final synthesis of ecstasy — is dealt with in chapter six.

Everything starts to come together in chapter seven, which explains how to make MDA, a drug that is chemically similar to ecstasy but produces hallucinogenic effects and doesn't have its cousin's empathogenic properties. Chapter eight presents what we've all been waiting for — five ways to synthesise ecstasy. Two of them involving converting MDA to MDMA, and the other three take a more direct route. For each method, *Ecstasy* also explains how to alter it slightly to produce the drug MDEA ("Eve"), which provides similar but less intense effects.

A final chapter deals with LSD, amphetamines, tryptamines, barbiturates, cocaine, and opium. The author just gives a few chemical tidbits, not nearly enough information to even attempt synthesising or extracting any of them. Those who are interested in getting more "hands-on" knowledge are directed to several sources of information.

I notice that *Ecstasy: Dance, Trance & Transformation* [below] says that this book has been "judged by manufacturers to be the best book on how to make MDMA." There is no higher recommendation.

Synthesis Books; $25
1992, 1995; oversized softcover; 90 pp
heavily illus; no ISBN

ECSTASY
Dance, Trance & Transformation
by Nicholas Saunders with Rick Doblin

In his book on ecstasy, Nicholas Saunders gives detailed attention to numerous aspects of the drug, including its physical, psychological and spiritual effects, its various uses, and its social aspects. While *Ecstasy: The MDMA Story* [below] focuses mainly on the drug's psychologically therapeutic uses, Saunders covers all the bases: improving relationships, problem solving, sexuality, artistic expression, martial arts, spiritual awakening, and more. He reports on a rabbi and several monks who use X. "Brother Bartholemew is a monk who has used MDMA about 25 times over the past 10 years as an aid to religious experience. Normally, he has taken it alone, but he has also taken it in a small group of like-minded people. He describes the effect as opening a direct link with God. While using MDMA, he has experienced a very deep comprehension of divine compassion. He has never lost the clarity of this insight, and it remains as a reservoir on which he can draw."

The sexual effects of ecstasy are a mixed bag. It appears that, on the whole, X strengthens the connectedness of lovers and improves some physical sensations, though it doesn't typically act as an aphrodisiac in the typical sense. "This sensual, rather than sexual, aspect of the drug gives rise to nonsexual 'orgies' at some parties, referred to as 'feely-feely' or 'snake slithering.' People indulge in group sensuous delights through caressing and slithering over one another, though I've only heard of this in Australia and California."

Saunders also takes a long, careful look at the negative aspects of X, including the evidence concerning brain damage, liver and kidney damage, heat stroke, addiction, paranoia, and panic attacks. Three chapters report on aspects of the rave/dance scene, which is virtually synonymous with ecstasy use. Other parts of the book look at the history of the drug and media reactions to it, how it's manufactured (no specific instructions are given), concerns about purity, laws surrounding X, herbal ecstasy, and how to take ecstasy more safely. Peppered throughout the book are short comments from users, and the final chapter contains fourteen longer accounts from people who have had major experiences while using ecstasy. They write about combating depression, experiencing the divine, facing death, rekindling love, overcoming cocaine addiction, and relieving physical pain. An annotated 36-page bibliography set in small type and a guide to other X resources help to assure that this is a superlative all-encompassing source of information on ecstasy.

Quick American Archives (Quick Trading Company); $19.95
1995, 1996; softcover; 282 pp
illus; 0-932551-20-3

ECSTASY
The MDMA Story
by Bruce Eisner

MDMA is a drug that has achieved widespread popularity due primarily to its most dramatic and usual effect — it produces empathy in users. "It softens defensiveness and gently removes obstacles to communication, so one speaks directly from the heart… MDMA also removes walls of isolation between individuals so that even strangers speak to each other in familiar, intimate ways. Insight and affinity-enhancing qualities evoked momentarily can be applied either to relationships and/or other matters of personal concern." Ecstasy's other main effect is that it steamrollers over your anxieties. "The de-stressing aspect is experienced mentally as well as physically; in certain instances, this can be dramatic. For most people, MDMA produces the sense of relaxation felt after several days of vacation."

Mainly because of its empathogenic effects, many therapists had their clients take ecstasy during sessions. MDMA therapy seemed quite promising. By allowing people to open up to other people and to themselves, X helped bring about breakthroughs in people's lives. It was used in couples' therapy because the partners would see each other with new eyes — they felt unconditional love for each other and ignored each other's faults and the anxieties brought about by the inherent uncertainties of any relationship. Therapists and users admitted that the so-called "hug drug" was not a panacea but a very helpful catalyst to the healing process. Of course, ecstasy therapy came to a crashing end in the US when the DEA laughably decided to make it a schedule-one drug, the same category as heroin and cocaine.

MDMA was synthesised in Germany in 1914. It was basically forgotten until the 1950s when the Army started doing toxicity experiments with it. (However, the book doesn't explain why the Army suddenly cared about a drug forgotten for 40 years.) In 1970, X started hitting the streets, and for fifteen years it managed to maintain a low profile. But in a series of events chronicled in detail, the DEA decided that it wanted to ban this non-addictive, helpful drug that only has minor side effects and a lower toxicity than many prescription drugs.

Besides discussing Adam's effects and history, this book contains first-person accounts of users, a chemical analysis, instructions for synthesising ecstasy (written at a very advanced level), a close examination of the drug's neurotoxicity, a thirty-page guide for users, and information on the revival of therapeutic research in Switzerland, which is letting mental health professionals use X and psychedelics to treat patients.

Ronin Publishing; $17.95
1989, 1994; softcover; 247 pp
illus; 0-914171-68-2

MARIJUANA & HEMP

BAKED POTATOES
A Pot Smoker's Guide to Film and Video
by John Hulme & Michael Wexler

When you're stoned, it's extremely important to watch the right movie. Watching the wrong one (what the authors call a "bad seed") can send you into a downward spiral of depression. This book acts as a guide to the best flicks to watch through the haze of pot smoke. Each one is described in irreverent and often hilarious terms, rated (on a scale of five pot leaves), and comes with a key that tells you if it's should be watched alone, will cause emotional trauma, requires no brainwaves, etc. Movies are divided into categories: "The Goes-Without-Saying List" (*Airplane!*, *Cheech and Chong's Up In Smoke*, *Die Hard*), "Reliable Sources" (*Aliens*, *One Flew Over the Cuckoo's Nest*, *Sixteen Candles*), "Unsung Heroes" (*A Brief History of Time*, *Destroy All Monsters!*, *Superfly*), "Risky Calls" (*Blue Velvet*, *The Fly*, Ronald Reagan's 1984 State of the Union Address), and "Bad Seeds" (*Eraserhead*, *Jurassic Park*, *Naked Lunch* (described as "Overwrought, self-indulgent, angst-ridden moose shit.")). Celebrities of sorts — such as Wavy Gravy and Steve Hager, editor of *High Times* — provide a few guest reviews. Several appendices list video distributors, tell how to cope with a bad seed, point out great scenes in otherwise non-baked-potato movies, and more.

Doubleday; $10
1996; softcover; 206 pp
0-385-47837-2

BROWNIE MARY'S MARIJUANA COOKBOOK & DENNIS PERON'S RECIPE FOR SOCIAL CHANGE
by Dennis Peron & Mary Rathburn

With grey hair, a grandmotherly aura of sweetness, and 70+ years under her belt, Mary Rathbun doesn't seem like the type to constantly confront authority, resulting in three arrests (the charges were dropped twice, and the first case resulted in a 30-day suspended sentence, community service, and probation). But "Brownie Mary" has indeed seen her share of legal troubles because of her commitment to the medical benefits of marijuana. She makes pot brownies for people with AIDS in San Francisco, and she is involved with the famous Cannabis Buyers' Club that provides marijuana to people who use it to treat medical conditions.

This book contains nine of Mary's recipes, including shrimp casserole, black bean soup, hemp seed salad dressing, and chocolate chip cookies. Unfortunately, Mary refuses to divulge the instructions for making the celebrated brown-

Mary Jane Rathbun and her stash.
Brownie Mary's Marijuana Cookbook.

ies. In the rest of the book long-time marijuana activist Dennis Peron tells about his efforts to liberate pot, including his founding of the Cannabis Buyers' Club and his crucial role in organising California's medicinal marijuana initiative, which passed in 1996. He also writes about his friend Brownie Mary's travails and triumphs and reprints tons of articles (with photographs) about Mary, himself, the Buyers' Club, and pot's medical effects.

Though the price of the book seems high, the proceeds fund efforts to use marijuana as a medicine.

Trail of Smoke Publishing (Californians for Compassionate Use); $15
1996; softcover; 95 pp
heavily illus; 0-9639892-0-0

CANNABEST HEMP CATALOGUE

Cannabest's catalogue is the first full-colour catalogue printed on hemp paper. (Hemp products are made from the stalk of the marijuana plant, which contains no psychoactive THC and is legal to import but not to grow.) They carry hemp clothes, accessories, and other products from several companies. Among the clothes you'll find are a bodice, bloomers, halter dress, kids' overalls, jumper, vests, shorts, tanktops, long- and short-sleeve shirts, a tie, poncho, scarf, kimono jacket, hair scrunchees, all kinds of hats, and more. Styles range from retro-Renaissance through Yuppie to tough-as-nails urbanwear. You do-it-yourselfers can buy hemp fabric by the yard. It comes in different styles and textures and can even be custom-dyed by Cannabest.

Other hemp items include backpacks, luggage, a wallet, purses, an apron, a fanny pack, a pillow case, twine and rope, carpet, lip balm, cooking oil, massage oil, salve, paper and envelopes, and sterilised hemp seeds. There are also books, videos, and magazines, plus a rubber stamp that says "I grew hemp" in a word balloon for stamping on the front of $1 bills.

Cannabest/1536 Monterey St/San Luis Obispo CA 93401
Catalogue: $3

CASTLING
by Rand Clifford

This big novel follows the adventures of Jim Ludwig. He loses his job because a urine test revealed pot, and he ends up as part of a secret, communal group trying to save the earth with hemp. Get ready to encounter lots of radical ideas, drugs, sex, personal politics, and enough dialogue for two or three regular novels.

StarChief Press; $20
1995; softcover; 543 pp
0-9647817-9-4

THE EMPEROR WEARS NO CLOTHES
Hemp and the Marijuana Conspiracy
(Expanded Edition)
by Jack Herer

Cannabis is the world's most useful and important plant. "The diverse properties of the scorned and condemned marijuana plant could provide sufficient clothing, oil, medicine, fuel, food, and shelter for all the peoples of the world, if completely legalised and commercialised... [Also,] hemp might prove to be the means of saving the planet (us) from acid rain, global warming and the depletion of our precious forests and fossil fuels."

For over 20 years Jack Herer has researched the many benefits of cannabis and the real reasons for its being illegal. What has come together is "a picture of a world being destroyed by a malicious conspiracy to suppress, not a 'killer-weed' but the world's premiere renewable natural resource, for the benefit of a handful of wealthy and powerful individuals and corporations."

Herer goes over the startling array of uses hemp has, including textiles, fabrics, paper, rope, art canvas, paints, varnish, lighting oil, clean fuel, food protein, building materials, smoking, a creativity-booster, and a key to economic stability and profitability. One of the more pointed facts that gets mentioned is that hemp saved the life of one of the men who tried hardest to wipe it out — President George Bush. We all know that during W.W.II Bush had to bail out of his burning airplane after a battle in the Pacific. What most people — including Bush himself — don't realise is that Bush's parachute webbing was made entirely of hemp, as was the stitching in his shoes and almost all of the ropes, rigging, and firehoses on the ship that pulled him out of the water. Also, parts of his airplane's engine were lubricated with oil made from hemp seed.

Another part of the book details the therapeutic uses of cannabis, including relieving and/or fighting asthma, glaucoma, tumours, nausea (from chemotherapy, AZT treatment, etc.), epilepsy, muscle spasms, multiple sclerosis, infections (including gonorrhoea and herpes), arthritis, dirty lungs, migraine headaches, emphysema, insomnia, and hundreds of other conditions.

Many studies have shown that marijuana has no pernicious effects. A 1981 study at UCLA examined ten people who belonged to the Zion Coptic Church and had each smoked *sixteen high-potency spliffs every day for ten years* (a spliff is equal to five American joints). The scientists found no difference between their brains and the brains of non-smokers.

So why is this wonderful plant illegal? Because it's too wonderful, and a lot of vested interests could lose money if it were easily available. The pharmaceutical companies would lose hundreds of millions to billions of dollars a year if people could grow a drug that's more effective than the over-priced stuff they sell. And they know it. Why else would they lobby the federal government to prevent research into marijuana's medical benefits? On top of that, they provide about half the funding of the "pro-family" anti-pot groups. Tobacco, liquor, and beer companies provide much of the rest. I wonder why...

Another powerful economic force that could get waylaid by cannabis is the textile/fabric industry. It was probably their machinations that got the plant outlawed in the first place. Manufacturers of paint and machine lubricants helped put nails in the coffin too. To help turn the public against pot, sensationalist newspapers and government officials erroneously reported that it causes violence (actually, the opposite is true). Most of these lies were also racist. Harry J. Anslinger, director of the agency that would eventually become the Drug Enforcement Administration, was one of the most despicable in this regard. "Anslinger pushed on Congress as a factual statement that about 50% of all violent crimes committed in the US were committed by Spaniards, Mexican-Americans, Latin Americans, Filipinos, Negroes and Greeks, and these crimes could be directly traced to marijuana... Not one of Anslinger's marijuana 'Gore Files' of the 1930s is believed to be true by scholars who have painstakingly checked the facts."

Harer also looks at the important role hemp has played throughout history, how the war against pot has destroyed our civil liberties and human rights, the flawed negative studies about marijuana, the suppression of the facts, and much more. A 108-page appendix (which is longer than the body of the book) reprints almost 70 documents, including "Marijuana Found Useful In Certain Mental Ills", "Hearing Before a Subcommittee of the Committee on Finance, US Senate, 1937", "DuPont Annual Report, 1937", "Protect Youth Against Dope", "Hemp for Fuel", "Administrative Judge Urges Medicinal Use of Marijuana", and "Voices for Legalisation". The book ends with 32 pages of ads for hemp products, books, videos, and periodicals.

The Emperor Wears No Clothes is an undisputed classic. Get it and you'll understand exactly why marijuana is so important and why it is so hated by the powers-that-be. (A version printed on hemp is available for $100. Of course, this price would be much lower if hemp could be grown in the US instead of having to be imported. Prices would also

fall if the industry as a whole were allowed to blossom.)
H.E.M.P.; $19.95
1985, 1995; oversized softcover; 268 pp
heavily illus; 1-878124-00-1

THE HEMP MANIFESTO
101 Ways That Hemp Can
Save Our World
by Rowan Robinson

Longtime hemp activist Rowan Robinson has put together this small book as a way to present the wonders of hemp in a concise, easy-to-understand manner. Each of the 101 pages in the main part of the book contains two or three paragraphs on a way that *Cannabis sativa* "has made, is making, or could make a positive impact on the world." The first half of the book focuses on the nonpsychoactive form of cannabis known as hemp, which has an incredible number of uses as fabric, fuel, food, etc. The second half of the book then looks at the medical, psychological, and spiritual benefits of the high-inducing form of cannabis known as marijuana.

In the first part of the book we find that hemp was used for the original US flag, the Declaration of Independence, the Constitution, the Gutenberg Bible, and the canvas of oil paintings by Rembrandt, Van Gogh, and other masters. Paper made from hemp is much, much more durable than paper made from wood pulp. Wood paper disintegrates in a century (and I have books that are turning yellow after just two years), but some pieces of hemp paper have survived over 2000 years. Hemp can also be used to make better fibreboard, insulation, building material (isochanvre "is as strong as concrete but weighs only one-seventh as much"), herbicide, clothing, ethanol, fibreglass, and more. Not only is hemp as strong as or stronger and more resilient than the substances usually used to make these products, it also has much less of an environmental impact when it is grown, harvested, and processed. "An acre of hemp yields four times as much fibre as an acre of trees, and no wildlife is destroyed in the process." On top of that, hemp is one of the world's best sources of protein and has been used a primary food by large parts of the world's population for thousands of years.

The second half of *The Hemp Manifesto* touts the various health benefits of marijuana: relieving the eye pressure of glaucoma, eliminating the nausea and lack of appetite from cancer chemotherapy and AIDS treatment, dilating the bronchial tubes of people with asthma, relieving pain caused by a number of conditions, as well as being an antibiotic, anticonvulsant, and anti-inflammatory. Not only does marijuana usually do a better job than the harsh pharmaceuticals used to treat these conditions, it is far less toxic, has practically zero side effects, and is drastically cheaper than patented drugs. It is also being used (off the record, of course) to treat depression and alcoholism. Furthermore, Mary Jane plays a role in many religious traditions, including Hinduism, Tantric Buddhism, Rastafarianism, and the Ethiopian Zion Coptic Church.

A few of the book's entries reveal what many people would consider surprising attitudes towards cannabis. For

You'd be amazed at what they're doing with hemp these days. *Hempworld*.

example, the US government grows marijuana and supplies it free of charge to people who need it for medicinal purposes. The programme stopped accepting new patients in 1992, but eight people still receive government-grown pot. Both the *Journal of the American Medical Association* and the *New England Journal of Medicine* have run articles supporting the medicinal use of marijuana. Some of history's most respected statesmen have recognised the supreme importance of hemp. "Thomas Jefferson believed hemp to be so important to the independence of the colonies that he secretly brought new varieties of it back from France, thus becoming the first cannabis smuggler on record. The profusion of hemp in the colonies provided an independent source of paper, clothing, rope, food, oil, and sails, and was one of the arguments Thomas Paine used in *Common Sense* to convince the colonists that they could secede from England."

In short, *The Hemp Manifesto* distils and crystallises every good thing about hemp and marijuana into one tidy little package. It is absolutely perfect for people who have heard how wonderful cannabis is but still have problems cutting through the decades of brainwashing about this "killer weed". I'm going to give my copy to my parents.

Park Street Press (Inner Traditions International); $5.95
1997; paperback; 105 pp
0-89281-728-3

HEMPWORLD
The International Hemp Journal

HempWorld describes itself as "the first 'capitalist tool' devoted to the modern hemp industry. *HempWorld*'s mission is to provide a forum for hemp entrepreneurs and to help nurture hemp back into the mainstream economy." The magazine's readers are consumers, "producers, manufacturers, importers, wholesalers, and retailers of hemp goods." Obviously this is *the* source for keeping tabs on the rising popularity of "the world's most useful plant".

HempWorld/PO Box 550/Forestville, CA 95436
Voice: 1-800-649-4421 [Visa, MC]
Email: sales@hempworld.com
WWW: www.hempworld.com
Single issue: North America: $8. Elsewhere: $10
Four issue sub (one year): $15. Canada: $20 Elsewhere: $35.

INTERNATIONAL DIRECTORY OF HEMP PRODUCTS AND SUPPLIERS
compiled & edited by James Berry

If you want to buy hemp products from retailers for yourself, or if you want to buy them from manufacturers and wholesalers for sale in your store or mail order business, or if you want fabric and raw goods so that you can become a manufacturer, this directory puts you in touch with the right sources. Over 160 entries list contact info and details for every kind of business dealing with hemp: sellers, distributors, importers, organisations, magazines, and others. Every type of product you could name is here, including shampoos, body oils, futons, towels, rope, wallets, purses, outdoor gear, paper, seeds, soaps, guitar straps, paints, hacky sacks, jewellery, insulation, caulking, food, candy, diapers, and all types of clothing. Indexes sort the entries by country, US state, product, and type of business.

For the more technically minded, statistical tables examine strength and elongation of various fibres, the dimensions of fibres and cells of vegetable fibres, and the physical properties of true hemp and sunn hemp fibres. Some introductory articles examine the commercial uses of hemp, especially paper and seed oil.

If you need an item — *any* item — made out of hemp, look no further.

The Message Company; $29.95
1996; softcover; 141 pp
illus; 1-57282-005-5

THE JOINT ROLLING HANDBOOK
Tips, Tricks and Techniques
(Expert Edition)
by Richard Kemplay

As any toker can tell you, rolling joints is an artform. At long last, there is an art instruction book that covers this neglected topic. Using step-by-step instructions in words and illustrations, *The Joint Rolling Handbook* will show you how to create a dozen different reefers. After a basic lesson in rolling, you'll learn how to make the Trembler, a quick and easy joint; Saturday Night Special, a classic that is easy to roll even for the minimally talented; the short and fat Magic Carpet; the Secret Agent, which looks like a tobacco cigarette; the Joker, a fairly easy cone-shaped number; the Crossroads, a complicated set-up that lets you smoke three joints at once; the Windmill, for brave souls who want *four* at the same time;

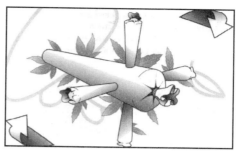

The Camberwell Carrot?
No, *The Joint Rolling Handbook*.

the Diamond, a wild joint that splits in the middle; the Tulip, which is a long roach with a big cone of pot on the end; and the Cannabis Cigar, formed by rolling uncured leaves around a Thai stick and coating the whole shebang with liquid resin. Other user-friendly sections cover handling the pot or hash itself, making roaches, selecting rolling papers, health tips, short and long-term effects, and the law.

This book will undoubtedly make you a hit among your friends while adding some variety and flash to your smoking style. Don't just sit there... get rolling!

Quick American Archives (Quick Trading Company); $9.95
1997; softcover; 61 pp
highly illus; 0-932551-23-8

MARIJUANA BEER
How to Make Your Own
Hi-Brew Beer
by Ed Rosenthal & The Unknown Brewer

If you're finding that Coors Light and Heineken are no longer packing a punch for you, perhaps you'll consider trying something a little stronger — marijuana beer. This short book opens with some general instructions for brewing your own beer. Given that a total of only seventeen pages are devoted to the subject, you'll probably want to get at least one of the eleven books on brewing that the authors list (unless, of course, you're already well-versed in the subject). After some instructions for preparing the pot, there follows recipes for ten marijuana beers, including Simple Head Ale, Hop Head Beer, Potted Porter, Headwiser, and Hammerhead Lager. Two of the recipes are fairly simple, while the others grow increasingly complex.

Once your "special brew" is done, you'll want something special to put it in, so the publisher has thoughtfully supplied 48 slick, green labels to glue onto your bottles. Each label shows a pot leaf, the "brand" of the beer ("Hi-Brew"), its nickname ("The Wacko One"), and the slogan: "When You're Having Only One".

Quick American Archives (Quick Trading Company); $14.95
1996; softcover; 54 pp, 16 sheets of labels
illus; 0-932551-22-X

MARIJUANA GROWERS HANDBOOK
Indoor/Greenhouse Edition (Revised)
by Ed Rosenthal

Ed Rosenthal — *High Times*' dean of pot growing — has created the seminal guide to raising Mary Jane in attics, basements, closets, greenhouses, or any other enclosed space that you can dream up. "The ideal area is at least 6 feet high, with a minimum of 50 square feet, an area of about 7 by 7 feet." However, it is possible to make do with less space. "The smallest space that can be used is a shelf 15-24 inches high." If you need to, you can even grow your plants lying on their sides.

Rosenthal's style is uncluttered and detailed... he tells you in plain English exactly what you must do and why. He discusses growing a variety versus growing one or two strains of marijuana, hydroponics versus soil gardening, when to plant, preparing the space, lighting, carbon dioxide, temperature, air and humidity, pH and water, nutrients, watering, containers, pruning, pests, breeding, harvesting, cloning, experiments (can birth control pills help pot grow faster?), and more. A plethora of pictures and diagrams let you see how everything should look.

One chapter is devoted to raising sinsemilla (a marijuana plant with no seeds), which is highly prized because of its increased potency. "In order for the flowers to ripen unseeded, they must remain unpollinated (unfertilised). Male and female flowers usually appear on separate plants. The males are removed from the space as soon as they are recognised." A special chapter on "Advanced Flowering" by Sam Selgnij let you use botanical knowledge — presented in 25 detailed tables and graphs — to produce bigger flowers and new clusters of flowers.

If you're going to grow indoors, this book will become your trusted companion.

Quick Trading Company; $19.95
1992; softcover; 232 pp
heavily illus; 0-932551-00-9

MARIJUANA LAW
by Richard Glen Boire

Defence attorney Richard Boire, a specialist in drug law, estimates that there are over 30 million pot smokers in the US and that in an average year 400,000 people will be arrested for some type of marijuana crime — use, possession, selling, etc. His book presents a comprehensive guide to your rights at every step of the way, from search through arrest to trial.

Boire looks at exactly what a prosecutor must prove when charging someone with a pot crime — including possession, sale, and transporting, being in a room where it's smoked, driving under the influence, and aiding and abetting a marijuana crime. When prosecuting for sale of weed, the Man must prove that you possessed it and intended to sell it. However, in many states merely offering to sell pot — even if you don't have any — is a crime. Boire also examines forfeiture law, in which all of your possessions can be taken away from you even if you are never charged with a crime (for more on this frightening topic, see the Fourth Amendment section of the Freedom chapter.)

The Fourth Amendment theoretically guarantees that our "persons, houses, papers, and effects" are safe "against

This bud's for you!
Marijuana Beer.

unreasonable search and seizure." This provides us with a lot of freedom, but there are many ways in which this right has been skirted (just look at the bill H.R. 666, passed by the House of Reps in 1995, which allows unconstitutionally seized evidence to be used in court as long as the seizure was made "in good faith".) Did you know that if a private citizen, acting on his or her own accord, breaks into your house, steals your pot, and gives it to the police, they can legally get a warrant to search your house? This has actually happened numerous times. Also, if hotel maids find pot in your room, it can be used against you. Private couriers, such as UPS and Fedex, are allowed to open your packages without cause. Police can also use information from citizen informants, confidential informants, narks, your own kids, mail order companies, and your garbage.

The author looks at the three types of encounters you can have with a police officer — contact, arrest, and that considerable grey area in between, known as detention. You can be detained if the cop has reasonable suspicion that you have violated a law, if you fit a "drug-courier profile", if you've been stopped at a roadblock, or in other situations. There are many instances in which a search and seizure is considered legal even when there's no warrant: after an arrest, at a US border, if you voluntarily allow a search, if the seized item was in plain view, etc.

Another chapter examines the searching of your vehicle, covering when you can be pulled over, when your car can be searched, probable cause, opening your vehicle's trunk, furtive movements, the plain-view rule, throwing pot from a moving car, roadblocks, and more. Remember that when you are stopped at a roadblock, an officer only has the right to quickly decide if you are intoxicated or otherwise breaking a law. If there is no reasonable suspicion, they must let you go. "In other words, a police roadblock allows the officers only to stop your vehicle. They cannot search you or your car without probable cause to believe that you are violating a law. Likewise, you retain every right to refuse to consent to an officer's request to search."

Further chapters examine searches of your home and

grounds, your Miranda rights, choosing a private attorney, and drug testing at work. Here's another helpful tip: If you're arrested, don't go back inside your house to get ID, change clothes, feed your dog, etc. The Supreme Court has ruled that cops are allowed to escort you into your home, where they can check for plain-view contraband.

An appendix of the book reprints the federal sentencing guidelines relating to marijuana. [Note: A massively expanded second edition has recently been published. Information below is for this new edition.]

Ronin Publishing; $15.95
1992, 1996; softcover; 288 pp
0-914171-86-0

MARIJUANA MEDICAL HANDBOOK
A Guide to Therapeutic Use
by Ed Rosenthal, Dale Gieringer, Tod Mikuriya, MD

Many other books in this section and the Marijuana section of *Outposts* have covered the incredible medical powers of cannabis, one of the most useful and beneficial plants in the world. With the passage of medical marijuana referendums in Arizona and California and the raiding of the San Francisco Cannabis Buyers' Club (all occurring in 1996), the heretical idea that the "evil weed" could actually help the human race was planted firmly in the national consciousness. Of course, President Clinton, drug czar General Barry McCaffrey, and other heartless government officials immediately manned their bully pulpits, exclaiming that pot is harmful and medically useless and implying that the countless people throughout history who have used it to relieve extreme nausea and pain (and other conditions) are either deluded or lying. Fortunately, you and I know who the real liars are.

Ganja guru Ed Rosenthal knows, too. Aided by the California director of NORML (National Organisation for the Reform of Marijuana Laws) and a practising psychiatrist who has researched the medical uses of cannabis for over 30 years — including a stint as director of marijuana research for the National Institute of Mental Health — he has put together this hands-on guide for people who want to use pot for health reasons.

The authors first address the question of safety. "Drug Enforcement Agency (DEA) Administrative Judge Francis Young wrote, in his decision recommending legalisation of medical marijuana, 'Marijuana, in its natural form, is one of the safest therapeutically active substances known to mankind.' Unlike other psychoactive drugs, including alcohol, aspirin, opiates, nicotine, and caffeine, it does not cause fatal overdoses... The government has never reported a death from cannabis use since it began keeping statistics."

After explaining how marijuana affects the body and mind, the authors present a thorough look at its medical benefits. It reduces nausea and stimulates the appetite, making it a godsend for people with cancer undergoing chemotherapy and people with AIDS who have AIDS wasting syndrome or are taking AZT. It has also been used for similar purposes by people with kidney disease, morning sickness, and anorexia nervosa. Among the other diseases and disor-

ders that pot fights are: epileptic seizures, muscle spasms, tremors, chronic pain, labour pain, arthritis, cramps, migraine headaches, inflammations, chronic itching, asthma, high eye pressure (glaucoma), insomnia, depression, and anxiety. The information is presented in a balanced manner. The authors note that although marijuana has been successful in preventing grand mal seizures in epileptics, it doesn't seem to do anything about petit mal seizures. It can benefit some people with AIDS, but it might depress the immune system... someone with strong immunity probably wouldn't notice, but it might be critical to a PWA [Person With AIDS].

The next chapter presents the real and mythological downsides of pot. Contrary to popular belief, it doesn't kill brain cells or damage chromosomes. On the other hand, smoking pot can cause similar problems to smoking tobacco in the long-term. When marijuana is smoked, it releases tars and other toxins that increase the user's chance of developing respiratory illness. Although an average joint is equal to 1.5 to 2.5 cigarettes, tobacco is still deadlier in practice. While very few users smoke more than one joint a day (and even that's uncommon), it's not unusual for cigarette smokers to go through a pack or more every day.

Assuming that you're an absolute beginner, the authors explain the potency of various plants and plant parts, growing indoors and out, and getting pot through buyer's clubs, people you know, or on the street. Of course, there's plenty of information on administering pot through ointments, smoking (joints, waterpipes, pipes, and vaporisers), and eating (recipes for marijuana cooking oil, brownies, soup, mashed potatoes, and other dishes are included).

Further material in this helpful resource includes a listing of California buyers' clubs, full texts of the Arizona and California initiatives, a look at how states can allow citizens to use pot despite the federal ban, a bibliographical review of the human studies on the medical use of marijuana, a glossary, and an extensive index.

Other books have revealed pot's amazing healing powers, but this is the first one written for people — particularly non-smokers — who want the practical information on how to get these benefits for themselves.

Quick American Archives (Quick Trading Company); $16.95
1997; softcover; 270 pp
illus; 0-932551-16-5

MARIJUANA QUESTIONS? ASK ED
The Encyclopedia of Marijuana
by Ed Rosenthal

Marijuana Questions? collects several years' worth of Ed Rosenthal's columns from *High Times*, in which he answers readers' questions about growing pot. These hundreds upon hundreds of questions and answers have been revised, expanded, and arranged into sections: "Cultivation Practices", "Indoor Cultivation Practices", "Outdoor Cultivation Practices", "Lighting", "Systems", "Cuttings, Clones, and Seeds", "Flowering, Harvesting, Pollinating and Seeding", "The Varieties", "Genetics Vs. Environment", "Insects and Pests", "Drying and Curing", "Smoking and Eating", and "Legal Implications", plus an eight-page glossary. Includes around 100 pictures.

Quick American Publishing; $19.95
1987; softcover; 294 pp
illus; 0-932551-01-7

MARIJUANA, THE LAW AND YOU
A Guide to Minimizing
Legal Consequences
by Ed Rosenthal, William Logan, Jeffrey Steinborn

Covering the same basic ground as *Marijuana Law* [above], this book tells you how to not get caught and what to do if you are pinched. It pools hundreds of real-life cases and little-known tips and tricks used by lawyers who specialise in pot cases. The first parts of the book deal with sentencing guidelines, informants, car searches, home searches, covering your tracks, getting arrested, and more.

Where the book really shines is in 100+ pages that tell you how to beat the rap. The first thing to do is hire a good lawyer, one who has successfully handled drug/pot cases. Attorney Bill Logan — who might just be the best pot lawyer in California — offers his six-point plan for defending a drug case. The first point is to look at the evidence and demand that it be introduced into the trial. In one case the evidence that was brought in was an empty bag. "The previously supplied photographs had shown 35 glass jars stuffed with beautiful buds, one pound in each jar. The evidence had shrunk to 28 pounds by the time it got to the Laytonville substation (I swear to God that the cops said, 'It loses weight when it dries'), and had 'dried' to nothing by court time." Other points are to visit the scene of the crime, talk to witnesses, and look at police reports, photos, video, and evidence lists.

You also learn about damaging the credibility of the prosecution's expert witnesses, personal use vs. sale, beating search warrants, undermining snitches, filing a civil rights action, using effective visual aids in court, and fighting forfeiture. The chapter "Guerrilla Trial Tactics" presents several sneaky (but legitimate) legal manoeuvres for lawyers to use. One thing that can tip the scale in your client's favour is to have a woman talk to witnesses, investigate, and testify at the trial. "For whatever nonsensical, stereotypical reasons, sometimes witnesses are more willing to let a female in the door... The reality is that the complexion of a case will be moderated by a woman testifying for the defence or serving as an advisory witness." In one case, the lawyer found out that the prosecution was in the habit of sitting at the wrong table. "We invoked the rule and made him move. He was obviously disoriented. The added benefit was that the judge, who had routinely relied on the prosecution for procedural guidance, was now looking to us."

Two appendices reproduce the DEA's "Cannabis Yields" report, which can be used to refute exaggerated prosecution claims, and the "Report of the Domestic Cannabis Eradication and Suppression Program", an inane, error-filled piece of work from the California Department of Justice.

Deciding whether to buy this book or *Marijuana Law* depends on which information is more important to you: *Marijuana Law*'s strength is its coverage of searches, seizures, and avoiding trouble, while the strength of *Marijuana, the Law and You* is the wealth of hard-edged information it

Absolute herb.
Marijuana Questions? Ask Ed.

contains on winning your trial.

Quick American Archives (Quick Trading Company); $24.95
1995; oversized softcover; 218 pp
0-932551-18-1

THE PHYSICAL, PSYCHOLOGICAL,
SPIRITUAL BENEFITS OF MARIJUANA
by Joan M Bello, MS

Most of the work published on pot's positive effects focus on the physical. Coming in a distant second, a few works talk about pot's spiritual potential, and I've seen even less about the psychological good that the herb can do. Joan Bello has done a remarkable thing by gathering many of the known benefits of marijuana into one book.

The very first paragraph of the chapter on physical benefits explains why pot is so good for you: "The wonder of marijuana is that it works in the body as an antidote to extreme swings. It does not stimulate. It does not depress. It does both at the same time... The simultaneous opposing action of marijuana is akin to balancing our entire system." MJ relaxes us when we are tense and in a hectic frame of mind, but it also picks us up if we are tired or relaxed. It enhances the functioning of both hemispheres of the brain, allowing us to become more creative and more perceptive. It also increases blood flow and dilates bronchial tubes, so more oxygen-rich blood gets to more parts of the body. Strangely, Bello doesn't specifically address pot's beneficial effects on nausea, glaucoma, pain, multiple sclerosis, and many other conditions.

Psychologically, pot enriches the perceptions of all five

senses, as well as eroticism, tenderness, and intuition. We become more insightful regarding our own and others' thoughts and emotions. Our subconscious motives and assumptions become easier to see. Some people complain that marijuana makes them sleepy or lethargic. "Is it possible that the 'slowing down' and the nap are the organism's turn toward health? A relaxed attitude is only harmful to the goals of a workaholic." A related complaint is that if everyone smoked grass, the world would stop functioning. Bello counters: "The world would certainly not fall apart, even if by some miracle, everyone did smoke pot. Imagine the possibilities for co-operation throughout the world that might take place if everyone somehow had a slightly higher consciousness, that included 'you as well as me.'"

This relates to pot's spiritual benefits. Cannabis puts us in an altered state that rejects materialism and focuses on "honesty and compassion". We become more aware of the interconnectedness of life and of the roles we are to play. By constructively using pot, we can achieve a more profound level of consciousness, vibrate at a higher level, direct energy up through our chakras — or however you prefer to think of it.

Bello makes pot sound like something of a panacea. She admits that most people only use Mary Jane recreationally, enjoying the relaxed feeling it gives them. However, if they started using it to purposely improve themselves, we'd be living in a better world.

This book also contains a history of marijuana and a large bibliography.

Lifeservices; $12.95
1992; oversized photocopied softcover; 60 pp
illus; no ISBN

POTHEAD CD-ROM

When you fire up the Pothead CD-ROM, you will find yourself in a 3-D environment that you can explore. By walking around, you'll enter interesting places (for example, hash bars rendered from photographs of the real ones in Amsterdam) and encounter eccentric characters, such as the little old lady offering you a marijuana brownie. You'll see lots of pictures of beautiful buds and trippy art, and your ears will be stimulated by hours and hours of ambient music, strange sounds, and people talking about their experiences with pot. Don't expect a linear, reference-style guide to cannabis, but rather an open-ended, non-goal oriented experience of exploration and discovery. *Pothead* has received numerous comparisons to *Myst* (perhaps it should've been named *Smoak*?). Works with Windows or Macintosh.

Happy Capitalist Productions; $19.95
1996; CD-ROM

WHY MARIJUANA SHOULD BE LEGAL

by Ed Rosenthal & Steve Kubby
In this well-reasoned critique, the authors present a concise look at — no surprise here — why marijuana should be legal. Their approach has two main thrusts. The first is to look at the many benefits of pot and hemp that are being tragi-

cally denied to us. The second is to look at the disastrous ramifications of keeping pot illegal. Mixed in with these arguments is an examination of who benefits from the outlawing of cannabis.

Several chapters look at the industrial uses of hemp, the medical uses of marijuana, and marijuana's extremely benign nature. These topics have been covered elsewhere in this section, so I won't rehash them. The authors do a good job of boiling the info down to a size that can be quickly read and understood.

Other chapters look at the terrible toll that marijuana prohibition is having on individuals and society as a whole. The outlawing of pot has triggered systematic violations of the First, Fourth, Fifth, Sixth, Seventh, Eight, Ninth, and Tenth Amendments. Billions of dollars' worth of private property are seized under suspicion of marijuana crimes (not to mention other drugs), yet eighty percent of people who have their property taken from them are never charged with a crime. Being convicted of some marijuana crimes allows the State to take your children from you. Hindus, Buddhists, Rastafarians, and others are not permitted to fully practice their religions without fear of going to prison. The War on Drugs has allowed the government to give itself police state powers, including violating due process, using the military against the citizens of the US, and shooting down unarmed planes that are merely suspected of carrying drugs.

Laws have been complete ineffective in curbing marijuana use. All they have done is fill up prisons with people whose only crimes were voluntarily buying, selling, or using a substance that makes them feel good. Not only does this give people a record for life and expose them to the violence and rape in prison, it takes an immense toll on the law enforcement and justice systems. "Nationwide, there were more arrests for marijuana than there were for arson, manslaughter, rape, stolen property, vandalism, and sex offences combined." Instead of catching and trying *real* criminals, cops and judges have to waste their time with pot smokers. Prisons are overflowing because of all the people sent there for cannabis-related offences.

This also wastes obscene amounts of government money. To cite just one example, over twenty federal agencies spend around $30 billion a year trying to enforce marijuana laws. On top of that, the federal and state governments could *make* an estimated $17 to $25 billion a year from taxes, fees, and licenses if marijuana were a legal crop.

Because growing marijuana is unregulated, it can contain all kinds of toxins. About half of all pot in the US comes from other countries, bringing with it the possibility of pests and disease that could devastate "legitimate" American agriculture. Because buying and selling marijuana is unregulated, people often place themselves in enormous danger from violent criminal elements, and children are able to buy pot as easily as adults.

These are just some of the authors' persuasive arguments, many of which haven't received a wide airing, even from people who favour marijuana's legalisation. For ethical, social, legal, economic, medical, industrial, governmental, and other reasons — as well as the general issue of personal freedom — ending pot prohibition is the right thing to do. This book makes that perfectly clear in just over 100 pages, making it — like *The Hemp Manifesto* [above] — the perfect gift for those who need convincing.

Thunder's Mouth Press; $9.95
1996; paperback; 118 pp
illus; 1-56025-110-7

ALTERING CONSCIOUSNESS WITHOUT DRUGS

ACCESS YOUR BRAIN'S JOY CENTER
A Natural Alternative to Using Alcohol, Nicotine, Drugs, or Overeating to Cope with Life's Pressures and Challenges
by Pete A. Sanders, Jr.

This book and cassette tape combination are aimed at helping you stimulate the parts of your brain that control anger, hurt, worry, and fear. The most primitive part of your grey matter — the limbic system — is responsible for these negative emotions, but there is a part of your brain that can override the limbic system and create elevated moods and feelings of well being. It's called the septum pellucidum, and it is this area that the book/tape triggers.

The author gives instructions for stimulating the pellucidum mentally and physically. Since it takes some practice to get the hang of it, the tape offers verbal guidance to aid you. The book contains examples of how to use this "Joy Touch" to assist in enhancing sex, quitting smoking, controlling weight, controlling pain, and more.

While the first part of the book deals with overriding the limbic system and stimulating your joy centre, the second half tells you how to clear away all the crud that built up in your limbic system over a lifetime. Sometimes the advice gets a little New Agey — with talk of "Soul Travel" and psychic connections — but even if you don't believe that those are the mechanisms in operation, the techniques are still useful. For example, in dealing with loss of a loved one (or prolonged separation), Sanders recommends mentally reliving all of the best moments with that person. "Whether you believe it is mere memory or Soul Travel, the bottom line is, it works." He also reveals ways to deal with rejection, betrayal, anger, worrying about family, depression, and more.

Free Soul; $27.50 ppd (book by itself: $20.05 ppd)
1994; softcover book and cassette tape in plastic case; 90 pp,

90 min
illus; 0-9641911-2-1

FLICKERS OF THE DREAMACHINE
The Definitive Handbook
edited by Paul Cecil

The Dreamachine is a very simple, low-tech device that has been found to produce profound visual experiences and altered states of consciousness. It was invented in 1960 by mathematician Ian Sommerville and groundbreaking artist Brion Gysin, best known for his influence on William Burroughs. Sommerville and Gysin had been reading a book called *The Living Brain*, which discussed the effects of flickering light on human perception and consciousness. Sommerville built the first prototype of a simple device based on the power of repetitive flickering, and Gysin further modified and perfected it. In its simplest form, it is a cardboard cylinder with precise shapes cut out of it. This cylinder is rotated by placing it in the centre of a record player turntable (remember those?) and is lit from within by a lightbulb hanging inside it. The user then sits with eyes closed in a dark room, putting his or her face close to the Dreamachine. This usually results in a dazzlingly beautiful display of colours and "archetypal" patterns inside the user's closed eyes.

In his seminal essay "Dreamachine", which is reproduced in this book, Gysin quotes from a letter Sommerville sent him in which the mathematician describes his initial experiments: "Visions start with a kaleidoscope of colours on a plane in front of the eyes and gradually become more complex and beautiful, breaking like surf on a shore until whole patterns of colour are pounding to get in. After a while the visions were permanently behind my eyes and I was in the middle of a whole scene with limitless patterns being generated around me. There was an almost unbearable feeling of spatial movement for a while but it was well worth getting through for I found that when it stopped I was high above the earth in a universal blaze of glory. Afterwards I found that my perception of the world around me had increased very notably."

Sommerville believes that the Dreamachine may tap into basic, shared areas of the human conscious. In his own seminal essay "Flicker" (also reproduced in this book), he notes: "The elements of pattern which have been recorded by subjects under flicker show a clear affinity with the designs found in prehistoric rock-carving, painting, and idols of world-wide distribution: India, Czechoslovakia, Spain, Mexico, Norway and Ireland. They are also found in the arts of many primitive peoples of Australia, Melanesia, West Africa, South Africa, Central America and the Amazon. Children's drawings often spontaneously depict them..." He also notes that the machine can create huge, moving patterns that look like Eastern mandalas.

Further probing of the Dreamachine and/or Gysin is provided by Genesis P-Orridge ("The Only Language Is Light"), Ian MacFayden ("Machine Dreams: Optical Toys & Mechanical Boys"), Ira Cohen ("Another Note in a Bottle"), Joe Ambrose ("The Dream Machine Queen"), Paul Cecil ("Inside Out: The Mysticism of Dream Machines"), and others.

A Dreamachine in *Flickers of the Dreamachine.*

Also included is a relevant excerpt from *The Living Brain*, which, you'll recall, heavily influenced Gysin and Sommerville. Finally — last but very definitely not least — you get a schematic and instructions so you can build your own Dreamachine out of cardboard.

CodeX; £7.95, $16US
1996; oversized softcover; 131 pp
illus; 1-899598-03-0

STONED FREE
How to Get High Without Drugs
by Patrick Wells & Douglas Rushkoff

It is a natural tendency for human beings to achieve altered states of consciousness. It feels good, we want to do it, and we're going to do it. The most obvious way to "get high" is through drugs, such as psychedelics and alcohol. Even many prudes, who would never dream of being "drug users", smoke cigarettes to calm down during stressful situations or drink coffee or Coke to catch a caffeine buzz.

But there are several problems with drugs. First, "They alter your consciousness by fucking you up." Though marijuana has some positive physical effects and LSD is not toxic, drugs as a whole really aren't very good for you, as anyone who has spent an entire day puking and dry heaving his or her lungs up can tell you. Second, the experience is always temporary and often hard to integrate into your day-to-day life. Third, drugs are really just a tool to altered consciousness. They mask the fact that you already have the keys to getting high within yourself.

Stoned Free is all about using those natural, drug-free methods to induce rushes, highs, and other altered states of consciousness. The first methods that are discussed use your eyes to get high. "One way of getting high on visuals is to look at something that initiates the optic experience of being high. Even if you have not been high before, the brain reacts to the altered vision by producing an appropriate altered consciousness." The authors give names and ordering info for several videotapes and software packages that use fractals, video feedback, and manipulation of raw images to create entrancing effects. They also discuss using strobe lights, staring at mandalas, and gently pressing your fingers on your eyelids, a technique practised by some shamans and monks.

Similarly, sound can be used to expand your consciousness. Follow the authors' instructions for doing simple chants. You don't need to have a voice like a Benedictine monk (Benedictines, incidentally, used chanting for this very purpose). Like other techniques in this book, this may sound corny and way too simple, but it actually works (for me, at least). I don't see God or anything like that, but it does produce a noticeable, profound state of relaxation bordering on bliss. This chapter also covers group chords, tuning forks, and prerecorded music.

Sex is also a very powerful means of achieving altered states. The key is to realise that sex engages the entire body and involves intimacy and the letting go of self. "For partners or even solo artists willing to accept the fact that sex is more than a bump and a squirt, an unlimited range of transcendental experiences awaits you." The authors give good basic introductions to Taoist sex, Tantric sex, and kundalini to get you pointed in the right direction. They mention that there are ways to produce mind-exploding orgasms, but then give details for only one method. For more techniques you are referred to a book published almost 25 years ago that is now out of print.

Another group of techniques centres on self-deprivation. "Deprivations are not penance. They are temporary closure, which allow other things to open." Specific techniques employ flotation tanks, temporary blindness, sleep deprivation, not talking, and fasting.

Among the many other varied methods that are covered

are meditation, yoga, dervish dancing, skydiving, using brain machines, getting back to nature, Zen koans, visualisation, lucid dreaming, and breathing techniques. Highly recommended.

Loompanics Unlimited; $12.95
1995; softcover; 157 pp
1-55950-126-X

TANKS FOR THE MEMORIES
Floatation Tank Talks
by Dr. John C. Lilly & EJ Gold

When you float on the warm saline solution in a sealed sensory deprivation tank, your sight, hearing, touch, and other senses are deprived of any input. With all of the physical senses turned off — the reasoning goes — the inner workings of your mind are allowed to come to the forefront. Many people experience incredibly real hallucinations while in these tanks.

Floatation tanks were invented by John C. Lilly, who also pioneered human-dolphin communication and has made other major contributions to the understanding of consciousness. In this book, he and his very private mentor — human potential movement pioneer EJ Gold — explain the history and uses of the tanks and how they affect your state of being.

The first three chapters are by Lilly… one is a lecture he gave in 1975 and two are articles from an obscure magazine called *Floatation*. In the first chapter, Lilly says: "All the average person has to do is get into the tank in the darkness and silence and float around until he realises he is programming everything that is happening inside his head. You are free of the physical world at that point and anything can happen inside your head because everything is governed by the laws of thought rather than the laws of the external world. So you can go to the limits of your conceptions."

The other five chapters are transcripts of Gold's lectures. Gold is — if anything — more esoteric and mystical than Lilly. At one point, he seems to be saying that you can use the tank not just to experience other realities while you're in it, but to actually change your day-to-day "non-tank" reality. "You can get a better concept of the experience by realising that the tank is genuinely your centre, that you're going home when you go into the tank. You're losing your imagery, you're ceasing to create a universe. You move into the tank and you think of another universe. You sit up, open the door and go out into that universe, and if it's the same universe as it is now for you, and it continues to be the same universe, you had better take a look at yourself, at your ability to move beyond the limits that you've set up for yourself."

Other subjects that Lilly and Gold cover include energy sources to the brain, self meta-programming, thinking in categories, other worlds, beliefs, habits, identity, and Alpha, Beta, Theta, and Delta states. This a vital book for all reality hackers and neuronauts.

Gateways Books; $12.50
1995; softcover; 152 pp
illus; 0-89556-071-2

C, by EJ Gold.
Tanks for the Memories.

MISCELLANEOUS

ABSINTHE
The Cocaine of the Nineteenth Century
by Doris Lanier

Absinthe is a bitter, green alcoholic drink that tastes like licorice [see *Absinthe: History in a Bottle*, *Outposts* p 68]. It contains the herb known as wormwood, which gives its users an altered state unlike that of normal alcohol. During the late nineteenth and very early twentieth centuries, absinthe became incredibly popular in France and New Orleans. Its most celebrated drinkers were the poets, writers, and artists from the Decadence, Impressionist, and other groundbreaking movements. The "Green Fairy", as absinthe was called, is now banned throughout the world because of its allegedly deleterious effects.

There is no doubt that absinthe wasn't exactly good for you, but the hysteria over "absinthism" seems to have been somewhat misguided. It is very likely that most of the bad short- and long-term effects of absinthe came from its incredibly high alcohol content (80%, or 160 proof), with wormwood playing a much lesser role. You wouldn't know it from reading this book, though. *Absinthe* provides a valuable detailed history of the drink, but it completely buys into the dominant view during absinthe's heyday that it was a horrible, debilitating drug that kills its users or drives them insane. Anybody familiar with the smear campaigns against marijuana and LSD will probably have grave doubts about the alarm raised in a December 1880 issue of the *New York Times*: "A French physician of eminence has recently declared that absinthe is ten times more pernicious than ordinary intemperance, and that it very seldom happens that the habit, once fixed, can be loosed. The same authority says that the increase of insanity is largely due to absinthe… Its immoderate use speedily acts on the entire nervous system in general, and the brain in particular, in which it produces organic changes with accompanying derangement of all mental powers. The habitual drinker becomes at first dull,

Ad for a French absinthe distillery.
Absinthe.

languid, is soon completely brutalised and then goes raving mad."

No doubt several writers and artists did drink themselves into an early grave with absinthe, but countless creative types have done that with all kinds of alcohol throughout the centuries. It just so happened that absinthe was the poison of choice for this group of radical visionaries. The author takes care to show the dependence on and effects of absinthe as they relate to Alfred-Henry Jarry, Paul Verlaine, Henri Toulouse-Lautrec, Vincent Van Gogh, and many others. However, she also talks about the positive aspects of the Emerald Enchantress — the users' glowing descriptions of their altered states and the great art they produced while under the influence.

Absinthe: The Cocaine of the Nineteenth Century reproduces a few absinthe-related works of art and other images in black and white. Visually, it can't hold a candle to *Absinthe: History in a Bottle*. As far as approaches go, *Absinthe: Cocaine* has much more textual information and takes a decidedly unromantic approach to the topic — which by itself may be a good thing — but at times it seems to border on Just Say No propaganda. *Absinthe: History*, on the other hand, sometimes seems to romanticise its subject (of course, the Green Fairy *does* have a strong mystique), but it makes a good point in questioning the severity of the non-alcohol-related effects of absinthe.

McFarland & Company; $29.95
1995; hardcover (library binding, no jacket); 188 pp
illus; 0-89950-989-4

BEYOND AA
Dealing Responsibly with Alcohol
by Clarence Barrett, J.D.

Clarence Barrett was an alcoholic who managed to permanently kick the habit in early 1959. He now offers his own approach to anyone who would like to either quit drinking or seriously decrease their consumption. The key to Barrett's method is willpower. "For many years it has been unfashionable, (totally unacceptable?) to mention the word **'willpower'** in the context of alcohol abuse, and particularly in connection with any treatment modality. Usually it has been summarily dismissed as moralistic, simplistic or naive, as though the reason for such summary disposition were readily apparent. Yet if there is a thread that connects all treatment approaches in the field of alcohol abuse it is that the drinkers must be persuaded, coerced, motivated or conditioned to change their behaviour from drinking to abstinence or at least controlled drinking."

Barrett reveals that alcoholics have an incredible amount of willpower, which they use to keep hitting the bottle. Skid row bums are amazingly resourceful in scraping together enough funds to buy some Mad Dog. While money isn't a problem for alcoholic executives, they show plenty of resourcefulness in hiding massive amounts of liquor and their liquor consumption from family, friends, and co-workers. "The fact is, they have **plenty of will power**, and have just been misdirecting it."

After discussing the nature of alcohol, different levels of drinking, the definition of alcoholism, the limitations of Alcoholics Anonymous, and the insights of Reality Therapy, the author gives specific advice for controlling your drinking or quitting completely and permanently. He doesn't pretend to offer any easy magic formula for you to achieve this goal. The main key to complete abstinence is taking the step of telling yourself that you will never drink another drop in any form for the rest of your life. "If you have decided for certain that you want to give up alcohol, and I mean really want to give up alcohol, then there is nothing that will or can force you to take a drink, for **you will do what you want to do**."

Positive Attitudes, Publishers; $11.95
1996; softcover; 151 pp
0-9630292-9-0

DISEASING OF AMERICA
How We Allowed Recovery Zealots and the Treatment Industry to Convince Us We Are Out of Control
by Stanton Peele

Ironically, Stanton Peele has become a leader in the addictions field by bucking the status quo. His main argument is that alcohol and drug use can become addictions, but addictions are not diseases. The current standard view — espoused by Alcoholics Anonymous, the medical community, and other powerful institutions — is that addictions are diseases and can be treated as such. Peele is fighting back against this tendency to "medicalise our personal and social problems."

The disease view of addiction contends that an addiction is akin to a parasite — it exists independently of a person's life, latching on to him and controlling his actions. He is totally unable to control his addiction, and, when intoxicated, unable to control any of his actions. This paradigm absolves the addict from any responsibility for his behaviour by reducing him to a helpless pawn.

Peele argues that an addiction is completely intertwined with the rest of a person's psyche. Addictions arise because of problems of a personal nature (e.g., marital discord) or a societal nature (e.g., alienation) or a combination of the two. "All addictions accomplish something for the addict. They are ways of coping with feelings and situations with which addicts cannot otherwise cope." The addictive experience can have several pleasurable effects, including: "Eliminates pain, uncertainty, and other negative sensations", and "Creates powerful and immediate sensations; focuses and absorbs attention".

So how do people get over their addictions without involving themselves in a medicalised programme? The answers are varied. Some people lose the need for chemical escape when they solve personal problems and feel more secure, less stressed, etc. Others come to a crucial point where their addiction clashes directly with some deeply held value, such as "God, health, self-control, a desire for the good opinion of others". Appropriate counselling for addictions would therefore help people identify and cope with their problems, emotions, etc. It would also express a clear disapproval for the addiction and hold people legally and personally accountable for all of their actions.

In the course of the book, Peele also discusses the origins of the medical model of addictions, the people and groups who claim to have a monopoly on the truth regarding alcoholism, the addiction treatment industry, addiction as an excuse for illegal behaviour, "creating a world worth living in" through the reestablishment of strong communities and values, and what we can learn from the experiences of John Belushi, Kitty Dukakis, Drew Barrymore, and Sid Vicious.

Lexington Books; $14.95
1989; softcover; 329 pp
0-02-874014-9

DRUG LEGALIZATION
For and Against
edited by Rod L. Evans & Irwin M. Berent

This anthology contains 24 essays which argue for and against drug legalisation. Many of the pieces are seminal statements, having been made when the idea of legalising drugs first came to the public's attention.

In 1989 economist Milton Friedman wrote an open letter to drug czar William Bennet in the *Wall Street Journal*, urging him to propose the legalisation of drugs. Friedman argues that this path will take the "obscene profits" out of drugs, decrease violence, and lessen the destruction of our liberty that is occurring in the name of the so-called War on Drugs. He alludes to a similar proclamation he had made in *Newsweek* seventeen years earlier: "Had drugs been decriminalised 17 years ago, 'crack' would never have been invented (it was invented because the high cost of illegal drugs made it profitable to provide a cheaper version) and there would today be far fewer addicts. The lives of thousands, perhaps hundreds of thousands of innocent victims would have been saved, and not only in the US."

Bennet responded with his own open letter to Friedman in the *Journal*. He wrote, "In my judgement, and in the judgement of virtually every serious scholar in this field, the potential costs of legalising drugs would be so large as to make it a public policy disaster." According to Bennet, whenever drugs are legalised, use and addiction have "skyrocketed". Most addicts don't seek treatment, so setting up widespread programmes wouldn't help. Also, Bennet thinks that people would continue to commit crimes to pay for drugs as well as their other expenses. He concludes: "At a time when national intolerance for drug use is rapidly increasing, the legalisation argument is a political anachronism. Its recent resurgence is, I trust, only a temporary distraction from the genuine debate on national drug policy."

Friedman then wrote his own response, "Bennett's 'Public Policy Disaster' Is Already Here", in which he blasts the czar's adherence to a failed approach. "More police, more jails, more stringent penalties, increased efforts at interception, increased publicity about the evils of drugs — all this has been accompanied by more, not fewer, drug addicts; more, not fewer, crimes and murders; more, not less, corruption; more, not fewer, innocent victims."

Invoking the ghost of Prohibition against alcohol is popular among debaters. This book contains two views on the issue. Political commentator Hodding Carter III's "We're Losing the Drug War Because Prohibition Never Works" centres mainly on the fact that when you make a substance illegal, you don't get rid of it, but you do bring about massive corruption. Prohibition ended in 1933, and Carter writes: "In my home state of Mississippi, it lasted for an additional 33 years, and for all those years it was a truism that the drinkers had their liquor, the preachers had their prohibition and the sheriffs made the money."

Harvard professor Mark H. Moore takes a contrarian position in "Actually, Prohibition Was a Success". He claims that "alcohol consumption declined dramatically during Prohibition." Cirrhosis death rates, hospital admissions for alcoholic psychosis, and arrests for public drunkenness and disorderly conduct all significantly declined. Regarding the role of organised crime, Moore says it existed before and after Prohibition, and that during that time violent crime did not increase. "The real lesson of Prohibition is that society can, indeed, make a dent in the consumption of drugs through laws."

The iconoclastic psychiatrist Thomas Szasz makes the most uncompromising argument for legalisation, basing his position on the belief that we must be allowed to determine what we put into our own bodies. He says that the War on Drugs is just another example of the search for scapegoats that has gone on throughout history. "In the past we have witnessed religious or holy wars waged against people who professed the wrong faith; more recently, we have witnessed racial or eugenic wars, waged against people who possessed the wrong genetic make-up; now we are witnessing a medical or therapeutic war, waged against people who use the wrong drugs."

Even if you are for legalisation and don't want to hear the pro-prohibition stance, you should get this book, because you can't counter the other side's arguments unless you know exactly what they are.

Open Court; $17.95
1992; softcover; 331 pp
0-8126-9184-9

THE IBOGAINE STORY
Report on the Staten Island Project
by Paul De Rienzo, Dana Beal, and Members of the Project

Ibogaine — an alkaloid derived from an African bush — has been shown to be amazingly effective in treating addiction to the most insidious drugs, such as heroin, morphine, cocaine, nicotine, and alcohol. Unlike methadone treatment, which replaces heroin addiction with methadone addiction, Ibogaine simply breaks the addiction. The majority of people stay off drugs for three to six months after just one dose of Ibogaine, and repeated doses result in even better results. This book tells the whole story of Ibogaine, including why this possible cure for addiction is being stymied by government agencies, the pharmaceutical industry, and hysterical anti-drug zealots who would apparently rather arrest or shoot addicts than help them kick their habits.

Autonomedia; $20
1997; oversized softcover; 348 pp
illus; 1-57027-029-5

JUST SAY NO TO DRUG TESTS
How to Beat the Whiz Quiz
by Ed Carson

The Fourth Amendment protects us against unreasonable searches and seizures of our "persons, houses, papers, and effects…" Ed Carson writes, "In 1791, when the Bill of Rights was ratified, it was not possible to search an individual's bodily fluids. Otherwise, I'm sure 'bodily fluids' would have been included in the Fourth Amendment." (It seems to me that drug tests also violate our Fifth Amendment right not to incriminate ourselves, although that right is guaranteed only "in a court". Presumably, then, employers are allowed to run roughshod over this Constitutional guarantee.) Carson sums up his mindset and reason for writing this book: "Your employer doesn't own you twenty-four hours a day, and if your drug usage doesn't affect your job, it is none of your employer's business."

Carson beat drug tests given to him by the military for eight years, so the techniques he gives are field-tested. He discusses what testing procedures are like and how the most commonly-used types of tests work. Thin-layer chromatography is the cheapest and least accurate test. Enzyme immunoassay and radioimmunoassay can test for the presence of ten drugs at a time. Gas chromatography/mass spectrometry is the most costly, and it is said to have 100% accuracy. It can tell exactly how much of every known drug or chemical is in the urine sample.

The crux of the book is the chapter that discusses how

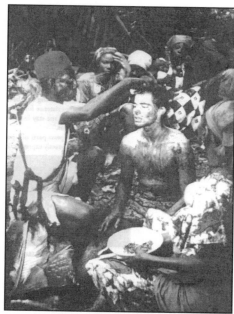

A Frenchman undergoes a traditional Ibogaine initiation.
The Ibogaine Story.

to beat the urine tests. Smuggling in someone else's urine is discussed, but most of the attention is on cleaning the drugs out of your system and legitimising any drugs that are found. The author discusses kidney shape-up, water dilution, fasting, exercise, and kidney shutdown. He lists the various drugs that tests detect and how long they can be detected after your last use. Cocaine usually won't show up five days after it is last used, while PCP will be detected for six months after just one use. Carson explores the best ways to flush the drugs out of your body, and if you're caught, how to explain their presence. For example, having a prescription for Tylenol 3 — which contains codeine — can explain the opiates that are found due to heroin use. Unfortunately, there is no discussion of fighting the results based on false-positives. (Drug tests often mistake legal substances for illegal ones, so if you test positive for amphetamines, you could say it was due to antihistamines. If the test detects opiates, you could say it was due to poppy-seed cookies, which are available at almost all bakeries.)

There's also a short, hopelessly incomplete chapter on beating breathalysers. The most informative part of the chapter reveals that many police flashlights are outfitted with breathalysers. When a cop pulls you over and shines a light in your face, he or she may be slyly taking a reading. The best things to do are roll your windows down early and don't talk directly at the flashlight. If you're taken in for a more accurate breathalyser, Carson's only advice is to stall.

Paladin Press; $12
1991; softcover; 39 pp
0-87364-624-X

LET'S BAN SMOKING OUTRIGHT!

by Patrick Griffin

Printed as a paperback the size of a cigarette pack, *Let's Ban Smoking Outright!* proposes the outlawing of all tobacco products. The author is a former three-pack a day man. "Apart from anything else, I was warned of the danger at least ten thousand times — that's if you count all the warnings printed on all the packs I cracked during roughly ten years of smoking. I am a man who ignored ten thousand warnings…"

In 1990, smoking killed 418,960 people in the US, which is more than the number of American battle deaths in World War I, World War II, Korea, and Vietnam added together. The number of years of "potential life" that were lost was 5,048,740, with 1,152,635 of those years coming from middle age, not old age. Since smoking is the number one killer in the US and it's preventable, shouldn't the government do something?

The author knows his proposal has its problems. "OK, it's a stupid, fascist, unnecessary, unworkable, historically discredited idea. But what's wrong with it?" Later he writes, "Banning a toxic substance, a deadly air-borne pollutant, and a habit-forming drug-in one! — can't be wrong." He realises that banning smoking would never get rid of it, only drive it underground, but that would be almost as good. Just like pot, people would still smoke tobacco, "But they would smoke it only at times, in places and under circumstances that allow dope smoking. Which, when you think about it, are pretty limited." This would cause smokers to almost become like heroin junkies. "Living on the margins, cringing from the law, endangering their loved ones, quietly destroying themselves — and not even having any fun doing it — smokers would inevitably begin to absorb some small part of the contempt we feel for other helpless addicts."

Obviously, I personally reject the author's proposal, but I was surprised that at least he did make a somewhat persuasive argument.

Ten Speed Press; $4.95

1995; small paperback; 56 pp

0-89815-685-8

M'HASHISH

by Mohammed Mrabet

Mohammed Mrabet is a Tangierian storyteller whose body of work has been translated by Paul Bowles. These ten stories are told in the simple manner of folktales, and I'm not sure if Mrabet is relating traditional yarns or if he made them up himself. Either way, they all deal with people who are *m'hashish* — that is, "full of hashish". Mrabet gives a well-rounded view of this state of intoxication, detailing the good, bad, and ambivalent effects.

A single man, Stito, and a married man, Kacem, are the main characters of "The Canebreak". Everyday they go to Kacem's house where his sexually-neglected wife fixes them dinner. Stito smokes hash (called "kif" by Mrabet), while Kacem gets blitzed with alcohol. One day, Stito pokes fun at his friend by asking him where his body stores all the booze he drinks. "Kacem laughed. And you? You don't get anything but smoke out of your pipe. I get the alcohol right in-

side me, and it feels wonderful. That's an empty idea you have, said Stito. Kif gives me more pleasure than alcohol could ever give anybody. And it makes me think straighter and talk better." It also lets him screw better, something Kacem's wife discovers after she strays from her alcoholically-impotent husband. Kacem finds out, but instead of getting angry, he kicks the bottle and hits the pipe. He stops being iron-fisted with his wife and starts having sex with her for the first time since they got married.

Hash doesn't come off in such a flattering light in "The Sea in the Street". A man goes to the market twice to pick up fish and then cooking oil for his wife, but spends most of his time smoking kif with the shopkeepers. When he finally gets back late in the evening, he's so stoned that he thinks the street has become the ocean. He takes his clothes off and jumps in, crawling through cactus patches and shit as he "swims" toward his house. "When his wife saw him naked, bloody, and smeared with excrement, her mouth fell open and she could say nothing." After recovering from her shock, she bathes him and puts him to bed. "In the middle of the night he began to call out to his wife: I've brought the oil! You can cook the fish now. I'm hungry."

Other stories include "The Datura Trees", "Allah's Words", "The Kif-Cutter's Story", and "Two Friends and the Rain."

City Lights Books; $8.95

1969, 1993; softcover; 79 pp

0-87286-034-5

ON DRUGS

by David Lenson

David Lenson is a professor of comparative literature, so he brings a "squishier", right-brained brand of thinking to the subject of drug use. He has written a basically pro-drug book (published by a university press!), in which he argues that the so-called War on Drugs is based on false ideas of human behaviour. The drive to become intoxicated is inborn, and that will never change. Any effort to override this innate urge will meet with as much success as the various laws that have prohibited sex acts. Lenson argues that "history has shown the state's inability to legislate the bloodstreams of its citizens."

Lenson weaves together many arguments about the true meaning and reasons behind anti-drug hysteria, many of which will be familiar to readers of drug literature. For example, drugs make a convenient enemy. Nixon first declared the War on Drugs as the Vietnam war ended. It waxed and waned, and then kicked into overdrive when the Cold War ended. Drugs became the new bad guy, the new threat that justifies increased government power. "Drugs seemed to have an alien origin, but could still be present in the most intimate corners of domestic life: in our bathrooms, our cars, our offices, and among our families — just like Communism."

One of the effects of the relentlessly negative mindset about drugs is that users often accept their criminal status and believe the condemnations that they will never contribute to society. "Perhaps the reason why a serious alcoholic like Winston Churchill was able to lead Britain through World War II and thereafter into the era of the Cold War was simply

A poppy bursting with "the milk of paradise".
Opium Poppy Garden.

that no one told him that his use of drink was supposed to disqualify him from political leadership."

Lenson thinks that the fear of drugs may come in part from our society's rigidly compartmentalised model of the mind. Drugs break down the barriers, making things a lot less certain, which is scary to control freaks who want consciousness to be neat and tidy. Because drugs alter the mind's functioning, they've gotten the reputation for being harmful and destructive. "If drugs simply killed the mind and/ or brain, why would anyone take them? Most common psychotropes bring changes in mental operations as certainly as they alter brain chemistry. But change is not death."

The prohibition of marijuana is perhaps the most troubling of all, given the plant's incredibly benign nature. Lenson sees something deeper at work. "But since there is no necessary connection of cannabis to violent crime, or to any breakdown of family life of the kind precipitated by alcohol or stimulants, or to the escalation of medical costs or harm to other people like that caused by alcohol and tobacco use, the illegality of this group of drugs has become a sort of a prolonged test case: can some activity be permanently illegal simply because the law declares it so, in the absence of any cogent rationale?"

On Drugs provides many intelligent, well-reasoned, and beautifully-stated arguments against anti-drug fervour and for what the author calls "a diversity of consciousness".

University of Minnesota; $21.95
1995; hardcover; 261 pp
0-8166-2710-X

OPIUM POPPY GARDEN
The Way of a Chinese Grower
by William Griffith

Part of this book is set up as the tale of Ch'ien, an eighteen-year-old man of Chinese descent who moves to Colombia to raise opium. His father gives him some family heirlooms, including poppy seeds and a diary written by Ch'ien's grandfather which gives instructions for opium cul-

tivation. Finally, after about 20 pages of Ch'ien's none-too-exciting adventures getting to his plot of land, the author delivers the goods. He tells us exactly how to raise and harvest poppies in the old Chinese way. "... [Ch'ien] knew his relatives had taught him a secret few other people in the world knew: the secret of how to milk almost one ounce of the precious raw opium from each plant." The author reveals this method. Our hero uses a special tool, but it sounds as though you could rig one up for yourself. The real downside is that it takes two months of daily, labour-intensive work to milk the plant for all it's worth.

A few pages from the family diary are reprinted. They contain more detailed instructions on how to milk, along with several illustrations of technique and the tools required (the cutter and the scraper).

After Ch'ien's tale and the pseudo-diary, several chapters discuss the more technical aspects of opium — botanical, pharmacological, and horticultural. This last chapter contains even more information on when and where to plant and how to milk. "The capsule is ready for milking 14-16 days or 18-20 days after flowering, depending on the variety selected. The capsule at this time has a blue-grey cast; the abscission zone has darkened where the flower petals were attached..." The best time for the daily milking is at midday, when the flow of opium is greatest. If you're going to grade your opium, only the first two milkings should be combined, because they contain the highest amount of morphine. The amount of codeine, however, stays constant.

Besides diagrams and molecular structures, this book also has around twenty pictures of different kinds of poppies at the various levels of growth, from seeds to the beautiful flower to the capsule bursting with "the milk of paradise" (to quote Samuel Taylor Coleridge).

Ronin Publishing; $14.95
1993; softcover; 78 pp
illus; 0-914171-67-4

PHARMAKO/POEIA
Plant Powers, Poisons, and Herbcraft
by Dale Pendell

Pharmako/Poeia provides an exhilarating and encyclopaedic look at plants that alter consciousness. Though it tackles its subject extensively, this book is not dry reference material. Its overall structure and its style are fluid and poetic... perspectives shift, voices change. Each chapter is a melange of flowing information on taxonomy, parts used, how it's taken, chemistry, effects, addiction, pharmacology, good/beneficial effects, toxicology, legalities, recipes, quotations, and more.

The author has developed his own classification system for drugs based on a mandala in which one type of drug slowly shifts into its neighbouring type, which shifts into the next type, and so on until you're back to the original category. The first category to be covered is thanatopathia: "In varying degrees, thanatopathics let you taste death." The two drugs in this category are tobacco and pituri, a shrub chewed by Australian aborigines.

The next category in the author's scheme is inebriantia — yeast, wine, barley, ale, hard liquor, aether, and "fossil

A mandala of psychoactive substances.
Pharmako/poeia.

fuels" (i.e., substances, such as gas, that are huffed). The inebriants offer a "return to 'just do it.' A return to what you desire, to beyond what you have been told you want, to what you really want. To do it. Yourself. Now. Leap, leap. License."

From there, we move into the rhapsodica (absinthe and dog grass), euphorica (opium and heroin), pacifica (kava kava), existentia (diviner's sage), evaesthetica (cannabis), metaphysica (nitrous oxide and numerous obscure plants). The back pages offer a glossary, an extensive reference section, and twelve pages of commentary on the main text.

No other drug book achieves the graceful blend of facts, ideas, observations, and opinions as *Pharmako/Poeia*. Its fuzzy, soft-edged approach reflects the shifting of consciousness that occurs when you take most of the substances it covers. Numerous illustrations — from fifteenth century woodcuts to botanical drawings of the plants — enhance the reading experience. Highly recommended.

If your drug of choice isn't included, don't worry — a companion volume, *Pharmako/Gnosis*, has been promised and should be out by the time *Psychotropedia* is. It will cover ayahuasca, DMT, peyote, ecstasy, toad venom, Belladonna, cocaine, coffee, and chocolate, among other substances.

Mercury House; $16.95
1995; oversized softcover; 301 pp
heavily illus; 1-56279-069-2

PLANT INTOXICANTS
A Classic Text on the Use of
Mind-Altering Plants
by Baron Ernst von Bibra

Published in 1855, *Plant Intoxicants* is the work of the Bavarian Baron Ernst von Bibra. Surprisingly liberal in his attitude towards drugs, von Bibra was among the first to put into writing information about the cultivation, preparation, and consumption of stimulant and inebriant plants. Specifically, he covers coffee, tea, Paraguayan tea, guaraná, chocolate, Fahan tea, khat, fly agaric, thornapple, coca, opium, lactucarium, hashish, tobacco, betel, and arsenic. Jonathan

Ott provides twenty-five pages of technical notes to clarify and update the Baron's findings.

Healing Arts Press (Inner Traditions International); $16.95
1995; softcover; 278 pp
0-89281-498-5

THE POLITICS OF CONSCIOUSNESS
by Steve Kubby

In *The Politics of Consciousness*, Steve Kubby frames the drug debate in no uncertain terms — you have an absolute, inalienable right to alter your consciousness however you see fit. By presenting the pro-drug position in these terms, he is placing freedom of consciousness along with freedom of speech, freedom of religion, etc. as a sanctified human right and American liberty. Enshrined in the documents that the US was built upon is the right to life, liberty, and the pursuit of happiness. Far from seeing himself as someone who is — to paraphrase our self-appointed guardians — destroying America through the scourge of drugs, Kubby considers himself a true patriot. Not only to we have an inherent right to put whatever we want into our own bodies, but the War on Some Drugs is shredding other valuable rights (particularly the Fourth and Fifth Amendments), and the illegality of drugs makes a mockery of the free market economy that America supposedly cherishes.

"The War on Drugs is in reality a War on Freedom. It is a war that brings misery to millions of Americans — far out of proportion to any real threat from the drugs themselves... Under the banner of the War on Drugs, we have subsidised criminal activities and created a police state, with more people behind bars than any other country in the world... Right now, at least 600,000 of our fellow citizens are rotting in American jails for acts that would never have been considered crimes until sixty years ago."

Kubby looks at the many ways in which the drug war is destroying the fabric of American society. For example, school programmes urge children to turn in their parents if they use drugs (does anyone remember the Hitler Youth Corps?). *Politics* quotes from a book on hemp to show how the DARE programme works: "[Children] are indoctrinated by DARE to wear red ribbons to show they are 'drug free' — a symbol borrowed directly from Big Brother's mind control methods in George Orwell's prophetic book, *1984*... Schools have sent pledge letters of a 'drug-free home' home to parents; lists are made available as to who had returned them signed, unsigned or not at all."

Kubby declares that if the radicals who founded the United States were alive today, they would not only be nauseated by the War on Drugs, they would be risking their necks by forcefully opposing it. "Thomas Jefferson would immediately convene a war crimes commission to investigate and punish those responsible for the jailing of more than 600,000 Americans. Benjamin Franklin would be building home-made Patriot missiles. George Washington and his men would be using those Patriot missiles to blow DEA choppers out of the sky. Sam Adams would be preaching revolution on college campuses. Ethan Allen would be burning US Customs boats."

Politics examines many other topics, including harsh mandatory sentencing for drug possession (many murderers get lighter sentences than people caught with LSD), the industrial uses for marijuana that could possibly save the world, the anti-capitalism nature of the drug war, the use of retroactive drug laws (despite the fact that *ex post facto* punishment is expressly unconstitutional), the criminalisation of nature, letting young people use drugs for Vision Quests or rites of passage, pot and psychedelics seen as sacraments, magic mushrooms in the Bible, and more.

Loompanics Unlimited; $18.95
1995; oversized softcover; 168 pp
illus; 1-55950-133-2

SHAMAN WOMAN, MAINLINE LADY
Women's Writings on the Drug Experience
edited by Cynthia Palmer & Michael Horowitz

For centuries, there has been an extremely powerful taboo placed on women using drugs, especially the drugs that are now legal (booze, tobacco, even coffee). While you read the drug literature now, it certainly seems that the world of pot, psychedelics, and hard drugs is another neighbourhood in Guyville. This book helps correct the imbalance by reprinting writings about drugs written by women. "*Shaman Woman, Mainline Lady* demonstrates that for a long time women have consciously sought the experience of getting high, and that they experimented courageously, lived dangerously, and wrote about it eloquently."

The book is divided into rough time periods. In the first section, the selections look at women from mythology and ancient history. Pythia, the Oracle at Delphi, was basically a shaman who answered questions of importance to the Greeks by going into a trance. It has been suggested that she chewed laurel leaves containing small amounts of cyanide. The fumes that she was said to inhale during her sessions may have been from burning bay leaves, henbane, or cannabis. Cleopatra is generally considered a "drug adept" and probably took mandrake root as a sedative. Some people have conjectured that the "apple" from the Garden of Eden might be symbolic of a psychedelic herb that Eve and Adam munched on, which made them "as gods".

The next section contains writings from women of the Victorian era. Elizabeth Barrett Browning — one of the greatest poets of all time — was an opiate addict from the age of fifteen. To help her frail constitution, she took morphine and laudanum (opium in an alcohol tincture) and was using an extremely high daily dose of the latter when she and Robert Browning met and fell in love. Elizabeth's poem, "A True Dream", is reproduced in the book. One verse reads: "I saw the drops of torture fall;/I heard the shriekings rise,/While the serpents writhed in agony/Beneath my dreaming eyes."

Even Queen Victoria herself got a little "hootered up", so to speak. During the birth of her fifth child, she was given chloroform. She wrote in her private journal, "Dr. Snow gave that blessed chloroform and the effect was soothing, quieting and delightful beyond measure."

Sisters are doing it for themselves.
Shaman Woman, Mainline Lady.

"Expatriates & Vagabonds" looks at women and drugs from the first half of the twentieth century. Mina Loy was one of the greatest poets of the Imagist movement. Her poem "Lunar Baedeker" "is one of the most perfect poems of drug-heightened perception ever written." The drug in this case is cocaine: "Cyclones/of ecstatic dust/and ashes whirl/crusaders/from hallucinatory citadels/of shattered glass/into evacuate craters".

"Mainline Ladies" focuses on women who use heroin; most of the writings are from the middle of the century. Legendary blues singer Billie Holliday was a user. She was constantly being tailed, harassed, set up, and arrested by narcs. For the last fifteen years of her life, Holliday went to private clinics in order to kick the habit, and some of those clinics actually tipped off the cops. In the excerpt from her autobiography, *Lady Sings the Blues*, she tells about getting busted after a show in 1947. She pulled up to her hotel in her chauffeur-driven car, and she knew her hunch that she was going to get "pinched" was right when she saw the lobby full of cops. Even though she had never driven before, she ordered the chauffeur to get out, and she jumped in the driver's seat as a fed noticed her. "As the Treasury agent came towards us, I stepped on the gas. He hollered 'Halt!' and tried to stop the car by standing in the road. But I kept driving right on and he moved. I pulled away through a rain of bullets."

The women in "Psychedelic Pioneers" explored inner space. Sometime in 1954 or 1955, famed experimental novelist, erotica writer, and libertine Anaïs Nin took a dose of LSD under the supervision of a psychiatrist. Her account of the experience is "one of the most superbly described trips in psychedelics literature." "The walls became fountains, the fountains became arches, the domes skies, the sky a flowering carpet, and all dissolved into pure space. I looked at a slender line curving over into space which disappeared into infinity. I saw a million zeros on this line, curving, shrinking in the distance…"

In the self-explanatory section "Beats and Hippies", there's a selection from underground comix artist Sharon Rudahl's *Acid Temple Ball*. In this psychedelic erotica novel, the "heroine makes love under the influence of eight or so different drugs or drug combinations." While tripping on LSD, the protagonist writes: "I am the earth from which he flowers, he is the river rushing into me, every muscle confirmed and created to this dance. Time is dead; we are the sacred image."

The final section collects writings from the 1970s. Marcia Moore wrote popular books on yoga and astrology. "But like most traditionally educated occultists, she viewed psychedelics as an inferior form of enlightenment. Ketamine changed her view." In *Journeys Into the Bright World*, she writes of her experiences with the anaesthetic: "This inner realm, full of sound, colour, and sensation was itself entirely formless. Here there could be no distinction between subject and object, this and that, I and thou. Only the vast nameless faceless process remained, churning on and on and on."

Other selections of non-fiction and fiction come from Charlotte Brontë, Louisa May Alcott, Edith Wharton, Boxcar Bertha, Laura Huxley, Margaret Mead, Susan Sontag, and dozens of others. The book is profusely illustrated with photographs, drawn portraits, etchings, comix, drug-induced art, and more. Truly a welcome addition to the literature.

Flashback Books; $15
1982; oversized softcover; 285 pp
heavily illus; 0-688-01385-6

TOTAL SYNTHESIS
by Strike

Total Synthesis presents complete, demystified, illustrated instructions for several ways to make ecstasy, MDA, amphetamine, and methamphetamine. Not only that, but it does so with such a fun writing style and sassy, mischievous sense of humour, that it's a pleasure to read simply for the sake of reading.

Things kick off with clear instructions for buying or making everything you'll need to start your own underground drug lab, including funnels, vacuums, fume hoods, and safrole, the base chemical for ecstasy that can be found in sassafras oil and other natural, unregulated substances. You'll also find a novice chapter explaining some very basic chemistry procedures.

The section "Strike's Top 10" is the heart of the book. In it, your intrepid author reveals recipes that require "the least amount of knowledge, effort, equipment, money, suspicion and danger… The following top 10 can all be performed on a counter top and are very hard to fuck up. The recipes use the least watched chemicals and offer the finest yields when all things are considered".

The next section serves up a few more recipes, which Strike judged to be "too restrictive or chancy" to make the top 10. "Build From Scratch" is a groundbreaking section that reveals numerous ways to make the intermediary chemicals for X and meth using freely available chemicals. This information is included just in case the government decides to outlaw or severely restrict sassafras oil and other natural sources of safrole. Final chapters discuss crystallisation, making various chemicals, and the legal implications of following this book's instructions.

Panda Ink; $30
1997; softcover; 145 pp
heavily illus; 0-9658291-0-3

WHITE RABBIT
A Psychedelic Reader
edited by John Miller & Randall Koral

White Rabbit is a first-rate collection of essays and fiction about drug experiences. Even though the subtitle includes the word "psychedelic", these 38 pieces cover a wide range of substances — heroin, opium, cocaine, absinthe, soma, LSD, DMT, hashish, yagé, morphine, ecstasy, and others. The experiences cover the range from beautiful highs and heightened states of consciousness to horribly bad trips and the hell of addiction.

One of the more unexpected testimonies comes from Jim Hogshire in "The Electric Cough Syrup Acid Test". After drinking eight ounces of a cough syrup containing dextromethorphan (DXM), he discovered that his reptilian brain had taken over. He drove to Kinko's copy shop around four in the morning and sat there trying to read a newspaper. "I found being a reptile kind of pleasant. I was content to sit there and monitor my surroundings. I was alert but not anxious. Every now and then I would do a true 'reality check' to make sure I wasn't masturbating or strangling someone, because of my vague awareness that more was expected of me than just being a reptile."

In "When the Going Gets Weird, the Weird Turn Pro", from *Fear and Loathing in Las Vegas*, gonzo journalist Hunter S. Thompson describes one of the most extreme instances of driving under the influence ever attempted. Hurtling towards Las Vegas at 90 to 100 miles per hour, Thompson and his attorney ingest over ten types of drugs while they're driving. "The trunk of the car looked like a mobile police narcotics lab. We had two bags of grass, seventy-five pellets of mescaline, five sheets of high-powered blotter acid, a salt shaker half full of cocaine, and a whole galaxy of multi-coloured uppers, downers, screamers, laughers… and also a quart of tequila, a quart of rum, a case of Budweiser, a pint of raw ether, and two dozen amyls."

Other selections (most of which are excerpts of larger works) include "In Search of Yagé" by William S. Burroughs, "The Man With the Golden Arm" by Nelson Algren, "Opium" by Florence Nightingale, "The Three Stigmata of Palmer Eldritch" by Philip K. Dick, "The Doors of Perception" by Aldous Huxley, "Kathmandu Interlude" by Terence McKenna, "Down the Rabbit-Hole" by Lewis Carroll, "Comedy of Thirst" by Arthur Rimbaud, "Coca" by Sigmund Freud, and many other vital pharmacological documents. This one is a must.

Chronicle Books; $13.95
1995; softcover; 288 pp
0-8118-0666-9

SEX

You are required to be either 18 or 21 to order almost every periodical or catalogue in this chapter. Not every book publisher requires this (books generally have more First Amendment protection than other media), though a lot of them, maybe even the majority, do need an age statement. To be on the safe side, always send a <u>signed</u> age statement when ordering anything from this chapter. Take note: Some titles under discussion may be hazardous to your liberty depending upon where you live.

PANSEXUALITY

Cover of one of *Black Sheet*'s most controversial issues.

ALTERNATE SOURCES

Alternate Sources is a gargantuan collection of contact information for over *10,000* alternative sexuality resources in over 40 countries. Everything you could ask for is listed: bars, archives, help lines, artists, mail order businesses (clothing, sex toys, publications, etc.), counsellors, BBSs, publishers, film festivals, health services, manufacturers, organisations, piercers, magazines, newspapers, bookstores, television production companies, Internet mailing lists, IRC channels, and even more. Just about every orientation, gender, practice, or kink you could name is covered. The body of the book is set up by geographical location. Two indexes — one by name and the other by category — will help you sort things out.

This book's massive scope comes at a price, however. Each entry is absolutely barebones. You get a basic category, contact info, and some symbols that indicate such things as general orientation or gender, non-profit or for-profit, wheelchair accessible, payment types, etc. Business hours are often listed for help lines and businesses with a physical location open to the public. Maybe a third of the entries include very short blurbs giving additional info.

Nonetheless, *Alternate Sources* is an amazing achievement. Get it for its breadth, and get one of the other guides in this section for depth. That way, you'll be covered.

Alternate Sources; $34Can, $24.95US, £21.99
1996; softcover; 454 pp
1-895857-09-0

THE BLACK BOOK

by Bill Brent & Black Books

The Black Book is just what you've been wanting and needing — a thick guide to every manner of sexual organisation, publication, catalogue, resort, service, etc. Approximately 800 listings give names, addresses, phone numbers, email ad-

dresses, Web URLs, methods of payment, and/or capsule descriptions that relate to all kinds of desires: gay, lesbian, bi, SM, fetish, body modification, transgender, and occasionally hetero. Need holistic gay/lesbian counselling? A club devoted to boots and the men who wear them? The House of Whacks? The International Association of Gay and Lesbian Martial Artists? A penis replicating service? A large selection of fetish clothing, piercing supplies, books, zines, or videos? They're all here, and more.

Listees do not pay to be included in *The Black Book*. They only have to complete a form, which ensures a large amount of listings. *The Book* also contains some ads and three indexes (topic, geographic, and advertiser). This is a truly indispensable resource.

Black Books; $20 ppd, Can/Mex: $24 ppd, Elsewhere: $28 ppd
1998; softcover; 256 pp
illus; 0-9637401-5-6

BLACK SHEETS

Put out by *The Black Book* impresario Bill Brent, the zine *Black Sheets* offers a "kinky, queer, intelligent, irreverent" look at sex. Each issue is chock-full of articles, interviews, photos, cartoonz, reviews, and other polysexual delights.

Issue 6 has pictures from the Folsom Fair and Dore Alley gay street fairs, an interview with Pat Califia, photos and an essay on a San Francisco mudfest, a listing of groups into messy fun, articles on self-torture, the short story "My Own Private Orgasm" by Lamia Dewlap, editor Bill Brent describing his recent first acid trip (complete with a picture), among other fun stuff.

Carol Queen road tests the female condom, Reality, and gives her reactions: "Midway through the fuck I became convinced that if I didn't reach down and hang on to the outer ring, the traction would pull the whole shebang into my cunt and my friendly co-researcher would be pounding his cock into an unprotected cunt (mine) with a twist of plastic down in its furthest reaches. In short, I found it a little hard to relax." Jim Sweet offers the male road test of Reality, which seemed to be more positive: "It was a very different experience inserting my naked penis into a plastic-lined vagina, and it felt wonderful! This was the first time in ages that my cock had been inserted, uncovered, into a pussy (or anywhere else, for that matter)."

Issue 8, playfully known as the "dead cow issue", is themed around leathersex/fetish/SM. Some of the best writing this issue includes "Guernica", a bi tale of a dystopia where SM is illegal (hmmm... present-day Britain, perhaps?); "Black Latex Clambake", a smothering story about a consensual torture scene; the good-for-a-laugh "Surrounded", which recounts having sex in the middle of a herd of steer; and the short poem "The Leatherdyke Meets the Animal Liberationist": "I know how it feels to be trussed,/Hung in the air like a piece of meat,/Expectant." The art quotient is particularly high, with great stylised SM shots from Todd Friedman, a set of photos from the Sexart show (one each from Eric Kroll, Craig Morey, Michael Rosen, Laura Johnston, et al), manly illustrations by Ted Erler and Nicholas Jordan, and even a fascinating clip art collage of all the kitchen implements that can be used for spanking.

Next up is "Whore Moan: The $ex Work I$$ue", crammed full of great writing. The line between fiction and non-fiction is especially thin in this issue, and I'm often not certain which is which. Two of the pieces deal with women having erotic massages with other women. A few detail the way the narrators got involved in the sex biz, whether as a male sex companion for university professors, a female nude dancer, or a sperm donor. Susannah Indigo turns in a fine story, "Do What You Love", about a woman who finds success fulfilling the fantasies of her rich Daddies, both male and female. The hapless sex worker in M. Christian's story can't win for losing when it comes to writing smut, starring in a porn movie, or posing for pictures. Thea Hillman debates whether she's a sex worker, since she is basically a writer of erotica; guest editor Steve Omlid reports on being a customer of lap dances in the Big Apple; and Neon Weiss reminisces about her hot encounter with a high-priced call girl. There's even more, but let me just say that you get more than your money's worth.

Issue 10 turned out to be the most controversial yet, dealing as it does with "Bestiality and Glamour!". Many of the "sex radicals" who read Black Sheets were pissed with Bill for daring to examine this highly unconventional orientation. It's a classic case of, "My sexuality is unfairly maligned and tragically misunderstood, but your sexuality really is sick and disgusting."

The issue is guest edited by Bill's snooty but adorable cat Judy, who chose to include Lori Selke's worshipful essay on that femme dominant Miss Piggy (complete with a drawing of the divine swine taking a riding crop to a certain frog's green ass!), a story about amusement park workers dressed in animal costumes getting it on (it contains many priceless lines, such as, "Lou the Kangaroo was sucking Billy Bunny's dick."), Carol Queen's thoughtful discussion of animal consent, an interview with a practising zoophile, the poem "Her Pussy", Heather Bradshaw's funny but nonetheless stomach-churning story about a woman and a cockroach, and a fascinating article about Koko, the first gorilla to be taught sign language, who developed crushes on her male trainers. Some of the wild art includes Benetton's ad of two horses bonking, Gordon Spurlock's anthropomorphic animal/men, and a centre spread of Judy herself. This issue was handled perfectly, with a lot of open-mindedness and just the right mix of humour, seriousness, explicitness, thoughtfulness, and bad taste. It's destined to become a classic in the annals of sexzines.

I misplaced (my grandmother told me never to say "lost") my copy of issue 11, damn it, but trust me — it was another winner. With the theme of "Bad Sex", it risked being labelled as sex-negative by humourless types because it admitted that things don't always happen the way they do in books and movies, with endlessly hard cocks, endlessly wet pussies, and endlessly horny people getting it on in perfect conditions.

Finally, the most recent issue as of this writing is "Sex Pioneers", which mainly deals with the swinging 1970s in San Francisco. Black Sheets subscriber Derek talks about busting loose in SF in the early 1970s, and Black Sheets editor Bill talks about doing the same thing in the late 1970s. Ian Ayres remembers the late poet fondly in the poem "Allen Ginsberg Gave Great Head". In two separate pieces, people talk about what it was like at the Catacombs (a fisting club) and the Hothouse (a gay pleasure palace), two legendary establishments which are no longer around. The centrepiece of the issue, though, is Bill's "Queer American Pie", a massive history of gay life in 'Frisco from just after WWII to the early 1980s, fleshed out with long quotes from people who were there and peppered with such images as an ad for the Cauldron piss club and a matchbook for South of the Slot, "a raunchy S/M bathhouse".

Black Sheets is one of precious few regularly appearing sexzines that offers explicit writing and art covering a wide range of orientations, genders, practices, and kinks. The cutting edge regularly draws blood within its pages. Highly recommended.

Black Books/PO Box 31155/San Francisco CA 94131
Voice: 415-431-0171
Fax: 415-431-0172
Email: blackb@queernet.org
WWW: www.blackbooks.com
Single issue: US/Can/Mex: $6. Elsewhere: $10
One year sub (4 issues): $20. Can/Mex: $24. Elsewhere: $36
Payment: cash, ck, mo, Visa, MC, Amex, Disc

DIABOLICAL CLITS

"If it's sexy, it's sacred," proclaims the pink cover of Diabolical Clits, a (so far) one-shot zine of pansexual erotica, edited by writer, artist, and performer Sandra Golvin. Experimental, daring, and very hot, these 23 stories and poems sustain an amazingly high quality. Some of my faves include "Kneeling", "Fantasia for Seventeen Instruments", "Robert", "Dybbuk", and "Look into My Eyes as You Fill Me (my lover doesn't come in my mouth anymore)". Highly recommended.

Diabolical Clits/ c/o S. Golvin/2219 Strongs Drive/Venice, CA 90291

Single issue: $6. Non-US: $7

Payment: cash, ck or mo made out to S. Golvin

EXHIBITIONISM FOR THE SHY
Show Off, Dress Up, and Talk Hot
by Carol Queen

Sex-positive activist and educator Carol Queen used to be shy, but she overcame it and found her own full, rich sexuality to explore. Now, she's going to help you. This isn't to say her book will turn you into a slut (unless, of course, that happens to be the direction you want to go). It will help you become more sexually self-confident and aware, which will benefit not only your partner (or partners) but also yourself. *Exhibitionism for the Shy* is about overcoming sexual shyness and projecting your sexuality in a confident, erotic, and arousing way. "It's about finding your inner turn-ons and expressing them." And it can be used by anyone — gay, lesbian, straight, bi, alone, partnered, etc.

Queen writes, "It is a pernicious myth that sex comes naturally." In our uptight, erotophobic society, we grow up in a sex-negative atmosphere. Information about sex is either withheld from us or comes in bits and pieces, sometimes incorrect. Most of the natural instincts we have towards sex are choked off at an early age. We're not allowed to get in touch with our sexual selves, so when it comes time to engage in sex, we may not know how to do it perfectly. "No wonder we can benefit from sex manuals, watching explicit movies, and listening to friends."

Exhibitionism, as Queen uses the term, isn't about wearing a trenchcoat and flashing people in the street. Her definition of the term is, "Deliberately presenting yourself in an erotic way for your own enhanced sexual arousal." In other words, you become an exhibitionist for you. "Our enjoyment and arousal in exhibitionism make it erotically powerful for us, as opposed to something we engage in simply to please or attract another." The key here, as always, is to tap into what turns you on, what makes you feel sexy, what gives you pleasure. Once you do this, you'll automatically become a sexier, more confident person capable of giving and receiving vast amounts of pleasure.

The other key to achieving your erotic potential is "talking dirty". This usually, but not always, involves four-letter words. What it always involves, though, is turning yourself on and opening communication between partners. You become more emotionally involved when you talk dirty. You learn to tell your partner exactly what feels good, what gets you off. You share your sexual fantasies and get to act them out.

Queen presents instructions for accomplishing all of this and more. She discusses finding sexy words that appeal to you, talking sexy on the phone, dressing up, using shyness to your advantage, awakening your sexual personas, un-

dressing for success, finding partners, swinging and group sex and working in peep shows (assuredly not for everybody, but if you're really adventurous…), talking with and listening to your partner, and much more. Queen gently walks you through all the steps, so don't worry, even if you're an absolute beginner.

The final parts of the book contain resource directory, a list of "dirty" words and phrases, over 50 erotic role-playing scenarios, and other helpful items. Oh, yeah — this book isn't only for the shy. The sexually brazen may learn a thing or two as well.

Down There Press; $12.50

1995; softcover; 241 pp

0-940208-16-4

PERCEPTIONS
The Journal of Imaginative Sensuality

This digest-size magazine begs for comparison to another omnisexual publication, *Libido* [*Outposts* p 85]. They both are the same size, have similar subtitles, have non-English quotations at the top of the masthead, and run fiction, poetry, essays, photos, and illustrations. Both are playful and fun and welcome all different orientations. The big difference, though, is that *Perceptions* doesn't just focus on sex. Notice the subtitle contains the word *sensuality*, not *sexuality*. Some of the magazine's writing, mainly its non-fiction, revels in non-erotic stimulation of the senses, a novel approach. And the writing that does concentrate on sex contains descriptions that involve the senses completely.

In the poem "Pathos", Joan Tammel writes: "So gently/ Your fingers stroke the strings of my heart./It sings. Deep, swiftly flowing, the moods of/Rachmaninoff ache inside me. Mozart, impulsively playful,/Strewed notes, rose petals from his darting fingers." Christy Rich employs some unique imagery in "Sex Was": "You read my body like sacred braille/ Silver tell-tale trail of your tongue/My moans a map for you to follow".

"Tight Spots #2: Nature Plays" by Robin St. Laurents is the first story I've read of sex between a human and a plant. During a camp-out with her female lover, a woman gets unbearably horny. While walking in a meadow, she comes across a plant that looks like a large cock. "Nectar began to flow freely as I raised my lips over the pointed, swollen tip, offering a better view. Dew-like drops anointed the pink crown as I brushed it with my nectar-dripping tunnel and my sighs rose into the air, sweet and raw, as if to tell the forest: See, you're not the only one who understands these things."

Among the non-fiction offerings, we have Bill Roberts' "Discoveries", which gives instruction for making decadent fudge. In "Touch", Manya Smith revels in tactile sensations: "I'm a fabric junky… I eat silk pie for smoothness. I need crunch in my casseroles… When I make love, it's textures against my tongue that make me wet, the soft flesh of earlobe, the downy nape of a neck, small hard nipples and wrinkled aureoles, wet chewy labia or hard spongy cock."

The curving illustrations of Nybor — featuring Satyrs and two women having sex — are quite striking. The photographs (almost all of which feature women) are competent but in general not very powerful. Part of the problem is probably that the photos look scanned... they have that funky pattern that desktop scanners can leave behind, and the tones are almost posterised instead of being rich and smooth. Other than this drawback, *Perceptions* makes a satisfying, sense-pleasing read. [All of the above selections are from Sample Issue 2.]

Perceptions/2111 Lido Circle/Stockton CA 95207-6014

Single issue: $5. Can/Mex: $6. Overseas: $9

Four issue sub (one year): $14. Can/Mex: $17. Overseas: $27

POLYSEXUALITY (SEMIOTEXT(E) 10)

edited by François Peraldi

This volume of the magabook *Semiotext(e)* has become an elusive classic since it was published in 1981. Thankfully, the publisher has reprinted it, so I would suggest grabbing it before it's gone again. Edited by a French psychoanalyst and containing works mostly by Frenchmen, this collection of stories and essays benefits from the fact that the French often seem to be 100 years ahead of everybody else when it comes to exploring sexual territory. That's not to say the Americans in this volume — William Burroughs, Peter Lamborn Wilson, and John Preston among them — are slouches when it comes to busting taboos.

Polysexuality presents a dense, all-inclusive examination of everyone's favourite subject: s-e-x. In the section "Animal Sex" Catherine Duncan writes about a woman who explores the Australian outback and has a sexual encounter with a feral dog. On a different note, nature-documentary filmmaker Frédéric Rossif is interviewed about sex and love in the animal kingdom.

The pieces in the "Alimentary Sex" section explore the pleasures of eating bodies and bodily fluids — cannibalism, semen swallowing, and "Coprophagy and Urinology". The last essay is by famed sadomasochist Terence Sellers, who explains the masochists' love for their Masters' piss and shit. "The superior can take no pride in such slaves, unless he or she regards their products with the same glamorised eyes as the masochist. Thus does their waste become the lowly one's nourishment; their filth cleanses the slave; their foulness seems a rare perfume. In this poor way, as well, does the slave ingest, and so possess, his beloved superior."

The sections towards the end of the book are made up of essays that take a post-modern, deconstructionist look at sexuality, gender, and related matters. Pornoisseurs will undoubtedly regard this as the most boring section of the book, but it does have its interesting moments. "To Destroy Sexuality" is a wonderful rant about capitalism's oppression of the body and sexuality. "We can no longer stand by idly while we are robbed of our mouths, our anuses, our sexual members, our guts, our veins... just so they can turn them into parts for their ignominious machine which produces capital, exploitation and the family... We can no longer not 'come' or hold back our shit, our saliva, our energy according to their laws with their minor, tolerated infractions. We want to explode the frigid, inhibited, mortified body that capitalism wants so desperately to make out of our living body."

The other 43 works in *Polysexuality* concern masturba-

It came and went. But mainly it came.
Pucker Up.

tion, transgenderism, SM, child sex, necrophilia, and more. Although some of the stories take the form of extended, explicit action, the vast majority of them are written at a demanding, literary level and many only have one short sex scene or none at all. The photographs interspersed among the stories depict war, death and destruction. In other words, don't expect this challenging book to be stroke-a-thon.

Autonomedia; $12

1981 (1995); oversized softcover; 300 pp

illus; 1-57027-011-2

PUCKER UP

Edited and published by Tristan Taormino (does she not have the coolest name in the whole world?), with much assistance from Karen Green, *Pucker Up* is "the zine with a mouth that's not afraid to use it." The emphasis is on "the fringe, the perverse, the irreverent." Tristan's statement of purpose will warm the hearts of those of us who enjoy the unorthodox: "Forget the watered-down, safely non-offensive mainstream press so obsessed with obscenity laws they won't publish anything interesting; we've got what the other's wouldn't dare print. We're here to push the envelope, fuck with people's boundaries, assumptions, and expectations, celebrate the renegades and the outlaws." Based on the four issues that have come out, *Pucker Up* is putting its money where its mouth is (and that's a lot of different places!).

In the premier issue, the fiction demonstrates genderfuck at its finest, whipping notions of sexual identity and orientation into such a creamy froth that you don't know what's what. In "Raw Meat" the self-proclaimed "King of the Heterosexuals" meets a woman who says she's a dyke who fucks guys anyway. They do some SM with her as the bottom, but when she wants to switch roles, he draws the line. She ends up getting him drunk, tying him up, and nailing him with a strap-on. "It was less than rape, but not by much. I wriggled and squirmed, groaned and broke into a cold sweat, but nothing would stop her. The more I fought the more brutal she became." "Jer's Combo" is about a three-way between a butch dyke, a gay guy, and a het-girl, while in "The Check Up" the narrator has a queer encounter with his dentist. A woman hires a male prostitute in "Like I Paid Him to", and excerpts from two of Red Jordan Arobateau's hardcore lesbian novels celebrate the uses of two bodily fluids — urine and breast milk.

The non-fiction is no less as daring. In one of the most controversial pieces *Pucker Up* has run, Laura Antoniou violates "SM correctness" by demolishing the oft-repeated phrase, "safe, sane, and consensual". "I don't want to negotiate everything to death, I want to be surprised, or surprise someone. I want to be afraid — I want to cause genuine fear... Passion, that's what I'm into, passion and blood and honour, so powerful it pounds through my veins and blinds me, so terrible I can't look away. Danger, Dementia, and Denial." Also, Tristan interviews some body modifiers, and Molly Weatherfield trumpets "The Pleasures of SM Pornography".

No sexzine would be complete without art, and *Pucker Up* delivers the goods, including Richard Kern's sexy women and Laure Weber's pictures of a woman masturbating with a vibrator and a man getting a blowjob from a blow-up doll. "White OJ" is a deconstruction of Simpson's famous mugshot, making him look Caucasian and feminine. "Screaming Man" Badbob — who did the cover for *Outposts* — contributes a couple of button-pushing panels from his first book.

The second issue carries on the consistently high level of work. Such on-fire talents as Sandra Lee Golvin ("Faggot Rant", "Remembering Daddy"), Linda Smukler ("Trash", "Little Girl"), D. Travers Scott ("Execution, Texas: 1987", "Love Inventory"), and Gerry Gomez Pearlberg ("On Bleaching My Hair", "Dyke Haiku") each contribute two or more pieces. Scott's "Jaymie" is so shocking that I wonder if anyone else would have the gonads to publish it, even though the ending does soften the blow. M. Christian's "Tricking" is great mistaken-identity genderfuck, "Death Rock" by Thomas R. Roche is a cool necro story, and an intense SM scene takes place completely online in Alison Tyler's "Fear".

On the non-fiction side, Wickie Stamps laments the taming of *Drummer*'s sexual content, and Robin Podolsky presents an intensely personal essay, "Losing It". The recently departed Kathy Acker and the vampiric Danielle Willis are both interviewed. This issue sees the start of a new feature, "Crush", in which Tristan, Karen Green, and an occasional guest express their lust for a celebrity... in this case, David Duchovny of *The X-Files*. Featured artists this time around include Kerry Allen and Sol Ray Sender.

The next issue contains three pieces from Transexual Menace cofounder Riki Anne Wilchins and two from Kitty Tsui. Gerry Gomez Pearlberg delivers more cracking good poetry, including "Spectrum":

We've eroticised the San
Genaro Ferris wheel, Temple
and the Fez. We've eroticised
fantasy play, sexy dreams and denim,
purple grapes and the aquarium,
taxi rides and bridges and
the Lower East Side,
the dark pause between street
lamps that ignite a bruising kiss.

"Louie Louie" by Mario Grillo is dark but humorous, Bree Coven brazenly tackles age play in "Daddy", and married couple Susan Sarandon and Tim Robbins are the targets of the "Crush". Tristan interviews Kembra Pfahler, lead singer of The Voluptuous Horror of Karen Black, while Karen Green and Pat Califia raise some eyebrows in their discussion, which is another of the most contentious pieces to run in *PU*. The issue reaches its climax with a reprinting of the entire first chapter of *Nearly Roadkill: An Infobahn Erotic Adventure* [reviewed below]. Visual treats this time include the butchy photography of Diana Morrow and lots of pictures of Kembra Pfahler.

Issue 4 is focused primarily on gender, with the centrepiece being a written and photographic guide to nine "gender icons" of New York, including poet Lovechild, drag king club creator Mo B. Dick, and Glennda Orgasm, who, among other things, made the documentary *Glennda and Camille Do Downtown* [reviewed below]. Among the writings are Kate Bornstein's "The Gyrl with No Name", which takes the form of a transcript of a police interview, "Passage" by Sandra Lee Golvin, "I Was Astride a Young Man" by Riki Anne Wilchins, "Cock" by Linda Smukler, and "The Proud & Masculine Porn Star" by Alvin Alfred Orloff. "Virus Logic," from D. Travers Scott, is one of those stories that stays with me, and I've found myself mentally replaying some of the sentences (especially the last two), kind of like a song I can't get out of my head.

Female-to-male transsexual photographer Loren Cameron and Chloe Dzubilo of the all-woman punk band the Transisters are interviewed, and Dennis Rodman gets "Crush"-ed. Featured artists Cameron and Michelle Serchuck provide most of the images.

There's actually more in each issue than I've mentioned here. I've left out the reviews of books, CDs, Websites, and sex toys, assorted artwork, *Hothead Paisan* comix, at least a dozen writings, and the profile at the end of each issue, not to mention the wild design schemes. Every *Pucker Up* is equivalent to a kickass anthology of material that proves we are in a Golden Age of sexual writing and erotic art. Regrettably, *Pucker Up* is on indefinite hiatus. Originally conceived to fill the gap left by the demise of *Frighten the Horses*, *Brat Attack*, the original *Taste of Latex*, and other stellar sexzines, *Pucker Up* might now leave a void of its own. It may come out of its coma yet, but even if it doesn't, it's still given us four wild fucks.

All the issues are still in print. I beseech you to buy every one of them.

Tristan Taormino, Pucker Up/PO Box 4108 Grand Central

Station/New York NY 10163
Email: puckerup@earthlink.net
Back issues: $5 each. Canada: $6 each. Elsewhere: $9 each
Payment: cash, ck made out to Tristan Taormino

Loren and Kayt come to Grips.
Stalemate, *Body Alchemy*.

GENDER

BODY ALCHEMY
Transsexual Portraits
by Loren Cameron

Loren Cameron is a former tomboy who started identifying as lesbian in high school and, around ten years later, began the process of physically becoming a man. Today, Cameron is a handsome, bearded, buffed post-operative transsexual man.

He started taking photographs of himself during his transformation in order to record the process for himself, family, and friends. With only a basic photography class for training, he took pictures with a no-frills camera, and within one year he had his own exhibition. More shows and publication in transgender, gay, lesbian, bi, photographic, and news publications soon followed. Cameron had touched a nerve by using his natural photographic skills to become the first transsexual to create a serious body of work documenting his life and the lives of other transmen. *Body Alchemy* collects 42 of these black and white images from 1995 and 1996.

Among the most powerful photos are the self portraits which open the book. Cameron reveals various aspects of himself in these shots (as well as the always honest commentary that accompanies them). In *Carney*, he reclines in a classic nude pose wearing only a fool's cap, indicating his role as jester in the uptight Court of Gender. The very next image, *De Profundis*, shows Cameron at his lowest point, tears running down his face and a gun to his head. In *Heroes*, he is at his proudest — head held high and chest out as he carries a flag that I think represents trans pride. *Testosterone* — Cameron angrily smashing a bottle on a chain-link fence — reflects the rage and violence that male hormone treatments often trigger, and *The Suit* shows him at his most suave, clutching a bouquet of flowers and decked out in a sharply tailored double-breasted suit. In the following three photos, which make up the chapter "God's Will", Cameron strikes three stylised poses while in the buff — looking at a scalpel, curling a dumbbell, and injecting testosterone into his hip.

The book closes with photos of Cameron and his partner Kayt, a striking biological woman who apparently identifies as a female-to-male butch lesbian who is involved with a transsexual man (talk about blurred boundaries!). They are shown holding each other nude on a fur carpet, crossing

swords and staring challengingly into each others' eyes, sitting in the back of a pickup truck, tucked under the covers watching the tube and eating popcorn, and — in the most powerful shot — arm wrestling while once again locking gazes.

The rest of the book is mostly comprised of Cameron's insightful portraits of other former women who are now men, including a bartender at a gay bar, a police sergeant, a single father of two, a skilled blue-collar worker, and a law professor. The chapter "Emergence" shows before and after photos of five men, including Cameron. "Our Bodies" breaks with the rest of work by being close-up documentary shots of the reworked genitalia and chest areas of several transmen.

Powerful from an artistic standpoint; revolutionary from a gender/sexual standpoint. Highly recommended.

Cleis Press; $24.95
1996; oversized softcover; 110 pp
heavily illus; 1-57344-062-0

BUTCH/FEMME
edited by MG Soares

In the text part of this book, MG Soares offers an overview of butch/femme identity, Judy Grahn writes about being butch, and Nisa Donnelly explores being a femme. Of the 46 black and white photos, a few are from the Lesbian Herstory Archives' collection of images from the 1920s-1950s, and the rest are from five lesbian photographers, including Joyce Culver and Eva Weiss.

Crown Publishers; $12
1995; small hardcover; 64 pp
heavily illus; 0-517-70222-3

GENDER OUTLAW
On Men, Women, and the Rest of Us
by Kate Bornstein

Kate Bornstein went from being a heterosexual man to being "a transsexual lesbian whose female lover is becoming a man..." Bornstein is now a playwright, author, and performance artist. Her book is a combination of autobiography, manifesto, and social critique.

Bornstein abhors the fact that society rigidly defines male and female. "The trouble is, we're living in a world that insists we be one or the other — a world that doesn't bother to tell us exactly what one or the other is." Society also has black-and-white views of orientation. "In my case, however, it's not so clear. I identify as neither male nor female, and now that my lover is going through his gender change, it turns out I'm neither straight nor gay."

Nicely but firmly, without a trace of anger, Bornstein examines the concepts of gender identity and why she thinks the rules need to be eradicated. She speaks of desire, revulsion, biological destiny, the ambiguity and fluidity of gender. Most people in society are addicted to gender, or more specifically, their gender roles. Addiction theory says that we get addicted in order to avoid something or make up for something that's lacking. We get addicted to being 100% woman or 100% man to avoid expressing ourselves fully. To avoid dealing with our own ambiguity and scary wants and needs.

In Chapter 3, Bornstein talks about what's on everybody's mind by this point. She gives a nuts 'n' clits description of her operation. "They lay the penis out, and make an incision down the length of it, pull the skin open, scrape out the spongy stuff, being very careful not to disturb the blood vessels and nerves… So then they take the tip of the penis and start pushing it in. Kind of like turning a sock inside out." Does she menstruate? Although Bornstein doesn't cramp or bleed, she does bloat, have mood swings, and goes through "seven days a month of raging PMS". Does she have orgasms? Yes, either by stimulation of the clitoris or the vaginal walls.

In another chapter she discusses her work with queer theatre. *Gender Outlaw* contains the full text of her play, *Hidden: A Gender*. In the final analysis, Bornstein sees her mission as the dismantling of gender. "I think it's time for us to use our status as Third [gender] to bring some harmony into the world. Like other border outlaws, transgendered people are here to open some doorway that's been closed off for a long time. We're gatekeepers, nothing more."

Vintage; $13
1994; softcover; 253 pp
illus; 0-679-75701-5

MISS VERA'S FINISHING SCHOOL FOR BOYS WHO WANT TO BE GIRLS

by Veronica Vera

In 1992 artist and sex activist Veronica Vera did an amazing thing. She created Miss Vera's Finishing School for Boys Who Want to Be Girls in New York City, and in doing so, she helped bring crossdressing aboveground. With playfulness and a 100% positive attitude, she took the shame out of what is still regarded by society-at-large as a "perversion". From the very start, the School was a success. Miss Vera writes that no sooner had she started it than "my pink Princess phone began to ring incessantly". She continues: "Not only had I put my well-manicured finger on the pulse of every cross-dresser's dream but I had tapped into the rich motherlode of the male psyche." Huge numbers of men, it seems, are just dying to liberate the woman trapped inside. As Miss Vera says, "For every woman who burned her bra,

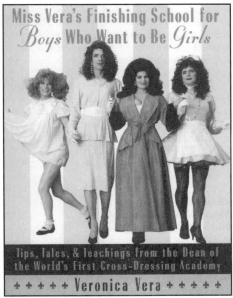

"For every woman who burned her bra, there is a man ready to wear one." *Miss Vera's Finishing School.*

there is a man ready to wear one."

After discussing her life, including the founding of the School, Miss Vera gives her thoughts on the psychology of gender and the needs that crossdressing fulfils (primarily, satisfying men's "Venus envy"), and she introduces us to some of her most outstanding students, including Jack, a pinstriped executive whose alternate persona is Sally Sissyribbons.

The rest of the book is devoted to giving specific advice and helpful hints regarding every aspect of releasing your "femmeself". Miss Vera discusses creating a complete personal herstory for your alterego, doing your hair (hair care, wigs), achieving a girlish figure (legs, hips, breasts, buns, corset, and getting rid of the bulge), applying make up ("Subtle is not in our cosmetic vocabulary"), developing a fashion sense (including a whole chapter on how to manoeuvre in high heels), performing household chores (for the homemakers and sissy maids in the class), speaking in a feminine manner (forget squeaky falsetto and go with soft, sensual, and husky), etiquette (including ladies room techniques), being a woman in public (passing, dealing with intolerance), and coming out to family and friends. An important chapter deals with the various aspects of sexuality that intersect with crossdressing, from getting in touch with female sexual energy, to identifying completely as a heterosexual woman, to having sex with your wife while in drag.

Miss Vera has a witty, assured writing style. Although she probably isn't going to give away all her trade secrets in this volume, she provides lots of concrete, pragmatic details. Men generally have larger joints than women, so it's a good idea to choose dresses that come down to at least the knee. A simple, inexpensive way to achieve realistic breasts is to stuff birdseed into the cut-off ends of stockings.

This book has been designed with care. It's filled with photos showing students in all stages of femaleness and maleness and every point in between. The wavy margins may take getting used to, but they add to the curvaceousness of the layout.

If you're interested in learning more about Miss Vera's Finishing School for Boys Who Want to Be Girls, you can check out their Website at www.missvera.com or call 212-242-6449 for a brochure and enrolment application.

Mainstreet Books (Bantam Doubleday Dell Publishing Group); $14.95
1997; softcover; 200 pp
heavily illus; 0-385-48456-9

READ MY LIPS
Sexual Subversion and the
End of Gender
by Riki Anne Wilchins

With righteous anger, a keen sense of humour, solid theoretical foundations, and an inclusive stance that's radical even among sexual/gender minorities, activist and organiser Riki Anne Wilchins bursts forth with an important, urgent addition to the burgeoning number of books on gender.

Many of Wilchins' best qualities and points can be found in the short second chapter "17 Things You DON'T Say to A Transexual". "**Don't #12. 'I hear you're a transsexual. When did you have surgery?'** Yes, and I hear you're a homosexual: when did you first suck cock? Ohhhh — it's not about sex." "**Don't #16. 'You look just like a REAL woman.'** How splendid, especially when you recall I'm composed almost entirely of compressed soy by-products. And you look just like a REAL transexual. Oh, I'm sorry, I didn't realise that was an insult."

The rest of the book is a similar blend of Wilchins' personal experiences and fiery opinions. She even manages to inject some post modern and Marxist ideas *without sounding like a post-modernist or a Marxist*. In other words, she's comprehensible!

Wilchins writes of numerous times she has been reproached and reviled, whether it was in childhood when her father informed her that boys don't use the word *divine*, or in adulthood when a group of SM lesbians pointed and laughed at her because she had a sex-change operation. She also relates other, more extreme examples of transphobia, including the rape and murder of Brandon Teena and an incident in which a emergency medical worker stopped trying to save a hit-and-run victim when he found that the apparent woman had a penis.

Wilchins' prescription is radical. In the most important and challenging part of the book — pages 67 through 71 — she admits that she is not so much interested in forcing the powers-that-be to grudgingly grant rights to transgendered people as she is in obliterating the concepts of gender and orientation. She writes that, "… I am at pains to point out, wherever I speak, that I am not a transexual, nor am I interested in a transgender rights movement, one which, unable to interrogate the fact of its own existence, will merely end

up cementing the idea of binary sex which I am presumed to somehow transgress or merely traverse… While I recognise how important it is to produce histories and sociologies of transpeople, I am wary of anything that might cement the category more firmly in place. I'd also like to investigate the means by which categories like transgender are produced, maintained, and inflicted on people like me. It's not so much that there have always been transgendered people; it's that there have always been cultures which imposed regimes of gender."

She points to the gay liberation movement as an example of changing tactics for the worse. "It is arguably the case that when the message of gay liberation changed from All People Are Queer to Gay Is as Good as Straight, the movement lost its revolutionary potential, its moral and redemptive centre. It ceded to the very oppressive system it formed to contest the terms of its struggle and allowed the system to dictate the terms of its resistance." Wilchins elaborates on many of these points in a later chapter, "Why Identity Politics Really, Really Sucks", but I feel these four pages make the case extremely convincingly on their own.

Other parts of the book address intersexuals, eroticism, Transexual Menace, the mainstream lesbian movement, "genderqueer kids", the Gay Games, how do you "feel like" a woman (or a man)?, and more topics. Wilchins also includes numerous pictures from protests and demonstrations, a chronology of the Transexual Menace and GenderPAC organisations, and a humorous, enlightening glossary.

Read My Lips is most highly recommended.

Firebrand Books; $16.95
1997; softcover; 231 pp
illus; 1-56341-090-7

SEX CHANGES
The Politics of Transgenderism
by Pat Califia

In *Sex Changes*, radical sex writer, practitioner, and activist Pat Califia applies her considerable talents to the subject of contemporary transgenderism, particularly transsexuality, in which people undergo medical changes (such as hormone treatments and surgery) to physically become — as much as possible — women (MTF transsexuals) or men (FTM transsexuals).

In separate chapters, Califia analyses the first wave of autobiographical writings by transsexuals — Christine Jorgensen, Jan Morris, and Mario Martino — and the second wave — Renée Richard, Mark Rees, Kate Bornstein, Lou Sullivan, and Leslie Feinberg's novel *Stone Butch Blues*. At the same time the first wave of transsexual autobiographies was appearing, the first group of doctors, psychologists, and/or sexologists were writing technical books about the desire to change one's sex. Although these professionals on occasion showed compassion or an enlightened attitude, for the most part they viewed "gender dysphoria" as pathological, a mental illness that could perhaps be cured by magnanimously granting sex-reassignment surgery. Califia notes "how very sad it is that even the people who viewed themselves as transsexuals' allies and advocates at

Violette Morris was an open crossdresser in the 1920s. *Transgender Warriors.*

the same time saw them as sick, delusional, and inferior people."

She continues her relentless critiques in further chapters by railing against transphobia within the feminist and lesbian movements and among gay male academics. Janice G. Raymond's influential 1979 book, *The Transsexual Empire*, is given an especially vigorous raking over the coals: "These extreme tactics and sloppy thinking are the marks of a fanatic. Although *The Transsexual Empire* is couched in academic language, it is obvious that Raymond is motivated as much by an irrational fear and loathing of transsexuals as she is of the niceties of feminist theory."

Further in the book, Califia examines the rise of transgender activism and takes a look at an important but oft-neglected topic — the partners of transgendered people. She ends with a probing essay on the possible futures of gender and transgenderism. Although there are no clear-cut solutions to the problem of rigid, intolerant beliefs regarding gender, Califia asks some important questions that point the way to a society of individuals who are simply allowed to be themselves: "Who would you be if you had never been punished for gender-inappropriate behaviour, or seen another child punished for deviation from masculine and feminine norms, or participated in dishing out such punishment? What would it be like to grow up in a society where gender was truly consensual?"

Cleis Press; $16.95
1997; softcover; 310 pp
1-57344-072-8

STRING OF PEARLS
Stories about Cross-Dressing
edited by Tony Ayres

At first, I was going to put this book in the Erotic Fiction section, but when I started reading it, I realised that wouldn't be a truly accurate reflection of its contents. *String of Pearls* contains fourteen stories by Australian writers about people who don the clothes of the biologically-opposite sex. This isn't always done for erotic reasons... sometimes the reasons aren't clear at all, as in "Butcher's Aprons". In this story by Alana Valentine, a woman is invited to a cryptic ceremony in which other women put on butcher aprons, grab a piece of offal (internal organs of farm animals), and take turns revealing a traumatic or embarrassing incident from their past. Paul Allatson's "Her Aviary" is a psychologically insightful story about a young man coming to terms with his missing mother.

In "Crystal" by Nick Enright, a male acting instructor has his students dress in drag as an exercise, and discovers powerful feelings for one of the men. "Supercollider" by Chad Taylor is a super-hot story about a man and a woman who wear various items of each other's clothing before, during, and after sex. In Catherine Lazaroo's lyrical "Instructions to My Seamstress", Lady Caroline Lamb disguises herself as a pageboy for her lover, Lord Byron. In one particularly compelling scene, while Byron is sleeping, Lady Lamb unwraps and fondles the dashing poet's infamous deformed foot. "When the last turns [of the bandage] dropped down, I held his bare foot with my bare hands, wanting for an instant to fling it away from me. The skin was soft and very pink, peeling in places. There was a faint, moist, almost putrid odour. It might have been an aborted piglet in my cradled hands, limp and misshapen. The foot was sharply turned in, creating a tender macerated cleft where the inner arch should have been."

Allen & Unwin; $16.95Aus, $13.95US
1996; softcover; 263 pp
1-86373-914-9

TRANSGENDER WARRIORS
Making History from Joan of Arc to Dennis Rodman
by Leslie Feinberg

Transgenderist Leslie Feinberg, author of the widely acclaimed novel *Stone Butch Blues*, has referred to this book as "the heart of my life's work". Undoubtedly, this book will be considered a watershed not just in Feinberg's life but in the trans movement in general. In a history lesson mixed with autobiography, indignation, and hope, *Transgender Warriors* tells the tale of people who have crossed or blurred gender lines throughout history. This is a tall order, since it covers people who were born male, female, and intersexed, people who crossdress, those who use surgery and hormones to bodily switch sexes, and those who use other means or combinations of means to violate the black and white picture of gender. But Feinberg handles it adeptly, weaving together the complex history of gender heresy.

Most Native American tribes had members who dressed as and acted like the opposite sex, and they were often treated with the utmost respect. Many tribes honoured them as special people who had much to teach. In fact, in many cultures the most spiritual people — shamans, priest/esses, and sacred dancers — were transgendered. And although the existence of a female Pope (Pope Joan) is thought to be legend, the Catholic Church has sainted a sizeable number of women who dressed as men.

Joan of Arc is a well-known transgenderist who displayed military prowess and courage, but there are many other such examples throughout history: the Basque conquistador Catalina de Erauso, the Napoleonic officer Liberté, and former King of Angola, Nzinga. In the late 1830s a large group of transvestite men calling themselves "Rebecca and her daughters" rose up in Wales to fight oppressive British taxes. The famous militant peasant movement called the Molly Maguires "'were generally stout active young men, dressed up in women's clothes,' according to historian Trench."

Feinberg also covers ancient Greece and Rome, Nazi Germany, Stonewall, women's liberation, the link (or non-link) between gender identity and sexual orientation, the biological aspects of sex and gender, the current state of transgender liberation, and, of course, the persecution of transgendered people throughout the ages. A final section contains pictures of and statements from over 30 people who are currently challenging gender norms, including two who paid the ultimate price for their individuality.

> Beacon Press; $16
> 1996; softcover; 226 pp
> heavily illus; 0-8070-7941-3

BDSM/ LEATHERSEX

AXFORDS CATALOGUE

Axfords is a British company specialising in back-lacing, boned corsets. Their slick catalogue is printed on large, heavy paper, and most of the photos are in colour. Models who don't mind showing some flesh present an amazing array of corsets, available in different colours, styles, and materials (satin, cotton, PVC, leather).

But the neo-Victorian fun doesn't end there. You can also get bloomers, French knickers, frilly blouses, half slips, a French maid outfit, the more modest parlour maid outfit, sheer nighties and negligees, plus a few things our ancestors never dreamed of, such as PVC bikini briefs.

> Axfords/82 Centurion Rd/Brighton, Sussex BN1 3LN/UK
> WWW: www.axfords.com
> Catalogue: £10
> Payment: international mo, UK cheques, Eurocheques, Visa, MC, Amex, Eurocard, Switch, Delta

BENEATH THE SKINS
The New Spirit and Politics of the Kink Community
by Ivo Dominguez, Jr

In these essays, Ivo Dominguez discusses spiritual, political, and sexual issues that are facing the evolving leather/BDSM/fetish community. He is doing so in order to promote discussion about commonalities and differences with this subculture. Essays include "Kink As Orientation", "Leatherphobia", "Pride Day: Where Should We Be?", "Butcher Than Thou", "Kink Nation: Identity Politics in Flatland", "National Groups: Why We Need Them", and "Soul Retrieval".

> Daedalus Publishing Company; $12.95
> 1994; softcover; 153 pp
> 1-881943-06-2

BITCHES WITH WHIPS
Dedicated to Female Dominance

Bitches With Whips is a slick, black and white magazine for dominant women and the people who love being beaten by them. In Volume 3 #2, Augusta Fury offers a testament to the allure of rope — as opposed to leather restraints or handcuffs — as a bondage device. She examines the bondage styles of three classic SM photographers and teaches you how to do a few rope tricks of your own. Scattered throughout the issue are photos from "Steel Exhibit: 130 Years of Steel Bondage Devices", which include an iron headcage, three-way handcuffs, and leg irons. Among the other features are an article on domestic violence in the SM community and several pieces of fiction.

Display ads for dominatrixes abound. Almost 40 women from California, Florida, New Mexico, Alaska, Ontario, and elsewhere promise that, "Your destiny will be decided in my dungeon," or declare: "The slave must not dare to disobey and shall not deny its servitude to the divine right of its superior." If you want to be treated like shit by a professional, this is the place to start looking.

> DM International/PO Box 16188/Seattle WA 98116-0188
> WWW: www.fetishsex.com
> Single issue: North America: $12. Overseas: $14.
> Four issue sub: $32. Overseas: $42
> Payment: ck, mo

THE BOTTOMING BOOK
Or, How to Get Terrible Things Done to You By Wonderful People
by Dossie Easton & Catherine A. Lizst

At first thought, it might seem like there's nothing to being a bottom/submissive in an SM relationship. Just lay (or hang) there and let someone torture the hell out of you, right? Well, as many people in the scene have noted, being a bottom is a complex role, and it may be more important in some ways than being a top.

Contrary to stereotypes, most bottoms feel very powerful during SM play. Co-author Dossie Easton explains it this way: "When I'm being flogged, early on I often come to a place where I need to stretch to take in the intense sensa-

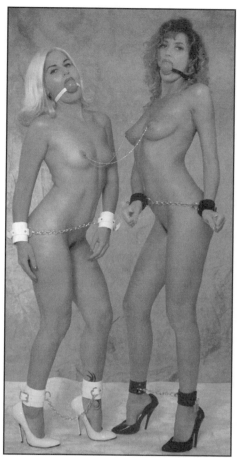

Centurians Whole Catalogue of the Bizarre.

tion, where I struggle and wonder if I can take it at all. That struggle seems to make me stronger, and soon I feel intense energy running through me, as if all the force with which the whip is thrown at me is injected into me, becomes my energy to play with. While my tops throw the whips at me as hard as they can, I take their power and dance in the centre of the storm." Bottoms also have other kinds of power. They can stop a scene at any moment, suggest a different form of punishment (sometimes), or even leave the top they're with.

The authors explain how to get the maximum enjoyment out of your submissiveness and how to uphold your responsibilities. What responsibilities, you ask? "You are responsible for knowing your limits and making sure your top knows them, for communicating clearly, explaining what you want, keeping agreements, supporting your top, and helping your top get his or her needs met." If you fulfil these obligations, you and your top should have a great time.

Of course, getting a top is a crucial part of being a bottom, and the authors tell you how to go about it. Then they lead you through negotiation, safety, and different kinds of

scenes and roles — bondage, pain, body modification, fetishes, authority scenes, regression, humiliation, mock resistance (kidnap, rape, etc.), gender play, and more.

A final chapter looks at SM and spirituality, and the bibliography offers a decent selection of books and magazines (but no organisations). Lastly, there's a poem, "When You Fuck Me I Become Enormous" — a paean to bottoming. Throughout the book are illustrations by Fish, who, as usual, has done a fantastic job with her highly kinky drawings.

Greenery Press; $11.95
1995; softcover; 123 pp
illus; 0-9639763-1-1

CENTURIAN SPARTACUS BOOK AND MAGAZINE CATALOGUE

This slick colour catalogue offers hundreds of books, comix, magazines, and catalogues covering SM/leather/fetish and transgenderism. Comix that are offered include *The Blonde Bondage Palace*, *Sabina: Mistress of Escape*, *Diary of a Dominatrix*, *The Leather Boy*, *Ex Libris Eroticis*, and a bunch of European stuff from NBM. The magazine selection is similarly international: *Dressing for Pleasure*, *Leather Obsession*, *Latex Maid*, *Rubber Nurse*, *Shiny International*, *The Rubberist*, *Glamour*, *Image*, *Secret*, *Kane*, *Cruella*, *<<O>>*, *Demonia*, *Skin Two*, *Club Caprice*, *Taffeta*, *TV Repartee*, *Transformation*, *Bizarre*, and many more. They carry from two to over a dozen back issues of each title. Absolutely the best selection of "perv" magazines I've seen.

Through the catalogues that Centurian sells, you can indulge your desire for fetish footwear, corsets, wigs, lingerie, leather, latex, sex toys, fetish videos, penis restraints, gags, hoods, and more bondage gear. The selection of books is less expansive, but again, Centurian carries material that is hard to come by in the US. Most of the books are published by Benedikt Taschen Verlag (*Eric Kroll's Fetish Girls*, *Stereo Nudes: 1850-1930*) and Glittering Images (*Bizarre Sinema*, *Marquis de Sade*). There are also some Bettie Page books and artbooks from photorealistic illustrator Hajime Sorayama.

Finally, Centurian offers a small selection of videos and bondage gear. This is a superb catalogue, definitely worth the price.

UTB/3540 W Sahara, Suite 094/Las Vegas NV 89102
Catalogue: $5

CENTURIANS WHOLE CATALOGUE OF THE BIZARRE

This big catalogue, mostly in colour, is packed with photos and printed on slick, heavy paper. It cost over $200,000 to produce, and it shows. It is the JC Penney Christmas Wishbook for jaded pervs. All your bondage needs will be met between its covers. (However, the catalogue contains only a minimum of equipment associated solely with SM, such as whips and paddles.)

Among the toys you'll want to play with:

☞ Wrist, ankle, and elbow cuffs
☞ Locking waist belts
☞ General purpose adjustable straps

☞ All kinds of collars, many with D-rings for attaching chains, cuffs, etc.

☞ Latex, leather, and authentic straightjackets

☞ A neck-elbow restraint

☞ A back-arm restraint

☞ Bondage mittens

☞ Spreader bars

☞ An iron yoke

☞ Handcuffs and thumbcuffs

☞ Lots of styles of blindfolds

☞ Corsets

☞ A variety of helmets (i.e., they completely cover the head)

☞ Hog-tie trainers

☞ Ball gags

☞ Penis gags. There are two types of penis gag. One kind has a dildo attached to the outside front, so your slave can pleasure you even if his/her hands and crotch are being restrained. The other kind has a smaller dildo attached to the inside front, so your slave will have a mouthful when being gagged.

☞ Pump gags. These have an inflatable little sack that fits in your slave's mouth. Just squeeze the pump a couple of times to fill up his/her mouth.

☞ Shoe or boot gag. Will hold the toe of a shoe or boot firmly and deeply in your slave's mouth.

☞ Over a dozen types of penis harnesses and sheaths.

☞ Medieval and post-modern chastity belts for men and women. Many of them come with attachable butt/vagina plugs.

☞ Behind-the-back arm binders

☞ Slave panties. This ingenious latex device is a hood with the mouth attached to the crotch of panties. Thus, the slave is forced to perform oral sex on his/her master.

This is an unparalleled collection of items for discipline disciples. And the catalogue itself is sure to become an underground collectors' item.

Spartacus/PO Box 429/Orange CA 92666

Voice: 714-775-0238

Fax: 714-971-7406

Catalogue: $29.95, plus $3 shipping ($9 for non-US)

Payment: cash, ck, mo, Visa, MC, Discover, Amex

CHASE PRODUCTS AND SERVICES CATALOGUE

Looking for some serious, hospital quality equipment for your medical and/or SM scenes? Chase has got all the supplies you need. They offer genuine medical equipment, but instead of selling to hospitals and doctors, they cater to people who just want to "play doctor".

You can get all kinds of supplies for catheterisation and enemasation — over a dozen catheters, syringes, trays, urine collection bags, enema tanks, flow meters, tubing, rectal nozzles, and more. Some of the medical instruments carried by Chase include dilators, urethral sounds, vaginal speculums, forceps, and tit clamps (OK, that's not a medical instrument… but it could be if you have a kinky doctor).

Body modifiers will find a large selection of body jewellery, although it isn't described in the catalogue. You have to call for details. If you want to enlarge your scrotum to the size of a softball or more, check out the scrotal inflation supplies.

Chase also carries some more general SM equipment, such as ass chains, butterfly boards, electrodes, restraints, stirrups, head stocks, foot stocks, a pillory, gallows, a jail cell, suspension items, and testicle crushers.

Extreme and hard-to-find items are Chase's speciality. If you have something special in mind, they may be able to make it or get it for you.

Chase Products/PO Box 1014/Novi MI 48376-1014

Catalogue: $2

THE COMPLEAT SPANKER

by Lady Green

This manual tells you most everything you need to know about smacking tails. Covers communication and mood, warming up, implements (hands, paddles, birches, etc.), positions, where and how hard to strike, potential problems, tips and tricks, finding people to spank with, cleaning your implements, resources, and more. Illustrated with line drawings.

Greenery Press; $11.95

1996; softcover; 87 pp

illus; 1-890159-00-X

CONSENSUAL SADOMASOCHISM
How to Talk About It & How to Do It Safely

by William A. Henkin, PhD, & Sybil Holiday, CCSSE

The authors of this book not only engage in SM but also have some academic and professional credits: William Henkin, PhD, is a psychotherapist and sexologist who is licensed in marriage, family, and sex therapy, while Sybil Holiday is a California Certified Safe Sex Educator and professional dominant. Together they have pooled their academic and real-world training to create an insightful, caring guide to practising SM.

The long introduction (28 pages) and the first chapter seem most appropriate for people who are just beginning SM or are considering engaging in it. The authors reveal how they got into the practice, discuss what SM is and is not, and explain the terms and concepts involved. The "SM glossary" contains brief definitions of over 60 terms, and the rest of the chapter gives lengthy explanations of such concepts as "top's disease", "smart-assed masochists", and "lifestyle DS".

The vast majority of the book, though, is taken up by the only other chapter, "Playing Safely", which weighs in at 150 pages. Not only do the authors specify exactly how to minimise the risk involved in over 50 acts — including dripping candle wax, caning, blindfolding, mummification, sexual penetration, and interrogation scenes — they also look at negotiations, safe words, meeting people, scenes that don't work, and the dangers of using SM scenes as psychotherapy, as well as some topics that don't really fit under the heading "Playing Safely" — social skills, dungeon etiquette, SM and spirituality, and Tantric SM. The book ends with a long annotated bibliography, short resources section, and extensive index.

I'd say that SM beginners would probably get the most out of the whole book, although the extensive look at safety offers important pointers for everybody.

Daedalus Publishing Company; $16.95
1996; softcover; 264 pp
1-881943-12-7

EROTEAK
Erotic Furniture for the Connoisseur

Eroteak sells finely-crafted, handmade furniture designed for BDSM purposes. They are all put together with an eye towards maximum restraining options. You can get pillories, benches, correction stools, a leg stretcher, a stocks bed, a "z bench", a rocking chair, and a large "X-cross" for crucifixions.

If you have something special in mind, they can make any sexual props you want. They'll be "expensive but perfect." Eroteak usually works in wood, but they will use metals, plastics, or whatever your heart desires. You can even have your furniture outfitted with winches and other mechanical gizmos.

Keep in mind that Eroteak can make not only sexual furniture, but magician's props, tables with hidden drawers, and any other specialised furniture needs you may have.

Eroteak/c/o 182 Denmark Rd/Lowestoft, Suffolk NR32 2EN/UK
Catalogue: £5

KINKYCRAFTS
101 Do-It-Yourself S/M Toys
edited by Lady Green with Jaymes Easton

Do you want SM equipment, but you don't feel like spending a lot? Or maybe you just enjoy crafts. Whatever the reason, you'll learn how to make all kinds of SM stuff with the detailed instructions in KinkyCrafts — adjustable ankle spreader ($50), ball crusher (under $5), bondage bench ($80 to $100), cat-o-nine-tails (under $5), fur mitt (under $10), labia stretcher (under $5), leather paddle (under $5), Nerf gag (under $2), nylon webbing sling ($30), spandex hood (under $10), and a suspension harness ($40). Each of the 101 items is accompanied by an illustration, a list of the necessary materials, tools, time needed, estimated cost, and step-by-step instructions. [A perfect-bound, softcover edition of this book is in the works and should be available in the first half of 1998. It will cost $15.95.]

Greenery Press; $19.95
1995; oversized plastic-comb bound softcover; 149 pp
heavily illus; 0-9739763-7-0

THE KISS OF THE WHIP
Explorations in SM
by Jim Prezwalski

This book is not a how-to book or a book for beginners to learn techniques. It is more interested in the "why's" of SM and in giving some general tips and ideas for those already versed in basic techniques. The book first intersperses the history of SM, the meaning of pain, SM ecstasy, and other basic topics with long comments from practitioners. Later on, there are ideas for getting the most out of each of your five senses, plus balance.

A very important chapter explores negotiations in detail. "Negotiation is one of those code words that everyone knows but few are really sure what it means. It's simply a meeting where each person expresses what they desire and want from the others and what they're willing to give in return. Most SM negotiations are on the level of a friendly chat."

In "Putting It Together" the author gives advice on incorporating improvisation, humour, irony, and creativity into your scenes. Of course, a chapter is devoted to safety considerations, with some of the most specific information I've seen in any SM book. There's also plenty of information on all kinds of diseases, from herpes and TB to AIDS.

Three chapters give pointers about a number of "specialities", such as abrasion, body modification, bondage, deprivation, whipping, clips and clamps, hot ash, electricity, and fisting. Finally, the author covers SM myths, SM metaphors, threats to SM (the ultra-right and commercialisation), and the three key figures in the early history of SM — Marquis de Sade, Leopold von Sacher-Masoch, and Richard von Krafft-Ebing. Appendices contain Sacher-Masoch's three slave contracts and one of his short stories.

Leyland Publications; $15.95
1995; softcover; 254 pp
0-943595-51-7

KPPT
Kinky People, Places & Things

A well-rounded SM magazine published by DM, a woman-owned business. In issue 4 #5, Jay Wiseman tells you everything you need to know about clamps — how to put them on, what to do once they're on, and how to take them off. He offers this reminder: "Clamps hurt continuously, even if the dominant forgets about them. Unlike whipping and spanking, which are labour-intensive, clamps require no ongoing effort on the dominant's part to cause pain. It's therefore easy to lose track of how much pain the submissive feels." There's a black and white photo review of Skin Two's Rubber Ball, featuring men, women, and transgenderists in various permutations of leather, studs, and chainmail.

"Self Bondage" is a completely unique, engrossing essay written by a man who managed to dress himself in an elaborate bondage outfit, attach a sucking device to his dick, hook shocking "buzzers" to his crotch and nipples, cuff his hands and feet, cut off his hearing and sight with headgear, and suspend himself in a crawlspace in his house, where he will be alone until the next afternoon. The only way he can get free is by managing to get the keys to his handcuffs, a difficult but supposedly not impossible task. Then he will have to struggle to get the other keys to free himself from his "cell". Once out of his self-imposed prison, he'll have to retrieve the keys to his "uniform" from a fence post at the back of his property. I got panicky just reading about his ordeal. Does he manage to get free before his wife comes home? I wish I knew, but the gut-tightening narrative is "to be continued".

KPPT has some of the more unusual personal ads I've ever come across. Take a gander at this one, headlined "Midwest Sub Slut": "Grandma, fat, old whore over 30 years experience in kinky sex with Dom males, groups, couples is available for sexual abuse & degradation, line ups, circle sucks, piss showers, TT [tit torture] VA [verbal abuse] BD/SM while voyeur mate videos. I'm 48, 4'11", 155#, 40B-34-44 with saggy cowtits, fat ass, big, fleshy, well-used cunt."

DM International/PO Box 16188/Seattle WA 98116

WWW: www.fetishsex.com

Single issue: North America: $10. Overseas: $12

Six issue sub (one year): $40. Overseas: $54

Payment: ck, mo

LEATHERSEX Q&A
Questions About Leathersex and the Leathersex Lifestyles Answered

by Joseph W. Bean

Joseph Bean has been involved in BDSM/leathersex for over thirty years as a practitioner (Top and bottom), lecturer, writer, columnist, and magazine editor. In this book he distils all of that knowledge through the use of actual questions that have been posed to him regarding SM and overlapping/synonymous practices. Most of the inquiries specifically regard gay leathermen, but almost all of the answers can be applied to leatherfolk of all genders. One guy asks: "Is it actually possible for a man to stick his whole arm, up to the pit, in another man's ass? Don't the intestines start curving around? And don't they stay in the lower abdomen, anyway, an area shorter than a man's arm?" Bean's answer begins: "Yes, the intestines do curve around, but haven't you ever had to reach around the leftovers and the cake to drag a bowl of olives from the back of the bottom shelf of the refrigerator? It's no problem to twist an arm around like a pretzel if you're getting to what you want."

The questions are divided into eleven thematic chapters covering novices ("How important is all the signalling by right and left coloured hankies, keys, collars, etc.?"), sex ("I want sex at the height of the scene, but most Tops relegate it to the straight time afterwards. How can I work this out?"), pain ("Is a bottom supposed to scream and howl when he's tortured? I feel better grinning — or usually not — and bearing it in silence, but this bothers the few tops I know."), extremes ("When you do breath control, how do you know when to let the bottom breathe again?"), relationships ("What if my Master orders me to do something my conscience says is wrong?"), safety ("How do you disinfect a bloody whip so it can be used again without carrying HIV from one bottom to another?"), and psyche and spirit ("Is it possible to have out-of-body experiences when I'm tortured… ?").

Leathersex Q&A ends with a brief booklist and a remarkably thorough index (16 pages!). For the merely curious or the real-life leatherlover, this book provides lots of great information.

Daedalus Publishing Company; $16.95

1996; softcover; 246 pp

1-881943-01-1

MISS ABERNATHY'S CONCISE SLAVE TRAINING MANUAL

by Christina Abernathy

Most of the how-to books dealing with the BDSM lifestyle, including those reviewed in this section, give instructions for such physical acts as bondage, whipping, hot wax dripping, and so on. Till now, no one had written a book on a very important but more sublime aspect of dominance and submission — the (obviously consensual) Owner/slave relationship. In this scenario, the submissive is completely under the control of the Dominant, performing every task that is required, from the menial to the erotic. This situation may last for just a few hours a couple of times a month, for an entire weekend, or — in the rarest and most extreme cases — twenty-four hours a day, 365 days a year. This special relationship may involve, at certain times, other aspects of BDSM — such as restraint or the giving and receiving of pain — but that is not its primary focus. It is mainly a very powerful relationship dynamic, and that is what Christina Abernathy covers in this slim book.

The first part of the book explains the training programme of a slave, with specifics regarding the initial interview, controlling the slave's bodily functions, forms of address for the Mistress/Master, submissive body postures, voice commands, forms of service (house work, personal attendance, sexual techniques, etc.), punishments and rewards, collaring a slave, marking a slave (piercing, branding, etc.), and clothing. In the second half of the book, Abernathy looks at the "nature and logistics" of these relationships, including the qualities of a good Dominant and a good submissive, different roles and relationships (house slaves, sex slaves, part-time, full-time, etc.), slave contracts, and "pre-nuptial agreements". The book ends with a listing of resources and reading material.

Greenery Press; $11.95

1996; softcover; 86 pp

0-9639763-9-7

MY PRIVATE LIFE
Real Experiences of a Dominant Woman

by Mistress Nan

Mistress Nan — a devoted wife and mother and a respected professional — has been dominating men and women for 30 years. In this book, she tells how she got into SM and recounts her most memorable scenes. In the first, from 1965, she tells us about the two types of men she encounters: "It takes about two lashes to discover whether you've got yourself a coward, or a so-called brave man. I love the cowards. You can make their flesh crawl just by looking at them. But I like the so-called 'tough guys' even better. I love to torture them and watch their alleged masculinity slowly disappear as they turn into snivelling, begging wretches."

"24 Hours in Hell" tells of one of Nan's most extreme

scenes, in which she mentally and physically tortured Alex, her female slave of many years, for a full day. Alex had been copping a majorly bitchy attitude lately, and Nan decided it was time to put a permanent end to that. She picked up Alex from her home, handcuffed her to the inside of the car, and drove her to the dungeon. At one point, she fastened Alex to an X-shaped cross with over a dozen belts and strap, then proceeded to whip the hell out of her. "'Where is your bravado now? Or are you only really challenging when you're a few miles away on the phone, making my life miserable. (Smack) Well, it's going to stop, now! (Slash) Yes, this is your scene, Bitch, but this is also your nightmare. And, most of all, this (smack) is (crack) my reality!' I began whipping in earnest. Her moans and cries became like that of a hurt animal, one with the sound of the whip, on and on. Eventually each breath was a sob, and my arm was tired." Later, she tied Alex up and left her in a dark room for an hour, stimulated her with vibrators, shocked her with a cattle prod, and force-fed her rice pudding, her most hated food. The iron-fisted tactics must have done the trick, because eight years later, Alex and Nan are still together.

All of the sixteen episodes are written so that we get inside Mistress Nan's head, feeling the charge she gets out of dominating, humiliating, and inflicting pain. Their detailed explicitness means that they can also be used as one-handed reading.

Daedalus Publishing Co; $14.95
1995; softcover; 196 pp
1-881943-11-9

PADDLES

A digest-sized Australian magazine that covers spanking, bondage, SM, fetishes, and similar concerns. It's illustrated with drawings and black and white photos of women and men getting paddled, caned, tied up, put in stocks, etc. Leonardo's drawings of a woman paddling her daughter for using her vibrator look just like the ultra-fundamentalist Christian comic tracts of Jack Chick.

The written offerings take the form of four fairly long stories, fictional and allegedly true. "A Full Session" is a fairly unconventional story about a mistress who ties up her man and makes him listen while she fucks another man in an adjoining room. She teases him about it, but did she really do it? He finds out the hard way when the stud comes into the room ready for more action, but the mistress won't put out anymore.

For all you Aussies, there's a scene report from the Casa de Camelot dungeon and over 30 personal ads. Not a bad little magazine, but not outstanding either.

Paddles/PO Box 524/Milsons Point NSW 2061/Australia
WWW: www.paddles.net
Single issue: Australia/NZ: $10Aus. Elsewhere: $10US
Six month sub: $54
Payment: US cash, ck, Visa, MC, Bankcard

THE SECOND COMING
A Leatherdyke Reader
edited by Pat Califia & Robin Sweeney

In 1981, the lesbian-feminist SM group Samois edited and published the first book by and for leatherdykes, *Coming to Power: Writings and Graphics on Lesbian S/M.* It was an important publication that helped to energise and solidify what had been a disparate quasi-community.

Fifteen years later, Samois co-founder Pat Califia and writer Robin Sweeney have put together a sequel that addresses issues that have arisen in the previous decade and a half, offers further looks at old issues, and provides some quality smut, all at the same time.

The 65 — count 'em, 65 — articles, essays, poems, and short stories (plus erotic photographs and a woodcut) cover an impressive amount of ground. Two sections — "Who Is My Sister? Challenging the Boundaries of the Leatherdyke Community" and "We Are Here Too: The Diversity of Perversity" — look at the struggles that transgenders, bisexuals, professional dominatrixes, Latinas, and the disabled have faced within the lesbian SM community, as well as the oppression of leatherdykes by the larger lesbian movement.

Another section contains articles on the use of fascist icons in SM, real violence among leatherdykes, and other weighty issues. There are also pieces on nitty gritty details of living the life ("Sex and the Single Submissive", "Sex Party Savoir Faire") and histories of several important women's SM groups, including Briar Rose, Lesbian Sex Mafia, Outcasts, and Female Trouble. Several sections offer poetry and fiction that range from grey hanky (the light stuff) through black hanky (the heavy stuff) to orange (anything goes) and beyond.

While no other book can have the effect that the original *Coming to Power* had, *The Second Coming* is a worthy successor. It's not content to simply be a "celebration" of lesbian SM... it asks some hard questions and stokes fires that will no doubt be burning in the leatherdyke community for years to come.

Alyson Publications; $12.95
1996; softcover; 380 pp
illus; 1-55583-281-4

SECRET MAGAZINE

One of the most celebrated of the "Europerv" magazines, and with good reason. Printed on amazingly heavy, slick paper, each issue has several articles on BDSM/fetish interests and portfolios from around seven radical artists, with one or two pages of work from a bunch of others. The artwork is simply amazing from technical, artistic, and erotic standpoints (it's pretty rare for erotic art to hit all three nails right on the head). In fact, *Secret* has so much breathtaking art that it almost seems unfair.

The scene-stealer of issue 8 has to be photographer Shinji Yamakazi. His opening photo shows a beautiful, nude Asian woman, amid dramatic lighting, wearing a bizarre neck and head brace. Another shot shows a woman, her face completely covered with blonde hair, in a fishnet bodystocking and black boots. She is sitting with her arms raised on a bed, while a long piece of rope that extends from beyond both sides of the frame wraps around her torso. A third picture, taken at a tilted angle, shows a woman in a PVC

One of the most celebrated of the "Europerv" magazines, and with good reason. *Secret magazine.*

eral others help keep *Secret* filled to the brim with excellent work.

This issue continues to prove that illustration — an often overlooked genre — is alive and thriving as an erotic art form. A series of drawings by Axterdam demonstrates some wild and woolly sex machines, Roy Tenidri creates an all-female world full of extreme bondage and penetration, and Timo Niemi/Roy creates a similar feminarchy clad in shiny black PVC.

With all this visual content, *Secret* still somehow finds lots of room for writings. Three articles look at the life and work of the Marquis de Sade, three others deal with corsets, one gives a history of SM in Japan, and several offer practical tips on a wide variety of activities — bondage, blood-drinking, being a slave, and more. Fictional delights are provided by a bunch of short stories, including "Der Klinik" and "The Offering". Maybe the most intriguing piece is by "Mr. Blowup", a British man with a fetish for inflatable rubber/latex clothing.

Secret lives up to its fearsome reputation and is quite simply a must-have.

Secret/PO Box 1400/100 Brussells 1/BELGIUM
Fax: 32.2.223.10.09
Email: secretmag@glo.be
WWW: www.secretmag.com
single issue: $20US; £10; 25DM; 500FB
4 issue sub: $70US; £40; 100DM; 2000FB
payment: cash (preferred by registered mail), Visa, MC, Amex, Eurocard, Diners Club, Access, Eurocheque in Belgian francs

THE SEXUALLY DOMINANT WOMAN
A Workbook for Nervous Beginners
by Lady Green

Yet another addition to the exploding body of literature on how to do SM. This one is a brief guide for women who are just getting into domination. It covers bondage, role-playing, and inducing pain, sensory deprivation, etc. There are also chapters on physical and emotional safety, the ten most commonly asked questions, things for your partner to keep in mind, a step-by-step guide for a basic session, and more.

Greenery Press; $11.95
1994; softcover; 91 pp
illus; 0-9639763-0-3

SM 101
A Realistic Introduction
by Jay Wiseman

This is probably the most detailed guide to SM acts that I've come across. It has 250 big pages crammed with very explicit instructions on a wide variety of topics. There are ten pages devoted to clamps alone. Among the many topics that are thoroughly covered — what SM is, consent and negotiation, "coming out" as a sadomasochist, finding partners of either sex, bringing SM into a relationship, tying someone up, hoods, gags, whipping, lubricants, hot/cold play, being a submissive, being a Dominant, safety, first aid, safer sex, anal play, electricity, finding help for problems (diseases, rape, sex addiction, etc.), SM resources (books, periodicals, clubs,

bodysuit and mask criss-crossed by chains that descend from the ceiling. If no publisher has released a book of Yamakazi's work yet, I demand to know why.

An artist named GRRR knows how to tap the forbidden reptilian pleasure centres of the brain with his/her occult-sexual ink drawings. One shows a beautiful woman with claws for feet who has all three holes being occupied by a horny tree. Another drawing depicts a woman sucking the grotesquely long nipple of a goat/woman while she literally gets the root from a tree-being.

Articles in this issue cover aquabondage (in which a submissive is bound and totally submersed in water), death by crucifixion, a beginner's guide to giving and receiving enemas, safety tips, the psychology of SM, and an interview with the SM band Sleep Chamber, whose show is enlivened by the antics of the "Barbitchuettes".

Issue 12 is graced by photos from some of the best artists in the biz. Trevor Watson turns in one of the sexiest gasmask shots I've seen, a superkinky medical examination scene, and two women, tongues touching, whose black and white face masks make them look like either bondage nurses or SM nuns. Barbara Nitke shoots grainy SM and bondage photos, my favourite being the one of a bored woman, leaning on a sink, who has a ho-hum expression on her face as she looks at the bound and gagged (with black electrical tape) nude woman trussed up on her kitchen counter. Masami Akita's shots of Japanese rope bondage are duly impressive. Todd Friedman, Plakidas, Alex D., Lindsey, and sev-

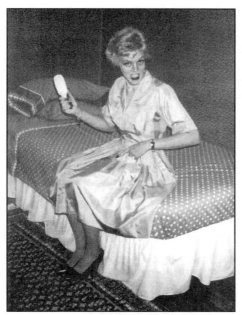

Whap! *Women Who Administer Punishment.*

videos, etc.), SM slang and abbreviations, and much more.

Greenery Press; $24.95
1992; softcover; 251 pp
no ISBN

THE TOPPING BOOK
Or, Getting Good at Being Bad

by Dossie Easton & Catherine A. Liszt

Written by the same team who brought you *The Bottoming Book* [above], this companion volume teaches you the art and science of being a top/dominant in an SM relationship. You must be like a maestro, carefully conducting the scene by constantly monitoring your bottom's reactions and adjusting your actions accordingly. You must learn how to go almost — but not quite — too far. How to keep upping the pain and/or humiliation to new, excruciating heights. How to push your bottom past his limits but not so far that you destroy him. You have to know when too much is just right and when too much is really too much. It ain't easy, but you have some accomplished guides to help you.

The authors elaborate on your rights and responsibilities as a top. A top's rights include the rights to clear communication, to expect support from your partner, to get your needs met, to receive constructive feedback. A top's responsibilities include your and your partner's emotional and physical safety, emergency preparedness, caring for your equipment, following through on your promises, and stating your needs, wants, and limits.

One especially important chapter for novice dominants answers the question, "How do you learn to do all this stuff?" You can join a club, get advice from seasoned tops, and maybe find a mentor. Another good piece of advice is to be

a bottom yourself: "… you can learn topping by bottoming, and paying attention to what works, and asking the top questions afterwards if you were too distracted (or happy) to pay attention to the technical details." You can also apply this philosophy by trying things out on yourself. "Put a clothespin on the web between your thumb and your forefinger to find out how intense the sensation is, or put it on your chest, or your nipple, or…"

The chapter "Shadow Play: Dark S/M" gives pointers for scenes that get into deep psychological issues. "Playing in parent/child roles is often deep play, as is playing out some personal trauma like child abuse, molestation or rape. Some players may use an S/M scene to explore historical oppression, like slavery, witch-burnings, the Inquisition or the Holocaust." These kind of scenarios are tricky to the extreme, but their successful completion can bring about emotional peace. "Many of us play rape scenes, and more than a few of us have actually been raped, so for some a rape scene is very deep play, searching for understanding, catharsis, healing or resolution."

Other parts of the book cover SM ethics, toys, finding bottoms, great real-life examples of scenes, SM spirituality, communication skills, keeping a scene going, when scenes go wrong, resources (clubs, publications, books), and more. Once again, *Brat Attack* creator Fish does a wonderfully perverted illustration job.

Greenery Press; $11.95
1995; softcover; 150 pp
illus; 0-9639763-5-4

WOMEN WHO ADMINISTER PUNISHMENT

Woman Who Administer Punishment (also called *WhAP!*) is for "maternally dominant" women and submissive men. Unlike most BDSM publications, the emphasis is on aprons, not leather. A light-hearted humour suffuses every aspect, from the article titles ("Fifteen Fun & Feasible Ways to Publicly Punish Your Husband") to the subverted quaint illustrations from the 1950s. The emphasis is on "Mommy Dearest" types who give their little men the spankings they so richly deserve (and crave).

In the publisher's note to the now unavailable issue 4, the women who create *WhAP!* write: "For many of us, there is nothing more sexually exciting than a man who is virile and successful in the outside world and at the same time on his knees for us at home." Editor Keri Pentauk gets specific about the physical and psychological punishments that *WhAP!* women mete out. "By physical punishment we mean, first and foremost, spanking. By spanking, we don't mean whipping or beating (necessarily), but traditional, 'hand or hairbrush to heinie' spanking, firmly, but lovingly administered; the kind that's [sic] takes place over a skirted knee; the kind that usually begins with protests and promises and ends with tears and admissions of guilt… Other more esoteric *WhAP!* disciplinary methods include — take a deep breath — panty and diaper punishments, repetitive writing assignments, role reversal (batteries not included), movement restraint (a term we prefer to 'bondage'), and, for lack of a better term, forced (insisted upon?) cross dressing."

The cover of issue 9 declares, "Men Are Dogs: Let's Train Them to Obey Us". The article inside says, "Good husbands, like good dogs, are the product of good breeding and proper training. And just as even the most surly and disobedient dog can be changed through obedience training, so can a difficult, rude, and unhelpful husband be turned into a model of consideration, kindness, and devotion — through the application of the principles of canine obedience training." The issue's top ten list features fateful phrases that were overheard at a WhAP! dinner party. "Yes, his suit is by Armani... but did he tell you that his undies are by Victoria? And if he keeps boasting, his spanking is going to be by Beth Anne." "When I buy a bar of soap I look for the best cleaning... when Gary goes shopping he looks for the best tasting." Other articles include "On His Best Behaviour... in the Bedroom: Sex Education for Husbands", "Female Family Values", "Beware the Girl Next Door", and instructions for delivering over-the-knee spankings.

The top ten list for the next issue sings the praises of the new crop of conservative women, such as Arianna Huffington: "Traditional values cheerleader gives lethal tongue lashings to liberal weenies," and Josette Shiner: "As an editor of the nation's most conservative newspaper, her pen is mighty as a hairbrush." Photo spreads show a matriarchal figure feeding her thirtyish husband while he wears diapers and a bib, a more modern dominatrix disciplining young men, and a gallery of the "femmes and dommes of film noir". Articles cover "Training Your Man to Service Your Pleasure", "Shame Arousal", "Managing Your Man's Money: His Li'l Assets Belong to You", and "The English Way".

Is WhAP! really a disciplinary, quasi-BDSM publication or is it a parody? I think it works well either way. It's always done with panache, visual flair, and reckless disregard for political correctness. Recommended.

Retro Systems/PO Box 69491/Los Angeles 90069
Voice/fax: 310-854-1043
Email: retrosys@hooked.net
WWW: www.whapmag.com
Issue 9: $9.95. Issue 10: $7.95
Four issue sub: $29. Canada: $39. Overseas: $49 [shipping charges apply to subscriptions]
Shipping: $4.95 per order. Overseas: 20% of order, $6 minimum
Payment: cash, ck, mo, Visa, MC, Amex, Disc

POLYAMORY

THE ETHICAL SLUT
A Guide to Infinite Sexual Possibilities
by Dossie Easton & Catherine A. Liszt

The authors of this book are unabashed, self-proclaimed sluts. This doesn't mean that they'll have sex with just anybody and everybody, but it basically means that they'll have sex with anybody they want to have sex with, following certain guidelines. Both of them have a peppy, infectious sex-positive attitude. "To us, a slut is a person of any gender who has the courage to lead life according to the radical proposition that sex is nice and pleasure is good for you. A slut may choose to have sex with herself only, or with the Fifth Fleet. He may be heterosexual, homosexual or bisexual, a radical activist or a peaceful suburbanite... A slut shares his sexuality the way a philanthropist shares her money — because they have a lot of it to share, because it makes them happy to share it, because sharing makes the world a better place. Sluts often find that the more sex and love they give away, the more they have — a loaves and fishes miracle in which greed and generosity go hand-in-hand to provide more for everybody. Imagine living in sexual abundance."

They also emphasise the ethical aspects of sluthood, which they describe as being rooted in pragmatism. They ask such questions as, "Are there any risks? Is everybody involved aware of those risks and doing what can be done to minimise them?" And, "How much fun is it? What is everybody learning from it?" Ethical sluts will always make sure that everybody is truly consenting (which includes no one being lied to or manipulated), that they are being honest with themselves, that everyone's feelings are being respected, and that the ramifications are being considered.

The term polyamory is basically used to describe caring, sexual/emotional relationships other than the standard monogamous couple set-up. Thus, swinging (swapping partners for sex) and other purely sexual encounters are often not considered polyamory (especially by the polys themselves). The authors of this book, though, want you to have it all. Besides traditional notions of polyamory (triads, quads, tribes), they also encourage you to explore swinging, one-night stands, group sex, having sex with friends ("fuck buddies"), and even having a relationship with just one other person if that's how you get your kicks. The point is, do what you want to do. Don't worry about how society will label you. Just worry about being true to yourself and honest with other people.

Most of the book gives specific advice for dealing with various issues. The authors, who speak from experience, describe various ways to be a slut, the skills you'll need (communication, honesty, planning, limit-setting, etc.), and how to truly enjoy sex. There are separate chapters devoted to dealing with various issues: boundaries, jealousy, love, conflict, health, childrearing, orgies, and finding partners.

It's refreshing to find a book that's as upbeat and happy about sex as this one is. It doesn't try to enforce any notions of which types of non-mainstream sexual relationships are acceptable and which aren't. As long as it feels good — and everybody involved, including yourself, is being respected — it is good. Hallelujah!

Greenery Press; $15.95
1997; softcover; 279 pp
1-890159-01-8

Übertriad. Lou Andreas-Salomé, Paul Rée, and Friedrich Nietzsche. *Three In Love.*

LOVING MORE
New Paradigm Relationships

The two dominant organisations devoted to polylove — the IntiNet Resource Center and Polyfidelitous Educational Productions — have teamed up to form the Abundant Love Institute, which publishes *Loving More*. This magazine explores the many flavours of polylove — triads (three-partner, committed relationships), group marriages, open marriages, intimate networks, expanded families, and all other "forms of multi-partner relating which are ethical and consensual."

The articles and essays reveal the ups and downs of being in sexualoving relationships with multiple people. In the Spring 1995 issue Bret Hill discusses some of the things he's learned about love and sex by living in a sexually open community of 100 people. "The key that I found is not trying to determine 'Am I poly?', 'Am I monogamous?', 'Am I fidelitous?' and act accordingly, but rather, to ask in each situation, 'What is required here?' To check with your body and heart and gonads and say, 'Can this go deeper?' and if so then to ask, 'Am I willing?' If you can say Yes to these questions, then make the offer — a practice of embracing chaos, a spiritual life indeed."

Loving More — and much of the polylove movement — is heavily infused with sacred sexuality. In "The Gift Is to the Giver", Adrielle Greenwood finds her male partner and her female partner making love and she joins them. "I reached down and caressed her soft hairy mound and swollen clitoris and touched his hard throbbing phallus. It aroused me to feel him inside her; when I touched the place where they joined, I felt moved by the Mystery, knowing how deep inside her sacred body he must be. This is the Source, the place where life begins, this joining of yoni and phallus."

Other articles examine sex in the lives of multi-partnered women, the history of the tribal Aluna community, Tantra and sexual healing, public sex, jealousy, and polylove pioneer

Gerald Jud. There are also reviews, personal ads, resources, and info on upcoming conferences.

Loving More/PO Box 4358/Boulder CO 80306-4358
Email: brett@lovemore.com
WWW: www.lovemore.com
Single issue: $6
One year sub (4 issues): $24. A subscription is included in membership fees of $49/year for individuals or $75/year for families. You also get discounts on books and conferences, access to ALI's network and library, an ad in one issue, and more.
Payment: ck, mo, Visa, MC

POLYAMORY
The New Love Without Limits — Secrets of Sustainable Intimate Relationships

by Dr. Deborah M. Anapol

Polyamory was originally published in 1992 as *Love Without Limits* [*Outposts* p 116]. Now it has been expanded and brought up-to-date with new resources and issues that were not addressed as thoroughly in the original. Since I've already reviewed the first incarnation of this book elsewhere, I won't go into detail here, except to say that it remains an accessible, non-threatening guide for anyone who would like to become involved in sexualove relationships other than the standard two-person-monogamy kind. You'll find chapters on the meaning of polyamory, ethics, deciding what's right for you, become polyamorous, coming out as a poly, "finding your tribe", the widespread benefits of polyamory, a new chapter on jealousy, and more topics. There is also an annotated 16-page poly bibliography and filmography, and a guide to organisations and online resources.

Intinet Resource Center (Dr. Deborah Anapol); $16
1997; softcover; 185 pp
1-880789-08-6

THREE IN LOVE
Menages a Trois from Ancient to Modern Times

by Barbara Foster, Michael Foster, & Letha Hadady

The past few years have seen a trend in which various sexual minorities trace their histories, showing that they have always been around and that many of history's most famous personages have been among their number. *Three in Love* is the first book to trace the specific polyamorous relationship known as the triad ("triad" is to three people as "couple" is to two people). Although the phrase in the book's subtitle, *ménages à trois*, is generally only applied to sexual encounters, here the authors primarily use it to describe sexualove relationships.

Scanning all of Western history, the authors (themselves a triad) devote each chapter to one to five menages, plus the occasional individual who engaged in several triads throughout his or her life. Among the people who are covered are Henry II, Jean-Jacques Rousseau, Casanova, the Marquis de Sade, Percy Shelley, Mary Shelley, Lord Byron, Friedrich Engels, Victor Hugo, Alexandre Dumas, Catherine the Great, John Stuart Mill, Friedrich Nietzsche, Sir Richard Burton, Butch Cassady and the Sundance Kid, Bonnie and Clyde, Henry Miller, Anaïs Nin, Salvador Dalí, Pablo Picasso, François Mitterand, Emile Zola, Franklin and Eleanor Roosevelt, various Kennedys, George Bernard Shaw, Eugene O'Neill, Radclyffe Hall, Ezra Pound, Joseph Goebbels, Marguerite Duras, Jean-Paul Sartre, Simone de Beauvoir, Ernest Hemingway, DH Lawrence, Greta Garbo, Clark Gable, Jack Kerouac, and Allen Ginsberg. Some of the triads push the definition of the term to the edge. Among the strangest are Adam and Eve and the serpent, and Clark Kent and Lois Lane and Superman.

Besides looking at the obvious subject of how these relationships were viewed by the rest of the world, particular attention is paid to the complex interpersonal dynamics within each triad. The chapter "Femme Fatale" covers the triads of pioneering psychoanalyst Lou Andreas-Salomé, who would become involved with Nietzsche, Sigmund Freud, philosopher Paul Rée, and poet Rainer Maria Rilke. The authors write that upon becoming attracted to the Russian preacher Hendrik Gillot, "Lou had discovered one leg of the triad she was to construct for the rest of her long life. She would be strongly attracted to an older mentor, feeling a pull that she claimed was due to her precognition of their intertwined fates. Next she would seek a brother or companion with whom she was more likely to surrender erotically. Salomé learned that her independence from any one man came from positioning herself between two men who loved her equally."

Rather than examine each relationship as if it occurred in a self-enclosed bubble, *Three in Love* examines its subjects as whole people, citing their contributions to society. Along the way, we're also treated to large doses of history, myth, religion, philosophy, and insight into art and literature. The writing isn't always as lively as I would prefer, but I have the feeling that this is because the authors were trying to write for the historical record. I think they've succeeded. Their book is an important contribution not just to polyamory but to the entire history of sexuality.

HarperSanFrancisco (HarperCollins Publishers); $25
1997; hardcover; 454 pp
illus; 0-06-251295-1

BOYLOVE AND GIRL-LOVE

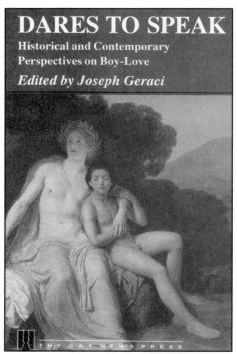

Cover painting is a detail from <u>Apollo, Hyacinthus and Cyparyssus Singing and Playing</u> (1831–1834) by Alexander Ivanov. *Dares To Speak.*

adolescent and preadolescent girls, along with some related subjects such as adult/child sex, adult/teen sex, and censorship. Surely the most controversial offerings are the photography books, featuring the work of Jock Sturges, David Hamilton, Sally Mann, Jan Saudek, and others who create underage nude images. The section of fine art books contains the work of Balthus, Graham Ovenden, and other artists who paint or draw girls in the buff. Erotic comix and manga (Japanese comix), postcards, and nudist videos round out the visual offerings.

Among the fiction — a surprising amount of which is from the big corporate publishers — you'll find *The Lover* by Marguerite Duras, *Nude Men* by Amanda Filipacchi, *Two Erotic Tales* by Pierre Louÿs, *First Love* by Joyce Carol Oates, *Belinda* by Anne Rice, *The Enchanter* and (obviously) *Lolita* by Vladimir Nabokov, and the *Too Young* anthologies of erotica. Real-life encounters are detailed in several books, including *Erotic Experiences of Girls and Men* and Duras's *The North China Lover*.

Of historical note are two books on Lewis Carroll, one on Mark Twain (rumoured to be a girl-lover), *Girl-Love and Girl-Lust in 19th Century England*, *Child Loving: The Erotic Child and Victorian Culture*, and *Passion and Power: Sexuality in History*. Sociological, psychological, and legal studies include *Paedophilia: A Factual Report*, *Long Range Effects of Child and Adolescent Sexual Experiences*, *Childhood and Sexuality: A Radical Christian Approach*, and *Ar-*

ALESSANDRA'S SMILE CATALOGUE

The illustrated catalogue for Alessandra's Smile, Inc. — formerly known as Ophelia Editions — offers almost 100 publications that have to do with the sexuality and eroticism of resting Images: Impolitic Art and Uncivil Actions. Issues of several periodicals are also available — Asia File, Paidika, uncommon desires newsletter, and Vogue Bambini.

Alessandra also puts out two supplemental catalogues. One offers copies of out-of-print books which run along the same lines as the main catalogue. Three bucks will get you the next quarterly list that comes out. The other catalogue has a small number of art books that focus on boys, usually in the nude. It can be had by simply asking for it when you order the main catalogue.

Alessandra's Smile is a unique operation. No one else is offering such a concentration of material focusing on one of the most staunchly forbidden aspects of sexuality. The proprietors must have nerves of steel and icewater in their veins.

Alessandra's Smile, Inc/PO Box 2377/New York NY 10185-2377
Catalogue: $3
WWW: www.alessandrasmile.com

BOYS SPEAK OUT ON MAN/BOY LOVE
edited by David Miller

The best-selling of the North American Man/Boy Love Association's booklets, this one in many ways is the most heretical. In it, twenty-five teens and preteens give their side of the story, explaining that their relationships with adult men were/are consensual, enjoyable, and very important to them. One contributor writes: "I am 18, and have been having sex with older men since I was 12. I was a pubescent sex fiend, always picking up men at the park, shooting off with them, then usually never seeing them again. Like other horny boys my age, I knew what I wanted, and I knew how to get it." In an interview, an 11-year-old Dutch boy talks about starting to have sex when he was eight or nine. "… first he asked me if it was okay. He said, 'If you don't like it, you've got to tell me.' And then he did this with his hand… he did that for a little while, a few days. Because I lived very close to him, I came by a lot. And finally, I think it was four weeks later, I did it to him, too. And two weeks later we had complete sex, almost every day we had sex, every day that I came."

Many of the relationships involve much more than sex, though. Greg in Philadelphia says, "I am 16 years old, and have been involved in a boy-man relationship since I was 12, and I am still with the same man. My life is far better now since meeting this guy four years ago. At first there was plenty of sex and fooling around with each other, and today we are great friends and continue to have great sex. I feel he sincerely loves me, and I love him. My relationship, although frowned upon by society, is the best thing that ever happened to me. You may use my name if you wish. I am proud of my relationship." A 12-½-year-old writes of his 23-year-old lover: "It's good to have him to love. He protects me and takes me out and treats me like I'm special. He never hurts me or tells me to do anything. He lets me make it clear to him when I want to do something… We never argue, and he treats me like a lover and friend, not a child."

This booklet also contains several articles on man/boy love, including "It's Adults Who Are Screwed Up About Sex" from Lesbian Gay Youth Magazine, "Teens Charge Cops

Threatened Them with Rape", and "I Know What I Am: Gay Teenagers and the Law".

NAMBLA; $3.95
1981, 1996; staple-bound booklet; 64 pp
no ISBN

DARES TO SPEAK
Historical and Contemporary Perspectives on Boy-Love
edited by Joseph Geraci

Dares to Speak reprints seventeen selections from Paidika, a Dutch journal devoted to paedophilia (attraction to pre-adolescents) and ephebophilia (attraction to adolescents). Paidika focuses almost exclusively on man/boy interaction, with the exceptions of articles that cover minors of both sexes and a special issue on woman/girl relationships (none of the articles concerning this practically unstudied topic is in this anthology, however).

The first section studies man/boy love from the ancient to the recent past in a variety of geographical areas. One cross-cultural article by Robert Bausman finds that in many societies throughout history these intergenerational relationships were accepted and even expected. In feudal Japan, boylove was practised and idealised by Samurai (who considered it "manly and heroic") and Buddhist clergy, whose vows of chastity forbade women but not boys. The behaviour appears as an ingrained part of society for centuries in classical Greece, New Guinea, the Melanesian Islands, the Azande tribe of Africa, and Morocco. The author quotes a 1926 book by an anthropologist as saying, "… it is common belief among the Arabic-speaking mountaineers of Northern Morocco that a boy cannot learn the Koran unless a scribe commits pederasty with him." Other articles in this section include a history of the Dutch pedophile liberation movement by the man who started it, "Celtic Pederasty in Pre-Roman Gaul", "The Irresistible Beauty of Boys: Middle Eastern Attitudes about Boy-Love", a short story by John Henry MacKay, and excerpts from A Defense of Uranian Love, a massive three-volume celebration of boylove published in 1928-30.

The book's second section looks at current concerns and attitudes. In an updated version of "The Hysteria Over Child Pornography and Paedophilia", which won the prestigious HL Mencken Award for investigative journalism in its original form, Lawrence A. Stanley states: "A number of experts who have observed the child pornography 'industry' from its beginning to its demise generally agree that the number of minors depicted in these magazines and films did not exceed between five and seven thousand world-wide. The children who participated in child pornography were not generally runaways, prostitutes, or drug addicts. They were also not the victims of kidnapping. Most were from middle-class homes and well-acquainted with the adult or adults for or with whom they posed… No children whose photographs appeared in child pornography magazines and films were ever known or even suspected to have been the victims of murder." Other selections include an interview with pre-eminent sexologist Vern Bullough, a look at the dramatic liberalisation of the Dutch age of consent law in 1990, a critical examination of the Satanic abuse panic, and a controversial interview with two of the most vocal proponents of false memory syndrome, the theory that most repressed memories of supposed childhood sexual abuse are bogus.

Dares to Speak presents lots of hard-to-find information on a radioactive topic. If you want to find out more about boylove for whatever reason (love it, hate it, curious about it), this is a crucial book.

The Gay Men's Press; £14.95, $19.95US
1997; softcover; 283 pp
0-85449-241-0

MICHAEL JACKSON WAS MY LOVER
The Secret Diary of Jordan Chandler
(Second Edition)
by Victor M. Gutierrez

OK, you can say I've sunk to new lows of tabloidism by choosing to review *Michael Jackson Was My Lover*, but I just couldn't resist covering a book that not only deals with an extremely controversial topic but is also total lawsuit bait. In fact, this book is so ripe for legal retaliation that even the publisher's *name* doesn't appear anywhere on or in it (although it does have an ISBN, which means the publisher is traceable). The copyright page contains the line, "Inscription No. 95.144 Santiago, Chile", which indicates that it was published in Chile, undoubtedly because no North American or UK publisher would touch it with a ten-foot pole. Perhaps Chile has much more lenient or ill-defined libel laws.

Investigative reporter Victor Gutierrez, who lives in Los Angeles, is probably the reporter with the most knowledge about the accusations concerning Michael Jackson's alleged attraction towards boys aged seven through thirteen. In fact, Gutierrez began his investigations into the matter three years before it made headlines all over the world. When the accusations involving Jordan Chandler — a boy who was eleven when he first started seeing Jackson — broke loose in the summer of 1993, it provided the journalist with the info he needed. Although Jackson eventually paid Chandler $20 million to keep quiet, the diary that Chandler had kept all through the relationship was leaked. Using this, plus legal documents and interviews with Jackson's former guards, housekeepers, child friends, and other people with first-hand knowledge, Gutierrez has put together an uncensored report that dispenses with words like "allegedly" and "supposedly" and often uses Chandler's own words to describe key events.

According to the book, when Jackson and Chandler went to Monaco in May 1993, they had their first sexual encounter (up to that point they had been making out) when they took a bath together. It is described entirely by Chandler himself: "'I could touch and feel his body. I felt his erect penis in my hands. Michael told me to keep touching it, that it felt incredible. As I did, Michael moved his hips towards me. He asked me to rub his penis and showed me how… We played this game until he put his hand over mine and together we began to masturbate him until he came on my legs and in the bath. He then made me sit on the edge of the bathtub and began to masturbate and then suck my penis.'"

Total lawsuit-bait, fresh from Chile.
Michael Jackson Was My Lover.

Later, Chandler is quoted explaining his relationship with Jackson. "'It wasn't the games we played or the expensive presents. It was the attention and love we received from Jackson,' declared Jordie to a close friend. 'On many occasions I tried to tell the therapist and the authorities that Michael never made me do anything I didn't want to but the authorities had told me that Michael had seduced me by buying toys and expensive presents. The attention and love he gave me was amazing. He always worried with details. He spent time with me. I was an important part of his life, a man that was so busy.'"

Gutierrez gives an extremely detailed narrative that describes the first times Jackson and Chandler met, their blossoming relationship, full descriptions of their alleged sexual activities, Jackson's treatment of Chandler's family, the legal action created by Chandler's biological father, the investigation of the charges, the criminal and civil proceedings against Jackson, and the aftermath. He also discusses other boys whom he claims Jackson had sexual contact with, including young actors. Mixed in with all this are extremely unflattering accusations of a non-sexual nature, including allegations that Jackson hates black people, that he is neglectful and even actively sadistic towards the animals in his private zoo, and that he wears a U-shaped prosthesis to give his nose shape because all the cartilage has been destroyed from repeated plastic surgery.

This book contains a long section of illustrations, including reproductions of the hand-written description and drawing of Jackson's penis that Chandler gave his father, a photo

Chandler took of Jackson wearing pyjamas and sitting on the boy's bed, a photograph from the infamous examination of Jackson's body by authorities (the photo, though, doesn't show Jackson's genitals but rather his eye area, demonstrating how black he is without all his makeup), and primary documents, including contracts, medical reports, and Chandler's original chronology of events.

Although there's no way to get this book from its mysterious publisher, it is available from Atomic Books [see Appendix A] and the online bookstore Amazon.com. This book is already very hard to find. If you want it, grab it before it completely disappears.

unknown publisher; $19.95
1996, 1997; softcover; 216 pp
illus; 956-272-305-4

NOT FADE AWAY
Selections from the NAMBLA Bulletin
edited by anonymous

The goal of the North American Man/Boy Love Association "is to end the oppression of men and boys who love each other." To that end, they work for the repeal of age of consent laws and for the social acceptance of the idea that minors are capable of engaging in consensual sexual and/or romantic relationships with adults.

Because of its stance, NAMBLA just might be the most hated and feared open membership organisation in the US. The authorities want it eradicated, the portion of the general public that knows about it hates it with a passion, and even many gays and lesbians scorn it. Among its more powerful, active enemies are the FBI, the UN, and the New York legislature. Even in many — if not most — radical circles, the name NAMBLA is anathema, instantly triggering derision and even outright hatred. There are a few exceptions. Camille Paglia, Allen Ginsberg, Samuel Delany, Kate Millet, Pat Califia, Scott O'Hara, Hakim Bey, and many founders of the gay liberation movement (including Harry Hay and Jim Kepner) have all voiced support for the group and/or its principles. Still, condemnation is often shrill and nearly universal.

Somehow NAMBLA has managed to survive for over twenty years. This booklet presents eighteen written pieces and numerous graphics from their Bulletin, the production of which has become their principle activity. One article discusses a landmark court ruling from 1981. A man who pled guilty to masturbating and fellating an eleven- and thirteen-year-old was found to be a "Sexually Dangerous Person" (SDP) and locked up in a maximum security prison for life with no parole. A Massachusetts judge reversed the finding that the man was an SDP and ruled that he may be placed in a different prison and will be eligible for parole at the usual time periods. Addressing the defence's contention that the boys consented to the encounters, the judge declared: "The evidence showed that the petitioner's sexual contact with boys was in consensual and mutually agreed upon circumstances… [and] there is no evidence of petitioner's propensity to inflict physical or psychological injury on others."

"'Victim' Joins NAMBLA" reveals that a sixteen-year-old who had been questioned in relation to the arrests of nine men on charges of having sex with underage boys is now an active member of NAMBLA, supporting the accused. "Baker stated, 'We must get these men out of jail, and we must get all these charges dropped. I don't want to see Karl, or any of the other men go to jail. If we (kids) have to go and protest in front of the court houses, then we will protest, but we do not want to see our friends go to jail.'"

In "Sappho Was a Right-on Pedophile", Linda Frankel points out that the spiritual mother of lesbianism had sex with her adolescent pupils. "The Unicorn", a column written by a self-proclaimed "eleven-year-old faggot" argues for the sexual rights of children. Other selections include "Police Threaten New Jersey Family", "The Masturbating Child", "The Politics of Ageism", Antler's poem "The Immortality of Boylove", and a review of the movie Pixote.

NAMBLA; $3.95
no date; staplebound booklet; 56 pp
heavily illus; no ISBN

THE PHOTOGRAPHER'S SWEETHEARTS
by Diana Hartog

The Photographer's Sweethearts is a most unusual novel. It is told from the point of view of a paedophile, but it's not at all what you'd expect. Instead of being written in a sensationalistic manner as a profoundly disturbing look into a diseased, psychotic mind, this story — based on the life of a real person — gives us a complex portrait of a man who desired to be in the company of children, in every way possible.

Louie Olsen was born in Denmark in 1879 (which accounts for the thick dialect in which this first-person narrative is written). In 1902, he left his homeland for Canada, in order to see for himself the beautiful forests of the North American West Coast. Eventually settling in California, he works as a lumberjack, despite suffering pangs of conscience for killing trees. We find that Louie is something of a mystic, a proto-New Age subscriber to herbal healing, Rosicrucian mysticism, and the belief that each one of us can become a Christ. He believes that his two purposes in life are to heal people and to see Yosemite. Louie is also a photographer. Using his bulky camera and glass plates, he takes pictures of virginal forests… and naked children. His goal is to collect these child nudes into a book. In explaining why he wants to do this, we get a glimpse of his feeling towards children: "In my young manhood a Vision came to me, that a picture book of nude, beautiful children would turn people towards appreciation for what the cosmos has given us, also teaching what the use of sex is, and the beauty of children."

Further insight into Louie's attraction comes after he has secretly watched a group of young cousins engaged in sex play on a river bank. After they leave, he walks to where they had been. "At every direction the landscape trembled in its Radiance. This am the true state of the earth, and children live this and am part of this trembling dance, a dance what grows in them so strong and fearless that they must leap and shout and tumble over each other, for they dwell still in the Kingdom of Heaven… Alas no more could I be as those children, blind to all but innocent life. In me then was a great longing to dwell with them in that Kingdom, knowing no other. And filling me now is sad joy, to have learned of these two worlds, what exist one within the other at all times."

Through flashbacks, letters to his younger brother Hans, and reprinted court documents, the book covers Louie's life from early boyhood almost to his death. During that time, he has sexual contact with many children and teenagers of both genders. He never forms a sexual or romantic relationship with an adult, although he feels comfortable around adults and has no problem relating to them. The one great love of his life was Kristjiana, a six-year-old Norwegian girl he met in Denmark when he was sixteen. Her mother found them naked on a beach, took the girl away, and Louie never saw her again.

The first time Louie got into trouble for his activities was in 1946 when he allowed two twelve-year-old boys and a six-year-old girl to have sex with each other in his apartment. This part of the story is told through transcripts of the boys' testimony and other official documents. As always, the author refuses to make things black and white for us. Louie claims that he never suggested or encouraged the children to have sex, that it was something they wanted to do themselves. In court, the questioning of the boys supports this claim, up to a point. However, Louie did help the girl off with her clothes after she told the boys she wanted to "do it," he told the boys how to have sex, and he rubbed lubricant on the penis of one of the boys.

This grey area runs throughout the whole book. Sometimes a child enjoys or actually seeks out Louie's attention, but at other times the child is scared or uncomfortable but Louie doesn't stop. At one point — during the book's only instance of Louie engaging in vaginal intercourse — he has sex with a sleeping girl, who he believes contains the spirit of his beloved Kristjiana. Most of the time Louie defends his actions — both to others and to himself — but occasionally there are moments when it appears that he is questioning the rightness of what he is doing. The most obvious instance occurs when he tells a woman he works for that he is going to die a terrible, painful death. She asks him whether or not, having foreknowledge of this event, he can avoid it. He replies: "Mam, I would not care to. At his End, if a man escapes justice he dont escape his own conscience and the Immutable Record it holds of wrong doing. This Record is gathered up in the desire body, to be read when the soul passes over to the First Heaven — and thereby will he suffer, till in deed he screams regret that his punishment might have been meted out while on earth."

The Photographer's Sweethearts is not easy reading in any sense of the word. Louie's unusual dialect and the narrative's constant shifting in time frames make this a fairly dense work to make your way through. Furthermore, its refusal to tell us what to think and its insistence that you draw your own conclusions will undoubtedly bother many people, but that's what makes this such a powerful and unsettling work.

The Overlook Press; $13.95
1996; softcover; 240 pp
0-87951-796-4

uncommon desires newsletter

Put out by the folks at Alessandra's Smile [above], *uncommon desires* is a digest-sized zine that deals with attraction to girls under eighteen. It offers an alternative to the hysteria and unrelentingly sex-negative attitudes that surround this topic, which is becoming more — not less — taboo with every passing day. The general tenor of this publication is that adult/adolescent relations need to be examined more openly and honestly, that sexual attraction to underage girls is natural and nothing to be ashamed of, and that the legal and social attitudes towards anything having to do with adolescent sexuality are ill-informed and unnecessarily harsh.

In the most recent issue (#26), attorney Lawrence A. Stanley carefully examines the US's little-known sex travel laws (similar laws exist in other countries). Under these laws, if you travel or make plans to travel to another country with even the *intent* of having sex with someone under sixteen — no matter what the age of consent is in that country — you have committed a felony. Even if you never have any sexual contact at all, you are looking at mandatory minimum sentences of eighteen months (if the other person is twelve to fifteen) or 108 months (if the other person is under twelve).

The issue also contains a review of and small excerpts from the book *Going All the Way: Teenage Girls' Tales of Sex, Romance and Pregnancy*, written by feminist Sharon Thompson and published by the highly respected Hill & Wang. Thompson conducted interviews for almost a decade with girls aged thirteen to seventeen and found that — contrary to what society would like to believe — they are horny and they often actively seek out older men for sex. Thompson writes: "What all the girls who went after adults said they wanted was sex. And while a few accounts ended in marriage or living together as well as with pregnancy, those were not the narrated goals. Sex was."

Other pieces include an article on underage prostitution, the supposedly true story of a man's paid encounter with a fourteen-year-old in an unnamed country, a badly written piece of erotica about a 23-year-old guy and a thirteen-year-old girl, some teen girl spanking experiences from the Internet, and a smattering of brief items highlighting laws, movies, and reportage regarding adult-teen sex. As with every issue, this one is illustrated with several photos of girls — usually nude — who are in the early stages of adolescence. A statement on the back covers explains, "None of the images contained herein is, or is intended to be, unlawful under federal law. Each image has been reviewed and approved by several attorneys and is reproduced as an example of lawful images on what is, for many people, an extremely confusing subject."

Due to the actions of the authorities, the unillustrated version of *udn* will be sent to the UK.

Alessandra's Smile, Inc./PO Box 2377/New York NY 10185
WWW: www.alessandrasmile.com/udn.htm
Single issue: $4.50. Can: $5. Elsewhere: $5.50
Six issue sub: $22. Can: $25. Elsewhere: $30

PORNOGRAPHY

LOVERS
An Intimate Portrait, Volume 2 — Jennifer and Steve

Candida Royalle's company Femme Distribution has consistently broken new ground by creating "feminist porn" films. These videos present the totality of lovemaking, showing each partner giving and receiving. The focus is on whole bodies, not just genitals... on foreplay, oral sex, screwing, orgasm, and other sex activities, not just come shots.

In the *Lovers* series, Femme devotes each film to one couple, delving into their sexual relationship. In *Volume 2* we meet Jennifer — a college-educated full-time stripper with a pierced nostril — and Steve, a West Coast filmmaker who sports a ponytail. The first part of the film cuts back and forth between the two of them separately talking about their professions, how they met, their first time, what they like about each other, and so on. Jennifer admits that she's a lifelong exhibitionist who wants every man in the world to want to fuck her. We see her performing an intense strip at her club. She fondles her breasts, puts her pussy right up to a patron's face, then fingers herself and lets him suck her finger.

The rest of the tape shows Jen and Steve doing all kinds of sexual things to each other, while they talk about their lovemaking in voice-over. She sucks his cock, he eats her out, they soul kiss deeply, they fuck in a number of positions. The heat gets cranked up a notch when we find out that Jennifer is a submissive who loves to be degraded and punished. The couple is not heavily into SM, with elaborate scenes, props, or costumes... what they're doing is basically bondage and discipline. Steve ties Jennifer's wrists together, spits on her, calls her names, smacks her ass, pulls her hair, acts out one of her rape fantasies, and commands her to be still while he tickles her with his mouth. At one point, when her hands are tied, he gets her turned on and then leaves, forcing her to masturbate if she wants any pleasure. Later on, Steve fists her and they have anal sex.

Lovers Volume 2 provides voyeuristic thrills and lots of heavy-duty, sweaty banging. (As far as I'm aware, it's also the first Femme film to show a male orgasm.) This is a vast improvement over the first tape in this series [*Outposts* p 82], mainly because Jennifer and Steve are likeable. It risks the wrath of many women because it shows that some women actually like being tied up, demeaned, and fucked roughly (as long as it's done by the right person). Being sexually liberated means having the kind of sex *you* want to have, no matter who might find it offensive.

Femme Distribution; $29.95
1994; VHS video; 75 min

MAKING IT BIG
Sex Stars, Porn Films, and Me
by Chi Chi LaRue with John Erich

Making It Big is the autobiography of gay porn director Chi Chi LaRue, a self-described "homosexual lad, effeminate of manner and portly in girth" who became "a 300-pound drag queen". After working in the sales aspect of the porn biz, LaRue started directing and quickly became a phenom. He has directed over 100 full-length sex films and helped revitalise the world of gay sex movies. In the first chapter, which is something of an introduction, LaRue very conveniently (for me) summarises the rest of his book: "I'll cover breaking into the business, giving an intimate firsthand account of how I did so; the science of making a porn flick, examining some of my own best and what I think made them good; revealing personal glances into the lives of the hottest boys in the business, some of whom I discovered, some of whom I merely had the lucky opportunity to work with; the fine art of drag, including creating and maintaining a look that will dazzle your fans; the timeless art of performing, working a crowd and projecting an authentic 'star' aura; the upsides and downsides of fame, including the uninhibited sex, the unchecked drug use, and the exotic flights of fancy to glamorous locations around the world; and, finally, a few thoughts on where we're headed and what's next for the industry I love. Fasten your seatbelt, sweetie, it's going to be a wild ride."

Alyson Publications; $12.95
1997; softcover; 268 pp
illus; 1-55583-392-6

MY SURRENDER

In this "couples friendly" film from Femme Productions, the curvaceous, short-haired Jeanna Fine plays April, the owner of a production company that makes videos of couples acting out their sexual fantasies. These tapes aren't for general consumption but are for the couples' own private viewing pleasure. While April is filming all this sex, however, she herself is celibate. There's a suitably good-looking fellow with Bon Jovi hair who she went out with, but she's pulled away from him because she's afraid of getting into a relationship.

April sits at her editing console, getting horny as she watches footage she's filmed and sighing over a videotaped message her would-be beau, Robert, has sent her, asking why she will no longer see him. In the first sex scene, April films a couple (who, like the others in this film, are real-life couples) playing out their fantasy scene of naughty schoolgirl and stern professor. After she tries to kiss him, "Professor sir" bends her over the desk and spanks her bum while verbally chastising this "nasty tart". Soon Kelly is on her knees — then on the desk — giving him a extensive, show-stopping blowjob up to orgasm. This scene rocks so hard because, besides possessing a mouth that would make Bill Clinton have a fit, Kelly is a technically proficient suckstress who obviously relishes what she's doing.

In the next scene, involving another couple, the woman is a stogie-chomping porn producer who gives the auditioning stud a workout on the casting couch. While editing this video, April falls asleep and dreams that Robert has come in and started making slow, passionate love to her, but she wakes up as the momentum starts to build. She then films the movie's third couple, a bald guy and a slinky brunette who pretend they're at the funeral for her husband, who is also the man's estranged brother. Grief turns to lust, and soon they're plowing right in front of the deceased's coffin. Finally, April realises why she's been running from Robert. She sends him a video explanation, and soon the two of them are getting it on in the movie's final scene.

With an imaginative narrative structure, some hot scenes (including a 100% BJ quota, the highest I can recall in a Femme film), a non-sexual cameo by the gorgeous Candida Royalle herself, and a good acting job by Fine (her "explanation scene", in particular, was surprisingly effective), *My Surrender* is just the ticket for anyone who wants explicit action tempered with some class.

Femme Productions; $29.95

1996, VHS videocassette; 80 min

PLATINUM CATALOGUE

Platinum specialises in videos and some magazines concentrating on five of your favourite kinks — enemas, foot worship, spanking, nude catfighting, and tickling. They also have a smattering of material on SM, rubber, leg and ass worship, transgendered people, and pregos. For those of you who want to practice what you watch, Platinum offers enema supplies and small selection of sex toys.

Platinum's catalogue is an eight page brochure that comes out quite often. The first one is free, but you have to pay to receive them regularly.

Platinum/4501 Van Nuys Blvd, Ste 215/Sherman Oaks CA 91403

Single issue: free

One year sub: $5. Non-US: $15

THE X FACTORY
Inside the American
Hardcore Film Industry

by Anthony Petkovich

Even those of us who enjoy good-ole hardcore pornography often don't know much about how it's made or what it's like to be involved in it. How does one break into porn? How long is a typical day? How much do you get paid? Do you really enjoy the sex? And, the most obvious question of all, what's it like when your job is to get laid all day? In *The X Factory*, freelance writer and long-time pornoisseur (since 1979) Anthony Petkovich penetrates America's heterosexual hardcore movie industry and brings back 26 interviews, all but five of which are with female stars, including Christi Lake, Danielle, Cumisha Amado, Nyrobi Nights, Saki, Nina Cherry, and Krysti Lynn. His manner is relaxed and natural, which helps bring out some interesting answers, and his questions range from raunchy through personal to political. He asks most of the women about their first sexual experiences, how they got into porn, and why they have or haven't gotten a boob job. He also probes the women about their favourite co-stars and scenes, and how they feel about performing a variety of sex acts, such as anal sex, double penetration, bondage, and girl-girl scenes. All the non-white actresses are asked about racism in the porn industry, and some of the women comment on men's control of the business. A few of the actresses talk about the other roles they play in the world of porn movies, including director and producer.

Of the remaining interviews, four are with male directors of porn (Gregory *New Wave Hookers* Dark, John *Fresh Meat* Leslie, Patrick *Sodomania* Collins, Bruce *Buttslammers* Seven), and the fifth is with camera operator Michael Cates. While I have read many interviews with porn stars and directors before *The X Factory*, this is the first interview I've read with someone who actually operates the cameras that are supposed to catch every last bit of gooey sex. In the three remaining pieces, Petkovich gives an insider's view of being on the set during the filming of three X films, including *World's Biggest Gang Bang 2* and *Buttslammers 6: Over the Edge!* "Kaitlyn's laying on her back now, her legs spread from coast to coast, her mouth gaping wide. Vicki sits on the mouth. As Kaitlyn munches muff, she slaps Vicky's jiggly ass cheeks. In the meantime, Suzie's [sic] works diligently on both of Kaitlyn's orifices — with both hands! The girls soon have Kaitlyn in the doggie position, her luscious (now oiled and shiny) creamy white ass fills up the camera lens. While Suzie plunges a purple-and-white streaked love popsicle in and out of Kaitlyn's pussy, Vicky services the captive's clit with a mini-vibrator."

As with most books from this publisher, *The X Factory* is absolutely stuffed with photographs. You literally can't open the book without seeing at least one picture, usually two, and sometimes more. There are breasts and butts a-plenty, with a generous amount of pubic hair and exposed lips visible. Because of British law, though, you won't be seeing any dicks or penetration.

Critical Vision (Headpress); £12.95, $19.95

1997; softcover; 208 pp

heavily illus; 0-9523288-7-9

XXX
A Woman's Right to Pornography

by Wendy McElroy

Wendy McElroy is a past president of Feminists for Free Expression (Canada), a pro-porn, pro-sex, anti-censorship feminist group. In *XXX*, McElroy elaborates on this pornography-friendly feminist stance, which may seem impossibly contradictory to those unfamiliar with it. Naturally, McElroy and others in the same camp defend porn's right to exist on First Amendment grounds, but their arguments go way beyond that. "I contend: Pornography benefits women, both personally and politically." McElroy goes on to expound five ways that porn benefits women personally and four ways it benefits them politically. In the personal realm: "It provides sexual information on at least three levels: it gives a panoramic view of the world's sexual possibilities; it allows women to 'safely' experience sexual alternatives; and, it provides a different form of information than can be found in textbooks or discussions."

On the political level: "Historically, pornography and feminism have been fellow travellers and natural allies." On the surface, that statement may not be apparently true, but that's because we've been brainwashed by the "feminist Puritans" who took over feminism in the 1980s. Pornography and feminism "both focus on women as sexual beings. Pornography dwells on the physical act itself; feminism examines the impact of sex upon women — historically, economically, politically, and culturally." McElroy's prescription is "for the feminist movement as a whole to become 'improper' and so outrageous as to suggest that sex can be fun and fulfilling. It is time to take sex out of politics and to put it back into the bedroom, where it belongs. Sex is a private choice, not a political matter open to a majority vote. it is a rebellious process of self-discovery."

But *XXX* is more than just theorising. Realising that she knew almost nothing about the porn industry, McElroy dove in headfirst, going to conventions and talking to producers and stars — male and female — of porn movies. She found that there is no more sexual coercion in the porn industry than in any other industry (every type of business has bosses who sexually harass female employees). The main problem is that the courts consider lawsuits by harassed sex workers to be frivolous. If porn were legitimised, the women would have the same protection as their counterparts in other jobs.

When talking to the women in the industry, McElroy discovered "the women I encountered were not victims. They were rebellious, a bit raunchy, shrewd at business, and they didn't take shit from anyone." While engaged in a casual conversation with the author, porn actress Veronica Hart railed at the notions of radical feminist Andrea Dworkin: "'I don't need Andrea Dworkin to tell me what to think or how to behave.' She seemed genuinely angry. 'And I don't appreciate being called psychologically damaged! I have friends in the business who call themselves "Anarchists in High Heels." They'd love to have a word with her.'"

In one chapter, McElroy gives a depressing history of the suppression of sexual speech in America, which denied women and men the right to read or write about contraception, venereal disease, marital rape, and other subjects crucial to understanding sexuality. Another chapter is devoted to interviews with women in porn, particularly those who are part of the sex positive movement — porn star Nina Hartley, feminist porn producers Candida Royalle and Crystal Wilder, Brenda Loew Tatelbaum (publisher of *EIDOS* [*Outposts* p 115]), and others.

XXX is a ringing defence of porn and a good introduction to the ever-growing pro-porn wing of feminism.

St. Martins; $12.95
1995; softcover; 248 pp
0-312-15245-0

OTHER SEX WORK

THE BROTHEL BIBLE
"The Cathouse Experience"
by Sisters of the Heart

The number of writings by and about sex workers has been increasing dramatically over the last few years, but, until now, I don't recall seeing a book written by someone who has worked as a legal prostitute in Nevada's brothels. Carole Rollins-Eddington (who uses the pen names "Ruby" and "Sisters of the Heart") went to work in the cat houses after earning three college degrees, becoming a PhD candidate at UC Berkeley, and co-owning a record production company, among other accomplishments. Surprisingly, she was 44 when she made the career move, and she stayed for four years, until she became physically and mentally burned out. The reasons she gives for becoming a prostitute are largely negative — fighting her mid-life crisis, trying to prove her sexual attractiveness, low self-esteem after years of emotionally abusive relationships and a recent physically abusive marriage, sex addiction, and more.

Still, her experiences as a brothel worker were not entirely negative. She reports that a lot depended on the working conditions and the relationship between the workers and management. "You can feel a warm, relaxed energy when there is harmony present in a house, or you can feel a coldness, hostility and tension when owners or management are more uncaring or calculating and treat the girls less humanely." Some of the places she worked were swanky, and in some she became close to some of the managers and other workers. In others, she reports being virtually a prisoner. "We were often times locked up in houses with sealed up and boarded windows, with no fresh air circulating or daylight allowed, with walls that had been ingrained with dirt from years of use. Imprisoned, by choice, for weeks at a time."

As for what kind of woman works at the houses, the author says, "We are human just like you. We have feelings, emotions and families. We grew up in rich, middle class and poor neighbourhoods. We come from all 'walks of life'. We arrive in Nevada from all over the world. We come for the money, the excitement and glamour — just like you do."

Rollins-Eddington explains what day-to-day life is like in the various brothels, the relationships between the workers (which range from sisterhood to back-stabbing), how men pick the women they want, how fees and acts are negotiated, the various sex acts that are performed, how much money the workers make (generally $2000 to $4000 a week and sometimes much more), and other topics. One chapter discusses the clientele the author dealt with — the old and young men, the men of various nationalities, and the "occasional hunks"; the New Age guru, the preacher's son with a disfigured face, the man who left a $2000 tip, and the guy whose dick was ten inches long while soft (he was politely asked to leave because no one would service him).

While the writing style could use technical improvement, *The Brothel Bible* easily earns its worth as an unprecedented inside look at the only legal form of prostitution in the US.

Sisters of the Heart; $12.95
1997; softcover; 119 pp
illus; 0-9657525-1-8
WWW: www.brothelbible.com

CALL ME MISTRESS
Memoirs of a Phone Sex Performer
by Natalie Rhys

At night Natalie Rhys, a conservative-looking 45-year-old systems analyst, becomes a steamy phone sex worker. In these explicit telephonic memoirs, she discusses her typical and atypical calls and adds her own keen insights into the motives of her callers and herself. She will do (and has done) just about any phone fantasy that her clients want. "Phone sex is a vehicle for expressing 'unacceptable' desires and needs, for exploring feelings and experiences that would be way too intense or too painful in real life. It is a way of stretching the limits, going beyond the boundaries of socially acceptable behaviour, without hurting anyone."

She describes the different types of callers she gets. Most of them are dull and easy to work with. Many clients are "low- to moderate-energy callers" who don't have much initiative or imagination. Other callers are lonely, bored, or curious, while others are demanding, invasive, or arrogant. The high-energy callers who actively participate in a give-and-take way are the ones that make the job worthwhile for Rhys.

Just as there are many types of callers, there are also many types of calls. The "standard call" is a five to seven minute affair with your basic "hot talk" and graphic descriptions of sex. Rhys has a hard time with the "pseudo-intimate call", where the caller wants a meaningful encounter with lots of foreplay and lovey-doveyness. "I feel intruded on: I need to save tenderness and affection for my own relationships." Other types of calls include the bisexual call, the angry submissive call, the strict or heavy dominant call, the transvestite call, and the story fantasy.

Rhys describes some of the themes she encounters fairly frequently, which may be surprising to many people. Pissing and shitting on the caller (or having them do it to her) happens quite regularly. Two themes that don't occur as often but still surface on a regular basis are incest and child molestation. Rhys does these kinds of calls because "I figure that if I can do the call effectively, perhaps it will keep the caller from acting out the fantasy." She also often deals with ethnic and age stereotypes, such as African American men are hung, Asian women are sweet and meek, and older women know how to get it on.

One chapter covers some of Rhys' more out of the ordinary callers, who want to have sex with animals, who love women's worn panties, or who claim to have 16-inch dicks. In the last three chapters, she discusses the power of sex and fantasy, what other phone sex workers are like, and how this line of work has affected her personally.

As to why Rhys does phone sex, she gives her answer while telling about one of her callers who wanted to do a fantasy about his daughter. She constantly considered terminating the call. "But as usual I was curious. I also don't like to turn away from anything: running away from things I find distasteful seems cowardly to me. I feel that I need to face and acknowledge everything that exists — the farthest reaches of human behaviour — if I am going to figure out what life and people are all about." Amen, Natalie.

Miwok Press; $8.75

1993; softcover; 122 pp
0-9637672-0-8

LIVE SEX ACTS
Women Performing Erotic Labor
by Wendy Chapkis

Live Sex Acts contains a series of essays that offer a sophisticated analysis of prostitution (and, to a much lesser degree, other forms of sex work). Wendy Chapkis examines the positions of sex radical feminists (such as Pat Califia), radical feminists (such as Andrea Dworkin), and libertarian feminists (such as Camille Paglia), offering a synthesis of these ideas that comes down in favour of prostitution but doesn't ignore the dark sides of the profession. The essays are filled with long, substantial quotes from people with various positions on the issue, including many prostitutes. Each essay is followed by at least two shorter essays written by some of these same people, including Nina Hartley, Annie Sprinkle, a victim of forced prostitution, an indentured brothel worker, the director of the Dutch Foundation Against Trafficking in Women, a high class call girl, street prostitutes, a porn magazine model, a phone sex worker, the sheriff of Santa Cruz, California, co-directors of the prostitutes' rights group COYOTE, and a window prostitute in Amsterdam.

Routledge; $16.99
1997; softcover; 248 pp
illus; 0-415-91288-1

THE LUSTY LADY
by Erika Langley

With her photojournalism career going nowhere slowly, Erika Langley decided to do a project on nude dancers. When she approached the owners of Seattle's famous Lusty Lady — a peep arcade owned and run by female ex-dancers — they told her that if she wanted to shoot, she'd have to work as a dancer herself. Langley did, and five years later not only does she still work there ten to twelve hours a week, but her remarkable project has finally reached the general public in the form of this book. With over 60 black and white photographs — most of them dotted with medium to intense grain — and Langley's candid personal narrative, *The Lusty Lady* offers an unrivalled glimpse at an inner sanctum of sex work.

What gives the photos their power is the fact that Langley became "one of the girls". Rather than always being an outsider looking in, she became an insider documenting her own world. She earned the women's trust and even friendship, and they dropped all self-consciousness around her. In the meantime, Langley was learning a lot about herself, a process that is described with honesty and humour in the text. While talking to another of the dancers, she says, "I thought at first I would do a documentary about nude dancers, but I didn't think about how it would affect me. How it's creepy sometimes, and boring often, and rarely glamorous. It's changed me, working here, I like my body better, but I watch my weight more. I'm still attracted to men, but some days I hate 'em here. And I never thought I was bisexual, but I only find myself feeling more curious and confused."

An unrivalled glimpse at an inner sanctum of sex work. <u>April</u>, *The Lusty Lady.*

Throughout the book, she elaborates on her evolving feelings toward her body, her sexuality, men, money, and the work she's doing, while also including thoughts from her co-workers regarding the same subjects.

The pictures themselves are up-close and personal. Most of them were taken in the Lusty itself, either in the dressing areas or in the central mirrored room where the women dance. A few of the photos were taken from the little booths in which the patrons deposit quarters so the sliding door rises and they can look through the glass at the women. Mostly, though, the photos of the women in action were taken from the unique vantage point of the room itself. We see several naked bodies at a time — which seem like many more due to the large mirrors that totally cover the walls — writhing, reclining, crawling, spreading, doing splits, wrapping around the lucite poles. In a few of the shots, the dancers get physical with each other, and in one especially memorable one, three of them start a game of nude Twister.

At least as many of the shots show what's going on behind the scenes. The women are dressing and undressing, applying make-up, resting on the couch, looking pensive, joking around, and occasionally engaging in sex. Above all, the images contain a surprisingly high amount of laughter, smiles, and camaraderie. This is due not only to the female management but also the fact that the dancers don't receive tips and don't have to hustle men for private dances. This lack of competition allows feelings of friendship and warmth to grow among many of the women.

A short section towards the middle of the book focuses on seven of the dancers, photographing each one in the outside world, at home, with family and friends, etc., while letting them express their thoughts and experiences regarding sex work and sexuality. This obviously helps to humanise them, but two of the most subtley engaging shots appear in the main part of the book… they show several of the women, dressed in their civilian clothes, simply chatting and laughing as they wait for a worker's meeting to start.

Langley has done a perfect job capturing various aspects of these women, herself included (several of the shots show her getting naked and quite lusty). I was expecting this book to make its subjects into flesh and blood human beings. However, based on other documentary-style photos of nude dancers I've seen, I was also expecting the sexuality to be toned down. To her credit, Langley includes lots of highly erotic shots, not letting us forget why it's called "*sex work*" in the first place.

In the burgeoning number of books on sex work, *The Lusty Lady* earns an important spot by having a dancer invite us into her guarded, tightly-knit world.

Scalo (DAP); $34.95
1997; softcover; 255 pp
heavily illus; 3-931141-59-4

RED LIGHT
Inside the Sex Industry
by Sylvia Plachy & James Ridgeway

Using over 120 photos from *The Village Voice*'s award-winning photographer Sylvia Plachy, and text from *Voice* correspondent and author James Ridgeway, *Red Light* provides an insightful look at some of the people who make up the sex industry in New York City. The general tone is one of honesty… sex work is, after all, simply a form of work, although it has its own unique set of ups and downs.

Plachy and Ridgeway cover a wide range of activities that fall under the general rubric of sex work. Besides the obvious choices of nude dancing, prostitution and porno movies, they also look at phone sex, adult magazines and zines, cyberporn (CD-ROMs, BBSs, etc.), professional domination, crossdressing services, sex toys, and erotic performance art. Ridgeway is careful to be non-judgemental in his writing. He uses lots of quotes — sometimes several paragraphs long — from the workers themselves, revealing the positive, negative, and above all, realistic aspects of what they do. A phone sex worker explains the sly ways she gets her customers to ask specifically for her when they call back. A porn actor talks about the time during a shoot when an actress grabbed his hard dick and started singing into it as if it were a microphone. Several dancers comment on the demands of their male audience. "'It gets to the point,' Kim, another dancer, says bitterly, 'where it's, "What do I have to do? Whip out my uterus?"'" Another dancer discusses why she commutes. "'I'm a suburban go-go girl. Have G-string, will travel. I'm the road warrior of go-go. I will not shake my clam in front of a tragically hip East Village audience for $35 a night when I can be doing the same in New Jersey for $300 a night.'" A former male hustler, who went on to open

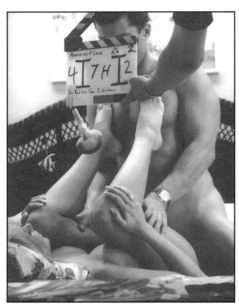

"It gets to the point," Kim, another dancer, says bitterly, "where it's, 'What do I have to do? Whip out my uterus?'" *Red Light*.

an erotic shaving service, talks about his days working for an escort service. "'It was vile… There was no sultry soundtrack. Blondie was not playing in the background. Richard Gere was nowhere in the picture. It was not *American Gigolo*."

Plachy's pictures capture the workers on the job, getting ready for and recovering from a day at work, and living the non-sex-related parts of their lives. In one shot done between takes, porn actress Lené is lying naked on a bed with her co-star kneeling between her legs as she talks to the director. A particularly revealing shot shows a woman with a very uncertain look on her face displaying her Greek goddess body to a beefy male in the foreground. *Screw* publisher Al Goldstein brandishes his rifle and pistol while sitting at his desk. A vampire dominatrix hovers over her slave, who is expectantly waiting to catch his Mistress's piss in a bowl on his chest. Ms. Rena Mason, a dominatrix, totally encases one of her submissives in concrete, only allowing him to breathe through a tube in his mouth. Gina, a male crossdressing performer, primps while wearing only pantyhose and high heels. A man hides his face, apparently in embarrassment, as a go-go dancer does her stuff right in front of him. A woman grabs a female dancer's calf and prepares to lick it at the lesbian Clit Club. At another club, a woman stuffs a tip into a male dancer's thong. A plastic surgeon who is popular among sex workers shows photos of his clients. In one shot we see Ivory fisting someone in front of a bunch of excited male and female onlookers at a bar. Then we see her at home, and it's almost impossible to tell that this tired, slightly vulnerable person is the same one who was in the other picture. In one of the book's final images, a social worker meets a prostitute on the sidewalk to tell her she's HIV-positive.

Even-handed and powerful in both pictures and words, *Red Light* is a surprisingly non-sensationalistic examination of the people who make up a part of the economy that remains hidden despite raking in billions of dollars annually.

powerHouse Books; $49.95
1996; hardcover; 255 pp
heavily illus; 1-57687-000-6

SEX WORK
Writings by Women in the Sex Industry
edited by Frédérique Delacoste & Priscilla Alexander

The mainstream feminist viewpoint is that sex work — prostitution, nude dancing, acting in porn, etc. — is horrible, degrading work that exploits individual women and undermines all womankind. The sex workers who wrote the over 50 essays in this book, however, offer a different take on things.

One of the best essays, "Good Girls Go to Heaven, Bad Girls Go Everywhere", does an exemplary job explaining why sex work is a positive, honourable career. The author — Aline — worked as a nude dancer and prostitute. One of her ancestors was a "witch" who was burned in Salem, and she is sure that if she had lived in those times, she would have met the same fate. "I've rejected motherhood, though I continue to 'mother' and nurture other human beings, and look forward to doing so throughout my life. I've enjoyed a career for over a decade nurturing and entertaining adult males… I contemptuously reject marriage, which all too often a form of unpaid, or indirectly paid, licensed, sanctioned, prostitution. Am I bound to become some kind of quasi-quaint old maid? Hardly. I'd rather suck cock than kiss ass!" In 1970 she became a topless dancer, discovering that it was fun and it made good money. "I much preferred exhibiting myself, flirting, showing off my body than working at some shit-job cleaning someone else's toilet for a poverty level income."

Of course, like any type of job, sex work has its downsides. Having to screw highly unappealing men is one of the drawbacks of prostitution, as poet and ex-prostitute Sapphire describes in "New York City Tonight": "It was makin' me wanna die vomit but the rent/tokens/dance classes/food/taxis/ clothes/telephone/gas/lites/books/food/rent/entertainment made me bite my lips an' say Oh baby/it feels so good/Ahhh/ oh yeah honey/do it daddy".

Although sex work is not inherently dehumanising, many of the social and legal attitudes that surround it make it that way. In her essay, Karen, a Bay Area prostitute, relates an incident in which a man wielding an icepick raped her for three hours and threatened to kill her. She escaped, and her friends were able to subdue the rapist till the cops showed up. "When I told them I wanted to press charges for rape, the officer would not take a police report." Their position was that "I was a prostitute and could not be raped."

In order to gain rights for sex workers, many current and former workers campaign for legalised prostitution and changes in attitudes surrounding all forms of sex work. This book contains information and statements from COYOTE (Call Off Your Old Tired Ethics), US PROStitutes Collective, and other organisations. Also included are the International Committee for Prostitutes' Rights World Charter and statements from the Second World Whores' Congress, which include the following denunciation: "… denial of human rights to prostitutes is publicly justified as a protection of women, public order, health, morality, and the reputation of dominant persons or nations. Those arguments deny prostitutes the status of ordinary persons and blame them for disorder and/or disease and for male exploitation and violence against women."

Other documents include "The Continuing Saga of Scarlet Harlot", "What Happens When You Are Arrested", "Leaving the Streets", "Confessions of a Feminist Porno Star", "Stripper", "The Social Consequences of Unchastity", and "The Red Thread: Whores' Movement in Holland".

Cleis Press; $16.95
1987; softcover; 349 pp
0-939416-11-5

SIX RACY MADAMS OF COLORADO
by Caroline Bancroft

Caroline Bancroft wrote histories of the American West from the 1920s through the 1960s. This booklet uses a breezy writing style to tell the stories of six women who ran bordellos in Colorado from the 1870s through the 1950s. Almost half the pages are devoted to Jennie Rogers, "Denver's Immoral Queen". She opened her first whorehouse on "the Row" (the town's red light district) in 1879, and immediately this beautiful, shrewd businesswoman made her establishment a huge success. Five years later she built the most lavish, opulent bordello in the city. "From that day in 1884 to 1909 she was the undisputed queen of the underworld."

Perhaps the most interesting character Bancroft covers is Laura Evins, a rough and tumble soldier of fortune who worked as a prostitute in the notoriously untamed mining town of Leadville. In 1896 she smuggled the payroll past striking miners to the ones who had stayed on the job. That same year, Evins and one of her colleagues went tearing through town in a horse-drawn sleigh. They smashed into the town's elaborate ice palace, destroying the ninety-foot tall, $200,000 structure. At a fashionable charity event held in nearby Central City, Evins attended dressed as a nun, and no one ever suspected that her true occupation wasn't as a bride of Christ. She eventually opened a successful house in Selida, which stayed in business for half a century, till the authorities shut it down in 1950. "Miss Laura was a hoyden — she specialised in pranks, wiles, peccadilloes and boisterous drunks — anything for a laugh. She was as unregenerate a sporting girl as you could meet… She swore, used bad language and was generous to a fault." She died just shy of her 90th birthday, still rolling her own cigarettes and telling her profanity-laden stories of the old days.

Six Racy Madams is a short, entertaining look at one of the most celebrated periods in the long history of prostitution.

Johnson Books; $3.95
1965, 1992; staplebound booklet; 64 pp
heavily illus; 0-933472-22-6

SOCIAL TEXT #37
edited by Anne McClintock

In this issue of the pomo journal *Social Text* from Duke University, the contributors examine sex work. Candida Royalle, founder of Femme Productions [see *Lovers, Volume 2* above], offers her thoughts on pornography, including why she started creating feminist porno films. "I wanted to show that it was possible to produce explicit porn that had integrity, I wanted to show that porn could be non-sexist, and I wanted to show that porn could be life enriching."

Jasmin, a German prostitute, offers some street-level observations about her profession in "Prostitution Is Work". "A girlfriend of mine works in Hamburg and got filed for taxes. She wrote back and argued that if she had to pay taxes, she would sue the government for being a pimp. She never heard from them again!" This parasitic relationship that the government has with whores creates a paradox. "Prostitution in Germany is a grey zone; it's not illegal, it's not legal. Men make the laws against us, but they also want to take our money."

Maybe the most intriguing essay is "Have You Seen Me?", one of the few that doesn't pertain to sex work. Marilyn Ivy deconstructs those mass mailings from ADVO that contain coupons for products and services along with information on a missing child. ""What at first might strike one as a simple public service announcement (indeed, that is how ADVO presents it) turns out to be an intense management of consumer desire and fear, complete with the fantasy bribe of the possible recovery of the missing child and the location of the missing consumer (and consumer object)."

Other pieces in *Social Text* #37 cover Annie Sprinkle's pornography and performance art, the censorship of a video documentary at a conference on prostitution, male submission/female domination, and the stigma of being a prostitute. There is also an interview with Mistress Vena and an essay by heterosexual crossdresser Robert/"Stella".

Duke University Press; $12
1994; softcover; 252 pp
illus; ISSN 0164-2472

WHORES AND OTHER FEMINISTS
edited by Jill Nagle

Can a person engage in sex work and still be a feminist? Can a woman exhibit her nude body for men, have sex with paying men, or make pornographic movies watched mostly by men and still consider herself a foe of the patriarchy? The more than 30 feminist sex workers who contributed in some form to this anthology show that it is possible.

One of the key philosophies that underlies this position is that it is the person who is *giving* the pleasure who has the real power. Orthodox feminism says that since the man has the money and pays for the woman "like a piece of meat" (whether she's flesh-and-blood or just an image in a magazine), the man has the power and the woman is the commodity. Sex writer and phone sex operator Marcy Sheiner felt that way for years, but after becoming a sex worker she became "newly inspired by actually being the object for sale, of knowing that men pay for the privilege of hearing my voice or reading my stories. And that's where I am today, without apology. All across the country men masturbate to the memory of my voice on the telephone wire, whispering nasty things in their ear, and their hot cocks throb in their hands… I cannot overemphasise the positive effect this has had upon my psyche: It makes me feel terrifically lush and powerful." Eva Pendleton strikes a similar note in "Love for Sale": "While some feminists argue that sex workers reinforce sexist norms, I would say that the act of making men pay is, in fact, quite subversive. It reverses the terms under which men feel entitled to unlimited access to women's bodies."

Another major component of sex-positive feminism is the desire to create pornography for women. The vast majority of porn has been created by men for men, but in recent years some women have tried to change that. In "First Ladies of Feminist Porn", editor Jill Nagle interviews Candida Royalle, who created the femporn film company Femme Productions, and Debi Sundahl, who founded a similar company, Fatale Video, as well as the pioneering lesbian sex magazine *On Our Backs*. They describe the ups and downs of creating porn for heterosexual couples and porn for lesbians by lesbians.

In her essay "Peepshow Feminism", Tawnya Dudash reveals the deep camaraderie and closeness among the performers at the Lusty Lady in San Francisco. "A dancer complained that although she had seen more vaginas since working at the theatre than ever before in her life, she still could not locate 'the hole you pee out of.' Other performers crowded around to point out on our own bodies this part of our anatomy. This kind of freedom does not exist at most places of employment…"

Other pieces include "In the Flesh: A Porn Star's Journey" by Nina Hartley, "We've Come a Long Way — And We're Exhausted!" by Annie Sprinkle, "The Littlest Harlot: Barbie's Career as a Role Model" by Tracy Quan, "Sex Radical Politics, Sex-Positive Feminist Thought, and Whore Stigma" by Carol Queen, "They Say I Write Sex for Money: The Dike Writer As Sex Worker" by Red Jordan Arobateau, "Showing Up Fully: Women of Colour Discuss Sex Work" moderated by Jill Nagle, "Working It" by Norma Jean Almodovar, "Inventing Sex Work" by Carol "The Scarlet Harlot" Leigh, "Organising in the Massage Parlour: An Interview with Denise Turner", and "Dancing Towards Freedom" by Siobhan Brooks.

This is probably the best single book you can get if you want to understand the pro-sex work, sex-positive feminist outlook.

Routledge; $18.95
1997; softcover; 291 pp
0-415-91822-7

SEX TRAVEL

ASIA FILE

Asia File is a very nicely laid out, digest-sized zine that gives practical information on obtaining commercial sex services in Asia. Sounds simple, right? Well, it seems that there are an awful lot of powerful people who don't want you to know these things, and they have given *AF*'s editor, Pan, a lot of grief. According to Pan, the trouble started when he was originally publishing in Canada, which has no bothersome First Amendment guarantees. The Sex Police seized his mail and charged him with publishing obscene material. Somehow, a Canadian vice cop running the bust got the US Post Office to send her mail they had seized from his California address. In April 1993 Canada dropped all charges against Pan and returned most of his US and Canadian mail. He has filed suit against the US Post Office and one of its officials for allegedly seizing his mail without a warrant. Pan is also suing over statements made by Canadian newspapers who covered the story, but reportedly never bothered to actually read *Asia File*. They accused Pan of being "an international pornography ring leader", and reported that child pornography charges against Pan had been dropped, when actually no such charges ever existed.

The fun doesn't end there, though. Pan's mail is being seized in Thailand, and letters he writes to his family are being seized by Canadian Customs and often held for months. When he arrived in Seattle in January 1995, he was detained by immigration officials for hours. He is being denied a new Canadian passport on "national security" grounds, and one of his friends has been questioned by Interpol.

All that just for publishing a friggin' zine?! Apparently so. What makes it so bad for Pan is that not only do the Puritans feel that *AF* is encouraging people to engage in prostitution and telling them exactly how to do it, it includes information on underage prostitutes. (Underage is actually a relative term. The age of consent in Thailand is sixteen, in Canada it's fourteen, and in the US it ranges from fourteen to eighteen.)

The info given in *AF* is very specific. You're supplied with directions, names, prices, etiquette, warnings, etc. For example, issue 6 has material on India. In the section on Bombay, you're warned to stay away from the Falkland Road area of the red light district and instead go to the Grand Road area (a map is provided). "The price is Rp100 [US$3] for a fuck or a blow, and Rp150 [US$4.50] for both. The girls are checked by doctors. You will also not be bothered like in gangster-controlled Sona Gachi (Calcutta). This is because prostitution is legal in Bombay and police patrol to keep order."

Similar details are given in this issue for Cambodia, Vietnam, Thailand, and the Philippines. Other issues also cover Laos, Malaysia, Singapore, Japan, and Chinatown. On top of that, *AF* is illustrated with black and white pictures of attractive Asian women.

Pan does admit that there are problems with forced prostitution in Asia, but he also shows something most people don't want to admit — a lot of prostitutes voluntarily choose their line of work. He offers a prescription for getting rid of the problems associated with commercial sex: "Legitimise recreational and commercial sex or suffer the consequences of gangsters and the State. Enforce stern punishments for kidnapping and rape. Pay cops well enough so they don't become crooks. And instead of hiding sex in the corner, celebrate it as divine."

Asia File/PO Box 278537/Sacramento CA 95827-8537
WWW: www.erotictravel.com
Email: asiafile@earthlink.net
Single issue: $12. Non-US: $13
Subscription (one back issue, one current, two future): $34.
Non-US: $37
Payment: cash (in registered mail), mo, ck

THE COMPLETE GUIDE TO GENTLEMEN'S ENTERTAINMENT, 1996 (North American Edition)

by Kinsley D. Jones & William A. Harland

If strip shows and titty bars are your passion, then you'll have to get your hands on this thick softcover guide to such establishments. No matter where in the US or Canada you happen to be, you'll find your neck of the woods covered by the more than 3000 listings in this guide. There's also a smattering of listings for Guam, Puerto Rico, Mexico, Croatia, France, Singapore, and elsewhere.

The listings for the US are broken down by state and city. The amount of details given about each club vary greatly, depending on how much information the club owner gave the authors. (They try to personally visit as many as they can, but they're only human.) At least half of them just list address and phone number, but others offer directions, type of entertainment, whether alcohol is served, hours, cover charge, food service, dress code, club capacity, and other info. Most of the clubs feature nude or topless dancing, but there are a few with go-go dancing and pasties dancing. Dress codes are usually "casual" or "none", but there are occasionally interesting stipulations. McDoogal's in Pasadena, Maryland, says, "No biker attire or bikes in parking lot." I'd like to see them enforce that one. The additional info sections tell about special deals ("free cover to all persons with military ID"), specific events (Jello wrestling), and additional services (lap dancing, table dancing).

This edition has a new feature — a twelve-page "Complete Guide to Ladies' Entertainment", that lists clubs featuring male dancing in seventeen states and two Canadian provinces.

The Complete Guide is also available on diskette for Windows.

The Complete Guide; $19.95 (book), $12.95 (disk)
1996; softcover; 575 pp
0-9636533-4-2

THE EROTIC WOMEN OF SOUTHEAST ASIA

A Gentlemen's Guide (Updated Edition)

by MacGruder Horn

This book is loaded with all the minute details you'll need to know in order to get laid like crazy in four Southeast Asian countries — Thailand, Philippines, Vietnam, and Indonesia. The bulk of the book is about Thailand, because, according to the author, it has the world's most beautiful women and your chances of having sex are excellent. Chapters 4 and 13 discuss some basic information for travellers to Thailand — such as visa requirements, currency, transportation, what to wear, etc. — and give a little background regarding the sex scene.

In Thailand there are around 200 bars that have stages packed with naked dancing women. Any of them can be yours for an entire night for $40. Blowjobs can be had for $8 to $60, with $20 being the norm. Maybe you'd like to make your own amateur porn tape with three girls… you can do it for a grand total of $65. This book covers a glossary of phrases Thai prostitutes use (with extensive explanations of what they mean), bargaining with hookers, deciding which one you want, avoiding STDs, dealing with problems, and scams you'll want to avoid. There's also a whole chapter on finding a Thai woman to marry.

Each of the next three chapters deals with one of the remaining countries. The Philippines remains a hotbed of sin and lust, even though it's only a shadow of its former self since the American military bases pulled up stakes. A whole night with a prostitute is only $20, a blowjob is $8, and under-18 girls are plentiful and legal. Prostitution is less open in Vietnam, but sex is only five bucks. However, the real reason to go to Nam is to find virgin wives. "There are so many young and beautiful virgin girls, who would give anything to marry with an American man, you're going to freak out." Finally, Indonesia doesn't even rate a full page. You can get some action there, but Thailand and the Philippines are definitely the places to go.

In the final chapters, the author relates some of his own true adventures and questions whether there really is an AIDS epidemic in Thailand. The book contains lots of the author's photos (some in colour) of Southeast Asian women in various states of undress.

PVS Publications; $29.95
1995, 1996; spiral-bound oversized softcover; 119 pp
illus; no ISBN

THE FIRST INTERNATIONAL RED-LIGHT GUIDE
To The Best Brothels, Bordellos & Sinbins of the World

by Dr. John Jekyl & Mr. Ed Hyde

The Red-Light Guide features information on 1000 sex establishments in fifty countries. Everything from tame topless dancing to getting your brains fucked out by two women at the same time is covered. You'll find the straight skinny on brothels, strip clubs, massage parlours, window brothels, swing clubs, live sex shows, and just about every other type of establishment you could want.

You couldn't ask for more of a global range. The authors explore Asia, Australia, New Zealand, the Caribbean, Canada, Central America, Europe, Mexico, Scandinavia, South America, and the US (with a special chapter for Nevada). This geographical completeness comes at a price, though. The information for some area can be pretty lean. Basically, if you're interested in men's establishments in North America, you should get the much more in-depth *The Complete Guide to Gentlemen's Entertainment* [above]. If you're hankering to sample the legalised prostitution of Nevada, get *The Official Guide to the Best Cathouses in Nevada* [below]. The entries for some countries, such as England and India, are annoyingly anaemic. However, if you're headed to Indonesia, the Philippines, Singapore, Thailand, Australia, Costa Rica, Germany, Spain, the Netherlands, or Mexico, then *The Red-Light Guide* will prove its worth. The authors relate the general atmosphere of the country and the attitudes towards sex, along with many of the major sex emporiums in each major city. Specific addresses and phone numbers are given, as are a general price range and the strengths and weaknesses of each establishment.

There is also some extra material of varying usefulness that can help the intrepid sex traveller. Among the most helpful of these approximately twenty sections are those that define the different types of sex establishments, warn about numerous scams and rip-offs, and list aphrodisiacs and libido-killers.

When you buy this book, you also get a free six-month subscription to the publisher's Website (normally $60), which contains updated information on the world's sex establishments.

Sinbins, Inc.; $29.95
1997; softcover; 233 pp
no ISBN

THE INTERNATIONAL PATRIARCHY'S (UPDATED) INTERNATIONAL BROTHEL-HAREM GUIDEBOOK

by A.S. Arne Saknussemm (a/k/a RJ Daniel)
This 18-page booklet was published by "The International Patriarchy: The Worldwide Brotherhood of Heterosexual — Straight — Males Who Oppose Feminists". The first five pages contain an anti-feminist, pro-men's rights, pro-Muslim rant. Ten pages are devoted to telling you about some brothels in various parts of the world. There are maps and specific instructions for getting to whorehouses in Seoul and four surrounding cities. Hamburg, Amsterdam, Bangkok, and several other cities get a few sentences each with some quick directions on where to find the girls.

The International Patriarchy; $29
1994; staplebound booklet; 18 pp
illus; no ISBN

THE OFFICIAL GUIDE TO THE BEST CATHOUSES IN NEVADA

by JR Schwartz
It still blows my mind that there's a part of the US where prostitution is legal. But legal it is — in all but four counties in

Nevada — and guess what? The United States hasn't crumbled and fallen yet. Neither has Nevada. In fact, the parts of Nevada where prostitution is illegal are the worst off. Rape rates in Las Vegas and Reno are sky-high. The reason sex-for-money is illegal in those two areas is because it would interfere with people gambling.

This completely updated edition of *Best Cathouses* gives you specific information on all thirty-six licensed bordellos in Nevada. Intrepid researcher JR Schwartz publishes addresses, phone numbers, house specialities, histories, maps, can't-miss-it directions, and more for each house of ill repute. Unfortunately he doesn't give prices. In the introduction he states that because the women are independent contractors, they do the negotiating, so it is completely up to each one. Prices "can run from a few dollars to as much as you have (and more), depending on what you're going to be doing together."

The Mustang Ranch, ten minutes outside Reno, is probably the most famous whorehouse in the world. It has 101 rooms, and it services more than 200,000 men per year. A working girl can easily earn $100,000 annually. "When you walk into the ballroom and see the opulence and lavishness of it, with the young alluring ladies standing there wearing the finest in fashion, the temptations that arise within you can become overwhelming. Like a kid in a candy shop, only this one is offering sex candy. And with it no future obligations, no crime ridden connotations, no guilt. Disease-free legal sex, and fun."

Around seven miles east of Carson City is the New Sagebrush Ranch, one of the most luxurious, cutting-edge cathouses around. It has "more than 72 party rooms, fantasy suites, a dance floor, two full service bars, Jacuzzis, and more beautiful women than you could possibly imagine to satisfy your every desire…" They take Visa, MasterCard, and American Express, and they have an on-site ATM. Besides that, the Ranch is a progressive employer. Each woman gets her own spacious room and private bathroom. She only has to work one week straight and can then take off for as long as she wants. Not a bad set-up.

Besides run-of-the-mill sex, some of the houses offer SM, watersports, rimming, anal sex, messy sex (whip cream, etc.), "Binaca blast" ("Woman performing oral sex with her mouth full of Binaca, cool and refreshing!"), and "Alka-seltzer" ("Sexual act performed by a woman inserting a moistened piece of Alka-seltzer in her, intending to create a fizzy climax.")

Schwartz writes in a frank, humorous manner (he obviously relishes his job), and he includes reproductions of brothel business cards, ads, and house menus. There's also a brief history of prostitution, a glossary, an index by town, and more.

JR Schwartz; $14.95
1995; paperback; 180 pp
illus; 0-9613653-0-7

WHORE STORIES

by Kurt Brecht
Kurt Brecht, the lead singer of Dirty Rotten Imbeciles, offers

unabashed reminiscences of over a dozen of his encounters with prostitutes all over the world. In Amsterdam, he went into an Asian woman's bedroom for a blowjob. He was lasting a long time, so she tells him he has to come soon. When he tells her that she'll have to screw him to get him to hurry up, she says it'll cost more. "'Fuck that!' I thought to myself. 'Get back to work!' I told her to suck faster. She still wasn't going fast enough, so I grabbed the back of her head and dribbled it like a basketball till I was done."

Another time, Brecht and the rest of the band went to a Mexican border town to get a prostitute for a friend who was having a birthday. When they negotiated the price for a cute *señorita*, she took him to a room across the street and he started to get scared. "He thought he was going to get mugged, or killed. So did everyone else, for that matter." But everything turned out just fine: "Eventually, he came back in, sauntered across the room, and gave me a big hug. He said he loved me. A good blow job can really do wonders for a man."

Other adventures told from a john's-eye-view include "Dial-A-Whore", "The Great Tijuana Fuck Fest", and "The Second Worst Whore I Ever Had". There are also three unlisted poems in the book, including "Night Deposit": "I tried/ To get you to give me head/You fell/Asleep instead/So I jerked off on you".

Dirty Rotten Press; $6
1993; softcover; 53 pp
1-879188-03-1

HOW-TO

GREENFIRE
Making Love with the Goddess
by Sirona Knight

Greenfire is a guide to using neo-pagan sex magic to dramatically improve your love life. "Through erotic guided fantasy, you will explore the concept of 'Greenfire' — the oneness of woman and man as represented by the sexual union of the Goddess and her consort. Contacting your divine nature through sexual expression deepens your sense of personal awareness and your connection with your lover and the Goddess... When you and your partner achieve oneness with the Goddess and her consort while making love, you begin to lift the veils that distort your everyday perceptions of life, sexuality, and spirituality, and you open the door to boundless magical possibilities." *Greenfire* offers eight fantasies/exercises in which you and your partner assume different aspects of the Goddess and the God.

Llewellyn Publications; $14.95
1995; softcover; 212 pp
illus; 1-56718-386-7

Fingering goes *both* ways.
The Guide To Getting It On!

THE GUIDE TO GETTING IT ON!
A New and Mostly Wonderful Book About Sex
by Paul Joannides and the Goofy Foot Press

Winner of the Firecracker Alternative Book Award 1997 in the sex category, *The Guide to Getting It On!* provides a light-hearted yet completely practical manual about sex. It's very humorous but not in a cynical way. It refuses to take itself seriously, yet it takes its subject very seriously, judging by the quality and quantity of information. (The chapter on finger-fucking alone is seventeen pages long!) It's basically aimed at straight people, although people of different orientations could benefit from specific chapters.

To give you an idea of the tone of this fun fuck guide, here is a quote from the chapter on penises: "When peeing alone a guy will often invent imaginary targets in the toilet to gun for. An especially fine time is had when a cigarette butt has been left in the commode. Floating cigarette butts are the male urinary equivalent of a clay pigeon." (OK, this passage doesn't directly pertain to sex, but it's a great example of the book's tone.) From the chapter on doing it in the booty: "Thanks to the inventiveness of the ancient Greeks, we now have things in our lives like politicians, lawyers, doctors and anal sex. The only one of these that should never cause you any pain is anal sex. If it does, you are doing it wrong…"

The first ten chapters deal with preliminaries, such as male and female equipment, orgasms, fluids, getting naked, and "dirty words" (this intriguing chapter questions why so many negative expressions involve sexual words: "Fuck you", "Suck my dick", "You're a pussy", etc.).

The next eleven chapters are the actual how-to part of the book. Specifically, they cover finger fucking, hand jobs, masturbating in front of your partner, nipple play, blowjobs, muff diving, massages, penis-vagina sex, anal sex (for him and her), and dildos and vibrators (the eleventh chapter is a general intro to oral sex). As always, you can expect clear, copious instructions presented in a fresh manner, reinforced by realistic line drawings that are neither clinical nor cartoonish.

The next 20 chapters (!) are a smorgasbord of facts, tips, and observations concerning homosexuality, religion, long-term relationships, kink (bondage, fisting, fetishes), masturbation, sexual fantasies, public sex, body images, sex during periods, sexual hygiene, birth control, abortion, diseases, premature ejaculation and other problems, explaining sex to kids, mental blocks to good sex, and even more.

There's a dizzying amount of material here, and the fact that it is presented with integrity but not dryness, a positive but not preachy attitude, is all the more amazing. Most books on how to have sex somehow manage to be as dull as a fix-it manual on plumbing (excluding the others in this section, of course), but this one has so much zest it makes you want to immediately practice what you've just learned.

Goofy Foot Press; $17.95
1996; softcover; 370 pp
illus; 1-885535-14-7

A HAND IN THE BUSH
The Fine Art of Vaginal Fisting
by Deborah Addington

Fistfucking, for the uninitiated, is the act of inserting one's entire hand into the anus or vagina (in the case of the anus, fisting may also include the wrist and forearm). Although anal fisting is still quite taboo and shrouded in secrecy, there is enough information available to at least get you experimenting on your own (for an example, see the *Trust Newsletter*, below). Vaginal fisting, though, is an even more mysterious topic, with only a few scattered articles or sections of books available for the curious. *A Hand in the Bush* is apparently the first book ever written on the subject.

Deborah Addington is an avid practitioner, both as receiver and giver. For the fistee, being handballed "offers a woman a sense of fullness that can't be had with any other item or activity." As the fister, Addington writes, "I feel reverent and honoured by my lover's acceptance of my presence so deeply inside her... I feel welcome, trusted, and entirely embraced."

After answering some basic questions, including many that deal with who can be fisted (given enough time, communication, and lube, almost any woman can receive, although pregnant and menopausal women should consult physicians first), the author discusses the importance of listening to your own body and to your partner. She gives an important anatomy lesson, discussing not just the cunt but all the muscles and structures that surround it (she also briefly covers the hand). Following some information on lubricants and latex gloves, it's onto the crux of the book: step-by-step instructions, with diagrams, for foreplay, insertion of the fingers one at a time, sliding in the rest of the hand, curling it into a fist, moving your fist in different ways, pulling your hand back out, and basking in the afterglow. Several positions are covered, as well as variations such as simultaneous fisting and, for the really adventurous, inserting both hands at once.

To give you more perspectives on this act, Addington includes poems and true-life vignettes on vaginal fisting from sixteen practitioners, meaning that this book also pulls duty as a short collection of handball erotica. Several appendices look at ejaculation and drugs as they relate to fisting, plus the solosexual pleasures of self-fisting. A brief resource

Give your lover a hand.
A Hand in the Bush.

listing for vaginal and anal fisting — and sexuality in general — closes the proceedings. All of this is enhanced by over 30 graceful line drawings featuring handballers of various genders.

When you write the only book ever published on a subject, there's not too much pressure on you to excel, but Addington has thoroughly covered all the bases. If you have the desire, this book is all you'll need.

Greenery Press; $11.95
1997; softcover; 102 pp
illus; 1-890159-02-6

HOW TO HAVE AN AFFAIR AND NEVER GET CAUGHT!
by Jay D. Louise

According to this book, 50 million Americans are currently involved in extramarital affairs and several million more are considering it. Another source I've read says that well over 90% of all men will cheat on a significant other (not necessarily a wife) sometime during their lives. With so many people straying, it's high time somebody wrote a book about how to do it right. This book can be used by men or women, and, even though it's written for married people, the advice will be useful to anyone in a monogamous relationship who wants to get a little on the side.

Author Jay D. Louise is something of an expert on the matter. Her husband consistently cheated on her for twelve years before running off with his mistress, and she has had a relationship with a married man. In the foreword she writes about how people reacted when she told them about the book she was writing: "There were individuals who questioned the condition of my morality. But I assured them, as I will you, that I make it a point to eat moral fibre for breakfast every single day. Unfortunately, one bowel movement and it's gone. That's nature for you."

Although this book (and the cartoons in it) contains a liberal dose of humour, it does offer lots of good tips for achieving high infidelity. After giving a historical and biological overview of cheating (almost no animal species are monogamous), Louise presents three chapters: "Misfortunes", "Mistakes", and "Mastery". For the most part, the first chapter discusses choosing your partner. Screwing around with someone who knows your spouse is a major risk. Another problem is getting involved with someone who will want you to leave you spouse or someone who will start stalking you. When the affair starts and you're in that giddy head-over-heels stage, don't act goofy and buoyant around your domestic partner.

Which leads to the next chapter, a compilation of mistakes that real-life lovers have made. People get in accidents, are photographed by reporters at social events, have their backs scratched to pieces, live next to nosy neighbours, leave evidence where it can be found, and, of course, get knocked up or catch STDs.

The most solid chapter is the final one, which lays bare the secrets of men and women — straight, gay, and lesbian — who have had successful long term affairs. And when I say long term, I mean five to thirty years! One of the keys is to develop emotional intimacy — sometimes for years — before any sex occurs. Another crucial element (and this goes for anything you do that needs to stay a secret) is to shut your big, fat mouth. Don't even tell your friends. Other tips, which are discussed fully, include — don't obsess about your new love, don't overcompensate or undercompensate your behaviour at home, don't create emotional distance from your spouse, don't produce any evidence (love letters, credit card purchases, etc.), develop a routine with your lover, and always put your family first. The book's afterword relates some final thoughts on diseases, suspicious people, and what to do if you get caught.

How to Have an Affair has a unique, humorous dustjacket. It shows a set of closet doors that actually open, revealing a naked, guilty-looking man grinning uncomfortably. If you take the jacket off, you'll find that the book itself has no words or markings of any kind on the outside, so you can read it anywhere without revealing what you're so interested in.

The publisher, Roxan Books, holds annual contests on "How to Have an Affair". They offer thousands of bucks in cash and prizes. Write to them for details (but don't use your home address, dummy).

Roxan Books; $17.95
1995; hardcover; 116 pp
illus; 0-9644789-0-0

THE NEW GOOD VIBRATIONS GUIDE TO SEX

by Cathy Winks & Anne Semans

Cathy Winks and Anne Semans work at Good Vibrations, the famous woman-run sex shop started by Joani Blank in 1977. They love their jobs, not only because they get to play with vibrators for a living, but because they get to help so many people take control of their own pleasure. Good Vibrations provides a "clean, well-lighted", friendly, sex-positive atmosphere for people of all orientations, genders, and walks of life to shop for sex toys, books, and videos. As staffers, Winks and Semans have fielded all kinds of questions through the years. When asked to recommend a sex manual, they could never do so wholeheartedly because every manual has its drawbacks. They decided it was time to take matters into their own hands and create a book that answered the most common questions about sex and pleasure but didn't have any of the pitfalls of the other books.

The Good Vibrations Guide to Sex is the result. It certainly fulfills the authors' goals of creating an accurate, practical, non-judgemental, inclusive, and frank book about sex, which is no small feat. Other sex books may focus on one orientation or play down certain sex acts, such as heterosexual anal intercourse. All previous manuals give short shrift to sex toys, as if they were only some side item instead of one of the main entrees in an active sex life. Some of the newer how-to books are being watered down in order to get wider distribution. The Good Vibes Guide corrects all these problems and many others. It's for everybody: "gay, straight, bisexual, young, old, novices, old-timers, singles, partnered, multi-partnered, pregnant, disabled, transgendered, terminally hip and sexually jaded."

The writing style is refreshingly straightforward. There's no feeling of sneakiness or dirtiness in the text, yet it's not clinical and detached either. It's like a couple of real close friends having a chat with you. They're telling you how things are done with the intention that you're going to try this stuff out yourself. Here's part of what they have to say about masturbation: "If you do it and you like it, keep doing it, with our blessing and encouragement... Masturbation is natural, healthy and brings us pleasure — why deny ourselves?"

On lubricants: "If all of life's minor inconveniences could be solved as cheaply, easily and enjoyably as the insufficiency of natural lubrication, the world would be a wonderful place. There's a dazzling array of options when it comes to lubricants."

On massage: "Don't break contact with the skin. Once you've started the massage, stay connected."

On cunnilingus: "Bear in mind that as your partner approaches orgasm, she'll probably appreciate it if you maintain a steady stimulation up to and through her orgasm. Many women need consistent, reliable stimulation to put them 'over the top', and if you test-drive a brand-new tongue stroke right before she's about to come, it may not go over too well."

On rimming: "The anus is highly sensitive and loaded with nerve endings, and there is no question that, physiologically speaking, it feels as good to have your anus kissed as to have your mouth kissed."

On vibrators: "Enhance your vibrator play by teasing yourself. Pay attention to your arousal level and turn your vibrator off intermittently."

The Guide also covers self-image, sexual anatomy, communication, mutual masturbation, anal and vaginal fisting, anal and vaginal intercourse, intercourse inhibitors, cock rings, Ben Wa balls, dildos, butt plugs, fantasies, group sex, watching porn, reading smut, phone sex, SM, bondage, blow-up dolls, condoms, and many, many more exciting topics. The resources chapter gives addresses of well over 100 groups, publishers, and retailers involved in sexual pursuits. The annotated bibliography and videography are thirteen pages long.

The text is interspersed with the italicised, uncensored comments of Good Vibrations' patrons, who tell what they do and why, in order to give a greater cross-sampling of activities and preferences. Of course, there is information on how to make the various sex acts safer (but not boring!), should you be in a situation, such as a non-monogamous relationship, where it's advisable.

The authors have covered their ground so thoroughly and lovingly, that *The New Good Vibrations Guide to Sex* is likely to become the sex manual by which all others are judged.

Cleis Press; $21.95

1997; oversized softcover; 300 pp

illus; 1-573440698

ORAL CARESS
The Loving Guide to Exciting a Woman
by Robert W. Birch, PhD

Sexologist and sex therapist Robert W. Birch has created an instruction manual for people who want to learn more about the fine art of munching muff. Much of the book is given over to discussions of eating out from moral, legal, and historical points of view. There are even poetic descriptions from a couple of normally opposing sources: the Bible (the Song of Songs) and Aleister Crowley ("Sleeping in Carthage"). Later, Birch examines the various positions that can be used — from behind, on her back, 69, face-sitting, etc. — and the advantages and disadvantages of each. Every other possible related matter is also addressed: hygiene, shaving, rimming (oral sex on the anus), women's sexual response cycles, menstruation, safe sex, using fingers and sex toys, different types of tongue and mouth moves, threesomes, moresomes, and much more. The book is charged-up by the presence of over 30 large b&w photos of men and women going down on their partners. These photos aren't at all coy... they show actual mouth/tongue-to-pussy contact, yet are much sexier than typical sex textbook photos.

If you're already a cunning linguist of some renown, you may pick up a trick or two from *Oral Caress*, but I think it'll be much more useful to people who have little or no idea what to do when they end up face-to-face with a quim.

PEC Publishing; $19.95

1996; oversized softcover; 136 pp

illus; 1-57074-307-X

SEX TIPS FOR STRAIGHT WOMEN FROM A GAY MAN
by Dan Anderson & Maggie Berman

Building on the assumption that no one knows how to please a man like another man, Dan Anderson tells straight women what he has learned from years of being a man and having sex with men. The genesis for this book occurred when Anderson gave some technical advice to his hetero friend Maggie Berman, who was having problems with an unresponsive lover. His tips worked so well, Berman told her friends to call him for pointers, and soon they realised they had material for a unique sex manual on their hands.

Among the things that will probably be news to a lot of women: Guys get hotter than hell when their armpits are eaten out. The inner thighs are another overlooked erogenous zone. Men are divided almost evenly between those who love nipple stimulation and those who don't care about it at all. When it comes time to take his cock out: "Whether it's boxers, briefs, or bikinis, lower the elastic so the penis comes out the top; don't try to pull it through the fly." When giving a handjob, keep one hand pressing around the base of his dick. "This constant, firm pressure on the base, about as much as it would take to push a heavy revolving door, directs the sensation to his penis, keeps it stiff and smooth, and has the added bonus of making his dick look bigger than a ballistic missile — at least from his point of view."

The authors stress that they key to a good blowjob is attitude. "He wants to feel that you are enthusiastically devoting your talents to making his penis happy, and that you're not just doing it because you had too much to drink." And, glory hallelujah!, there's even a whole chapter devoted to stimulating guys' balls, which are often criminally ignored. There's even mention of the perineum (i.e., the taint), a part of the body that is cold-shouldered even more often than the nuts.

The chapter on intercourse contains some interesting and unusual positions, and "'Do Not Enter' Alternatives" has ideas for sex contact other than oral/anal/vaginal. There are also pointers on personal appearance, your boudoir, sex toys, condoms, dealing with requests you're not comfortable with, and getting picked up ("If you're in a bar with a male friend of any persuasion, it's superimportant to keep scoping the room so other guys know you're not attached.").

The main thing that bugs me about this book is that sometimes the authors overgeneralise or display a decidedly non-progressive attitude. In the chapter on sex toys, they say that if your man wants you to strap on a dildo and nail him, "our advice is to say 'so long' right now." So much for being open and accepting of each other's desires. I guess straight people are only allowed to have certain kinds of sex. Also, visuals showing how to perform some of the more unconventional positions would've been nice, but what do you expect from a book that will only print a cartoonish drawing of a hand performing manual sex on a *vibrator*? And, speaking of handjobs, the authors only cover one stroke, implying that that's all you'll ever need.

While *Sex Tips* does have a lot of good things to say, it isn't the one book that will turn you into a world-class lover.

Still, it is a step in the right erection, especially if you're clueless or incompetent in the sack.

ReganBooks (HarperCollinsPublishers); $16
1997; small hardcover; 178 pp
illus; 0-06-039232-0

SUPERMARKET TRICKS
More Than 125 Ways to Improvise Good Sex
by Jay Wiseman

You don't necessarily have to spend big bucks on sex toys to have wild thrills. If you know what you're doing, you can use easily-available items as a springboard into super sexual sensations. To be honest, when I first heard about this book, I didn't have high hopes for it. I thought it would be full of clichés about stuff like cucumbers and whipped cream. I'm glad to say I've been proven wrong. *Supermarket Tricks* does venture into the highly obvious at times, but it offers enough thoughtful ideas to add at least several tricks to anyone's repertoire.

The suction cups that come in snake bite kits "can create very interesting sensations when moistened and applied to the nipples. After the cups are removed, the expanded tissue becomes very sensitive to whatever 'follow-up' sensations you care to apply." Wearing sunglasses during sex can make the act more impersonal and, to some people, more exciting. Mirrored shades also let your lover see himself/herself in action (a neat twist to the mirrors on the ceiling theme). Running the backside of a chilled knife across your lover's skin can create a very intense cutting sensation. Blowjobs can be made more exciting for the recipient if you have some toothpaste in your mouth. "Pepsodent has something of a cult following, as does Close Up."

Twenty-four of the tricks involve SM or at least some form of bondage. If you are into whippings, try a bicycle inner tube. It can be inflated to various levels for a variety of sensations. And remember, cutting boards make great paddles.

A special section explores the risky activity of playing with menthol (contained in cough drops, arthritis creams, and other products). Over 20 pages are devoted to safety tips for SM and erotic power play. Even though this book is meant mainly to explore the erotic potential of everyday objects, this section is as complete as you will find in most books devoted to SM. Other sections cover general tips for tricks, sexual problems, and alternative sexuality resources.

Supermarket Tricks will show you how to spice up your sex life quickly and inexpensively. Who would've thought that your neighbourhood grocery store could be such a den of iniquity?

Greenery Press; $11.95
1995; softcover; 115 pp
0-9639763-6-2

TRICKS
More Than 125 Ways to Make Good Sex Better
by Jay Wiseman

Tricks is a compilation of easy-to-do activities that will spice up your sex life and produce new enjoyable sensations. Jay Wiseman picked up these hints and tactics from gay, lesbian, straight, and bi associates, sex workers, and his own experiences. Tip #9 ("The Nays Have It") reads in part: "When performing cunnilingus, position your lips or tongue over her clitoris, then rapidly shake your head from side to side." Hooker's Trick #2 advises, "To help make the guy come, use your fingertips to lightly tap the underside of his scrotum every minute or so." Another hooker's trick, for creating a knock-out orgasm, is to hold a bag of pepper under a man's nose so he sneezes at the moment of climax.

"A Peachy Idea" lets women in on one of Mother Nature's secrets: "One young lady told me that a peach pit, when used while still wet and slick, is excellent for clitoral stimulation. (Be careful of its sharp, pointy end!) She said its combination of smoothness, roughness, and wetness made it feel a lot like a tongue." A man's orgasm may be delayed if you sit between his legs while servicing him. "Many men have difficulty reaching orgasm if their legs are spread apart."

A special section (also included in *Supermarket Tricks*, above) discusses at length tricks using menthol. After that, a series of essays cover the Madonna/Whore Complex, nonoxynol-9, the riskiness of various sex acts, lubricants, nightstand supplies, what to do if a condom fails, and more. Resource sections offer contact information for groups involved in alternative sexuality and sex-related problems (abuse, diseases, etc.).

Greenery Press; $11.95
1992; softcover; 108 pp
no ISBN

TRICKS 2
Another 125 Ways to Make Good Sex Better
by Jay Wiseman

This sequel to *Tricks* provides more easy ways to spice up your sex life. When doing "The Remote Control Blow Job", "the man being fellated takes the hand of his partner — I suggest using the partner's left hand if they're right handed — and puts their forefinger in his mouth. He then does to his partner's finger what he would like them to do to his cock, and the partner reacts accordingly." For "Play Her Like a Violin" — "Rub a longish hair back and forth across her clit like a violin string." Also includes sections on spanking tricks, safer sex, SM, lubricants, problems, alternative sexuality resources, and more. [A perfect-bound softcover edition at the same price is slated for release in mid-1998.]

Greenery Press; $11.95
1994; plastic comb-bound softcover; 116 pp
no ISBN

THE ULTIMATE GUIDE TO ANAL SEX FOR WOMEN
by Tristan Taormino

Anal sex has been stereotyped as an activity that occurs almost exclusively among gay men, but anyone with an asshole can play... indeed, many people of varying genders

Figure 12:
Spooning

Venus and Uranus.
The Ultimate Guide to Anal Sex for Women.

and orientations have been using the back door, and it appears that the ass's popularity is on the rise. Tristan Taormino (she of *Pucker Up*, *Best Lesbian Erotica*, *Ritual Sex*, and more) has written the first book especially for women who want to discover a new frontier of erotic delight, whether as the explorer or the explored.

First, Tristan dispels myths about anal sex, including the gay myth mentioned above, plus the beliefs that it's messy and painful and that women don't enjoy it. To the notion that the asshole was never meant to be eroticized, she counters, "The anus and rectum are full of sensitive, responsive nerve endings, and the stimulation of these nerve endings and penetration of the rectum can be intensely pleasurable — and orgasmic — for men and women. Furthermore, women's G-spots and perineums can be stimulated during anal sex, and men may experience stimulation of the bulb of the penis and the prostate gland through anal penetration."

The chapter "Our Asses, Ourselves" is an illustrated look at the anus and its surrounding exterior and interior anatomy for women and men (as throughout the rest of the book, Fish does an excellent job providing multiethnic, multigender drawings), while the subsequent chapter examines desire, fear, communication and other psychological/emotional aspects of anal sex.

"Anal Penetration" is, of course, the key chapter, letting both partners know what to expect, the best ways to proceed, and the basic positions for this type of intercourse. "Tools of the Trade" covers some purchases you'll probably want to make, from lubes and safer sex paraphernalia to butt plus, vibrators, dildos (including strap-ons, for women who want to give), and anal beads (for the notorious Briggs & Stratton effect). The chapter on shaving and enemas details these procedures because some people may want to feel as clean and smooth as possible and because these acts can be erotic on their own.

Tristan devotes a chapter to each of the other anal pos-

sibilities: masturbation, anilingus (oral sex on the anus, aka rimming), fistfucking (inserting the hand and possibly more of the arm into the anus), SM, and gender play (for example, a lesbian couple pretend that they're gay men or, with a straight couple, the woman pretends she's a het man giving it to his squirming girlfriend). A chapter on STDs and keeping your ass healthy, a resources guide, and an index round out the proceedings.

Even though this book is primarily aimed at women, most of the information it gives applies to everybody. If you have a booty or you have a lover who does, then you too can get in on the fun. Tristan will gently take you by the gland and show you how it's done.

Cleis Press; $14.95
1998; softcover; 152 pp
illus; 1-57344-028-0

SACRED SEX

LESBIAN SACRED SEXUALITY
by Diane Mariechild & Marcelina Martin

This book is a sumptuous exploration of the spiritual aspects of women having sex with women. Coauthor Diane Mariechild states up front that this form of sacred sex is no different from any other. "Sex is sex. It is not our partner's gender that makes our sex sacred. It is the consciousness that we bring to our sexual acts that makes them sacred, whether we are making love to ourselves or with a partner. Lesbian love is sacred when it is visionary, interconnected, and transformational."

Among the 27 pieces of poetry and prose from other people is Jeanne Jullion's "a mother's orgasm at the beginning of her day", which starts: "the purity of orgasm/burns me clean/my body extends/into a single spike/of purest pleasure". In "letters to kate", Joan Iten Sutherland writes: "yr thighs are milky white streaked with sweet red blood they are koi slipping through my fingers. the water's surface is far above."

Lesbian Sacred Sexuality is enhanced by gentle, light green-tinted black and white shots of eleven couples making love, often in outdoor settings surrounded by nature. The women represent a wide variety of ages, body types, and races (although the majority by far are white) and are given the opportunity to speak their feelings. Jill — the only person in the book photographed without a partner — says that, "Nature is not out there to be called in, but is and always was a part of me. Touching my body sweetly I touch all life. The teacher I seek, the externalised truth I have found in Nature is within me as well. My own sacred body is Her gateway, and only my conditioned mind prevents me from knowing the authentic experience of Her."

Beth echoes a theme that runs throughout the book —

Patti worships at the Temple of Beth.
Lesbian Sacred Sexuality.

emotional release, often accompanied by crying. "I cry about seventy-five percent of the time we make love. It is feeling love on a really deep level and it just wells up from inside and I cry. It is like an emotional orgasm." She also reveals: "When Patti and I were first making love we called it worshipping; worshipping the other person, her body, her spirit, her soul. We both got off on my name, which in Hebrew means house of worship. Patti called it worshipping at the temple of Beth."

Wingbow Press; $24.95
1995; oversized softcover; 140 pp
heavily illus; 0-914728-81-4

SACRED SEX
by anonymous

The *Sacred Symbols* series is a set of small, square, hardcover books that use an attractive layout, colour illustrations, and brief text to illuminate the religious and spiritual symbols of ancient Egypt, the Maya, Taoism, and so on. This volume contains 78 illustrations that take a omnicultural look at the astonishing number of ways humans have merged sex and spirit, a concept that currently seems foreign to Western society as a whole.

Creation myths often take on sexual overtones, including cosmic eggs, primal wombs, and outright intercourse between Mother Earth and Father Sky, all of which are covered. The Sun has been revered as a male fertility symbol, as evidenced by the Aztec terra cotta figure, Bronze Age drawing, and fifteenth-century illuminated Italian manuscript that each depict a man with the Sun shining from his groin. We also learn that, "The jade lady of Taoism, Lan T'sai-ho, is portrayed in swirling lines suggestive of organic forms and

therefore of the *yin* essences of the world. Her association with jade — regarded as the solidified semen of the dragon — is potent indeed." Other two-page sections include "Sexual Landscapes", "Goddess", "Cosmic Twins", "Vulva", "Kali", "Satyrs", "Castration", and "Paradise Regained". Unlike other books in this section, this isn't a look at how to achieve sacred sex for yourself but rather a survey of the concept throughout times and cultures.

Thames and Hudson; $10
1997; small hardcover; 80 pp
heavily illus; 0-500-06027-4

SECRETS OF WESTERN TANTRA
The Sexuality of the Middle Path
by Christopher S. Hyatt, PhD

Occultist Christopher Hyatt lays out a modified form of the sacred sex practices known as Tantra. By following these specific instructions, he claims, you can achieve spiritual enlightenment, besides having great sex. Although he explains the philosophies behind this form of Tantra, he doesn't get bogged down in mysticism, instead preferring to give clear directions.

"Many forms of Tantra are restrictive and limiting, focusing on holding back and holding in. Western Tantra is completely different. Its focus is on melting and giving, using only small amounts of holding to make the Gift more beautiful and complete. Western Tantra holds the belief that complete Orgasm is freeing, and energising. In fact, the methods are designed with that result in mind. The outcome of following the creative and liberating path of Middle Path Sexuality (MPS) is enlightenment and the creation of what I term the Magickal Child. This 'Child', whether physical or spiritual will become the leading edge of the new human race the planet is creating."

New Falcon Publications; $14.95
1989, 1996; softcover; 191 pp
1-56184-113-7

SENSUAL CEREMONY
A Complete Tantric Guide to Sexual Intimacy
by Kenneth Ray Stubbs, Jr

Kenneth Ray Stubbs is a teacher and student of Tantra, a sexual-spiritual school of thought that comes from Hinduism and Buddhism. Tantra teaches us to embrace our sensory experiences and surrender to the moment, using physical sensations as a gateway to transcendent, mystical experiences. Stubbs has developed a ceremony — the Secret Garden Ceremony — based on Tantra.

The instructions for the ceremony make up the majority of the book. As in Stubbs' other books, the writing is a gentle, flowing hybrid of poetry and prose. You are free to modify the ceremony as you see fit — it can last minutes or hours. You can use just one part of it, making that the entire ceremony. You can make it sexual and/or orgasmic or not. Some of the accessories you may want to employ are music, oils, lotions, soaps, bathing accoutrements (loofas, pillow head rests), feathers, favourite fabrics, and massage tables.

The first step of the ceremony is guided imagery. "Never express judgement, anger, or impatience/through voice or actions/Laughter as a shared joy, however, is a delight/Let your voice/be soft and gentle/almost as if lullabying an infant". Besides giving basic guidelines, he presents a detailed imagery scenario involving communion with nature. You can use it as a springboard for your own scenarios.

The next chapter will instruct you on giving your partner ecstasy through food and drink. Sparkling nectars, fruits, nuts, whipped cream, candies, and other edibles are presented in detail. Stubbs describes imaginative ways to prepare, arrange, serve, and feed the culinary delights to your lover. A special section covers having messy fun with your food and drink in the bathtub.

The following chapter deals with ceremonial bathing, with a special section on the art of foot bathing. "Take off her shoes and socks/Since most people are not used/to having this done for them/you may have to use gentle, verbal persuasion". The last chapter on the Secret Garden Ceremony gives a brief but adequate overview of Tantric massage techniques. For more advanced training, see *Tantric Massage* [below].

The final two chapters explore Tantric exercises for couples and people by themselves. One of the things couples can do together is "mapping", which involves rating the relative pleasure of various sensations on various parts of the body (using a scale of plus three to minus three). Solo techniques include powerful breathing patterns and self-massage.

Sensual Ceremony is illustrated with black and white and coloured pencil drawings that aren't intended so much to graphically depict the techniques in the book as they are to enhance the general ambience.

Secret Garden; $18.95
1993; oversized softcover; 112 pp
illus; 0-939263-10-6

TANTRIC MASSAGE
An Illustrated Manual for
Meditative Sexuality
by Kenneth Ray Stubbs, Jr

In this revised version of *Erotic Massage*, Kenneth Ray Stubbs shows you in detail how to give a blissful, beautiful full-body massage to your partner. Simply stated, massage is "patterned touch". (Unpatterned touch for pleasure is often referred to as a caress.) When giving or receiving a massage, you should let go of the present and the future, of all expectations, and, as this book says, "Be/Here/Be/Now".

After giving basic instructions on preparation, accessories, and general pointers, *Tantric Massage* guides you through 78 strokes (and variations). Every part of the body is given attention: back, shoulders, thighs, ankles, soles of the feet, arms, hands, fingers, torso, breasts, nipples, scrotum, penis, clitoris, G-spot, neck, scalp, ears, eyes, lips, and more. There is a special section that teaches you how to spread sexual energy all over your partner's body after you've performed genital massage.

Each stroke is accompanied by at least one detailed il-

An eighteenth-century crystal carving representing a phallus and an egg. *Sacred Sex.*

lustration showing you how and where to place your hands and fingers. Arrows indicate how to perform the stroke. If a stroke has more than one part, very often each part will have its own illustration. Stubbs' lyrical, minimal prose will tell you the rest..

Secret Garden; $18.95
1989, 1993; oversized softcover; 112 pp
heavily illus; 0-939263-09-2

TANTRIC MASSAGE VIDEO

Tantric Massage Video was created as a companion to the *Tantric Massage* book [above]. There is no narration or voice-over instruction. It is simply one hour of Stubbs wordlessly performing massage on a woman and on a man. If the accompanying mid-tempo synthesiser music isn't to your liking, you can always turn down the volume and play whatever you desire.

The video goes through all the strokes in the same order as the book (a few new genital strokes are included). You not only watch each movement being performed, you also get to see the overall "dance" of massage. Each seemingly effortless stroke leads smoothly into the next, which seamlessly merges with the next, and so on.

You could probably just get this video and learn a lot about *Tantric Massage*. However, if you're serious about it, you'll need to get the book, too.

Secret Garden; $19.95
1989, 1994; VHS video; 60 min

WOMEN OF THE LIGHT
The New Sacred Prostitute
edited by Kenneth Ray Stubbs, Jr

This book is not about prostitutes as we normally think of them. In ancient times there were women, often called temple prostitutes, who helped people advance spiritually through sex. Although such positions have been formally abolished, women who do basically the same sort of thing are still around today. "Their bodies are their temples, to which they invite others. Their purpose is to support a deeper discovery of the spiritual flame that burns within us all. Sexual energy, in a broad sense, is this flame."

The nine women in this book have different backgrounds and different approaches, but the common denominator is that in some sense they exchange spiritually-charged sex for money. Each of them contributes an essay in which she explores her life, her beliefs, and her erotospiritual practices. Every essay is prefaced by a long introductory essay by editor Kenneth Ray Stubbs.

Pleasure activist Carol Queen, who is (or was) a call girl, smashes some of the myths of prostitution. She was not forced into it. She was in complete control of her clients. She met many smart, self-assured women who were call girls. Queen learned that even though most whores and their clients don't know about ancient sacred prostitution, it resonates unconsciously in their actions. "At first I was surprised to open the door to men I had never met before and find that they were already erect, but now I see this as a body understanding on the client's part that his desire will be accepted and affirmed. He does not feel desire for a particular person, but the sort of desire, I am certain, that ardent worshipers brought to the temples, desire to connect, to know eroticism as powerful and good."

Stephanie Rainbow Lightning Elk was born a Catholic of European ancestry, but she has become a shaman in the Native American tradition. Specifically, she is a FireWoman — her shamanistic energies focus on sexuality, which is viewed as the central point of spiritual, mental, emotional, and physical growth. "In the olden days a young person was given a choice of working with a FirePerson who helped educate and awaken sexuality in harmony with spirituality. In today's world, adult initiates come to me for the same ceremony."

The other women who contribute are a porn star, a sex surrogate, a meditation teacher, a group sex hostess, an artist, a masseuse, and a nurse. Of all the available books on sacred sex I've seen, this one gives the most in-depth yet accessible view of the topic, so it's highly recommended for newbies. It'll give you old-timers a lot to chew on, too.

Secret Garden; $14.95
1994; oversized softcover; 255 pp
0-939263-12-2

PRIVATE PARTS

AT YOUR FINGERTIPS
The Care & Maintenance of a Vagina
edited by Hysteria

Brought to you by the feminist humour magazine *Hysteria*, this collection explores the lighter side of pussies. These 28 essays poke good-natured fun at menstruation, the menopause, sex, gynaecologists, urinating, and other quim-related matters. In "What IS a Douchebag?" Laura Allen Sandhu looks at the air of purposeful vagueness that surrounds feminine hygiene. Concerning the question in the title, she wonders: "Why is it an insult to be called one? And why do you never see one lying on somebody's coffee table?"

Cathy Crimmons continues that line of thinking in "Vaginal Fashion: What's In and Out". She takes the makers of menstrual products to task: "Why don't they have pictures of girls throwing coffee cups at their husbands and boyfriends, or clutching their abdomens in agony? Ads for headache and indigestion-related products show people grimacing or holding their heads. What's currently on the drugstore shelves is more notable for its amusement quotient than its aesthetic value or integrity: Kimberly-Clark's New Freedom pads, for example show a woman in sensible khaki hiking pants jumping up for joy. Did she just get her period, or buy a Toyota?"

A cartoon by Nina Paley shows a woman in a bandanna singing "On the Rag Again". The first verse goes a little something like this: "On the rag again/I can't wait to get on the rag again/I'll get cramps but at least my P.M.S. will end/Yeah I can't wait to be on the rag again."

Hysteria Publications; $7.95
1994; softcover; 111 pp
illus; 09629162-6-9

THE BREAST
An Anthology
edited by Susan Thames & Marin Gazzaniga

This unassuming little book contains 46 writings exploring and celebrating breasts and their relationship to women and society. The writings in this mammary opus cover every possible aspect of the subject in tones that range from light-hearted to serious. But even when the subject is anything but funny, the writers often inject some humour. In "Tabula Rasa", Karen de Balbian Verster writes about her breast cancer treatment: "Every morning at nine o'clock I get my tits fried. Just one, actually. The right one. When I'm done I'm going to have a radiation barbecue. Cook the burgers right on my chest."

Caroline MB Paul's essay "Threshold" is a very unusual piece of writing, impossible to neatly summarise. Paul is a paramedic who often performs CPR. She speaks of the technical beauty of the human chest and of the strange intimacy between her and the people she tries to resuscitate. She describes in detail one particular case in which she unsuccessfully did CPR on a 60-year-old woman. "My hands fuse with her chest. I imagine life dripping into her through my sprawled fingers. I am a thick, awkward intravenous tube. With each press her chest makes a place for me, the skin parting and heating up under my palm, the breasts falling to the side like arms opening wide in welcome."

"Vunder-bra" is a funny, hyperbolic slap at the Wonder Bra. "Vunder-bra! Given by the Gods, machine washed in nectar, re-engineered with micro-chip technology, the legally non-binding, gentlemen-preferred bra, made from forty-something pieces of fine lace, cotton, and removable pads, lovingly stitched by the lumpenproletariat of countries you would never let your daughter go to… And it's fully guaranteed to put your nipples in his face. Pander to his desperate need for sex with anyone, then loathe him for his lecherous demands; the childishness of his leering at others wearing the same bra; his failure to appreciate the part Feminism plays in your life."

The laugh-out-loud funny "A New Boom and Bust Theory" is a radio transcript of San Francisco's *Chris Clark Show*. A caller brings attention to a previously unrecognised trend — "that in politically conservative, repressive times big breasts on women become popular and in liberal, free-wheeling times small breasts become popular." He goes on to theorise that breast size popularity is not due to the political climate, but conversely, the political climate is based on society's breast preferences.

Other essays, stories, and poems talk of breast-feeding, getting mastectomies, getting implants, being flat-chested, developing breasts during puberty, dancing topless, using tortillas as a bra (!), and more. This is a worthy anthology for an important part of the body. I give it an A (cup).

Global City Press; $14
1995; softcover; 242 pp
0-9641292-8-0

DECIRCUMCISION
Circumcision Practices and Foreskin Restoration Methods
by Gary M Griffin, MBA

As you'll find out in this book, the practice of mutilating the penises of babies and adults has been fairly widespread for about 4000 years. The earliest known circumcisions occurred in ancient Egypt, perhaps as an initiation rite into adulthood or the priesthood. The author traces this barbarous surgery across time and culture. Circumcision was not widespread in Britain until the last half of the nineteenth century when it was touted as "cure" for the widespread "problem" of masturbation. Luckily, when socialised medicine came to the UK, it wouldn't pay for the removal of foreskins, so rather than parents paying their own money, circumcision stopped being popular.

As late as the turn of the century in the US, only 10% of men were clipped. However, during World War I routine circumcision was required for American soldiers in a weird attempt to prevent them from catching VD. Having a cut dick thus became a macho status symbol. As hard as it is to believe, men actually volunteered to undergo this operation so they could be like their war heroes. Of course, men who were circumcised had their sons circumcised, and it snowballed into the situation today, where approximately 60% of new-born males are butchered.

A rather unnerving chapter demonstrates in words and drawings the ways in which foreskins are cut off. Next, the author discusses the pros and cons of circumcision, shattering many myths in the process. Finally, before the discussion of decircumcision begins, there is a brutal chapter on "female circumcision" and some of the more extreme practices done to males (Australian aborigines slice open the bottom of the penis from the glans to the scrotum).

Although methods to restore the foreskin apparently haven't been around as long as methods to remove it, there are records of men trying to regain their lost tissue as long as 2100 years ago. Today, there are surgical techniques to recreate the foreskin. The author covers these procedures in detail but warns that this operation is still considered "risky and experimental". Should you still want to try it, contact info is given for several physicians who perform the procedure.

A much safer and cheaper way to get your foreskin back is to do it yourself non-surgically. This book details a simple method that will work for almost every man. "All you need to start with is a roll of tape. In summary, your objective will be to draw the skin from the penis as far as it will go up on the glans and then tape it in place. Over a period of months, new skin cells will be generated to fill in the stretched epithelial spaces, and you will develop a fully-functional and natural-looking foreskin similar to the one you were born with." Full details and illustrations are given for this months-long process that requires daily attending.

It may take well over a year, but you can eventually get back a part of your body that was painfully taken from you without your consent.

Added Dimensions Publishing; $16.95
1991; softcover; 108 pp
illus; 1-897967-05-7

PENIS ENHANCEMENT SURGERY
A Self-Help Guide for Men
by Faiz Ansari

If you'd like to make your dick bigger, you've got two basic routes: non-surgical and surgical. For the straight dope on methods in the former category, check out *Penis Enlargement Methods* [*Outposts* p 95]. But if you don't mind going under the knife, *Penis Enhancement Surgery* is the book (endorsed by the American Academy of Phalloplasty Surgeons, by the way) to help you explore medical options.

Faiz Ansari explains the two primary types of operation and shows how they are performed. Elongation, which involves severing two ligaments, typically adds three-quarters of an inch to one and a half inches in length and requires that you wear weights several hours a day for at least four months after the operation. Girth enhancement, which is performed by removing fat from an area of the body and injecting it into *der penis*, can increase thickness by up to 50%. A downside to this procedure is that your body can reabsorb the fat. Liposuctioned fat transfer can result in a 60% to 80% reabsorption rate, but the rate is much lower (around 10%) with dermal graft transfer. The procedures are fairly costly — around $4000 for lengthening and $4500 for dermal graft transfer.

In one chapter, Ansari offers several before and after photos of men who definitely got what they wanted. Then, in the following chapter — aptly titled "Your Worst Nightmare" — he talks about what can go wrong. Pictures of cocks that look like they've been through a meat grinder drive the point home. Ansari reprints other published articles on penis enhancement surgery — "The Battle for the Bulge", "Surgeon

Helps Men Inch Toward Greater Self-Esteem", and "How a Risky Surgery Became a Profit Center in Los Angeles" — and stories from patients. Three of the guys had successful procedures and are happy, while the fourth didn't gain anything in the crotch area but did get $6000 lighter in the wallet.

Several chapter are actually interviews with or articles by surgeons who work on penises. They discuss how the operations are done, what you can expect afterwards, what can go wrong, etc. Things are wrapped up with a list of answers to frequently asked questions and contact information for certified Phalloplasty doctors. For current information, you can visit the author's Website at http://www.penis-enhancement.com.

Faiz Ansari; $25
1997; softcover; 100 pp
illus; no ISBN

TESTICLES
The Ball Book
by Gary Griffin, MBA

Testicles could be subtitled *Everything You Ever Wanted to Know About Nuts But Were Afraid to Ask*. Gary Griffin — the force behind Added Dimensions Publishing — is an admirer of balls, and he wants to share the results of his fascination with you. You'll learn about all there is to know about size, semen, the scrotum, ejaculation, injaculation (a Taoist technique), orgasm, sperm, fertilisation, castration, dysfunction, and enlargement techniques.

Among the basic facts:

☞ Testicles are divided into 250 compartments.
☞ The average size of a testicle appears to be 1.5 inches long and one inch wide.
☞ Healthy testicles can reach the size of cue balls and even larger.
☞ "The average human testicle weighs between ten and fifty grams, depending upon genetics and race."
☞ "95% of a man's testosterone is produced in his testicles…"
☞ Less than 5% of semen is produced in the testicles (the rest comes from the prostate and the seminal vesicles).
☞ Most men ejaculate a teaspoon or two of come.
☞ Men with one testicle can still ejaculate normally and have kids.
☞ The only thing you can do to increase your load is to avoid coming for several days, but even that won't increase the volume very much.
☞ There's no way to enlarge your testicles, but there are three main ways to enlarge your ballsac — saline infusion, vacuum pumping, and surgical procedures.
☞ You can also get free-swinging, low-hanging balls by lengthening your ballsac through leather thong wraps, ball stretchers, weighted ball bags, and a parachute strap with weights.

Griffin devotes a chapter to each of the last two topics,

complete with instructions and mail-order resources for the necessary apparatuses. He also provides photos of several men with extremely low-hanging scrotums and freakish nutsacs that are almost as big as footballs. If you want to go totally over the edge, take a gander at the African tribesmen with testicular elephantiasis and the circus performer with two functioning penises and scrotums and a third arm growing out of his groin.

Balls have always played second fiddle to the penis itself. *Testicles* is the only book to bring them out into the limelight. Consider it a seminal work.

Added Dimensions Publishing; $16.95
1992; softcover; 96 pp
heavily illus; 1-897967-09-X

SOLOSEX

THE ART OF AUTO-FELLATIO
(Oral Sex for One) (Fourth Edition)
by Garry Griffin

Guys, you know how you've always said that if you could give yourself a blowjob, you'd never leave the house? Well, here's your chance to put your meat where your mouth is. Gary Griffin has written a complete guide to performing oral sex on yourself. Since most men cannot easily suck themselves, the key is to increase limberness and flexibility. Griffin presents an exercise and stretching routine that should have you ready to blow your own horn in a matter of weeks or months. He also shares another limbering-up programme, developed by Jack Stark, who founded the "monosexuality movement".

There are at least six auto-fellatio positions, all of which are presented. Two of them are by far the easiest and most popular. The plow position involves lying on your back and bringing your legs and hips up over your head. In the over easy position, you sit down and bend from the waist. The other positions — such as the lotus — are extremely difficult, and you almost have to be a contortionist to do them.

Over one-third of the book is made up of letters from self-suckers who describe their exploits in dripping detail. Along similar lines, *Auto-Fellatio* has dozens of uncensored pictures of men going down on themselves. Finally, there is a resource section that includes titles of over 100 auto-fellatio films and several magazines that often include it in their line-up of sex acts. Griffin also gives instructions for a "blow pipe", a home-made device that can give you some of the sensations of blowing yourself if you can't yet reach it on your own.

Added Dimensions Publishing; $9.95
1988, 1994; softcover; 96 pp
heavily illus; 1-897967-11-1

CELEBRATE THE SELF
The Magazine for the
Solo Sex Enthusiast

Celebrate the Self is a publication for men who enjoy masturbating. The attitude here is that jacking off isn't some poor substitute for sex but an enjoyable form of sexual contact. The men who write to *Celebrate* — their letters make up a large part of each issue — are gay, straight, and bi. Some even define themselves with a new term — solosexual, meaning that they "adopt masturbation as their primary and most cherished sexual outlet." Steve in Denver writes: "Ten years ago, I began to find solo sex to be the most exquisite way for me to play. Today, as a creative, accomplished artist, I find I am falling more and more blissfully in love with myself with each passing day."

In one section readers describe an imaginative, endless variety of ways in which they get themselves off. In Volume 3 #4 John from New Jersey describes one of his techniques: "When my cock is hard up against my abdomen, I place each thumb on its respective nipple and my index finger of each hand on the underside of my skin-covered cockhead, and I begin an up and down sort of strumming motion of my two thumbs on nipples and the index fingers on cockhead…" TJ in Vermont tells about his experiments with brinkmanship (stopping right as you're about to come) in the previous issue. He'll stroke himself for three or four hours, stopping right at the brink 60 to 70 times.

Other regular sections of this magazine offer information on sexual and overall health, news blurbs on sex and freedom and other topics, video and book and product reviews, and more. Although the written content caters to all orientations, all but one of the photos are of men.

Factor Press/PO Box 8888/Mobile AL 36689-0888
Voice: 1-800-304-0077
Single issue: $4
Six issue sub (one year): $19.95. Can/Mex: $23.95. Elsewhere: $34.95
Payment: cash, ck, mo, Visa, MC

FIRST PERSON SEXUAL
Women & Men Write About
Self-Pleasuring
edited by Joani Blank

First Person Sexual is a collection of forty written pieces concerning the most common sexual practice of all, masturbation. Considering that this is a near-universal form of sex, it's amazing how little has been written about it. Sex educator Joani Blank has put together this anthology to help bring solosex (a/k/a masturbation, self-pleasuring) out of the closet and establish it as legitimate form of sex. Forty people — most of them not professional writers — contributed primarily non-fiction pieces on their own experiences and thoughts concerning masturbation.

At first, it might seem that a bunch of people writing about jerking off would make for a repetitious, one-note collection, but this is not at all the case. As with all my favourite anthologies, *First Personal Sexual* reveals an incredible array of experiences, writing styles, approaches, and angles. From straightforward accounts of masturbation sessions to personal histories to meditations on the subject to efforts to cope with shame instilled at an early age, Blank has covered a surprising amount of territory.

In "Behind the Shower Door" Rowen Michaels gives a chronological account of her solosexual experimentation throughout her entire life. It starts with, "I discovered exactly what my pussy was for when I was just twelve years old"; moves to, "The collection of pornography I had stolen from other places all indicated that women loved *big* things inside them and I worked persistently to fit bigger and bigger objects inside myself, looking for the ultimate 'high.'"; and ends with, "Now I suppose I'm a bit stodgy in my masturbation habits. I always do it in my room with my door closed, although I welcome the variety of doing it in different parts of the house when I know I won't actually be interrupted."

Several of the contributors discuss masturbatory episodes that left large imprints on their sexuality. BD Mann reveals, in "Confession of a Jerk-off", that when he was a teenager, he had a secret spot in the woods where he would play with himself for hours on end. One day he was caught by two girls around his age who blackmailed him into jerking off while they watched, an episode which he describes in pulse-quickening detail. "An Apt Student" is Maggie Michaels' account of being introduced at age eleven to the wonders of self-pleasure by her cool thirteen-year-old cousin Julie. Although Julie told Maggie to think about a man while touching herself, Maggie realised that her cousin's presence was much more inspiring. Some of the contributors talk about the guilt that was pushed on them as children. Molly K. Flanagan was around eleven when her mom walked in on her masturbating with a vibrator she had rigged out of an electric toothbrush. "She screamed hysterically and kept right on screaming as she ran down two flights of stairs to the basement where Dad was in his den." Luckily, her father and Alfred Kinsey assured her that what she was doing was perfectly normal, and she didn't seem to bear any psychological scars from the incident, if her subsequent actions are any indication.

In "Tight Jeans" Jill Nagle lets out a female secret: tight jeans provide an exquisite, unnoticed form of public masturbation. "We sit, lean, stand, and walk about our lives, discussing anything but the garment that happens to be fucking us at the moment. The perfect secret." "Sermon" by M. Christian is a hilarious, unapologetically belligerent rant: "Let's get this straight — we all do it. Sure, yeah, right: 'not me' you say. Sit the fuck down and shut the fuck up. We all do it. Nuns do it, dogs do it, bees do it, Newt Gingrich and Jesse Helms do it (God what a thought!)."

Elsewhere, female-to-male transsexual Mark Wilson tells about post-operative masturbation; Julia/dolphin Trahan puts the lie to the idea that people with disabilities "don't have sexualities"; Shannon Rene talks about masturbating her brains out while pregnant, especially during the last four weeks, and about doing herself on stage at the Crazy Horse theatre; Emile Zarkoff talks about his first time with a blow-up doll; Annie Sprinkle speculates on what might have been on the missing eighteen minutes of the Watergate tapes;

Thea "jilling off" in a photo by Victoria Heilweil.
I Am My Lover.

and Antler contributes a poem about the joys of jerking off as an adolescent boy.

If any book can help bring self-pleasuring out of the closet, this one can. Honest. Funny. Tender. Brash. Unashamed. Sexy. *First Person Sexual* is all of this and more. Most highly recommended.

Down There Press; $14.50
1996; softcover; 176 pp
0-940208-17-2

I AM MY LOVER
Women Pleasure Themselves
edited by Joani Blank

As the second strike in their masturbatory one-two punch [see *First Person Sexual* above], Joani Blank and Down There Press have created *I Am My Lover*, which documents the solosex sessions of a dozen women. Once again, the aim is to bring self-pleasuring out of the closet. To demystify it and treat it with the same positive, respectful, joyous attitude that should surround all forms of sex. The primary goal is not to titillate you, although you may very well find yourself titillated as a secondary effect (this is sex, after all). Instead, the six photographers want to give you non-embellished, true-to-life depictions of how several women actually give themselves pleasure.

In keeping with this strategy, a fairly wide range of women are photographed. Although some of them would be considered very attractive by conventional standards, none of them conform to the big-titted, perfectly-toned mannequin look so prevalent in porn aimed at straight men. Some of them are older, plumper, or hairier than your run-of-the-mill "bombshell".

Each of the photographers brings a different approach to the subject. Ron Raffaelli uses lots of grain, motion blur, and dramatic lighting to create the moodiest set of photos, although Phyllis Christopher comes close. Craig Morey and Victoria Heilweil include a large percentage of shots focusing directly on the bodies — particularly the genitals — of the women, while the others primarily take whole-body shots. Michael Rosen and Annie Sprinkle offer the sharpest, most documentary style photos with ordinary lighting.

The women, too, exhibit their unique styles. Thea masturbates with a big ol' wand vibrator while her cats look on.

Julia uses only her fingers. Miriam focuses mainly on her large breasts. Kim doesn't engage in penetration, while Vicki usually has a finger or a slim lucite dildo inside her. All of the women get down with themselves indoors, except Barbara, who prefers a forest clearing.

At the beginning of each spread, most of the women discuss their feelings and experiences regarding solosex. Ellen describes one of her techniques in detail: "Third finger, right hand. No toys. Such a distinctive, specialised touch to the clitoris. Slow, light, liquid, finger on top. Slight pressure to the side; circle, circle, circle. Almost ready for orgasm, retreat a bit for more touching pleasure..." Barbara writes, "My first masturbation to orgasm was on the day of my Holy Communion; it happened outdoors with a tree that I used to climb. It was my first real sexual, spiritual experience, and it was with Nature, not the Church."

Down There Press; $25
1997; oversized softcover; 103 pp
heavily illus; 0-940208-18-0

MORE JOY...
An Advanced Guide to Solo Sex
by Harold Litten

Harold Litten's book *The Joy of Solo Sex* [*Outposts* p 93] was a groundbreaking how-to manual for men who want to improve their masturbation technique. In *More Joy...*, Litten continues, extends, and advances his instructions for those who believe that solosex is one of their most important — or *the* most important — sexual activities.

One chapter relates three different forms of "brinksmanship", which involves stimulating yourself almost but not quite to the point of orgasm. The "whole-body high" is a way of playing with yourself while indefinitely delaying orgasm in order to stir up the entire body's sexual energy. Another technique involves repeated ejaculation without full orgasm, and the final one lets you stay on the crest of orgasm for minutes to hours. Needless to say, all of this takes some serious practice, which is why this book is called "an advanced guide".

Two chapters are devoted to toys and games. First, you'll learn about some of the basic helpers, including oils, baby powder, coconut cream, aloe vera, Vick's Vapo Rub, straps, rings, feather dusters, condoms, showers, and food. Then you'll move into more sophisticated activities — autointercourse (sticking your dick into your anus), depilation (hair removal), sounds (objects inserted into the urethra), piercing, and using vacuum pumps, vibrators, and other more expensive toys.

For your added pleasure, you might try spanking it with at least one other person present or masturbating in a public place, either with or without an audience. Litten also relates scenarios in which you are given a handjob by another person, which isn't technically solosex, but it is still jerking off.

The concluding chapters move beyond physical techniques to involve the mind and even the spirit. "Make the Next Time Your First Time Again", "Altered States", and "The Mystic Experience: Sex and God" can make masturbation a profound, moving, mind-blowing experience.

Not only is *More Joy...* helpful for men, but it's also utterly appropriate for anyone who wants to give more pleasure to their penised partner. Not only that, but at least half the book is not "dick specific", meaning that women could learn how to pleasure themselves more, too.

Factor Press; $12.95
1996; softcover; 190 pp
0-962531-8-7

ANNIE SPRINKLE

ANNIE SPRINKLE'S POST-MODERN PIN-UPS
Pleasure Activist Playing Cards
by Annie Sprinkle

Performance artist, photographer, writer, porn star, and all-around erotic Renaissance person Annie Sprinkle is one of the leaders of the pleasure activist movement, a group of people (mainly women) spreading the word that sex is fun, healthy, and spiritual. This message should be self-evident, but it's a sad commentary on our erotophobic, sexually-dysfunctional society that it needs forceful repeating.

Sprinkle has advanced the cause of pleasure in a number of ways, including her inventive, feminist erotic photography. Her photographs of other pleasure activists often take the form of updated pin-ups... in which the subjects are in full control, choosing their poses and props. To take this postmodern twist on a typically male institution one step further, she and Katharine Gates teamed up to create a deck of cards using these sex-positive pin-ups. The result is a revolutionary "nudie deck" that functions as a game, as art, as porn, and as an overview of the movement.

Each suit is devoted to a different kind of activist. The spades are pleasure artists, such as Italian performance artist Diviana Ingravallo, who is pictured raising her sheer skirt to reveal the only other thing she is wearing — a strap-on dildo. Ecstatic activists — who fight the politics of repression — are featured in the hearts. The three of hearts is Susan Manson, a porn star and dedicated anarchist (her motto: "Give me liberty or give me head!"). She is pictured sitting nude on a steel stool in a tiled room. Her legs are spread to reveal a shaving cream-covered pussy. On her torso, "Shave me" is written in foamy cream.

The thirteen women in the clubs suit are sexual performers. Koy Puss, the blonde lead singer of Glamourpuss, is pictured naked, singing into a microphone while she lays on a layer of purple feathers on a pink floor. The final suit, diamonds, portray erotic entrepreneurs. Chastity Church, a high-class call girl and actress, shows up on number eight, wearing only a pretty smile, daisies in her hair, nipple rings,

and tattoos, including a set of ferocious teeth on her outer labia. That leaves the four jokers (the first printing of the deck had two), including Sprinkle herself in a self-portrait that shows her spreading her legs while picking her nose.

The production values on the cards are top-notch. The sharp, full-colour pictures are printed on slick, heavy, oversized cards. Along with the deck you get a 64-page booklet in which Sprinkle gives short, gossipy biographies of the women on the cards. This alone is a valuable document.

Suitable for playing strip poker or solitaire, framing, or jerking off to, *Annie Sprinkle's Post-Modern Pin-Ups* succeeds on all fronts.

Gates of Heck; $20
1995; deck of 56 cards & 64-page booklet
heavily illus; 0-9638129-3-9

LINDA/LES AND ANNIE
The First Female-to-Male Transsexual Love Story

Les Nichols was born a girl. She was always attracted to other girls, and eventually became a femme lesbian. At twenty-nine, she joined the Army, started wearing men's clothes, and became butch. She began taking hormones and eventually decided to go all the way. Twelve operations and $50,000 later, Linda had become Les.

Nichols does indeed look like a man. He's got short black hair, sideburns, a moustache, three-day beard growth, and tons of tattoos. Repeated surgery removed Nichol's breasts and created a patchwork penis. The flesh from the lower abdomen was removed, turned inside out, and skin grafts were wrapped around the outside. Two round saline sacs were inserted into the mons to make testicles. Les's female genitalia was left unmodified, so he still has a vaginal opening and a clitoris.

Annie Sprinkle and Nichols met at a party. They instantly fell for each other, and Nichols decided that Annie would be the first person to test-drive his new dick. She excitedly accepted the offer, and the two of them had the encounter filmed for posterity and this video.

Although Nichols' penis receives sensations, in order to get erect, a hard plastic rod must be slid into his hollow penis at the base. But as soon as he and Annie start to hump, the rod slides out the top. While Annie and Les are in the kitchen cutting the tube down to size, Annie suddenly bursts into tears, crying for the pain felt by Les and all the other people who don't love the bodies they're born with.

They return to their lovemaking, but, unfortunately, the shorter rod slides out also. Les sticks his thumb into his penis, but this leads to other complications. Finally, they end up having oral and digital sex and rubbing their pussies together.

Linda/Les and Annie is a quality, sex-positive production that avoids any hint of sleaziness. Its simple style and uncensored sex scenes make it a must-see. You won't be able to tear your eyes away.

REW Video; $39.95
VHS video; 32 min

SLUTS AND GODDESSES

Annie Sprinkle's *Sluts and Goddesses* video workshop has become one of the seminal works of the sex-positive movement. Its aim is to instruct you on releasing the sluttish and goddess-like aspects of your sexuality in order to build self-confidence and acceptance, increase your sexual pleasure, and even grow spiritually.

Sprinkle and her multi-ethnic female facilitators merrily demonstrate dozens of ways to drop your inhibitions and have fun with yourself and/or your partner(s). The video starts with techniques to primp and pamper your bod, including facials, wet clay, wild makeup, jewellery, body painting, and shaving. You can dress up as whoever you desire — an enema nurse, a Girl Scout, a latex lover, or a man. Sprinkle advises: "Awaken your Inner Slut by stepping into some high heels."

After you're looking your best, you can have fun as the women show you how to dance, make sounds (sing, yell, etc.), and make your own porn. "Go ahead — show some pink." We are invited to do yoga by following along with Amy, but that might be difficult since Amy is an extreme contortionist.

"Probably the single most important key to sex I've yet discovered," says Sprinkle, "is conscious rhythmic breathing." Most of us breathe in a shallow manner, taking in just enough air to stay alive. "The more you breathe, the more you feel and the more you become alive." Three types of breathing are demonstrated — breath of fire, bliss breath, and group breathing, which may give you "breath orgasms".

Before you have sex, it's good to do some sexercises to get the erotic energies flowing through your body. Sprinkle and two of her cohorts go through the Ecstatic 8, Sugar Shack Shake, Womb Wave, Vag-a-lift, Doggy Dip, and others. Jane Fonda never worked out like this (not on camera, at least).

An absolute requirement for becoming a slut or goddess is getting to know your pussy. Examine it with a mirror. Use a speculum to look up inside. Smell it. Taste it. "Your pussy is your friend."

In the next segment of the video, Sprinkle and her friends get down to it. They demonstrate vibrators, strap-ons, toe-sucking, bootlicking, spanking, rimming, 69, dick/dildo stroking, getting double-fingered, threesomes, and various sexual positions. Anyone who says that female ejaculation is a myth should be forced to watch as Sprinkle shoots a clear load of girl-jizz at least three feet, splashing the two women who are fingering her.

Besides that jaw-dropping moment, this tape has also become famous for the five-minute orgasm that Sprinkle revels in with the help of a vibrator and two hands. She screams bloody murder as a line graph charts the ups and downs of intensity she is experiencing. During this "megagasm", Sprinkle clears out her emotional garbage — fear, anger, and frustration. She reminds us: "Orgasms are a path to truth and the meaning of life."

Elsewhere on the tape, we are taught about subtle energy orbit, prayer, ritual, the Goddess spot, kegels (pussy muscle exercises), and the all-important masturbation. Sprinkle and her crew are obviously very comfortable with each other and are having a blast making this video. The special effects and production tricks might be cheesy in someone else's hands, but these sluts and goddesses make it work for them. With a lot of humour and panache, they show how you can live up to your vast erotic potential. A+.

REW Video; $39.95
1992; VHS video; 52 min

XXXOOO
Love and Kisses From Annie Sprinkle [Two Volumes]
by Annie Sprinkle

If you're looking for a unique way to keep in touch with the people in your life, you might consider getting these collections of postcards (30 in each volume) featuring photographs and other art created by or featuring Annie Sprinkle. I'm not sure how many of these cards would make it through the postal system without being seized, so perhaps you can just keep them as a relatively inexpensive collection of Sprinkle's art, including some of her most famous pieces.

Among the works of art you'll see in Volume 1 are Annie doing her "Bosom Ballet", a "Tit Print" she made by inking one of her breasts and using it as a stamp, Annie's "Yin-Yang Breasts", "Annie Sprinkle's 101 Uses for Sex", a pussy decked out in flowers and greenery, Dutch sexual anarchist Cora Emens licking her own toes, "40 Reasons Why Whores Are My Heroes", the Aphrodite Award for Sexual Service to the Community (one way to deserve it is to "Donate a mercy fuck"), Annie having her famous five-minute "Energy Orgasm", "A Public Cervix Announcement" which features a close-up of a cervix (strangely, it's not Annie's), and photos of other sex pioneers, including Lydia Lunch, Linda Montano, and Lily Burana. Also included is the reality-based "Anatomy of a Pin-Up Photo", which shows Annie looking glamorous but tells the real story with arrows pointing to various areas of her body. These arrows reveal: "Bra is a size too small to make my breasts look bigger"; "Corset makes my waist 4 1/2" smaller, but I can't breathe", "Haemorrhoids don't show, thank goodness!". [ISBN 1-889539-00-7]

In the second volume, there's a self-portrait of Annie spreading her legs as she sticks a finger up her nose, a shot of Annie's friend Katharine as a nude, crucified Jesus, a picture of a vagina covered with the contents of two eggs, an eerily-lit masturbation shot, a poem Annie typed with her ass, a set of lactating breasts, "Annie Sprinkle's Fuck You Note", "Things I Put In My Twat", A *USA Today*-style graphic showing the amount of cock Annie has sucked, portraits of several more sex radicals, and "Miss Sprinkle's Guidelines for Sex in the 90s". [ISBN 1-889539-01-5]

Both volumes of *XXXOOO* are carefully designed and produced. The whole thing is printed in colour on ultra-heavy postcard stock. Each postcard takes up about two-thirds of a page, with the other third containing Annie's text and a smaller reproduction of the image (so you'll still be able to see it even if you send the postcard).

Gates of Heck; $11.95 each
1997; small softcovers; 60 pp each
heavily illus

TUPPY OWENS

CONSENTING ADULTS

This newspaper from Tuppy Owens and her organisation, the Sexual Freedom Coalition, contains the latest sex-positive news and views from Britain.

The second issue covers sex workers' experiences, Pervefest, S/M Pride, "Naturism: Why British Nudists Are Not Radical", "Nightlife: How to Throw a Great Sex Party", gay rights in Britain, a national petition to legalise all forms of sex between consenting adults in the UK, the Erotic Oscars, Sex on the Internet, "Censorship: Police Proposals to Classify Porn", sex on drugs, sex therapy, and sex and disability.

SFC/PO Box 4ZB/London W1A 4ZB/ENGLAND
WWW: www.sfc.org.uk/adults/default.htm
Four issue sub (one year): $50, £20 UK, £25 Europe

HIGH TEAS
Twelve "Easy to Feed Each Other" Recipes
by Tuppy Owens

This tiny book contains a dozen recipes for food that is especially enjoyable as a prelude to sex. Ultimate angels is "traditionally luxurious fare" that involves salmon, pineapple, caviar, milk, eggs, cinnamon, and garlic clove. Owens' advice on eating this dish reads, in part: "It begs to be devoured on soft cushions near the sofa, in a room bathed in mellow music and very soft lights."

Messy spare ribs is another meal, but these are to be enjoyed in a less laid-back manner than ultimate angels. They are to be put in floating bowls and eaten in the bathtub. "Use the smaller bowls for the bones, the bath water as finger bowls and your bodies as napkins."

Other recipes include carpaccio, satay, piccata alla pecorina, chicken in mint, and nut flan. On the page facing each recipe is an erotic black and white photo that has been hand-tinted in colour. Oddly, all the photos are of women. Won't straight and bi women and gay and bi men be cooking with this book, too?

Tuppy Owens; $10, £5 Europe, £3.50 UK
1990; tiny hardcover; 25 pp
heavily illus; 1-872819-01-X

THE POLITICALLY CORRECT GUIDE TO GETTING LAID
by X [Tuppy Owens and friends]

In order to be politically correct these days, you have to stifle your sexual urges. After all, thinking of people in a sexual way demeans them, right? Flirting with and chatting up prospective partners is degrading to all involved. "But relax, we've caught you cadging a quick look over your vegeburger and now, with this guide, will ensure you get laid safely, AND remain TPC (Totally Politically Correct)."

This mini-book (3.5" x 4.5") is set up so that each two-page spread has bite-size text on the left page and a trenchant cartoon on the right. In the first spread, Owens tells it like it is: "Denying that you have sexual desires for people of the opposite, or same gender, will never make the world a better place for any of us." The facing cartoon shows a woman saying to a nervous guy: "My Tuesday group says I should stop repressing my desires and get a good shafting. Are you up for it?"

Among the advantages of sex are that it heals, it makes you a more whole and harmonious person, it's a conservation measure (because it generates heat), etc. Owens' advice for getting laid ranges from politically correct — don't rule people out because of disability, age, or appearance — to politically incorrect — getting slightly drunk can open you up to do things you've always wanted but were to afraid to try. She also discusses overcoming guilt, communicating openly, having sex with friends ("Caring about the sexual needs of your friends and seeing to them in moments of dire frustration is a PC ideal."), achieving androgyny, avoiding games, and more.

Because the information in this book is presented in such small bursts, it doesn't make a good manual for specifics on how to get laid or what to do once you're being laid. Owens' main purpose is to fire off short bursts of ideas to get you thinking. And laughing. And screwing.

Tuppy Owens; $10, £2.50 UK, £5.50 Europe
1992; tiny paperback; 92 pp
heavily illus; 1-872819-08-7

THE SAFER SEX MANIAC'S ADDRESS BOOK
by Tuppy Owens

Do you want an address book that goes beyond cutesy designs and "respectable" solid colours? Acknowledge your sexual side with this slim address book from Tuppy Owens. It looks conservative on the outside (except for the title), but inside is a ton of sexual information along with space to write the names, addresses, phone numbers, etc. of the important people in your life.

Each of the 23 sections (X/Y/Z and P/Q are combined) opens with a work of art by an artist whose name starts with the letter of that section. For example, F shows a drawing by the eighteenth-century artist Peter Fendi. The artist's biography (which is included for all twenty-three of them) states: "Despite his short career, he was one of the official artists at the court of Emperor Franz Josef I of Austria, and his pictures of strangely pneumatic ladies and their acrobatic lovers may well have been ordered by a decadent member of the Viennese court."

On the next one or two pages, Owens gives capsule biographies of people who are important for sexual reasons. Among the hundreds of entries: Charles Baudelaire, Robert Crumb, Honeysuckle Divine, Alfred Kinsey, Anaïs Nin, and Veronica Vera.

The space for each of your entries is preceded by a sexual word, written in a style that reflects its meaning (*semen* uses dripping wet letters). Some of the words in the L section are *loose, limp, legendary, latex lover, leather queen, load licker,* and *libidinous.* Just be careful which of your friends you put next to which word!

A thin vertical strip along the side of each page presents an interlocking series of sexual illustrations. Each section has a different strip.

Nice idea, well-executed. If you use this book, you'll want excuses to refer to it, so you might actually keep in better touch with family and friends.

Tuppy Owens; $20, £6 UK, £7.50 Europe
1989; small, thin hardcover; 160 pp
heavily illus; no ISBN

FRANK MOORE

ART OF A SHAMAN
by Frank Moore

Frank Moore is a sacred sex shaman, a performance artist whose rituals are designed to get participants in touch with themselves and enhance their sexuality, personal relationships, and other intense aspects of their lives. *Art of a Shaman* was originally presented as a speech at New York University's "New Pathways in Performance" conference. In it, Moore lays down his philosophies regarding the power of performance and art and what he's trying to achieve with his rituals.

Moore was born with cerebral palsy, and his parents were told that he had no hope of a normal life and should be placed into an institution. They rejected this view of their son. By doing this, they became Moore's role models in going against the grain. He rejected the cultural expectations that were heaped on him and decided to live life on his own terms. In an ironic way, Moore's disability helped him. "I was never under pressure to be good at anything, to make money, to make it in 'the real world', to be polished — and the other distractions that modern artists have to, or think they have to, deal with. So I could focus on having fun, going into taboo areas where magical change can be evoked."

The reason Moore started doing performance was not to express himself. "It was simply the best way I saw to create the intimate community which I as a person needed and that I thought society needed as an alternative…" In these performances, the line between artist and audience is erased. The cast and the audience mingle and participate together, with Moore acting as "a channel through which a whole host of factors actively can mix together, creating a performance, creating a community, creating change."

Art of a Shaman contains descriptions of a number of Moore's widely divergent performances. During his brief stay in New York City, he developed a performance called Inter-Relations. "Inter-Relations was focused on clothes…

undressing, dressing, exchanging clothes, using clothes to tell your life story. After I did it a number of times, I began to realise that I could never predict what the performance would be like. The cast, in street clothes, came in with the audience. Everyone sat on the floor, so there was no way to tell who was the cast and who was the audience. So when the cast started to do their unspoken ritual, members of the audience slowly copied the actions, even undressing in slow motion."

inter-relations; $5
1991; staple-bound oversized softcover; 46 pp
no ISBN

CHEROTIC MAGIC
by Frank Moore

Cherotic Magic attempts to relate Frank Moore's overarching philosophy of life/reality/sexuality into a framework that you can apply to your life. "At first, it looks like it is about the relationship between an apprentice and a master teacher in an intense journey into the magical secrets of reality alchemy. This level is true. But suddenly the apprentice turns into you, and the teacher turns into your lover, the magical other. The apprenticeship transforms into your relationship to life. This reveals the powerful creative force of universal trust and deep love. The student/teacher relationship transmutes into your every relationship."

The basis of *Cherotic Magic* — the way I understand it — is connecting to yourself and the people around you. The main way to do this is to get your Chero flowing. Chero is Moore's name for the life energy/life force/orgone/libido (in the original sense of the word) that flows through each of us. One of the best ways to get your Chero charged is through eroplay, which is pleasurable touching for its own sake. Eroplay is the same as foreplay, except that it does not lead to intercourse or orgasm. By using Chero, we can shape our own realities, heal ourselves and others, and perform other life-changing activities.

Cherotic Magic is extensively illustrated by LaBash, whose swirling, interconnected collage-like drawings are designed to offer a visual equivalent of Moore's written message.

inter-relations; $15
1990; plastic comb-bound oversized softcover; 109 pp
heavily illus; no ISBN

THE CHEROTIC (R)EVOLUTIONARY

The Cherotic (r)evolutionary is the zine of Frank Moore and friends. Carol A. Queen contributes a true story to Volume 1 #4. In "Warm Silk" she vividly describes spending the day in an extremely turned-on state and then masturbating like a fiend that night. "I love the wave of crazy horniness that washes over me when I'm alone, separate from any love or lust I feel for a woman or a man, that makes me want to straddle the bedposts. I love the frantic attempt to incorporate the whole world into my cunt, a juicy itch that can't possibly be scratched from the outside." Other offerings include the poem "Jesus Lives on Haight Street", comments on Native American sexual attitudes, paintings by Joanna Pettit,

Hallucinogenic sex from Michael LaBash.
Cherotic Magic Sex.

and photos by Annie Sprinkle. Volume 1 #5 has a long inter-view with Paul Krassner by Moore, a poetic tribute to Billie Holiday, a review of Annie Sprinkle's Post Post Porn Mod-ernist show, and much more.

inter-relations/PO Box 11445/Berkeley CA 94712
Single issue: $5
no subscriptions

OTHER SEXUAL VISIONARIES

GLENNDA AND CAMILLE DO DOWNTOWN

In this half-hour film drag queen Glennda Orgasm (alter ego of Glenn Belverio) and anti-feminist feminist scholar Camille Paglia engage in escapades throughout downtown New York while dishing about various topics, including beauty contests, Lolitism, omnisexuality, date rape, and more. Glennda sports a fashionably loud dress, medium-length blonde hair, Cleo-patra eyeliner, and a Valley girl drawl. Paglia looks more conservative with her short greying hair, a white tee-shirt, and a black unstructured jacket. She is famous for her brand of loud pro-porn, pro-sex feminism, presented in her books *Sexual Personae* and *Vamps and Tramps*.

The dynamic duo start off in front of a fountain in Wash-ington Square Park. Paglia explains, "We're here to trash, essentially, the feminist establishment and all anti-sex porn folk... This is anti-Andrea Dworkin Day" (referring to the most virulent anti-porn feminist in the world). She reiterates her famous credo: "Pornography and art are identical for me."

"A day without pornography," Glennda chimes in, "is like a day without sunshine."

Paglia loves to talk, as this video clearly demonstrates, and Glennda usually has to interrupt to get her two cents in. While still in the park, Paglia declares, "Drag queens are the dominant sexual persona of this decade." When Glennda tells her that some people complain that male crossdressers mock women, Paglia replies that, on the contrary, "Drag queens have preserved the power of women."

The terrible twosome start their journey, encountering a sidewalk table set up by Women Against Pornography (WAP). This is undeniably the high point of their adventure. After seeing the cameras filming the event, the WAP women demand that they be turned off. Meanwhile, Glennda is gawk-ing at one of their protest posters, which shows a cover of *Hustler*: "Camille, look at the picture. Oh my God, that's hot. Wow!" Paglia asks, "Where can we get some of that?" Things heat up rapidly, with Paglia raking WAP over the coals at the top of her lungs, while a crowd of New Yorkahs gather round. "You're afraid," she taunts the WAPsters. "You guys are real tough aren't you, when no one's contradicting your ideas?... You're anti-art, anti-sex, anti-everything. You people can go to hell!... This is bullshit! Bullshit!" WAP and a bystander attempt to fight back, but Paglia simply steamrollers them.

Next, the two end up in front of Stonewall, where Paglia gets on her knees and kisses the ground. She and Glennda take the opportunity to bash the mainstream gay rights move-ment, which often tries to marginalise drag queens and leatherfolk. They agree that the movement has been taken over by Yuppy whitebread who lack philosophy and vision. Paglia reminds Glennda that it was the drag queens who first fought back against the cops during the Stonewall riot. Paglia also gets in some more licks against feminism. "Femi-nist rhetoric is based on the victimisation of woman. Woman as victim. Drag queen philosophy is based on the idea of woman as dominatrix of the universe."

The next stop is Gay Pleasures bookstore, where Paglia says that gay male pornography is "the hottest porn there is", because it's so brazen and unashamed. Lastly, our rab-ble rousers chat near the Hudson River, by the decrepit pier that is a well-known sex spot, especially for gay men. Paglia manages to get in some more highly flammable statements concerning her ideas about date rape.

Even though *Glennda and Camille Do Downtown* is mostly talk — wacking WAP was the only truly adventurous moment — it's still a rip-snortin' good time.

Glenn Belverio/S.O. Productions; $19.95
1993; VHS video; 29 min

REAL LIVE NUDE GIRL
Chronicles of Sex-Positive Culture
by Carol Queen

At last we have a sorely-needed collection of essays by Carol Queen. Her credits as a sexual commentator are impecca-ble: she's an admittedly kinky, submissive, exhibitionistic bi-sexual sex worker who works at Good Vibrations, writes a column for the California sex newspaper *Spectator*, co-hosts a weekly public access show for the prostitute rights group

COYOTE, wrote *Exhibitionism for the Shy* [above], and co-edited the one-of-a-kind anthology *Switch Hitters: Lesbians Write Gay Male Erotica and Gay Men Write Lesbian Erotica* [below]. To top it off, she will soon be earning a PhD in sexology.

True to the sex-positive movement, most of Queen's writings are based on her own experiences. The level of candidness reaches a high point with the very first selection, "Dear Mom: A Letter About Whoring", which takes the form of a letter to Queen's deceased mother. In it she tries to explain to her mom why she became a prostitute, but she also ends up explaining to all of us why sex in general became such an important part of her life. Queen's mother never allowed herself to experience her own sexual nature, probably because she didn't come to terms with being molested by her older brother. Queen writes: "Sex was so profound a problem to you that it became a path for me, mingling growth and individuation, spirituality and materiality, passion and politics."

Of all the best-known sex-positive activists, Queen seems to be one of the most active when it comes to scrambling notions of orientation and desire. Again, this goes back to her own life. As she grew up, she was attracted to guys and then to girls. She came out as lesbian even though she slept with men… but not just any men — gay men. "For years I refused to look at a dick on a straight man, but a fag's penis was a different appendage altogether." She also discovered that she preferred gay porn to all other types. "I had to listen to what made my pussy wet, not what was said in Mary Daly study groups." This mixing of boundaries is explored in several essays.

Queen's jobs as a prostitute and a peep show worker have given her plenty of insight into the human libido. In fact, that's a large part of why she became a sex worker in the first place. "I'm a sexual anthropologist at heart, kind of a highfalutin' voyeur." Interestingly, Queen admits to being turned on by many of the things she's done in the line of duty, which flies in the face of the "men are dogs, I do it strictly for the money" stereotype of sex workers. One of the most insightful essays is "Through a Glass Smudgily: Reflections of a Peep Show Queen". At the peep show, a person (usually a man) would enter a booth. Behind a glass barrier, Queen would do what he asked — strip, masturbate, talk dirty, etc. You'd think that patrons would simply jerk off while watching her, but on her first day alone Queen had a patron who indulged in an incest fantasy, another who dominated her verbally, and a third who had her watch as he put a gigantic dildo up his ass.

Elsewhere in this wide-ranging collection, Queen discusses performing on-stage with Annie Sprinkle, rails against circumcision, praises butch lesbians and strap-on dildos, relates the delights of being spanked, introduces us to the man who opened China's first sex shop, and says farewell to the late "supermasochist" Bob Flanagan. Not bad for a self-described "recovering shy person"!

Cleis Press; $14.95
1997; softcover; 200 pp
1-573440736

SEXWISE

by Susie Bright

Following *Susie Sexpert's Guide to Lesbian Sex* and *Susie Bright's Sexual Reality* [both *Outposts* p 89], *Sexwise* is Bright's third book of insightful essays on sex, life, and culture as refracted through a sex-positive lens. The most confrontational essay is "Dan Quayle's Dick", in which Bright gives a detailed account of fucking the former Vice President. Of course, in the end we find out that it was only a wet dream. The part that stuck out most in my mind, though, was Bright's perceptive and sympathetic observation of Quayle's love for his daughter. When interviewed on CNN, he had said that even if his daughter decided to abort her pregnancy, he would support her decision. The next day, Marilyn Quayle was in an uproar, declaring that if pregnant, her daughter would carry the baby to term. "Marilyn must have carried her pregnancies to term, and raised small children, during times that were not altogether to her liking. She resented it and, like every other repressed mother, she was determined to pass on her suffering to her daughters — particularly her eldest daughter, who brought a light to her husband's eyes that he may have stopped sharing with his wife a while back."

In "How To Make Love To A Woman: Hands-on Advice From a Woman Who Does", Bright gives straight men a few tips on seducing women. After all, lesbians and straight men both "are hung up on girls" and "vie for the same joy". Her initial advice concerns "the look", in which you use your eyes to openly express interest in a woman. "If she doesn't want you, she'll complain to her friends about how you 'objectified' and 'degraded' her, but ignore all that crap. Calling a man a sexist interloper is just a trendy way of stating an old-fashioned sentiment: 'He's not my type.' When a dyke gets an unwanted ogling from another dyke, we don't use political pejoratives. We just say, 'Over my dead body.'"

In other essays, Bright puts in her two cents about Madonna, Stephen King, Nicholas Baker (author of *Vox*), Dr. Ruth, Camille Paglia, Jimi Hendrix, radical feminist Catherine MacKinnon, "gay radar", women's erotica, and more. She also interviews Erica Jong, porn director Andrew Blake, and former Black Panther Elaine Brown.

Cleis Press; $10.95
1995; softcover; 127 pp
1-57344-002-7

SUSIE BRIGHT'S SEXUAL STATE OF THE UNION

by Susie Bright

Since the release of her first book of essays — *Susie Sexpert's Lesbian Sex World* — Susie Bright has become perhaps the world's foremost sexual commentator. Along the way, she also created the pathbreaking *Herotica* series and edited the first four volumes, co-founded and co-edited the courageous lesbian erotic magazine *On Our Backs*, and continues to edit the seminal *Best American Erotica* series. In a way, her latest book is her most important yet. Susie Sexpert provides shoot-from-her-hips commentary about the touchiest of subjects in a way that tears away the veils of conformity and hypocrisy… but she's always done that. What makes this book so important is that it was published by the huge corporate machine known as Simon & Schuster, a tentacle of Paramount Productions, which in turn is a subsidiary of the multinational media behemoth Viacom.

Since Bright's previous books of commentary have all been published by the independent Cleis Press, this move is certain to raise cries that our beloved badgirl has sold out. This argument is not without some merit, but I see being published by a giant media conglomerate as a two-sided thing. Yes, the Man is using Bright to line his pockets with more filthy lucre, but also keep in mind that Bright is using the Man to get her unabashedly sex-positive message to the masses. Because of Simon & Schuster's massive distribution and promotion power, people in suburban shopping malls are being exposed to ideas such as, "We know how to say no to sex in fifty different languages, in every mood, place, and time, but it's clear why it rings so hollow and aching sometimes — we never learned to say yes to sex, without duress, without a fall from grace." People looking for the latest Danielle Steele opus in the new releases section of McChain Bookstore will thumb through Bright's book and learn that, "When I first discovered vibrators, I had vibrator races: I would see if I could come in under a minute, and then laugh like a maniac when I succeeded." And, "It's ironic: even though butt-fucking is popularly associated with gay men in today's sexual culture, it is in fact heterosexuals who have gone wild about their asses."

Are the calcified brainstems of John and Jane Q. Public ready to hear Bright slag Christianity, admit that she's tasted her menstrual blood, or talk about getting fisted by a butch lesbian on the street in front of a gay club? Well, ready or not, here she cums. The topics that Bright sounds off about read like a list of hot-button issues: abortion, AIDS, anti-Internet hysteria, the "born-again virgin" movement, gay marriage, female beauty, SM, cybersex, anonymous sex, sexual fantasy, gender, violence, and pornography. But no matter how explosive her opinions, Bright never comes across as abrasive. She sounds like your younger sister, who always says exactly what's on her mind but manages to be endearing anyway.

I haven't heard any reports concerning whether or not Simon & Schuster refused to let Bright address certain topics, but as far as I can tell, she hits fairly hard and covers all the bases. I realise that no single book is going to transform our crusty society into an erotic autonomous zone, but if *Sexual State of the Union* causes just a few people — who might otherwise never have been reached — to unhook their mental chastity belts, then it's done a very fine service indeed.

Simon & Schuster; $12
1997; softcover; 256 pp
0-684838508

SEXUAL FICTION & POETRY

BEST GAY EROTICA SERIES
edited by various

With the inaugural volume *Best Gay Erotica 1996*, the editors purposely went about selecting only those stories that disposed of the conventions of gay male porn, whether through inventive plots, structure, language, points of view, or insights. Co-editor Scott Heim (who shared the decision-making process with Michael Ford) writes in his introduction: "I made the stipulation that each piece had to stray from my preconceptions and admittedly ingenuous expectations… There are only so many synonyms for *cock* and *cunt*. Only so many retellings of the well-hung TV repairman; the moustachioed traffic cop willing to accept a good, imaginatively perverse bribe; the pair of naughty nursemaids caught sixty-nining in the storage room." Among the seventeen stories are "First Shave", "Ganged", the HIV+ tale "The Last Blowjob", the Marine-screwing "Whiskey Dicks", "Good in Tension", "Loveth Thou Me, Boy?", and the excellent coming-of-age story, "Playing Solitaire". [$12.95; 1996; 180 pp; 1-57344-052-3]

Even though *Best Gay Erotica 1997* was put together by two new editors — Richard Labonté and Douglas Sadownick — the mission has obviously remained the same. All of these stories have something to offer besides just a fuck'n'suck. "Cocksucker's Tango" is Justin Chin's meditation on performing oral sex. "The very first time I had a cock in my mouth, I gagged so hard, I vomited so much I scared myself. The man I was sucking fled the toilet stall. At that moment I decided that I would never gag again, no matter how large or mean the next cock got. I practised with fat marker-pens, broomhandles, shampoo bottles, beer bottles, carrots, cucumbers." In "Je T'aime, Batman, Je T'adore", Robin professes his desire for his superhero partner, and in "The First Branding Journal", a man writes about branding his submissive. "Sex With God" is a humorous yet powerful story about rejecting organised religion, and "Lance as a Redneck Spiritual Adept" is a highly experimental short piece about the connection between sex and spirituality. Scott O'Hara's "Social Relations" — which was supposed to be published in O'Hara's own anthology from Masquerade Books, but they didn't have the nerve to publish it — deals with early adolescent sexuality and unrealised incestuous desire. [$14.95; 1997; 201 pp; 1-57344-067-1]

The 1998 volume of *BGE* will be co-edited by Richard Labonté and Christopher Bram. I'm already sure that it will be a must-have.

Cleis Press; softcovers

BEST LESBIAN EROTICA SERIES
edited by Tristan Taormino and others

The Best Lesbian Erotica series is not content to merely be a collection of the "greatest hits" of the past year in the genre of lesbian sex fiction. It ambitiously strives to include works that defy convention and break new ground. Thus, *BLE* doesn't just recap the past year but is helping to move erotic writing ahead.

In the first volume, *Best Lesbian Erotica 1996*, the editors — Tristan Taormino and Heather Lewis — are attempting to erase boundaries of gender and orientation, to show that sexual identity is fluid and unpredictable. These stories are ones that challenge assumptions and confront fears. In fact, notions of what "lesbian erotica" is supposed to be are tossed out the window — the authors are not necessarily lesbians, and the stories don't necessarily contain lesbian sex, although most of them do. Some of them prominently feature men, and a good number of these tales are dark, violent, and disturbing. Among the many standouts are "Healy", "Semiraw", "The Little Macho Girl", "Addict Girl #1: Drug-free Afternoon", "Chelsea Thirteen", "Bird", "The Angel at the Top of My Tree", "Pumpkin Pie", and "Confessions of a Blood Eater". It's not hyperbole to say that this book really does push limits. [$12.95; 1996; 197 pp; 1-57344-054-X]

Best Lesbian Erotica 1997, which sees Jewelle Gomez join Tristan for editing duties, takes a different tack. While the previous volume emphasised the forbidden currents of sexuality, this one gives voice to erotic desires of women who often have to struggle to be heard — African Americans, Latinas, Asians, Native Americans, Jews, the disabled, blue collar workers, and others. While it again proves that the sexual is political, *BLE 97* doesn't become watered down in political correctness (Tristan would *never* let that happen). After all, this is *Best Lesbian Erotica*, not *Best Leftist Erotica*. The action is always hot and boundaries are frequently pushed, although most of these selections stick to a more traditional narrative style than the entries in the 1996 volume. Among the pieces that stayed with me after I had read the collection are the sauna encounter "Steam" by Jeannine De Lombard, the seemingly autobiographical "Like a Virgin" by Julia/dolphin Trahan, "Adventures in Dick Sucking, or Why I Love to Suck Butch Cock: An Oral History" by Bree Coven, Cecilia Tan's rapid-fire "Penetration", and Robin Bernstein's utterly original "Virgin's Gift", about a Jewish lesbian high-schooler who fantasises she's a Hasidic Jewish man deflowering his wife on their wedding night. [$14.95; 1997; 194 pp; 1-57344-065-5]

The next instalment of *BLE* will be co-edited by Jenifer Levin, author of *Water Dancer* and *Love and Death & Other Disasters*. As a high school pal of mine used to say, "I can't hardly *wait!*"

Cleis Press; softcovers

BETWEEN THE CRACKS
The Daedalus Anthology of Kinky Verse
edited and with photos by Gavin Dillard

Doesn't just recap the past year, but is also helping to move erotic writing ahead. *Best Lesbian Erotica.*

While *Ritual Sex* [below] is the best collection of sex writings I've ever read, *Between the Cracks* is undoubtedly the finest collection of erotic poetry I've ever read. Come to think of it, I really haven't read very many collections of erotic poetry, but that doesn't matter... I'm not sure how an anthology *could* be better than this one. Gavin Dillard — porn star, writer, poet, photographer — has set out to create a central repository for the most important verse to deal with unorthodox sex. He has searched high and low, gathering poems from the famous, the infamous, and the unknown, from ancient times till yesterday, from the obvious to the obscure, the sublime to the ridiculous. Together they form not only an unparalleled treasure trove of erotic poems but also a map of human sexuality.

To be included in this collection, a poem has to examine some form of non-standard sex. Dillard explains his criteria in the introduction. Oral sex, anal sex, group sex, prostitution, watching porn, and sex with youth were all considered too universal a part of the sexual spectrum to warrant inclusion on their own. Non-consensual encounters were cryptically left "out of the realms of kink." So what did make it in? Bondage, SM, clothing fetishes (leather, latex, Levis, shoes, etc.), crossdressing, scars, tattoos, fistfucking, dildos, food, autofellatio, piss play, scat, assholes, scent, feet, biting, motorcycles, cars, guns, bloodlust, suicide, and more. As if that weren't enough, *Between the Cracks* deals with the subjects that make most other erotic publishers shake in their boots — necrophilia, bestiality, and incest. And although intergenerational sex isn't represented as a category, it still makes appearances, as in "Skullcups Vs. Boymouthcups" by Antler and "Masturbation" by Cheryl Townsend.

There's such an overwhelming amount of material here — around 300 poems — that I hardly know how to approach it for a review. I think I'll just point out a few of the more intriguing selections from the book to give you an idea of the range of topics and approaches. In "Mouse" by Trebor, the narrator starts out downloading online porn images and ends up getting pleasure with his computer's mouse.

> By the time I got it up my ass
> the screen saver was on
> which just happened to be a white mouse in a maze
> As I squirmed, files started opening
> fonts turned bold
> there were preferences and commands
> tools and windows
> the control panels all went down

Belinda Subraman writes in "A Pentecostal Neighbour" of asking the title character what it's like to speak in tongues. After she responds that it's like a climax, "I ask her if she's/relaxed afterwards,/she says yes./I ask her if she/smokes a cigarette,/she smiles/and touches the bible/like a lover's cock." Thaddeus Rutlowski's "Sock Man" is one of many entries that is not technically a poem but a short prose piece written in a quasi-poetic style. The narrator goes to the laundromat in his apartment complex and steals strangers' socks from the dryer, then races to his apartment. "I waste no time in defiling the socks. I nibble them with my lips, soak them with my spit, then take out my argyle buster and work them over till they need patches. When I am totally spent, I return them to the dryer."

"Yellow Fever" by Selena Anne Shephard and Andy Plumb is a short poem about an old man sitting in the centre of a circle of guys who are pissing on him. "He opens his mouth wide/and takes a drink of bittersweet pee/it goes down like fine wine". Meanwhile, back in 1871, the Decadent poets Paul Verlaine and Arthur Rimbaud were similarly teaming up to write "Sonnet to the Asshole". " It's a swooning olive chute, an enticing vent,/A tube where the heavenly praline makes its decent,/A feminine Canaan clammy with gobs of cum."

Many other famous poets of the past make appearances. While you shouldn't be surprised to see Sappho or the lusty Roman Catallus, your schooling may not have prepared you for poems by Emily Dickinson, Walt Whitman, and Edgar Allan Poe. Bet your teacher never told you that Poe's world-famous lament to his deceased child-bride, "Annabel Lee", ends with a veiled reference to necrophilia, which becomes obvious when you know about it: "And so, all the night-tide, I lie down by the side/Of my darling, my darling, my life and my bride,/In her sepulchre there by the sea — /In her tomb by the side of the sea."

Another type of famous person makes an appearance in "The Night Keanu Reeves Kicked Me in the Face" by Michael Gregg Michaud. The star of *Speed* has a broken ankle and is relaxing at a table in a night-club. The narrator pretends to lose a contact so he can crawl on the floor until he's just inches from Reeve's injured tootsie. "I moved so close I could smell/the dryness, the staleness of his foot./I wanted to take each little dusty kicker/slowly into my mouth,/let my tongue roll between each gummy bear,…"

Of the fourteen poems on incest, two of the best are "Thomas", Vytautas Pliura's painful tale of a boy's desire for his younger brother, and a much shorter untitled poem by editor Dillard: "I remember my brother making a deal with me, that if I would let him do it to me, he would let me do it to him./Well I did. But he didn't." The equally candid poems about animal sex include three by Deena Metzger. In "Moon in Taurus", she writes of being surprised as a bull tenderly sucks on her hand. "I have dreamed this animal but not his gentleness, not that I would herd with him, not that I would wish him to nudge my flanks, his skin slouched over his bones, a tent of a beast, not that he would drive me forward/head down/hungry/through the/night fields."

Finally, Dillard deserves a special commendation for rescuing Aleister Crowley's gloriously filthy erotic poetry from obscurity. The Beast 666 is best known for his work with magick and the occult, but the half dozen poems here show that he was no slouch when it came to pornography. To wit, these lines from "Leah Sublime":

> Rub all the muck
> Of your cunt on me, Leah
> Cunt, let me suck
> All your glued gonorrhoea!
> Cunt without end!
> Amen! til you spend!
>
> Cunt! you have harboured
> All dirt and disease
> In your slimy unbarbered
> Loose hole, with its cheese
> And its monthlies, and pox
> You chewer of cocks!

With further contributions from Pat Califia, Allen Ginsberg, Michael Lassell, Edmund Miller, Scott O'Hara, Gerry Gomez Pearlberg, Linda Smukler, Elissa Wald, and dozens of others, rest assured that *Between the Cracks* has achieved its goal of codifying and preserving pervy poetry. It's as close to definitive as a collection of omnisexual verse can be.

Daedalus Publishing Company; $18.95
1997; softcover; 354 pp
illus; 1-881943-10-0

THE BOOK OF ORGASMS

by Nin Andrews

In this witty, insightful collection of short short stories/meditations, orgasms are considered as living creatures who are very important to us and who bring us transcendent experiences. According to these 45 microtales — most of which are not even a page long — orgasms choose us. They float above people, resisting the call as long as they can. Eventually they swoop down into the body, but then leave almost immediately. Most orgasms don't like humans, but some do. Some orgasms are jerks, some are shy, some are selfish, and some are nice.

In "Teaching the Orgasm to Speak" the narrator talks to an orgasm. "Every human is an instrument to be played by an orgasm, she says. Some make no noise. Others produce an alarming array of discordant notes and can frighten away even the most determined orgasm. But the best sort of human has perfect pitch and can carry orgasm and person alike to a world from which there is no return."

The orgasm used to be a creature in the same way as a fish or a bird, according to "The Orgasm in Ancient Times". But one day a man captured her, put her in a cage, and tried to feed her fruit and wine, which she refused. She slowly withered away until she was only a sound. "Ever since then, she had been invisible and fleeting, slipping through the eager hands of lovers... She seeks revenge upon men and women, visiting them in their sleep and sweeping their minds clean of reason with a single puff of her warm breath."

"Notes on the Orgasm" presents some things to keep in mind. "The orgasm will peel you like an orange. You may feel exposed, raw, even wounded. The orgasm wants you to live life without the rind." "Many dislike the speed of orgasm, the way she comes and goes and takes all she can get. The orgasms cannot help herself. She has no tomorrow."

Asylum Arts; $8.95
1994; softcover; 64 pp
1-878580-69-8

BREATHLESS
Erotica
by Kitty Tsui

This collection of 26 erotic lesbian stories has its ups and downs. "vanilla and strawberries" seems by-the-numbers, but "i go out walking" is the highly unexpected story of a butch, with a strap-on dildo slung over her shoulder, who walks naked through a festival attended by 150,000 women. The story of a woman approaching an unapproachable woman in "unforgettable" doesn't really go anywhere, but "the girl loves garlic" — one of many stories heavily involving food — opens up new vistas. "Her clitoris rises to meet my hand, hard and tough, like a clove of garlic. I sink down to her, mouth open, tongue ready. I grip her with my mouth, massage her clit with my lips. I bite into her with my teeth, drawing blood. The metallic tang of it fills my senses. Pleasure sweeps over me as the sharp taste of garlic explodes in my mouth." Other highlights include "a femme in butch clothing", which is partly a contemplation of women and partly of food; "the abduction of Shar"; "the cutting", about a woman getting her first cutting on her breast; "the foodie club"; "damn safe sex"; and "Daddy and her girl".

Firebrand Books; $9.95
1996; softcover; 151 pp
1-56341-072-9

DARK EROS
Black Erotic Writings
edited and annotated by Reginald Martin, PhD

This anthology of erotic writing, put together by a co-editor of *Erotique Noir*, contains over 100 stories, poems, and essays from African-American writers. Selections include "C:\Back Slash\Merge", "Do Ya Got Some Blow?", "Electric Lover", "coffles: a suicide note", "Orgasm Notes", "Hurt Me", "Ode to My Sweet Sexy Brown", "Pussy Ann Trouble", "Forty-Five Is Not So Old", "Nzinga Astral Travels", "Sweat Burns", "Dear Lord, I Lift the Covers", "Why I Play with My Cunt", and "*Cajunto Sabor*".

St. Martin's Press; $25.95
1997; hardcover; 405 pp
0-312-15508-5

DOING IT FOR DADDY
Short and Sexy Fiction About a Very Forbidden Fantasy
edited by Pat Califia

These 22 taboo-bustin' short stories explore one of the most deeply buried aspects of the collective sexual unconscious — daddy fantasies. Most of these stories concern SM daddy scenes in all kinds of variations — gay, lesbian, straight, transgendered, submissive daddies, and more. In Carol Queen's "The Leather Daddy and the Femme, Part One: After the Light Changed" a woman passing as a man picks up a gay leather Daddy. As the action gets hotter, the Daddy discovers he's been duped, but keeps going anyway. The woman says to him: "'I'm no ordinary boy, Daddy, and I'm no ordinary woman. Do you want it? Just take it.' There is so much power in being open and accessible and ready. So much power in wanting it. That's what other women don't understand. You'll never get what you want if you make it too hard for someone to give it to you."

John Preston's "Birthday Boy" features a twenty-two-year-old man and his male partner, who's old enough to be his real father. It's the young man's birthday, and he and his domineering Daddy are about to celebrate. "He was real good about rolling the rubber out over my cock. I was all hard and ready when he whined, 'Daddy, please let me suck your dick!' 'You just spread 'em like you know you're supposed to,' I said, and I said it sharply enough that he knew better than to fool around anymore."

Pam Parker's untitled story breaks with most of the others because the lesbian narrator talks about fantasies involving her real dad. "There was a period of time — I remember it as being not very long — when I imagined my father with me in bed as I jerked off." "Family Man" by Jay Shaffer pushes things even further by describing a sexual encounter between a father and his adult son.

Other stories include "Our Father", "Long-Lost Brothers", "Forbidden Game, "What We Make, What We Are", and "It Takes a Good Boy to Make a Good Daddy". *Doing It For Daddy* is one of the most fiercely controversial collections of sex stories to be published in a long, long time.

Alyson Publications; $11.95
1994; softcover; 240 pp
1-55583-227-X

THE EROTIC READER
Selected Excerpts From Banned Books

This double cassette set lets you hear a man and a woman lustily reading from six Victorian sex novels. Includes *The Diary of Mati Hari*, *Flossie*, *Pauline the Prima Donna*, *Memoirs of a Young Don Juan*, *Confessions of an English Maid*, and *The Loins of Amon*. Just the thing for long commutes to work.

Passion Press; $16.95
1995; two cassettes
1-886238-00-6

EXTREMES
by Lizbeth Dusseau

Lizbeth Dusseau used to write for Masquerade but now publishes all of her work through her own company, Pink Flamingo Publications. The territory she has staked out generally has to do with dominance and submission, bondage and discipline — including lots of spanked bare bottoms — with women on the receiving end of male ministrations. *Extremes* is a collection of eleven short stories that break with this mould, mainly describing the exploits of self-assured, ferociously-willed women who unapologetically want to fuck their brains out.

Like much of what Lizbeth writes, most of *Extremes* is one-handed reading, but she has a flair for language that allows her to transcend the simple "stroke book" label. These stories have the power to turn the reader on, but they also have the power to make you appreciate a beautifully written passage or a clever turn of a phrase. "Garden Party" opens: "A tiny tendril of ivy wound its way up the thigh of the naked stone as if to make this bold woman of granite shy, the way it covered that place between her legs where — if she were alive — she'd accept the offerings of men." In "I Never Complain About a Gangbang", a woman goes into a porno theatre and starts getting hot and heavy with one of the men there while the other guys watch:

> Climbing off his lap, I wait as he takes out his cock. I see the size and cringe happily, realising how full I'll feel to have this one driven up my cunt. Descending to it, I feel the head enter where it's wet. A little dance at the top, I listen to him groan, then I sit right down so the full thick prick is way deep inside. We bounce together as his hands reach around to grab my breasts and hang on while he thrusts hard. I'm groaning, leaning back exposing more of me, taunting the boys in the theatre with what they can't have.

"57 Chevy" is a wet dream of a story about a guy who stops for a gorgeous, horny, willing woman sitting on the hood of a 57 Chevy that is parked by the side of a desolate desert highway. He gladly gives her some roadside vaginal, anal, and oral sex, as she directs the action. In other stories, a woman uses all of her orifices to full advantage while committing corporate espionage, a lawyer gets back at her husband — who's now too busy with cyberporn to bone her — by charging other men for hot sex, and two women engage

in a passionate relationship that seems doomed because of the untameable recklessness of one of them. The poems in this volume, written by Lizbeth's husband, contrast with the stories by providing less explicit, less specific celebrations of sexuality.

I masturbated once while reviewing this book, and I could probably have done it again by the time I finished, but I've still got a lot more reviewing to do, so I'll save my energy!

Pink Flamingo Publications; $9.95
1996; staple-bound softcover; 131 pp
no ISBN

FRIENDLY EROTICA
A Question of Boundaries
edited by Heide Brown & Jay Mussell

"Middle-aged hippies" Heide Brown and Jay Mussell decided to put together this anthology after they noticed that a large number of erotica collections featured stories that disturbed them because of their use of "dominance, abuse, and violence". While it's true that there are some (quite few, actually) stories out there that feature non-consensual encounters, the editors are also upset by consensual activities such as sadomasochism, which they lump together with sexual abuse as "indicators of cultural decline". Obviously, this attitude is going to immediately turn off and piss off a large number of people who might otherwise be open to a book of sexual writings. Wanting to create a collection of easy-going erotica is itself a good idea, since not everybody's taste runs toward pain and power, but the division of consensual sexualities into "healthy" and "unhealthy" strikes me as more than a little, well… unhealthy.

Nonetheless, taking *Friendly Erotica* for what it is — a collection of sexual stories and poems in the *Yellow Silk* vein — I think that it has its good moments, but it has lots of subpar moments too. This isn't too surprising when you consider that, "The call for submissions went out to friends and was passed on to friends of friends." Almost none of the writers here is professional, which doesn't mean that they're not good, but they probably haven't had a chance to hone their craft. For example, things get stilted when the main character in "Breaking the Link" wonders if he should try to dig through his porn tape collection for a video of guys performing auto-fellatio: "'No, I have a good one there already — another day I will enjoy watching the guys sucking themselves off.'"

Strangely, some of the stories themselves are uneven in quality. "Elderlove" is an important story in that it involves the sexuality of senior citizens, but it doesn't pick up steam till over halfway through. The sex scene in "Three Little Pieces" is so-so, but the part where the couple watches two dragonflies have sex is great.

Friendly Erotica is at its best when the contributors stretch their imaginations. The main premise of "You and Fish" is the similarity between the narrator receiving little kisses all over her body and the way it felt when little fish rubbed against her when she once went skinny-dipping. The connection between food and sex isn't new, but the prose poem "Food Is Such Sexy Stuff" does a fantastic job of showing the erotic nature of edibles. "New bread rising, soft as breasts and but-tocks for me to caress and pinch and sink my hands into…/ Eggplants like the pregnant bellies of black women shine with full promise."

Martin Park Communications; $14.95Can, $14.95US
1996; softcover; 123 pp
0-9680271-0-5

HEROTICA
A Collection of Women's Erotic Fiction
edited by Susie Bright

The first volume of the now legendary *Herotica* series helped to establish "feminist erotica" as a distinct, powerful sub-genre of porn. In the intro, editor Susie Bright provides a witty look at sexual material as it has related to women's desires in the past and present. "I began my pursuit of women's erotica looking underneath my girlfriends' beds. Stashed away, but within arm's reach, I discovered back issues of 'men's' maga-zines, Victorian-era ribald short stories, trashy novels with certain pages dog-eared, plain brown wrapper stroke books that seemed to have had a previous owner, classics like *The Story of O* or *Emmanuelle*, and even serious critiques of pornography that were paper-clipped to fall open to the 'good parts'."

Herotica attempts to gather together those far-flung pock-ets of pornorotica under one cover. Obviously, not every person's taste can be covered in one book, but Bright has chosen an eclectic variety of stories, because, as she has said, "Some women want the stars, some the sleaze." This collection runs the gamut of orientations, situations, loca-tions, orchestrations, and stimulations. But always, a woman (or women) and her desires are the focal point.

A woman dresses her girlfriend up in stockings, a garter belt, high heels, and a robe in "Shades of Gray". Then the lovemaking commences. "I love the taste of her. I rub my face against her lips as they open beneath me, blooming. I moan into her as her foot finds its way between my legs… Her clit moves beneath my tongue. As she begins to come, I follow. The surface of my skin has expanded and each touch of silk, or skin, or suede, sends me further out until I am too far to call back. We finish with a passion that will leave bruises."

The passion in "Shaman's Eyes" by Nancy Blackett strikes a more demure note. The young women in a Native American village are doing the maiden dance, in which they choose male partners for life. The main character nervously approaches the warrior she has fallen in love with, and finds that things are not as they appear.

Although reviewers quoted on the back cover trumpet the stories in *Herotica* as unpredictable and non-formulaic, I found a large number of them to be basically by the num-bers. Woman fucks her demanding boss at the office. Woman fucks another woman on a subway train. Woman fucks her roommate's sensitive yet studly brother. (Perhaps when this book first came out a decade ago, having women engage in these otherwise stereotypical scenarios was radical.) About half of the stories, though, do throw some nice curve balls. Sex educator Isadora Alman offers a refreshing change of

"My pussy grabbed that seat so hard, I could almost smell the plastic meltin'!" *Hog Heaven.*

pace in "Big Ed", in which a giant, hairy Southern mountain man gets in touch with his feminine side. In the science fric-tion story "Visit to the Mighoren", a female scholar from earth visits a bordello stocked with dashing men of the human variety.

Down There Press; $10.50
1988; softcover; 150 pp
0-940208-11-3

HEROTICA [Cassette Version]
edited by Susie Bright

This double cassette set features readings of ten of the sto-ries from *Herotica* [above], plus an afterword from Susie Bright. Blake C. Aarens, Tweed, Angela Fairweather, and Sharon Cheralyke read "Pickup", "Night Travelers", "Just a Bad Day", "Sex Education", "Jane's Train", "Police Protec-tion", and others.

Passion Press; $16.95
1995; two cassettes
1-886238-02-2

HOG HEAVEN
Erotic Lesbian Stories
by Claressa French

Claressa French writes her lesbian erotica with an easy, play-ful style and a flair for inventiveness. These twelve stories are divided into four sections based on their explicitness: PG-13, X, XX, and XXX. The story in the first category could be read by "your Aunt Minnie", while the two stories in the last category "are only for those readers who have never heard of (or have chosen to ignore), P.C.-ness."

We're going to skip the first category ('cause if you're not gonna go all the way, why go at all?) and jump right into the hard stuff. "For Myself" wears an X-rating. It's one of the few erotic stories I can remember reading in which all the sexual action is masturbation. OK, there have been other stories, but the main character usually ends up having an elaborately described fantasy about another person, so it may as well be two people fucking. But in this story, French lovingly describes a woman whose relationship just ended giving pleasure to herself in the bathtub. She lowers herself into the tub "so that my breasts become islands rising from the rosy reef of my body. My palms raft over them, teasing the nipples that jut up through the foam like knobs of coral. At last, under the sea, my thighs open, and my fingers swim down, sleek dolphins, to explore the cleverly concealed cave below…"

The triple-X stories are "Sister Mary Clitoris" and "Traffic Jam". In the latter story, the tough-talkin', truck-drivin' female narrator tells about the sights she sees from the vantage point of her rig. One day she was stuck in an interstate traffic jam beside a gorgeous high-class woman driving a red Cadillac convertible. She honked the horn at the truck driver to get her attention, and pulled her skirt above her waist. "At first, in the dusk, I thought she had the biggest bush I'd ever seen. Then I realised it was the back of someone's head! Holy shit! Someone was going down on her! My pussy grabbed that seat so hard, I could almost smell the plastic meltin'!"

French's fiction proves that creativity, slippery-smooth writing, and a high turn-on factor can co-exist in the same sex stories.

The Crossing Press; $10.95
1994; softcover; 116 pp
illus; 0-89594-660-2

IMMORTALITY

by Kirsty Machon

In these twelve stories by Kirsty Machon, death and sex intertwine. The writing has a hip, snappy sensibility but it can also be lyrical. "It was late. It was dark and smoky. I had come here with the express intention of getting stupidly laid. Or laid by someone stupid. Anyone — I didn't care — as long as I could throw them out the morning after without having to worry about tea or fruit juice or consequences. Or conversations" (from "Bottom of the Harbour"). "She was leaning over a black beer. She had fuck off hair, redder than the lips of John the Baptist. Her skin was soft and paper thin. A patrician daughter gone wrong. Hardly my type. And yet I bought her a drink and bent to kiss her mouth. She tasted of too-ripe berries. Later, she slid her latex fist into my cunt, drawing honey" (from "The Euphoric Pleasure of Speech"). "… Jackie had died in a long-winded agony, drawn out over weeks with KS bubbling in his throat to full orchestral accompaniment, and lurid visions of the baby Jesus" (from "State of Shock.) "Forgiven" opens: "That the blood spilled like gems on the pavement surprised no one."

Despite being mainly about sex and death, these sto-

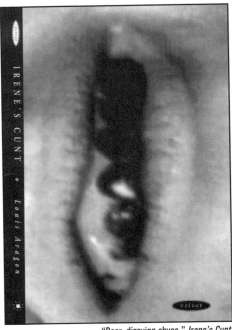

"Dear, dizzying abyss." *Irene's Cunt.*

ries don't often portray either one in graphic detail, and when they do, it's over quickly. The emphasis is more on atmosphere, a gloomy canvas Machon fills with decay and depression. In "Cliffhanger" a boy is in love with his older brother, a tough kid who gets involved in a murder. In "Forgiven", a woman's girlfriend is gunned down in the street. A woman finds the body of a murdered female weather announcer and becomes obsessed with her in "Butterflies, Baby". "Eight Legs of the Devil" concerns a guy who bashes a transvestite to death. "Death Became Him", the story of two sisters raised by their aunt, begins with a description of a boy's body floating in a river:

> He had floated all night. Borne by the current, filling slowly with gases and blind creatures taking him apart. Molecule by sweet molecule. At night, as he found his way to saltier waters, these tiny creatures, phosphorus bright, edged toward him. Bearing him along on a raft of moving light. Curiously lovely.

Like a car wreck that makes you look despite yourself, Machon's short, sad tales demand that you read them even as you pop another Prozac.

BlackWattle Press; $14.95Aus, $10.95US
1996; softcover; 126 pp
187524322-4

IN HER I AM

by Chrystos

Chrystos writes lesbian poetry and poetic prose that combine two approaches that are often segregated: flowery, weepy-eyed descriptions of physical love and down'n'dirty descriptions of hot fucking. Usually you either get one or the other. With Chrystos, you get both, and they're two great tastes that taste great together.

An example of the softer side of erotica can be found in the opening poem, "You Ask Me for a Love Name", which starts:

> I name you moon bird diamond frost night fruit
> tender flag bramble nest vision bread proud eye
> I call you flying your tongue lifts me radiant
> fills lost places

"Song for a Lakota Woman" is one of the poems that emphasises Chrystos's ethnic heritage: "You turned to me with tiny wildflowers in your hands/murmuring softly *Winyan Menominee/Anpetu Kin Lila Wasté*". A note at the end provides a translation: "*Menominee woman, you are good & beautiful*".

On the other side of the coin, you've got "Hold Me Down": "Fuck me with your strap on/till my pussy sucks/Screaming to let me free I want you/to hold me there in that sharp grasping/before exploding/Grab my hair & wrap it around your fist". Chrystos' playful sense of humour comes through in "She Left Me a Note/saying *I DID NOT lick your panties/must have been my dog/who left them lying in the hallway*".

In Her I Am is a strong collection that shows the spiritual *and* the physical sides of sex. You've got to just love someone who writes poems titled "O Honeysuckle Woman", "Soft", and "Tenderly Your", as well as "I Suck", "Hot My Hair Smells of Your Cunt", and "I Like a Woman Who Packs".

Press Gang Publishers; $12
1993; softcover; 91 pp
0-88974-033-X

IRENE'S CUNT
by Louis Aragon

Irene's Cunt was first published anonymously in France in 1928. We now know that it was written by surrealist poet Louis Aragon, and it can be considered a companion to another piece of outrageous surrealist erotica written in the same year — *Story of the Eye* by Georges Bataille [*Outposts* p 100]. At last, this lost classic has been translated in full into English (becoming the first book published in the English language to contain "cunt" in the title). The story concerns a man who returns to a French town to forget a doomed love affair and becomes obsessed with an imaginary woman's genitals. "Don't be afraid of moving your face closer to this place — and already your tongue, the chatterer, is restless — this place of delight and darkness, this patio of ardour, in its pearly limits, the fine image of pessimism. O cleft, moist and soft cleft, dear dizzying abyss."

Creation Books; $12.95
1996; softcover; 88 pp
1-871592-54-2

LIMERICKS NAUGHTY AND GAY
by (the late) Dr. Fey

A collection of over 180 gay-themed limericks written by Donald Dimock, who is still among the living though he uses the pen name "(the late) Dr. Fey". Like any anthology of this type of poetry, there are hits and misses. To give you a taste, here are a few of the more valiant attempts:

> The astrologer studied and crammed.
> He thought and he said, "I'll be damned!
> I think that most fairies
> Are probably Aries
> Because they so like to be rammed."

> A man who got drunk in Scotts Bluff
> Went looking one night for strange stuff.
> He woke up at noon
> Next to a baboon
> Which kissed him and asked, "Strange enough?"

> There once was a fellow called Milt
> Who said to a Scot named MacCrilt
> "I can see at a glance
> You've no underpants.
> I can tell by the tilt of your kilt."

Fey's limericks are accompanied by 29 whimsical though slightly amateurish line drawings of naked young men.

Factor Press; $6.50
1995; softcover; 60 pp
heavily illus; 0-9626531-9-5

MATRIARCHY
Freedom in Bondage
by Malcolm McKesson

The illuminated erotic novel *Matriarchy* is the work of 87-year-old outsider artist Malcolm McKesson. In 1961, through the support of his wife, McKesson was able to completely withdraw from the world, secluding himself as he worked on his art. In the introduction, Tony Thorne says of these images — almost 80 of which are reproduced in this book — "His voluptuous, anonymous, androgynous figures seem to emerge from a soft muffling darkness, taking on form like a photographic plate slowly yielding an image. These mysterious, indistinct, courtly marionettes pose, merge, bow and submit in a dream landscape where unknown rituals are enacted in a state of erotic trance."

Most of *Matriarchy*, though, consists of McKesson's written story of Gerald, an eighteen-year-old Manhattanite, who, while on a ski trip in 1929, meets the wealthy Miss Gladys von Gunthardt. By the end of the first page of McKesson's narrative, delivered in a matter-of-fact style, Gerald is already sitting with Gunthardt in the parlour of her mansion. She invites him to stay for dinner, saying, "'But first let us change the relation between us and play that you are my dear child and I am your loving mother.'" By the end of the third page, Sally the maid has dressed Gerald as a dainty little girl. Gunthardt declares that from now on he will be known as Little Rose, and from there she leads the narrator on a life that involves being his Mistress's 24-hour-a-day, seven-day-a-week submissive. He is put on a regimen of extreme sissification, submission, and servitude, which he throws himself into with relish. His mistress explains to him: "'You are to be my little girl and study beauty in everything. When you have passed the test, you shall wear pretty dresses and serve me in public ways. But do not fear for your native sex, dear child — you shall be at times my little man child, at others my little girl. Yet you will always delight in the feminine, which will become your true nature. As a young man, you will forever be my dependent and rejoice in my service. As a young lady, you will rejoice in your beauty and guard your virginity.'"

Gerald is often whipped in order to "curb his manly nature". At one point, one of his Mistress's friends absconds with him and uses him sexually. Soon after he returns, his sister joins the household as Gunthardt's companion and protégé. Gerald is "forced" to be her servant, too. I won't tell you exactly how the book ends, but let's just say that everyone lives happily ever after.

Matriarchy is an unusual contribution to the BDSM literature. Dealing with an extreme, basically non-sexual Mistress/slave relationship, it lovingly presents subject matter that is all but impossible to find elsewhere.

Heck Editions (Gates of Heck); $14.95
1997; softcover; 191 pp
illus; 0-9638129-7-1

MEETING THE MASTER
An Exploration of Mastery, Slavery, and the Darker Side of Desire
by Elissa Wald

Each of Elissa Wald's eight short stories are perfectly cut dark gems of psychological SM. Rather than take the over-the-top approach, she comes at her subject from a more subtle — and very insightful — vantage point. The emphasis is as much on emotional politics as it is on sexual action, maybe more so. "Ruby and the Bull", for example, is about a couple in which the man is the top and the woman is the bottom. There is one SM/sex scene, but the story focuses on the relationship as a whole. Bull reads Ruby's private journal and finds more facets to his girlfriend than he had previously seen, but he pays a price.

"The Resolution" doesn't have any sex scenes at all. It revolves around the undying love a woman feels for the gay man she befriends when they both work at a circus. He has sex with her once in a while when he gets frustrated, but their relationship is mainly deeply Platonic. When she finds out that he has AIDS, he reassures her that he got it after they last had sex. "'I'm not worried,' I said. I was, though. I worried that I might not have it. And that he wouldn't allow me to get it. From him, anyway. But then, I could work on him. Bring him around. He believed in things like this. Love without limits, suicide pacts..."

Unfortunately, this edition of *Meeting the Master* cuts out Wald's sixteen poems, which were in the prior version that she self-published. Still, I will mention them here, because I reviewed the original version and because I think that Grove/Atlantic should have kept the poems. Segregate them in an appendix if you must, but don't delete them. (Many of these poems have been included in the wonderful *Between the Cracks*, above, so you'll still be able to enjoy them)

As in her stories, Wald displays a similarly keen eye for hard-edged emotions in her poetry. "Sufferer" celebrates the joys of misery:

I've caught my own eyes in the mirror —
Bright and shiny, aglow,
Just before the tears flow:
I've never seen anything clearer.
In dark moments like these I believe
There is nothing so beautiful
As me
When I grieve.

Similarly, "The Joy of Woman's Desiring" maps the painfully delicious side of another feeling that is usually seen as undesirable and negative — unfulfilled lust. "Oh, I wouldn't trade this passion for consummation;/Wouldn't have you be mine, mine to collar and flaunt/And surrender the quivering joy of: I want."

Don't be fooled by my placing this book in the erotic fiction section... it's not stroke material. *Meeting the Master* is unlike any other collection I've read — highly cerebral, complex, and erotic.

Grove/Atlantic; $12
1996; softcover; 224 pp
0-802135501

THE MISTRESS AND THE SLAVE
by anonymous

The Mistress and the Slave is another classic SM novel rescued from the brink of obscurity by the erotica dealer/publisher Delectus Books. It was originally published in France around 1903, and published in English in 1905 by the daring Erotica Biblion Society.

The story concerns a wealthy young man in Paris who becomes involved with a beautiful dominating woman from the wrong side of the tracks. Despite its dated language and style, the book still packs a wallop due to its explicitness, brutality, and an SM relationship that seems thoroughly modern. Anna toys with George, humiliating him and denying him pleasure. While on their way to wager at horse races, George gets excited and starts grovelling for attention. Anna curtly replies: "Don't excite yourself. You are going to make a pig of yourself. Listen. If you win at the races, you shall sleep with me, and I promise you a delicious night."

Anna subjects George to every torture at her disposal. "She frigged him till the blood came, for a nothing, and inflicted on him the supreme humiliation, soiling his face with her excretions... For hours Aïscha and the maid, Claudine, rubbed, pinched and beat him. Then they tickled his loins and balls with peacocks' feathers. When Anna came back, she made him spend by a few jerks of her wrist."

But Anna's control over her slave goes far beyond the physical. She instructs him: "'But, my child, you don't seem to understand what a mistress is. For instance: your child, your favourite daughter, might be dying and I should send you to the Bastille to get me a twopenny trinket. You would go, you would obey! Do you understand?' — 'Yes' he murmured, so pale and troubled that he could scarcely breathe."

Eventually, Anna makes George come so much that his penis haemorrhages and becomes useless. Having gotten all the fun out of him that she can, she ties him up and kills him in a most unpleasant way.

Delectus Books; £19.95, US: $34.95
1903, 1995; hardcover; 156 pp
1-897767-09-9

NEARLY ROADKILL
An Infobahn Erotic Adventure
by Caitlin Sullivan & Kate Bornstein

On the Internet, you can be whomever you want to be, limited only by your own skill (and your ability to cover your tracks). I personally know someone who has developed three different personas — one female and two male — that he uses in chat rooms, and each of them is accepted as an actual human being. The ability to switch gender, age, race, and other characteristics is one of the strongest allures of the Net. It also calls into question many dynamics of human relationships as you wonder whether the person you're chatting with (or having cybersex with) is male or female or transgendered, gay or straight or bi, fifteen or fifty, gorgeous or unattractive, etc. Part of you desperately wants to be able to pin down these other people, while another part of you realises that, in many ways, it doesn't truly matter.

With *Nearly Roadkill*, the inherently vague, fluid playground of cyberspace is given the treatment it deserves. Gender heretics Caitlin Sullivan and Kate Bornstein have crafted a highly experimental novel that follows the online exploits of Scratch and Winc, two people who delight in bamboozling everyone — including each other — about their identities. Even we, the readers, are unsure of their genders, ages, and other fundamentals. Just when you think you've found a clue, there's a counterclue that points in the opposite direction.

Scratch and Wink surf the Net, engaging in cybersex, SM scenes, and philosophical debates with each other and many other characters. The basic plot revolves around the "Registration", which is the government's plan to get everyone who is online to register their true identities so that they can always be tracked… in the name of preserving law and order, of course. Our heroes refuse to Register, making them online outlaws.

Almost all of the action takes place as dialogues in chatrooms or as email messages, with a little standard narrative being supplied by Toobe, a friend of Scratch and Winc. At one point, Scratch is in a chatroom with someone who hopes that "ze" (a genderless pronoun) is female:

AWESOME: You a guy or a girl?
Scratch: Does it matter?
AWESOME: I'm pretty loose about most things, but I don't fuck no dudes.
Scratch: Ah, that's a shame, hon. You'd probably enjoy it if you loosened up. That's OK, I'm not

anything tonight.
AWESOME: I take it you enjoy watching guys together. No, I don't think I would enjoy it, and yes, I am pretty loose.
Scratch: I enjoy lots of things, like guys who can be receptive, as it were. :)

In the first of their encounters, Scratch adopts a female persona and Winc a male:

Winc: ::on my knees in front of you . . . looking up into your eyes::
::cock throbbing::
::precum glistening with your juices on my cock::
Scratch: Whatcha gonna do for me now, huh?
Winc: ::swallowing hard:: I . . . I want to lick your cunt . . . want to taste you, fuck you with my tongue. ::breathing hard::
Scratch: Lie back down . . .
Winc: ::not moving, looking at you::
Scratch: ::Straddling your face . . . pressing my pussy into your mouth, hands on floor on either side of you::
Winc: ::moaning into your pussy::
Scratch: ::dropping my body onto your chest::
Winc: ::kissing up and down your lips:: ::lapping you with the broad of my tongue::
Scratch: yesssssss

When future histories of erotic writing are set down, I think that *Nearly Roadkill* will be seen as a truly original novel that broke new ground in both style and subject. Naturally, I highly recommend it.

High Risk Books (Serpent's Tail); $13.99, £8.99
1996; softcover; 385 pp
1-85242-418-4; www.nearlyroadkill.com

PAINFUL PLEASURES
by anonymous

Again, a lost classic of flagellation erotica is rescued by Delectus Books. *Painful Pleasures* was originally published by the shadowy Gargoyle Press of New York in 1931. It contains two discussions, eight "genuine letters", and five short stories regarding corporal punishment and discipline being meted out to guys and dolls by cold, unyielding women. Includes the eighteen original illustrations by Francis Heuber.

Delectus Books; £19.95
1931 (1995); hardcover; 283 pp
illus; 1-897767-03-X

PLEASURE IN THE WORD
Erotic Writing by Latin American Women
edited by Margarite Fernández Olmos & Lizabeth Paravisini-Gebert

Over the past ten years there's been a movement afoot for women to "reclaim their erotic voices" in a patriarchal society that has defined sex almost exclusively through men's desires. And when it comes to male-dominated societies, things don't get much more manly than Latin America, where machismo is the order of the day, and girls and women are reminded, "Flies don't enter a closed mouth." Therefore, the 68 writings in this collection represent exceptionally daring breaks with the social order.

The 32 contributors hail from all over the Spanish-speaking regions of the Southern hemisphere: Argentina, Mexico, Chile, Brazil, Nicaragua, Uruguay, Puerto Rico, Honduras, Cuba, and elsewhere. They cover various orientations, practices, and approaches — joyous, sad, funny, horny, political, tender, violent.

"Lyrics for a Salsa and Three Soneos by Request" by Ana Lydia Vega displays pyrotechnic language. "There's a holy feast day fever of fine asses on De Diego Street. Round in their super-look panties, arresting in tube-skirt profile, insurgent under their fascist girdles, abysmal, Olympian, nuclear, they furrow the sidewalks of Río Piedras like invincible national airships." One of Ana Istarú's many fine poems, "III", uses unashamed female sexuality as a weapon against the legacy of colonialism and male violence:

> I kill it and kill it again
> with my sex open and red,
> cardinal cluster of my happiness,
> from this America incarnate and inflamed
> the Central one, my America of rage.

In other selections a middle-age woman reflects on her relationship with a much younger man ("Woman Sitting on the Sand"), a woman relishes the sameness ("my lover, my sister, my likeness") of her female lover ("Ca Foscari"), a girl is raped by one of her father's farm hands (excerpt from *The Spotted Bird Perched High Above Upon the Tall Green Lemon Tree*), and Alejandra Pizarnik graphically recounts the torturous activities of Erzsebet Bathory ("The Bloody Countess").

Pleasure in the Word is an exceptionally strong collection, but, like a lot of literary erotica, it will usually stimulate your brain more than your groin.

White Pine Press; $19.95
1993; hardcover; 283 pp
1-877727-31-8

PORNO PEN
A Networking Resource for the Sex Publishing Community

If you're hoping to have your writings about sex published, you must get *Porno Pen*, which is the only zine of its kind in the US, as far as I'm aware. Each issue lets you know of 20 to 25 outlets for your work, be it fiction, article, essay, or personal experience, for all orientations and genders, although most of the publications are asking for gaylesbitrans material. Past issues have contained publishers/editors seeking everything from sexual science fiction to erotica by and about Jewish women to articles for the *Encyclopedia of American Gay Culture*.

Besides listing anthologies, magazines, and zines seek-

ing sexual writing, *Porno Pen* also makes writers aware of other things that may interest them: awards, agents, events, writers' groups, books on writing erotica, job openings, etc.

Black Books is providing a much-needed service with *Porno Pen*, and I hope that this useful zine continues to grow.

Black Books/PO Box 31155/San Francisco CA 94131
WWW: www.blackbooks.com
Single issue: $3. Non-US: $4
Six issues: $14. Non-US: $20

PRIMITIVE
by Lizbeth Dusseau

In this recent novel by Lizbeth Dusseau [see *Extremes*, above], the fair Camille accompanies her stepfather and his biological daughter, Lydia, to a sparsely populated little island in the South Seas. Camille is a sheltered Pollyanna who is horrified by her stepsister's wanton sexuality. Stuck on this remote island for one or two years while Lydia's father studies exotic plants, the young women react to their new situation differently. Camille wants to live cautiously, while Lydia humps the sailors who come into port and then gets involved with a white painter, Llewellyn, who's been living on the exotic isle for years (*à la* Paul Gauguin).

Lydia enjoys tormenting her prudish sister, who is actually jealous of Lydia's popularity with the menfolk and her freewheeling carnality. Lydia, in turn, is jealous of the loving, unconsummated relationship that Camille has developed with one of the sailors. In an act of treachery, Lydia helps Llewellyn kidnap Camille and turn her into his sex slave.

Camille discovers the forceful lust that she had kept bottled up inside of her, as her captor and his two male native servants turn her on so much that she begs to be deflowered in every way possible (along the way, she is also slapped, whipped, tattooed, and pierced).

> I dread the first prick in my ass. But I need it there with this ache running deep.
>
> "Oh, my loves, please," I utter quietly. My psyche is consumed with the desire.
>
> So ready for this offensive breach, I feel him near. Llewellyn. He looms behind my ass, his hands on my two cheeks as Kee and Michal pull away.
>
> "You want this place violated?" he murmurs, as one hand pulls around me, pinching a hardened nipple. I hear the message he speaks clearly in my half delirious brain, how he conquers me again, and I beg to be sodomised with as much desire flowing as flows through me when I seek my pussy fucked.
>
> I can't lie, my body would defy my words so I whisper back, "I want you there."
>
> He prods the gently worked back channel with a finger, and I feel it as a sharp attack. I lurch forward so he withdraws, only to have him grab my ass more forcefully and shove two fingers deep.
>
> "Don't deny your passions, ever," he says to me, as I feel those fingers finally withdraw to be replaced at my anus by the pulse of his cock's head.

As usual, Lizbeth has created action that will have you reaching to unzip your pants, described it in evocative language that sets it well above typical "stroke material", and added an interesting story with layers of psychological conflict between the characters.

Pink Flamingo Press; $9.95

1997; staple-bound softcover; 132 pp

no ISBN

RITUAL SEX

edited by Tristan Taormino & David Aaron Clark

It was released without any fanfare and I have yet to see it reviewed, but *Ritual Sex* is easily one of the best anthologies of erotic writings I have ever read. It might even be *the* best. When I read any sex collection — especially one with 35 selections — I am expecting two things: 1) At least 20% of the stories will be duds. 2) There will be two, maybe three, standout stories that etch themselves into my head. The rest will fall somewhere between those two poles. *Ritual Sex* blew those expectations out of the water. First of all, there isn't a single dud. Don't ask me how the editors did it, but none of these stories, essays, or poems could be considered weak. On top of that, there are at least *ten* standout pieces. As I look back over the table of contents, the titles jump out at me — "The Supreme Homage", Genesis P-Orridge's eloquent ode to jism-covered faces; the raw brutality of Peter Sotos's "Full Blown"; Carl Watson's hallucinatory "This Supreme, Sarcastic Succulence Called Death"; Will Tracy's historical/mythological essay "Pasiphae: The Woman Who Fucked Bulls"; Lawrence Schimel's sexual encounter with Jesus, "Calvinism"; the single-page intensity of Kate Bornstein's "Blood..."; the non-stop racial abuse and manrape of Samuel Delany's "Down by the River" from *Hogg*; the gender- and orientation-blending "Faggot Rant" by Sandra Lee Golvin; Robin Podolsky's painfully personal tale of emotional healing, "Dirty". There are others, but suffice it to say that just about every selection deserves an individual mention.

Besides being powerful on their own, all of the pieces tie together so well that *Ritual Sex* becomes even stronger than the sum of its already-strong parts. The range of genres, tones, approaches, and subjects represented is a textbook example of the word *eclectic*. The overall theme here is the intersection of sex with spirituality, religion, ritual, and/or magick. This is extraordinarily fertile ground and what grows from it is diverse and enlightening (and occasionally, just plain scorching). Whether it's step-by-step instructions for sacred sex ("Yoni Massage Ritual"), an explicit story about a doubting priest and a mysterious stranger ("Revelation"), a look at homophobia among Native Americans ("Physical Prayers"), or a scalpel-precise rant about religious hypocrisy ("The Catholic Religion as a Sadomasochistic Cult"), these writings never fail to hit a nerve by demonstrating that two of the most important aspects of our lives — sex and spirit — are so intertwined that they cannot be separated. In her introduction, Tristan Taormino writes: "People often investigate religion for the same reasons they turn to sex: to help make sense of our complex, fragmented, ever-changing identities

and lives; to pay homage to personal spirits, deities, and even demons; to take a soulful journey inward, searching for personal enlightenment and spiritual transformation... Both sex and spirituality help us confront and explore mortal hopes and fears, desires of the flesh, life-and-death questions for our souls."

If there were any justice in the world, *Ritual Sex* would be getting much, much more attention than it has been. But there isn't, so just go and buy a copy without further ado. It's an instant classic.

Rhinoc*eros* (Masquerade Books); $6.95

1996; paperback; 386 pp

1-56333-391-0

SEVEN HUNDRED KISSES
A *Yellow Silk* Book of Erotic Writing

edited by Lily Pond

Apparently, the fifteen-year-old erotic magazine *Yellow Silk* has morphed into a yearly book. In this, the first volume, editor Lily Pond presents over 60 short stories and poems that stay true to the magazine's sensibilities. *Yellow Silk* is more concerned with what goes on *around* sex than with sexual acts themselves. Most of the writing is imbued with eroticism, but the eroticism comes more from descriptions of desire, the intricacies of the human mating dance, and the use of evocative language than from sex scenes, which are usually either slyly skipped or described in broad brush strokes. This isn't everyone's cup of tea, but if you like your sex writing refined and flowery, no one does it better than *Yellow Silk*.

The selections in *Seven Hundred Kisses* include "Coyote and the Shadow People" by E. Beth Thomas, "New York Public Library" by Jill McDonough, "Apollo and the Seven Whores" by Carlos Fuentes, "If the Rise of the Fish" by Jane Hirshfield, "The Life of the Body" by Jane Smiley, "Two or Three Things I Know for Sure" by Dorothy Allison, "Vespers" by Timothy Liu, and "Trust Muscle" by Leasa Burton.

HarperSanFrancisco (HarperCollins Publishers); $14

1997; softcover; 273 pp

0-06-251484-9

SEXUALITY & MASQUERADE
The Dedalus Book of Sexual Ambiguity

edited by Emma Wilson

The twenty-one stories and novel excerpts in this literary anthology are meant to show that desire crosses boundaries and destabilises categories, particularly with regard to gender and orientation. To a large degree, in fact, desire is dependent upon — or at least greatly enhanced by — ambiguity and uncertainty. Includes selections from Anaïs Nin, Virginia Woolf, Honoré de Balzac, Marguerite Duras, Djuna Barnes, Angela Carter, Émile Zola, Marcel Proust, Roland Barthes, Sylvie Germain, Gustave Flaubert, Oscar Wilde, Jean Genet, and Michel Foucault.

Dedalus; £8.99, $13.99

1996; softcover; 274 pp

1-873982-07-0

SLAVE LOVER

by Marco Vassi

Slave Lover is one of the hot, taboo-busting novels written during the period 1970-1976 by Marco Vassi, who has earned comparisons to Henry Miller and has been called the foremost erotic writer of our time. This story concerns the travails of several women who are kidnapped and held in a mysterious compound where they are forced to engage in all kinds of sexual acts.

Second Chance Press; $16.95

1993; softcover; 192 pp

0-933256-89-2

SUNBELT STORIES

by V.O. Blum

Finding a great but obscure book like *Sunbelt Stories* is one of the most exciting aspects of writing *Psychotropedia*. Somehow I stumbled across a single Webpage advertising this collection of three stories by VO Blum. Not long after that, the page disappeared, but — in a rare display of forethought — I had written down the address of the bookstore that was acting as the book's distributor. When I finally got my hands on a copy, I was delighted to find a talented writer with a wicked imagination.

The book's centrepiece is the 75-page story "Sperm Boy". A wealthy Republican widow with cervical cancer hears reports that the semen of Catholic Albanian men can reverse cancer. Desperate for a cure, she hooks up with just such a man, who proceeds to inject her with his "miracle cure". As things unfold, we realise that the point of the story is more about the woman's sexual awakening than about her fight against cancer. The sex in "Sperm Boy" is usually spelled out but not in graphic terms (with the notable exception of the final scene). It is actually a story *about* sex rather than a sex story, if you know what I mean. Blum has a distinctive voice, writing in a short, almost clipped, style that somehow manages to be graceful and occasionally poetic.

"The Farm" concerns life at a shadowy facility where babies are made (the old-fashioned way) to be sold on the black market. The shortest story, "Whale Song", is not about sex. It is a monologue being spoken by a whale. This creature speaks of the "Whalacaust" perpetrated by humans against cetaceans. But the message goes way beyond a simplistic accusation of the human race as the narrator looks at the role that whales and dolphins have played in their own demise and then speculates on their future evolution and their role in the universe.

Unexpected, uncategorisable, and unlike anything else I've read.

Diesel: A Bookstore; $7.95

1994; softcover; 151 pp

illus; 0-9620886-1-7

SURFING THE CONSCIOUS NETS

by Timothy Leary

Surfing the Conscious Nets, Timothy Leary's first and last novel, is set up as a series of postings to a computer network. The central character, who does most of the posting, is Huck Getty Mellon Von Schlebrugge, a bisexual African American man currently imprisoned in a mental hospital because of his manic-depression. Huck gets messages from two people — Dr. Richard Alpert and Dr. Susan Sarandon. By questioning him about his recent activities, they get him to reveal the story's main plot — his search for the perfect aphrodisiac.

Huck claims to have led a charmed life — exclusive schools, world-wide modelling, a successful music career — that resulted in massive amounts of sex, but he eventually got tired of it. "At this point I find that my sexuality (how shall I put it?) becomes very elitist and selective. I no longer feel that incessant, throbbing teenage desire to fuck or be fucked by any or all consenting warm bodies in the vicinity. A one-night bland is lust or bust depending on my feelings toward the person, my emotional state, the ebb and flows of manic-depression, the effects of any illegal or prescription medication, and my period of heat. <u>Tom Cruiser I'm not, if you catch my drift.</u>"

Huck questions several scientists but all are tight-lipped about aphrodisiacal drugs, which are a forbidden area of study for "serious" medical researchers. While in West Germany, he sees a live sex show starring a stud who indefatigably bangs women all over the stage, but his companions refuse to divulge the drug that makes him a fuck machine. Finally, he finds out that the Southern California Sexual Dysfunction Clinic is experimenting with yohimbine on human subjects, so he volunteers. First, they need to take some readings using a "Peter-Meter". Huck gets a little carried away and ends up destroying the machine, which doesn't endear him to the scientists. When he starts demanding they give him the sex pills anyway, they refuse. He goes bonkers and is committed to the mental hospital.

While he's relating his quest, Huck also brings up some other problems and concerns. For one thing, he's in trouble for supposedly sexually harassing a student nurse who was interviewing him. Even worse, he's uncovered a conspiracy to steal and store human brains in the lower levels of the mental hospital. Huck also finds time to digress into such topics as Einstein vs. Newton, the Vatican's porn collection, hackers, Timothy Leary, and the LSD revolution of the 1960s.

Besides being the first book I'm aware of that was written entirely as a series of online exchanges, the design of *Surfing* is unprecedented, too. Each page represents a Macintosh/Windows screen. The backgrounds, which change with each chapter, are chaotic, fractalish designs. Along with the jagged text, each screen/page contains digitally manipulated photos and illustrations of — among other things — Einstein wearing shades, Cary Grant's head on the Mona Lisa's body, a woman sensually licking a circuit board, and William Burroughs surrounded by floating brains. Robert Williams contributes a number of his hyperkinetic paintings to the mix. The whole swirling visual stew is printed in hypnotically bright colours on superslick paper.

It goes without saying that *Surfing* is a groundbreaking artistic experiment. Whether or not it succeeds as a work of literature is not quite as obvious.

Last Gasp; $16.95

1995; oversized softcover; 125 pp
heavily illus; 0-86719-410-3

SWITCH HITTERS
Lesbians Write Gay Male Erotica and Gay Men Write Lesbian Erotica
edited by Carol Queen & Lawrence Schimel

In this literally unique anthology, gay men were called upon to write hot stories involving lesbians, lesbians to write stories about gay men, and a few bisexuals to write about the opposite sex. The result is a high quality collection (grade: A-) of sweaty stories that usually hit the nail on the head so perfectly, you wouldn't realise that they were the result of literary cross-dressing. As in all top-flight anthologies, the approaches are as varied as possible. Kevin Killian's "Renga" is a beautifully written story about a married, bisexual female poet trying to write a poem in the Japanese form known as *renga*. She's having trouble getting past the first line but finds inspiration in the form of a sultry maid who works at the writer's colony she's visiting. "Indeed, Lee Ann's legs were perfect, faintly muscular, her kneecaps like two china door-knobs, the dimples behind them moist beneath my passionate kisses."

At the opposite end from the exquisite "Renga" is "Predators" by Wickie Stamps. In the first half of the story, Jamie, who likes rough trade, is telling his friend/lover about an encounter he just had with two guys in an alley. There was a little bit of violence and some insults, but it was exactly what Jamie wanted. After relating his tale, he heads to a bar and proceeds to get into another rough encounter in an alleyway. This time, though, he's picked a huge, angry homophobic man who beats the shit out of him, then fucks him. "As Jamie lay crumpled against the wall with his pants down around his knees, he could feel the man staring at him. Then he felt the stranger's warm piss spray all over his shivering body. Before walking out of the alley, the stranger kicked Jamie squarely in the balls."

We see that gay men and lesbians can write erotica that features each other, so we know the experiment was a success. But a deeper question is, can this writing bring any kind of insights? Can it add freshness to the genre and allow writers to address issues they couldn't if they stuck to their own genders? The answer is yes. Lawrence Schimel's "Dry Run" eroticises the notions of pregnancy and motherhood and the actual act of artificial insemination. "The Pussy Pier" by William J. Mann concerns two lesbians in their early thirties. One of them has enjoyable encounters at the pussy pier — an area underneath a dock where women have anonymous, unapologetic sex — while the other is horrified by this "objectifying", politically incorrect form of sex, which she associates with gay men. Perhaps a field trip will change her mind?

Other contributors include Thomas Roche, Marco Vassi, Cecilia Tan, Larry Townsend, Laura Antoniou, Lucy Taylor, D. Travers Scott, and Pat Califia. Taken together, they prove that a good erotic writer can approach sex from any angle and make it work.

Cleis Press; $12.95

1996; softcover; 191 pp
1-57344-021-3

TORN SHAPES OF DESIRE
Internet Erotica
by Mary Anne Mohanraj

When Mary Anne Mohanraj was an undergraduate, her boyfriend persuaded her to start using her college Internet account. She eventually gravitated to the two main Usenet groups devoted to erotic writing — alt.sex.stories and rec.arts.erotica — and realised that she could write smut that was better than most of what was being posted. She was right. Her contributions to the groups earned her so much positive feedback that she kept at it, started a Webpage to archive her writings, and eventually was approached by a publisher. Along the way, many of Mohanraj's stories were either reprinted or commissioned for a large number of magazines, zines, and anthologies. She is probably the first writer whose career was "made" on the Internet.

Torn Shapes of Desire contains around two dozen stories and fifteen poems spanning the period 1992 through 1996. Although it might be tempting to dismiss this collection as "gimmicky" because it's most obvious marketing angle is that it contains sexual material originally from the Internet, *Torn Shapes* is actually an impressive collection that stands on its own. Even though its author found success in an unorthodox manner, she definitely deserves her accolades. Mohanraj writes with grace and sophistication. Her style would be right at home in the erotica litzine *Libido*... despite the literary sheen, she doesn't mind getting down and dirty on a regular basis. You'll find the words *penis*, *vagina*, and *semen*, but you'll also see *cock*, *cunt*, and *cum*. Mostly, though, what you'll find are non-formulaic plots, imaginative forms, and a positive view of sexuality in various forms, although the premiere orientation is hetero.

"Jinsong" takes the form of a poetic email exchange between a lonely guy and a girl who just broke up with her boyfriend. In another story, a blindfolded woman's sexual fantasy comes true, courtesy of her boyfriend. One of the light-hearted pieces in the book is "Fleeing Gods", about a certain Greek deity who doesn't know what to do when he approaches a woman of the Nineties and she, instead of trying desperately to flee, welcomes the carnal encounter.

Another thing I like is that, as gentle as she usually is, Mohanraj isn't afraid to delve into the dark side of sex. "Charlie" is told from the point of view of a woman who is unapologetically committing adultery. In "Letter Found Near a Suicide", a high school student laments over the unrequited love/lust for another student that eventually leads to suicide. "Diana" caused something of a stir because of the erotic death (shall we say "snuffing"?) of one of its characters. The short piece "Meditation on Human Relations" is a powerful monologue on the nature of rape. "... you might even want to try pulling a train, with your body out there and it's theirs and yours all at once and incandescent but you get a little anxious and so embarrassed to mention it, 'cause while it's all right nowadays for women to like sex, they're not supposed to like sex that looks like rape and they're not supposed to like sex that might be degrading, and they're especially not supposed to wonder if they might actually like rape after all…" And we won't even get into the story about a twin sister and brother…

On the whole, the author's poetry is less explicitly erotic and more coy, even romantic. Many of the poems sigh over lost loves or unfulfilling relationships. Then again, others are quite sexy, such as "Mango", "You'll Understand When You're Older, Dear", and "Renewal": "I am a garden, love, run wild and fertile under your caress./No gardener could better train these creeping vines/and scattered blooms."

Torn Shapes is rounded out by an interview with a panel of Internet sex writers led by Mohanraj and a dozen relatively tame black and white erotic photos of women by Tracy Lee. For more of a taste, check out the author's Website at http://www.iam.com/maryanne.

Intangible Assets Manufacturing; $14.95
1996; softcover; 128 pp
illus; 1-885876-03-3

WHITE STAINS
by Anaïs Nin and Friends

Believe the hype. If the literary detectives are correct, then the re-publication of *White Stains* really is an event of historical significance. The story behind this book begins back in the 1930s, when Texas oil millionaire Roy Johnson — who claimed to have read every sex book in the English language — would pay one or two dollars per page for erotica written especially for him. It is well-known that Anaïs Nin was the main writer who did Johnson's bidding, creating feminist erotica half a century before that concept was recognised.

Nin was part of a circle of other writers, known as the Organisation, who also cranked out literary porn for private collectors. Henry Miller — Nin's colleague and lover — was part of this circle, as was Robert De Niro Sr. (a poet and father of the actor). Although Nin's hand can be seen heavily in *White Stains*, it's possible that these stories were written round-robin style by the Organisation, in order to alleviate the monotony of writing stroke material.

White Stains was published anonymously in 1940. It was almost certainly originally meant for Johnson, but conniving publishers often bootlegged the Organisation's work. One of these unauthorised copies made it into the hands of Delectus, and a lost classic has now been brought back into the world.

The book consists of six short stories and a sex manual. The stories are poetic but explicit, and, fitting the period in which they were written, more than a little quaint. *White Stains* gets off to a coy start with "Alice", a story about a couple spying on another couple making love in the country. While peeking at the action, our lovebirds become horny and start getting frisky. "'OO-oo-oh!' gasped Alice, and fell to kissing me wildly. Needless to say, I kissed wildly back. Her hand held something hard and stiff, and her treatment of it was as skilful as it was delicious."

Nin and her compatriots dispense with the euphemisms in "Florence". The title character is working at a New York firm, when a handsome young buck gets hired. He leads

Stories of male erotic power.
SexMagick2.

Miss Florence to an empty bedroom used by the night watchman, where he seduces her and plies her with cider. He had only ended her virginity with a few strokes when the firm's junior partner, who has the hots for Florry, barges in and tosses the coming boy out of the room. Not missing an opportunity, the knight in shining armour says to the still-prone woman: 'Oh dearest Florence, you know I would never have done this act to you; your purity would have always been safe with me. But now, if it is gone, and you surely know if his seed did touch you, if it has, then come and lie in my arms, and we will love to the very heights of heaven.' Being a sucker for a good line, she agrees.

By the time we get to the story "Cunts", all pretence has been stripped away. It opens with these words: "Pretty young girls have nice tickly little cunts between their legs for ardent young men to stuff their pricks into. Let any young man see a young girl's pretty, hairy cunt, and watch how his prick will come up standing!" The story ends with this advice: "Girls, after you have been fucked by a nice, lovely boy with a big, thick prick, you will enjoy living, and nothing in the world will give you more satisfaction than letting your cunt be used now and then — not too often — for a sweet-delicious fucking."

The 60-page manual "Love's Encyclopedia" appears to be a modification of the nineteenth century classic *The Horn Book*, rewritten in more blunt language. It has sections on the history of sex, sexual organs, five methods of fucking, the art of seduction, birth control, faking virginity on the wedding night, and more.

White Stains is a highly prizable addition to the canon of Anaïs Nin, Henry Miller, and vintage erotica in general.
Delectus; £19.95; US: $34.95
circa 1940, 1995; hardcover; 203 pp
1-897767-11-0

CIRCLET PRESS

THE BEAST WITHIN
Erotic Tales of Werewolves
edited by Cecilia Tan

This anthology of four stories — two long and two short — presents the sexual possibilities of lycanthropy. "The Killing of the Calf" is a daring story about a female werewolf and a female wolf. The two of them have sex while the werewolf is in human form. "And so we kissed: the strong tongue of the wolf, licking and licking the inside of my mouth, and my head thrashing and my throat making little puppy sounds, opening and playing, running my little human tongue around Timor's teeth, sucking the wolf's lips, soft on one side and fur on the other." During their lovemaking, the human becomes one with the wolfpack, and she finally makes up her mind about whether to stay with the pack or return to her human lover.

In "Alma Mater" a future world leader is saved from dying in a blizzard by a female werewolf. She suckles the wounded soldier and the two have sex, with her turning into a wolf in the middle of it. Like the protagonist in "The Killing of the Calf" he must decide whether or not to stay with his lupine lover.
Circlet Press; $7.95
1994; softcover; 103 pp
1-885865-01-5

GENDERFLEX
Sexy Stories from on the Edge
and In-Between
edited by Cecilia Tan

These dozen stories use the possibilities inherent in science fiction to create interesting situations in which gender is mixed, matched, blended, bent, broken, and erased. In her introduction, editor Cecilia Tan writes: "Does this sound sexy to you?… Switching from female to male with a quick swipe of a software card. Plugging in a nine-inch pierced cock that feels like your very own. Trading it in for a smaller/wider/longer one to fit your mood. A devil-throated high priestess in high heels with a foot-long schlong… A hermaphrodite exhibitionist with a golden cock and velvet depths to plumb. Visiting a world where the most intriguing gender of all is 'I'm not telling.'"

Circlet Press; $12.95
1996; softcover; 203 pp
1-885865-12-0

SEXMAGICK 2
edited by Cecilia Tan

In *SexMagick* [*Outposts* p 101], six women wrote stories offering a feminine take on erotic power as a key to liberation. This time around, it is primarily men looking at their erotic power as a way to achieve bonds and lasting connections. "I, Slimerod" is a humorous tale narrated by a demon (actually, as Slimerod says, "Dammit! I'm not a demon… I'm an imp of the tenth degree."), who is ordered by a magician to possess a beautiful woman. Conveniently, the woman's boyfriend is an exorcist who rebukes the foul denizen of the netherworld though the ritual use of sex. "'I think it's time for the rod treatment,' he tells her. She spreads herself to receive him. One hand eagerly guides the cylinder into her and I find myself moving up and down on top of it as he thrusts and withdraws. A deep lunge and my head smashes against her sternum. And again! And again!"

In "The Night of Pan" by Kenneth Deigh, the god Pan, who personifies raw animalistic lust, is summoned to a pagan ritual by a priestess. A mask of the Horned God and a strap-on dildo made of bone — inherited from a German witch — turn an uptight lesbian into a bisexual sex machine in "Jack-a-roe" by Raven Kaldera. The oppressive society envisioned by Thomas S. Roche in "The Arrows of Devotion" is run by women. Men stage a revolution for their independence, and the brother of the rebel's leader must decide whether he will become the permanent submissive of his mistress, a sorceress who can help the men if she gets her way. The other stories are "The Magic of Sexual Beings" by Robert Knippenberg, "The Perfect Beauty" by Gary Bowen, "Dragon's Fire" by Jack Dickson, and "Fleeing Gods" by Mary Anne Mohanraj.
Circlet Press; $9.95
1997; softcover; 143 pp
1-885865-09-0

S/M FUTURES
edited by Cecilia Tan

These ten stories imagine what directions SM might take in the future, as it reacts to medical, technological, political, and other changes. "Dark Fiber" by Thomas S. Roche is one of the stories that features a cyborg made for pleasure — called a girldroid in this case. She is tied in to the massive central computer of her creator, Black Corporation. Through the miracle of artificial intelligence, this machine has achieved consciousness, but it is lonely. Enter Hans Jurgen, Jr., who — for reasons I won't try to explain — has had his brain partially wired to Black Corp's system. This way, when he does his thing with one of the company's masochistic girldroids, he'll feel her pain in a feedback loop. He starts his scene with Reseta, the 'droid: "In one second Jurgen knows Reseta's darkest desires, her most powerful needs, the sensation of being fisted on a silken bed, the agony and pleasure of the flogger across her bare back, the ecstasy of being laced into a corset and suspended on a cross, tormented by clothespins and cut by razors, and always, always, the knowledge that she can never be taken by anyone, can never be dominated because she can never lose control. Except to the system, which protects her." The Black computer manages to shanghai Jurgen's mind, so it gets the pleasure of doing Reseta, and she gets to know what it's like to be totally dominated.

"Hands of a Dark God" blends spirituality and technology into a fable about a master and slave who act out their scenes for an audience. Only the audience doesn't just watch, they feel the bottom's physical sensations through headsets they wear. The master isn't just any ol' master, though — during performances, he is possessed by the god of death. "Then he begins to move his ass towards the strokes with a slow sensuous motion. The welts have become maroon, purple, blue, the colour of rich wine. On this space he lives moment to moment, dying and being reborn between every stroke. I drink his pleasure like I drink his pain. I, psychopomp of the endorphins, have taken him past the Gate, and Valhalla awaits."

Circlet Press; $12.95
1995; softcover; 169 pp
1-885865-02-3

VIRTUAL GIRLS
by Evan Hollander

Evan Hollander's erotic science fiction stories have been published in loads of men's magazines. This volume collects five of his ten-page stories (the man is consistent), including one that was previously unpublished. In "The Zero Gee Spot" a space pilot is flying a collection of art to an outpost on Venus Colony IV. The only person accompanying him is a beautiful but stone-cold female curator. After they fly through a strange energy field, they become nymphos in space. Floating in zero gravity, she gives him a blowjob and finishes him by hand. "The first wad of cum flew the length of the cabin and splattered against the navigation console. The second wad splashed against one of the cabin's portholes some twelve feet away."

"Sex in Time" explores the erotic possibilities of a time machine. Brenda has sex with Bill because she's heard he's a great lay, although you wouldn't know it from his nerdy exterior. However, he's got a secret weapon. He's a physicist who's developed a small device that can replay the last five seconds in a loop three times. When Brenda comes from being eaten out, Bill kicks his machine into action:

"'Yes,' she screamed, 'Oh, yes... Ohhh...'
"'Yes,' she screamed, 'Oh, yes... Ohhh...'
"'Yes,' she screamed, 'Oh, yes... Ohhh...'"

Circlet Press; $6.95
1995; softcover; 57 pp
1-885865-04-X

EROTIC COMIX

ANGEL CLAW
by Moebius & Alexandro Jodorowsky

Within the pages of this really big hardcover book, comix legend Moebius displays dozens of finely crafted drawings of sexy, kinked-out subject matter. Filmmaker Alexandro Jodorowsky — best known for his "metaphysical anti-Western movie" *El Topo* — adds brief, lyrical prose beside the images, creating a narrative about a young woman who explores the more unorthodox aspects of her sexuality. She gets covered in blood falling from above, wears shackles and a leash attached to the ceiling, sucks a tentacle, plays with her piss, pushes needles through her nipples, tangles tongues with a hooded man, grasps the erection of a god, grows a cock and balls, has sex with an angel, and does even wilder things.

NBM; $19.95
1996; way oversized softcover; 69 pp
heavily illus; 1-56163-153-1

ATTRACTIVE FORCES
by Robert Edison Sandiford & Justin Norman

Using a diffused, soft black and white style of painting, Justin Norman visually interprets three short stories by Robert Edison Sandiford, all of which end up with an African American man and woman having steamy sex.

NBM; $9.95
1997; oversized softcover; 52 pp
heavily illus; 1-56163-193-0

CATHEXIS
by Michael Manning

Before *The Spider Garden* and *Hydrophidian* [below] introduced the world at large to the rampant erotic power of Michael Manning's comix, the artist self-published his own work. *Cathexis* collects numerous sequences, illustrated stories, and single panels from 1987 to 1992.

NBM; $12.95
1997; oversized softcover; 102 pp
heavily illus; 1-56163-174-4

COLEY RUNNING WILD
Book One — The Blade and the Whip
by John Blackburn

Often appearing in the *Meatmen* anthologies, John Blackburn's character Coley is a pretty, buffed, hung Adonis who is literally a sex god. Narcissistic and hedonistic, Coley employs his eternally-hard cock to plunge into the willing orifices of countless male and female lovers, although he definitely prefers the former.

In the adventure "Return to Voodoo Island" Coley ventures back to the voodoo practitioners who turned him from a mere mortal into an irresistible, unstoppable sexual pow-

A different kind of teacher/student meeting.
Countdown: Sex Bombs.

erhouse. He's accompanied by his porn star colleague and lover Lon, his director Harry Lance Larue, and their female friend Kit, who feels unrequited love for the self-absorbed Coley. The blonde porn god with pierced nipple manages to get in a three-way with another guy and a woman and perform a voodoo sex dance with a hot biracial woman before being kidnapped by some natives. They take him to the lair of the Black Widow, an evil voodoo priestess who drains the life force out of young men by sucking their dicks till they die. Happily, our hero uses his twelve-inch rod to defeat his nemesis. Afterwards, Coley gets into an all-male threesome and, later, Kit sucks him during an animalistic ceremony.

The second adventure, "Idol of the Flesh", starts with Coley getting interviewed and photographed by Jennifer Collins, a freelance writer on assignment for a skin magazine for women. She decides she wants to write a book on the young libertine, but in order to do it, she has to go along with Coley's wild impulses. To test her out, he takes her on a high-speed motorcycle ride (he, as usual, is bare-ass naked), and they end up at a church. Coley often has sex with the young priest who resides there, and they end up doing each other on the altar. When an elderly priest catches them, Coley's friend sneaks off to the rear of the chapel and hangs himself. In his rage, Coley trashes the church and sets it on fire. He and Jennifer speed away on the motorcycle, as she goes down on him. After a run-in with a brutal policeman, Coley is bailed out by a mysterious stranger who wants to use him as a human sacrifice in a rite to an ancient death-god.

A final section of the book contains unpublished drawings of Coley and illustrations that were used only in the limited edition publication of *Return to Voodoo Island*.

EROS Comix; $14.95
1995; oversized softcover; 140 pp
heavily illus; 1-56097-214-9

THE COLLECTED HORNY BIKER SLUT, VOLUME 1

This book collects the first three issues of one of the messiest, gooiest comix in existence — *Horny Biker Sluts*. The head Biker Slut is a tall, insatiable brunette with a pneumatic body. She'll gladly fuck anything that moves, and kick some ass in the process. Throughout her adventures, pants go down and dicks go up in non-stop fashion.

The stories are drawn by several different people, but they have one thing in common — they're 100% triple-X material. Big veiny dicks shoot loads. Hot girls are covered in come. Every gushing orifice is gleefully penetrated.

"Four Cheeks on Hot Vinyl" is a typical episode. The main Slut and her sometime partner in grime are hitchhiking in a deserted desert. A car comes along, and having found a better way than "thumbing" a ride, the Slut flashes her giant melons. In the car is a suburban couple who quickly engage the Sluts in some roadside sex, which ends up in a four-way with the wife getting fisted. As soon as the action is over, the couple leaves the Sluts spent by the side of the road. For the next vehicle that come along, Slut #2 bends over. A van comes screeching to a halt and a rock band jumps out. They proceed to gangbang the willing women and, once again, leave them stranded. Finally, they spread their legs for a third try at getting picked up, and get taken in by the police car that comes by. In the final panel, our two heroines are at the jailhouse, getting reamed in the keisters by the boys in blue.

Last Gasp; $16.95
1995; softcover; 120 pp
heavily illus; 0-86719-422-7

COUNTDOWN
Sex Bombs

by Hiroyuki Utatane

Proving once again that the Japanese are masters at effortlessly making mincemeat of taboos, this work of manga will knock your socks off. It contains the first eight issues of the *Countdown: Sex Bombs* comic series, drawn in trademark manga style, with lots of strange angles, unusual cropping of frames, exaggerated motion lines, and hardcore sex. Hiroyuki Utatane has redrawn many panels especially for this American printing, due to censorship of the originals in Japan.

Starting things off with a bang is the most debauched of the stories, "Lonely Night Bird". The beautiful Sana — complete with impossibly round eyes, mondo breasts, and a wasp waist — is waiting for her father. Her younger stepbrother, Suo, waits on her hand and foot and calls her "Mistress". When Daddy comes home, Sana and Suo engage him in a three-way, rendered in gushing, triple-X detail.

In "Sweet Lips", a student-parent-teacher conference turns into another soaking *ménage à trois*. A music teacher and her student tickle the ivories in "Ad Libitum", and "Regarding Temptation" features more incest, this time close encounters between cousins. One wordless episode — unlike the others, drawn in traditional Japanese style — portrays a woman having sex with a dragon.

This is a must for people who demand erotic content that — besides being perfectly rendered — is more than a little outrageous.

EROS Comix; $19.95

1996; oversized softcover; 144 pp
heavily illus; 1-56097-231-9

THE CONVENT OF HELL

by Noe Barreiro

The Convent of Hell does a great job exploring a favourite erotic theme — nuns gone bad. Really bad. In this painted, hardcore comic, a Spanish convent becomes a den of gooey carnality. From the opening sequence, we know that things are a little "different" with these nuns. One of them has been caught masturbating, so she is tied down while the sexy Mother Superior mercilessly shoves a donkey-sized dildo into her as punishment. The Mother then heads back to her cloister and masturbates furiously while thinking of the sister she just fucked practically in half.

When the nuns accidentally discover a door in the basement, they pry it open despite a warning that it could lead to demonic realms. Sure enough, as soon as the portal is opened, seven long, thick penis-tentacles come snaking out and grab a nun. Some of the tentacles hold her down and strip her while the others violate her mouth, cunt, and ass. The slithering cocks are finally beaten back by the other nuns, not including Mother Superior, who is masturbating furiously.

The door is barred, but that night Mother Superior sneaks down and opens it, summoning Beelzebub. A giant horned goat-being with an unnaturally humongous schlong shows up and fucks the sister silly. Another nun comes in, but Satan controls her mind, and soon they are locked in a three-way. From there, the convent turns into a non-stop orgy, with a memorable scene in which a buxom nun is crucified and, while on the cross, she gives Satan a blowjob and is eaten out by Mother Superior.

This comic is completely blasphemous and hotter than hell.

NBM; $9.95
1997; oversized softcover; 59 pp
heavily illus; 1-56163-192-2

GULLIVERA

by Milo Manara

Fans of giant women, rejoice. European erotic comic master Milo Manara reinterprets *Gulliver's Travels* his own special way in this full colour comic. Gullivera just so happens to be a curvy babe with full lips, a tiny button nose, and curly brown hair that cascades halfway down her back. After getting dumped off her floating air mattress while sunbathing nude, she climbs aboard a deserted boat that just happens to have been sitting offshore. A violent storm tosses her onto a beach in Lilliput. When she comes to, she has been tied down while on her back in a spread-eagle position by the Lilliputians, who are small enough to fit in her hand. She gains the King's favour when he forms a military parade to march under the "arch" of her standing with her legs planted wide apart. But then she pisses off the Queen by pissing on her to put out a fire in the royal palace.

Gullivera jumps on her boat and sails away, only to dock in a land where the denizens are giants and she is as small as a Lilliputian. A man and a woman find her on the beach.

Walking softly in Lilliput. *Gullivera.*

She has some fun rubbing against the guy's finger, but the girl gets jealous and once again Gullivera is headed out on her ship.

Her next port of call is the land of the Yahoos, a breed of intelligent, talking horses. When one of them tries to get frisky with her, our heroine once again takes off, only to end up on a floating island populated by women. After they engage in some spanking, Gullivera beats a hasty retreat and finally ends up home.

For whatever reasons, Manara chose to let this opportunity slip through his fingers. With a woman who was a giant, then small, then with horses, then in a Sapphic paradise, he could have explored endless sexual possibilities. Unfortunately, Gullivera seems to be a nun in training who hardly takes advantage of her opportunities. The only exception is a full-page coloured-pencil drawing at the very end of the book that shows Gulli lustily embracing a gigantic, veiny cock.

NBM; $13.95
1997; oversized softcover; 72 pp
heavily illus; 1-56163-170-1

HYDROPHIDIAN

by Michael Manning

In this sequel to *The Spider Garden* [below], Michael Manning once again employs his talents in creating a stunning erotic fable. This time the exquisitely rendered, genderfucked action takes place in Hydrophidian, the realm of the Water Snake Clan, who appeared in the orgy scene of *The Spider Garden*. The incestuous twin sisters Squamata and Lichurna Serpentine rule this murky kingdom populated by water "naiads", who wear fetishistic, black latex mermaid outfits that only show their bulbous breasts and bottoms.

next page, an ugly sicko is disrobing. He says to the crying, bound woman next to him, "Baby, lucky for you I bought 'I Piss on Your Grave'... How else would I have gotten these ideas!!" In the strip "Like a Sex Machine", a hot waitress takes a quadruple amputee veteran home with her. She and three of her friends then pull out his teeth, stick him in a hole in the bed so only his head is showing, and then force him to eat their pussies. You'll also find several instances of nuns and priests having sex, a woman in a clusterfuck with four rabbis and Jesus, a menstruating porno actress, Santa Claus getting laid, two witches fucking Elvis's corpse, a dominatrix sticking a man in the oven, a porno film featuring Lobster Boy in a gangbang, and the rape scene from *A Clockwork Orange* reworked so that Bob and Elizabeth Dole are the victims.

If you like your sex comics to stomp on all notions of propriety, you'll have to get *I Piss on Your Grave*.

Sophie Cossette; $3
1996; comic book format; 28 pp
heavily illus, no ISBN

LUMENAGERIE
by Michael Manning

Lumenagerie presents 58 mostly full-page drawn portraits of the denizens of Michael Manning's bizarre, fetishistic kinkworld [see *The Spider Garden* and *Hydrophidian*]. Genders are fractured and combined; humans, animals, and aliens intermingle; the bondage is extreme; and the sex is wild and explicit. These otherworldly erotic beings are presented in seven categories, including "Domina: the keepers of the human beasts", "Gynandros: those 'of doubtful sex'", and "Servus: rubber slaves".

NBM; $11.95
1996; oversized softcover; 72 pp
heavily illus; 1-56163-151-5

MARIE-GABRIELLE
by Pichard

Pichard is a European master of SM comix. *Marie-Gabrielle* is his most extreme creation, and is one of the most unyielding works of its genre. The action takes place sometime in the 1700s and centres around the Ste. Madeline De La Redemption convent. In this hellhole, nuns with perfect cheekbones mercilessly torture the young women sent to them for the worst crimes imaginable — masturbation, fornication, adultery, and missing church. Of course, this is for the women's own good. If they suffer enough, they will be pardoned for their transgressions. As the theologian P. Baudran once wrote: "It's an essential tenet of Christian morality that sin must be expiated through punishment. All that was touched through sin must be purified through penitence."

Approximately the first half of the book concerns Cunegonde, a young woman who is caught playing with herself by her mother. She is sent to the convent of pain. Eventually, she is "adopted" by Countess Marie-Gabrielle and her husband. Marie is caught having an affair, and then it's her turn to spend half the book being physically abused by the sisters.

"Are you quite sure it's Elvis? I had imagined him a lot fatter!" *I Piss on your Grave!*

Verio, a human male visitor at Hydrophidian, engages in a three-way with a naiad and the reptilian Lichurna. Afterwards, the horse-humanoid Gion licks the naiad clean. Around that time, Squamata returns from a decadent vacation at the Spider Garden. Following custom, she's stolen a slave from the Garden and brought her back to be relentlessly used. While the slave is being orally serviced by Gion, she is made to tell what she knows of a Garden concubine named Sasaya, who used to belong to Verio. She tells of a scene in which Sasaya was bound in an extremely tight wasp corset and suspended in a web of chains, while Shaalis — the hermaphrodite "Mastress" of the Spider Garden — fucks her in the ass. In a story within a story within a story, Shaalis tells Sasaya of how her former master, Verio, was made to pleasure the Tengu Matriarch and her jealous sons. Finally, as Gion sucks himself, Verio despairs that he'll never see Sasaya again.

Once again, Manning has hit the nail on the head with a sumptuous, self-contained mythos taking place in a universe that revolves around kink.

NBM; $9.95
1996; oversized softcover; 64 pp
heavily illus; 1-56163-167-1

I PISS ON YOUR GRAVE!
by Sophie Cossette

In this black and white collection of stories and single-page artwork by Sophie Cossette, you'll find that the subject matter is as subtle as the title. Forget about notions of political correctness... they're about to get fucked. The opening page is a gruesome rendition of Elizabeth Bathory going down on a woman who has evidently been tortured to death. On the

The Far Side... of the bed.
Rina's Big Book of Sex Cartoons.

The non-stop punishment heaped on these women and their fellow inmates defies the imagination. They are bound with ropes and chains into physically impossible positions. One woman hangs from the ceiling by her ankles with a weight attached to her long hair. Another is shackled around the wrist and ankles in a bent over position. She is chained to a post by the ring through her nose, and a padlocked metal device holds her mouth open. Two others are led around by clamps on their tongues and nipples. While naked and bound, the women are savagely beaten with whips and canes, often in public. They are given forced enemas. They are made to lick latrines clean. Every orifice is violated with whips, brooms, and other objects. Their outer pussy lips are padlocked closed. They are confined for days on end in impossibly small cages.

Words haven't been invented that can convey the depths of brutality and ruthlessness that *Marie-Gabrielle* reaches.
NBM; $15.95
1977 (1995); oversized softcover; 141 pp
heavily illus; 1-56163-138-8

MEATMEN
An Anthology of Gay Male Comics, Volume 16

Another instalment of some of the rudest, raunchiest all-dick comix being published. In Jon Macy's "Penetrating Heaven" Satan is horny as hell. He puts angel wings on one of his flunky demons and sets him up as a decoy. Soon a real angel swoops down to help his supposed comrade. He is cap-

tured and taken to Beelzebub for an unholy alliance.

Elsewhere, that mysterious rebel Jonny Shadow has an encounter in a dark alley. As a crowd of toughs gather around to watch, he starts insulting them, so they use him, then tie him up in the open for everyone to see. In the latest adventure of Jack Masters: Private Dick, Jack saves a young man who witnessed a murder.

On the lighter side, in the cartoon-style "Jayson's Dream Man", Jayson almost steals his female roommate's date. Kurt Erichsen's four-panel strips offer humorous takes on gay life. One recurring character goes up to people in public and announces: "Hi! My name's Jeff. I'm gay!" When a man grabs him around that waist and says, "So am I," Jeff replies: "Wait a minute! That was a **political** announcement!"
Leyland Publications; $15.95
1995; oversized softcover; 158 pp
heavily illus; 0-943595-44-4

RINA'S BIG BOOK OF SEX CARTOONS
by Rina Piccolo

In her third collection of cartoons, Rina Piccolo examines sex within the universe of her quirky single-panel cartoons. Try to imagine Gary *The Far Side* Larson after he's ingested a big helping of oysters, GHB, and green M&Ms... then you'll have some idea of the territory Piccolo covers. In one of 86 cartoons, labelled as "A Scene from Leave It to Beaver", Ward walks in the door and says, "Hello, boys — where's the beaver?" His two sons reply, "She's in the kitchen making sandwiches."

While climbing up the Empire State Building, King Kong realises: "Hey, my penis fits perfectly in this window." In another panel, Dorothy, Toto, the Scarecrow and the Cowardly Lion find the Tin Man and a Tin Woman stuck while screwing. The Tin Man yells: "Well don't just stand there — **get the oil can!**"

Some guys hanging out on a sidewalk are waving to a man and a woman on the opposite side of the street. One of the guys says to the others, "That must be Fred's new girlfriend — you guys wanna go over and meet her or do you wanna just wait for the video?" Elsewhere, a princess is saying to a toad: "... and if I kiss you and turn you into a prince, is there any way we can keep that tongue of yours?"
Laugh Lines Press; $8.95
1997; paperback; 85 pp
heavily illus; 1-889594-02-4

SHE-MALE TROUBLE #2

The gloppy, extra-hardcore comic *She-Male Trouble* is a collection of stories and single panels by various artists. All of them follow the sexploits of two very horny people — they look like beautiful, curvaceous bombshells, except for one thing... they've got huge dicks. In John Howard's extremely raw story "Pinched", Kate and Kaz are doublefucking the hell out of a woman who's agreed to "work off" her brother's gambling debts. A cop bursts in and arrests them for siccing their pit bulls on anti-porn protesters. Once they've been taken downtown, they're subjected to an enjoyable body cavity search. The cops think they'll teach the "freakos" a

Saving the world from being humped to death. *Sin 7*.

lesson by throwing them in with a bunch of guys, but the She-Males set their cellmates straight: "Y'see, we ain't the ones locked up in here with you… y'all are locked up with us!" I leave the ensuing action to your imagination (even though the comic doesn't).

"Coming Attractions" by James Burchett is a delicately shaded pencil-drawn story about three She-Males living in the future. They go to a theatre showing a sex film that allows viewers to somehow merge with it (and each other). The She-Males and dozens of men and women engage in an epic clusterfuck that fills the entire theatre.

Four more spurting adventures fill out this instalment of *She-Male Trouble*.

Last Gasp; $3.95
1994; comic book format; 40 pp
heavily illus; 0-86719-264-X

SIN 7
Sodomina
by Tony Luke

Mina is a nymphomaniacal prostitute in London who works the streets for her love of sex and money, not because she needs to in order to survive. In her spare time, she creates experimental dildos, vibrators, and sex machines, including the Orgasmatron, which harnesses brain waves to create sexual sensations in the receiver. It just so happens that Mina's pussy is actually an interdimensional doorway, and during the Orgasmatron's trial run, she becomes so erotically charged that a being calling itself Scratchman, the God of Fuck, manages to come through the portal. He wreaks havoc on London, declaring that he will eventually hump the world to death. It's up to Mina to discover her true nature and — with her previously unknown sisters from another di-

mension — put a stop to Scratchman's sexual conquest. Tony Luke uses an impressive punk style that mixes splattered black and white, fuzzy greys, photographs, computer-generated backgrounds, and negative printing to create a maniacal graphic style perfectly suited to its maniacal storyline.

NBM; $9.95
1997; oversized softcover; 60 pp
heavily illus; 1-56163-194-9

THE SPIDER GARDEN
by Michael Manning

This decadent cybergothic porn fable should have "masterpiece" printed right on the cover. Erotic artist Michael Manning, who had already developed a following among the sexual adventurers of the San Francisco scene, is heavily influenced by Japanese prints. At times he uses his lines sparingly, and other times he provides fine details — sometimes using both approaches within the same panel.

The story centres on a beautiful hermaphrodite named Shaalis who rules over a stunningly-rendered, fetishistic Never-Never Land, inhabited by insectoid robot creatures and servants who wear ball gags and tight leather dresses with the derrieres cut out. Some of these servants are men and some are women, but all of them have cantaloupe breasts and beautiful feminine faces.

In the first segment Shaalis breaks in a new female concubine, provides forbidden pleasures for a horse-being, and fends off a would-be assassin. In the second, longer, part of the book Shaalis hosts an intergalactic orgy, inviting representatives of the Water Snake Clan, Sisters of the Black Halo, and Women of the Simoom, Veil of Heaven. They engage in an indescribable banquet of debauchery featuring tentacles, lit candles, whips, impossible positions, serpent tongues, bondage, and graphic penetration of every orifice.

Manning has managed to create an entire libertine mythos that lives up to the publisher's claim of "pressing the boundaries of sexuality." *Spider Garden* has set a new standard for erotic comix and for erotic art in general. Most highly recommended.

NBM; $11.95
1995; oversized softcover; 95 pp
heavily illus; 1-56163-117-5

SWEET SMELL OF SICK SEX
by Sophie Cossette

With full colour covers and black and white inner artwork, this collection of Sophie Cossette's comic art (most of which was originally published in *Screw*) is a follow-up to *I Piss on Your Grave* [above]. Although it has its moments, it just doesn't live up to its predecessor. The best work is the series of full-page panels called "Twilight Zone's Twisted T.V.", which imagines X-rated version of classic shows. Jeanie (as in *I Dream of…*) is on her knees, sticking her bottle inside Samantha Stevens of *Bewitched*. Meanwhile, two dogs — who have the heads of Jeanie's Master and Darin Stevens — are screwing. In other panels, Bettie Page pulls out Ed Sullivan's massive schlong onstage, Batman and Robin al-

The Tijuana Bibles, Volume 1.

most get their dicks chopped off while watching Catwoman masturbate, the Flying Nun gets it on with African tribesmen, the Munsters and the Addams Family go at it, and the Honeymooners have a cannibalistic barbecue orgy. The issue's centrepiece is an twelve-page telling of the murder of Judy Dull by 1950s serial killer Harvey Glatman. Dull had been the favourite model of bondage illustrator John Willie, one of Cossette's biggest influences. It's an ambitious effort, but it never quite comes together.

Sophie Cossette; $5
1997; comic book format; 28 pp
heavily illus, no ISBN

THE TIJUANA BIBLES
America's Forgotten Comic Strips,
Volume 1
edited by Michael Dowers

"Tijuana Bibles" is the name given to a genre of pornographic comics that flourished earlier this century. Each booklet contained eight pages' worth of pure, raunchy fucking and sucking. The Bibles began appearing in the late 1920s or early 1930s and faded away by the 1950s. It's been estimated that as many as 2000 titles were produced, and that at their zenith of popularity, twenty million copies were being cranked out yearly. "The little booklets were drawn in attics, printed in garages on cantankerous machinery, and distributed surreptitiously from the back pockets of shady vendors in alleyways and in dimly lit rooms."

Almost without exception, Tijuana Bibles are badly drawn, badly written, amateurish, and filled with lame humour. They're also completely explicit, showing hard-ons, spread lips, spurting dicks, and all kinds of penetration. In a typical example of the genre, "The Interview", a dorky-looking guy at a publishing company sees the hot new intern and says (and I quote): "Holy fuck! I've been waiting for an intern like you for a long time." He whips out his stiffy and they immediately start having sex. Then another guy in the company comes along, takes the woman away, and they start humping. The first guy is angrily holding his throbbing rod when another beauty walks in to apply for an internship. They immediately start screwing on the floor, and the first woman comes back in. In the final panel, the first guy is getting blown by the original girl while he licks the newcomer's ass. The second man exclaims: "Dear God! The perfect so-

lution! We'll take them both!" And there you have it. An important but often overlooked aspect of the history of sex publishing.

This first volume contains fifteen of these little wonders, including many that involve famous comic characters (Superman, Captain America, Flash Gordon, etc.) and celebrities (Ginger Rogers, Errol Flynn, Elvis Presley, and others). The original Bibles are extremely rare. I recently found a used bookstore selling them for $20 *each*. This book and others in the series are the only realistic way to enjoy these historical gems.

EROS Comix; $12.95
1996; softcover; 128 pp
heavily illus; 1-56097-223-8

UNDERTOW
by Kiki Kjaer

A verrrrrry sensual, delicately drawn comic about a yuppie woman who gets away from it all at the beachhouse of a girlfriend and her husband, only to be introduced to the pleasures of nudism, Sapphic sex, threeways, and fourways.

NBM; $8.95
1997; oversized softcover; 44 pp
heavily illus; 1-56163-185-X

THE YOUNG WITCHES
by Solano Lopez & Barreiro

South American artist Solano Lopez provides one of the unfortunately more tasteful entries in the EROS Comix series. *The Young Witches* is about a secretive sect of man-hating women who worship Ishtar. The cult died out with the invasion of monotheism, but it was later resurrected as a way for women to use their psychic powers to take control of the world away from men.

Young Lillian Cunnington is the daughter of one of the Ishtar worshipers, and as such, possesses extraordinary psychic powers. She is sent by her incestuous aunts to the "Institute", where she's taught to use her abilities. Her gorgeous elder classmates just love having their way with her, but she manages to fend them off. She's interested in the male gardener, but the head mistress arranges for Lillian to catch him getting gangbanged by a bunch of students. "I hope this convinces you once and for all what the true nature of men really is," sneers the mistress.

During the disgusting insemination ritual used to keep the sect going, the "honoree" chickens out, and Lillian sticks up for her. The schoolmarm gets pissed and engages luscious Lillian in a duel to the death.

The back of the book contains a short, full colour story. A mysterious stranger enters a woman's bedroom and starts to have his way with her. A woman (roommate? sister?) in another room comes rushing in. She struggles with the guy, but ends up kissing him. Both women then bang the intruder silly and proceed to go at each other.

The Young Witches includes a lot of full and semi-nudity. However, the sex scenes are handled discreetly, meaning that there's no hardcore imagery — nipple sucking is the only sex act that is graphically portrayed.

EROS Comix; $16.95
1992; oversized softcover; 104 pp
heavily illus; 1-56097-202-5

2 HOT GIRLS ON A HOT SUMMER NIGHT
by Hooper & Wetherell

2 Hot Girls on a Hot Summer Night comes at you with both barrels blasting. This comic is really just an excuse to show two women who are built like brick shithouses having a fuckathon. There are four Sapphic sequences here, starting in the present day and going backwards through time.

The first one takes place in 1992, when a woman gets back from a month's vacation in Morocco and has a special homecoming with her lover. In the next episode, from 1955, a woman visits her aunt in London. When she arrives, Auntie isn't home but a maid with gravity-defying bazoombas is. Then we go back to 1898 to the home of a drunken, oafish English aristocrat. Again, a gorgeous maid enters the scene and then the man's dissatisfied wife. The final episode jumps all the way back to 1080, when an Anglo-Saxon princess-witch and a fair maiden do some magic on each other. We find out that the witch has performed a ritual that will bind the women together in their future lifetimes.

Throughout the whole book, the reincarnated lovers go at it with gusto, using tongues, fingers, vibrators, dildos, ice, and a cucumber. Some of the props include a ladder, a kitchen table, and a barrel-for-two filled with water. This black and white comic is a blisteringly hot little number that covers a millennium of luscious lesbian karma.

EROS Comix; $10.95
1992; oversized softcover; 82 pp
heavily illus; 1-56097-203-3

EROTIC AND NUDE ART

THE AGE OF INNOCENCE
by David Hamilton

The Age of Innocence has rapidly become one of the most controversial and embattled books in America. It is a quasi-retrospective of the work of David Hamilton, a British photographer who has been taking pictures of nude or partially nude adolescent girls — with their full consent and eager co-operation, plus the consent of at least one parent — for almost thirty years. Unlike the work of Jock Sturges, another photographer who often shoots unclothed adolescents, Hamilton's work has an unmistakable erotic edge. The seductive and coy looks. The repeated posing of the girls with their

Currently one of the most controversial books in the US, it could possibly be outlawed. *The Age of Innocence.*

arms stretched over their heads, making their breasts even perkier. The fact that almost all of the models are beautiful and that every one of them has full, sensuous lips. The shots where the viewer is looking down on a girl stretched across a bed.

Of course, there are no pictures of sex or "lascivious display of the genitals", the two key elements of child pornography. The girls' sexual natures are revealed much more subtly. Yet, for all its eroticism, *The Age of Innocence* does not come off as exploitive. Because while there are seductive and coy looks, the more than 200 photographs also reveal a myriad of other expressions — proud, self-confident, strong, sly, uncertain, happy, filled with wonder. Out of Hamilton's extensive body of work, he has chosen for this book his most vibrant and psychologically revealing images. Sometimes he has been criticised for artistic and emotional vacuousness in his work. Based on some of his other books I've seen, these charges may not always be off the mark, but overall these photos — almost all of which were taken in the studio with one model in each shot — are artistically strong and most often reveal the models as individuals. Though Hamilton is primarily focusing on the erotic natures of his subjects, the general atmosphere is one of celebration, not exploitation. Of forthrightly revealing and revelling in the youthful blossoming of sexuality. Of daring to show the desires, feelings, and allure of human beings who are well on their way to becoming women.

This attitude is reflected in the short quotations that accompany each picture. Some of them address beauty and sexuality in general, but most of them focus specifically on youth. Many are from poets, such as WB Yeats: "The innocent and the beautiful/Have no enemy but time"; "The rosebud beginning to glow on her face…"; "And finding her beauty such power has got,/Her heart pants for something — she cannot tell what." John Dryden: "Take me, take me, some of you,/While yet I am young and true;/Ere I can my soul disguise;/Heave my breasts and roll my eyes." Shakespeare: "On a day, alack the day!/Love, whose month was ever May,/ Spied a blossom passing fair,/Playing in the wanton air." Lord Byron: "Where the virgins are as soft as the roses they twine./ And all, save the spirit of man, is divine." Oscar Wilde: "Lily-white, white as snow,/She hardly knew/She was a woman, so/Sweetly she grew". A surprising number of quotes come from the diary kept by Anne Frank, who chronicled not just her experiences hiding from the Nazis but also her coming of age: "I think what is happening to me is so wonderful, and not only what can be seen on my body, but all that is taking place inside"; "Who would ever think that so much can go on in the soul of a young girl?"

It goes without saying that there are quite a few people who, as usual, do not agree with me. These people — primarily fundamentalist Christians (as well as a few liberals) and their pals in the government — are doing what they can to make sure that you can't see *The Age of Innocence* and similar work. In the fall of 1997, two famous fundies urged their followers to go into bookstores and rip up the books of Jock Sturges. The faithful did so in at least 20 bookstores, including those located in New York City, Dallas, Denver, Oklahoma City, Colorado Springs, and Franklin, Tennessee. Four people were arrested in the Dallas incident, although, inexplicably, police chose not to arrest the vandals in most of the incidents. The fundies also griped about the work of Hamilton and Sally Mann (her book *Immediate Family* has photos of her three young children in the nude), although I'm not sure if their books were also burned… oh, excuse me, I mean shredded.

Goaded by fundies, district attorneys across America are deciding whether or not to press some kind of charges regarding books by Hamilton and Sturges. In November of 1997, the nation's largest bookseller, Barnes & Noble, was indicted by a grand jury in Tennessee for distributing *The Age of Innocence* and Sturge's books *Radiant Identities* [Outposts p 202] and *The Last Day of Summer* in an area open to minors. The charges officially state that the two books may constitute "obscene material". Then, in February of 1998, an Alabama grand jury indicted Barnes & Noble on 32 counts of selling "child pornography" (the charges specifically involve *The Age of Innocence* and *Radiant Identities*). Later that same month, *another* Alabama grand jury indicted Barnes & Noble on three more "kiddie porn" charges stemming from the same two books. Around this time, UPI broke the story that the Department of Justice is investigating whether the work of Hamilton, Sturges, and "other photographers" who create underage nudes violates federal law.

Naturally, all of this controversy has done wonders for sales of the books. As I write this, *The Age of Innocence* is currently the best-selling art book at Barnes & Noble (they have admirably refused to stop carrying it). It is also the third best-selling non-fiction hardcover at Amazon.com, the company whose name is synonymous with online bookselling. As usual, the censors are their own worst enemies. Thousands upon thousands of people who would have gone their whole lives without even hearing the name David Hamilton are now gazing at his photographs of nude teenage girls.

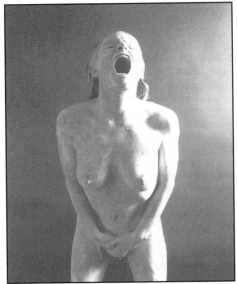

An eclectic exploration of sexuality, sensuality, and nudity. Kura Shouting, *Beauty/Reality*.

Still, we shouldn't let this wonderful irony divert us from the fact that these books may be banned in parts of the US or the country as a whole. I suggest you buy a copy before the Art Police and the Sex Police make sure you can't. And although in general I believe that books should be purchased from independent booksellers, might I suggest that you thumb your nose at the censors and support Barnes & Noble by buying it from them?

Note: Authorities in the UK have been seizing this book and the people who own it.

Aurum Press; $45
1995; oversized hardcover; 214 pp
heavily illus; 1-85410-304-0

BABY DOLL
by Peter Whitehead

"Peter Whitehead is probably best known for the films he directed in the Sixties. These include *Charlie Is My Darling* (1965), the first, and best, depiction of the Rolling Stones, shot when the band were on the brink of stardom; *Wholly Communion* (1965), a documentary account of the Beat poetry performances at the Albert Hall; and *The Fall* (1968), a depiction of the occupation of Columbia University in 1967." In 1972, he and a beautiful nineteen-year-old heiress referred to only as Mia ensconced themselves in a chateau in Southern France. For one month, they ingested psychedelics, took photographs, and — one would presume — got in on like rabbits.

The photos from these "lost four weeks" have never previously been published. Almost 100 of them are contained in *Baby Doll*, printed on slick, pitch-black paper, which is fitting since all of the pictures look like they were taken in the dark with only a (usually) frontal source of light. Swimming in this murkiness are contrasty, grainy images of the blonde Mia, usually nude or partially nude, often with a subtly uncomfortable expression on her face.

The pictures have a stiff, formal experimentalism about them. They look as if Whitehead was simply playing with different positions, lighting, reflection, exposure times, motion blur, etc. to see if he could stumble onto something interesting. Occasionally, he did. In one powerful picture, Mia looks as though she might have been crying. She is topless, keeling on the ground facing the camera, while a topless female mannequin towers behind her. In an abstract shot, all we can see is Mia's alabaster ass glowing in the background as her legs — wrapped in black-and-white-striped stockings — slither out of the darkness at us. Early in the series, we see Mia's head, wrapped in a wide blindfold that leaves only the tip of her nose and her pouty lips visible, in front of the peculiar bars of her Edwardian cot. The image is partially reflected in a slick surface at the bottom of the frame.

All in all, though, the pictures are too detached and coldly experimental to be gripping. *Baby Doll* has more interest as a historical or aesthetic document than as an erotic one.

Velvet Publications (Creation Books); £12.95, $17.95US
1997; oversized softcover; 87 pp
heavily illus; 1-871592-78-X

BEAUTY/REALITY

by Tony Ryan

Tony Ryan is a photographer living on a small island far south of the Australian Mainland. In this relatively secluded environment he has managed to create a body nude artwork unlike any other I've seen. Every single image deserves its own short essay (which, in fact, is what Ryan provides), because each one goes off in a different direction, gently exploring a different type of person or different mood. It's an eclectic collection that maintains consistency due to Ryan's smooth, sharp style of black and white photography and his ability to capture the warmth and humanity of his subjects.

Most of the people appear nude, but to label this entire book as erotic art doesn't seem accurate. Many of the images certainly reflect that designation, yet others contain a relaxed nudity. Some are explorations of innocence, and others could best be described as sensual, rather than sexual. Of course, many images combine these approaches or walk the fine line between them, making for some challenging work.

One of the most outright erotic shots is *Kura with Cream*, showing a woman with cream running from her throat, over her beasts, into her pubic hair. She cups one frothy breast and licks cream from the index finger of her other hand. In *Kura and the Carnage of Nature*, shot four years prior, the same model is covered in raspberry jam, and her neck and wrists are wound with pearls, seashells, and studded leather.

The other most openly sexy shots involve Hannah, a lithe yet chesty young woman who looks barely post-adolescent. Her calves and armpits are trimmed with a fair amount of hair, which actually adds to her wildchild animalism. *Hannah at the Window II* is a beautifully lit masturbation shot done in front of a glowing window. In an image that captures the power of pure, simple nudity, Hannah is sitting on her spread legs, back arched, throwing her head back. In *Hannah and Nellie*, Hannah and another nude young woman engage in a passionate kiss in the woods.

The nude portraits of most of the other women are not as blatantly erotic, requiring you to make of them what you will. *Patricia* shows a topless woman wearing jeans and an arm tattoo, with her black leather jacket slung over her shoulder. Her slumped posture indicates a defiant yet slack attitude, while her face betrays a softness and unsureness. Small-breasted Jane has a mad glint in the one eye that peeks out from under a wild mass of hair. Sarah looks straight up at the ceiling and grabs her own breasts so forcefully that it hurt her (according to the accompanying text). *At Mary's Place II* shows a large woman draped across a couch in a classical nude pose. *Michelle I*, taken with the sun shining through the trees, does a wonderful job showing the beauty of a heavily pregnant woman.

Men don't figure heavily in Ryan's work, but they are there. The first in a series of images of Jason shows him hugging his knees while sitting on the ground. He is only wearing a black tee-shirt, and his cock is visible through the space between his shins. In *New Clippers* — the only shot featuring a male couple — one man, sitting on the edge of a bathtub, plays with his partner's ass and dick while getting his head shaved.

Several of the photographs explore the connection between mother and child. In one, a toddler tentatively reaches out for his mother's powerful body as she stretches and gazes out the window. Several of the shots involve breastfeeding of infants and toddlers. In an interesting case of synchronicity, just before I discovered Ryan's work, I had been leafing through a long out-of-print book that collected material from three New York underground sex newspapers put out in the late 1960s/early 1970s. Amidst pages of uninspired barely-erotic photography, I suddenly came across an elegant shot of a woman breastfeeding a baby. I thought to myself, These days, who would have the unflinching nerve to publish such a photo in a book that contains a high amount of sexuality. Tony Ryan, that's who! He addresses the subject directly. "Breastfeeding — especially in public — blurs the distinctions between human and animal, sex and sensuality. In a culture that fetishises the human breast and at the same time worries feverishly about any connection between children and sex there is bound to be tension and embarrassment (yet another burden for women in a patriarchal society)." In another controversial shot, a nude mother in the background looks on while her unclothed nine-year-old twin daughters apply make-up to each other. This juxtaposition of tawdry, completely adult faces on little girl bodies makes this perhaps the most jarring shot in the book.

I seem have to gone on more than I planned to about Ryan's work. As I mentioned, though, he explores so many facets of sexuality, sensuality, and nudity in this one book of 60 photos, that this review could easily keep going. There are many other images that I feel are worth mentioning and commenting on individually, but I'll stop now and simply tell you to get *Beauty/Reality*. It was printed as a limited edition of 800, and I don't think there will be any more, so hop to it! To see some of the shots from this book, plus many others, go to Ryan's Website at www.imalchemy.com/Tony.Ryan/.

Tony Ryan; $29.95US
1997; oversized softcover; 96 pp
heavily illus; 0-646-28011-2

BIG TOWN, LITTLE TOWN
Nudes for the Urban Environment
by Frank Wallis

This book features 20 black and white nudes by photographer Frank Wallis. The shots were taken in public areas of Manhattan, including the financial district, Greenwich Village, the subway, a library, and an Ivy League college. The mission: "I wanted to contrast the natural beauty of a woman with the magnificence of the man-made environment."

Wallis' model, Sheila, generally wears a simple one-piece dress. In most of the shots she lifts the bottom half or lowers the top half (or both) to reveal that she's wearing nothing underneath. I'm guessing this has to do mainly with the logistical problems of getting totally starkers in public. However, it definitely adds to the forbidden, voyeuristic thrill of the photos, as if Sheila is quickly flashing us before a passerby comes along. She's very pretty, but in an approachable, down-to-earth way, rather than a glamslam/supermodel way. She's got long legs, perky breasts, and a nice caboose.

In one shot, she's peeling off her dress as she walks away from us in the Village. She uses her skirt to polish a car in another image, giving us a fabulous booty shot. In one picture that reeks of urban alienation, a despondent and 100% nude Sheila is leaning against a phone booth near Wall Street. One of the book's interior shots shows Sheila exposing herself in a college classroom. The book's final image, one of the strongest, looks at Sheila from a dramatic lower angle as she pulls her skirt up in front of a gigantic monument to PT Barnum.

Besides the finely produced images on glossy paper, Wallis provides some background on the shoots, an interview with Sheila, and technical information on how the pictures were shot. He has also created a related video, *Naked in San Francisco*, in which he filmed naked women frolicking in the City of Angels. (The video is $29.95, plus $3 shipping.)

Frank Wallis; $11.95
1994; oversized, staple-bound softcover; 29 pp
heavily illus; 0-9638332-8-6

THE BODY EXPOSED
Views of the Body — 150 Years of the Nude in Photography
edited by Michael Köhler

The Body Exposed is based on a sweeping German exhibition that surveyed the history of nude photography. Curator/editor Michael Köhler is to be commended for his non-elitist approach to the subject. He writes in the preface: "Both exhibition and catalogue, therefore, insist on rejecting the conventional distinction between aesthetically significant nudes and aesthetically insignificant representations of nakedness.

Instead, the approach chosen here has no preconceptions."

The first section goes way back to 1865, almost to the birth of practical photography, the period in which daguerreotypes were taken. Believe it or not, photographic pornography wasn't invented in the 1950s by *Playboy* but has been around for over one and a half centuries. "Académies" reprints over fifteen academic nude studies taken from 1855 to 1900, while the next chapter examines more lascivious images from the same period.

The book's first departure from the norm is its chapter of ethnological photography (*National Geographic*-style "naked natives") from 1860-1920. During the first two decades of this century, a photographic movement called Pictorialism attempted to ennoble photography and prevent it from being desecrated by hacks. This was done mainly through diffusion created by a soft-focus lens. The results, as shown in this book, are hauntingly beautiful. Around the same time, France saw the explosion of "naughty postcards", which get their own chapter.

"The New Vision" shows the heavy experimentalism of Man Ray and others from 1920 to 1940. At the same time, an opposing movement was occurring in which objectivity was the goal. Edward Weston and Imogen Cunningham were among its practitioners.

The next big surprise is the quick survey of photojournalism featuring nudity, including famine victims and a prison strip search. "Advertising" features characteristically immodest Swiss ads, like the one for Care cologne featuring full frontal male nudity.

"Contemporary Glamour" has sixteen pictures from 1960 to 1980 showing off Marilyn Monroe, Andy Warhol's Factory, and a hooded woman in leather and chains. "Playmates" shows three decades of photography from men's magazines, mainly *Playboy*.

"The Nude Portrait" claims to be about straightforward, non-erotic nude shots, so John Swannell's portrait of a starvation model trying to look sexy in lingerie and Peter Hujar's photo of a man jerking off don't seem to fit in. Images of a more daring and imaginative nature are featured in the last two chapters. Charles Gatewood captures a pantyless woman raising her skirt in public, Wilhelm Loth presents a bold portrait of his model's knees, and Jan Bengtsson captures a very old couple making love.

The Body Exposed tries to cover so much territory that it ends up giving only a cursory examination of each subject area. It's not concerned with being a who's who of big name photographers, so don't expect Helmut Newton, Robert Mapplethorpe, or Joel-Peter Witkin. It does earn points in its presentation of neglected areas of nude photography. Still, there's a lack of daring in the majority of this material. If you can only get one or the other, I'd heartily recommend getting *The Body* by William A. Ewing [*Outposts* p 162] instead.

Edition Stemmle (D.A.P.); $29.95
1986, 1995; oversized hardcover; 208 pp
heavily illus; 3-905514-47-8

BODYSCAPES™
by Allan I. Teger

Allan Teger is a trained psychologist and untrained photographer. He was drawn to photography as part of his mystical quest to capture the idea that two realities can exist simultaneously, but for a while he was uncertain how to do this. "I remember the moment that the idea for Bodyscapes came to me. I was thinking that the shape and structure of the universe repeated itself at every level and suddenly I had the image in my mind of a person skiing down a breast."

Teger's lightly brown-tinted photos show people, animals, buildings, and vehicles interacting with their environment — the human body. He doesn't use any kind of darkroom or digital manipulation to get his images… they are simply miniatures placed on real female bodies. The illusion is pulled off due to the subtle lighting which gives the images an ambiguous atmosphere (is that a human torso or a dusky plane?) and usually casts the props in silhouette, masking details that might give away their tiny stature. Also, the judicious use of depth of field — in which background objects appear out of focus — helps to distort the sense of scale.

The image on the cover of the book is a good representative of the rest of the work. A fisherman is standing on a flat surface, casting his line into a deep, dark bellybutton. *Downhill Skier* shows a skier crouching as he begins to slide down the side of a mountainous breast. In *Harvest*, a man with a scythe is about to trim some pubic hair while a windmill looms in the background. Two infants go ga-ga over a gigantic nipple in *Babies*. Breasts make another appearance in *Mermaid*, which shows a transparent mermaid perched on a wet mam, looking out to "sea". Pubic hair plays an even bigger role in Teger's work, acting as a stork's nest, a desert oasis, a grazing area for cattle, and a divot for a golf tee.

Another bodily part takes centre stage in *Moon Shot*, which shows a rocket heading for a cratery surface (Uranus?). In *Marathon*, four runners are making their way across a long leg, and a construction worker uses a jackhammer on some pearly white teeth in *Dental Work*. The book's closing image, *Erector Set*, shows a crane getting into position to move a seemingly gigantic penis.

With *Bodyscapes*, Teger has managed to forever blur the distinction between the body and the larger world that surrounds it. Once you see his work, you may never look at a sand dune (or a breast) the same way.

Shade Tree Press; $26.95
1995; oversized softcover; 87 pp
heavily illus; 0-9638703-7-8

BUNNY'S HONEYS
Bunny Yeager, Queen of Pin-Up Photography
by Bunny Yeager

In the early 1950s, Miami model Bunny Yeager did lots of cheesecake work. She decided to try her hand on the other side of the camera, and, in doing so, became one of the most important erotic photographers of all time. She took some of the best-known pictures of Bettie Page, and virtually defined the early look of *Playboy*. With the exception of Page, Yeager never worked with professional models, shooting only women she happened to meet in public. By the late

1970s, Yeager's style was considered old fashioned, but she refused to become more explicit. She stopped shooting female figures. Luckily, the renewed interest in her work has convinced her that her style is still appreciated, so she has once again started photographing women.

This sumptuous volume presents Yeager's work with almost 50 models. Most of them get two pages, a few get four, and Page gets six. They're wearing home-made bikinis, hot pants, or nothing at all. Since most of these shots were made when showing pubic hair could get you busted, it is conspicuously absent most of the time, although it does make a few appearances.

It is apparent that Yeager's models are amateurs. It's not that they look uneasy — it's just that they're so unsophisticated and, well, wholesome. Almost all of them are the archetypal girl next door. Sandy Bowman's huge brown eyes give her the startled fawn look. The statuesque, raven-haired Lorna Carroll looks like someone you could easily start chatting with, even when she's standing bare-ass naked behind a tall houseplant. Blonde Marci Lane looks like the cliché kid sister. Not all of Yeager's models are so full of innocence, though. Six-foot Jackie Miller cuts quite an imposing figure, and the black and white shot of Kiki Kaiser fondling her own breasts while making an orgasm-face must have raised a few eyebrows.

These photos are the beautiful legacy of a bygone era. That tableaux of slightly bright pastels and supersaturated warm light sends me reeling back to my youth when I would look at my contraband vintage *Playboys*. But Yeager's pictures are more than just a nostalgia trip. They're a kinder, gentler porn that provides a nice balance to the harsher material of today.

Benedict Taschen Verlag; $24.99
1994; oversized softcover; 160 pp
heavily illus; 3-8228-9329-3

CITY OF THE BROKEN DOLLS
A Medical Art Diary, Tokyo 1993-96
by Romain Slocombe

Two things strike me as extremely noteworthy about Romain Slocombe's work. First of all, I just love it when someone devotes their art to a very specific, personal, and outrageous erotic obsession that they have. In the case of Slocombe, this devotion is for Japanese women wearing bandages and casts. Which leads to the second noteworthy aspect — the brazen disregard for notions of seemliness. By photographing broken and occasionally bruised women, Slocombe makes himself ripe picking for people who will be upset by the implied violence towards his models or the notion that incapacitated women are attractive to men who want someone they can easily dominate and control. But Slocombe knows what turns him on, and he's not going to let others' opinions get in the way of that.

The women in these almost 100 black and white photos wear varying amounts of medical supplies, and the pictures range from being blatantly erotic to appearing so benign that you wouldn't recognise their true nature if it weren't for the context of the whole book. In one shot, a petite young woman

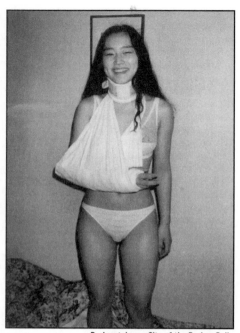

Broken taboos. *City of the Broken Dolls.*

dressed in ordinary dark clothes is wearing a neck brace and looking noncommittally at the camera. In another, a woman in a schoolgirl uniform — her head bandaged and her left arm in a cast — attempts to walk on crutches in her hospital room. In one of the few shots of unknown women whom Slocombe happened to see in public, a plainly-dressed woman with her right arm in a cast and sling walks though a crowd outside a subway station.

Other pictures are explicitly sexual. Two shots show a woman wearing a lacy bra and light-coloured panties standing against a wall. Both of her arms are in casts past the elbow and supported by slings. Bandages encase her thighs. The look on her face — half-closed eyes, slightly parted lips — is ambiguous, signifying pain or horniness, or both. Elsewhere, a woman with two broken arms, finger splints, a knee bandage, and Band-Aid under her left eye is lying on her hospital bed, allowing us to see the crotch of her panties underneath the edge of her gown. A woman with a by-now typical array of bandages, casts, and a neck brace licks the end of a double-headed dildo. In the next picture, she is attempting to reach inside her silky panties, which proves difficult since her cast covers all but two fingers.

A few pictures spill over into straightforward bondage and SM. A nurse wearing a neck brace is gagged and tied in a wheelchair. In another image, a nurse wearing arm-length leather gloves fastens a studded harness onto a prone woman wearing a neck brace, arm and leg bandages, and a shiny black bikini.

City of the Broken Dolls will have considerable appeal to people who are into BDSM or those who are attracted to disabled people. But although it overlaps with these two ar-

eas, it charts its own unique course. Anyone who is aroused by broken taboos will want *Broken Dolls.*

Velvet Publications (Creation Books); £12.95, $17.95
1997; oversized softcover; 106 pp
heavily illus; 1-871592-81-X

DIARY OF A THOUGHT CRIMINAL
by Mark I. Chester

Radical sex photographer Mark Chester has been taking pictures of men and women since 1981. He principally aims his lens at gay men who are into SM/leather, creating a body of work that has caused more than its fair share of controversy. The images are black and white shots done in a studio, featuring men who are, for the most part, muscular and defined without looking like they spend the majority of their waking hours at a gym. They generally pose alone, either naked or wearing the accoutrements of their sexuality — leather hoods, biker caps, leather vests, big-ass boots, and nipple chains. But the thing that really makes these shots different is the presence of hard dicks. In the majority of shots where a cock is visible, it's erect. Sometimes it's because its owner or someone else is stimulating it, but usually it's hard for no immediately visible reason. In the slyly named "Zoltan with Pole", we have a dramatically lit shot of a nude man, obviously a bodybuilder, clenching a bamboo pole in his left hand. This would look like many other well-done, classically shot male nudes, except that Zoltan's cock is jutting straight out from his body. The presence of hard-ons makes these pictures confrontational. These guys aren't just here to be looked at. They're aroused and they want to fuck.

In other shots, Jeff has pulled down his spandex shorts and is stroking himself, Kai leans over to tie his boot while sitting on a stool, a young man holds the American flag aloft while his balls and erection rest on a pillar, one man encases another in a formfitting bodybag, Craig moons the camera, Jack is caught making an orgasm-face, Pat masturbates and grimaces in agony while Mad Dog tattoos his nipples, and a man — dressed in a spandex hood and tights, boots, and a leather vest — has his hard dick tied by a leather rope that runs up and loops around his neck. The lone shot to feature a solitary woman shows Shelly, perfectly nude, with her hands clenched behind her head. The only other woman is shown entwined with a man in *Nude Foot.* Perhaps the most out-of-place, yet moving, photo is entitled *Cal — In memory of dead friends.* It shows a nude, pot-bellied man turned away from the camera with his hands grasping the back of his head. Even though we can't see his face, the slump of his shoulders and his downturned head make his grief palpable.

Probably the most challenging images are the series entitled *Robert Chesley — ks portraits with harddick & superman spandex.* The subject is Chester's deceased friend and lover, the playwright Robert Chesley. The purple lesions of Kaposi's sarcoma are visible all over his torso and arms as he goes from wearing jeans to putting on tights and then a Superman outfit with the crotch cut out to expose his erection. In the sixth, final shot of the series, he is bound in rope but manages to play with himself anyway. These photos were

Mark Chester's photos are among the few that go to
the extremes of sexual provocativeness and
political/social provocativeness in one fell swoop.
Jacob, *Diary of a Thought Criminal.*

banned from an exhibit called *X: Works That Dare Censorship* that was held as part of the Festival for Freedom of
Expression. Isn't the hypocritical irony here as strong as it
could possibly be? The organisers of an event that directly
confronts censorship engaged in censorship. I'm not even
sure what people found so objectionable. Yes, at first it is
jarring to see someone with HIV/AIDS portrayed so blatantly
as a sexual being, but after the initial jolt wears off, why would
you want these images banned? Are people with HIV/AIDS
not allowed to have sexualities? Are they only allowed to be
portrayed in political settings as activists or in hospital settings as martyrs?

It is exactly these kind of strong reactions and important
questions that Chester's work evokes. His are among the
few photos that go to the extremes of sexual provocativeness and political/social provocativeness with one fell swoop.

Mark I. Chester; $30 [hardcover: $50]
1996; oversized softcover; 63 pp
heavily illus; 0-9627616-2-1

DIRTY WINDOWS
by Merry Alpern

It's common practice among photographers to make shots
appear as if they were taken without the subjects' knowledge. Porn magazines get a lot of mileage out of this Peeping Tom approach, but you know good and well that it's completely staged. The "hidden" photographer is giving instructions to the models, who have all signed release forms. *Dirty*

Windows, though, is another story. The pictures it contains
really were taken without the subjects' knowledge or permission.

During the winter of 1993-94, an unadvertised, unofficial men's club opened in a housing building on Wall Street.
Photographer Merry Alpern's friend Norman lived in a loft in
the same building. "He showed me how the configuration of
his loft space enabled a view across the airshaft, into two
small grimy windows, one flight down, maybe fifteen feet
away." Those two windows showed the tiny women's bathroom in the illicit club. Peering in from her hidden perch,
Alpern took pictures of executives and hookers having sex,
doing drugs, urinating, and exchanging money.

The black and white pictures are intensely grainy. So
much so, in fact, that I wonder if it was completely because
of Alpern's film or if she added special effects in the darkroom. Either way, the grain adds to the whole seedy, voyeuristic ambience of the images. Every page has the same
basic set-up: The frame of the window is the frame of the
picture. Through the small double panes of glass we see
anonymous bodies engaging in hedonism.

The pictures can be divided into several categories. Probably the largest category is the shots of prostitutes. Women
in gaudy lingerie, only panties, or wearing nothing at all hover
in many of the frames. As in all the shots, faces are rarely
visible. (Not only does this increase the impersonal mood of
the pictures, it avoids lawsuits.) A subcategory of this type of
shot shows the scantily-clad working girls counting their
money.

Other shots show the men decked out in their suits and
ties, after a hard day at the office. Some have their dicks
hanging out taking leaks, and others seem to be talking. In
the third type of shot, the denizens of the bathroom are snorting coke or, less often, sucking on crack pipes. Finally, there
are pictures of the two parties meeting to do some business.
Several shots show hard-ons wrapped in condoms. In the
most decipherable image of a sexual act, we get a profile
shot of a woman on her knees giving a blowjob. A bunch of
murky pictures show the hookers bent over, as the execs
give it to them from behind.

Dirty Windows provides a naughty sensation like no other
book or magazine I've ever seen. The thrill of spying on these
people while they're engaged in illicit activities is undeniable. This book is genuine voyeurism at its artistic *and* sneaky
best.

Scalo (D.A.P.); $39.95
1995; oversized hardcover; 111 pp
heavily illus; 1-881616-58-4

ERIC KROLL'S FETISH GIRLS
by Eric Kroll

At last, we have a much-needed collection of the photos of
Eric Kroll, one of the all-time masters of fetish photography.
These 200 black and white and colour shots are remarkable
for the unusual poses of the models and the bizarre outfits
they wear. It's not often you see a picture of a woman in
thigh-high leather boots and a sheer leotard bending over
and biting her own knee. Among the many standouts in this

book:

- A pouting brunette wearing a huge hairbow and a straightjacket.
- A crouching woman in a leather bodysuit walking on her hands and feet (all four which are wearing high heels).
- Annie Sprinkle dressed as a ballerina/fairy/Easter bunny while pinching one of her nipples.
- A woman — dressed in a leather bra, corset, and gloves, fishnet stockings, and Kroll's trademark eight-inch heels — aiming a crossbow at a kneeling man.
- A topless cutie stretching the waistband of her black and white horizontally-striped pantyhose (another Kroll trademark)
- A short-haired blonde wearing only high heels and a chastity belt balancing precariously on a stool
- A metallic redhead wrapped in green and red Saran Wrap
- An Asian woman smoking a cigarette between her toes
- A blindfolded blonde — her bare torso covered in feathers — holding a leash attached to the collar around her neck.

Benedict Taschen Verlag; $24.99
1994; oversized softcover; 199 pp
heavily illus; 3-8228-8916-4

ERIC KROLL'S BEAUTY PARADE

by Eric Kroll

This second lavishly-produced collection of photography from Eric Kroll shows the photographer's move away from fetish fashion and more towards purely sexual images that are "confrontational, hopefully disturbing". Despite Kroll's intent, though, these photos still display an abundance of outré clothes and props. Leather corsets. Collars and manacles. Red, six-inch platform shoes. Strap-on dildos. Rope. Vibrantly coloured Saran Wrap. Boxing gloves and headgear. A protective mask worn by fencers. Neon red "Caution" tape across the pussy. Smoke rings. An artificial arm. Plastic cone collars worn by dogs who have had operations so they won't gnaw their stitches out. A woman on a bed masturbates with the condom-encased heel of a high-heel shoe. Another has a wooden circle, supporting a snifter of brandy, around her neck. A blonde wearing a girdle flogs a brunette shackled in a doorway.

As usual, Kroll uses models who are unorthodox lookers. They aren't the freeze-dried models-in-a-can who are used interchangeably in mainstream sexual photography. A few of them violently confront staid notions of physical attractiveness... two examples being Kimberly Austin — a single-leg above-the-knee amputee who is herself an accomplished photographer — and a thin women with a shaved head and tattooed aureoles.

The models often find themselves in unique positions and unusual situations. A redhead in a sheer maid outfit sucks on a doorknob. A topless brunette with a leather gun holster stands with her full weight on a man's chest, digging her

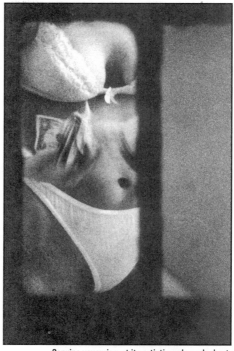

Genuine voyeurism at its artistic <u>and</u> sneaky best.
Dirty Windows.

high heels into him. A completely nude woman rubs her pierced labia against the horn of a horse saddle. Another nudie literally stands in a bookcase, with the shelves cut for her neck, torso, and legs. A woman kneeling in a corner wearing a dunce cap waits for a spanking. A pantless blonde straddles the fin of a 1950s car. Wearing only cowboy boots, a brown-haired woman stands in a prairie while the curious cattle behind her look on. A beautifully severe mistress gives a finishing school lesson in walking elegantly to a man dressed in a maid costume who's balancing a book on top of his head. A model with a straw in her mouth leans over to take a sip out of a toilet. Another woman, dressed in a long black dress and shoes on her hands, drinks from a metal bedpan (no liquid or solid matter is visible, though). A grey-haired woman is bound to the frame of a cart used by bellhops to carry luggage. A blonde attaches a clothespin to one of her breasts, which are sticking out the top of her yellow rubber miniskirt. A standing woman bends completely in half to suck the dildo that's strapped to her knee.

In the unexpectedly revealing introduction, Kroll gives some insight into the life of an erotic photographer. "Today, when I walk into a room filled with women, they either hate me because I've taken their photograph (they think I've become rich and, therefore, ripped them off) or hate me because I haven't taken their photograph (they I think I think they are not beautiful enough)." "I'm always looking for a double-jointed woman, a professional ice-skater, or a female tightrope walker. But it's the attitude that is most important."

Never a dull moment at Kroll's studio.
Eric Kroll's Beauty Parade.

"The woman I chose [to photograph in Flagstaff, Arizona], Amber, was so fresh and unsophisticated, that for the first time, a model made me feel like my ideas were weird. That was refreshing. In San Francisco, New York, Paris, Amsterdam or Berlin it is impossible to shock a woman."

Benedict Taschen Verlag; $29.99
1997; way oversized hardcover; 192 pp
heavily illus; 3-8228-8601-7

EROTIC ART VIDEOS BY
MARK I. CHESTER

Gay erotic photographer Mark I. Chester (see *Diary of a Thought Criminal*, above) hosts shows of sexual art in his gallery. He creates videos of these shows, focusing on every individual work of art and giving background on the artist and commentary on the work. These are admittedly raw documents, filmed on a camcorder with no editing and narrated during the actual shooting. Some of them cover SexArt, the yearly pansexual erotic art exhibition that displays the work of around twenty photographers, painters, sculptors, filmmakers, and others. Other tapes document shows by single artists and shows with a gay theme. Send a self-addressed stamped envelope for a list of videos.

Mark I. Chester; $25 each

EROTIC PHOTOGRAPHY
An Exhibition

edited by Demarais Studios
Erotic Photography is a collection of black and white photo-

graphs from a national competition held in 1981. Whoever selected the pictures in the exhibition evidently has quirky taste in eroticism, making this book different from most others of its kind. Overall, the emphasis is not on making you drool but on showing the possibilities, and perhaps the limits, of photography as a messenger of eroticism.

This is evident in the very first of the 96 photos, which is one of the most subtle. *Sports Fans* shows six men queuing up to have a peek inside a house through a couple of windows. We are unable to see anything through the windows, so there's no telling what's going on inside. If it weren't for the fact that this photo is in a book of sexual images, would you even know what it was about? You might, but that would mainly be a product of your imagination. So is this pictures erotic? In the end, each person has to make his or her own choice.

Makalu throws another curveball. In the centre of the frame, a German shepherd has mounted a black Labrador. Despite being engaged in such an activity, he is viciously snarling at another black lab, who seems much more interested in a tiny white poodle than in the dog being poked. In *Statuetory Rape*, a slob has his hands up a mannequin's shirt, copping a big feel of polyurethane breast. Freud would have loved *Barns*, which features one of the most phallic silos you'll ever see, complete with a domed head with a slit in it.

One of Charles Gatewood's photos, taken in a lounge, shows the archetypal dirty old man pulling down a plump woman's shirt and sucking on her right breast, while she and another man laugh. In an untitled shot by Roger Hyman, a somewhat out-of-shape naked man sits on the floor with his legs spread at the camera. He's in a room filled with medical equipment, and he's inhaling some serious gas through a mask over his face. An old man on a park bench seems happy indeed as a gaggle of naked hippie chicks fawn over him in *Discovering a New Life*.

Many of the pictures take a more direct approach to eroticism. *Daniel's Sister* is an extraordinarily grainy picture of a woman in a small black evening dress stretched across the backseat of a luxury car. One leg is raised, her head is thrown back, and she is leisurely touching herself above the left breast. *An Evening at Home* is a solarized image of a female hand gracefully reaching for the bulge in a man's briefs. In a strangely eerie backlit shot, a woman masturbates by letting the bathtub faucet flow between her legs. In the epic shot *Monoliths*, the camera, positioned at a very low angle, records two hard dicks bursting from the ground to be framed by a brightly-lit sky.

Erotic Photography comes across as very unprepossessing, but it manages to deliver something that not many books can promise — a different way of looking at things.

Demarais Studios; $12.95
1981; oversized softcover; 102 pp
heavily illus; 0-9607462-1-8

EROTICA
Drawings

by Jean Cocteau

Jean Cocteau was an avant garde poet, filmmaker, playwright, and visual artist. These simple drawings of stylised men portray Cocteau's friends, lovers, acquaintances, and fantasies. Some of his figures — such as a rakish sailor leaning against a wall — are tame, while others are completely explicit. In #34 a masturbating man is having an orgasm. Drawing #50 depicts a man squatting on another man's cock as he throws his head back and comes in ecstasy.

Other drawings, especially those toward the end of the book, are more abstract and definitely not erotic. In #98 a maitre d' extends his hand... his palms form the profile of a woman with long hair. A person of indeterminate gender whose head, neck, and chest look like a maze is the subject of *Tattooed Head*.

A few of the drawings record Cocteau struggling to break free from his celebrated opium addiction. Particularly memorable is #17, which shows a man on his back, head hanging off the bed, eye bulging out. His right hand remains undrawn, and where his left hand should be is a criss-cross pattern.

Peter Owens (Dufour Editions); $45
1991; oversized hardcover; 109 pp
heavily illus; 0-7206-0822-8

EROTICA UNIVERSALIS
by Gilles Néret

Erotica Universalis boldly reclaims sexually explicit art from the shadows and basements of prudish mainstream art history. Journalist and historian Gilles Néret refuses to let erotic masterpieces collect dust in the backrooms of museums... he drags them out into the light in one of the most important collections of sexual art ever published. Over 750 paintings, drawings, engravings, etc. (almost every medium except photography) — ranging from prehistory to the 1980s — forever dispel the idiotic notions that 1) graphic depictions of sex are a recent invention and 2) that art can't be pornographic (and vice versa).

The earliest artworks are rock drawings from circa 5000 BCE depicting human/animal hybrids with humongous schlongs. In one, a man with a spear is threatening a rabbit creature. In the other, some kind of creature is nailing a woman in the missionary position. The ancient Egyptians may have walked goofy, but they knew how to get it on. One of the images shows the Pharaoh getting a blowjob while Anubis looks on. Greek groping, hot and heavy scenes from Pompeii, and Medieval woodcuts and manuscript illuminations round out the first section.

The next part of the book, covering the Renaissance and the Golden Age contains a large number of works by famous artists. A detail of the Sistine Chapel by Michelangelo contains the earliest known depiction of fistfucking. Rembrandt created not only three sexual drawings — including one of a monk getting laid — but also a depiction of a urinating woman (thought to be his wife). Albrecht Dürer drew four less explicit images, including *The Rape of Amynome*.

This book certainly doesn't skimp on material. It reproduces 20 of Agostino Caracci's intricate engravings of mythological beings — satyrs and nymphs, Venus and Mars —

The Temptation of Saint Anthony, 1878, by Félicien Rops.
Erotica Universalis.

having sex. There are also 33 drawings from the *Academy of Ladies* series by an anonymous artist in 1680, eleven anonymous prints from Boccaccio's bawdy masterpiece *Decameron*, and 39 orgiastic and cruel engravings from the Dutch editions of Marquis de Sade's *Justine* and *Juliette*.

The most surprising section reveals the bawdy drawings from the French Revolution, which were used as vicious satire. One portrays La Fayette riding a giant cock and balls as if it were a horse, while Marie Antoinette strokes its shaft. Mainly, the drawings present aristocrats, military men, nuns, and friars in compromising situations.

The Romantic era brought giant penises and Satanic imagery into play. *The Virgin's Dream* — an anonymous engraving from 1840 — shows four women playing with huge disembodied cocks. A series of lithographs from 1848 reveal a variety of activities, including three instances of bestiality. A colourful sequence of scenes by Peter Fendi depicts big-bootied women getting plugged in a number of increasingly acrobatic positions.

The section of erotic Art Nouveau contains some of the most arresting imagery in the book. The elegant curving lines of these artists bring a grace and elegance to every work, even *Lysistrata Defending the Acropolis*, which shows a woman farting at a wizened old man. The Satanic paintings of Félicien Rops are show-stoppers, especially *The Temptation of Saint Anthony*, which depicts the crucifixion of the buxom Eros.

The diversity of modern erotica fills the book's last section. Gustave Courbet's photorealistic painting *The Origin of the World* is what we would today call a beaver shot. It was created in 1866. At the turn of the century, Auguste Rodin —

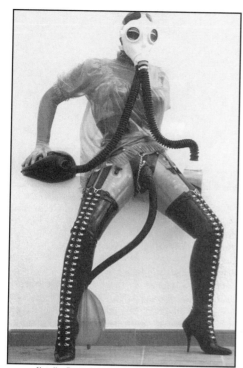

Natalia: Favourite Leisure Dress by Jo Hammar. Filled to bursting with the absolute best erotic photography in the world ... *Fetish Photo Anthology, Volume 2.*

famed sculptor of *The Thinker* — painted four spread-eagle shots. Henri de Toulouse-Lautrec did a doodlish line drawing of two pigs bonking. A few of Picasso's erotic engravings are here, as well as his painting *Pissing Woman*. If you're only familiar with Salvador Dalí's paintings, you'll be wholly unprepared for his bestial line drawing featuring a woman, a lion, a dog, a sheep, a frog, and other animals in a quasi-daisy chain. There are lots of stiff drawings of illicit sex, including SM, from the 1930s and 1940s. Other artists represented in this section include Jean Cocteau, Edgar Degas, Gustav Klimt, George Grosz, Jean Dubuffet, and Tom of Finland.

If you don't get this book, there will be a giant, gaping hole in your erotic library.

Benedict Taschen Verlag; $24.99
1994; softcover; 757 pp
heavily illus; 3-8228-8963-6

FETISH PHOTO ANTHOLOGY, VOLUME 2

edited by Jürgen Boedt

As usual, when *Secret Magazine* decides to do something, it does it big. *Secret*'s editor and publisher, Jürgen Boedt, has assembled this second massive anthology of photography relating to bondage & discipline, SM, and fetishes for leather, latex, PVC, and other shiny/stretchy material. The black and white work of 61 photographers is reproduced here

in oversized format. Although you'll see many well-known Americans — Todd Friedman, Justice Howard, Eric Kroll, Craig Morey — this anthology's strengths are its inclusion of lesser-known talents and its internationalism (photographers hail from Germany, France, Belgium, the US, Britain, Austria, Switzerland, Canada, and Japan).

Here is a sampling of the more than 300 photos included:

☞ A woman in a very shiny PVC scuba suit (complete with mask and fins) stretches out on the floor

☞ A blonde woman in a body armour corset with two-inch spiked nipples

☞ A leather nun using her teeth to tug on one of the strands of a dildo-handled cat o' nine tails

☞ An abstract shot of an alabaster ass mushrooming out of a black leather corset

☞ A brunette woman in a tight, shiny miniskirt standing in a bathtub, pushing a prone woman underneath the water

☞ A close-up of a woman wearing an elaborate leather gag. The image looks as though it was printed on weathered concrete

☞ A naked tattooed woman with barbed wire winding loosely around her body

☞ A close-up side view of a heavily pierced dildo heading for the open mouth of a woman with a heavily pierced tongue, nose, and ear

☞ A woman doing something indeterminate to the body of a hooded man tied to a cross

☞ A woman using a man on all fours as her dinner table as she eats spaghetti and drinks wine. In another shot, she's bound his hands behind his back, put a corset on him, and has made him get down on his knees to service her orally

☞ A blonde woman in a shiny black body suit with the front torso ripped away gently tongues a rose

☞ A naked man in a studded collar and a naked woman wearing a black mask blow fire out of their mouths

☞ Two blonde women lean towards each other for a kiss. The one standing up is wearing lingerie. The other in sitting naked on a toilet.

☞ Two men in leather pants and gasmasks kneel on either side of a PVC goddess on a pedestal. She is wearing a full bodysuit, her legs are held together by six leather straps, and tubes run from her nostrils to behind her head

☞ A tight shot of a female crotch creates a jarring juxtaposition with manly leather chaps and delicate, lacy panties

☞ A brunette wearing only fishnet stockings, nipple rings, and goggles is tied to a dentist's chair as a female dentist prepares a wicked instrument

☞ Daniel Hayes Uppendahl contributes several amazing close-ups of modified bodies: a woman's pierced back is laced up like a corset; one prong from a fork slides through a hole beneath a man's lip; a chain used to walk dogs is attached through the ring in a man's throat; a delicate silver necklace forms a triangle when threaded through the rings on three nipples at the edges of the photo

☞ A hose running from a woman's crotch spews a liquid, which she receives in her wide-open mouth

☞ A seductive nurse dressed in a white rubber uniform sucks on a large syringe

Fetish Photo Anthology, Volume 2, is filled to bursting with the absolute best erotic photography in the world. Even the weakest material is still a pleasure to look at, and the numerous show-stoppers will melt your mind. It's pretty expensive, but if you're going to drop big bucks on a book of sexual art, make it this one.

Secret; $70US
1997; oversized hardcover; 232 pp
heavily illus; 1336002002

IN DEFENSE OF BEAUTY
by Tom Bianchi

Photographer Tom Bianchi has become famous for his male nudes. But because he only photographs the most handsome and buffed men in the world, he has generated controversy among gay men who accuse him of "lookism" (i.e., elitism based on physical appearance). In this essay, he defends his choice of models and presents 34 of his black and white photos. "[P]eople who find fault with beauty, who trivialise it by assuming a negative quality in it, diminish themselves. The ability to appreciate beauty in others is a prerequisite to express it in oneself."

Crown Publishers; $12
1995; small hardcover; 63 pp
heavily illus; 0-517-70223-1

LARRY TOWNSEND'S PHOTO COLLECTION
edited by Larry Townsend

If you're used to only seeing women trussed up in bondage shots, this slim softcover book will throw you for a loop. Instead of damsels in distress, you get dudes in distress. These black and white shots show naked men tied, bound, chained, roped, clamped, and crucified. In one photo, a guy has been bound to an X-cross with 18 leather straps. In another, a man is chained to an old-fashioned rack and is being stretched by a near-naked leatherman.

There's a frontal shot of Randy Storm with his arms spread, nipples clipped, and balls in a vice (literally). In one of the most extreme shots, a man is standing with his hands cuffed behind his back. A chain from the ceiling encircles his neck. Also from the ceiling, two cords tug hard on his nipple rings, and a wire fastened to the floor pulls on the Prince Albert through his cockhead.

A few pages of pictures were taken during a slave auction in Tennessee. Slaves are shown tied to the railing of a bridge. In other shots, three guys shave each other's pubic hair.

Larry Townsend; $12.95
1992; staple-bound oversized softcover; 48 pp
heavily illus; 1-887684-01-6

Octavia (93681.7). Gaze upon the upper 0.1 percentile of the population. *Linea*.

LINEA
Thirty Five Nudes
by Craig Morey

When I first saw Craig Morey's book *Studio Nudes*, I was taken aback by the intense beauty of his erotic photography. Using minimal props and clothing, he photographs gorgeous women against a draped background in his studio. There is nothing elaborate or ornate about his style, yet he manages to produce some of the most mesmerising erotic art I've ever seen. Of course, it helps that his models are in the upper 0.1 percentile of the population when it comes to physical attractiveness. But Morey knows how to make the most of their looks, taking photographs with tones so rich, you can almost feel the flesh. The models strike highly stylised poses that highlight the lines of their flawless physiques.

Linea contains 35 of Morey's nudes from 1988 to 1996 (nine of them previously appeared in *Studio Nudes*).

☞ A profile shot shows a woman wearing a black hat with attached veil — the stereotypical headwear of a grieving widow — cupping her breasts, her eyes closed, and her head held high.

☞ A large-breasted woman has cocooned herself from her ankles to mid-thigh with thick rope.

☞ Another woman in a leather corset and collar has her hands manacled above her head

☞ A woman gazes directly into the camera through the filmy black material she has wrapped around her head.

☞ A muscular black man does a push-up while a white woman lays on him with her back against his.

☞ A woman with very short black hair sits on her feet, her back to the camera.

☞ A seated blonde leans forward and grabs her ankles.

☞ In one of the shots that capture an aspect of the model's personality, an Asian woman with long raven tresses stares at the camera with a demanding, slightly pissed-off expression.

The main drawback of *Linea* is that it is a small hardcover, with most of the images printed 3¼ to 3½" wide and

3½ to 4" tall. Still, it's a relatively inexpensive way to enjoy Morey's work. If you order a copy directly from him for $35, it will be signed, dated, and inscribed to you. [See Appendix B for his address.] To see some of his work online, head to www.moreystudio.com.

Korinsha Press; 1500Yen, $20US
1996; small hardcover; 48 pp
heavily illus; 4-7713-0227-8

MAIA
Prometheus
by Marcelo Maia

In this very small hardcover, Brazilian-born photographer Marcelo Maia presents 49 of his nudes of muscular black Adonises. Maia uses jet black backgrounds and only enough light to barely illuminate his subjects, who are always (with one exception) completely undressed and posing without props. The lighting is angled in such a way that whole land-scapes are created by the play of shadow along hardened torsos and broad backs.

Some of the shots are abstracted figure studies, focus-ing on specific parts of the body, usually abs, pecs, and/or cocks. Other shots pull back some to reveal faces that are thoughtful, seductive, relaxed, or distant. Despite the formal-ism in Maia's work, the shots that show the men's faces cap-ture their humanity and feelings. The close-up portraits are especially powerful. Each of these fifteen images presents the model as a unique individual — one looks subtly con-frontational, another looks blissed out, yet another looks wise, and a fourth is almost smiling bemusedly.

In his introduction, Maia says of his art: "I hope that by showing the world what I think is beautiful, I am somehow doing good. That beauty will somehow become the magic sword that cuts through prejudices, leaving behind archaic ideas like the ashes after a purifying fire…"

Stonewall Inn Books (St. Martin's Press); $13
1997; small hardcover; 54 pp
heavily illus; 0-312-15166-7

NEW YORK GIRLS
by Richard Kern

Richard Kern has become legendary in non-mainstream circles for his films and photographs. In the 1980s he and Nick Zedd — with help from their friends Lydia Lunch, Lung Leg, David Wojnarowicz, and others — created brutal short films that were dubbed the "Cinema of Transgression". Dur-ing this time, and continuing to the present, Kern was also taking photographs of women in his New York apartments. This book presents over 200 of these photos, half in black and white and half in colour.

Although some of the women Kern shot are gorgeous, almost none of them are beauties in the classic sense. There are no safe, sanitised, generic centrefolds here. All of these chicks have an edge to them. Many of them are tattooed and pierced in various places, but the edginess results from something more undefinable — an unusual facial structure, an "imperfect" but still dangerous body, and — of course — the way Kern captures them on film.

There are no safe, sanitised generic centrefolds here. All of these chicks have an edge to them. *New York Girls.*

A perfect example is the first photo in the main body of the book. It shows a brown-haired woman with her hands behind her head, looking up into the camera. Some hair is falling into her right eye, and a Marlboro with about half an inch of ash dangles from her thick lips. She is bathed in a harsh, pinkish neon light coming from her left side, and her right side is illuminated by green neon. A swollen nipple — almost flooded out by the glare — is visible in the lower right corner. Other shots include:

☞ A short-haired blonde — wearing only black stiletto heels and white mid-thigh stockings — is curled so that her shoulder blades are on the floor, her ass is sticking straight up, and her knees hit the floor beside her head.

☞ A glistening-wet brunette stares into the camera as she gives her plump breasts a good squeeze.

☞ A naked blonde carries a limp brunette dressed only in combat boots.

☞ In one of several pictures of girls with guns, a blonde in a police hat, black stockings, and a blue shirt that's falling off aims a pistol with her right hand and clenches her strap-on dildo in her left.

☞ A crouched woman drinking from a bowl on the floor looks up at the camera, as water runs from her pouty lips to the bowl.

☞ Several photos that are likely to be the most controversial in the book suggest violence. In one close-up, a blonde with two huge black eyes glares into the camera while her out-of-focus breasts dangle in the background.

☞ A naked woman completely covered in metallic green body paint crouches in a room painted the same colour as she is.

☞ A brunette clenches her fists in her long hair and pulls the flesh near her left shoulder with her teeth.

☞ A naked brunette with her panties around her ankles sits on a toilet in a public bathroom.

☞ In the most explicit of several shots involving candles, a woman in black stockings and outrageous platform shoes bends over away from the camera, displaying a lit candle sticking out of her pussy.

☞ A large number of pictures, most of which are grouped together, show women in bondage. In one, a blonde strikes a cliché "glamorous" pose while completely wrapped in some sort of plastic tubing that criss-crosses her entire body.

☞ A woman wearing a corset is suspended from the ceiling by rope tied around her ankles.

☞ A clothed brunette turns her left cheek to the camera to show a lizard crawling up her face.

Kern presents the unpolished, raw side of erotic photography, a medium that very often gets so caught up in trying to achieve technical perfection that it loses sight of the unadorned earthiness of its subject matter. *New York Girls* reminds us how nice it is to get back to basics.

Benedict Taschen Verlag; $29.99
1996; oversized hardcover; 208 pp
heavily illus; 3-8228-8180-5

NOTHING BUT THE GIRL
The Blatant Lesbian Image
edited by Susie Bright & Jill Posener

Pictures of women engaging in sexual acts with each other have been around a long time… almost as long as photography itself (just look at some collections of nineteenth century erotica for the proof). However, up until very recently, these pictures were always taken by men. It was only in the 1970s that women who identified as lesbians began creating erotic photographs, and it wasn't until the early 1980s that this art blossomed in the book *Coming to Power*, the magazine *On Our Backs*, and other daring independent publications. The photographers usurped the male gaze, producing lesbian visions though the eyes of actual lesbians. Amazingly, these photos ran into (and continue to run into) resistance and hostility — not just from expected quarters — but from feminists and even lesbians. In daring to expose sexuality — especially butch/femme identities, SM, and penetration — these photographers and those tiny outlets that published their work had to hurdle every conceivable obstacle from every direction. This book is the first to collect a representative sampling of this scattered and suppressed body of art in one place.

Bright, who is a cofounder and former editor of *On Our Backs*, and photographer Jill Posener have divided the 153 images into four subject sections and five sections devoted to specific artists. The "Dyke" section contains a smorgasbord of imagery, including a portrait of a naked Rubenesque brunette smoking a cigarette on a deserted downtown sidewalk at night; Honey Lee Cottrell's *Bulldagger of the Season*; a post-masturbatory photo of a relaxed woman with a deformed hand; Jill Posener's billboard "modification" of a Gatorade ad so that the bottles above the slogan "For That Deep Down Body Thirst" are labelled "LESBIANISM"; Chloe Sherman's affectionate image *Jew Dykes: Ali and Tai*; a negative-printed, voyeuristic shot of two women engaged in oral sex on the hood of a car that's parked on a Washington DC overpass; and a wonderfully simple shot of a standing woman taking a piss in a meadow.

"Cunt" contains pictures that focus primarily on the vulva (or, in the case of Phyllis Christopher's portrait of Tribe 8's lead singer, Kim Breedlove, a dildo sticking straight out of her jeans). Tee A. Corrine's *Isis in the Sky* superimposes a gigantic white-haired pussy in the sky over a line of trees. In an early shot (from 1978) Corrine captures the moment just before a woman's mouth meets her lover's mound, and Morgana Gwenwald challenges notions of depersonalisation in *Incorrect View of the Beloved*.

The photos in "Butch" examine the masculine side of lesbianism. Some of the subjects directly imitate male celebrities, including Tito Jackson (*Fire* by Jennie Sullivan) and Elvis Presley (*Elvis Herselvis* by Phyllis Christopher). Other times, the subjects appear to be generic males. In fact, just by looking at it, you'd probably swear that a man is the subject of Della Grace's from-behind shot of a Navy sailor's broad back and slim hips. In *Lesbo Gang Bang*, two butches manhandle a distraught femme at a bar.

"Sex" shows it being done in a variety of ways, from the SM ass-paddling of *In the Ice House* to doggie-style humping on a beach in *Sex in the Dunes*. From the passionate kiss and nipple-tweaking of *Yvette and Annie I* to the tender embrace of Katie Niles' untitled shot from 1978. From the explicit fistfucking of two of Morgan Gwenwald's pictures to the afterglow of Gon Buurman's untitled photo. Blood-letting, group sex, oral sex, and masturbation are also represented.

The other sections of the book each offer a portfolio from an important photographer: Tee A. Corinne, Honey Lee Cottrell, Della Grace, Morgan Gwenwald, and Jill Posener. Grace displays her pictures of tough and tender skinheads, Posener has a shot of oral sex in a public bathroom, Corinne shows her psychedelic mandalas featuring the female body, Cottrell took a picture of the senior citizens known as Foxy Frances and the Vixens, and Gwenwald's sly photo of two sets of legs — one in stockings, the other in pants — tells the story of a butch/femme picnic turned lusty.

Every section, as well as the book itself, is introduced by an insightful essay by Bright, and direct quotes from the photographers run through the margins. Corinne provides an important reference by compiling a bibliography of erotic lesbian photography.

Expertly laid out and carefully produced, *Nothing But the Girl* is a pioneering document. Naturally, it will bring tears of joy and drops of excitement to most lesbians, but it is also one of a few books that must be in the library of *anybody* who's into erotic art (or sexual politics or freedom of expres-

Jardin Tropical. Enter Irina Ionesco's realm of Byzantine and Baroque artifice, with touches of Victorianism, SM, cyberpunk, and kitsch. *Nudes.*

sion). Be sure you buy the hardcover version I have reviewed (check the ISBN below against the number of any copy you might buy). For whatever reason, the softcover edition of this book (and, from what I can gather, the British edition) have deleted five of the most controversial photographs: Gwenwald's fisting pictures, Grace's shot of four women buzzing a fifth one, Posener's image of outer labia being pulled apart, and Claire Garoutte's portrait of a woman who has been made into a human loom by needles and string. Grab the American hardcover version before it goes out of print.

Freedom Editions (Cassell); $29.95
1996; oversized hardcover; 144 pp
heavily illus; 1-86047-001-7

NUDES

by Irina Ionesco

Shooting for over 30 years, Romanian-born Irina Ionesco creates her own elaborate fantasy world of eroticism and fills it beautiful women. It's a realm of Byzantine and Baroque artifice, with touches of SM, cyberpunk, and kitsch. There's a heavy feel of Victorianism, but the details are too modern to make it simply retro. Ionesco has created her own decadent mythology... it seems like every woman has a distinct role — princess, aristocrat, villain, demon, temptress, prophet, executioner — but everything's occurring in a parallel dimension so we can't quite grasp it. In her introduction, Ionesco writes, "I can only imagine eroticism in its metaphysical dimension. I adore all that is excessive, dreamlike,

curious. So I have adopted as my own these words by Baudelaire: 'In art, only the bizarre is beautiful.'"

The photos, all back and white, are printed one to each oversized page, often as a full bleed. Two facing images, on pages eighteen and nineteen, show how varying Ionesco's imagery can be, even while seeming all of a piece. In the left picture, a woman — with pierced nipples and bellybutton and an elaborate tattoo that winds along her right hip and lower abdomen to her shaved pussy — is wearing only a studded collar and thigh-high leather boots. She supports herself on a stool, looking at the camera with an expression that seems slightly seductive but is basically hard to read. On the facing page, a seated woman is wearing stockings supported by garters, a huge lace bow around her neck, a flowing fur coat, and a flapper girl hat from the Roaring Twenties. Her pale face has a vacant, faraway look.

In another photo, a woman whose face is framed by white gossamer stares at us. On her chest is a lace doily with a doll's head suspended in the centre. A long needle juts out of the doll's neck. Many of the women wear elaborate headdresses that are difficult to describe but appear to be made out of fake pearls and other baubles attached to wire and string. I would swear that one of them is wearing Christmas tinsel. Another has her whole head snugly covered with gauze, and around her neck and shoulders is the "bubble wrap" that's used to cushion packages sent through the mail.

One photo shows a caped woman wearing lamé gloves and sharp, six-inch finger extensions holding a hand around her throat. A topless woman bites the blade of a long stiletto. A vampiric woman holds out a voluminous Victorian dress. A pantless brunette sits with a circle of 30 roses between her parted legs. A woman with a face painted like a harlequin has a huge flower covering her forehead and a rose between her lips.

The book ends with ten photos of Ionesco's daughter Eva ("She was one of the main threads to weave their way through my work. She belonged to that cell I had created, a matrix, a world unto itself, a world representing the Dream.") taken throughout her adolescence. In one she looks at us through a feather she is holding. In another, with strange symbols painted on her face, she pulls open her fishnet shirt.

While these images may be too coolly detached for some tastes (including mine), Ionesco's artistic talent and singular vision have won her a huge following.

Edition Stemmle (D.A.P.); $49.95
1996; oversized hardcover; 143 pp
heavily illus; 3-908162-52-1

PREGNANT NUDES

by Catherine Steinmann

In these twenty-five exquisite photographs, Catherine Steinmann captures "the inherently dramatic figure of a woman soon to bring a new life into the world." Each lush black and white photo (most of which have a brown tint) is reproduced on a separate, oversized page.

All of these nude subjects are in the late stages of pregnancy, with seriously swollen bellies and breasts. Plate 18 shows Steinmann's predominant style — suffused, grainy pictures with an ethereal air about them (reminiscent of Joyce Tenneson's work). The subject in the photo is sitting in a white wicker chair at a forty-five degree angle to the camera. Her head is turned to look at the viewer, but the top part of her head has been cropped. Plate 17 also retains a soft, otherworldly glow as it pictures a woman wrapped in filmy material lying on her side.

Plate 4 is from the more literal end of the spectrum. It is a sharp, simple shot showing a women in profile from the middle of her face down to mid-thigh. Her bulging white belly makes a stark contrast with the black background it is set against. A couple of the photographs feature the husband of the woman pictured. In Plate 13 a woman is on her back, and her husband lies beside her on his side. His upper arm is on her abdomen, and her left hand is on his.

Pregnant Nudes presents an impressive and — as far as I've seen — unique body of work. You can see several of the images at the artist's Website: users.tuna.net/Cath48/.

Catherine Steinmann; $30
1994; oversized softcover; 54 pp
heavily illus; 0-9640297-0-7

SCENARIO
The Art Photography Magazine

This hugely oversized magazine from England is a bonanza of high-quality contemporary and classic photography, at least 90% of which is erotic/nude. The other less than 10% comprises portraiture, urban landscapes, etc. Bob Carlos Clarke has an extensive portfolio in issue 2. His comments on the nature of his work are interesting... he calls sexual imagery "a delicate conspiracy between the imagination and the evidence." Later he says, "The erotic image is an illusion — just marks on paper. The best photographers are the most convincing illusionists, the ones to whose version of the truth we most readily succumb." His photographs are impressive: a profile of a woman dressed only in a short metallic top and a headpiece of feathers. A back shot of a nude, muscular man. A topless woman with scratchy brown tinting all over her body and face. A short-haired woman in thong panties crouched on all fours with a glass tabletop across her back. A heavily scratched picture of two women in a steamy embrace.

Claudia Bohm is undoubtedly the most extreme artist featured. She says: "I include everything that frightens me in my pictures. Then it is gone." Frightening, indeed. One picture shows a huge, green woman with a praying mantis' head about to have missionary-position sex with a man flat on his back. In another shot we see a bald woman, whose neck and face have been painted stark white, with the stem of a pink rose piercing one side of her neck just below the jaw and coming out the other side. Blood runs from the punctures. My favourite image is the portrait of a large-eyed, bald woman who has a small octopus wrapped around her head.

John Swannel's shots are all tinted in a warm brown bordering on amber. They show nude women hunched over on a large sphere; wrapped in a wet, clingy fabric; reclined on a riverbed of rocks; and more. Extremely intriguing are Calum Colvin's "Seven Deadly Sins", a series of photographs

The golden age of Tokyo's sex business.
Tokyo Lucky Hole.

made with toys, shells, postcards, comics, dung, and all sorts of knickknacks. Guntur Blum turns in a couple of straight-on shots of iron-pumping, nude men. China Hamilton's picture of a naked brunette woman straddling a tree stump at the beach is a definite stand-out.

Other artists who grace these pages include Robert Mapplethorpe, Man Ray, Albert Watson, fetish photog Christopher Mourthé, Charles Roth, and Tony Butcher. *Scenario* is an outstanding piece of work. Many of the pictures are so big and beautiful, they're suitable for framing, which is exactly what I've done.

Scenario/PO Box 900/Croydon, Surrey CR9 5ZQ/England
Email: scenario@scenario-magazine.co.uk
WWW: www.scenario-magazine.co.uk
Single issue: £12 + shipping [UK: £2. Europe: £3. US: £5]
Four issue sub: UK: £46. Europe: £56. Overseas: £66
Payment: cheques in Pounds sterling, Eurocheque, Visa, MC, Amex, Delta, JCB

TOKYO LUCKY HOLE
by Nobuyoshi Araki

This fat book is filled to bursting with Nobuyoshi Araki's black and white photographs documenting the golden age of Tokyo's sex businesses from 1983 to 1985. Araki and the editor of the magazine that published his work would troll the city's no-panties coffee shops, peep rooms, massage parlours, strip clubs, live sex shows, and other, sometimes very strange, sex spots. Around *1000* pictures show women dancing, lapdancing, massaging, giving blowjobs, having sex on stage, relaxing, posing for the camera, and doing other things that usually involve nudity. An amazing chronicle of a free-spirited time that came to an end in February 1985, thanks to new laws.

Benedict Taschen Verlag; $29.99
1997; softcover; 704 pp
heavily illus; 3-8228-8189-9

TOM OF FINLAND
edited by anonymous

A nice selection of 130 of Tom of Finland's drawings, action shots, and sequences, all featuring the most muscled, hung, hypermasculine dudes in all of erotic art. Includes sections on Navy men, bikers, and construction workers/lumberjacks; reprints of dozens of covers, including many of the publications featuring Kake; a complete reprint of *Kake 10: Raunchy Truckers*; pictures of Tom himself; and biographical timeline.

Benedict Taschen Verlag; $12.99
1992; oversized softcover; 80 pp
heavily illus; 3-8228-9342-0

TOM OF FINLAND EXHIBITION, 1994-1995

In 1994 a Berlin museum hosted a three-month retrospective of the late Tom of Finland, "the Norman Rockwell of gay erotica". Tom is renowned throughout the world for his thousands of drawings of ruggedly handsome, massively muscled men who are hung with dicks that would make a mule weep with envy. In Tom's world everybody is perpetually horny, constantly hammering away at each other.

This lovingly-produced book from the exhibition contains many of Tom's best, most famous, and most controversial works. Drawings from early in his career depict effeminate men, but that didn't last long. Soon he was creating images of leatherbikers in orgies, guys fucking in locker rooms, and tough cops getting blown.

Different sections explore various aspects of Tom's work. Some group his drawings by theme — lumberjacks, the circus, or black men. "Definitely Not Vanilla" presents some of Tom's harshest material, including depictions of rape. Anyone who thinks that men are never pictured as the objects of brutality in porn have never seen the picture of two guys in fascist uniforms chaining a man to the wall by his cock and balls, shoving a billy club up his ass, and making him perform oral sex. In one of the many quotes from Tom that run throughout the book, he says, "The whole Nazi ideology, the extremism, is hateful to me, but nevertheless I had to draw them — they had the sexiest uniforms!"

Elsewhere, there are photos of some of Tom's models alongside the drawings based on them, as well as reproductions of preliminary sketches and drawings. This book also contains pages from Tom's humorous scrapbooks and the covers he did for the Finnish magazine *Biker News*. Of historical interest are the panels from his earliest extant erotic story and the final, unfinished pieces that were on his drawing table when he died of a stroke brought on by emphysema in 1991. Finally, there is a chronology of Tom's life, an essay on his importance, and photographs of the man himself.

This retrospective is a crucial part of any ToF collection.

The Tom of Finland Foundation; $20
no date; oversized softcover; 63 pp
heavily illus; no ISBN

TRUE BLOOD

by Charles Gatewood & David Aaron Clark

As soon as I took it out of the large envelope it was shipped in and quickly flipped through it, *True Blood* immediately

"The Norman Rockwell of gay erotica."
Tom of Finland.

became one of my all-time favourite erotic photography books. All you have to is look at the cover to realise that this book will take you where no others have. A pretty blonde woman with huge greenish eyes and an ample chest looks at us with a neutral, perhaps slightly bemused, expression. So far, this isn't out of the ordinary. The two hypodermic syringes stuck in her eyebrow are a little unusual, though. And the three hypo needles in her left ear and the six needles through her *throat* might give you pause. The barbed wire wrapped around her wrists and across her chest is also an unusual touch. But what will probably grab your attention most is the presence of blood in this sexy picture. It's running down from the woman's eyebrow, trickling along her nose, and drying on her full lips. It's speckled across her milky chest. Her hands and forearms are positively caked with it. Welcome to the transgressive world of bloodplay.

Using the mostly full-colour photography of Charles Gatewood — a famed chronicler of body modification and the sexual underground — and the evocative texts of David Aaron Clark — author of *Juliette: Vengeance of the Lord* and co-editor of *Ritual Sex* — this oversized book presents the world of people who love to bleed, to cut, to be cut, and to drink the liquid of life. In one photo spread over two full pages, a feminine-looking man with a crimson cross smeared on his forehead watches as a woman squirts a syringe filled

Charles Gatewood lets it bleed.
True Blood.

with blood into her mouth. Her almost-closed eyes and the ecstatic countenance on her blood-encrusted face relate the bliss she is experiencing.

A few pages later, a thin, pale woman has pulled her dress back and is cutting straight lines into her thigh with a razorblade. Her upper right arm already bears five similar cuts. What the psychiatrists would call self-mutilation and mental aberration is recast as an important intimate ritual. The opposing page contains a close-up of the woman's leg, with blood bubbling up from her thin incisions. Clark's text — which always interprets the photos but never describes them in literal terms — reads: "An unknown alphabet suggests itself with each new string of crimson beads. Her own personal language. Come to save her."

The most painful photos would have to be the series showing a woman using an X-acto knife to carve a large pentagram and another symbol into a man's entire upper back. In the first photo, she is doing the actual cutting. Clark writes: "Every time she forces open a door between the sticky pores of his flesh, his body shudders with the headlong thrust of his spirit trying to surf its way on the pounding blood waves of his heart, frantically seeking the limitless space outside, reverberating with the one-second-off vibrations of an ethereal nether sphere where crueller angels wait, patient in their loving fury, instruments of infallible joy gleaming with sunspot measure." In the second photo, she holds an ornate bowl up to his back to catch the scarlet river flooding down. Finally, he bows low as she squats above him, pissing on his back.

If you're squeamish, you'll want to avoid this book at all costs. But if you're entranced by blood — or just by extreme

body and sex rituals in general — you'll be in haemoglobin heaven.

Last Gasp; $19.95
1997; oversized softcover; 64 pp
heavily illus; 0-86719-443-X

WATERDANCE
by Howard Schatz

I would venture to guess that acclaimed photographer Howard Schatz has created a book of erotic/nude photography that does not have a single predecessor. His daring idea was to photograph professional dancers — mainly those who perform ballet — underwater. The results are perhaps the most amazingly beautiful art covered in *Psychotropedia*.

Dancers, of course, have stunning bodies and are able to move with a precise grace and flow that the rest of us can only marvel at. By putting them underwater, their suppleness and lyricism are multiplied to a near infinite degree. As the introduction states, with these 110 colour photographs Schatz "offers us a ravishing glimpse of the ecstasy of pure beauty, of bodies without bounds, and pyrotechnics without penalty."

It is a testament to Schatz's talent and vision that he was able to convince most of these dancers — whose numbers include some of the world's best — to pose completely nude for him. The woman bare their all for these photos. The men do, too, but due to strategic positioning, there are no penises on display (except in one instance). Even if these shots weren't done so beautifully underwater, this book would be worth the price just to have the unprecedented chance to drink in the limber, finely-tuned bodies of unclothed world-class dancers.

Luckily, Schatz has made the most of his subject matter. In *Underwater Study #4*, the pale, lithe body of Katitia Waldo floats against an almost-black background. Her fiery red hair curls around her face, as a piece of red chiffon in her left hand forms a tight arc. *Underwater Study #23* is a back shot of Yuri Zukov — naked as the day he was born — with his left leg pointed straight down, his right leg bent so that his toes touch his left knee, his right arm straight out from his side, and his head above water.

Underwater Study #149 is a close-up of Cindy Storman's torso draped in billowy red chiffon. When *Underwater Study #193* was snapped, Shannon Lilly was apparently upside down just under the surface of the water. Wearing only ballet slippers, she is walking with her toes pointed. Her head is arched back, and her arms extend gracefully upward. The picture is presented inverted, so it looks like she is delicately walking on water. *Underwater Study #119* is one of about a dozen photographs that feature the dancers together. Tiffany Heft and Nikolai Kabaniaev are torso to torso with their right arms around each other, left arms thrown behind them.

Because of its sheer beauty and the fact that its approach is without precedent, *WaterDance* is most highly recommended.

Amphoto (Graphis Press); $24.95
1995; oversized softcover; 176 pp
heavily illus; 1888001208

WHAT SHE WANTS
Women Artists Look at Men
edited by Naomi Salaman

Although the history of erotic images is a long and varied one, it has a monstrous gap in it… the veritable absence of erotic representations of men by women. *What She Wants* is an attempt to address the situation. By gathering photographs from 64 female American and European artists, the editor (and curator of the show that the book represents) shows that some women have been busy picturing their desires.

But this book is not a collection of pretty, naked men. The images run the gamut — prurient, subtle, abstract, and weird. Some might not be considered erotic if they were viewed apart from this book, and others are best taken as comments on gender and sexual politics. There are few orthodox black and white figure studies. Instead, the artists have experimented with angle, composition, texture, and media (including X-rays, cloth, and collage).

The photograph on the cover — *Abroad* by Diane Baylis — shows a man's hairy body set against a skyscape of fluffy clouds. His penis appears to have been flattened and rolled up like one of those party noisemakers that unravels when you blow into it. Let's hope that this is trick photography. *Untitled I* by Sarah Pucill is a parody of Man Ray's famous *The Prayer*, featuring a guy's hairy ass instead of the smooth female one in Ray's photograph.

Other works include:

- *Venus De Milo*: an armless man dressed in jeans and a bra.
- *Untitled (Light Box)*: a female hand pinching a male mannequin's nipple.
- *User Friendly*: male hands are typing on a computer; a big dick is coming out of the monitor's screen.
- *Close-up*: an extreme close-up of the intersection between a man's thighs and butt.
- *Buyaka*: a buff guy smiling a little nervously at the photographer.
- *Headless*: a harshly front-lit shot of a man masturbating. The head of his penis is covered by his hand, and his other head has been cropped out.
- *Man in Tights*: an extreme upward angle shot of a man wearing pantyhose.
- *Pure* and *Enmesh*: photographs of men's torsos that have intricate geometric patterns cut out of them (the photos, not the torsos).
- *Whatever Tickles Your Fancy*: a latex glove on a man's foot.
- *Overstep*: someone's foot squishing a man's cock and balls.
- *The Sink*: a side view of a man's stomach and penis as he pisses into a sink.
- *Cockerel Cock I*: The legs of a naked sitting man come towards us. In front of his cock is… a cock (of the poultry variety).
- *Sammy*: A brown-tinted shot taken from behind a dog standing on its back legs. Its tail looks just like a long penis.
- *Still, Flying*: Two butterflies perched on a dildo.
- *Other Chambers*: A woman's hand buried up a man's keister.
- *Liason*: A hand in a velvet glove gripping a hard-on. One cuff of a pair of handcuffs is around the wrist. The other is clenched around the base of the penis and one testicle.

Five essays at the front of the book analyse the photos, erotic art, men as sexual objects, "the penis and the phallus", and the purposes of the book. As Cherry Smyth writes in her essay: "'What She Wants' establishes a site for women to take their pleasure seriously, eschewing market demands for images replete with fake seductiveness, which fail to 'clitillate'. The show attempts to chart current changing masculinities and situates 'want' back into the discourse of straight feminism, beyond the tortured defensiveness of anti-porn feminism and the laissez faire transgression of some pro-sex representations."

What She Wants is one of the strongest collections of erotic art I've seen. Highly recommended.

Verso; $17.95

1994; oversized softcover; 160 pp
heavily illus; 0-86091-656-1

WOMEN EN LARGE
Images of Fat Nudes
by Laurie Toby Edison & Debbie Notkin

In case you haven't noticed, 99.9% of female erotic photography — from the self-consciously artistic to the joyfully smutty — portrays slim women. This isn't too surprising, since society considers skinny to be sexy. Curves are appreciated, but only in certain places on an otherwise sleek toned body. This penchant for thinness has reached its logical extreme with the invasion of models such as Kate Moss, the waif that launched a thousand lunches.

Women En Large was created as a direct challenge to this paradigm. Sure, these photos of nude fat women will appeal to the so-called "chubby chasers", but this is not niche porn, meant for people with a certain fetish. A radical expansion of the aesthetics of female attractiveness is the ambitious goal here. The creators of the book proclaim: "We will no longer let society define beauty!"

The women in these black and white photos by Laurie Toby Edison range from fairly overweight to out-and-out huge, with most of them leaning towards the latter half of the spectrum. The shots are divided evenly between sharp and low/medium grain. The models are doing what most models in erotic photos do — reclining on a bed, posing against rock formations, stretching on the floor, looking pensive, staring playfully into the camera, taking showers together, and so on. Its jolting to see such massive women within the framework of traditional erotic photography.

Debbie Notkin's essay, "Enlarging and Society", is a manifesto of the fat-positive movement (also called the size acceptance movement). "Self-hatred is a horrifyingly-inexpensive commodity in this culture for all genders, races, and lifestyles, but for fat teens the immediate price is minuscule; your ongoing reasons to despise yourself are written on your 'pretty face' and measured in the size clothes you buy off the rack. If you have to shop at a 'fat store' because other stores don't sell clothes you can wear, hating yourself is easier still."

Books in Focus; $24.95
1994; oversized softcover; 116 pp
heavily illus; 1-885495-00-5

MISCELLANEOUS

AMERICAN SEX MACHINES
The Hidden History of Sex at the U.S. Patent Office
by Hoag Levins

When we think of the US Patent Office, most of us don't think of sex, but for 150 years designs for sexual devices have regularly made their way into the stodgy storehouse of inventions. Hoag Levins takes us on a rollicking ride through this uncharted territory — the Patent Office's version of the Vatican's porn collection. Along the way, not only will we be amazed and entertained, but we'll also get a lesson in society's attitudes towards sex, because in every patent, the inventor must "describe the problems or deficiencies that their invention is designed to correct."

One of the chapters that is particularly enlightening when it comes to uncovering America's Puritan streak is "America's Assault on the Solitary Vice", which reveals inventions designed to discourage playing with oneself. Michael McCormick's anti-masturbation device (1897) was worn around the waist. The penis was inserted through a hole. Over the top of this hole hung an "awning" with spikes on the bottom, designed to puncture the penis if it got hard. "In the case of an 'irresponsible' person who needed to be involuntarily restrained from participating in the solitary vice, McCormick noted that the 'appliance can be permanently secured to him... (with) a fastening strip of some permanent character, like sticking plaster.' In 1903 Albert Todd patented an electrical harness that would encase some poor soul's dick. If he got hard, the device could either sound an alarm or send an electrical shock powerful enough to cause "burning of the flesh".

"Anti-Rape Technology" is a surprising chapter on the sometimes very forceful devices that allow women to resist sexual attacks. Some of the items include weapons to repel attackers, such as the ring filled with noxious chemicals that can be sprayed into a rapist's face. The most surprising, though, are the intravaginal devices. Alston Levesque patented an item that looks like a large ring, which is inserted into the vagina. When a penis goes through the ring, small

A radical attempt to expand the boundaries of beauty.
Women en Large.

blades pop out along the interior, lacerating the penis when it is moved backwards. A similar concept is behind the Vaginal Harpoon Tube. "Shaped like a vagina-lining sheath, its far end consisted of a plastic plug embedded with one to three two-inch surgical steel shafts fitted with double harpoon barbs at their points."

Among the many other types of sexual gizmos that have kept inventors feverishly busy are abortion devices, condoms, female contraceptives, erector rings, penile splints, penile inserts, bras and other breast-supporters, breast implants, vibrating sex toys, coital harnesses, sex furniture, safe sex inventions (such as dental dams), and more. Levins does a wonderful job covering patents in all these areas, ranging from the prosaic to the absurd, and along the way gives a history lesson for each type of device. Hundreds of drawings and diagrams from the patents are included, so you can see for yourself the bra with electrical nipple stimulators, the zippered condom, and the water-powered vibrator.

Adams Media Corporation; $9.95
1996; softcover; 284 pp
heavily illus; 1-55850-534-2
WWW: www.levins.com/sexmachines.html

ANTI-GAY
edited by Mark Simpson

No, *Anti-Gay* isn't a collection of writings by Pat Buchanan, Jerry Falwell, and their ilk, although it may be considered at least as controversial by many people. *Anti-Gay* contains essays by gay men, lesbians, and bisexuals who are directly challenging gay orthodoxy. The inside flap of the dust jacket sets the tone immediately, asking us if we've ever wondered, "Why most gay culture these days is mediocre trash?" and, "Why being gay is like being a member of a religious cult, except not so open-minded?"

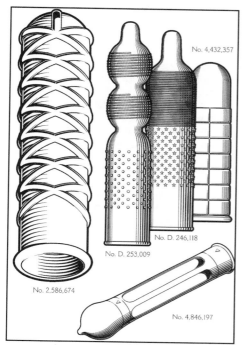

Condom patents or 1950's science fiction rockets?
American Sex Machines.

Within any community or subculture, there is always a party line to toe, but — luckily — there are always people who won't conform to those unofficial rules, mores, and expectations. Some of the most vocal dissenters from mainstream gay and lesbian views are gathered here. In "Gay Dream Believer: Inside the Gay Underwear Cult", editor Mark Simpson writes: "Isn't it just fabby to be gay? Gay is, after all, good, and everyone fortunate enough to be gay is, of course, glad — when they're not too busy feeling proud. Which is perfectly understandable since gays, as we all know, have the best clubs, the best drugs, the best underwear shops and the best time… All things considered, it's so fabby being gay, that it's difficult to imagine what it must be like to be straight. Imagine the suffering of those poor souls who are doomed by some accident of genetics or underdevelopment of that brain lobe which regulates aesthetic potential not only to never be able really to appreciate *Ab Fab* or carry off wearing a silver thong but also never able to come out."

Many of the essays don't poke fun at the herd mentality within the gay community but, instead, fight against essentialist notions of sexual orientation. Peter Tatchell opens "It's Just a Phase: Why Homosexuality Is Doomed" with this powerful thought: "The ultimate queer emancipation is the abolition of homosexuality and the eradication of the homosexual." Although on its surface this idea may bring a tear of joy to Jesse Helms' eye, Tatchell is actually referring to the idea that being a "homosexual" or a "heterosexual" is a concept that originated in the recent past. "Our modern Western forms of lesbian and gay identity, sexual behaviour, relationship patterns and sub-culture are relatively recent developments. The notion of queers as a group of people distinct from straights is notably new." Since the idea of sexual orientation has been culturally constructed, Tatchell foresees the possibility of it being obliterated. "Perhaps, eventually, there will come a moment in the development of human civilisation when defining oneself as lesbian or gay will cease to have relevance or meaning. Maybe homosexuality as a distinct and exclusive sexual orientation will be transcended — as will its mirror opposite, heterosexuality. Instead, the vast majority of people will be open to the possibility of both opposite-sex and same-sex fancies and no one will give a damn about who loves and lusts after whom."

Other contributions include "Forbidden Fruit" by Lisa Power, "Indigestion: Diagnosing the Gay Malady" by Jo Eadie, "Confessions of a Gay Film Critic, or How I learned to Stop Worrying and Love *Cruising*" by Paul Burston, "Gay Culture: Who Needs It?" by Toby Manning, "Move Over Darling: Beyond the Daddy Dyke" by Suzanne Patterson and Anne-Marie Le Blé, and "A Case for the Closet" by Bruce LaBruce and Glenn Belverio/Glennda Orgasm.

Freedom Editions (Cassell); $16.95
1996; small hardcover; 172 pp
0-304-33144-9

BARBIE'S QUEER ACCESSORIES
by Erica Rand

It's hard to imagine a more perfect stereotype of what an American woman is supposed to be than the Barbie doll. She's got blonde hair, a thin waist, a large chest, a boyfriend, tons of material possessions, and a spunky can-do attitude. Mattel has spent untold sums promoting this white-bread image since their wonder-girl was introduced in 1959. Although there have been career-oriented and multi-ethnic Barbies, these have still been presented in rather limited ways and still within the larger context of the chick who has everything. The author thinks that these Barbies were created more out of necessity than the goodness of anybody's heart. "So Mattel gave Barbie careers only when these become necessary signals of a girl who can do everything. It gave Barbie racial diversity when the number of consumers who might consider this feature was seen to be sufficiently large, although in such a way as to enable people who don't look fondly on racial diversity to ignore or bypass diversity Barbies."

Despite — or perhaps because of — these carefully crafted images, Barbie is ripe for subversion. With all of her well-crafted, sanitised roles, Barbie makes a useful way to make a point. By creating "unauthorised" images for her or putting her in situations that such a nice girl would never find herself in, it can make social commentary in a humorous way. For example, the AIDS-zine *Diseased Pariah News* did a full page parody ad for AIDS Barbie ("with Malignant Lymphoma and Gynaecological Complications"). Reproduced in this book, it shows three naked Barbies… one of them has lesions all over her legs and an IV in her arm. Another zine, *P.C. Casualties*, dreamed up a new line of Barbies, including "Battered Barbie — Burdened with small children. No marketable skills and no assets. Self-esteem sold separately."

The author also examines how Mattel has presented Barbie, particularly how they handle those thorny issues surrounding the doll — her sex life, her anatomy, her unrealistic beauty, etc. One of the questions Mattel constantly has to deal with is why Barbie doesn't come with panties (except when she's decked out in a short skirt). "I can conceive of an argument that Barbie doesn't need panties because she is not anatomically correct; since she (is a representation of someone who) has no apparent sources of moisture, odour, or menstrual leaks, she doesn't need panties. But that would thrust Barbie's lower orifices into the conceptual spotlight along with her already troublesome breasts, not to mention raising a series of very weird questions: Would a plastic orifice be more likely than a smooth surface to generate olfactory hallucinations?"

The other main section of the book is based on testimony of adults regarding how they reacted to Barbie and what meanings they gave to her when they were children. Some used the dolls to act out sexual fantasies; others became violent with theirs. One woman's childhood friend repeatedly put nipples on Barbie with a magic marker. The reactions of most of the women were mixed and often ambivalent, but one thing was constant — Barbie was an extremely important part of their childhoods.

Barbie's Queer Accessories is a fascinating look at the "unofficial" side of one of the world's most powerful pop culture icons.

Duke University Press; $16.95
1995; softcover; 213 pp
illus; 0-8223-1620-X

BETTER SEX THROUGH CHEMISTRY
A Guide to the New Prosexual Drugs
& Nutrients!

by John Morgenthaler & Dan Joy

The same individuals who introduced the world at large to smart drugs [*Outposts* p 67] have now revealed sex drugs and nutrients for all to see. "The compounds covered in this book can enhance sex drive, erection, frequency of orgasm, intensity of orgasm, stamina, vaginal lubrication, skin sensitivity, personal enjoyment of sex, and even intimacy and emotional intensity. They may also effectively treat sexual difficulties such as premature ejaculation, loss of interest, impotence, and difficulty achieving orgasm."

Unlike something like the spurious Spanish Fly, though, none of these substances will screw up your body in order to produce their effects. As a matter of fact, all of this stuff is good for you in other ways beside sex. Some have anti-ageing properties, others can improve memory and cognition, and still others can fight depression.

Better Sex gives details about ten drugs and nutrients that will unleash the sex machine in you. You'll find out not only how a substance works and the scientific and anecdotal evidence of its effects, but also how to obtain and use it.

Taking choline and vitamin B-5 increases the amount of acetylcholine in your body. This neurotransmitter controls the nerve transmissions involved in sexual response. By having

more of this compound, you can go at it longer and with more gusto. Large doses of niacin (vitamin B-3) often cause people's blood vessels to dilate, which causes a "niacin flush", similar but more intense than "sex flush". "People who use niacin prior to sex remark about its ability to increase sensation, and not just in the genital area. Skin-to-skin contact all over the body during a niacin flush can be extraordinary."

The prescription drug Bromocriptine is used primarily to treat Parkinson's disease, but it has a staggering number of other uses, including increasing capacity and duration of hard-ons, increasing frequency of orgasms in women, and stimulating interest and desire in both genders. GHB, a natural substance present in every cell of your body, can help with erections, give women more intense orgasms, and increase libido, emotional bonding, and intimacy. (Its misuse, coupled with lots of misinformation, has resulted in a media/governmental smear campaign against this new bogeydrug.)

The other substances covered in detail are L-arginine, tyrosine and phenylalanine, L-dopa, yohimbe and yohimbine, and deprenyl. The concluding chapter briefly discusses several other natural and synthetic compounds that seem promising and need to be studied further.

Smart Publications; $14.95
1994; softcover; 224 pp
0-9627418-2-5

THE BISEXUAL RESOURCE GUIDE
(Second Edition)

edited by Robyn Ochs

This amazing book gives contact information for over 1500 bi groups and gaylesbi (glb) groups and periodicals worldwide, with the lion's share of the entries located in the US. The *BRG* covers groups in Australia, Belgium, Canada, Japan, Norway, South Africa, and sixteen other countries, as well as international groups. The almost 100 pages' worth of entries for the US are divided up by state. Almost all entries have addresses and some include phone numbers and email addresses. Over half contain brief descriptions. There are also addresses for a couple dozen email discussion lists.

Here's a sampling of the diverse resources presented: The Q-Krew, a Portland, Oregon, social activity group for glb youth (under 21); BREATHE (Bisexual Revolutionaries Engaged in Art To Heal the Earth), a performance play group for artists; Proper Pronoun Productions, which markets music by openly glb singers & songwriters; Gay, Lesbian or Bisexual Employees at Intel (GLOBE); Quaker Bisexual Group; Alternative Wrestlers Europe, a gay-bi wrestling organisation; *Bi Girl World*, a zine; Off Pink Publishing Collective; Coming Out Pagan; Boise Bisexual Network; Digital Queers; Bi Alcoholics Anonymous; and *Wavelengths*, a magazine exploring the intersection of glb and science fiction/fantasy.

The Guide also has listings of bi books and periodicals, movies with bi characters, upcoming conferences, and anthologies and periodicals calling for contributions. This is undoubtedly the most comprehensive bi-guide available.

Bisexual Resource Center; $11.95 ppd
1997; softcover; 200 pp
illus; no ISBN

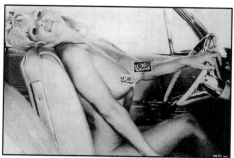

Publicity photo for Russ Meyer's <u>Mondo Topless</u>, starring Babette Bardot. *Bizarre Sinema!*

BIZARRE SINEMA!
Sexploitation Filmmakers
by Riccardo Morrocchi and others

A loving look at seven filmmakers who specialised in nudie-cuties, ghoulies, roughies, kinkies, and other forms of sexploitation movies. Covers Russ Meyer (*Faster, Pussycat! Kill! Kill!*, *Beneath the Valley of the Ultravixens*), David F. Friedman (*The Erotic Adventures of Zorro*, *A Smell of Honey, a Swallow of Brine!*), Herschell Gordon Lewis (*Bloodfeast*, *Scum of the Earth*), and Doris Wishman (*Nude on the Moon*, *Deadly Weapons*). Don't expect the minimal three-language text to be detailed... the real attraction here are the hundreds of stills, publicity shots, and posters from these movies featuring truckloads of chesty women — often in sexual or sadistic situations — wearing their birthday suits.

Glittering Images; 70.000 lira
1995; oversized softcover; 158 pp
heavily illus; no ISBN

THE BLOWFISH CATALOGUE

The catalogue put out by the fun-loving sexual upstarts at Blowfish offers a fine selection on pleasure-positive goodies in many sexual flavours. In the "Objects D'Art" section you'll find pink and black triangle pendants, the Wondrous Vulva Hand Puppet, political buttons ("I'm Polyamorous, and I Vote"), rubber stamps, T-shirts with Medusa (instead of snakes for hair, she has penises). Their selection of the best toys and supplies continues to grow. Choose from vibrators, collars, cuffs, blindfolds, silicone and acrylic dildos, dildo harnesses, Avanti and Reality condoms, oils, lubes, oral sex dams, Honey Dust ("A unique, edible, ever-so-silky body powder with a sweetly delicious flavour..."), and more.

Blowfish offers an impressive selection of fiction, non-fiction, and art books, including *The She Devils*, *The Petticoat Dominant*, *Nothing Sensible: Erotic Haiku*, *My Life As a Pornographer*, *Bisexual Politics*, *The Mistress Manual*, *SM101*, *Anal Pleasure and Health*, *The Advocate Advisor*, *Reclaiming Sodom*, and *Early Erotic Photography*. There's lots of material from Daedalus, Circlet, Greenery, Shaynew, Taschen, and other gutsy publishers. A nice selection of comix, too, including *Omaha the Cat Dancer*, *Spanish Fly*, *Story of O*, *Dyke Strippers*, and *The Spider Garden*. Among the seventeen magazines for sale: *Blue Blood*, *Fat Girl*,

Splosh, *Bad Attitude*, *Black Sheets*, and *Secret*.

The large selection of videos guarantee that there'll be something worth watching on the boob tube. The documentaries and instructional vids are the best: *How to Have a Sex Party*, *Let's Talk Anal*, *The Gay Man's Guide to Safer Sex*, *Welcome to SM*, *Magic of Female Ejaculation*, and *Porn Star Confidential*. In case you're just in the mood for a down 'n' dirty fuck film, almost all of which are hetero, you can get *Debbie Does Dallas*, *Painful Mistake*, *Enema Bandit*, *Lilith Unleashed*, *Bathroom Sluts*, *True Legends: Porn Superstars*, *New Wave Hookers*, *Where the Boys Aren't*, *Dirty Little Cartoons*, or *Genital Hospital*. With the incredible amount (99%?) of worthless porn movies on the market, it's nice to have the Blowfishies select the cream of the crop for us.

Every item is well-described, often with a splash of humour. It's obvious that the 'Fishies aren't some money-hungry corporation hocking crappy sleaze, but a small group of iconoclasts who know what they're doing and love hocking *great* sleaze. To make their illustrated catalogue even more enjoyable, they include a bunch of erotic poems and stories. Highly recommended.

Blowfish/2261 Market St #284/San Francisco CA 94114
Email: catalog@blowfish.com
WWW: http://www.blowfish.com/
Catalogue: US/Can: $3. Overseas: $5 or 6 IRCs

BLUE BLOOD

Blue Blood is the magazine of gothic-punk erotica. It mixes the Middle Ages, Victorianism, the post-apocalypse blues, punks, piercings, vampires, and omnisexuality into a slick treat for those people who like to read erotic material while lying in their coffins. Volume 2 #2 opens with an expansive, well-designed review section that covers everything from the zine *Lezzie Smut* and the porn flick *What's a Nice Girl Like You Doing in an Anal Movie?* to Sister Machine Gun's industrial album *The Torture Technique* and *Hustler's* sister magazine *Barely Legal*.

Most of the fiction has something to do with music. In "#1 with a Bullet" the female drummer for a band gets it on with a guy who is probably a werewolf, and he avenges her beaten brother. An unbelieving singer conjures Mary Shelley for some painful phantasmagoric sex in "Pipe Dreams". "Bombshell" is about a night in the life of a dyke dancer at a club.

The three photo spreads have something for every orientation. Two women in leather and metal have their way with a third woman in the back of a limo. A chick with bright fuchsia hair dyes a guy's hair to match hers, he shaves her pussy, and then they condition each other in a variety of positions. Gloomy black and white shots, some tinted blue, make up the final pictorial in which a punk guy has a rendezvous with another he-punk and then is taken to task by a dominatrix.

Blue Blood is breaking new ground with its unique brand of gothporn.

Blue Blood Magazine/2625 Piedmont Rd. Suite 56332/Atlanta GA 30324
Fax: 714-668-0517

WWW: www.hallucinet.com/blueblood/
Single issue: $8. Non-US: $12
Three issue sub: $22. Non-US: $33
Payment: ck, mo, Visa, MC, Amex, Disc

BODY PACKAGING
A Guide to Human Sexual Display
by Julian Robinson

Body Packaging is a sumptuously illustrated guide to what our clothing reveals about our sexuality (and the sexual attitudes of the surrounding society). Clothing historian and avant garde designer Julian Robinson's thesis is that "clothing and other forms of body decoration were never designed to conceal, or even to protect the body from the wear and tear of everyday life, but were primarily intended to render the body more sexually attractive." Later he elaborates: "But time and some long-forgotten rituals have gradually transformed attention-seeking garb into a form of concealment. Thus it can be fairly argued that our current modesty about our bodies is the result and not the cause of our present mode of dressing."

Robinson's survey of the hidden meanings of clothing and other body adornment spans times and cultures, from ancient Egyptian royalty to Kenyan tribes to the Dallas Cowboy Cheerleaders. In the chapter "Historical Perspective" we find that padding various parts of the body is not a recent invention nor has it been limited to women. "During the 17th and 18th centuries many men of fashion added thigh and calf pads to the inside of their hose to enhance the appeal of their masculine legs and padded the crotch area to simulate a perpetual erection — a most attractive feature for the many women of the royal courts who apparently craved continual sexual indulgence." During that time it was also popular for women to rouge their nipples and shave their pubic hair into decorative shapes, such as hearts.

The section of crossdressing notes that in England in the 1500s, women were not allowed to act in the theatre, so men and boys played female roles. "In fact there were several famous theatrical companies which specialised in training and disciplining young boys in the art of female impersonation for the stage. These boys — generally from well-established theatrical families — were taken into training as actresses at an early age and instructed in the art of makeup, feminine gestures, wearing female apparel, voice control, and many were castrated in order to retain their high voices and youthful looks."

Among the many other topics covered in this wide-ranging book are lingerie, wedding dresses, swimsuits, black leather and chains, uniforms, 1930s Hollywood, public nudity in the 1960s, makeup, perfume, tattoos, scarification, the Beatles, James Dean, Twiggy, Brigitte Bardot, fashion magazines, clothing as a political statement, and the future of fashion.

Elysium-Sunset; $32.95
1988; oversized hardcover; 208 pp
heavily illus; 1-555-99027-4

DHAMPIR
Child of the Blood
by VM Johnson

VM Johnson is active in the leather/SM community, but this autobiographical book is not what you'd expect. Johnson is a real-life vampire, a Child of Lilith, a drinker of blood. In a rare move, she explains what it is like to be a "dhampir".

Two-thirds of the book is composed of letters Johnson has written to her "daughter". This isn't her daughter in the biological sense, but in the vampiric sense — she is a grown woman whom Johnson initiated into the Clan of Lilith. Johnson's letters cover just over the first year of her "cub's" new life. Apparently, Johnson initiated her cub during a leather conference in Toronto. She writes: "I watched you come alive this weekend. I have a feeling the mara [Scandinavian term for female vampire] that has emerged from within you will be slow to go back inside and keep silent. You've done me proud these last five days. There were very few big wigs at conference who weren't wearing your mark by Sunday's end. It became one of the event's most sought-after souvenirs."

As Johnson writes letters to her new vampire progeny, we see exactly how a true vampire lives, loves, and feeds. Contrary to popular wisdom, vampires do not feed on the unwilling, and they have respect for those they feed upon. Well, female vampires, anyway. "Our males would feast and let their food fall prey to the arms of death. I have no desire for the tasty morsels that give me life to lose their own life force. Neither must you. Food is needed. Food nurtures, and is nurtured in return, not cast aside as an empty carcass. When you are ready to hunt for yourself, it is more than blood you must seek to nurture your body. Quest for a soul to enthral, a spirit to merge with your own power, a fountain from which you can drink again and again."

Vampires are not repelled by crosses (they belong to many religious traditions, including Christianity); they do have reflections; they can go out in the sun, although they are sensitive to sunlight; they are susceptible to disease; they find the smell and taste of garlic offensive; they don't steal souls; they do have heightened senses. And, of course, they have the physical, emotional, and spiritual need to drink blood. In the last third of the book, which comprises entries from Johnson's diary, she talks about how overwhelming this need can become. "I hunger. Thanks to Michael, I need badly. My blood is racing and my head is pounding loud enough to drown out everything but my need for blood. I backed my Mistress up against a wall a few minutes ago. For a brief moment all I could see was perfect flesh and my next meal. It wasn't until she screamed that I came to my senses. I will dine on stranger, friend, or foe. In this advanced state of blood lust, the carnivore must be free to find its prey."

Other shorter sections of the book relate the origin of the Dhampir (they descended from Adam's first wife, Lillith), a glossary of terms, and the vampire's Commands of Conduct ("Honor The Blood, and those who share it").

Mystic Rose Books; $8.95
1996; softcover; 139 pp
illus; 0-9645960-1-6

DIAPER PAIL FRIENDS

Ever feel like chucking your responsibilities as a grown-up and reverting to the infant state? *Diaper Pail Friends* is the newsletter for men and women who do just that and for the people who play their "parents". It also caters to people with related and overlapping interests, such as plastic pants, bedwetting, humiliation, spanking, enemas, and sissification. In each forty- to fifty-page, stapled issue, people write in with their infantile experiences. Rick (a/k/a Susie) writes in issue 82: "I like my Baby Heaven diapers wet, covered with Gerber plastic pants and frilly girl's panties. A little girl's dress which is short enough to show that I need changing, a ribbon in my hair and a pacifier in my mouth are nice, too. So what that at 6'2" I look a bit imposing, it's what's inside that counts!"

Elsewhere, there is party news, book reviews, questions, opinions, and a roster of members, with detailed descriptions of what they're into and personal contact information. *DPF* also offers a bunch of merchandise, including stories, videos, and clothing. All of this is presented in great detail in the group's thick catalogue, which is also available on the Web. Among the adult-size baby clothes you can get are crawlers, sleepers, onesies, rubber pants, coveralls, and diapers of all descriptions, plus pacifiers, bottles, and other paraphernalia.

DPF/38 Miller Ave, Suite 127/Mill Valley CA 94941
Email: babytom@well.com
WWW: www.dpf.com
Catalogue: free
Single issue: $7
Six issue sub (one year): US/Can: $30 if you're listed in the roster; $39 if you're not. Elsewhere: add $20

DIVA
Cine Sex Stars
edited by Riccardo Morrocchi & Stefano Piselli

Diva is a guide to the sexy female actresses of the 1950s, 1960s, and 1970s, done in the lavish pictorial style that the Italian publisher, Glittering Images, specialises in. The editors are unashamed of their admiration of and lust for these sirens of the silver screen. They generally stay away from such obvious sex symbols as Marilyn Monroe and Brigitte Bardot, instead focusing on women who didn't achieve quite such high status.

In the opening chapter on Hollywood bombshells, there are photos of Jayne Mansfield, Mamie Van Doren, Julie Newmar, the Italian Silvana Pampanini, Sophia Loren, Barbara Nichols, and Jane Russell. In most of the shots, the women are scantily clad… only a few reveal it all. However, starting with the second chapter, major nudity comes to the forefront and stays there. In "Ultrabreastedvixens!" we are treated to shots of famous B-movie/sexploitation starlets (including many gravity-defying women from Russ Meyer's movies), such as Uschi Digart, Babette Bardot, Chesty Morgan, Candy Samples, Blaze Starr, Tempest Storm, Francesca "Kitten" Natividad, and Bettie Page.

The next chapter focuses on women from horror movies of the 1950s through 1970s — Ingrid Pitt, Barbara Steele, Barbara Shelley, Maria Rohm, and others. From there it's on to the leggy stars of the Italian sex comedies and erotic thrillers that had their heyday in the 1970s. The entire next chapter, "So Buxom, So Depraved, So Cruel…", is devoted to Dyanne Thorne, the chesty star of some of the greatest sexploitation flicks ever made: *Greta the Torturer*, *Ilsa, Harem Keeper of the Oil Sheiks*, and *Ilsa, She-Wolf of the SS*. The final chapter pays homage to the first-generation porn actresses. There are explicit and action shots of Linda Lovelace, Vanessa Del Rio, Annie Sprinkle, Marilyn Chambers, Veronica Hart, Seka, Annette Haven, and many others.

The text — written in English, Italian, and French — gives brief descriptions of the highlights of each actress's career. The bibliography has information on autobiographies, biographies, and photography books, and a long filmography lists the best movies of over 150 sexbombs, including many not covered in the body of the book. Located after each chapter is an explicit and sometimes violent four-page comic, based on the women in the preceding chapter.

Glittering Images; 60.000 Lira
1994; oversized softcover; 104 pp
heavily illus; no ISBN

EMERGENCY CONTRACEPTION
The Nation's Best-Kept Secret
by Robert A. Hatcher, MD, and others

When this book was published, almost no one knew about emergency contraception — methods of preventing pregnancy after unprotected intercourse has occurred. It wasn't advertised. Most people were unaware that such a thing existed. Even a lot of doctors — including gynaecologists — weren't familiar with the concept. This book was part of an effort to fill this gap in knowledge, and it has worked quite well. Sometime in 1998, a drug marketed specifically as an emergency contraceptive is supposed to become available in the US, and in February of 1998, Washington State became the first state to allow pharmacists to dispense birth control pills as emergency contraceptives without a prescription.

Emergency Contraception covers the five main methods of preventing unwanted pregnancy on "the morning after". "These five options can be used anytime within several days after sex and will significantly decrease the chance that you will become pregnant." As the name suggests, these methods should be used only in emergency situations — such as if a condom breaks, if a rape occurs, or if you get caught up in the heat of the moment and don't use any protection. They should not be used as your only means of contraception, unless you want to be called Mommy or Daddy real soon.

The most common form of emergency contraception is emergency contraceptive pills, which are actually nothing more than ordinary birth control pills. The difference is that you take a higher-than-normal dose of them within 72 hours of intercourse. They work by either preventing fertilisation of an egg or by not letting a fertilised egg attach itself to the wall of the uterus. Using the Pill in this way will decrease your chances of pregnancy by 75%.

The second main method of emergency contraception

is the insertion of an intrauterine device (IUD). IUDs are well-known as long-term contraceptive devices, but if inserted within five to seven days after risky intercourse, they offer an even more effective solution than taking emergency contraceptive pills.

Other options include birth control minipills, which contain no oestrogen; the synthetic hormone danazol, which has not been shown to be very effective; and Mifepristone, also known as RU 486 or "the abortion pill". Mifepristone acts differently than the other methods. Although it can prevent an egg from lodging in the woman's body, it is also capable of dislodging an implanted egg (thus, its nickname).

For each method, the team of contraceptive experts who wrote this book tells how it works, how to use it, possible side effects, and — most importantly — where to get it. They include a state-by-state directory that lists the phone numbers of over 1000 doctors, clinics, and student health services that dispense emergency contraception.

The authors estimate that if these techniques were widely used, they would prevent almost 1.7 million unintended pregnancies and 800,000 abortions every year! Now that a company has applied to the FDA for approval and a state has relaxed its regulations regarding dispensation, the strangely neglected practice of emergency contraception might finally get the recognition it needs.

Emergency Contraception shattered the silence on an important and empowering reproductive health issue. It belongs on the shelf of everyone who is heterosexually active. This book just might save your heinie.

Bridging the Gap Communications; $12.95
1995; paperback; 236 pp
illus; 0-9638875-3-X

THE ENEMA AS AN EROTIC ART AND ITS HISTORY

by David Barton-Jay

When David Barton-Jay was eight, he received his first enema. By the time he was twelve, he was giving himself enemas for the intense sensations it gave him. Ever since then, he has used them as a means of sexual pleasure.

His erotic attachment to this procedure drove him to create this mammoth book — a cornucopia of words and pictures celebrating the enema's erotic potential. After relating his experiences with the cleansing apparatus, Barton-Jay reprints the writings of men who share his desires. "A flood of love fills me with the water, love for the enema master who is now asserting his right to own me. Slowly, ever so slowly I am swelling, distending. I wish to swoon away with love as I grow increasingly swollen with water. My gut, each membrane, is stretching as I grow fuller and fuller, my belly not mine, my insides a stranger's. He may kill me this way, but I assent because I love him."

"The Allure" examines references to enema eroticism in modern fiction (Marco Vassi, Samuel Beckett, Aldous Huxley), men's magazines, pop culture, and the writings of sexologists. The next chapter examines the history of the procedure, starting in ancient Egypt. "There is a well-known legend that the Egyptians derived their conception of the

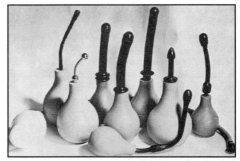

"A lovely garden of bulbs."
The Enema as an Erotic Art and Its History.

enema from an observation of a procedure practised by the ibis, a wading bird. It was believed to blow water from the Nile into its rectum." The accompanying drawings show the ibis doing its thing. From there, we are treated to a cross-cultural tour of the practice, complete with photographs of Africans administering enemas with a gourd and with a reed. The human race's ingenuity in this regard boggles the mind.

For those who want to take the plunge, one chapter tells you how to give yourself an enema and another offers instructions for couples. To aid in your education, there are dozens of explicit photographs of a male couple and a male-female couple giving each other enemas while stimulating each other with hands and mouths. During those times when you only want to read about the experience without participating, chapter seven offers several erotic short stories about close encounters of the tubular kind.

Among the literally hundreds of illustrations — ranging from the medical to the prurient — we see an apparatus for tobacco smoke enemas, a Medieval illuminated manuscript showing a gymnastic enema, an eighteenth century copperplate depicting a wigged gentleman doing the deed to a prostitute in a brothel, an aquarelle from the late-1800s showing a doctor cleaning out a Rubenesque woman, a 1930s illustration of a woman giving an enema to another woman, a photo of a young man using a hose attached to a humongous, six-foot cooler of sudsy water, enema porn from the early twentieth century, and panels from erotic comix depicting forced enemas. Most amazing of all is the photo gallery of the author's private collection of paraphernalia, including a "white enamelled enema can with rim and pitcher-style handle trimmed in cobalt-blue", glass nozzles, dildo nozzles, extra-long colon tubes, a double barium balloon catheter, and a device for administering urine enemas.

For those who know the allure of the bag and the tube, this veritable enema encyclopaedia is a godsend. Its omnisexual, centuries-spanning scope, its superb design and illustration, and its sheer massiveness mean that it is a must-have for aficionados. (A brochure about the book is available for $1, in case you'd like to find out more before you buy, and you can also get a preview online at www.sover.net/~dbjay3/. A limited number of slightly damaged copies are being offered for $39.95 each.)

The DBJ Projects; $54.95
1982; oversized softcover; 335 pp
heavily illus; 0-910409-00-5

THE EROTIC IMPULSE
Honoring the Sensual Self
edited by David Steinberg

From David Steinberg — who brought us the sumptuous and uplifting *Erotic by Nature* [*Outposts* p 106] — comes another collection of sex-positive ideas and attitudes. The sole mission of *The Erotic Impulse* is to pay homage to the beauty, the power, and the naturalness of the human libido. In his introduction, Steinberg asks: "What happens when you follow the erotic muse wherever it may lead, follow with your eyes open but with complete trust, lust, love, and wonder? What happens when you fully open yourself to the erotic life force, even when it leads you into territory that is as unpredictable as it is delightful, as unsettling as it is exciting? What if you give the erotic impulse the right-of-way, only defining as perverted what blocks its flow? What if you reject the pervasive notion that there is something wrong with your erotic feelings and desires — something wrong with being interested in erotic matters too much, too strangely, or too differently from what other people consider proper?" There is no single answer to any of these questions, but the contributors provide many clues and signposts.

The first section of the book provides some general examinations on the nature of the erotic impulse, from the analytical approach of Jack Morin's "The Four Cornerstones of Eroticism" to Michael Venura's highly personal reflection of how Elvis, Marilyn Monroe, Jesus, and Dracula shaped his sexuality (in "The Porn Prince of Decatur Street"). Pioneering psychoanalyst Rollo May speaks of "daimonic" aspect of the libido, and Greta Christina uses humour to highlight a surprisingly ambiguous matter — exactly which actions qualify as "sex"?

Located in the section on the erotic imagination is Richard Goldstein's essay "Pornography and Its Discontents". Although I don't agree with every point the author makes, it is one of the most perceptive writings concerning its subject that I have ever read. While discussing porn from a social standpoint, Goldstein dares to admit that it often arouses him. "The personal is what's missing from critiques of pornography. D.H. Lawrence doesn't say that, by propelling him toward masturbation, smut leaves him drained; instead, he informs us that it leaves the body 'a corpse, after the act of self-abuse.'"

The section on erotic initiation contains "Discovering the World of Sex" by Henry Miller, "A Warm Emotion Which He Could Not Name" by Gore Vidal, "Bringing Up Children Sexually", "Another Coming Out Manifesto Disguised as a Letter to My Mother", a tale of bumpy teenage lust, and a novel excerpt about sex between a fifteen-year-old boy and 36-year-old woman.

Other prose pieces throughout the book include "The Roving Erotic Eye" by Camille Paglia, "Eroticism in Women" by Anaïs Nin, "What Turns Her on?" by Susie Bright, "Eroticism and Taboo" by Paula Webster, "The Masculine Con-flict" by Nancy Friday, "The Ballad of Sexual Dependency" by Nan Goldin, "The Horse of Desire" by Robert Bly, "The Religious Suppression of Eros" by Robert T. Francoeur, "Erotophobia: The Cruelest Abuse of All" by Marty Klein, "Going Public" by Betty Dodson, "Erotic Power and Trust" by Carol A. Queen, "How Dare You Even Think These Things?" by John Preston, "The Prayer of Conjugal Love" by Kevin Regan, and "Bodhi Is the Body" by Marco Vassi. Each section ends with a poem or two, including works by Allen Ginsberg, James Joyce, ee cummings, Anne Sexton, and Leonard Cohen.

An anthology of uniformly high quality and thought-provoking writings, *The Erotic Element* is a key text for understanding and accepting our sexual natures.

Jeremy P. Tarcher/Putnam (David Steinberg); $13.95
1992; softcover; 322 pp
0-87477-697-X

THE EVOLUTION OF DESIRE
Strategies of Human Mating
by David M. Buss

"We grow up believing in true love, in finding our 'one and only.' We assume that once we do, we will marry in bliss and live happily ever after. But reality rarely coincides with our beliefs. Even a cursory look at the divorce rate, the 30 to 50 percent incidence of extramarital affairs, and the jealous rages that rack so many relationships shatters these illusions." Why is love this way? Why are we attracted to certain people but not others? Why is sex so damn important? Why is staying together so damn hard? The greatest philosophers and poets — not to mention just about every other person who has ever lived — have wrestled with these questions without coming up with any definitive answers. Now it's time for evolutionary theorists to take a crack at it. (Besides this book, you can check out several similar ones that came out within a year of each other: *What's Love Got to Do with It?: The Evolution of Human Mating* by Meredith F. Small, *Eros and Evolution: A Natural Philosophy of Sex* by Richard E. Michod, *The Sex Imperative: An Evolutionary Tale of Sexual Survival* by Kenneth Maxwell, *Anatomy of Love: A Natural History of Mating, Marriage, and Why We Stray* by Helen Fisher, and *The Red Queen: Sex and the Evolution of Human Nature* by Matt Ridley.)

After studying the mating behaviour of over 10,000 people in thirty-seven cultures all over the world, psychologist David Buss has some provocative theories. Most of our feelings and behaviours regarding love, sex, and procreation have deep roots in our evolutionary past. This can help explain why men and women are worlds apart in their views. One of the main reasons why most women are notoriously choosy about their partners has to do with the simple fact that a single act of intercourse can place a nine-month burden on a woman, not to mention nursing and nurturing the child after it's born. "Because women in our evolutionary past risked enormous investment as a consequence of having sex, evolution favoured women who were highly selective about their mates. Ancestral women suffered severe costs if they were indiscriminate — they experienced lower reproductive success, and fewer of their children survived to reproductive age. A man in evolutionary history could walk away from a casual coupling having lost only a few hours of time."

Men's ideals of female beauty vary from culture to culture in certain ways, but there are features that have been found to be universally attractive, such as full lips, good muscle tone, high energy level, and clear, smooth skin. "These physical cues to youth and health, and hence to reproductive capacity, constitute the ingredients of male standards of female beauty." Following this line of reasoning, the much-derided fixation on young, beautiful people that exists in our society is not a sign of modern discrimination but an innate leftover from the early days of humankind.

Other topics include what women look for in men, men's status as it relates to women's beauty, homosexual mate preferences, lust, sexual fantasies, casual sex, attracting a partner, the functions of sexual jealousy, ways to keep competitors at bay, rape, sexual harassment, infidelity, loss of desire, menopause, and harmony between the sexes. Since love and sex are such impenetrable enigmas, any new ways of looking at them can help shed some light. *The Evolution of Desire* may even help you start to understand some of the perplexing aspects of your screwy love life.

BasicBooks (HarperCollins Publishers); $14
1994; softcover; 262 pp
0-465-02143-3

Wildlife photography in *Fetish Times* [UK].

FAT GIRL
A Zine for Fat Dykes and the Women Who Want Them

Photographs, erotic stories, poems, interviews, essays, and resources celebrating large lesbians and dealing with society's anti-fat bias. Features in issue 4 include "What's So Sexy About Fat Women?", "Fat Watch", "A Fat, Vulgar, Angry Slut", "Confessions of a Fat Sex Worker", "You're Crazy, Your Life's Outta Control, & You Should Go to Weight Watchers", an interview with Jewelle Gomez, and "Barbarism in the Cemetery".

Fat Girl/2215-R Market St #193/San Francisco CA 94114
Email: solo@sirius.com
WWW: http://www.fatso.com/fatgirl
Single issue: US/Can: $5. Elsewhere: $7
Four issue sub: US/Can: $20. Elsewhere: $28

FETISH TIMES [US]

Fetish Times, a tabloid sex paper, started publishing in 1973 and is still going strong. Around 25 of the 40 pages in each issue are given over to photos, photos, and more photos. Text, such as movie reviews and even the letters page, is always accompanied by pictures.

These aren't just any pictures, mind you. They're grainy black and white images of good-looking naked women engaged in fetish activities. The issues I saw (261 and 262) both had pictorials of catfights, tickling, bondage, spanking, and foot worship. The watersports pictures are explicit, showing enemas being inserted. The bondage fare is pretty light, featuring a woman struggling in ropes and a bound woman

with a ball gag being licked by a chick. There is no hardcore SM here. Everybody in the tickling shots seem to be thoroughly enjoying themselves. The foot licking photos are pretty steamy, especially when the women suck their own toes. Issue 261 has a special surprise — lactating breasts, including some groovy stop-action images of squirting milk.

Each issue also has an interview with a dominatrix (with photos of her plying her craft) and movie reviews. All the videos that are reviewed are available from *Fetish Times'* publisher, so bad reviews are scarce. The ads in the back offer phone services, catalogues, and videos, devoted to all kinds of fetishes, including many I didn't see covered in the rest of the paper — SM, transsexuals, infantilism, small breasts, etc.

Fetish Times certainly doesn't skimp on content. Page after page of big photos means that kinksters will not be let down. I definitely give it two nozzles up.

B&D Company, DBA Platinum/4501 Van Nuys Blvd, Ste 215M/Sherman Oaks CA 91403
Sample issue: $6 worldwide
Twelve issue sub (one year): $40. Non-US: $75

FETISH TIMES [UK]

This beautifully-executed British magazine explores BDSM, fetishes, and related pursuits (sex parties, sex and drugs, erotic smoking, etc.) with gusto and light-hearted humour. *Fetish Times* delivers quality articles and images on an impressively wide range of topics. Especially when it comes to the writing (fiction and non-fiction), this is one of the best magazines of its type.

Fetish Times/BCM Box 9253/London WC1N 3XX/UK

WWW: www.erotica.co.uk/
Single issue: UK: £8. US: £9
Four issue sub: UK: £28. US: £32.

THE FORTEAN TIMES BOOK OF WEIRD SEX

compiled by Steve Moore

The British magazine *Fortean Times* [*Outposts* p 190] has spent over twenty years chronicling the strange, puzzling, and goofy aspects of our world. And nothing brings out the strangeness, puzzlement, and goofiness of the human race like S-E-X. Drawing on *Fortean Times* and its huge unpublished archives, *Weird Sex* presents around 400 blurbs that show the wackier side of humanity's favourite activity.

In the chapter on embarrassing accidents, we read about an impotent California man who was fitted with a penile implant prototype that worked by remote control. "Unfortunately, the 52-year-old patient got a lift every time his neighbours used their electronic car doors." Elsewhere, there's the story of a man addicted to the African drug khat — known for its aphrodisiacal qualities — which he chewed all day long. In 1992 he went to his doctor complaining that he had been having forty orgasms a day! A week later, he could no longer get it up. He kicked the khat habit but remained impotent. "His doctor was reported as saying she believed he had used up his entire lifetime's supply of orgasms in that one month."

If you think a guy getting his dick chopped off is an isolated occurrence, the wince-inducing chapter "Bobbitted" will set you straight. Among the eleven incidents related is one of a Welsh preacher who cut off his own penis and threw it into a fire "so he could devote all his time to preaching…" In July 1993, a wife in North Carolina took a different tack — "she doused her sleeping husband's penis with nail-polish remover and set fire to it." He refused to press charges.

Again proving that men of the cloth do the darndest things, a preacher in El Paso in 1994 was so upset with his noisy congregation, that he mooned them during the middle of one of his sermons. Getting people to use contraception to control population growth can be tricky due to religious and social attitudes, but Kurdish rebels in south-eastern Turkey have come up with a very strange reason not to use intra-uterine devices. They claim IUDs are used for spying.

Some other nuggets: "A Swedish taxi driver was jailed in October 1994 for leaving the meter running while he had sex with a woman customer and billing her for £5,600." "A psychiatric survey carried out by Wisconsin researchers into the reasons for nose-picking discovered that 0.4% of those surveyed did it for 'sexual stimulation.'" "The most ancient corpse to be involved in a potential case of modern necrophilia is that of 'Otzi', the 5,000-year-old man found in a glacier in the Italian Alps. Shortly after he was found, 10 women came forward and asked if they could be inseminated with his sperm."

John Brown Publishing; £4.99 ppd. US: $11 ppd. Elsewhere: £5.50 ppd
1995; softcover; 126 pp
illus; 1-870870-65-4

THE GIRL WANTS TO
Women's Representations of Sex and the Body

edited by Lynn Crosbie

In this hard-to-pin-down collection, 39 women — ranging from post-modern post-feminists through riot grrrls to pioneers from the 1960s — use fiction, essays, poetry, song lyrics, comix, and photos to offer bold views of sex and related issues. The book's subtitle is misleading. It makes *The Girl Wants To* sound like a collection of cryptic pomo essays "deconstructing" gender, sexual politics, etc., but it's actually much more straightforward and earthy than that. As Trish Thomas writes in "Fuck Your Ex-Lover": "Don't get me wrong./ I've intellectualised up the/feminist ass/with the best of them./ But all that theoretical masturbation/never got me a warm body in my bed."

In "Not Your Bitch", Cassie Jameson rails at men who keep women down and the women who let themselves be kept down. "So call yourself a Riot Grrrl and start making as many scenes as you deem necessary to be understood. Realise you are a rad female because you are not the image this male-dominated society wants you to be. You don't owe anyone but yourself anything. So fight like a girl and take no shit!"

Of course, fun guilt-free sex is present in spades. In the futuristic story "For the Love of a Good Toaster" a woman gets off with a blender. "Her fingertips brushed over the five Bermuda Pink buttons announcing incremental increases in speed. June savoured their names on her tongue: purée, whip, blend, liquefy, and frappé." In "Erotic Fragments", Ramabai Espinet writes: "Our lovemaking is rock and sand and water, he sucks and bites my breasts until I am half-dead from delight and fear of what will happen next, such is love, such should be love forever."

Other pieces include Kathy Acker's "New York City in 1979", Pamela Des Barres' groupie memoir "The Dirty Minds in '69", Xaviera Hollander's "The Three-Way", Lydia Lunch's "Cruel Story of Youth", Erica Jong's "The Long Tunnel of Wanting You", Ellen Flander's photo-story "Lesbian Peep Show", Carel Moiseiwitsch's woodcuts, Fifth Column's song "All Women Are Bitches", and Julie Doucet's feminine hygiene comic "It's Clean Up Time!"

Chock full of good material and designed with flair, *The Girl Wants To* is a powerful, diverse document on the current state of sexual politics and sexual fun.

Stoddart Publishing; $17.95US
1993, 1997; oversized softcover; 210 pp
illus; 1-551990113

GOLD 'N STREAM

Gold 'N Stream is the publication of the Yellow Hanky Men club and is only available if you are a member. This digest-size magazine is for guys who are into golden showers (i.e., fun with urine) with other guys. It contains lots of stories and illustrations (and one photo) about being pissed on, drinking "lemonade", playing with urinals, and so on. One of the members describes the joys of taking a leak, comparing it favourably to coming: "A good orgasm can take from a minute to a day to achieve, and that build-up can be real hot. But after a few seconds of release, and that familiar high, you usually need down time. Relieving the pressure in your bladder provides relaxation without having to take a nap. A good piss can last as long as a minute, and cleans you out, leaving you ready for your next boner."

You also get ads for videos and personal contact ads from men around the country who are into pissplay.

Winter Publishing/PO Box 80667/Dartmouth MA 02748
One year membership and sub: $35; non-US: $50
Send an SASE for an application

A GUIDE TO AMERICA'S SEX LAWS

by Richard A. Posner & Katharine B. Silbaugh

It hopefully will come as no shock to most people that the self-proclaimed "freest country on earth" is filled with laws regulating one of the most private aspects of life — sexuality. What may surprise you is that there are only a tiny number of federal sex laws… each state is free to set its own penal code regarding various sex-related acts. This has resulted in a crazy-quilt of unequal, contradictory, and often discriminatory laws. Oh, did I mention stupid and fascistic laws, too? Yep, they're here in spades.

A Guide to America's Sex Laws is exactly what the title says. A verbatim reprint of the statutes for every state (and Washington DC) broken down into the following areas: rape and sexual assault (including marital exceptions), age of consent for sex and for marriage, sodomy, transmission of disease, public nudity and indecency, fornication and cohabitation, adultery, abuse of position of trust or authority, incest, bigamy, prostitution, possession of obscene materials, bestiality, necrophilia, obscene communications, and voyeurism. (In case you're not familiar with these and other sexual/legal terms, there's also a helpful glossary at the back of the book.)

Each chapter starts with a two-page introduction explaining the activity, looking at how it has historically been treated under Common law, and examining patterns in modern US laws and court cases. The bulk of the chapter is simply a listing of the laws themselves. It can make for dry, repetitious reading in many places, but it also yields fascinating insights into the urge of authority to regulate and curb sexuality. For example, in the District of Columbia, Georgia, Idaho, Massachusetts, Minnesota, Utah, Virginia, and West Virginia it's a misdemeanour for an unmarried man or woman to have sex, even if he or she is a consenting adult and doing it in private. Lest you think that these are all crusty, archaic laws enacted a century ago, be amazed that many of them were passed relatively recently (e.g., Idaho in 1972).

It seems that most people are under the impression that the age of consent in the US is universally eighteen. Not so. "In the vast majority of states the age of consent is either fifteen or sixteen." In Hawaii the age is fourteen. The laws in most states also take into account other factors, such as the exact age of the younger participant (which could mean the difference between a misdemeanour and a felony), the age difference between the participants, the kind of act (sexual intercourse vs. sexual contact), and, more rarely, other factors, such as whether the younger participant was "chaste".

In a typical display of inequity, Idaho's codes make it a felony for an adult to have sexual intercourse with a 16- or 17-year-old female, but there is no law against having sex with a male of that age.

Among the most indefensible sex laws are those against "sodomy", which usually refers to anal and oral sex. Some state laws use this as a way to ban homosexual acts. To wit, in Arkansas it is a misdemeanour to engage in "any act of sexual gratification involving the penetration, however slight, of the anus or mouth of a male by the penis of another male; or the penetration, however slight, of the anus or vagina of a female by any body member of another female." The law is silent about heterosexual acts of the same sort. This isn't usually the case, though. It is a *felony* for anyone — regardless of gender or orientation — to engage in oral or anal sex in Georgia, Idaho, Louisiana, Maryland, Massachusetts, Michigan, Mississippi, Montana, North Carolina, Oklahoma, Rhode Island, South Carolina (anal sex only), Utah, Virginia, and Washington DC (which would mean that — if the allegations are true — President Clinton and Monica Lewinsky committed repeated felonies). "Sodomy" is a misdemeanour in six other states. (Less than a handful of states make exceptions for married couples.) Same-sex penetration only is a misdemeanour in an additional five states. In an effort to cover all the bases, Washington DC law not only makes it a felony to penetrate the mouth or anus of another person, but also goes on to forbid "carnal copulation in an opening of the body other than the sexual parts", which presumably also rules out ears, eye sockets, nostrils, and belly buttons.

After seeing how many commonplace sex acts are banned, it's surprising to find out that some states have no laws against other forms of sex that are generally thought of as extremely distasteful. Every state in the Union makes incest a felony, except Rhode Island, which has no law against it. Almost half the states (22) have no laws concerning sex with animals, and 35 states are silent on the issue of sex with corpses, although necrophilia may be prosecutable on other grounds involving disrespectful treatment of human remains. Wisconsin law simply says, "All sexual assault crimes apply whether a victim is dead or alive at the time of the sexual contact or sexual intercourse."

As I mentioned, by its very nature this book is not the most readable in the world, but it is absolutely essential for anyone seriously interested in sexual freedom. It also could be used by sexually active people — especially the sexually adventurous — as a "where to live" guide.

University of Chicago Press; $14
1996; softcover; 243 pp
0-226-67565-3

HAIR TO STAY

Does your nose wrinkle at the practically bald women in 99% of porno and fashion magazines? At these shaved, depilated women who have removed the hair from every part of their bodies except their heads? Do you long for a more natural look? Fear not, for there is a place for you to feast your eyes on furry female flesh. *Hair to Stay* is a zine devoted to hairy and hirsute women.

One of the most frequently banned books of the 1990s. *Heather Has Two Mommies.*

In each issue you get fiction, articles, video reviews, black and white photos, and personal ads concerning women who don't own a razor. Issue 3 has an essay in which a man who loves hairy women comments on his attraction. "One of the true pleasures in life is seeing a beautiful woman raise her arms and expose her lush, tick [sic] and lovely unshaven armpits. My dream is that someday, shaving will go out of style and all women will reveal their true, natural hair." In another essay, Pam Winter explains the difference between hairy women and hirsute women. The former are those who let their leg, underarm, and pubic hair grow unchecked. The latter are those women who have hair in unusual places, such as backs, butts, and knuckles.

A column of hair sightings in the media will alert you to not only to "speciality" magazines and videos but also hairy chicks in mainstream flicks, such as Juliette Lewis in *Natural Born Killers* and Bette Midler in *The Rose*. The pictures are nude shots of women with the bushiest bushes you've ever seen, some of which spread to their bellybuttons. Sometimes the models are just showing off their underarm hair, and one woman displays her hairy crotch, legs, pits, and moustache.

This is just the t(h)icket for you followers of follicles.

Winter Publishing/PO Box 80667/Dartmouth MA 02748
WWW: www.winterpublishing.com/hairtostay.html
Single issue: $12. Canada: $13. Elsewhere: $17
Four issue sub (one year): $40. Canada: $50. Elsewhere: $70
Payment: cash, ck, mo, Visa, MC, Amex, Optima, Disc

HEATHER HAS TWO MOMMIES

by Lesléa Newman & Diana Souza

Heather Has Two Mommies is one of the most controversial, frequently-banned books of the 1990s. According to *Banned Books Resource Guide*, during the battle to have it removed from the Mesa, Arizona Public Library, some ninny said that it is "vile, sick, and goes against every law and constitution." (This inane comment simply offers proof of Justice Hugo Black's comment: "The layman's constitutional view is that what he likes is constitutional and that which he doesn't like is unconstitutional.")

For such a powderkeg of a book, *Heather* is awfully unassuming. It's a thin, large format children's book. Each big page has a few simple sentences and a black and white illustration drawn in a flat perspective. Despite being listed in this chapter, it's not about sex per se. The story concerns a little girl whose parents are lesbians.

In typical children's book style, it tells how Heather's mommies met, fell in love, and moved in together to raise a family. "Kate and Jane went to see a special doctor together. After the doctor examined Jane to make sure that she was healthy, she put some sperm into Jane's vagina. The sperm swam up into Jane's womb." Soon Heather is born. The story fast forwards to when Heather is three, and her parents take her to a cool, progressive day care centre (they call it a "play group"). All the children draw pictures of their widely varying families. One kid has a mom and stepdad; another has a single mom and a little sister; another has two dads; another has a mom and dad and two siblings. The teacher tells them, "Each family is special." When Heather's moms pick her up, she shows them her picture, and everybody is happy.

Heather is part of the Alyson Wonderland series, all of which have caused a general uproar. Other titles include *Daddy's Roommate*, *Gloria Goes to Gay Pride*, *The Duke Who Outlawed Jelly Beans*, and the Dr. Seuss-like *The Daddy Machine*.

Alyson Wonderland (Alyson Publications); $8.95
1989; oversized softcover; 33 pp
heavily illus; 1-55583-180-X

HELLO, I LOVE YOU!
Voices from Within the Sexual Revolution

edited by Jeanne paslé-green & Jim Haynes

This book does a valuable service by documenting the thoughts and actions of 48 people who — at the time — were participating in the ongoing Sexual Revolution/free love movement. In these vignettes they offer their feelings, opinions, hopes, fears, and sense of fun and excitement. Remember, these were the pre-AIDS glory days, when if it felt good, you did it! Well… it wasn't quite that simple, as Jeanne paslé-green notes in the introduction. "My main definition of sexual liberation is freedom of choice. I am afraid that a lot of people think that sexual liberation means to fuck all the time and to fuck with a lot of people. That concept causes a great deal of fear and anxiety. Real freedom means choice; choice of people, choice of situations, choice of sexual expression. It involves the tremendous responsibility of knowing yourself and being honest and open in order to make those choices…"

Nudist, therapist, and teacher Carolyn Demirjian gives a negative review of swinging parties: "I found a lot of people carrying the same old armours, the same masks, and playing the same games as the sexually repressed. The guys seem to feel that they have to ball every chick in the room to prove they have balls, and every chick has to make every guy fall in love with her so she can say no, to prove that she is selective."

Germaine Greer, author of *The Female Eunuch*, says in an interview: "Yes, I was once married... for three weeks. That's how I found exactly what the institution of marriage was about... I thought that maybe we could make a marriage that belonged to us instead of the status quo. BULLSHIT!"

I have to chuckle at the quaint naïveté of Valida Davila, who writes that lack of sexual expression as a child "does impair bodily functioning and cause individual unhappiness and even anti-social behaviour — these to such an extent that sex repression is now recognised as a major cause of crime and juvenile delinquency." Not that Davila is wrong (in fact, I agree)... I am laughing because I want to know who the hell — besides Wilhelm Reich, hippies, sex radicals, and others on the fringe — "now recognises" sexual repression as a "major cause" of problems. Certainly not mainstream society, which is as busy repressing now as it ever was.

Kay Johnson, a painter and poet, offers a thought-provoking essay about the longing for love, touch, and sex. She feels that our souls love every single living creature — humans and animals — and that this love is properly expressed through touching, cuddling, and kissing. In what seems to be an anti-sex stance, she feels that sex is actually a perversion of this higher, purer form of love. "But it is not sexual union the soul is after. It is some chemical interchange from skin to skin, from being to being, from proximity to proximity, from sitting next to each other, from sleeping in the same bed."

Among the other offerings: Germaine Greer does a memorable feminist rant against the missionary position, Jeanne d'Arc says that receiving anal sex is a common denominator that both men and women can share, Joan Glenn discusses having her boyfriend sexually initiate her teenage daughter, sixteen-year-old Daryl Marshak offers the most entertaining free love rant in the book, and Pat Bond, founder of the Eulenspiegel Society, reveals his thoughts on SM liberation.

Although some of the pieces may come across as dated, *Hello, I Love You!* is still a fantastic document. Not only does it illuminate an important and misunderstood aspect of recent history, its openly "sexual anarchist" position is still relevant and can teach us a thing or two about sex, intimacy, and freedom. Most highly recommended.

Times Change Press; $7.95
1977; small softcover; 173 pp
0-87810-032-6

"HOW I GOT INTO SEX"

edited by Bonnie Bullough, RN, PhD, et al

What leads a person to devote his or her professional life to sex? This collection of over 40 answers to that question gives us insight into the lives and minds of sexologists, sex educators, activists, prostitutes, writers, a therapist for sex offenders, and others who are involved with sex to a much larger degree than the average person. Most of the academic sexologists have degrees in another field, such as psychology, sociology, medicine, and even theology. Together, they give us intimate portraits of the forces that drive someone into the field of sex. Among the contributors are

- Elizabeth Rice Allgeier, editor of the *Journal of Sex Research*
- former cop, call girl, and prostitute rights activist Norma Jean Almodovar
- husband and wife team Bonnie and Vern Bullough, who have published over 50 books on sexuality
- sexology journalist Jan Morris Dailey
- transsexual educator Dallas Denny
- pioneering feminist and sexual liberationist Betty Dodson
- famed psychiatrist Albert Ellis, who co-founded the Society for the Scientific Study of Sex
- Catholic priest and sexologist Robert T. Francoeur
- Kinsey researcher Paul H. Gebhard
- the late Gary Griffin, writer and head of Added Dimensions Publishing
- Ronald R. McAllister, one of the leading designers of sex toys
- swinging pioneer Robert McGinley
- Ted McIlvenna, founder of the Institute for Advanced Studies in Human Sexuality
- John Money, one of the most important sexologists of all time
- cross-dressing pioneer Virginia Prince
- Barbara Roberts, "who professionalised the use of sexual surrogates and for a time served as a surrogate herself"
- Kenneth Ray Stubbs, writer and head of the Secret Garden Publishing house

Since each of these essays is about the writer reflecting on his or her own life, it can be a self-indulgent, less than thrilling reading experience. Still, there is much insight peppered in these autobiographical pieces. This one is only recommended for serious students of sexuality.

Prometheus Books; $29.95
1997; hardcover; 480 pp
illus; 1-57392-115-7

HOW THEY DO IT
From Cats to Bats and Sharks to Frogs. How They Mate

by Robert A. Wallace

Ever wondered how octopuses, pigs, fleas, seahorses, wasps, penguins, lizards, lobsters, and 40 other animals — mammals, insects, sea creatures, and more — engage in sex? You haven't? Then you need to either develop a healthy curiosity about the world around you or quit lying.

When you want to learn how animals other than yourself get it on, grab ahold of this book. Although there is an impressively wide range of ways in which animals do the nasty, one of the themes that runs through a disturbingly high number of entries is how violent, painful, and even fatal the act can be. Rhinoceroses have a particularly harsh mating ritual. The male and female will beat the living hell out of each other for an hour. Then they really get rough, and it's at this point that one may get injured or killed. Finally, as they're starting to get tired, the female will decide if the male is worthy. If so, they'll engage in over an hour of sex.

Octopuses often are brutal with each other before and during sex. It's not unusual for the male to lose an arm during the erotic melee. Unbelievably, sometimes the male's penis will get ripped off during the violent mating ritual, but it will somehow find the female's vagina on its own! I kid you not. When a male bedbug mounts his mate, his spiked penis can't reach her vagina, so he literally stabs her in the back and delivers his load there. Somehow the sperm eventually migrates through her tissues to the ovaries.

The male flea has a complex organ "loaded with spines, braces, and hooks" that often tears up the female. Of course, it's well-known that cats have backward-sloping dick barbs that hurt the female when a mating couple disengages. Male porcupines have a trick that isn't violent but seems pretty degrading: "… when he gets within six or seven feet of her, he begins to drench her with short spurts of urine (a good trick in itself, since not many animals can urinate with an erection, and six feet is not bad in any case)." Platypuses have a reputation for being bizarre, and their mating habits aren't going to help that image. It's not a fully-accepted fact, but it appears that during sex the male punctures his struggling mate with barbs on his legs. These sharp spurs deliver poison that calms and intoxicates the female. It would appear that even non-human animals commit date rape.

Not all animal couplings are this unseemly, though. Penguins mate for life. A female will search through a whole colony, singing a song, until she finds her mate, whom she recognises by the song he sings back to her. The two will generally waddle off to a secluded spot, have a peaceful consensual quickie, and that will be the extent of their boffing for the year. Not too different from many married human couples, apparently.

In anticipation of the question that must be on everybody's mind by now — yes, this book has pictures. Almost 30 of them, as a matter of fact. You really haven't lived until you've seen two snails screwing.

Quill (William Morrow & Co); $8.75
1980; softcover; 172 pp
illus; 0-688-08718-3

KISS FOOT LICK BOOT
Foot, Sox, Sneaker & Boot Worship/ Domination Stories, Volume 1
edited by Doug Gaines/The Foot Fraternity

These 30 pieces are supposedly true stories of gay men who have foot fetishes or enjoy having their feet worshipped. This fetish often branches into footwear, socks, even jockstraps — the more soiled and smelly, the better. These stories are pure raunch, so unflinchingly nasty they'd make Tom of Finland blush.

In the inventive "Licking Tony's Circus Boots", a bi guy, a foot-worshipping gay guy, and two het girls end up in a four-way. "Debbie's mouth bobbed the raw length of my cock as I sucked onto [sic] Eric's big toes. A bitch was sucking me as I worshipped the feet of a man, sucking his long, hard,

Hard-assed yet cheeky. *Lezzie Smut.*

round, sweaty toes."

One of the harshest stories is "'Kiss My Reebok Like You'd Kiss Your Girlfriend'", in which the narrator insults his alleged friend and goes to his friend's house the next day to beg forgiveness. Instead, his friend ties him up, humiliates him, beats him, and otherwise tortures him. "All of a sudden, I felt steel spikes touching my exposed ball sac. Mark pulled the underwear off my face and ripped the tape from my mouth. I was lying on my back so the first thing I saw was Kent's face smiling down at me. It was his golf shoe I felt bearing down on my balls. 'Give me a good reason not to squash your pathetic little nuts with my golf spikes…' Kent said."

Leyland Publications; $14.95
1995; softcover; 189 pp
illus; 0-943595-57-6

THE LEGENDARY ENDOWMENT PROJECT
by Gary Griffin

This unusual book chronicles in words and unbelievable photographs the existence of human penises that measure at least nine inches along the top while erect. Some of them are quite a bit larger than that, including one that clocks in at 10¼" while soft and 11½" hard. The guys they're attached to each answer a 37-item questionnaire that asks how satisfied they are with their size, what their ideal size is, if they've found underwear and condoms that are comfortable, the reactions their schlongs have received, etc.

Added Dimensions Publishing; $16.95
1995; softcover; 104 pp
illus; 1-879967-16-2

LEZZIE SMUT

A very well-done dyke zine that manages to be rough and hard-assed while still maintaining a cheeky sense of humour. The photography includes butches, femmes, transgenderists, body modifiers, bald women, and "fat girls". Issue 7 opens with a bang — the inside front cover is an *extreme* close-up of a pussy's inner lips being pulled open. Features include the feedback column "Smutsters Have a Say About: Gender", the essay "Quim, Tabletops & G-Spots", the poem "Dildo Discourse II", and the short story "Flirting With a Sexual Demon" ("I lean over, slipping the belt around her throat and pulling her head back towards my face. 'It ain't over till the fat bearded lady makes you scream, sweetheart.'"). Issue 6 has four short stories and five photo spreads. Each issue also has "Censorship Watch", which keeps tabs on Canada's censorship of queer and SM material.

Hey Grrrlz! Productions/Box 364, 1027 Davie St/Vancouver BC V6E 4L2/CANADA

Single issue: US: $7. Canada: $7Can. Elsewhere: $10US

Four issue sub: US: $28. Canada: $22Can; Elsewhere: $40US

MEAT
True Homosexual Experiences From S.T.H. , Volume 1
edited by Boyd McDonald

In the 1970s and 1980s, *Straight To Hell: The Manhattan Review of Unnatural Acts* was the most unabashed publication of true gay encounters being published. Readers sent in their adventures involving casual, usually anonymous sex, cutting right to the chase and holding nothing back. *Meat* — which had been unavailable for years — is the first anthology of writings from *Straight To Hell*, with most of the material coming from the rare early issues.

The over 200 encounters that are recounted here achieve a sort of transcendence. The descriptions of fucking, sucking, piss-drinking, and other acts are so non-stop and so absolutely unapologetic, that *Meat* achieves a libertine Nirvana. It isn't about sex. *Meat* is sex.

One reader writes: "Real connoisseurs of the male body love not only the flesh, but its products as well — sweat, piss, shit, farts, snot, toejam, earwax. Hell, I'm a born cannibal. I could suck the marrow from a man's bones and if I should ever happen upon a fresh corpse, I might do just that."

In one fairly typical letter, a guy tells about his experience in a New Orleans gay bar during Mardi Gras. "I sucked 7 cocks that evening: next year I'll start earlier and suck more. I got 5 loads (2 didn't want to unload but wanted to go from mouth to mouth). At times, those of us who were on our knees waiting for cock resembled hungry birds waiting to be fed. And what delicious big worms. Not a sour load in the bunch — all sweet and delicious."

Gay Sunshine Press; $14.95

1981 (1994); softcover; 190 pp

illus; 0-917342-78-X

NAILS TALONS AND CLAWS

NTC is a newsletter for devotees of frighteningly long finger-nails and toenails. Each issue contains several photos of women with wicked claws, but NTC is photocopied, so the images aren't exactly crisp and colourful, although they reproduce acceptably well. Most of the 22 or more pages are text — letters, true-life encounters, musings, etc.

One reader wrote in issue 4 about his experiences getting scratched by almost a dozen professional dominatrices. Mistress J told him: "My nails are about an inch-and-a-half long and extremely sharp. Are you sure you want to be scratched? I can make you bleed like a pig!" Upon going for a session, he reports, "Her nails were very sharp and I bled a lot!"

Most of the next issue reprints readers' letters. One guy wrote on his interesting variation to this attraction: "I have, what you might call a balloon fetish. What I mean is I like to watch women with long sharp fingernails pop balloons!" Another reader writes about his first girlfriend, who had incredibly long toenails. "When we were having sex (she was very flexible) and I was inside of her she bent her legs back at the knees and scratched my crotch area with her long toenails. I went insane!"

Frank, the nail-lover behind *NTC*, keeps the mood very open, excited, and chatty. Demonstrating a true love for his fetish, he has set up a video trade. Send him a nail fetish video, a blank videotape, and few bucks, and he'll copy any of 36 of his tapes for you.

NTC/PO Box 1081/Bedford Park IL 60499

WWW: www.ntcweb.com

Single issue: $4

Four issue sub (one year): $12. Non-US: $20

NATURE'S BAN
Women's Incest Literature
edited by Karen Jacobsen McLennan

Contrary to popular opinion, women have been writing about incest for more than just the last few decades. This unprecedented collection gathers together 41 of these stories, poems, and personal recollections, spanning eight centuries. Thirty of the selections involve father-daughter incest, with a few of those also dealing with brother-sister incest. Some deal with uncles, and one mainly involves a sexual encounter between mother and son. "Seven selections, all poems, elude a strict definition of incest but express a resistance to patriarchy in the language of incest trauma. The economic, political, or spiritual world is described in the terms of feminine violation."

By far the earliest selection is "The Two Lovers", a poem written in the twelfth century by Marie de France. There is a gap of 400 years before the creation of the next entry, Marguerite de Navarre's "Story Thirty" from her epic *Heptaméron*. Another sizeable gulf of about 240 years separates this story from the next two, "The Death of Amnon" by Elizabeth Hands in 1789 and an excerpt from *Marian and Lydia* by Susanna Haswell Rowson in 1791. From here things become a little more evenly spaced, with eight selections from the 1800s, ten from 1900 up to 1970, seven from the 1970s, and six each from the 1980s and 1990s.

The editor believes that there were certainly more works

written by women about incest prior to this century, but they were probably never shown to anyone or, if shown, rejected for publication. The novella *Mathilda* by Mary Shelley — included in this anthology — is a perfect example. Although the author of *Frankenstein* and wife of Romantic poet Percy Bysshe Shelley had literary clout, her publisher (who happened to be her father) refused to publish her fictional letter from a woman whose father had molested her... in fact, he refused to even return the "disgusting and detestable" manuscript to her. It remained lost and unpublished for 140 years, until its publication in 1959.

In "Bubba Esther, 1888" Ruth Whitman relates what her grandmother told her shortly before she died — that her uncle had molested her when she was seventeen: "still ashamed, lying/eighty years later/in the hospital bed,/trying to tell me,/trembling, weeping with anger". The Chinese father in "Mr. Tang's Girls" by Shirley Geok-Lin Lim has trouble dealing with his four daughters' developing sexualities, especially that of his eldest, the surly seventeen-year-old Kim Li. In one scene, she is clipping her toenails in the same room that her father is in. "She moved her skinny legs and shot a look at him slyly as if to catch him staring. If she weren't his daughter, he thought, he could almost believe she was trying to arouse him. But he couldn't send her out of the room without admitting that she disturbed him. Once he had watched a bitch in heat lick herself and had kicked it in disgust. He watched her now and was nauseous at the prospect of his future: all his good little girls turning to bitches and licking themselves."

Other contributors include Emily Dickinson, Louisa May Alcott, Virginia Woolf, Mourning Dove, Sylvia Plath, Alice Walker, Maya Angelou, Anne Sexton, Toni Morrison, Ntozake Shange, and Dorothy Allison.

Northeastern University Press; $16.95
1996; softcover; 394 pp
1-55553-253-5

THE NECROEROTIC

You knew it had to happen sooner or later — an erotic zine for necrophiles. (In case you're not up on all the different varieties of sex, necrophiles dig dead people.) The production values on this typed, stapled Xeroxzine are nil, but that only adds to the forbidden flavour. I mean, wouldn't a colour glossy necrophilia magazine seem not quite right? Besides, *The Necroerotic* more than makes up in content what it lacks in style.

In my limited exposure to this brand of sexual attraction, I've noticed there are two kinds of writings on necrophilia. The first kind is a calm type in which a corpse is used sexually, but it's basically a gentle encounter. In the second type, the necrophile is brutal. He or she prefers cadavers of people who have died in horribly violent ways, and may mutilate the corpse as part of the sex act. The creator of this zine, John, decidedly falls into the second category.

He describes his fantasy necro-sex partner as a girl who has been mercilessly beaten, mutilated, and violated by a serial killer. He's even kind enough to include a drawing of his dream date. A short story called "Funeral Parlour Fun" is

about a mortician who has sex with one of his "clients" and then desecrates her body in such a revolting manner that even *I* am not going to go into any further detail.

John provides information on exactly which articles in the *American Journal of Forensic Medicine* will appeal to necros. There is also a reprinted interview with a necrophile, a look at the legalities of necrophilia, news reports of corpse-lovers (mostly from *Weekly World News*), and true stories of John going to open-casket funerals to have a look and possibly cop a feel. An article on the front page brings word of the first rally in support of the legalisation of necrophilia. True, it was only John and a friend who participated, and it only lasted three minutes, but, hey — it's a start!

John/PO Box 92303/Warren MI 48092
Single issue: $2
"Do NOT address inquiries to 'The Necroerotic'!"

NICE GUYS DON'T GET LAID
by Marcus Pierce Meleton, Jr.

Have you ever noticed which guys are constantly getting dates, getting laid, being pursued by women? Right, it's the assholes. The more of a jerk a guy is, the more women are attracted to him. The more he lies to them, cheats on them, stands them up, emotionally (or even physically) abuses them, and embarrasses them in public, the more they cling to him and come back for more. Meanwhile, the nice guys, who are romantic, chivalrous, thoughtful, and caring, can barely manage to get a date and have an even tougher time getting some action.

Someone has finally gotten the nerve to bring this phenomenon kicking and screaming into the light. Forget *Men Are From Mars, Women Are From Venus*, Marcus Meleton has written what just might be the most important book on relationships ever published. He wrote it for two reasons. First of all, he is by his own admission a nice guy, although it's not like he never gets laid. Second, he got tired of seeing women moaning about men who are jerks even as they enter relationships with those very jerks.

Nice Guys Don't Get Laid has a multiple choice test that you can take to see what kind of guy you are. You will fall into one of five categories: 1) Mama's boy: "If I ever got married I would... have to have Mother's approval." 2) Mr. Psycho: "If I ever got married I would... lock her in a closet to keep her away from other men." 3) Mr. Average: "If I ever got married I would... be faithful, maybe." 4) Mr. Nice Guy: "If I ever got married... I would be forever faithful." 5) Mr. Abuse: "If I ever got married I would... be faithful at least the first week or until the first opportunity to score, whichever comes first." Since the first two types are very rare, Meleton only discusses the last three in detail.

Here's his definition of nice guy: "A term used by women to depict a male who is courteous, considerate, and dependable and therefore undesirable as a mate." But don't women dream about men who are sweet and sensitive, who always bring flowers? Sure they do, but Meleton emphatically warns: "DON'T CONFUSE MEN WOMEN DREAM ABOUT WITH MEN WOMEN ATTACH THEMSELVES TO." Because women invariably fall for Mr. Abuse. "To him women are good for only one thing. This makes him very successful as women seem to fall for his indifference, non-acceptance, and undependability. Of course not all women fall for this type, but enough do to keep him too busy to care about the rest."

So what's a nice guy to do? Simple. Become a total bastard. You'll be a stud instantly. Meleton spends a lot of the book teaching pathetic Mr. Nice Guys how to become the "walking disasters" that chicks dig. For example, if she says, "I like guys who are sensitive," you reply, "So what?" If she says, "You are so considerate," you ask, "This lunch is on you, isn't it?" But you can't stop there. You must reprogram your personality using the techniques in this book. You have to become angry, egotistical, immature, irresponsible, unhappy, and/or unstable. You also must learn that most women have at least one characteristic — self-deprecation, martyrdom, need-to-take-care-of, or need for a challenge — that can be used to Mr. Abuse's advantage.

Women can also get some use out of this book, especially the chapter on finding and using nice guys. "Is your car broken? He'll fix it. Do you need some boxes moved? Give him a call."

This book is a great wake up call to both sexes. According to the author, men have used it to become much more popular with the ladies. Some women, on the other hand, have read it, recognised themselves, and actually stopped dating assholes. Not many books can claim such powerful results.

Sharkbait Press; $7.95
1993; softcover; 93 pp
heavily illus; 0-9635826-0-7

THE NOOSE LETTER

This publication is only for members of the Hangman's Noose Club. Both the Club and its publication are for gay men who are turned on by descriptions of torture, mutilation, and execution. Issue 5 has eighteen stories in which men are hanged, shocked, drowned, beaten, raped, impaled, left out in the desert to be eaten by wolves, etc. In the story "Navy" a sailor and a mysterious older man take another sailor out to sea, where they handcuff him and fuck him roughly. They tie one end of a rope around his ankles and the other end to a cement block, which they push overboard, dragging their captive underwater. He struggles against his restraints, but it's no use. "I tried not to breathe in, but couldn't control another gasp and water seared down my throat, then more. I suddenly felt euphoria, I didn't care, nothing mattered. I knew I was dying down here in deep water, but it didn't matter, and I drifted into unconsciousness and death."

There are also reviews of extreme but consensual SM videos (nutcrushing, fisting, hot wax, etc.) and mainstream movies that feature men being tortured or executed. If you're interested in swapping violent material or meeting people for consensual torture sessions, there are a surprising number of personal ads awaiting your response.

Issue 5 is the last issue of the Noose Letter under this publisher. Rick Winter is shutting it down purely because of legal pressure. He's been told by several attorneys that this publication is total lawsuit-bait. He's afraid that if some

For the snuff fetishist. *Noose Letter.*

dumbass out there gets hurt or killed trying something described in the *Noose Letter* and then says he got the idea from the magazine, Winter could get his pants sued off. Keep this in mind, First Amendment defenders — free speech is being choked not just by legislation but by litigation too.

Future issues will be published by Dragon Publishing/ 2442 Market St #170/Seattle WA 98107. Send them an SASE (or an email to lthrcowby@sisna.com) with an over 21 statement in order to receive a membership application. Membership costs $50/year and includes four issues of *The Nooseletter* plus other goodies.

Winter Publishing/PO Box 80667/Dartmouth MA 02748
Send an SASE to find out about availability of back issues

THE ORAL MAJORITY

This digest-sized magazine is for members of the Light Blue Hanky Men, a private organisation for gay men who love to suck or get sucked. Each issue is filled with stories, artwork, and comix with oral fixations. Issue 3 has a comic from the Hun, whose style is kind of like Tom of Finland but with a much more cartoony feel. In this episode, Sig, the new waterboy for a varsity football team, discovers that he has many duties that weren't in his job description.

There are also personal ads and one of the longest guide to handkerchief codes I've ever seen. Wearing a dark pink hanky in your left back pocket indicates that you like to torture tits, while wearing it in your right means that you like to have your tits tortured. A brown lace hanky means you have an uncut cock or are looking for one. The list goes on to include 45 more colours and a few non-hanky codes, such as a vacuum cleaner bag (cock pumping) and a teddy bear (cuddling).

Winter Publishing/PO Box 80667/Dartmouth MA 02748
One year membership and sub: $35; non-US: $50
Send an SASE for info

ORAL SEX
Bad Taste and Hard to Swallow?

by Vernon Coleman

This sequel to *"I Hope Your Penis Shrivels Up!"* collects hundreds more questions and answers from Dr. Vernon Coleman's immensely popular column from Britain. Most of the subjects have to do with sex, but I would estimate that at least one-fourth of them are non-sexual in nature.

A man writes in that he thinks the two women living next door to him are lesbians. He asks in wide-eyed wonder, "What do lesbians do together?" After Coleman finishes raking this dolt over the coals, he concludes: "You sound [like] an odious, nosy little toe rag and I think you should get back to masturbating in the lavatory with a copy of your wife's underwear catalogue perched on your knees."

One letter goes a little something like this: "I am 18 years old and I think about sex all the time. Am I abnormal?" Coleman replies: "No. Cherish your youthful fantasies and enjoy them to the full. In a few years' time all your waking hours will be spent worrying about mortgage rates, blocked drains and German measles."

On the non-erotic side, a small business owner talks about a black female employee who's chronically tardy and absent and has a bad attitude. He's told her he's going to fire her, but she's threatened to sue him for racial and sexual discrimination. Coleman says to go ahead and fire her and complain to the police if she uses blackmail.

Common themes that run throughout Coleman's books are men with small penises, women with small or overly-large breasts, lonely people, and pissed-off prudes. An amazing number of people simply want reassurance that they're not perverts or freaks. The good doctor has an almost libertine attitude, so he is often very supportive. His anti-authoritarian tendencies become prominent when bluenoses complain about his language, his subjects, or his readers. In one reply, he tells someone who thinks transvestites should be locked up that, "I'd rather sort sewage bare handed than shake hands with someone like you."

Blue Books; £9.95
1995; softcover; 237 pp
1-899726-02-0

PSYCHOPATHIA SEXUALIS
The Case Histories

by Richard von Krafft-Ebing

In the late 1800s, Doctor Richard von Krafft-Ebing wrote several editions of his landmark work, *Psychopathia Sexualis*. In this modern translation of the final edition, the doctor provides case histories of 238 people with sexual proclivities other than mainstream heterosexuality: sadism, masochism, homosexuality, exhibitionism, coprolagnia (ingesting urine, shit, etc.), nymphomania, fetishism, paedophilia, crossdressing, bestiality, necrophilia, "anaesthesia" (total lack of interest in sexual activity), "sexual delirium", and others.

Psychopathia is a pioneering book because it was one of the first that sought to formally study and catalogue sexual behaviours. One of its most interesting aspects is that Krafft-Ebing blatantly injects his own moral beliefs into the text. In

Case 81, he writes: "At eighteen he yielded to the impulse. To his utmost delight, he found a woman who would urinate in his mouth. He then had coitus with the vile woman. Since then, he felt the necessity to repeat the disgusting act every four weeks." Other subjective words such as "immoral", "loathsome", "natural", and "normal" make regular appearances. As Terence Sellers — author of *The Correct Sadist* — points out in her introduction, today's psychologists may use more neutral language, but we still have many of the same attitudes towards sexual "deviation".

Here are a few highlights of the more unusual cases:

Case 22: "A certain Gruyo, aged forty-one, with a blameless past life, having been three times married, strangled six women in the course of ten years. They were almost all public prostitutes and quite old. After the strangling he tore out their intestines and kidneys through the vagina."

Case 189: "Of good ancestors, highly cultured, good-natured, very modest, blushed easily, but always the terror of the family. When alone with a male, regardless of whether he was a child or a man, or old man, whether handsome or hideous, she would at once strip him naked and vehemently and violently urge him to sat[e] her lusts."

Case 211: "His wife kept a milk-shop. Again and again he could not resist the temptation to completely submerge his genitals in the milk. In the act he felt lustful pleasure, 'as if touched with velvet'. He was cynical enough to use this milk for himself and the customers."

Velvet Publications (Creation Books); £9.95, $14.95
circa 1888, 1997; softcover; 251 pp
1-871592-55-0

REAL CATFIGHTS

edited by anonymous

It won't win any awards for its writing, but this staplebound collection of fights between women makes up for it with its unashamed enthusiasm. Over 125 people answered the publisher's call for true descriptions of fights between women, and, although it's impossible to determine the veracity of each story, there is no doubt that they were not "faked" by professional writers wanting to give the impression of real-life letters. The writing is often of poor to average quality, with lots of grammatical and spelling mistakes. But this only adds to the underground feel of this politically incorrect fetish.

The recountings of female fisticuffs range from just a few sentences to a page and even longer. Divided into sections based on where the fight happened (street, school, parties, etc.) or who was involved (lovers, wives, or the woman telling the tale), some patterns can readily be seen. There's lots of slapping, hair-pulling, and screaming. Most of the fights involve a loss of clothing, which often seems to be the real objective, rather than truly hurting the opponents. Often the victor will purposely strip the loser in order to humiliate her. A few fights are much more vicious, with punching, kicking, and other efforts to inflict real damage.

In a typical account, Tony from Rhode Island writes that he and his roommate went outside when they heard shouting in the parking lot of their apartment complex. Outside was a group of young women, and two of them started mixing it up. The larger one threw the petite one to the ground, straddled her, and tore open her blouse. "The bigger girl then ripped the bra off the little one and threw it to her friends who were laughing and making fun of her victim. With her arms pinned by the knees of her foe, the petite one couldn't cover her big breasts as they jiggled with every effort to dislodge the one on top. Her nipples were puffy and pink and very erect. Seeing this the big girl began to slap the milky white breasts of the little one making the skin turn a bright red with every stinging slap. The little one screamed and cried even louder. The big girl was obviously getting into this as she smiled and laughed every time her hands connected with the swollen crimson breasts that were at her disposal."

USA Publications; $19.95
1995; oversized stapled-bound softcover; 103 pp
no ISBN

THE RELUCTANT EXHIBITIONIST
by Martin Shepard

Dr. Martin Shepard is a psychoanalyst. During the 1960s he got tired of conventional tactics and started leading encounter groups. He also did LSD and, being a Tantric explorer, engaged in lots of sex, even with his patients. When these memoirs first came out in 1972 (under the title *A Psychiatrist's Head*), Shepard was stripped of his license to practice medicine by the New York Board of Regents. The sole reason was the revelations contained in this book. He appealed and on the last day of 1983 was reinstated.

Shepard engaged in the typical Counterculture awakening, becoming liberated through experiencing bisexuality, threesomes, LSD, pot, and Taoism. He describes his adventures, their effects, and the philosophy behind them with equal up-frontness, calling it like he sees it. In the chapter in which he tells the prisoners he's counselling that he sucked a man's cock, they tease him. He writes: "Poor, sad, dumb motherfuckers. They just don't seem to realise that it's all okay. That if you're horny you have to get it off one way or another."

At one point early in the book, he's engaged in a threesome with his reluctant wife and another man. "Seeing her buttocks rise rhythmically to take his cock into her, watching her glide and slide along its shaft, I felt that I had never seen a more beautiful or harmonious motion in my life… Copulation and its ripples of motion were at the heart and soul of the universe."

From there Shepard goes on to a series of *ménages à trois*, foursomes, and outright orgies. Amongst all this humping, he talks about his father, his days right after med school, and the reactions of various people to his manuscript in progress. In the end, he finds out that free love is just another bunch of hype: "But of all the pitches — of all the illusions — I suppose that sexual freedom is the greatest seducer. Find orgastic happiness — drop your load whenever you wish — and the world is your oyster. And of course it is not."

The Permanent Press; $5.95
1978, 1985; paperback; 244 pp
0-932966-57-8

THE SCAT TIMES

If you join Brown Hanky Men, a club for gay/bi men into scat, you'll get this zine of fiction, articles, and artwork. For those not in the know, scat is the erotic attraction to shit. The premiere issue of *The Scat Times* has reviews of several videos (only one of which is dung-related), a light-hearted look at society's relationship with crapola, an article on the Tom of Finland Foundation, and seventeen personal ads. Rick Winter's story is about a guy's first time eating another man's #2's.

Winter Publishing/PO Box 80667/S Dartmouth MA 02748
One year membership and sub: $35; non-US: $50
Send an SASE for an application.

SEX AND MATRIARCHY
by Victor Woodhull

This is the kind of book I love to see. It stands the common, accepted wisdom right on its head, and it does it in a way that makes a good case. Victor Woodhull's unorthodox belief is that women hold the real power in society. The key to their power is the giving or withholding of sex. Most men simply cannot get sex, or — if they can — it is only through Herculean effort and sacrifice. On the other hand: "No sex-seeking woman could fail to find a partner within a single day if she set her mind to it." The men who get sex — the "alpha males" of our primate society — are very few in number: the powerful, the rich, and those who have learned how to manipulate women into the sack. This relatively small proportion of the male population monopolises a high percentage of the female population. Many of the men who are left behind are simply worker drones, cannon fodder, etc. to be exploited by the powerful alpha males who run the show and get all the women.

Woodhull estimates that approximately 27 million American men are suffering from sexual deprivation, which he defines as "an absence of sexual fulfilment for long enough time to result in emotional imbalance and/or behavioural deviance." It may sound like a joke, but Woodhull believes that this withholding of sex contributes to many of society's problems. "Although it will be denied by the many who believe abstinence to be virtuous, the unfortunate answer is that many sexually deprived individuals suffer psychological warping that, collectively, causes society's gears to grind. All of us pay a price, for sexual deprivation leads people to behave in uncivilised ways, from use of demeaning sarcasm to rape and even mass murder."

In this key paragraph, Woodhull outlines his most important concepts: "In counterpoint to feminists who view the world through a filter that makes it look like men run everything for their own interests, we'll don the equally valid filter that *women* are actually, though quite subtly, in control. It is *they* who 'created' the macho male through their own eugenic mating choices over aeons of evolution, who breed fighting men to plunder on their behalf while dying early by the hordes, who decide who among men will be allowed full sexual lives, who blame men for the world's mess while manipulatively hoarding the key to balance and sanity under their skirts. But we blame them not, for they are rarely even conscious of their controlling role. We only wish to work with them to create a better world for all."

In the rest of the book, he shows specifically how women manipulate men, inspects the extremely unbalanced "sexual economy" of America, offers advice for the sexually-deprived male, and proposes some macro level solutions, including legalising prostitution, allowing insurance plans to cover the use of sex surrogates, providing voluntary, *reversible* chemical castration for men, increasing the female libido through chemicals or genetics, using reproductive technology to change the gender ration to 1:2 or 1:3 male to female, prohibiting discrimination in choosing sex partners, and promoting gay sex as an acceptable and desirable practice. [Check out the publisher's Website for chapter one of the book.]

Moniker Media; $10.95
1995; softcover; 178 pp
0-9643190-0-4

SEX & REALITY
The Time Has Come!

By Meha Mondaito

This book is so bizarre that I can't even explain it. In the foreword, author Meha Mondaito writes: "This work examines the effects of the Judeo-Christian religion on present-day human sexuality from the tripod vantage point provided by Taoism, Confucianism and Buddhism, and reinterprets Christ's mission on Earth." Seems like a fairly up-front explanation, but the book is way weirder than this statement of purpose would have you believe. Besides Eastern religious thought, Mondaito also mixes in feminist, masculinist, Freudian, Jungian, post-modern, and other strains of thought I can't identify. It makes for a highly original, idiosyncratic stew that will leave most of us scratching our heads.

I definitely like Mondaito's overarching viewpoint: "Philosophers have long sought one single phenomenon that underlies all others. I say in this book that human sexuality is that one, single, underlying phenomenon." However, soon after she says this, things get hairy. In fact, this may be the last easily comprehensible thing she says. Chapter two is titled "Genesis: The Story of Human Life Called an Outline of Sexual Ethics". In the third paragraph, Mondaito states:

We call the place from which human life issues the WOMB. This word is made up of four letters or elements necessary to bring forth life.
W (women, the positive or female principle)
O (all else or constant vehicle, nothing or nothingness)
M (man, the negative or male principle)
B (birth, or child, a moment in the process of becoming.)

She goes on to expound: "The negative principle, or Devil, being non-being *per se*, WOMB, (in Christian dogma previously known as God), must and does give up a portion of its being to again give birth. This birth process is called 'giving up of life' (knowledge), because it requires a form of death, a sacrifice of self. That portion of WOMB available for

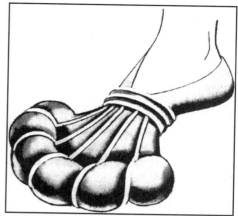

The scarpine, or "bear's paw," first emerged in late fifteenth-century Germany and was later outlawed by the English as obscene. Each toe, separately pocketed, represented a phallic member. *The Sex Life of the Foot and Shoe.*

such purpose is signified by its last letter. In giving up B, WOMB is left written, WOM, but it has at the same time created 'AND' or another WORD. WOM *and* B. B now represents the negative-principle that produced God and the Devil in the original event, as well as WOMB as a concept." From reading further in the book, I can tell you that things don't get much more lucid than that. I'm not going to say that this isn't a worthwhile book, but be aware that you're going to have to work damn hard to understand Mondaito's labyrinthine theories.

New Falcon Publications; $14.95
1996; softcover; 192 pp
1-56184-082-3

SEX FROM AAH TO ZIPPER
A Delightful Glossary of Love, Lust, and Laughter

by Roger Libby, PhD

This sex-positive book offers refreshingly humorous and enthusiastic definitions of hundreds of sexual words. Its goal is to reclaim the erotic vocabulary from sexophobic prudes and neutered academics, breathing new joyful life into lustful language. "If there ever was a time to laugh about sex and immerse ourselves in orgasms, it is now. There is no rational basis for putting off orgasms until all STDs are conquered... We are elated to offer *Sex From Aah to Zipper* as part of a conspiracy against those who would censor our orgasms. We can network with kindred spirits to promote more, better and safer sex if we use words which facilitate a happy outcome."

The second entry (after "aah") is "Abstinence: The strangest of all sexual perversions, this is the sometimes voluntary but always frustrating avoidance of orgasms. Abstinence doesn't make the heart grow fonder, since the long term practice of this sort of self-denial is unnecessary, unhealthy, unnerving, unthinkable... well, you get the picture."

Pornography is principally defined as: "Whatever moralists label as too sexy." A blow job is "An oxymoron if ever there was one, since it is neither blowing nor a job. It is, however, great 'work' if you can get it!" "No" is "An overused word." And a "sex maniac" is "Anyone who wants more sex than you do."

What is the author's answer to "the battle between the sexes"? Simple: "Let's negotiate a 'piece' treaty, and celebrate each other's differences instead of fighting over them." What's "D.W.A."? "Driving While Aroused. Fun, but can result in a ticket, accident, injury, or death... Masturbation or fucking while parked are two forms of autoeroticism we favour."

On the down side: Although the entries are written in an "orientation-neutral" manner as much as possible, the numerous illustrations that involve two people always show a het couple. Also, the author propagates the untrue belief that *fuck* is an acronym for "Fornication Under Consent of the King." Puhleeeeeze!

Playful Pleasure Press; $11.95
1993; softcover; 171 pp
heavily illus; 0-9635353-4-X

SEX IN PUBLIC
Australian Sexual Cultures
edited by Jill Julius Matthews

Although various aspects of the American sex-positive movement are becoming well-known (in alternative circles, at least), most of us in the US probably don't know what's happening along similar lines in Australia. There are probably a lot of people in *Australia* who don't know what's happening in Australia either, and this book helps fill this gap.

The first three essays are general in their focus: a scattershot look at sex and gender in Australia's media, an examination of "screen sex" (movies, the Net, and virtual reality sex), and an informative rundown of the laws regulating the sex industry in Oz. The country has approximately 16,000 sex workers (90% are female) who receive a total of 240,000 visits per week. There are no federal laws concerning prostitution, and the laws in the states and territories vary widely. In 1993, the Australian Capital Territory repealed all laws concerning prostitution, and New South Wales is almost as liberal. The other parts of the country are more strict, with Queensland being the most authoritarian. This state also has the harshest censorship laws. "All sexually explicit and sexually simulated books, magazines and videos are banned."

Three essays deal with an extraordinarily taboo topic that is almost completely ignored everywhere: the sexuality of people with HIV/AIDS. "Sex and the Single T-cell" focuses on the uproar that sex-positive, HIV-positive photography and writing have caused, paying particular attention to the most confrontational artist in this area, the late David McDiarmid. Several of these contentious images are reproduced, including McDiarmid's magazine cover spoof, *Plagueboy*, which featured headlines such as "Forty-ish, Fabulous & Full-Blown", "Tips on Remembering Your Own Name", and "Half-Dead and Hot".

Logo for *The Sphincterian Quarterly*, periodical of the American Sphincter Society.

Two other essays concern the struggles that defiantly erotic imagery has caused: "Stirred Heart and Soul: The Visual Representation of Lesbian Sexuality" and "Lesbian Erotica and Impossible Images". Judith Ion examines the lesbian separatist communities of New South Wales, which formed in the 1970s and are still flourishing. The other essays from Down Under are "Grief and the Lesbian Queer/n: A Love Story", "Bisexual Mediations: Beyond the Third Term", "Dangerous Desire: Lesbianism as Sex or Politics", and "I Was a Teenage Romance Writer".

Sex in Public is an excellent book recommended for anyone who wants to be informed on how progressive sexual attitudes are faring in countries besides the US.

Allen & Unwin; $24.95Aus
1997; softcover; 220 pp
illus; 1-86448-049-1

THE SEX LIFE OF THE FOOT AND SHOE
(Updated Edition)
by William A. Rossi

Concept: Podiatrist William A. Rossi presents an in-depth look at the eroticism of feet and shoes, throughout history and into the present.

Overriding Idea: "The foot is an erotic organ and the shoe is its sexual covering."

Fields consulted: Everything from medicine and sexology to fashion and mythology.

Approach: Comprehensive and serious, but with a light-hearted touch, as evidenced by chapter titles such as "Walking Is a Sex Trap", "Thank Your Foot for Sex", "Tread on Me", and "Cinderella Was a Sexpot".

Specific Subject #1: The direct role of the foot in sexual activity. While in London, the author was taken to a brothel that, besides offering all the usual services, specialised in women who were trained in the art of podophiliac sex. The madam explains: "It can take all kinds of forms: having the penis massaged by the girl's feet; or putting the penis between the girl's feet; or sucking the toes of the girl; or using the big toe to insert into the vagina; or holding or kissing the girl's feet while they're being laid."

Specific Subject #2: Our motives for wearing shoes. "We wear shoes chiefly for sex-attraction purposes — to send out sex signals, consciously or subconsciously." Although our first reaction might be to say that shoes primarily serve the functional role of protecting our tootsies, the good doctor scoffs at this notion. "What could possibly be functional about snug or tight shoes, high heels, platform soles, backless shoes, pointy toes, strippy sandals, and shoe ornaments?" They make no functional sense. But they do make sex sense. "Fashion is essentially an aphrodisiac."

Other Topics Covered: the foot's sexual nerves, shoe rituals, Chinese footbinding, biological reasons for foot appeal, shoe designers, shoe ads, the four categories of women's footwear ("sexy, sexless, neuter, and bisexual"), the phallicism of the foot, high heels, the harmful effects of shoes, standards of foot beauty, walking as a form of sexual communication, foot lovers, shoe lovers, the desire to be trampled, podocosmetics, reflexology, and taboos concerning bare feet and certain types of footwear.

Notable Illustrations: photos and X-rays of women's bound feet, amusing drawings of bygone footwear, a woman wearing thigh-high "lattice boots".

Drawbacks: Lack of references within the text. Occasional subtle implication that foot fetishists are abnormal. High price tag.

Obvious Audience: foot fetishists, podiatrists (medical foot fetishists), shoe sellers (retail foot fetishists).

Bottom Line: A wonderfully well-rounded look at an aspect of sex that hasn't been the subject of many books.

Krieger Publishing Company; $28.50
1976, 1993; softcover; 265 pp
illus; 0-89464-756-3

THE SPHINCTERIAN QUARTERLY

Published quarterly by the American Sphincter Society, *The Sphincterian Quarterly* is a long, slim periodical, shaped like a pamphlet, for people — particularly men — who adore men's anuses. It contains fiction, non-fiction, personal ads, illustrations, and photos focusing on fingering, rimming, anal sex, enemas, and other asshole eroticism. The photography is always particularly amazing. The first issue has a close-up of a Duracell battery (D-cell) being pushed up a guy's ass, and the next issue has lots of pictures of fingerfucking. The most visually impressive issue so far, though, has been the third, which has close-ups of feathers, a condom, a GI Joe-sized action figure, a hook with a key hanging from it, and three small American flags all protruding from assholes.

Publication of *SQ* has been suspended but will probably resume in the fall of 1998. For information, send $1.00 to the address below or inquire by email. If you'd like to buy back issues, all three are still available for a total of $6, postpaid ($9, outside the US).

The DBJ Projects/PO Box 14692/Ft. Lauderdale FL 33302-4692
Email: dbjay3@mindspring.com

Smoke gets in your eyes. *Smoke Signals.*

SMOKE SIGNALS
A Monthly Newsletter Devoted to the Smoking Fetish

A periodical for people who dig women who smoke. Each issue has black and white photos of women puffing away; reviews of movies, TV shows, and magazines; listings of female celebrities who light up; personal ads; real-life experiences; and more.

Smoke Signals/500 Waterman Ave, Suite 193/E Providence RI 02914

Twelve-issue sub: $39.95. Can: $44.95. Elsewhere: $60
Single issue: $5

SPLOSH!
The Wet and Messy Fun Mag

Splosh! has been making quite a splash in alternative circles recently. Perhaps that's because it's a fun erotic magazine that joyfully celebrates an unusual but apparently growing obsession — getting erotically messy and/or soaked. Generally, every issue has three colour spreads, one for each of the main brands of sloppiness — mud, water, and miscellaneous slop, such as food and paint. (The outside and inside of the front and back covers also have colour shots.) In issue 24 three cuties wade into a mudpit that comes up to midcalf. They gradually lose their clothes and become more and more caked with mud till finally only their faces remain untouched. During this sludgefest, the women wrestle a little, grope each other, entwine their bodies, and bend over for the camera.

Issue 25 features a two-page photo-essay of Karen, decked out in a nice wedding dress, slowly submerging herself in a pool. She floats around a little, slicks her hair back, then climbs out with the dress clinging to her bod. Another section in the same issue chronicles an epic foodfight be-

Leading the goo-ed life. *Splosh!*

tween two saucy wenches. It starts out with Sammy-Jane plastering a custard pie onto April's kisser. She smooshes two more pies on either side of her head, dumps two cans of spaghetti over her, and pours a can of rice pudding down the back of her panties. She gets April on the floor and covers her in custard before grinding a strawberry cream pie into her face. Since turnabout is fair play, the grody April belts Sammy-Jane with custard pies, coats her in baked beans, and dumps a jug of spaghetti into her panties. In the *pièce de résistance*, S-J streams a can of golden syrup over April's now naked body and licks it off her breasts.

The rest of the magazine contains black and white shots embedded in articles and reviews. Issue 18 has a write-up of the Aquantics, a three-day muckathon. An article in issue 25 follows the making of a messy movie.

Splosh! also has ads for gloppy/wet movies, photo sets, zines, and organisations, as well as personal contact ads. Make no mistake, this has become a full-fledged subculture. Get in on the slime!

Splosh!/12, Leonard Road/Redfield/Bristol BS5 9NS/UK
WWW: www.splosh.co.uk
Single issue: Europe/UK: £8.00. US: $15.50. Elsewhere: £9
Four issue sub (one year): £28
Payment: UK ck, mo, traveller's cheque payable to Net Result
Available in the US from Atomic Books, Last Gasp, and others

SPORTSDYKES
Stories from On and Off the Field
by Susan Fox Rogers

Sports have played a unique role by providing a sense of community for many lesbians. The zine *Girljock* [*Outposts* p 88] was one of the first official acknowledgements of this connection. Now *Sportsdykes* provides another touchstone for the athletic lesbian subculture.

The opening piece is "How Girljock Are You?", a tongue-in-cheek quiz. One question asks: "In your code of ethics, pulling hair is a) a nasty foul; b) just part of the game; c) a strategy for winning; d) a come-on." Another question: "Which nickname comes closest to yours? a) Sunblossom; b) Feather; c) Mommy Sir; d) Hairball; e) Meat."

The section "Empowerment" contains essays on the feelings of belonging, camaraderie, and self-esteem that sports brings. Deborah Abbott, in "Of Hightops and Home Plates", tells of being a jock despite having a bum leg from childhood polio. Things were wonderful as a child. "Nobody seemed to notice or care that I had one leg in a metal brace and wore only ugly brown hightop shoes. My friends walked a little slower for me, and Missy, who was the fastest sprinter and most ruthless slider, was my pinch runner." In junior high, she underwent a bunch of painful leg operations that made sports impossible, so she became an intellectual. In her early thirties, she became a jock again through swimming, and with the prodding of her lover, she kayaks, rafts, and boogeyboards.

Another section looks at the politics of Sapphism in sports. Victoria A. Brownworth examines the effects of antilesbian discrimination. "Women in college sports can — and do — lose scholarships because of their sexual orientation." Professionals also have a lot to lose. "Product endorsements, prize money, and positions as coaches, trainers, or sportscasters after retirement are all threatened."

The section on heroines includes three pieces on Martina Navritolova and a comic by Joan Hilty in which she eagerly looks for signs that two members of the US Olympic women's volleyball team are lovers. The sex section has a field report from Roxxie of *Girljock*, who states that in the lesbian and gay leagues of "some sports, so much happens off court, it's amazing the games ever get played."

Other entries include looks back at tomboy days, short stories, and an interview with a lesbian hockey team leader.

St. Martin's Press; $8.95
1994; softcover; 238 pp
illus; 0-312-13187-9

THE STORY THE SOLDIERS WOULDN'T TELL
Sex in the Civil War
by Thomas P Lowry, MD

If you're a Civil War buff or know someone who is, then you've probably seen first-hand the staggering number of books that have been written about every conceivable (and inconceivable) aspect of that conflict. Hundreds of books have been published about the Battle of Gettysburg alone. But until the publication of this book, no one had set down a detailed account of the sexual lives of the soldiers. This blindspot is so conspicuous, that it led Thomas Lowry to write facetiously in his introduction: "There was no sex during the Civil War. Everyone knows that." He then spends the next

A popular daguerreotype from the Civil War era. *The Stories the Soldiers Wouldn't Tell.*

200 pages proving himself wrong.

The first-hand material regarding the predilections of Johnny Reb and Billy Yank are not exactly bounteous, since the boys were hesitant to write about such things, and when they did, family members often destroyed any mention found in letters and diaries. But by using the surviving writings, newspaper articles, military documents, and other sources, Lowry has filled in the final missing piece in the lives of the Blue and the Gray.

A New Hampshire soldier wrote in a letter home, "We cannot get anything here but fucking and that is plenty." As this indicates, prostitution was extremely widespread during the War Between the States. Many military men complained of being stationed in Sodoms filled with whorehouses, but of course, many more men were taking advantage of the situation. In fact, Nashville and Memphis both legalised prostitution for a short while. They were hoping to regulate it and cut down on venereal diseases, which were spreading like wildfire.

Homosexuality was not uncommon among the men. One Illinois soldier wrote to a friend in Tennessee about an unusual occurrence. At one point his company picked up a new enlistee. "The boys all took a notion to him. On examination, he proved to have a Cunt so he was discharged. I was sorry for it, for I wanted him for a Bedfellow." Amazingly, there are no records of any soldier being disciplined for "sodomy" or "buggery", although we know that six Navy sailors were court-martialed for their encounters.

Although some Civil War scholars have actually said that rape was non-existent during the war, we know conclusively that this is so much blarney. "Confederate rapists are somewhat harder to locate than Union ones, since unknown persons set fire to the Confederate Army court-martial records about the time of Lee's surrender, but a survey of less than 5 percent of the Federal court-martial records, preserved in the National Archives, have yielded more than thirty trials for rape." Some of the soldiers who were found guilty of rape were executed.

Any deluded souls who think photographic pornography is only a few decades old will be dismayed to learn that the lads on the front were buying scads of nudie and hardcore photos and explicit novels that were printed to look like Bibles. The more adventurous could buy condoms and dildos through the mail.

Other highly entertaining subjects that are covered include bawdy songs sung by the soldiers, ribald tales, cursing among the enlisted, contraception, social diseases, Walt Whitman's sex with soldiers, Abraham Lincoln's sexual orientation, and the private lives of officers, generals, and Army clergy. A centre section contains pictures of VD hospitals in Nashville, soldiers who are eaten up with syphilis, a woman who secretly served as a soldier, and a few nude pix (including a spread shot) that were circulating among the troops.

Even if you're not especially interested in the Civil War, you'll find *The Story the Soldiers Wouldn't Tell* to be fascinating for its eye-opening historical insights into sex.

Stackpole Books; $19.95
1994; hardcover; 214 pp
illus; 0-8117-1515-9

TRUST
Handballing Newsletter

This 20-page quarterly newsletter is for men who are into fistfucking with other men (for those who don't know: fisting involves the insertion of the entire hand and perhaps even the forearm into an anus (or a vagina)). *Trust* covers the fisting scene, technique, preparation, videos, upcoming events, and more. Personal ads from around the country put out the call for people into handballing, including variations such as punching, double-fisting, elbowing, and "outdoor spiritual fisting".

Trust/PO Box 14697/San Francisco CA 94114
Single issue: $5
Four issue sub (one year): $25. Canada: $26. Other: $30

WET SET
The Magazine for "Accident Prone" Adults

Wet Set is a slick, digest-sized magazine for people aroused by adults who piss on themselves. Each issue has around 20 black and white pictures, mainly of women who have had accidents. Sometimes they're wearing jeans with dark, upside-down-V stains starting at the crotch. Other times they're dressed in diapers or sopping panties. Issue 10 has a picture of a guy, dressed in huge diapers, sucking on a pacifier. The previous issue shows a man taking a leak on a woman's chest.

The letters section is fascinating. Readers tell about their urinary experiences, ranging from a woman who lets her husband change her used diapers to a man who wets his pants in public because it excites him. One man writes about a woman he dated who took a whiz on his hand while he was playing around with her in a movie theatre.

In issue 9, Patches — creator of a popular Website devoted to golden showers — tells about her piss-soaked life. In her college days, to raise money for textbooks, she went to a bar that had a secret contest. If a woman could put out a candle by leaking through her panties, she would get $100. Patches won easily. In fact, the candle almost floated away.

Each issue also has soaked fiction, a question and answer column, and contact ads, so you can cross streams with that special someone.

WSP/PO Box 392/Turramurra NSW 2074/Australia

WWW: www.wetset.net

Single issue: $10US

Four issue sub (one year): $38US

Payment: cash (all currencies accepted), ck (from any country), mo (no postal money orders, though), bank cheque/draft, Visa, MC, Bankcard

WHAT WILD ECSTASY
The Rise and Fall of the Sexual Revolution
by John Heidenry

When it comes to the Sexual Revolution, the images that seem to reside in the public consciousness are of naked, acid-drenched hippies making love, not war, or — a few years later — coked-up dancing queens with IUDs and preening guys wearing big gold chains engaging in strange mating behaviour at the disco. But there is much, much more to the Revolution than that. It was a time of such massive social, cultural, medical, legal, economic, literary, and artistic change that our current society is irreversibly different because of it and always will be.

Former *Penthouse Forum* editor John Heidenry has created a massive history of this period, starting with the first rumblings in 1938 when Alfred Kinsey began interviewing people for his unprecedented study of human sexual behaviour, to the beginning of the Revolution in 1965 when Masters and Johnson's *Human Sexual Response* and Bob Guccione's *Penthouse* were unleashed on the world, to the aftershocks and backlashes that are still being felt today. In the midst of all this, we are told about sex magazines *Playboy*, *Hustler*, *Screw*, *Suck*, and *Straight to Hell*; skin flicks *I Am Curious (Yellow)*, *Deep Throat*, and *Caligula*; the groundbreaking books *Sexual Politics* by Kate Millet, *The Joy of Sex* by Alex Comfort, and *The Hite Report* by Shere Hite; personalities such as erotic writer Marco Vassi, porn star John Holmes, sex activist/artist Annie Sprinkle, radical feminist Andrea Dworkin, "father of the modern dildo" Ted Marche, sexologist John Money, and Roberta White, the first person to undergo sex change surgery in the US; pivotal events, including the Stonewall riot, the invention of the birth control pill, and the "discovery" of the G-spot and female ejaculation; as well as sex communes, the SM movement, the Hellfire Club, AIDS, and dozens of other topics.

Forgoing a dry recitation of facts, Heidenry uses a highly anecdotal chronological approach to tell his story. This style allows the happenings to retain a freshness and even leads to some suspense, especially when you're not familiar with the events he's describing. On the downside, the author's style can at times become *too* detailed. When describing Marco Vassi meeting his lover at a dingy East Sixth Street apartment, he writes, "As soon as he walked into the building, he felt a deep dirty thrill going right down to his anus." Hmmmm… if you say so. Frustratingly, several episodes end quite abruptly, leaving you wishing for some sort of conclusion. Finally, some subjects receive scant coverage. I would have particularly liked to have read more about Olympia Press and the prostitutes' rights movements, both of which are covered only in passing. Then again, *What Wild Ecstasy* does provide lots of scarce information (for example, I was particularly glad to learn more about sexual anarchist Willem de Ridder and the notorious publications he was involved with — *Suck*, *Finger*, and the aborted *God*), so, in the final analysis, this is a worthwhile overview of a tumultuous period in America's collective sexual development.

Simon & Schuster; $26

1997; hardcover; 416 pp

0-684810379

WHEN PASSION REIGNED
Sex and the Victorians
by Patricia Anderson

Currently, the word "Victorian" is a synonym for "prudish". We are under the impression that British society from 1840 to 1905 was extraordinarily uptight and sexually repressed. So dainty were the Victorians' sensibilities, we're told, that they put trousers on their pianos, so they wouldn't have to see uncovered legs of any kind. If historian Patricia Anderson has her way, this perception will change drastically. Her book, *When Passion Reigned*, demonstrates that we've got it all wrong. The Victorians dearly loved sex, and it was present in almost every aspect of their lives.

Of course, the pornographic novels from that period are famous, but they were not widespread. Anderson shows the open sexuality in a wealth of songs, poems, valentines, advertisements, and romance novels that were widely circulated among the common people but are now known only to scholars. From these we see that the Victorians relished sex, passion, and desire, but their celebrations of carnality were not as graphic or commodified as in today's world. "Most Victorians lacked the notion of sexuality as a subject for clinical, professional, or otherwise explicit discussion. They allowed sex a life of its own by preserving a measure of silence about it. With almost reverential circumspection, they protected and sustained a mystique of acutely pleasurable naughtiness. They preferred engaging euphemism over the language of the clinic, suggestive reticence over verbal exhibitionism. Misunderstood by later generations, this preference for the combined joys of sex and silence gave rise to the myth of Victorian prudery and repression."

The penchant for euphemisms can be seen in a lot of the popular fiction of the day. "In describing Bella's beauty, Charles Reade gave loving attention to her mouth. Searching his imagination, he saw 'two full and rosy lips. They made a smallish mouth at rest, but parted ever so wide when they smiled, and ravished the beholder.' In writing *Taken by Storm*, the author gave his hero Ainsley a constant desire to 'sip the nectar' from Beryl's 'pretty' and 'quivering' lips." A typical Valentine of the period contained the following verse: "How prized the coral and the shell,/And beautiful the pearl,/Who can the hidden treasures tell,/O'er which the soft waves curl."

The theatre was another place in which female sexuality was flaunted. "High kicks, lewd winks, provocative body language — all were permissible, indeed expected, behind the footlights."

Anderson brings the results of her research home by suggesting that maybe it's we — and not the Victorians — who have the real problems dealing with sex. "But as the nineteenth century progressed and turned into the twentieth, sex increasingly attracted the professional attention of legislators, doctors, educators, Freudians, and the like. They sorted and separated it into categories and behaviours. They analysed, labelled, and discussed it. In the process it began to acquired a new dimension of abstract meaning — and began to lose substance as a powerful and complete human experience."

When Passion Reigned is a startling and convincing revision of a generally unquestioned aspect of sexual history.

BasicBooks (HarperCollins); $15
1995; softcover; 209 pp
illus; 0-465-08992-5

THE WILD ANIMAL REVUE

Proving that there is a publication for every desire — no matter how frowned upon by society — *The Wild Animal Revue* is a zine for people interested in bestiality, either as a spectator or a participant.

Issue 11 examines and reproduces the fantasy art of Frank Franzetta, who often deals with non-explicit "beauty and the beast" themes. There are detailed reviews of a trilogy of Brazilian donkey films — *Donkey, Donkey Love*, and *Donkey Dong*. They feature smouldering women, horny burros, specially-written musical scores, professional titles and credits, and lots of slapstick comedy. "Directed by Di Angel, they have more artistic merit than most of the current network television productions."

A reader writes about seeing a live show in Mexico in which a woman had oral and vaginal sex with a donkey. Another unnamed reader supplies a country-by-country look at live animal/human sex shows. The Netherlands is a hotbed of this activity. "You name it, if you've got the money, they've got a show for you." Spain has monkey shows, Norway uses reindeer, and in Southeast Asia you can see slithery sex with snakes and eels. Eastern Europe is seeing an influx of dog-sex tapes. The only action going on in the US and Canada is "impromptu and underground".

The letters section has accounts from female readers on their encounters with goats, a Doberman, and a Shetland pony. One reader writes in detail of how she and her friends have orgies with her Labrador. There are two pages of personal ads from men and women looking to exchange tapes or get together with other people into "animal training".

The centrespread of the magazine is a colour reproduction of a naked woman hugging a miniature mule. Like all the other photos in *The Revue*, it is not explicit. Although some of the pictures show female (and animal) nudity, there is never any sexual contact.

Farm News/PO Box 608039/Orlando FL 32860
Single issue: $10

THE BODY

AIDS

AIDS
by Peter Duesberg, PhD, & John Yiamouyiannis, PhD

Peter Duesberg has become famous for theorising that HIV does not cause AIDS. In this book, he and a scientist with a similar viewpoint explain this theory and the evidence in clear, nontechnical terms. Duesberg's beliefs boil down to this: "… the use of recreational drugs and DNA-inhibiting chemotherapies such as AZT, ddI, ddC, and hydroxyurea are sufficient to explain all AIDS victims with the exception of haemophiliacs, whose AIDS is explainable by impurities in the transfusion fluids. Duesberg does not believe that cancer, weight loss, and dementia can result from the depression of the immune system. Furthermore, Duesberg concludes that the reason AIDS is more prevalent in HIV-positive individuals is because 1) those groups at highest risk of getting HIV, for example homosexuals, are also the largest users of recreational drugs, and 2) once a person is found to be HIV-positive, they are likely to be given one of the drugs like AZT, which will depress the immune system and thus cause AIDS."

Co-author John Yiamouyiannis' view is essentially the same but differs on two counts. First, he feels that cancer and other AIDS diseases can result from immunodeficiency. Also, he believes that recreational drugs and AZT cause AIDS but must almost always be accompanied by other factors that damage the immune system — bad diet, environmental factors, certain over-the-counter or prescription drugs, etc. Occasionally, these other factors may be enough to cause AIDS on their own.

The authors show the many faults of the theory that AIDS is caused by a virus. For one thing, some people have AIDS but are not HIV-positive. Conversely, there are over 12 million people who have HIV but do not have AIDS. In some of these people the level of the virus is above that of people who do have AIDS. Despite researching HIV more than all other viruses combined, no one has been able to cure AIDS with antiviral drugs or "induce AIDS by injection of chimpanzees with HIV viruses grown in culture."

AIDS also covers such topics as the number of HIV-positive people (which was the same in 1994 as it was in 1984), the theory that HIV is not new, the age distribution of AIDS, the low rate of HIV among prostitutes who don't use drugs, AIDS in haemophiliacs and other transfusion recipients, AIDS in Africa, government funding for AIDS research, and more.

If you want a clear, concise guide to the hypothesis that HIV doesn't cause AIDS, you can't do better than this book. You might also want to check out other books Duesberg has authored on this topic, including *Inventing the AIDS Virus* and *Infectious AIDS: Have We Been Misled?* (You can get further, up-to-the-minute info at Duesberg's Website, www.duesberg.com.)

Health Action Press; $15
1995; softcover; 194 pp
illus; 0-913571-05-9

AIDS AND SYPHILIS
The Hidden Link
by Harris L. Coulter

Like the authors of *AIDS* [above], Harris Coulter believes that AIDS is the result of an immune system that has already been weakened by other factors. "The AIDS virus is probably little more than another 'opportunistic' infection of an already destroyed immune system — at the most a 'co-factor' which may possibly give rise to AIDS when combined with other factors. This is already known to be true for PCP. The *Pneumocytis carinii* is found in more than 95 percent of healthy persons and is life-threatening only in the individual with a defective immune system."

The main contention of this book is that having syphilis is a major contributing factor towards getting AIDS. A large number of people who have AIDS also had (or have) syphilis. Coulter maintains that this is not a coincidence, but is in fact a causal relationship. "In the first place, AIDS and AIDS-related conditions often resemble syphilis, leading to diagnostic confusion." Also, syphilis can be transmitted through blood transfusions, which could account for people who got AIDS that way, especially since blood is rarely screened for syph. Some babies are born with AIDS, but Coulter contends that this is probably congenital syphilis.

If AIDS and syphilis are so connected, then why doesn't almost every person with AIDS also have syphilis in their background? Because tests for syphilis are notoriously unreliable. "We suspect that if all AIDS patients were given the full battery of serological and treponemal tests for syphilis, the incidence would be found to 'approach 100 percent.'"

The book ends with two interviews with Joan McKenna, who was the first person in the US to rigorously study the AIDS-syphilis connection, and Stephen Caiazza, who was the first American doctor to treat AIDS patients with penicillin.

North Atlantic Books; $8.95
1987; softcover; 132 pp
1-55643-021-3

THE ANARCHIST AIDS MEDICAL FORMULARY
A Guide to Guerrilla Immunology
by Charles R. Caulfield with Billi Goldberg

Charles Caulfield wrote the column "HIV News" for the *San Francisco Sentinel* in 1992 and 1993. In this collection of essays adapted from those columns, Caulfield and Billi

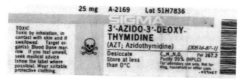

25 mg   A-2169   Lot 51H7836

SIGMA

TOXIC
Toxic by inhalation, in
contact with skin and if
swallowed. Target or-
gan(s). Blood Bone mar-
row. If you feel unwell,
seek medical advice
(show the label where
possible). Wear suitable
protective clothing.

3'-AZIDO-3'-DEOXY-
THYMIDINE
(AZT; Azidothymidine)   (30516-87-1)
Desiccate   C₁₀H₁₃N₅O₄
Store at less   Purity 99% (HPLC)
than 0°C   For laboratory use only. Not for
                      drug, household or other uses.
                      · 9315AET

Fw 267.2

AZT label.
AIDS.

Goldberg examine alternative AIDS therapies, report on breakthroughs in immunology, and trash the way the government and the medical establishment have responded to the crisis.

Caulfield was diagnosed with AIDS in January of 1994. He has dedicated himself to telling people about possible treatments from the AIDS underground and fighting the heartless, hamstrung bureaucracy that doesn't do enough to save people's lives. Twenty of the essays mercilessly slam the AIDS establishment. Seventeen essays report on some of the more promising ways to boost the immune system, including antioxidants, Vitamin A, Chinese medicine, the experimental drug Acemannan, Hypericin, and DeVeras Beverage. Five of the articles discuss DNCB, a well-known topical solution that is also a chemical used in the photography industry. When DNCB is applied to the skin, it increases the number of immune cells. Although the promise of this substance is widely known in the medical community, DNCB is not being formally investigated and probably never will be. Its incredibly low cost ($2 for a month's supply) and the fact that it can't be patented means that there is no profit in it, so the establishment scientists are staying away from in droves. However, you can get DNCB cheaply and without a prescription from the resources listed in the back of this book.

The resources section also lists contact information for organisations offering six other alternative treatments, as well as further information. A fifteen-page glossary rounds out the book's important offerings.

North Atlantic Books; $12.95
1993; softcover; 155 pp
1-55643-175-9

EMERGING VIRUSES
AIDS and Ebola — Nature, Accident or Genocide?

by Leonard G. Horowitz, DMD, MA, MPH

Could the HIV virus have been manufactured as a biological weapon and then accidentally or purposely released into the world? It's a theory that has become popular in many circles, and now Dr. Leonard Horowitz has created the most massive, well-documented assembly of evidence ever published in support of this idea. In this monumental book he tells of his own quest for answers as he weaves together information about pharmaceutical companies, the cancer establishment, the military-industrial complex, biological warfare scientists, the World Health Organisation (WHO), the CIA, the Sloan Foundation, Henry Kissinger, Dr. Robert Gallo, President Nixon, President Ford, and many other players in this murky, complicated scenario of genocide. If you

believe in the man-made HIV theory or at least hold that it's a strong possibility, *Emerging Viruses* will give you more ammunition to bolster your position. If you scoff at the notion that HIV was artificially created, withhold any out-of-hand dismissal until you read this book. You won't be so cocky once you see how much evidence exists.

Obviously, it's next to impossible to encapsulate 500 pages of complicated sleuthing in a short review, so let me point out just a few of the most cogent facts. In 1970, the Department of Defence requested and received $10 million to start a biological warfare programme to specifically create new diseases that would destroy the immune system. *Emerging Viruses* contains two pages of verbatim testimony from the appropriations hearings that were held before Congress. Among other things, the DOD representative says: "Within the next 5 to 10 years, it would probably be possible to make a new infective micro-organism which could differ in certain important aspects from any known disease-causing organisms. Most important of these is that it might be refractory to the immunological and therapeutic processes upon which we depend to maintain our relative freedom from infectious disease."

One of the main functions of the WHO is to enable scientists world-wide to have access to viruses for study. One of the WHO's publications reports that between 1968 and 1974, its greatest concern was "slow viruses". In particular, it mentioned two such viruses that attack the nervous system of sheep and one that causes Vonu, an incredibly rare disease (found only in New Guinea) that results from eating human brains. Horowitz asks: "When in history has helping cannibals been a world priority?" However, this interest makes more sense when you realise that these slow viruses cause problems remarkably similar to HIV/AIDS. Maybe the WHO scientists were so incredibly interested in these obscure diseases for biological warfare purposes.

Retrovirologist Robert Gallo is generally credited with discovering the HIV virus. Horowitz reveals damning evidence that Gallo might have actually *created* the virus a decade before he "discovered" it. During the mid-1970s Gallo's lab — which is part of the National Cancer Institute (NCI) — proudly published papers trumpeting the fact that it had made AIDS-like viruses. Furthermore, it is known that the NCI "was the principal beneficiary of the $10 million DOD AIDS-like virus contract." Another suspicious fact is that, according to Randy Shilts' acclaimed book *And the Band Played On*, "Gallo all but sabotaged international research efforts to isolate the AIDS retrovirus."

On top of that, the NCI ran the Special Virus Cancer Program during the 1960s and 1970s, in which they gave grants and contracts to several institutions to study AIDS-like viruses and vaccines. Horowitz reproduces eighteen pages of grant descriptions and research reports filed by those taking part — Bionetics, Merck, Hazleton, the University of California, the Public Health Research Institute of New York, and the Massachusetts Institute of Technology.

Emerging Viruses also focuses on the dreaded Ebola and Marburg viruses, albeit to a much less degree than HIV. Horowitz notes that two of the world's leading experts in monkey virology have declared that Ebola and Marburg were artificially created. Suspiciously, in 1969, after Henry Kissinger called for the development of new diseases for biowarfare, he ordered the CIA to conduct covert operations all over Zaire and Angola, the two areas in Africa that have been hit hardest by Ebola (and AIDS).

In this review I've only managed to barely scratch the surface of what *Emerging Viruses* reveals. I recommend it most highly. You'll never think of AIDS the same way again.

Tetrahedron, Inc.; $29.95

1996; hardcover; 556 pp

illus; 0-923550-12-7

HIV/AIDS RESOURCES
The National Directory of Resources on HIV Infection/AIDS: The Professionals' Reference, 1996-97 Edition

Even though this huge directory doesn't offer alternative information on AIDS, it contains so much helpful, practical information that I wanted to include it anyway. As big as the telephone book for a fair-sized city, this book contains addresses, phone numbers, fax numbers, names of administrators, and capsule descriptions for thousands upon thousands of resources for people with HIV/AIDS (or people who think they might have it).

Part One is a guide to resources on a federal level. Information is given for all areas of the federal government that have anything to do with AIDS — the Executive branch, the Department of Health and Human Services, Public Health Service, Centres for Disease Control and Prevention, the FDA, the National Institutes of Health, Department of Defence, Senate Committees, and House Committees. Following that is contact information for nation-wide, private, non-profit organisations, such as American Civil Liberties Union Lesbian and Gay Rights AIDS Project, American College Health Association, Hospice Association of America, and the Ryan White Foundation.

Part Two is broken down by the fifty states and Washington DC. At the beginning of the section for each state is info on state-wide Health and Human Services offices, mental health services, medical services, community services, and education/prevention organisations. Then, each state is broken down into counties, and information for the above types of services is given for each and every county. In case you don't know what county you're dealing with, an index references the names of over 3500 cities and towns with the county in which they're located.

Obviously, *HIV/AIDS Resources* is aimed at AIDS organisations, medical facilities, libraries, etc., so check with them if you need this book.

Guides for Living; $110

1995; oversized softcover; 660 pp

1-885461-02-X

INNOCENT CASUALTIES
The FDA's War Against Humanity
by Elaine Feuer

In 1989 the True Health company tested its nutritional supplement on people with AIDS, and that clinical trial produced the most successful results of any study of nutrients *or* drugs on AIDS patients. Yet the FDA has done everything it can to destroy True Health. Midway through the 180-day study, the company held a press conference to announce the dramatic results that were already being achieved. "*All thirty patients who were infected with either HIV or AIDS had shown remarkable reversal and/or remission of their infections; T-4 cell counts doubled and tripled, and many patients were able to function and lead normal lives.*"

Shortly thereafter, two FDA agents visited Richard Stokely, head of True Life, at the company's headquarters. He believed that agents were there to congratulate him and discuss possible government funding of further studies. He quickly found out that what they really wanted was to stop the clinical trial and shut down True Health. "At first the FDA officials insisted that True Health's nutritional study had been released too soon; they also expressed concern over the amount of money True Health was charging test patients for the product. Stokely told them it was being supplied free of cost, as were the medical tests and Dr. Pulse's services. Whereupon the investigators decided that the nutritional supplement should be classified as a drug since it was a possible 'cure' for AIDS. [Agent] Ken Davis asked Stokely if he wanted to proceed with a drug classification, but Stokely immediately declined. To designate True Health's nutritional product a drug would be as ludicrous as writing a prescription for Vitamin C. Moreover, it takes about twelve years and $231 million to go from the synthesis to the approval of a new drug."

When it became apparent that Stokely wouldn't back down, the agents concocted some excuse to embargo 283 quart bottles of aloe vera juice (a completely natural product available in every health food store in the world), which was being used in the AIDS study. Several days later, one of the agents paid a visit to the doctor who was overseeing the clinical trial. "As he browsed through AIDS test patients' files, he told Dr. Pulse and his assistant, Elizabeth Uhlig: 'It is against God's law to save those gays.' Martinez later repeated the exact same statement to Stokely."

Innocent Casualities details True Health's battles with the FDA and the FTC (Federal Trade Commission), as well as how the company started, the specific results of its amazing AIDS study, the media's bias against True Health, and where the company stands right now. Because of a court order, "True Health was forced to refrain from selling or giving their products to AIDS patients as a treatment for AIDS, to stop giving the product out as they had been, free of charge, to the patients who had participated in the test." Technically, they might be able to sell the nutrient without making any specific health claims about it, but the small company is financially drained and fears further governmental harassment.

In the second part of the book, the author offers a succinct look at the FDA's disgraceful history of using police state tactics against nutrients while letting the public take dangerous medicines. She also provides a nice overview of non-mainstream ideas about AIDS and the politics that sur-rounds the condition. Several appendices cover nutrition, clinical studies of essential fatty acids, and more.

Dorrance Publishing Company; $15
1996; hardcover; 180 pp
illus; 0-8059-3819-2

REAPPRAISING AIDS

This short monthly newsletter from The Group for the Scien-tific Reappraisal of the HIV/AIDS Hypothesis is the only regu-lar publication I've seen that's fully devoted to exploring al-ternative ideas concerning AIDS, mainly the hypotheses that HIV is only partly responsible or not responsible at all for causing the disease.

The Group/7514 Girard Ave #1-331/La Jolla CA 92037
WWW: www.virusmyth.com/aids/reappraising/index.html
Twelve issue sub (one year): $25. Non-US: $35

THE RIGHTS OF PEOPLE WHO ARE HIV POSITIVE

by William B. Rubenstein, et al

As part of its series that spells out the exact legal rights of various groups, the American Civil Liberties Union has cre-ated this thick guide to the rights of people who have HIV. Using a question and answer format, it covers a large number of areas: HIV testing, confidentiality, public health measures, liability for transmission of HIV, health care, private insur-ance, public benefits, planning for incapacity and death, fam-ily law, discrimination (with regards to housing, employment, public places, and access to health care), and special cir-cumstances (in schools, in prisons, immigration, and intra-venous drug use). Among the many, many questions that are answered:

☞ "Does the law permit testing of individuals without informed consent?"

☞ "In what circumstances, if any, can a health care provider breach a person's confidentiality so as to warn third parties who may be at risk of contracting HIV?"

☞ "What are the elements of a negligence claim against a supplier of blood or blood products, and have such claims been successful?"

☞ "Can insurance companies impose limits on the amount of coverage provided for HIV-related treatment?"

☞ "Must a couple be HIV-tested to get a marriage license?"

☞ "May restrictions be placed on the infected child's freedom to attend school?"

Southern Illinois University Press; $13.95
1996; softcover; 392 pp
0-8093-1992-6

CANCER

BREAST CANCER
Poison, Profits, and Prevention

by Liane Clorfene-Casten

Statistics imply that one in eight women will develop breast cancer sometime in her life. The number of women who have died from breast cancer since 1960 (950,000) is much greater than the number of Americans who have died in all wars fought this century (617,000). And almost half of these can-cer deaths occurred in the ten-year period from 1981 to 1991.

Investigative reporter Liane Clorfene-Casten exposes what she considers the main causes of this epidemic: chemi-cals and radiation. She believes that 70% of breast cancer cases are caused by artificial, toxic substances in the air, water, food, and elsewhere. Furthermore, she says that "the leaders of the 'war on cancer' have known this for decades and have refused to deal with this information." To back up that statement, she cites numerous scientific studies, often performed by the medical establishment, that are practically unknown to the general population. "In 1964, the World Health Organisation (WHO) concluded that 80 percent of cancers were due to human-produced carcinogens." Exam-ple two: "In a Connecticut study, levels of PCBs and DDT were 50-60 percent higher in the breast tissue of women with breast cancer than in women without breast cancer." Example three: "The EPA found that US counties with waste sites were 6.5 times more likely to have elevated breast can-cer rates than counties that did not have such sites."

Among the most insidious cancer-causing agents are DDT and related chemicals, polychlorinated biphenyls (PCBs), dioxins, synthetic human hormones, bovine growth hormones, nuclear radiation, and xenoestrogens (harmful chemicals that mimic oestrogen in the body). The author examines each of these substances and traces the ways in which they enter the human body — pesticides, lawn care products, workplace contamination, nuclear power plants, nuclear bomb tests, x-rays, hormone replacement therapy, etc. She also acknowledges the smaller roles that she feels other factors — such as obesity, family history, and exces-sive alcohol consumption — play in breast cancer.

A chapter is devoted to each of three poisons masquer-ading as something else. The synthetic hormone tamoxifen — which has been classified as a carcinogen by the WHO — is being touted as a possible *preventative* for breast can-cer. Mammograms, which use radiation to scan the breast for tumours, can help cause cancer and are of dubious value anyway. Then, of course, you have silicone breast implants, supposed enhancements that are being implicated in se-vere health problems.

A particularly hard-hitting portion of the book exposes deceitful politics, conflicts of interest, and outright failures of the US government (the EPA, USDA, and FDA), the cancer establishment (the National Cancer Institute and the American Cancer Society), corporations (drug companies and chemical companies, which are sometimes one and the same), and the media in owning up to the environmental causes of breast cancer and doing something about it.

This powerful book ends with suggestions for protecting the public health through public action and for protecting your own health through individual action.

Common Courage Press; $18.95

1996; softcover; 341 pp

1-56751-094-9

THE BURZYNSKI BREAKTHROUGH
The Century's Most Promising Cancer Treatment and the Government's Campaign to Squelch It

by Thomas D. Elias

Dr. Stanislaw Burzynski has developed an anti-cancer therapy that has achieved astounding success rates. He introduces antineoplastons — naturally-occurring peptides — into people with cancer, and quite often the cancer is slowed or completely eliminated. Burzynski found that the blood and urine of healthy people contains peptides that are lacking in people with cancer. When these peptides are put back into the body, they can return cancerous cells to their normal, healthy state of functioning.

Thomas Elias tells of this unorthodox but successful treatment by focusing in-depth on several patients who have been cured of cancer and by looking at other evidence that antineoplastons often work. "In late 1996, he [Burzynski] submitted 28 current brain tumour cases for review by independent radiologists at the Southwest Neuro-Imaging centre in Phoenix. The results reported by independent radiologists: Thirteen patients saw their tumours shrink by more than 50 percent, while three more had significant improvement but less than a 50 percent reduction. Then he submitted 17 cases for evaluation by Dr. Robert Burdick of the University of Washington. Results: almost half were complete remissions. These results were achieved for brain cancers that are almost always fast-growing and deadly."

Like many practitioners who get results by using natural, alternative methods, the Doc has been hounded by the Food and Drug Administration. In early 1997, he was brought to trial in US District Court on over 70 counts of insurance fraud and interstate commerce of an unapproved drug. This was the fourth time in twelve years that the FDA tried to indict Burzynski, and this time they finally got they wanted. However, the trial ended in a hung jury, and the court ordered an acquittal on the fraud charges. He was retried that May on the interstate commerce charges and was again acquitted.

Besides writing of the results Burzynski has achieved and the trial that resulted, the author also tells of Doctor B's life, his struggle to continue healing desperately sick people, and the endless harassment and smearing he receives from the medical establishment, which involves "elements of personal vendetta, industry betrayal and apparent dishonesty at the highest levels of America's scientific institutions."

If you want clear, detailed information on an alternative

At a rally, Dr Burzynski holds a patient whose life he saved.
The Burzynski Breakthrough.

cancer therapy that often works and on the repercussions that this has triggered, *The Burzynski Breakthrough* is the book for you.

General Publishing Group; $22.95

1997; hardcover; 294 pp

illus; 1-57544-018-0

THE CANCELL CHRONICLES
Why Is a Possible Cure for Cancer Being Suppressed?

by Louise B. Trull

CanCell is a substance that thousands of people claim has rid them of cancer. It's been around since the 1940s and has been distributed free of charge since the beginning. Its creator is a Michigan metallurgist named Edward J. Sopcak. (OK, at first it does seem weird that an expert in metals may have cured cancer, but you have to remember that many of the greatest discoveries and inventions of all time — some say over half — have come from people working outside their fields of expertise. The reason is simple: not having been formally trained in a subject, they haven't been locked into the orthodoxy that surrounds that subject. They haven't been told that certain things are "impossible", so they go ahead and do them.)

Sopcak was basing his work on the advances of James V. Sheridan, a chemist who felt that energy flows trigger cancer. He devised a substance, Entelev, that used chemicals to alter these flows. Entelev has reportedly been successful in curing cancer and other diseases. Sheridan says that over 100 people have been cured of AIDS and fifteen of genital herpes with his creation.

Sopcak feels that Sheridan is definitely on the right track, but that it is vibrational frequencies that are adversely affecting cells. With this in mind, he created CanCell. At first it was identical to Entelev, but gradually Sopcak modified it. Now it works by altering the vibrations of cancerous cells. These two men manufactured and shipped their substances to people who requested them for around 50 years. They have not made a single penny from their creations, and thousands of people say they have been cured of cancer.

Of course, no good deed goes unpunished, so the FDA and the cancer establishment have had fits about CanCell and Entelev. After many battles, Sheridan obeyed a 1989 court order and stopped helping people get rid of cancer.

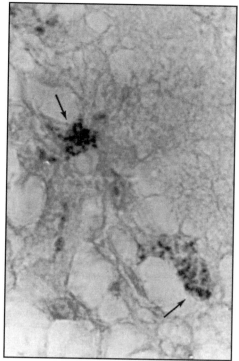

The darkened areas represent possible cancer microbes.
The Cancer Microbe.

tiple sex partners, and high stress.

Some mycobacteria are known to cause TB and leprosy, and Cantwell believes that another kind is responsible for cancer. He has, in fact, found the "cancer microbe" in several types of cancer, both by observing it under the microscope and growing samples in cultures. As further evidence of cancer's bacterial nature, Cantwell points out that Kaposi's sarcoma (KS) is an extremely rare form of cancer that used to strike only men of Jewish, Italian, and Greek descent. Yet it is the second most common opportunistic disease to invade people with AIDS. Since AIDS depresses the immune system, KS must be infectious. What else would explain its prevalence?

This mycobacterium also cause other diseases, including scleroderma (a fatal hardening of the skin and internal organs), sarcoidosis, and AIDS itself. (For more information on Cantwell's theories about AIDS, see *AIDS: The Mystery and the Solution* and *Queer Blood: The Secret AIDS Genocide Plot* [*Outposts* pp 151 & 153].)

Throughout the book, Cantwell weaves in details of his personal life, and he examines the work of other medical iconoclasts — Wilhelm Reich, Antoine Bechamp, and Virginia Livingston — whose work followed paths similar to his own. The book ends with 19 full-page microphotographs, four in colour, that plainly show the cancer microbe in diseased tissue and laboratory cultures.

Aries Rising Press; $19.95
1990; softcover; 283 pp
illus; 0-917211-01-4

Sopcak disobeyed his cease and desist order in 1990 but finally relented in 1992. He's currently appealing against the ruling.

The CanCell Controversy also reprints a report by Sheridan that explains how Entelev/CanCell works (it was written when they were identical substances). There is also testimony from a dozen people who say that CanCell cured them, along with corroborating testimony from their physicians. Finally, and perhaps most importantly, this book tells you how you can obtain CanCell for free. A small outfit in Michigan — whom I admire more than I can say — is making sure it stays available. Plus, there are instructions for using CanCell effectively.

Hampton Roads Publishing Company; $9.95
1993; softcover; 149 pp
1-878901-76-1

THE CANCER MICROBE
The Hidden Killer in Cancer, AIDS, and Other Immune Diseases
by Alan Cantwell, Jr, MD

Medical orthodoxy says that cancer is not a contagious or infectious disease and that it has no bacterial cause. Dr. Alan Cantwell vehemently disagrees, saying that cancer is caused by a mycobacterium. This bacterium is always present in people's cells, but it only gains the upper hand when people punish their bodies' immune systems through bad diet, mul-

CANCER THERAPY
The Independent Consumer's Guide to Non-Toxic Treatment and Prevention (Revised Edition)
by Ralph W. Moss, PhD

This thick guide reports on the efficacy and safety of 80 unorthodox cancer treatments. The author is careful to present a balanced picture, showing when a treatment hasn't achieved wonderful results, as well as when it has. The nearly 1000 references that he provides all come from peer-reviewed mainstream medical journals that are widely respected by orthodox professionals. In other words, it's hard to argue with the results presented in this book.

A chart in the front of *Cancer Therapy* lists all the therapies covered along with the cancers they've been most effective in combating, so if you're interested in a particular kind of cancer, you can jump right to the most appropriate treatments. The methods — each of which is dealt with separately — are divided into groups: vitamins, including A, B, and D; minerals, including calcium, lithium, and zinc; herbs, including aloe, essiac, and Hoxsey therapy; diets, such as macrobiotics; "From Earth and Sea", including algae, coenzyme Q, and mushrooms; "Less Toxic Drugs", such as arginine, DMSO, and urea; electromagnetism, including heat therapy and photo therapy; immune boosters, such as krestin, MTH-68, and thymic factors; and less documented modalities, such as CanCell, carnivora, and Naessens (714X). Each treatment is followed by full medical references, and each section is followed by a resource section, which tells how to get the substances or where to have the therapies performed.

To give an example of the kind of information you'll find — the chapter on ginseng tells of a Korean study in which rats were fed a carcinogen, along with one of four food substances. Of the "control" rats, who weren't given any of the food substances, 44% developed cancer. But only 3.4% of the ones who were given ginseng and a carcinogen got the disease. In Japan, ninety people with cancerous tumours were treated with a new microwave heating system, which raised the temperatures of their tumours to above 107°F (42°C). "Two-thirds of the tumours either partially or completely regressed." Obviously, not all the results presented in this book are that wonderful, but I wanted to make the point that many of these treatments are very promising.

In *Outposts* I told everyone who had cancer or knew someone who did that they must get a copy of *Options*. This time around, I make the same urgent recommendation for *Cancer Therapies*.

Equinox Press; $19.95
1992, 1994; softcover; 523 pp
1-881025-06-3

DRESSED TO KILL
The Link Between Breast Cancer and Bras
by Sydney Ross Singer & Soma Grismaijer

It's an established fact that certain articles of clothing can be detrimental to health. High-heeled shoes cause leg and back problems. Tight underwear and pants are supposedly contributing to the drastically reduced sperm count among the male population. And the wasp-waist corsets popular in the nineteeth century could mess up women internally. One piece of clothing, though, has escaped notice as a potential health risk until now. The authors claim that there is substantial evidence that bras trigger breast cancer and other problems.

The main problem is that bras constrict the lymphatic system within the breasts. Less oxygen and other nutrients get to the cells, and toxins build up in the tissue. "Human breasts have developed over hundreds of thousands, if not millions, of years without constraint. It has been biologically impossible to adapt to bras in the short time since their invention. Women's breasts were clearly not designed by nature to be shaped the way bras try to shape them."

There is much evidence that indicates the existence of a bra/cancer connection. As women get older, the potential for breast cancer increases, which makes sense if toxins are building up over a woman's lifetime. Breast cancer is more prominent among Western industrialised countries, where bras are an unquestioned part of everyday life for almost all women. As other countries become more Westernised, their breast cancer rates increase. Breast cancer is the most common form of cancer among women. "In our culture, no part of the female body is as highly constricted, or constricted for as long a time each day, as are the breasts." Around 90% of women will experience a breast lump, the vast majority of which are benign. Many of these benign

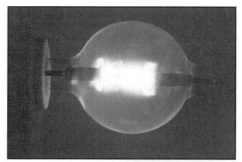

The Rife Beam Ray Device in action.
Resonant Frequency Theory.

lumps are sacs filled with — guess what — lymph fluid.

To further test their hypothesis, the authors conducted a year-and-a-half long survey. They interviewed 4500 women in five major American cities. Approximately half the women had been diagnosed with breast cancer and half hadn't. "[W]e learned that women who wear bras twenty-four hours a day have a 125-fold greater chance of getting breast cancer than do women who do not wear bras at all, and a 113-fold greater chance of getting breast cancer than do women who wear bras for less than twelve hours daily. This is anywhere from 4 to 12 times greater in significance than the connection between cigarette smoking and lung cancer!"

The authors spend a good deal of time discussing why breasts and bras are so important to our society, and the sexual and fashion factors involved in bra wearing. They also make recommendations for decreasing your chances of developing breast cancer from bras. The best solution, of course, is to quit wearing them. If you can't, the authors give tips on minimising the time you do wear bras and how to select ones that fit properly.

Avery Publishing Company; $11.95
1995; softcover; 192 pp
0-89529-664-0

QUESTIONING CHEMOTHERAPY
by Ralph W. Moss, PhD

Instead of promoting alternative cancer treatments, this book takes a look at what is wrong with one of the most popular mainstream treatments — chemotherapy. This form of treatment had its modern start in the chemical warfare research that took place during World War II. Researchers found that a new form of mustard gas had a deleterious effect on cells, so a Yale anatomist had the idea to inject it into mice with tumours. That led to more experiments with different substances, resulting in the chemotherapy industry that's in place today.

Despite what the medical establishment would have you believe, "chemo" is, on the whole, an ineffectual and damaging process. Ralph Moss, who began his career as a science writer at a cancer centre, indicates that many doctors are highly aware of this fact. "I heard the widely used drug BCNU jokingly referred to as 'Be seein' you,' and 5-FU as 'Five Feet Under.'" If you read an oncology nurse's manual for precautions to take when preparing chemotherapy drugs, you'd think they were handling nuclear waste. The manual "warns that cytotoxic agents pose a 'significant risk' of damage to the skin, reproductive abnormalities, haematologic problems, and of liver and chromosomal lesions... Nurses are instructed to protect themselves with long-sleeved gowns, face shields or goggles and latex surgical gloves, which should be changed every half hour."

Even more unbelievable is the fact that some cancer drugs can actually accelerate the cancer, and others — are you ready for this? — can *cause* cancer. "To give just one example of carcinogenicity, doctors looked at one-year survivors of ovarian cancer from five randomised trials. The incident rates for acute nonlymphocytic leukaemia and for pre-leukaemia were about 100 times more common in women who got the drug melphalan than in those who received no chemotherapy."

Moss examines in detail the effectiveness of chemotherapy in fighting almost 50 types of cancer, including breast, colon/rectum, lung, and ovarian. With a few exceptions — and even they are not too encouraging — clinical trials reveal that chemo is ineffective and is not of any survival benefit.

Other parts of the book cover the multibillion dollar chemo industry, unintentional bias and outright fraud in clinical chemo trials, methods of decreasing the side effects of chemotherapy, questioning your doctor, and the major drugs used in the treatment.

Equinox Press; $19.95
1995; softcover; 214 pp
1-881025-25-X

RESONANT FREQUENCY THERAPY
Building the Rife Beam Ray Device

by James E. Bare, DC

In the 1930s, Dr. Royal Rife created a device that cured people of cancer. According to the short introduction in this book: "Dr. Rife's device was tested in a 1934 clinical trial performed by Medical Physicians associated with the University of Southern California, at the Scripps Ranch in California. The results of this research test were that 14 out of 16 people in the test were pronounced cured of their Cancer in 60 days. The remaining two people were pronounced cured in the next 60 days." On top of that, the device also was credited with curing cataracts.

The technology driving Rife's amazing invention somehow got lost and has only now been possibly recreated. James Bare believes that he has developed a device that, while it may not be exactly what Rife used, is very close and produces results that are as good or better than its predecessor. Both devices use electrical resonance. In Bare's device, a transmitter (in the form of a CB radio) puts out audio and radio waves, which are amplified, and then fed into an antenna tuner. The tuner sends the waves into a plasma tube, where they are modulated with light waves, and these three types of waves create a form of energy known as plasma. It is the plasma that travels into the patient's cells, bypassing the cells' natural resistance to out-

"After a romantic weekend in Mexico, Ralph called to tell me: 'I love the asymmetry of your chest.'"
Dani & Ralph, *Winged Victory.*

side stimuli. Harmful cells and micro-organisms are destroyed or devitalised (i.e., most of their activities are stopped). Bare's experiments on cells and animals — and other people's experiments on humans — indicate that this device is helpful in treating cancer, herpes, Lyme disease, influenza, pain, joint inflammation, and other diseases and disorders. (For more info, see Bare's Webpage at http://www.rt66.com/~rifetech.)

This book presents clear, complete instructions for building and using the Rife/Bare device. It can be constructed with easily obtainable off-the-shelf components (CB, linear amplifier, antenna tuner, plasma tube, square wave generator, and various smaller parts) that cost $890 to $1000 total. Building this device isn't supposed to be terribly difficult, but it's definitely over my head. From what I can tell, though, it should be within reach of an amateur electronics buff. Bare walks you through every step, lists sources for the components, and then discusses various ways to use what you've built (best frequencies for various purposes, duration of exposure, etc.). The instructions are augmented with numerous diagrams and photographs. Because this book is photocopied, the photos aren't exactly crystal clear, but they are adequate.

Bare also puts out a videotape, *The Beam Ray Device: Construction, Operation, and Effects on Selected Micro Organisms* [$20 + $4 shipping; 100 minutes]. The first half of the tape shows actual footage of protozoa being destroyed by the plasma emanating from a Rife/Bare device ten feet away. The second half shows you how to build and use the device.

Bare's device is still highly experimental and can be dangerous if misused, but if you'd like to carry on the crucial, life-saving work of Rife, this is your best opportunity.

James E. Bare, DC; $25

1995-1997; oversized comb-bound softcover; 133 pp

illus; no ISBN

WINGED VICTORY
Altered Images — Transcending Breast Cancer

by Art Myers and others

When Art Myers — a fine art photographer and physician — found out that his wife had breast cancer, an idea was born. He wanted to take portraits of women whose breasts had been operated on. But not just any type of portraits... they had to be topless or completely nude shots. They had to show women who are not at all ashamed or upset by their scars or missing breasts.

The result is *Winged Victory*, which contains black and white photos of fifteen women who have had breast cancer. Some of them had reconstructive surgery and now have a breast with deep scars. Others are missing one breast, and several had radical double mastectomies. Tanya, wearing a huge grin and a tuxedo, has her shirt pulled open to reveal the breastless left side of her chest. Karen, a radiologist, stands topless next to a mammography machine that she operates. In one of several shots involving couples, Richard reaches around and "cups" the chest of his wife Andrea, who had her breasts removed. Both of them are laughing. Yavonne is the subject of the two photos that are overtly sexy, defiantly making sure that her scarred left breast is prominent. Bodybuilder Lisa shows off her well-defined form, which includes a supple breast on one side of her chest and a chiselled "pec" on the other side. Besides these straightforward portraits, there are seven other shots that are moody, abstracted mastectomy nudes.

Maria Marrocchino contributes several poems on dealing with breast cancer, and the subjects of the photos offer their comments, which are usually touching or humorous, sometimes both at the same time. Dani, whose left breast was removed, says that "after a romantic weekend in Mexico, Ralph called to tell me: 'I love the asymmetry of your chest.' I smiled and laughed to myself — thinking of how hard he must have thought to come up with the perfect compliment." One of the most arresting shots is of Dora, an 83-year-old Christian grandmother, and her husband of 60 years, Cy. She, perhaps inadvertently, offers the whole reason for the creation of this book. "While I was in the hospital shortly after surgery, Cy's aunt was sitting by my bedside. I remember her saying, 'Whatever you do, Dora, never let anyone see your scar, and especially never let Cy see it.'" In *Winged Victory*, all of these women have triumphantly defied Cy's aunt and everyone who thinks like her, showing that breasts are not a prerequisite of beauty or confidence.

Photographic Gallery of Fine Art Books; $24.95

1996; oversized softcover; 56 pp

heavily illus; 1-889169-00-5

ALTERNATIVE HEALTH

ACCEPTING YOUR POWER TO HEAL
The Personal Practice of Therapeutic Touch

by Dolores Krieger, PhD, RN

Therapeutic Touch is the name of a technique that Dr. Dolores Krieger developed by combining several ancient healing practices involving the laying-on of hands and the redirection of energy flow. This practice is now taught in universities throughout the US and seventy other countries. It involves "only the explicit, conscious direction and modulation of natural human energies..." TT is not a miracle cure — "it is simply an opportunity to actualise the natural human potential to help or heal yourself or others."

Therapeutic Touch has four main benefits. It causes rapid relaxation, clinically reduces pain, accelerates the healing process, and alleviates psychosomatic illnesses. Krieger explains the underlying principles of TT and gives detailed descriptions of the methods used in feeling human energy fields, assessing them, and directing them with three major techniques and several spin-offs. After presenting the general uses of TT, Krieger tells how to work with seven conditions, including pregnancy, PMS, and AIDS. There are lots of instructional diagrams for you to refer to, as well as exercises to centre yourself, increase your sensitivity, manipulate energies, work with a partner, and more.

Bear & Company Publishing; $14

1993; softcover; 199 pp

illus; 1-879181-04-5

THE BACKYARD MEDICINE CHEST
An Herbal Primer

by Douglas Schar

We Americans spend billions of dollars a year on over-the-counter remedies for all our aches, pains, and other relatively minor bodily problems. The funny thing is, mother nature has already come up with treatments for these conditions. Herbalist and gardener Douglas Schar has written a witty, user-friendly guide to the herbs that can cure what ails you.

The book is divided into sections dealing with digestive problems, respiratory problems, female problems, nervous problems, skin problems, and problems with muscles, joints, and the back. Each section is subdivided into chapters that cover a specific ailment, such as diarrhoea, nausea, flu, allergies, PMS, muscular pain, headache, insomnia, poor complexion, and fifteen others. For each one, Schar tells what is actually causing the ailment and which single herb will best get rid of it (an illustration of each herb is included). He then discusses the properties of the herb, why it works, how it's

The*Backyard*
MEDICINE CHEST

An
Herbal
Primer

By *Douglas Schar*

Mother Nature's Rx.
The Backyard Medicine Chest.

resistant to drugs. Suddenly, pneumonia, tuberculosis, and ear infections are becoming deadly again. In *Beyond Antibiotics*, the authors discuss this and other reasons to stay away from antibiotics — they also kill friendly bacteria, they suppress your immune system in the long run, they can cause yeast overgrowth, they may contribute to Chronic Fatigue Syndrome, and more.

There are many things you can do and not do to make your immune system stronger. One chapter examines the obviously important subjects of nutrition and food. It's no surprise that most of us need to eat more nutritious food and less junk. But it's surprising to learn what may be bad for us. "Excessive consumption of cow's milk may be one of the major factors contributing to susceptibility to common infections." Our environment contains many threats to immunity — parasites, heavy metals, mould, pesticides — that we can reduce to a degree. The chapter on lifestyle shows the roles of touch, sleep, smoking, alcohol, prayer, meditation, and other factors on our immunity. Other topics covered by the authors include stress, anger, meaningful relationships, laughter, vitamins, herbs, plant oils, homeopathy, and chiropractic. Chapter 11 offers non-toxic treatments for fourteen conditions that are usually treated by antibiotics, including acne, the flu, and sore throat.

North Atlantic Books; $18.95
1993; softcover; 342 pp
1-55643-180-5

been used throughout history and different cultures, how you should use it, and how to get it (whether by buying it and/or growing it). He also throws in some personal anecdotes testifying to the plants' effectiveness.

It turns out that the leaves and root of the marshmallow plant are great for treating irritated skin brought on by boils, abscesses, burns, bedsores, stings, etc. In fact, marshmallow is well known for being able to "magically" draw out insect stingers and splinters embedded in the skin. It also relieves the resulting pain. Schar's nephew got stung by a swarm of hornets, and he applied the herb. "A Virginia hornet sting can hurt a grown-up for days, and for kids it's even worse. I am happy to report that my nephew's pain went away completely within two hours' time!"

The book also contains methods for making tinctures and base cremes. Keep *The Backyard Medicine Chest* in your medicine chest instead of all those overpriced chemicals.

Elliott & Clark Publishing; $12.95
1995; softcover; 159 pp
illus; 1-880216-28-0

BEYOND ANTIBIOTICS
50 (or So) Ways to Boost Immunity and Avoid Antibiotics

by Michael A. Schmidt and others

It's no secret that antibiotics are bad news. Even the mainstream media are reporting that massive overuse of antibiotics for decades has resulted in strains of bacteria that are

DIMENSIONS OF RADIONICS

by David V. Tansley with Malcolm Rae & Aubrey T. Westlake

The radionic method of healing theorises that we exist in a vast sea of etheric energy, which flows around us and through us. All of us, in fact, have etheric bodies in addition to our physical bodies. Medical problems arise when the flow of etheric energy is disturbed or interrupted. "The procedures of radionic diagnosis and treatment then, are a means by which the practitioner can determine what factors lie within the mental and astral bodies and the etheric form, which serve to hamper and distort the flow of energy from the soul by way of the chakras. In doing so the way is opened for the practitioner to give very real aid to the incarnated soul by removing those blockages to energy expression which lie on the mental, astral and etheric levels."

Dimensions of Radionics is considered a classic, even the "Bible", of this form of healing. David Tansley supplies the theoretical background, explaining the intricate web of energy that makes up all of reality, while Malcolm Rae focuses on the applied aspects of the field. You'll learn to build devices that can detect and analyse the ethers. After a diagnosis is made, the instruments can be used to project energy at the patient, or therapy involving gems, colour, flower essences, vitamins, tissue salts, or homeopathy can be employed.

Brotherhood of Life; $17.95
1977, 1997; softcover; 214 pp
illus; 0-914732-29-3

HOME CHIROPRACTIC HANDBOOK AND VIDEO

by Dr. Karl V. Holmquist, Chiropractor

It is possible to do most forms of alternative healing at home by yourself. Generally speaking, though, chiropractic is an exception to this rule. According to Dr. Karl Holmquist — who has given over 100,000 adjustments during his 20 years of practice — chiropractic is a vicious cycle that keeps you dependent on trips to your chiropractor. In a revolutionary move (and one that has upset more than a few of his colleagues), Holmquist now teaches us how to adjust family, friends, and ourselves.

Home Chiropractic Handbook tells you everything you need to get cracking. After presenting basic ideas on the "chiropractic philosophy, science, and art", Holmquist gives an illustrated lesson on the anatomy of the spinal column, the vertebrae, the ribs, the pelvis, related muscles, and how the spine connects to bodily systems (glandular, nervous, digestive, etc.). The next chapter acquaints you with how the spine feels and what you are feeling when you place your hands in certain areas.

The bulk of the book gives instructions for forty chiropractic techniques. For each technique, there is a full page photograph and the following information: which misalignment it's used for, how to place hands and fingers on the spine, the direction of the movement, pressure, force, speed, and more.

In order to have somewhere to apply these techniques, the author explains how to make a simple correcting table. He also advises when you should see a professional chiropractor and how to choose a good one. The two final chapters give further advice on achieving optimum health, including the roles played by your mind and emotions.

The accompanying videotape is a professional production which demonstrates how each technique in the book is performed. Every move is viewed from at least two camera angles. Holmquist also covers a few techniques not in the book that you can use to adjust yourself. The video is essential to fully understanding how each technique is safely and effectively performed.

One 8 Publishing; $69.95
1985; softcover; 194 pp
1991; VHS videocassette; 100 min
heavily illus; 0-935081-00-3

NATURAL ALTERNATIVES TO PROZAC

by Michael T. Murray, ND

Over six million people regularly take the prescription drug Prozac, which is intended to fight depression. Unfortunately, there are some downsides to the drug. Its reported side effects — particularly the ability to trigger violent and/or suicidal behaviour in some users — are alarming. Also, there is evidence that it is no more effective than many other older (and cheaper) anti-depressants. Natural Alternatives to Prozac covers these topics in the first chapter (for more detailed information see Talking Back to Prozac [Outposts p 170]). It also proposes a new model for depression, discusses how to uncover easily reversible organic causes of depres-

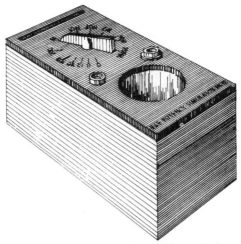

The Mark III Potency Simulator.
Dimensions of Radionics.

sion, and looks at the crucial roles of lifestyle factors (smoking, drinking, exercise) and nutritional factors (vitamin deficiencies, too much refined sugar) in depression. The final sixty-three pages examine in detail five natural substances that combat depression — St. John's Wort, kava, ginkgo biloba, amino acids, and melatonin. For each, the book covers how it works, dosage, safety issues, clinical studies and case histories demonstrating effectiveness, and more.

William Morrow and Company; $20
1996; hardcover; 227 pp
0-68814684-8

NATURAL HEALING FOR SCHIZOPHRENIA
A Compendium of Nutritional Methods

by Eva Edelman

Eva Edelman believes that almost every single case of schizophrenia is caused by some sort of biochemical imbalance. The brain is either deficient in certain nutrients or is being overloaded with toxins (or both). In this book, Edelman looks at natural methods being used to correct these problems.

Nutritionally-oriented medical researchers, in such fields as orthomolecular and biochemical medicine, have developed biotypes, which are classifications for people based on aspects of their biochemistry. These researchers claim that 80% to 95% of schizophrenics fall into at least one of four biotypes and that, after being treated properly, 90% of them recover from schizophrenia. Two of the biotypes involve either an oversupply or an undersupply of histamine, a brain neurotransmitter and neurohormone that plays a crucial role in mood, appetite, sleep, thought, metabolism, and immunity. In the third biotype, pyroluria, the person has an excess of urinary kryptopyrroles, which depletes the body of zinc and vitamin B6. People who fall into the final biotype have allergies to food or other substances that cause swelling and other damage to the brain, especially the cerebrum. For each of these biotypes, Edelman provides identifying physical and mental tendencies and symptoms, as well as treatment recommendations.

Around 10% to 15% of schizophrenics don't fit neatly into any biotype, but are nutritionally deficient in a variety of ways. Part two of this book looks at over 20 vitamins, minerals, and electrolytes that are often present in low quantities in schizophrenics. The roles, sources, and side effects of each one are discussed.

Other sections examine problems that may overlap the main causes of schizophrenia or that may cause symptoms of schizophrenia. Neurotoxins such as caffeine, alcohol, pesticides, lead, and free radicals can disrupt the brain's activities in a number of ways. Certain illnesses — candida, syphilis, lupus, epilepsy, endocrine disorders, and others — can trigger mental symptoms that are almost indistinguishable from schizophrenia.

Further topics that are covered include autism, depression, neurotransmitter imbalance, toxic treatments for schizophrenia, physical and mental tests, the definition of schizophrenia, the struggle of nutritional treatments to gain acceptance, and more. A resources section lists alternative treatment centres, diagnostic labs, and organisations.

Edelman has done a spectacular job presenting lots of detailed information in a way that can be easily understood and applied. Moreover, the book's design is not only pleasing to the eye, but also assists in clearly conveying the concepts. This book is a must if there is a schizophrenic in your life.

Borage Books; $24.95
1996; oversized softcover; 202 pp
illus; no ISBN

NATURAL HORMONE REPLACEMENT FOR WOMEN OVER 45

by Jonathan V. Wright, MD, & John Morgenthaler

For most women, the ebb and flow of hormones (most notably oestrogen and progesterone) that began in puberty will begin to change when they reach their early to mid-40s and, by the time they hit their 50s, it will be so altered that their periods will stop, marking the end of their reproductive stage of life. This infamous change of life, menopause, often brings with it a number of unpleasant effects, including hot flashes, decreased sex drive, vaginal thinning and dryness, irregular sleep, poor memory, mood swings, and depression. In the long run, this radical hormone change leads to an increased risk of cardiovascular disease (by far the leading cause of death in women who have been through menopause), cancer, osteoporosis, and senility.

In order to avoid these possible effects, millions of women undergo Oestrogen Replacement Therapy (typically with the drug Premarin®) or Hormone Replacement Therapy (typically with Provera®). As the authors of this book demonstrate, there are many problems with these forms of treatment. The overarching problem is that they don't actually use hormones, but rather synthetic forms of hormones. While they apparently do lessen the chances of cardiovascular disease and osteoporosis, these drugs have been shown to increase the risk of developing uterine and breast cancer. They can also trigger such side effects as bloating, nausea, anxiety, and vaginal discharge. Some forms of oestrogen used in replacement therapies are actually horse oestrogen, which is metabolised differently in the human body and can lead to all kinds of problems.

The solution to this quandary is blindingly simple — replace the missing hormones with the same *natural, human* hormones. The authors show us the studies and testimonials that prove that Natural Hormone Replacement provides all of the benefits of its synthetic equivalent, with hardly any of the side effects. NHR reduces the long term risks of menopause and alleviates the symptoms. (The medical evidence of this has been around for decades, but it has been ignored because natural hormones are not patentable, so the medical industry can't make much, if any, money from them.) If all of this sounds good to you, read this book in order to find out — in clear, nontechnical terms — exactly what natural hormones are, how you should use them, where you can get them, and how you can find a doctor who will prescribe the ones that are available by prescription only.

Smart Publications; $9.95
1997; softcover; 128 pp
illus; 0-9627418-0-9

OXYGEN HEALING THERAPIES
For Optimum Health and Vitality

by Nathaniel Altman

This groundbreaking book examines the impressive research demonstrating that bio-oxidative therapies (more commonly called oxygen therapies) are effective in treating cancer, immune disorders (such as AIDS and candida), heart and circulatory disease, asthma, migraine headaches, and other disorders. The root cause of these problems is that people's cells are starved for oxygen, mostly due to air pollution, tobacco smoking, processed and preserved food, stress, radiation, and poor breathing.

The process of oxidation occurs when oxygen atoms combine with other atoms. In our bodies, this process creates molecules that attack viruses and bacteria. Oxygenation is a related phenomenon that refers to the saturation of various components of the body with oxygen. This process helps our bodies get rid of toxins.

Exactly what to these therapies do? "Bio-oxidative therapies accelerate oxygen metabolism and stimulate the release of oxygen atoms from the bloodstream to the cells... When large amounts of oxygen flood the body, germs, parasites, fungi, bacteria, and viruses are killed along with diseased and deficient tissue cells. At the same time, healthy cells not only survive but are better able to multiply."

The author explains the history, principles, successes, and limitations of the two kinds of bio-oxidative therapies. He examines in detail their uses in treating cardiovascular diseases, cancer, and HIV/AIDS, and he covers over 30 disorders — everything from senile dementia to snakebites — in lesser detail. His facts come from world-wide practitioners as well as studies published in medical journals, including *Lancet* and *Cancer*.

Despite this, mainstream medicine hates these therapies. "Ozone… has been used extensively in Europe for over 30 years to treat a wide variety of medical conditions, including heart disease, cancer, and AIDS. However, medical doctors in the United States and Canada who use bio-oxidative therapies are often persecuted by state medical authorities and medical societies. Some have even had their practices closed down."

Should you want to try these therapies yourself, the author lists addresses of several groups that can give you more information and help you find a practitioner. He also spends a good deal of the book describing a holistic health regimen to use along with the therapies. It includes body purifications, an oxygen-rich diet, aerobic exercise, vitamins, minerals, and mind/body healing.

Inner Traditions; $12.95
1995; softcover; 201 pp
illus; 0-89281-527-2

PLANT SPIRIT MEDICINE

by Eliot Cowan

Using herbs and other plants to heal and maintain health is a popular practice in the US and all over the world. However, herbalist and acupuncturist Eliot Cowan reminds us that we have lost the deeper meaning of natural healing. Native healers believed that it wasn't actually the plant doing the healing but instead the spirit in the plant. Today, when we pop our ginger or Echinacea capsules from the health food store, we don't even think about the deeper, original meaning behind what we're doing.

Cowan — who is the designated successor of an elder Huichol Indian shaman and plant spirit healer — teaches us how to get into contact with the spirits of the plants. "There is only one active ingredient in plant medicines — friendship. A plant spirit heals a patient as a favour to its friend-in-dreaming, the doctor." But you don't need exotic Amazonian shamans to make use of the plants/spirits. "If you want to meet the most powerful healing plants in the world, just open your door and step outside. They are all around you."

Swan*Raven & Company (Blue Water Publishing); $13.95
1995; softcover; 187 pp
0-926524-09-7

SEEING WITHOUT GLASSES
Improving Your Vision Naturally

by Dr. Robert-Michael Kaplan

According to Dr. Robert-Michael Kaplan, weak eyesight and other eye problems can be corrected using natural, inexpensive methods — eye exercises, nutrition, and attitude adjustment. People with normal vision who suffer from eyestrain will also be able to benefit from these measures.

Kaplan says that people are addicted to their glasses and contacts. "Lens prescriptions become stronger over time, which leads to greater and greater dependency on the corrective devices, which is as insidious in its own way as a dependency on sugar, drugs, or alcohol." But the doc is not suggesting that we throw away our glasses and contacts… we should use them as therapeutic tools for better vision. By getting a prescription that is slightly weaker than 20/20, you will force your eyes to keep trying to see more sharply.

You should be aware that your eyes are biofeedback mechanisms. Your vision can vary according to your stress, anger, diet, exercise, breathing, and more. By "paying attention to what you're eyes are saying", you can improve your life and your vision.

Kaplan continues with this line of thought by theorising that your physical vision reveals something about your inner perceptions. If you are nearsighted perhaps you have a fear of seeing the world around you or your future. The answer is to "Reach for your dream. Push outward." Another problem created by attitude comes when you allow yourself to believe that you've got a "vision problem." You become programmed that your eyes will get "worse", which only starts a vicious cycle.

Even if you're not too sure about all this talk of "attitude" and "mind's eye", *Seeing Without Glasses* can help you with its suggestions for nutrition and exercise. Eating healthily and exercising keeps the blood and nutrients flowing, both of which help your vision. You should also avoid bodily reactions to processed sugar and flour that can temporarily decrease your vision by fifty percent or more.

Over 60 pages are devoted to a multi-faceted programme to improve your vision. Most of the programme involves twenty-one exercises that relieve stress on your eyes, increase blood flow, break bad vision habits (staring intensely too long), increase your eyes' movements, and train your eyes and brain to work together.

The end of the book has the results of a clinical study in which Kaplan's vision programme significantly improved the subjects' eyesight. There is also a bibliography, a list of suggested reading material, and a resources section.

Beyond Words Publishing; $12.95
1994; softcover; 171 pp
illus; 0-941831-97-3

YOUR BODY'S MANY CRIES FOR WATER
You Are Not Sick, You Are Thirsty!
(Second Edition)

by F. Batmanghelidj, MD

Our bodies are 75% water, and our brains are 85% water. With that much H_2O making up our bodies, we should be drinking lots of it, but most of us don't. According to Dr. F. Batmanghelidj, this constant state of dehydration is responsible for most of the diseases and disorders that afflict us.

Dyspeptic pain — heartburn, gastritis, and duodenitis — is the most important sign that a person is dehydrated. Batmanghelidj says that simply drinking more water is the only treatment you need for these problems. (If your pain is caused by an ulceration, then diet modification is also necessary to promote healing.) The author has successfully treated over 3000 people with dyspeptic pain in this manner. One such case was a young man with an extremely inflamed ulcer. After eating lunch, he was racked by crippling pain. Over the next ten hours, he took three tablets of prescription medication and drank a whole bottle of antacid, but it didn't do any good. When the doctor got there, the man was semiconscious and groaning, curled up in the foetal position. Doc made him drink a few glasses of water, and he recovered within twenty minutes.

Dehydration also causes the brain to react as if you are under severe stress. The resulting anxiety and depression can be alleviated with water. Unfortunately, many people react to this perceived stress by drinking alcohol, which only causes more dehydration, especially in the brain cells.

Drinking water can also help with weight loss. This is because the body's demands for water are often interpreted by the brain as hunger. If you get enough water, you won't feel "hungry" as much and will cut back on your eating.

Other problems that are caused by chronic dehydration (and can be fought by drinking water) include arthritis, headaches, neck and back pain, high blood pressure, asthma, allergies, diabetes, and perhaps — to some extent — AIDS.

Batmanghelidj lays out an optimum water-drinking regimen, which is fairly simple. "Your body needs an absolute minimum of six to eight 8-ounce glasses of water a day." And when he says water, he means water. Not coffee, tea, or anything with caffeine. Juices are only second rate. You need to drink water, and it doesn't have to be the expensive bottled kind. Unless your drinking water is heavily contaminated, straight out of the tap is preferred, because of its bacteria-killing chlorine. The author tells the best times to drink your *agua* and relates some other water-related health tips.

Like *Your Own Perfect Medicine* [below], this book offers the simplest, cheapest, most unregulated method available to cure and prevent a host of health problems.

Global Health Solutions; $14.95
1995; softcover; 200 pp
illus; 0-9629942-3-5

YOUR OWN PERFECT MEDICINE
The Incredible Proven Natural
Miracle Cure That Medical Science
Has Never Revealed
by Martha M. Christy

What would you do if you knew that you could easily get your hands on a powerful healing substance that is free, easily available, and completely unregulated? Well, I'll tell you what the medical profession would do... they'd keep it a secret. The Health Police don't want you knowing about a substance that undermines their authority and doesn't profit anyone. Very bad for business.

But this book spills the beans. Or should I say, spills the urine? Yep, your pee is "your own perfect medicine". I know this statement violates generally held attitudes and beliefs concerning urine, but the author says that these prejudices are the results of misinformation and a general uptightness about bodily fluids. If we examine what medical science knows but isn't telling about urine, we will find the truth. "Scientists have discovered that urine, because it is actually extracted from our blood, contains small amounts of almost all of the life-sustaining nutrients, proteins, hormones, antibodies and immunising agents that our blood contains". Far from being a nasty combination of our bodies' wastes, urine is sterile and contains a plethora of medically vital substances.

Modern researchers have been studying the effects or urine for almost 100 years, and they have come up with some amazing results. The book's longest chapter provides details on 44 clinical trials, experiments, and physicians' observations that confirm the power of urine and/or urea, a salt which is the primary organic solid of urine. In 1936, the American Proceedings for the Society of Experimental Biology included a paper by two doctors who report that urea destroys polio and rabies viruses. Several studies have shown that urine/urea can fight cancer. In 1957 a doctor reported in a symposium that urea had destroyed a brain tumour in two hours. A 1969 study published in *Science* had this to say about retine, a urine extract: "Smaller doses of retine inhibit growth of the tumours, while bigger ones actually make the tumour regress." Used orally, intravenously, or topically, urine/urea also had these effects: healed infected wounds and burns, killed bacteria, displayed anti-ageing properties, and cured or relieved symptoms of asthma, allergies, various skin problems, migraines, arthritis, meningitis, gonorrhoea, and other diseases and disorders. Although urine's anti-viral and anti-bacterial properties make it a natural for fighting HIV/AIDS, no trials have yet been reported.

Another chapter contains anecdotal evidence — namely, testimonials from people who claim that their urine has healed them. Several people with HIV/AIDS report beneficial effects. A 38-year-old man says that his fatigue and gland swelling disappeared after commencing urine therapy (which is the only treatment he uses). "When urine therapy is skipped for more than two days, gland swelling and fatigue return." Another man reports that after four months of urine therapy, his T-cell count went from 285 to 489.

A woman says that urine therapy cured her of chronic yeast infection and constipation. Another person relates that the sebaceous cysts on her face and neck — which never responded to any medication or cream — disappeared permanently after three weeks of rubbing urine on them. A diabetic reports that she dramatically decreased her insulin dosage after ingesting her urine.

The all-important chapter six teaches you how to employ urine therapy at home. There are detailed instructions for collecting the urine and using it several ways, both internally and externally. Questions about dosage, administration, side effects, and different disorders are answered.

Other chapters examine why urine therapy is being kept from the general public, the history of urine therapy, and how the author cured her excruciatingly painful medical conditions (including an "incurable" one) with her urine. They don't call it "number one" for nothing, you know.

Futuremed; $19.95
1994; oversized softcover; 221 pp
0-9632091-1-6

MEDICAL MAYHEM

ASPARTAME (NUTRASWEET™)
Is It Safe?

by HJ Roberts, MD

Aspartame — better known by its brand-name NutraSweet — is used in over 4000 products. Over 100 million people in the US currently eat it. But is it safe? The answer, according to Dr. HJ Roberts, is not on your life.

Roberts looks at the evidence — including clinical studies, questionnaires, reports filed with the FDA, and observation of his own patients — that aspartame may be linked to a distressingly large number of health problems. The most major of these includes epilepsy, anorexia, gastrointestinal disorders, heart problems, diabetes, allergies, Parkinson's disease, Alzheimer's disease, brain tumours, as well as birth defects, impaired intelligence, and behavioural problems in babies born to women who eat aspartame during pregnancy. Not all of the possible effects of aspartame are this severe. The most frequently reported reactions are temporary but still troubling: headaches, seizures, impaired vision, dizziness, atypical unexplained pain in various areas of the body, rashes, fatigue, depression, personality change, confusion, and memory loss. Other noted reactions include diarrhoea (sometimes bloody), slurred speech, ringing in ears, tremors, irritability, insomnia, severe sleepiness, heart palpitations, nausea, hives, marked weight loss, and increased urination.

This book contains many case reports of individuals who have bad reactions to aspartame, which go away when they stop ingesting it. Then, to prove it was aspartame that caused their problems, they will start ingesting it again (the author calls this "rechallenging"). The symptoms resume almost immediately, and then subside when the person quits again. Here is a typical case report in the chapter on psychiatric and behavioural reactions: "A 43-year-old lawyer quit several jobs because of presumed 'job-related depression'. He drank three or four cans of diet cola daily. He also had suicidal thoughts, extreme irritability, 'anxiety attacks,' and personality changes. He deduced this aspartame beverage to be the cause after rechallenging himself four times. His complaints improved 'immediately' every time he avoided it."

Further chapters explore other troubling aspects of the artificial sweetener. There are signs that any adverse effects of aspartame may be much more severe in current or former alcoholics, or even in non-alcoholics who have recently had an alcoholic drink. Also, aspartame may have significant interaction with many other common drugs, including anti-depressants and insulin. Children and the elderly might be especially susceptible to negative effects.

A very revealing chapter looks at how aspartame made it to the marketplace and stayed there. It examines the PR, vested interests, questionable research, FDA failures, and bureaucratic obstacles that surround the sweetener. Two other chapters reveal the struggles of patients, consumers, and consumer groups to discover and disseminate the facts. Finally, there is a chapter on alternatives to aspartame.

Given the amount of artificially-sweetened food and drink that is consumed, this is an incredibly important book that affects every one of us, either directly or indirectly through family and friends. I only wish that this book would be updated to provide us with even more information.

The Charles Press, Publishers; $16.95
1990; softcover; 315 pp
0-914783-58-0

BITTERSWEET ASPARTAME
A Diet Delusion

by Barbara Alexander Mullarkey

Bittersweet Aspartame is a collection of columns written by Barbara Mullarkey, who also edits and publish the journal NutriVoice, from the Wednesday Journal in Illinois. "Aspartame may go down in history as the most harmful food additive that the FDA has permitted in the food supply. When Americans finally ferret out the complete truth, it might rival the stories of Watergate, the Challenger chaos and the Iran-Contra crisis."

In the front of the book is an FDA document listing the symptoms that were reported to them as having been caused by aspartame. There are over 90 symptoms listed, including 1558 counts of headaches, 669 of dizziness or problems with balance, 551 of vomiting and nausea, down to one each of anaemia, conjunctivitis, and change in sexual function.

The columns — written from 1984 to 1993 — provide a running account of Mullarkey's quest to look at the reported negative effects of aspartame, call the government (especially the FDA) into question over its inaction, and deal with flak from NutraSweet, who constantly rebut her columns. To Mullarkey's great credit, she reproduces these responses in full.

The titles of her columns include "Independent Study Shows Potentially Serious Aspartame Effects", "FDA Claims 'No Basis' for 3,660 Aspartame Complaints", "Long List of Flaws in FDA's Investigation of Aspartame", "What's In a Label? At Times Inaccuracy and Confusion", and "Scenes from the Best Little Aspartame Symposium in Texas". "Drinking Woes at the White House" alerts us to reports that 1) President Clinton chain-drinks Diet Coke, and 2) he suffers from some commonly reported aspartame side effects.

NutriVoice; $11
1993; oversized softcover; 76 pp
illus; 0-944366-00-7

THE DOCTORS' CASE AGAINST THE PILL
25th Anniversary Updated Edition

by Barbara Seaman

Barbara Seaman is the founder of the women's health movement. At the end of the 1960s, she wrote a book that exposed the dangers of the birth control pill. For this, she was ridiculed as some sort of religious reactionary, and she lost her job writing for women's magazines because of advertiser pressure. However, her book triggered Senate hearings that ended up requiring the warning inserts in every package of the Pill.

The Doctors' Case contains a complete reprinting of her original book. In it she shows that, as is so often the case, a drug that's being touted as a panacea has a much darker side that its makers don't want you to know about. The biggest health risk of the Pill was blood clots. British studies in 1968 reported a "highly significant" rate of hospitalisation and death among Pill users as compared to non-users. In 1968 the FDA reported that 27 women in America had died from lung clots caused by the Pill. Furthermore, many otherwise healthy young women started dropping dead of strokes from "unknown causes". In almost every case, they were on the Pill.

The Pill was also suspected in instances of cancer, heart disease, diabetes, birth defects, miscarriages, jaundice, rheumatism, cataracts, depression, decreased sex drives, and hair loss. An increase in seizures had been noted among some women with epilepsy who take the Pill. After coming off the Pill, some women had irregular periods and some stopped menstruating completely. Many are infertile.

Seaman examines the shocking story of how the Pill came onto the market. The original Pill was tested on Puerto Rican women, the vast majority of whom dropped out way before the studies were complete. In the end, the FDA granted approval for the Pill based on trials in which only 132 women took the drug continuously for a year or more! As the *Washington Post*'s drug industry specialist Morton Mintz pointed out in 1969: "For one thing, 132 is a smaller number of women than, this year alone, will die from clotting induced by the Pill." Three of the young subjects even died during the trials, but no autopsies were performed.

A new chapter towards the end of the book examines the Pill as it is in 1995. It's changed a lot since the rest of the book was originally published. "The levels of oestrogen and progestin are only a fraction of what they were." The Pill is much safer now, but it continues to have its problems. It is still being implicated as a cause of permanent infertility, strokes, heart attacks, high blood pressure, and cancer. It has just recently been linked to two types of inflammatory bowel disease. Also, despite industry claims that the pregnancy rate is less than one percent among women who correctly use the Pill, Seaman says the rate is actually 2%.

The final chapter, "Norplant: The Contraceptive You're Stuck With", looks at this birth control method, in which six matchstick-sized capsules are put into the woman's arm. They slowly dissolve over a roughly five-year period, releasing levonorgestrel, a synthetic progestin. Some problems that have been reported so far: headaches, depression, acne, loss of hair, nausea, and nipple discharge. Seamans says that 4% of women of normal weight will become pregnant during the five years they're on Norplant. Eighteen percent of these pregnancies are ectopic (outside the uterus). Furthermore, "We learned long ago from the example of

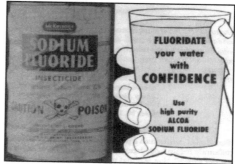

Fluoride – your friend or deadly poison?
Fluoride: The Aging Factor.

DES-exposed babies that hormone exposure in utero can lead to cancer and severe reproductive abnormalities, many of which will not be apparent until after puberty."

Hunter House; $14.95

1995; softcover; 258 pp

0-89793-181-5

THE COT DEATH COVER-UP?

by Jim Sprott

Sudden Infant Death Syndrome (SIDS) — which is referred to as "cot death" in New Zealand, where this book was published — is a baffling occurrence that has killed around one million babies world-wide since it was recognised in 1953. The medical establishment is at a loss to explain or prevent SIDS (the most popular theory says that it's accidental suffocation), but chemist and forensic scientist Jim Sprott is sure he has the answer. Cot death is actually a form of unintentional poisoning by nerve gases. Based on his own research and that of a British scientist, Sprott believes that SIDS is caused when a common household fungus forms a chemical reaction with any of three chemicals that are commonly found in crib mattresses: phosphorus, arsenic, and antimony. These reactions form toxic gases that kill the child.

The Cot Death Cover-Up? explains how Sprott and others put the pieces together and documents their struggle to get the medical establishment, the media, and parents to listen to their message. They also examine the evidence for their hypothesis, from both a chemical standpoint and an epidemiological standpoint. They point out that instances of SIDS dropped, but did not disappear, when parents started laying babies to sleep on their backs instead of their stomachs. This is because the gasses are heavy, and babies who are sleeping face up are not breathing nearly as much of the gasses. For a long time, SIDS was almost unheard of in Japan, but is now starting to rise. This is because Japanese babies used to sleep on untreated cotton futons, which contained no harmful chemicals. "Recently, however, as Japanese parents have started to adopt western babycare practices, mattresses, etc., the cot death rate in Japan has started to rise. It has been noted that when Japanese families emigrate to the United States their cot death rate rises to that of the local population."

The official reaction to the nerve gas hypothesis has been less than enthusiastic. It appears to be the typical reception the medical establishment gives to most boat-rocking theories, especially one that might have the potential to end SIDS and, thus, derail the whole charity/research gravy train that has built up around the phenomenon. Also, makers of crib mattresses have been none too happy with this theory, although British manufacturers have very quietly reduced or eliminated the presence of the three offending chemicals.

Sprott's urgent suggestions to parents: "Mattresses should be wrapped in thick, natural-colour (not black) polythene sheeting or surgical rubber sheeting." The sheeting should be taped so that it is airtight on top of the mattress but allowed to "breathe" underneath. It should then be covered with a cotton underblanket. Exact instructions are given on the inside back cover of this book.

Penguin Books (NZ) Limited; NZ$18, £6
1996; softcover; 191 pp
0-140-26198-2

DYING FROM DIOXIN
A Citizen's Guide to Reclaiming Our Health and Rebuilding Democracy
by Lois Marie Gibbs and the Citizens Clearinghouse for Hazardous Waste

Dioxin is a harmful chemical compound that is usually created as a result of burning waste. We ingest this highly toxic junk from our food, air, and water, and it has been implicated in cancer, reproductive problems, birth defects, skin disorders, diabetes, heart disease, liver damage, nervous system damage, impaired immune response, and other health problems. This book spells out exactly what dioxin is, where it comes from, how it affects us, and — in a detailed 150-page section — how to organise to stop this form of poisoning.

South End Press; $20
1995; softcover; 381 pp
illus; 0-89608-525-2

FLUORIDE
The Aging Factor
by Dr. John Yiamouyiannis

Dr. John Yiamouyiannis is a tireless opponent of fluoride, and, according to the biographical blurb on the back of this book, he is responsible for stopping fluoridation of water in some areas of the US and abroad. Why would he be so hostile towards a supposedly beneficial substance? For starters, fluoride is a poison. There are several cases on the books of children swallowing fluoride gels during dental teeth cleanings and dying horrible deaths. Although outright death is uncommon, children having bad reactions is not. "Surveys show that over 6% of the children receiving fluoride treatments at the dental office complained of side effects, including nausea and vomiting, either immediately or within one hour following treatment."

Less concentrated doses of fluoride — contained in drinking water in various parts of the world — have more subtle long-term poisonous effects. At levels as low as one part per million, fluoride causes the breakdown and irregular formation of collagen, a protein that "serves as a major structural component of skin, ligaments, tendons, muscles, cartilage, bones and teeth." This artificially-induced shortage of collagen results in frail bones, bad teeth, weak tendons, wrinkles, arthritis, as well as such reactions as rashes, diarrhoea, lethargy, migraines, inflamed mouths, gastrointestinal disorders, weakened immune systems, genetic damage, and more. "Government facilities such as Argonne National Laboratories (1988) and the National Institute of Environment and Health Sciences (1990) have shown that fluoride causes cancer… Animal studies showing fluoride-linked increases in bone cancer and oral cancer have been confirmed by human studies (1991-1993)."

But everybody knows fluoride does have one beneficial effect — it's good for your teeth, right? "Still — and the US Centres for Disease Control and the British Ministry of Health admit this — no laboratory study has ever shown that the amount of fluoride added to drinking water is effective in reducing tooth decay. Furthermore, they admit that there are no epidemiological studies on humans showing that fluoridation reduces tooth decay that meet the minimum requirements of scientific objectivity." Scientists at the Environmental Protection Agency have also shown that fluoridation doesn't help teeth. The author admits that the one place in which fluoride might fight tooth decay is in toothpaste. But even then the results are not outstanding and debatable.

So how did this toxic substance become the alleged friend of our teeth, and why is it still being dumped into the water supply in parts of the US and other countries? It's long been suspected by conservatives that fluoridation is a communist plot to sneakily introduce "socialised medicine". However, Yiamouyiannis builds a strong case against greedy capitalists, rather than utopian socialists. "Fluoride is an industrial waste product." Specifically, it is a by-product of the production of aluminium and phosphate fertilisers. When these industries mushroomed in the 1920s and 1930s, they began poisoning the environment, people, and animals with fluoride. Eventually, public and governmental pressure forced the companies to do something. Part of the solution was to sell fluoride as rat poison and insecticide, but that wasn't getting rid of enough. "Dr. Gerald Cox of the Mellon Institute (the Mellons were owners of the Aluminium Company of America — ALCOA) solved this problem: Dump the waste fluoride into public drinking water. Tell the people it will reduce tooth decay." This started a chain of events involving other industrialists, the media, and government officials which has resulted in the present situation.

The author gives advice on how you can stop fluoridation and protect yourself in the meantime. He recommends not using toothpaste that contains fluoride. If you live in an area with fluoridated water, you should get a purifier or drink distilled water. This may sound extreme, but Yiamouyiannis warns: **"The low levels at which fluoride exerts its deleterious effects indicates that there may be no safe level of fluoride."**

Health Action Press; $14.95
1993; softcover; 294 pp
illus; 0-913571-03-2

THE GREAT POWER-LINE COVER-UP
How the Utilities and the Government Are Trying to Hide the Cancer Hazards Posed by Electromagnetic Fields
by Paul Brodeur

Could electromagnetic fields (EMFs) from electricity substations, transformers, powerlines, and other equipment cause cancer? A lot of evidence points towards yes, and the possibility has caused some commotion in recent years. EMFs have a disturbing effect on the body: "... every molecule in the brain and body of a human being standing in a strong alternating-current power-frequency magnetic field, such as is given off by any high-voltage or high current power line, will vibrate to and fro sixty times a second — a phenomenon called entrainment, which, in turn, has been shown to alter the normal activation of enzyme and cellular immune responses in ways consistent with the promotion of cancer."

Investigative reporter Paul Brodeur examines the phenomenon and its ramifications. He tells the story of neighbourhoods plagued by impossibly high cancer rates and what the residents have done about it. Along one 250-yard-long street with just nine houses in Guillford, Connecticut, seven adults and children have developed cancer in the past few years. Children at Montecito Union School in California get leukaemia and lymphoma at *fifteen times* the normal rate. According to a local paper, when shown this cluster of cancer, the programme manager of electromagnetic research at the Department of Energy said, "If I were a parent, I would get the hell out."

Such a moment of candour is a rare thing. It's amazing to watch government officials — from local school officials to the Bush administration — wiggle and squirm and deny the obvious while people, including children, are dying. The CDC has said that cancer clusters near power substations are probably just due to chance. The EPA prepared a report that classified EMFs as a probable carcinogen, but the report was emasculated by an EPA bigwig after he met with White House officials. The report was still fairly damning, though, so the Bush administration did what it could to delay its release.

Despite government denials and corporate propaganda, evidence continues to mount. In November 1993, "Dr. Dana Loomis, an epidemiologist at the University of North Carolina at Chapel Hill announced that a study of 27,882 women who had died of breast cancer between 1985 and 1989 showed that women working at jobs with exposure to electromagnetic fields had experienced a forty per cent higher breast-cancer death rate than women working in non-electrical jobs." Another study has shown that women under 55 who live near powerlines have three times the breast cancer rate as those who don't. Four studies done from 1988 to 1993 show that men exposed to EMFs on the job got breast cancer at four to six times the normal rate.

The author feels that mounting evidence, lawsuits, jury verdicts, and out-of-court settlements will eventually lead to enough public outrage that the government will be forced to admit the disastrous effects of EMFs and do something

meaningful about the situation.

Little, Brown, and Company; $12.95
1993, 1995; softcover; 351 pp
0-316-10911-8

HEART FRAUD
The Misapplication of High Technology in Heart Disease
by Charles T. McGee, MD

Dr. Charles McGee exposes the problems with the way doctors treat coronary artery disease, which kills more Americans than any other disease. First of all, angiograms — the test used to detect coronary artery disease — are highly inaccurate and usually unnecessary. This was reported in major medical journals but has been ignored by physicians. An amazingly accurate form of testing has been around for twenty years, but it is used only for research purposes. Second, over 600,000 coronary bypass operations and balloon angioplasty procedures are performed every year, but there is no evidence that they extend life. Most artery obstructions can be cleared up through diet, exercise, meditation, giving up smoking, and other such changes in lifestyle.

MediPress; $11.95
1993; softcover; 263 pp
illus; 0-9636979-4-3

IMMUNIZATION THEORY VS. REALITY
Exposé on Vaccinations
by Neil Z. Miller

You gotta love the succinct and decidedly clear way the publisher summarises this book on the back cover: "Take a trip into the shadowy underworld of vaccine theory, where live viruses are brewed in diseased animal organs prior to being 'stabilised' with chemical compounds and carcinogenic substances, prior to being injected into *your* healthy child." That pretty much sums up the way vaccines are created.

In his follow-up to *Vaccines: Are They Really Safe and Effective?* [below], Neil Miller continues to show that vaccines are inherently dangerous substances with a very low success rate. After looking at the history of vaccines (many epidemic diseases have died out when people *stopped* getting vaccinated *en masse*) and flaws in vaccine theory, Miller shows the reality. In 1986 Congress passed a law that, among other things, established a system for doctors to report side effects of vaccinations on patients. Despite the fact that the FDA admitted that 90% of doctors don't report vaccination reactions, the system still logged over 34,000 adverse reactions in three and a half years. "These figures include hundreds of cases of irreversible brain damage and over 700 deaths."

Furthermore, Congress has set up a fund for children who are killed or permanently damaged by vaccines. The fund is supported in part by taxes placed on vaccination fees. As of the beginning of February 1995, the fund had paid out more than $522 million and is expected to owe over *$1.7 billion* on vaccinations performed before 1998 alone. The US government has proof positive that large numbers of people — mainly children — are being killed and damaged by vaccines, but they never say a word about it. In fact, all they ever do is push harder for mandatory vaccination, with "universal vaccination" being the Clintons' deadly mantra.

Another chapter examines whether the polio vaccine introduced AIDS to humans and whether Gulf War Syndrome is caused by the experimental vaccines that the government tested on American troops. One heart-rending chapter tells the stories of children and families who have been devastated by the effects of vaccines.

The longest part of the book, "Ploys", enumerates the many methods used to hoodwink and pressure the public into thinking vaccines are safe and effective, including denial, double talk, gimmicks, bribes, skewed statistics, fraud, intimidation, scare tactics, euphemisms, and more.

Elsewhere, Miller reprints pleas to health and government officials for new vaccination policies, examines what can be done to improve the situation, reveals the ingredients in popular serums, and offers further references.

Because of Miller's books and similar information I've read, I no longer receive vaccinations of any type, no matter how much the government tries to convince me that "this year's flu epidemic is going to be three times as bad as last year's!" (Have you ever noticed that they say that *every* year?)

New Atlantean Press; $12.95

1996; softcover; 157 pp

illus; 1-881217-12-4

THE MERCURY IN YOUR MOUTH
The Truth About "Silver" Dental Fillings
by Quicksilver Associates

"Silver" dental fillings — also known as amalgam fillings — are actually at least 50% mercury, which is the deadliest element next to plutonium. The controversy over possible harmful effects of these fillings even reached the mainstream media at one point, and dentists were quick to reassure everybody that the 100 million amalgam fillings they were putting into people's teeth every year are perfectly safe. Their theory is that once the fillings have solidified, the mercury cannot escape in any form. This book says that they are wrong.

Numerous independently performed scientific studies have established that mercury amalgam fillings are unstable. "**Mercury vapour is continuously released from amalgam fillings in measurable quantities, from the moment the fillings are inserted into your teeth**. This mercury vapour is inhaled and swallowed, and is absorbed into every part of your body." The experiments that demonstrate this "have been published in the most highly respected and most stringently peer-reviewed scientific journals."

The Mercury in Your Mouth looks in detail at several of the most important of these studies. It also examines a meta-study that was done in which two dentists analysed the results of six different studies involving 1569 patients. In each of these studies — performed around the world — people had their mercury amalgam fillings replaced with fillings that don't contain mercury. The results were astounding. "**86% of the fatigue sufferers, 87% of the headache victims, 91% of those with depression and 88% of those with**

dizziness reported cure or improvement after the removal of their amalgam fillings." Even those conditions that showed the least improvement still improved by 50%, and other conditions improved by 70% to 97%. Even 75% of the people with multiple sclerosis reported some relief of their symptoms.

Symptoms of toxicity caused by mercury fillings include depression, dizziness, headaches, irritability, memory lapses, allergies, bleeding or receding gums, fatigue, gastrointestinal illnesses, high blood pressure, and kidney problems. There is also evidence that mercury may lead to MS, Alzheimer's, leukaemia, Lupus, infertility, birth defects, a damaged immune system, and other grave health problems.

After looking at how harmful mercury and mercury amalgam fillings are, the book helps you determine if you're being poisoned by your fillings and, if so, how to have them removed. Resources in the back of *Mercury* include a bibliography, news clippings, and a list of dentists and physicians who are knowledgeable about amalgam toxicity.

Quicksilver Press; $14.95

1994, 1996; softcover; 197 pp

0-9643870-0-X

RACKETEERING IN MEDICINE
The Suppression of Alternatives
by James P. Carter, MD, DrPH

Racketeering in Medicine documents the way the medical/pharmaceutical establishment — with the aid of the government — has actively worked to discredit and eliminate alternative therapies and persecute the people who practice them. "Investigations against alternative practitioners follow a pattern of arrogance, dogmatism, deprivation of constitutional rights and a might-makes-right attitude. To suppress alternative medicine, Organised Med[icine] resorts to bad behaviours: disinformation, smear campaigns of libel and slander, harassment, unwarranted IRS audits, enticement of patients and family members to sue doctors (even offering financial payment to do so), entrapment by undercover agents posing as sick patients who may persistently beg for alternative treatments, illegal wiretaps, and break-ins and records theft."

The author provides lots of actual examples to support his accusations. A minor example that demonstrates the government's arrogance has to do with American International Hospital, which publicly adopted the use of magnets as therapy for skin and bone problems. "They were visited by an FDA official, who after his tour, was quoted as saying to the research physician, 'You've got a nice office and a nice home. If you want to keep them, quit promoting and advertising the therapeutic use of electromagnetic fields.'" In another example, a dentist had his license revoked because he removed a patient's toxic mercury amalgam fillings and replaced them with composite materials in order to alleviate the pain of her rheumatoid arthritis. He was accused of practising medicine.

The type of persecuted treatment that the book covers in the most depth, though, is chelation therapy. Used to treat heart and circulatory problems and cancer, this form of medicine involves the IV-drip administration of EDTA, a synthetic amino acid. Despite evidence that it works very well against some disorders, it has been the subject of a prolonged attack by the medical establishment. The root cause, as always, is money. "The patent of EDTA expired years ago. It is now a generic drug — any company can manufacture and sell EDTA. The [treatment] programme also includes supplementation with various nutrients (also not patentable). Such doctor's orders sharply contrast with expensive, highly profitable, patentable drugs with their typical 800% markup for heart disease."

Other chapters include "Does Medicine Have a Bad Attitude?", "Is There a Secret Team?", "Doctor Hunting", "Doctor Bashing", "Will You All Rise? Kangaroo Court Is Now In Session", "The Attack Dog: The Role of the FDA", "Our Health Care Crisis: The Hidden Causes", and "The Rejection and Legal Quarantine of Medical Hypotheses".

Hampton Roads Publishing Company; $12.95
1993; softcover; 374 pp
1-878901-326-X

ROOT CANAL COVER-UP
A Founder of the Association of Root Canal Specialists Discovers Evidence That Root Canals Damage Your Health. Learn What to Do
by George E. Meinig, DDS, FACD

Dentist George Meinig is a pioneer of root canal operations, which save teeth by scraping out the pulp in the root canal and replacing it with a filling substance. He is spreading the word that the operation that he helped to make widespread — as it is being practised today — may endanger your health. The problem is that your teeth's dentine (the extremely hard substance under the enamel) contains miles of microscopic tubules. These tubules are home to some very nasty bacteria that escape into the bloodstream of the teeth's sockets. Having a root canal increases the ease with which these bacteria make their way into the rest of your body.

Dr. Meinig claims that these teeth bacteria are still causing a large number of problems today, even though most dentists and doctors believe that since antibiotics arrived, these infections are no longer a problem. The bacteria attack the heart and circulatory system most often, causing at least sixteen bad conditions. The doc tells of a nine-year-old girl who had been bedridden for five years due to inflammation of the lining of her heart. A culture was taken from the pulps of two of her baby teeth and injected into three rabbits. Each of them developed heart inflammation and one developed rheumatism. "One of the rabbits developed the greatest enlargement of a heart ever seen."

Bacteria from your teeth can damage the kidneys, joints, eyes, brain, ovaries, testicles, stomach, and any other organ, gland, or tissue. These bacteria also damage the immune system, which can lead to all sorts of problems. Pregnant women should be especially wary of infected teeth and root canals, because foetuses are very susceptible to these bacteria.

Meinig presents numerous clinical studies and case studies that back up his assertions. Much of the research was

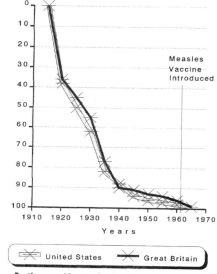

Deaths caused by measles decreased by more than 95% **before** the vaccine was introduced. *Vaccines.*

performed over 25 years by top dental and medical minds under the auspices of the American Dental Association, and it is extensively documented in the professional literature.

By incorporating what has been learned, you can minimise the risk to yourself if you do get a root canal or have had one. Meinig advises that most infected teeth should instead be removed, along with the periodontal ligament and part of the bony socket. People dealing with an infected tooth would be well-advised to check out this book before submitting to a root canal.

Bion Publishing; $19.95
1994; oversized softcover; 239 pp
illus; 0-945196-19-9

TORN ILLUSIONS
Fully-Documented, Private and Public Exposé of the Worldwide Medical Tragedy of Silicone Implants (Second Edition)
by Pamela Stott-Kendall

Almost as soon as Pamela Stott-Kendall received her silicone breast implants, she started experiencing major medical problems. "What followed was a ten-year nightmare of physical pain and personal agony. Pamela lost her health, husband, home, job and the formative years of her children's lives because of her illness. Ravaged by the effects of silicone on her immune system, she became an invalid, suffering respiratory problems, convulsions, bouts of paralysis as well as brain seizures while beads of silicone travelled undetected through her body." In this book, she not only gives a harrowing account of what silicone did to her, she relates her massive research which has uncovered loads of evidence that silicone is far from the "inert chemical" that its manufacturers claim it is.

The problem is that silicone gel slowly seeps out of breast implants and into the body, while a certain percentage of implants completely rupture. Even the saline-filled implants aren't safe because their shells — as with almost all breast implants — are made of silicone, which sloughs off. But the menace goes well beyond breast implants. Silicone is also being used for implants in hips, jaws, wrists, penises, and other parts of the body. Approximately eleven million Americans and an untold number of people world-wide have silicone devices inside them.

The author lays out the charges loud and clear. Silicone is not inert but is instead "both biochemically active and destructive." It insidiously causes a host of health problems and can even lead to death. Children of mothers with implants are developing silicone-related problems and diseases. "By the 1960s, implant manufacturers were well-informed of: the perpetual leakage of silicone gel through the porous shells of all implants; the frequency of spontaneous shell ruptures, which release massive quantities of gel; the ability of any uncontained silicone to travel throughout vital organs and glands inside the body; and its capacity to cause serious illness. This information was withheld from the Food and Drug Administration (FDA); from physicians; and from those women who would become implant recipients." For its part, the FDA went for decades without regulating or issuing requirements for silicone use in humans. When the FDA finally asked to see the research in 1991, it found that the implants were not proven safe.

Stott-Kendall supports her accusations with research, including reports from the mainstream medical community and the FDA's own publications. Here is just some of the research she found (minus the references, which are included in the book):

☞ "Mayo Clinic urologists have identified silicone particles and foreign body granulomas in seventy-two percent of twenty-five patients with urinary and penile prostheses."

☞ An FDA notice, "which appeared in a 1990 Federal Register publication, stated that 'other silicone implants [in addition to breast implants]… have been documented to produce sarcoma and other forms of carcinoma in humans.'"

☞ "… silicone has been used as an anti-foam agent in a device that oxygenates a patient's blood during cardiac bypass surgery. In these cases the silicone particles' entrance into the body blocked capillaries and caused tissue damage. In a study of fourteen patients who underwent open-heart surgery aided by a bubble oxygenator, eight were found to have silicone droplets in their blood. Five of the fourteen cases proved fatal; silicone was detected in the brains and kidneys of these fatalities."

☞ "As early as 1981, there have been medical literature reports of mortal liver disease resulting from exposure to silicone tubing."

☞ "In studies of implants retrieved, Dr. Blais reports the presence of organisms 'never before found in

the human body.' The micro-organisms that are isolated from breast implants fall into these categories: fungi, water-borne bacteria, micro-bacteria, sulfate metabolising bacteria, anaerobic bacteria and pseudomonas. The latter pathogen, pseudomonas, is associated with lethal hospital-contracted infections capable of causing death."

☞ "Of the numerous abnormalities that are detected in silicone-implanted women, incredibly, none fit into any diagnostic category of any known neurological disease."

Suffice it to say that this a book that the silicone implant industry wishes had never been written. It is absolutely essential if you want to find out what all the superficial news stories on breast implant court battles leave out.

Debcar Publishing; $17.95
1994, 1997; softcover; 279 pp
0-9652783-0-1

VACCINES
Are They Really Safe and Effective? — A Parent's Guide to Childhood Shots
by Neil Z. Miller

In the US and many other industrialised nations, childhood vaccines are a compulsory and unquestioned part of life. The problem is, there are many reports and studies — most of them from the mainstream medical community — that show that vaccines are dangerous, ineffective, and/or even deadly.

A vaccine is a liquid that contains a weakened form of the disease that it is allegedly protecting you against. The presence of this disease forces the body to create antibodies to fight it. If the full-force disease shows up, the antibodies will repel it (at least that's the theory).

The first part of this book examines each of the supposedly mandatory vaccines — polio, diphtheria, measles, German measles, mumps, tetanus, and whooping cough. We find out that between 1923 and 1953, incidents of polio had decreased by 47% in the US and 55% in England. Yet *after* mass inoculation with the original vaccine developed by Jonas Salk, the incidents of polio actually *increased*, perhaps more than doubling in the US. In Massachusetts the incidents of polio went from 273 in the year before massive use of the vaccine to 2027 the year after! In European countries that refused to implement organised inoculation, the polio epidemic ended on its own. "Doctors and scientists on the staff of the National Institute of Health during the 1950's were well aware that the Salk vaccine was ineffective and deadly. Some frankly stated that it was 'worthless as a preventative and dangerous to take.' They refused to vaccinate their own children. Even Dr. Salk himself was quoted as saying: 'When you inoculate children with a polio vaccine you don't sleep well for two or three weeks.'"

News about the other vaccines is no more comforting. "The measles vaccine may cause ataxia (inability to co-ordinate muscle movements), learning disability, retardation, aseptic meningitis, seizure disorders, paralysis, and death. Other researchers have investigated it as a possible cause

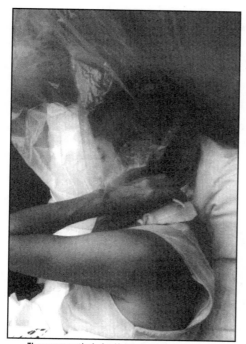

The proper method of self-deliverance using a plastic bag.
The Art and Science of Suicide.

certify that a child is in danger from inoculation. Nevertheless, parents who don't vaccinate their children are sometimes harassed by social workers and courts. "Ironically, parents have lost custody of their children and were accused of
child abuse — 'shaken baby syndrome' — when their babies had seizures or went into a coma following vaccinations." (For more information on conscientiously objecting to
vaccines, you can order copies of your state's vaccine laws
for $4 from New Atlantean Press.)

New Atlantean Press; $8.95
1994; softcover; 79 pp
illus; 1-881217-10-8

SELF-
DELIVERANCE

THE ART AND SCIENCE OF SUICIDE,
CHAPTERS 1-5

by the Right to Die Society of Canada

This series of five booklets gives minutely-detailed instructions for ending your own life. Each booklet, referred to by
the publisher as a "chapter", covers a separate means of
self-deliverance. The reasoning behind creating a separate
publication for each method is that 1) you only pay for the
method you're interested in, instead of getting a whole book
filled with methods you don't want to use, and 2) the publishers can update each chapter as new information becomes
available without having to reprint an entire book. The drawback is that if you're unsure of which method you're interested in — or if you just want to buy them for your library of
forbidden info — then you've got to shell out $50 for the
whole set. Nevertheless, if you want the real hardcore steps
for taking yourself out, this is what you need.

*Chapter One: Self Deliverance & Plastic Bags — Intro-
ducing the Customized Exit Bag™* (15 pp). Killing yourself
solely by overdosing on barbiturates is not a good idea. You
can end up in a coma before death, or you can not die at all.
To do it right, you need to also put a plastic bag over your
head as you drift off. This booklet details the many problems
and failures that can occur with a standard bag, then it introduces a solution. As bizarre as it may sound, the Right to
Die Society of Canada has developed what they call the Exit
Bag. This plastic bag is specially constructed so that it provides the right size, strength, and structure to insure maximum chance of death. This booklet gives instructions along
with photographs of how to use your Exit Bag, but it doesn't
tell you about how to O.D. on drugs. For that, you have to
buy another booklet, natch.

Chapter Two: Nitrogen and Other Inert Gases (11 pp).

or co-factor for multiple sclerosis, Rye's syndrome,
Guillain-Barre syndrome, blood clotting disorders, and
juvenile-onset diabetes." The DPT vaccine (for diphtheria,
pertussis, and tetanus) contains one carcinogen (formalde-
hyde) and two toxins (thimerosal and aluminium phosphate).
A study done at the University of Nevada School of Medicine found that of 103 children who died of SIDS (Sudden
Infant Death Syndrome), 70% had received the DPT vaccine within the previous three weeks.

The second section of the book exposes the facts about
several newer vaccines, including influenza, hepatitis B,
pneumonia, and smallpox. Following that, the author looks
at the possible long-term effects of vaccines. Not much study
has been done in this area, but there are indications that
inoculations damage the immune system and cause genetic
mutations. Vaccinations are the leading cause of encephali-
tis (inflammation of the brain), which leads to developmental
disabilities. Because vaccines are often cultured in animal
tissue, they may introduce new diseases into humans. (This
is one of the most popular alternative theories about how
HIV/AIDS started.) Vaccines may also cause autism, hyper-
activity, drug abuse, and violent crime.

The last section is a smorgasbord of information, covering individuals who are likely to react badly to vaccines, doctors who refuse to report fatal vaccine reactions, the causes
of vaccine reactions, promoting vaccine safety, and more. It
turns out that no vaccine is truly compulsory. Most states will
let parents refuse to vaccinate their children based on personal, religious, or philosophical grounds, or if a doctor will

The Right to Die Society of Canada conducts original research into new and better ways to commit suicide. Among their groundbreaking discoveries is the use of inert gasses, such as nitrogen, helium, and argon. Breathing in high concentrations of inert gases is apparently a good way to go, since it quickly depletes the brain of oxygen but does not produce a feeling of suffocation. "Loss of consciousness thus typically occurs with no discomfort — and often with no warning." Unfortunately, this promising method has not been tested out on humans. This booklet recounts the results of nitrogen euthanasia on animals and cases where humans accidentally died of inhalation. However, this suggested method for self-deliverance is sketchy and not recommended.

Chapter Three: Carbon Monoxide for Self-Deliverance (19 pp). Breathing in heavy concentrations of carbon monoxide should, under perfect circumstances, lead to a painless and quick death. This method is often used by Jack Kevorkian on the people he is assisting. The catch is, to be done right, pure CO should be administered from a canister through a gasmask. Many people kill themselves by breathing in car exhaust fumes — a modus operandi examined in detail in this booklet — but this is an imperfect method. Plus, emission control standards for new cars may make it almost impossible. If you want to try it, *Chapter Three* will tell you how, while warning you of the consequences if you screw up.

Chapter Four: Barbiturates Revisited (11 pages) explores the use of the sedatives known as barbiturates. Lethal doses are hard to determine — and will vary from person to person anyway — but this booklet lists the most recent estimates in this department. It also mentions other substances that might help the process along (such as champagne) and the effects that a barb overdose has. Because the death could take from six hours to several days, it's recommended that you also use a plastic bag over your head.

Chapter Five: Tricyclic Antidepressants — A New Look (11 pp). The major problem with trying to suicide with barbiturates is that they are no longer prescribed very often. Tricyclic antidepressants, on the other hand, are still very easy to get by prescription (they're even available over-the-counter in Mexico). They're also quite toxic, especially the older forms, usually causing death in 12 to 24 hours. In this booklet, you'll find estimates of the lethal dose of several tricyclics. As with barbiturates, it's a good idea to supplement these drugs with a plastic bag.

Last Rights Publications; $10 each
1996 & 1997; staplebound booklets
illus, no ISBNs

DEPARTING DRUGS
An International Guidebook to Self-Deliverance for the Terminally Ill
by anonymous

Apparently created by many of the same people responsible for *The Art and Science of Suicide* [above], *Departing Drugs* is an earlier guide to the most effective ways to commit suicide. After a number of short sections on depression, legal warnings, shelf-life of drugs, ingestion of drugs, a pre-

suicide checklist, and other topics, *DD* gives detailed instructions for five self-deliverance methods: plastic bags and a sedative, barbiturate overdose, overdose of chloroquine (an anti-malarial pill available over-the-counter in many countries, including the UK), orphenadrine pills overdose, and propoxyphene (painkiller) overdose. When employing an overdose method, the book also recommends taking sedatives and/or anti-sickness pills, using a plastic bag over your head, and washing down the pills with booze, for maximum effectiveness. Several tables list the lethal doses for various recommended drugs, and there are pages upon pages listing chemical and brand names for drugs in twenty-two countries.

The less preferable methods of hypothermia, carbon monoxide poisoning, and fasting are also covered. Another section tells you why you should steer clear of such uncertain methods as electrocution, shooting, wrist slashing, and aspirin overdose. A pull-out section in the middle of the booklet contains two examples of "do not resuscitate" notes that can be left somewhere near you when you attempt to end your life.

Last Rights Publications; $12
1993; staplebound booklet; 68 pp
illus; no ISBN

...OR NOT TO BE
A Collection of Suicide Notes
by Marc Etkind

For a different kind of anthology, check out Marc Etkind's *...Or Not to Be*. Etkind has assembled over 130 suicide notes from people famous and unknown, presenting them along with intriguing background information. Before the 1700s, suicide notes were practically unheard of. As literacy rates rose in the eighteenth century, some people decided to leave their parting thoughts. The burgeoning newspaper industry printed these notes, and the public clamoured for more. Etkind writes that "... newspapers gave potential suicides, for the first time in history, access to a mass audience. The suicide using his note could now craft his death to achieve sympathy, revenge, or posterity. Suicide was now self-expression." The first chapter of the book contains many of these early notes, the oldest being from 1743. In an interesting aside, Etkind observes that despite the radical changes that have taken place in the last three centuries, the reasons and psychological states evidenced in suicide notes have stayed the same.

The notes cover a wide range of attitudes and emotions, which are at times conflicting. The perfect example is this brief note: "Dear Betty: I hate you. Love, George". One man wrote a note to his dog: "Bow wow and good-bye, Pepper." Disgraced biologist Paul Krammerer wrote in part, "Simplest and cheapest would be to use the body in a university dissecting laboratory. I would actually prefer to render science at least this small service in this way. Perhaps my esteemed colleagues will find in my brain a trace of the qualities they found missing from the expressions of my intellectual activities while I was living." A kamikaze pilot wrote a haiku before his first (and last) mission: "Like cherry blossoms/In the spring/

Let us fall/So pure and radiant." Jo Roman argues in her note for what she calls rational suicide. "More than a decade ago I concluded that suicide need not be pathological. Further, that rational suicide makes possible a truly ideal closing of one's life span… Life perspectives clouded by the vagaries and fears of open-endedness become crystal clear."

Among the notes of note are those from Virginia Woolf, Kurt Cobain, Sylvia Plath, Dorothy Parker, Adolf Hitler, philosopher Arthur Koestler and his wife Cynthia, people who burnt themselves to death in protest at the Vietnam War, the first person to commit suicide by jumping out of an airplane, people who dove off of the famed Golden Gate Bridge, members of the People's Temple of Jim Jones, and failed actress Peg Entwistle, who leapt from the "H" in the famous Hollywood sign.

A few of the entries are not truly suicide notes. OJ Simpson wrote a note but never attempted to kill himself, and Ken Kesey wrote a fake suicide note when he was being pursued on drug charges. Vince Foster's note is valid only if you accept the theory that he killed himself. Some "notes" were actually delivered as speeches, including those by Yukio Mishima, Jim Jones, and Pennsylvania state treasurer Bud Dwyer, who shot himself in the mouth during a press conference. One whole chapter is devoted to suicide *diaries*, including those of photographer Diane Arbus and Italian writer Cesare Pavese. There's even a remarkable set of entries by non-famous people who kept writing as they were in the process of dying from poison.

Etkind's remarks add to the insights gained by reading the notes. He points out that although the Bible mentions suicide, it never condemns it. It wasn't until the fifth century that Saint Augustine declared dying by one's own hand a sin. Research has shown, "Women who use birth control pills attempt suicide more often than those who use a diaphragm." The suicide rate is lowest during December and highest during May and June, showing that holidays don't have anything to do with suicide. After Marilyn Monroe died, the suicide rate increased twelve percent (this copycatting is known as the Werther effect, from the suicidal hero of Goethe's *The Sorrows of Young Werther*).

In his introduction, Etkind apologetically proffers that this collection is valuable because of the chance it gives us to understand people who commit suicide. He leaves out two facts. First, reading these notes appeals strongly to the voyeur in us all. Second, suicide notes can be treated as a fascinating, if crass, literary genre. These are the final bursts of creativity from individuals who are about to end their own lives. They may not be the most virtuosic examples of writing, but they are one of the most brutally direct.

Riverhead Books (The Berkley Publishing Group); $10
1997; softcover; 116 pp
1-57322-580-0

SEDUCED BY DEATH
Doctors, Patients, and the Dutch Cure (Revised Edition)
by Herbert Hendin, MD
The debate over whether or not to legalise physician-assisted suicide and euthanasia rages in the US and other countries. The debate is often framed in theoretical terms concerning the rights of the patient. What would really happen, though, if these practices were legalised? The Netherlands gives us the answer, because in that country assisted suicide and euthanasia are legal and commonplace. Dr. Herbert Hendin shows that this legalisation has unleashed unexpected consequences and has actually given more power to *doctors* and less to patients, as doctors suggest death without exploring other alternatives, base their decisions to kill patients on issues that should be irrelevant (such as whether the patient can continue to pay for treatment), and even kill patients without consent.

W.W. Norton and Company; $14.95
1997, 1998; softcover; 304 pp
0-393-31791-9

EMBRACING DEATH

AZRAEL PROJECT NEWSLETTER
This is *the* networking resource for death junkies. Whether you are into the spiritual, literary, artistic, musical, or other aspects of the Angel of Death (a/k/a Azrael), this newsletter will give you plenty of leads. The Statement of Purpose reads: "The purpose of the Azrael Project is to put forth the word of the Angel of Death and thereby conquer fear through understanding. To make people aware of the essential nature of Death, and to help mankind see their universe through His eyes in order to gain a macrocosmic understanding of both, Life and Death. To view the world from neither side of eternity, but rather from the threshold between the dimensions of space and time. To reconcile Life with Death, rekindle precarnate memory, and replace fear with love."

In the most compelling section, readers write about their encounters with the Great Equaliser. Sometimes Death appears as a hooded Grim Reaper, an androgynous winged being, or an unseen energy force. In Volume 4 #2, one man relates that when he was eight, he was by himself when he fell through some ice and almost drowned. He grabbed on to something that was poking him. It turned out to be the Reaper's scythe. "Death actually saved my life, and I have felt His presence with me ever since."

There are three pages of small type listing addresses and interests of readers who would like to hook up with people of a similar bent. Some of the interests listed include cemeteries, vampires, occult, magick, gothic music, dark eroticism, necrophilia, and one instance of "death by drowning". Two sections contain reviews or blurbs about death

Uncle Tim — flower power till the end.
Design for Dying.

books, zines, music, art, organisations, and other sundry items, such as handmade wooden coffin boxes. Poetry, fiction, ads, and a calendar of events round out the wonderfully macabre offerings.

Azrael Project Newsletter is put out by Westgate Press, publishers of several books on Azrael and other necromantic subjects. Westgate Press is the publishing arm of the Westgate Gallery, which displays and/or sells fine art, prints, posters, sculptures, artefacts, books, and other items revolving around the Angel of Death. They're open Tuesdays through Saturdays, 12:30 PM until 5:30 PM, and other times by appointment.

Westgate Press/5219 Magazine St/New Orleans LA 70115

Single issue: $3

Two issue sub (one year): $10

Westgate Press catalogue: free

DESIGN FOR DYING

by Timothy Leary with RU Sirius

By now the sex-positive movement — led by Susie Bright, Annie Sprinkle, Carol Queen, and many others — has become well-known among nonconformists. Their message that sex is natural, exciting, and non-shameful is hopefully encouraging lots of people to get rid of their hang-ups. I believe that Timothy Leary — the reality hacker best known for promoting LSD during the 1960s — may help to create the *death-positive* movement. When he was diagnosed with prostate cancer in January 1995, Leary refused to go into isolation and die in solemn privacy. In fact, he did the opposite... he made his impending death an event, a party even. He invited a constant stream of friends, colleagues, and in-

terviewers to his abode to laugh, talk, reflect, and trip. He told them exactly how he was feeling and what he was going through. He openly discussed how much he was looking forward to his "ultimate trip". By doing so, he actively demonstrated that death, like sex, is natural, exciting, and non-shameful. In the introduction to *Design for Dying*, published posthumously, he writes: "Personally, I've been looking forward to dying all my life. Dying is the most fascinating experience in life. You've got to approach dying the way you live your life — with curiosity, hope, experimentation, and with the help of your friends." Perhaps Leary's words and deeds won't inspire a full-fledged movement (after all, you can screw your brains out for decades on end, but you can only die once), but hopefully they will help some people see their deaths in a different light.

In *Design*, which was largely written while Leary had the cancer and was then ironed out by *Mondo 2000* founder RU Sirius, Uncle Tim gives you clues, suggestions, and pointers for designing your own death, as well as living your own life. In fact the first of the three sections in this book doesn't have to do with dying — it has to do with "Living". Leary gets extremely heavy in these chapters, positing his final, updated thoughts on the nature of self, the nature of reality, and the meaning of life. I won't even attempt a summary here, except to say that it's a melange of game theory, quantum physics, chaos theory, cyberspace, DNA, space colonies, evolution, psychedelic substances, archetypes, cybernetics, language, group therapy, mutation, and much, much more.

In section two, "Dying", things become more lighthearted. The title of the first chapter, "Dying? Throw a House Party!" should give you an indication of where things are headed. Leary writes that he was "thrilled" when he got the news he was dying, and he posted a sign in his home that read, "The mother of all parties." "It's wonderful having everybody come and pay tribute before you die, in a spirit of joy and friendship — no morbidity, please. Instead of treating the last act in your life in terms of fear, weakness, and helplessness, think of it as a triumphant graduation. Friends and family members should treat the situation with openness, rather than avoidance." Leary further advises us to stay out of hospitals, which he calls "vicious, alienating death factories." At home, you can do drugs, snuggle up with someone, and have visitors whenever you want.

Leary goes on to describe the media circus that ensued when his design for dying became known, the taboos that societies and religions have placed on death throughout history, and some of the people who are currently challenging that taboo (Elisabeth Kübler-Ross and Jack Kevorkian). He offers some practical advice for reprogramming your feelings towards death and "experimenting with dying" through out-of-body experiences, near death experiences, and psychedelic trips.

In the final section of the book Leary looks at alternatives to dying. Some of these methods include preserving all or parts of your body through deep-freezing (cryonics), transferring your consciousness to a computer or cyborg, repairing your declining body with molecule sized machines (nanotechnology), and other radical solutions that are either brand-new or are not yet available.

To wrap up the book, Sirius writes about how Leary ultimately chose to die, and various friends and family — John Perry Barlow, David Byrne, Ram Dass, Laura Huxley, and Rosemary Woodruff Leary among them — reflect on what they learned from Leary's death and recall their favourite memories involving him.

HarperEdge (HarperCollins Publishers); $24.00
1997; hardcover; 239 pp
0-06-018700-X

HOW TO DIE AND SURVIVE
The Interdimensional Travel Manual
by Angela Browne-Miller

Angela Browne-Miller believes that dying is a form of interdimensional travel. Anytime you travel somewhere you haven't visited before, it's bound to make you a little jittery, perhaps even frightened. With death, it's even more nerve-wracking, since there is no round-trip ticket (with the possible exception of near-death experiences). Miller wants to prepare you for this ultimate trip. She says that the lessons she teaches also apply to any major transitional experience in life and can benefit people who are grieving for loved ones.

The basic framework for dealing with these great changes is a series of seven "LEAPs", which stands for "light-energy-action-process". Each LEAP represents a new shift in consciousness that allows you to see things differently and prepares you for the next LEAP. "All death LEAPs, large and small, are great shifts in awareness... The realisation that a LEAP in one's awareness has taken place is key to mastery of death... Again, the LEAP is a movement from one dimension of reality to another. A LEAP is most effective when consciously constructed and purposely fuelled. Then the LEAP lasts, becoming more than a brief insight, becoming a spiritual elevation, a solid stepping stone in your ascension into higher consciousness."

The first LEAP, "Embracing", is summarised as, "Accepting, feeling ready for, fully moving into the death (or shift) out of a dimension or a phase of life or out of the physical body." From there the LEAPs proceed through Quickening, Willing the Exit, Leaping to the Next Dimension, Ascending, Catharting Beyond, Metascending, and Achieving Metastasis and High Metaxis. "High metaxis is the greatest of all LEAPs: from wherever you are, right now or at any given moment, right into the most divine realm of the highest, purest, clearest Light."

Along the way, Miller goes into great depth about each level with 56 short chapters, including "Learning How to Die", "Releasing Attachments", "Dissolving the Self: At the Membrane", "Detecting Portals and Gateways", "Dying with Purpose", and "Harvesting Death for Freedom". Each chapter includes at least two, and usually more, exercises that will allow you to put the book's teachings into practice. For more information on her approach, check out the Metaterra Website at www.metaterra-link.com.

Truth Seeker Publications; $27.95
1997; softcover; 324 pp
illus; 0-7872-3705-1

Don't play with dynamite.
Death Scenes.

IMAGES OF DEATH

DEATH SCENES
A Homicide Detective's Scrapbook
edited by Sean Tejaratchi

Jack Huddleston was a homicide detective with the Los Angeles Police Department from 1921 to the early 1950s, back when the City of Angels was *noir* incarnate. He kept a six-inch thick scrapbook of crime scene photos, morgue shots, and other gruesome images of suicides, homicides, and accidents. *Death Scenes* is a reprinting of around 300 of the most interesting and startling pages from the hard-boiled copper's collection. His original typed and hand-written notes accompany the brutal photos.

One chapter contains images of accidents, including a woman who burned to death while smoking in bed, a boy and girl who played with dynamite that exploded, a car accident victim's decapitated head sitting upright in the middle of the road, and victims of a couple of hit-and-run accidents. The suicide chapter opens with a blood-drenched man slumped on a sofa. His right hand still holds a gun, and his temple contains a hole. Other photos show a man who plunged out of a courtroom window after being sentenced to death for murder, Jean Harlow's husband collapsed on the floor of a bathroom, what's left of a man's face after he used a shotgun on himself, and a Japanese man who apparently committed *hara-kiri* by stabbing himself in the throat. The first of ten pictures of people who hanged themselves contains one of Huddleston's few (weakly) humorous captions: "JUST A LITTLE THROAT TROUBLE".

The book's longest chapter is devoted to homicides. The caption under one picture indicates that the 91-year-old man's throat was cut by his 83-year-old wife because she saw him talking to a female neighbour. Another image shows a woman who was killed and then fucked by her husband. Among the other scenes: movie cowboy Tom Bay killed by his girlfriend, three children killed with a hammer by their mother, a two-week-old baby whose head was cut off by his mother, a woman who was cut into four pieces by another woman, three of Albert Dyer's victims, and several dead policemen and bootleggers. It's a tough call, but perhaps the harshest shot is the torso of a woman whose head and hands have been chopped off.

The book's last chapter shows morgue photographs of people who died in all kinds of ways — car accidents, knife attacks, buckshot in the chest, dog attack, split skulls, and suicide. The first chapter presents material different from all the others. Apparently Huddleston also collected photographs of anything unusual, such as a shrunken head from Borneo, hermaphrodites' genitals, a man with elephantiasis of the testicles, a kitten using a chamberpot, and a man with advanced leprosy being treated at LA County Hospital.

This is perhaps the most ruthless, unrelenting book you'll ever lay eyes on. As Katherine Dunn says in her superb, insightful introductory essay: "The evidence that the crimes of Jack Huddleston's era were as brutal and deranged as anything that happens today offers a grim lesson in the nature of the human animal." Highly recommended.

Feral House; $19.95 (signed, limited edition hardcover: $39.95)
1996; oversized softcover; 168 pp
heavily illus; 0-922915-29-6

The picture they said could *NEVER* be shown..

The *Bloodiest* thing that ever happened in front of a camera!!

SNUFF

The film that could only be made in South America... where Life is *CHEAP!*

The most transgressive cinema of all.
Killing for Culture.

KILLING FOR CULTURE
An Illustrated History of Death Film
from Mondo to Snuff
by David Kerekes & David Slater

The idea of being able to watch someone die holds a morbid fascination for us. It's been said that death is the most powerful taboo of all. If that's true, then images of death are even more forbidden and revealing than hardcore pornography.

Killing for Culture is a comprehensive survey of death on film, whether faked or genuine, accidental or planned. The first part covers motion pictures based on death, starting with the most infamous one of all — the 1976 flick *Snuff*. This favourite target of feminists actually began life as *Slaughter*, yet another worthless piece of garbage made by husband and wife exploitation filmmakers Michael and Roberta Findlay. They shot it in Argentina in 1971, and it was such a stinker that even the distribution company who bought it wouldn't release it. But a few years later a plan was hatched. The distributors had a fake murder tacked on to the end of the film, then anonymously leaked stories to the media that true snuff films existed, including one that had come into the US from South America. The media went crazy and public curiosity was piqued. Right on cue, *Snuff* — "The film that could only be made in South America... where life is CHEAP!" — was released. The rest is history.

The next chapter meticulously covers several movies with plots revolving around snuff films — *Peeping Tom, Emannuelle in America, Hardcore,* and *Last House on Dead*

End Street. The final section of this chapter examines *Cannibal Holocaust,* David Cronenberg's *Videodrome, Henry: Portrait of a Serial Killer,* the satirical *Thrill Kill Video Club,* and the totally over-the-top *Man Bites Dog* (which you really should rent).

The middle section of the book is the longest. It covers "mondo films", those shockumentaries that include clips of real and fake carnage, among other strange and disturbing footage. The film that jump-started the whole genre is, of course, *Mondo Cane,* which features a woman breast-feeding a pig, geese being force-fed, religious penitents lacerating their legs, children polishing skulls, and people being killed by bulls. Following this movie were *Mondo Daytona, Mondo New York, Mondo Topless, Mondo Bizarro, Mondo Sex, Taboos of the World, Slave Trade in the World Today,* ad nauseam. The 1980s saw the invasion of the *Faces of Death* series and a slew of imitators, all showing nothing but pure death and mutilation. As the book makes plain, most of the footage in these kinds of films are either fake deaths, the killing of animals, autopsies, or archival accident footage. Not too many of them contain much genuine, recent human death caught on tape.

The theme of chapter six, "Babylon", is the integration of art and death. It discusses splatter zines, music videos using real or staged death footage (from SPK and Hijohkaidan, but surprisingly no mention of Nine Inch Nails), grotesque performance art, films that utilise actual death footage, Nazi atrocity documentaries, the slaughter house documentary

The Blood of the Beasts, and the Rolling Stones concert film, *Gimme Shelter*, which features footage of a fan being stabbed to death by Hell's Angels during the concert at Altamont.

The most interesting part of the chapter deals with a short Japanese film called *Flower of Flesh and Blood* (the second in a series called *Guinea Pig*). This movie features a man dressed as a Samurai who captures a young woman, ties her to a bed, cuts off her hands, arms, and legs, slices her wide open, plays with her intestines, beheads her, and sucks on her eyeball. *Guinea Pig 2* has gained fame, not only for its savagery, but also because Charlie Sheen was so distraught after seeing it that he alerted the FBI. The Feds were already on the case, as it turns out, and they eventually concluded that it was not a true snuff film. Apparently there are some people who still believe that it's genuine, but, having seen it, I can tell you that it is very gruesome but utterly unconvincing. (If you want to judge for yourself you can get it for $20.95 post-paid from the Catalogue of Carnage in the AlternaCulture chapter. They refer to it simply as *Guinea Pig*.)

The next chapter is a detailed cataloguing of actual deaths that were captured on tape. R. Budd Dwyer, former Philadelphia State Treasurer, shot himself in the mouth during a press conference (he's the subject of Filter's song, "Hey Man, Nice Shot"). Chris Chubbuck, a local news anchor in Florida, blew her head off during her morning show. In a rare on-screen murder, Emilio Nunez emptied his revolver into his ex-wife, whom he blamed for the suicide of their daughter. Several people have died while shooting movies, including Vic Morrow and two children in *Twilight Zone: The Movie*, Brandon Lee in *The Crow*, and several stuntmen.

The book's final chapter examines the enigma of snuff films. In its proper sense, a snuff film is footage in which a person is purposely murdered for the benefit of the camera. But such films are slippery beasts, and are probably urban legend. Everybody claims they exist, many people claim to have seen them or know someone who has, but when push comes to shove, there has never been a single instance of a verifiable snuff film. [See also *Gods of Death*, Merry Mischief chapter.] The authors provide a history of alleged snuff films and the hysteria surrounding them.

Killing for Culture is a bold, far-reaching overview of the most transgressive cinema of all. It describes the plots of many of the movies in excruciating detail, and it contains hundreds of movie posters and gruesome stills from the footage being described.

> Creation Books; $17.95
> 1994, 1995; oversized softcover; 353 pp
> heavily illus; 1-871592-20-8

TRAUMA CODE
On the Scene with Fire and Rescue
by Sonny Shepherd

Although *Trauma Code* gives numerous nods to emergency rescue workers in its title, dedication, captions, etc., there really is one reason, and only one reason, to get this book — to see black and white photos of mangled corpses. Over 120 full-page pictures show what's left of people who died in bad ways. Amid the twisted wreckage of a car, we see charred objects barely recognisable as human bodies. A man with the top half of his head completely blown off by a gunshot reclines in his underwear and socks. A woman's twisted body rests on the railroad tracks where she was run over by a train. A head lies on its side next to the elevator shaft where the victim was decapitated. An elderly man's head is smooshed like a tomato when a car door is forced closed on him. Several bloated bodies wash up on river banks.

Not every shot features gruesome stiffs, though. A small percentage show the remains of vehicles, such as a truck on its side in a river or a small airplane that smacked into a building. One arresting picture shows rescuers administering oxygen to an unconscious cat, which, along with some guinea pigs, was the only survivor of a house fire.

Not everyone's cup of tea, but if you're a gorehound, it's much cheaper than a medical textbook. The new printing of Trauma Code has improved production values with a hinged spine and extra varnish for an ultra glossy look.

> Raven Entertainment; $19.95
> 1996; oversized softcover; 130 pp
> heavily illus; 0-9655450-6-7

MORE ON DEATH

AFTER THE FUNERAL
The Posthumous Adventures of Famous Corpses
by Edwin Murphy

"Most biographies end with the death and burial of their subject... This is a book that begins where biographies leave off." Every once in a while, the body or part of the body of a famous person continues to have interesting adventures after its owner has kicked the bucket. *After the Funeral* investigates the unpredictable fates of thirty-five people's remains. When the philosopher of freedom Thomas Paine was buried, one of his most ardent admirers, the radical reformer William Cobbet, dug up the body without permission. He paraded it around England in order to raise money for a monument to Paine. When that scheme unsurprisingly failed, he left the corpse to his bankrupt son, who lost it. Its whereabouts remain unknown. You'll also read about the travails of Francisco Goya's skeleton, Mozart's head, Richard the Lionhearted's heart, Abraham Lincoln's corpse, Albert Einstein's brain, and Dorothy Parker's ashes. Unfortunately, the illustrations only show the people when they were alive or their resting places, and not what they looked like after the funeral.

> Citadel Press (Carol Publishing Group); $9.95
> 1995; softcover; 248 pp
> illus; 0-8065-1599-6

THE BIG BOOK OF DEATH
by Bronwyn Carlton and 67 comic artists

Take an entertaining look at death, with 67 comic sequences written by WFMU talk show host Bronwyn Carlton and illustrated by mainstream and underground comic artists. Each one- to six-page vignette, done by a different artist, covers some aspect of death — capital punishment, murder, suicide, disease, physical disposal, cemeteries, and so on.

The brooding "Look Out! It's the Killer Postman" presents a history of mail workers who snapped and returned fellow employees to their Sender. In a very flat, high-contrast style, Batman artist Mark Wheatly tells of Typhoid Mary, the cook who spread typhoid to literally thousands of people, causing dozens of deaths in New York at the beginning of the century. Richard Sala applies his unique, pointy style to eight strange cases of death. "In 1981, Kenji Urada became the first person killed by a robot when he was disassembled by an automated assembly machine."

Other topics that are dealt with include firing squads, teen suicide, war, spontaneous human combustion, cryonics, the Vienna Funeral Museum, organ donation, cannibalism, necrophilia, and famous last words. *The Big Book of Death* doesn't shy away from gruesomeness, yet it manages to achieve a high level of dark humour. Don't fear the Reaper — laugh at him!

Paradox Press; $12.95
1995; oversized softcover; 223 pp
heavily illus; 1-56389-166-2

THE FORTEAN TIMES BOOK OF STRANGE DEATHS
compiled by Steve Moore

For over 20 years the excellent British magazine *Fortean Times* [*Outposts* p 190] has chronicled the unexplained, unusual, and utterly bizarre aspects of our world. Its section "Strange Deaths" is particularly delightful for those of us with a morbid curiosity and sense of gallows humour. This book collects hundreds of the best short pieces from that section and is therefore an unparalleled compendium of the weirdest ways in which people have bought the farm.

Strange Deaths opens with the only picture in the book, and it's worth more than a thousand words. It shows an ill-fated tryst between a man and a hen. A bricklayer in Spain abducted the fowl and was having his wicked way with it by a riverbank when his movements dislodged a granite boulder that fell on the couple, crushing them to death instantly.

The rest of the freaky fatalities are divided into 21 chapters covering death by machine, human sacrifice, suicide, cannibalism, guns, cold weather, etc. The chapter on deaths caused by animals contains the case of a Spanish woman who had gone fishing. "She was trying to free the hook from a fish's mouth in July 1983 when the fish jumped out of her hand and into her mouth. She choked to death as it wriggled down her throat."

One of the most unbelievable chapters deals with deadly coincidences. "Moped rider Erskine Lawrence Ebbin was knocked off his machine by a taxi and killed in Hamilton on 20 July 1975. It was the same taxi, with the same driver,

Going out in style.
Going Into Darkness.

carrying the same passenger that killed his brother Neville, on the same day of the previous year. Both brothers were 17 at the time, and had been riding the same moped in the same street."

I could go on and on — telling you about the women who killed her husband because he was possessed by Mickey Mouse, the Chinese psychic who beheaded a boy as a sacrifice for the correct lottery number, the gravedigger who dropped dead and tumbled into the grave he had been preparing, or the chess grandmaster who was electrocuted by the computer he had just beaten three times in a row — but suffice it to say that this book proves that there *is* something funny about death.

John Brown Publishing; £4.99
1995; softcover; 128 pp
illus; 1-870870-50-6

GOING INTO DARKNESS
Fantastic Coffins From Africa
by Thierry Secretan

In most industrialised countries, for a few grand you can be buried in a super-deluxe, hermetically-sealed, velvet-lined, cushioned titanium coffin. Not only is this a colossal waste of money, it's incredibly boring. But in the Accra region of Africa, they know how to go out in style. The custom-made coffins used by the Ga tribe reflect the people who are buried in them. With lots of big colour photos and a little text, *Going Into Darkness* presents eight such coffins, each one carved to resemble something wholly unexpected — a lion, an eagle, a chicken, a sardine, an onion, a cocoa pod, a boat, and a Mercedes Benz. Each coffin is the subject of a short photo essay, showing the recipient on his death bed, the construction of the coffin, the funeral service, and the burial itself.

Thames and Hudson; $24.95
1995; oversized softcover; 127 pp
heavily illus; 0-500-27839-3

TOMBSTONES
Seventy-Five Famous People and Their Final Resting Places
by Gregg Felsen

Tombstones presents glossy colour pictures of the places that house the remains of 75 writers, artists, actors, politicians and other well-known people. Memorials to the deceased range from the nondescript tombstones of James Dean and Washington Irving to the elaborate monuments of Al Jolson and Abraham Lincoln. Along the way there is also the statue of Stonewall Jackson perched on top of his tombstone, the carved obelisk of John Wilkes Booth, Karl Marx's imposing tombstone with an equally imposing bust of him on top, Emily Dickinson's elegant marble tombstone, the Celtic cross of Andrew Carnegie, the simple marker of Wyatt Earp and his wife, the extravagant circular stone-and-marble monument of George Eastman, George Gershwin's mausoleum, the heart-shaped tombstone of Jayne Mansfield, Elvis Presley's tomb at Graceland, the 2200-year-old Greek vase containing Sigmund Freud's ashes, the detailed statue of James Joyce sitting cross-legged on his tombstone, and the metal markers over Frank Lloyd Wright's original grave, done in his signature style.

Each full-page picture is accompanied by a short, punchy biography of the grave's occupant. While these bios reveal some interesting facts about the people's lives and deaths, there is barely a word spoken about the gravesites themselves. Since the monuments to the dead are the focus of the book, this is a glaring and frustrating oversight. I'd like to know why the carved scroll that takes up two-thirds of Herman Melville's tombstone is glaringly blank. Was that a symbolic move, or did nobody ever get around to chiselling an epitaph? Why did Walt Whitman choose to be buried in a mausoleum that looks like a structure from Stonehenge with a pyramid on top? And who paid for the stylised angel that flies on the massive gravestone of Oscar Wilde, who died in poverty?

Tombstones succeeds as a visual guide to the resting places of famous people, but it fails as an informational guide.

Ten Speed Press; $19.95
1996; oversized softcover; 153 pp
heavily illus; 0-89815-860-5

VOICES OF DEATH
Letters and Diaries of People Facing Death — Comfort and Guidance for All of Us
by Edwin Shneidman

Using letters, diaries, interviews, suicide notes, and his own observations, Edwin Shneidman — co-founder of the Los Angeles Suicide Prevention Centre — tries to provide us with the thoughts and feelings of people for whom death is imminent. By listening to what they say as they stand at death's door, maybe we can gain some insight into the fate that awaits us all.

One chapter looks for clues in suicide notes. Shneidman reprints and comments on notes that indicate the suicide was caused by hate, love, shame and disgrace, fear of going insane, traumatic rejection, or ambivalent emotions.

In a similar vein, the next chapter deals with documents written by people who knew they would be soon be facing a violent death, including Jewish people in Nazi concentration

Hooks, tridents, skewers, and holes.
Beyond Belief.

camps and German soldiers sent on a suicide mission. There are also letters written by prisoners — John Brown, Bartolomeo Vanzetti, and others — on the eves of their executions. Chidiock Tichborne, who was executed for conspiring to kill Queen Elizabeth in 1586, wrote a poem in the Tower of London: "My tale was heard, and yet it was not told;/My fruit is fall'n, and yet my leaves are green;/My youth is spent, and yet I am not old;..." I think it's safe to say that the world didn't lose a great poet that day.

Other chapters deal with the thoughts of people with terminal illnesses, people who have survived suicide, old people, and loved ones left behind. Thanks to its large amount of primary documents, *Voices of Death* provides an intriguing glimpse into the minds of those who are about to depart this vale of tears.

Kodansha America; $12
1980 (1995); softcover; 206 pp
1-56836-112-2

BODY MODIFICATION

BEYOND BELIEF

There isn't an introduction, a back cover blurb, or even any captions to give us some orientation concerning these 72 photographs. All I can tell you is that they depict numerous acts of heavy-duty body manipulation and modification. Perhaps the single most common act portrayed is the insertion of an object through the mouth via holes in each cheek. In one series, a man with Sanskrit (I think) characters tattooed across his throat inserts a silver skewer through his face. In

348 • Psychotropedia

another picture a woman with a spike through her nose glides a fairly thin little trident through another woman's cheeks. Another man ups the ante by criss-crossing a prong from two large tridents through his mouth. Later we see the same guy with the *handle* of a trident — which must have a diameter of at least half an inch — pushed through the holes in his cheeks.

In a series of photos interspersed throughout the book, large hooks are inserted into a man's back, and a guy dressed like Pinhead from the *Hellraiser* movies hoists him until he is suspended with his entire body perpendicular to the ground. Another series shows a man with a Tank Girl tattoo on his left pec inserting scads of hypodermic needles along his arms, chest, legs, and forehead. Afterwards, he displays a tray filled with a pile of the bloody needles. The other pix show similar instances of people with hooks, tridents, skewers, and other objects embedded in various parts of their anatomies.

The photos are almost all in colour, printed on heavy, glossy paper. Quite a nice treat for the low price.

The Wildcat Collection; £6 postpaid, $10 postpaid

1996; staple-bound softcover; 48 pp

heavily illus; no ISBN

BODY ART

This square-backed, bookstyle magazine on body modification earns points for its high production values (most photos are in colour) and its broad range, which includes subjects like genderblending and body painting. Issue 20 has interviews with tattoo artist Juli Moon and the founder of Gauntlet and *PFIQ*, Jim Ward. There are photographic profiles of several people with unusual tattoos, including a man whose back is covered in gorillas and a woman who has an arrow running up the side of her torso onto the back of her upper arm. The article "The Third Gender" was written by a woman who has become androgynous through shaving her entire body and having her breasts removed. (Two pictures of the author accompany the article). Probably the most striking photos in this issue are of the winners of the Annual Body Painting Competition. The winner was Gillian Farnsworth, who painted her body to look like an anatomical drawing that shows all the muscles and tendons. Other winners include a man who looks like a cross between a cheetah and a cyborg, a woman with a beautiful sky scene painted on her upper body and face, and a woman who looks like she's wearing Spiderman's costume as designed by Keith Haring.

Issue 21 has more body painting, photos by Housk Randall, images from the 1870s of the Tamil people of India, and photos from the book *The Illustrated Woman*. A series of full-page photos from the portfolio of Frederic Karikese is the highlight of the issue. Karikese sets up dramatic shots of "a post-apocalyptic world peopled by haunting figures." None of his models have permanent body modifications, but they all wear outrageous quasi-cyberpunk costumes. One woman has wires taped to her bare chest, three lines of a language that looks like Sanskrit scrawled across her belly, black leather arm bands with giant screws sticking out of them, and four hypodermic syringes holstered on her leg.

Body Art is an impressive magazine, but I don't know if it's worth the huge cost of having it sent to the US.

Publications Limited/PO Box 32/Great Yarmouth, Norfolk NR29 5RD/UK

Single issue: US Surface: $27. US Air: $31. UK: £8. All others Air: £11.50

Four issue sub (one year): US Surface: $70. US Air: $90. UK: £30. All other Air: £44

Payment: US ck, UK ck, Eurocheque, Visa, MC, Eurocard, Access

THE CHAMELEON BODY
Photographs of Contemporary Fetishism
by Nicholas Sinclair

A flood of body mod photography books has been hitting the market over the last three or four years (with no apparent end in sight), but this one stands apart from the crowd. Photographer Nicholas Sinclair is not a member of the subculture, but he is a famed portraitist. Proving that a true artist can work wonders even with a subject he's new to, Sinclair took these amazing black and white pictures within a year of being exposed to the modern primitive movement. Two things make them spectacular. One is Sinclair's ability to take crisp, understated pictures that let the subjects elegantly present themselves. The other is the choice of body enhancements that his subjects use. Where the current glut of books tends to make certain mods repetitive, these images show that there is always something new and exciting that can be done on the human canvas.

Suzy affixes shiny stars and baubles in symmetrical patterns to her beautiful face. They are complemented by her silver earrings, nose-ring, and labret piercing. The white feathers in her hair, black feathers on her shoulders, three diamond-studded collars, and overwrought diamond necklace give the impression of an upper crust woman gone Goth. Similarly, Polly combines such disparate elements as a jewelled broach affixed to her shaved head, a silver collar and armband, chunky rings, a partial corset, a studded leather bikini bottom, and a Red Sonja-style armoured bra into a most unsettling and provocative vision.

Christine Bateman and Fia Berggren don't appear to have any permanent body modifications, but they dress in such wildly elaborate SM-cyberpunk outfits that you may not even notice. The bizarre headgear Berggren wears in two pictures looks like it came from *The City of Lost Children* or a Terry Gilliam movie.

Enzo Junior's perfectly chiselled body and face might make you think he's actually a Greek marble statue, except Greek statues don't have rings through their nipples and navel. Dicky Dick is completely covered in tattoos, including his face and head, and he sports numerous facial piercings, with silver jewellery through his eyebrows, nose bridge, septum, lips, and cheeks. A photograph of three naked bald-headed men who look like they're caked in dry mud is spooky as hell. Elsewhere, Peter Mastin — who resembles Nosferatu, is formally clad in a British officer's uniform, although I don't think the spikes through his nose and the tops of his ears are military issue. The silver crosses and cruci-

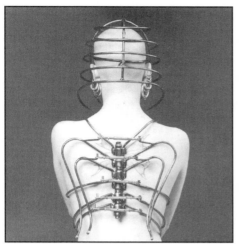

There is always something new and exciting that can be done on the human canvas. Polly, *The Chameleon Body*.

fixes pinned to Darryl Carlton's face and body contrast sharply against his ebony skin.

Performance artist Franko B does some wild stuff, mainly through fetishising disabilities and medical equipment. In one shot, his pale, powdered body is in a wheelchair. In another, he's leaning against a wall — nude except for leg braces and shoes — clutching an enema bag. The most extreme picture shows him walking down a hallway with a cane. He has an oxygen mask over his face, an IV sticking in his right arm, and a catheter that attaches to a urine bag.

Other photos showcase gasmasks, a beaked and feathered leather mask, and insectoid metal contraptions that wrap around people's heads, arms, and torsos.

The 64 photographs are bracketed by the essays "The Chameleon Body" and "Fetishism's Culture". The latter, with its look at the radically subversive power of sexuality, is especially interesting.

The Chameleon Body ranks as one of the four or five best books of body modification photography I've ever seen.

Lund Humphries; $55
1996; oversized hardcover; 112 pp
heavily illus; 0-85331-696-1

THE EYE OF THE NEEDLE
by Pauline Clarke

Pauline Clark, founder of the Piercing Association United Kingdom has created this large photo book devoted strictly to piercing. Over 250 pictures — more than half in colour — show people with jewellery in just about every body part that can have a hole put in it: ears, noses, lips, nipples, navels, tongues, inner and outer labia, clits, dicks, scrotums, and so on. Most of the subjects have other modifications, mainly tats. A lot of the photos, which were mainly taken at events and clubs, seem like a routine cataloguing of the various ways in which the body can be pierced. Occasionally there is something quite out of the ordinary, like a heavily-pierced

and painted scrotum with eleven rings through it, ears with at least eighteen rings, and a woman with inch-long nipples and inner labia that hang a good three inches. The choice of subjects is impressively egalitarian, with large people, old people, and others who don't have perfect bodies getting the same space as those who do.

Clarke's text examines each type of piercing and offers some general thoughts on the subject. A few people, including some pioneers, explain why they got pierced and what it means to them.

PAUK; £15
1994; oversized softcover; 124 pp
highly illus; 0-9521175-0-9

FLASH FROM THE PAST
Classic American Tattoo Designs, 1890-1965
by anonymous

Hundreds upon hundreds of vintage tattoo designs reproduced in colour in a horizontally formatted book. None of the tats featured are on people but are ink and water-colour on paper or illustration board (these were kept in tattoo shops for customers to browse). There are tons of variations on dames, Jesus, the American eagle and flag, roses, hearts, snakes, panthers, devils, Native Americans, and so on.

Hardy Marks Publications; $30
1994; softcover; 107 pp
heavily illus; 0-945367-13-9

GAUNTLET CATALOGUE

If you have an artificial hole, Gauntlet has something to fill it. The internationally-renowned piercing palace puts out a catalogue of jewellery for your every piercing need. Some of the jewellery is multi-purpose, such as barbell studs, L-bars, circular barbells, weights, and lots of rings. Captive bead rings come in an extremely wide variety, and jewelled rings are set with diamonds, emeralds, opals, etc.

Other jewellery is more specific for a certain piercing, including ear, eyebrow, tongue, lip and cheek, nostril, septum, navel, nipples, foreskin and penis, scrotum, labia, clit, and clitoral hood. Among the more unusual pieces offered are a captive ring with a spearhead weight, tusks that go through the septum, and nipple shields. You can also get forceps, piercing needles, insertion tapers, ring expanding pliers, jewellery boxes, and other tools of the trade.

Almost all of the jewellery comes in a variety of gauges (thicknesses), lengths, and diameters. Some are available in different metals — gold, surgical stainless steel, niobium, and sterling silver. A full colour two-page spread at the front of the catalogue has photographs clearly depicting all the types of piercings.

Gauntlet Customer Service/2215-R Market St, Box 801/San Francisco CA 94114
Voice: 1-800-RINGS2U (746-4728)
Fax: 415-252-1407
WWW: www.gauntlet.com
Catalogue: $5 (refundable with jewellery purchase)
Age statement (21+) required

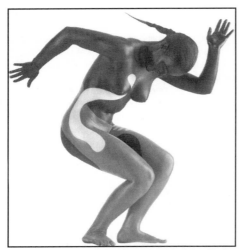

Christián Abelli's handiwork in *Painted Bodies*.

PAINTED BODIES

by Roberto Edwards

This humongous ten-pound book presents a lush look at a non-permanent form of body modification that appears to be growing in popularity. Body painting truly utilises the entire human body as a canvas, creating amazing aesthetic and erotic effects that are not achievable any other way.

Photographer Roberto Edwards invited forty-five Chilean artists to paint one or two models using special paints he had been developing for years. He then photographed these models against solid white or black backgrounds, making them pop out even more than the beautiful colours coating their bodies already do.

Edwards' images are presented on thick, glossy pages measuring a whopping 11" by 14". The models are female, except for a handful of males, and conform to widespread notions of beauty, with a couple of notable exceptions. The paint that they wear has been applied in the largest range of colours, tones, patterns, textures, and images you could imagine. A few are solid colours... dark grey or Smurf blue from head to toe. One woman is dark greenish-black with an eerie yellow mask painted onto her face.

Francisco de la Puente's model is off-white with Miró objects on her torso and calves. A leafy twig sticks straight up from her hair bun. The dry, cracking paint caked on one of the men makes him look like a sun-baked stretch of desert. Many other artists chose to follow a "back to nature" approach. A particularly effective instance involves a model who is mostly covered in shiny gold paint posing with vegetables. Would you believe that a woman draped over a large gourd or holding two heads of cabbage while gazing confidently at the camera could be sexy? It's true. Patricia Israel's butterfly women are quite spectacular to behold, too.

A brown-haired woman is painted with a circus motif, and her bush forms the mouth of a clown. Christián Abelli gave her model an olive green foundation, with orange flowing up her lower body. Another woman is chewing-gum pink

with blue "ribbons" wrapped around her legs and an apple over her right breast. Perhaps my favourite of all is the "Geisha", whose front is stark white with black Japanese characters running down her body. Her back is pure black with white hieroglyphics.

A few artists created pretend clothing. One model with a face like a mime artist looks like she's unzipping a black bodysuit. Another looks like she's in an old Vaudeville act, while a blonde appears to be wearing a conglomeration of leather and lace.

This is such an amazing collection that I'm sorry to see it priced out of reach of most people. I don't foresee very many libraries acquiring it, so I'm not sure who's going to be buying this lovely but pricey collection.

Abbeville Press; $75

1996; greatly oversized hardcover; 335 pp

heavily illus; 0-7892-0268-9

PFIQ

Put out by the fine folks at Gauntlet, *Piercing Fans International Quarterly* covers its subject completely and graphically. Every issue is filled with no-holes-barred photography showing off the latest in neo-primitive handiwork. Issue 43 has pictures of a woman who had her third nipple pierced (it's located directly below her left breast) and a man with a pierced throat. An interview with controversial piercer Jon Cobb includes a photo of a uvula piercing he performed. Cobb, who is known for doing unconventional and extraordinarily tricky piercings, is a self-taught piercer who uses "free-hand style" (i.e., almost no tools). He has also put an apadravya (vertical bar) through the base of his penis and an ampallang (horizontal bar) through the nape of his neck, disconcertingly close to the cranial nerve.

Issue 44 features a series of interviews, titled "Body Mod for Modified Bodies", that puncture more taboos than you can shake a Prince Albert at. Four of the five interviewees are pierced transgenderists — two are female-to-male, one is male-to-female, and one is a pseudo-hermaphrodite (i.e., "although a person will have most if not all the internal organs of a female, they will externally appear more male"). Close-up shots of their pierced genitals are included, so you can see exactly what's going on. The fifth subject of the series is a woman who pierced her left nipple and had breast reduction surgery.

Other articles in the issue look at body modification on the Internet, the SM cut-paper art of Joseph Bean, Folsom Street Fair, and how to pierce the tragus (the lobe just outside the ear canal).

Gauntlet Customer Service/2215-R Market St, Box 801/San Francisco CA 94114

Voice: 1-800-RINGS2U (746-4728)

Fax: 415-252-1407

Four issue sub (one year): $40. Canada, Latin America, Europe, Africa: $48. Asia and Pacific Rim: $52

Signed age statement (21+) required

PFIQ has been seized by Customs in Canada, the UK, Australia, New Zealand, and Japan

Unusual body mods abound in *Spheres of Adornment*.

PIERCING WORLD

A quarterly magazine on body piercing. Each issue contains around 60 photos — most in colour — of people with multiple and/or inventive piercings, most of whom also have tattoos. Articles cover different types of piercings, reports from body modification expos, and profiles of piercees.

PAUK/153 Tomkinson Rd/Nuneaton Warks CV10 8DP/UK

Single issue: UK: £4; US: £6

One year sub (4 issues): UK: £16; Europe: £20; Elsewhere: £25

SAILOR JERRY COLLINS
American Tattoo Master

edited by Donald Edward Hardy

The late Jerry Collins was "the foul-mouthed owner of a dimly-lit tattoo parlour in Honolulu's sleazy Hotel Street Sailortown area." He was an ingenious, inventive tattoo artist who took the best techniques of his mentors, added his own innovations, and thus became a master of the art.

Donald Edward Hardy corresponded with Collins from 1969 until Collins' death four years later. Those letters form the basis of the text in the book. They give an interesting portrait of a fun-loving yet ultra-conservative, racist man who truly loved what he did. Here are his thoughts on a colleague who was attacked at his studio. "He got hit on the head with a big coke bottle and robbed, in Jax, so he decided to give it up rather than take a chance on getting killed. What he should have done is blown that punk's asshole out with a shotgun full of buckshot. Makes them think, when they reach back to wipe their ass and it is gone, and they have to piss through a hole in their armpit." On one of his best customers: "Stays sober, and that is indeed a blessing compared to some of these creeps that have to get boozed up before they get guts enough to get on the bench." On tattooing women: "I tell them honestly that I would rather put one on their snatch

for free than put one on their arms for twenty dollars."

Of course, it's the tattoos that are most important here, and *Sailor Jerry Collins* is filled with hundreds of them. Probably a little less than half of them are on people, and the rest are on paper. One shows a sword through a heart, with a banner that says "Death Before Suck-Ass". Another one with the same design has a slightly different banner: "Death Before Castration". Continuing in the macho mode, another work is a picture of a booze bottle, a woman, and an anchor. The banner reads: "Stewed Screwed and Tattooed". One of the weirdest tats is on a guy's chest... just under his neck is a dotted line over the words, "Cut on Dotted Line". Other examples of Collins' handiwork include Jesus wearing a crown of thorns, Hula girls reclining by the sea, a ten-foot dragon winding all over a woman's body, plenty of mermaids, a tombstone that reads, "Better Dead Than Red!", Japanese floral and water scenes, King Tut, trigrams from the *I Ching*, a Sanskrit mantra, Poseidon, a pair of eyes on buttcheeks, and lots and lots of nekkid dames.

Hardy Marks Publications; $30

1994; oversized softcover; 168 pp

heavily illus; 0-945367-11-2

SPHERES OF ADORNMENT

by Pauline Clark

The follow-up to *The Eye of the Needle* [above], *Spheres of Adornment* takes a pictorial look at a wider variety of body modification practices. Visually, it's a much stronger book. Most of the photos are in colour, printed as full-page bleeds, and were taken in a studio, as opposed to candid shots or "hold still for a second and let me take your picture" shots taken at events (although there are some of those).

The book's main sections are based on a particular kind of mod — hair and facial adornment, fetish dress, tattoos, and body jewellery — but, of course, there is overlap since a lot of people have more than one kind. Some of the highlights include a bald guy with Sanskrit tattooed on his dome, a woman with a metallic sculpture on her head, numerous tats of famous men (Charles Bronson, David Bowie, Vincent Price, Winston Churchill), a woman's gorgeous back tattoo of a mermaid and a merman having sex, a heavily pierced grandfather type, a graceful shot of a woman with flowers tattooed on her shoulder holding an arrangement of flowers, a guy with metal spikes coming out of his head, lit birthday candles inserted through a woman's nips, a sleek male torso with chains attached to pierced nipples and cock, a series of pawprints tattooed up a woman's thigh, and super close-ups of a heavily pierced scrotum and vulva. There is also a photo of the most inexplicable tattoo I've ever seen. A woman's back is covered in a black and grey scene depicting an elephant stomping to death a tiger that has just killed a baby elephant. Somebody must really like *The Trials of Life*.

What little bit of text there is discusses the origins of different piercings, introduces each section, and deals quickly with a few other topics.

PAUK; £20

1996; oversized softcover; 152 pp

heavily illus; 0-9528179-0-X

NUDISM

FAMILY NATURISM IN AMERICA
by Iris Bancroft

Despite the word "family" in the title, this book is actually a general look at the history and present state of nudism in the continental US and Canada. The book's assertion is that nudism has made great strides in becoming more accepted and widespread. "Like civil-rights protesters nation-wide, nudists have risked (and sometimes sought) arrest in order to force courts to deal with the inequities of present laws. They recognise the right of dressed society to have 'textile' beaches, but they feel they deserve some good beach areas for nude swimming and sunbathing. They look forward to the day when, as in Europe, nude and clothed beaches will exist side by side with nothing more than a low wire fence separating the two. And that day seems closer now than ever before."

The text examines the groundbreaking camps and associations that challenged society's uptight notions as far back as the 1930s, some of the laws and court cases that have worked for and against nudists, and the rise of luxurious clothing-optional resorts. Occasionally the writing overgeneralises and becomes sappy and insulting to the intelligence: "Boat and resort owners quickly discover that nudists are well-behaved, responsible people who take care of the property they rent." "Sometimes nude sunlovers do encounter dressed vacationers on a wilderness path. However, most such meetings are friendly and provide the nudist/naturists with an opportunity to tell new people about the benefits of their lifestyle."

Of course, over 50% of the book is devoted to hundreds of colour pictures of people in the buff laughing, playing, swimming, sunbathing, hiking, getting massages, and just having an all-around great time.

Elysium-Sunwest; $24.95
1988; oversized softcover; 96 pp
heavily illus; 0-910550-54-9

LIVING NAKED AND FRUGAL
A Handbook for Parsimonious Nudity
by Paul Penhallow with Marilyn Lovell

In this manifesto and instruction manual, the late Paul Penhallow — a retired professor from Syracuse, New York — makes a tempting case for chucking your worries, your expenses, and your clothes by living at a nudist resort. In a relaxed yet enthusiastic style, he explains all the benefits, which include security. "Theft and pilferage are somehow just not compatible with living naked. Once inside the gate, locks are often forgotten as sort of 'clothing for doors.'" Another plus is the simple freedom that comes from naturism. "The instant you separate from all your tags and labels you become anonymous, just another plain face (or bare ass) in the crowd. You become so totally yourself that your 'good

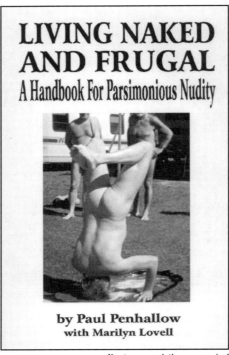

LIVING NAKED AND FRUGAL
A Handbook For Parsimonious Nudity

by Paul Penhallow
with Marilyn Lovell

No stress, no clothes, no worries!
Living Naked and Frugal.

buddies' who depend on shields, labels, and uniforms (whether military or corporate) would do a classic Marx brothers triple-take and still have to ask if that human in the buff in front of them is really you." Also, and perhaps most important from a purely practical standpoint, is the money factor. "My fees for a whole year at the resort where I now live are $1600. That is, I am living in a three-bedroom, two-bath trailer, and for a full year's access to all the facilities of a luxury resort I am paying less than three months' rent on my old one-bedroom apartment. And I'm living naked!"

Penhallow then devotes a separate chapter to each of the four maxims for living that he has developed: "Accept Yourself" (learning to feel comfortable when you're starkers), "Respect Others" (interacting with others at a nudist resort), "Live Simply" (inexpensive ideas for shelter, furniture, food, etc.), and "Relax Daily" (getting massages, working on creative projects, watching the world go by, and other activities of a "REAL life"). He ends with a listing of nudist facilities in 32 states where you can begin your new life.

Loompanics Unlimited; $8.95
1997; softcover; 91 pp
illus; 1-55950-165-0

"N" IS FOR NAKED
The Nudists from "A" to "Z"
by Ed Lange

This picturebook was originally published in 1961. It is almost totally comprised of around 100 pictures, most in b&w,

some in colour. The book is divided into 26 sections, each one based on a letter of the alphabet and a word that starts with that letter. For example, the chapter "V Is for Volleyball" has four shots of nudists engaged in their favourite sport.

"N" Is for Naked really must have been written for young children, because what little writing the book contains is so dippy that it would insult anyone over five. Not only that, but the syntax has been tortured so brutally it should apply for amnesty. Check out the first chapter: "A Is for Air… the stuff you breathe and can't see but feels good blowing over your skin unless you go indoors if it turns cold or maybe put some clothes on." Here's another example: "L Is for Looking… which is what eyes are for and then you want to touch but sometimes you can't if you are small or even after you grow up sometimes." The hell trying what you are to say?

Elysium-Sunwest; $21.95
1961, 1994; oversized softcover; 63 pp
heavily illus; 1-55599-052-5

NUDIST MAGAZINES OF THE 50S AND 60S, BOOK 3
by Ed Lange

This is the third volume of the popular series that reprints pictorials from nudist magazines published in the 1960s (with just a nod to the 1950s). Fifteen pieces are reproduced, totalling over 160 photos (including 16 pages in colour). The emphasis seems to be international… besides a guide to early foreign nudist magazines, there are reports from France, Denmark, Switzerland, and elsewhere in Europe.

"The Naked Lunch" — from *Nude Living*, December 1963 — reveals that, even though the French are considered to be sexually liberated, some nude paintings created in the nineteenth century caused outrage. Gustave Courbet dared to use live models for his nudes. "In 1853, his Bathers had created such a scandal at the Salon that Napoleon III struck the canvas with his riding crop in a gesture of disgust, while the Empress was heard to call the women 'Mares!'"

Elysium-Sunwest; $24.95
1995; oversized softcover; 95 pp
heavily illus; 1-55599-051-7

MISCELLANEOUS

ANIMAL INGREDIENTS A TO Z
(Second Edition)
compiled by the EG Smith Collective

If you're a vegetarian, a vegan (a person who doesn't eat or use any animal-derived products including meat, eggs, honey, etc.), or just someone who's trying to lessen her intake of animal products, this guide will help you decide what's OK and what's off limits. The longest chapter lists over 150 substances and comments on how they are used, whether they involve animals and, if so, what alternatives exist. We find that when pollen is collected from bees, their legs are often ripped off by the trap doors. One pound of the red pigment carmine can involve the deaths of 70,000 cochineal beetles. Shellac is "[o]btained from the bodies of the female insect Tachardia lacca." Gelatin — in everything from pudding and cake to cosmetics and photographic film — is made by boiling various body parts of cattle and hogs.

Two similar chapters list over 300 animal-derived products and over 500 that are usually obtained from animals. (These entries are not accompanied by any further information). Another chapter names 150 specific beers and other alcoholic beverages that are vegan-safe. An extremely helpful chapter examines the sources of nutrients, such as carbohydrates and vitamins, for vegans, while others expose myths (maple syrup doesn't contain pork fat) and refer you to books, Internet resources, and world-wide organisations concerning vegetarianism, veganism, and animal rights.

AK Press and E.G. Smith Press; £4.95, $6.95
1995, 1997; softcover; 87 pp
1-873176-59-7

AMOK JOURNAL
Sensurround Edition — A Compendium of Psycho-Physiological Investigations
edited by Stuart Swezey

A staggering collection of articles mainly from medical, psychiatric, and scholarly journals and texts exploring some of the most extreme areas in which the mind and the body meet. Inside this revelatory book you will read about autoerotic fatalities, which are deaths that occur when people masturbate in ways that cause super-intense orgasms (usually this involves cutting off the oxygen supply while coming); trepanation, the act of drilling or chipping a hole in one's skull for medical or spiritual purposes; Gualtiero Jacopetti, the director of *Mondo Cane* and other "shockumentaries"; South Pacific cargo cults; Neue Slowenische Kunst (NSK), a radical artistic collective from Slovenia; self-mutilation (including self-castration and gouging one's eyeball); amputee fetishes; the effects and uses of infrasound; hallucinations in hostage situations; lycanthropy, the condition in which people think that they're animals; a woman who masturbated with a deer tongue; a man who gave himself a concrete enema; and more. Because the Amoksters don't believe in being coy, they have generously included many photographs, including death scene photos of autoerotic fatalities, frontal pictures of men who have cut their penises and/or scrotums off, and a woman drilling a hole in her own skull.

Amok Books; $19.95
1995; oversized softcover; 476 pp
illus; 1-878923-03-X

BONES OF CONTENTION
Controversies in the Search for Human Origins (Second Edition)
by Roger Lewin

Rather than merely looking at different theories of how *Homo sapiens* evolved, *Bones of Contention* digs deeper, examining the controversies and disputes that occur within the paleoanthropology community when new hominid fossils are found. Every time a scientist unearths a new type of fossil and declares it a part of the human evolutionary tree, other scientists attack it for reasons that are professional (they don't agree with the new theory) and sometimes personal (paleoanthropology is filled with cantankerous, often bitter, rivalries). Sometimes it's hard to tell the difference between the two, since scientists of all types are sometimes so wedded to their theories that they won't rationally entertain alternative explanations.

Bones examines four particularly contentious disputes — the Taung Child, Rama's Ape, the KBS Tuff controversy, and "Lucy" — and the lives of two prehistorians who have been at the centre of much controversy, Louis Leakey and his son, Richard Leakey. Some of these controversies have been basically settled, while others (especially Lucy) continue to divide paleoanthropologists. But the author says that one thing is for certain — this branch of science will always remain one of the most dispute-filled because it touches on the most sensitive of issues: who we are and where we came from.

University of Chicago Press; $18.95
1987, 1997; softcover; 366 pp
illus; 0-226-47651-0

CANNIBALISM
From Sacrifice to Survival
by Hans Askenasy, PhD

The first comprehensive history of the practice of eating human flesh. Hans Askenasy examines the history of cannibalism around the world, looks in detail at reasons for cannibalism (famines, accidents, religious ritual, sadism, etc.), and probes the fascination with cannibalism in myth, literature, and the media. He covers the Aztecs, New Guinea, the Andes plane crash of 1972, Countess Bathory, Jeffrey Dahmer, *Eating Raoul*, and much more.

Prometheus Books; $26.95
1994; hardcover; 268 pp
illus; 0-87975-906-2

DEMONIC MALES
Apes and the Origins of Human Violence
by Richard Wrangham & Dale Peterson

Scientists and philosophers used to believe that the human race was the only type of animal that would seek out and kill an adult member of its own species. In certain species, two males will sometimes get violent during rutting season, but the fight stops when one backs down. Members of some species will fight to the death when one feels threatened by the other's presence. But it seemed than humans were the only ones who killed without being provoked, for reasons that didn't have to do with immediate survival. In January 1974 that perception changed forever. It was then that a member of Jane Goodall's research centre in Gombe, Tan-

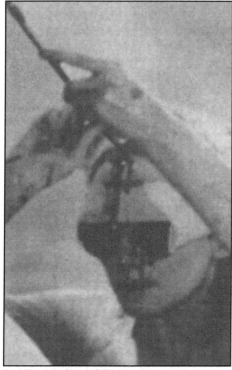

Head like a hole: Amanda Feilding's self-trepanning, recorded in her film <u>Heartbeat in the Brain</u>. *Amok Journal.*

zania, watched as a group of eight chimpanzees walked with determination out of their own territory and into that of a neighbouring chimp community. There they found Godi, a twenty-one-year-old male, in a tree by himself. They chased him. One of the attackers jumped on him and held him down while the others savagely beat him for ten solid minutes. He was gravely injured and in agony when they left. He was never seen again, and is believed to have died. After that, the human race realised that its closest cousins can be needlessly brutal and bloodthirsty, too.

It has also been discovered that the human race doesn't have a monopoly on sexual violence, either. Male members of several kinds of primates, if spurned by a female they're interested in mating with, will beat and then force themselves on that female. The authors even recount a jaw-dropping event that occurred at a scientific camp that was studying orang-utans in Borneo. A young male orang-utan actually raped the camp's female cook! Rape also exists outside of the primates, most notably in elephant seals, scorpion flies, and several species of duck.

The authors of this book apparently don't have a particular grand unified theory about why primates, including humans, are so aggressive or why violence is overwhelmingly a male pursuit. But they do offer some large pieces of the puzzle. At one point they write: "If emotion is the ultimate arbiter of action for both species [chimps and humans], then

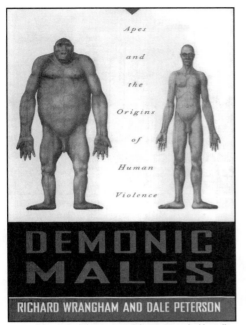

Humans don't have a monopoly on unprovoked brutality.
Demonic Males.

what kinds of emotions underlie violence for both? Clearly there are many. But one stands out. From the raids of chimpanzees at Gombe to wars among human nations, the same emotion looks extraordinarily important, one that we take for granted and describe most simply but that nonetheless takes us deeply back to our animal origins: pride." As soon as they make such a statement, though, the authors often point out exceptions to it or show how other factors play crucial roles, too. Over the course of the book, we learn about the closeness between chimps and humans, warfare among primitive peoples, the non-existence of perfectly peaceful societies, violent women, patriarchy, intelligence, infanticide among gorillas, territorialism, conformity and group identification, sexual selection, and many other strands.

In the final analysis, the authors suggest that male domination and brutality is perhaps not inevitable. We may yet see a human society that — like that of the bonobos primates — is gentle, equitable, and not based on power and force.

Houghton Mifflin; $24.95
1996; hardcover; 350 pp
illus; 0-395-69001-3

ECSTATIC BODY POSTURES
An Alternate Reality Workbook
by Belinda Gore

While studying works of non-Western art, including cave paintings and small stone sculptures, anthropologist Felicitas Goodman noticed that certain body positions and postures appeared repeatedly in different times and cultures. After some experimentation, she realised that these postures aren't random expressions of the artists' creativity but recordings of specific rituals. They reveal ways we can position our bodies in order to achieve altered states.

"What this book presents is a method for achieving ecstatic trance and its attendant visionary experiences… If a specific posture represented in one of these artefacts is combined with rhythmic stimulation, be that by drum or rattle, the body temporarily undergoes dramatic neurophysiological changes, and visionary experiences arise that are specific to the particular posture in question." Each one of the 40 postures explained in this book will trigger remarkably similar experiences in different people. For example, people in the Bear Spirit posture, used for healing, often report being held or engulfed by a bear that comforts them and takes away toxins and other garbage. Many others report being clawed open by the bear and having their pain escape through the "wounds". There is almost never any physical pain accompanying this process, however.

This book presents details on 40 postures which must be replicated exactly in order to have the desired effects. The positions are divided into seven categories — healing, divination, metamorphosis, spirit journeys, living myths, celebration, and initiation: death and rebirth. Each posture is accompanied by two detailed line drawings — one showing an ancient artefact using the position and the other showing a person assuming that position. The text explains where the posture originated, how it is used, what kind of experiences it triggers, and exactly how to do it yourself. All of the information is based on Goodman's twenty years of research with shamanic body postures, including holding regular workshops in which thousands of people have used these positions.

One posture, which involves laying on your back with your left arm over your eyes, often transports people to the Lower World. Assuming the posture of one of the drawings in the famous Lascaux Cave in France transports you to the Sky World. Replicating the position of a stone pipe effigy carved by the Adena Indians can help the seeker find answers to questions, especially about health and healing. By imitating an ancient Ecuadorian figurine with its legs crossed and its tongue completely extended, you can experience metamorphosis into other life forms.

Ecstatic Body Postures is an intriguing and perhaps very important book. Could it be that the keys to shamanic journeys have been right under our noses (or right before our eyes) for thousands of years?

Bear & Company; $20
1995; oversized softcover; 285 pp
illus; 1-879181-22-3

EXPLORING THE SPECTRUM
The Effects of Natural and Artificial Light on Fundamental Biological Processes and Health
by Dr. John N. Ott

Dr. John Ott is one of the founders of the science of photobiology, which studies the effects of light on living things. These two documentaries present some of his findings. They were obviously produced as educational films for classroom use… the narration, camera angles, and black spots blipping on screen are dead give-aways. I suppressed my urge to start a paperwad fight and settled down to watch what turned out to be an interesting presentation.

Ott got into his line of research through his hobby of filming plants using time-lapse photography. He not only time-lapsed flowers such as tiger lilies and morning glories, but he also filmed some plants, including pumpkins, continuously over periods of years. He noticed that some plants wouldn't bloom or bud under certain lights, so he would switch lights and achieve good results. In fact, he was able to get disease-ridden tomato plants to produce tomatoes.

Using time-lapse microphotography, Ott studied pigment cells from a rabbit's retina. He was doing research on the side effects of tranquillisers, but he noticed that the colour of the lighting he used to illuminate the slides had a much greater impact on the cells than the drugs did. With red light, the cells weakened and ruptured, while with blue light they contorted and went haywire. Under standard incandescent lighting, the cells were sluggish and showed almost no activity. When a little ultraviolet light was added, they started dividing again.

Later, Ott began to experiment with animals. Mice that spent weeks under pink fluorescent lighting developed spots and severe lesions on their tails, but mice raised in direct sunlight had normal tails. When mice from the first group were put into direct sunlight, their tails eventually returned to normal. But after six months under a pink light, the mice's tails shrivelled up and fell off. Mice living under purple fluorescent light lost their fur and developed lesions on their bodies.

Further studies have shown that male rats — who often eat their young after their mates give birth — are gentle and fatherly when living under full spectrum fluorescent lights. Mice with tumours have been shown to live longer when receiving a wider spectrum of light. Time-lapse photography of a first-grade class showed that when the lights were replaced with full spectrum lights, a hyperactive boy calmed down and began participating in class. He had been diagnosed with a learning disability, but after the new lights were installed, he learned to read within 90 days.

Ott presents convincing evidence that lighting plays a major role in how living things function and behave. His documentary contains a lot of time-lapse photography, meaning that not only is it informative, but it's also fun to watch. There'll be a quiz on this tomorrow. [Note: *Exploring the Spectrum* is also available in European PAL format.]

Orgone Biophysical Research Laboratory (Natural Energy Works); $29.95
1975, 1994; VHS videocassette; 80 min
0-9621855-2-3

GROWING OLD IS NOT FOR SISSIES II
Portraits of Senior Athletes
by Etta Clark

Growing Old Is Not For Sissies presented photos and pro-

Ninety-one-year-old Helen Zechmeister can deadlift 200 pounds. *Growing Old Is Not For Sissies.*

files of senior citizens who totally defy our expectations by being extremely active, healthy, and physically fit. In this sequel, photographer Etta Clark presents posed shots (and a few action shots) of around 100 athletes whose ages range from 52 to 100, with most of them in their 70s and 80s. A number of them were featured in Clark's first book, so we get to see through side-by-side photos how they've aged over the past ten or so years. Among these elderly jocks are a 77-year-old female fencer, an 83-year-old male rough-water swimmer, a 91-year-old female weightlifter, a 94-year-old female dancer, an 83-year-old male surfer, an all-woman dance troupe with an average age of 70, an 80-year-old male skier, a 68-year-old male ultra-marathoner (races of 100 miles), 68-year-old married bungee jumpers, and a 100-year-old female aerobics instructor.

Pomegranate Artbooks; $22.95
1995; oversized softcover; 117 pp
heavily illus; 0-87654-478-2

HERBAL ABORTION HANDBOOK
The Fruit of the Tree of Knowledge
by Uni M. Tiamat

Although abortion is still technically legal, that is becoming a moot point. Because of the fear of extreme tactics by some "pro-lifers", doctors who perform abortions are becoming a rare breed. Most medical schools no longer teach the procedure, and, if they do, it is often not required. It's getting harder and harder to get an abortion, and it's not inconceivable that the Supreme Court could reverse *Roe v. Wade*.

Given this situation, Uni Tiamat has decided to uncover a body of knowledge that has been for the most part forgotten. Women have used plants to induce abortions for millennia, and it is with this power that women can reclaim their bodies. Some of the pros of herbal abortion, as listed in this book, are that herbs are natural and believed to have fewer side effects than pharmaceuticals, most abortive herbs are easily accessible, the cost ranges from nothing to minimal, you don't run the risks of a clinical abortion (infection, perforated uterus, etc.), and, of course, you take control of your own body and life. The cons are that herbal abortion works

MULTRUM TOILET

(Garbage chute not shown)

Don't let your waste go to waste.
The Humanure Toilet.

best when done before eight weeks, effects of the herbs on the foetus and pregnancy are unknown should your herbal abortion not work, and if you have an incomplete abortion, you will have to get a clinical one.

The first section of the *Handbook* has background and general information regarding herbal abortions — when they're best performed, how to prepare, what to expect, what to do if the abortion is incomplete, finding assistance and support, gathering and buying herbs, and more. The author also gives a simple programme to follow, which includes exercising and taking lots of vitamin C, to help you not become pregnant if you have unprotected sex during your fertile time.

The second section gives the low-down on 20 herbs that can be used for abortions, including aloe vera, garlic, mistletoe, mugwort, rosemary, and saffron. These herbs work in different ways. Some, such as rue, prevent the fertilised egg from attaching to the uterine wall, so that it is flushed out with the next period. These kind of abortifacients are considered to be the safest and most effective. Other herbs work by imitating oestrogen, relaxing the uterus, or contracting the uterus.

For each herb, the author relates the botanical name, common names, parts used, medicinal uses, effects on the body, what it contains, a description, herbal lore, cultivation, gathering, preparation, dosage, signs of toxicity, and "words to the wise". Every herb is accompanied by an illustration.

The final section has a reading list, index, first aid for poisoning, and addresses for mail order herb suppliers, botanical gardens, organisations, cotton menstrual pads, and more.

The Herbal Abortion Handbook is an extremely important book. I recommend that everyone who may be in need

of an abortion one day get a copy. Powerful knowledge is crucial for self-reliance.

Sage-Femme; $16.95
1994; staple-bound softcover; 78 pp
heavily illus; 0-964520-3-7

THE HUMANURE HANDBOOK
A Guide to Composting Human Manure
by JC Jenkins

It's a shame to let our waste go to waste. If you're taking the things you read in *Psychotropedia* to heart, then you're already drinking your urine [see *Your Own Perfect Medicine*, above]. But what to do with the other half of the equation? "The simple truth is that we shit every day and we should be returning that organic material back to the soil," says the author. By flushing instead of recycling, we create disposal problems and unhygienic conditions while depriving the topsoil of vital nutrients that are now being supplied by petrochemicals.

With solid research and a good amount of (toilet) humour, homesteader JC Jenkins presents *the* groundbreaking work on reclaiming an important, abundant natural resource that we literally flushed away. He estimates that "… the US population today produces approximately 228,125,000,000 pounds of faecal matter annually. That's 228 billion pounds." After showing us many convincing reasons why we need to change our ways (for example, "It takes between 1,000 and 2,000 tons of water at various stages in the process to flush one ton of humanure."), Jenkins shows us how. His methods are always low-tech and thoroughly hygienic. He covers various types of toilets, including commercially available models, but he goes into the most detail about sawdust toilets, which are elegantly simple to construct and use. Composting gets two chapters, which cover having a good blend, the carbon/nitrogen ratio, building a compost bin, monitoring the compost, and then putting it to use. A separate chapter deals with pathogens and how to avoid them.

Using plenty of photos, cartoons, drawings, sidebars, and tables, Jenkins makes putting your shit to good use a painless process.

Jenkins Publishing; $19
1994; oversized softcover; 198 pp
highly illus; 0-9644258-4-X

OFF THE RAG
Lesbians Writing on Menopause
edited by Lee Lynch & Akia Woods

Over forty lesbians share their thoughts, feelings, and experiences regarding the "change of life". "An Ode to Estrogen", "Menopause and the Gift of Healing", "Hot Flash to Warm Glow", "Desire Perfected: Sex After Fifty", "Kotex, Tampax and Vitamin E", "Free! Free! Free!", "The Period: A Sequel", "Toward a New Understanding of the Importance of Eating Weeds", "Trapped in Jello", and "Hormonic Convergence".

New Victoria Publishers; $12.95
1996; softcover; 232 pp
illus; 0-934678-77-4

THE RE/SEARCH GUIDE TO BODILY FLUIDS
by Paul Spinrad

Displaying a level of candour approaching 100%, Paul Spinrad has written a book that openly discusses all of the substances (fluids, solids, and gases) that our bodies produce. His good-natured romp through faeces, farts, vomit, urine, snot, saliva, tears, eye gunk, earwax, smegma, toe cheese, bellybutton lint, dandruff, milk, semen, vaginal secretions, female ejaculate, sebum, sweat, and menstrual blood enthusiastically examines all the minutiae surrounding these taboo topics.

Spinrad designed a bodily function survey that was filled out by 106 people. He discusses the results in the appropriate sections throughout the book. The answers are revelatory. After all, do you know how many other people wipe themselves the way you do? Forty-four percent of the respondents said they reach around their backs and wipe from bottom to top, while 11% said they reach between their legs and wipe top to bottom. Six percent wipe top to bottom from behind their backs, and four percent wipe bottom to top between their legs. Ever wondered how many other people share your habit of nosepicking? According to the survey, 96%!

Speaking of slimy material, Spinrad offers nutritional information regarding semen. "Its chemistry varies widely, but in rough numbers, 3.5 ml of semen [an average ejaculation] contains 11 mg. carbohydrates, 150 mg. protein, 3% of the US RDA for copper and zinc, 7% of the RDA for potassium, less than one calorie, and only 3 mg. cholesterol and 6 mg. fat."

In the late 1800s Joseph Pujol became one of the most popular entertainers in Paris. His act consisted of farting. But not just your run-of-the-mill tooting... he could break wind in tenor, bass, or baritone. He would put a tube up his anus and use it to smoke a cigarette and play the flute. For his finale, he blew out gas lights from a distance. Another amazing fart fact you'll learn: "Farts-to-be can sometimes actually be seen as dark cloudy areas on X-rays of the pelvis."

Spinrad also delves into constipation, fossilised turds, motion sickness, urine therapy, trying to urinate with genital piercings, feminine protection products, Thomas Crapper, excrement in religion, bodily functions in literature and cinema, sanitation in Western history, and more.

Although *The RE/Search Guide to Bodily Fluids* is humorous, it's also a very important book. It marks the definitive outing of an unexplored bodily taboo.

RE/Search Publications (Juno Books); $15.99
1994; oversized softcover; 148 pp
illus; 0-940642-28-X

SHATTERING THE MYTHS OF DARWINISM
by Richard Milton

It seems as though the only people who have ever attacked Darwin's theory of evolution are Christians who believe that if they destroy Darwinism, it will somehow automatically prove that their creation mythology is really the way things hap-

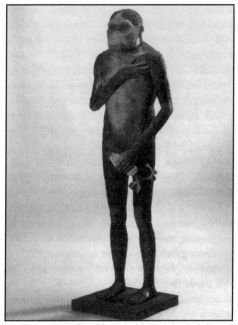

Inaccurate replica of <u>Australopithecus</u> in London's Natural History Museum which supports Darwinism but ignores actual fossils. *Shattering the Myths of Darwinism.*

pened. The problem, though, is that there really *are* humongous flaws in Darwin's theory. Further complicating matters is that Darwinism itself has become an ideology that is protected and promoted just as irrationally as any religious dogma. What we need is a person with a science background and no vested interest in promoting religious beliefs to provide a sound critique of evolution orthodoxy. Richard Milton — design engineer, scientific journalist, Mensa member, and 20-year-member of the Geologists' Association — is that person.

Milton is careful to state up front that he objects to Darwinism on empirical — and *not* religious — grounds. He believes that it is quite likely that evolution is a reality. However, he absolutely does not believe there is even a shred of worthwhile evidence to support Darwin's particular view of evolution, which says that species evolve due to the processes of natural selection ("survival of the fittest") and chance mutation. Among the major holes that Milton pokes in the Darwinian religion: "... recent research into the age of the Earth has produced evidence that our planet could be much younger than had previously been thought: existing methods of geochronometry such as uranium-lead decay and radiocarbon assay have been found to be deeply flawed and unreliable; the extent of genetic change by selection has been found experimentally to be limited; bacteria can be induced in the laboratory to mutate in a direction that is beneficial to them — without generations of natural selection; only a catastrophist model of development can account for important Earth structures and processes such as continental drift and most fossil-bearing rock formations — most of the Earth's surface in fact."

Using a relaxed pace and a pleasing tone, Milton goes on to look carefully at these and other challenges. He demonstrates that even if the earth is 4,600 million years old — the commonly accepted age — this cannot be enough time for life to have formed and evolved to reach the stage it has. Furthermore, methods of dating the earth have been shown to be so unreliable that they are basically meaningless. When push comes to shove, no one has any idea at all how old the earth is. Elsewhere, Milton scientifically shows us what creationists have been screaming all along: there really isn't any evidence of a "missing link". Although Darwinism rests on the idea that there are transitions between the major steps in evolution, no one has found any fossils demonstrating a transition between the animal kingdom and mammals, between mammals and apes, and between apes and humans.

Shattering the Myths is fascinating and intellectually exciting. It shows us the wizard behind the curtain and reminds us that even the most widely accepted theories are just that — *theories*. If you want to see a sacred cow of science expertly sliced and diced before your very eyes, this is the book to get.

Park Street Press (Inner Traditions International); $24.95
1992, 1997; hardcover; 311 pp
illus; 0-89281-732-1

SUSPENDED ANIMATION
Six Essays on the Preservation of Bodily Parts
by F. Gonzalez-Crussi

In these six essays pathologist F. Gonzalez-Crussi writes about skeletons, dissection, medical models, tissue specimens, pickled foetuses, and other examples of body parts that are preserved after their owners die. The writings are not intended as academic lectures but as missives of medical philosophy.

When the author was an intern at a Catholic hospital, he had to examine "products of conception", tissue — perhaps containing an embryo — that is expelled during spontaneous abortions. He uses this circumstance to reflect on the debate among ancient scholars with regard to when life begins. From there, he discusses the quasi-mystical role of the placenta. The afterbirth is capable of developing by itself, without an embryo. "Little wonder that in many cultures this organ is viewed as the foetus's 'double,' its shadow or twin brother. Physiologists tell us that the placenta subsumes the functions of all the major organs before birth, thereby lending a certain air of scientific respectability to the wildest contentions of myth and folklore."

In "Nature's Lapses" the author meditates on mutations and malformations. Throughout the ages, aberrations of nature have been blamed on debauchery, pregnant women's imaginations, supernatural influences, and diseases. God has been blamed for deformed babies, and many philosophers have sought to implicate or exonerate the Supreme Being for this. Science is helping reduce nature's anomalies, but Gonzalez-Crussi writes: "Congenital malformations

Skeleton(s) of conjoined twins.
Suspended Animation.

will always exist, because genetic material is eminently plastic: it is made to undergo mutations and transformations... Science and technology will always endeavour to minimise the errors, without altogether suppressing them."

Suspended Animation contains nine glossy colour photographs of skulls, a plaster cast of a hydrocephalic child, the wax head of an albino man, the skeleton of conjoined twins, and other corporeal objects.

A Harvest Original (Harcourt Brace & Co); $16
1995; oversized softcover; 151 pp
illus; 0-15-600231-0

A TOILET PAPER, OR A TREATISE ON FOUR FUNDAMENTAL WORDS REFERRING TO GASEOUS AND SOLID WASTES TOGETHER WITH THEIR POINT OF ORIGIN
by Rachel Mines

A light-hearted little booklet that examines the words "arse", "fart", "shit", and "turd". Rachel Mines reveals the etymology, literary occurrences, and current usage of each forbidden part of our language. "There is scanty but thought-provoking evidence that the word ["shit"] might be an essential part of our very human nature; not only do flight recorders from downed aircraft often reveal a despondent 'Shit!' from the pilot moments before impact, but Washoe, a chimp trained in American Sign Language, spontaneously transformed the matter-of-fact noun into a pejorative when annoyed with her trainer."

Anvil Press; $4.95
1991; small booklet; 40 pp
illus; 1-895636-00-0

WHAT YOUR DOCTOR CAN'T TELL YOU ABOUT COSMETIC SURGERY

by Joyce D. Nash, PhD

Dr. Joyce Nash, a clinical psychologist, underwent a successful radical facelift in 1991. To her dismay, she found that she was completely unprepared to deal with the physical pain and emotional trauma of the operation. In this book, she doesn't advise against surgery but instead tells you in no uncertain terms what you can expect from such operations.

"Nothing the doctor says fully prepares you for the physical and psychological trauma of cosmetic surgery. Almost always, the pain is underestimated... There is unforeseen pain, unfamiliar pain. Pain, together with the inevitable bruising, swelling, general discomfort, and interruption of daily routine that accompanies cosmetic surgery, can trigger psychological trauma. Reaction can range from a vague sense of loss to full-fledged grief, anger, and depression. A temporary identity disturbance can occur — even psychosis in rare instances. Sometimes initial euphoria gives way to a downward emotional slide." Nash emphasises that she is not out to relate plastic surgery horror stories. She simply wants you to be prepared for all the repercussions, at least some of which you will encounter.

Besides dealing with the short and long term effects of surgery, this book helps you decide whether you should have an operation in the first place. Nash looks at the numerous conscious and unconscious motivations and expectations that you might have. Sometimes therapy might be a better choice than surgery.

An especially eye-opening chapter peels away the mystery surrounding cosmetic surgery by giving nuts and bolts descriptions of over fifteen procedures, including facelifts, breast augmentation and reduction, buttock-thigh lifts, cheek implants, chemical peels, collagen injections, liposuction, penis enhancement, hair transplants, and tummy tucks. Other chapters examine the social taboos surrounding plastic surgery, the reactions of family and friends, and dissatisfaction with the results.

New Harbinger Publications; $13.95
1995; softcover; 221 pp
illus; 1-57224-032-6

WHAT'S IN YOUR COSMETICS?
A Complete Consumer's Guide to Natural and Synthetic Ingredients

by Aubrey Hampton

As this books points out, if you care about what you're putting into your body, you should also care about what you're putting on your body. Aubrey Hampton has been making herbal cosmetics since he was nine, when he learned the craft from his mother. In 1967 he started Aubrey Organics, which produces over 200 natural cosmetic products that are sold in almost every health food store in the US, as well as all over the world.

Hampton has assembled an encyclopaedic guide to the good stuff and the garbage that you will find in products for hair, skin and body care. The first chapter is a 170-page

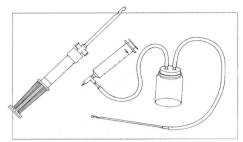

The DEL-EM™ kit for menstrual extraction.
A Woman's Book of Choices.

guide to over 1000 natural and synthetic ingredients in cosmetics. You'll finally be able to learn the nature of ceteareth-3, cottonseed oil, ferric chloride, hexamethylenetetramine, PHDs, xylenol, and zinc oxide. On the down side, all EDTAs are toxic and should be avoided. On the up side, PABA — best known as a UV-blocker in sun-protection lotion — can also slow down hair loss and prevent grey hair.

Chapter two is a 90-page chart listing information on well over 150 herbs. Each entry relates the plant's folk uses, parts used, extracts, typical substances it contains, cosmetic uses, properties and other uses, similar plants, and more. Among the things you'll find out: liquorice root can help boost the immune system in people with AIDS, nettle juice may stimulate hair growth, and the hips from a certain type of rose "can reduce wrinkles and help burns and even make some scars disappear".

The next chapter reveals "the fine art of reading a cosmetics label." Hampton gives a side-by-side comparison of the labels from a natural shampoo and a synthetic shampoo and from a natural moisturiser and a synthetic one. He also shows the typical ingredients that will be in natural and synthetic products. The final chapter contains instructions with illustrations and photos for natural skin care (including cleansing, moisturising, and massaging) and natural hair care.

Odonian Press; $11
1995; softcover; 317 pp
illus; 1-878825-45-3

WHY I AM AN ABORTION DOCTOR

by Suzanne T. Poppema, MD with Mike Henderson

Suzanne Poppema is a Harvard-trained abortion doctor who is recognised as one of the world's leading experts on terminating pregnancies. In this book, she rips away the mystery surrounding the procedure, explaining why doctors specialise in abortion, why women choose to end their pregnancies, what happens during an abortion, and what goes on in abortion clinics. She also discusses dealing with threats of terrorism and the promise of RU-486 ("the abortion pill") and "morning after" solutions (see *Emergency Contraception* in the Sex chapter for more on these topics).

Prometheus Books; $26.95
1996; hardcover; 266 pp
1-57392-045-2

A WOMAN'S BOOK OF CHOICES
Abortion, Menstrual Extraction, RU-486

by Rebecca Chalker & Carol Downer

Women have been purposely ending their pregnancies from time immemorial, using whatever means they have available. Nothing is going to stop this. As the authors make clear, "Regardless of the outcome of future Supreme Court decisions, abortions will continue to be done."

Given the inevitability of abortion, the authors decided to write a clear guide to the various options open to women. The first three chapters are devoted to medical abortions. Chapter one gives advice on finding a good abortion provider. It covers abortion prices, fake abortion clinics, Medicaid payment for abortions, parental consent, clinic picketers, comparison shopping, etc. The second chapter lists addresses and phone numbers for abortion clinics, groups that do referrals, public policy organisations, financial assistance and loan funds, and international resources. The third chapter exposes abortion myths. For example, the authors claim that abortions are not dangerous. "One salient fact that the anti-abortion movement cannot afford to acknowledge is that childbirth is 11 times more dangerous than early termination abortion." The chapter also discusses sonograms, counselling, local and general anaesthesia, abortion terminology, how abortions are done, complications, and more.

Several chapters cover the history, legality, and practice of menstrual extraction (ME), an at-home abortion procedure done by laypeople without professional medical equipment. "On or about the day that a woman expects her menstrual period, the contents of the uterus are gently suctioned out, lightening and greatly shortening the expected period. If an egg has been fertilised in the preceding weeks, it will be suctioned out as well." Contrary to reports in the mainstream press, ME cannot be done by a woman on herself. It must be performed by at least one other woman who knows exactly what she's doing. The authors say that the best way to learn is to join or form an informal group devoted to women's health and ME. This close-knit group will get to know each other well, buy the necessary equipment, and learn how to do ME from books and videos (and hopefully an experienced mentor). Fairly explicit instructions are given, along with illustrations, for performing an ME; however, the authors caution that this book by itself will not give you enough knowledge to do the procedure. But it is a starting point.

Herbs and other at-home procedures are covered in the next two chapters. The authors explain the success rates, risks, and advisability of herbal abortions, catheters, digital irritation, drugs, caustic substances, hangers, physical injury, and other methods. The final chapter looks at RU-486, the "abortion pill".

Sections in the back of the book tell what practitioners need to know about abortion complications, list suggestions for further reading and study, and describe exactly how to make a Del-Em™ extraction device from parts that are readily available from mail-order laboratory and scientific supply companies.

Four Walls Eight Windows; $13.95
1992; softcover; 271 pp
illus; 0-941423-86-7

ALTERNACULTURE

UNDERGROUND OVERVIEWS

Madge comes out of the closet in The Inevitable Truth! by Antonio Ghura. *Critical Vision.*

CRITICAL VISION
Random Essays and Tracts
Concerning Sex Religion Death
edited by David Kerekes & David Slater

This selection of writings is culled from issues one through five of the notorious British publication *Headpress: A Journal of Sex Religion Death* [below]. Not only is this volume valuable because those early issues of *Headpress* are unavailable, but also because these articles have been updated to bring you the latest word on heretical and insane topics.

The opening article — a 50-page epic titled "Thrill to Stories of Graphic Lust!" — documents the history of underground sex comix from the appearance of R. Crumb and S. Clay Wilson's *Snatch Comics* in 1968 to the late 1980s, with just a nod towards the 1990s. It's generously illustrated with single and multiple panels from the comix, including Britain's extremely daring *Truly Amazing Love Stories.*

"Mr. Punch: Sex-Killer Puppet — Traditional Sadean Atrocities for Children" takes a hard look at the beloved puppets Punch and Judy. It's amazing that this puppet show has been entertaining children since at least 1827 through the present day, considering the fact that Punch is a homicidal psychopath who beats to death his own child, wife, neighbour, a servant, a beggar, the Devil, and anyone else who gets within range.

Other articles cover the social and religious ramifications of the Black Plague, the real story behind the Sunset Strip Murders (was the wrong man convicted?), the Miracle Healing Crusade, the Children of God sect, the novelist Evelyn Waugh, and England's outlaw publishers, Savoy. Almost a fourth of the book is devoted to previously unpublished letters that were sent to European and American porno magazines but were rejected for being too bizarre. These letters are interesting for the shocking insights into the depravity and illiteracy of John Q. Public that they provide. "I have a store to tell you once my gril friend and I were going on a trip wen she started to get vere horne so said way dont you suck my dick and so she did then it got me horne so I poled over and she sat on my face and let a big jusie orgazem in my mouth." Reading a few of these letters can provide some base entertainment, but almost 60 pages' worth is way, way too much.

Except for this overdose of moronic porn letters, *Critical Vision* provides some great material on three of our most powerful hot-button subjects (i.e., sex, religion, death). And

the cover shot, showing a sculpture of a decomposed face, is a nice bonus.

Headpress; £11.95; $19.95
1995; oversized softcover; 251 pp
heavily illus; 0-9523288-0-1

CULT RAPTURE
by Adam Parfrey

In this follow-up to *Apocalypse Culture* [Outposts p 121], Adam Parfrey continues to explore the most bizarre and extreme strains of thought coursing through the social psyche. This time around, Parfrey writes most of the material himself. "From Russia, With Love" is his journey into the sordid world of businesses that procure submissive foreign wives for American men. "To my surprise, the mail order bride business confirmed feminist tracts pillorying the male's dehumanising regard of the female as commodity." Wielding his laser-accurate wit, Parfrey tells it like it is: "Nakhoda (translation: 'Godsend') is one such Moscow-based agency that sends photos and vital statistics of aspiring Amerikanskis to stateside businesses like Scanna, which supplies North American men with spiral-bound books displaying the exotic merchandise. Page after xeroxed page, Kohl-smudged nubiles stare uncertainly and even grimly at hope of a 'better life.' The pathos is even more overwhelming than a trip to the pound."

Around one-third of the book examines right wing, anti-New World Order sentiments through articles on Bo Gritz and Linda Thompson. *Cult Rapture* contains the full text of Thompson's infamous "ultimatum" — which she sent to all members of Congress — demanding that they do several things, including repeal the Brady Bill, NAFTA, and the Fourteenth, Sixteenth, and Seventeenth Amendments. If Congress did not comply by the end of the second week of their new session in September 1994, Thompson declared that all the militias in the US would come armed to Washington DC and "you will be identified as a Traitor, and you will be brought up on charges of Treason before a Court of the Citizens of the this Country." (Needless to say, the plan never materialised.) This part of the book also contains Parfrey's incisive examination of Oklahoma City bombing facts that the media conveniently never explored and an article on Dick Kramer, an artist whose photorealistic paintings of SWAT and other tactical teams swinging into manly action have earned him a cult following.

Other articles by Parfrey examine the UNARIUS Movement, radical feminist Andrea Dworkin, freak shows, shock treatment, the president of the fan club for Elvis' last girlfriend, I CAN (a group of disabled people who live together and have constant sex), the man who killed a hairdresser and an opthamologist because they were helping dark-haired, dark-eyed people look "Aryan", and the battle between the Keanes, the couple who gave the world the weepy-eyed waifs that were so popular from the 1950s through 1970s. And if that isn't enough, you also get "scum rocker" GG Allin's last interview, conducted by Parfrey a few days before Allin drowned in his own puke after snorting "four bags of New York white."

Cult Rapture is illustrated with over 50 photos, including a pickled two-headed baby and a federal agent who looks suspiciously like Timothy McVeigh. The book's full colour frontispiece is a gruesome painting by apocalyptic artist Joe Coleman.

Feral House; $14.95
1995; softcover; 371 pp
illus; 0-922915-22-9

FUNERAL PARTY, VOLUME 2
A Celebratory Excursion into the Beautiful Extremes of Life, Lust & Death
edited by Shade Rupe

This eclectic, large-format book takes us on a romp through some of the most transgressive art, writing, and culture being created. While the first volume of *Funeral Party* — now sadly out of print — was a sight to behold, the second volume is even better. From a purely aesthetic standpoint, the production values are superb and the design is bold and beautiful, unusual but not overly experimental. Getting past outward appearances, the material in *FP2* is an amazing trip through the areas where sex, violence, and death commingle. But don't get the idea that because this is a glossy book, it waters down its content. The material being pre-

Mark Frierson's poster for an art show based on *Cult Rapture*.

sented here is among the most extreme you are ever likely to find. Much of it is so unyielding, that there are only a few publishers who would even touch it.

Things kick off with a look at the art of Trevor Brown, an enormously talented painter who mixes extreme SM, torture, medical fetishes, death, Japanese schoolgirls, dolls, and innocent yet menacing sexuality into powerful images that sear into your frontal lobes. In one painting, a little girl of about five — although, looking at her hands, she might really be a doll — is strapped into an electric chair. "Nipple Injection" — reproduced in the full-colour 16-page centre section — shows a woman with full facial bandages and a neck brace opening her white shirt to receive a hypodermic shot in her right areola.

FP2 also looks at the gruesome work of Milo Sacchi, who makes sculptures out of the bodies and body parts of dead animals he gets from slaughterhouses and roadsides. Mike Kuchar is known for his bloody illustrations of surrealistically well-endowed men being tortured, and Spanish artist Miguel Angel Martín contributes a spare comic about a teenage girl who wreaks bloody havoc aboard a Nazi-controlled spacestation. Turning to other areas of the arts, Ulli Lommel — director of *Tenderness of Wolves* and *Holy Joan of Balboa* — is interviewed, and Joseph Mauceri examines the new theatre company carrying on the gruesome tradition of Grand Guignol.

Philip Nutman interviews horror writer Jack Ketchum, who is famous for not turning away when the action becomes brutal. Ketchum also contributes a story ("The Work"), as do several other literary terrorists, including Colin Raff ("Winter Travelogue"), Lucy Taylor ("Punishment"), Amy Grech ("Dead Eye"), Rob Hardin ("Knives for a Narcoleptic"), Marlene Leach ("Moments of Time"), John Shirley ("Answering Machine"), and Thomas S. Roche ("Viva Las Vegas"). There are also some essays, including "Pathology Report" by LD Beghtol, and the lyrics to Whitehouse's "Just Like a Cunt (Kinderwhore Version)" by Peter Sotos, the late twentieth century's Marquis de Sade.

Examinations of the decadence of Berlin between the wars, America's sleaziest sex tabloids, the male-snuff publication *Nooseletter*, and a bunch of reviews round out the wild offerings.

If the absolute extremes of the human condition are your cup of tea, do not under any circumstances miss the *Funeral Party*.

Rude Shape Productions; $17.95
1997; oversized softcover; 144 pp
heavily illus; 1-890528-00-5

HEADPRESS
The Journal of Sex Religion Death
edited by David Kerekes

Since issue 8 was reviewed in *Outposts* [p 124], Headpress has changed format and now appears three times a year as a book. It still covers the same heady, psychosexual territory, and, as always, contains pages of book/zine/video/audio reviews and is filled with demented, sexy visuals.

Headpress 13: Plague: Covering the concept of "plague" are two articles in which Howard Lake entertains the idea of a modern-day plague and David Kerekes surveys movies and books based on outbreaks of deadly, highly-contagious diseases. *Headpress* continues its mission of charting post-alternative culture with looks at the movies *Crash*, *Hustler White*, and *Traces of Death 3*, the porno genre of cumshot compilations, the lesbian SM stage musical *Voyeurz*, crappy old albums, and vintage printed matter on SM. Simon Whitechapel examines the possibilities of using nanotechnology to control people's minds, and David Greenall cruises the Bay Area but somehow doesn't get involved in any sex. [£4.95, $7.95; 1996; 0-9523288-8-7]

Headpress 14: Suicide: The articles that focus most directly on the theme of self-deliverance are Simon Whitechapel's fascinating meditation on three ancient suicides and Howard Lake's irreverent (to the say the least) look at the much more recent *hari-kiris* of porn actresses such as Savannah and Shauna Grant. Along the same X-rated lines are an on-the-scene report from the *World's Biggest Gang Bang 2*, a look at the significance of the bestiality flick *Animal Farm*, and an interview with progressive pornster Nina Hartley. Moving from porn films to underground films, *Headpress* also covers Larry Wessel, creator of *Taurobolium* and *Ultramegalopolis* [reviewed elsewhere in *Psychotropedia*], two underground documentaries, Richard Stanley's *Brave*, and *Nekromantik* director Jörg Buttgereit's experiences as a juror at the International Festival of Fantasy Cinema. Among the other gems you'll find in this treasure chest are an interview with Mr. Lifto from the Jim Rose Sideshow Circus, a tour of Hollywood's sites of sex and scandal, an interview with *City of the Broken Dolls* photographer Romain Slocombe, and thoughts on Christianity's "destructive obsession with sex". [£4.95, $7.95; 1997; 1-900486-00-8]

Bondage Hippies in *Plague: Headpress 13*.

Headpress 15: War in Heaven: This time around, Simon Whitechapel examines the evidence that Jack the Ripper was performing an occult ritual through his murders, Annabel Chong — central attraction of *The World's Biggest Gang Bang* — is interviewed at length, and Howard Lake analyses Jerry Springer's talk show in "The Best Li'l White Trash Freakshow in Chicago!" Other pieces look at accidents, a Peruvian cemetery, the overlooked sci-fi TV series *U.F.O.*, "crap Brit movie" *What's Good for the Goose*, and the best ass of the 1970s, which belonged to Agnetha Fältskog, "the blonde masturbation fantasy in ABBA". [£4.95, $8.95; 1997; 1-900486-01-6]

As of writing, there has been a **Headpress 16: Human Gargoyles** [£4.95, $8.95; 1998; 1-900486-02-4], while the latest edition is **Headpress 17: Into the Psyche** [£4.95, $8.95; 1998; 1-900486-04-0]. **Headpress 18: The Agony and the Ecstasy of Underground Culture!**, destined for release in January 1999 [£8.50; 1999; 1-900486-05-9], will see an increase to 144 pages.

Headpress; softcover; 96 pp/144 pp; heavily illus
individual issues: see above
two issue sub: £16. Europe: £18. US: £25

RAPID EYE 3
edited by Simon Dwyer

This is the third volume in a series of books that document some of the more outré aspects of art, religion, sex, and politics [see the second volume in *Outposts* p 122]. Subjects include filmmaker Kenneth Anger, William Gibson, author Stewart Home, filmmaker Maya Deren, visual artists

Gilbert and George, performance artist André Stitt, the eroticism of the crucifix, freak films, *Stranger in a Strange Land*, cryptography, the aesthetics of porn, the Process Church of the Final Judgment, and the Sisters of Perpetual Indulgence, an order of gay male nuns. Besides being chock full of good subversive information, every instalment of *Rapid Eye* is brimming with equally subversive images.

Creation Books; £14.95, $19.95
1995; oversized softcover; 250 pp
heavily illus; 1-871592-24-0

CYBERCULTURE

Tim Leary gets wired.
Chaos and Cyberculture.

ANARCHY ONLINE
net sex/net crime
by Charles Platt

Science fiction author and *Wired* correspondent Charles Platt has been involved with computers and the Internet for quite awhile, and in *Anarchy Online*, he reports on some of the more recent controversies in cyberspace. The title may seem a little on the sensational side, but, realistically, it's not too far from the truth, although government forces are starting to extend their iron fists into cyberspace. The book's cover promises us "The truth behind the hype", and it's surprising to see that this claim is as accurate as it can be ("truth", of course, is a very slippery concept). Another refreshing aspect is that Platt knows what he's talking about, so we don't have to put up with an author who's confused about the concepts of Usenet, IRC, hacking, and other cyberstuff. In fact, Platt does his best to succinctly explain these things just in case the unwired read his book.

A little over half of *AO* is devoted to sex on the Net and all the trouble and hand-wringing this combination has caused. Platt spends about forty pages discussing the infamous study by Marty Rimm — swallowed whole by *Time* magazine in a cover story — that claimed that hardcore porn is all-pervasive on the Internet. This study and the resulting story by *Time* proved immensely damaging to the reputation of the Net in the eyes of the general public, legislators, the media, and other people who spend little or no time online. In a clear and detailed manner, Platt demolishes Rimm's study, showing how and why his research methods were so badly flawed that his report is utterly useless. For example, Rimm made the laughable assertion that 83.5% of the pictures posted to Usenet are pornographic. A more sane methodology reveals that only around 5.8% of *all* posts to Usenet could be considered "adult" in nature. Platt goes on to discuss the subsequent Rimm-reaming that ensued, including revelations of Rimm's previous stint as an advisor to porn BBSs, telling them how to maximise profits.

Platt goes on to cover other issues and famous episodes involving net sex, including the question of liability, the Amateur Action BBS, paedophiles and kiddie porn, filtering software, the Guardian Angels' Netwatch, Robert Carr's BBS, and Jake Baker's online story in which a teenage woman — who is given the same name as a female student at his college — is raped, tortured, and killed by her brother and his friend. Some other issues — such as spam, hate groups, electronic money, and the notorious list "Top 75 Reasons Why Women (Bitches) Should Not Have Freedom of Speech" — are also discussed, although they don't directly relate to net sex. Platt gives time to various viewpoints, but he always comes down on the side of free expression.

The other part of the book delves into computer crime — hacking, cracking, phone phreaking, pirating software, creating viruses, and even stealing video from satellites. Many famous names are here: Kevin Mitnick, Dark Fiber, the Legion of Doom, *Phrack*, *Tap*, the book *Cyberpunk*, Operation Sundevil, the Michelangelo virus, the Good Times hoax, and others. Once again, Platt pushes aside government/media hysterics and tries to give a more rational view of hackers and related folk. He stresses that when you look at how much damage has really been done by hackers, you see that it's relatively little, especially compared to crime in the "real world", and it's done by a relatively small number of individuals compared to the subculture as a whole. "Most human beings simply choose not to be vandals or murderers. Society works on a co-operative basis of self-restraint that we take for granted. But where hackers are involved, we lose this faith in human nature. We tend to assume that they don't know the meaning of self-restraint and will use their skills in the worst possible way. Why? Because they're not like us. They have the bogeyman aura, the mad-scientist image. They're alien and inscrutable. They set themselves apart from society. Their skills seem like black magic."

Naturally, *Anarchy Online* is already in need of updating, but that's an inevitable problem when you're writing a book on a medium that sees major changes on a weekly basis. It is an excellent hype-deflating look at what's really happening in cyberspace.

HarperPrism (HarperCollins Publishers); $14
1996; softcover; 367 pp
illus; 0-06-100990-3
WWW: www.charlesplatt.com

CHAOS AND CYBERCULTURE

by Timothy Leary

This whopping big book collects over 40 works by Timothy Leary, the late 1960s drug guru and 1990s cyberdelic shaman. Most of these essays, articles, and interviews have never been collected in book form, although some of them appeared in earlier forms in *Timothy Leary's Greatest Hits*. Uncle Tim tackles sex, drugs, personal freedom, countercultures, death, religion, guerrilla art, and other cool topics.

In the preface, Leary celebrates individuality and the beautiful chaos it triggers. "Individualistic thinking is the original sin of the Judaeo-Christian-Islamic Bibles. It sabotages attempts by the authorities to order Chaos. The first rule of every law-and-order system is to trivialise-daemonise the dangerous concepts of Self, Individual Aims, and Personal Knowledge. Thinking for Your Selves is heretical, treasonous, blasphemous. Only devils and satans do it."

Leary is a techno-optimist who thinks that personal computers and the Internet are the key to the next step of evolution. However, he doesn't think that computers in and of themselves are so critical… it's our brains that are of tantamount importance. Computers are merely the catalyst for tapping our grey matter's full potential. Leary admits that our brain power is already there and some individuals have managed to tap it without computers. "Imagine what James Joyce could have done with MS Word or a CD-ROM graphic system or a modern data base! Well, we don't have to imagine — he actually managed to do it using his own brainware."

In the essay "Hormone Holocaust", Leary looks at the different things that turn people on in various cultures and time periods. In Arab countries women are wrapped from head to toe in robes, but they still have a most powerful allure — their eyes. "I learned this in 1961 when Allen Ginsberg, William S. Burroughs, and I started flirting with a Moroccan singer in a Tangier café, and suddenly found ourselves being pulled into enormous, luscious nymphomaniac brown eyes as warm and melting as chocolate-pudding vaginas. I'm talking about two X-rated, hard-core eyeballs whose wet nakedness was demurely veiled by skilfully fluttering eyelids."

Other pieces cover Yuppies, LSD, ecstasy, the decline of casual sex, pranks, artist Robert Williams, Republican militarism, *The Last Temptation of Christ*, and interviews with William Gibson and Leary's goddaughter, Winona Ryder. *Chaos and Cyberculture* is imaginatively designed. It borders on the chaotic but manages to have a semblance of order that keeps it readable. If you can handle *Wired* and *Mondo 2000*, you can handle this book. If you can't… well, good luck with the next millennium.

Ronin Publishing; $19.95
1994; oversized softcover; 274 pp
heavily illus; 0-914171-77-1

Stelarc with Laser Eyes, Third Hand, and Amplified Body.
Escape Velocity.

ESCAPE VELOCITY
Cyberculture at the End of the Century — An Unforgettable Journey into the Dark Heart of the Information Age

by Mark Dery

The rise of high-tech has provided fertile ground for nonconformists to breed brand new subcultures, forms of art, and streams of subversive thought. Cyberculture critic Mark Dery has become the first person to write a book covering all of the major elements of the "Information Age counterculture". Despite the movie-of-the-week melodrama inherent in the book's subtitle — not to mention its use of that meaningless marketing word "unforgettable" — Dery has managed to walk a fine line, carefully explaining and commenting on what's going on without gushing about it or putting it down.

The book's first section examines the "cyberdelic" subcultures, which fuse the counterculture of the 1960s with the cyberculture of the 1990s. "Cyberdelia reconciles the transcendentalist impulses of sixties counterculture with the infomania of the nineties. As well, it nods in passing to the seventies, from which it borrows the millenarian mysticism of the New Age and the apolitical self-absorption of the human potential movement."

Performance artist Stelarc is featured in the first chapter of the "Cybernetic Body Art" section. The Australian Stelarc often tries to bridge and blend the boundary between technology and his body. "A welter of thrrrups, squeals, creaks, and cricks, most of them originating in Stelarc's body, whooshes around the performance space. The artist's heartbeat, amplified by means of an ECG (electrocardiograph) monitor, marks time with a muffled, metronomic thump. The opening and closing of heart valves, the slap and slosh of blood are captured by Doppler ultrasonic sound transducers, enabling Stelarc to 'play' his body."

Dery interprets what these denizens of cyberculture are saying about life in a world that's becoming more hyper-technologised by the day. Some of the people are optimistic techno-utopians who see all this wild new technology as the key to liberation or even transcendence. Others are sounding a warning that our new relationship is a "Faustian bargain with technology" in which our servant will suddenly become our master. Many cybernauts express a combination of those two views.

Other topics that are downloaded in this sprawling investigation include cyberpunk science fiction, cyberpunk music, *Mondo 2000*, technopagans, smart drugs, the warring robots of Survival Research Laboratories, biomechanical artist HR Giger, virtual reality sex, cyberporn, cyborgs, downloading consciousness into a computer, and more.

As always, reading about subcultures is never as informative as reading material written by the subcultures, but *Escape Velocity* nonetheless has a lot to offer.

Grove/Atlantic; $15
1996; softcover; 376 pp
illus; 0-8021-3520-X

THE HAPPY MUTANT HANDBOOK
Mischievous Fun for Higher Primates
by Mark Frauenfelder, et al

This handbook — concocted mainly by the forces behind *bOING-bOING* and *Wired* — aims to help cheerful nonconformists get beyond blow-dried consensus reality and have some fun while frustrating "normals". To find out whether you're a happy mutant, a normal, or an unhappy mutant, the authors have provided comparison charts. Happy mutants laugh at authority, normals fear authority, and unhappy mutants hate authority. A happy mutant "Uses computer tech for fun and empowerment", a normal "Works as a keypunchin' meatbot for megacorporation", and an unhappy mutant "Downloads 'tasteless skin diseases' GIF files". As far as movies go, happy mutants like *Brazil*, normals like *Sleepless in Seattle*, and unhappy mutants like *Faces of Death*. Got the idea? If not, you must be a normal.

The Handbook has lots of ideas for hacking reality and chipping away at the dominant paradigm. There's a short article on pirate radio and TV. Like many of the articles, it is only a barebones intro to the subject at hand followed by resources that will help you if you want to go all the way. Another article encourages you to come up with your own logo and slogan. With the help of copy shops, you can put your personal logo on T-shirts, bumper stickers, etc., thus undermining the power of McCorporations who want to possess your consumerist soul.

The next step in beating the marketing drones is to cover their products with the stickers provided in the book (well, they aren't actually stickers yet... you need to colour photocopy them onto stickyback paper). There's a bright yellow starburst that screams, "SUCKS LESS", a symmetrical grey starburst that says, "Obsolescence Guaranteed in Three Months", and a USFA (US Food Administration) stamp that

New warning stickers for the workplace.
The Happy Mutant Handbook.

proclaims: "Fewer Insect Parts By Weight Than the Leading Brand". Along similar lines are the official-looking warning signs you can apply where necessary, such as your workplace. A bright yellow label warns: "Caution: Small Mind Sector. Displays of Enlightenment May Carry Risks for Individuals".

There are also a few features on pranks, those little kicks in the ass of conformity. A series of ideas from the alt.shenanigans Usenet group will help you to befuddle the masses. When riding a subway or an elevator: "Bring a Chia pet in on a leash and talk to it, pet it, and kiss it."

The chapter "Better Living Through Silicon" will be useful only to those who are already online. There are trading cards that act as a field guide to net.bozos, those jerks who make online life so irritating. Pranksters will get good use out of the instructions for attaching any email address to your messages. Of course, there's a guide to cool sites on the Net, but it's already hopelessly obsolete.

The Happy Mutant Handbook is a great idea, and with a stellar list of contributors and a mutated design scheme, it is a tasty treat for your simian brain. It's at its best when it gives instructions and tools for disrupting the status quo, and I hope that the promised future volumes are heavier on the DIY factors.

Riverhead Books (The Berkley Publishing Group); $15
1995; oversized softcover; 205 pp
heavily illus; 1-57322-502-9

THE SOUL OF CYBERSPACE
How Technology Is Changing Our Spiritual Lives
by Jeff Zaleski

The Internet is having, and will continue to have, a humongous impact on society. Other new technologies — such as virtual reality and artificial intelligence — haven't yet had a resounding effect on the world, but they undoubtedly will when they eventually fulfil the promise they show. Besides affecting us socially, culturally, politically, sexually, and artistically, such radical new developments are bound to have an effect on us spiritually. *The Soul of Cyberspace* looks at how these technologies — particularly the Net — are leading to new forms of worship, spiritual seeking, and proselytising.

Several chapters cover the migration of large mainstream religions into cyberspace. Judaism, Islam (mainly Sufism), Christianity, Buddhism, and Hinduism each get a chapter, which includes interviews with cyberreligion pioneers and a detailed look at some of the online areas created for that belief system. Other chapters have a broader focus, looking at the spiritual and religious implications of artificial intelligence, artificial life, and virtual reality. A chapter on community deals mainly with Twelve-Step programmes online, and another chapter explores the concept of "sacred cyberspace".

In a moment that sums up this book rather well, the author asks the Sufi master Sheikh Hisham Muhammad Kabbani why he has created a Website for his foundation. In slightly awkward English he replies: "Because you know that always spirituality is high-tech. Spirituality is a kind of energy transmission from human beings to each other, if we are able to receive it, because human beings are receivers and transmitters at the same time. This is what we see also on the Internet and in the sophisticated equipment nowadays — that everything receives and transmits. So we want to show people that Sufism is a way of communication through energy that can move from one person to another through spirituality."

HarperSanFrancisco (HarperCollins Publishers); $22
1997; hardcover; 284 pp
0-06-251451-2

COUNTER CULTURE

THE ABC-CLIO COMPANION TO THE 1960S COUNTERCULTURE IN AMERICA
by Neil Hamilton

ABC-CLIO puts out, among other things, a number of fine books that give library-level reference treatment to many radical topics. This volume is a 400-entry encyclopaedia chronicling the rebellious American youth culture in the late 1960s and early 1970s. Some of the entries include:

- ☞ Art: Fluxus, *Easy Rider*, *Hair*, Poster Art, San Francisco Mime Troupe, Andy Warhol, Jules Feiffer
- ☞ Music: The Beatles, Jefferson Airplane, Janis Joplin, Joan Baez, Miles Davis, Grateful Dead, Motown, Velvet Underground
- ☞ Writing: James Baldwin, Norman Mailer, Allen Ginsberg, Rod McKuen, New Journalism, JRR Tolkien, *Trout Fishing in America* by Richard Brautigan
- ☞ Personalities: Twiggy, Timothy Leary, Lenny Bruce, Benjamin Spock, Ken Kesey, Jane Fonda, Charles Manson
- ☞ Politics: American Indian Movement, Free Speech Movement, Black Panthers, Cesar Chavez, Angela Davis, Abbie Hoffman, Diggers, Weather Underground, New Left, Gloria Steinem
- ☞ Drugs: marijuana, magic mushrooms, STP, LSD, *The Doors of Perception* by Aldous Huxley
- ☞ Publications: *The San Francisco Oracle*, *The Realist*, *Los Angeles Free Press*, *Ramparts*, *Rolling Stone*, *The Whole Earth Catalogue*
- ☞ Events: Democratic National Convention of 1968, Altamont, Kennedy and King Assassinations, 1967 March on the Pentagon, Be-In, Vietnam War, Woodstock
- ☞ Places: Haight-Ashbury, I and Thou Coffee House, Kathmandu
- ☞ Groups: Hell's Angels, Jesus Freaks, Yippies

The book also covers various things that came into being before the 1960s but ended up having a large influence on the Counterculture — Reichian psychology, *The Second Sex* by Simone de Beauvoir, *Mad* magazine, William Blake, and the *I Ching* being a few examples.

Although many of the topics will be familiar to anyone who's even halfway knowledgeable about the 1960s, the author covers some aspects of the Counterculture that haven't become as ingrained in our mass consciousness. The Brown Berets were a group of militant Mexican Americans modelled after the Black Panthers. "As it did with other activist groups, the federal government infiltrated the Brown Berets and encouraged them to commit violent acts that would disparage the movement. In one famous incident, a Brown Beret, Eustacio Martinez, attacked a US senator by kicking him and damaging his car. Martinez turned out to be an undercover agent."

Five days after the Kent State massacre, the same thing happened at Jackson State College, a primarily black university in Mississippi. After racial tensions had been flaring, a group of students set fire to a dump truck. They threw rocks and bottles at police, who open fire on them with no warning shots, killing two students and wounding twelve. "Overall, the tragedy received limited media attention, a situation that infuriated many blacks who believed the unbalanced cover-

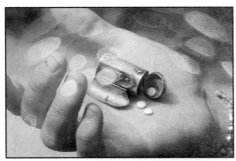

The legendary and much-missed Orange Sunshine LSD. *The Summer of Love.*

age between Jackson State and Kent State underscored society's racism."

Over fifty photos, a chronology of 1960-1973, an extensive bibliography, a listing of Websites, and a detailed index round out the groovy offerings.

ABC-CLIO; $60
1997; hardcover; 392 pp
illus; 0-87436-858-8

SCRAPBOOK OF A HAIGHT ASHBURY PILGRIM
Spirit, Sacrament & Sex, 1967-1968
by Elizabeth Gips

Elizabeth Gips was a hippie in the centre of the Countercultural universe — San Francisco's Haight and Ashbury Streets during the "Summer of Love". "I started out in high heels and a mink coat going to look at the 'weirdos'. I ended up with very little, another sadhu wandering around America... I mean, it was hard, man, and it was heaven. It was groovy, and it was sad. It was a pendulum swing between nirvana and hell. But through it all we were reaching for spirit."

Scrapbook contains portions of Gips' diary, poems, drawings, essays, and other things she wrote at the time. It makes a great snapshot of the era as experienced by a person who lived it. Through it, we can see the idealism and the hopefulness that permeated the movement.

Gips is very concerned with the spiritual side of life. She writes in the intro: "Spirit underlay all the experiments in sex, in music, in politics, in psychotropic sacraments and family relationships. It was toward spirit that we yearned. It was to Spirit that we committed our energies."

Part of what makes the book so interesting is that Gips writes very openly about her struggles to live up to her own ideals. At one point, she feels frustrated because she is not achieving cosmic oneness with her partner when they have sex. "I don't know why I think it is my fault, but it is as though there were a deep dark well inside of me that nothing can quite fill up. The well is isolation, aloneness. All I really want is to feel together as one and to let our sex together be an expression of that unity. Oh, well. Frustration."

A lot of *Scrapbook* will seem hokey to us now ("Death is no mystery only we have closed ourself off from digging it."),

but at least the hippies were attempting to understand themselves, their world, and the nature of reality. And, if they couldn't achieve those lofty goals, they were sure as hell going to have fun trying!

Elizabeth Gips; $15
1991; oversized softcover; 223 pp
illus; 0-9639056-0-0

THE SUMMER OF LOVE
Haight-Ashbury at Its Highest
by Gene Anthony

Gene Anthony spent the Summer of Love (from November 1965 to January 1967) at Haight and Ashbury Streets in San Francisco, the epicentre of hippiedom. Hundreds of photographs that he took are reproduced in this book, along with some explanatory text. Dozens of people, groups, and events associated with the hippies are pictured — the Grateful Dead, artist Michael Bowen, the Diggers (an anarchist do-good organisation), the Charlatans, Hell's Angels, Allen Ginsberg, Timothy Leary, Grace Slick, Janis Joplin, Lenny Bruce, George Harrison, the Free Clinic, Hippie Hill, the Psychedelic Shop, the Fillmore Auditorium, Orange Sunshine LSD, *The Oracle*, the Love Pageant Rally, and the Human Be-In.

Last Gasp; $19.95
1995; oversized softcover; 176 pp
heavily illus; 0-86719-421-9

WHAT A LONG STRANGE TRIP IT'S BEEN
A Hippy's History of the 60's & Beyond...
by Lewis Sanders

First published in 1989, this is an overview of the 1960s by someone who was there and remembers it (wait a minute, doesn't that mean he wasn't really there?). Lewis Sanders is an unrepentant, unreformed hippie, and his reminiscences are considered by many to be the definitive history of the era when the love was free and the LSD was great.

Sanders writes in a quasi-stream-of-consciousness style that unleashes fact after fact but still manages to stay on task and give you a complete sense of what he's talking about. He begins his tale by placing the hippies in the tradition of society's outsiders — poets, hermits, shamans, etc. More directly, he traces the hippies' lineage to jazz musicians. "These cats blew, & blew, & blew, & blew and knew what they were doing. They had done it once before in Jericho, and were here to try again... It was in the haze of the reefer-filled jazz clubs of the 20's, 30's, & 40's that the first true Blows Against the Empire were heard..."

Next came Jack Kerouac and the Beats: "Speed was the key, rushing nowhere in particular, just straight into the eye of Eternity." The final piece of the puzzle was LSD. "That such a tiny piece of matter could deprogram the countless years of bullshit which had been fed to us by so many normals was astounding."

Sanders sees the assassination of JFK as the defining event that kick-started the counterculture. Kennedy was cool. He smoked pot, dropped acid, and wanted to bring the troops home from 'Nam, but he "got X'd by members of the CIA & Cuban exiles group, with assistance from the Mob & US intelligence & law enforcement agencies, backed by the Texas oil cartel upset at Kennedy's plan to repeal the 27.5% oil depletion allowance." Then LBJ came into power and escalated the war, despite assurances that he would do the opposite.

From here, Sanders launches into a rollicking, authority-bashing tale involving the Vietnam War (including a sorely needed history of Vietnam from 1884), Richard Nixon (whose name is almost always prefaced with "that son-of-a-bitch"), music, poetry, Tim Leary, the assassination of Robert Kennedy, Students for a Democratic Society, the FBI & CIA, the Yippies, the Black Panthers, the American Indian Movement, the Free Speech Movement, the 1968 Democratic Convention, the Kent State Massacre, George McGovern, Watergate, Patty Hearst, and much more.

But Sanders' magical history tour doesn't end with the Vietnam War. He keeps chugging through the rest of the 1970s and the 1980s. Ronald Reagan "played the role old & bumbling, but that's exactly how he had to play it to get away with things he did and not get impeached or jailed." There are big chapters on Iran-Contra and the War on Drugs, Operation Desert Storm, and George Bush. According to Sanders, George Bush once gave the finger to a reporter who dared to ask him about his cosy relationship with Manuel Noriega.

The action moves right into the early 1990s, with Clinton's lies, Waco, NAFTA, and Croatia. In the end, Sanders reminds us that the future is ours. "Meditate, materialise Peace, non-violently resist criminal authority, feed the hungry, OM intently, dose lightly. The more people who work for Peace, the more peaceful the future will be."

Miscellaneous documents at the end of the book discuss JFK's assassination further and give a long list of heroes (White Buffalo, John Lennon, Gore Vidal), martyrs (Malcolm X, Abbie Hoffman), villains (Agnew, Ed the Sleaze Meese), and sell-outs (Jerry Rubin, Greg Allman).

Still Steaming Press; $13.95
1989, 1994; softcover; 236 pp
0-9643083-0-4

ZINE BOOKS

ANSWER Me!
The First Three
by Jim & Debbie Goad

Husband and wife team Jim and Debbie Goad have an all-inclusive — shall we say multicultural? — philosophy. It doesn't matter if you're white, black, yellow, or red, male or female, gay, straight, or bi, disabled or nondisabled — they still hate your stinking guts. All those superficial characteristics don't mean anything — beneath it all you're still an asshole. The Goads practice equal opportunity hatred in their insanely popular zine, ANSWER Me! [Outposts p 138], proving that the long tradition of powerful literary misanthropy lives on.

This collection reprints the entire first three issues of ANSWER Me! — "the Genesis, Exodus, and Leviticus of the 'Bible of Hatred.'" In his introduction, Jim explains: "Anger is an art form, but not everyone's an artist. Just as there are poor lovers, there are poor haters. For better or worse, I happen to be gifted with a rare degree of anger. Can't quite get away from the thunderclaps in my head." Jim supplies most of AM!'s articles ("Twelve Steps to Hell", "Ho Chi Minh's Revenge") and interviews (David Duke, Iceberg Slim), while Debbie handles the out-and-out rants ("Nothing But Enemies", "The Homeless Can Eat Shit") and prank calls (to Jack Kevorkian and a suicide hotline). They write a few of the articles together, and other people supply the rest.

AK Press; $13.00
1995; oversized softcover; 316 pp
1-873176-03-1; heavily illus

THE BOOK OF ZINES
Readings from the Fringe
edited by Chip Rowe

This is one of three multi-zine anthologies that came out almost simultaneously (the other two are The Factsheet Five Zine Reader and A Girl's Guide to Taking Over the World, below). While looking at these books, the first thing that comes to mind is that I'd hate to have been one of the editors. Imagine trying to choose just 170 to 200 pages of material to reprint from the tens of thousands of zines that have been published. It's like being told to create one meal that will represent all of the world's cuisines… it's an impossible task. Still, all three books make worthy attempts (each in a different way). At least the editors of A Girl's Guide had a narrower range (girl zines) to work with, but The Book of Zines and The F5 Zine Reader had to choose from every zine in existence.

Chip Rowe, creator of the popular zine Chip's Closet Cleaner [below], winnowed his choices down to eighty-three. The word "quirky" is often used to describe zines in general, which is a pisser because it doesn't do justice to the huge range of approaches and topics in the zine universe. However, that word definitely fits the majority of these selections. Rowe has selected pieces from the more whimsical and idiosyncratic areas of zinedom. Many of the pieces examine pop culture, especially the retro stuff: "Before Nintendo" from Reign of Toads, "Family Circus of Horrors" from Underbelly, "Why the Seventies?" from It's a Wonderful Lifestyle, "Two Minutes Batchat with Adam West" from Hitch, "Drills on Film" from Chip's Closet Cleaner, "KISS Memories" from Mommy and I Are One, "The Truth About Fonzi and Mrs. C." from TV Grind, and "The Brutality of 'Little House on the Prairie'" from Rollerderby. Other articles look at flukey topics — "Armour Pork Brains in Milk Gravy" from Beer Frame, "Milkcrate

Sports" from *Milkcrate Digest*, and "Fruitleather Underwear" from *Ben Is Dead*.

Most of all, though, the primary requirement for the pieces is that they be humorous. Most of the articles already listed are infused with light-hearted humour, and many others are strictly for laughs: "A Day in the Life of Matt's Hair" from *ecdysis*, "Final Exits for Aquatic Species" from *Meanwhile…*, "Deviant Bowler Signals" from *The Secret Handsignals of the DBA*, and "Eleven Ways to Annoy the Person Next to You on the Bus" from *15 Minutes*. The only piece to cover conspiracies and cover-ups (or anything overtly political, for that matter) is actually a parody of JFK conspiracy theories, "The Verbivore JFK Assassination Diorama" from *Verbivore*. It's not that the world of conspirology couldn't use some lightening up, it's just that I wish at least one article covering real-world malfeasance had made it in. A small percentage of the contributions do give serious consideration to weightier topics such as growing old, fat liberation, romantic relationships, and the mind-altering effects of large doses of DXM (found in cough syrup). Introductions to each selection, info on how to get the zines, and — glory be — an index make the book more valuable.

If any of this sounds disapproving, it isn't meant that way. It just has to do with personal taste… I prefer a more even ratio of humour/whimsy and seriousness. However, if you're looking mainly for the lighter side of zines, *The Book of Zines* does a marvellous job of crystallising it in 83 short selections.

Owl Books (Henry Holt and Company); $14.95
1997; softcover; 180 pp
heavily illus; 0-8050-5083-3

THE FACTSHEET FIVE ZINE READER
The Best Writing from the Underground World of Zines
edited by R. Seth Friedman

When the future of the famous *Factsheet Five* — the zine of zine reviews, the closest thing to a centralised hub that exists in the zine world [*Outposts* p 121] — was in doubt, R. Seth Friedman took over as editor, publisher, and chief reviewer. Prior to this foolhardy act he was an avid zine reader and had published one of his own. Now he estimates: "I've probably read fifty thousand zines in the last ten years." In short, no one has more access to zines than Seth does. This undoubtedly made the Herculean task of selecting 72 articles, essays, musings, comics, and other writings even more impossible than it already was, but Seth has made the best of it.

The F5 Zine Reader attains a representative balance of the far-flung zine world. As far as approaches go, some pieces are light-hearted, a few are purely humour, and still others are completely serious (but not, of course, in the boring, academic sense of the word… rather, in a lively and urgent way). The subject matter is likewise very eclectic. Of course, everyone will have nits to pick concerning topics that were overdone, underdone, and completely ignored, so there's no point in going into my personal checklist.

Several of the articles are investigations of topics most people wouldn't think of investigating: Freakies cereal ("The Real Freakies" from *Freakie Magnet*), Jerry Lewis' unreleased Holocaust movie ("Thus Spake Cinderfella" from *Hermenaut*), Hello Kitty ("The Skinny on Hello Kitty" from You *Sank My Battleship!*), Jack Chick's rabidly Christian fundamentalist comics ("Picking Up (Jack) Chicks" from *Schlock*), the connection between the Beat movement and jazz ("The Invisible Link" from *Long Shot*), the politics of music formats ("Hey Sony — What Makes CDs So Popular?" from *Sony Free*), disreputable Popes ("The Bad Boys of the Vatican" from *DIS*), the world's worst train wrecks ("Choo Choo Crash Bang" from *Murder Can Be Fun*), and the medicinal and psychedelic properties of toad venom ("Venom: Poison or Panacea?" from *Eye*).

Naturally, many essays document private obsessions — collecting eight-track tapes ("Diary of a Mad Tracker" from *8-Track Mind*), travelling off the beaten path ("The Best of Roadside Journal" from *Out West*), eating olives ("I Love Olives" from *Cooking on the Edge*), shooting guns ("Places to Shoot, Things to Shoot" from *Gun Fag Manifesto*) — and personal experiences — living in a rough part of New York City ("24 Hours in Hell's Pantry" from *Ersatz*), growing up as a manic-depressive, dope-shooting, suicidal, homosexual teenager ("I Was a Manic-Depressive, Dope-Shooting, Suicidal, Homosexual Teenager" from *babysue*), being a sex worker ("I Was a Phone Sex Girl" from *Snevil*), donating plasma ("Plasma Donation: Lazy Man's Dream or Needle-Ridden Nightmare?" from *Hitch*), and leaving hair bleach on too long ("The Day My Hair Fell Off" from *Bust*).

Some other outstanding pieces include the AIDS-blood exposé "Murder by Charity" from *Mouth*, supermasochist Bob Flanagan's masturbation rant "Why" from *Chemical Imbalance*, "Side Effects of Living: 25 Reasons to Drink" from *Pinch Point*, "Foreskins Forever! Circumcision Is Mutilation!" from *batteries not included*, an anti-War on Drugs piece from *Claustrophobia*, and "Transgressive Hair: The Last Frontier", about a woman who refuses to shave her thick beard, from the mystical-Jewish-feminist zine *Lilith*. A brief history of zines, introductions to each selection, and a guide to getting the zines that are excerpted round out the offerings.

Seth has created a challenging, well-balanced anthology of zine material that's as good as you could ask for, given the overwhelming nature of the task.

Three Rivers Press ((Crown Publishing (Random House)); $14
1997; oversized softcover; 192 pp
heavily illus; 0-609-80001-9

A GIRL'S GUIDE TO TAKING OVER THE WORLD
Writings from the Girl Zine Revolution
edited by Karen Green & Tristan Taormino

The dynamic duo behind the pansexual zine *Pucker Up* [reviewed in the Sex chapter] have assembled some of the best material from Riot Grrrl, postfeminist, do-me feminist, dyke, and just plain personal zines put out by women. As I expected from these two radicals, the 72 selections in this collection are subversive, pissed, loud, and blunt. There are some moments of humour, but overall this is the least light-hearted of the zine-book triplets [see the two immediately preceding reviews].

The book starts with one of many pieces about sex — "Learning to Fuck" from *Diabolical Clits*, which opens: "On my forty-first birthday I learn how to fuck you." In "Jesus Kick" (no relation) from *youtalkintame?*, Julene Snyder confesses her lust for the Messiah, and Lovechild reveals "Why I Play with My Cunt" (from *Brat Attack*). Erika Langley talks about dancing at the Lusty Lady in an article from *Blue Stocking*, and an anonymous *Pawholes* contributor talks about a typical night stripping.

Several powerful pieces involve family. In *Bust*'s "Farewell, Father", "girl" reveals that her father is dying. "Or I guess he is slowly disintegrating, dissolving into an ever simpler form of life, his body gradually letting go as his million tiny veins give way one by one, clotting and popping, failing him as he fails us." "The Electra Company", again from *Bust*, is an unexpectedly touching tribute by Lotta Gal to her dad. "My father ruined me. No — not that way. It's just that, well, he's such a great guy, and, much to my dismay, far greater than most of the men I've dated. This is a problem."

Other articles cover pregnancy ("The Double Blue Line: When the Positive Pregnancy Test Brings No Joy" from *hip Mama*), menstruation ("Menarche Hell" from *Pasty*), panic attacks ("'Wednesday Night…'" from *Alien*), eating disorders ("there is something horribly, terribly wrong…'" from *Pisces Ladybug*), self-hatred ("Self-Hate" from *Scrawl*), body modification ("Tough Girls, Navel Girls, and Warrior Women" from *Pucker Up*), weight ("The Fat Truth" from *Fat Girl*), religion ("Do You Believe in God?" from *Looks Yellow, Tastes Red*), misogyny ("Sexists on the Net" from *Kusp*), men ("Men?: I Thought I'd Let Them Speak for Themselves" from *Bust*), feminism ("Ode to a Feminist" from *H2SO4*), racism ("Asian FUCKING Stereotypes" from *Bamboo Girl*), arming yourself ("Girl Gun Safety" from *Not Your Bitch*), rape ("The War of Rape" from *Battle Dress*), celebrity encounters ("I Just Met Tory Amos" from *Rats Live on No Evil Star*), and pop culture ("Hello Kitty" from *Ben Is Dead*). There are also interviews with Lydia Lunch, Pagan Kennedy, filmmaker Trinh T. Minh-ha, and Leslie Mah from Tribe 8. Extra goodies include an intro from actress/singer/writer Ann Magnuson, notes on the contributors, and a guide to girl zines.

The writing in *A Girl's Guide* is mostly powerful and excellent, but I was surprised by how bleak the book is as a whole. I realise that women face numerous obstacles and tough issues, and, by all means, these should be dealt with in a brutally honest fashion. But where are all the accomplishments? Where are the fun aspects of being a girl? The anger and confusion born from being female in our society are here — as they should be — but somehow the joy got shoved aside.

St. Martin's Griffin (St. Martin's Press); $14.95
1997; softcover; 229 pp
heavily illus; 0-312-15535-2

I CHECK THE MAIL ONLY WHEN CERTAIN IT HAS ARRIVED

A Collection of Letters from People I Didn't Know, 1986-1994
edited by Andy Jenkins

In 1986 Andy Jenkins created *Bend*, a zine originally devoted to skateboarding and music. Using the time-honoured method of self-publishing known as "using your employer's stuff" (in the business world it's called "corporate pilferage"), Jenkins went for 15 issues. The sixteenth issue is actually this book, a collection of mail Jenkins received during the *Bend* years from people he didn't know at the time.

Some of the mail is from one of Jenkins' two current partners in crime, Spike Jonze, director of the videos for "Sabotage" by the Beastie Boys, "Buddy Holly" by Weezer, and "California" by Wax. Mark Lewman, creator of the zine *Chariot of the Ninja*, is the other member of the trio. Together, the three have created *Dirt* ("little brother to *Sassy* magazine"), two skateboard companies, a film script, and other projects. One of Jonze's letters starts, "We are driving drivers. Enclosed is my hair that has been falling out. I collected it from around the car. Kevin [Wilkins] has only lost his temper 19 times so far. We are very proud." In a letter written the next year (1991), he writes, "Some freaky street girl threw a dime at me and this freaky street guy chased her — called her a 'fucking slut.'"

Some of the most compelling, non sequitur-laden correspondence comes from one Thomas Campbell. He writes: "Hey, this is Thomas, I'm on a volcanic rock, it's mean, it's green, it's a '70's machine. Blatant Donnyism. I play on big hunks of individual molecules, peddle my mover of me across the dog-forsaken jungle, lick the tops of tables in a lizard tongue. Hang out with nice grandmas." Susan Lapper of Ontario sends in updates of her life written in short, clipped sentences: "And so. I continue to listen to disco and liking it. Finished school for this year. Did well. Got myself a boy that I have actually liked for more than a month."

Each letter lists who sent it, when it was received, and objects that were enclosed with it, if any. Some items include a lizard tail, an Andy Griffith trading card, and a rejection letter from the Christ of the Hill Monastery in Blanco, Texas. Some of the more unusual postcards, envelopes, and illustrated letters that Jenkins received are reproduced.

I love *I Check the Mail*. Everything about this book is just so right — the concept itself, the selection of letters, the inspired layout and design, the foreword and intro, even the freaking copyright page! Jenkins has banged the gong perfectly. Definitely one of the coolest books I've come across.

Bend Press; $8.95
1995; softcover; 107 pp
illus; 0-9643598-0-4

MAKE A ZINE!
A Guide to Self-Publishing Disguised as a Book on How to Produce a Zine
by Bill Brent

Bill Brent — publisher of sexzines, including *Black Sheets*, and the biennial pansexual resource guide *The Black Book* [see the Sex chapter for both] — has now published a book telling how you too can self-publish. He approaches the topic of creating zines and other publications from every possible angle you could ask for. (All of the material pertains to zines, and quite a bit of it also applies to books, pamphlets, etc.) You'll learn about getting material ("Interviews", "Contributors"), physically creating the zine ("Layout and Type", "Production", "Photos, Illustrations, and Prepress", "Printing and Paper"), getting it to the people ("Postage and Freight", "Sales", "Barcodes"), legal matters ("Copyrights and Related Topics", "What You Must Known About Libel"), personal concerns ("Stress, Burnout, Inspiration, and Creativity", "QUITTING?"), practical concerns ("Money", "Organization", "'Selling Out'"), and special topics ("E-Zines", "Sex Zines and Queer Zines"). Brent's easy-going style, personal experiences, and attention to detail — whether he's talking about pull quotes, sales calls, or creativity — make it feel like a knowledgeable friend is talking to you.

Several valuable appendices list boatloads of alternative, zine-friendly, and sex-positive stores; large and small distributors; catalogues that sell zines; books and articles on zines and general self-publishing; zine info online; publications that review zines; and more. Making this book even more of a great reference is the detailed five-page index, a feature that is all too often left out of non-fiction books put out by alternative presses.

Make a Zine! contains so much hands-on, nitty-gritty information, that it could very easily become the most ragged book in any ziner's library.

Black Books; $10
1997; softcover; 191 pp
illus; 0-9637401-4-8

NOTES FROM UNDERGROUND
Zines and the Politics of Alternative Culture
by Stephen Duncombe

Notes From Underground represents the first scholarly book-length study of zine publishing. Author Stephen Duncombe is an assistant professor at SUNY, which gives him egghead cred, and a political radical and zine writer/editor/publisher, which gives him street cred. He tries to walk the line in his book, showing knowledge and enthusiasm regarding zinedom but also offering balanced analysis. To his credit, he forgoes stodgy writing and references to other academic research and instead writes in an engaging manner using plenty of quotes from the zines themselves.

After a brief discussion of the question which has no answer ("What is a zine?"), Duncombe examines the people who make zines. Overwhelmingly he finds that zines are created by people who just don't fit in. "Zine writers may be shy, awkward, and lacking social skills, but there is more to the loser label than this. Zine writers are self-conscious losers; they wear their loserdom like a badge of honour. Mike Appelstein proudly displays rejection letters from jobs he has applied to as a writer in *Writer's Block*, and in *The Olecatronical Scatologica Chronicle*, Jokie Wilson reprints his letter of rejection from an art school." Ziners use their zines to write about their lives, no matter how mundane they may be, to express their personal views on all matters, to

have complete freedom to express themselves, to create their own identities, often by purposely doing the contrary of what society expects of them.

The chapter "Community" examines various ways zine publishing has formed a ziner subculture as well as helping bond other subcultures, such as Riot Grrrls. Duncombe makes some great points about the herd mentality that afflicts many subcultures supposedly based on individualism. In order to belong to a certain rebellious subculture, you often have to dress a certain way, listen to certain music, hold certain beliefs, etc. But by doing this, you are no longer being a true nonconformist.

The next chapter is devoted to the topic that is on everyone's mind, "Work". Most ziners respond to work with contempt, calls for sabotage, or the urge to slack. The final part of the chapter looks at the subject from a different angle, examining the reason for creating a zine: love vs. money.

With the chapter "Consumption", Duncombe shows how zines approach our consumerist culture. Some of them simply make fun of or rail against conspicuous consumption. Others appropriate bits and pieces of culture, such as fanzines that publish "slash" (fan-written fiction that involves sex between male characters in a TV series, the most famous example being Kirk/Spock). *Beer Frame* takes a unique approach by examining in detail items that are either too arcane or commonplace to usually warrant much attention.

"Discovery" chronicles the ups and downs of the mass media's misguided, half-witted infatuation with zines, which moves us into "Purity and Danger". Here Duncombe expressly deals with the overriding theme of the book: Can a zine — or any other product — truly be rebellious "in a commercialised society in which all culture — especially rebellious culture — is gobbled up, turned on its head, and used as an affirmation of the very thing it was opposed to." He thoughtfully examines the inherent problem in zine publishing: do you keep yourself pure and uncompromising, thus staying broke and only reaching a limited number of people, or do you "sell out" and make your zine more marketable, which can increase profits and the number of people who see your message, but can result in a watering down of content to make it more palatable to the mainstream?

In "The Politics of Alternative Culture", the author thoughtfully submits that it's easy to see what zines stand against, but what do they stand *for*? "Zines, as part of an adversarial subculture, face a political obstacle. Politics require solidarity, planning, and a vision, while what unifies the underground is *a negation of what is*."

In a sure to be controversial conclusion, Duncombe writes: "The underground's search for authenticity is a failed project. But without this futile struggle they would give in to something far worse — the tyranny of the here and now. Zines and the underground culture from which they come are a lie that gives direction and sustenance, solidarity and a sense of accomplishment. Against a world dragging you back, they keep you moving forward."

Verso; $19
1997; softcover; 240 pp
illus; 1-85984-158-9

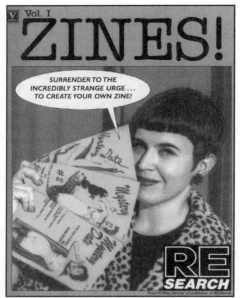

In the tradition of pamphleteering and resistance bulletins.
Zines! Volume 1.

'ZINE
How I Spent Six Years of My Life in the Underground and Finally... Found Myself... I Think

by Pagan Kennedy

From 1988 to 1993, Pagan Kennedy, author of the short story collection *Stripping and Other Stories* [*Outposts* p 228], put out a zine that was eventually called *Pagan's Head*. Written (mostly), printed, and distributed informally to friends and acquaintances by Pagan herself, it was all about... well, Pagan. It belonged to that subcategory known as personal zines, in which people write about the stuff that happens to them, their likes and dislikes, their childhood, etc. This genre of zines generally inspires the same sort of reactions as coconut, Howard Stern, and gangsta rap — people either love it with all their heart or they wish it'd disappear off the face of the earth.

Pagan's Head is no different... you'll either love it or hate it. I myself dig it (in fact, I'm spending way too much time reading it when I need to be moving on to other reviews), which is surprising considering that my overall personal zine tolerance is fairly low.

Pagan displays a high-level of self-absorption. The level is so high, though, that you realise it must be a form of self-deprecation, a pomo kind of irony that says that you know you're unimportant by acting as if you are important. Or something like that. In issue two she writes: "What I really wanted [from life] was to be standing on a balcony over a crowd of millions all yelling with one voice the name of their saviour, 'Pagan, Pagan, Pagan.' I wanted to be Gandhi without having to spin my own cotton; Florence Nightingale without getting blood on my hands; Florence Henderson without hav-

ing to do the Wesson commercials."

Pagan's honesty and self-mocking humour are especially evident in all the new material she wrote especially for this book. In the prologue, she writes that during the *Pagan's Head* years, she existed on two levels: "On the one hand, I was just another out-of-whack, directionless woman trying to muddle through her late twenties; on the other hand, I was the star of my own story, a story illustrated by cheesy clip art and half-assed cartoons and photos chosen because they make me look like I had high cheekbones. On the one hand, I was a frustrated writer, receiving rejection letters from *The New Yorker* for my short stories; on the other hand, I was a publishing dominatrix who demanded my readers send me money, toys, and fan letters — and I got them."

'Zine is an enjoyable book, even if somebody else's changes of hair colour, relationships, and thoughts on the *Partridge Family* don't rank extremely high on your scale of important things. Like all good personal zines, it brings out the voyeur in the reader. It also reminds you that you're not the only one with a confusing and plodding life.

St. Martin's Press; $15.95
1995; softcover; 184 pp
heavily illus; 0-312-13628-5

ZINES!, VOLUME 1

by V. Vale

With this volume, the redoubtable V/Search Publications (one of the successors to the defunct RE/Search Publications) sets its alternaculture-mapping sights on the world of zines. Like most publications in the V/RE axis, *Zines! 1* takes a deep but not overly broad look at its topic through extensive interviews with the people who are making things happen. In this case, that means the creators of ten zines — *Thrift Score* (thrift store shopping), *Beer Frame* (weird product reviews), *Crap Hound* (clip art as social commentary), *Housewife Turned Assassin* (Riot Grrrl), *Meat Hook* (Riot Grrrl), *X-Ray* (zine-making as an art form), *Mystery Date* (social mores for women in America, 1940s through 1960s), *Outpunk* (queer rock), *Fat Girl* (large lesbians), and *Bunnyhop* (parodying pop culture). Additionally, there is an interview with Ramsey Kanaan of AK Distribution, a workers' collective that distributes and publishes all kinds of subversive material.

V/Re founder V. Vale interviews all the ziners personally. He asks many of them some general questions, such as why and how they started doing their zines, why doing a zine is important, what they think of the mainstream media's coverage of zines, etc. But mostly he talks to them not so much about their zine as about their zine's subject matter. For example, one interviewee is Paul Lukas, who publishes *Beer Frame*, a zine which reviews the world's most unusual as well as commonplace products (sauerkraut juice, musk-flavoured lifesavers, toothpick dispensers, Hydrox cookies). Vale and Lukas talk extensively about product packaging and design — bizarre packaging, failed packaging, and so on. "I also wrote an obsessive piece about the new M&Ms colour. They added blue, but they didn't tell anyone this meant they were eliminating tan — which had been my favourite colour! Consumers had been invited to vote on blue, but

slant.

because a girl's
gotta do what
a girl's gotta do.

number five.

Mimi Nguyen's <u>Slant</u>.
Zines!, Volume 2.

they didn't say they were going to eliminate a colour — I regarded this as a kind of election fraud. I spoke with a lot of people in their office about this." The interview with *House-wife Turned Assassin* co-creator Sisi, whose parents are Mexican immigrants, hardly mentions the zine at all, instead focusing on Sisi's thoughts and activities concerning the struggles of women, Mexican-Americans, and Chicanos.

Nico Ordway provides an important history lesson about self-publishing that puts zines in the larger context of pamphleteering, early Jewish printing, William Blake's books, anarchist publishing, the "little magazines" of the early twentieth century, Dadaism, the resistance bulletins of W.W.II, and science fiction fanzines of the 1950s. Following that is a ten-page collection of quotes from zines and a zine directory. As you've come to expect from Vale, *Zines! 1* is attractively designed and chockablock with killer graphics and zine excerpts.

V/Search Publications; $18.99
1996; oversized softcover; 184 pp
heavily illus; 0-9650469-0-7

ZINES!, VOLUME 2
by V. Vale

This time around, V. Vale delves further into the world of self-publishing by interviewing twelve more movers and shakers. The first quarter of the book takes on the theme of work, featuring Pete of *Dishwasher*, Keffo of *Temp Slave*, and Julie Peasley of *McJob*. The, shall we say, unorthodox attitudes towards work exhibited by these ziners is apparent in this quote from Dishwasher Pete: "I'm *addicted* to that feeling of quitting: walking out the door, yelling 'Hurrah!' and running through the streets. Maybe I need to have jobs in order to appreciate my free leisure time or just life in general." In his

interview, Keffo says, "... I'm not one of those idiots screaming: 'American jobs first!' *I'm not for jobs at all.*"

Other interviewees known principally for one zine are the creators of *8-Track Mind* (eight-track tapes and other analogue forms of audio), *Tiki News* (the preservation of tiki bars, statues, masks, etc.), the e-zine *Arthur Cravan* (devoted to the quasi-Dadaist "boxer-poet-wild man-provocateur"), and *Murder Can Be Fun* (death and disaster examined rigorously yet humorously). There are also chats with several people who have been involved with numerous zines or other self-publishing projects: three members of the Revolutionary Knitting Circle ("a mostly teenage feminist collective"), Mimi Nguyen (*Aim Your Dick*, *Slant*, and *Race Riot*), Bruno Richard (creator of over 50 books and 100,000 graphics since 1976), John Held, Jr. (pioneering mail art coordinator), and Candi Strecker (creating zines — including *It's a Wonderful Lifestyle* and *Sidney Suppey's Quarterly and Confused Pet Monthly* — since 1979).

Also in *Zines! 2* are an article by Nico Ordway on proletarian novels ("the voices of the social underclass"), two pages of zine reviews, and another zine directory. Do I even have to tell you that this book has a wonderful layout, tons o' illustrations, and scads of excerpts?

V/Search Publications; $14.99
1997; oversized softcover; 148 pp
heavily illus; 0-9650469-2-3

MISCELLANEOUS

BARBARA GOLDEN'S GREATEST HITS, VOLUME 1
by Barbara Golden

Talk about hard to classify, this book/CD combo is a cookbook, a poetry book, a diary, and a CD of joyously bawdy songs rolled into one and illustrated with drawings and photos. It all represents the passions of Barbara Golden, a self-described homebody and Pacifica Radio DJ who loves cooking, drawing, writing poetry, making music, and — I would venture — having sex.

In this collection of "tasty recipes and tasteless songs", you'll find recipes for over 50 dishes, including Baba's Muffins, Broiled Fish, Frosted Chocolate Chip Squares, Liver Not to Be Believed, Mum's Cheese Blintzes, and Super Stew. While you're cooking up a storm, throw the 19-track CD in the player and sing along with Barb solo or with her group WIGband (lyrics and music are included in the book). In "Tampon Rag", Golden goes a capella: "And if you guys have the vampire lust,/You really really must satisfy that urge,/Give those qualms a purge/Go down on blood city/Where the sauce is the boss/I said the sauce is the boss and you can use the string for dental floss!"

The synth-driven "Clit Envy" is a nyahh-nyahh directed at men: "Doesn't wobble while you walk/Doesn't hang there while you talk/Doesn't rise and make a scene/A clit's what you want,/On your team." In the slow, sultry blues of "Trashy Girls", Golden reflects on the good bad life: "Trashy girls love TV/Vibrators in their bed/Remote control, silk wrapper/Their honey gives them head".

Sex, food, and rock and roll. What more do you want?

Burning Books; $24.95

1994; spiral-bound softcover; 112 pp

heavily illus; 0-936050-12-8

BEAT SPEAK
An Illustrated Beat Glossary
by Ashley Talbot

Although useful as a guide to about eighty terms used by the Beat Generation, *Beat Speak* is actually more of a show-case for the addictive artwork of Ashley Talbot, who is prob-ably better known by the triangle with a line through it that she uses instead of her name. (In her defence, she was us-ing her glyph way before a certain eccentric musician changed his name to a symbol.)

The left page of each spread in this oversized, beauti-fully-produced book contains a term hand-drawn by Talbot in imaginative lettering, a typed definition, a hand-drawn number (not the page number, but the term number), and a background illustration reminiscent of Picasso or Miró. The right-hand page contains a nearly full-page illustration of the term being defined. Talbot's style sometimes has the weird angles and distortions of Cubism and other times a more orthodox, angular cartoon approach. She deals strictly with black and white… no shades of grey whatsoever, making her art quite sharp and immediate. It's an approach that works well with its subject matter.

Some of the terms you'll see defined are "blast crap" (smoke pot), "to freeze" (to snub someone), "to be gassing someone" (to be telling an entertaining story), "to lay on" (to give a gift), "H" (heroin), "ofay" (a white person), "a poke" (a wallet), "sides" (vinyl albums), and "trim" (cunnilingus).

Water Row Press; $29.95

1996; oversized hardcover; 170 pp

heavily illus; 0-934953-45-7

BIZARRE

At last, a magazine with ultra-high production values that unabashedly covers the most unusual, controversial, and just plain weird aspects of our world. With its slick paper, full-colour printing, and professional (yet visually exciting) lay-out, you might think that *Bizarre* is a mainstream magazine. But you'll realise that impression is completely wrong when you read the heavily illustrated articles on the Circus of Hor-rors, aphrodisiacs, highly alternative sexualities, movies cen-sored in Britain, stigmata, travelling to the world's most dan-gerous places, Russia's human organ underground, pubic hair sculpting, British street gangs, undersea shark photo-graphy, Voodoo sacrifices, and Hong Kong porn, to name just a few topics. Each issue opens with several full page repro-ductions of the most attention-grabbing photos in the world,

"Hipster: someone who knows the score."
Beat Speak.

including a Pakistani man with a snake crawling up his nose and out his mouth and an Israeli motorcyclist getting thrown straight into the air during a traffic accident. Highly recom-mended.

UK: Bizarre Subscriptions/Customer Interface/Bradley Pavilions/ Bradley Stoke North, Bristol BS32 OPP

Voice: 01454-620070

Single issue: £3

6 issue sub (one year): £15. Europe: £17. Elsewhere: £19

US: Bizarre Subscriptions/3330 Pacific Ave, Suite 404/Virginia Beach VA 23451-2983

Voice: 1-888-428-6676

6 issue sub (one year): $23.75

Payment: ck payable to John Brown Publishing Ltd, "all major credit cards"

WWW: www.bizarremag.com

BUST
The Voice of the New Girl Order

So I'm sitting here trying to think of a way to describe *BUST*. Feminist humour? No, it's not like *Hysteria*. It's younger and hipper. Postfeminist? Probably, but what the hell does that mean? Riot Grrrl? Definitely not. It lacks the anger of that unofficial movement, although it might be considered tan-gentially related. Well, I guess there's no easy categorisa-tion. I think a male letter-writer in issue 5 summed it up as well as can be expected: "It's good to know that women are as confused as men about What It All Means, but even bet-ter to know that you're having a lot of fun figuring it all out."

BUST's most likely audience is Generation X women, but older and younger women and even men are enjoying it, too. It's fun and fresh and disrespectful without being mean-spirited. Issue 5 is about "My Life as a Girl". It's packed full of nostalgic looks back at the grade school and junior high years. Tricia Warden offers a documentary-style essay on her landmarks towards womanhood: growing breasts, then pubic hair, starting to menstruate, having sex, and finally, having orgasms. Miss X describes her tumble into "the sticky abyss known as teeny-bopperdom", complete with David Cassidy and Simon LeBon. In "Perchance to Dream", Dixie LaRue tells about her series of attempted suicides in a way that somehow manages to be funny. "I actually downed a bottle of twenty-five or so pink St. Joseph's Children's Aspirin. This required more courage than you might imagine, as I famously feared and detested their chalky saccharine taste… Anna Karenina in barrettes and knee socks, I mashed up the aspirin in a spoon with water the way my mother did."

On the musical side, there are interviews with members of Veruca Salt, Luscious Jackson, the Cramps, Tsunami, Come, and the Wedding Present. There's a section on the best books about girlhood, including *The Diary of Anne Frank* and *Are You There God? It's Me Margaret*. Reviews (that aren't afraid to throw punches) of music, movies, books, and TV shows round out the offerings. High on oestrogen and low on dogma, *BUST* isn't just one of the best girl zines out there… it's one of the best zines, period. Unfortunately, the Girl issue is unavailable, but the Motherhood and Sex issues are still waiting for you.

BUST/PO Box 319, Ansonia Station/New York NY 10023
Single issue: $4.50
Four issue sub (one year): $14. Canada: $18. Overseas: $20
Payment: cash, ck, mo (made out to CASH)

CATALOGUE OF CARNAGE

This thick catalogue offers well over a thousand horror-related goodies that you'll be hard-pressed to find anywhere else. You can get realistic foam rubber replicas of various bodily organs; gothic pewter jewellery, clocks, belt buckles, flasks, steins, etc.; coffin boxes; all kinds of clothing encrusted with skulls; necklaces that look like strings of tiny bones; skeleton and rotting corpse kits; trading cards; Easy Rider jewellery; sculptures of deformed foetuses; resin statues of horror creatures; latex armour; bizarre and disturbing masks; scripts for 200 movies; handcuffs; books and raw materials for making your own horror props; movie posters; actual human bones and skeletons; noir candles; and even more necrotic items. If you want some unusual T-shirts, look no further. These tees feature serial killers, skulls and skeletons, Japanimation hero Akira, Countess Bathory, horror movies, deformed babies, freaks, a piercing chart, and so on. Got around $3,000 burning a hole in your pocket? Then you can order life-size, free standing replicas of Predator, Alien, or Pumpkinhead that are cast from the original moulds.

The most exciting part of the catalogue, though, has to be the incredible selection of videos. They've got things I've only heard whisperings about. And many of their movies are uncut versions, containing scenes you'll never see otherwise. Feast your eyes:

☞ *Aviation Disasters, Volume 1*

"Are you listening to me now?"
DIY Feminism.

☞ several John Woo films
☞ *The Suckling*: movie about a foetus that gets flushed down the toilet but comes back to life to kill women about to get abortions
☞ *Guts of a Virgin*: ultraviolent Japanese flick filled with rape, torture, and mutilation
☞ *Salò*: Uncut version of Pier Paolo Pasolini's swan song, widely considered the most unwatchable movie ever made
☞ *The Anal Dwarf*: hardcore porn loop that allegedly stars Herve Villechaze (Tattoo from *Fantasy Island*)
☞ Celebrity Porn: skin flicks allegedly featuring Linda Blair, Barbara Streisand, Elvira, and many others
☞ *Cocksucker Blues*: the legendary, almost unobtainable Rolling Stones documentary
☞ *Guinea Pig*: the pseudo-snuff film that had Charlie Sheen and the FBI up in arms
☞ The infamous Go-Go's bootleg tape, in which the wasted girl-band harass roadies
☞ The even more infamous Rob Lowe sex tape
☞ Bud Dwyer's press conference suicide video
☞ Several tapes of Howard Stern uncensored
☞ Videos of an actual embalming, an autopsy, and an exorcism that the Vatican declared genuine
☞ An hour and a half of footage cut from *Apocalypse Now*
☞ *Behind Convent Walls*: rare Italian lesbian nun

movie

☞ *Splatman*: hardcore Batman spoof that Warner Brothers has tried to wipe off the face of the earth

☞ John Wayne Bobitt's porno movie, *Uncut*

☞ Complete 5½ hour version of *This Is Spinal Tap*

☞ Live stuff from GG Allin, KISS, Nine Inch Nails, Genitorturers, and others

☞ *Confessions of Linda Lovelace*: features outtakes from *Deep Throat* and pre-1972 loops

☞ An episode of *Ren & Stimpy* that was too violent to be aired

Foxx Entertainment Enterprises/327 W Laguna/Tempe AZ 85282
WWW: www.qualia-net.com/foxx/
Catalogue: $5. Non-US: $10

CHIP'S CLOSET CLEANER

Put out by Chip Rowe — editor of *The Book of Zines* [above] and an editor at *Playboy* — every issue of *Chip's Closet Cleaner* is a grab bag of yummy goodies for your brain and funny bone. The most recent issue (#13) contains a fond tribute to *The Six Million Dollar Man*, an unusual article on basketball written by two feminists for *Oui* (they never published it), a revealing look at those "12 CDs for the price of one" mail order music clubs, a tour of the most boring exhibits of the Smithsonian, and guides to maintaining your privacy, fighting junk mail, and ripping off the Post Office.

Candi Strecker reviews books from the subgenre of librarian porn: *The Librarian Loves to Lick*, *Horny Balling Librarian*, *Bang the Librarian Hard*, and similar titles. In one weirdly entertaining article, Rowe sent questionnaires to people who have the same names as famous personalities and then publishes their responses. A couple of sections of *CCC* contain bits and pieces collected from zines, magazines, newspapers, the Net, and elsewhere. In an article in the *Baffler*, an elevator repairman admitted that the "door close" button doesn't do anything. "It's just a pacifier," he says. An interview in a Boston newspaper revealed that comix artist Robert Crumb turned down *$100,000* to draw a single illustration for a Toyota ad.

Rowe keeps most, if not all, of the contents for *CCC* back issues starting with number 5 on his Website. Some of the articles you can read online include "Liz Phair-O-Matic", "Sex with My Computer", "How to Get Out of Jury Duty", "How to Cheat on the SAT", "Stories I Wrote at 16 to Be Like Kurt Vonnegut", "Why Women Are the Default", and "Play Music on Your Phone".

Chip Rowe/PO Box 11967/Chicago IL 60611
Email: chip@playboy.com
WWW: thetransom.com/chip/cleaner/index.html
Issue 13: $3. Issue 11: $2

DIY FEMINISM

edited by Kathy Bail

The editor of *Rolling Stone*'s Australian incarnation has assembled a spiffy collection of 26 writings and numerous comix and graphix by a new generation of women who are redefining what it means to be feminist. Among them are "Riot Grrrls, guerrilla girls, net chicks, cyber chix, geekgirls, tank girls,

Rolling a joint on a cop car in Amsterdam.
Get Lost!

supergirls, action girls, deep girls", plus femocrats, do-me feminists, and some new strains of thought yet to be identified. They bring a hipper, more radical and streetsmart sensibility to their mothers' feminism. In her intro, Kathy Bail writes of Old School feminism: "The legacy of these efforts is double-edged: younger women assume their rights to the resulting opportunities yet they regard feminism as a prescriptive way of thinking that discourages exploration on an individual level. The word 'feminism' suggests a rigidity of style and behaviour and is generally associated with a culture of complaint. Young women don't want to identify with something that sounds dowdy, asexual or shows them to be at a disadvantage. They don't want to be seen as victims."

This view is captured perfectly in one of Jasmine Hirst's contributions. A grainy photo shows a tough, pretty, bleached-blonde woman nude except for thigh-high boots. She leans very provocatively at the camera, her face wearing a pissed-off expression. The text on the image says: "You touched me when I was six. Come touch me now… motherfucker." A T-shirt designed by Janet English — singer and bass player of Spiderbait — reproduces the silhouette of a buxom woman seen on the mudflaps of countless trucks. The large, chunky text underneath it screams: "SUCK MY PENIS ENVY!"

Some of the writers discuss their feelings about appearance and the politics of looks. Julie Bennett — creator of the zine *The Jellybean Ranch* — comments on the supermodel standard of beauty. "Linda Evangelista is a freak. Every single gene came up aces in the ideal notion of beauty in the late twentieth century. I don't know much about biology, but I do know that there's a lot of genes involved in getting a human unit together. Surely the odds must be a million to one of getting them ALL right on? So you and I, we're normal."

Unfortunately, most of the writings are not as powerful or as original as the above material indicates (although most of the visuals are first-rate). I longed for fresh approaches, different angles, vibrant writing styles, and even whole new topics. (Speaking of topics, I am dumbfounded that none of the pieces in the book deals with sex. Sexual harassment, rape, and abuse — yes. But not a single thing about healthy, consensual sexuality.) Not all the writing is mundane — "geekgirl" is quite interesting, "Politically Correct" has grit, and "Black Sistas" shines light on the experiences of aboriginal women. I just don't think that the prose as a whole lived up to its potential, especially when compared to the artwork.

Allen & Unwin; $19.95Aus
1996; oversized softcover; 211 pp
heavily illus; 1-86448-231-1

ESOTERRA
The Journal of Extreme Culture

EsoTerra chronicles the place where necromanticism, Nazism, fascism, Satanism, the occult, and other dark tendencies meet music, art, and literature. Add the unexplained and some miscellaneous strangeness, and the whole mass congeals into an intriguing investigation of the surreally extreme. Issue 5 is the big Satanic music special, with interviews of Marilyn Manson (from the pre-fame days), Blood Axis, Electric Hellfire Club, White Stains, Christian Death, and Whitehouse. The interviews are very well conducted — the interviewer asks short, pointed questions and then stands back while the subject talks at length.

In "Love Among the Tombs", Leilah Wendell discusses one profession that can provide opportunities for the frustrated necrophile — becoming a forensic archaeologist: "… we necromantic types have been misunderstood and vilified for ages. While it's okay for science to 'fiddle with the dead', it's an act of grave abhorrence (no pun intended) for the rest of us to do the same. Go figure!"

Karen K. Taylor reports from the opening night of Adam Parfrey's deranged museum exhibition, Cult Rapture, which focuses on the apocalyptic declarations of all kinds of extremists. There's also an essay called "After the Deluge" by the infamous Process Church of the Final Judgement. Other items cover cattle mutilations, the use of runes by Hitler's SS, and HP Lovecraft's mythos.

Issue 6 delves into Norwegian Black Metal, one of the most extreme musical forms around, plus interviews with Alan Moore, Genesis P-Orridge, Strength Through Joy, Iain Banks, and Peter Whitehead. The current issue (#7) investigates the genre of Dark Ambient with Endura, Mother Destruction, Allerseelen, and Master/Slave Relationship. Other articles cover necrophilia, cults, the process, and apocalyptic artist

Two members of the Swiss goth band Lacrimosa.
Hex Files.

Joe Coleman.

EsoTerra is a satisfying read. Recommended for fringe-o-philes.

EsoTerra/410 E Denny Way, #22/Seattle WA 98122
Single issue: $6.25. Non-US: $8
Two issue sub (one year): $12. Non-US: $16

GET LOST!
The Cool Guide to Amsterdam
(Fifth Edition)
by Joe Pauker

If you go to Amsterdam, and you're young, adventurous, or just want to have a damn good time, you *must* have this travel guide with you. In just over 100 pages, it tells you exactly where you can have every one of your needs met, from food and lodging to sex and drugs. Joe Pauker's street-level tone sets the mood perfectly as he gives you the straight, no-bullshit dope on all the places that the other, more staid travel guides leave out.

Cheap, or at least reasonable, is the name of the game here. For accommodations, you can stay at a hostel, a camp site, or one of the less-prohibitive hotels in town. Transportation includes renting bicycles, inline skates, mopeds, or cars; using taxis or public transportation; and getting around on the water. When you get hungry, consult the guide for the best supermarkets, health food stores, street foods, all night eating, free samples, restaurants offering good deals, and other places to get a bite. Cool people and poseurs will want to hit all the cafes, while just the cool people will want to frequent any or all of the 22 coffeeshops listed. At these establishments, you can choose from a world-wide selection of marijuana and hashish and then smoke it right there or take it with you! Pauker describes the coffeehouse Homegrown Fantasy this way: "For years, this well-known coffeeshop has had a good reputation for both the quality of their weed and the relaxed atmosphere of their shop. They have a large, tasty selection of Dutch grown grass and a couple of types of hash. I like it here best in the day time when the light is soft and time just seems to slow... right... down. Be sure to visit the toilet where the black light makes your teeth glow and you pee look like milk!"

If you're still not done with drugs, there are eight shops that sell pot seeds and growing equipment, and half a dozen stores offering magic mushrooms, which are also legal. (Just don't try to take any of this stuff out of the country.) Should good old rotgut be your drug of choice, consult the listing of 19 bars.

If you're wanting to purchase non-drug goods, *Get Lost!* has an impressive chapter listing ten markets, sixteen bookstores, thirteen record stores, clothing stores, head shops, a tattoo studio, and some extremely specialised shops, including ones that carry only toothbrushes, holograms, or old sunglasses.

You can hang out at a number of parks, gardens, libraries, skateboard areas, saunas, dance clubs, or live music venues. If you're wanting some culture, you can go the mainstream museums listed, but for alternaculture, pay a visit to the Sex Museum, the Erotic Museum, the Hash Marihuana Hemp Museum, the Torture Museum, the Tattoo Museum, the Museum of Fluorescent Art, or several other cultural institutions. For other forms of entertainment, visit the many independent moviehouses or tune in to some pirate radio stations. Finally, when it's time to get yer ya-yas out, *Get Lost!* tells you where to find the prostitutes, peeps, live sex shows, sex shops, and fetish parties.

Other practical information placed throughout the book includes important Dutch terms and phrases, currency exchange, a warning about pickpockets, and phone numbers for emergencies, information, and embassies. Updates to *Get Lost!* can be found on the Web at http://www.xs4all.nl/~getlost.

Get Lost Publishing; $13, £6.95, Nlf14.50
1997; softcover; 104 pp
illus; 90-802561-4-5

GET LOST!
The Cool Guide to San Francisco
by Claudia Lehan

Just as they did for Amsterdam, Get Lost Publishing presents an alternative travel guide for another of the world's coolest cities, San Francisco. Once again, the focus is on taking you to the unusual, fun, and non-touristy spots while helping you minimise expenses. Covers places to sleep (hostels, hotels, camping), getting around (public transportation, bikes, scooters), food (fruits and vegetables, 24-hour supermarkets, breakfast, restaurants), cafes, headshops, cannabis buyers' clubs, shopping (books, magazines, music, body modifica-

"You will imagine yourself feeling the inextinguishable flames of hell, in which the souls of the damned will burn forever as though sealed in bodies of flame." *Intense Device.*

tion), parks, beaches, museums (Alcatraz, Exploratorium, Tattoo Art Museum), performance art, music (free concerts, dance clubs, raves, commercial-free and pirate radio stations), bars, independent film theatres, sex shops, peep shows, and more.

Get Lost Publishing; $13, £6.95, Nlf17.50
1997; softcover; 96 pp
illus; 90-802561-6-1

HEX FILES
The Goth Bible
by Mick Mercer

Mick Mercer — founder of purportedly the first Goth zine, *ZigZag* — has put together this surprisingly big, bountiful guide to Goth culture, a music style/clothing style/lifestyle involving graveyards, vampires, gargoyles, bats, full moons, absinthe, arsenic, old lace, crushed velvet, the night, capes, corsets, pitch black clothing and hair, ghostly pale makeup, and other aspects of the macabre. On top of that, Mercer also covers the related leather/fetish and pagan subcultures, although to a lesser degree.

Hex Files is one gigantic, annotated listing of Goth resources. Periodicals and bands are by far the most numerous entries, but there are also listings for individuals (photographers, poets, organisers, etc.), organisations, clothing and jewellery sources, and businesses (booksellers, record labels, etc.). Almost every one of the gazillion entries is described (albeit briefly), and contact information is given. The sections on the UK and the US are easily the most expansive, but there are also resources for Australia, France, Germany, Indonesia (!), Malta, South Africa, and many other countries. Besides putting you in contact with the children of the night, *Hex Files* lets you see them through hundreds of striking black and white photos. No telling how many truckloads of black ink were used to print these illustrations.

Man, you just gotta love the band names: Master/Slave Relationship, Inkubus Sukkubus, Look Back in Anger,

DRAG

New York's answer to Mardi Gras.
Masked Culture.

Monica's Last Prayer, Pretentious Moi?, And Christ Wept, Faith & Disease, Sativa Luv Box, Rosewaterelizabeth, Ultracherry Violet, Burning Dollhouse, Girls Under Glass, Angina Pectoris, Love Is Colder Than Death…

The Overlook Press; $23.95
1997; oversized softcover; 230 pp
heavily illus; 0-87951-783-2

INTENSE DEVICE
A Journey Through Lust, Murder & the Fires of Hell
by Simon Whitechapel

Simon Whitechapel — quite possibly one of the most well-read persons on the planet — regularly graces *Headpress* [above] with his compelling articles and essays on all manner of things subversive and arcane. *Intense Device* contains fifteen of these gems, all of which are being published here for the first time.

Whitechapel delves into numerous, far-flung subjects, sometimes within the same article. In fact, I think he's at his best when he's finding the surprising connections between seemingly unrelated things. The most obvious example has to be "Gilt by Association: From H.P. Lovecraft to Electronic Distortion by Way of the Malayalam Alphabet", which starts out thus: "What's the link between a 1930's horror writer, an over-used font, and an industrial metal band from Yorkshire?" I won't attempt to retrace the train of thought here, but suf-

fice it to say that there is a connection.

"Endgame: Mass Psychology, Astrophysics, and Ragnarök" starts out examining the Book of Revelation, moves into scenarios involving meteors slamming into the earth, segues into a discussion of how society would handle news of an impending colossal meteor collision, and then becomes a philosophical rumination on the nature of human suffering as Whitechapel wonders if there is possibility of "arguing that rape and slaughter before and after a giant meteor strike could be morally negligible or neutral or even acceptable as artistic or existential acts." Likewise, "Golden Laughter: The Hidden Meaning Behind an Imperial Pervert's Ignominous Death" is ostensibly about the Syro-Roman emperor Heliogabalus, but it spends much time discussing solar cults and holy castration.

Not all of the author's writings are so free-flowing, though. Most of them stick to a given topic, although Whitechapel usually does manage to bring in various angles and references from all over the board. Some of these articles cover the history of dildos and vibrators from ancient Greece to today, conceptions of Hell, novelisations of movies, the Marquis de Sade's writings, Jack Chick's virulently Christian comix, the strange airplanes that Germany built towards the end of W.W.II, the homoerotic appeal of Rugby, and farting as it relates to Sir Richard Burton, Pythagoras, and de Sade.

Whenever I see the name Simon Whitechapel, I know I'm in for a treat. He is truly a rogue scholar of the subversive aspects of history and society.

Critical Vision (Headpress); £10.95, $19.95
1997; softcover; 188 pp
illus; 0-9523288-9-5

MASKED CULTURE
The Greenwich Village Halloween Parade
by Jack Kugelmass and others

The Greenwich Village Halloween Parade is New York's answer to Mardi Gras. It's every bit as wild as its Cajun cousin, as these 100 large colour photos attest. Onlookers gawk as revellers parade through the streets on the one night during which many of society's rules are suspended. There's a heavy drag queen presence, with guys dressed as ballerinas, French aristocrats, nuns, and showgirls. Three men are shown with urinals attached to their torsos and graffiti scrawled across their shirts. Paraders also dress as cows, Shriners, ghosts, witches, bloody madmen, giant tubes of lipstick, and Ronald Reagan with his dick hanging out. One woman is wearing a wedding dress, and a baby doll is seen coming out from between her blood-streaked thighs. The accompanying text describes the action on the street and the preparation behind the scenes, often using the words of the revellers themselves.

Columbia University Press; $42
1994; oversized hardcover; 216 pp
heavily illus; 0-231-08400-5

BELIEFS

NEW RELIGIOUS MOVEMENTS

E: REFLECTIONS ON THE BIRTH OF THE ELVIS FAITH
by John Strausbaugh

John Strausbaugh takes a serious look at an unorganised and unofficial new religious movement — the worship of Elvis Presley. Although the subject may seem funny, this book is not a joke. Elvis has literally been deified by legions of fans, and *E* looks at Elvis' followers, pilgrimages to the "shrine" of Graceland, "holy" relics and altars, "the King's ministers" (Elvis impersonators), sightings of Live Elvis and Dead Elvis, alleged miracles wrought by Dead Elvis, Elvis' Christ complex, and Elvis lore. "At one of his very last shows, in June of '77, just two months before he died, he muttered five enigmatic, oracular words that many believers would take as a coded farewell. 'I am,' he mumbled, 'and I was...' And then he paused, murkily, and the show stumbled forward."

Blast Books; $12.95
1995; softcover; 223 pp
illus; 0-922233-15-2

THE GODS HAVE LANDED
New Religions from Other Worlds
edited by James R. Lewis

This book is supposedly the first comprehensive, scholarly examination of the religious dimension of belief in UFOs. "Chapters range from analyses of the religious meanings attached to this phenomenon by the larger society to surveys of specific movements that claim inspiration from 'Space Brothers' and other extraterrestrial sources."

John A. Saliba provides the most far-reaching essay, approaching the subject from a variety of angles. In one of the most revealing sections, he looks at the seven major themes that UFO belief has in common with traditional religious belief: "(1) mystery; (2) transcendence; (3) belief in spiritual entities; (4) perfection; (5) salvation; (6) worldview (the ascription of meaning and purpose to the universe); and (7) spirituality." Saliba states, "The attributes of UFO occupants are generally those ascribed to supernatural beings, spiritual entities, or gods, who differ from mere humans in their intellectual, spiritual, and mortal state... Perfection, immense power (often used for healing purposes), and omniscience are among the common qualities of UFO occupants." Referring to salvation, he later writes, "The mission of UFOs is frequently described as one of redemption. Among the more common themes contained in messages from aliens

Was he the King or the King of Kings? *E.*

are the cure of all diseases, the deliverance from the destructive forces of atomic power, and the transportation to a new planet where there will be complete security, wealth, and co-operation."

In another essay, John Whitmore looks specifically at the religious overtones and undertones of the abductee experience. New religions expert J. Gordon Melton surveys the history of UFO contactees. Although the *modern* contactee movement began in the 1950s, he examines all known claims of alien contact prior to that decade, starting with Emanuel Swedenborg in 1758!

Other essays specifically examine new religious movements that are based on UFOs/aliens — Unarius, the Raelean movement, and the "Bo and Peep cult", which would later become known world-wide as the infamous Heaven's Gate when most of its members snuffed themselves in 1997. Further topics include parallels between the spreads of Spiritualism and UFO religion in New Zealand, the ways in which Judaeo-Christian theologians have dealt with the possibilities of alien life, and a review of the sociopsychological perspectives that have been applied to the contactee phenomena. The book ends with exhaustive, 80-page listing of literature regarding contactees.

State University of New York Press; $19.95
1995; softcover; 348 pp
illus; 0-7914-2330-1

A cover of a book on Sensual Meditation from the Raelean Movement. *The Gods Have Landed.*

THE KEEPERS OF HEAVEN'S GATE
The Millennial Madness —
The Religion Behind the Santa Fe
Suicides
by William Henry

Starting on March 24, 1997, the news was dominated by the mass suicide of a religious sect that came to be known popularly as Heaven's Gate. Thirty-nine people living communally in a mansion in Rancho Santa Fe, California, used barbiturates and plastic bags to off themselves so they could be reincarnated aboard a spaceship that was tagging along with the Hale-Bopp comet as it passed earth. Written in prose that often comes from the indigo/violet end of the spectrum, if you know what I mean, this book looks at the ideas held by Heaven's Gate (and some other sects, such as the Order of the Solar Temple and Aum Shinrikyo) and demonstrates that they are neither new nor uncommon.

The group's worldview is a melange of the Book of Revelation, Gnosticism, Messiahism, Millennialism, prophecy, planetary alignments, aliens, archetypes, the appearance of comets, and various other occult and mystic beliefs. These things are not recent inventions, and they sure aren't unique to Heaven's Gate. In fact, a whole lot of people put credence in at least some of the things on this list. (Other topics covered don't seem to relate directly to the matter at hand. Francis Bacon, the founding of the US, *E.T.*, the promise of the Web, and the author's New Agey feelings about the possible future evolution of the human race don't contribute to our understanding of the sects.)

The author sheds some much-needed light on these connections, but be warned: he's not exactly objective. He constantly uses the pejorative word "cult" instead of "sect", and at one point he calls the group a "cybercult", an extremely misleading bit of sensationalism that the mainstream media lunkheads used, too. He also admits that he shares many of the core New Ageish beliefs of Heaven's Gate — UFOs, reincarnation, etc. — however, he won't go as far as they did. "The difference between Marshall Applewhite and me is that I'm not prepared to die for this belief. In order for me to trade my earthly life for life aboard a spaceship it would take incontrovertible evidence that something greater waited on the other side." In the end, this seems to me to be the *only* difference between the mainstream New Age movement and the Heaven's Gate sect. Those 39 people were willing to walk it like they talk it.

In the end, *The Keepers* feels like numerous books in which a Christian from a mainstream denomination criticises fundamentalist Christians for twisting the beliefs to the extreme. There is no critical examination of the underlying beliefs of Heaven's Gate, just an admonishment that they took those beliefs too far.

Earthpulse Press; $12.95
1997; softcover; 152 pp
1-890693-00-6

MOON SISTERS, KRISHNA MOTHERS, RAJNEESH LOVERS
Women's Roles in New Religions
by Susan Jean Palmer

In this book, Susan Jean Palmer takes an objective look at the role women play in seven new religious movements (NRMs): the International Society for Krishna Consciousness (ISKCON), the Rajneesh Movement, the Unification Church (a/k/a Moonies), the Institute of Applied Metaphysics, Northeast Kingdom Community Church, the Institute for the Development of the Harmonious Human Being, and the Raelean Movement. Relying almost completely on interviews and other first-hand sources, she also looks at why women join these movements in the first place.

ISKCON represents a polarisation of the sexes and a de-emphasis on sex. "In ISKCON men advance spiritually through celibacy and nonattachment; women advance through motherhood and devotion to their husbands in the tradition of stridharma, the wifely duty of submission to the husband and the bearing of sons." So that husbands and wives don't become too attached to each other and screw up their karma, marriages are arranged and sex is done only for procreation after performing elaborate six-hour rituals.

The Raelean Movement is a "UFO contactee cult" founded in 1973 by a French race-car driver. He claims that humans have been genetically engineered by aliens, and that we stand on the brink of either nuclear annihilation or a vast upward shift in consciousness. If we evolve, we will inherit the aliens' technology and be able to individually replicate ourselves through our DNA, achieving immortality. "Women in the Raelean Movement define themselves as the sensual friends and 'playmates' of the Raelean men, who are themselves encouraged to develop the feminine qualities necessary for the 'Age of the Apocalypse.'" This

A Krishna Consciousness bride.
Moon Sisters, Krishna Mothers, Rajneesh Lovers.

group is one of the few that encourages sexual experimentation, sexual ambiguity, and homosexuality. "[The women] reject the institution of marriage, tend to postpone or veto childbearing, are open to expressing their sensuality with other women, and live on an impermanent (but often long-term) basis with the lover of their choice." Given the group's androgynous stand and its insistence that men and women are completely equal, Palmer was surprised to find the relative scarcity of women in leadership roles. Much of the chapter examines this contradiction.

In the final two chapters, Palmer compares the diverse roles of women in these movements, finds the commonalities, and draws some conclusions. "Our data suggest that the innovations in sex roles and sexual mores presently developing in NRMs, far from representing a conservative reaction against 'mainstream' experimentation and feminism, might more accurately be characterised as offering even more extreme, intensified, and diverse versions of the ongoing experimentation already occurring outside these utopias."

Syracuse University Press; $16.95
1994; softcover; 297 pp
illus; 0-8156-0382-7

A PIECE OF BLUE SKY
Scientology, Dianetics and
L. Ron Hubbard Exposed
by Jon Atack

Jon Atack was heavily involved with the Church of Scientology™®© for nine years but left after becoming disillusioned. He has amassed a huge collection of Scientology documents — official publications, bulletins, court records, correspondence, and memoranda — and has interviewed scores of ex-Scientologists. Using this information, he has created a highly detailed and *extremely* unflattering account of the Church of Scientology, its founder L. Ron Hubbard™®©, and Dianetics™®©, a psychological self-help system invented by Hubbard. *A Piece of Blue Sky* is sweeping in its scope. It covers Atack's personal experiences with the Church, Hubbard's entire life, the creation of Dianetics and Scientology, the history of the Church, and Scientology's teachings, including supersecret, upper-level material. A special section looks in detail at Scientology's numerous legal battles, both as plaintiff and defendant.

Lyle Stuart (The Carol Publishing Group); $21.95
1990; hardcover; 433 pp
0-8184-0499-X

THE PIED PIPERS OF HEAVEN
Who Calls the Tune?
by L. Kin

The teachings of the Church of Scientology are revealed gradually, as members move from one level to the next. These doctrines — especially the upper level material — have been the subjects of fierce legal battles since they were released without authorisation onto the Internet. The Church claims that they are copyrighted trade secrets, while critics wonder how in the world the "holy scriptures" of a group that calls itself a religion can be considered "trade secrets". The publication in book form of these teachings would surely result in massive, unending lawsuits for publishers in the US, the UK, or just about anywhere in the world. However, the German government has been waging a war with the Scientologists. It appears to me that the government's actions have definitely gone too far, becoming an indefensible attack on religious freedom. However, this backlash against the highly litigious Church has enabled the publication of a series of books by L. Kin.

In *The Pied Pipers of Heaven*, Kin reveals many of the teachings and techniques of Scientology, but he's not doing it from a critical standpoint. Rather, he's approaching matters from a "Freezone" perspective. Freezoners believe that the fundamental teachings of Scientology and its founder, L. Ron Hubbard, are correct but that the Church has corrupted, distorted, monopolised, and added to these basic truths. This is more or less the same as people who believe that Jesus spoke the truth but that the machinery of Christianity has almost completely destroyed his original message. Kin analyses the core ideas of Scientology and fits them into a larger picture of metaphysical/occult beliefs throughout history.

Kin is an auditor unaffiliated to the Church, and he apparently believes in the process of auditing, in which a trained person (the auditor) helps the auditee discover what painful past experiences are currently interfering with her ability to achieve her potential. This may sound straightforward, but it involves such concepts as "thetans", thought beings who are constantly messing with us, and "Genetic Entities", the bio-electric field that surrounds each of us. It was created by thetans but has achieved something like a life of its own.

Apparently, Kin is somewhat less sure about the upper level teachings, which describe where humans, thetans, and the rest of the gang came from. He qualifies his support of these ideas, but still feels the need to give us notice: **"Warning: Anyone reading on beyond this point does so at their own risk!"** What follows is a history of the world according to Scientology, which really does read like a work of science fiction. It involves a character named Xenu, the leader of the Galactic Federation, which was comprised of 76 planets. Xenu was a despot who tried to seize complete power over the Federation, but luckily he was stopped. However, he did manage to bring billions of thetans to earth and then drop H-bombs in volcanoes in order to get rid of them. I could go on, but I think you get the idea. Believe me, it gets quite byzantine and even more bizarre.

Kin has written three more books, all published by the same German press. *Scientology, Volume One: More Than a Cult?* [$20] lays out the complete history, beliefs, and ideas of Scientology. *Scientology, Volume Two: A Handbook for Use* [$35] gives clear instructions for the procedures, such as auditing and e-metering, performed by Scientologists. In *From the Bottom to the Top: The Way Out* [$30], the final volume, Kin combines the fundamentals of Hubbard's thoughts with his own to present a path to spiritual liberation and enlightenment.

If you can get past the author's belief in these basic ideas, his books present a much-needed examination of some of the most jealously guarded information of our time.

Edition ScienTerra (ScienTerra Book Service); DM40,00, $34
1994; softcover; 354 pp
3-922367-28-3

THE RASTAFARIANS
(Twentieth Anniversary Edition)
by Leonard E. Barrett

A special edition of the pioneering study of the Rastafarian movement, a new religion indigenous to Jamaica. Rastafarianism is a millenarian sect that hold the following tenets: the late Halie Selassie — former Emperor of Ethiopia — was the messiah; Ethiopia is the promised land for blacks; all blacks will eventually be repatriated to Ethiopia and will rule the world; marijuana is sacred; and all oppression is wrong. The author examines this movement, from its prehistory to the mid-1980s, including its tenets, impact, and spread around the world.

Beacon Press; $15
1977, 1997; softcover; 314 pp
illus; 0-8070-1039-1

REVELATION X
The "Bob" Apocryphon — Hidden Teachings and Deuterocanonical Texts of J.R. "Bob" Dobbs
translated by The SubGenius Foundation, Inc.

If you've never encountered the Church of SubGenius before, nothing I can say will prepare you for it. It is a hyperactive, super-detailed parody of organised religions, new religions, and New Age beliefs. Yet, it goes beyond making fun

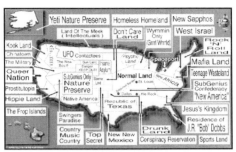

The America(s) of the future, according to the Church of the SubGenius. *Revelation X.*

and actually becomes a replacement for those things. As someone (perhaps a SubGenius) once asked: "Is it a joke disguised as a religion, or a religion disguised as a joke?"

The centre of the SubGenius theology is J.R. "Bob" Dobbs, the quasi-messiah who has come to save US from THEM. "'BOB' DOBBS encompasses The Total Vision, The Ultimate Program, The Final Answer, The Incontrovertible Greed, and the Endless Excuse." One of the ultimate goals of a SubGenius member is to achieve 'Slack'. In a revealing interview, Dr. Drummond (the "Overman") expounds on the nature of Slack. "Compared to Slack, the bliss of Transcendental Mediation is like walking on flaming rock-salt after you've cut the skin off your feet with rusty razor blades. It's like excreting a ball of tangled rusty fishhooks and swimming backwards through a sea of acid with a thousand mosquito bites on every square inch of your body."

Revelation X is 1000 pages of screeds, rants, social satire, jokes, antic art, mystical truths, and the keys to reality frappéd in a blender and then pressurised into 208 pages. Within it you will learn about The Conspiracy, God vs. aliens, alien orifices and their discharges, life after the end of the world, the bleeding head of the world cup golfer, regaining your lost Yeti powers of psycho-consciousness, purity through smut, the necessity of performing "deviant" sex, and why you should "Visualise world armed insurrection". Confused? Good, that's as it should be. "We don't seriously expect **ANYONE** to understand Dobbs, and WHOEVER CLAIMS TO IS LYING!"

Fireside (Simon & Schuster); $14.95
1994; oversized softcover; 208 pp
heavily illus; 0-671-77006-3

SEX, SLANDER, AND SALVATION
Investigating the Family/Children of God
edited by James R. Lewis & J. Gordon Melton

The Family (formerly called the Children of God) is an extremely controversial new religious movement. It was the first group to be the primary target of an anti-cult group, and the behaviour-manipulation technique known as deprogramming was developed specifically for use on its members. In 1984 its Island Pond village in Vermont was raided by 150 government officials and agents, who arrested 110 adults and took 112 children — who the state claimed were being abused — into custody. "The court held that 'the state failed to present any specific evidence of abuse,' and ordered all of the children to be released. After a thorough examination by the social service case workers, no evidence of any abuse of any kind could be found."

This collection of sixteen essays on the Family was co-edited by J. Gordon Melton, author of the towering three-volume *Encyclopedia of American Religions*. Melton is extraordinarily tolerant of new religions and studies them in depth, so I trust him to provide a clear portrait of his subject, unclouded by hysteria over groups with unusual beliefs. This anthology draws together work by authorities on religion and the sociological aspects of religion, many of whom were allowed open access to the Family's literature and communal homes.

"The Family: History, Organisation, and Ideology" offers a good introduction to this sect and its founder, former evangelical Christian pastor David Berg. In the late 1960s, he organised a radical religious group variously called Teens for Christ, the Children of God, the Family of Love, and now simply the Family. It incorporates a millennialist outlook, aggressive recruitment, and communal living. Members are required to read the Bible and the daily writings of Berg (known as "MO letters"), which are considered to be on the same level of importance as the Bible.

The group's attitudes toward sex have always provoked bitter controversy. Melton's essay, "Sexuality and the Maturation of the Family" examines this changing aspect of the sect's beliefs. From the start Berg held the monogamous mixed-sex married couple to be the ideal. Sex within marriage was seen as healthy and fun. Masturbation, nudity, and some forms of non-marital sex were allowed, but birth control, abortion, and male homosexuality were roundly condemned. Berg's pronunciations on children's sexuality were a reaction to his own repressed upbringing: "They [children] should learn that the pleasurable feeling that emanated from their sexual parts, even during the prepubescent years, were normal and should be enjoyed without threats of punishment or the imposition of guilt."

In 1974 Berg created the doctrine of Flirty Fishing, in which female members were to flirt with men outside the Family in order to draw them into the fold. The flirtation could involve drinks or kissing or — sometimes — sexual intercourse. Berg wrote: "Every one of you girls who spreads out your arms and your legs on the bed for those men are [sic] just like Jesus, exactly like Jesus!" From 1978 to 1983 the Family was under a doctrine of very liberal sexual freedom, although a large percentage of the membership didn't take advantage of it. During 1983, Berg started issuing MO Letters that have made the Family's sexual beliefs much more mainstream.

Other essays in this wide-ranging, detailed book include "Psychological Assessment of Children in the Family", "From 'Children of God' to 'The Family': Movement Adaptation and Survival", "New Religions and Child Custody Cases", "Today's Jackboots: The Inquisition Revisited", and "Island Pond Raid Begins New Pattern". Appendices contain a breakdown of the Family's racial makeup and an interview with two fe-

male members who practised Flirty Fishing.

Academic Research; $14.95
1994; softcover; 299 pp
0-9639501-2-6

SNUFF IT
The Quarterly Journal of the Church of Euthanasia

The Church of Euthanasia is one of the newest and fastest-growing fringe religions. The Church's main stance is that the earth is overpopulated and getting worse by the day. The answer is to take any action — as long as it's voluntary — that's needed to thin the population and prevent more births. Thus, it follows that the Church's Four Pillars are Suicide, Abortion, Cannibalism, and Sodomy. They also endorse masturbation and oral sex as ways of getting sexual pleasure without any danger of breeding. The Euthanasiacs' sacred animal is the lemming, and RU-486 ("the abortion pill") is considered a sacrament. Their motto, which has sold well over 20,000 bumperstickers, is, "Save the planet — kill yourself." Not only has the Church been gaining popularity, but the IRS has granted it tax-exempt status, meaning that it is now a legally-sanctioned religion.

Snuff It is the Church of Euthanasia's publication. Issue #2 features an interesting letters section. A transgenderist writes: "It's the duty of every drag queen, T.S., T.V. and crossdresser to get a straight boyfriend and keep him away from girls of breeding age." Another reader sings the praises of masturbation: "Any spoo that lands outside of a human reproductive system is heroic spoo."

The articles and essays examine American thought control, urine therapy, overpopulation problems, crossdressing, Columbus, and a 14-year-old member of the Church. The back pages feature holy relics you can buy from the CoE, including T-shirts, bumperstickers, posters, and music from the Church's label, Kevorkian Records. The back cover features the Church's poster graphically depicting the Four Pillars, as well as Jesus suffering on the cross. Remember: "Jesus died for our sins — and so should you."

Church of Euthanasia/PO Box 261/Somerville MA 02143
Email: coe@netcom.com
WWW: http://www.paranoia.com/coe
Single issue: $3
Six issue sub: $10

SPYING IN GURU LAND
Inside Britain's Cults
by William Shaw

For one year William Shaw — who often writes features for *Details* — plunged himself into the world of Britain's new religions. Pretending to be a spiritual seeker with no ulterior motives, he became involved with several unorthodox sects, sometimes to the point of being accepted as a member. He managed to infiltrate Chrisemma, the Eminent Theater Journey, the Society for Krishna Consciousness, the Aetherius Society, the School of Economic Science, and the Jesus Army.

Shaw refuses to buy into anti-cult hysteria, and instead

takes the radical approach of actually trying to understand these unusual groups. By pretending to be a new recruit, he was able to see the way each sect works from the inside. His narrative is always exciting, often funny, and — above all — enlightening. He presents a nuanced view of all the aspects of each "cult" — the positive, the negative, the fun, the scary, the weird — and refuses to draw easy black and white pictures for us.

The chapter on Shaw's experiences with the Jesus Army is a great example of showing the good and bad aspects of a sect. The JA is an aggressively fundamentalist Christian group whose members mostly live in communal arrangements, giving all their income to the common purse. It's one of the fastest growing religious sects in the UK, and one of only three branches of Christianity on the rise in Britain.

Early on, Shaw goes to a meeting at one of the JA's houses. He is the only outsider jammed into a room of 30 people, who start playing guitars, bongos, and tambourines, singing Jesus songs, and speaking in tongues. Tom, a man who befriended Shaw, asks God to open Shaw's heart because, "He is thirsty for you." During a quiet moment of prayer, Tom asks Shaw to immediately and completely join the Jesus Army. Shaw's explanation of how he felt is one of the most important parts of the book: "It is like standing on the edge of a cliff, knowing how easy it would be to jump. It is not that I am genuinely tempted to join new Zion, it is simply that the same sense of awesome, vertiginous possibility is there. At this moment I could leap. Tom is presenting me with the rare possibility most of us never consider; right now, in just a few moments, I could abandon my job, my former life, all my friends, my possessions, my frustrated ambitions, my overdraft, my mortgage, everything, and disappear into this new fervent evangelical monasticism. Their reassuring world is ready to wrap itself around me. There is a thrill to being presented with the chance to tear everything you know into little shreds."

The next evening Shaw talks to a woman who was involved in a similar movement for nine years, and it is here that one of the many negative aspects of these sects is revealed. "She said for all those nine years she hid the guilt that stemmed from the feeling she could never believe strongly enough. It used to affect her badly. She felt that there must be something lacking in her, not to be able to believe as strongly as all her church friends did." She still feels guilty for leaving, even years later. A member of her former church had killed himself years ago, and she is convinced it was over the guilt of not being able to believe strongly enough.

Spying in Guru Land is — as far as I'm aware — a wholly unprecedented book. Never before has an objective, curious outsider penetrated several so-called cults and sent back thoughtful reports on what it was like on the inside. This is a very important book.

Fourth Estate; £6.99
1994; softcover; 230 pp
1-85702-329-3

WHY AMERICANS BELIEVE IN CULTS?
by Dan Friedman

This stapled report is a reprinting of an article from *Practice: The Journal of Psychology and Political Economy*. It refutes the idea of "cults", saying that nonmainstream religious groups are simply misunderstood and vilified. "The belief that groups of people holding unconventional views do so because their minds are controlled and that they, in turn, have the power to control the minds of unsuspecting or unwilling others is relatively new in America."

This article looks at the history of religious diversity and tolerance in America from the colonial days till the present, tracing how this "anti-cult" attitude arose. It also looks at the motivations and allegations of the Cult Awareness Network and other similar organisations that "have proven very successful in propagating — and profiting from — this intolerance."

Castillo International; $3
no date; stapled; 36 pp

PAGANISM/ WICCA

AMERICAN DRUIDISM
A Guide to American Druid Groups
by Daniel Hansen, Msc.D.

In this book, Daniel Hansen, a self-identified Druid, provides a remarkably clear lesson on the three main forms of Druidism. The paleo-Druids were the originals. Hardly anything is known about them, and what is known comes from about thirty references made by ancient historians. They appeared in the late Iron Age and, contrary to the popular conception of Druids as mystics, they were apparently the scholars, judges, philosophers, and priests of the ancient Celtic people. This form of Druidism died out around the fifth century CE.

The meso-Druids appeared around the year 1700. Having very little in common with its ancient namesake, this Druidism was mainly an esoteric belief system that attracted Hermeticists, Rosicrucians, Freemasons, and other occultists. It lasted for two centuries, and then all but died out right after World War I.

Neo-Druidism appeared in the US in 1963, and, strangely enough, it started as a humorous form of protest. Carleton College in Minnesota had a rule that all students must attend chapel of some sort. To protest this enforced religious practice, some students created the Reformed Druids of North America, which held faux religious services. The next year, Carleton abolished its rule about attending chapel, but the Reformed Druids kept going because some people had apparently found something of value in the new belief system. Other Druid organisations began appearing, and before long, a new religious movement had been born. It is this form that *American Druidism* is most concerned with.

Hansen attempts to explain what the neo-Druids believe, but since it is a relatively unofficial, unorganised movement, that is not an easy task. "For some, Druidism is a viable alternative religion with rites, rituals, and a pantheon of Celtic deities, Nature spirits, and honoured ancestors. For others, Druidism is simply a philosophy to bring one closer in tune with the forces in Nature and the cycles of the year and of life." Neo-Druidism is heavily influenced by Wicca, and some elements are combining it with Christianity, Buddhism, or Native American beliefs. Hansen examines the further similarities and differences among neo-Druids in several chapters on sigils, magic, conversion, Arch Druids, Celtic Wicca, and "Fear of the Burning Times". A chapter is given to each of nineteen currently active neo-Druid groups — including the American Druidic Church, Ar nDraoicht Fein, Divine Circle of the Sacred Grove, the International Druidic Society, and the Church of Y TylwythTeg — and contact information is given for all of them plus dozens of others in the US, UK, and Ireland.

Despite the many typos, *American Druidism* is well-written and refreshingly straightforward about its tangled subject matter. It's an excellent introduction to this form of neo-Paganism.

Peanut Butter Publishing; $14.95
1995; softcover; 180 pp
0-89716-600-0

GREEN EGG
A Journal of the Awakening Earth

Green Egg is put out by the Church of All Worlds, a neo-Pagan sect named after the organisation in Robert Heinlein's *Stranger in a Strange Land*. Issue 108 focuses on family values. In "Pagan Family Values", Anne Newkirk Niven describes four basic values for pagans to pass on — compassion: "emphasising our connection with all living beings", respect: "valuing the opinions, ideas, and decisions of ourselves and others", celebration: "making every day special", and honour: "being true to yourself, to what you believe, and to the God/dess". Fathom Hummingbear ponders the sense of community created by covens and tribes. "As we grow more attuned to our inner Nature, I expect we will more often choose to live in extended families or multi-family communities, and to get more of our cultural information through festivals and tribal-level communications rather than big universities and television."

Is it possible to be Jewish and Pagan? The Judeo-Pagans who contributed to issue 107 think so. David Myriad explains, "Monotheistic Judaism has strong Polytheistic Pagan roots. This was a wondrous realisation, since it allowed me to connect my spirituality with my ancestral and cultural Pagan traditions." The lusciously-named Pollyanna Flowerthighs elaborates: "Now, years later, I find out all the good stuff they [mainstream Judaism] left out of our school-

"*Fatherhood*".
Pagan family values. *Green Egg*.

ing. Such as the Shekina — the female indwelling spirit of God, Jewish meditation, the Sabbath Queen, moon rituals, the mysticism of the Kabbalah, to say nothing of the centuries of folklore, occult, and magical practices."

Issue 109 has several articles on Hellenic Paganism, including a statement of belief from a current follower of this ancient Greek religion. The modern Hellenes worship the Twelve Olympian Gods, "and we must underline here that Hellenism honours and worships not only 'forces and energies' of Nature (as almost all Pagan religions do) but also abstract Ideas, such as Harmony, Eunomia, Justice, Injustice, Freedom, Beauty, Luck, etc. For us, the Ideas are alive and have form; they are deities that simply 'show themselves' through the functions of the human mind."

Besides lots of articles on the diverse aspects of Paganism, each issue also has poetry/song lyrics, fiction, reviews, calendar of events, Pagan news, and a list of Church of All Worlds "nests" around the world.

Green Egg/PO Box 488/Laytonville, CA 95454
Email: webspinners@caw.org
WWW: www.caw.org/green-egg/index.html
Voice & Fax: 707-984-7062
Single issue: $5
Six issue sub (one year): $28. Canada: $42. Latin America: $51.
Transatlantic: $58. Transpacific: $63
Payment: ck, mo, Visa, MC

INSIDE A WITCHES' COVEN
by Edain McCoy

Whether you are a Witch/Wiccan wishing to join or create a coven, or just a curious outsider, this book by a Witch who's been practising since 1981 is a lucid, simple guide to covens. A coven is simply a group of Witches who gather to practice their beliefs together. "Like other religious organisations, covens today may serve social and cultural functions, but their primary purpose is still spiritual. We join covens to worship, to revel in the presence of the divine, and to seek the ancient mysteries and celebrate creation." Covens are organised along various lines: hierarchical or more egalitarian, Traditional or Eclectic, skyclad (nude) or ritually dressed, teaching or non-teaching, single gender or mixed, etc.

Within these pages, you'll learn about the different kinds of covens, how to find the one that's right for you, the interview process, the initiation rites, developing relationships within the coven, magick and healing rituals, festivals and observances, networking with other covens, feuding with other covens ("Witch wars"), teaching others, keeping secrets, banishing members, leaving a coven, creating a coven, dissolving a coven, and many more practical, real-world topics. Since actual rituals and practices vary so much within Wicca, just as in any religion, the author lays out the fundamental beliefs and general practices, filling in the picture with a few specific details that may or may not apply to your case.

Although *Inside a Witches' Coven* provides lots of information that will be new to outsiders, don't expect the author to reveal anything very hush-hush. The promotional copy on this book states that you'll discover "inner circle secrets that covens vow to keep to themselves", but that's only a half-truth. We aren't told the actual secrets, only what topics in general are kept secret. For example: "Methods of invoking deity, names of deities, and the names and manner of calling on other spirits or elementals who regularly assist the coven."

In spite of this misleading promise, this book is still quite valuable for anyone who would like to know more about the main form of organisation of one of the most misunderstood and vilified belief systems in existence.

Llewellyn Publications; $9.95
1997; softcover; 206 pp
1-56718-666-1

WICCA
The Ancient Way
by Janus-Mithras & others

Wicca is a short, introductory book for outsiders who would like to understand what Wicca is really about, as opposed to the hype and hysteria that surround it. "A Traditional Witch is someone who has dedicated herself to the service and worship of Our Lady the Great Mother Goddess of Many Names and Many Forms, and of the Great Horned One, Her Consort." (Note that a Witch can be a woman or a man.) Being pantheistic, Wiccans believe that the Gods are everywhere, in all things (or at least, all things natural). "The Witch, in looking to her Gods sees no fixed traditional image, but instead looks to what is around or inside her at any given moment. The Witch is constantly aware that the very ground she steps upon, the wind that blows through her hair, and the warmth of the Sun are all very much alive and as aware of her as she is of them."

Another chapter provides a general look at the Three Degrees (no specific, secret information is given out). "The Three Degrees are actually three stages of the candidate's development from the darkness of ignorance to the spiritual light of her identity with the Gods." The First Degree corresponds to the Goddess, and the Second Degree to the God. In the Third Degree, the two are integrated, embodying "their inseparability as the Ancient Harmony, from which they never depart and which is their meaning, upon which we mortals in our blindness and ignorance project the fiction of Him or Her, Male or Female, and so on, making God in our own image."

Other chapters explain the Mighty Ones, the training of a Witch, the protectors of the Craft, and the grand Sabbath: All-Hallows Eve.

IllumiNet Press; $5.95
1994; softcover; 64 pp
illus; 1-881532-02-X

A WITCH'S BREW
by Patricia Telesco

Beverages are an important but oft overlooked part of Pagan spirituality. This unique book contains recipes for 236 "spiritually symbolic" alcoholic and non-alcoholic drinks. These brews can "give you an emotional lift, ease a minor illness, deepen the meanings of your rituals and celebrations, or magically aid goals such as increasing psychic awareness, fertility, productivity, or luck."

The first part of the book covers the history of brewing, the religious and medicinal uses of beverages, brewing and magic, and serving vessels, toasts, creative touches, and more. Types of drinks presented in the alcoholic section include beers/ales, cordials/liqueurs, wine and wine coolers, fruit and vegetable wines, meads, punches, tea and coffee spirits, seasonal brews, and spirits for health. In the non-alcoholic section you'll find flower drinks, dessert drinks, juices, sodas, malteds, punches, teas, coffees, seasonal beverages, "soft" beers and wines, and drinks for health.

The recipes make my mouth water — dandelion beer, traditional mulled ale, heather honey cordial, May wine, old-fashioned egg nog, yule glogg (pretty unappetising name, I know), mulberry wine, honeyed honeysuckle, and orange joy juice. Besides the ingredients and instructions (obviously), each recipe lists the beverage's magical attributes. Strawberry-banana stimulation is for, "Sexual potency, stamina, fertility, physical pleasure", and rose geranium oracle helps with, "Prophesy, well-being, insight, love, service to others." Most of the recipes also include instructions for variations, and some have "helpful hints".

A final section has a resources guide, glossary, bibliography, and appendices, plus appendices on brewing folklore, deities of brewing, and the magical properties of the ingredients used in the drinks. Monotheism never tasted this good!

Llewellyn Publications; $16.95
1995; oversized softcover; 268 pp
illus; 1-56718-708-0

NEW AGE

BEAUTY AND THE PRIEST
Finding God in the New Age
by Reverend Patrick McNamara

Ordinarily, this book probably wouldn't end up in *Psychotropedia*, but I've known the author for several years. In fact, I knew him before he was "the author", back when he was "Father Pat", a most unusual Catholic priest. Patrick had always questioned things and bent the rules as a priest, but as time went on, his vistas started expanding to include such heretical areas as spirit channelling, reincarnation, psychic surgery (during which the healer inserts his hand into you without any instruments), Native Mexican shamanism, and Native American healing. Finally, he committed the greatest heresy of all — he fell in love and got married. This was what finally caused him to leave the Church.

In this book, he talks candidly about his life, concentrating especially on the journeys and meetings that introduced him to these new, decidedly un-Catholic ideas. Although anybody with an interest in the New Age will find his story interesting, Patrick aims many of his comments at other Catholics who may be looking to "move beyond" the Church. He hasn't, however, abandoned the Church but rather tried to integrate some Catholic/Christian and New Age beliefs. Although this is blasphemy to the Church, it is par for the course to the New Age movement, which is really just an eclectic blend of various beliefs anyway. "Truth comes from the Native Americans, from Catholics, from Hindus, from the rain forests of the Amazons. Truth is in all people's hearts." Patrick tells each of us that "you are a Spiritual being on a human pathway. That pathway must become Sacred because of who you are. You are a channel of God! You are the earthen vessels. You are here this lifetime to get it right, to accept your divinity and not get caught up in all this world's illusions. You have the keys of understanding a healthier, happier, holier way."

Ozark Mountain Publishers; $14
1997; softcover; 218 pp
illus; 1-886940-01-0

CONVERSATIONS WITH NOSTRADAMUS, VOLUME 1
(Revised Edition)
by Dolores Cannon

Past life hypnotherapist Dolores Cannon claims to have contacted Nostradamus. The famed seer explains to her his cryptic quatrains and gives more information regarding upcoming events. Like so many others, Nostradamus sees troubled times ahead. He discusses the rise of the anti-Christ, the assassination of the Pope, the destruction of the Catholic Church, World War III, natural disasters, the fall of the anti-Christ, and much more. There are two other volumes available in this series. The second one [0-9632776-1-8,

Slumming Pleiadians attempt to help earthlings, the destructive bumpkins of the universe. *Earth.*

$14.95] covers the creation of AIDS, weather control technology, the earth's axis shift, space aliens, and more on the anti-Christ and WWIII. In volume three [0-9632776-3-4, $15.95] Nostradamus talks more about the axis shift, disasters, aliens, and the anti-Christ, plus upcoming technology and problems with the world's economies and stock markets. There are also police composite sketches showing what the anti-Christ and his mentor will look like.

Ozark Mountain Publishers; $14.95
1989; softcover; 326 pp
0-9632776-0-X

EARTH
Pleiadian Keys to the Living Library
by Barbara Marciniak

This book is another addition to the vast genre known as channelled material. Barbara Marciniak claims to channel Pleiadians, and she, her sister, and a friend put out a newsletter of these teachings called *The Pleiadian Times*. For this second book of Pleiadian platitudes, they have gathered together the voluminous, unstructured channellings of the extraterrestrials and attempted to put them in some sort of order.

The Pleiadians' message is pretty straightforward New Age thinking. "It is our intention to assist you in creating a new vision — a vision that inspires you to live and love on planet Earth… As threads unravel to reveal your celestial heritage, do not become entrapped by a glamour from the heavens, for you too are on a star, reflecting and radiating light to worlds seeking the solutions to their own creations. Your task at this point in time is to activate the Living Library of Earth, to restore Earth and the human version of life to the forefront of creation."

In the distant past, the Pleiadians came to Earth to create "an intergalactic exchange centre of information." Representatives from many different alien races sent their DNA to the Pleiadians' master geneticists, and they used it to create human beings and other animals. But now our reptilian aspect has become tyrannical. We've forgotten our true nature, and the aliens are here to help us wake up. The Earth is a storehouse of information (the Living Library referred to earlier), and if we can tap it, we can save ourselves and help save the universe. The Pleiadians give advice on how to do this — through toning, ditching TV, getting back to nature, embracing the Goddess, opening your heart, having sex, and more. All in all, not a bad regimen to embrace, even if you don't believe it will lead to a glorious new age.

Bear & Company; $12.95
1995; softcover; 253 pp
1-879181-21-5

A MAGICAL UNIVERSE
The Best of Magical Blend Magazine
edited by Jerry Snider & Michael Peter Langevin

The magazine Magical Blend, which began publishing in 1980, can basically be classified as a New Age magazine, although that doesn't tell the whole story. It covers more territory than typical "fundamentalist" New Age publications, and it deals with topics, such as drugs and cutting-edge technology, that generally don't fit into the movement.

A Magical Universe collects 29 of the best pieces to appear in the magazine so far. Most of the material is made up of interviews. Lots of interviews. Dead Grateful Dead member Jerry Garcia talks about spirituality and music, Julia Cameron discusses getting creative juices flowing, Robin Williams yaps about the power of comedy, Sasha and Ann Shulgin pontificate on exploring the mind with psychedelics, Stanislav Grof looks at LSD and consciousness, Jacques Vallee theorises about extraterrestrials, Whitley Strieber raps about Roswell and alien visitation, Timothy Leary expounds on "mind-altering software", Jaron Lanier ruminates on Virtual Reality, Riane Eisler rails against the system, medical doctor Larry Dossey promotes the power of prayer, and Douglas Rushkoff points out media viruses. Other interviewees include Celestine Prophecy author James Redfield, Way of the Peaceful Warrior author Dan Millman, neo-Pagan author and organiser Zsuzsanna Budapest, and psychologist and shamanic initiate Alberto Villoldo.

The articles cover a similarly wide ground: being of service, Virtual Reality as a form of altered consciousness, experiences with Australian aborigines, addictive behaviour, and "The Importance of Being Offensive" (by John Cleese). Natalie Goldberg writes about the lessons to be learned from some unusual monks. "There is an order of Buddhist monks

in Japan whose practice is running. They are called the marathon monks of Mount Hiei. They begin running at one thirty A.M. and run from eighteen to twenty-five miles per night, covering several of Mount Hiei's most treacherous slopes… The monks run all year round. They do not adjust their running schedule to the snow, wind, or ice… In fact, when they run they carry with them a sheathed knife and a rope to remind them to take their life by disembowelment or hanging if they fail to complete their route."

Swan Raven Company (Blue Water Publishing); $15.95
1996; softcover; 272 pp
illus; 0-926524-39-9

THE PYRAMID COLLECTION

Evidently, Pyramid is doing all right for itself selling jewellery, books, CDs, and other items related to New Age spirituality, because their slick, full-colour catalogues come constantly, especially during the second half of the year. Although they sell some New Age music, subliminal tapes, and books on alternative health, sacred sex, Taoism, etc., the real reason to get this catalogue is for the other merchandise. They offer all kinds of paraphernalia related to faeries, sun & moon, Native Americans, paganism, Wicca, astrology, Egypt, Eastern religions, and more. Even if you don't practice any of this stuff, you'll still see some goods that you just have to have.

The jewellery is incredible. The most recent catalogue offers an ankh pendant carved out of fiery red brecciated jasper that has been secured by a satin cord to a brass I Ching coin. There's also a gold-plated brooch shaped like a rendering of Salvador Dalí's highly stylised signature. You can also get a Christian cross pendant inset with the Yin-Yang, Om symbol, the Star of David, Triskelion, Pentagram, and Solar Cross. How about a pewter pin in the shape of a hand signing "I love you" with a heart-shaped piece of red jasper in the palm? Or maybe you'd like a Southwestern bracelet inlaid with carnelian, mother-of-pearl, malachite, sugilite, turquoise, onyx, red onyx, and lapis lazuli.

If jewellery's not your speed, you can get a Yin-Yang table, a potion bottle, gargoyle bookends, a South American rainstick, edible love oils, an Australian aboriginal boomerang, a King Tut clock, a lead crystal goblet with a pentagram etched on it, crystal balls, vials, and Boji stones from a natural North American pyramid. Prices are fairly steep but not exorbitant.

The Pyramid Collection/PO Box 3333, Altid Park/Chelmsford MA 01824-0933
Catalogue: free

RADICAL SPIRITUALITY
Metaphysical Awareness for a New Century
by Dick Sutphen

According to Valley of the Sun publishers, Dick Sutphen started the self-help audio tape movement in 1976. Since then, he has created subliminal audio and videotapes and self-hypnosis video tapes… over 400 in all. He also has penned several books and gives popular seminars. This book presents his basic spiritual teachings, which might be described as anti-New Age New Age. He trashes what he calls the "foo-foo" aspects of orthodox New Ageism and its "wishful thinking", such as angel and alien communications.

He advocates a more practical, grounded spirituality that mixes metaphysics, Zen Buddhism, and human potential concepts. One of the fundamental principles of his beliefs is that negative thoughts need to be integrated, not ignored and denied as the basic New Age philosophy would have it. Repressing your negative thoughts doesn't get rid of them, it only drives them into your subconscious where they'll manifest as unnecessary arguments and hostility or, in the long term, ulcers, cancer, etc. To integrate your negative emotions, you have to recognise that they're rooted in issues created in this life or others.

This leads into Sutphen's other major topic — karma. By understanding what has happened to you in past lives and in this one, you can see why you're experiencing negativity and how it's affecting you. Once you understand, you can integrate these emotions and become self-actualised.

Sutphen spends two chapters on sex and one on sex and relationships. His is an accepting view of sexuality — he feels as long as everyone is consenting, it's OK. He frequently gets questions from "seekers" who are homophobes or who believe that sex is an obstacle on the path to spirituality. He replies brilliantly: "Celibacy is demanded by most cults, and encouraged by many religions, so you think it's spiritual. These organisations know that sex is such a powerful force, it can not be successfully repressed. When followers fail to contain their sexuality, they feel guilty, which is just what the guru/priest wants. It is easier to control guilty people." Over time, the members' guilt leads to loss of self-esteem, and they come to believe that the guru/priest offers the only hope for salvation.

Sutphen continues to grind up New Age cows by saying that there is no such thing as selfless service, that pornography isn't a bad thing, that horror movies are spiritually good for you, that you don't have to be vegetarian to be spiritual, that the Harmonic Convergence was baloney, and other provocative things. He presents a heretical brand of New Age thinking that I recommend all seekers examine.

Valley of the Sun Publishing; $12
1995; softcover; 214 pp
0-87554-583-1

CHRISTIANITY

THE BIBLE TELLS ME SO
Uses and Abuses of Holy Scripture
by Jim Hill & R & Cheadle

You're probably familiar with Shakespeare's quote, "Even the devil can cite scripture for his purpose." This book proves it. It shows that throughout history, the Bible has been used to back up diametrically opposing political, religious, cultural, and moral stances. Various sections examine how the Bible has been quoted to *justify* and to *oppose* slavery, war, homosexuality, the ordination of women, the marriage of priests, capital punishment, prayer in schools, medical advances, and environmentalism. These sections contain the contradictory quotes from the Good Book itself, as well as text exploring how these ideas have been trumpeted by religious and political leaders. Other sections show how the Bible has been used to give divine credence to many negative and positive positions — to persecute Jews, Catholics, and blacks, to execute "witches", to oppose masturbation and abortion, to justify the physical punishment of children, to define the terms of marriage, to oppose the consumption of alcohol, to prove that the earth is the centre of the universe, to empower and liberate the poor, and to justify civil rights for African Americans.

Anchor Books (Bantam Doubleday Dell Publishing Group); $12.95
1996; oversized softcover; 159 pp
heavily illus; 0-385-47695-7

BLOOD ON THE ALTAR
Confessions of a Jehovah's Witness Minister
by David A. Reed

Jehovah's Witnesses are forbidden by their religion to receive blood transfusions. They claim that, based on their particular Biblical interpretations, transfusions "violate Moses' command to remove and dispose of blood from kosher meat... Therefore, to 'partake' of them would be not kosher but cannibalism." The author — who was a Witness for thirteen years, eventually becoming an elder — sees this prohibition as tantamount to large-scale murder. He estimates that 7,000 to 16,800 Witnesses die each year by refusing to receive blood. Since the head Witnesses handed down this law in the mid-1940s, we could extrapolate that 364,000 to 873,600 people have needlessly died (this is assuming the Witness population has stayed roughly the same). Worst of all, Witnesses will not allow their children to receive blood transfusions. (What's more, it's also a sin for Witnesses to allow their *pets* to get blood.)

The author rails against the cruelty and stupidity of this lethal prohibition. He shows just how meaningless this Biblical interpretation is by looking at the arbitrariness of this and other medical bans. In 1931, the men who run the Jehovah's Witnesses from the headquarters in Brooklyn suddenly decided that vaccinations were against Moses' law. But, lo and behold, in 1952 they reversed themselves, dropping the ban. Are we supposed to believe that God had a change of heart? Similarly, the men in power made a life-ending proclamation one day in 1967 that organ transplants were a grievous sin unto the LORD. But thirteen years later — after an untold number of deaths — they decided, oops, that they had been mistaken and once again graciously allowed people to receive organs. The ban on transfusions didn't start until the mid-1940s. The sect had been around for approximately 65

Sacred Allegory, Jan Provost's fifteenth century painting of Jesus and his bride, Mary Magdalene. *Bloodline of the Holy Grail.*

years by that time, with members getting blood transfusions that saved their lives, but literally overnight, the human beings who run the show decide that it is God's will for people to die based on a typically vague passage in the Bible.

The arbitrary nature of the matter is further exposed when the author lets us in on a secret — Witnesses can receive certain *components* of blood. For example, pregnant women with Rh incompatibility can receive Rh immune globulins, and haemophiliacs are kindly allowed to get Factors VIII and IX. However, nobody can receive plasma, white or red blood cells, platelets, or whole blood from another person. How about having your own blood taken and stored for later use? Talk about splitting hairs: if your blood is removed from your circulation, no matter how briefly, reintroducing it is a violation of God's law punishable by damnation. However, if an apparatus, such as a heart-lung machine, is used to take the blood and return it without interrupting circulation, that's OK with the Almighty.

The author digs into the history of the Witnesses, showing how they came about and what brought on the various bans on medical treatments. He looks at the toll taken by the transfusion ban, and ends by noting that instead of relaxing their rule, the Witnesses have become more militant. A 1991 article in *The Watchtower* concerning courts ordering a transfusion to be performed "suggests that a JW patient should 'avoid being accessible for such a court-ordered transfusion by fleeing the scene, or else follow the example of the twelve-year-old girl mentioned earlier who had been taught to "fight any court-authorised transfusion with all the strength she could muster, that she would scream and struggle, that she would pull the injecting device out of her arm and would at-

tempt to destroy the blood in the bag over the bed.""'"

Prometheus Books; $24.95
1996; hardcover; 285 pp
1-57392-059-2

BLOODLINE OF THE HOLY GRAIL
The Hidden Lineage of Jesus Revealed
by Laurence Gardner

Laurence Gardner is a leading authority in the Byzantine field of sovereign and chivalric genealogy. He holds a number of impressive titles including Presidential Attaché to the European Council of Princes and the Jacobite Historiographer Royal. He has used his extensive knowledge of more than 2000 years of European and Middle Eastern genealogy to come up with this intricate look at a long-suppressed historical fact: Jesus and Mary Magdalene had children, and their bloodline is in existence today. Additionally, Jesus's brother James also begat a lineage that still survives.

Because of his reputation and his persistence, Gardner was granted access to Sovereign, Noble, Chivalric, and Church archives and repositories that are rarely, if ever, seen by anyone other than the people who own and maintain them. He has seen many documents that have routinely been suppressed and denied over the centuries. From these and other sources, he has put together a history of Jesus's and James's bloodlines set against a background of emperors, popes, kings, queens, knights, saints, the Holy Roman Empire, the Knights Templar, Joan of Arc, the Inquisition, wars, revolutions, skulduggery, and other grand elements of history. If you're wondering what the Holy Grail in the title has to do with all this, Gardner explains that the phrase "Holy Grail" is actually a corruption of the word *Sangréal*, the name for the bloodline that includes Jesus and James.

If you want to experience the grandeur and intricateness of Gardner's tale, you'll have to read this big book yourself. But allow me to go right to the heart of the matter and relate what everyone's dying to know. Jesus and Mary Magdalene married in 30 CE and had three children: a daughter named Damaris and two sons: Jesus and Joseph. Daughters were not permitted to carry on the royal bloodline, which was a responsibility that fell to the firstborn son. Unfortunately for the *Sangréal*, Jesus Junior's first son, Galains, was a life-long celibate. That meant that the royal bloodline went to Jesus Senior's and Mary's younger son, Joseph. Joseph begat Josue. Josue begat Aminadab. Here the lineage of Jesus intersects with that of his brother, because Aminadab got with James's great-great-great granddaughter Eurgen. Eventually, this lineage produced King Arthur and many of his knights, including Lancelot, Galahad, and Gawain. The book's final chapter, "The *Sangréal* Today", is a letdown. It doesn't give a detailed listing of people who are currently descended from Jesus but instead focuses mainly on Scotland's House of Stewart, which is partially descended from King Arthur's father and, thus, Jesus himself.

Bloodline of the Holy Grail makes for a fascinating recasting of history. Gardner writes with such authority and assuredness that it's easy to take seriously his claim to have discovered the truth about Jesus.

Element Books; $18.95

1996; softcover; 491 pp

illus; 1-86204-111-3

BROTHERS OF LIGHT, BROTHERS OF BLOOD
The Penitentes of the Southwest
by Marta Weigle

The Penitente Brotherhood is one of the more interesting and misunderstood aspects of Christianity. "The Brothers of Our Father Jesus, commonly known as the Penitentes, are men of Hispanic descent who belong to a lay religious society of the Roman Catholic Church... The Brotherhood's Headquarters are in Santa Fe, and the organisation's greatest strength is in northern New Mexico and southern Colorado."

The Brotherhood developed among Spanish pioneers in northern New Mexico in the late 1700s. They were basically isolated from centres of Spanish culture and were in hostile territory, so their Catholic beliefs morphed into something similar but different. The Penitentes are slavishly devoted to mutual aid through good deeds and charity and to the Christian belief that humans are unworthy beings born to suffer. They piously observe the Passion (i.e., suffering) of Jesus and are repentant to the extreme. It is these harsh forms of penance that have caused the Brotherhood to be scorned and persecuted. Although they have apparently stopped such rituals, they used to flagellate themselves and perform mock crucifixions. Rumours exist that nails were used, but the consensus from reliable sources, including photographs, is that the men were lashed to the crosses with rope. Before these rituals, two other Penitentes would drag a crude wagon which carried a wooden statue of the angel of death. This earned the group a reputation as death worshippers, when actually the "death cart" was just a reminder of mortality.

Brothers of Light, Brothers of Blood is the most complete book available on this secretive sect.

Johnson Books; $18.95

1976; softcover; 319 pp

illus; 0-941270-58-0

THE CHRISTIAN CONSPIRACY
How the Teachings of Christ Have Been Altered by Christians
by Dr. L. David Moore

The history of Christian belief is far from neat and tidy. Especially for the first 500 years of its existence, "Christianity" was a morass of conflicting beliefs, sects, and doctrines. Of course, there are various denominations today that disagree with each other over such technicalities as when baptism should occur or exactly how Armageddon will take place, but in the early days, even the most basic, fundamental Christian doctrines were up for grabs. So who decided what beliefs were to become unquestioned dogma and which ones were to become heresy? It certainly wasn't God. It was a bunch of men with highly political motivations.

A rare shot of Penitente cross-bearers sometime in the 1920s.
Brothers of Light, Brothers of Blood.

As theologian David Moore makes clear, these men ignored the original teachings of Jesus and created Christianity in their own image. They assembled the books of what is now called the Bible based on their own motives (which usually had to do with holding power over the people). "By the end of the first 500 years of the Church's existence, the Church had not only defined Christ, they had required his followers to accept those definitions. In addition, the Church defined the followers as being a loyal subject of the supreme Church." Jesus preached a direct, personal relationship with God, but the Church altered this message by placing itself between the Christian and God/Christ. "Jesus said, '... he who does not believe will be condemned.' [Mark 16:16]. Augustine brought the Church squarely into this by saying that '... those who do not receive the Sacrament [of Baptism] shall be condemned.'"

Moore examines how the early Church changed and corrupted messages regarding the nature of Jesus, the definition of a Christian, salvation, the soul, intolerance, world affairs, reincarnation, karma, angels, sex, and more. Importantly, he also looks at how these tainted messages are often still an accepted part of Christianity. For example, reincarnation and karma were widely accepted in Jesus's time, many prominent early Christian theologians openly believed in the concepts, and nothing in the Bible rules them out. Moore isn't clear on how the concept has come to be reviled by Christians, but it has a lot to do with the misinterpretation of a few parts of the Bible.

Moore gives a fascinating history of how the New Testament was formed. For over three centuries after Jesus, there were lots of Christian writings floating around, many of which had been written or sponsored by Apostles. The Church decided that it needed to develop an official canon, so after lots of wrangling some of these writings were put together to form the New Testament in 367 CE. The books that these men decided should be included are now considered "the inspired Holy Word of the LORD", and the ones they didn't like ended up in history's garbage can. The final decision was to include the Gospels of Matthew, Mark, Luke, and John, but the Gospels written by two other apostles — Thomas and Peter — were chucked. Interestingly, the Revelation of John was adopted as the Holy Word, was later rejected as part of the New Testament, and then was reinstated by the end of the seventh century. Moore gives a description of fifteen books that — even through they were widely considered sacred — didn't make the final cut. Inexplicably, he ignores the highly relevant topic of how the books that were accepted were altered by people other than the authors.

The Christian Conspiracy also gives details on the five Ecumenical Councils, during which it was decided what Christian belief is and isn't. These meetings were heavily political. The final Council was called by Emperor Justinian — who wanted a unified Christianity in order to consolidate his power over the Roman Empire — and was not attended by the Pope or any Western bishops. A massive appendix gives summaries of all the major streams of thought in early Christianity that were stamped out by the politically correct councils, including Pelagianism, which taught that people have free will, and Arianism, which taught that "God was so unique that he could not be divided or diminished in any way and as a consequence, Jesus Christ was less than God."

Moore declares that he is a Christian and that his book is meant to peel away the distortions that have been heaped on Jesus's message. But whether or not you believe in his underlying thesis that Jesus is divine, this book mercilessly exposes how the machinations of men have come to be blindly accepted as the unquestionable word of God Almighty.

Pendulum Plus Press; $14.95

1994; softcover; 347 pp

0-9635665-2-0

THE CRIMES OF JEHOVAH
Selections from the Bible
by Mark Mirabello, PhD

These 100 quotes from the King James version of the Old Testament show Jehovah/Yaweh at his most brutal and barbaric — selling children into slavery, killing babies, ordering women burned alive, telling soldiers to rape women, demanding human sacrifice, causing cannibalism, ordering massacres (including genocide), killing people with haemorrhoids (1 Samuel 5:6), slaughtering over 200,000 people, using foul language, showing favouritism, and saying that disabled people aren't allowed at altars or in sanctuaries.

See Sharp Press; $2.50

1997; staplebound booklet; 34 pp

1-884365-13-2

THE DARK SIDE OF CHRISTIAN HISTORY
by Helen Ellerbe

The idea for this book originally came to Helen Ellerbe when she was in the familiar situation of having an acquaintance ramble on about how great and beautiful Christianity is and how it's sown peace and understanding throughout the world. Ellerbe thought, "Puhleeeze!" How can someone ignore the Crusades, the Inquisition, European and American witchhunts, the torture and slaughter of other assorted infidels, and the rampant hatred that Christianity hath wrought? In response, she prepared a short presentation to reveal the

Torturing buxom young women was all in a day's work for these men of God. *The Dark Side of Christian History.*

other side of the coin, the one no believer wants to admit. She realised that there was so much material — and it was kept so far from view — that she expanded it into this book.

In the intro, she lays bare Christianity's fruits: "It is a legacy that fosters sexism, racism, the intolerance of difference, and the desecration of the natural environment. The Church, throughout much of its history, has demonstrated a disregard for human freedom, dignity, and self-determination."

How did this start? In the first few centuries of Christianity, there were actually a huge variety of sects that held widely divergent views on the nature of Jesus and God, the role of women, obedience, and other crucial issues. One of these groups is what Ellerbe calls orthodox Christians… they believed in a jealous, angry male God who must be feared and obeyed. His truth can only be dispensed through middlemen called priests. At the opposite pole were what we call the Gnostic Christians, who believed in a loving, all-encompassing God who is very tolerant. They felt that we can directly experience the divine, and women played active roles in these churches. Needless to say, these two camps hated each other. The orthodoxers thought that the Gnostics were heretics who should be killed. Interestingly, some Gnostic thought managed to creep into the Bible, such as Luke 17:21, in which Jesus says that "the Kingdom of God is within you."

So how did orthodox Christianity come to be the dominating force within the religion? By making Christianity palatable to the Romans, so that it eventually became the official religion of the Empire. At first, Christianity was a fringe "cult" that was hated by the Romans, mainly because Christians refused to accept the Roman pantheon of gods and wouldn't recognise the Emperor as a god. To become accepted, they did whatever they had to do. "They revised Christian writings and adapted their principles to make Christianity more acceptable. They pandered to Roman authorities. They incorporated elements of paganism. Orthodox Christianity appealed to the government, not as a religion that would encourage enlightenment or spirituality, but rather as one that would bring order and conformity to a faltering empire."

The rest, as they say, is history. Although decadence is routinely blamed for the fall of the Roman Empire, it was actually *after* Christianity became the state religion that Rome came crashing down. As the Church came to dominate Europe, civilisation entered the Dark Ages. The Church, through the repression of knowledge and the burning of libraries and intellectuals, set back science, art, literature, and the study of history.

As the Middle Ages dawned and humanity again began to take strides forward, the Church reacted by unleashing the Crusades, the Inquisition, and missionaries, who went all over the globe with orders from the Pope to kill or enslave indigenous people who would not convert. Then came the witch hunts, which claimed over 100,000 lives. Children were not exempt — girls as young as nine-and-a-half and boys ten-and-a-half could be found guilty of witchcraft and tortured. Younger children, who could not be accused of witchcraft, were tortured to extract information that would be used against their parents. "A famous French magistrate was known to have regretted his leniency when, instead of having young children accused of witchcraft burned, he had only sentenced them to be flogged while they watched their parents burn."

Christianity set the stage for our modern world by making God a cold, distant figure that does not exist in nature. Thus we became alienated from the natural world and began to treat it with disrespect. Christianity also solidified the concepts of struggle, domination, control, and unyielding, top-down authority. "Power and authority should, in the eyes of the orthodox, be exercised only by those at the top of the hierarchy."

The Dark Side uses lots of primary documents from Christians to back up its points (even though these inhumane actions speak for themselves). One shorter example is St. Clement of Alexandria's typically misogynistic quote: "Every woman should be filled with shame by the thought that she is a woman." There are also lots of woodcuts and illustrations depicting Christianity's brutal legacy. Most highly recommended.

Morningstar Press; $12.95
1995; softcover; 221 pp
illus; 0-9644873-4-9

THE JESUS CONSPIRACY
The Turin Shroud and the Truth About the Resurrection
by Holger Kersten & Elmar R. Gruber

The authors have come to a unique conclusion after studying the Shroud of Turin, that mysterious piece of cloth that allegedly swathed Jesus after he was crucified and which is somehow imprinted with the image of a man. This new theory states that Jesus was still alive when he was taken down from the cross. The evidence is in the image itself and the fact that there is an image at all. The authors meticulously explain how they arrived at this judgement, and they implicate the Vatican in covering up what they know to be truth because of its potential to destroy Christianity. The centre section of the book contains several photos of the shroud and religious iconography.

Element Books; $14.95
1994; softcover; 373 pp
illus; 1-85230-666-1

Does this building contain Jesus' body?
Jesus Lived In India.

JESUS LIVED IN INDIA
His Unknown Life Before and After the Crucifixion
by Holger Kersten

Holger Kersten claims to have found evidence that Jesus travelled to India and became a Buddhist master, that he survived the crucifixion and returned to India, and that he was buried in the capital of Kashmir, where his tomb still exists. Sections include "Kashmir the Promised Land", "Buddhist Thought in the Teachings of Jesus", "Miracles — of Jesus, and in India", "Was Jesus Entombed Alive?", and "The 'True' Jesus in Islam".

Element Books; $14.95
1986, 1994; softcover; 264 pp
illus; 1-85230-550-9

THE LOST GOSPEL OF Q
The Original Sayings of Jesus
edited by Mark Powelson, Ray Riegert, & Marcus Borg

The "Gospel of Q" was written during the sixth decade of the Common Era, only twenty or so years after Jesus is said to have died. Thus, it is much older than the four Gospels that were selected for the New Testament and, as such, it is said to contain the unvarnished words of Jesus before they were distorted by various factions. An actual copy of this document has never been found, but it has been pieced together from other sources. Like the Dead Sea Scrolls, this ancient work has been known only among scholars, who have not been anxious to release it to the rest of the world. This book presents it to the public for the first time.

Ulysses Press; $15
1996; small hardcover; 126 pp
1-56975-100-5

THE MOST DANGEROUS MAN IN AMERICA?
Pat Robertson and the Rise of the Christian Coalition
by Robert Boston

The author critically examines Pat Robertson and his Christian Coalition, "one of the most powerful religious-political movements in American history." He shows the scary amount of influence the group has — especially on the Republican party — at state and national levels, and he reveals

Robertson's plan to turn America into a fundamentalist Christian theocracy. Especially enlightening is the chapter documenting Robertson's attitudes towards feminism, race relations, gays and lesbians, and other religions, including mainstream Christians ("Robertson once asserted that more than half of all Protestants who attend services every Sunday are not really Christians and that they are going to hell because they are not 'born again.'").

Prometheus Books; $16.95
1996; softcover; 248 pp
1-57392-053-3

THE PETITION AGAINST GOD
The Full Story of the Lansman-Milam Petition
by Pastor A.W. Allworthy

In December 1974 a Petition for Rulemaking was filed with the Federal Communications Commission asking them — among other things — to no longer allocate reserved educational FM bands and TV stations to "religious 'Bible,' 'Christian,' and other sectarian schools, colleges, and institutes". Within nine months, over 700,000 letters of protest had been mailed to the FCC. That total is now up to 30 million, and the letters are still coming. Every once in a while, some ill-informed Christian group urgently warns its members that the FCC is considering a petition to ban Christian programming, and the letters flood in anew.

The authors filed the petition in all seriousness. However, when they saw the reaction it provoked, they decided to have some fun, which is why they wrote this book. You see, "Pastor A.W. Allworthy" is actually Lorenzo Milam, co-author of the petition. This whole book is presented as having been written by a gravely concerned Christian, when actually it's just Milam having fun with the faithful.

"Allworthy" claims to have met Milam and his co-petitioner, Jeremy Lansman, by pretending to be on their side. He offers this description: "Not only is Milam grossly fat, but he is constantly sniffing and slobbering. Where Lansman has a slight lisp, Milam speaks as if he were a fog-horn, and often grunts… I have some doubts as to how he is able to feed his wife (who is as tiny as he is big) and the seven or nine children that troop in and out at all hours."

The Petition Against God contains the entire text of the petition, responses from religious broadcasters, and the "joyous FCC decision", which rejected the petition's demands. Also included are letters from members of the flock, most of whom misunderstood and thought that the FCC was considering banning all religious programming from radio and TV. One man in Minnesota wrote to the Commission: "Dear Sirs, please dont take the christian broadcast off i think American people should have some rights. i'm not getting nasty but i'm getting mad. it's just that i don't want things that well hurt christ!"

"Christ the Light Works" (Mho & Mho Works); $3.95
1975; softcover; 149 pp
illus; 0-917320-07-7

SNAKE OIL
Kooky Kontemporary Kristian Kulture

Snake Oil takes a cynical look at the idiotic, tacky world of Christian televangelists. Ranging from light-hearted criticism to hard-hitting facts, the articles crucify Kenneth Copeland, Benny Hinn, Robert Tilton, the Bakkers, Pat Robertson, and other "kooky kristians". In issue 4, "High Times with Paul and Jan" pokes fun at the bewildering couple behind Trinity Broadcasting Network, presently the world's dominant Christian channel. "Paul and Jan Crouch of Trinity Broadcasting Network are very often described by those first encountering them as 'like Jim and Tammy — only weirder.' Indeed, the Crouches, with their ultra-gaudy sets of Louis XIV furniture, red carpet, and flocked wallpaper, make Jim and Tammy look downright restrained by comparison. Dallas Morning News columnist Steve Blow aptly dubbed Jan Crouch 'Tammy Faye Antoinette' with her gobs of make-up, froufrou dresses, and mounds of silvery purple hair." (The cover of Snake Oil shows Jan as a dominatrix stepping on her slave, Paul, who is dressed in leather and chains.)

Other features include a cut-up assembly of pictures and text straight from the propaganda of Dr. O.L. and Miss Velma Jaggers, founders of the Universal World Church; a travelogue of Christian sites (Christian Broadcasting Network, Jimmy Swaggart Ministries, etc.); and an article on a loud, obnoxious TV preacher who has faced eleven child molestation charges and, according to a police report, beat his roommates — a 71-year-old invalid and her retarded son.

Snake Oil is the number one guide to the new pastime called Recreational Christianity, which includes watching television preachers for their absurd entertainment value.

Snake Oil/6110 E Mockingbird #102374/Dallas TX 75214
Current issue: $3 cash
no subscriptions

WHAT COLOR WAS JESUS?
by William Mosley

Despite phrasing its title as a question, this book declares in no uncertain terms that Jesus was black. For proof, it turns to the only Biblical passages that physically describe Jesus, which "depict God Himself or the Son of God with hair like 'wool,' and with bodily parts the colour of 'brass' and 'amber' (cf. Ezekiel 1:27 & 8:2; Daniel 7:9; Revelation 1:14-15)." It also looks at the genealogical lineage of Jesus given in Matthew and Luke. The author says that these "have a significant bearing on the fact that Christ Jesus had Black (African), that is, Hamitic ancestors."

The next parts of the book examine the role of black Jesus throughout the world and how — despite such things as the thousands of statues throughout Europe depicting Mary and the infant Jesus as black — Jesus came to be portrayed as white. The author says that portraying Jesus as white has been devastating to the black community. It has alienated them from their Saviour and imposed a feeling of inferiority. "One of the mandates of Black theology, according to James H. Cone, is to end the reign and worship of a White god in the Black community. Not to do so would be tantamount to accepting the doctrine of White supremacy and White racism for which it is the foundation. Without tongue in cheek, Cone asserts: 'The White God is an idol, created by racists… and we Black people must perform the iconoclastic task of smashing false images.'"

African American Images; $6.95
1987; softcover; 67 pp
illus; 0-913543-09-8

WHAT GOD HAS REVEALED TO MAN
The Genuine Word of God As Revealed by the World's Holy Books and the World's Holy Men
This little booklet is completely blank inside.
See Sharp Press; 35 cents
no date; small booklet; 12 pp
no ISBN

WHAT THE BIBLE REALLY SAYS ABOUT HOMOSEXUALITY
Recent Findings By Top Scholars Offer a Radical New View
by Daniel A. Helminiak, PhD

Recently, some theologians have been offering radical interpretations of the Biblical passages that deal with (or allegedly deal with) homosexuality. These scholars use the historical-critical approach of Biblical interpretation, which attempts to find out what passages meant in the time and culture in which they were written and whether those messages still apply today.

Probably the most notorious passage in the Bible dealing with the issue is Leviticus 20:13: "If a man lies with a male as with a woman, both of them have committed an abomination; they shall be put to death, their blood is upon them." Ultra-fundies love to use this passage to call for the death penalty for homosexuals. (What I love to point out is that this passage doesn't mention women, so those who use it to condemn lesbians are 100% wrong. Hee hee!) If we look from the historical perspective at why gay sex was so reviled, it yields an unexpected answer. "Among the early Israelites, as Leviticus sees it, to engage in homogenital sex meant to be like the Gentiles, to identify with the non-Jews. That is to say, to engage in homogenital acts was to betray the Jewish religion. Leviticus condemned homogenital sex as a religious crime of idolatry, not as a sexual offence, and that religious treason was thought serious enough to merit death." Therefore, the author contends, this passage is now irrelevant.

Later in Leviticus there is a list of rules called the Holiness Code that also forbids male-male sex, along with tons of other acts (including having sex with a menstruating woman). The penalty for all these indiscretions, however, is to be ejected from the land of Canaan, not to be killed. So which punishment applies in this contradictory situation?

The author also looks at the widely differing ways in which two words have been translated. Does *malakoi* mean "catamites", "the effeminate", "boy prostitutes", "sissies", or "masturbators"? Does *arsenokoitai* mean "sodomites", "sexual perverts", "practising homosexuals", "male prosti-

tutes" or "paedophiles"? The answers, as always, depend on the prejudices of the translators.

Other parts of the book similarly examine every Biblical reference to homosexuality, as well as the prohibition against sex with angels and the Bible's supposed advocacy of heterosexuality.

Of course, for those who don't believe in the Bible, this won't make any difference. But those who do believe in it will be faced with new evidence that may undermine the foundation of their "Godly" hatred and intolerance.

Alamo Square Press; $9.95
1994; softcover; 121 pp
0-9624751-9-X

MILLENNIALISM

ARMAGEDDON 2000
by Kenneth Rayner Johnson

A new entry in the ever-growing field of apocalypse prediction literature. Kenneth Rayner Johnson's first doomsday book, *The Zarkon Principle*, has become something of a classic since its publication in 1975. In this major expansion and reworking of that book, Johnson demonstrates that many of his predictions have already come true and expands on his prophecy that the world as we know it will end in the year 2000. By analysing religious scriptures of the world, occult and magickal literature, other prophecies, unexplained phenomena, meteorology, chaos theory, and related areas, the author has come up with several end-of-the-world scenarios — collision with a giant comet or a huge bunch of antimatter, ecological catastrophe, nuclear annihilation, being swallowed by a black hole, the sun turning into a Red Giant, or the invasion of hostile space aliens.

Creation Books; $14.95
1995; softcover; 248 pp
1-871592-27-5

MILLENNIUM, MESSIAHS, AND MAYHEM
Contemporary Apocalyptic Movements
edited by Thomas Robbins & Susan J. Palmer

This collection of sixteen papers by scholars sheds light on various specific aspects of the current upswing in apocalyptic/millennialist thinking. The first three essays concern the theoretical aspects of studying apocalypticism and are for heavy thinkers only. The final essay in the first section looks at reactions within the Baha'i sect to fifteen years of failed prophecies.

Next comes a series of papers on a fascinating phenomenon, the rise of *secular* millennial thinking. Even though the most obvious apocalyptic thought systems are based on religious or spiritual beliefs, many don't involve supernatural elements. One essay covers the survivalist and militia movements, which see the end of the world as we know it coming from nuclear war, government crackdown, and other political causes. Earth First! and its vision of environmental armageddon is covered in another essay. John M. Bozeman's piece on "technological milenarianism" examines eugenics, cryonics, and space colonisation, each of which is championed by "groups strongly holding the opinion that technology will bring about a new golden age in the near future that will create a substantial, and permanent, fundamental improvement in the human condition." The section's last essay points out the "feminisation" of millennialist movements, in ways that range from increased female leadership to visions of women as "world saviours and rulers of the future".

The third group of essays examines apocalyptic thinking within four of the more established religions — Catholicism, Seventh Day Adventism, Mormonism, and fundamentalist Christianity. The latter paper provides an overview of the unnerving movement known as Christian Reconstructionism, whose followers are hell-bent on creating a theocratic government, economy, and legal system based completely on Old Testament principles.

The last group of essays offers insights into why apocalyptic groups — namely, the Branch Davidians, the Order of the Solar Temple, the Aum Shinrikyo, and the Christian Identity Movement — often become violent, either towards the rest of society or towards themselves.

M, M, & M is worth reading for those who are seriously interested in millennial madness and don't mind putting up with academic writing styles.

Routledge; $18.95
1997; softcover; 334 pp
illus; 0-415-91649-6

WELCOME TO THE END OF THE WORLD
Prophecy, Rage, and the New Age
by Teresa Kennedy

In *Welcome to the End of the World*, Teresa Kennedy attempts to analyse spiritual milleniallism — particularly as it now exists — in psychological and sociological terms. She doesn't push a certain viewpoint, and she's not concerned over whether or not any predictions will come true. Instead, she looks at why we as a society are all tied up in knots about the approach of the year 2000.

The first section, "Prophecy", examines some of the more famous prophets and prophecies of history, along with the general personality types of prophets. The purpose, though, isn't to provide a crash course in predictions but to analyse why these prophets and their utterances resonate with so many people. "The point is that most of us, no matter what our personal notions of the future, are more comfortable affirming the prophetic 'powers' of a long-dead fifteenth-century courtier or some discarnate being from Alpha Centauri than we are owning our capacity for enlightenment — our own power to draw upon inner knowledge — to predict and therefore to shape our future."

"Rage" contains four chapters on the roles that widespread fear, alienation, and paranoia play in millennial thinking. "Rage develops because on a fundamental level we know that we do not exercise the degree of control over our lives and destinies that we are 'supposed' to… Seemingly 'stuck' in our lives, we begin to project — to suspect that the change we crave will come necessarily from some unstoppable outside force — god, nuclear war, the intervention of hostile extraterrestrial intelligence, the earth tilting upon its axis, etc."

"New Age", the final section, focuses on the New Age movement and related strains of thought in which followers try to gain back some of the control they feel they have lost. "Afflicted as we are by collective paranoia, we manifest increased spirituality either in purification movements (self-improvement and wellness), in otherworldliness (angels, aliens, and other 'rescuers'), or by embracing the magical-thought systems of 'lost' cultures and indigenous religions — believing perhaps that the answer lies not in looking to the future, but somewhere in the past."

Most of what Kennedy has to say is interesting, and perhaps accurate, food for thought. However, most of it isn't terribly groundbreaking. Her analysis is occasionally surprising, as when she says that obsessive-compulsives are the people behind most our current "purification movements", whether it's to stamp out porn and casual sex, help people end their addictions, or clean up the environment. As with many books I review, this one is a good primer if you're unfamiliar with the general concept (in this case, the psychology of millennialism), but you should look elsewhere for more insightful analysis.

M. Evans and Company; $19.95
1997; hardcover; 188 pp
0-87131-817-2

SATAN & COMPANY

ANTICHRIST
Two Thousand Years of the Human Fascination With Evil
by Bernard McGinn

Throughout history, the human race has sought to understand "evil". One of the most simplistic ways to understand all the dark tendencies that course through our psyches is to personify them, either as a supernatural being (e.g., Satan) or as a human being (e.g., the anti-Christ). This book focuses on the latter legend, which involves a person who is complete, 100% evil. The concept has its precursors in Second Temple Judaism and came into full being among members of the fledgling Jesus movement in the second half of the first century CE. From there, it has continued for almost 2000 years, and is once again gaining in popularity as we head for the end of a millennium. The author not only looks at the anti-Christ legend in all its guises, but examines what it says about the human race's relationship to evil and why it overlaps so much with another set of beliefs — apocalypticism.

HarperCollins Publishers; $18.00
1994; softcover; 372 pp
illus; 0-06-065282-9

BIOGRAPHY OF SATAN
Exposing the Origins of the Devil
by Kersey Graves

A reprinting of Kersey Graves's 1924 book in which he looks at ancient personifications of evil, paying special attention to where Christianity got its ideas of Satan and Hell. Graves argues that the concepts of a supernatural being devoted to evil and a place of eternal damnation were not a part of pre-Christian Judaism. The Old Testament makes no mention of either of these things. When the word "devil" appears in the Old Testament, it is always in the plural and refers to the gods of the "heathens", and "hell" actually is the word for "grave". Graves argues that Satan and Hell were developed by the early Christian priesthood to keep the people in line.

· The Book Tree; $13.95
1924 (1995); softcover; 163 pp
1-885395-11-6

PACTS WITH THE DEVIL
(Second Edition)
by S. Jason Black & Christopher S. Hyatt, PhD

In *Pacts with the Devil*, two decades-long students of various magick and occult practices give an unvarnished history of the Left-Hand Path (a/k/a Black Magic) in Western civilisation and then tell you how to get in on the action.

The first part of the book examines the history of this dark esoteric tradition. If anyone in Europe during the 300 years after the Renaissance "practised magic", it was most likely to be the kind covered by the authors. Specifically, attention is focused on the epicentre of such practices — France in the late 1700s. During this time, the aristocracy was filled with secret society members, sorcerers, alchemists, and outright Satanists. Three important grimoires became popular during this period: *The Grimorium Verum*, *The Grand Grimoire*, and *The Constitution of Honorius*. The authors also examine blood sacrifice, parallel beliefs in the East, and the history of belief in the devil.

The second part of the book contains step-by-step instructions for re-enacting the rituals laid out in the grimoires mentioned above. (You'll be happy to know that animal sacrifice is replaced by sexual rituals involving the "sacrifice" of bodily fluids.) It all involves lots of sigils, invocations, recitations, conjurations, etc. I'm still not sure if the authors truly

Papal Antichrist as wild man. Melchior Lorch (1545). *Antichrist.*

believe that actual evil spirits are being contacted or if they see these pact rituals as a metaphor for invoking your own personal power. At one point they write: "This material represents what is normally considered 'black magic,' since the spirits it pretends to consort with are admittedly demons." Despite other similar statements, there are many times when they imply that actual demons are being contacted.

Whether or not you take all this literally, *Pacts with the Devil* provides detailed knowledge on this surreptitious branch of esotericism.

New Falcon Publications; $14.95
1993, 1997; softcover; 285 pp
illus; 1-56184-058-0

THE SATANIC MASS

This CD is a re-release of the classic recording of a Satanic Mass, taped live at the Church of Satan in 1968. Speaking over an organ that is sometimes bright and sometimes brooding, the late Anton LaVey — founder and High Priest of the Church — conducts an eleven-part Mass. LaVey stands in front of an "altar" (which is actually a nude, beautiful priestess) and tolls a bell nine times while turning counterclockwise. He invokes Satan: "In the name of Satan, Ruler of the Earth, King of the World, I command the Forces of Darkness to bestow their infernal power upon us. Open wide the Gates of Hell and come forth from the Abyss." Next comes the Drinking of the Chalice and the Benediction of the House. Then LaVey calls by name several demons and devils, and the congregation repeats each name.

LaVey recites the Fourteenth Key in the ancient Enochian language, and conjures a curse against someone who has wronged a member of the Church. You'll notice strange noises towards the end of this ceremony. The liner notes explain: "The guttural ululations of the demonic inhabitants

MISCELLANEOUS

Astaroth, a lord of perverse eroticism who presides over the Witches' Sabbath. *Pacts with the Devil.*

of the Infernal Empire can be heard as the High Priest concludes his invocation and summons them up from the Pit to carry out his diabolic command."

After reciting the Seventh Enochian Key, LaVey performs a ritual in which he casts an enchantment on a man with whom a female member of the congregation wants to fulfil her lustful desires. Next, LaVey Satanically baptises his three-year-old daughter, Zeena. The Mass ends with a Benediction and LaVey tolling the bell nine times.

In the next part of the recording, LaVey reads the Prologue and Verses One through Five of the "Book of Satan", from the *Satanic Bible*. In Verse Three, he espouses the Church's individualistic attitude: "Hate your enemies with a whole heart. And if a man smite you on one cheek, smash him on the other! Smite him hip and thigh, for self-preservation is the highest law!"

The CD concludes with a track not on the original vinyl recording, "The Hymn of the Satanic Empire, or The Battle Hymn of the Apocalypse". In the first part of this track, LaVey forcefully proclaims the creation of a Satanic utopia, while relaxed synthesiser strains play in the background. After this ends, wait a few minutes and you'll come to a hidden track — an instrumental piece of great pomp and circumstance.

Amarillo Records; $15
1968; compact disk; 55 min

AGHORA
At the Left Hand of God
by Robert E. Svoboda

Aghora is an extreme and highly misunderstood Left Hand spiritual path within Hinduism. "Strict renunciation is the prerequisite, extreme enough to purify the aspirant through and through. Only when purity is perfected is the aspirant assigned rituals which to the untutored observer might seem hedonistic or 'sinful.' Aghora is not indulgence; it is the forcible transformation of darkness into light, of the opacity of the limited individual personality into the luminescence of the Absolute." This book explores Aghora through one of its most well-known practitioners, Vimalananda.

Brotherhood of Life; $19.95
1986 (1995); softcover; 327 pp
0-914732-21-8

AMERICA'S ALTERNATIVE RELIGIONS
edited by Timothy Miller

There are some books that you know are going to be important when you first see them. *America's Alternative Religions*, a big, impressive-looking volume, fits this category. After opening it, you find that your initial judgement was right.

Inside this weighty tome, you will find articles that give something incredibly rare — basically non-biased information about 42 nonmainstream religions. Most of the major new religions (often called "cults") are covered — the Unification Church ("Moonies"), the Church of Scientology, Hare Krishna, ECKANKAR, the People's Temple, the Branch Davidians, and others. There are also articles on Anabaptism, Christian Science, Unitarian Universalism, Mormonism, Pentecostalism, Christian Identity, Hinduism and Buddhism in America, Black Islam, Sufism, Santería, Voodoo, Rastafarianism, Theosophy, neo-Paganism, channelling, hippie communes, Satanism, UFO religious movements, and new Native American religions. Each chapter is written by an expert in the field who attempts not to pass judgement on the belief system, but simply report on its history, tenets, and the controversy it has caused.

You'll learn many fascinating things from this book. The history of the Seventh Day Adventists, and its offshoot the Jehovah's Witnesses, is a study in failed prophecies. William Miller predicted that by March 21, 1844, Christ would return. When Jesus stood the human race up, Miller predicted October 22, 1844, was the real date. Again, Jesus pulled a no-show and this non-event has become known as "the great disappointment". Charles Taze Russell, apparently not learning from the past, said that Jesus had already returned invisibly in 1874 and that the final apocalyptic cataclysm would occur in 1878. Then 1881. Then 1914. Russell died two years later, extremely disillusioned. The Witnesses kept predicting, though: 1918, 1925, 1975. After this last date failed to

"Open wide the Gates of Hell and come forth from the Abyss." *The Satanic Mass.*

produce results, over one million followers left the sect.

The Branch Davidians were actually formed over 60 years ago. Victor Houteff, a Seventh Day Adventist, became disillusioned with the church in 1929. He felt the leaders had betrayed the group's basic teachings, so he started challenging him. In 1934, they booted him out, and he and his followers formed the group that would become known as the Branch Davidians. Bouteff believed that Jesus would be returning literally at any moment and that it was his duty to decipher the Seven Seals in the Book of Revelation and gather together the 144,000 elect "who would be delivered at the Second Coming of Christ when sinners would be destroyed and the Kingdom of David would be erected in Palestine."

The chapter on Satanism reveals that when Anton LaVey founded the Church of Satan in 1966, he promoted it through a topless night-club he opened called Witches' Sabbath. Susan Atkins (aka Sharon King), who would later become a key member of the Manson Family, was one of the dancers. The Church of Satan attracted several celebrities into its ranks, including Sammy Davis Jr., Jayne Mansfield, Christopher Lee, and Kim Novak. The chapter also covers a dozen other Satanic sects, including the Temple of Set, the Universal Church of Man, and The Process.

For all of us students of unusual belief systems, this rich resource is to be treasured. It's easily worth twice the price.

State University of New York Press; $24.95
1995; oversized softcover; 474 pp
0-7914-2398-0

THE COMPLETE STORY OF THE COURSE
The History, the People, and the Controversies Behind
A Course in Miracles™
by D. Patrick Miller

When *A Course In Miracles* was published in 1976, it was hard to imagine that it would eventually sell over one million

copies in its English language version alone, be incorporated into several best-selling books, spawn over 2000 study groups around the world, and, in essence, create a whole industry that includes ministries, teaching academies, service organisations, a Usenet group, Websites, and more. It is one of the most important spiritual movements of current times, based on the breadth and depth of its influence, yet no one has ever written a balanced examination of it until now. In this book, investigative journalist D. Patrick Miller looks at "its history, the fundamentals of its message, profiles of its major teachers and interpreters, and a survey of its diverse applications as well as the critical reactions and controversies the teaching has engendered". Despite the fact that he has studied and benefited from the Course, Miller strives to be objective. His book is not born out of a need to convert people but out of his innate curiosity. He wants to understand the history, the message, the achievements, and the shortcomings of this understudied movement.

"*A Course in Miracles* is a self-study curriculum that guides students towards a spiritual way of life by restoring their contact with what it calls the Holy Spirit or 'internal teacher.' The Course uses both an intellectual and experiential approach within its 650-page Text, 500-page Workbook of 365 daily meditations, and 90-page Manual for Teachers." It was written over seven years by Helen Schucman, a research psychologist, who claimed that it was dictated to her by a "Voice", which identified itself as Jesus. The Course encourages people to constantly practice forgiveness and — using Christian language but an Eastern philosophy — to view the physical world as an illusion and the spiritual world as the only true reality. Although these teachings have inspired a movement, it is a complete informal one. "There is no centralised religion or membership institution built around the Course, and no 'guru' widely accepted as an embodiment of the teaching."

Miller writes in detail of the life of Schucman, the events that led to the writing on the Course, how it got published, the ways it has spread. He also examines the lives of two people who have written extremely popular books based on Course principles — Jerry Jampolsky (*Love Is Letting Go of Fear*) and Marianne Williamson (*A Return to Love*). He then examines the foremost Course teaching academy, looks at whether the Course is a form of psychotherapy, and lists "some core characteristics that it shares with the world's most ancient and revered religious traditions."

Things get a little more hairy in the next two chapters, devoted to criticisms of the Course. The first chapter looks at why many Christians despise it. Although couched in Christian terms, on many crucial points it has a message exactly opposite to that of the Bible. Naturally, this makes it false and probably "Satanically inspired". The other chapter examines non-Christian critiques of and attacks on the Course, including those of the chief critic — archetypal psychologist James Hillman; the authors of *The Guru Papers*, who see it as a form of brainwashing; and many people who are turned off by its Christian, patriarchal language.

The next chapter contains fourteen essays by people who are studying the Course, and this part of the book seems undeniably propagandistic. All of the people have had wonderful insights and have often changed their lives because of these teachings. While there is nothing wrong with hearing from people whose lives have been enriched, I think essays from disillusioned or disappointed ex-students would have been in order. The closest thing to criticism comes from an attorney who loves the Course's psychological insights but rejects its metaphysical teachings.

Miller wraps things up with his thoughts on where the Course fits in with contemporary spirituality and a listing of Course resources, including teaching centres, service organisations, Websites, and online discussion groups.

Fearless Books; $15.95

1997; softcover; 255 pp

0-9656809-0-8

CRIMES OF PERCEPTION
An Encyclopedia of Heresies and Heretics
by Leonard George

What we have here is a massive guide to a large number of beliefs that are usually labelled as "heresies". Of course, heresy can be a slippery concept. The author offers his definition in the introduction: "A heresy is a crime of perception — an act of seeing something that, according to some custodian of reality, is not truly there. Heresy, therefore, is always relative to an orthodoxy. Every tradition has its heresies; from the perspective of those conventionally labelled heretics, the orthodox themselves are heretical." Making things even harder to pin down is the fact that yesterday's heresy can become today's orthodoxy. This is why *Crimes of Perception* includes an entry on Jesus, who was considered a heretic of the first degree by the authorities of his day. In order to limit the scope of this already huge book, the author decided to cover three areas: Christian heresies, Jewish heresies, and the occult, which is considered heretical by just about every established religion. Not included are heresies of a non-Western and non-religious nature.

What's left are 600 entries, including Adamites, groups who shed their clothes in order to return to an Eden-like innocence; Anabaptists, which include the Amish, Mennonites, and Hutterites; the Book of Mormon; the Councils of Constantinople, which helped decide the versions of Christianity that would become orthodoxy and those that would become heresy; John Dee, the astrologer and alchemist of Queen Elizabeth I's court; Gnosticism; the Gospel of Thomas; Matthew Fox, the renegade priest whose "creation centred spirituality" has recently gotten him into trouble with the Vatican; the Inquisition; Monophysitism, an ancient Christian heresy which taught that Christ had only a divine, and not a human, nature; necromancy, which involves contacting the dead in order to foresee the future; Ordo Templi Orientis, an organisation that practices sex magic; Origen, a third century Christian church father who promoted reincarnation and sacrilege; David Reubini, one of the false messiahs in Jewish history; snake handlers; *Treatise on Angel Magic*; and Roger Williams, who "established the colony of Rhode Island as a haven of spiritual freedom."

You'll find world famous heretics such as the Knights Templar, Joseph Smith, Aleister Crowley, and Joan of Arc next to relative unknowns such as Paul of Samosata — a third-century bishop who taught that Jesus started life as an ordinary human and was later "adopted" by God — and the Brothers and Sisters of the Free Spirit, who believed that once they achieved spiritual perfection, they could do anything they wanted without sinning or breaking the law, because such concepts no longer applied to them.

Despite the author's scholarly thoroughness, he writes in a highly readable style laced with dry humour. For example, in the entry for the Fifth Monarchy Men, an English sect that believed that Jesus was going to return soon and start the fifth divine kingdom on earth, he writes: "After a while, some believers became impatient and tried to help the Lord along by provoking riots in London."

The only thing that seems to be missing is any mention of current new religious movements. *Crimes* covers such groups in the past, including the defunct Oneida Community, which practised Christianity mixed with a form of free love, and the bizarre Forest Brotherhood, a Swiss sect that worshipped the "divine" genitals of its founder in the late 1800s. Puzzlingly, there is no mention of the Branch Davidians, the Unification Church, or any other modern group that is widely considered heretical. This might have something to do with the fact that the Reverend Sun Moon owns the publishing house that puts out *Crimes of Perception*, but I still can't figure out the benefit of not mentioning any new religions.

Despite this strange drawback, *Crimes of Perception* is a fascinating and unparalleled treasure trove of religious thought that has been damned by the authorities. It has become one of the mainstays of my library on unorthodox beliefs.

Paragon House Publishers; $29.95

1995; oversized hardcover; 368 pp

1-55778-519-8

THE ENOCHIAN WORKBOOK
A Complete Guide to Angelic Magic
by Gerald & Betty Schueler

Enochian Magic has its beginnings with John Dee, Queen Elizabeth I's court astrologer. Together with his psychic partner Edward Kelly, Dee recorded the Enochian language as it was presented to them by angels. There wasn't much interest in their work until the late 1800's, when a mysterious group called the Hermetic Order of the Golden Dawn, of which Aleister Crowley was a member, began investigating the Enochian system of Magic and adding to it. This book is the first guide to Enochian Magic written for novices.

It is divided into 43 short lessons that gradually guide you through the learning process. Some lessons tell you how to invoke the deities in the Watchtowers and Aethyrs. You'll also learn how to make magical weapons, amulets and talismans, magic squares, and magic circles; how to charge talismans, consecrate weapons, make magical signs, invoke an Enochian angel, and scry with crystals; and how to use the Enochian tarot for divination or meditation.

For your further edification, each of the main sections has questions and suggestions for things to do. There are plenty of illustrations, including colour plates of the four Watchtowers. Appendices present, among other things, some numerology and warnings about the dangers of Magic.

Llewellyn Publications; $19.95
1993; oversized softcover; 309 pp
illus; 0-87542-719-7

JESUS AND BUDDHA
The Parallel Sayings
edited by Marcus Borg

Despite the fact that Jesus and Buddha were separated by 500 years and 2000 miles — and despite the fact that one is the embodiment of Western religious thought and the other epitomises Eastern religious thought — they said a number of remarkably similar things. According to the writings that are more or less supposed to be records of their utterances, these two men held almost the same philosophies regarding compassion, wisdom, materialism, temptation, salvation, the future, and other topics.

This book highlights these stunningly equivalent thoughts by putting them on facing pages — Jesus on the left and Buddha on the right. We learn that Jesus said, "Why do you see the splinter in someone else's eye and never notice the log in your own?", while Buddha said, "It is easy to see the fault of others and hard to see one's own." In the Gospel of Matthew, Jesus is recorded as saying, "Truly I tell you, if you have faith the size of a mustard seed, you will say to this mountain, 'Move from here to there,' and it will move; and nothing will be impossible for you." Meanwhile, the Anguttara Nikaya quotes Buddha thusly: "A monk who is skilled in concentration can cut the Himalayas in two." The two were also alike in declarations that leave me cold, including setting themselves up as the way to salvation. Jesus: "Everyone who lives and believes in me will never die." Buddha: "Those who have sufficient faith in me, sufficient love for me, are all headed for heaven or beyond."

The sections entitled "Miracles" and "Life Stories" demonstrate how much the lives of both men mirror each other. Mark 6:48 relates that, "When he saw that they were straining at the oars against the adverse wind, he came towards them early in the morning, walking on the sea." Amazingly, the Anguttara Nikaya says of Buddha: "He walks upon the water without parting it, as if on solid ground."

While the more than 100 parallel quotes are the centrepiece of the book, an introduction by the editor — progressive Christian and new wave Jesus scholar Marcus Borg — provides a more in-depth look at the similarity of the two men, their thoughts, and their legacies. Borg also delves into how these correspondences came about. He briefly mentions the radical theories that Buddhist thought was known in Jerusalem or that Jesus travelled to India during his "lost years", but in the end he opts for a more mystical explanation. Both of them had similar life-transforming experiences of enlightenment around the age of thirty. "From this new way of seeing flowed their wisdom teaching about the way: a perception of the way we typically live, a perception of the

An Enochian god-form.
The Enochian Workbook.

alternative way of being, and the path/process leading from one to the other." This explanation seems inadequate and almost circular to me, but nevertheless, the similarities are definitely there. Make of them what you will.

Ulysses Press; $19.95
1997; hardcover; 258 pp
1-56975-121-8

THE ORIGINAL HANDBOOK FOR THE RECENTLY DECEASED
by Claude Needham, Ph.D.

A label affixed to the front of this book warns that it is only for dead people. If you ignore the warning and open it anyway, you will find a most unusual book… a tongue-in-cheek, thoroughly Americanised version of the Tibetan Book of the Dead, which teaches you how to get along in the afterworld (referred to as "bardo"). Chapters include "Etiquette During One's Funeral", "What Should I Expect in the Bardo?", "Fun Games To Play When You Are Dead", "Interfacing With Local Lifeforms", "How to Put Up With Eternity", and "High-Power Plasma Containment System Maintenance and Repair".

Gateways Books; $12.50
1992; softcover; 132 pp
illus; 0-89556-068-2

PSYBERMAGICK
Advanced Ideas in Chaos Magick
by Peter J. Carroll

Peter J. Carroll is an advanced practitioner of a type of magick called Chaos Magick, which seems a lot like ordinary magick, except that it emphasises and incorporates chaos theory, quantum physics, and postmodernism. "Some philosophers and psychologists bemoan the disintegration or fragmentation of the self in the contemporary world. We celebrate this development. The belief in a single self stems from religious monotheisms having only a single god. Let us throw out the baby with the bath water."

PsyberMagick is divided into 60 sections, each one comprised of a chapter and a commentary on that chapter. Fortunately for those of us who like information in bite-size nuggets, no chapter or commentary is more than a page long and most are only half a page. Each chapter presents an idea or concept as a poem, riddle, equation, experiment, etc. The commentary on the facing page then offers a more literal explanation.

In the first commentary to deal directly with magick, the author writes: "Everything works by magick; science represents a small domain of magick where coincidences have a relatively high probability of occurrence. Half of the skill in magick consists of identifying probabilities worth enhancing." One of several chapters on politics comments on conspiracy theory and chaos: "Conspiracies exist all right:/But Fuckup mostly rules the outcome."

PsyberMagick rails against all systems of conformity — "Our Glorious Simian Heritage/Obeisance, obeisance, obeisance!/Offering your arse in submission/To the bull ape of the troop." — including some that might seems surprising — "Magick will not free itself from occultism until we have strangled the last astrologer with the guts of the last spiritual master."

In other parts of the book, Carroll covers the six dimensions, spells, divination, money, chaocracy, liberty vs equality, the Illuminati, New Age-ism, dogs, specific rituals, and Spinwarp theory, which involves subatomic particles.

New Falcon Publications; $12.95
1995 (1997); softcover; 127 pp
illus; 1-56184-092-0

THE RELIGIOUS BELIEFS OF OUR PRESIDENTS
From Washington to F.D.R.
by Franklin Steiner

These days it isn't hard to find examples of Christians pointing to past Presidents as paragons of religious virtue. But are these current perceptions based on the truth or have they become distorted through time, like so much of history? In 1936 Franklin Steiner attempted to set the record straight with this thoroughly-researched book.

Despite claims to the contrary, it appears the George Washington was not particularly religious. "Washington never made a statement of his belief, while his actions rather prove that if he was not a positive unbeliever, he was at best an indifferentist. We have seen that he was not a regular attendant at church services — rather an irregular one... That Washington did not commune is established beyond all doubt by reputable witnesses... Bishop White says Washington did not kneel during prayer." Combing the Father of Our Country's writings for clues yields little to support any definitive classification. "Most important of all, there stands out the fact that while in Washington's writings there is nothing affirming or denying the truth of Christian revelation, there is also nothing inconsistent with Deism." So, it is probably what GW didn't say that is the most revealing: "In his letters to young people, particularly to his adopted children, he urges them upon truth, character, honesty, but in no case does he advise going to church, reading the Bible, belief in Christ, of any other item of religious faith or practice."

Abraham Lincoln was one of the two most brazenly unreligious Presidents. He never belonged to a church and didn't believe in the divinity of Jesus or the Bible. "In 1846, when he was a candidate for Congress against a Methodist minister, the Rev. Peter Cartwright, his opponent openly accused him of being an unbeliever, and Lincoln never denied it." John T. Stuart, a member of Congress from Illinois and Lincoln's first law partner, offers this revealing insight: "Lincoln went further against Christian beliefs than any man I ever heard: he shocked me." Colonel James H. Matheny, Lincoln's friend and political manager, said that Honest Abe was an "infidel".

Like Lincoln, Founding Father Thomas Jefferson was a freethinker. He believed that Jesus and the Bible had many good things to say and offered some important rules for living. However, he adamantly rejected all supernatural aspects of Christianity, such as the divine nature of Jesus and the Bible. He writes, in Volume Four of *The Writings of Thomas Jefferson*, that the Gospels of Jesus's life are "a ground work of vulgar ignorance, of things impossible, of superstitions, fanaticisms, and fabrications." Jefferson was upset by the close-mindedness and hypocrisy he saw in many so-called Godly men, and he often lashed out in frank terms. "Millions of men, women, and children, since the introduction of Christianity, have been burned, tortured, fined, imprisoned; yet we have not advanced one inch toward uniformity. What has been the effect of coercion? To make one half the world fools, and the other half hypocrites; to support roguery and error all over the earth."

Steiner also examines the beliefs of many Presidents who were religious, such as Presbyterians Jackson, Polk, and Cleveland, Baptist Warren Harding, and Quaker Herbert Hoover. Some Chief Executives were religious but not members of any church — including Andrew Johnson, Grant, and Hayes — and others had religious views that are hard to ascertain, including Madison, Monroe, and Van Buren.

Prometheus Books; $16.95
1995; softcover; 190 pp
0-87975-975-5

SANTERÍA GARMENTS AND ALTARS
Speaking Without a Voice
by Ysamur Flores-Peña & Roberta J. Evanchuk

Santería — more properly referred to as Lucumi or Orisha worship — is an Afro-Cuban religion. It's rooted in the spiritual practices of Nigeria and took shape in Cuba during and after the slave trade, where practitioners introduced many elements of Catholicism. Santería has moved into the US, and is now the fastest growing African-based religion in the country. It is principally known to outsiders for its sacrifice of animals, a practice upheld by the Supreme Court in 1993.

Orisha worshipers believe in a single God, Olodumare, who created everything, including around 200 Orishas. These beings are "divine entities that care for creation and act as God's agents." Like the Catholic saints and ancient gods and goddesses, different aspects of creation are represented by different Orishas. Ogun is the Orisha of war and industry, Babalú Aye is the Orisha of infectious diseases, and Oshun

Shiva's followers may keep their arms raised non-stop for 12 years. *Shiva*.

represents love, sweetness, and sexuality. Each human being will be watched over by one Orisha for his or her entire life. There are two major divination systems that allow humans to communicate with the Orisha.

This book contains 42 colour plates showing the beautiful, ornate paraphernalia of Orisha worship. The outfits are all very satiny and are decorated with lots of colourful, sparkling material and cowrie shells, a seashell that plays an important part in the religion. To give you a better idea, the garments are very reminiscent of what the Beatles are wearing on the cover of *Sgt. Pepper's Lonely Hearts Club Band*.

An altar to Ibeji, the protector of children, is a cornucopia of brightly-coloured streamers, candy, dolls, and party favours. The centrepiece of an altar to Obatala, the Orisha who created humans, is an exquisite, intricately-carved ivory dagger.

Besides these beautiful photos, *Santería Garments and Altars* also contains background information on the religion itself.

University Press of Mississippi; $15.95
1994; softcover; 72 pp
heavily illus; 0-87805-703-X

SHIVA

by Paula Fouce & Denise Tomecko
The Hindu god Shiva is the oldest god and millions still wor-

ship him. He has many facets… he is the one who destroys the world at the end of each cycle of creation, yet he is also a god of love. "He became popular as the great ascetic whose meditation keeps the world in existence, and as the protector of animals. Also loved as the Lord of Procreation, His symbol became the linga, the male reproductive organ."

Shiva is primarily a picture book. Over 100 colourful photos show all aspects of Shiva worship, including statues, carvings, altars, temples, festivals, and followers. The most attention-getting chapter shows yogis practising extreme forms of self-denial and self-torture. One practitioner is standing on his feet continuously for twelve years. When he gets tired, he leans against a padded swing hanging from a tree branch. One of the most difficult — yet allegedly rewarding — austerities is for a yogi to keep his arm held pointed upwards non-stop for twelve years. The authors don't mention how long the yogi in the picture has been at it, but his arm has become atrophied from lack of use and draining of blood. A couple of yogis are shown with huge rocks hanging from their penises. This proves that during their initiation, their nerves were severed. Human belief systems never fail to amaze me.

Brotherhood of Life; $20
1990; oversized softcover; 133 pp
heavily illus; 974-869743-6

TOTAL FREEDOM
The Essential Krishnamurti

J. Krishnamurti
I have the feeling that many readers of *Psychotropedia* are instantly sceptical — or at least extremely wary — when they encounter anything having to do with a spiritual "leader" or "master". Good. This is as it should be. But it's important to realise that just about everybody has at least some good points to make. When it comes to "spiritual leaders", J. Krishnamurti seems to have his act together more than most.

Krishnamurti was born in a small town in India in 1895. When he was quite young, the leaders of the Theosophical movement proclaimed that he was the prophesied "World Teacher" — the reincarnation of Jesus and Buddha — and took him to England to prepare him for his role. At the tender age of sixteen, he was made head of the Order of the Star in the East, an organisation created to spread the teachings of this new saviour. But in 1929, Krishnamurti did an amazing thing. He simply walked away from all of it. He proclaimed that he was not the World Teacher and then dissolved the Order. He spent literally the rest of his life (till he died aged 90) espousing his ideas through writings and lectures, attracting the attention of countless people, including many famous personages, from quantum physics founder David Bohm to pioneering erotic writer Henry Miller. Yet he refused to start a movement or accept any disciples, even though many were eager to follow him.

Total Freedom collects over 30 speeches, writings, journal entries, and interviews spanning Krishnamurti's entire post-messiah life. (The title refers to his constant proclamation: "My only concern is to set humanity absolutely, unconditionally free.") The first selection in the book is the speech

Santa Claus (Sinte Klaas) before Coca-Cola got to him.
When Santa Was a Shaman.

Krishnamurti gave to 3000 of his followers when he dissolved the Order of the Star of the East. The speech is called "Truth is a Pathless Land", and that title has become the best known of his quotes because it so eloquently summarises his anti-dogmatic approach to spirituality. The speech itself remains the simplest, most direct expression of Krishnamurti's general ideas. "I maintain that Truth is a pathless land, and you cannot approach it by any path whatsoever, by any religion, by any sect… Truth, being limitless, unconditioned, unapproachable by any path whatsoever, cannot be organised; nor should any organisation be formed to lead or to coerce people along any particular path… A belief is purely an individual matter, and you cannot and must not organise it. If you do, it becomes dead, crystallised; it becomes a creed, a sect, a religion, to be imposed on others… Truth is narrowed down and made a plaything for those who are weak, for those who are only momentarily disconnected. Truth cannot be brought down; rather, the individual must make the effort to ascend it." Later, he reiterates: "If an organisation be created for this purpose [to lead people to spirituality], it becomes a crutch, a weakness, a bondage, and must cripple the individual, and prevent him from growing, from establishing his uniqueness, which lies in the discovery for himself of that absolute, unconditioned Truth."

In "Freedom from the Known", he boils it down: "All authority of any kind, especially in the field of thought and understanding, is the most destructive, evil thing. Leaders destroy the followers and followers destroy the leaders. You have to be your own teacher and your own disciple. You have to question everything that man has accepted as valuable and necessary."

In other selections, Mr. K discusses learning how to think in new ways, abandoning your ideas about "searching" and

"seeking" (because this paradigm automatically assumes a division between the seeker and that which is sought), becoming truly aware, living life to the fullest, and many other topics including love, sex, education, creativity, ambition, revolution, fear, and reality. He may not always be easy to understand, and I don't agree with everything he says, but Krishnamurti is most definitely worth listening to.

HarperSanFrancisco (HarperCollins Publishers); $18
1996; softcover; 378 pp
0-06-064880-5

THE WAR BETWEEN THE PATRIARCHY AND THE PAGAN GODDESS
Numerology and the Original Authors of the Bible
by R.J. Daniel

According to R.J. Daniel, the authors of the Old Testament worked a secret numeric code into their writings. This code "is being revealed to men in order that they will gain 'self-knowledge and understanding' and join the crusade to bring about the international triumph of monotheism and Patriarchy over radical feminism, goddess worship, pagan idolatry, polytheism and homosexuality."

The original writers of the Old Testament discovered a divine numerology — arranged by God — and this somehow made them realise "the pagan belief in many gods was false." When they wrote the books of the Old Testament, they used this numerology to advance monotheism and patriarchism. The authors of the New Testament, however, abandoned this message and the numerology that went with it and instead focused their message solely on Jesus.

A large part of the book gives instructions for interpreting people's characters through numerology. By applying the numerological codes to a person's full name and birth date in various ways, you can determine their "character (soul) traits". There are nine such traits and each one has a positive and negative side. For example, a person with the third positive trait has developed his creativity and imagination and is optimistic and friendly. A person with the third negative trait has no developed talents or skills and is deceitful and frivolous.

The International Patriarchy; $29
1993; softcover; 121 pp
illus; 03-033-06-7

WHEN SANTA WAS A SHAMAN
The Ancient Origins of Santa Claus and the Christmas Tree
by Tony van Renterghem

In this fascinating book, Tony van Renterghem — who bears a distinct likeness to his principal subject — traces the historical development of Santa Claus, as well as the Christmas tree, the Yule log, mistletoe, and other Christmas customs. As it turns out, every last one of them has its origins in ancient pagan religions. Santa is really the latest incarnation of the wise shaman who is in touch with nature. Among the many branches on the Jolly One's family tree are Pan,

Odin, Robin Goodfellow, Zwarte Piet, the Dutch Sinte Klaas, Saint Nicholas, and many others. The figure we now think of as the one and only Santa Claus — the fat, jolly, bearded man in a red and white suit — is actually a modern, corporate creation. That particular Santa was created in 1931 by the Coca-Cola Company. This would explain the colours of Santa's suit, hat, and beard... they're also Coke's trademark colours.

Renterghem believes the Christmas tree is a representative of the Tree of Fire archetype. Supposedly, burning trees (and bushes) have become an important part of the human race's mythology because our ancestors first came into contact with fire when lightning bolts torched trees. The electric lights we now wrap around trees are a dim reminder of the ancient ceremonies in which trees were ignited. The lighting of the Yule log is a more direct descendent of this custom. Pine trees had a special significance to our ancestors because they stayed green during even the harshest winters, when the rest of nature shut down. Ivy, holly, and mistletoe also became revered for this reason.

When Santa Was a Shaman is filled with illustrations showing the evolution of Santa, the Christmas tree, etc. through ancient times, the Middle Ages, the Victorian era, and into the modern age of commercialisation. If you'd like to cut through the hype and get back to the true heathen meaning of the Christmas celebration, put this book on your wish list.

Llewellyn Publications; $16.95
1995; softcover; 194 pp
illus; 1-56718-765-X

WHY I AM NOT A MUSLIM

by Ibn Warraq

A groundbreaking and brazenly courageous work, *Why I Am Not a Muslim* is the first book-length criticism of Islam ever published. The author — a former Muslim — casts a critical gaze on all aspects of this religion:

- Muhammad's life: "... the picture that emerges of the prophet in these traditional accounts is not at all flattering. Furthermore, Muslims cannot complain that this is a portrait drawn by the enemy."
- the totalitarian nature of Islamic law: "Islamic law has certainly aimed at 'controlling the religious, social and political life of mankind in all its aspects, the life of its followers without qualification, and the life of those who follow tolerated religions to a degree that prevents their activities from hampering Islam in any way.'"
- the oppression of women: "Women are inferior to men under Islamic law; their testimony in a court of law is worth half that of a man; their movement is strictly restricted; they cannot marry non-Muslims."
- the violation of human rights in Islamic regimes: "We have seen what punishments are in store for transgressors of Holy law: amputations, crucifixion, stoning to death, and floggings."
- the treatment of other heretics and freethinkers: Atheists "do not have 'the right to life' in Muslim countries. They are to be killed."
- the suppression of other religions: "Non-Muslims living in Muslim countries have inferior status under Islamic law; they may not testify against a Muslim. In Saudi Arabia, following a tradition of Muhammed who said, 'Two religions cannot exist in the country of Arabia,' non-Muslims are forbidden to practice their religion, build churches, possess Bibles, etc."
- Islamic colonialism and conquest: "Although Europeans are constantly castigated for having imposed their insidious and decadent values, culture, and language on the Third World, no one cares to point out that Islam colonised lands that were the homes of advanced and ancient civilisations, and that in doing so, Islamic colonialism trampled underfoot and permanently destroyed many cultures."

Why I Am Not a Muslim has similarly harsh words for the Koran, Salman Rushdie's death sentence, the total rejection of democratic principles in Islamic regimes, and other topics. Fully documented with almost 700 endnotes and a 300-entry bibliography, this is an unprecedented and devastating critique of one of the world's biggest religions. It's a crying shame that the author had to risk his life to write it.

Prometheus Books; $25.95
1995; hardcover; 410 pp
0-87975-984-4

THE UNEXPLAINED

UFOS & ALIENS

THE ALIEN ABDUCTION SURVIVAL GUIDE

by Michelle LaVigne

Reports of abductions by aliens have skyrocketed in the past few years, to the point that there are now psychiatrists who specialise in "abductee therapy". Personally, I'm not sure what's going on, but I refuse to rule anything out. Perhaps these people (or at least some of them) really are being physically transported to a spaceship, medically (even sexually) examined, implanted with tracking devices, and released. If this is indeed the case, then obviously these people will need some kind of assistance coping with their experiences.

Michelle LaVigne, who claims to have been repeatedly abducted since early childhood, has written a book to help abductees deal with their fears and feelings and feel more in control of their lives. Her book is "a guide to coping with — and maybe even thriving in — the perplexing world of alien abduction phenomena. It is a practical look at problems faced by abduction experiencers, and includes some solutions to these problems that have been tried and really work."

The first thing LaVigne does is examine the different "types" of abductee that form the Secret Community (her collective term for people who've been abducted). One-timers only get taken by aliens once. Quick in/Quick outs may get picked up repeatedly, but their time aboard the spaceship is brief. Astral abductees have their souls removed from their bodies and placed in a host body aboard the ship. Gemini people are the ones who are taken many times and stay on the ships for extended periods, during which they may be assigned roles as teachers, controllers, or empaths.

Many abductees go through cycles of emotion, such as wanting to know everything about UFOs and abductions, and then feeling upset and repulsed by the subjects. Other people go through a different cycle: "Many go from feeling like lab animals used in some horrible experiment to feeling like much loved pets or cherished children, then back to feeling like lab rats again."

LaVigne addresses many of the fears abductees have. The fears include wondering if the ETs will kill you, if they'll abduct everyone you know, if you've had sex with them, and if everyone will think you're crazy. She discusses coping with these fears, gaining control, getting help, and looking at the spiritual aspects of the situation.

Other sections focus on childhood experiences, some of the tests and procedures the aliens may perform on you, and myths and misconceptions about the aliens. For example, aliens can physically talk, they have smooth warm skin, and abductions can be pleasant, enriching experiences. Finally, there is a glossary, reading list, and resources guide.

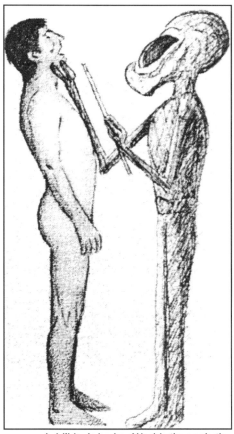

Jack Weiner's drawing of his abduction examination.
The Allagash Abductions.

Wild Flower Press (Blue Water Publishing); $11.95
1995; softcover; 113 pp
illus; 0-926524-27-5

ALIEN IDENTITIES
Ancient Insights into Modern UFO Phenomena

by Richard L. Thompson

Alien Identities points out in great detail the amazing parallels between modern UFO literature and the Vedic literature (the ancient, holy scriptures of India). The Vedic writings overflow with descriptions of flying machines (called *vimanas*) and the otherworldly races who use them.

According to these ancient accounts, there are 400,000 races of humanoid beings living throughout the universe, with humans being among the least powerful. Most of the other races possess powers (*siddhis*) including the abilities to read thoughts, see or hear at great distances, levitate, teleport objects, control minds, become invisible, abduct human beings, and enter another being's body and control it. Another type of unusual being that appears in later Vedic literature is the *yantra-purusa*, a "machine-man", which seems to parallel our ideas of robots and cyborgs.

Interstellar and interdimensional travel is also mentioned frequently. "In Vedic society, it was understood that travel to other worlds is possible. This could involve travel to other star systems, travel into higher dimensions, or travel into higher-dimensional regions in another star system. It was also understood that it is possible to leave the material universe altogether and travel through a graded arrangement of transcendental realms."

Furthermore, the *vimanas* usually have characteristics that are attributed to flying saucers. They move irregularly, become invisible, land on cliffs or water, and sometimes appear as huge "floating castles" which the author likens to descriptions of mother ships. *Vimanas* are sometimes shot down by "arrows" that blaze like the sun and home in on the sound of their targets.

The author provides a massive survey of the key themes in modern UFO reports and then ties them in with similar occurrences in the Vedic literature, often quoting the scriptures directly. His detailed comparisons seem to point to one of two conclusions: either the ancient Indians were actually visited by aliens, or the UFO archetype is so ingrained in the human race's collective unconscious that it was showing up in nearly identical forms thousands of years ago.

Govardhan Hill Publishing; $19.95
1993; softcover; 492 pp
0-9635309-1-7

THE ALLAGASH ABDUCTIONS
by Raymond E. Fowler

In 1976, four men, including identical twins, went on a camping and canoeing trip in the Allagash Waterway in northern Maine. All four men claim that they were abducted by aliens and taken aboard a UFO. (The movie *Fire in the Sky* was based on this incident.) In this book, Raymond Fowler presents this case as unmistakable proof that would "stand up in court" that alien abductions do occur.

The four men had journeyed into a remote wilderness area and had run out of fresh meat. Their fishing that day hadn't produced anything, so in desperation they tried night fishing. They paddled out around a quarter mile from shore, their only light coming from a large fire they had built on shore. Chuck sensed something strange. His notes of the event read: "I became aware of a feeling of being watched. I turned toward the direction from where I felt this and saw a large, bright sphere of coloured light hovering motionless and soundless about 200-300 feet above the south-eastern rim of the cove." Jack Weiner writes: "At a distance of maybe 200 or 250 yards away, rising out of the woods, was a very large, bright, pulsing, spherical light. It was not making any noise at all!"

One of the men flashed his flashlight at the object and it started moving towards them, projecting a beam onto the water. They paddled like mad for the shore with the object

chasing them. After reaching land, they got out and calmly watched as the object hovered for a few minutes and left. To their surprise, the fire, which should have burned for at least a couple of hours, was just a lump of glowing embers. They thought the whole incident had lasted 15 to 20 minutes, but during that time they had been taken aboard the spacecraft.

Fowler and a colleague performed hypnotic regression on all four men at separate times in order to find out what happened during the missing time. Selections from the transcripts of all the sessions are reprinted in this book. Each of the men tells a very similar story of bulbous-headed creatures stripping them and physically examining them, paying special attention to their penises and taking semen samples. Further sessions showed that the aliens had been visiting the men for years before their Allagash encounter.

One of the freakiest aspects of the case is the strange lump that suddenly appeared in Jack's calf. He had an operation to remove the strange pink tumour that he says was about the diameter of a nickel. His doctor couldn't figure out what the tumour was, and he told Jack he was having it sent to the Centre for Disease Control for analysis. When the results came back, Jack's doc nervously evaded giving any specific answers, only saying that they still weren't sure what they were dealing with. When Jack went to get his medical records for Fowler to study, he found that his tumour had never been sent to the CDC, but had instead gone to the Armed Forces Institute of Pathology in Washington, DC. To this day, Jack doesn't know what was taken out of him.

The abductees have also experienced terrifying nightmares since the incident. Making this case a little more nerve-wracking, Chuck Rak lives on an isolated ranch, yet after his second hypnosis session, he caught trespassers on his property three times in two weeks. The day after the last trespasser, his house was buzzed by an unmarked black helicopter.

Fowler concludes that the abductions are unarguably real. The men's corroborating stories, their experiences afterward, their physical scars, and other evidence all point to an actual phenomenon.

Besides written testimony, *The Allagash Abductions* also include photographs of the physical after-effects and many drawings by the abductees.

Wild Flower Press (Blue Water Publishing); $16.95
1993; softcover; 347 pp
illus; 0-926524-22-4

BEYOND ROSWELL
The Alien Autopsy Film, Area 51 & the U.S. Government Coverup of UFOs
by Michael Heseman & Philip Mantle

Two UFO researchers offer an extensive look at everything that is known about the Roswell crash and its aftermath, including the recent "alien autopsy" footage and the mysterious Area 51 facility, which is said by some to house flying saucers and alien bodies. The authors firmly believe that a spacecraft did crash in early July 1947 in Roswell, New Mexico, and that the government has been covering up this fact (along with numerous others related to UFOs).

Rather than simply rehash everything that's already been said about this most famous of UFO cases, the authors add a lot of new information to the mix. In 1995 Michael Heseman interviewed the daughter of one of the German scientists who was called upon to examine the wreckage. Friedrich August Kueppers was "a physicist who worked for the aircraft builders Martin Co. (later Martin Marietta), then for government military projects." His daughter, who was twelve at the time, recalls: "*Daddy called, as usual from a place he was not allowed to divulge. He was enthusiastic, said, 'At last we can prove that extraterrestrials exist.' I jumped for joy. Mother could foresee what effect that would have on our church and faith. On the next day daddy called again. That was the day the army took back the story (8 July 1947). 'Liars, damned liars,' he said angrily, 'we know better. Don't believe them. They do exist!'... We knew that he was in New Mexico, for the lady on the telephone exchange said so automatically every time he called.*"

The authors also drop a bombshell by claiming that there was another saucer crash in the general area one month before Roswell. Although this has been briefly alluded to in the past, apparently no ufologist has fully looked into this matter. Evidence indicates that on May 31, 1947, a craft crashed near Socorro, New Mexico, about three-and-a-half hours west of Roswell. While investigating the site, they found what they believe are traces of the actual impact point. As far as the alien autopsy footage is concerned, they believe it is real, but that it shows the dissection of one of the creatures retrieved at the Socorro site, not Roswell.

Beyond Roswell is filled with photographs, sketches, reproduced documents, maps, and frames from the alien autopsy. Several appendices offer further information, including medical opinions about the autopsy film and a discussion by Dennis W. Murphy of the debris shown on the film.

Although the Roswell crash appears to have been done to death, this book manages to wring out yet more clues and leads. It is obviously a vital work on this watershed event.

Marlowe and Co; $24.95
1997; hardcover; 307 pp
heavily illus; 1-56924-781-1

CASEBOOK ON THE MEN IN BLACK

by Jim Keith

The Men in Black have become an integral part of the ufology scene. They are purported to be sinister figures who interrogate UFO witnesses about what they've seen and often threaten them into keeping silent about it. In this book, conspiracy researcher Jim Keith gives a detailed look at this bizarre phenomenon.

It turns out that MIB are not newcomers to the field of the unexplained. Ominous figures wearing black appear throughout mythology and folklore of many cultures, including Medieval Europe, where they were thought to be demons or the devil himself. Mysterious strangers have often been noted at historically important moments, passing on wisdom to politicians and philosophers alike. Keith speculates (heavily) that these beings are the mirror image of the

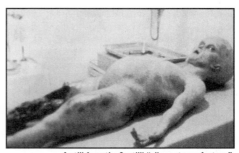

A still from the Santilli "alien autopsy footage".
Beyond Roswell.

MIB. While the MIB work to suppress knowledge and truth, these other mysterious beings help promote human progress.

Most of the book, though, is devoted to encounters with Men in Black that have occurred since the 1940s. Sometimes they show up by themselves, in pairs, or in larger groups. Sometimes they wear black suits, plain clothes, or military uniforms. But they always know more than is seemingly possible about a person's encounter with a UFO. In 1967, an Ohio man allegedly hit a UFO that was parked on a dark road. The UFO vanished, but a small lump of metal remained on the street. The man was interrogated twice at his house by MIBs. During the second incident, they "requested the piece of metal, whose existence was only known to Richardson, his wife, and senior members of the civilian group APRO, the Aerial Phenomenon Research Organization. Richardson told them that it had been given to APRO for analysis. The Men in Black threatened him, saying, 'If you want your wife to stay as pretty as she is, then you'd better get the metal back.'"

Most of the encounters with MIBs involve ordinary people who saw UFOs, but Keith reports that famous people have had encounters too. Malcolm X wrote of being visited by a mysterious man in his jail cell. Rauschning, the former governor of Danzig, reported that Hitler told him of meeting a frightening man who he felt was a more advanced form of human being. Naturally, MIB figure in the JFK assassination. You can supposedly see a MIB in Dealy Plaza in the first few frames of the Zapruder film.

Keith offers various explanations for the MIB: supersecret government agents, aliens, hoaxes, delusions, members of occult lodges, supernatural beings, agents of the Vatican, or goons for some other earthly power that we're not aware of. Of course, different cases might fall into different categories. Some are definitely hoaxes, and others would seem to involve government agents. No matter what the explanations are — even if the MIB don't exist at all — this is an intriguing aspect of UFO and conspiracy lore.

IllumiNet Press; $14.95
1997; softcover; 222 pp
1-881532-11-9

CONTACT FORUM

Contact Forum is a newsletterish magazine for the discussion of human/alien interaction. The underlying philosophy is that aliens do exist, and that they are visiting earth and abducting people. Although the purpose of the *Forum* is ostensibly to look at contact from various angles, most of the material sees this contact as something positive. Volume 5 #1 contains the second part of an interview with Lyssa Royal, author of *Preparing for Contact* and other books. She says: "I think that the contact experience is the single most important and significant phenomenon that is occurring on the planet at this time. If you look at it in a more unionist perspective, then it's a part of ourselves reaching out to ourselves. That is a tremendous force of transformation. If you look at it like the ETs are something totally outside ourselves contacting us, then that in and of itself is life changing, world changing, and our planet will never be the same. No matter how you look at it, we can use this phenomenon to better ourselves and our world." The other main features in this issue are an essay on using discernment when confronted with paranormal claims and an article integrating Native American prophecies and beliefs in alien intervention.

An earlier issue, Volume 4 #2, was primarily concerned with the "Kidnapped by UFOs?" episode of the public television show *Nova*. Abduction experts John Mack and Budd Hopkins both write detailed responses to the biases and inaccuracies they felt the show contained, and the show's producer is given a chance to respond in an interview. Elsewhere in the issue, a surgeon in California claims to have removed three alien implants from two patients.

Wild Flower Press (Blue Water Publishing)/PO Box 2875/Rapid City SD 57709
Voice: 1-800-366-0264 (Visa, MC, Disc)
WWW: www.bluewaterp.com/~bcrissey
Single issue: send a self-addressed 6"x9" or larger envelope with $3 (in the US), $4 in Canada), $5 (elsewhere)
One year sub (6 issues): $18.50. Canada: $23. Elsewhere: $26.75

EXTRA-TERRESTRIAL FRIENDS AND FOES

by George C. Andrews

If you accept the idea that aliens are visiting earth, the next question becomes, "Why are they here?" This book examines the different types of beings that are coming here and what their motives are. Actually, that's what the book claims its mission is, but it mostly covers other aspects of the alien question. Various chapters deal with Wilhelm Reich's involvement with UFOs, the Nazis' contacts with UFOs, mysterious happenings at Lake Tahoe, the alien origins of the visions known as the Miracle of Fatima, the Dulce Papers, and various disinformation and censorship regarding UFOs. While a lot of this information is certainly interesting, it doesn't directly address the question of which aliens are here for what purposes any more than most other UFO books do.

One of the chapters that tackles the question head-on is "Tentative Taxonomy of Extra-terrestrial Humanoids". The details come from a woman who claims to have been repeatedly abducted, and are backed up by many other abductees. The two types that are discussed in detail are the Procyonians — known as "Swedes" or "Blonds" — and the Rigelians — also called "Grays". "This type of humanoid

A Reptilian, drawn by an abductee.
The God Hypothesis.

is performing most of the animal mutilations and human abductions, has made a secret deal with our government, and was in contact with Hitler. They derive nourishment — absorbed through their pores — from the glandular secretions and the enzymes extracted from the animals they mutilate. Our government permits such activities partially because of its acute fear of these beings, and partially because it is under the delusion that they will give us technical information enabling us to attain military superiority over the Russians in exchange for permitting the mutilations and abductions." The Procyonians, on the other hand, are a helpful race who want humans to learn to get along. A large part of another chapter, "An Explosive Exchange", examines more of the Rigelians' activities.

Extra-Terrestrial Friends and Foes also branches into some territory that has little, if anything, to do with UFOs: US government drug-running, Native Americans for a Clean Environment, and the CIA connections of Marc Lepine, who massacred fourteen female students at the Polytechnical College of Montreal in 1989.

I was disappointed that this book didn't attempt to catalogue and explain the "many types" of aliens it says are all around us. Instead, it focuses on only two species in a minority of the book, and contains all kinds of other information in the larger part. However, if you look at it simply as a general book about the UFO phenomenon — rather than a consumer's guide to aliens — it is a fascinating read.

IllumiNet Press; $14.95
1993; softcover; 359 pp
illus; 0-9626534-8-9

FROM ELSEWHERE
Being E.T. in America — The Subculture of Those Who Claim To Be of Non-Earthly Origins
by Scott Mandelker, PhD

The alien abduction scenario is becoming old hat. The newest trend to reach a relatively widespread level is to claim that you actually *are* an alien. Scott Mandelker publishes a newsletter for people who believe that they are in reality Star People. In this book, he offers the first investigation of this intriguing subculture through in-depth interviews with 22 of its members. Obviously, Mandelker believes wholeheartedly in this phenomenon, so don't expect to find any scepticism. On the other hand, he does admit that there is no proof one way or the other about these people's beliefs. Operating under the assumption that they truly think they come "from elsewhere", Mandeleker examines their lives and beliefs.

There are basically two kinds of Star People. Wanderers are E.T. souls who incarnate at birth into a human body. Walk-ins are E.T. souls who take over the body of a human being (with that person's permission) sometime during the person's life. Not all Wanderers and Walk-ins have alien souls, though. A minority claim that they originally come from the Angelic Kingdom, a level of reality populated by non-physical beings who are "[r]esponsible for maintenance of the planet/solar system and the development of consciousness."

Based on channelled information, Mandeleker estimates that there are 100 million Wanderers on earth. Because memories of past existence are wiped clean at birth, people have to slowly come to the realisation that they have E.T. souls. "Their awakening almost always comes gradually and follows a long period of loneliness and alienation. And, although this transformation dawns slowly, afterward any deep desperation is lifted and it seems like the final link in a long chain has finally appeared." The vast majority of Wanderers are currently "Sleeping Wanderers", who haven't yet realised their true nature.

The basic reason why these aliens have taken on human bodies — according to most of the book's interviewees — is to aid the human race. They want to help people see their divine oneness with all that exists and move to a higher level of consciousness.

From Elsewhere also covers how these people came to realise their nature, how they establish a sense of identity, how it affected their family and friends, how it affected their sex lives, what they think of the media's representation of aliens, and what the future holds for the human race. A questionnaire devised by the author can help you determine if you are a Sleeping Wanderer.

Whether or not you believe in this book's premise, it is an intriguing and groundbreaking addition to the literature on aliens.

Bantam Books (Bantam Doubleday Dell Publishing Group); $5.99
1995; paperback; 288 pp
0440222869

A probable German secret craft photographed over South Africa in the early 1950s. *Man-Made UFOs, 1944–1994.*

THE GOD HYPOTHESIS
Extraterrestrial Life and Its Implications for Science and Religion
by Joe Lewels, PhD

The God Hypothesis examines how scientific and religious paradigms could be restructured to account for UFOs. The author first envisions a fairly new view of reality based on quantum physics and the holographic theory of the universe, then shows how flying saucers, alien abductions, and other paranormal phenomena are perfectly at home in this worldview. Lastly, he reinterprets the Christian view of history as having been caused by godlike alien beings.

Wild Flower Press; $18.95
1997; softcover; 335 pp
illus; 0-926524-40-2

KEEPERS OF THE GARDEN
by Dolores Cannon

One of the most popular theories about aliens is that they somehow created us humans and have been involved with our development ever since. In this scenario, we are a garden, and the aliens are the gardeners. Dolores Cannon — a psychic investigator and hypnotherapist — had performed thousands of past life regressions without bumping into any sign of the human race's extraterrestrial origins. One day, she unexpectedly ended up doing a session with Phil D, a 28-year-old owner of an electronics repair business.

It turns out that Phil has spent every past incarnation as an alien. Towards the end of his third session with Cannon, he saw a strange, otherworldly scene that upset him. As they handled this aspect of his regression, he became comfortable enough to explore the scene. "It's windy… sandy and dusty. I feel it and see it. The sky is somewhat reddish-orange tinted. I'm standing outside a spacecraft. There's a clearing where we landed. I'm looking at the spire. It's to my right." Phil, it turns out, is a member of another species bringing supplies to a scientific outpost in a remote part of the galaxy.

Phil describes his people as small, slight, light-skinned, and androgynous. They have big bald heads with no nose. Their mouths are only for breathing because all communication is telepathic. They live in an easy-going society where no one causes any problems (it sounds too close to *Brave New World* for comfort).

Most of the rest of the book is a transcription of Phil's sessions in which he describes in detail his spaceship, alien cities, his society's politics, economics, and social structure, the aliens' intervention in earth's affairs, the origin of different races on earth, human evolution, dinosaurs, other types of aliens, aliens on earth, and more.

After Cannon had completed this book in its original form, Phil was abducted by aliens. This led to more sessions in which Phil discovered that extraterrestrials had been contacting him throughout his life.

Ozark Mountain Publishers; $15
1993; softcover; 287 pp
0-9632776-4-2

MAN-MADE UFOS, 1944-1994
50 Years of Suppression
by Renato Vesco &
David Hatcher Childress

It is this book's argument that UFOs are not spaceships piloted by beings from other planets but are instead supersecret aircraft created by humans. The flying saucer story is one of suppressed technology, not alien life forms. The modern era of UFO sightings is generally said to have started soon after World War II. According to the authors, this is because of the radical new technology that had been developed just before and during that conflict. Germany in particular had been at the forefront of creating ultra-advanced aircraft and anti-aircraft technology.

Germany experimented with an explosive gas that would blow up enemy fighters. They had tentative plans to develop an electromagnetic weapon that would cause plane engines to conk out. One weapon that was used was the windkanone, a projectileless cannon that shot blasts of air that could disrupt and bring down planes at a distance of up to 650 feet.

During the war, Allied fighter pilots frequently reported seeing glowing objects flying alongside their planes, yet radar would show nothing. These Foo Fighters — as they came to be called — were remote-controlled turtle shell-shaped craft that were meant to disrupt aircraft instrumentation. However, the Third Reich put them into use before they were fully functional.

The Nazis didn't stop there, though. They also developed anti-gravity propulsion systems. The authors even go so far as to make the claim: "Towards the end of the war, the Germans had developed interplanetary craft with no moving parts which were capable of going to the moon or Mars."

It's now a well-established fact that at the end of WWII, the US intelligence community gave refuge to many Nazis, who were put on the American payroll in the effort to fight communism (this shameful scheme is known as Operation Paperclip). Part of this deal, according to the authors, also included handing over technological secrets. Besides the US, Britain and Russia managed to get their hands on German flying craft and began to build their own. This research has continued into the present, as evidenced by the mysterious

The site where the Roswell craft was allegedly found.
The Randle Report.

sightings around Area 51 in Nevada.

After WWII, many Nazis escaped to South America (an undoubtable fact) and perhaps to Antarctica (a hotly-debated theory). Some areas of South America that are concentrated with Nazis have heavy UFO activity. In fact, the existence of flying saucers is a widely accepted part of life in that part of the world.

The authors conclude: "What becomes clear to researchers into man-made UFOs and early German discoid craft is that this technology is real, 'Above Top Secret', and is possessed by various groups on this planet today. Not only are the Americans and British said to have this technology but so do such countries as Russia, China, France, Italy, Israel, and Chile. Private corporations, individuals, and agencies are also claimed to possess 'craft.'"

Man-Made UFOs casts new light on the whole modern history of UFOs, also covering topics such as early American sightings, Project Blue Book, suction aircraft, British and Canadian aeronautical advances, rumours of a hidden colony of scientists in Venezuela, and more. There are scores of photographs and diagrams of experimental aircraft and UFOs, including pictures of Foo Fighters and flying disks buzzing military jets.

Adventures Unlimited; $18.95
1994; softcover; 436 pp
heavily illus; 0-932813-23-2

PROJECT BLUE BOOK EXPOSED
by Kevin Randle

After the first wave of modern UFO sightings ended in 1947, the military began a series of investigations, which eventually became known as the Air Force's Project Blue Book in the early 1950s. This investigation — the US government's only admitted involvement with the UFO phenomenon — was officially ended at the end of 1969. Prolific UFO author Kevin Randle believes that Project Blue Book was always intended to calm the public with disinformation instead of actually searching for the truth behind flying saucers. In this book, he presents what is claimed to be the first examination of the Project by a non-biased outsider, with particular emphasis on thirteen UFO reports that the Air Force either explained away or couldn't explain at all.

On October 2, 1961, a private pilot taking off from Utah Central Airport at noon saw a metallic disc-shaped object hovering approximately two to three miles away from him. He approached it twice, but both times it evaded him. Several people on the ground at the airport confirmed seeing the object. At first, the Air Force said that the witnesses had seen Venus or a research balloon. The pilot responded to reporters with disbelief: "'The object I saw was saucer-shaped, had a grey colour, and moved under intelligent control. I got within three miles of it, and that is a lot closer than Venus is. I have seen a lot of balloons too, and this was no balloon.'" When the final report was written, Blue Book came up with a third explanation — everyone had seen a sun dog, which is a light caused by the sun reflecting off ice crystals in the atmosphere. Randle sees this as clear-cut case in which a flying craft of unknown origin was given a patently absurd explanation, and the case was closed.

Not every case that Randles examines could have been an alien craft, though. For example, on January 7, 1948, Captain Thomas Mantell of the Kentucky National Guard became the first person to die while chasing a UFO. Although the military officials who investigated couldn't have known it at the time, the object that Mantell pursued was undoubtedly a huge balloon, called a Skyhook, used for high-altitude research. "Clearly, in 1948, without knowledge of the existence of the Skyhook project, they should have declared the case to be unidentified. But rather than that they kept manipulating the data to provide multiple answers to the case. Even if the evidence didn't fit the facts as they knew them, they chopped and cut until they did fit, and by doing that, created an air of suspicion about their investigations."

Project Blue Book Exposed also contains a twenty-page history of Blue Book, a glossary, a bibliography, and a summary of most of the hundreds of Blue Book cases that were officially labelled as "unidentified".

Marlowe & Company; $22.95
1997; hardcover; 282 pp
1-56924-746-3

THE RANDLE REPORT
UFOs in the '90s
by Kevin D Randle

In *The Randle Report*, flying saucer sleuth Kevin Randle digs deep to find out what's going on with recent UFO/alien cases and to unearth new clues in older, "classic" cases. Although Randle is not a sceptic, he apparently isn't afraid to call it like he sees it, even if his beliefs question the validity of various famous cases. He pronounces the "alien photos" that were published in *Penthouse* to be undeniable fakes, and says that the Travis Walton abduction is "little more than a hoax". He also comes to the conclusion that Ray Santilli's much-ballyhooed "alien autopsy footage" is also bogus. "He [Santilli] has done everything in his power to prevent researchers and investigators from learning the truth. He has misrepresented, from the beginning, exactly what was on the film. When caught in a misstatement, he changed it to make it consistent. When evidence he submitted was challenged, he withdrew it and never mentioned it again. When

It Conquered the World, one of several sci-fi "It" movies made during the '50s. *Saucer Attack!*

evidence was presented that challenged him, he changed the evidence or blamed someone else. And when people asked for the film to analyse, and when Kodak volunteered to analyse the film for free, Santilli decided he couldn't trust them."

Randle goes on to cast a harshly probing light on other aspects of the Roswell case, the Shag Harbour UFO Crash of 1967, the famous MJ-12 documents that point to a government committee on UFOs, the Gulf Breeze photographs of 1987, the Air Force's final report on Roswell, and the blood-sucking Chupacabras first reported in Puerto Rico. He doesn't declare all of his subjects to be hoaxes or, at least, foundationless — he does, for example, think that the Space Shuttle footage of an object that suddenly changes direction and speed might show an alien craft — but throughout almost the whole book, he takes a decidedly contrarian viewpoint.

M. Evans and Co; $19.95
1997; hardcover; 231 pp
illus; 0-87131-820-2

ROSWELL
A Quest for the Truth
by John A. Price

John Price is a lifelong resident of Roswell, New Mexico, and the former head of the UFO Enigma Museum. He is as familiar with the Roswell crash as anyone, having talked to many of the people who played a role in the crash, as well as the family and friends of those people. Some of them claim to have seen the saucer remains and the alien bodies. In this book, he reveals what he has learned.

Truth Seeker Company; $19.50
1997; softcover; 213 pp
illus; 0-939040-01-8

SAUCER ATTACK!
Pop Culture in the Golden Age of Flying Saucers
by Eric Nesheim & Leif Nesheim

Saucer Attack! is a lavishly illustrated collection of pop culture artefacts primarily from the "golden age of flying saucers", which is roughly the two decades from 1947, the year that allegedly saw the Roswell crash and Kenneth Arnold's historic sighting of flying saucers in Washington state. Approximately 200 movie posters, toys, and covers of books, comics, and magazines — all reproduced in vivid colour — take us on a tour of what happens when marketers and Martians have close encounters with the public's imagination.

The earliest entry is an illustration of a Martian from the November 1897 issue of *The Cosmopolitan*, which ran HG Well's *The War of the Worlds* as a serial. Among the other most important and interesting items on display are the issue of *Amazing Stories* that introduced Buck Rogers, the first issue of *Fate* (with a cover story on Kenneth Arnold), George Adamski's book *Flying Saucers Have Landed*, Li'l Abner flying on a spaceship in the famous comic strip of the same name, an issue of *Mechanix Illustrated* that reveals "How the Flying Saucer Works", actual flying saucer patents from the 1950s and 1960s, the first edition of the novel *The Body Snatchers*, a poster for the original movie version of *The Thing*, the poster for *Earth Vs. The Flying Saucers*, UFO salt and pepper shakers, issue number one of *Flying Saucers* comic, a *Lost in Space* lunchbox, and a wind-up Robby the Robot toy from *Forbidden Planet*.

A loving and visually arresting examination of the pop side of ufology.

General Publishing Group; $16.95
1997; oversized softcover; 127 pp
heavily illus; 1-57544-066-0

SPACE ALIENS FROM THE PENTAGON
Flying Saucers Are Man-Made Electrical Machines
by William R. Lyne

This book has the same basic premise as *Man-Made UFOs, 1944-1994* [above]. Namely, that the Nazis developed flying saucers during WWII, and this technology was subsequently improved upon by US scientists. Therefore, since all alleged spacecraft are of human origin, there are no aliens visiting earth.

The author claims to have had Top Secret clearance in Air Force Intelligence and to have turned down a high-ranking job in the CIA because he had come to resent government secrecy, especially about the true nature of UFOs.

In this book he says that the brilliant inventor Nikola Tesla

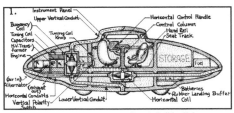

How to build a flying saucer.
Space Aliens from the Pentagon.

created the flying saucer before 1900. "The American government helped the Nazis steal the invention from Tesla (who hated the Nazis), and by 1937, the Nazis were developing it at Los Alamos, New Mexico (then called the 'p2' project), under the direction of the Baron Werner Von Braun, with the collaboration of Dr. Robert Godard." After 1937, the US government helped the Nazis, the Trilateral Commission, and the Illuminati move the project to Germany. The Germans couldn't get their saucers (known as Foo Fighters) to work right, so in 1945 they traded the technology to the US in exchange for certain favours, including amnesty for many Nazis, including Mr. and Mrs. Hitler. "Adolf Hitler and Eva Braun were daringly rescued from the Berlin Bunker by a flying saucer... The 'Hitlers' even visited America on the invitation of L.B.J. to visit 'Hemisfair', the World's fair at San Antonio, Texas, in 1967."

The US government — acting on behalf of the Illuminati and Trilateral Commission — immediately started a massive disinformation campaign meant to hide its involvement with flying saucer technology. It spreads disinformation that UFOs are alien spacecraft, natural phenomena, mass hallucinations... anything to confuse and cloud the issue. Science fiction films and the New Age movement are creations of the secret government, meant to further dupe the people.

The author also relates some of his own troubles, including having his ideas stolen from him by the Patent and Trademark Office, which he says is a front for the secret government to steal valuable new technology and then malign the inventors. In another series of incidents, he found out that a supposed friend was actually a "Man in Black" sent to intimidate him into not writing this book. A final section of the book contains plans for building your own UFO propulsion system.

A new, expanded edition of *Space Aliens From the Pentagon* is in the works and may be out by the time you read this.

Creatopia Productions; $24.95
1993; oversized softcover; 244 pp
illus; 0-9637467-0-7

SPACESHIPS OF THE PLEIADES
The Billy Meier Story
by Kal K. Korff

Eduard "Billy" Meier is a Swiss farmer who claims to have been in continual contact with aliens from the Pleiades star system for over 20 years. He has taken 1000 photos and twelve videos of what he says are visiting spacecraft, and has snapped pictures from on board the flying saucers while travelling through time and space. Meier has also allegedly received thousands of pages of instructions and wisdom from the aliens, which he passed on to many of his followers. In this book, Kal Korff presents his massive investigation of Meier, his followers, and his evidence (including rock and metal samples from the Pleiades) and has declared the whole matter to be the most elaborate UFO hoax in history. Many of Meier's photographs — including some previously unpublished ones — are included.

> Prometheus Books; $25.95
> 1995; hardcover; 439 pp
> illus; 0-87975-959-3

At right, space alien Valiant Thor.
Stranger at the Pentagon.

STRANGER AT THE PENTAGON

Dr. Frank E. Stranges

According to the author, in March 1957 a space alien named Valiant Thor, who looked like a normal human male, landed in Virginia after leaving his home planet, Venus. He met with President Eisenhower and all the brass at the Pentagon, advising them on the coming troubled times for the earth and how aliens would help us. Dr. Frank Stranges, a minister, was contacted by someone in the Pentagon to meet with Thor. In this book, he tells all about the alien's three-year visit to earth and includes seven pictures of him.

> Inner Light Publications; $9.95
> 1967, 1991; softcover; 127 pp
> illus; 0938294-66-0

THEY KNEW TOO MUCH ABOUT FLYING SAUCERS

by Gray Barker

Gray Barker was a researcher and writer who covered UFOs and other Fortean topics starting in 1952. He became the chief investigator for a leading UFO organisation of the time, the International Flying Saucer Bureau. When the Bureau suddenly announced that the UFO mystery had been solved and then closed its doors, Barker found out that the group's founder had been intimidated into silence by mysterious men dressed in black. In this book, originally published in 1956, Barker elaborates on his investigation into this occurrence, as well as other people who claimed to have been threatened after learning too much about flying saucers. This is the book that started the whole Men in Black phenomenon.

> IllumiNet Press; $12.95
> 1956, 1997; softcover; 256 pp
> 1-881532-10-0

UFO DANGER ZONE
Terror and Death in Brazil — Where Next?

By Bob Pratt

The country of Brazil is a hotspot for UFO activity, but perhaps because of technical difficulties (and a tendency to ignore non-industrialised countries), these cases aren't often covered by ufologists. Bob Pratt has ventured into the remote small towns and forests of Brazil to talk directly with over 1700 people regarding 200 cases. In this

groundbreaking book, he presents his exclusive information on dozens of these cases, which often involve forced abductions, terrorisation, brutality, and even murder on the part of the aliens.

> Horus House; $16.95
> 1996; softcover; 356 pp
> illus; 1-881852-14-8

THE UFO INVASION
The Roswell Incident, Alien Abductions, and Government Coverups

edited by Kendrick Frazier, Barry Karr, & Joe Nickell

In this collection of 40 articles (all but one of them reprinted from *The Skeptical Inquirer*), a platoon of naysayers poke holes in various aspects of the UFO/alien phenomenon. As other books in this chapter show, sceptics can be as dogmatic, arrogant, and irrational as true believers, but in general I enjoy reading what the hard-nosed doubters have to say because — even if I don't believe that they've definitively closed the case (which is often their claim) — they can bring up many good points that can help create a more balanced look at the subjects.

In "The 'Top Secret UFO Papers' NSA Won't Release", Philip J. Klass offers an alternative explanation concerning the National Security Agency's refusal to release 156 documents relating to UFOs. This stonewalling has been trumpeted by ufologist Stanton Friedman as prime evidence of a "Cosmic Watergate". Given the dates of the documents — 1958-1979 — Klass says it's most likely they are intercepted communications from Soviet Bloc countries. They probably contain references to sources, facilities, and methods that are unknown to the governments of those countries. Their release would also reveal exactly which cryptographic codes were cracked by the NSA.

The much-discussed "alien autopsy" footage takes a drubbing from Trey Stokes, who has done special creature effects for *Species*, *The Abyss*, and *Robocop II*. His article "How to Make an 'Alien' for Autopsy" tells exactly how he

"Betty is helped into the barrel, as light beings repair the hole in the crystal lake." *The Watchers II.*

thinks the alleged space creature was constructed and how the alleged autopsy was filmed. Discussing the part of the film where the skull is cut open and the brain removed, he writes: "First, we use our blood-tube scalpel on the scalp. We cheat just a bit and skip the moment where the skull is first exposed to allow for any needed touch-up work, then let our actors peel the scalp back... Skipping the actual removal of the skull cap, we shoot the removal of the brain from a low angle where the skull can't be seen. We throw one of our organs in there and roll camera as the organ oozes out."

Other unbelieving articles include "New Evidence of MJ-12 Hoax", "The 'Roswell Fragment' — Case Closed", "A Surgeon's View of the 'Alien Autopsy'", "The Big Sur 'UFO': An *Identified* Flying Object", "3.7 Million Americans Kidnapped by Aliens?", "No Aliens, No Abductions: Just Regressive Hypnosis, Waking Dreams, and Anthropomorphism", "The Crop-Circle Phenomenon", and "Searching for Extraterrestrial Intelligence".

> Prometheus Books; $25.95
> 1997; hardcover; 315 pp
> illus; 1-57392-131-9

UFOs OVER AFRICA
by Cynthia Hind

In the field of ufology, there's a scarcity of information about Africa. Cynthia Hind, co-ordinator for Mutual UFO Network's (MUFON) Africa branch, continues to correct that oversight with this, her second book on the subject. She contends that there are many UFO sightings and alien encounters occurring in Africa, but in many areas residents don't realise what they're seeing or, if they realise the significance of it, they don't know where to report it. Other times, UFOs and aliens are regarded as ghosts or some other form of spirit.

Hind relates her interviews with witnesses of several key events, including the La Rochelle case in Zimbabwe, a man who met aliens aboard a spacecraft near Cape Town, several sightings by pilots, and the Ariel School incident, in which a large group of children claim to have witnessed a UFO land and its occupants disembark. She also analyses a hoax concerning a UFO supposedly shot down over Botswana, and several chapters deal with abductions, complete with missing time, physical aftermaths, and sexual violation.

Although there don't appear to be any cases with the significance of Roswell or Gulf Breeze, this book is the only one currently available to fill in the ufological gap of an entire continent.

> Horus House Press; $15.95
> 1997; softcover; 254 pp
> illus; 1-881852-15-6

THE WATCHERS II
Exploring UFOs and the Near-Death Experience
by Raymond E. Fowler

In this sequel to *The Watchers*, Raymond Fowler uses further extensive hypnosis sessions with abductees Betty Andreasson Luca and Bob Luca — plus information from other cases — to draw many parallels between the experience of UFO abduction and the Near-Death Experience. Fowler's unique conclusion is that "death may be the ultimate UFO abduction experience!"

> Wild Flower Press; $18.95
> 1995; softcover; 389 pp
> illus; 0-926524-30-5

HIDDEN POWERS

THE ASSOCIATIVE CARD CODE
by Katharine Cover Sabin

Katharine Sabin is a psychic who — according to several articles — has made hundreds of predictions that have come true. This is provable because she sends her predictions through Western Union telegrams so that they are officially dated. It is claimed that these telegrams show her predicting problems with space flights, the time and severity of San Diego earthquakes, Ted Kennedy's "problem" at Chappaquiddick, and much more.

Working outside the mainstream of parapsychology research, Sabin claims that she has performed positive, repeatable experiments with ESP, and — even more importantly — that she can teach anyone to achieve precognition. Sabin employs a form of external ESP, which means that she uses a divinatory tool — in this case, cards — as an aid. She developed a code (the "K Code") that gives each card a meaning. By shuffling and laying out the cards, you can see what they are saying. Later, she developed another, more powerful code that not only makes personal predictions but predictions of a national and international scope as well. This new code — the "Associative Card Code" — is the basis of this book.

The system is based on a set of cards called Gypsy Witch Fortune Telling Playing Cards, which are put out as a children's game by the US Playing Card Company. When Sabin saw them, she felt that the written messages they contained

Steve Bisyak strolls across 15-feet of coals measuring 1,546°F. *Firewalk.*

were too simplistic to be of value, but the cheesy illustrations of common objects on each one could be a powerful tool. For example, the picture of the key denotes ownership or the solving of problems. The meaning of most cards will depend on the cards surrounding it during divination. The tower represents a building. "With the FLOWERS, it is a hospital, for we take flowers to the hospital. With the LILIES, it is a church; with the COFFIN, a morgue; with the BOTTLE, often a cafe or bar; with the BOOK, a school; with legal matters, a courthouse; with the PIG, it is often a restaurant."

Sabin reveals the meanings of every card in the deck. Since you use the deck in conjunction with two decks of regular cards, she also gives the meanings of the standard cards. After giving exercises in interpretation, she tells you how to shuffle, deal, and layout the cards in simple and complex patterns. She also gives instructions for using the cards to answer very specific personal questions and to predict world events.

Each copy of *The Associative Card Code* comes with a Gypsy Witch deck.

The Mindreach Publishing Company; $40
1968, 1994; 8.5"x11" paper bound in a presentation binder and a deck of 54 cards; 59 pp
illus; 1-884715-03-6

FIREWALK
The Psychology of Physical Immunity
by Jonathan Sternfield

Jonathan Sternfield is a writer who has firewalked twice. The fact that he did it without injuring himself, along with the fact that thousands of other people have safely done it, sparked a desire to find out more about this seemingly impossible feat. How long have people been firewalking? Why do they do it? Most importantly, how do they do it successfully, and what does this reveal about our minds and bodies?

Sternfield tells us about his own firewalks, first with master motivator and seminar guru Tony Robbins, and then with a Zen master. He gives a fascinating history lesson of firewalking. The Bible has many references to the phenomenon. Throughout the Middle Ages, Christians in Europe walked the walk for a variety of reasons. In 1007 the German Empress Kunigunde was accused of adultery by her husband. To prove her fidelity, she chose a literal trial by fire. "In the Cathedral of Bamberg, the fire was lit, the Mass said and the iron heated. Accompanied by two bishops, the empress carefully and deliberately walked over nine red-hot plowshares, stepping off the last one with no injuries whatsoever." Firewalking and other rituals involving close contact with fire — mainly as a part of religious ceremonies — have occurred in Asia, Africa, India, Australia, the Pacific Islands, South America, and among Native North Americans and Pentecostal Holiness Christians. A centre section of the book contains photographs of ten firewalks, both past and present.

Sternfield further explores the topic by examining individuals who do much more than walk across fire. They stand in fire, hold their hands in flames, and hold red-hot coals. Steve Bisyak holds the record for longest firewalk (126 feet) and hottest firewalk (1540°F with three-inch flames).

Many theories have been offered to explain firewalking. One of the most popular says that firewalk materials are usually poor conductors of heat. This explanation is often combined with the Leidenfrost effect, which says that the feet are protected by water vapour in the spheroidal state. Other theories say that there is a special way of walking that minimises contact, that endorphins deaden the pain, that walkers use pain-deadening drugs or apply chemicals to their feet, or that people achieve altered states during their walks.

Sternfield leans towards the latter explanation. "Firewalking, then, appears to be an expression of faith. From another perspective, it is an expression of mind over matter, an alteration of the properties of the human body through the action of psychology alone." Somehow our minds are able to alter the normal properties of our bodies, perhaps utilising various life energies, to create a resistance to fire, pain, and other stimuli.

In the end, the author sees firewalking as a way of fulfilling human potential. By demonstrating to ourselves the amazing power of our minds (and by overcoming the fear of firewalking in the first place), we recognise the vast potential that we have just barely begun to tap.

Berkshire House, Publishers; $12.95
1992; softcover; 236 pp
illus; 0-936399-04-X

FLYING WITHOUT A BROOM
Astral Projection and the Astral World
by DJ Conway

Flying Without a Broom is a complete guide to travelling in the astral realm. The author teaches you how to get there, what you can do while you're there, how to get back, and how to remember your travels. She gives instructions for astral travelling during meditation and during sleep (which most of us do anyway). You can choose a spirit guide to help you in your journeys, which is a good idea since there are lots of things to learn, like protecting yourself from lower-level spirits.

While you're travelling, you can do many things, such as visit the Akashic Records, which holds records of every human's past lives, among other knowledge. You can travel forwards or backwards in time using any of five methods. The author gives specific instructions for visiting Atlantis, Lemuria, early America, the Oracle at Delphi, the Library of Alexandria, and other hot destinations. Or you can drop in on wizards, witches, shamans, or ancient gods and goddesses who may impart wisdom and forgotten knowledge. You can also visit friends and lovers in the present.

Speaking of lovers, the author devotes a chapter to the safest sex of all — astral sex. "This astral relationship can have all the same tenderness, warmth, and satisfaction of a physical one. Since your senses on the astral plane are more intense than on the physical, you will discover new and enhanced feelings." You must choose your psychic lover(s) with care, though. Don't become an easy astral lay. "If you don't care how you get your astral sex, then you'll get what you deserve. It won't be a pleasant experience. You will find that you opened yourself to the advances and misuses of any low-level entity that comes along."

Advanced uses of these powers include healing, working magick, and defending yourself against the dark side. The author gives directions for various powers and methods within each one. With astral magick, for example, you can perform rituals for health, prosperity, spiritual growth, divination, love, justice, and more.

The book concludes with a five-page glossary and a bibliography.

Llewellyn Publications; $13
1995; softcover; 218 pp
1-56718-164-3

MIND TREK
Exploring Consciousness, Time, and Space Through
Remote Viewing
by Joseph McMoneagle

In 1970 Joseph McMoneagle had a near-death experience, and by the end of the decade, he was trying to tap into some of the powers of the mind that had been revealed to him during his experience. He went to the paranormal research centre SRI-International, where he developed his skill of remote viewing (RV). This is a form of ESP in which you "see" things that are not perceptible to your five ordinary senses. You target something or somewhere that you want to sense, and the images, feelings, signs, and symbols flood into you. "Any person, group, association, thing, circumstance, object, event, occurrence, thought, place, belief, or concept can be

Dr Shiuji Inomata works on a machine called the JPI that uses magnets to tap into space energy.
The Coming Energy Revolution.

targeted… All past, present, or future times, and all existent realities can be targeted. Even someone else's fantasies can be targeted."

This is different from having an out-of-body experience. In such cases, some part of you actually leaves your body and travels to a destination. Remote viewing is a process that's much harder to define… you don't actually go anywhere but somehow sense what you're targeting. In some of the exercises McMoneagle has done, someone has given him longitude and latitude co-ordinates of a well-known site. He then focuses and, with help from a partner asking him questions, he pinpoints the landmark he was given. After several months, he claims that he's been correct half the time and has had a few truly outstanding viewings, such a zeroing in on the St. Louis Arch and the Devil's Tower in Washington.

McMoneagle gives tips and exercises for people who want to tap their remote viewing powers. To do so, you must learn how to relax, become centred, open your awareness, and communicate intuitive perceptions. It takes approximately a year and a half of daily training to become good at remote viewing.

The author claims to have viewed "how the Great Pyramid was built, the Crucifixion, the assassination of President Kennedy, UFOs, and life in the year 3000." He's currently writing a second book that will tell exactly what he saw regarding these events and other similarly intriguing ones.

Hampton Roads Publishing Company; $10.95
1993; softcover; 231 pp
illus; 1-878901-72-9

PSYCHIC WARRIOR
Inside the CIA's Stargate Program —

The True Story of a Soldier's Espionage and Awakening

by David Morehouse

The CIA has officially admitted to developing a programme for "remote viewing" — a psychic phenomena in which the "viewers" somehow transcend time/space to witness events in other locations in the past, present, or future. David Morehouse, who was one of these remote viewers, tells what is was like working in this programme, what he saw, why he left, and the troubles he's faced since becoming a whistleblower (including a court-martial, tapped phones, and attempts on his life).

> St. Martin's Press; $6.99
> 1996; paperback; 258 pp
> illus; 0-312-96413-7

UNORTHODOX SCIENCE

THE COMING ENERGY REVOLUTION
The Search for Free Energy

by Jeane Manning

Although the scientific establishment doesn't believe it, many inventors have come up with ways to create energy that don't rely on oil, gas, nuclear power, or any other orthodox fuel or process. Some of these technologies involve "free energy", which refers to ways of harnessing the sea of energy that supposedly flows throughout the universe and the earth. Other technologies involve the creation of energy from similarly controversial sources.

Convinced that these technologies are real and that their implementation is only a matter of time, the author describes their developments and the principles behind them, primarily by focusing on the inventors who pioneered their use. She describes the concept of free energy, and talks about the earlier energy iconoclasts, such as Nikola Tesla, John Keely, Thomas Moray, Lester Hendershot, Wilhelm Reich, and others.

Most of the book concerns contemporary mavericks, including eight men who are working on free energy devices. Ken Shoulders uses static electricity and plasma to create Charge Clusters, doughnut-shaped groupings of 100 million electrons that give off thirty times as much energy as it takes to produce them. A lot of the other inventors use some form of rotating magnets to create a practically unlimited amount of energy.

Another section of the book examines the work being done on radical forms of energy creation that don't involve free energy. These technologies include cold fusion, "the joining, or fusing, together of atoms at room temperature ac-

companied by the release of excess energy"; hydrogen as fuel; harnessing the heat in the atmosphere; hydropower that works with the current, instead of damming it up and causing environmental disaster; and a hydrosonic pump that creates shockwaves in water.

The book's final section looks at the promise that such limitless, easy-to-obtain forms of energy hold for the human race, and why these developments are being stymied. These inventors have been the targets of break-ins, destroyed equipment, funding cut-offs, government-ordered secrecy restrictions, threats, and violence. Fellow scientists are either too arrogant or too afraid to get involved with them. The oil, gas, and nuclear industries are terrified of being put out of their multi-trillion dollar business by these new technologies. Governments are afraid of the unforeseeably radical effects that would hit society. Other inventors are their own worst enemies, acting in a secretive, paranoid fashion that assures their ideas will never get anywhere.

The author has the uncanny ability to make these revolutionary, highly theoretical theories easily understandable. I'm sure she's oversimplifying to a degree, but this is still the clearest explanation of free energy and related topics that I've ever seen. Add to that an amazing international resource list and a glossary, and *The Coming Energy Revolution* becomes one of the best unorthodox science books you can get.

> Avery Publishing Group; $12.95
> 1996; softcover; 246 pp
> illus; 0-89529-713-2

THE FREE-ENERGY HANDBOOK
A Compilation of Patents and Reports

compiled by David Hatcher Childress

A free energy device is a motor, generator, or propulsion system that does not run on fuel or any "external prime mover" such as water or wind. The power to run these devices would instead be created by somehow harnessing the energy of forces we already know about — such as magnetism — or forces that are presently unknown (at least to orthodox science) — such as the natural energies that some people theorise are constantly flowing around the earth and universe. If a device could be powered in this way, it would cost almost nothing to run and would not be dependent on foreign oil or strong winds or any other uncontrollable factors.

The Free-Energy Device Handbook reprints dozens of important documents relating to this Holy Grail of radical scientists. By far the earliest entry is by Peter Pengrinus, who is believed to have developed the "first known and recorded permanent magnet motor in 1269". A collection of diagrams and short articles shows some of the research performed by Nikola Tesla, the most famous free energy pioneer.

The report "Non-Conventional Energy and Propulsion Methods" takes a quick look at space power, superconductors, magnetic motors, nuclear batteries, inertial propulsion, electrogravitics, and kinetobaric propulsion. Other articles and reports examine in detail the one-piece Faraday generator, macroscopic vacuum polarisation, the Adams pulsed electric motor generator, the homopolar "free energy" generator, the Worthington magnetic motor, the Swiss M-L converter, unified particle theory, and electric charge generation by space rotation.

Another section reprints diagrams and application information from a bunch of patents relating to free energy — the flux switch alternator, the pulse capicitator discharge electrical engine, method and apparatus for generating a dynamic force field, electromagnetic levitation, and the ionocraft. The final two sections have several news clippings and a look at free energy devices in pop culture, such as comics and science fiction, which is a light-hearted way to end a very heavy book.

> Adventures Unlimited; $16.95
> 1995; oversized softcover; 306 pp
> heavily illus; 0-932813-24-0

FUEL FROM WATER
Energy Independence With Hydrogen
(Sixth Edition)

by Michael A. Peavy

According to Michael Peavy, it is possible to run cars, planes, homes, and factories with hydrogen fuel from water. Because the only by-product of burning hydrogen fuel is water vapour, using it would help the planet immeasurably, besides eliminating our dependence on non-renewable forms of energy. On top of that, hydrogen is non-toxic, can safely be transported through pipelines, and has three times more energy per unit weight than gasoline. Hydrogen has some disadvantages — such as a higher range of flammability when mixed with air — but, overall, it is still a serious alternative.

Fuel From Water is not a popularised treatment of the subject. Most of the material is a highly technical look at the hows and whys of producing hydrogen (including making it from waste), storing hydrogen, modifying engines to run on hydrogen, creating electricity from hydrogen, hydrogen as a supplementary fuel, catalytic burners, hydrogen for homes, and safety considerations. Over 150 charts, diagrams, and photos accompany the text.

With 75% of the world's oil reserves in the Middle East, and the US expected to drain its natural gas deposits in eighteen years, it would be wise to seriously investigate the possibility of making fuel from water.

> Merit, Inc.; $20
> 1995; oversized softcover; 251 pp
> heavily illus; 0-945516-04-5

PULSE OF THE PLANET #4
Research Report and Journal of the
Orgone Biophysical Research
Laboratory

This huge yearly magabook centres on the work of unorthodox scientist/psychoanalyst/healer Wilhelm Reich. Reich was part of Sigmund Freud's inner circle during the creation of psychoanalysis. Like Carl Jung, Reich broke with his mentor and went off in radical directions. Reich's main discovery — which influenced almost everything else he did — was that all natural things have a life energy, called orgone, which

An experimental vertical take-off aircraft.
UFOs and Anti-Gravity.

flows through them.

He theorised that orgasms are good for you because they release blockages of orgone in your body and let the energy flow freely. Fascism, he said, results when a society sexually represses its youth, thus blocking their orgone and turning them into maladjusted control freaks. He also experimented with controlling the weather and healing diseases — including cancer — by manipulating orgone. Despite (or because of) the fact that he was often successful in ridding people of cancer, he was harassed by the Food and Drug Administration, which eventually had him thrown in jail, where he died. Under a US court order in 1956, Reich's laboratory equipment was smashed to pieces and his books were burned. Sickeningly ironic is the fact that some of these same books had likewise been burned by the Nazis, whom the US had defeated just a decade earlier.

Pulse of Planet offers articles on Reich and his work, current studies of life energy, new theories and observations, and related matters. Issue 4 has three articles by Reich — including "Experimental Investigation of the Electrical Function of Sexuality and Anxiety" — plus "Wilhelm Reich in Denmark", "Why Is Reich Never Mentioned?", "The Biophysical Discoveries of Wilhelm Reich", and "The Jailing of a Great Scientist". Articles not specifically about the man cover Three Mile Island, abuses of power by the FDA, and research into possible causes of AIDS besides HIV.

Ten departments report on science, nuclear power, environment, economy, health, and other subjects from a Reichian perspective. There are also book reviews, reports on Reichian research, a listing of recent articles and other material relating to orgone, and more.

The group that puts out *Pulse* also offers a catalogue of books, videos, and devices relating to Reich, orgone, and tangential subjects. The catalogue costs $2.

> Orgone Biophysical Research Lab (Natural Energy Works); $20
> 1993; oversized softcover; 173 pp
> illus; 1041-6773

TIME TRAVEL
A New Perspective
by JH Brennan

JH Brennan believes that time travel is possible, and indeed already has occurred/is occurring/will occur (hey, verb tenses get a little tricky, if not meaningless, when you're dealing with time travel). In the first part of this easily readable book, he examines some of the tantalising clues that time travellers have left behind, such as a metal nail, a pot, a vase, perfect metal spheres, and even a human footprint that have all been found embedded in rock layers 600 million to 2.8 billion years old.

The second section of the book examines precognition as a form of time travel, time as a fourth dimension, cases of people travelling back in time by accident briefly, the influence of gravity, black holes, wormholes, logician Kurt Gödel's theory of time travel, skeletons of modern humans found in strata three to four million years old, subatomic particles that travel through time, and various other aspects of physics. Brennan concludes that the concept of time travel does not violate Newton's physics, Einstein's theory of relativity, or quantum mechanics.

The final section gives instructions for an experiment that has allegedly allowed groups of people to travel back in time. Five to twenty people gather and do exercises that will calm them emotionally and charge them psychically. While focusing on an object from the time period to which they want to travel, a member of the group leads them back verbally. The others will follow, and everyone will be surprised that they are all having the same experience.

Llewellyn Publications; $12.95
1997; softcover; 216 pp
illus; 1-56718-085-X

TOWARDS A NEW ALCHEMY
The Millennium Science
by Dr. Nick Begich

In this book, Dr. Nick Begich exposes the world at large to the ideas and inventions of Dr. Patrick Flanagan, an inventor who works with energies, particularly biological energies. When he was twelve, Flanagan created a device that could instantly detect any missile launch or atomic bomb blast within an 8000-mile radius. Not only did he win the science fair, the Pentagon adopted his technology.

A few years later, he invented a device called the Neurophone® (much to my annoyance, this name is followed by a trademark symbol every single time it appears in the book.) "The Neurophone® is an electronic device which transmits sound through the skin to the brain, by-passing the normal hearing channels. The device converts sound waves into digitised electronic signals which have a wave form and timing configuration, which can be deciphered and understood by the human brain. The internal hearing, or mental sound imprinting, is delivered to the brain intact just as it was transmitted. The electronic signal is fully perceptible as if the sound were heard through the ears." Begich actually uses the device himself. "I placed the electrodes between my thumbs and forefingers and instantly I could

hear the music as if it were playing in the centre of my head." He relates the history of the device from its creation, when Flanagan was fourteen, to its restriction on security grounds by the National Security Agency (which was subsequently overturned after lengthy court battles) to its current digital incarnations.

Flanagan also worked on the US Navy's Dolphin Communication Project, and he claims that they developed a device that converted human language into dolphin language and vice versa. On top of that, he has created a revolutionary air purification system, a form of water that provides extremely efficient delivery of nutrients to cells and removal of toxins from cells, and he has successfully experimented with pyramid energy and related forces.

Several appendices take more technical looks at some of Flanagan's inventions, including the patents for the Neurophone and the Electro Field Generator.

Earthpulse Press; $14.95
1996; softcover; 179 pp
illus; 0-9648812-2-5

UFOS AND ANTI-GRAVITY
Piece for a Jig-Saw
by Leonard G. Cramp

A reprint of a 1966 book in which a ufologist looks at various ideas and theories regarding anti-gravity, then speculates on the technology alien spacecraft would have to be using to account for the UFOs that witnesses have sighted. The author attempts to keep the tone as conversational as possible, but the material becomes quite technical in places (which can be a good or bad thing depending on your level of understanding). Includes lots of photos, illustrations, and diagrams.

Adventures Unlimited Press; $16.95
1966 (1996); softcover; 388 pp
illus; 0-932813-43-7

UNIVERSAL LAWS NEVER BEFORE REVEALED
Keely's Secrets — Understanding and Using the Science of Sympathetic Vibration (Revised Edition)
edited by Dale Pond

John Keely (1827-1898) was an inventor who has become an idol of unorthodox science. He isn't quite up there with Nikola Tesla, but he's definitely holding his own. Keely's claim to fame is his development of Sympathetic Vibratory Physics and many inventions based on this paradigm. *Universal Laws* serves as an advanced Keely reader, with 91 old and new articles, including some from the man himself.

A transcript of Dale Pond's lecture "Sympathetic Vibratory Physics" is the only beginner's level introduction to Keely's ideas here, but, for some reason, it is located about one-third of the way into the book. Pond says of this type of physics: "It is the science of Harmony, or Oneness. It holds the concept that all comes from One Source, One Force. It maintains that the fantastic array of things and activities throughout the universe are related in a simple manner. This simple basis of relativity is called vibration. It has long been recognised that everything in the universe vibrates. Thus, a study of vibrations is the study of the very foundation of Nature... Unlike dogmatic, cold science, Sympathetic Vibratory Physics does not isolate one phenomena from another but accepts and shows the inter-connectivity between all things and forces." Keely was able to use this approach to release huge amounts of energy from atoms through subtle means that did not give off radiation or cause other problems. He was able to transmute energy and matter, making advances in disintegration, levitation, telescope and microscope design, and the treatment of mental "illness".

Keely proposed 40 laws governing vibrations, and each of those laws is revealed here along with further commentary from Pond. Other articles from Pond cover gravity, ultrasonic energy, music, polarity, vibration vs. oscillation, and the secret of Keely's infamous motor, which Pond and a colleague were able to recreate. Among the articles by Keely are "Levitation", "The Chord Settings of Life", "The Role of Atomic Forces in Healing", "The Basis of a New Science", and "Gravity" (with Edgar Cayce). Further articles by other people discuss Keely's theories or their meetings with him.

Arranged haphazardly and without a concise overview of Keely and his contributions, *Universal Laws* isn't a book for the idly curious. But if you want serious, hardcore knowledge concerning Keely's ideas and inventions, this is a must-have.

The Message Company; $19.95
1990, 1995; softcover; 285 pp
heavily illus; 1-57282-003-9

MISCELLANEOUS

ABLAZE!
The Mysterious Fires of Spontaneous
Human Combustion
by Larry E Arnold

When spontaneous human combustion (SHC) occurs, a person is engulfed in flames that have no outward source. The body catches fire internally, and the person is reduced to a pile of ash. Like all such bizarre phenomena, many people don't even believe it exists, but SHC has always struck me as one of the best-supported aspects of the paranormal. *Ablaze!* takes an impressively thorough look at this enigma.

One of the most amazing things about fires attributed to SHC is that they completely reduce the body (or most of the body) to a pile of ash in minutes. The human body is extremely resistant to fire. Cremation usually employs temperatures of 2200°F for 90 minutes and 1700°F for an additional 60 to 90 minutes. (The hottest house fires are almost never more than 1700°F, and rock turns to lava at 1800°F.) Even

John Keely and some of his inventions.
Universal Laws Never Before Revealed.

after all of that, though, a cremated body still has chunks of bone and skull. Furthermore, people who get burned up in the hottest type of fire known — a thermite fire, which melts steel beams — can still be identified. But people who die by SHC are literally piles of ash. In the space of a few minutes, they are burned into a fine powder. No known form of fire can explain this total damage.

Another spooky fact is that this impossibly hot fire does either minimal or *no* damage to objects immediately surrounding the person who burns. People have flamed up in small apartments, beside wooden furniture, even on chairs and beds, yet all of it is lightly scorched or undamaged. Sometimes objects in the immediate vicinity go up in flames, but usually they do not. Even more amazing, many victims' clothes are still intact. Sometimes they're partly burned or described as "smouldering", but they haven't been burned to ashes like the body they covered. In numerous cases, victims' hair — which should ignite like so much hay — is also unburned.

Very often victims of SHC didn't smoke and were not near any sources of flames or significant heat when they caught fire. In some cases, the people were last seen alive just minutes before they became piles of ash. Occasionally, there are witnesses to the event, as in the case of Robert Bailey, a homeless alcoholic in England. On September 13, 1967, a group of people saw a light in an abandoned building and called the fire apartment. Fire Brigade Commander Jack Stacey and his crew arrived to find Bailey already dead. According to Stacey himself, who was interviewed by the author, a blue flame was jetting from an opening in Bailey's abdomen. "'The flame was actually coming from the body itself,' asserted Stacey, "from *inside* the body. He was burning literally from the inside out!'"

Besides examining all known or suspected cases of SHC from the thirteenth century to the present (including many that have never been reported in any other SHC literature), the author also looks at what might cause the phenomenon, commonalities of people who have died this way, false reports of SHC, people who have spontaneously combusted and survived, people who claim to have been burned by UFOs, corpses that have mysteriously caught fire, SHC in literature, and more. A centre section contains fifteen gruesome photos of people who were seemingly victims of SHC. It's hard to imagine a book covering its subject more thoroughly than *Ablaze!*.

M Evans and Company; $24.95
1995; hardcover; 498 pp
illus; 0-87131-789-3

ADVENTURES UNLIMITED CATALOGUE

This heavily illustrated catalogue offers hundreds of books and videos on an array of unexplained topics — lost cities, ancient civilisations, exotic lands, Atlantis, Mu, mysterious phenomena (e.g., crop circles), alternative science, free energy and Tesla, anti-gravity, ancient science (e.g., harmonics, ancient high-tech), extraterrestrial archaeology, alternative health, conspiracies, alchemy, philosophy and religion, and UFOs and ETs. A sampling of books includes *Lost Cities of Atlantis, Ancient Europe & the Mediterranean, Riddle of the Pacific, In Secret Mongolia, The Harmonic Conquest of Space, Somebody Else Is on the Moon, World War III According to Nostradamus, Living Water,* and *Grand Illusions: The Spectral Reality Underlying Sexual UFO Abductions, Crashed Saucers, Afterlife Experiences, Sacred Ancient Sites, and Other Enigmas*.

Adventures Unlimited/303 Main St, PO Box 74/Kempton IL 60946
Catalogue: US/Can: $1. Elsewhere: $5

ALTERNATIVE SCIENCE
Challenging the Myths of the Scientific Establishment
by Richard Milton

In his earlier book *Shattering the Myths of Darwinism* [reviewed in The Body chapter], Richard Milton used empirical evidence, common sense, and a hard look at the facts to deal a serious blow to one of science's most unquestionable dogmas — the theory of evolution. In this book, he uses the same approach to kick the teeth of a number of other scientific ideologies. The scientific establishment and its funders have rigid ideas about what science should study and what it shouldn't. Those mavericks who try to seriously and scientifically investigate "taboo" topics are often demoted, fired, cut off from grants, ridiculed and attacked, or expelled from the ivory towers of Science.

What the establishment doesn't want to admit and, thus, what you may never hear, is that there has been much credible, empirical evidence gained through scientific experimentation supporting such outcasts as cold fusion, psychokinesis, telepathy, biological energy, the mind/body connection, and alternative medicine. Milton clearly spells out the research supporting these phenomena, as well as the reactions this research has unleashed.

Much of the book examines the hows and whys of scientific close-mindedness. "In its more subtle form, the taboo reaction draws a circle around a subject and places it 'out of bounds' to any form of rational analysis or investigation. In doing so, science often puts up what appears to be a well-considered, fundamental objection, which on closer analy-

The remains of Helen Conway, who appears to have spontaneously exploded in 1964. *Ablaze!*

sis turns out to be no more than the unreflecting prejudices of a maiden aunt who feels uncomfortable with the idea of mixed bathing... In its most extreme form, scientific tabooism closely resembles the behaviour of a priestly caste who perceive themselves to be the holy guardians of the sacred creed, the beliefs that are the objects of the community's worship. Such guardians feel themselves justified by their religious calling and long training in adopting any measures to repel and to discredit any member of the community who profanes the sacred, places, words or rituals..." Besides the topics listed above, the author uses scads of other examples from the present and the past to specifically show these reactions in action.

Scientists sneered that the Wright Brothers couldn't have possibly flown because, according to their calculations, human flight is impossible. The *New York Herald, Scientific American,* and the Army all declared them hoaxers. It wasn't until five years after the first flight that President Teddy Roosevelt ordered a public exhibition, and Orville and Wilbur were vindicated. Similarly, white-coats publicly lambasted Edison because the electric lamp he invented could not exist. You would think that today's scientists would learn from their humiliated predecessors and be willing to rigorously scrutinise any invention, idea, or theory. Hopefully, *Alternative Science* will provide a step in that direction, and if it doesn't, at least we laypeople will realise that there are more scientific discoveries being made than we're aware of.

Park Street Press (Inner Traditions International); $14.95
1994, 1996; softcover; 266 pp
0-89281-631-7

A French chemist, born in 1818, appears on a TV screen from the Great Beyond. *Conversations Beyond The Light.*

BOOK OF THE DAMNED
by Charles Fort

Charles Fort is one of the central figures in the study of the unexplained. In the early twentieth century he catalogued tens of thousands of strange phenomena that could not be explained by the known laws of science. He called this type of data "the damned" because it was fated to be ridiculed or simply ignored by the scientific establishment. Although much of the information Fort drew together was verifiable, it often made mincemeat of widely-held scientific "facts" and, thus, scientists would rather ignore it than admit that their theories are inadequate or wrong.

Book of the Damned, originally published in 1919, was Fort's first collection of bizarre phenomena. Rather than present them in list form using a dry, academic writing style, Fort created an interlinked, demanding, yet humorous narrative that relates the incidents and comments on them. In this edition of the book, the original text from the 1919 edition has been restored.

An article in *Science* tells of a block of limestone that supposedly fell from the sky onto Middleburgh, Florida. Fort comments: "The writer, in *Science*, denies that it fell from the sky. His reasoning is: There is no limestone in the sky; therefore this limestone did not fall from the sky. Better reasoning I cannot conceive of — because we see that a final major premise — universal-true — would include all things: that, then, would leave nothing to reason about — so then that all reasoning must be based upon something not universal, or only a phantom intermediate to the two finalities of nothingness and allness, or negativeness and positiveness." Other reports of strange things falling from the sky include frogs, fish, mussels, snakes, flocks of dead birds, rocks, silk-like substances, and strange, fibrous materials.

Fort never misses an opportunity to artfully put down close-minded scientists: "Stranglers of Minerva. Desperadoes of disregard. Above all, or below all, the anthropologists. I'm inspired with a new insult — some one offends me: I wish to express almost absolute contempt for him — he's a systematistic anthropologist."

Throughout the book, Fort discusses hundreds of strange things, including ancient coins, giant footprints, tiny prehistoric tools (around a quarter-inch long), unknown planetary bodies, spots moving across the sun, dark days, unexplained lights on the ocean, strange prints in fresh snow, and UFOs of all descriptions.

John Brown Publishing; £9.99
1919 (1995); softcover; 322 pp
1-870870-53-0

CONVERSATIONS BEYOND THE LIGHT
With Departed Friends and Colleagues by Electronic Means
by Dr. Pat Kubis & Mark Macy

Forget about trying to communicate with the spirit of a dead person through a channeller or by having them materialise in front of you. It's time to get wired! There is a relatively new branch of paranormal studies being developed called Instrumental Transcommunication (ITC). "Today, using high-tech communication, the 'dead' are now transmitting information to our scientists in pictures, text, and voice via television screens, computers and telephones," as well as radios, tape recorders, and fax machines.

The Transcommunication Study Circle of Luxembourg (CETL) is on the forefront of this kind of research. In November 1992, Ernst Mackes — a close friend of the people who run CETL — died. A little over two months later, one of the computers at CETL printed out a message from Mackes, which read in part: "At the moment I am sitting here under a roof of exotic palm tree leaves. I am trying to focus my thoughts into a sort of typewriter which is sitting in front of me on the glass plate of a small bamboo table." A month later the computer's hard drive suddenly contained a scanned picture of Mackes as a young man.

On January 27, 1994 Dr. Konstantin Raudive — a paranormal researcher who had been dead 20 years — called George Meek, a researcher in the US. Meek was prepared and switched on his tape recorder as he answered the phone. "What he then heard was to be the first taped telephone conversation from the astral plane to the United States." Raudive told him: "This is the beginning of a new story, a new chapter, George."

As surprising as it may seem, the idea of electronic communication with the dead isn't new. In 1903 a French ethnologist was the first to record spirit voices. When a Siberian shaman he was visiting went into a trance, several voices spoke directly into the horn of the scientist's phonograph. In the 1920s, Thomas Edison — inventor of the motion picture camera and phonograph — worked on an invention that could record the voices of the dead but died before finishing it.

According to the authors, the dead have now set up a communication centre called Timestream Labs for the express purpose of communicating with the living on earth through electronics. Their goals are to prove to us that there is life after death, to convince us that "we are all one", to let the greatest minds of all time help us socially, scientifically, and medically, and "to help man understand the role of ani-

Illustration of an ancient bronze figurine from Asia Minor.
Historical Evidence for Unicorns.

mals on Earth and also to help animals".

Conversations gives transcripts of all sorts of messages the CETL has received. A photo section contains 23 images, including photographs that were supposedly beamed from the Great Beyond onto the CETL's computers and TV screens. A good portion of the book details exactly what the afterlife is like according to the spirits at Timestream. One chapter tells how you can perform these kinds of experiments, but it only covers capturing voices on audiotape. Then again, that's probably the only type of communication that needs preparation. If a spirit wants to talk on the phone, it'll just call you. If it wants to communicate via computer, you'll find the message on your hard drive the next time you boot up.

This is a fascinating book about an underpublicised aspect of the paranormal.

Griffin Publishing; $12.95
1995; softcover; 173 pp
illus; 1-882180-47-X

DISNEYLAND OF THE GODS
by John A. Keel

John A. Keel is one of the pre-eminent investigators of the unexplained. He writes in an irreverent and humorously cynical manner, bashing not just dogmatic sceptics but occasionally dogmatic believers, too. He knows some strange things are going on, but he isn't wedded to any theory that explains them (or explains them away). In this collection of essays he writes about Charles Fort, obsessed debunkers, the Egyptian Pyramids, radio communications with aliens, people who are struck by lightning, mysterious crime waves, reports of strange creatures, bizarre explosions, UFO abductions, why science has found no bones or artefacts dating from the period 25,000 BCE to 15,000 BCE, and more.

IllumiNet Books; $9.95
1988, 1995; softcover; 174 pp
1-881532-06-2

HISTORICAL EVIDENCE FOR UNICORNS
by Larry Brian Radka

The existence of unicorns has been relegated to mythology and folklore, but this book reveals intriguing evidence that this classification might not be correct. Larry Brian Radka presents written and visual references to one-horned beasties thoughout the ages.

A lot of the references come from the Bible, a book in which Radka believes completely, or from Bible-based studies of history. There are seven direct Biblical mentions of unicorns, all in the Old Testament. Numbers 23:2 says: "God brought them out of Egypt; he hath as it were the strength of the unicorn." Although these mentions are interesting insofar as the Bible can be taken as a historical document, many people will want more much more proof, and Radka delivers it.

Aristotle makes reference to two types of one-horned animals. "There are… some animals that have one horn only, for example, the oryx, whose hoof is cloven, the Indian ass, whose hoof is solid. These creatures have their horn in the middle of their head." Julius Caesar spoke of an "ox shaped like a stag" with a tall straight horn in the middle of its forehead. Pliny the Elder, the Greek physician Ctesias, and the Roman naturalist Aelian also wrote of the existence of similar creatures. In 1567 Vincent Le Blanc, who travelled Asia extensively, wrote of seeing unicorns first-hand, and the Elizabethan traveller Edward Webbe wrote in 1590, "I have seen, in a place like a park adjoining unto Prester John's Court, three score and seventeen unicorns and elephants all alive at one time, and they were so tame that I have played with them as one would play with young lambs."

Some of the evidence presented doesn't refer to horses with a horn on their heads — which is how we think of unicorns — but rather to other types of one-horned animals which no longer exist. The ancient stone which contains the laws of the Babylonian King Hammurabi has an extremely interesting entry which starts: "If a man hires an ox and it breaks off its horn…" Notice that the singular word *horn* is used, as opposed to *horns*. Several hieroglyphics from Egypt show hard-to-identify domesticated animals with one horn. Artwork left behind by the Assyrians also shows horse-like animals with one horn. (All of these ancient representations are reproduced in this book.) The last chapter looks at the one-horned animals that exist today — rhinoceroses, narwhales, and a bizarre type of bird in the Amazon valley — but doesn't offer any clues to the current existence of a unicorn horse.

Historical Evidence for Unicorns provides numerous thought-provoking leads for anyone interested in cryptozoology. The author's overtly Christian orientation colours his presentation of almost all the evidence and will surely be off-putting to those who want a more objective examination, but there's still a good deal to be learned here.

The Einhorn Press; $15
1995; softcover; 152 pp
heavily illus; 0-930401-81-6

THE LAST SKEPTIC OF SCIENCE
(Revised Edition)
by René

René was a member of Mensa who apparently got on other members' nerves by incessantly questioning scientific orthodoxy. In this collection of essays, billed as "the book Mensa tried to stop", he offers all manner of heretical proofs and "unproofs" regarding astronomical, geographical, physical, and chemical matters. I can't pretend that I understand everything he's saying, but someone well-versed in the sciences will be able to appreciate his challenges.

Most of *The Last Skeptic* concerns gravity. In the chapter "Gravity Doesn't Suck" René demonstrates that Newton's theory of gravity is impossible. In order for the Moon to orbit the earth and not get drawn to the Sun, the earth's gravitational pull must be stronger than the Sun's. However, René uses a basic formula to calculate relative force, showing the Sun's pull is over twice as powerful. "My 'Unproof' has knocked the cornerstone from under Newton's celestial mechanics, Einstein's relativity, Hubble's expanding universe and the Big Bang. They will also have to throw away black holes, quasars, giant explo-lapsing stars, neutron stars, super strings and hundreds of other useless theories."

René also takes on nuclear power, subatomic particles, light, the earth's composition, the Ice Age, magnetism, the earth's rotation, and the general close-mindedness of scientists and other geniuses who are wedded to certain theories. Although the book gets fairly technical, it is suffused with a conversational writing style and a sense of humour.

R. René; $21
1990, 1995; oversized softcover; 182 pp
heavily illus; no ISBN

MAPS OF THE ANCIENT SEA KINGS
Evidence of Advanced Civilization in the Ice Age
by Charles A. Hapgood

Charles Hapgood believes that the existence of certain old maps points the way to many heretical conclusions: 1) Before historical records began — perhaps as early as the Ice Age — there were civilisations whose inhabitants explored the globe; 2) these seafarers had advanced navigational instruments; 3) they also possessed knowledge of latitude and longitude, and "the spherical trigonometry of map projections"; and 4) they visited the coast of Antarctica when it had no ice.

The evidence for this, needless to say, is not airtight. However, Hapgood presents the case that although the original maps made by these ancient people have been lost or destroyed, copies of them that were made in the Middle Ages, the Renaissance, and later still survive. He looks in detail at several amazingly accurate maps, including the Piri Re'is map of the Americas from 1513, the Oronteus Finaeus world map of 1531, the Hadji Ahmed world map of 1559, Mercator's map of the Antarctic from 1569, and a stone map of China carved in 1137.

Other portions of the book specifically examine the scientific implications of the maps, the nature of the civilisation(s) that spawned the original maps, geographical tables, a large bibliography, and more.

Adventures Unlimited; $19.95
1966; 1996; oversized softcover; 320 pp
heavily illus; 0-932813-42-9

THE NEW INQUISITION
by Robert Anton Wilson

Robert Anton Wilson — reality hacker and guerrilla ontologist — launches a devastating attack against what he calls "fundamentalist materialism". His argument is that very often science is nothing more than a religion, and anyone who dares to question the scientific orthodoxy is branded as a heretic. Scientists will cling jealously to their particular beliefs and dismiss anyone out of hand who questions them. Wilson shows this intolerance in action. "I shall exhibit learned men behaving with the bigotry of Mississippi lynch mobs, distinguished scholars conspiring to suppress dissident opinions, savants acting like circus clowns or hooligans."

Wilson effortlessly explains the frailty of knowledge and the uncertainty of "truth". (It may take a little effort to understand him, though.) We can never really know anything for certain. But we assume that we can all the time. "Even 'the' is a metaphor — it assumes the world is divided the same way our minds divide it — and seems to have been a very hypnotic metaphor indeed. In terms of human tragedy and suffering, think of what has been provoked by generalisations about 'the Jews' and 'the blacks.' More subtly, remember that 'the length of the rod' seemed to be a perfectly meaningful and objective phrase until Einstein demonstrated that a rod has various lengths — length^1, length^2, etc. — depending on its velocity and the velocity of the galoot who is trying to measure it."

Wilson also mercilessly drubs the Center for Scientific Investigation of Claims of the Paranormal (CSICOP), James Randi, Martin Gardner, and other "New Fundamentalists". "Mr. Gardner has an infallible method of recognising real science and of recognising pseudo-science. Real science is what agrees with his Idol and pseudo-science is what challenges that Idol. Colin Wilson has written, 'I wish I could be as sure of anything as Martin Gardner is of everything.'" Wilson defends the ideas of Wilhelm Reich, Rupert Sheldrake, Nikola Tesla, ufologists, and other heretics. This is not to say that he defends them as being right... rather, he defends them against being summarily dismissed as absolutely wrong. Wilson has as little patience with "true believers" as he does with dogmatic naysayers.

Besides giving the unexplained some credibility, *The New Inquisition* will blast open your reality-tunnel by helping you learn how to question everything you think you know. Read it and you'll look at everything around you in a new way.

New Falcon Publications; $14.95
1987; softcover; 243 pp
1-56184-002-5

PYRAMIDS OF MONTAUK
Explorations in Consciousness
by Preston B. Nichols & Peter Moon

Pyramids of Montauk is the third book of a trilogy [see *The Montauk Project* and *Montauk Revisited*, *Outposts* p 188] that explores the research that supposedly took place at the Air Force base in Montauk Point, New York. The Montauk Project, as it's called, began in 1933 when the military was trying to make the *USS Eldridge* invisible to radar. Somehow, they made the ship invisible and teleported it (this event is referred to as the Philadelphia Experiment). At the Montauk Base, research continued into ways to warp the space-time continuum and control people's minds.

In this book the authors reveal that there are small, ancient pyramids in the Montauk area. Montauk is a powerful energy point that is somehow "connected" to Egypt, Atlantis, and Mars. It occupies an important spot on the energy grid that covers the earth and, as such, is an interdimensional gateway. As it turns out, Montauk has been considered an important place by many secret societies and mystery sects. To the Montauk Native Americans it was sacred land, but early this century it was stolen from them by the courts. The experiments that have been performed there for the purposes of war are considered crimes against the human race and "crimes against the grid".

The authors fully explore the history of Montauk, its mystical significance, and the power that exists there. It's a long, winding journey that includes the Sumerians, Kali, Napoleon, Aleister Crowley, the Nazis, Ian Fleming, and many other things. But the story doesn't end with the official closure of the base. The authors share evidence — including underground tunnels, a particle accelerator, and radiowave transmissions — that indicates that Montauk is still in operation.

Sky Books; $19.95
1995; softcover; 256 pp
illus; 0-9631889-2-5

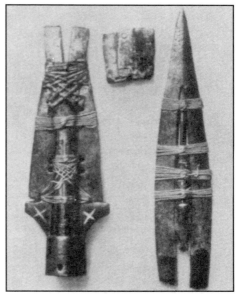

This is allegedly the spear that pierced Jesus' side. *The Spear of Destiny.*

SCIENCE FRONTIERS
Some Anomalies and Curiosities of Nature
compiled by William R. Corliss

The Sourcebook Project is an incomprehensibly titanic effort by William Corliss to catalogue thirty volumes' worth of scientific anomalies — phenomena that cannot be explained adequately or at all by the current "laws" of science. Since 1976, the Project has also published a newsletter of short entries documenting anomalies from the world's scientific literature. *Science Frontiers* collects all 86 issues, organises the contents by subject field, and indexes the whole thing. These 1500+ entries from 1663 sources (accompanied by 417 illustrations) cover the fields of archaeology, astronomy, biology, geology, geophysics, psychology, chemistry, physics, math, and esoterica.

This is the kind of book that I could get lost in for days, but I'll try to pick out just a few shining examples. A British neurologist tells of many people who have virtually no cerebral cortex yet have no mental impairment. In fact, a student at Sheffield University has an IQ of 126 and has won honours in maths despite the fact that his cortex is a millimetre thick, instead of the usual 4.5 centimetres. "Although the deeper brain structures may carry on much of the body's work, the cortex is supposed to be a late evolutionary development that gave humans their vaunted mental powers and superiority over the other animals. If the cortex can be removed with little mental impairment, what is it for in the first place?"

Mysterious, extremely loud booms have been heard off the Eastern coast of the US for decades. Several government-sponsored investigations have failed to draw conclusions. "A recent example occurred on June 24, 1981, when the coastline of North Carolina, South Carolina and Georgia was hit by a house-shaking boom. No supersonic jets were in the area, seismographs recorded no earthquakes, and no man-made explosions had occurred, according to a careful check."

Since 1905, birds have been attracted to a one-kilometre stretch in the small Indian village of Jatinga. They arrive at night and become immobile after landing. They refuse to eat — starving themselves to death — and will not move even to avoid capture. This phenomenon "peaks in September and October, as the monsoon season wanes, with as many as 500 birds, from some 36 species, dying each night."

Besides having great entertainment value, *Science Frontiers* will expand your ideas about reality like almost no other book. Read it and be amazed at how much we don't know.

The Sourcebook Project; $18.95
1994; oversized softcover; 350 pp
heavily illus; 0-915554-28-3

SECRETS OF COLD WAR TECHNOLOGY
Project HAARP and Beyond
by Gerry Vassilatos

Filmed in 1922, <u>Nosferatu</u> is still one of the creepiest vampire movies of all time. *The Vampire Book.*

Based on patents and research papers, this book — unfortunately written in turgid prose — describes the hidden history of communications and weapons technology that utilise aural energy, electromagnetic pulses, extremely low frequencies (ELF), ray beams, Tesla's ideas, X-rays, gamma rays, and similar phenomena. It offers a deep examination of HAARP technology, claiming that it is not a weapon, weather modifier, or mind control system.

Borderland Sciences; $15.95
1996; softcover; 324 pp
illus; 0-945685-20-3

THE SPEAR OF DESTINY
The Occult Power Behind the Spear
Which Pierced the Side of Christ
by Trevor Ravenscroft

Here we have a recounting of the intriguing legend of the spear that pierced the side of Jesus. When Jesus was on the cross, he was about to be horribly beaten by Romans who were under orders to break his bones (this was done to foil the prophecy that the Messiah shall have no broken bones). Not wanting to see anyone tortured so cruelly, a Roman soldier at the scene slid his spear in between the fourth and fifth ribs on the right side of Jesus' chest. At that moment, the spear was allegedly infused with incredible powers. Trevor Ravenscroft tells what has become of this holy relic (in which he apparently believes).

The spear was owned by a succession of conquerors and leaders. It went through the hands of Mauritius, Constantine the Great, Theodosius, Alaric the Bold, Aetius, Theodoric (who used it to turn back Attila the Hun), Justinian, Frankish General Karl Martel, Charlemagne, Otto the Great, Frederick Barbarossa, and dozens of others. Eventually Hitler located the spear, and most of the book focuses on his use of it.

A museum in Austria housed the spear, and this was Hitler's main motive for taking over that country. Upon travelling to Vienna, he went to the museum and claimed the spear as his own. It was then that he dropped all pretence

and went full steam ahead with the Holocaust and his plans to conquer the world. "It was admitted at the Nuremberg Trials that the decision to go ahead with the plans for the 'final solution' dated from the night of Hitler's triumphant entry into Vienna."

When Leningrad fell, and the future of the Nazis was uncertain, Hitler ordered the spear moved to a permanent hiding place. The SS decided that the best place would be in the tunnels 900 feet under the Nuremberg Fortress. Nuremberg got pounded by an air raid that destroyed the Fortress, exposing the secret entrance to the tunnel. It was quickly camouflaged, but in April 1945 Nuremberg was taken by the Allies. Soldiers discovered the tunnel and the heavily fortified vault that contained the spear. On the last day of April, the US became the next possessor of the spear that pierced Christ. Months later, nuclear bombs were dropped on Japan. In 1946 the spear was returned to the Viennese museum where Hitler first saw it, and that is where it remains.

Samuel Weiser; $12.95
1973; softcover; 384 pp
illus; 0-87728-547-0

THE VAMPIRE BOOK
The Encyclopedia of the Undead
by J. Gordon Melton

J. Gordon Melton is best known for his towering, even-handed three-volume survey of American religions, so I was surprised to see he had written a book on vampires. Luckily, he brought the same depth and definitiveness to this book as he has to his others. *The Vampire Book* is truly monumental. Over 800 pages cover every aspect of haemoglobin addicts you could name — history, folklore, literature, movies, music, comics, and real vampires. Each of the 375 detailed entries are referenced, and the longer entries are actually essays that could stand on their own.

One such entry is "Music, Vampire". "More than one hundred vampire songs have appeared in contemporary music in the last decade, ranging from the superlative to the execrable." The nine-page essay looks at song with obvious vampire lyrics, songs with oblique vampire lyrics, songs that are allegedly vampiric, songs that mention vampires, and songs on soundtracks to vampire movies. Musicians that have recorded songs in the first category include Siouxie and the Banshees, Concrete Blonde, Bauhaus, Alice Cooper, Grim Reaper, and others.

The incredibly creepy movie *Nosferatu* was made in 1922 without permission of Bram Stoker's estate. Stoker's widow sued the movie studio and won, destroying all their copies of this now-classic piece of cinema. Luckily, at least one complete copy of the movie survived and was released in 1984.

Despite the fact that Dracula's best-known physical feature is his fangs, according to the entry "Fangs", the vamps portrayed by Bela Lugosi, Lon Chaney Jr., John Carradine, and Max Schreck (from *Nosferatu*) didn't sport sharp canines.

The entry "Crime, Vampiric" contains some fascinating anecdotes. In 1960 a man in Argentina "was arrested after more than 15 women said someone had entered their bedroom, bit them, and drank their blood." In 1987, "A jogger in San Francisco Park was kidnapped and held for an hour in a van while a man drank his blood."

Other entries include: "African American Vampires", "Bats, Vampire", "Christianity and Vampires", "Elrod, P.N.", "Hammer Films", "Humour, Vampire", "Ireland, Vampires in", "*Journal of Vampirology*", "Kali", "Psychological Perspectives on Vampire Mythology", "Rice, Anne", "Vampira", and "Werewolves and Vampires".

The back of the book has a resource section that includes addresses for — are you ready? — eight zines and eighteen fan clubs solely devoted to the TV show *Dark Shadows*. An unbelievable annotated vampire filmography goes on for 54 pages and includes such gems as *I Bought a Vampire Motorcycle*, *Robo Vampire*, and *Rockula*. Melton also lists 23 pages of vamp novels and seven pages of vampire dramas.

Suffice it to say that this is *the* reference book on vampires. It makes all the others look anaemic. And it's got a low price tag.

Visible Ink; $16.95
1994; softcover; 852 pp
illus; 0-8103-2295-1

WHAT REALLY CAUSED THE DINOSAURS' DEMISE?
A Question of Increasing Gravity
by John West

Dinosaurs ruled the earth for approximately 140 million years, and then, in the relative blink of an eye, they were wiped out. The cause of the great lizards' demise is a hotly debated subject. The three most common theories are that a meteor slammed into the earth and changed the climate radically, the climate changed for another reason, and an exploding star cooked the dinosaurs with radiation.

John West has a different theory. Dinosaurs can't exist in today's world because our 1g gravity field would make it physically impossible. In the larger dinosaurs especially, there is no way blood could get to the brain. Also, when they bend over to take a drink, the vessels in their head would burst. "It is also apparent that the flying reptiles, some with estimated wingspans of over ten feet, would not have been anatomically equipped for flight in a 1g gravity field." According to some palaeontologists, the gravity field would have had to be 0.27g to 0.33g for the dinos to function comfortably.

Shifting land masses and oceans and the partial melting of the North Pole have caused polar shifts and changes in the earth's magnetic and gravity fields many times in the past. Approximately 240 million years ago, such events paved the way for the rise of the dinosaurs. Then when these major events happened again 65 million years ago, the dinosaurs couldn't handle the increased gravity and rapidly died.

After West relates these ideas, the book takes a rapid and unexpected turn. The author refutes Darwin's theory of evolution using fossils and research from the *Bible-Science Newsletter*, among other Christian sources. "The fact that dinosaurs and early humankind existed contemporaneously, and that advanced plants, trees, etc., also existed at the same time, leaves no doubt that mankind is indeed a creature of Creationism."

Things get even more unpredictable from there. West starts discussing free energy, anti-gravity technology, Wilhelm Reich's orgone energy, AIDS, Lyndon LaRouche's government drug-running theories, the international banking conspiracy, the suppressed truth about the Moon, extraterrestrials, crop circles, and other such topics, many of which don't have much to do with gravity and dinosaurs.

Veritas Press; $24.95 (Australian)
1996; spiral-bound oversize softcover; 151 pp
illus; no ISBN

COMIX CARTOONZ & OTHER GRAPHIX

ACTION GIRL COMICS

edited by Sarah Dyer

From the creator of the zine *Action Girl Newsletter* comes this anthology series of all-ages comix by female artists. Like most collections, the styles and subject vary widely, as does the quality. In the premier issue, the best bits involve "'A' Girl" lazily floating downstream, a crow hanging around a corpse, a young woman who takes a dip in a reservoir, a former punk rocker who's burdened with a baby, and the Action Girl series of paper dolls. In the other issues I have here before me, some of the good stuff includes Patty Leidy's look at her continuing infatuation with Godzilla, a folktale from the Bahamas about a man whose wife is secretly an egret, and a fishhead woman who is given mind control pills that turn her into a Nazi [issue 5]; "How I Became Beautiful", Jen Sorenson's surprisingly non-angry tales of being a grocery store cashier, and Melissa MacAlpin's multimedia story about buying some of her deceased neighbour's belongings [issue 11]; and the adventures of Action Girl and Ultra Girl, which take up almost all of the twelfth issue.

Slave Labor Graphics; $2.75 each
1994-1997; comic book format; 24 pp each
heavily illus
WWW: www.houseoffun.com/action/index.htm

THE ADVENTURES OF MENG AND ECKER

by David Britton, Kris Guidio, Michael Butterworth

At last, a giant oversized collection of the best material from the world's most invective, deliberately offensive comic book, *Meng & Ecker*. In case you're not familiar with this series, please read the reviews of *Meng & Ecker* and its companion series, *Hardcore Horror: David Britton's Lord Horror*, below. These comics are based on the universe originally created by David Britton in his confrontational novel, *Lord Horror* [reviewed in the Fiction chapter], in which the British Lord Horror (based *extremely* loosely on the real-life Lord Haw Haw) and his henchmen, Meng and Ecker, search the world for Hitler, who survived World War II. In the comic series based on them, Meng and Ecker take on a life of their own. In each issue, Britton writes, Kris Guidio painstakingly draws, and Michael Butterworth edits a series of misanthropic, amoral, vulgar, nihilistic adventures where more sacred cows are slaughtered than at McDonalds' processing plants in India.

No other comic is so good at being so bad. As one of the characters comments about Meng and Ecker: "Even 'bad taste' wouldn't stay in the same room as these fuckers." In someone else's hands, *M&E* could turn into a pitiful, tail-spinning exercise in hateful masturbation. But the writing is so excellent, the artwork so untouchable, the production values so high, and the dark humour so perfectly pitched that it becomes a crowning achievement of transgressive art.

On these 256 large pages you will find many of the dynamic duo's greatest hits — including pieces from the first three issues, which have been banned and burned in Britain — plus 60% new material. Among the joys you'll discover: M&E try to resurrect L. Ron Hubbard with some of his stored sperm, Meng hops into bed with Prince Charles and Princess Diana, the boys sell pastries laced with HIV, Meng gives birth to twins and Ecker shoots them, the terrible twosome dine at the Planet Auschwitz restaurant, Ecker turns into a giant piece of shit and gets a job as a bobby, Meng runs a seminar on improving your rape technique (hey, didn't I warn you that this stuff was extreme?), and lots and lots of people are fucked and/or killed. Along the way, many historical figures, religious figures, modern celebrities, cartoon characters, Lord Horror himself, and Chief Constable James Anderton make appearances. Textually, noted science fiction author Brian Stableford explains the family of books and comix revolving around Lord Horror, Carolyn Horn contributes a short story about M&E, and a reprinted article from *GQ* gives a brief history of Savoy, the publishers of Lord Horror/Meng & Ecker material.

The drawback of this collection is that three of the best scenes in the series — which show Meng screwing Margaret Thatcher's corpse, coming on Garfield, and holding Constable Anderton's severed head — are not included. Because of these unfortunate omissions, you'll have to buy at least some individual issues of *Meng & Ecker* to revel in their full glory, but this collection is perfect for those who want to experience the world's most outrageous comic book without spending $45 for the compete series (which is impossible to get anyway, since issue 1 is out of print). Of course, for Lord Horror completists, this is a must.

Savoy; $20.95; £9.99
1997; oversized softcover; 256 pp
heavily illus; 0-86130-099-8

ALL I EVER NEEDED TO KNOW I LEARNED FROM MY GOLF-PLAYING CATS
A Collection of
Tom the Dancing Bug Comic Strips
by Ruben Bolling

Actually, this anthology of the weekly comic strip *Tom the Dancing Bug* has nothing to do with golf, cats, or learning all you ever needed to know. The title is a parody of all the copycat books on those three topics that continually sell in the jillions, while works of real merit are ignored.

As far as I can tell, the title *Tom the Dancing Bug* is a misnomer too, since I can find no traces of an insect cutting a rug. So what the heck *is* all this about? Well, anything and everything as long as it's treated humorously. *Tom* traffics in social, political, and cultural satire, but it also examines trick-or-treating, relationships, and childhood fears. In one strip entitled "Endangered Species and Their Press Agents", Barb Pecota — the PR agent for manatees — says, "So I said, 'I see the cover of *Time*! I see the Discover Channel! But **come on! Move** a little! Jump through hoops! **Pep up**, for God's sake!'"

In other instalments you'll find a translated conversation between two twentysomethings that consists of almost nothing but the word "dude" said different ways, a look at American attitudes towards Canada ("DID YOU KNOW?: Canada actually has its own government?"), a parody of *Forrest Gump* featuring a human-like primate, a news conference where aliens announce the real reason they're here: "to introduce you to an exciting new delicious snack food — Meatloaf-On-A-Stick™!", a conference in which gays and lesbians secretly continue to implement the dreaded "homosexual agenda", the unexpected results of decriminalising murder, and the Disneyfication of several heavy books, including Kafka's *The Trial* and Marx's *Das Kapital*.

> NBM; $7.95
> 1997; softcover; 80 pp
> heavily illus; 1-56163-183-3

AS NAUGHTY AS SHE WANTS TO BE!
by Roberta Gregory

Bitchy Bitch is a permanently PMSed, oestrogen-filled terror who hates men but wants to fuck them anyway. Think of a hetero Hothead Paisan and you're on the right track. Drawn in a manic doodle style with frizzy hair, sagging breasts, and a pissed-off expression, Bitchy stalked the pages of Roberta Gregory's *Naughty Bits* comic. Now, the raunchiest of those escapades have been brought under one cover.

In "Bitchy Bitch Gets Laid" our protagonist gets ripped off at an overpriced Yuppie supermarket and decides to unwind with a cucumber. Afterwards she answers a personal ad. Lo and behold, she ends up with a toad. One thing leads to another, which results in decidedly unexciting sex — he's got bad breath, he doesn't have any condoms, he pressures her to go down on him but doesn't return the favour, and he falls asleep right after coming. While walking home, she grouses: "Guess I know why all the other women in this country are obsessed with food. Shit… I shoulda killed the li'l bas-

Panels from Wet and Wobbly Prostrate Potatoes, *B.A.C.*

tard…" In her other adventures, BB tries going to church, turns 40, and discovers that her date from hell is now working at her company.

The second part of the book has four non-Bitchy stories from early issues of *Naughty Bits*. "Crazy Bitches" is a female revenge fantasy that makes Thelma and Louise look like domestic goddesses by comparison. A gang of five women tie up a man, shove a cucumber up his ass, take turns riding him, bite his dick off, shove it in his mouth, and then shit on his face.

As a bonus, you get "War of the Muses", which marks Bitchy's first appearance. She's only in a few panels at the beginning of the story, but she definitely makes her mark. As she walks along fuming at the world, a little girl says to her, "Oh, things can't be all that bad. Remember…God loves you." Bitchy knocks her down and starts stomping her. She says, "Now I feel better! Or I did… Now I feel just as bad again and now worse because I just broke my heel on that little girl's face!"

> Fantagraphics Books; $9.95
> 1995; oversized softcover; 87 pp
> heavily illus; 156097-182-7

B.A.C.
Bad Art Collection
by Jhonen V.

For rapid-fire absurdity and non sequiturs galore, all bathed in pitch black humour, you simply can't beat Jhonen Vasquez's *Bad Art Collection*. Each self-contained, single-page comic contains 24 small square panels filled with strange violence, scatology, and antisocial sentiments drawn in the purposely cheesy style of the "Happy Noodle Boy" segments from Vasquez's comic *Johnny the Homicidal Maniac* [see the Comix chapter]. Strips include "Umbilical Death Noogies", "Licking the Rancid Corpse Thingies", "Wet and Wobbly Prostate Potatoes", "Bean Infested Fecal Sausage", and "Nailing the Crotch of the Token Fat Boy". Highly recommended.

> Slave Labor Graphics; $1.95
> 1996; oversized comic book format; 16 pp

BAKER STREET
Children of the Night
by Guy Davis & Gary Reed

The *Baker Street* series of comix takes place in an "alternate" London. World War II never happened, and the Victorian Era has carried over into the present. Baker Street — made famous by Sherlock Holmes — is the centre of England's radical youth movement, meaning that this comic is inhabited by an odd hybrid — Victorian punks.

Children of the Night collects five issues of *Baker Street*. The main character is Sue, an American who has come to study medicine at Wisteria University. She earns her keep by being the live-in maid of two punks who own a bookstore — Samantha, a man who crossdresses, and Sharon, an ex-inspector for Scotland Yard who now solves crimes independently (*à la* Sherlock). The plot revolves around a series of Ripper-like murders. Somebody's been slashing rapists but has moved on to killing men who haven't been accused of rape. The police suspect a gang of female punks known as the Inquisition, but Sharon is sure it's not them. Meanwhile, a female punk gets snuffed in an apparently unrelated murder. Again, the cops have a suspect, but Sharon knows it was someone else.

The plot is suspenseful, and the characters are fully fleshed out and believable. Although both mysteries are solved by the end, the murderers never answer for their crimes. It's a dark ending to a dark story.

Caliber Press; $14.95
1993; oversized softcover; 171 pp
heavily illus; 0-941613-43-7

BAKER STREET
Honour Among Punks
by Guy Davis & Gary Reed

Honour Among Punks is the first collection of the *Baker Street* comix. It starts out drawn in a less gritty, more "comic bookish" style than its successor [above], but by the fourth issue it's achieved the *noir* look. The story revolves around two mysteries that seem unrelated in the beginning. First, after years of relatively peaceful coexistence, the punk gangs of Baker Street are at each other's throats, and bodies are turning up everywhere. Second, someone's been stealing art from museums and passing off forged versions of the missing pieces. Sharon — the punk Sherlock Holmes — is on both cases, and she finds out that they may be closely related.

An end section contains two smaller stories about Sue's stay in the hospital during Christmas and Sue, Sharon, and Samantha's run-in with (apparently) the real Sherlock Holmes.

Caliber Press; $14.95
1993; oversized softcover; 191 pp
heavily illus; 0-941613-42-9

THE BIG BOOK OF WEIRDOS
by Carl Posey and 65 artists

In this collection, 65 comic artists each do a two- to five-page biography of a "weirdo". These are the crackpots, visionaries, eccentrics, crazed geniuses, and madmen who have livened up history. Many of them are famous — Ivan the Terrible, Lawrence of Arabia, Rasputin, Edgar Allan Poe, Ambrose Bierce, Harry Houdini, Salvador Dalí, Henry Ford, Howard Hughes, and J. Edgar Hoover. Others — such as Wilhelm Reich, Nikola Tesla, and William Burroughs — are well-known primarily in unorthodox circles.

From the neurotic who invented autobiographical comix. *Binky Brown Sampler.*

Feliks Dobrin — the artist of the first comic published in the Ukraine — tells the story of Edward Leedskalnin. In the 1920s and 1930s, Leedskalnin built a castle out of sea coral without any assistance. Claiming to know how the pyramids were built, he somehow moved three-ton slabs by himself. This bizarre structure, which he says he built for a mysterious woman who may have been imaginary, still stands in Homestead, Florida.

Rick Parker — who does the *Beavis and Butthead* comic for Marvel — handles the case of Walter Freeman, the doctor who "perfected" the lobotomy. Freeman developed his own tool for severing the nerves of the frontal lobe — a long, thin, gold-plated pick that he carried in a special velvet case. Giving the patient only a local anaesthetic, he would insert the scraper through an eye socket and into the brain, where he would haphazardly scrape with gusto. "Each lobotomy cost about $1000 — although Freeman sometimes did assembly-line lobotomies — for $25 bucks a head!" He ended up performing over 3500 such operations before one of his patients beat him to death in his office.

Paradox Press; $12.95
1995; oversized softcover; 223 pp
heavily illus; 1-56389-180-8

BINKY BROWN SAMPLER
by Justin Green

Justin Green invented autobiographical comix in the late 1960s. Robert Crumb and Art Spiegelman credit this not very well-known neurotic with starting them down the same path, which is now well-worn by the likes of Chester Brown, Mary Fleener, et al. Green's pen and ink alter-ego is Binky Brown, an obsessed, self-torturing guy who was raised Catholic.

The 1972 classic "Binky Brown meets the Virgin Mary", reproduced in uncut form, is an epic telling of Bink's life. It opens with him playing ball in the house and accidentally

The Statue of Liberty is now just an ugly woman attacked by the plague.

Hurrah death and destruction!!

WWII ends a little differently in Planet of the Jap by Suehiro Maruo. *Comics Underground Japan.*

destroying a statue of the Virgin Mary. Binky talks to grass, entertains his sisters with his penis, and has his first orgasm. He recounts his Catholic school daze, including being kissed by a former nun, living in fear of the "fascistic penguins", and wondering if his Jewish uncle was going to rot in eternal damnation. He's suddenly transferred to a public school that's 90% Jewish, and he doesn't fit in at all. "Jewish kids were smart! Instead of mouthing back dogmatic bullshit to a teacher, they could think and ask thought-provoking questions."

As the increasingly compulsive Binky enters adolescence, a light ray emanates from his crotch at certain times. If this light ray hits a church or any holy object, it is a horrendous sin. Binky starts thinking more and more sexual thoughts, which leads to non-stop, snowballing guilt. Eventually his fevered thoughts reach critical mass and he realises it's time for a showdown with Our Blessed Virgin for control of his own life.

Other shorter works in this collection look at Binky's decision to become a cartoonist, a one panel drawing of purgatory, the history of typography, and Binky's interest in his friend's mother. "Great Moments in Alcoholism" recounts how Green's dad told Frank Sinatra and his noisy entourage to shut up in a Las Vegas night-club in 1968. The book ends with some Binky rarities, a long essay by Green, and a few pages of colour comix.

Last Gasp; $16.95
1995; oversized softcover; 96 pp
heavily illus; 0-86719-332-8

THE BOOK OF MR. NATURAL
Profane Tales of That Old Mystic Madcap
by R. Crumb

Spanning thirty years, this collection contains twenty-six of Robert Crumb's stories starring the squat, bearded guru, Mr. Natural, and his neurotic foil, Flakey Foont.

Fantagraphics Books; $12.95
1995; oversized softcover; 126 pp
heavily illus; 1-56097-194-0

CAVE MAN
Evolution, Heck!
By Tayyar Ozkan

In these twenty-eight strips, comix artist Tayyar Ozkan (*World War III*, *Heavy Metal*, *Big Book of…* series, *Bushwhacked*, etc.) silently demonstrates just how little the human race has changed since the prehistoric days. Each one starts by examining the adventures of some Neanderthals, while the concluding panel jumps to a parallel situation in the modern world that brings the point home.

One of the most direct strips is the opener, which shows several Cro-Mags staring in wide-eyed wonder at lightning. Others are mesmerised by the fires that the lightning starts. Still another group is in awe over the Sun, and others are bowing in worship to the Moon and stars. Soon the four groups are arguing with each other over the power and worthiness of their various objects of worship. The disagreements turn nastier, and eventually the groups are clubbing and stabbing each other to death. The final panel switches to a desolate modern-day landscape littered with skulls, bones, and religious artefacts: a cross, Bible, menorah, Buddhist statue, totem pole, sword covered with Arabic characters, etc.

Another strip takes a swipe at the savagery of eating meat, while a related one asks why we slaughter and eat some animals but adopt others as pets. Another draws the obvious parallel between prehistoric and current men who beat their mates, terrorise their kids, and enjoy getting in fights. The inanity of war, torture, littering, and male/female relations are also highlighted through this unusual history lesson. In the end it becomes clear that we're still a bunch of violent, warlike, horny, hungry, primitive primates.

NBM; $9.95
1997; oversized softcover; 64 pp
heavily illus; 1-56163-175-2

THE CHERRY BOMB REVOLUTION
by Mike Diana

The Cherry Bomb Revolution is one of Mike Diana's post-arrest works (for the full story, see *The Worst of Boiled Angel*, below). It concerns Cherry the Clown, whose soft drink — Cherry Bomb Soda — has ten times the caffeine and sugar of regular sodas. Three teenagers are enjoying this refreshing drink when one of them keels over. After slitting his throat open with a dissection kit, his friends find that he choked to death on a razor-edged piece of metal with Cherry the Clown's face engraved on it. The two boys break into

Cherry's factory, where they are taken prisoner. One of them is sentenced to die, and the other is brainwashed into becoming a follower of Cherry, who wants to lead a master race made up entirely of clowns. Will the boys escape a horrible, violent death? Yeah, right.

This comic was printed in a limited edition of 666 signed and numbered copies. The cover is a six-colour silk-screen done by hand. Once this printing sells out, it will never be republished, so grab this rarity while you can.

Mike Hunt Publications; $10 postpaid

1995; oversize comic book format; 18 pp

heavily illus; no ISBN

Carl Jung on Acid.
Cruel World Graphicomix.

THE COLLECTED OMAHA
The Cat Dancer, Volume 3
by Reed Waller & Kate Worley

Contains issues 7 through 10 of *Omaha*, a comic about a nude dancer who happens to be an anthropomorphised cat. Although there are a few explicit sex scenes, the narrative is heavy on plot and characterisation. This volume also contains a previously unpublished sequence showing how Omaha became a stripper and met her best friend, Shelley.

Fantagraphics Books; $14.95

1995; oversized softcover; 136 pp

heavily illus; 1-56097-161-4

COMICS UNDERGROUND JAPAN
edited by Kevin Quigley

Comics Underground Japan is the book that followers of extreme manga have been waiting for. Kevin Quigley has gathered together work from thirteen Japanese practitioners of comic art and translated them into English for the first time. In his introduction he writes, "An enormously wide variety of manga is churned out every week in Japan, but no matter how unique it may seem to the foreign reader, the vast majority of what's published is right down the middle of the road." What distinguishes the selections in this anthology is that they are subversive, idiosyncratic, and often unapologetically strange.

The opener, "Hell's Angel" by Yoshikazu Ebisu, tells of a salaryman who is so exhausted from a day at work that he can barely walk home. After graphically warning him of what could happen if he fell into the busy street, a woman offers him a piggyback ride. She carries him, but he notices that they don't seem to be moving. Suddenly, she has turned into the skeleton of some sort of reptilian creature, while the man has begun to shake and sweat profusely. That's where it ends. More fathomable is Ebisu's "It's All Right If You Don't Understand", in which salarymen willingly submit themselves to violence and degradation — even to the point of death — at the hands of their bosses, while society unofficially condones this inhumane treatment.

In "Don Quixote #1", drawn in a sparse doodle style by Yasuji Tanioka, a talking cockroach taunts a prisoner awaiting execution. Hideshi Hino is in fine form with his dark tale of circus freaks and a clown named "Laughing Ball", who can do nothing but laugh. "Mercy Flesh (Jiniku)" is a really, *really* weird tale of a rich family that traps Buddhas and then

locks them in cages with a girl who waits on them. But even that isn't as outlandish as Muddy Wehara's "Bigger and Better", in which every panel is a two-page spread of epic strangeness. Two men in suits — the "Chief Director" and his lackey — ride a giant turtle and giant frog to their jobs working for the new President...a Martian whose office is in the mouth of a whale.

Many of the stories are drawn in a cute style of manga generally intended for children, a move that belies their bizarre storylines. In "Selfish Carol's Summer Vacation", a wide-eyed schoolgirl girl knifes her friend, apparently because the dead girl had B.O. "Cat Noodle Soup" is drawn in the innocuous style of Hello Kitty, but I don't think Kitty ever tangled with Death and had her soul stolen.

As far as artistic rendering and sweeping vision are concerned, "Planet of the Jap" by Suehiro Maruo is the book's standout. In this alternative history, Japan and the other Axis powers win World War II. The Japanese invade the American mainland, drop nuclear bombs on LA and San Francisco, publicly behead General MacArthur, and occupy America, while the troops engage in wanton murder and rape. Although on the surface this would appear to be a revenge fantasy, it's actually a savage jab at Japan's militarism.

Comics Underground Japan is highly recommended.

Blast Books; $14.95

1996; oversized softcover; 225 pp

heavily illus; 0-922233-16-0

CRUEL WORLD GRAPHICOMIX #1
by Jim Blanchard

A collection of sixteen sequential comix, single-panel illustrations, and conceptual pieces from Jim Blanchard. "A Trip to the Hardware Store" is drawn with thin lines and no grey shading or solid black inking. It has the sparse, empty feel of instructional diagrams that come with large items you have to put together yourself. Unfortunately, the storyline isn't nearly as interesting as the artistic style.

"The Tush-Hog" is drawn in a more orthodox style. In it Blanchard recounts the travails of an ugly but nice construction foreman he worked under. "Crimesexy" is a series of 30 mugshots drawn in a realistic style. Next to each person is a short quote indicating the nature of his or her crime: "...any john who wants to eat me is as good as dead...", and, "...you can't just say when a man is drunk and a woman is

Julie Doucet returns to leave her mark on the convent she attended as a teenager. *Dangerous Drawings.*

lying...that's first off..."

The most intriguing piece is "The Execution of Carl Jung". The typed text below the panels, written by George Petros, incorporates the actual words of Carl Jung as he is being interrogated about playing footsie with the Nazis. Just before his questioning begins, Jung takes a hit of LSD. As the interrogation proceeds, the space around Jung becomes saturated with geometric patterns and strange objects. Finally, the officer puts a bullet through Jung's skull, but he's so blissed out, he probably doesn't even notice the difference.

Beef Eye; $3.50
1993; oversized comic book; 40 pp
heavily illus; no ISBN

CRUMB-OLOGY
The Works of R. Crumb 1981-1994
by Carl Richter

Detailed information on 544 items from 1981-1994 containing the work of first-wave underground comix master Robert Crumb, including every appearance of his art in comic books, magazines, tabloids, anthologies, and other books (including non-English versions), plus cards, posters, CDs, calendars, written material, exhibitions, theatre, film, and material about Crumb. Bound in burnished leather with the title and a Crumb self-portrait stamped in gold foil on the cover.

Water Row Press; $39.95
1995; oversized hardcover; 82 pp
illus; 0-934953-24-4

DANGEROUS DRAWINGS
Interviews with Comix and Graphix Artists
edited by Andrea Juno

In *Dangerous Drawings*, former RE/Searcher Andrea Juno interviews fourteen artists who create subversion when their pen or pencil touches paper. The majority of interviewees write and draw comix: Art Spiegelman (*Maus*), Chris Ware (*ACME Novelty Library*), Julie Doucet (*Dirty Plotte*), Emiko Shimoda (various manga), Dan Clowes (*Eightball*), Chester Brown (*Yummy Fur, Underwater*), Phoebe Gloeckner (published in numerous comix), Aline Kominsky-Crumb (*Twisted Sisters*), Diane Noomin (*Twisted Sisters*), Keith Mayerson (*Horror Hospital Unplugged*), and Ted Rall (a syndicated strip of social/political commentary). A couple of the interviewees — GB Jones and Eli Langer — are strictly graphix artists who don't create comix, while many of the others, such as Shimoda, Gloeckner, and Reid, do both sequential and single images.

In keeping with Juno's interviewing style, these discussions cover the personal (childhoods, the autobiographical nature of the work, opinions on various topics) and the professional (themes, styles, inspirations behind particular pieces). Julie Doucet seems quite unguarded in her interview, letting a lot of self doubt show through. After Juno assures her that her current work is as powerful as her older work, Doucet says, "Well, that's good, I worry a lot about that. Sometimes I do think, 'Why would people want to read about all this?'" An interesting exchange takes place between Juno and Dan Clowes when she asks him whether his male characters reflect his attitude towards men:

> *Clowes:* I can't even comment on something like that... It's for somebody else to psychoanalyse me and —
> *Juno:* It's for me to —
> *Clowes:* — write me off as a pathetic, horrible loser.

Besides insights into the personalities behind the pictures, *Dangerous Drawings* often reveals the intended meanings behind works. GB Jones explains that she draws female versions of the Tom of Finland men because she "wanted to criticise an aspect of the gay male scene which sees cops and military men as sex objects." She continues: "It's time to fetishize the *revolutionary*, rather than the police person. I think authority figures have been fetishised enough. Society is fucked and we've got to destroy it! [laughs]".

Other artists talk about the reactions their work has triggered. Although her work is critically acclaimed and influential, Aline Kominsky-Crumb remarks, "I've had zero response to most of the work I've put out." Art Spiegelman reveals that his most controversial work wasn't the Holocaust tale *Maus* but his cover for the *New Yorker* that showed an anthropomorphised rabbit being crucified on an income tax return. "The *New Yorker* lost advertising. That cover really got me in trouble. The real offence of it was that I was a Jew commenting on Christians. Nail him to the cross one more time.

Children's books meet an artist with cutting-edge sensibilites.
The Day I Swapped My Dad For Two Goldfish.

I got much more hate mail for that than for anything else I ever did — pencil-scrawled 'we'll get you' letters."

The large pages of *Dangerous Drawings* are packed with artwork from the interviewees. Many of their most famous and important creations are reproduced, including Jones' *I Am a Fascist Pig* series, Doucet's strips on menstruation and becoming a man, the drawings that got Eli Langer busted on child porn and obscenity charges, pages from Chester Brown's early *Yummy Fur*, a drawing from *Pinocchio the Big Fag* by Mayerson, and Phoebe Gloeckner's medical illustration of fellatio. Plus, there are old and recent photos of the artists themselves, just in case you ever wondered what the people responsible for the drawings look like.

Juno Books; $24.95
1997; oversized softcover; 223 pp
heavily illus; 0-9651042-8-1

THE DAY I SWAPPED MY DAD FOR TWO GOLDFISH

by Neil Gaiman & Dave McKean

At last, children's books meet an artist with cutting-edge sensibilities. Neil Gaiman (of *The Sandman* fame) tells the story of a boy who trades his father for two goldfish. When his mother finds out, he and his little sister are forced to go to his friend's house to undo the trade. Trouble is, his friend has traded the father in question to another kid for a guitar. And so it goes....

Dave McKean — who has worked with Gaiman before (on *The Sandman* and *Death: The High Cost of Living*) and illustrated Stephen King's *Wizard and Glass: The Dark Tower, Volume 4* — retains the fairly simple lines of most children's book illustrations, although they are imprecise and very rough around the edges. They are washed through with heavily textured colours that look they were applied by first putting the paint on rough paper and then pressing it onto the illustrations. On some pages you can still see faint print from where a newspaper was used. The crude, hand-lettered font further enhances the messy, childlike feel of the whole pro-

duction.

In the end, the narrator gets his father back and swears that he will never trade him again, but he doesn't seem to have truly learned his lesson....

Borealis (White Wolf Publishing); $21.99
1997; oversized hardcover; 56 pp
heavily illus; 1-56504-944-6

DIXIE #2

This is the second instalment of the adventures of Dixie (Dicksee) Do Mae, the free-spirited Southern belle whose favourite movie is *Shaft*, favourite band is King Missile, and favourite architecture is "anything involving Ionic columns". In one adventure, Dicksee and all her friends have a great time drinkin', screwin', and downin' mushrooms at their favourite hangout, Beer Hut. In another episode, Oolah takes swanky Brad back to her trailer, dresses him in a French maid outfit, and makes him do chores before servicing her. In "Dixie Challenge #1: See Who Can Get Dicksee the Stonedest", we see the Bible Belt bimbo puffing five joints with Twila Mae, getting shotgunned by Jimmy, and smoking Sparky's "Kevorkian bong". The best part of the comic is the episode concerning Dixie's search for the "detachable penis" of King Missile's lead singer.

Lisa Brosig; $4
1995; comic book format; 32 pp
heavily illus; no ISBN

DREAMLAND JAPAN
Writings on Modern Manga

by Frederik L. Schodt

Frederik Schodt's previous book, *Manga! Manga!* [*Outposts* p 198], has become the definitive work on the Japanese comic form. *Dreamland Japan* updates and expands his original 1983 study, making it an equally essential purchase for the manga fan. In this book, he doesn't discuss the history of the medium (which has been thoroughly covered in his first book) but instead looks at issues, themes, artists, and publications that have appeared in the last 13 years.

After examining the general characteristics of manga and what the medium has to offer, Schodt looks at manga conventions and fans, the debate over what to call Japanese comix, the future of manga, the misleading (to Western eyes) representation of Japanese physical characteristics, and some contentious issues that have cropped up: pornography, violence, and racism.

Another chapter looks at the magazines that crank out manga for the masses, including *June*, which features stories about gay men created by and for women, and *Weekly Boys' Jump*, one of the world's best-selling weekly magazines (it has a circulation of five to six million copies. For comparison, *Time* has a circulation of around four million). Next, Schodt examines eleven manga artists — including traditionalist Hinako Sugiura and controversialist Suehiro Maruo — and a dozen specific works — *Emperor of the Land of the Rising Sun*, *Criminal Defense Stories*, *Banana Fish*, and *Doraemon (The Robot Cat)*. There's also a section devoted to manga put out by the now infamous Aum sect, ac-

The bizarre world of *Frank* (left).

cused of nerve-gassing Tokyo's subways. A separate chapter explores the legacy of the late Osamu Tekuza, a revered figure often referred to as "the God of Comics".

"Beyond Manga" examines the influence manga has had on anime (Japanese animation), the intersection of manga and novels, digital manga, and more. Finally, Schodt takes a look at manga in the English-speaking world, including American-created manga and Japanese manga being translated into English. Reference material at the end of the book covers publishers of Japanese comix in English, magazines that often feature translated manga, and a huge bibliography.

Like its predecessor, *Dreamland Japan* contains hundreds of illustrations (including an 8-page colour insert), ranging from the cartoony to the realistic, kiddie fare to sexy stuff, true romance to Zen mysticism.

Stone Bridge Press; $16.95
1996; softcover; 360 pp
heavily illus; 1-880656-23-X

EYE OF THE BEHOLDER
by Peter Kruper

"Eye of the Beholder" by comic artist Peter Kruper, who also did *Give It Up!* [below], made history when it became the first strip to appear regularly in the *New York Times*. It was then syndicated to alternative papers across the US, and now we have this collection of 44 instalments. Each wordless, black and white strip consists of two parts. First, there are four panels on the right-hand page. Turn the page and you see the fifth and final panel, which "explains" the preceding panels. This last image is what gives "Eye" its flair. Sometimes the first panels are four images seen through somebody's (or something's) eyes. It's up to you to guess who's doing the looking before you turn the page. In one strip, we see a busy city full of tall buildings, loud noises, and choking fumes. With each panel the city slowly fades away. Turn the page, and we see a woman peacefully meditating. In some cases, the viewer is an inanimate object, such as the ATM bank machine that sees a man nervously checking over his shoulders and a woman screaming in surprise.

Other segments tell a story with a twist at the end. Panel one: Cigar-chomping store owner watches as a truck delivers a large box containing merchandise. Panel two: Owner convinces a nicely-dressed couple that they need his product. Panel three: Couple takes stereo out of the box in their nice apartment. Panel four: Empty box is on sidewalk in front of building waiting to be picked up with the rest of the garbage. Panel five: A homeless man is sleeping inside the box in an alley.

NBM; $8.95
1996; softcover; 94 pp
heavily illus; 1-56163-159-0

FOREIGN EXCHANGE
by George Dardess

Foreign Exchange is a full-fledged novel told in comic format. With delicate drawings that border on whimsical, George Dardess tells the story of Alvin, a student at a multiracial high school. Alvin's extremely religious mother and Vietnam vet father decide to host an exchange student named Rudi. When Alvin and the other kids see him, they realise he's a dog with a huge nose and fringy mane of hair. The school's janitor also realises that Rudi is canine, but all the authority figures — parents, teachers, etc. — think he's a boy.

The students decide to play along by acting as if Rudi is human, and he slowly becomes more humanised and more popular. Alvin never liked Rudi, and his negative feelings only grow as Rudi becomes a big man on campus. While playing baseball, Alvin beans Rudi, sending him into a coma. By the time he comes out of it, he's a human being. Eventually, Rudi is faced with his past life as a dog. He must reconcile what he has been made into (human) with his true nature (a dog), but he isn't very successful.

Foreign Exchange is an enjoyable parable about the power other people's expectations have over us.

Austen Press; $12.95
1994; softcover; 141 pp
heavily illus; 0-9638052-9-0

FRANK
by Jim Woodring

Frank — the cute, buck-toothed, puffy-cheeked quasi-cat drawn by Frank Woodring — has developed a devoted following. Drawn without any dialogue, the *Frank* comix follow their namesake as he has weird adventures in a fantasy world that looks just enough like our own to give us a vague orientation but is bizarre enough to kill any hope of understanding what's going on. In that sense, Frank lives in a dream world, with an internal consistency and a set of logical rules...but we'll be damned if we can figure out what those rules are.

In "Frank's Faux Pa", a larger version of Frank — who we'll assume is Frank's father — pays him a visit and together they walk to a building made out of a giant gourd. Once inside, Frank's dad taps on a large urn with a stick, and an extraordinarily skinny humanoid with a face like a crescent moon pops out. Dad shakes its hand, winks at it, and points to Frank. After the moon-creature checks Frank's face, it brings out a device that looks like an elaborate set of eggbeaters. Frank cranks the device, causing his face to change shape. The moon-being gives him a toy gun that shoots suction-cup darts. Frank pops a quasi-mannequin in the face with a dart, and it tips over, revealing a message that reads, "And you call yourself a gentleman."

After Frank and his dad leave, a truly disturbing pig-man (who appears in several stories) enters the building and says something to the moon-creature. The creature jumps on the pig-man's back, beating him with two billy clubs as it rides him across fields, over a pyramid, and into a large orb-shaped building. On a raised floor is another giant urn being guarded by a sleeping beast with a hundred eyes. The moon-creature makes the pig-man bite the eye-creature's tail, causing the creature to chase the pig-man out of the building. He runs until he collapses from exhaustion. Frank and Frank Sr. see the sleeping pig-man, and Frank's face turns back to normal as a tear trickles down his cheek. Frank brings a pillow and blanket for the pig-man as Frank's dad expresses his frustration. The end. What the hell does all that mean, you ask? I ask the same thing.

In other episodes — several of which are printed in bright colour, the majority in black and white — Frank creates a dozen copies of himself, guts a giant moustached fish that never stops smiling, swallows a gigantic egg, goes to a party for the dead, gets a pet that looks like a cross between a small house and a loaf of bread, walks along the bottom of the sea, tangles with a bunch of living hammers, rides on a vehicle that looks like a ribcage mounted on a skateboard, and has several more run-ins with the pig-man.

Fantagraphics; $14.95
1996; oversized softcover; 96 pp
heavily illus; 1-56097-153-3

FRANK PHANTOM #1
For the Love of Björk
by Frank Phantom

The main story in this comic is an "elaborate valentine" to the musical alternachick Björk, "the most beautiful woman in the world". It is narrated by a deranged man named Mr. X, who we will assume represents the author. In the story, an old, ugly female mad scientist has a plan to make herself beautiful by stealing Björk's face and brain. Needless to say, this nefarious plot is foiled, and Mr. X concludes by singing a little ode to his unattainable Icelandic love.

"Black Punks Primer" talks about the difficulties facing a black person who becomes a punk; "She" is the darkly poetic story of a guy's encounter with his mysterious soul mate; and "Love Letters to Death" is a meditation on the power of women who are "99% sex incarnate".

Mike Hunt Publications; $4 postpaid
1994; comic book format; 32 pp
heavily illus; no ISBN

GIVE IT UP!
And Other Short Stories by
Franz Kafka
illustrated by Peter Kuper

Peter Kuper, cofounder of the radical poli-comic magazine *World War III*, illustrates nine of Franz Kafka's short stories in stark black and white. His simple, abstracted figures swim

Euro-alienation meets American alienation. *Give It Up!*

in inky darkness. Comics legend Jules Feiffer captures the essence of the book so perfectly in the intro, that I will yield the floor to him: "...Kafka's stoic Euro-alienation meets and merges with Kuper's thoroughly American rock and roll alienation. Our alienation is noisier, more raucous than theirs. Americans expect to be winners even as we lose, so we scream. Central Europeans expect to lose, so they shrug. In these pages, Kuper gives us the screaming shrug."

"A Little Fable" kicks off the anthology with an unnerving metaphor for life. The main character is a briefcase-carrying human/rat hybrid in a suit and tie. He moans that at first the world was so big that he was afraid. "I kept running and running, and I was glad when at last I saw walls far away to the right and left..." This Everymouse is content to enter a little enclosed maze of brick, but he finds that the walls narrow quickly. Eventually, he comes to a trap that he knows he must run into. But before he can, a cat appears over from over the wall and eats him.

"Give It Up!" is a typically Kafkaesque tale of confusion and helplessness. A man walking through a generic urban landscape is late for an appointment and, becoming disoriented, gets lost. He sees a big, hulking policeman with a face like an armoured tank and naively asks for directions. The giant bullyboy presses Everyman against the wall and screams in his face, "Give it up! Give it up!"

Other somewhat cryptic stories in this collection concern a hunger artist, a murderer, a human bridge, and a philosopher who thinks that by understanding a spinning top, he can understand everything.

NBM; $14.95

1995; hardcover; 64 pp

heavily illus; 1-56163-125-6

GO NAKED #1

This collection of black and white comix is fucked in the head, even by underground comix standards. A high number of them have an extraordinarily raw, messy style. I don't understand what's going on or why it's going on in most of the pieces, but that's the point. The absurdity quotient is off the scale.

Bruno Richard and Gary Panter team up on perhaps the sloppiest, most impenetrable comic sequence I have ever seen. Just slightly more comprehensible is the squiggle explosion drawn by Savage Pencil. At least I can tell what it concerns — a demented duck practising necrophilia. "Pee Dog" is hopelessly adolescent (if even that) in story and art, but somehow this story of a male dog who grows eight breasts has a charm of its own. The purposely hokey and shittily-drawn "Smiley the Hobo" is about a bum who sings songs with animals in the forest.

In Kazimieras Prapuolenis' creation, "Slugogo: The Cartoon Has Been", an old horny derelict who bears an uncanny resemblance to Sluggo from the *Nancy* comic strip asks his girlfriend to wear a black wig of pointy hair with a bow. Later, he thinks he sees "Nansee" in an apartment window, and he accosts her, only to find out that he saw a crossdresser.

Go Naked isn't going to appeal to everyone, even fans of underground comix. It pushes the insanity and artistic chaos inherent in the medium to its outer limits.

Last Gasp; $7.95

1993; oversized staple-bound softcover; 59 pp

heavily illus; 0-86719-209-7

HARDCORE HORROR
David Britton's Lord Horror
by David Britton, Kris Guido, and others

David Britton's controversial novel *Lord Horror* [see the Fiction chapter] take place in a parallel world where Hitler survived World War II. The title character is based loosely on Lord Haw-Haw (né William Joyce), who left Britain during W.W.II to broadcast Nazi propaganda from Germany. The five-part comic series *Hardcore Horror* acts as sort of a prequel to the novel.

Horror is drawn as an imposing, somewhat rakish figure, with chiselled features, multiple earrings, and an explosion of hair blasting off from the very top of his otherwise shaved head. He is super-suave and always in control of every situation. Horror broadcasts radio diatribes against Winston Churchill and the rest of the authoritarian British government, making him Churchill's number one target.

In issue 1 Horror speaks at a socialist rally and is almost assassinated by cops (acting under the orders of Churchill), but his brother — the famed author James Joyce — rescues him. In the next issue, he takes on the "Tick Tock Men", robot warriors that Churchill has sent against him. In this issue, the artwork has become much more detailed and elec-

Banned in Britain.
Hardcore Horror No 1.

trifying. Many panels are so powerful that each one could stand alone as a work of art.

By the time we get to issue 3, the artwork has become dizzyingly forceful, standing head and shoulders above almost all other comix. Horror has been invited by Adolf Hitler to come to Germany, where he can broadcast his opinions of England without fear of reprisal. In keeping with the over-the-top manner of *Hardcore Horror*, Hitler is drawn wearing black leather and a swastika earring, with half his head shaved. It turns out, though, that Horror has a little problem with the Nazi mindset. When he comes across several Brownshirts beating the hell out of an old man, he slices them to ribbons with the straightrazors he carries for self-defence. When Hitler gets word that Horror has become disillusioned after seeing what Nazism is about, he almost has him killed but decides instead to send him to "a rest camp in Poland" called Auschwitz. From there, Hitler promises, Horror can continue to broadcast.

Issue 4 takes a distinctly different turn. It is composed almost entirely of full-page panels that don't seem to be telling a chronological story. Instead, they are snapshots of Horror's stay at Auschwitz. True to his word, Hitler is letting Horror do his show from the concentration camp. The artwork shows Horror broadcasting and brooding amidst the carnage of the camp. One panel shows Horror crucified with barbed wire. In another, he has split open a Nazi with his razors.

The final issue is the biggest departure of all. It consists of nothing but stark, incredibly detailed panoramic drawings of the concentration camps. Dead bodies are all around, but nothing living can be seen in the desolation. Blank white

Hell Baby just wants a mommy.
Hell Baby.

rectangles appear on every page. They were supposed to contain narration, but after seeing the artwork, the publishers realised that text was superfluous. The comic ends with fifteen full-page photographs of mutilated corpses.

Hardcore Horror has been banned in Britain. The British government was so horrified by the violence and human suffering (and anti-British sentiment) portrayed in the illustrations, photos, and accompanying short stories in the comic that in July 1995 — following a four-year legal battle — the series was found to be obscene. However, it is still being made available in the UK, as well as the rest of the world.

Savoy; $4.99 each
1990; oversized comic book format; ranges from 38 pp to 54 pp
heavily illus

HELL BABY

by Hideshi Hino

Hideshi Hino's first work of manga to be translated into English — *Panorama of Hell* [*Outposts* p 194] — was so original and outlandishly nightmarish, that I knew it would be a hard act to follow. *Hell Baby* proves my instincts were right. This story concerns a rampaging demon-baby that terrorises a Japanese town. It's pretty damn gruesome all right, but the "monster loose in city" cliché can't compare to *Panorama*'s storyline about a demented artist who paints with his own blood.

In the beginning of the story, a woman gives birth to twins. One is normal, but the other is a twisted monster humanoid with fangs. The father ditches the little mutant in the world's largest garbage dump, located outside the city. The baby dies, but is brought back to life by a mysterious bolt of lightning. Gnarled, deformed, and oozing with worms and maggots, the misunderstood Hell Baby wants a mommy. When she is seven, she is visited in a vision by an old hag, who tells her to go to the city and take revenge against the human race, which has rejected her. She goes on a terror spree, ripping off an old man's arm, tearing a boy limb from limb, etc. — all rendered in loving manga-style detail. Finally, the girl finds her family and must decide whether or not to kill her perfect little twin sister.

This is still a good purchase for the fan of ultraviolent manga, but it can't compare to the author's previous work.

Blast Books; $10.95
1989 (1995); softcover; 190 pp
heavily illus; 0-922233-12-8

HEY SKINNY!
Great Advertisements from the Golden Age of Comic Books

by Milles Beller & Jerry Leibowitz

Those wonderful miners of pop culture at Chronicle Books have done it again. This time they've exhumed and saved for posterity those dippy ads in comic books from the 1940s and 1950s. These ads are before my time — I grew up with a new generation of idiotic ads in the 1970s — but I can still appreciate the naïveté they represent. I say naïveté because the ads are laughably blatant in their promises that these cheeseball items will change your life and make you popular with the opposite sex. Of course, ads are still making those same promises, but it's often in a slicker, more implied way.

There's nothing subtle about the ad in which a bumbling idiot is trying to find a cigarette and matches for a swell girl who wants to light up, when all of a sudden Rico Suave is on the scene with his glamorous $1.98 "all-in-one cigarette lighter and full-pack case personalised with your name". The next thing you know, this discerning woman is dancing with her nicotine Romeo and saying, "What a man!"

In a similar vein is the famous Charles Atlas ad that gives the book its title. After a "bag of bones" becomes a buff dude thanks to a FREE book from Charles Atlas, he decks some guy who once pushed him around. A beach bunny clings to his python-like arm, squealing, "Oh, Joe! You <u>are</u> a real he-man, after all."

Of course, there are products to help all you unsure girls out there attract a man, so you won't become lonely old spinsters. A sad-faced girl thinks, "I'm certainly missing a lot of fun, and dates, too. If only I could play the piano the way Betty does." Betty, of course, is nearby tickling the ivories and being fawned over by suitably-impressed men and a woman. Mary sends her $1.98 to Dean Ross Piano Studios, and before you know it this reincarnated Mozart has to fend off men with a stick.

Many of the ads are for toys that will give you hours and hours of enjoyment — cosmic vision helmets, rubber masks, jet-propelled speed boats, ant farms, Nutty Putty, jet rocket spaceships, professional batons, and more cheap junk. Others are for those too-good-to-be-true schemes, such as getting a live monkey at "almost **NO COST**" or getting all kinds of neat stuff for "selling just one 40 pack order of seeds at 15¢ a pack."

Interestingly, some of these items will look eerily modern. How about the creme that will make your pimples disappear and keep you from becoming a laughingstock? Or the art lessons that will turn you into a fabulously successful modern-day Michelangelo? Some things never change, especially gullibility.

Chronicle Books; "only $10.95"
1995; oversized softcover; 95 pp
heavily illus; 0-8118-0828-9

HORROR HOSPITAL UNPLUGGED

by Dennis Cooper & Keith Mayerson

This graphic novel takes the story "Horror Hospital" by wildman Dennis Cooper and tells it through the lens of Keith Mayerson's ever-changing, high-octane art. The basic plot is a typical rock and roll fable: Horror Hospital is a no-talent band with a handsome, "who-gives-a-fuck?" lead singer — Trevor Machine — whose inane lyrics are about how much the world sucks. The group gets lucky when they pen a tribute to River Phoenix, and a stoned Courtney Love is tricked into singing it as a duet with Trevor. Geffen Records is plotting to sign up the band so they can release this "anthem of a generation" and then drop Horror Hospital once they've used up their one-hit quota. Adding some twists to this well-worn storyline is Trevor's realisation that he's gay, which leads him to become involved with his first boyfriend and to fend off (or not) the advances of several interested men.

Although the story makes some interesting points about the search for sexual identity and the heartlessness of the rock 'n' roll biz, the real draw is Mayerson's awe-inspiring art. He effortlessly jumps from style to style, yet somehow makes it all hang together. You literally never know what the next page will bring. A stereotypical comicbook style with thin lines and no shading. A more developed approach with shading. Detailed realism. Swirling surrealism. Doodles. Pure abstraction. Pseudo-water colour paintings. And any combination thereof. The ruggedly handsome Geffen executive is always drawn in heavy, inky lines. Trevor's first sexual encounter with his boyfriend is done in the style of romantic manga. Horror Hospital's final performance takes on a menacing air when it's rendered in scratchboard.

Mayerson throws in heaps of visual tricks, such as drawing dialogue inside characters' mouths and giving Trevor 46 faces to indicate his struggle to say "I love you" to his boyfriend. Keep an eye out or you might miss goodies like Boo Boo giving a blowjob to Yogi Bear, a hypodermic syringe sticking in Courtney Love's eye in one panel, and Trevor's T-shirt that reads "hclef I" (that's "I felch" written backwards).

Horror Hospital Unplugged is a monumental triumph for the graphic novel. It shows the huge potential of the medium, not to simply retell a written story as a literal series of drawings, but to use the art to expand on the story, to do things that the written word can't.

Juno Books; $24.95
1996; oversized softcover; 256 pp
heavily illus; 0-9651042-1-4

I NEVER LIKED YOU

by Chester Brown

This anthology of issues 26 through 30 of Chester Brown's comic *Yummy Fur* deals with Brown's adolescence. All the pages are stark black. Floating in them are the story's panels, sometimes as few as one small one on a page. The narrative is broken into lots of abruptly-ending vignettes, that, when taken together, form the episodic story of Brown's life from fourth grade through high school. Much of the storyline centres around girls. Carrie, who is a slender beauty, likes Chester a lot, and he likes her, but he's got much stronger

True tales of the shaky teenage years.
I Never Liked You.

feelings for Sky, a heavier girl who likes him but is less obvious about it. Carrie's good-looking, aloof sister Connie seems to like Ches, too. He finally gets the nerve up to tell Sky he loves her, but he never asks her out, which leads to much confusion.

Of course, confusion is what *I Never Liked You* is all about because that's what the teenage years are all about. Chester and the girls wrestle each other, but they never kiss. Chester refuses to use cuss-words, and the other kids tease him incessantly about it. Chester's mom acts kind of strange and she eventually checks into a mental hospital.

Brown's willowy drawing style seems perfect for capturing the shaky teenage years. He creates an awkward lyricism that rings true with anyone who's had a goofy adolescence.

Drawn and Quarterly; $12.95
1994; softcover; 185 pp
heavily illus; 0-9696701-6-8

JACK THE RIPPER
A Journal of the Whitechapel
Murders, 1888-1889

adapted by Rick Geary

Rick Geary — a comix artist and illustrator whose work has appeared in *National Lampoon*, *Heavy Metal*, Dark Horse comics, and the *New York Times* — interprets the Jack the Ripper murders as recorded in the 24-volume journals of an unknown British man who followed the case very closely. The book opens with the murder of a prostitute known as Polly on August 31, 1888 and continues through a murder in July of the next year that was somewhat Ripperesque but may not have been the work of Saucy Jack.

Geary's Victorian style nicely captures the feel of the times, and he paces the story well. It's quite a page-turner even though we all know how it ends — with no killer being captured. Using the journals of the anonymous Brit as the framework for the story adds new facets to the familiar tale. For example, he lists the various cockamamie theories that were floating around at the time. A panicky nation was conjecturing about Thugees from India, German hill people, Satanists, Voodoo practitioners, anarchists, and an ape that escaped from a travelling show.

NBM; $14.95

1995; hardcover; 64 pp

heavily illus; 1-56163-124-8

JOHNNY THE HOMICIDAL MANIAC

by Jhonen Vasquez

Here we have one of my favourite comic series of all time. Johnny the Homicidal Maniac (you can call him "Nny" for short) is an impossibly skinny, sadistic, homicidal twentysomething who prefers slashing to slacking. The briar patch of black hair on the very top of his head and the dark rings around his madman's eyes give him a deranged countenance that matches his personality. He is constantly being badgered by two evil Pillsbury Dough Boys and a rabbit he nailed to the wall.

Unlike the similarly ultraviolent *Milk and Cheese* [below], put out by the same publisher, Johnny's escapades of murder and torture aren't played strictly for laughs. There is often a disturbingly plausible rationale for his actions. In the premiere issue, Nny explains to a man taking a door-to-door survey: "Whether in a suit or in a loincloth, people are ignorant little thorns cutting into one another. They seem incapable of advancing beyond the violent tendencies which, at one time, were necessary for survival." He then jams a pencil into the survey-taker's skull and throws his body out the window. In the next issue, Nny explains to a man he's torturing: "My days are less enjoyable because of people. You will be the effigy I burn, infused with all that makes them the detestable little goblins they are. You won't really burn, though: ripped to strips is more accurate." But Nny isn't all bad. In a move that gives him just a touch of humanity, he seems to like the little kid next door, named Squee.

In further issues, Nny slaughters a coffeeshop full of the Cool People [issue 3]; he seems to kill himself [issue 4]; two of his victims attempt an escape [issue 5]; Nny meets God, raises hell in Heaven, and visits Hell [issue 6]; and he meets a fan of his work and says goodbye to Squee [seventh, final issue].

Besides following the adventures of Nny, *JTHM* also contains "Happy Noodle Boy", a primitive, sticklike comic drawn by Johnny himself. In one episode that showcases Noodle Boy's delusions, weird language, creative name-calling, and non sequiturs, he is attempting to become a cult leader (or something like that) when a dog yaps at him. He screams at it: "Cease your barky noise making!! Join my legion of darkness, my frowny face empire!!!!" He grabs the dog and lifts it over his head: "Squeely bladder fuck!! Now my plan comes to fruition!! Minutes of planning, finally, my toes wiggle!! I anoint thee!!! I do not copulate twinkies! Yaaargh!!"

Another comic sharing space with Nny and Noodle Boy is "Wobbly Headed Bob". Bob is like Johnny in that he looks down upon the human race, but instead of channelling his feelings into homicidal rage, he wallows in the pain. A walking existential crisis, Bob copes with his knowledge of the world's cruelty by informing starry-eyed couples that love is a lie and otherwise inflicting happy people with depression.

Finally, each issue of *JTHM* contains an episode, drawn in the "Johnny" style, which doesn't have to do with him or any of the other characters. A guy shits his pants while on a date. Incompetent aliens abduct a man and force him to have sex with a chicken. Stuffed animals slaughter a family.

Dark and oddly depressing but containing wit and depth, *JTHM* is simply a great comic. Go, Johnny, go! [You can buy the issues separately or in one volume with additional material: *Johnny the Homicidal Maniac: Director's Cut*. $19.95.]

Slave Labor Graphics; $2.95 each

1995-1997; comic book format; 24 pp

THE JOY OF SOY
Vegetarian Cartoons

by Vance Lehmkuhl

In the only collection of its kind, Vance Lehmkuhl presents 87 cartoons that support the vegetarian/vegan lifestyle (and occasionally poke good-natured fun at it).

☞ An older woman leading a Thanksgiving prayer says: "and last, the turkey, for which we all — except **Charlene**, to whom the wondrous bounty of your creation just isn't good enough — thank you. Amen."

☞ A man says to his wife in exasperation, "Will you please tell your son he's **allowed** to eat animal crackers?"

☞ A man walks into a hospital room and sees a woman breastfeeding a baby. He says, "I thought you said you wanted to raise him vegan!!?"

☞ Two girls with unsure expressions on their faces are looking at a turkey. One of the says, "I've heard it tastes just like gluten."

☞ A diagram dissects what's really in a hamburger, including "faecal matter that will 'cook out' at 155°F", "sweat from restaurant workers", "not more than 8% insect parts", and "just a smidgeon of Secretariat".

Other cartoons look at where vegetarians draw the line concerning what they will and won't eat, skewer the "more veggie than thou" attitude, and laugh at having to cope with carnivores.

Meat-eaters probably won't "get" or want this book, but *The Joy of Soy* has the vegetarian market cornered.

Laugh Lines Press; $8.95

1997; paperback; 90 pp

heavily illus; 1-889594-03-2

KICKING THE HABIT
Cartoons About the Catholic Church

by Rina Piccolo

Recovering Catholic Rina Piccolo turns her sweetly cynical wit onto her former religion. Somehow she manages to poke fun at nuns, priests, bishops, popes, and Jesus without being mean-hearted or viciously sacrilegious (well, usually…).

In the first of the single-panel cartoons (printed on the book's cover), two nuns are praying in a wheatfield, while the scarecrow they're kneeling in front of says, "Look, for the last time…you've got the wrong guy!!" In the first cartoon in the book itself, a nun answers the phone: "Good morning, 'Church of Our Lady of the Holy Grace with the Gaping Bloody Wound Through Her Heart of Infinite Agony and Pain-Ridden Anguish Who Falls Splitting Her Head on the Stones of the Fiery Abyss of the Perpetual Flames of Torment, Fear and Vexation' Accounting Department, can I help you?"

Another panel shows Noah & Company aboard the ark. Brandishing a clipboard, he asks, "Okay, who copulated today?" His wife and one of the monkeys are the only two who raise their hands.

An extremely bow-legged angel angrily says to his brethren who are laughing at him: "You'd walk funny too if you spent the winter with a Christmas tree up your ass!"

The scene: an open casket funeral. A devout priest says to a woman sitting in the front row, "Sorry about your husband, Mrs. Gladstone. I guess you just weren't praying hard enough." Elsewhere, a priest is in a park, throwing bread crumbs to the pigeons. One of them flails its wings, fulminating to the rest of the flock: "Eat! Eat, my children!! For this is the body of Christ!"

Like Piccolo's other collection that was published at the same time (*Rina's Big Book of Sex Cartoons* [see the Sex chapter]), *Kicking the Habit* has its falls from grace, but overall it's a great collection. Any book that causes me to laugh out loud repeatedly has to be recommended.

Laugh Lines Press; $7.95
1997; small softcover; 93 pp
heavily illus; 0-9632526-7-4

MENG & ECKER
Lord Horror's Creep Boys
by David Britton, Kris Guido, and others

Released simultaneously with *Hardcore Horror* [above], *Meng & Ecker* is an eponymous comic about Lord Horror's amoral henchmen. Meng dresses in drag, espouses racism, enjoys killing people at the slightest provocation (or none at all), and is so horny that he "would fornicate with a diseased aidsrat." Ecker is much more subdued but still manages to get his kicks.

Issue 1 of *Meng & Ecker* has the distinction of being the first comic banned in Britain. Since then that honour has been bestowed upon the first three issues of the (so far) nine-part series. The cover of the first issue shows Meng holding a bloody knife and the decapitated head of ex-Manchester Police Chief James Anderton, who led the legal harassment of Savoy. In one of the stories inside, Meng goes on a savage killing spree in order to get meat for the tea rooms that he and Ecker operate.

In "Meng and Ecker Halt the Decline of English Lit" [issue 2], the boys attend a lecture by a panel comprised of four British authors who are held in the highest regard. Meng and Ecker are sickened that their tepid, unimaginative work is considered the best Britain has to offer, so they decapitate each author and replace his or her head with the noggin of a truly talented writer. After Meng rips off Martin Amis' head, Ecker replaces it with "writer, Victorian time-traveller, and surrealist body-builder" William Hope Hodgson. They also save Salman Rushdie from an assassination attempt.

"Sometimes I offend myself when I'm drawing it."
Meng & Ecker.

One panel in the third issue shows Meng screwing a corpse that looks suspiciously like Margaret Thatcher. He says: "Phew! This KY came in handy. That old granny was as dry as a mole's arse. Christ! I think I'm going to have to get a fucking foreskin transplant." Later, he sticks it to Constable Anderton.

Issue 4 provoked legal action from United Features Syndicate. Even though *Meng & Ecker* is filled with cameos by cartoon and comic characters — from Mickey Mouse to Tank Girl — apparently they shouldn't have messed with a certain overweight, bulge-eyed feline. In a two-page section, Meng grabs a cat who heavily resembles Garfield, comes all over him, and then holds him up by the tail while the semen flows into his own mouth. Savoy settled out of court with UFS for a four-figure sum.

In other issues, "social services counsellor" Lord Horror solves people's problems by killing them [#5], Meng gives birth [#7], Meng is dismembered and his balls are eaten in an exotic restaurant [#8], and Meng's chip-off-the-block daughter comes for a visit [#9].

Issue 7 contains an interview with Kris Guido, who did the art for *Meng & Ecker* and the first four issues of *Hardcore Horror*. When the interviewer asks him if he thinks *Meng & Ecker* is pretty gross, he replies: "Sure. Sometimes I offend myself when I'm drawing it. It's vile. Of course it's vile, but it's theatrically so, at least. You'd have to be either brain-dead or a police officer to take it seriously....I think David [Britton] sees Meng & Ecker as products of the dark lands you'd probably find in any big city; two regular sorts who become worse than their environment, but they keep smiling instead of taking it seriously." Currently, all issues but the first are in print and available, even in Britain.

Savoy; $4.99 each
1989-1995; oversized comic book format; 36 pp to 70 pp
heavily illus

MILK & CHEESE

by Evan Dorkin

Take a carton of milk and a wedge of cheese, anthropomorphise them, fill them with rage, sociopathic attitudes, and a tendency towards violence, and what do you have? Milk and Cheese: "Dairy Products Gone Bad". In one of the statements that the pair are fond of making, Milk proclaims: "Heed well our verbs and pronouns! We are homogenised hatred! Thirty-two ounces of unpasteurised impatience! Wake up America! It's Howdy Doddy time!!! Don't laugh! We're serious! We'll kick your lousy ass!" Cheese adds: "And we're just the guys to do it, too…" Elsewhere, Cheese says, "I wish I had a baseball bat the size of Rhode Island so I could beat the shit out of this stupid ass planet!"

This comic series has become extremely popular, because who can resist food substances who act our most antisocial fantasies?: getting into a flaming shish kebab duel at a fancy restaurant, smacking a mailman in the head with a six-pack of empty beer bottles because he never brings anything good in the mail, terrorising a courtroom while on jury duty, starting a revolution, driving a car through the front of a trendy club that wouldn't allow them in, throwing bowling balls at people while at the bowling alley, demolishing a crappy mall record store, and burning New York City to the ground, all of which takes place in the first issue.

In the opening page of the second issue (which is actually known as "the other number one"), Milk asks "why didn't you buy our last comic? Are you so totally stupid? You must be new to this country!" Cheese continues the berating: "Really! What the hell's wrong with you? Can't afford a lousy two-fifty? Ten quarters! Why don't you just slit your wrist if you're so poor?" From there, they proceed to scare an old woman to death and take her purse, beat a man whose name they picked out of a phone book, literally kick a screaming baby out of a movie theatre, kill a bunch of hippie poseurs ("Make hate, not love!"), and go "on the road" as a couple of brutal beatniks.

Other lowlights include: pinning Santa underneath a burning Christmas tree and slaughtering animal experimenters ("Ha! Look! Specimen loses communication abilities when struck with a Louisville Slugger!") [in the third number one issue]; setting a folk singer on fire and breaking bottles over people's heads at a wine tasting [fourth number one issue]; handing out cabbages, syringes, urine samples, used condoms, cockroaches, and tequila at Halloween and opening up their own body modification business to pierce people through the head with hangers, tattoo The Last Supper using broken gin bottles, and toast a guy's scalp with a flamethrower ("Third degree burns are 'in'!") [the first second issue]; helping out with a blood drive in their own special way and attempting to stalk third-rate celebrities [issue 666]; going on a violence-laced drinking binge and starting a cult but

Society Is To Blame! in *Milk and Cheese*.

then killing all their followers for being losers ("There are many roads to Heaven's Gate, my friends — but yours just happens to be out our window!") [issue seven].

If absurdist violence pulled off with panache by a couple of well-spoken yet uncivilised characters is what you crave, I'd suggest a big helping of Milk and Cheese.

Slave Labor Graphics; $2.75 each
1991-1997; comic book format; 24 pp each
heavily illus
WWW: www.houseoffun.com/m&c/index.htm

MURDER CAN BE FUN

edited by Craig Pape

Based on John Marr's obsessively researched, darkly humorous zine of disasters, death, and crime, *Murder Can Be Fun* [*Outposts* p 143], this series of the same name tells your favourite tales of mayhem through comic art. The premier issue relates the 1944 circus fire that killed 168 people, the worst train wreck in US history, the Great Boston molasses flood, the Triangle Factory fire of 1911, and the Port Chicago explosion, which was the largest man-made detonation in history up to that point. It accounted for 20% of all the African American casualties of World War II.

Issue 2 is an all-star affair with a look at the deaths of Bruce and Brandon Lee, Carl Switzer (Alfalfa from *The Little Rascals*), Black Panther Huey Newton, Bob Crane (from *Hogan's Heroes*), Ernest Hemingway, Jayne Mansfield, and John Holmes, plus the shooting of Andy Warhol and the downfall of Fatty Arbuckle. In the following issue, four artists take extremely different artistic approaches to the cases of postal employees who went on homicidal rampages.

Bizarre murderers are the focus of issue 4, and the next instalment covers dead musicians, including jazz trumpeter Chet Baker, members of the Band and Chicago, and Karen Carpenter. The latest ish, #6, is devoted to zoo bloodbaths. Besides looking at numerous instances of animals maiming and murdering patrons, it also introduces us to an elephant that accidentally killed three hippos. Jeff John and John Marr

The homicidal lesbian terrorist is back!
Revenge of Hothead Paisan.

blow the whistle on zoo secrets: zoophiles who sneak in at night for some wild sex and animals who become enamoured of the zookeepers.

Slave Labor Graphics; $2.95 each
1996-1997; comic book format; 24 pp each
heavily illus

THE NARRATIVE CORPSE
A Chain-Story by 69 Artists!
edited by Art Spiegelman & R. Sikoryak

The Surrealists used to play a game called Exquisite Corpse, which consisted of each person writing a sentence while only having the previous sentence as a frame of reference. The resulting narrative was filled with the odd juxtapositions that the Surrealists loved.

The beautifully-designed *Narrative Corpse* applies the same method to comix. Sixty-nine artists participated in the experiment by supplying three panels about the adventures of a stickman. The catch is, the artists were only allowed to see the three panels that came immediately before theirs. Among those contributing are Peter Bagge, Lynda Barry, Chester Brown, Charles Burns, R. Crumb, Julie Doucet, Mary Fleener, Bill Griffith, Matt Groening, Gilbert and Jamie Hernandez, Aline Kominsky-Crumb, Gary Panter, Savage Pencil, Spain, Art Spiegelman, and S. Clay Wilson. Two of the most surprising appearances are those of old school legend Will Eisner and *Beetle Bailey*'s creator, Mort Walker.

As you might guess, this stellar cast creates a story that is so disconnected and jarring, there's really no point in trying to summarise the whole thing. Let's just say that at blinding speed "Sticky" has sex with the earth (and knocks her up), becomes the target of a hooker, is heralded as the messiah, gets a second mouth, wins an Oscar, falls in love with a Japanese starlet, sucks a mermaid's nipple, possesses the meaning of life, gets beaten by cops, gets split into two beings, is force-fed psychiatric drugs, and gets thrown out of a window by the Mob. Whew!

There never was — and probably never will be — another comix jam session like this one. Taking five years from conception to completion, *Narrative Corpse* is a treasure for any comix fan.

Gates of Heck and Raw Books; $25
1995; oversized softcover (9" x 16.25"); 18 pp
heavily illus; 0-9638129-4-7

PALESTINE
A Nation Occupied
by Joe Sacco

A collection of the first five issues of Joe Sacco's comic *Palestine*. Using an entertaining style with lots of unusual angles, Sacco shows what life is like under Israeli occupation in Palestine. He paints a picture of a day-to-day existence filled with violence and the constant threat of violence, torture, and police state tactics. Although written from the viewpoint of Palestinians, this comic shows why both sides feel the way they do.

Fantagraphics Books; $14.95
1994; oversized softcover; 144 pp
heavily illus; 1-15097-150-9

REVENGE OF HOTHEAD PAISAN
by Diane DiMassa

Look out all you homophobes, macho men, and assorted creeps — Hothead Paisan, the homicidal lesbian terrorist, is back, and she hasn't mellowed with age! If anything, this self-described "gun-totin', axe throwin', take-no-prisoners, queen of my world, angry pissed-off bitch on wheels" has become even more of your worst nightmare. This sequel to *Hothead Paisan* [*Outposts* p 193] contains issues 10 through 18 of the comic zine and some new material, including a short glimpse of Hothead's birth. As a male doctor pulls the raging dyke from the womb, he megalomaniacally declares: "Look!! I'm the giver of life!! I'm the alpha and the omega!! Me!!" Baby Hothead replies, "Dream on fuckface!" and slices his head off with a scalpel. She's been homicidal since day one.

One of HH's major escapades this time around begins when she wanders into a courtroom during a rape trial. The three accused men are questioned by their lawyer: "Did you rape anyone, boys?" "Nope." "Uh-uh." "No." "No further questions!!" After dismissing his clients, he says: "I now call the pathetic snatch to the stand." As you can guess, things only go downhill from there. The rapists go free, so Hothead kidnaps them one at a time (after killing their lawyer with a stick of dynamite). She chains them up in her dungeon. Two of them get their spines ripped out through their assholes, and the third one gets his dick guillotined.

In between the homicidal actions, the suicidal thoughts, and HH falling in love, *Revenge* works in lots of acrid satire of the patriarchy. Hothead's TV flashes the message, "If you ain't got a dick, you ain't shit." She sums up her position nicely when she says: "Go ahead! Give me a choice between breeding, accelerated ageing, living with an orangutan, and maid duty for life **OR** autonomy, black boots, multiple orgasms, cats instead of kids, people who say what they mean, and nothing stopping me from doing whatever I wanna do…and guess which one I'll pick?"

Cleis Press; $16.95

1995; oversized softcover; 211 pp

heavily illus; 0-57344-016-7

REVERBSTORM

by David Britton, John Coulthart, Michael Butterworth, and others

Reverbstorm is the current cycle of comix within the *Lord Horror* series [see *Hardcore Horror*, above]. Once again, Horror is in the thick of things, along with his wife Jessie Matthews and his brother James Joyce. The setting is Torenbürgen, "an imaginary city overshadowed by the manic zeitgeist of Adolph Hitler's Germany and created from the unearthly tectonics of Auschwitz." It's hard to say exactly what the plot is or even describe the action. James Joyce wears a hat with several long straight razors tucked in the band. Occasionally the hat comes to life and calls him names. Horror engages in SM and continue his radio diatribes. At one point, in issue 6, he "plays" a humongous keyboard instrument that tortures people in various ways when the keys are pressed. Interspersed in the action are dental photographs and Picasso's work, especially the war atrocity painting *Guernica*.

Each issue starts with several full page illustrations, photographs, and combinations thereof. Number 5 contains a highly grainy, Xerox-like photograph that appears to show Picasso, Joyce, Ezra Pound, and Lord Horror standing together. The next issue has a drawing of Matthews pissing into Horror's right eye. At the end of every issue, several pages of creatively laid-out text follow the further adventures of Horror.

It practically goes without saying that John Coulthart's pen and ink work continues the amazingly high level of sophistication and power that we've comes to expect from this series. Every panel is a visual treat, and many of them are individual works of art. They form the basis of each issue's rich tapestry of illustrations, photographs, high art, poetry, music, text, and quotes from famous figures woven together in a smooth design scheme and printed on high-quality, glossy paper. Calling this a comic is almost a misnomer. Think of it as a highly experimental graphic novel being published in serial form.

As with every new work of graphix or fiction within the Lord Horror mythos, *Reverbstorm* dazzles while offering more questions than answers. Someday, I swear, I'm going to figure the whole thing out.

Savoy; £2.95

1993-1997; oversized comic book format; 48-52 pp each

heavily illus

ROARIN' RICK'S RARE BIT FIENDS

by Rick Veitch

Roarin' Rick Veitch — "the world's most overworked cartoonist" — has been drawing superhero, fantasy, and horror comics for around a decade, and he's been fascinated by his dreams since he was six. In *Rare Bit Fiends*, his two obsessions meet and fuse, becoming an illustrated dream journal

Roarin' Rick's Rare-Bit Fiends.

that's "written by my unconscious sleeping mind and drawn by my waking self."

Veitch does a fine job capturing the non-linear, alogical aesthetic of the dreamworld. His style is more or less straightforward — the drawing is realistic, and the use of panels gets pretty creative at times but nevertheless manages to be linear. This orthodox use of form focuses attention on the bizarre content. Each dream only lasts one or two pages, but there are no subheads or titles or anything else to let us know that for sure. Are we really starting on a completely new dream, or did Veitch's dream just jump tracks suddenly?

In the premiere issue, an old lady walks up to Veitch on a path in a park, says "Hello", and proceeds to inspect his teeth. A Southern Colonel in the Civil War swims to the bottom of a lake to pull out the giant bathstopper at the bottom. A naked woman sits at a table in the middle of a mall flooded in six inches of water. She says, "You know me." George Stephanopolis calls to iron out last minute details about the President's appearance at Veitch's house: "The Secret Service will be coming in to plant a row of weeds in your backyard." In an epic panel, Veitch hears the voice of God and writes down what he hears, but his writing looks like gibberish. And that's just scratching the surface of this one issue.

In other issues a secret weapons system melts the world, people visit the Bob Dylan Museum, Veitch turns into Superman, Egyptian statues come to life, Robert Crumb gets his face removed, and Veitch visits a hotel in India where visiting ghosts perform in the bar.

In addition to Veitch's nocturnal adventures, each issue contains several pages of dream comix from other artists,

You can never be too direct.
Rude Girls and Dangerous Women.

and an enthusiastic letters section where readers talk about their dreams, give tips on remembering them or becoming lucid, and contribute comix of their own dreams. In addition, every cover of *Rare Bit Fiends* is a magnificent, hypnotic piece of full-colour eye candy, suitable for framing. A superb comic. [Helpful hint: The first eight issues have been collected into the book *Rabid Eye*, available for $16.95, postage paid. Outside the US, add $2 for Airmail.]

King Hell Press/PO Box 1371/West Townshend VT 05359
Single issue: $4. Non-US: $5
Six issue sub (half year), mailed First Class with backing board: $24. Non-US: $28
Payment: ck, mo

RUDE GIRLS AND DANGEROUS WOMEN
by Jennifer Camper

In the outrageous dyke world of Jennifer Camper's comic strips, nothing is sacred and you can never be too direct. In "How to Get Laid", the narrator suggests hitting on the bride in a wedding and saying, "Ya wanna eat my pussy?" in front of the crowd. Camper gives advice on eight types of "women to avoid at the bar". One says, "Hey bitch — I bought you two drinks, so don't tell me you're going home with someone else!" Another one says, "No — I'm not bisexual. I'm a lesbian who sleeps with men."

One strip demonstrates "naughty things to do with communion wafers", including: "Stella uses them for pasties in her strip show." Men's stupidity is put on display in "Het Boys Say the Darndest Things", and a jerk gets Bobbitized by a switchblade-packing superhero in "Ironwoman's Safety Tips for Gals". "Jailbirds" explicitly shows what happens when a horny lesbian goes to prison, and "Aphrodisiacs" is a poetic celebration of sexual enhancers: "This '66 Mustang's ever so cute,/It's smooth & it's fast & it's kicky,/Though the leather seats show all the stains/And the gear shift gets awfully sticky." In one of the many strips on power and privilege, we see a clean-cut white boy griping: "OK! OK! So I've always gotten any job I've wanted, and I could live anywhere I went, and was treated with respect by store clerks, and cops, and even strangers on the street! But now everyone else wants to live that way, too!"

Camper has got an impeccable eye for human foibles and hypocrisies. Add to that a wicked sense of humour and a cast of multi-ethnic lesbians, and you have a winning talent.

Laugh Lines Press; $8.95
1994; softcover; 90 pp
heavily illus; 0-9632526-5-8

SECRET LANGUAGE
by Molly Barker

Secret Language is set up as a series of small, square panels, one per page. The drawings are all done in black ink that is applied so heavily it often forms a scratchboard effect. Underneath some of panels is a line of a poem.

The basic theme is that of people dealing with and trying to overcome their loneliness and alienation. In "Heads" a woman is watching a documentary that shows a squirrel trying to escape a forest fire by burying its head. By the end of the series, the woman has wrapped herself completely in a blanket, indicating that sometimes we try to deal with the fires burning around us in the same way. "Inwardly" is more cryptic, but it's apparently about a homeless woman who fondly remembers her childhood and finds solace by playing the harmonica and laying in fields underneath the stars. In "Dream" a young woman hears her grandfather's corpse singing.

"Fathoming", perhaps the best part of the book, starts out by lamenting the dreariness and stagnation of modern life. Drawings of people on a subway car, in an elevator, and walking along the street without interacting are accompanied by the lines "sometimes it's hard to see through/or make waves./it's almost the same song everywhere." There is a sanctuary, however, but it's not what you might expect — the library:

a gathering place
a last quiet ocean
of wandering thoughts
...
there's a feeling of caves
all joined up.
people collect and diverge
drifting seekers
are delving
and brushing by.

City Lights Books; $12.95
1997; small hardcover;
heavily illus; 0-87286-328-X

SKELETON KEY [Two Volumes]
by Andi Watson

Skeleton Key follows the interdimensional adventures of Tasmin Mary Cates, a bored high school Gothgirl who lives in a small Canadian town called Garfield. In the collection of the first six issues, *Beyond the Threshold*, we're introduced to Tasmin and the bizarre skeleton key that she found in a costume she bought from a thrift store. She discovers that

Lamenting the dreariness of modern life.
Secret Language.

the key unlocks doorways to other dimensions. During her first, brief time through, she accidentally brings someone back with her. Kitsune is an Asian girl approximately her own age who appears completely human except for having a fox's tail. As they become fast friends, they enrol Kitsune in school, deal with dumbass jocks, go to parties, and fight a pillow monster from another dimension. Meanwhile, the creeps who lost the skeleton key have tracked it to Tasmin. During the struggle to get the key from her, she, Kitsune, and a friend of theirs named Yale get taken to another dimension. [$11.95; 1996; 96 pp; 0-943151-12-0]

The second volume, *The Celestial Calendar* (containing issues 7-18), picks up with Tasmin and Kitsune by themselves in a new dimension. They first run into the "Super Deformed Circus Troupe", who draft them into fighting the Redcaps. Then they, among other adventures, stay at a creepy boarding school, rescue Yale, fight an undead hockey team, and Tasmin resists a forced marriage to a root beer heir. While this is going on, Tasmin is turning into a giant pillow *and* she looks like she's become immaculately pregnant. [$19.95; 1997; 192 pp; 0-943151-15-5]

With its fun plotline and appropriately cute all-black and all-white (no grey) artwork, *Skeleton Key* is an enjoyable romp.

Amaze Ink (Slave Labor Graphics)
oversized softcovers; heavily illus

SPOTS

by S. Clay Wilson

Spots contains almost fifty of S. Clay Wilson's tasteless single-panel comix, many of which appeared in *Screw* in the 1980s. A mugger bashes a guy over the head with his huge dick, a woman holds a pistol to the elephantine boner of a rapist, a woman pisses on a man's head, a woman eats a zombie's rotting penis, a snot vampire sucks on a woman's nostril, a pirate chokes his captive lassie with his huge schlong, and so on. The easily offended need not apply.

Last Gasp; $15
1989; softcover; 61 pp
heavily illus; 0-86719-349-2

SQUEE!

By Jhonen Vasquez

Thus begins a new comic series by Jhonen Vasquez, creator of *Johnny the Homicidal Maniac* [above]. *Squee!* mostly follows the traumas of a little boy named... Squee, who first appeared in the *Johnny* series. One of the standout pieces in issue 1 concerns the problems that can occur when trying to go to sleep in a big, dark room — Squee is confronted by two groups of aliens, who argue over which of them will get to abduct the young lad for their "hideous experiments". The other A+ goes to "Meanwhile... There's a New Toy", which doesn't involve Squee. It features a parody of the antiseptic Tickle-Me Elmo doll called Tickle-Me Hellmo. This popular toy has 20 features, including "Hellmo giggles when squeezed", "Secretes substance inducing vicious rash and temporary blindness", "Starts reciting goth poetry", and "Summons local monkeys to brutalise child". It looks like we can expect more wonderfully-drawn dark hilarity from Vasquez for quite a while.

Slave Labor Graphics; $2.95
1997; comic book format; 24 pp
heavily illus

STAND BACK, I THINK I'M GONNA LAUGH...

by Rina Piccolo

This book of cartoonz presents humorous single-panel takes on various themes — sex, relationships, PMS, men, religion, popular culture, and general kookiness. Rina Piccolo seems to be gently poking fun at her subjects, rather than spewing venom. In one cartoon, the caption reads, "Mrs. Winchester finds a positive outlet for frustrated negative energy." We see a matronly old woman sewing throw-pillows that say, "Fuck you", "Fuck the whole world", and "Bastards". Another panel shows "The worst little whorehouses in Texas", with names like Mom's, McSex, Ugly Puss, El-Frigid-elle, and John 3:14. In another, when faced with an impossibly huge ball of yarn, one cat asks the other: "Did we do any drugs today?"

One of my favourites shows a clown at a kid's birthday party saying to Mom, "Before we start the party, Mrs. Reynolds, I must warn you of my deep dark psychotic side that comes out from time to time..." Piccolo's occasional flair for the gross is evident in the surgery scene in which the fork-wielding doctor says: "It's so chunky, I'll have to use a fork." One panel simply contains a bottle with the label: "This product has not been tested on cute fuzzy animals. We use big ugly ones that stink."

If you like your humour dark and pointed but tempered with a certain gentleness, you'll dig Piccolo's work.

Laugh Lines Press; $8.95
1994; softcover; 94 pp
heavily illus; 0-9632526-3-1

WOLFF & BYRD: COUNSELORS OF THE MACABRE [Three Volumes]

by Batton Lash

Here's an intriguing idea for a comic. Follow the adventures of two lawyers who specialise in cases involving the supernatural. Alanna Wolff and Jeff Byrd, "Counselors of the Macabre", represent all kinds of monsters and scary creatures as they get mired in the biggest nightmare of all — the court system. *Wolff & Byrd* has been a weekly strip since 1979 — appearing in *The National Law Journal* starting in 1983 — and a comic book since 1994.

Case Files, Volume 1 collects the first four issues of the comic book. The barristers' very first client is a hulking shamble of plant matter named Sodd, who is accused of "reckless endangerment, destruction of property, and inciting a riot at the botanical gardens." It quickly becomes apparent that Batton Lash is fond of puns (is that name itself a pseudonymous pun?), which is great because I am, too. Among some of the groaners that are unleashed within the space of just three pages: "... to us, it's just a nervous client shaking like a leaf", "He has roots in the community, your honour", "I hope you go out on a limb for your client", "Your client's ass is grass... and I'm the lawnmower", "Just don't believe everything you hear through the grapevine!" In other cases, the counsellors have to deal with a dog that came back from the dead, a haunted house, zombies who were fired from jobs that were supposed to be "for life", a professor who was translating Tibetan incantations that caused him to permanently levitate, and a cryptkeeper accused of graverobbing. [1995; 93 pp; 0-9633954-1-6]

In *Case Files, Volume II* (issues 5 through 8), the squires get involved in paranormal proceedings involving Count Dracula (who wants all the imitators out there to stop using his name), a modelling agency that uses occult powers to keep its star model, and the continuing saga of Sodd. On a more personal level, Wolff and Byrd both find possible love interests, and their receptionist must fight off the advances of a smitten interdimensional alien. [1996; 90 pp; 0-9633954-3-2]

The third volume reprints issues nine through twelve, in which the hearse-chasers represent a woman who was artificially inseminated with Satan's sperm, a man who's being divorced because he literally turned into a "snivelling blob of jelly", a stand-up comedian who has his own personal laugh track because of a gypsy's curse, and a guardian angel who negligently allowed his charge to hurt himself. [1997; 90 pp; 0-9633954-4-0]

Since *Wolff & Byrd* has a wide audience among lawyers, it pokes very gentle fun at the profession instead of setting its phasers on kill. Still, aside from corny puns, it's filled with a sly, sophisticated humour that many people outside the profession would enjoy.

Exhibit A Press; $9.95 each
softcovers; heavily illus

"Beware the creatures of the night — they have <u>lawyers</u>!" *Wolff & Byrd.*

A WORLD WITHOUT HOMOSEXUALS

by Jason Ross

In this series of 82 single panel cartoons, Jason Ross takes a satirical look at a future in which gays and lesbians have been eradicated and all of their contributions have similarly gone up in smoke. The Religious Right and other bigots are in full control of the theocratic government. What would happen in such a situation? Well, let's see...

In one cartoon, all the women at a fashion show are dressed in frumpy, no-waist, polka-dot dresses with doilies for collars. Obviously, fashion has taken a nose-dive. We see Rush Limbaugh sitting alone at his desk, his hands over his face. He's thinking: "Oh shit!... Oh shit!... Without a crew... I don't have a show!" At the Academy Awards, a hooded Klansmen is the presenter: "... And the winner for best original screenplay goes to... *Fitted Sheets: A Love Story!*" In music stores, Anita Bryant's record is sold out, but stacks of Madonna, Grace Jones, and Broadway musical albums have been put in the 1¢ sale bin.

In an effort to find a new group of people to hate, a crowd of protesters gathers. One has a sign saying: "Read the Bible. God hates tall people!" Elsewhere, the Mardi Gras parade has dwindled down to six revellers. At a performance of *The Nutcracker*, a flying female dancer is about to hit the floor. The caption asks, "Who will catch the ballerinas?"

In one of the most interesting extrapolations, a line of pregnant women is forming outside First Christian's Birth Termination Depot #21A, for "homo-gene positives only!" The caption reads: "Once the gene connection was confirmed, the Religious Right was faced with a CHOICE." Now there's a catch-22, eh?

Road Kill Press; $10
1994; softcover; 95 pp
heavily illus; 0-9641408-1-0

GET A PRIZE IN EVERY BOX OF JESUS FREAKS CERIAL!! MCD '91

Some of the *Worst of Boiled Angel*.

THE WORST OF BOILED ANGEL

by Mike Diana

In March 1994 Mike Diana was convicted on three counts of obscenity for making and distributing issues 7 and "Ate" of his zine, *Boiled Angel*. This makes him the first comic artist in US history to be arrested because of his art. Diana was sentenced to serve three years probation, pay a $3000 fine, do 1300 hours of community service, undergo psychiatric evaluation at his own expense, and stay at least ten feet away from children. The most disturbing aspect of his persecution is that he is not allowed to draw anything that could be considered obscene, even if it's for his own pleasure and not intended for publication. To enforce this thought control, police are allowed to make unannounced, unwarranted searches of Diana's home whenever they feel like it.

Because of the small number of copies of *Boiled Angel* that were printed, most people have never been able to see what the uproar is about. *The Worst of Boiled Angel* fixes

that. Within its 224 oversized pages you can bask in amazing tales of mind-numbing sociopathic brutality taken from all eight issues of *Boiled Angel* and its predecessor, *Angel Fuck*. Diana's single panel works and sequential comix — as well as some work by guests — depict everything that scares the shit out of society at large: bestiality, necrophilia, rape, child molestation, incest, torture, mutilation, cannibalism, sacrilege, Satanism, and more, presented alone or in various combinations.

Diana's innocent, "doodlesque" style of drawing creates a visual paradox with its subject matter. Here's a typical story. In "Baby Fucked Dog Food!" a man adopts a boy named Scott. As soon as they're out of the adoption agency, the man says to him: "You didn't think I adopted you outta love did you? How could I even think of loving a fuckin misfit orphn [sic] like you? Da only thing I'm gonna love is fuckin yer hot little ass!" When they get home, he does just that. The next day he makes Scott a slave at his dog food factory, where he uses a special process. He buys unwanted babies from prostitutes, screws them to death, throws the remains in the shredder, and out comes dog food. Scott and his stepdad's dog, Spot, become good friends, and Spot kills his master. The story ends with Spot nailing Scott.

Among the written offerings are a story by and interview with convicted killer GJ Schaefer, an interview with serial killer Ottis Toole (partner of Henry Lee Lucas), anti-Jesus Christmas carols, several ultraviolent short stories, and the official report of the psychiatrist who examined Diana for his trial. He writes of *Boiled Angel*: "The material appeals to the outraged and outrageous, the angry, the psychopathic, the sexually mentally disturbed, and to those whose warped concept of sexuality requires the stimulation of such fantasies." This shrink gives Diana's work publicity that money just can't buy: "As a personal note, in my thirty-seven years of practice in psychology, I have seen pornography and other forms of obscene depictions. With the exception of one murder case in which I was involved, these pictures are the worst I have ever seen, even more destructive than those I had viewed in the murder case alluded to." I couldn't possibly give this book a higher recommendation than that.

Mike Hunt Publications; $16.95
1996; oversized softcover; 224 pp
heavily illus; no ISBN

ART
PHOTOGRAPHY

BODY AND SOUL
by Andres Serrano

Photographer Andres Serrano has become one of the best-known controversial artists. He's part of that unholy quartet of outlaws (Karen Finley, Robert Mapplethorpe, and Holly Hughes being the others) whose government-funded work helped trigger the whole National Endowment for the Arts debacle.

The photograph that became practically a household name (if you had the guts to say it out loud) was *Piss Christ*, a portrait of a crucifix submerged in Serrano's urine. Senator Alfonse D'Amato (R-NY) tore this work of art to shreds on the Senate floor in May 1989. Christian groups went ballistic, and the hysteria hasn't subsided yet. I saw a news programme on a Christian TV network in summer 1995 that talked about the 1987 photograph as if it had just come out yesterday. (The best part was watching the attractive anchorwoman stumble on the name of the photograph.)

Serrano took his lumps from nonconformist circles too. He was accused of being a shockmeister. Some underground commentators were saying that he had no talent. Spencer Tunik, another great taboo-breaking photographer, even did a shot of a nude female model whose torso bore the words: "Andres Serrano — Jesus Christ, you piss me off."

In defiance of both the mainstream and the underground, I am here to tell you that Serrano's work is great. *Piss Christ* was no fluke, no half-assed attempt to capitalise on controversy. This oversized, lushly-printed retrospective of Serrano's career proves it.

First, let's turn to the photograph in question. If you didn't know the name of the piece or the story behind it, you would think it's simply a gorgeous, haunting rendition of a crucifix. It's taken from a low angle, about 45 degrees to the right of the cross. The whole tableaux is an orange-red that's being lit from the side. The light hits mainly the top of the cross and Jesus' head and torso, giving off a diffused golden glow. Lots of tiny bubbles permeate the scene. It's quite effective.

Looking at the rest of the book, we see that this is far from the first or last time Serrano worked with religious icons, bodily fluids, or a combination thereof. *Heaven and Hell* features two people. On the left is a naked woman whose hands are tied above her head. Her head is thrown back, and blood is streaming down her torso. On the right, turning away from the tortured woman, is a priest dressed in a blood red hat and robes. It's an odd juxtaposition. The image is divided neatly in half, and neither character seems aware of the other's presence. Another photo, *Pietà*, shows a hooded, sorrowful woman holding a gigantic, bloody fish that's been

Heaven and Hell, 1984 — Further reflections on religion from the creator of Piss Christ. *Body and Soul.*

gutted.

There are many abstract shots of vital fluids. *Milk, Blood* shows a white rectangle next to a red rectangle. *Yellow River* seems like a sunset shot on a beach looking out to sea, but is actually Serrano's urine. *Bloodscape IX* is an eerily lit shot of blood, and *Semen and Blood* presents a mixture of those two fluids in a way that is reminiscent of fractals. *Untitled XIV* and *Untitled VII* are blurry white streamers set against a black background. Only when you read the subtitles do you realise what you're looking at — *Ejaculate in Trajectory*.

Several photographs show religious or Greek statues surrounded by an extremely bright but suffused yellow light. The objects themselves — which include a female bust, a crucifix, and the goddess Nike — are glowing red. Another series shows black religious statues — *The Last Supper*, *Mary* — in a clear liquid with thousands of bubbles coating their surfaces.

Several works from the mid-1980s involve dead animals. *The Scream* is a picture of a coyote hanging from a noose (the coyote was dead before Serrano got it). *Cabeza de Vaca* is a profile of a cow's head on a wooden pedestal, and *Meat Weapon* shows a muscular man brandishing a raw leg of lamb as if it were a machine gun.

The Nomads series consists of six psychologically revealing portraits of homeless men shot against a black background in the New York subways. The controversial *Klan* series shows close-ups of several male and female KKK members dressed in their quasi-ecclesiastical robes and hoods. Sparse close-ups of nuns and friars constitute most of *The Church* series. Perhaps Serrano's most brutally unnerving series is *The Morgue*. He presents factual images of men, women, and a child who have died of meningitis, drowning, burning, eating rat poison, and — the most horrifying of all — beaten to death by police. The book ends with some atypical nude shots taken in Budapest.

Serrano's work is crisp to the extreme, with every last detail clearly presented. He has a rigorous documentary style that breathes life into his subjects. Although his work is visually the opposite of Joel-Peter Witkin's, Serrano does have something in common with the "Photographer of the Grotesque". They both create aesthetically beautiful works devoted to the most shocking subjects.

Serrano's elegant pictures easily mix life and death, the sacred and the profane, the body and the soul, so that we can see how intertwined they really are. It's a message that many people find disturbing, but it needs to recognised.

Takarajima Books; $50
1995; oversized softcover; 128 pp
heavily illus; 1-883489-11-3

HORRIPILATIONS
The Art of J.K. Potter
by JK Potter

I've always been a big fan of photomontage, and I admire the works of Scott Mutter and Jerry Uelsmann. The problem is, their images, while surreally beautiful, are slightly on the mundane side. I've longed to see what would happen when photomontage met an artist with messed-up sensibilities. I found my answer with JK Potter.

Potter creates photomontages for magazine and book covers and interiors. His work is used mainly by publishers of dark fantasy, horror, and science fiction, but even if you generally don't care for such genres, you'll still relish Potter's work if your tastes run along *noir* lines. There are no bug-eyed monsters or busty damsels in distress here. Potter explores the dark side of the psyche, the forces inside us that are always bursting out. The perfect example is *Evil Twin*, which depicts a man being violently choked. The hand around his neck leads to a forearm that suddenly morphs into the head of the man being choked.

Potter's work often explores the transmutation of flesh, as is demonstrated in "Transformations", one of the most powerful chapters in the book. *Big Mouth* shows a woman whose entire face, from chin to forehead, is a gigantic screaming mouth. *Toe-Headed Boy* is pretty self-explanatory. One of Potter's many collaborations with punk/writer/performance artist Lydia Lunch, *Strange Contemplation*, starts with Lunch's tattooed foot and ankle, leads to her calf, her bent knee, her thigh, which seamlessly becomes her upper arm, leading into her bent elbow, her forearm, and her hand, which is cradling her disembodied head.

Mermaid at Low Tide is a blue-tinted black and white shot of a beautiful mermaid with glowing eyes stranded on a rocky beach. *Dark Angel* shows a black-shrouded woman with wings standing in front of the Le Notre garden in the Palace of Versailles. *Reverend Satyr* is a portrait of a priest who has a normal left side of the face but whose forehead, nose, and right side of the face are that of a satyr.

Among my favourite shots is the series of three tinted photographs showing a blonde woman whose lower body is a tree (*Rooted*), an arm (*Katrina*), and the gaping jaws of an alligator (*The Succubus*). The image I find the most disconcerting is *Licking the Nightmare*. The left two-thirds of the frame is filled with a man's open mouth. He is sticking his tongue out, and on the end of his tongue is a man's head, which is licking the tongue of a woman in the right side of the

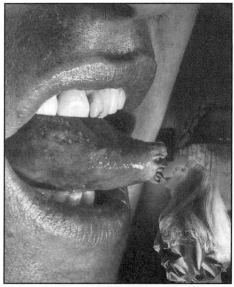

I've longed to see what would happen when photomontage met an artist with messed-up sensibilities. Licking the Nightmare, *Horripilations*.

picture.

Besides taking photographs and transforming them into montages, Potter also builds many of the objects in his work. The insect-like silvery robot of *Box Maker* (which was an illustration for William Gibson's *Count Zero* when it was originally published in *Isaac Asimov's Science Fiction Magazine*) is made up of tripods, toenail clippers, spoons, a piece of a chandelier, and other found objects. The grotesque creature in *Mr Lovecraft* was created with a cucumber, a horse vertebrae, starfish, octopus tentacles, and a glass eye.

Despite the amazing technical feats Potter pulls off in these images, he shuns cutting-edge technology for old school photography methods — dodging and burning, printing negatives, double exposing, solarising, etc. The most new-fangled device he uses is an airbrush. In the true experimental spirit of photography, many of his effects are accomplished during the actual taking of the picture. For example, the eerie lighting in *The Road Back to the Past* was accomplished simply by rocking the camera during the exposure.

Horripilations is a first-class presentation of the work of a criminally talented artist. It is beautifully printed on thick semi-glossy paper and contains around 130 images, including many that were previously unpublished. The text by Nigel Suckling sheds light on Potter's life and art. Each photomontage is accompanied by a caption that reveals the symbolism, technical details, and anecdotes behind the image.

US: The Overlook Press; $29.95
UK: Paper Tiger (Dragon's World); £12.95
1993; oversized softcover; 128 pp
heavily illus; 0-87951-613-5

William Vollmann's outsiders in the flesh.
Open All Night.

NEON NEVADA

by Sheila Swan & Peter Laufer

A photographic review of over 100 neon signs from the neon capital of the world, Nevada. These colour photographs were taken in 1977-1978 and in the early 1990s. The earlier photos show many signs that are no longer in existence. Accompanying text examines the history of neon in Nevada, how signs are made, and the future of this modern art form in Nevada.

University of Nevada Press; $19.95
1994; oversized softcover; 96 pp
heavily illus; 0-87417-246-2

NEUROTICA
The Darkest Art of J.K. Potter

by JK Potter

This second collection of JK Potter's wicked photomontages takes us further down dark roads of the psyche. In fact, the cover image, *Mouth of the Maw Shark*, comes directly from one of Potter's nightmares. A naked woman covers her face as a giant mouth opens up from just below her nipples to her bellybutton. From out of this gaping maw slithers a finless great white shark. This image may have been created in the artist's nightmares, but now it's sure to show up in ours, too.

One of the creepiest images I have *ever* seen is also one of Potter's simplest. An extreme close-up shows a frontal view of a man's open mouth, including lips, tongue, and teeth. A pair of sinister eyes peer out at us from the back of the throat, just behind the man's tongue. Potter comments: "I am always reminded of this picture whenever I have a sore throat."

Obeahman shows a man whose face morphs into an African mask with brightly glowing eyes. In several works, creepy nude women are inserted into pictures of bleak places, such as Pere Lachaise cemetery in France, a Gothic pulpit from the Victoria and Albert museum in London, and the ruins of Lincoln Beach. Nine mostly nude shots of the bewitching horror writer Poppy Z. Brite show her in a tattered and torn antique dress as a ghost, with three heads, and with a hand for a lower body.

Soul Effigy presents a woman whose head is gone, replaced by two hands clasping a large, smooth egg. In *Hand of Doom*, a giant disembodied hand with a snarling male face for a palm floats above a skeleton lying on the cracked ground. Sprawled across a bed, a woman's shapely legs, ass, and lower back flow smoothly into another woman's shapely legs, ass, and lower back in the aptly titled *Quadruped*. In *Horror House*, a skull is faintly superimposed onto a shot of an unpainted Victorian house.

Some images show seamless human/animal combinations, such as *Chihuahua Man*, *Mr Armand Dillo*, *Piranhaman*, and *Zebra Centauress Watching Ostrich Sex*. A woman's entire body morphs into the body of an octopus in *Xeethra*. A related work, *Lasher*, depicts a man opening his mouth, with a long, slimy octopus tentacle unfurling instead of a tongue.

The 110 images in *Neurotica* prove once again that JK Potter can creep us out like no one else because, instead of relying on scary monsters and other external forces, he reimagines our most important possession — our body — in ways that make the most grotesque distortions seem possible.

The Overlook Press; $27.95
1996; oversized softcover; 127 pp
heavily illus; 0-87951-687-9

OPEN ALL NIGHT

by Ken Miller with text by William T. Vollmann

In *Open All Night*, photographer Ken Miller shows us the actual people who populate the writings of William T. Vollmann [*Outposts* p 226]. Vollmann writes fiction and nonfiction based on his experiences with neo-Nazi skinheads in San Francisco, hookers and pimps in the Tenderloin, and alcoholic street people on Haight Street. Thanks to *Open All Night*, we get to peer into the eyes of these social outsiders. Vollmann reveals in his introduction that Miller is disgusted by beauty, riches, and all things middle class. "A thug hideously tattooed, a street witch whose rat-familiar peers out from between her breasts, a stinking bum who pisses in Ken's sink — these are the people who will open the shutters of his heart to maximum aperture, like a high school girl who was just given a rose."

In each of the 43 two-page spreads, one of Miller's photos fills the right-hand page. On the facing page is a relevant short excerpt from one of Vollmann's books, including *Butterfly Stories* and *Whores for Gloria*. The most menacing picture shows a group of skinheads standing in a room brandishing weapons — a lead pipe, a hatchet, guns — for the camera. Vollman's quote is from "The White Knights": "'Politics,' I once heard a conservative say, 'is the exercise of power. Power is the ability to inflict pain.' By this criterion the skinheads are among our most spontaneous politicians. Let us assume, then, that being spontaneous they are light of heart." In a humorous picture, a skinhead makes a distorted face by pulling his cheeks out with his ring fingers and turning his nose up with his middle fingers. Another shot shows a toddler who is just learning to walk being supported by an unseen adult whose arms are covered with tattoos of a naked woman and S. Clay Wilson's Checkered Demon.

One of the dozen or so pictures of prostitutes shows a naked woman sitting on a bed while the shirtless man next to her shoots up. Other pictures show two grizzly drunk guys in the mouth of a tent, a couple of Thai prostitutes, Thai kick boxers fighting, a naked man who's had 23 years of shock therapy, and a young blonde woman wearing a leather collar and a chain mail bikini top. [Also available in softcover from Penguin. $25; ISBN 0879516488.]

The Overlook Press; $40
1995; oversized hardcover; 91 pp
heavily illus; 0-87951-571-6

PLAYING WITH THE EDGE
The Photographic Achievement of Robert Mapplethorpe
by Arthur C. Danto

One of the world's pre-eminent art critics offers a surprisingly sympathetic look at Robert Mapplethorpe's photography. Arthur Danto examines Mapplethorpe's aesthetics, his messages and meanings, the controversy he ignited, and his place in the history of art. Reproduces twenty-three of Mapplethorpe's photos, including flowers, bodybuilder Lisa Lyon, child nudes, a self-portrait in drag, a self-portrait with a bullwhip up his ass, *Jim and Tom, Sausalito* (a hooded man pissing in another man's mouth), and *Man in Polyester Suit* (with his dick hanging out).

University of California Press; $24.95
1996; hardcover; 198 pp
illus; 0-520-20051-9

RAISED BY WOLVES
by Jim Goldberg

This fat monster of a book is crammed full of photographs taken by Jim Goldberg as he documented runaways and other homeless kids living on the streets of Hollywood and San Francisco. Over a period of ten years, he gained their confidence and was allowed to capture every aspect of their lives on film. As you might guess, this ain't a feel-good book.

"At Flynn squat I find Darby asleep in a bush. Hippie Dave is living in a box, trying to slam a crushed Valium pill in his arm with a blunted point. He keeps missing his veins so he gets red bumps. We climb up the hill and eat the Nutter Butters that Hippie Dave found in the trash." This is a typical episode related by Goldberg during the process of shooting. Another description, of life at the Paradise Hotel in Frisco, is more of the same: "The door is kicked in at Rhonda and Jill's. Hubba. There are other girls staying there, all whores

tricking for rocks. Jill has a black eye. Apparently Rhonda is paranoid and beating up on her. Crystal says she just had a seizure from smoking too much crack. They are all bored."

The hundreds of mostly black and white pictures are the visual equivalent of these relentlessly hopeless journal entries. Two kids leaning over the hood of a sheriff's car. A fire blazing in a dumpster outside a multi-level parking garage. A close-up of one hand flicking a lighter and the other holding a crack pipe. A guy holding onto a rail and puking on the sidewalk. One teenager pinning another one to the street while a couple of people look on. A drag queen hooker standing on a street corner. A shirtless boy, all skin and bones, lying down on the star-covered sidewalk outside the Chinese Theater. Three guys and a girl shooting heroin. A young girl with "LOST GANGSTA CRIP" tattooed on her back. Four kids lounging around the most squalid shithole of a room you've ever seen. A pretty girl whose hand is covered in purple lesions. A kid aiming a pistol out a window at a passer-by on the sidewalk below.

Some of the portraits of the kids appear alongside their hand-written notes. A short-haired girl sniffs a rose. Beside her is inscribed: "I want to get married and have at least four kids with 10 dogs, and live in a mansion with a jungle greenhouse with a pet jaguar." Next to an old school picture of a young boy, Robert writes: "MY MOM AND DAD REEJECT. ME ThEY TOOK A hAMMER TOO MY LEG. AND BEATED ME--BRIAN DAMAGE. TheRE iS NO LOVE IN MY LIFE. ThiNGS ARE ALL WRONG. I SUCK DiCK FOR$$$."

The kaleidoscope of images — blurry and focused, grainy and sharp, panoramic and close-up, at all different angles — creates a collage effect that gives a more well-rounded feel for life on the street (of course, looking at pictures could never come close to letting us feel what it's like to live it. But they're powerful enough to make me be thankful for everything I have.) The written documents — journal entries, scrawled notes, bits of dialogue, a letter from Children's Hospital, a doodle of a girl being raped by her dad — all add up to a street-level view of this ignored aspect of the American Scream.

Scalo (D.A.P.); $45
1995; oversized softcover; 319 pp
heavily illus; 1-881616-50-9

THE SACRED HEART
An Atlas of the Body as Seen Through Invasive Surgery
by Max Aguilera-Hellweg

Medical textbooks and journals have a cult following in certain subcultures. Looking at clinical photographs of surgery, tumours, and accident victims may sound crass and base, but it's actually quite fascinating because it reveals an important aspect of our world that remains hidden from most of us. Even if we own nothing else, each of us possesses one thing — our body. Yet the inner functionings of this ubiquitous wonder are only dealt with in the most abstract terms. Few people want to or have the opportunity to get an unadulterated look at what goes on under the hood. That's why medical photography has developed an unexpected follow-

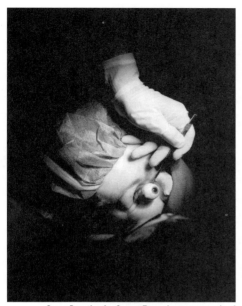

Organ Donation for Cornea Transplant, an example of medical photography as high art. *The Sacred Heart*.

ing. I could be wrong, but I believe it was JG Ballard who once said that these photos are a form of pornography. They reveal in no uncertain terms the most intimate functionings of the body.

Well, if *Techniques of Cardiac Surgery* is the equivalent of *Debbie Does Dallas*, then *The Sacred Heart* is *Libido* or the work of Jeanloup Sieff. Same subject matter, wildly different approaches. Max Aguila-Hellweg is the first person to purposely take graphic medical photography to the level of art form. In this book, 44 surgical procedures are documented by the unblinking eye of the camera. The images are explosions of reds, pinks, and fleshtones swimming in the centre of a black sea. I'm not sure how Aguilera-Hellweg did it, but each picture — most of which are printed as full-page bleeds — brightly illuminates the body part being photographed, while the rest of the area is pitch black. It looks as though all the lights in the OR were turned off and then a narrow spotlight was put on the surgical area, but this would seem to be extraordinarily dangerous to the patient. Many of these pictures were clicked in the very midst of an operation, so I doubt that the lights were turned out. Perhaps Aguilera-Hellweg achieved the effect in the darkroom. No matter how it was done, though, the results are haunting, moody, and bloody.

In *Organ Donation for Cornea Transplant*, a surgeon has gently scooped an eyeball out of a donor. The orb stares straight ahead just an inch away from the now empty cavity that used to contain it. The focus of *Tumor Associated with Liver Disease* is a white, roundish mass a little smaller than a tennis ball that sits amid the glistening pinkish organs of a torso that's been opened wide. One of the more gently disturbing images shows a young woman's eyelids being sewn

shut prior to craniofacial surgery.

In *Breast Lift, Nipple and Areola* a pair of gloved hands pulls apart a breast that has been completely cut open like so much raw meat. In the middle of this bloody mess sits an undisturbed nipple and areola. Another shot shows two thin metal rods gracefully pulling a clump of visceral matter from a bodily opening. The title says it all: *Uterus and Tumor Removed via the Vagina*. The more euphemistically titled *Penile Implant Surgery* features an unassuming penis that has been cut open right where it meets the scrotum. In a later shot, we see a surgeon's finger sticking in this gaping wound.

If you want to test your mettle, check out *Face Peeled Back (Side View)*. This is one in a series of photos showing the skull reconstruction of a woman with a hereditary deformity. In order to work on the top half of her noggin, the doctors made an ear-to-ear incision over the top of her scalp, then peeled back her face. You get to see the completely exposed skull of a living human. In *AIDS Autopsy: Brain*, not only is the corpse's face pulled back, but a portion of its skull has been removed too. A wet pink brain protrudes from what was once face.

Other procedures that are documented in this book range from the prosaic (bunion removal) to the exotic (Siamese twin separation), including spinal cord injury, removal of plaque from the cartoid artery, surgery to relieve epilepsy, heart procurement for transplant, skin grafts, a Caesarean birth, hip replacement, and laser eye surgery.

The Sacred Heart is a pioneering book that finds queasy beauty in the most corporal of subjects.

Bulfinch Press (Little, Brown & Co); $50
1997; oversized hardcover; 127 pp
heavily illus; 0-8212-2377-1

UNTITLED
by Diane Arbus

Diane Arbus is one of the most respected photographers of all time. During the 1960s, she did portrait and glamour photography for magazines such as *Esquire* and *Harper's Bazaar*, but towards the end of the decade she had become a photographer of what she called the "bloodied people", those who exist at the fringes of society. Her images were black and white snapshots of midgets, nudists, transvestites, the homeless, retarded people, and, one of her favourite obsessions, twins. Reaction to this work was mixed at first — some people were quite hostile towards it — but she has now been recognised as a visionary. She committed suicide in 1971.

From 1969 until her death, she travelled to homes for mentally retarded people and took photos of the residents. She had thought of making a book out of the project, but died before any plans were made. Thus, most of the 51 photographs in *Untitled* remained unpublished until now. As always, Arbus shot her subjects straight on, with them looking at the camera. There's nowhere to run, nowhere to hide… you must gaze directly into the eyes of people who make most of society very uncomfortable.

Arbus was careful never to let her images become some kind of freak show, and this is apparent in *Untitled*. She doesn't invite us to gawk at her subjects — instead, she hu-

<u>Still Life</u>, Marseilles, 1992. *Witkin.*

manises them. A lot of the people in the photos are in masks or full costumes (apparently half of the pictures were taken on Halloween). In one photo, a line of five women in "good witch" costumes smile and wave their magic wands at the camera. In another, a girl in a Casper mask and a boy in a home-made masquerade mask walk hand-in-hand across a lawn. Among the non-Halloween images is one of a woman, who looks at least 50, clutching a doll and some other toys. In another picture, a woman with the face of a middle-age woman and the body of a young girl laughs hysterically while pointing to something outside the frame.

In most of these pictures, the people are unguarded and usually appear to be unselfconscious. Because of this, Arbus may have achieved what she always wanted to show in her art — a purity and humanity that only the bloodied people can possess. This is probably why she wrote of these pictures, "Finally, what I've been searching for."

Aperture; $50
1995; hugely oversized hardcover (11.25" x 14.25"); 112 pp
heavily illus; 0-89381-623-X

WEEGEE'S PEOPLE
by Weegee

Weegee (real name: Arthur Fellig) is one of the most important photographers of the century. He started out as a freelance photojournalist, combing New York's mean streets during the 1940s, looking for crimes and disasters. He had an uncanny knack for being at the right place at the wrong time and snapping gritty shots of the Big Apple's underbelly. These pictures were collected in the book *Naked City* (1945), which brought instant fame, fortune, and women to Weegee. He was then in demand as a glamour photographer for *Vogue*, *Life*, etc.

Weegee accepted his new role and snapped pictures of glamorous clubs, debutante balls, and the "beautiful people". However, being Weegee, he couldn't resist trolling the "earthier" sections of town, taking pix of the homeless, the working poor, Bohemians, jazz musicians, party-goers at after-hours clubs, and so on. These are the photographs that are collected in *Weegee's People*. The chapter "Society" contains most of the glitzy pictures. It seems someone had forgotten to get Weegee a ticket to an opera opening,

so he snuck in with none other than Mrs. Cornelius Vanderbilt. Interestingly, Weegee had to shoot these pictures with infrared film because if he used a flash he'd "get the bum's rush", to use his phrase.

"The Park Bench" shows the denizens of benches in Washington Square Park in Greenwich Village. Weegee captures lovers making out, men playing chequers, an old man covered in birds, a woman with a cat in her purse, and a Bill Cosby-lookalike blowing bubbles. "The Sidewalk" contains two of the most memorable pictures. One shows the cheesiest character you've ever seen holding up a slogan that a beer company was test-marketing. The other shows "the walking department store", an old man who has pinned pipe cleaners, toilet scrubbers, cheese graters, and other junk onto his coat. The homeless and destitute take centre stage in "A Place to Sleep", while hep cats boogie in "Saturday Night."

Weegee's flat, grainy pictures have extremely high contrast. They use a blinding flash to cut through the darkness and freeze a moment perfectly, whether it's a prima donna laughing at a joke or a drunk bum about to fall over. It's obvious that Weegee loves all kinds of people. As he writes in the introduction: "Here's my formula — dealing as I do with human beings, and I find them wonderful: I leave them alone and let them be themselves…"

Da Capo Press; $13.95
1946, 1988; softcover; 238 pp
heavily illus; 0-306-80242-2

WITKIN
edited by Germano Celant

Joel-Peter Witkin has become known as the Photographer of the Grotesque for good reason. His photographs are elaborately-staged productions that centre on amputees, hermaphrodites, pre-operative transsexuals, dead animals, Siamese twins, severed heads, still-born babies, and other beings and objects that make people uncomfortable. Witkin manages to take even his most shocking and repulsive subjects and make them into photographs that are beautiful, at least in the technical sense. More than any other photographer, he has endeavoured to record his own bizarre universe, creating a mythos populated by the macabre, the misunderstood, and the rejected.

Witkin uses a long, laborious process in order to make his photographs look like dark brown, tinted, scratched daguerreotypes. It may take weeks of intense work to get just one photograph the way he wants it.

OK, enough talk. Let's take a look at some of the 113 plates that are reproduced, representing Witkin's work from 1973 to 1994.

☞ *Carrotcake I, New Mexico, 1980*: A nude, unbelievably obese woman wearing a frilly white mask masturbates with a carrot.

☞ *Madame X, San Francisco, 1981*: Resembling a transgendered Venus de Milo, Madame X strikes a regal pose, revealing that s/he has no arms, full breasts, and a penis.

☞ *Woman with a Severed Head, New Mexico, 1982*:

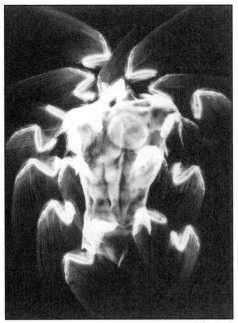

x=001, *X=T.*

A topless woman wearing a black veil cradles an old man's decapitated head.

☞ *Portrait of Holocaust, New Mexico, 1982*: A nude, obese woman lies on her side. She is holding three foetuses by their legs.

☞ *The Kiss (Le Baiser), New Mexico, 1982*: The severed heads of two old men (who look like twins) are embraced in a lip-lock.

☞ *Testicle Stretch with the Possibility of a Crushed Face, New Mexico, 1982*: A man is tied laying face-up on a board. His scrotum is being stretched to an inhuman length by a leather strap attached to a rope. The rope goes through a pulley on the ceiling, and on the other end are several barbell weights, which hang over the man's head.

☞ *Savior of the Primates, New Mexico, 1982*: A monkey wearing a mask is tied crucifixion-style to a cross.

☞ *Eunuch, New Mexico, 1983*: A dog wearing a strap-on dildo is mounting a man who is wearing fake breasts and holding a hacksaw.

☞ *Feast of Fools, New Mexico, 1990*: A lavish setting of grapes, gourds, seafood, severed hands, a severed foot, and a dead toddler.

☞ *Man without a Head, 1993*: A somewhat overweight man sits in a corner wearing nothing but socks. There is a big, gaping hole where his neck and head should be.

Final sections contain listings of Witkin's awards, individual and group exhibitions, books, catalogues, articles, and permanent exhibitions, which are housed in more than 24

institutions, including Bibliothèque Nationale in Paris, the Metropolitan Museum of Art, the Smithsonian, and the Museums of Modern Art in New York and San Francisco.

Scalo (D.A.P.); $75
1995; oversized hardcover; 272 pp
heavily illus; 1-881616-20-7

X=T
The Art of X-Ray Photography
by Seiju Toda

Just when you thought you knew every unorthodox method of photography — infrared film, solarisation, pinhole cameras — along comes one of Japan's most accomplished designer/artists and does something that has never been done before. Seiju Toda has used an X-ray machine as a fine art camera. These 39 images, taken over a period of five years, go right through the outer surfaces of their animal and human subjects "into their 'inner space'… where the essence of 'life' resides." The spectral beauty brought out by the X-rays hitting Toda's unusual conglomeration of objects ensures a visual experience like no other.

At the top of the fifth plate (*x=005*) are two wings from a toy fighter airplane. Extending to the bottom of the plate are the bones from three heron legs, encased in filmy elliptical objects. The next plate shows a tall, narrow wooden cabinet housing the intertwined skeletons of eight pit vipers.

x=008 is a close-up of two monkey hands pressed together in prayer. In between them is the slithering skeleton of a viper. Continuing with the primate theme, *x=011* contains the ghostly images of a wooden model of futuristic apartment buildings, each of which houses a monkey finger. The next plate features the same model, X-rayed at a slightly lower angle, but this time it's filled with the upright skeletons of another eight vipers.

The enigmatically beautiful skeletons of sting-rays form the basis of two of the book's most powerful images. In *x=020* a Y-shaped balsa wood structure seems to rise out of the image towards the viewer. A sting-ray "swims" out from each branch of the Y. The next plate contains the angelic image of a giant sting-ray superimposed on nine large sperm-shaped sculptures.

No doubt you'll be wondering about the story behind these images, so thankfully Toda explains how they were made and provides traditional photographs of his props. Art critic and historian Max Kozloff attempts to put it all in perspective with his essay "Metaphysics of the X Ray."

Fittingly, the book itself is as elaborate as its unprecedented subject matter. It measures a whopping 12" x 17", so it's not going to fit on your bookshelves. You could put it on your coffee table, but there's a chance that it's as large as your coffee table, leaving you with few options. The images have been painstakingly reproduced as duotones on glossy paper that's as thick as magazine cover stock. Twenty-six of the X-rays are printed as full page bleeds, and the remaining third are massive foldouts that are a foot-and-a-half wide.

Naturally, such a lush book of exquisite photography is going to cost you a humerus and a femur. See if you can wheedle a nearby well-funded library (if such a beast exists) into buying a copy.

Hudson Hills Press; $75

1995; hugely oversized hardcover; 161 pp

heavily illus; 1-55595-080-9

FILM

DESPERATE VISIONS
The Journal of Alternative Cinema,
Volume 1: Camp America
by Jack Stevenson

The first volume of this "journal" (which in form and content is really a book) is devoted to three impresarios of trashy, sleazy cinema — John Waters (*Pink Flamingos*, *Hairspray*, *Serial Mom*) and the Kuchar Brothers, twins George and Mike (*Pussy on a Hot Tin Roof*, *Hold Me While I'm Naked*, *Sins of the Fleshapoids*). The first part contains an essay on Waters, 65 pages of interviews with him, and separate interviews with four members of his entourage: Divine, Mink Stole, Mary Vivian Pearce, and Miss Jean Hill. Part two has an essay on the Kuchar Bros., separate interviews with each of them, and a look at actress Marion Eaton, best remembered for *Thundercrack!*, a 1975 underground bisexual porno horror film. Plus an extensive filmography and loads of pictures, including some from the directors' rare early movies.

Creation Books; $17.95

1996; oversized softcover; 256 pp

illus; 1-871592-34-8

IMMORAL TALES
European Sex and Horror Movies,
1956-1984
by Cathal Tohill & Pete Tombs

From the mid-1950s to the mid-1980s, European filmmakers produced an outrageous crop of films that mixed terror and eroticism. They were influenced by everything from Surrealism, Romanticism, Decadence, and *fantastique* cinema to pulp fiction, early horror movies, and sex comics. "Because of this, these bizarre flicks defy simple pigeon-holing. They're too lowbrow to be considered arty, but too intelligent and personal to be described simply as Euro-trash. They're a curious hybrid, milking the dynamicism of popular literature and comic books, combining it with the perverse romanticism of real Art."

Immoral Tales is a definitive history and critique of this fuzzy genre, which encompasses *Terror Creatures from Beyond the Grave*, *Horror of Spider Island*, *Erotic Witchcraft*, *Hercules' Challenge*, *Spermula*, *Pick-Up Girls*, *The Bare-Breasted Countess*, *Paris, Oh, La La!*, *Slow Slidings of Pleasure*, and *Behind Convent Walls*. The book starts with

Judex, *Necronomicon*.

a history of the horror film, showing how it was transformed in Europe by the addition of eroticism. The chapter "The European Experience" devotes about ten pages each to Italian, German, French, and Spanish contributions to the genre.

After that, six directors are each given a chapter: the "lowbrows" Jess Franco, Jean Rollin, and José Larraz and the "arty types" José Bénazéraf, Walerian Borowczyk, and Alain Robbe-Grillet. An appendix gives information on dozens of additional directors, stars, writers, and others involved in European erotic horror cinema. Another section in the back of the book traces the concurrent history of the European adult comic book.

Like any worthwhile book on B-movies, *Immoral Tales* is lavishly illustrated with hundreds of movie posters and stills, many of which contain nekkid ladies. A centre section has sixteen pages of full colour reproductions.

St. Martin's; $17.95

1995; oversized softcover; 272 pp

heavily illus; 0-312-13519-X

NECRONOMICON
The Journal of Horror and Erotic
Cinema, Book One
edited by Andy Black

Andy Black's highly-respected magazine *Necronomicon* has now become a heavily-illustrated, glossy yearly book. The first instalment contains eighteen articles scrutinising and interpreting directors, actors, and specific movies that fall into the genres of horror or erotica/porn. The writing goes way beyond fans just talking about why their favourite movies are so cool. The contributors analyse themes, symbols, and techniques used in these films, which is groundbreaking, since horror and erotic movies are usually considered beneath such serious attention. The essays can get kind of stilted and dense with references to psychoanalysts (Freud,

The choicest schlock around. *Slimetime.*

Jung, Lacan, et al), film theory, and feminist theory, but they're never stodgy (this is a book from Creation, after all).

In "Once Upon a Time in Texas: *The Texas Chainsaw Massacre* as Inverted Fairy Tale", Mikita Brottman writes: "Whereas the majority of horror films, by affording their audiences uncanny glimpses of the fairytale's animistic universe, lead them through the dangers of adolescent sexual predicament, reinforcing the culture's taboos in a ritual display of rule-breaking, *The Texas Chainsaw Massacre* instead serves to mislead, misdirect and confuse its audience in a bewildering nightmare of suggested bloodshed and violence." Xavier Mendik's essay, "From 'Trick' to 'Prick': Porn's Primitive Pleasures" states, "While not wishing to deny the essentially exploitative and misogynistic nature of many pornographic images, Linda Williams' account of films such as *Deep Throat* and the Marilyn Chambers vehicle *Behind the Green Door*, has pointed to the way that such texts concentrate on the expression of women's desires, thus creating a 'female' space that is lacking in most mainstream films."

Other articles include "*Daughters of Darkness*: A Lesbian Vampire Film", "Marco Ferreri: Sadean Cinema of Excess", "*The Evil Dead*: From Slapstick to Splatshtick", "*Psycho/The Birds*: Hitchcock Revisited", "The Other Face of Death: Barbara Steele and *La Maschera Del Demonio*", "Crawling Celluloid Chaos: HP Lovecraft in Cinema", "*Last Tango in Paris*: Circles of Sex and Death", "Herschell Gordon Lewis: Compulsive Tales and Cannibal Feasts", and "*The Bride of Frankenstein*: Sexual Polarity and Subjugation".

Creation Books; £11.95, $16.95US
1996; oversized softcover; 191 pp
heavily illus; 1-871592-37-2

PASOLINI
Forms of Subjectivity
by Robert S.C. Gordon

A Pasolini scholar interprets all of the work of the controversial, gay, atheistic, anti-fascist creative genius Pier Paolo Pasolini: his journalism, essays, poetry, prose, and films.

Oxford University Press; $72
1996; hardcover; 324 pp
illus; 0-19-815905-6

SLIMETIME
A Guide to Sleazy, Mindless, Movie Entertainment
by Steven Puchalski *et al*

From 1986 till 1989, the zine *Slimetime* offered up searing, stinging, and even approving reviews of hundreds of bizarre films from the past and present. This book collects over 400 reviews from the zine. It isn't meant to be a comprehensive encyclopaedia of celluloid strangeness, but rather an entertaining and highly personal selection of some of the choicest schlock around — Frank Zappa's *200 Motels*, Andy Warhol's *Bad* and *Trash*, *The Blue Eyes of the Broken Doll*, *Dolemite*, *Ganjasaurus Rex*, *Godzilla Vs. The Bionic Monster*, *Killer Shrews*, Dennis Hopper's ultra-rare *The Last Movie*, *Matango: The Fungus of Terror*, *Naked Angels*, *The Sadist*, *Salvation! Have You Said Your Prayers Today?*, and *The Undertaker and His Pals*.

Puchalski and co rarely hold back in their opinionated reviews:

Fat Guy Goes Nutzoid!!: "Lloyd Kaufman and Michael Herz strike again with this stinkwad of a film, which Troma scraped off the Men's Room floor and decided to distribute. It's as bad as you can imagine. Maybe worse. John Golden directed and let's hope somebody blinds him with hot pokers before he gets the chance to pick up another movie camera."

KISS Meets the Phantom of the Park: "Damn it! *Damn* it! AVOID THIS MOVIE AT ALL COSTS, GOD-FUCKING *DAMMIT*!!!"

The Incredibly Strange Creatures Who Stopped Living and Became Mixed-Up Zombies: "I've been searching for this cult item for several years, and now that I've found it is there any way of losing it again?"

The Toxic Avenger: "But Troma Pictures, the scuzzbag operation who virtually revitalised the rip-off drive-in movie with junk like *Stuck on You* and *Screwballs*, has actually pulled a winner out of their toilet bowl this time around. Sure, no cliché is left unsoiled and it looks like it was edited together with a dull steak knife and a stapler, but that's half the fun..."

But not every movie is slagged off. Puchalski actually has kind words to say about the mainstream flick *Heathers*, and he catches everyone completely off-guard by heaping praise on the Monkees' only feature film, *Head*. He declares that it is "one of my top five favourite motion pictures of all time." He goes on: "Well, I saw this film for the first time about 15 years ago. Since then I've sat through *Head* half a dozen times on the screen and another dozen times of video, and as far as I'm concerned, it's The Monkees' own *2001* — their *Yellow Submarine* — their *Godzilla vs. The Thing*. Not just a good film, not just a weird film, this is one of the most cleverly-conceived masterworks of the LSD era. And would you believe me if I also said it was one of the few most cerebral *and* hallucinogenic movies ever made?"

Slimetime ends with Puchalski's detailed histories of three outlaw genres — biker movies, blaxploitation films, and psychedelic drug flicks — earlier versions of which were originally published in *Shock Xpress* magazine.

Headpress; £12.95, $19.95; OUT OF PRINT
1996; oversized softcover; 199 pp
heavily illus; 0-9523288-5-2

SOMETHING WEIRD VIDEO CATALOGUE

Thousands upon thousands of exploitation and sexploitation movies for only $20 each! It's hard to believe that this many wonderfully crappy movies ever got made, but the proof is right in front of your eyes in this 120-page catalogue that's crammed with three to ten illustrations on every wildly-designed page. You can choose from several decades' (but mainly the 1960s and 1970s) of schlock, sleaze, hack work, gore, youthsploitation, drugsploitation, shockumentaries, nudie-cuties, softcore teasers, sci-fi skin flicks, whore stories, Mexican wrestling, bikers, nymphos, and sex, drugs, and violence.

Among the things that caught my eye: Twelve psychosexual horror movies by Brazilian cult director Coffin Joe, including *This Night I Will Possess Your Corpse* and *Hallucinations of a Deranged Mind*. *Mondo Balordo*, a patently fake Italian shockumentary, narrated by Boris Karloff. *White Slaves of Chinatown*, the first of the three "Olga films", about a sadistic woman who keeps babes in bondage in her torture chamber. Several all-but-impossible to find Ed Wood films, including his last opus, *Necromania* (1971). *Indian Raid, Indian Made*, a 1969 flick starring the beachball-breasted Morganna, better known as baseball's Kissing Bandit.

Murder in Mississippi, a harsh 1965 movie that tackles the subject of murdered civil rights workers more bluntly than *Mississippi Burning*, which was made more than two decades later. *Satan's Bed*, a twisted grindhouse feature with Yoko Ono in a starring role. *Teaserama*, "the Holy Grail of Girlie Flicks", is Irving Klaw's long-lost movie that features pinup queen Bettie Page in her only starring role. Several burlesque films, including three starring Tempest Storm. A 100 volume series of nudie-cutie compilations. Twenty-nine volumes of under-the-counter fetish sex loops. Fifty volumes of hardcore loops, stag films, and peeps from the 1950s, 1960s, and early 1970s, and six volumes of triple-X stags from the 1920s through 1940s.

Plus, you won't want to miss *The Pigkeeper's Daughter*, a classic of the hillbilly sexploitation subgenre; *The Beast That Killed Women*, about a homicidal gorilla that invades a nudist camp; *Nude on the Moon*, "Man discovers a NUDIST CAMP on the MOON!"; *Illegal Wives*, a thinly-disguised anti-Mormon exploitation film from 1939; *Alice in Acidland*, a psychedelic 1960s movie; and *Killer Snakes*, "an

over-the-top Hong Kong horror/sex/kung-fu flick".

Not only is the catalogue profusely illustrated with bare-breasted bimbos, but it's also a treat to read. These sleazehounds obviously love what they're doing and have gone to the ends of the earth to bring you obscure celluloid sickness. They describe each movie, sometimes briefly and sometimes in detail, but always in a fun, light-hearted manner. They also let you know the movies' directors, stars, alternative titles, and release dates.

SWV Catalog/PO Box 33664/Seattle WA 98133
WWW: www.somethingweird.com
catalog: $5

TOTEM OF THE DEPRAVED
by Nick Zedd

Concept: Autobiography of Nick Zedd.

Who: Nick Zedd is the prime mover of the Cinema of Transgression, an important underground movement that messed with people's heads in the 1980s. His films include *They Eat Scum*, *Thrust in Me*, *Fingered*, *Whoregasm*, and *War Is Menstrual Envy*.

Approach: Nasty, nihilistic, unbridled, hedonistic.

Cast of Characters: Lydia Lunch, Lung Leg, Rick Strange, Slick, Nazi Dick, GG Allin.

On His Parents: "We didn't get along too well when I was a teenager, but for some reason they couldn't bring themselves to disown me even though I got busted for drugs, burglarised houses, and once stole a bubble gum machine. My younger brother Jon turned out to be quite normal."

On His Art: "I have tried to release my id in my films — to express something beyond words — my own confusion and horror, joy and ecstasy at being alive. These deformed, brilliant, and beautiful entities are shadows of light and sound made to cut through the hypocrisy to which you and I are conditioned."

On Sex with a Woman Named Casandra: "I practically devoured her, biting, ripping and bruising her all over. She had a unique proclivity for absorbing pain that cemented us together for nine months."

On Drugs: "The sight of a thin metal spike as it impaled a thick blue vein made me feel closer to the death that I wanted."

Credo: "I have always felt that it is better to give ulcers than to receive them."

Verdict: Not nearly enough details on the making of the films to satisfy people wanting to learn about the Cinema of Transgression, but it makes an interesting, though depressing, read.

2.13.61; $12
1996; softcover; 163 pp
illus; 1-880985-35-7

UNDERGROUND FILM
A Critical History
by Parker Tyler

Originally published in 1969, *Underground Film* is recognised as one of the most important books on avant garde film ever published. Film critic Parker Tyler was at the time almost the only critic who championed such films. In this book he analyses the work of Kenneth Anger, Aubrey Beardsley, Stan Brakhage, André Breton, Luis Buñuel, Jean Cocteau, Maya Deren, Marcel Duchamp, Man Ray, Alain Robbe-Grillet, and Andy Warhol, as well as The Beatles' *Yellow Submarine*, the beatnik *Pull My Daisy*, Yoko Ono's *Number Four*, the documentary *Titicut Follies*, *Passages from Finnegans Wake*, *I Am Curious (Yellow)*, and many more. Includes 31 pages of film stills, including some of the most notorious scenes from the movies.

Da Capo Press; $13.95
1969, 1995; softcover; 282 pp
illus; 0-306-80632-0

Tribe 8 is San Francisco's all-dyke punk band.
Angry Women in Rock, Volume 1.

MUSIC

ANGRY WOMEN IN ROCK, VOLUME ONE
by Andrea Juno

Concept: Andrea Juno — one half of the former RE/Search Publishing team and the mastermind behind *Angry Women* [*Outposts* p 238] — conducts extensive interviews with over a dozen of the most radical women in rock and roll.

Overriding idea: "Rock'n'roll has always been a haven for the image of the outlaw, making it a natural place where the boundaries of proscribed femininity can be transgressed. Girls can be bold, brash and loud; all the things they were taught not to be."

Interviewees: Jarboe (the Swans), all the members of Tribe 8 ("San Francisco's all-dyke punk band"), Joan Jett, Kathleen Hanna (Bikini Kill), Valerie Agnew (7 Year Bitch), Lois Maffeo (Lois), Naomia Yang (Damon & Naomi), Kendra Smith (formerly of Opal, which became Mazzy Star), "The All-American Jewish Lesbian Folksinger" Phranc, Candice Pedersen (co-owner of K Records), Bettina Richards (founder of Thrill Jockey Records), Chrissie Hynde (The Pretenders), and June Millington (cofounder of Fanny, the first all-woman band to be signed to a major label).

Interview Topics: making music, selling out, playing shows, musical tastes, the business side of music, the male domination of rock and roll, feminism, sex, gender, pornography, drug use, violence, the Riot Grrrl movement, the media, spirituality, much more.

On Live Shows: Tribe 8 discusses their notorious antics in which singer Kim Breedlove takes off her shirt and wears a 10-inch dildo hanging out of her pants. She invites straight men to come up onstage and suck it during the show. Later she'll pull out a knife and chop it off. "I *really* love to have a big, hunky, straight guy with a five-day beard growth sucking my dick, and have the crowd look at that: me topless with my big rubber dick down that straight guy's throat. I want

them to see *that*, because that really freaks them out and turns the whole power thing upside down. It threatens them, and I want them to feel threatened."

On Musical Training: Valerie Agnew of 7 Year Bitch: "When I first started taking lessons at a Seattle drum school, I remember my teacher saying, 'You know, a lot of women have problems with their upper arm strength. You have to be very careful about tunnel carpal syndrome and make sure you hold your sticks correctly, because two months down the line, a lot of women drummers find the stress of their muscles is too much.' I remember thinking, 'That's a complete crock of shit!'"

Illustrations?: Wall-to-wall, with a couple of memorable shots of a big white guy with a shaved head giving Kim Breedlove an onstage blowjob.

Bottom Line: Because of its narrower focus, generally not as important as *Angry Women*, but still a vital document on the past and present oestrogenisation of the overwhelmingly adolescent male world of rock and roll.

Juno Books; $19.95
1996; oversized softcover; 224 pp
heavily illus; 0-9651042-0-6

BACKSTAGE PASS
Interviews with Women in Music
by Laura Post

Laura Post conducts short interviews with 40 women who are making music in a variety of genres — alternative rock, bluegrass, jazz, folk, folk-rock, blues, world music, pop, and other styles and permutations. Interviewees include Ani DiFranco, Joan Osborne, the Chenille Sisters, Marianne Faithfull, Phranc, June Millinton, Laura Love, Vicki Randle, Moe Tucker (of the Velvet Underground), Kristen Hersh of Throwing Muses, and jazz guitarist Mimi Fox. A short intro, discography, and a photo flesh out each interview.

New Victoria Publishers; $16.95
1997; softcover; 222 pp
illus; 0-934678-84-7

BOOTLEG
The Secret History of the Other Recording Industry
by Clinton Heylin

When you love a group or a solo artist so much that you've tracked down everything they've released yet you still want more, what do you do? You find the stuff they haven't released... at least, they never intended it to find its way to the outside world. Bootleg consists of live recordings, demos and alternate takes of officially released songs, and — most precious of all — songs that were recorded but never made available in any form. Bootleg recordings have unofficially played an important role in the history of rock and roll. They are so widespread and so cherished by fans that they have spawned a subterranean industry, a hidden mirror of the official rock industry.

The first rock bootleg album was *Great White Wonder* by Bob Dylan, appearing in the summer of 1969. This unassuming collection of home recordings and Woodstock performances spawned what would become a $250 million industry that puts out 2000 new releases each year. Some bootleg works — Prince's *Black Album*, the Beach Boys' *Smile*, and the Rolling Stones' "Cocksucker Blues" — have taken their place among rock and roll's most legendary recordings.

Rock writer Clinton Heylin presents a history that's as massive and far-ranging as the subject it covers. He offers a thorough examination of twenty-six years of unauthorised rock — the bootleggers, the sellers, the fans, the artists, the legal battles, and, of course, the recordings themselves. *Bootleg* also contains the often creative album covers for over a hundred releases.

Unexpectedly, it turns out that Heylin is a defender of bootleg. Despite the sobbings of the corporate world that it loses millions annually to bootleg, it is probably not financially damaging. Someone who likes, say, U2 enough to buy a bootleg, already has all of their official releases. It's not an either/or situation. The reason this fan turns to bootleg is because she's already exhausted the band's "legitimate" body of work. "The bootleggers are the ultimate free-marketeers, giving fans what they want — and to hell with the wishes of the artist or the record company." Bootleg recordings can also serve an important function by showing how an artist originally intended an album to sound. For example, *Get Back* contains the Beatles' simple, back-to-the-basics tracks that were subsequently muzaked by Phil Spector when he turned them into *Let It Be*.

With its encyclopaedic breadth and detailed focus on every aspect of the subject, *Bootleg* is the book that the underside of rock and roll deserves.

St. Martin's; $16.95
1994; softcover; 441 pp
illus; 0-312-14289-7

EXPERIMENTAL MUSICAL INSTRUMENTS

This friendly, completely unpretentious magazine is devoted to "the design, construction and enjoyment of unusual sound

Trade Mark of Quality logo. *Bootleg*.

sources." The instruments they cover may be already-existing but obscure, newly created, or not even instruments at all. Volume 10 #3 covers the alfalfa viola, a single-stringed instrument; the Apache violin; the tubulong, "a set of tuned metal tubes mounted marimba-style for playing with mallets"; aeolian instruments, which are stringed instruments that produce music when the wind blows through them; pyrophones, instruments that use flames to heat glass tubes which then produce sounds; the use of bamboo in instruments; and Franco Piper, a turn-of-the-century South African who could, among other things, juggle six banjos while playing a tune on them. As the neck of each banjo fell into his hands, he would play the correct one or two notes to keep the song going in perfect time.

The next issue has articles on nature recordings; the Stroh violin, which looks like a cross between a violin and a horn; Johannes Bergmark, a musician who has created over thirty wild instruments; the Lautenwerk (or lute-harpsichord), a keyboard stringed instrument; hunter's game calls; the trigon incantor; and speed bump music. In the latter article, the author tells of a novel idea his friend had for making music. "In particular, Tim was telling me about his interest in the hum that is produced when a car runs over a series of small speed bumps. The pitch of the hum is altered according to the speed of the vehicle, the size of the bumps, and the spacing between bumps. He wondered if it would be possible to arrange the raised patterns so that they would produce a sequence of pitches (a melody) as a vehicle rolls over them."

Naturally, each issue has reviews of recordings, instruments, videos, and books. And there are plenty of photos, illustrations, and diagrams of the instruments in question. *EMI* also puts out a yearly tape of music played on unorthodox instruments. On the tapes ($8 each) that are currently available, you'll hear people making sounds from chemical light absorption spectra, stone pillars in Hindu temples, ceramic whistles, flower-pot-o-phones, a VW-Beetle-Harp, Vox Insecta, underwater electric guitar duets with sea mammals, a feedback machine, a nine-string guitar, metal tongue drums, a Waterharp, game calls, a fire organ, shell trumpets, and several instruments that play themselves. It's hard to imagine that any music lover or musician with even a hint of creativity wouldn't love *Experimental Musical Instruments* and its tapes.

Experimental Musical Instruments/PO Box 784/Nicasio CA 94946
WWW: windworld.com/emi
Single issue: $6
Four issue sub (one year): $24. Can/Mex: $27. Overseas: $34

FAIR USE
The Story of the Letter U and the Numeral 2
by Negativland

Fair Use is a bulky anthology of material relating to one of the best known wars between art and commerce. In 1991, SST Records released the single "U2" by Negativland, a band of self-described noisemakers. The single contained two versions of "I Still Haven't Found What I'm Looking For", which incorporated part of the song of the same name from the immensely popular Irish band U2.

Negativland had come into possession of unauthorised outtakes from Casey Kasem's countdown show, *American Top 40*, and decided to build an experimental sound collage around these profanity-filled gems. At one point, while introducing a song by U2, Kasem is naming the band members when he suddenly erupts: "This is bullshit, nobody cares… these guys are from England and who gives a shit?!" Later he lashes out at his crew: "OK, I want a goddam <u>concerted</u> <u>effort</u> to come out of a record that isn't a fucking up-tempo record every time I do a goddam <u>death</u> dedication! It's the <u>last</u> goddam time, I want somebody to use his <u>fuckin'</u> brain to not come out of a goddam record, that is, uhh, that, that's up-tempo an' I gotta talk about a fuckin' <u>dog dyin'</u>!"

Negativland figured that since Kasem had been talking in part about U2, they should incorporate some of that group's music into their song. Without obtaining permission, they used 35 seconds from "I Still Haven't Found What I'm Looking For". They also threw in some CB radio clips and other cultural refuse. To take the prank even further, the cover of "U2" was designed to look at first glance like a U2 release, although further examination would reveal the record's true nature.

Before they could blink, Negativland and SST were slammed with a 180-page lawsuit by Island Records, U2's label. They claimed that the single was a violation of copyright and trademark laws because of the unauthorised sample and the misleading cover. Island won its suit and ordered all copies of the single as well as anything used to produce the single to be sent to it for destruction. As for Kasem, he was upset about his off-colour comments being used but refrained from legal action. He did, however, threaten to sue if "U2" ever saw the light of day again.

Negativland has always vehemently defended its single on the grounds of "fair comment, parody, and cultural criticism, which the copyright law specifically allows." "U2" is part of a large issue — whether it is acceptable to incorporate the work of other artists into a new work without asking permission. In their first press release concerning the lawsuit, Negativland writes: "Perceptually and philosophically, it is an uncomfortable wrenching of common sense to deny that once something hits the airwaves, it is literally in the public domain. The fact that the owners of culture and its material distribution are able to claim this isn't true belies [sic] their total immersion in a reality on paper. Artists have always approached the entire world around them as both inspiration to act and as raw material to mould and remould. Other art is just more raw material to us and to many, many others we could point to. When it comes to cultural influences, ownership is the point of fools."

Fair Use covers all of the above issues and more by reprinting over 80 documents, including press releases, selections from the lawsuits, letters and faxes from the various parties, an interview with U2's guitarist Edge, attorney letters, magazine articles, and much, much more. The first section of the book is a complete reprinting of the contested magazine *The Letter U and the Numeral 2*, which details SST's lawsuit against Negativland. An appendix contains a dozen documents — such as "Mocking the Monopoly of Copyright" and "The Economy of Ideas" — pertaining to the right to freely incorporate other artistic works into a new and unique work. A final section offers, among other things, a transcript of the "U2" single, a Negativland discography, and the addresses and phone/fax numbers of all involved parties.

As if that weren't enough, *Fair Use* comes packaged with a CD of Negativland's new works of parody/collage/appropriation — the same kind of material that got them into trouble in the first place. Included are samples of Muddy Waters, Marilyn Quayle, Led Zeppelin, *The Little Mermaid*, Rush Limbaugh, Taco Bell, Larry King, the Chipmunks, U2, and Casey Kasem.

Seeland (Negativmailorderland); $20
1995; oversized softcover and CD; 270 pp
heavily illus; 0-9643496-0-4

INSTANT LITTER
Concert Posters From Seattle Punk Culture
compiled by Art Chantry

Instant Litter presents a giant selection of concert posters from Seattle's underground music scene in the late-1970s and early-1980s. Given the disposable nature of the medium (very often not even the bands and artists kept copies), these almost 200 posters are as near to a definitive collection as you can hope for. Bands that are represented include the Enemy, Refuzor, the Fags, Bad Brains, the Avengers, Young Scientist, Student Nurse, 3 Swimmers, Bunnydrums, and Wall of Voodoo. Each poster is accompanied by information — the band, the location, the year, the medium used, the printing method used, and measurements. Most are reproduced in black and white, and seven are in colour.

Real Comet Press; $10
1985; oversized softcover; 112 pp
heavily illus; 0-941104-15-X

Bad Brains/Life In General concert poster by Dennis White.
Instant Litter.

KOMOTION INTERNATIONAL SOUND MAGAZINE

Komotion is an all-volunteer artists' collective. With their performance space, recording studio, and magazine/CD combo, a variety of musicians, writers, and all kinds of other artists can get their work before larger audiences than if each were struggling separately. Issue #8 of the magazine/CD *Komotion International* combines the talents of over 20 people. On the magazine side of the equation is an interview with George Collier, author of *BASTA!: Land and the Zapatista Rebellion in Chiapas*; an essay on our compulsion to label ourselves; a couple of articles on creativity; a poem called "Mazzy Star Video Meditation"; a long review of *33 Revolutions Per Minute* by Marxman; and collages by Freddie Baer and Johann Humyn Being. An essay called "Word" looks at the imposition of order onto art. "Before 1800 (a rough cut-off date) musical pieces consisted of loosely outlined chord progressions and melodies with which the musicians took improvisational liberties not unlike those of jazz musicians today. After 1800, with the 'Beethoven revolution', musicians existed solely in the function of the composition, which was now finally fully written out… The composer became God."

The accompanying CD has thirteen tracks that exhibit a rare eclecticism. You might not expect to hear the angst-ridden dance-industrial of Headlock alongside the beautiful *a capella* (well, almost) harmonising of Charles Dentel. Or the Peruvian music of Inkari along with the good ol' loud rock 'n' roll of Strawman. Or the futuristic night-club sound of President's Breakfast on the same disk as the Caribbean rhythms of a group called, well, Caribbean Rhythms.

But all of that is here, plus Sunbear, Lisa Palty, Three Mile Pilot, A Subtle Plague, Mat Callahan, Plum, and Ultra Violet Candy.

Komotion International/PO Box 410502/San Francisco CA 94141-0502
Email: komotion@c2.org
Single issue: $10
Four issue sub: $20

MAN'S RUIN
The Posters & Art of Frank Kozik
by Frank Kozik

Frank Kozik is perhaps the foremost rock poster artist. His big, bold creations featuring pop culture icons, disturbing imagery, and bright cartoon colours have alerted the world to performances by Helmet, Nine Inch Nails, the Supersuckers, Gas Huffer, Killdozer, the Lunachicks, Nirvana, Danzig, Red Hot Chili Peppers, and almost every other 1990s punk or alternative band of renown.

Kozik uses the time-honoured tactic of appropriating our culture's visual imagery, putting it in a blender, and then straining it through a filter that marks it distinctively his own. The first part of the book displays almost 100 of Kozik's offset posters from 1981-1990. Most of them are black and white or have one additional spot colour. Already Kozik's themes have become apparent. A ghoulish poster for Scratch Acid shows a needle being injected into a disembodied eyeball resting in a bedpan. A transgendered Virgin Mary on a Jane's Addiction poster is one of many heretical images, and an appropriated nude photo of Jayne Mansfield shows up on a poster for Thee Hypnotics.

Most of the rest of *Man's Ruin* contains Kozik's silk-screen posters, which display his more well-known style of hyper-hues. His first silk-screen poster — for the Butthole Surfers — shows a cartoonish kid with a tab of LSD on his tongue. He's shooting a bird with his left hand and holding a meat cleaver with his right. A poster for Helmet and L7 takes Lee Harvey Oswald's face from the famous picture where he's getting iced, and makes it look like he's singing into a microphone. Charles Manson makes numerous appearances. His deranged face hovers above two blond children in a poster for Jesus Christ Super Fly. Also turning up several times are Kozik's super-sexy female demons, their hard bodies coloured completely red from the tip of their tails to the tips of their horns.

Additionally, you'll view Kozik's fine art (which look like his silk-screens but are more detailed), album covers, seven-inch covers, and picture disks. All printed on slick black paper to make the raging colours leap off the page and tear into your eyeballs.

Last Gasp; $24.95
1995; oversized softcover; 95 pp
heavily illus; 0-86719-397-2

RNA
Ribonucleic Ambience
by Michael Mantra

Normally I don't really get into ambient music, but Michael

Mantra's *RNA* is different. It was created for maximum chill-out effect, and that's exactly what it does. The mellow, lush soundscapes got me so relaxed while I was trying to write, that I had to stop listening to it. I felt like just nodding off in front of the computer. The effects are supposed to be even more intense with headphones. If you're looking for something to completely soothe your stressed-out self, this is it.

Tranquil Technology Music;
1994; compact disk

SATAN TAKES A HOLIDAY

by Anton Szandor LaVey

The eighteen tracks on this CD feature Anton LaVey — founder of the Church of Satan — playing keyboards. LaVey is recognised as a virtuoso organist, and in these songs, he uses synthesisers for a full, rich effect, proving that despite their bastardisation by musical lightweights, they are viable instruments.

The collection is surprisingly peppy and upbeat. Surprising, too, is the Infernal One's selection of songs, which includes burlesques, circus music, and Hollywood musical numbers. The title track — written by band leader Larry Clinton in 1937 — appears twice, first as an instrumental, and later in a smoky night-club treatment with vocals by Blanche Barton.

In several tracks, such as the 1953 German love song "Answer Me" and the Laurel and Hardy number "Honolulu Baby", LaVey half sings, half recites the lyrics. Nick Bougas provides deep, rich vocals for five tracks, such as the sweeping operetta piece "Softly, As in a Morning Sunrise"

"Band Organ Medley" is a suite of four swirling numbers often used on merry-go-rounds. LaVey and Bougas create a faithful rendition of "Dixie" "as it might have actually been heard during the Civil War, complete with rebel yell." The disk ends on a more sombre note... "Satanis Theme" is an original dirge composed by LaVey for the 1968 film *Satanis*.

Amarillo Records; $15
1995; compact disk; 71 min

SAVOY WARS

Savoy not only pushes the envelope with comix such as *Hardcore Horror* and *Meng & Ecker* [see the Comix chapter] and in fiction such as *Lord Horror*, they also release convention-defying rock and roll. This CD collects ten of their singles, most of which feature PJ Proby, a larger-than-life, obsessive, alcoholic singer who was quite popular in the 1960s (especially among teenage girls) until his pants somehow kept splitting open during concerts. Barred from almost all venues, he sank into relative obscurity before being resurrected by Savoy.

The CD's first track, "Blue Monday", splices together the New Order song of the same name with Bruce Springsteen's "Cadillac Ranch". The cover of the single is one of Savoy's most controversial pieces of artwork. It apparently shows former Police Chief of Manchester James Anderton's head exploding, surrounded by all sorts of epithets. It was intended as commentary on Anderton's intolerant attitudes, but it helped get Savoy labelled as hate-mongers.

Phil Collins' song "In the Air Tonight" is given a massive deconstruction, with African percussion, lots of strings, and over-the-top vocals by Proby. "I'm on Fire" by Bruce Springsteen gets similar treatment. Proby croons like Elvis reincarnated over an overblown string section. Other remakes — which are often so altered that even musicians who originally performed them might not recognise them — include "Sign O' the Times" (Prince), "Garbageman" (the Cramps), and "Raw Power" (Iggy Pop).

One song is credited to Meng and Ecker. "Shoot Yer Load" is a techno track sung by D'nise Johnson of Primal Scream and Rowetta, formerly of the Happy Mondays. The lyrics are comprised mostly of, "Shoot your load/Let it go" and, "He's a motherfucker/Cocksucker".

Another original song is the epic "Hardcore: M97002", which clocks in at just under sixteen minutes. A percussion track stomps away while Proby and a woman echo each other's raunchy lyrics. The songs opens with: "There ain't no such thing as rape when you're wearing a Superman cape." Other lyrics include "Telly Savalas uses his bald head as a phallus", "What a knob that boy has", and "I am a dick-licker/I am a cunt-lover". What helped catapult this record to fame is that the lyric sheet claims that the female singer is Madonna. The English tabloids went into a frenzy and Madonna threatened to sue. Chalk up another successful prank for Savoy.

Savoy; $20.98
1994; compact disk; 70 min

SEX & DRUGS & ROCK & ROLL

edited by Chris Charlesworth

In these days of sappy popmeisters and flaky middle-of-the-road rock, it's easy to forget that, to a large degree, rock is — or is supposed to be — about hedonism. This amazing collection of around 500 photographs captures the sex, the booze and other drugs, the nudity, the juvenile antics, and the recklessness that is rock and roll.

The pictures come mostly from the 1970s and 1980s, featuring everyone from the towering legends of rock to punks, from metalheads to pop singers:

☞ David Bowie goes down on Mick Ronson's guitar during a concert.

☞ Rob Halford of Judas Priest — done up in leathers — brandishes a whip.

☞ Siouxsie (of the Banshees) poses in outrageous makeup, fishnet stockings, one thigh-high boot, a leather bikini, and a swastika armband.

☞ The Who's late drummer Keith Moon reclines among dozens of empty bottles of beer and other alcohol.

☞ In a publicity photo, Throbbing Gristle poses behind a table topped with dozens of shiny dildos.

☞ Bob Marley takes a hit off a big ol' pipe.

☞ Years before Courtney Love arrived on the scene, Debbie Harry gets down and shows audiences her panties.

☞ David Lee Roth plays with a blow-up doll on stage.

Madonna struts down the runway in a Gaultier dress with the breasts cut out.

Of course, a lot of shots show naked women. Freddy Mercury of Queen autographs a woman's bare ass. Frank Zappa is carried and groped by seven adoring topless women. Mick Jagger and Jerry Hall, both shirtless, embrace for the camera. Alice Cooper's bandmate pours booze over a woman's pendulous bare breasts. Sometimes the artists themselves get naked… Wendy O'Williams displays her bod several times, and Grace Slick takes her shirt off at an outdoor concert.

But naked men make a showing, too. In a frontal shot, Sex Pistol Sid Vicious pulls down his pants to prove that he doesn't wear underwear. Elton John and Angus Young (from AC/DC) moon the camera in separate photos. Lux Interior of the Cramps shows his stuff on stage, and Iggy Pop poses in the buff for a publicity picture. Not quite 100% naked, the Red Hot Chili Peppers perform in their infamous tube socks (which they don't wear on their feet, dig?).

A lot of these shots will make you wince in embarrassment, and others will have you laughing at the idiocy of the musicians, groupies, and sycophants, but taken together they're a great testament to the untamed, Dionysian circus called rock and roll.

Bobcat Books (Book Sales Ltd); £12.95, $19.95US
1993; oversized softcover; 192 pp
heavily illus; 0-7119-3445-2

THE SHIT OF GOD
by Diamanda Galás

Avant garde vocalist Diamanda Galás has been called a "one woman sonic event". In his introduction, Clive Barker describes "how her voice — ONE MOMENT SERPENTINE, THE NEXT A JUGGERNAUT — carries her audience on a journey into primal regions, where intellectual analysis and even aesthetic judgements become redundant. All you can do is listen and feel." *Keyboard* magazine once said of her, "With astounding vocal abilities spanning three octaves, three languages, and a wider sonic palette than most synthesisers, there's little in Heaven, Earth, or Hell that she can't put forth in song." Galás howls, moans, and soars about the bleakest of subjects, especially the AIDS plague, death, and insanity.

The Shit of God contains lyrics to 26 of Galás' songs and three prose pieces. "Let My People Go" opens with the lines:

The Devil has designed my death
and he's waiting to be sure
that plenty of his black sheep die
before he finds a cure.

O LORD JESUS, do you think I've served my time?
The eight legs of the Devil now are crawling up my spine.

In "No More Tickets to the Funeral" from the *Plague Mass* performance, she writes:

And on that holy day

And on that bloody day
And on his dying bed he told me
"Tell all my friends I was fighting, too,
But to all the cowards and voyeurs:
There are no more tickets to the funeral
There are no more tickets to the funeral."

Unfortunately, not all of Galás' lyrics translate so well onto paper. While it might be amazing to hear her sing "Hee Shock Die" on the highly experimental *Schrei X*, reading it isn't quite the same: "WOOH/WOOH/WOOH/WHEE/WHEE/WHEE/WHEE/WHEE/WHEE/WHEE/WHEE/WHEE AH IH OO IH OO AH". Thankfully, lyrics of this type are in the minority.

The sixteen photographs in *The Shit of God* show that Galás takes her physical appearance to extremes, much the same way she does with her vocals. In some shots she's severe and downright scary, while in others (such as the Annie Liebowitz photo of her crucified, nude except for a cloth draped across her crotch) we see that she can also be unconventionally gorgeous.

High Risk Books (Serpent's Tail); $16.99
1996; small hardcover; 135 pp
illus; 1-85242-432-X

VIERUNDZWANZIGSTELJAHRSSCHRIFT DER INTERNATIONALEN MAULTROMMELVIRTUOSENGENOSSENSCHAFT

This international journal, usually referred to as *VIM* for obvious reasons, is devoted exclusively to the Jew's harp, also called the jaw harp and the scacciapensiere. The editor prefers to use the term "trump". Whatever you call it, it's still a folk instrument that is held between the teeth while being plucked with the finger (do I hear someone giggling out there?). I enjoy the sound of the trump even though I've only heard it on "Join Together" by the Who and being played by Snoopy in a *Peanuts* cartoon.

Issue 4 has an article on the career and playing style of trump master Obediah Pickard, who led the popular bluegrass family band the Pickards from 1927-1930. "Monsieur Le Vaillant Wows the Hottentots" chronicles the adventures of an eighteenth-century zoologist as he travels deep into Africa, mesmerising the indigenous peoples with his trump playing. Phons Bakx writes about a hit single of house music titled "Poing", which prominently features a sampled trump. Other articles examine tonal resources of the trump, two high-calibre trump makers (with their addresses), and several books on the subject. The final part of the issue is a facsimile reproduction of an 1833 book titled *A Sketch of the Life of C. Eulenstein, the Celebrated Performer on the Jews' Harps*.

VIM/601 N White St/Mt Pleasant IA 52641
Issues 4 and 5: $9 each anywhere in the world

WIRELESS IMAGINATION
Sound, Radio, and the Avant-Garde
edited by Douglas Kahn & Gregory Whitehead

Perhaps the most neglected area of avant-garde art is sound experimentation. Although the Futurists, Dadaists, Surreal-

Lyrics from the "one-woman sonic event".
The Shit of God.

ists, and such notables as John Cage, William Burroughs, and Antonin Artaud have pushed the artistic envelope through their use of non-musical or quasi-musical sound, it is not often discussed as a distinct form of radical art. *Wireless Imagination* collects sixteen essays that aim to correct this oversight.

"Marcel Duchamp's Gap Music: Operations in the Space Between Art and Noise" examines what Duchamp was getting at with his "musical compositions" and his ready-made sculptures. In his compositions of notes played randomly, the emphasis was on "the noise that lies in the intervals between the notes or the gaps left empty between the sounds." Duchamp believed that it was the gaps — and not the notes themselves — that were the true art.

"The Ear That Would Hear Sounds in Themselves" is about radical composer John Cage's work from 1935 to 1965. In *Imaginary Landscape No. 1* a gong beater is swept across the bass strings of a piano while two phonographs play a record containing test tones. The speed of the phonographs is varied and the stylus is raised and lowered at various intervals. *4'33"* is Cage's most controversial piece. "In *4'33"* no sounds are produced by the performer, who simply sits quietly in front of the piano for four minutes and thirty-three seconds, opening and closing the piano lid to indicate the pieces three 'movements.'"

Other articles include the Futurist manifesto "La Radia",

which has never previously been published in English, and Arseni Avraamov's performance instructions for *The Symphony of the Sirens*, in which a whole city used foghorns, factory whistles, and sirens to recreate the sounds of the October Revolution.

The MIT Press; $19.95
1992; softcover; 455 pp
0-262-61104-X

PUNK

FLIPSIDE

Flipside is a big ol' thick magazine crammed full of news, views, and reviews relating to punk and related genres/hybrids. A line-up of columnists, reader letters, interviews, a big review sections, and tons o' ads let you know who's touring, who's recording, who's got new releases, who sucks, who hates whom, and so on. In just one issue (#99) you'll read about Celibate Rifles, Turbonegro, Tunnelmental, the Drags, Chixdiggit, the Paper Tulips, Red Aunts, Mike Watt, Anti-Flag, Toadies, Neurotic Boy Outsiders, the Lunachicks, the Wynona Riders (my favourite band name), and lots more.

The interviews are often revealing. Nobody seems to hesitate in opening up to *Flipside*'s interviewers. In the interview with the Supersuckers, Dan Siegal talks about the music industry and their place in it: "There's so much real bullshit out there, bands that are products of record labels, manufactured bands to make money, and we just simply aren't that. We're just four fucking losers doing the best we can." George Clinton, the tireless force behind Parliament Funkadelic, gives a great interview that proves that he is indeed the funkiest man on earth. Interviewer Gerry Fialka says to him: "George, you've been doing music for over forty years and still going strong…" He replies: "Just getting started. It takes that much foreplay to be funkin' really right. You need about forty years of foreplay, then you can really stick it to 'em."

But music isn't all *Flipside* is about. There's a section of real short zine reviews, and some of the columnists also write about zines they love or hate. In issue 99 Killjoy urges readers to help kill the Omnibus Counter-Terrorism bill, which threatens to put the kibosh on a few more of our rights. (She also conducts an interview with *moi*.) "Just Say Know!! DXM for You and Me" reveals how to extract the morphine analogue DXM from over-the-counter cough and cold remedies, and a double interview with Bob Dobbs (*The Perfect Pitch*) and Paul Krassner (*The Realist*) reveals some intriguing thoughts about power and political structure.

All this plus a blaring full-colour cover for only $12 bucks a year? It's a steal.

Flipside/PO Box 60790/Pasadena CA 91116

Single issue: $2.50. Can/Mex: $3. Eurasia: $4. Others: $5
Six issue sub (one year): $12. Can/Mex: $25. Eurasia: $35.
Others: $40
WWW: www.indieweb.com/flipside/

THE GREAT BRITISH MISTAKE
Vague 1977-1992

Vague is an anarchist zine that covers the punk scene. The brainchild of Tom Vague, it has become legendary, or at least legendary enough to warrant this greatest hits collection covering issues 1 through 21, with the majority of the material coming from 1979-1985. The book is divided into sections covering various subgenres of punk.

The first section, on punk and post-punk, has a pathetic review of a Joy Division show and interviews with the Ramones and the Clash. Whenever one of *Vague*'s contributors writes something particularly trite, Tom Vague has no qualms about inserting a disparaging comment into the story. Usually, he'll write: "(Too embarrassing! Ed.)"

The next section is on sex punk, with an article on and an interview with Adam and the Ants. In one article, the writer and his friends are trying to get into a club in Wales to see the Ants, when they get mixed up in a feud. "… I remember Tim getting a kicking on the floor. I grabbed his assailant and explained to him that Tim was alright. He seemed to understand so I let him go, whereupon he headbutted me and his mates proceeded to headbutt me out the hall. Simultaneously, Martin and Tim are getting similar treatment, while Taz is trying to get Chris out from under a table." There's also material on Bow Wow Wow and Siouxsie and the Banshees.

The section on anarcho-punk and positive punk covers Crass, the Church of the SubGenius, *Viz* Comics, and a death threat from a British sailor upset by Vague's views on the Falkland Islands war. The section on cyber-punk has a communiqué from Genesis P. Orridge, an interview with Psychic TV, and an article on *Decoder*, a movie about the insidious effects of Muzak.

The articles continue to move through post-modern punk (post-industrial no wave, noise, hardcore, and hip-hop art punk), post-postmodern punk, and Situationism. Tom Vague offers a lengthy and very informative article on Situationism that covers the Strasbourg University scandal of 1966, the student uprising of May 1968, the Angry Brigade, King Mob, and the Sex Pistols. The back of the book gives a bibliography of the first 23 issues of *Vague* (with reproductions of all the covers) and all of Tom Vague's articles that have appeared in other fanzines.

AK Press; $11.95
oversized softcover; 114 pp
heavily illus; 1-873176-72-4

MAXIMUMROCKNROLL

Maximumrocknroll is another of the chief punk fanzines. Like *Flipside*, above, *MRR* has lots of reader letters, columnists writing on all kinds of topics, scene reports, interviews, and reviews (music, zines, books) out the keister. Issue 146 has features on Nailed Down, the Riverdales, the McRackins,

The Weirdos and uninvited guest vocalists.
Search and Destroy.

Y.A.P.O. (Youth Against Political Oppression or Young And Pissed Off), 10-96, Spanakorzo, Underhand, and the record label TPOS. From the interview with the Bristles: "*MRR*: How do you guys feel about successful punk bands like Green Day or Nirvana or Rancid? Aaron: We hate them because they're not us. Fuck them. Anthony: They just suck anyway… *MRR*: So, how are your shows anyway? Andy: They suck. Aaron: Why don't you come and watch, asshole. You're getting on my nerves, interviewer boy."

MRR also gives some coverage to non-punk genres, as long as they're light years away from the mainstream. Issue 146 has an interview with Empress of Fur, who are described thus: "The band (who have every line in Elvis's '68 comeback special memorised) twang-out vicious rockabilly-burlesque, while perma-pouting front-woman Venus RayGun is like both Elvis and Ann-Margret in *Viva Las Vegas* morphed into one shapely body."

Maximumrocknroll/PO Box 460760/San Francisco CA 94146-0760
Single copy: US/Can/Mex: $3. UK/Europe: $5. Australia/Asia/Africa: $7
Six issue sub: US/Can/Mex: $18. UK/Europe: $33. Australia/Asia/Africa: $42

SEARCH AND DESTROY
The Authoritative Guide to Punk Culture — The Complete Reprint [Two volumes]
edited by V. Vale

From 1976 to 1979, V. Vale — who would later go on to found the redoubtable RE/Search Publications — edited, published, and wrote most of the seminal punk fanzine *Search & Destroy*. Published as a tabloid, all eleven issues are reprinted in their entirety at 90% of their original size in these two volumes. Instead of focusing strictly on the music through record and concert reviews, Vale used interviews — a technique that would become a RE/Search hallmark — to find out who was making the music.

Volume 1: #1-6 contains interviews with a veritable who was who of punk/new wave: Crime, Vermilion (Mary Monday), Clive Langer (Deaf School), Iggy Pop, Penelope (the Avengers), the Ramones, Nickey Beat (the Weirdos), the

Clash, Devo, the Zeros, Tom Verlaine (Television), the Damned, Blondie, Patti Smith, Mumps, Stiv Bators (the Dead Boys), Helen Wheels, the Screamers, Suicide, Talking Heads, the Dickies, Throbbing Gristle, Buzzcocks, Pere Ubu, and others. Scattered throughout are lyrics from many of the bands, "Politics of Punk", "The Complete Residents Handbook", a history of anarchism, some concert reviews, and ads for albums, concerts, and record stores. [1996; 0-9650469-4-X]

Volume 2: #7-11 offers up interviews with Devo, Dick Envy, DNA, Cabaret Voltaire, Roky Erickson, the Clash, Mick Farren (the Deviants) the Dils, the Mutants, the Cramps, Siouxsie and the Banshees, Pere Ubu, Patti Palladin, the Flesheaters, the Enemy, Dead Kennedys, Ray Campi and His Rockabilly Rebels, the Zeroes, Television, D.O.A., Exene (X), Steve Jones (Sex Pistols), Karla Michelle Du Plantier (the Controllers), and bunches of others. Vale expanded his reach during this half of *Search & Destroy*'s lifetime by interviewing many nonmusicians, including John Waters, Amos Poe, David Lynch, Russ Meyer, JG Ballard, and William Burroughs. Other offerings include an article on black humour, punk musicians relating their dreams, "Politics of Punk", and more lyrics and ads. [1997; 1-889307-00-9]

This is the authentic punk experience — representing the West Coast/San Francisco wing of the movement — captured as it happened. *Search & Destroy* is faithfully reproduced the way it was first sprung upon the world… written on a typewriter, chock-full of raw, under- and overexposed photographs presented in a bold, rough design scheme.

V/Search Publications; $19.95 each
hugely oversized softcovers; 148 pp each
heavily illus

MISCELLANEOUS

THE ART FORGER'S HANDBOOK
by Eric Hebborn

Eric Hebborn was one of the greatest art forgers of all time. For years this English artist fooled "experts", museums, collectors, auctioneers, and others in the international art world into thinking that his creations were actual works by Brueghel, Piranesi, Rubens, Van Dyck, Augustus John, and other second-tier Old Masters. In this book, he gives detailed instructions on how to create your own forgeries. This is no shabby confession in which he just tells us basically what he did but leaves out the practical information. No, here he divulges the innermost secrets for creating a painting or drawing that will be officially judged as a work by an Old Master.

Chapter after chapter gives the low-down on paper, watermarks, inks, drawing instruments (quills, metal pens, etc.),

charcoal, chalk, pastels, signatures, monograms, canvases, pigments, oil paints, underdrawing, mounting, staining panels, creating cracks, and fooling experts, dealers, and collectors. You'll find out exactly which twelve colours of paint you need, how to lower tone in oil paintings, where to find old paper, and how to mix varnish like the Masters used. Hebborn leaves nothing to chance. For example, he warns that new paint can stay relatively soft for decades, causing obvious authenticity problems. A way around this is to use paint mixed with a synthetic resin, allow the painting to dry for at least a year (nobody ever said forging was a quick way to make money), then bake it in an oven at 210-220°F (100-105°C) for two to three hours. The one thing the author doesn't get into is how to actually draw or paint like a famous artist. You'll have to develop that skill on your own through practice and study.

But Hebborn discusses more than just how to forge. He also reveals ugly truths about the art world, showing that matters aren't as cut and dried as you might think. "How the experts sometimes choose artists to fit certain pictures was told to me by the late Harry Ward Bailey who was for some time Christie's representative in Rome. When cataloguing a number of pictures for a sale of minor paintings there are usually a number of pictures whose authorship can only be guessed at., and in these cases the method of guessing has been known to be this. A number of authorities gather together, each having a volume of E. Bénézit's monumental *Dictionnaire des peintres, sculpteurs, dessinateurs et graveurs* (*Dictionary of Painters, Sculptors, Drawers and Engravers*) (1960). They close their eyes, each opens their volume at random and points to a name. Names are compared and the most likely one is adopted."

The jacket of *The Art Forger's Handbook* cryptically mentions that the book was completed just before the author died "under mysterious circumstances". They don't elaborate, but some checking has revealed that Hebborn's body was found on January 11, 1996, on a street in Rome. He died of a head wound, and authorities were launching an investigation, although I don't know what conclusions they've reached, if any.

Hebborn may be gone, but his pseudo legacy lives on. Fortunately, he let us know his secrets before being dispatched.

The Overlook Press; $35
1997; hardcover; 206 pp
illus; 0-87951-767-0

ART ON THE EDGE AND OVER
Searching for Art's Meaning in
Contemporary Society 1970s-1990s
by Linda Weintraub

If you're confused about the meaning and worth of avant-garde art — such as large blocks of lard, telegrams announcing what time the artist got up each day, or naked people rolling around with meat products — then this book can provide some background, clarification, and interpretation. Each of the 35 chapters is devoted to an artist who represents a radical new aspect of art from the past three decades. For-

Untitled Turkey XV, 1992 by Meyer Vaisman.
Art on the Edge and Over.

going art critic gobbledegook, the authors attempt as far as humanly possible to explain in clear language what the artists are doing.

The book's first section looks at three themes — nature, the self, and the communal self — that are addressed by many cutting-edge artists. Wolfgang Lieb creates art with pollen. It often takes him an entire season to painstakingly collect enough pollen for one piece. The artist On Kawara has created a ten-volume set of books titled *One Million Years (Past)* that simply lists every single year from 1969 back to 998,031 BCE. The second ten-volume set lists every year from 1980 to 1,001,980. The French artist Orlan is attempting to become a completely new person. "Her goal is to transform herself so fundamentally that she legally warrants a new identity. This change is actual, and it is permanent. She works on her internal self through intense psychoanalysis. At the same time she reconstructs her outer self through elective surgical operations."

Section number two looks at some of the more unusual processes being used by artists, such as creating a work of art entirely by machine (Rosemarie Trockel) and simply buying items and placing them on shelves (Haim Steinbach). The next section examines unorthodox media, including the urine of Andres Serrano, the menstrual blood of Carolee Schneemann, and the cutting-edge technology of Toni Dove. Next, the authors examine some of the purposes of new art. This includes Barbara Kruger, who uses the techniques of advertising and propaganda to agitate for gender equity, and Jeff Koons, who "blatantly proclaims his greed, lust, and ambition and recommends them as the means to achieve happiness."

Finally, there is a section on alternative aesthetics. This can involve the use of a sense, such as smell, that is usually not involved in art, or it can involve something harder to define — the inconsistency of Gerhard Richter's style(s) or the homeliness of Mike Kelley's old, soiled stuffed animals that were purchased from thrift stores. Sherrie Levine challenges the aesthetic of originality by taking photographs of other artists' photographs and presenting her photos as works of art. One of her theories is that photographs are taking the place of actual experience, and are therefore legitimate subjects for photography. The authors ask: "Of all the places around the globe that you can identify, how many have you actually visited? How many do you know through photos?"

Featuring beautiful design and layout, superb production values, and scads of images — including Serrano's *Piss Christ*, Koons' *Michael Jackson and Bubbles*, Gilbert and George's *The Edge*, and other well-known avant-garde works — *Art on the Edge and Over* serves as a great explanation of radical new directions in art and as a field guide to some of the most intriguing artists of our time.

Art Insights; $22.50
1996; softcover; 264 pp
heavily illus; 0-9651988-1-2

BRUSH FIRES IN THE SOCIAL LANDSCAPE
by David Wojnarowicz

The late David Wojnarowicz easily mixed photography, acrylic paints, spray paint, found art, text, and other media into works that made searing statements about mortality, AIDS, sex, and oppression. He grew up a gay man on the mean streets of New York, hustling for a while, and then turning to art. He poured his rage over the horrible abuse he suffered as a child and society's hatred of homosexuality into collages, montages, and other single- and mixed-media pieces.

Each work in his eight-part *Sex Series* uses a large photograph printed as a negative for the background, inset with one or more circular photographs. At least one of these photos is a reversed printing of a sex act appropriated from anonymous porn. One of the works in the series has a large ship as its main image and a shot of a man going down on another man in the upper right of the picture. Another work shows a train going through the mountains accompanied by images of oral sex, blood cells, cops in riot gear, and a fragment of a newspaper article about two gay men being stabbed and beaten. The sex shots are cropped as circles to give the feeling of "examination and/or surveillance" through a microscope, telescope, or binoculars. Wojnarowicz peels away the outer covering of society to see what's going on underneath.

Another one of Wojnarowicz's most infamous works is the Xerox collage *Untitled (Genet)*. It shows outlaw French author Gene Genet standing in a crumbling church where a comic book commando is machine-gunning angels. On the wall over Genet's left shoulder is an image of Jesus shooting heroin. Wojnarowicz defended the junkie Christ against attackers in this way: "... I thought about what I had been taught about Jesus Christ when I was young, and how he took on the suffering of all people in the world, and I wanted to create a modern image that, if he were alive physically before me in the streets of the Lower East Side, I wanted to make a symbol that would show that he would take on the suffering of the vast amounts of addiction that I saw on the streets."

Among the other works reproduced in this book:

☞ A series of five photos of a snake catching and eating a frog.

☞ *Fuck You Faggot Fucker:* Against a background of a world map, two male figures kiss. Small photo vignettes show naked men, and in the bottom centre is a torn scrap of paper covered in homophobic doodling.

☞ Black and white shots of Mexican mummies, made from super-8 film stills.

☞ *Bad Moon Rising:* Against a background of dollar bills of varying denominations, trees grow from the headless body of Saint Sebastian. Two vignettes show male-male oral sex and two others show a house being vaporised by an atomic bomb. Three circles contain a clock with no hands, red-blood cells, and half clock/half red-blood cells.

☞ *Untitled (Buffalo):* a picture of several buffalo running off a sheer cliff and falling to their deaths. This shot was used as the cover for a U2 single.

Several friends and acquaintances of Wojnarowicz — including his lawyer David Cole and performance artist Karen Finley — contribute essays about the man and his art.

Aperture; $35
1994; oversized hardcover; 83 pp
heavily illus; 0-89381-567-5

CAN CONTROL

Can Control is the magazine for getting the latest, straightest news on the graffiti subculture. Each issue is mostly colour and black and white pictures of trains, subways, busses, buildings, walls, overpasses and other areas of urban canvas covered in outlaw art. Features include interviews, letters, and comix. The slang is thick and heavy, so don't expect to understand everything that's being said unless you're in the scene yourself. There are lots of references to writing, bombing, kinging, tags, throw ups, pieces, legals, scribs, toys, heroes — each of which has its own distinct meaning.

Issue 8 contains — besides the usual crop of great photos — interviews with the legendary Zephyr and the band Tres Flores, step-by-step instructions for 3-D graffiti, and a special section of subway and freight train graffiti. The next ish is 100% devoted to freights — over 60 pictures and no text articles.

"The First Annual Black and White Bombers Only" issue has an interview with three writers from LA. TOOMR talks about the life: "I know Gangsters who have the balls to go out shooting, but don't have the balls to go out on a bridge or the freeway. They give Me, Saber & GK allot of credit for doing that. We go to all the neighbourhoods, go thru gang land, get shot at, chased by cops or hero's. This shit is crazy." There's also a section where writers explain what motivates them. NZONE says, "I Bomb because I Crave Fame." For RISKYONE it's more fundamental: "To know I'm alive." And

Seize the night.
Carpe Noctem.

POWERONE revels in the subversive message it puts out: "So society doesn't forget who has the real power in this country, the numbers, strength, mental capability, manner, and weapons to run your bullshit."

Because art publishers have put out a few book on graffiti in the last few years, the medium has gained a little more acceptance, but it's still generally shunned by the art world and considered vandalism by society at large. *Can Control* proves that graffiti really are art. The writers have undeniable talent, but instead of slaving away in a studio to sell a single painting to one person, they give their art freely to the public. Their work becomes even more impressive when you ask yourself this: How good a job would Michelangelo have done on the Sistine Chapel if he had had to constantly worry about running from gang members or getting his head busted by cops?

Can Control/PO Box 61069/Seattle WA 98121-6069
Single issue: $7
Four issue sub (one year): $19. Non-US: $21
Payment: US money orders only

CARPE NOCTEM

The hedonistic phrase *carpe diem* translates literally as "Seize the day." *Carpe noctem*, therefore, urges us to "Seize the night." It's a fitting title for this visually enticing magazine that covers every type of Gothic art — music, sculpture, writing, comix, movies, paintings, etc.

Volume 2 #2 reproduces four pages of work from RH Phister, whose medium of choice is graphite on Egyptian cotton with stitches, glass beads, and other objects added for effect. These photorealistic drawings mostly depict people whose flesh is becoming undone, like a pair of worn-out

Levi's. Also featured are Terrence Craven, who creates sculptures that look like alien insectoids; "Le Petit Mort", a pictorial of the most beautiful and elaborate sculptures in French cemeteries; "Fondling the Intestinal Meat Niblets", a hilarious, non sequitur-filled comic about a "faeces vampyre"; darkwave group Trance to the Sun; comic artist Frank Miller; special effects artist Screaming Mad George; and more.

Volume 2 #3 reveals the dark erotic photography of David Penprase, an interview with Clive Barker, *Faust* comic artist Tim Vigil, *The Prophecy* director Greg Widen, Goth photographer Clovis IV, a member of the "industrial-tinged ethno ambient" band Muslimgauze, and even more. Unfortunately, these two issues are now out of print. I don't mean to be a tease, but I want to give you an idea of the ground *Carpe Noctem* covers. Hopefully these issues will someday be reprinted, and until then, Xeroxes of past articles are available.

The latest issue, Volume 4 #2, covers typically wide ground. Caitlin Kiernan, the Goth author of *Silk*, is the only writer profiled. Musically, there are interviews/articles dealing with Brian Williams of the one-man-industrial/ambient/experimental-band Lustmord, darkwave band Sunshine Blind, ethereal rockers Autumn, and Zoar, who play "Music for the New Dark Age".

Among the visual artists featured are Stephen Fitz-Gerald, who sculpts bodies out of pieces of metal; Alex Ross, who paints comix for DC; fantasy illustrator Brom; and filmmaker Lynne Stopkewich, creator of *Kissed*, the instantly infamous movie that sensitively portrays a female necrophile. Stopkewich says, "Part of the reason why I chose the story was that I was absolutely and utterly terrified of death. It's almost like forced therapy! [Laughs] Confronting the thing that terrifies you most and not only deal with it, but eroticise it. I just loved the character for her braveness in that respect; that she is so 'unafraid of death' that she crawls into bed with it." There are also reviews of some of the best Film *Noir* and transgressive movies ever made, plus recent books, CDs, computer games, and fashion. Photos from the Highgate Cemetery in London, a *Johnny the Homicidal Maniac* comic, some short fiction, and a look at the Gothic wonderland Castle Blood in Pennsylvania help complete the offerings.

The Dark Romantics behind this publication have a flair for design that's distinctive but not overtly experimental. *Carpe Noctem* is the premiere art/culture magazine for girls and boys who only come out at night.

Carpe Noctem/260 S. Woodruff Avenue Suite 105W/Idaho Falls
ID 83401
Email: carpenoc@carpenoctem.com
WWW: http://www.carpenoctem.com
Single issue: $6.75
Six issue sub (one year): $20

CELLBLOCK VISIONS
Prison Art in America
by Phyllis Kornfeld

Some of the most vital and creative art you'll ever see is made by prisoners. When people are incarcerated and have

Nelson Molina's soap carving, No One Cares.
Cellblock Visions.

such huge amounts of freedom taken from them, they'll often turn to the freedom afforded to them by creativity. Most prisoner artists are self-taught, which often leads to highly original works that directly express inner feelings.

In *Cellblock Visions*, Phyllis Kornfeld — who has worked as an art activities co-ordinator for men and women incarcerated everywhere from county jails to death row — collects 92 works of prison art (42 in colour), along with extensive text on the artists themselves, the roles that art plays, and the forms that it takes behind bars. Sometimes it seems that there is too much text, crowding out more or larger reproductions of artwork.

Some of the pieces use traditional media, such as painting and drawing. Dennis Smythwick's *Room with a View and the Many Different Shapes of D.L.S.* plays with bright geometric shapes; Braulio Valentin Diez uses coloured pencils to create fantastical creatures; Arthur Keigney's prison scene, *Walpole*, is reminiscent of an illustration in a children's book; and Michael Rinaldi's work reminds me of Mike Diana, both in its hyper style and sexual/violent subject matter.

Other works take unorthodox forms. There are short sections on tattoos and interior design. Showing that the creative urge cannot be stifled, prisoners often use cigarette packages (*Kools Purse* by Leland Dodd), newspaper (a newspaper house by an unknown artist), and soap *(No One Cares* by Nelson Molina is a soap sculpture of people walking by a prison) as their mediums. Another form of art that seems to be unique to prison is toilet paper sculpture. "Dominic Vincenzo-Thomas, doing twenty years to life for murder, makes toilet paper sculptures refined to the delicacy of porcelain figures. 'I was the tier man, a glorified janitor. An inmate threw wet TP at a C.O., it was all over the wall and I had to take it down. It was hard and it kept its shape. The rest is history.'"

Princeton University Press; $35
1997; oversized hardcover; 112 pp
heavily illus; 0-691-02976-8

CIRCUS AMERICANUS
by Ralph Rugoff

Ralph Rugoff is an art critic for *LA Weekly*, but his 40 penetrating essays in this book don't cover art as we normally think of it. Instead, they focus on the wider world of visual culture — PR media events, strange museums, theme parks, the human body, public art, and much more.

"Excremental Journey" examines the strange appeal of sewage plants, particularly LA's gargantuan Hyperion Waste Treatment Plant. Rugoff notes that Aldous Huxley and Victor Hugo have waxed eloquent concerning such facilities. "Perhaps it's their inherently egalitarian nature that endears sewers to liberal thinkers — like death, a sewage treatment plant is a great equaliser. In Hyperion's primary sedimentation tank, your shit meets the Reagans', and nobody's waste gets special treatment."

Every July in Los Angeles, the Sheriff's department publicly destroys the enormous cache of weapons — guns, knives, blackjacks — that it has seized during the previous year. In "Gun Rites", Rugoff writes: "However seemingly straightforward, this simple drama yearns to reach beyond mere PR fluffery to become a full-blown ritual, partly obsessive and partly carnivalesque, and dedicated to restoring safety to our public spaces. If Spielberg were producing it, a hole in the ground would open with a roar, spitting flame and sulphur, and the forces of good would then dispatch the evil weapons to the underworld."

The author offers some harsh reviews of the bizarre LA County Sheriff's Museum and the whitewashed Richard Nixon Library and Birthplace. Of the latter, he says: "It's not always clear… whether the multi-media exhibits in the presidential Graceland were designed to restore Nixon to grace or to entrap him within a kitsch hallucination. More pointedly, the NLB is also a model for the ongoing museumisation of America, a conspiracy of vitrines and touch-screen video monitors that one day, if we're lucky, will allow us all to become the curators of our own lives."

Rugoff also casts his probing eye on golf courses, auto shows, Sea World, artist-prankster Robyn Whitlaw, Interstate 105, the Scientology Collection, the Liberace Museum, bodybuilding, supermodels, Mexican Wrestlers, plastic surgery, nudism, and forensic photography. He consistently manages to go below the visual surface and tell us what the objects we see tell us about ourselves.

Verso; $19.95
1995; oversized softcover; 215 pp
heavily illus; 1-85984-003-5

CONFESSIONS OF THE GUERRILLA GIRLS
by the Guerrilla Girls

Calling themselves "the conscience of the art world", a group of anonymous feminists known as the Guerrilla Girls have been outing the racism and sexism of museums, galleries, critics, curators, etc. since 1985. Their two main weapons are masks and posters. They wear gorilla masks during their demonstrations and press conferences not only to protect their identities but to make themselves memorable through outrageous humour.

Their posters, which get pasted all over New York, LA, and other bastions of the art world, pointedly demonstrate the extraordinary exclusion of female and minority artists from the mainstream art world. One of the GG's first strikes was a

Jesus Milhouse Nixon.
Circus Americanus.

poster with the headline: "These galleries show no more than 10% women artists or none at all." Underneath is a list of 20 galleries. A similar poster listed 22 art critics who write about one-person shows by women 20% of the time or less (some never write about women). Another proclaims: "Only 4 commercial galleries in N.Y. show black women. Only 1 shows more than 1."

A poster that ran as an ad on New York busses shows a picture of a reclining female nude wearing a gorilla mask. The text reads: "Do women have to be naked to get into the Met. Museum? Less than 5% of the artists in the Modern Art Sections are women, but 85% of the nudes are female." In 1991, the Girls expanded their attacks to include homelessness, the Gulf War, and rape.

Confessions presents slick, colourful reproductions of over 50 of the GG's posters, as well as their fliers, their newsletter *Hot Flashes* [*Outposts* p 209], and other projects. Within this visually attractive book is an essay on the group, an interview with several members, positive and negative mail they've received, photos of their demonstrations, and four postcards. Expect an acid-tongued follow-up, *The Guerrilla Girls' Bedside Companion to the History of Western Art*, by the time you read this.

HarperCollins Publishers; $18
1995; oversized softcover; 95 pp
heavily illus; 0-06-095088-9

DADA
Art and Anti-Art
by Hans Richter

Dada was a radical art movement that lasted basically from 1915 to 1923, flourishing in several major cities and counting as its diverse adherents a number of painters, sculptors, photographers, filmmakers, graphic artists, writers, poets, and what we today would call performance artists. But Dada was never a formal school of art with defined subject matter, approaches, etc. It was actually more of an art ethic which stood for the eradication of the old and the creation of something profoundly new.

Painter and filmmaker Hans Richter was one of the founders of the movement, and in this book he offers a unique viewpoint for understanding this turbulent era of art. He states that art historians are confused by Dada because it is so

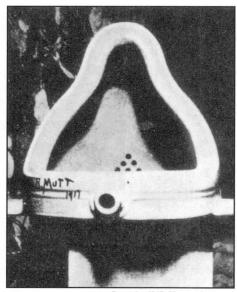

Fountain, 1915, Marchel Duchamp.
Dada: Art and Anti-Art.

self-contradictory, sprawling, and purposely obfuscatory. Rather than try to "clean up" Dada and place it in an easily understandable pigeonhole, Richter embraces the confusion and weirdness of the movement, carefully explaining the various ideas and ideologies promoted by the different artists. "Dada invited, or rather defied, the world to misunderstand it, and fostered every kind of confusion. This was done from caprice and from a principle of contradiction. Dada has reaped the harvest of confusion that it sowed. However, this confusion was only a facade. Our provocations, demonstrations and defiances were only a means of arousing the bourgeoisie to rage, and through rage to a shamefaced self-awareness. Our real motive was not rowdiness for its own sake, or contradiction and revolt in themselves, but the question (basic then, as it is now), 'where next?'"

Dada in its most extreme form was found among the Berlin faction. "They followed the play-instinct wherever it led them and paid no heed to God or man, art or society, but only to their own unrest, THEMSELVES, the need for change. So, when Dada gradually assumed the positive social function of rousing the public from its sleep and making it conscious of its own banality, the presence of a social and cultural purpose was in itself a sign of decadence. Dada in its pure state was pure revolt, ANTI-EVERYTHING!"

Richter divides his narrative by city — Zurich, New York, Berlin, Paris, Hanover, and Cologne — with brief looks at post-Dada and neo-Dada, and he employs personal memories, interviews with old acquaintances, documents from the period, and 179 visuals (artwork, magazines, fliers, portraits, etc.) to tell the story. His personal involvement with Dada means that he has lots of lively anecdotes that add depth to our understanding of the artists. Although Berlin painter George Grosz was an extreme leftist, he was disgusted by

the way communism was being practised. One night he was having dinner with his wife, the author, and a man who had just returned from the Soviet Union. "Obviously with the intention of pleasing Grosz, the traveller spoke of how wonderful he had found everything in the USSR. This went on for a while, Grosz becoming more and more taciturn. Then, totally without warning, he reached over and punched his unsuspecting table-companion full in the mouth."

Dada is a perfect introduction to a confusing but hugely important and fascinating aspect of avant garde art.

Thames and Hudson; $14.95
1964, 1997; softcover; 246 pp
heavily illus; 0-500-20039-4

DEAD MEAT
by Sue Coe

Artist Sue Coe managed to penetrate the secrecy and denial that surrounds the meat and dairy industries by gaining entrance into slaughterhouses, meat farms, feedlots, and egg factories. She would often get in because she knew someone who knew someone who worked there. Occasionally she had to flat-out trespass. One owner even threatened to kill her. She was never allowed to bring a camera or videocam, and sometimes even her sketchpad was forbidden. Somehow, despite these conditions, she managed to create dozens of drawings and paintings depicting the ways in which we get our meat, milk, and eggs. It isn't pretty.

Throat Cutting, an illustration from a veal slaughterhouse in Montreal, depicts a calf that's been hanged by its back legs. A man has slit its throat vertically starting at the top of the chest, and blood runs over the creature's face. The calf is drawn in a simple style that almost makes it look cartoonish, while the slaughterer's face is represented in detail, symbolising the man's viewpoint that the animal he's killing isn't really a unique, living being. In the text on the opposite page, Coe explains, "The animals are forced into the restraining pen, two at a time. The veals can see their comrades having their throats cut. The calves' eyes become practically white. Foam is pouring out of their mouths. The man with the stun gun waits until there is enough space in the conveyor belt to receive the newly stunned veals. A large metal bolt strikes through the animal's skull." Veals take longer to die than most livestock, so they are hoisted up by a chain and their throats are slit, usually causing them to die in five minutes.

Another dark, dank drawing from a second veal slaughterhouse in Montreal shows two workers apparently talking in the foreground while blood pours from the throat of a suspended calf, and two more calves await the same fate in a holding pen that's not big enough for both of them. "One stunned veal swings toward us, hanging upside down, chained by the legs. I have seen a lot of animals not properly stunned before throat cutting, but this one is stunned. It's a misconception that animals are dead at this stage. It's important that the heart pumps the blood out of the animal once its throat has been cut." After having their throats slit, they are sent down the line where their heads are cut off. "As I watch, I see one veal that is about to be decapitated — alive. Although almost completely drained of blood, this veal

"As I watch, I see one veal that is about to be decapitated – alive." Veal Slaughterhouse, *Dead Meat*.

has come out of the stun, which means that there was not enough electricity or the captive bolt did not hit the right point."

The brooding painting *Live Baby Chicks as Fertilizer* shows the broken, bloody bodies of little chicks strewn across a field being ploughed by a tractor-driving farmer. In *Hatchery*, a man tosses a crateful of live chicks into a dumpster. Coe and animal rights activist Lorri Bauston visited a Pennsylvania hatchery with a dumpster in back. The two climbed inside looking for living chicks. "The male baby chicks are discarded as soon as they are hatched. They have no use, no value, since they cannot lay eggs. And it would cost too much to euthanize them. So they are tossed into the dumpster alive. But it is too late for us to rescue any chicks — the sun is just too hot. On the top layer of corpses, flies are eating the chicks' eyes... Gene Bauston, cofounder of Farm Sanctuary, told me that sometimes the baby chicks are ground up alive and thrown on the fields as fertiliser. Walking along a ploughed field, you can sometimes find a chick, still alive, with no legs or wings."

One particularly harrowing image, *Debeaking*, shows a man sticking a young chicken's beak into a small press, which comes down and cuts off the bird's beak. A wastebasket full of waiting victims is to his left, and a wastebasket full of chickens bleeding from their faces sits on his right. The chickens are debeaked so that when they are stuffed into tiny cubicles (depicted in *Egg Machines*) they won't peck each others' eyes out, although they still try.

While the suffering of the animals is the overriding theme, Coe also explores other problems, such as the greed of the owners. *Butcher to the World* depicts a fat executive clenching two bags of money, which drip with blood, while standing on top of a pile of animal corpses. The dehumanising effect

that slaughter has on workers also crops up. Alongside a sketch of a man skinning a lamb, Coe writes, "He says to me 'I don't think of these animals as living beings. I think of them, as a librarian thinks of books, as an auto worker thinks of car parts, this is a factory'."

Other illustrations, paintings, and rough sketches show kids playing soccer with a bloody pig's head, a screaming pig being tackled by workers as it tries to escape, piglets getting their tails clipped off, a swollen cow's udder being relentlessly pumped by a milking machine, an assembly line of chickens who are hanged upside down before being killed and defeathered, a man whipping a downed calf, pigs with cancerous tumours, goats being selected for slaughter, flies swarming over butchered cows, horses being whipped at a horse slaughterhouse, and a man holding a McDonald's bag being followed by the ghosts of all the animals he's eaten.

This a very powerful book that, with pictures and words (including a long introductory essay by Alexander Cockburn), pulls back the veil on a bloody industry that shuns scrutiny.

Four Walls Eight Windows; $40, £30
1996; oversized hardcover; 136 pp
heavily illus; 1-56858-050-9

THE DISASTERS OF WAR
by Francisco Goya

This series of Francisco Goya's etchings, known collectively as *The Disasters of War*, stands as one of the most brutal, uncompromising visual representations of war ever created. These 83 plates depict the rebellion of Spanish nationalists against French imperialism in 1808, which led to the Peninsular War. Goya witnessed some of the scenes personally, and he based the rest on other people's accounts. When the etchings were finally published, thirty-five years after Goya died, a friend of his prepared short, often cynical captions from Goya's notes. The book became a classic denunciation of the absurdity of war.

Many of the plates show soldiers dressed in fancy uniforms battling soldiers wearing commoners' clothes. In Plate 2 several of these men are stabbing each other with bayonets, spears, and knives. The caption reads: "With or without reason". Plate 8 shows a crumpled horse lying on the ground with its rider pinned beneath it. The caption notes, "This always happens". In the next plate a French soldier is engaging in the age-old military tradition of raping a woman, but an old lady is sneaking up behind him to plunge a knife into his back.

While standing amid a pile of dead bodies, the Spanish fighter in Plate 12 is either vomiting or spitting up blood. The caption coldly says, "This is what you were born for." In the etching captioned "Charity", several men are throwing naked bodies into a mass grave. Plate 33 depicts three French soldiers spreading the legs of a naked man. A fourth soldier is using a sword to butcher his groin. The harshest image, Plate 39, shows a small tree. Lashed to the trunk are two men whose genitals have been chopped off. On one branch, a headless and armless torso is hanging upside down. Its arms are hanging further down the branch, and its head has been placed upright on another branch. The sarcastic caption comments on this mutilation: "Great deeds — against the dead!"

The plate that sums things up the best is number 32, which shows three French soldiers pulling the legs and pushing on the back of a man who is hanging from a tree. The captions asks simply, "Why?"

Dover Publications; $7.95
1967; oversized softcover; 95 pp
heavily illus; 0-486-21872-4

FREAKS GEEKS & STRANGE GIRLS
Sideshow Banners of the Great American Midway
by Randy Johnson and others

With the publication of the lavish, beautifully designed *Freaks Geeks & Strange Girls*, sideshow banners have been consecrated as another medium — like graffiti or rock and roll posters — that is now being appreciated as an art form, whether the ivory tower intellectuals give their approval or not. Over 150 colourful cloth banners have been reproduced within these oversized pages, sometimes on an extra-large gatefold. Ten articles by "literary freaks, computer geeks & strange contributors" explore and explain tattooed people, fat people, anti-drug shows, banner artists, the "lure of the sideshow", and more.

The introduction explains that for a long time sideshow banners were considered to be nothing more than cheap advertising. "They earned their keep. Once the show folded or the attraction bolted, they were instantly obsolete as paintings (unless they were recycled for other shows), and were used instead for their value as tarps. They sopped up oil under trucks, they were cut up for scrap, discarded." The only reason any survived is because a few artists and collectors recognised their aesthetic value and saved them from a less than noble fate.

The many banners you'll see in *Freaks* advertise such wonders as Otis the Frog Boy, the Great Marlowe ("Strong as a Lion"), Nuba the Ferocious Black Leopard, Alligator Boy, Emmett the Armless and Legless Boy, Dickie the Penguin Boy, Albino Girl, Vickie Condor the 4 Legged Girl, Huey the Pretzel Man, Marie the Armless Girl, Rubber Skin Man, an African Witch Doctor, Zoma the Sadist, an 88-pound man, the "only 3 legged football player in the world!", a "bone crushing anaconda", waltzing dogs, fire eaters, contortionists, fat men and women, midgets, and snake charmers. A few advertise such non-wonders as tattoo artists, a palm reader, and the dope shows designed to scare people away from drugs (one poster shows a woman holding a bloody scimitar and warns: "Anything can happen if your trip is a bummer! Remember Charlie Manson and Sharon Tate!").

Hardy Marks Publications; $30
1995; oversized softcover; 169 pp
heavily illus; 0-945367-19-8

GOOD TASTE GONE BAD
The "Art" of Mitch O'Connell
by Mitch O'Connell

A collection of artwork from Mitch O'Connell, who has liv-

Sideshow banner by Snap Wyatt.
Freaks Geeks & Strange Girls.

ened the pages of *National Lampoon*, *Spy*, *Playboy*, and other magazines with his bold, dynamic illustration style that often makes the characters pop right off the page. *Good Taste Gone Bad* includes several comic stories, such as "Mitch Makes a Pitch", in which an aspiring screenplay writer tries to sell a stogie-chomping Hollywood producer on an idea, and "Spider in the Hairdo!", a treatment of one of the most famous urban legends. Single panel work includes the sci-fi tribute "This Island Earth", a poster for the play *The Betty Page Story*, and "Jimmy's Wet Dream", one of the many works that incorporates kitschy pop culture imagery — in this case, the heads of famous cartoon and comic women on the bodies of bikini babes.

Good Taste Products; $12.95
1993; oversized softcover; 88 pp
heavily illus; 0-9639762-0-6

THE GRAPHIC WORKS OF EDVARD MUNCH
by Edvard Munch

Edvard Munch is best known for *The Scream*, a violently coloured painting whose gaunt central character is the embodiment of modern alienation and confused terror. The lithograph version of that masterpiece is here, along with 89 other black and white works in various media. Many of them embrace dark subjects — death, vampires, loneliness, grief — but even the ones that deal with lighter subjects are done in an unrelentingly dark and morose style. Included are a mezzotint of a ghostly, topless woman wearing a hood and collar, an etching of a naked woman squeezing the blood from a heart all over her feet, a lithograph of a cabaret show, a drypoint of a naked woman embracing a skeletal figure, a woodcut of a woman's head silhouetted against a beach, an etching and aquatint of a little girl (?) clenching her fists and grimacing beside the corpse of her mother, and *Anxiety*, an extraordinarily inky woodcut of a group of men, women, and children whose skeletal faces stare bleakly at the viewer.

Dover Publications; $11.95
1979; oversized softcover; 101 pp
heavily illus; 0-486-23765-6

FROM THE FILES OF MITCH O'CONNELL

Maximum kitsch.
Good Taste Gone Bad.

THE HISTORY OF FORMERLY SALTY AREAS

by Timothy Patrick Butler

Timothy Patrick Butler's 68 pen and ink drawings map a menacing subconscious terrain inhabited by all manner of outcast beings — from skeletons and demons to unnamed humanoid and bestial creatures. The attention to fine detail makes it seem as though Butler is actually viewing each nightmarish scene and recording it for us. Except for a few solid black areas, he shades using the time-honoured techniques of stippling, hatching, and cross-hatching.

Nobis Invitvs depicts a stooped, winged skeleton in a trench coat and stovepipe hat feeding crows the way an old person might feed pigeons. A full moon hangs low in the sky, while a winged demon looks on. In *The Slug Lord* we see a giant slug dressed in an aristocratic outfit surrounded by the accoutrements of his office. Two small reptilian beings sit on the floor pointing accusingly at each other.

A cross between a bull, a warthog, and a demon with a hard-on rips the entrails out of a small dragon in *Land Carnivore*. One of my faves is *The Death of Don Bread*. A being with tentacles instead of legs and a loaf of bread for a head is using a large knife to slice his own noggin.

In one of the most openly erotic drawings, *Customer Service*, an obese, hung, hooded executioner is being serviced three ways. A cute fairy-girl is massaging his dick, a grinning lump with an arm is using a feather to tickle his balls, and a smaller lump with an arm five times the length of its body is pushing a dildo up his ass. The sexuality strikes a much more threatening note in *Even the Moon Conspires Against Us* — a giant goat-legged demon smiles wickedly as he grabs a little girl and picks her up.

Some of Butler's work can be viewed on his Website

(http://users.aol.com/thesaltlik/). You'll also find a listing of the numerous magazines that contain Butler's art. Usually they're porn, Satanic, death metal, or gruesome art magazines, although I find that these pieces aren't as brutally confrontational as that might imply. Their classic style makes them seem more like the works of Bosch and Dürer (two of Butler's influences) than modern necroporn art.

Timothy Patrick Butler; $12
1994; oversized softcover; 77 pp
heavily illus; 0-9644469-0-1

HR GIGER'S RETROSPECTIVE, 1964-1984

by HR Giger

In the introduction to this overview of twenty years of HR Giger's artistic life, his publisher eloquently captures Giger's approach: "He has alighted in his own unique universe. A universe where organic and inorganic forms are shaped by the 'Bio-mechanical aesthetic'; the dialectic of man and machine, where flesh and bone join magma and metal in synergistic ballet. Steel girders support, and conduits flourish. Human forms grow fluid and metamorphic, evolving into a new realm, both disturbing and sublime."

This book presents some of the Swiss surrealist's most important work in a year-by-year fashion. It starts in 1964, when we see little Indian ink drawings of whimsical humanoid creatures Giger did while in his second year of art school. The next year, Giger created black polyester sculptures of alienesque lifeforms and more involved drawings of bizarre beings. In the following year, Giger created some amazingly detailed, dense drawings that give the first solid indications of where his art was headed. From there, it's on to Giger's first work designing movie aliens (for the short film *Swiss-Made 2069*), his *Passages* series (about openings in the mechanical landscape around us), his first acrylics, his work on the movie *Dune*, his designs for *Alien*, his subsequent fame, and, finally, some of his biomechanical images from 1983. The year 1984 doesn't contain any of Giger's work, instead reproducing photos of the artist with his mother and shooting at targets.

For each year, there is some information regarding Giger's artistic output and his personal life. *Retrospective* ends with an exhaustive listing of Giger's solo exhibitions, works on permanent display, prizes and awards, original prints, books and articles by and about him, and more.

Morpheus International; $19.95
1997; oversized softcover; 116 pp
heavily illus; 1-883398-29-0

JUXTAPOZ

Juxtapoz is a slick, full-colour magazine devoted to "lowbrow art", strange art, and experimental art — but none of that high-falutin', purposely clever, cryptic avant-garde stuff (OK, maybe a little). Just highly-talented people honestly pursuing their own unique visions.

The spring 1995 issue features the oil paintings of Mark Ryder, who creates purposely kitschy canvases inhabited by Barbie, sad-eyed waifs, hula dancers, pink flamingos, and, occasionally, disconcerting things like demons and severed heads. His painting on the cover — which depicts a human-size ginseng root giving birth via C-section to a blue-rabbit-stuffed-animal — proves that art can shock you without sex or violence.

The same issue features Spencer Tunik, whose specialty is photographing nude people in public. In one picture, thirty people got naked and laid down in a zigzag line in the middle of the street in front of the United Nations building in New York. The author of the article accompanying the photos dubs it "artistic terrorism at its best". Also in the issue is the airbrushing of Rick Griffin, the miniature urban installations of Michael McMillen, and the graffiti of Twist.

The centrepiece of the next issue is a mondo fourteen-page visual history of the rock poster from Elvis and Jimi Hendrix through KISS to Sonic Youth and Gas Huffer. Other highlights include Rick Kern's photography, Kimberly Austin's pseudo-daguerreotype nudes, Neon Park's acrylic on masonite paintings, and Jason Mercier's pop culture mosaics made from coloured noodles and beans.

The Fall 1995 issue again proved to be an eclectic visual treat. How can you beat a magazine that has the awe-inspiring psychedelic/metaphysical/Tantric paintings of Alex Gray, the rude crude antics of S. Clay Wilson's Checkered Demon, and the magic marker courtroom illustrations of Walt Stewart under one cover? And that's just for starters.

An article in the Fall 1996 issue gives a fascinating history of the sacred symbol known as the swastika. This hooked cross has become so associated with Nazism that Western society has forgotten that it has been around for over 3500 years and exists in almost every culture. Its name comes from the Sanskrit word for "well-being". "Examples of this cross, which traditionally holds the meaning of environmental balance, harmony and good fortune, can be found in the artefacts from the Hittites of Asia Minor, Greece, Rome, Persia, India, Babylonia, Egypt, Scotland, Ireland, Russia, Poland, and Balinesia, to Celtic, aboriginal North American, Meso-American and South American civilisations. The Jain Buddhists make the sign of the swastika. You can see the hooked cross in the wailing wall in Jerusalem. The United States Army's 45th division used it as a logo from 1929-1939." The article is accompanied by over two dozen pictures of the swastika being used in non-Nazi ways in everything from its appearance in Native American and Hindu artwork to a Canadian women's hockey team who used it as their symbol in 1916 and a 1920s swastika-shaped watch fob emblazoned with "Coca-Cola" (the company denied its existence, but here it is, plain as day).

Spring 1997 covers, among other things, the "museum quality T&A" of Glenn Barr, the best new graffiti, and Stanislav Szukalski, the greatest unrecognised sculptor of the twentieth century. The summer 1997 issue is one of the best, with coverage of Coop, Gilbert Shelton (best known for the *Fabulous Furry Freak Brothers*), tattoo artist Don Ed Hardy, the awe-inspiring work of Viennese Fantastic Realist Ernst Fuchs, the Jim-Henson-on-acid lifeforms of Krystine Kryttre, and the unapologetically bizarre panoramas of eccentric jani-

Pals, 1966 by JM.
The Museum of Bad Art.

tor Henry Darger.

The regular four-issue subscription price for *Juxtapoz* is $14.50, but they've been charging a mere $10 for over two years now. Snap up this total steal while you still can.

Juxtapoz/PO Box 884570/San Francisco CA 94188-4570
Voice: 415-822-3083
WWW: www.juxtapoz.com
Single issue: $3.95. Canada: $4.95
Four issue sub (one year): $10 (for now). Canada: $18.50.
Elsewhere: $25
Payment: ck, mo, Visa, MC

THE MUSEUM OF BAD ART
Art Too Bad to Be Ignored
by Tom Stankowicz & Marie Jackson

In 1993, antique dealer Scott Wilson started the Museum of Bad Art in order to collect, preserve, and promote an overlooked genre of art — art that sucks. But not just any sucky art qualifies for inclusion, mind you. It has to be art that sucks in a good way. Allow me to explain. Any jerk can pick up a paintbrush and create a worthless piece of crap. But this book is not a collection of paintings done by the incompetent. Most of the works appear to have been created by people who had at least a modicum of talent but not the discipline or the vision to use their talent in a meaningful way. Wilson explains the crucial factors he looks for when deciding if a work is right for the Museum: "some evidence of artistic control, lack of perspective, garish colour choices, unusual subject matter, and an inappropriate frame."

The paintings are often found in flea markets and garage sales. The MOBA has a steadfast rule that it will pay no more than $6.50 for any piece. Once purchased, the works of art may be exhibited at the Museum's physical location in Dedham, Massachusetts, on its CD-ROM, at its Website

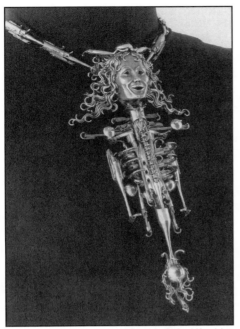

Medusa by Richard Mawdsley.
The New Jewelry.

(http://www.glyphs.com/moba/), or in travelling exhibitions.

This book is a logical outgrowth of MOBA's commitment to giving bad art the exposure it deserves. Herein, you'll find an old woman in a field of flowers, two doves kissing on a thin tree limb, Mary Todd Lincoln painted on lace, a battle from the American Revolution, a dancing animal at a circus, a clown and his monkey friend, a paunchy executive wearing only his briefs, and over 30 other disquieting works. Each piece is accompanied by mock-serious art-crit commentary, and a similarly tongue-in-cheek end section looks at MOBA's history and activities.

Andrews & McMeel; $14.95
1996; oversized softcover; 108 pp
heavily illus; 0-8362-2185-0

NEOISM, PLAGIARISM & PRAXIS

by Stewart Home

Stewart Home, author of the class war novel *Red London* [*Outposts* p 141], is one of the leading theoreticians and spokesmen for British avant-garde movements of the 1980s. This collection of his writings records for posterity the thoughts and actions behind Neoism, Plagiarism, the Art Strike, and other manifestations of anti-culture culture.

Home was part of the Neoist Alliance, a loose-knit group of artists who mainly used audio, video, and performance art and were influenced by Futurism, Dada, Fluxus, Mail Art, and Punk. The Dada influence can be seen clearly in the Neoists' desire to completely undermine and destroy the religious, political, social, and artistic status quo. But while the Dadaists were anti-everything, the Neoists had a vision of what they wanted — to foster ugliness and degeneracy, to incite class warfare, to lower people's morals.

Two of the Neoists' biggest complaints are that "hardback fiction has no social value whatsoever and is, in fact, a form of mental pollution" and that British mainstream authors of little worth are monopolising the publishing industry. In June 1993, the Neoist Alliance sent a leaflet to authors, editors, agents, and other movers and shakers in England's literary establishment. The polemic opened with the lines: "When 'high art' hack Robert Burns hanged himself, the literary establishment responded by wringing its hands. One year on, it's high time book bores like Salman Rushdie, Martin Amis and Julian Barnes wrung their own necks. To encourage these parasites to top themselves and simultaneously celebrate the Richard Burns suicide anniversary, the Neoist Alliance is organising a psychic attack on the book trade."

In the late 1980s, after Home had left the Neoists, he called for an Art Strike. All artists were to stop creating work from January 1, 1990, to January 1, 1993, in order to protest against the commercialisation of art. Or something like that. Although many people promoted the idea of the Art Strike, Home was one of the very few people who actually struck. "I not only ceased writing, producing graphics, organising events and playing the guitar — I also stopped promoting the Art Strike."

Other essays look at Karen Eliot, Plagiarism, Neoist pranks, Fluxus, the parallels between terrorism and avant garde art, and much more.

AK Press; $18.95
1995; softcover; 207 pp
1-873176-33-3

THE NEW JEWELRY
Trends + Traditions (Revised Edition)

Peter Dormer & Ralph Turner

Like all art forms, jewellery has its radicals and its experimentalists. This impressive book contains 262 photographs (129 in colour) documenting the most unusual and creative body ornamentation ever made. The first two sections cover "mainstream" jewellery, which is defined as work that "is familiar in its function even where the design and materials are novel. The jewellery is usually comfortable and practical to wear, although clearly, in breaking away from the staleness of department-store ware, it breaches some conventions." Basically, this is stuff you'd recognise as jewellery even though it gets pretty wild.

The first section covers mainstream abstract jewellery. There's a gold pendant that looks like something MC Escher might have made. Joelle Levie has created a Plexiglas bracelet and necklace that look like they came straight out of the Jetsons. Another necklace is a stiff square of painted steel. There are also bracelets made out of hundreds of intertwined red, white, and blue rubber bands, and cream-coloured armbands made from papier-mâché. One set of pins looks like a colony of sperm in search of an egg. Paul Derrez's neckpiece resembles a short lampshade around the model's shoulders.

An essential look at the unofficial artist of the apocalypse. *Mommy/Daddy*, *Original Sin*.

The next section looks at more literal mainstream figurative work, which portrays recognisable objects. Richard Mawdsley's incredibly elaborate *Feast Bracelet* is a silver contraption that looks like a table set with cutlery, glasses, food, and a bottle of wine. Gijs Baker has created an audacious neckpiece that makes the wearer look like a big rose. *Medusa* is a detailed ten-inch silver reproduction of the head and upper skeletal system of the famous Gorgon.

The third section, "Jewelry as Theater", is where things go bonkers. These are true avant-garde ornaments that you wouldn't wear in a million years. For instance, Caroline Broadhead's see-through nylon neckpiece engulfs the model from her shoulders to above the top of her head. It looks like she's wearing a giant Slinky. One of Otto Künzli's brooches appears to be a gift box stuck on the lapel of some guy's jacket. Another one looks like five bricks taken out of a wall. You modern primitives will want to take note of the blue aluminium spike worn through the earlobe.

The final section examines the more radical directions jewellery has taken since the book was originally published in 1985. Adele Piper's gold-plated wavy headpiece is something the god Neptune would wear. Jared Taylor's handpiece could pull double duty as brass knuckles. The series of brooches called *Bugs* have bodies made of aluminium foil with pins, hooks, blades, and sparkplugs stuck in them.

The New Jewelry also contains several essays and short biographies of all the artists whose work is featured. It's a top-notch book. If you like jewellery, you'll love it. If you've never really thought about it, it can make you see jewellery in a whole new light.

Thames and Hudson; $24.95
1985, 1994; oversized softcover; 216 pp
heavily illus; 0-500-27774-5

ORIGINAL SIN
The Visionary Art of Joe Coleman
by Joe Coleman and others

At last, a book that does full justice to one of the most gifted, untamed artists of our time. Based on talent, vision, and eccentricity, Joe Coleman is on a par with many of the painters enshrined in the pantheon of Western art. He may never be recognised as such, though, or it may take several decades after his death to do the trick, because of the extreme nature of his work.

In his art and his life, Coleman utterly rejects the normal and the banal, finding meaning in life's extremes. He identifies with the outsiders, the dispossessed, the reviled, and even the sociopathic. His vivid, incredibly detailed tableaux are filled with the disfigured, the insane, serial killers, petty criminals, misanthropes, tortured writers, extremists, and others on the fringe. The canvases seethe with decay and are often filled with violence.

Many of Coleman's paintings are large portraits of a famous outsider surrounded by numerous smaller images relating to his or her life. (These smaller images are so detailed that each of them could be a painting on its own.) *Descent into the Maelstrom of Edgar Allan Poe* shows the famed author surrounded by his mother, his stepparents, his wife/cousin, a raven, Annabel Lee, Hop Frog, The Conqueror Worm, Baudelaire, Poe's cottage in the Bronx, a scene from a dream he had in which a demon sawed off his mother's legs, and other images that figure in Poe's life. Other personages who receive similar treatment include unrepentant, sadistic serial killer Carl Panzram, Ed Gein (the basis for *Psycho*), schizophrenic outsider artist Aldolf Wölfli, the Elephant Man, John Brown, hillbilly Anse Hatfield (of the famous Hatfield and McCoy feud), Jayne Mansfield, Jesus, and Sigmund Freud.

Each of these famous people represents an archetype. Coleman sees Poe as the doomed son/lover, Wölfli as the divine madman, the Elephant Man as the deformed shadow-self, Mansfield as the temptress, and McCoy as the dark father. In his essay, Harold Schechter writes: "As an archetypal artist, Coleman instinctively knows that primordial images always put on the garb of the here-and-now, that 'visionary' works are those which manage to render the perennial meanings of myth in terms of the present moment."

Other paintings depict scenes populated by anywhere from eight to dozens of strange characters. *Immaculate Conception* shows several provocatively dressed people with gruesome skin diseases sitting in a room with four horribly deformed babies (including one with two heads). Among the details you'll notice are a magazine opened to an advertisement for menstrual pads, a bottle of Kaluha, a vagina-like insect creature, and four separate appearances of the Virgin Mary.

A few works are directly autobiographical. The epic canvas *Mommy/Daddy* shows Coleman's parents as two halves of the same being, surrounded by people and scenes from the artist's life. *Hellhound on My Trail*, which depicts Coleman walking out of an industrial wasteland and out of the picture itself, represents the painful end of a five-year romantic relationship.

Even when the paintings don't seem to be explicitly about Coleman, though, they contain autobiographical elements. An assembly of details from several paintings show that Coleman's mother and father reappear in various forms. A quote in Jim Jarmusch's essay reveals just how personal all of this art is. Coleman compares painting to raising devils and says, "I can only raise the ones that I identify with... I'm interested in the parts of them that reflect myself."

Original Sin is lavishly produced, containing colour plates of 26 paintings along with enlarged details from most of them. Many other works and details are reproduced in black and white. The essays by three admirers and critics reveal many facets of Coleman's life and art, and the accompanying visuals include artwork that influenced Coleman, biographical photos (his parents, his work as a performance artist, etc.), and the Odditorium, his personal collection of bizarre items, including a pickled one-eyed pig, a lock of Charles Manson's hair, a cast of a Thalidomide victim's arm, a Victorian wheelchair, and opium pipes. For your further edification, a section in the back of the book provides the keys to decode the meanings of all the images in nineteen of the paintings.

An essential look at the unofficial artist of the apocalypse.

Heck Editions (Gates of Heck); $29.95 [hardcover: $50]
1997; oversized softcover; 144 pp
heavily illus; 0-9638129-6-3

OUT FROM UNDER
Texts By Women Performance Artists
edited by Lenora Champagne

Out From Under is a collection of written pieces from nine female performance artists, including three of the most well-known — Karen Finley, Holly Hughes, and Laurie Anderson. In "The Constant State of Desire", Finley rails at Yuppie/executive types who have a superficial liking for performance art because it adds a little rebellion to their otherwise conformist lives. "So I open up those designer jeans of yours. Open up your ass and stick up there sushi, nouvelle cuisine. I stick up your ass Cuisinarts, white wine, and racquetball, your cordless phone and Walkman up your ass. And you look up at me worried and ask 'but where's the graffiti art' and I say 'up your ass.' And you smile 'cause you work all day and you want some of the artistic experience, the artistic lifestyle for yourself after work and on weekends."

In the selections from the seven-hour piece *United States*, Anderson offers brief vignettes about playing games when she was a child, dreaming she was President Carter's lover, and getting her palm read. In one section, she recalls living in West Hollywood when the Hollywood Strangler was killing women. Every night on TV there was a panel discussion on the topic. When a policeman was identified as a suspect, the chief of police appeared on the panel. "He said, 'Now, girls, whatever happens, do not stop for a police officer. Stay in your car. If a police officer tries to stop you, do not stop. Keep driving and under no circumstances should you get out of your car.' For a few weeks, half the traffic in LA was doing twice the speed limit."

Other pieces include "My Brazil" by Rachel Rosenthal, "Getting Over Tom" by Lenora Champagne, and "The Survivor and the Translator" by Leeny Sack.

Theatre Communications Group; $12.95
1990; softcover; 191 pp
illus; 0-55936-009-7

POP CULT PRODUCTS CATALOGUE

This colour catalog offers all kinds of items bearing the artwork of such wild talents as Kim Deitch, Clive Barker, Robt Williams, XNO, Jim Woodring, James O'Barr, and others, with more being added all the time. Items include silkscreened and embroidered T-shirts, hats, backpacks, posters, prints, limited edition art, and original art. Why wear stupid corporate T-shirts and clutter your walls with generic art when you could have images of sultry she-devils licking ice cream cones or glue-sniffing teenagers hallucinating?

Bess Cutler Gallery/PO Box 1380/York Beach ME 03910
WWW: www.besscutlergallery.com
Catalog: $2

PSRF
The Photostatic Retrofuturist

This zine is put out by Lloyd Dunn, who was formerly with the Tape-beatles and is now part of that group's successor, Public Works. Dunn's work focuses on plagiarism, appropriation, detournement, sampling, collage, parody, and other similar approaches to art that filter or combine elements of existing culture in new ways. Forget black metal and noise, this is *the* outlaw form of music (and, less commonly, it involves other forms of art). It doesn't violate moral standards but, rather, intellectual property laws. Several practitioners, such as Negativland and John Oswald, have had their work suppressed, and just about every artist in this loosely defined genre is in constant danger of meeting that same fate.

PSRF contains news, ideas, manifestos, and examples pertaining to these various forms of plunder art. Issue 48 contains the declaration "Public Works Means Reality for the 3rd Millennium", which states: "Step by step, Public Works allows the liberation of plastic form among all formats; and the creation of a fractalised, kaleidoscopic cosmos of forms of their own. The spatio-temporal conception binds together and interbraids fragments of meaning and creates a context nutritious to mentation just as, in another period, the uncovery of the rules of perspective did when they used a single stationary point to aid naturalistic representation." This article is followed by "Our Common Bond", which cleverly weaves text through page after page of found photographs used without permission. The text is a philosophical treatise on the ways in which art and inventions give form to ideas.

A tongue-in-cheek article by former Tape-beatle John Heck tells the allegedly true story of that group's demise, and another writing by him decries wageslavery while relating his adventures as a waiter. Elsewhere, Bill Brown tells us about his parody of Nike's ads, Dunn gives his thoughts on the concept of "amedia" ("We use media as disrespectfully as it tries to use us"), the Unknown Neoist reports from the First Congress of the New Lettrist International, Dunn

Part of the Palace Ide'al, built by one person over the course of 33 years. *Raw Creation*.

reviews printed and audio material dealing with anti-copyright art, and Spencer Selby offers a long list of experimental poetry/art magazines.

PSRF-Static Output/PO Box 8832/Iowa City IA 52240
Email: psrf@detritus.net
WWW: soli.inav.net/~psrf
Single issue: $5. Non-US: $7
Four issue sub: $15. Non-US: $20

RAW CREATION
Outsider Art and Beyond
by John Maizels

As editor of *Raw Vision* magazine since 1989, John Maizels has been heavily involved with art created by people who are self-taught. This includes artwork by people considered clinically insane, by sane social outsiders (eccentrics, hermits, etc.), and by folk artists. The common denominator is that these creators are not formally trained… their work flows directly from their imaginations with little or no thought about "correct" techniques, theoretical foundations, public opinion, fashionableness, or any rules of the art world.

Maizels looks at the history of outsider art, from its early admirers to its recognised status as a group of genres to its influence on formal artists to its surging popularity today. Over a third of the book deals specifically with the art of the mentally ill, one section looks at "visionary environments" made by artists, and various chapters examine contemporary folk art in the US, "marginal art", self-taught art in the non-Western world, and unusual objects created by outsiders.

Along the way we are treated to hundreds of stunning works of art (the vast majority reproduced in colour) done in wild, fantastic styles that cover a huge spectrum of approaches. Several works are by Aloïse Corbaz, who was permanently institutionalised in 1918. "Executed in coloured pencil, her drawings are dominated by a single flowing, rounded feminine presence. Bare-breasted and resplendent, the figure is often accompanied by an upstanding young escort in fine uniform. Sometimes the two figures, male and female, are linked together in embrace, even sharing the same mouth or eyes. The eyes on all her figures are simple blue ovals that seem to be both blinded and staring; deep blue pools contrasting with the warm pinks and reds that flow around them."

James Hampton was a night janitor in Washington DC. When he died, a little storage space he rented was cleaned out. "Within this shabby space was discovered a creation that Hampton had been working on for the last fourteen years: the *Throne of the Third Heaven of the Nations Millennium General Assembly*." Hampton was a religious man who had been inspired by the Book of Revelation to make this construction. "It consisted of a mass of handmade shrines, pulpits and altars symmetrically flanking a large throne; the walls displayed a series of tablets proclaiming the names of the prophets and disciples… His material included cast-off furniture (the altars and main structure of the throne were made from old tables and chairs, the throne itself from an old armchair), old lightbulbs, carpet rolls and cardboard. Practically all of the nearly two hundred elements in his creation were covered in shining gold or silver metal foil, some smoothly, others with a crumpled texture."

French postman Ferdinand Cheval built an unendingly elaborate palace out of rocks he collected while delivering mail for 33 years. Similarly, Rodia — an Italian immigrant to America — spent 33 years building three soaring, weblike towers and six shorter ones with pieces of metal he found wrapped in wire and cable. The entire interior of Danielle Jacqui's home is covered in intricate embroideries and paintings. Folk artist Jimmy Lee Sudduth paints with mud, adding ground up leaves and berries for their pigments. Augustin Lesage is one of the few artists in the book who uses the traditional medium of oil paints on canvas, letting the voices in his head tell him how to paint gigantic, intricate canvases.

Raw Creation is likely to be considered the definitive look at this fascinating aspect of art and of creativity in general.

Phaidon Press; $69.96
1996; oversized hardcover; 240 pp
heavily illus; 0-7148-3149-2

RETINA DAMAGE
by Jim Blanchard

A way oversized collection of Jim Blanchard's solo work and his collaborations with Chris Kegel and Daniel Heidebrecht. Blanchard's heavily detailed pen and ink images usually combine abstract repetitive patterns with grotesquely distorted people and other beings. The opening piece shows ancient symbols, South American designs, and snake-like objects bursting from the forehead of a human skull. Another drawing combines Mayan symbolism with the technological feel of circuit boards to create some sort of shaman/computer being (well, that's how I interpret it).

Another work (almost none of them has a title, so bear with me) shows a skeletal being reminiscent of Grateful Dead artwork being embraced by a giant spider. The *Tremendous Demands of 'True' Love* shows two bizarre lizard-aliens with cigarettes engaged in oral sex (I guess). The book's finale is a four-page jigsaw collage featuring a range of styles, including comic book, op art, realism, neo-Victorian, doodles, and altered photographs.

At a measly five bucks, *Retina Damage* makes a nice visual treat.

Beef Eye; $5

1991; oversized softcover; 28 pp
heavily illus

RIVER OF MIRRORS
The Fantastic Art of Judson Huss
by Judson Huss

When speaking of painter Judson Huss, his admirers often bring up the names of the Masters of European art. Filmmaker Terry Gilliam goes so far as to call him a "new Old Master", and I have to concur. Had Huss been born on the Continent 150 to 300 years ago, we would probably be seeing his works in art history textbooks and the Louvre. For now, we can see it in *River of Mirrors*.

Many of Huss's works fit right in with the oeuvre of Bosch, Dürer, and their compatriots. In the brown ink drawing *The Pilgrim*, a balding, weary man clad in a simple robe tied at the waist with rope is trodding along a path in the countryside. Slung over his right shoulder is a sack with a grotesque troll-like beastie sticking its head out. Huss's caption gives some insight into the symbolism of this picture: "Damnit! Wherever the road may take us, we are obliged to carry our character with us." The oil painting *Return from Africa* is a sweeping canvas showing a heavily armoured knight riding his steed on a grassy plain. What makes the image so startling is that the knight is atop a rhinoceros, not a horse.

The Mojave Triptych is a detailed three-part painting depicting a desert filled with strange creatures among rock formations that have faces. In the centre of the scene, a naked man who looks like a sad Julius Caesar holds a chain that leads to the collar on a small woman with whip marks criss-crossing her back. A giant chrome scorpion with a man's face scuttles towards the couple. In the left panel a man with an urn for a head and angry faces on his knees huddles in a corner. A powder-white asexual humanoid is reclining on a large satin pillow, listening to headphones that plug into its bellybutton. It is looking sadly into a huge oval mirror being held by a screaming woman who has an arrow in her back. Meanwhile, on top of a cliff, a disrobing woman whose legs are through the fingerholes of a gigantic pair of scissors is about to snip the stilts of a midget.

Things take a decidedly more ominous note in *P.U. 239.05.94 [Plutonium]*, a tempera painting of a gaunt zombie-like being dressed in a flowing reddish-orange robe and a crown of barbed wire. Over his upturned, gaunt right hand floats a giant uranium atom, while his left hand points to a mushroom cloud. He is flanked by two soldiers wearing armour and gasmasks, one holding a sword and the other clutching small missiles. The oil painting *Indoctrination* shows three men in ecclesiastical robes and headgear nonchalantly using a long silver rod to puncture a bound man's eardrum.

In a few paintings, such as *Natural History* and *Isa Flore*, Huss seems as though he is a reincarnated Pre-Raphaelite. *The Reconciliation* — an interpretation of the Beauty and the Beast theme — shows an ethereal fair maiden in a lovely blue dress sitting in the woods as a hairy brute tenderly lays his head on her knee.

Many other classic styles are employed, always filtered through Huss's own unique vision. The bright colours and

Ecce Homo by a modern Master.
River of Mirrors.

slightly abstracted details of *The Transformation of Saint George* gives the European subject matter an Oriental feel. Goya would've been proud to paint the fiery *The Discovery of Plutonium*, and the highly symbolic *Ecce Homo* reminds me of Botticelli.

Huss take the best techniques of the past, fantastic subject matter, an outlook that can be whimsical, threatening, or hopeful, and combines it all with a level of talent and craftsmanship that many people have written off as dead. *River of Mirrors* is highly recommended, even more so when you consider that it's large enough for the pages to be cut out and framed, making it a gallery in a book.

Morpheus International; $24.95
1996; oversized softcover; 96 pp
heavily illus; 1-883398-17-7

UNE SEMAINE DE BONTÉ
by Max Ernst

Une Semaine de Bonté (*A Week of Kindness*) by surrealist Max Ernst is one of the masterpieces of collage. Ernst took woodcut illustrations from old catalogues, pulp novels, and magazines, then recombined them into 182 bizarre, morbid scenes. Each one seems to be telling a story that we can never know. They are tantalising glimpses into a disturbing world of dark dreams that provide more questions than answers. Why is an apparently dead man with the head of a rooster hanging from a tree by his trousers while a woman in the foreground has her breast groped? Who is the man with an Easter Island head sitting in the restaurant with a drunkard and giant insects? Why are a woman and a dragon prostrating themselves before a man with bird wings sprouting out of his back?

Dover Publications; $10.95
1976; oversized softcover; 212 pp
heavily illus; 0-486-23253-2

SEPTEMBER COMMANDO
Gestures of Futility and Frustration
by John Yates

Renegade graphic designer John Yates — founder of the Stealworks media guerrilla group — appropriates the imagery that surrounds us and adds his own stinging commentary. As he says in the introduction, "It's the stealing of an over-the-counter culture made popular by thieves. It's the subtle weaponry of the mass(acre) media acquired and redefined for bluntly defined intervention. It's a Citizen Caine mutiny in which the media supplies the pictures and Stealworks supplies the war. Praise the PowerPC and pass the ammunition."

Each of the 70 full-page graphics in the main part of September Commando follows the same format: A black and white photo gives us the visual. Large white text in black rectangles above and below the picture gives us the bite. A picture of schoolkids with their hands on their hearts, looking attentively at the American flag, says: "PLEDGE ALLEGIANCE TO INDOCTRINATION". In another image, a man is duking out a Klansman holding a microphone. The caption reads: "FREEDOM OF SPEECH AND JUST TAXATION".

"YOU ARE THE MACHINERY AND THE MONKEY WRENCH" surrounds a shot of interlocking gears. Another of Yates' creations contains the famous shot from *Independence Day* where a hovering UFO blows the White House to smithereens. The text declares: "PROOF OF ALIEN INTELLIGENCE". A picture of a man perusing a wall covered in handguns is accompanied by the caption: "FREEDOM OF CHOICE I CAN LIVE WITHOUT".

The last 14 pages reproduce the CD covers and interiors Yates has done for Alternative Tentacles, Allied, AK Audio, and other highly independent record labels.

AK Press and Active Distribution; $11.95
1996; oversized softcover; 95 pp
heavily illus; 1-873176-52-X

SHATTERED FORMS
Art Brut, Phantasms, Modernism
by Allen S. Weiss

People who are insane, extremely eccentric, and socially isolated often produce incredible art. Jean Dubuffet recognised this work as a quasi-category of art called "art brut" ("raw art"). He wrote, "We are witness here to a completely pure artistic operation, raw, brute, and entirely reinvented in all of its phases solely by means of the artists' own impulses." In typical academic prose, the author analyses some of the major works of art brut, looks at how modern artists have incorporated their style, and tries to figure out where art brut fits into the world of art. Some particularly interesting chapters examine art brut in the forms of writing, music, sound art, movies, and architecture. Includes just twenty-one illustrations.

State University of New York Press; $24.50
1992; hardcover; 158 pp
illus; 0-7914-1117-6

"A Citizen Caine mutiny in which the media supplies the pictures and the Stealworks supplies the war." *September Commando.*

THRIFT STORE PAINTINGS
edited by Jim Shaw

This book collects around 200 paintings that were found in thrift stores. There is absolutely no commentary, no introduction, not even a back cover blurb. We can only assume that these paintings are meant to represent naive/folk art, found art, and/or "crap chic", that trend towards appreciating things that are so bad they become good in a weird way. Get ready for reproductions of abysmal works showing a murky green street corner barely lit by three street lamps, a close-up of a hand on a Bible, a child's lamp with an elephant for a base, ugly clowns, a 1950s robot attacking two women, a platinum blonde woman wearing a tight red dress in a blue room, a turtle smoking a cigarette, a pink poodle approaching a fire hydrant, portraits of lots of homely people, and more dreck.

Heavy Industry Publications (D.A.P.); $29.95
1990; oversized softcover; 205 pp
heavily illus; 1-879158-01-9

WILD WHEELS
by Harrod Blank

Cars can be a medium for their owners' self-expression. Some people hang fuzzy dice from the rear-view mirror, and others affix catchy bumperstickers. But there are a small number of people out there who take a much, much more creative approach to vehicular expression. In *Wild Wheels*, filmmaker Harrod Blank presents forty-two drivers who have turned their means of transportation into elaborate and bizarre works of art.

The "Cowasaki" is a three-wheel motorcycle that has been modified to look like a cow with wheels. "[I]n order to put gas in it, one has to lift up its tail and stick the nozzle in its rear end!" In a related move, the "Hippomobile" is a 1971 Ford Mustang convertible that has been overlaid with a 600-pound brass and copper hippopotamus. It has a built-in P.A. system that plays "the groaning sound of mating hippopotami."

As its name implies, the "Grass Car" is completely covered — top to bottom, end to end — with live, growing grass. Its owner admits that it is high maintenance: "I have to water it every day…" While in a mental institution, an Alabama man says God told him to put faucets on his car. Shortly after he heard this voice, his life got much better, so he immediately began affixing faucet handles and nozzles to his big, olive green Chevy.

A cab driver in Seattle has carved hundreds of blocks of wood into small buildings and glued them to the roof of his car. The book doesn't say it, but it appears as though this miniature cityscape is loosely based on part of Seattle's skyline. The rest of the car's exterior is painted to resemble an aerial view of a city

Other vehicles that are documented include "Button Car", "Cosmic Ray Deflection Car", "Fruitmobile", "Jesus Truck", "Mirrormobile", "Our Lady of Eternal Combustion", "Unidentified Moving Object", and "Wrought Iron VW". Each set of wild wheels is pictured with its owner (who is often just as eccentric as the car or truck itself) in a full-page photo. On the facing page is the story behind the vehicle and its owner, and one to three smaller pictures. *Wild Wheels* is a well-done tribute to yet another underrecognised art form.

Pomegranate; $18.95
1994; oversized softcover; 95 pp
heavily illus; 1-56640-981-0

www HR GIGER COM

by HR Giger

In this book, biomechanical artist HR Giger — who achieved world-wide fame as the designer of *Alien* — was given free reign to put together a collection of his creative output from the last 30 years. Selected, designed, and written by the artist, *www HR Giger com* mostly stays away from the famous airbrush paintings that have been reproduced in many other books (including *HR Giger's Retrospective, 1964-1984* [above]), instead displaying an astounding variety of other works, including ink drawings, acrylic and oil paintings, rough sketches, album covers, posters, watches, pins, sculpture, furniture, interior design, and more.

"A Feast for the Psychiatrist" is a series of twelve drawings based on Giger's dreams. *Birth Machine* is a cutaway illustration of a pistol in which the bullets are strange little beings wearing huge goggles. *Zodiac Sign Scorpio* is a nickel silver sculpture of a female leg that turns into an arm, which is giving a hypodermic injection to itself in the back of the knee. Several paintings are reproduced as stereograms that appear to be 3-D when viewed properly.

One chapter depicts in photos and drawings the bars Giger designed in Tokyo and Chur, Switzerland. Another chapter deals with the controversies that have resulted from three of his sexually explicit series, including "M. de Sade". Gratifyingly, the images from all of the series are reproduced so that we can judge for ourselves. Elsewhere, Giger presents his design work for the film adaptation of Ralf König's comic, *The Killer Condom*.

Three pages show people who have been tattooed with Giger artwork. In a similarly worshipful vein, a New Jersey chiropractor completely redid a Harley Davidson 1990 Fat Boy to look like it came straight out of a Giger painting. In another chapter, Giger displays works by other artists from his personal collection. He has originals by Ernst Fuchs, Joe Coleman, Dado, S. Clay Wilson, and Salvador Dalí.

A series of photos throughout the book shows famous people sitting in Giger's *Harkonnen Capo Chair*, a metallic throne that looks like the exoskeleton of a large alien. Among those having a seat are artist Joe Coleman, pleasure activist Annie Sprinkle, tattooist Spider Webb, Slymnestra Hyman of the band Gwar, photographer Irina Ionesco, actor Quentin Crisp, and a perfectly nude Natasha Henstridge, the actress who played Sil in *Species* (another movie Giger designed).

Also included in this hefty book are an autobiography of Giger's early life illustrated with snapshots, a biography of his professional life, and a listing of solo exhibitions, prizes and awards, books, interviews, film work, and more.

This collection contains numerous works that have never before been published or are not available in any other book. Taken from all media at all phases of Giger's life, they prove that his talents stretch way beyond his signature technorganic pieces. As we've come to expect from this publisher (Taschen), they have crammed an embarrassment of visual riches onto thick, glossy paper and managed to offer it for about half the price you'd expect. If you want the work that Giger is principally known for, you should probably get *Biomechanics* or *Necronomicon 1* and *2* (all published by Morpheus International), but if you want a full picture of his achievements, *www HR Giger com* is what you need.

Benedict Taschen Verlag; $29.99
1997; oversized hardcover; 241 pp
heavily illus; 3-8228-8567-3

FICTION ESSAYS & POETRY

SPECULATIVE FICTION

BLACK LEATHER REQUIRED
by David J. Schow

A baker's dozen of short stories from David Schow, a horror writer often associated with the splatterpunk movement. Schow's gut-level writing crackles with energy as it delivers tales of shocking violence and sex straight to your frontal lobes. The shock therapy begins right away, with the first lines of the first story, "The Shaft": "I made it to the rail just in time to watch Chiquita destroy an aluminium umbrella table, face-first, five stories below the balcony on which I stood. She missed the pool by a good ten feet. Until I saw her brains splatter all over the sun deck I hadn't realised she'd had any." Unfortunately for the narrator — a drug courier — the woman that jumped because of his dare was the girlfriend of a drug lord. He has to skedaddle to Chicago to stay alive, or so he hopes.

"Life Partner" is a necrophile love story with some good psychological insight. When JJ's asshole live-in boyfriend dies in their bed, she leaves him there. She remarks to a girlfriend, "'He's a changed man, Cecily. He's there for me.'" Her boyfriend's new state also improves their love life: "They made love every day, sometimes more than once, at all sorts of hours. Their shared bed had transformed into a domain whereupon JJ's sexuality had finally caught fire and burned hot."

Other stories include "Kamikaze Butterflies", "Scoop Makes a Swirly", "Jerry's Kids Meet Wormboy", "A Week in the Unlife", and "Where the Heart Was".

Mark V. Ziesing; $29.95
1994; hardcover; 246 pp
0-929480-29-5

THE BRAINS OF RATS
by Michael Blumlein

Dr. Michael Blumlein's anthology *The Brains of Rats* is clas-sified by the publisher as horror, and he is often published in science fiction magazines, but if you're expecting these tales to fall into either of those genres, you'll be caught off guard. They don't fit into any category I'm aware of. Some of them might be kin to New Wave science fiction, a late 1960s/early 1970s movement in which JG Ballard, Harlan Ellison, and other experimentalists pushed the form and content of the genre so far that it became something other than science fiction.

For instance, take the title story. It's basically a mono-logue in which the narrator, who is a doctor and medical researcher, relates his thoughts on gender in a stream-of-consciousness style. He discusses Joan of Arc, a married patient who caught gonorrhoea, his own desire to be a woman, the genetic basis of gender, domestic violence, Pope Joan, the *SCUM Manifesto*, penile implants, his wife, his daughter, rats' brains (which are very different between the sexes), and related topics. The only hint of science fiction comes when the man mentions that his laboratory has cre-ated a virus that will cause every foetus in the world to de-velop as the same sex. That sex will either be male or fe-male depending on his choosing. Although he finds this thought disturbing, he says: "But I think it shall have to be one or the other." We never find out if he lets the virus loose and, if so, which gender he chooses, because that's not the point of the story. The point seems to be that women and men are so irreconcilably different that they may as well be two entirely different species. "The Brains of Rats" is an oddly powerful work that belongs in its own genre.

The most stunning piece in the book has to be "Tissue Ablation and Variant Regeneration: A Case Report". The fact that Blumlein is an MD becomes apparent in this story, which takes the form of a report written by a doctor. He describes in clinical detail the complete surgical dismemberment of former President Ronald Reagan while the Gipper is alive and unanesthetised. To tell you why Reagan is excruciat-ingly cut into pieces would be to give away the ending, but let's just say that this is the most cold-bloodedly vicious po-litical satire since Jonathan Swift's "A Modest Proposal". This infamous story alone is worth the price of the book.

"Shed His Grace" is another medically-detailed stand-out story. This time the main character is bombarding him-self with images from a bank of sixteen video screens in his apartment. After watching a mind-numbing array of surgery footage, the Olympics, and Ronald and Nancy Reagan, he performs an operation on himself. Dismemberment and operations are at the forefront again in "Bestseller", about an author who donates body parts for money.

On the non-medical side, "Keeping House" is an extremely well-crafted story about a woman's slow decent into madness. "The Wet Suit" tells of a son coming to terms with his late father's peculiar practices, and "The Thing Itself" is a moving story about love and death.

Blumlein writes with a self-confident deliberation. His style is unhurried, which is not to say that it is at all slow or boring. It simply moves along with an easy grace, building up until either 1) you get nailed with a powerful ending or 2) the story simply stops, leaving you to figure out the point (and, yes, there is one, but you may have to search for it). The only problem is that these stories were published in the 1980s, and I haven't seen anything new from this talented author in several years. Michael Blumlein, where are you?

Dell Publishing; $5.50
1989, 1997; paperback; 230 pp
0-440-21373-8

GHOST OF A CHANCE

by William S. Burroughs

This novella was originally published in 1988 in a very limited edition by the Whitney Museum. Luckily it has been resurrected from obscurity by High Risk Books. In his inimitable style, the late William Burroughs serves up an environmental warning, but don't worry... although the message is loud and clear, it's presented in such a peculiar manner that it won't seem too manipulative.

I'm not going to pretend that I understand everything that happens in this book, but basically it goes down like this. The first part of the story involves the pirate Captain Mission and the anarchist utopian community he set up on Madagascar around the early 1700s. Mission has accidentally discovered an ancient structure that turns out to be the Museum of Lost Species, which contains a member of every extinct species.

The members of the Board — a small group that runs the world by sowing chaos and disharmony — are upset that Mission has created a community where everyone lives in peace with each other and with nature, all without any kind of laws. They send an agent provocateur to disrupt things and destroy the Museum.

The second main part of the book skips to the near future. It seems that the Museum of Lost Species also contained viruses that were thought to be extinct, but because of the Board's interference, these new diseases are escaping. The earth gets devastated by one fatal disease after another... the Christ Sickness causes people to think they're the Messiah. An unnamed disease covers people's bodies in suffocating, wriggling hair. The Roots is a condition where plants take over the body: "... his skull becomes a flowerpot for stunning brain orchids that grow over dead eyes and idiot face while the skin slowly toughens into bark."

Burroughs knows where to place the blame for these extinctions and unleashed diseases — on the crude, oafish human race. Misanthropy oozes out of passages such as this one: "Beauty is always doomed. 'The evil and armed draw near.' Homo Sap with his weapons, his time, his insatiable greed, and ignorance so hideous it can never see its own face."

Ghost of a Chance is illustrated with seventeen abstract paintings by Burroughs, which lose something when reproduced in black and white.

High Risk Books (Serpent's Tail); $14.99
1988, 1995; small hardcover; 59 pp
illus; 1-85242-406-0

HOT PLANET

by Michael Burns

Hot Planet is the first novel in a three-part environmental fable. Early in the next century, all the polluting gases that trap heat in the atmosphere have reached critical level, causing the "greenhouse effect" to occur. Temperatures all over the earth are rising — the mercury is close to 100 over much of the US even though it's almost Christmas. Australia sets a record for the highest temperature ever recorded: 145°F. But worst of all, the Antarctic is in the mid-seventies and climbing. The glaciers are starting to melt, and by mid-May they could be completely gone, a condition that would raise ocean levels by 200 feet. If this were to happen, continents would lose most of their coasts, and many islands, such as Hawaii and Japan, would be partly submerged.

The novel's main character, an Australian scientist named Jonathon Holmes, is convinced that the rise in temperatures is no "heat wave" but a sign that the greenhouse effect has kicked in. He tries sounding the alarm but has a hard time convincing people. Eventually, the authorities become convinced that he is a violent extremist. Meanwhile, a group calling itself the Defenders of the Planet has been waging eco-sabotage in the US.

While all this is going on, the governments of the world, led by the US, realise that the planet is about to flood, and, naturally, they try to suppress the story to prevent a panic. Eventually, the media get wind of the cover-up and try to expose it.

Hot Planet is extremely well-written and enjoyable, a page-turner in the truest sense of the world. Although the author clearly wants to warn us about global catastrophe, his book isn't a thinly-disguised piece of propaganda. It's an expertly-crafted novel that stands on its own. The many threads of the story — which involve Dr. Holmes and his daughter, the Defenders of the Planet, scientists around the world, and the highest levels of government — are deftly woven together. Sermonising is kept to a minimum, and there's plenty of action. Not only environmentalists, but anybody who likes novels with intrigue and excitement, will enjoy *Hot Planet*.

Planet Press; $9.50
1994; softcover; 316 pp
0-9639345-0-3

AN IDOL KILLING

by Mark J. White

Five decades hence, in an ecologically ruined Britain, the rock star and radical eco-activist Empti Vee is about to be snuffed during a concert. A genetically altered groupie, members of Internal Security, and a cybernaut are the other main players in this cyberpunkish novel.

AK Press; $12.95, £7.95
1997; softcover; 222 pp
1-873176-89-9

SCIENCE FICTION EYE

Given the first two words of its name, the magazine *Science Fiction Eye* is different from what you'd probably expect. You might naturally assume the *SF Eye* would be filled with science fiction stories. Actually, they are few and far between. Each thick issue is packed mainly with non-fiction by SF writers, giving them an opportunity to write articles and essays that may otherwise never be published. The contributors are almost all from the new schools of SF and related genres, such as Cyberpunk, slipstream, avant pop, etc.

Bruce Sterling and Paul Di Filippo are regular columnists, pontificating on whatever deserves pontification — Ishmael Reed, Parisian Bohemians, electronic text, the Russian space programme, overlooked magazines of the past that published SF. Each issue also sees a new guide to alternaculture from Richard Kadrey, author of the *Covert Culture Sourcebook*s.

In addition to these three regulars, Charles Platt speculates on "upstream speculation", Takayuki Tatsumi and Larry McCaffery have an email discussion on "the theoretical frontiers of 'fiction'", Lyle Hopwood looks at HIV/AIDS and David Memmott responds, Dan Joy interviews Brian Eno, Steve Erickson writes about his novels, Bruce McAllister remembers working in Disneyland in 1965, Michael Roessner gives a surrealistic history lesson of San Jose, California, and several writers review books. There's even more than that going on… and that's just one issue (#12).

In the next instalment, Charles Platt interviews Extropian founder Max More, Ken Jopp points out the human race's evolutionary retardation, John Shirley meditates on violent imagery, Takayuki Tatsumi chats with David Blair (director of *WAX*), Don Webb promotes "mysterious science fiction", and Steve Kelner reflects on the mind and brain in SF. Highlights of issue 14 include "Techno-Erotic Pagans Sucking the CPU Teat, or 'Yes, Momma, the Milk has Gone Sour and My PC Is Obsolete'" by Michael Hemmingson, Nancy Collins' rant on reproductive technology ("Attack of the Billion Dollar Babies"), an interview with Philip K. Dick, an examination of Oz illustrator John Neill, and forty pages of reviews, including some written by William Gibson, Paul Di Filippo, Don Webb, and John Clute.

Each chunky issue of *SF Eye* comes wrapped in an eye-catching colour cover and crammed with great writing accompanied by top-notch artwork (including collages by Freddie Baer) incorporated into a bold design scheme. If you want to read what the brashest SF writers have to say about their field and just about everything else, open the *Eye*. It's helping science fiction achieve its potential as a form of literature that matters.

SF Eye/PO Box 18539/Asheville NC 28814
Email: eyebrown@interpath.com
WWW: www.empathy.com/eyeball/sfeye.html
Single issue: $5, plus $2 shipping for 1 or 2 issues, $3 for 3 to 6.
Overseas shipping is $8 and $15, respectively
Three issue sub (one year): $12.50. Overseas: $20.

SPLATTERPUNKS II
Over the Edge
edited by Paul M. Sammon

Splatterpunk is horror fiction taken to its illogical extreme. It blends heavy metal, misanthropy, slasher flicks, and gore into a stew that's hard for many people to take. But Splat does more than simply shock — it confronts. It holds a dark mirror in front of your face… then it breaks it over your friggin' head. The stories in this anthology aren't afraid to look at our deepest fears and basest instincts.

Unlike the first *Splatterpunks* anthology, this one has lots of female writers, who provide different — but no less harsh — voices and viewpoints from those of their male counterparts. "Cannibal Cats Come Out Tonight" by Nancy Holder is about two best friends who sing in a rock band. Dwight is an outcast brutally abused by his hate-filled father, and Angelo is the archetypal high school cool dude. While becoming blood brothers, they discover that blood tastes good, and, later, that flesh tastes even better. "It was so terrific he fainted. It was like the best kind of acid; it was psychedelically delicious." They start killing and devouring women. One day they fall in love with the same girl, but Angelo eats her by himself, and things are never the same after that.

Pandy, the anti-heroine narrator of "Pig" by Gorman Bechard, is a members of "PIGS — a group of pumped-up, pumped-out babes who'd infiltrate the drug dens, and whatnots, by whatever means possible, then open fire." In the beginning of the story she gets picked up by a dealer who takes her back to his place for some smack and sex. After shooting up, they begin to fuck: "… he's humping and groaning and sweating and mumbling some sort of shit in Spanish — find the pig in this picture." Right as he's coming, Pandy does the deed in a reverse snuff scene in which the guy gets the short end of the barrel. The next day, she and her partner get hired by a reverend to whack an underground abortionist (abortion being illegal in the future) who terminated his twelve-year-old daughter's pregnancy. When they go to make their hit, though, they realise that it's the reverend who needs his clock cleaned, setting the stage for a revolting feminist revenge.

"Accident D'Amour" by Wildy Petoud is the bottomlessly bleak story of a jilted woman… another revenge fantasy. The narrator is knocked up by a guy who leaves her. She sews her vagina shut. "Shut your forever hungry maw, pussy. Forever." Gangrene eats away at her body, and she stops eating and washing. Around six months she gives birth: "My belly exploded in a splatter of rotten flesh and curdled liquids, and she emerged, leaning on the ruined meat, her sharp-clawed, thin arms coated with slime and pieces of me." The narrator sends her bouncing baby daughter out to retrieve daddy for a very special family reunion.

Other writers in this collection include Kathe Koja, Nancy A. Collins, Lucy Taylor, Clive Barker, Nina Kiriki Hoffman, Elizabeth Massie, Wayne Allen Sallee, and Poppy Z. Brite. On the non-fiction side, there's an interview with Brian de Palma by Martin Amis, the rant "Nothing but Enemies" from *ANSWER Me!*'s Debbie Goad, and an interview with Anton LaVey, founder of the Church of Satan, by *ANSWER Me!*'s Jim Goad.

File under "N", for nihilism and nightmares.

TOR (St. Martin's Press); $14.95

1995; hardcover; 416 pp

0-312-85786-1

TRANSGRESSIVE WRITING

BIG GURL

by Th. Metzger & Richard P. Scott

This is a photocopied version of the near-legendary horror novel *Big Gurl*. It's a completely over-the-top, splatter-filled tale about a huge psychopathic killer with the body of a woman and the mind of a demented little girl. In the opening scene, Big Gurl catches the meter man outside her house, drags him inside, and tortures him to death with bug spray, rope, a corset, a lawnmower, and fertiliser. Things only go downhill from there.

Ziggurat; $10

1989; staple bound oversized softcover; 65 pp

no ISBN

EDEN, EDEN, EDEN

by Pierre Guyotat

Eden, Eden, Eden has been hailed by prominent post-modernists and avant-gardists as a unique work of literature, a book that has no precedent, although it is informed by the Marquis de Sade, Antonin Artaud, and Gene Genet. The whole book is one long sentence — it is strung together mostly by semi-colons but also by colons. It tells the story of a prostitute boy, Wazzag, in an apocalyptic zone of Algeria during a civil war. He and other characters (including animals) engage in a dizzying series of brutal, degrading acts of sex and/or violence.

Here is a representative, though relatively tame, passage: "shepherd squeezing nomad's thin thighs; scent of camel-dung rising from penis lifted up in shepherd's chapped hand ; shepherd placing lips on dry pubic fleece : line of sweat glistening along fold of thigh, shepherd grabbing encrusted balls in one hand, other masturbating short member-tiny veins, stretched by erection, simmering against

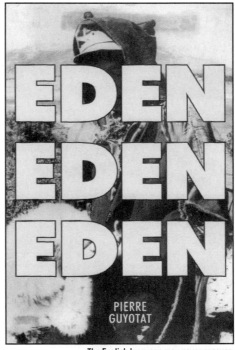

The English language may never recover.
Eden Eden Eden.

cheek ; nomad tensing legs ; jissom spurting, shepherd rolling back tongue into throat ; jissom, heavy, fresh, filling mouth ;..."

Evidently, Guyotat has decided to not only continue the heritage of French transgressive writing but also to live his life in an extreme manner. In his teens he fought in France's colonial war with Algeria. He encouraged fellow soldiers to desert, and his punishment was to spend three months in a hole in the ground. He once became so engrossed in his writing that he stopped eating. After losing half his weight, he slipped into a near-fatal coma.

When *Eden* came out in 1970, it was immediately banned by the French government and remained illegal for eleven years. Creation's 1995 edition marks the first time it has been translated into English. The language may never recover.

Creation Books; £7.95, $13.95

1995; softcover; 163 pp

1-871592-47-X

THE EYES

by Jesús Ignacio Aldapuerta

Like Pierre Guyotat [see *Eden, Eden, Eden* above], Jesús Ignacio Aldapuerta has written some of the most brutally confrontational fiction since the Marquis de Sade. Aldapuerta was born in 1950 into an extremely rigid Catholic family in Seville. He completely rejected religion and all of society's rules about propriety and decency. Spending part of his life in Central and South America and the Philippines, Aldapuerta

Emetic fables from the Andalusian de Sade.
The Eyes.

is rumoured, perhaps baselessly, to have engaged in various murky criminal activities. In 1987, he died by immolation when he apparently set his apartment and himself on fire, but rumours persist that he was snuffed by outraged Catholics or drug dealers. Another rumour says that he didn't die at all… the body in the fire was his lover's, and Aldapuerta is now in Central America working on his masterpiece, a recreation of Sade's lost work *The Days at Florbelle.*

The eleven stories in *The Eyes* are the first widely available English translations. They rank alongside Sade and Georges Bataille as among the most blasphemous, scatological, black-hearted works ever to see the light of day. As the back-cover blurb eloquently puts it: "More than stories, they are the apocalyptic scriptures of an atheist madman who worshipped at a shrine dedicated in blood and semen to both Eros and Thanatos."

"Indochine" is about an American lieutenant in Vietnam who has a freshly-killed local prostitute brought to his quarters once a week. He places her body on top of a map of Indochina and has sex with the corpse. "At orgasm, he was fucking not the undernourished body of a teenaged refugee whore, but an entire nation. In her he was fucking all the recent dead, all the thousands, the tens of thousands killed in the week since he had last fucked a dead Vietnamese whore."

In "Ying and Yang" a resident of an unnamed frozen wasteland comes across a crashed plane. Its passengers — all Japanese women — are dead and perfectly preserved, so he decides to have some fun with a new kind of art. Using his knife, he cuts out a variety of organs from the women and arranges them in patterns. "The organs were like enor-

mous jewels, very cold and hard and beautiful in his hands. He hunted amongst the corpses, piling ten minutes' worth of *matériel* to one side of where he intended to work, and then slowly laying out the patterns, metre-wide whorls and zigzags on the ice, trying to find the most pleasing combination of colours and shapes, the hard red fists of hearts beside the fat white tubes of intestine section, the fat glossy shells of kidneys beside the intricate glittering venation of single small lungs."

The previously unpublished "Pornoglossa" is probably the most nauseating piece in the whole book. It is set up as a "glossary for a language highly suitable for the composition of ultra-violent sadistic pornography." Because it is written like a dictionary, there is no plot or anything else to dilute the experience of reading one act of sexual violence after another. "ka-: to set fire to the pubic hair"; "khe: the (unraped) female anus; âmgkhe: male anus"; "li-: to bite off a nipple"; "mra-: to pour hot liquid into wounds; to urinate into wounds"; "raí: to use an empty eyesocket as a sexual orifice, e.g. after eyegouging"; "tsle: sound made by flesh tearing free under pincers; wound left by this". There are about a hundred more such definitions, but I think you get the idea.

Welcome to hell.

Headpress; £5.95, $10.95
1995; softcover; 88 pp
0-9523288-3-6

HOGG
by Samuel Delany

Hogg might just be the most brutal and (for most people) unreadable book reviewed in this chapter. *The Eyes* and *Killer Fiction* come close, but I think *Hogg* noses them out. This may seem somewhat surprising, because this novel was written by one of the most respected, influential science fiction writers of all time. Samuel Delany occupies a unique position in the field, because — as far as I am aware — he is the only first-tier SF master who is African American, and he is the only one who is openly gay. He has won scads of Hugo and Nebula Awards for his short stories and novels, many of which are considered classics: *Babel-17*, *Dhalgren*, *Triton*, "Aye, and Gomorrah", "Time Considered as a Helix of Semi-precious Stones", and others. Delany has also earned a reputation for his critical writings, and he is now a professor of comparative literature at the University of Massachusetts.

During his long career, Delany has written three pornographic novels: *Equinox* [*Outposts* p 98], *The Mad Man*, and *Hogg*. The latter was finished in 1973, around the same time as *Dhalgren*, a dense, experimental novel that has a devoted following. For over two decades, *Hogg* was rejected for publication by numerous publishers, giving it the widespread reputation of being "unpublishable". Luckily (or not, depending on your viewpoint), FC2 has the intestinal fortitude to release this work of darkness to the world.

The novel is narrated by an eleven-year-old boy who is never named but generally referred to as "cocksucker", because that's what he loves to do. He meets up with a huge, decidedly uncivilised guy named Hogg. "'They call me Hogg 'cause a hog lives dirty. I don't wash none. And when I get hungry, I eat my own snot. I been wearin' these clothes since winter. I don't even take my dick out my pants to piss most times, unless it's in some cunt's face. Or all over a cocksucker like you.'" By profession, Hogg is a "rape artist" — it's the same general principle as a hit man, except he is paid to rape women. Now, before you become extremely upset about the nauseating mind that would dream up something as unthinkable as a rape artist, realise that such people actually exist. In the early 1960s, Delany spoke with an acquaintance of an acquaintance who actually did this for a living.

Hogg and the narrator are soon hired for three jobs and are told to bring in some extra guys. Here is where we meet Nigg, Dago, and Denny, three of the novel's other main characters. Soon all of them are brutally gang-raping the three women (and the disabled twelve-year-old daughter of one of them) for their clients, action which Delany describes in precise step-by-step detail. Afterwards, Denny goes on a mass murder spree, and the narrator gets taken away from Hogg by Big Sambo, who likes to have sex with his daughter, but Hogg gets him back.

Hogg and just about every other character are the most id-driven, uncaring sacks of shit you'll ever run across. The novel is filled with their non-stop fucking, sucking, raping, killing, maiming, piss-drinking, and shit-eating. The bodily fluids, incest, and racial epithets flow thick and heavy.

Denny really began to pump. With one hand he must have been feeling Hogg's dick. The other grappled my hair. His legs were shaking against my chest. He pushed his cum out with three little grunts, and I felt his ass relax, my mouth filling with slopping salts. (It wasn't whiskey, either.) My cheeks filled and I swallowed, but it still leaked down my chin. Finally it got so he'd plunge, I'd spurt; all over Hogg's hand and Denny's pants. He was still grunting and slipping it way in and saying, "Jesus Christ, oh shit, oh yeah! Oh yeah, goddamn, oh shit!" I heard the others come up, laughing and joking:

"Hey," the wop said. "Watch this. Denny gets so excited, you can…" The wop grunted. Denny's pants came open. "Somebody workin' on Denny's pecker, an' anybody can fuck 'im." Denny staggered, grunted again. "See…" the wop said, breathing a little hard. There was a secondary rhythm in Denny's shove now. I came off Denny right onto the nigger's black dick, which loosed urine against my cheek. "Hell," the nigger said, chuckling. And kept on chuckling. And kept on pissing.

Delany has said that *Hogg* is "an aggressive novel — an attack on the reader." Consider your ass kicked.

FC2; $11.95
1995; softcover; 219 pp
1-57366-011-6

KILLER FICTION

by GJ Schaefer as told to Sondra London

Ex-policeman Gerard John Schaefer was convicted of killing two young women, and he is suspected of murdering at

G.J. Schaefer gave this sketch to Sondra London back in 1991 as a proposed cover for *Killer Fiction*.

least twenty others. While he was in prison (where he was murdered by another inmate in 1995), his former girlfriend, Sondra London — who is now romantically involved with convicted serial killer Danny Rolling — wrote to him about collaborating on a book. Schaefer agreed, and the result was two books of his writings that London published under the imprint of her business, Media Queen.

Both of those books plus extra material have been combined in this edition of *Killer Fiction*. It contains gruesome stories that Schaefer wrote before being arrested (they helped convict him of the killings), as well as stories he penned while in the pen. Also included are Schaefer's drawings of hanged women, his poems, and dozens of letters he wrote to London while incarcerated. True crime writer Colin Wilson supplies a foreword, and London provides a fifty-page essay on Schaefer, entitled "The Serial Killer Who Loved Me".

The stories, written in the first person, involve the narrator selecting a female victim, brutalising and raping her, then killing her. Occasionally he'll mutilate and/or have sex with the corpse. Here is a typical passage from "Blonde on a Stick":

"If I do what you want will you let me go?" There was a thread of hope in her question. I severed it deftly.

"No. But if you treat me real nice I won't cut off your nipples before I slit your throat."

She stared at me in mute apprehension. She began to tremble, the wetness glistening at her crotch and spreading downward almost to her knees. Then she leaned forward and vomited on the back seat.

I seized her long blonde hair and dragged me toward me. She knelt in the grass wheezing and coughing and spitting. I gave her a minute to collect herself, then took out my throbbing erection.

Even Colin Wilson, who has read and written about the most heinous human behaviour for much of his life, admits that he was unable to read more than bits and pieces of

Killer Fiction. He says, "Schaefer suffers from a kind of hali-tosis of the soul, and the stench quickly induces disgust."

Feral House; $14.95
1997; softcover; 291 pp
illus; 0-922915-43-1

POETRY

GIRL'S GUIDE TO GIVING HEAD
by Sheri-D Wilson

Surprise, this is actually a book of poems, not a manual on oral sex. Performance poet Sheri-D Wilson's verses on the ups and downs, simple joys and pains in the ass of life crackle with wit and energy. In "Mister P.M.S. (Post Modern Syndrome)", she writes that the title character "Named his computer James Dean/'Cause it was always crashing" and "Is scared of becoming an abandoned Coke machine/You can't get parts to, not worth the fix". "Men-Ming-Ming-Mang" contains the memorable lines: "It's been so long since I've been laid/I have to wear pants so my legs don't grow together", and, "He said: I love you, but I'm not IN love with you/And I said:/I'm IN love with you, but I don't LIKE you/So don't get so uptight".

Most of Wilson's poems have a strong rhythm that isn't found too often in contemporary poetry. "Airplane Paula, or All the Telephones at the San Francisco Airport Have Video Screens" practically sings itself:

Airplane Paula waves a fan dance plume
Her nine inch nails dig a Cleopatra tomb
Disco user friendly with a belly pierced for love
Biohazard blonde, forty thousand feet above
Supersonic post-bionic aerosolly hair
She's the lip stream dreamstress
Where Jackals only dare
She stirs her shadow drink in a shifty flagrant flare
With a petrified swizzle that's the boner of a bear
Out there, out there

In "Egg Bank: A True Story", the narrator is having Christmas dinner with her family when her 98-year-old grandmother asks her if she's ever going to have a kid. She facetiously answers that she's going to have her eggs taken out and frozen. From now until she's 80, she's going to ask men with features and traits she likes to jerk off into test tubes. Then she'll put the eggs back in and fertilise them with a mixture of sperm carrying all the best traits, "Like the ingredients of a made-from-scratch Duncan Hines batter". It's "The perfect love child recipe". As the poem draws to a close, the narrator momentarily gets serious: "After asking everyone I know why they would have a child/Nobody has come up with a

"It's been so long since I've been laid / I have to wear pants so my legs don't grow together." *Girl's Guide to Giving Head*.

good enough reason/For having one".

Other selections include "The Gangster Cleaning Lady", "MacSex", "Conversations with a Jealousy Junkie", "The Grass Is Always Blonder on the Other Side of the Fence", "The Day I Married Elvis", "P3: Bunsen Burner Breakdown", "Cannibal Rant", "Mall Animals", "Wild Hearses Couldn't Keep Me Away", and "I Got Dumped by the Devil (My Trip Through Purge-atory)".

Arsenal Pulp Press; $14.95Can, $12.95US
1996; softcover; 163 pp
1-55152-031-1

GOTHIC DREAM
by Carmen Willcox

Another beautifully made, thoughtfully presented book of Carmen Willcox's poetry [see *Luminarium* below]. There aren't as many poems this time — seventeen — and there seems to be more of a focus. Unfortunately, that focus is on the waste of time known as love. "I have lost - without possessing,/my young dreams/on love's pyre tossed." Once again, the poems are enhanced by Medieval and Victorian drawings, and the book is printed on pink paper with purple covers.

Carmen Willcox; $6
1995; spiral-bound softcover; 44 pp
heavily illus, no ISBN

HARD CANDY
by Jill Battson

Jill Battson — described as a "Hero of New Poetry" and a "high priestess of the spoken word" — performed at over 200 poetry readings and similar events in 1996, organised the Canadian poetry contingent for Lollapalooza, and produced the Word Up! series, which has been released as a book, CD, and video. Somehow, she manages to find the time to write her own poetry, which is presented in *Hard Candy*, her first book.

Divided into eight themed sections — each named after a type of candy and dealing with a subject such as relationships, death, or family — this collection has words that are often sweet but subjects that are usually jawbreakers. Various poems deal with emotionally and sexually comforting a bald-headed, battered woman ("Kathy"), refusing to take care of a parent with multiple sclerosis ("This Is My Mother Now"), the cycles of menstruation and fertilisation ("Fallopio"), the similarities between boxing and love ("Pugilistic Relationship"), attending a lover's funeral ("Woodbridge Memorial Gardens"), a young man running away from home and becoming a hustler ("Hitching"), and burning down a church ("Church Fire")

"174 Chances" looks at each menstruation as another sign that a chance to have a child has been missed:

And then there is this
the mucal substance between our thumb and
index finger
stretching away against the biological countdown
to the next millennium
snappy or loose dictates who are
what we could be

"Time and Tide" is written by a baby being born:

Sucking and tearing
my safe home
is contracting me into the world
…
I am dressed in swaddling bands
restrained pupa in bloodstained cloth
among the trash of a trawled ocean
lucky to find land
when others have kissed cold porcelain
or smothered in the blackness of garbage

Hard Candy is a hopeful and sad look at all the things that matter most: birth, death, love, sex, family, friends, the promises and perils of living.

Insomniac Press; $11.99Can, $9.99US
1997; softcover; 107 pp
illus; 1-895837-01-4

KINKY

by Denise Duhamel

Add Denise Duhamel to the growing legion of writers and artists who — much to the chagrin of Mattel — are slagging the Barbie doll. In this series of 43 poems, Duhamel takes a mocking look at real and fictitious Barbies, creating unau-

thorised scenarios that puncture the plastic princess and offer social commentary.

Sex plays a big role in these alternative takes. "Marriage" opens: "Barbie wonders if it's cheating/when she dreams of fashion doll boyfriends/Mattel never made for her to play with." Barbie and Ken exchange heads in "Kinky". "The two dolls chase each other around the orange Country Camper/unsure what they'll do when they're within touching distance./Ken wants to feel Barbie's toes between his lips,/take off one of her legs and force his whole arm inside her." In "Tragedy", Barbie and Ken find out that they're actually supposed to be sister and brother.

In "Barbie's Gyn Appointment", "There's nowhere for him to take a pap smear,/but Barbie's gynaecologist suggests a D and C,/a hysterectomy, then a biopsy, just to be sure." "Barbie as Mafiosa" finds her engaged in some highly illegal business. "When she's slipped the bag of cocaine,/Barbie ducks into her favourite alley./She pulls her head off and fills herself up/as though she's as innocent as a shapely salt shaker." "Buddhist Barbie" finds her unsurprisingly agreeing with the notions that, "All is emptiness", and, "There is no self." "Oriental Barbie", "Hispanic Barbie", and "Black Barbie History" note how similar the ethnic Barbies are to the standard Aryan Barbie. "Black Barbies look exactly like White Barbies./Identical moulds, not unlike uniform squares/of Nestles' Dark and Alpine White chocolate bars."

In other poems, the Pink One goes to therapy, joins a Twelve Step programme, enlists in the military, survives World War III, engages in SM, converts to Mormonism, almost joins a convent, goes through Beatnik and hippie stages, worries about her German past, and becomes the Antichrist. If Barbie thought math was hard, it's nothing compared to the real world.

Orchises Press; $12.95
1997; softcover; 90 pp
0-914061-61-5

THE LARGER EARTH
Descending Notes of a Grounded Astronaut

by David Memmott

A cycle of 22 poems by Rhysling Award-winner David Memmott. "The Grounded Astronaut Searches For The Godman Down By The Tracks Having Fallen Off His High Horse", "The Grounded Astronaut, Betrayed By His Own Words, Searches For Ghosts Among The Holograms But Can Only Find The Juggler Of Life Birds", "The Grounded Astronaut Accidentally Releases The Earth Goddess From The Meat Locker Where She Was Locked In By Logical Empiricists To Tame Unruly Passions".

Permeable Press; $9.95
1996; softcover; 104 pp
illus; 1-882633-18-0

LIFETAKER

by Bill Shields

Bill Shields is a Vietnam vet who writes poetry that directly confronts the demons that war and its aftermath have cre-

"I sang dead lovers' names like bloodied
daisy chains." *Luminarium.*

himself or a fictional character?) who gets wounded in 'Nam. After hitting his mom and then his dad, the young man rushes out of the house, ends up at a recruiter's office, and signs up for duty. He gets wounded in the face, losing his ears and lower jaw. "Almost 19 years old and wrapped into a VA hospital bed, shitting blood and worms. My face was wrapped in a hospital towel — part of a cheekbone still oozed pus & rice paddy slime." The rest of the poem is filled with powerful images: a nurse puking when she takes his bandages off the first time, orderlies feeding him through a tube, smelling the pus running down his face, not having enough privacy to masturbate, his mom shaking when she visits, his dad drinking away his disability cheques…

It's the perfect antidote for people who harp on the nobleness and glory of war.

2.13.61 Publications; $11
1995; softcover; 116 pp
1-880985-30-6

LUMINARIUM
In Search of the DreamChild
by Carmen Willcox

Dreams, the night, the moon, opium, taffeta, angels, flickering candles, and death's caress flow through Carmen Willcox's 55 dark, gentle poems. As someone who loves the night, I can relate to the way her verse revels in nocturnal mysteries and enchantment.

"Journey" opens with these lines:

*And so we come
full Circle.*

*Gargoyles and Angels
with stone souls
and prophecies.*

*Dream-haunted Shadows
And platinum clouds
that drape the
pomegranate-tinted sky.*

In "Radiance", the narrator befriends a dove:

*But one darkest day
I found you*

*As a sleeping angel
might lie — still*

*Beautiful — but cold,
Softest white wings
stretched out
as if on one last
eternal flight
— welcoming the unknown.*

ated in him. This, his third collection, contains numerous brief poems that often make up larger poems. The grouping of poems referred to as "1994" are among his most revealing and brutally honest. In the poem "the day I catch my soul falling through a throat", he writes: "Vietnam is shit 24 years after the fact/it's been my worst excuse for being no damn good/ /no damn good at all". In "the steel canopy" he describes himself as "an ex-drunk, an ex-addict/a permanent stupid Vietnam veteran". He continues:

*there is no one to call at 2:12 a.m.
when the phone line has been gnawed by the dead*

*but if I could
would you answer?*

I wouldn't

In "Die Motherfucker: An Opera", a vet is preparing to shoot his sleeping wife. "Young women & baby Vietnamese jumped his eyes, tore the hair right out of his heart. Humiliated, the man stuck the magnum back in his underwear drawer & laid back down beside the woman he so wanted to bloody." Later, Shields describes a scene in Vietnam. A soldier carrying three human heads rests in a burned-out village. "He had two hours to kill. 3 heads to talk to & a cramp to work out of his hand. The cigarette was snuffed out on the man's head. He slept briefly, fingers wound around the hair of a man, another man & a woman./ /Then he cut their faces off."

The book closes with "Son of a Bitch", a long no-nonsense poem that economically tells of a man (is it Shields

One of the most gripping images comes from "Seduction": "Ensnared in the sacrament of delirium/dazzled beyond lamenting/ /I sang dead lovers' names/like bloodied daisy chains".

Luminarium has been lovingly crafted. The poems are heavily illustrated with woodcuts and Pre-Raphaelite drawings. The cover is a heavily textured paper, the endpapers are a translucent peach, and a piece of vellum has been tipped into the front. The pages are extremely light pink paper. It's a good lesson in the way books should be created, so that not just the words but also the object itself reflects devotion and care.

Carmen Willcox; $8
1992; softcover; 88 pp
heavily illus; no ISBN

OVER THE INTERSTATE LINES OF THE MIND
by Bob Zark

Poet, posterist, and punk rocker Bob Zark lets loose with 45 raging poems, expressing disgust at conformity, materialism, hipsters, gas station convenience stores, animal experimenters, censorship, and more.

> *the average postage stamp it can really show*
> *what's going on in the streets*
> *what's really going on you know*
> *a stamp depicting violence and rape*
> *wouldn't that be amazing*
> *a stamp showing under the table*
> *deals being cut corrupt folks on the take*
> *why not talk shit like it is right on*
> *the average postage stamp*
> (from "the average postage stamp")

Also available is a cassette with Zark reciting the poems over bass, percussion, samples, and sound effects. His expressive, slightly amused delivery style and Anthony Sepulveda's creative use of sound make the tape more powerful than the book.

Panic Button Priest; book: $7.95; tape: $5.95; both: $12.95
1995; softcover; 55 pp
heavily illus; book: 1-88649-602-1; tape: 1-88649-603-X

SEX WITH GOD (Expanded Edition)
by Thomas O'Neil

Sex With God is a book-length free verse poem, a realistic portrait of the ups and downs of a relationship, a hard look at AIDS, and a stinging attack on religious hatred and hypocrisy. The first part of the book — "Sex With God" was published by itself to much critical acclaim in 1989. It concerns O'Neil — a white Irish Catholic writer from the Midwest — who journeys through New York's sex scene, where he meets and falls in love with Brian, a black Protestant ex-Marine. The poems about having sex, setting up house, celebrating birthdays, and so on are interspersed with poems about orgies in the Vatican, paedophile priests, and gay saints.

The second, new part of the book is called "The Ashes of Eden". Brian has contracted AIDS, and this causes O'Neil

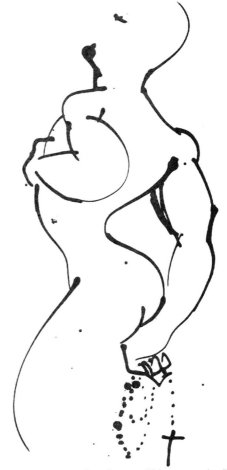

"... at least you didn't wear a condom."
Sex with God.

to take an even harder look at God and religion. "Will the Catholic Jesus, dressed/in a radiant Christian Dior gold gown,/really meet me on Judgement Day/when I am finally ravished from AIDS/and say, 'It's OK, kid. Actually, I'm proud of ya./At least you didn't commit one mortal sin — /at least you didn't wear a condom.'" The book is illustrated with dozens of minimalist drawings by Ty Wilson.

Wexford Press; $6.96
1994; softcover; 161 pp
illus; 0-9622398-1-X

'52 PICK-UP
Scenes from the Great Conspiracy — A Documentary
by Peter Klappert

This book bills itself as "a poem in 52 scenes, 2 jokers, and an extra ace of spades". It is so heavily experimental that I can't even begin to make heads or tails of it. One page contains **ENCYCLOPEDIA BRITANNICA** sinks" written three times. The next page simply says, "Removal from office by depilatory." On the next page, two phrases are written side by side: "Sympathetical mummies." and "*half an aspirin of sperm/a gallon of eggs*".

Orchises Press; $5
1984; softcover; 122 pp
0-914061-02-X

FC2

THE BOOK OF LAZARUS
by Richard Grossman

One of the most formally experimental of all the books published by FC2, *The Book of Lazarus* is a big jigsaw puzzle that you must mentally assemble. The main part of the book that will help you get your bearings is the section titled "Emma", which sticks out like a sore thumb because it's a 130-page, traditionally-structured novella in the midst of almost 500 pages of experimentalism. It's narrated by Emma O'Banion, a woman whose father deserted her and her mother over twenty years ago, when Emma was a girl. Out of the blue, she receives a call from her dying father. When he dies, Emma is thrown into a mystery as she tries to untangle who her father was, and how she could possibly have an older brother that she never knew about. Her father, it seems, was involved with several violent far-left political groups — including the fictitious People's Liberation Front — in the 1960s, and his past has caught up with him. Unfortunately, it might be catching up with Emma, too.

The rest of the book, which fleshes out the decades-old events that Emma discovers, is actually the scrapbook kept by the man who is supposedly Emma's brother, Robert Lazarus. It contains numerous photographs of people who died while saving someone else's life (one member of the People's Liberation Front kept these pictures as a "Hallowed Hall of Heroes"). There are also several pages of political and philosophical aphorisms by another one of the group's members ("A nuclear weapon is as mystical as a flower." "Capitalism teaches men to worship money; democracy teaches men to worship capitalism."). That's just the tip of the iceberg — a ransom note, New Year's resolutions, childlike drawings of stick figures, a single 69-page stream-of-consciousness sentence, various letters, love notes, a poem by Robert, and other material are also included. Not only does this fill in the details of the O'Banion/Lazarus saga, it indirectly tells us what became of Emma herself.

The Book of Lazarus manages to give us the best of both worlds: the challenge of high experimentalism and the satisfaction of a tightly plotted mystery.

FC2; $19.95
1997; hardcover; 494 pp
illus; 1-57366-029-9

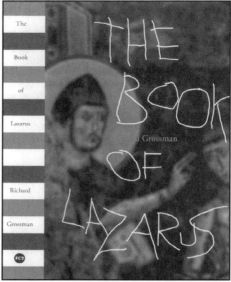

A big jigsaw puzzle that you must mentally assemble. *The Book of Lazarus*.

BLOOD OF MUGWUMP
A Tiresian Tale of Incest
by Doug Rice

A thick, profane, profound prose style in the tradition of James Joyce and William Burroughs is employed to tell a tale of an incestuous clan of Catholic, gender-shifting vampires.

FC2; $8.95
1996; paperback; 140 pp
illus; 1-57366-018-3

CHICK-LIT: ON THE EDGE
New Women's Fiction Anthology
edited by Cris Mazza & Jeffrey DeShell

This collection of new writing mines the thriving vein of post-feminist literature. The intro by Cris Mazza explains what this term means in her eyes (I'm going to quote a lengthy paragraph because I believe her definition of post-feminist writing could become the definitive one): "It's writing that says women are independent & confident, but not lacking in their share of human weakness & not necessarily self-empowered; that they're dealing with who they've made themselves into rather than blaming the rest of the world; that women can use and abuse another human being as well as anyone; that women can be conflicted about what they want and therefore get nothing; that women can love until they hurt someone, turn their own hurt into love, refuse to love, or even ignore the notion of love completely as they confront the other 90% of life. Postfeminist writing says we don't have to be superhuman anymore. Just human."

Jan Nystrom's "The Young Lady Who Fell from a Star" is a deconstruction of *The Wizard of Oz*. In 22 small sections, the author mixes facts about the making of the film with thoughts on its meaning. One of the facts Nystrom relates is, "The horses of a different colour are painted with Jell-O. This makes things difficult because the horses lick each other colourless between shots." One of her insights into the movie is, "Desire is a foolish thing but only Toto understands this. Dorothy wants to get back to Kansas where one day is just like the next and the landscape is as flat and bland as a pancake. The Tin Man wants a heart so he can be jealous and devoted."

"Reading" by Kim Addonizio is a purposely disoriented monologue in which the narrator is in bed with a fever, reading a barrage of disturbing and violent articles and books. S/he reads these things rapid-fire in small pieces in order to induce disorientation and hallucination. "You might feel, for example, like you're at home in your own bed with fever when you're really dying in a hospital, blind from everything you've tried not to see."

Other stories deal with a random attack on a woman, a girl who has a strange encounter with the "cat lady", a daughter who kills the children she's supposed to watch while her mom is working, and a mysterious woman who comes to work at a salon. The stories in *Chick-Lit* manage to be experimental but still accessible. A very strong collection.

Black Ice Books (FC2); $11.95
1995; softcover; 205 pp
1-57366-005-1

CHICK-LIT 2
No Chick Vics
edited by Cris Mazza, Jeffrey DeShell, Elisabeth Sheffield
In the follow-up to *Chick-Lit* [above], eighteen women contribute cutting edge and often experimental literary excursions that explore women's lives from a standpoint of power, not victimisation (i.e., "no chick vics"). Includes "*see also* Random", "SixLips", "Mammals", "Word.edu", "The Many Tenses of Wanting", "Rat Mother", "The Imaginary Wars of Bellford County", and "CAUTION: Sharp Object".

FC2; $11.95
1996; softcover; 225 pp
1-57366-020-5

DEGENERATIVE PROSE
edited by Mark Amerika & Ronald Sukenick
This anthology contains around thirty pieces of writing that completely do away with all of the "rules" of writing. As co-editor Mark Amerika explains, *Degenerative Prose* is "anything that re-synthesises wild, hybridised forms of prose including fiction, faction, friction and non-diction."

"SIM2\RE.LA.VIR" is the most radically deconstructed of all the pieces. At least part of it has something to do with a VIRtualhypernovel called *RE.LA.VIR*. Here's a passage:

Suture What: i went to the Palac
e i wore d ark cri mson rubb
er appliance to assfuck glos glos glos
sed silk i want to 8
over eight

In "Both Feeds in the Middle Kingdom" Steve Katz writes about a most unusual object in the Imperial Museum in Taipei, which houses treasures of Chinese civilisation. "From the endless jade collection the most prized single piece, among all the chalices and bowls exquisitely carved, the coolly glowing bracelets and hair-pieces figured with elaborate detail, is one simple hunk of jade carved to resemble a slab of pork. It sits in its own glass cube, in its own case, on its own pedestal, lit softly with a spot from the ceiling."

At first glance, "Contributors' Notes", the last piece in the book, appears to be a listing of the people who contributed to this anthology, but it's actually a humorous work of fiction by Bayard Johnson. One of the entries reads: "**Richard 'Speck' Bartkowech** lives in LA, just bought a gun and is about to become unglued. 'Die, Fucker' is his first published essay."

Other writings include "Eight Adult Males: A Neuropsychological Drama", "The SprayGun Mondo Vanilli Interview", "The Story of O and Couch Patrol: Two Superbly Barbed Semiotic Training Wheels, an Interview [Rough Draft]", "Rapidly Approaching Virginity", "Tanky Ferlustungs", and "They Used to Beat Me Up When I Was Young But Now They Don't Do It".

Black Ice Books (FC2); $9
1995; softcover; 148 pp
illus; 1-57366-008-6

DISTORTURE
by Rob Hardin
Distorture won the 1997 Firecracker Award, Fiction Category, for its eroticised physical and psychological violence described in evocative, often lush prose. Dysfunctional interpersonal relationships lead characters to become abusers or the abused. "*Burned by the stove, I became a pyro*" ("Hemorrhage"). "As my tormentors knew, the boy who feels is flayed. But every familiar who ever scarified my nerves has died twitching on a homely davenport or easy chair, with innards restrung like assets in secret accounts" ("Blood and Void"). "Confused women cling to your sadism as if to an oxygen mask. Tense and pressing, their feelings encircle your personality until you become part of their emotional respiratory system" ("Punishment Masque").

Sex and violence are ways to escape and retaliate. "Like Pollack, Masson & Van Gogh, certain artists grow convinced of failure: frustrated, mute, they are compelled to slash their canvasses. It is the same thing with the artist of the body: mutilation becomes his last vain attempt at transcending captivity" ("Definitions for the Dungeon"). "For outsiders like us, sex is a snuff film for hypocrisy — an all-American *Salò*, where the stereotypes of sin die in interesting ways" ("Punishment Masque"). "Violence is porn, and porn is the head cleaner of the human mind" ("Twenty-Five Reasons for Liking Horror"). "'Hold still, baby,' she whispered as she cut him. 'I wanna show you what it's like to lose your mind'" ("Interrogator Frames").

People, places, and things are described in terms of decadence, death, and decay. "The city was a sitz-bath of Madagascar Hissing Cockroach innards, of crumbling pre-Ruskin brownstones, of heat and sweat and mucous and

"Violence is porn, and porn is the head cleaner of the human mind." *Distorture.*

yet it was too sterile" ("BlowHo"). "She was a sugarpale streetcorner whore with eyes like cracked blue marbles and a smile frosted as white as windshield mist" ("Torn from Me"). "… a couch of solid apricot, canopied in cadaver grey to deflect thoughts of death or discorporation; finished with a mixture of peach varnish and pasteurised XYY semen; and speckled with the treated blood of suicidal donors" ("Val Demar's Pear").

Rarely have different types of violation and degeneration been described as beautifully as in the 26 stories of *Distorture.*

FC2; $9
1997; paperback; 206 pp
illus; 1-57366-027-2

MEXICO TRILOGY
by D.N. Stuefloten

Three short novels: *Maya*, about three actors abandoned on a film set; *Ethiopian Exhibition*, in which a city in Ethiopia pretends to be the tourist resort of Puerto Vallarta; and *Queen of Las Vegas*, about a director shooting a porn film in the mountains of Mexico. When FC2 was lambasted on the Senate floor as a vile publisher that uses government money (through the National Endowment for the Arts), this was one of the books that were specifically named as outrages.

FC2; $12.95
1996; softcover; 298 pp
1-57366-019-1

III PUBLISHING

ANARCHIST FARM
by Jane Doe

George Orwell's *Animal Farm* used the format of animal fable to show that communism is ruined by greedy leaders and revolutions fail because the new system soon imitates the old one. *Anarchist Farm* uses the same device — talking animals — to show how a consensual anarchist utopia could work.

III Publishing; $10
1996; softcover; 190 pp
0-886625-01-8

DECONSTRUCTION ACRES
by Tim W. Brown

In describing this novel, Lance Olsen (author of *Burnt*, below) used the phrase "wholesome subversion". Although — like all oxymorons — this seems impossible, it is an accurate description of this story set in a small Midwestern college town called Jasper. The protagonist is known as Underdog, a nickname that has stuck with him since his second grade Halloween party. On his first day in college at Jasper, his dorm-mate finks on him for smoking pot, and Underdog is expelled.

Our hero gets a job at a copy shop and rents a room at a boarding house, leading to all sorts of wild situations. Judy Baine — the corn-fed, brick shithouse daughter of the boarding house's owner — has gone crazy for Underdog and wants to screw him at every possible moment. Underdog, however, is falling for Ione Twayblade, a young widow whom Judy constantly refers to as "that flat-chested bitch with no ass". Judy, you see, begins to anonymously harass the interloper Ione, who wonders if it might be Underdog who's secretly stalking her.

Meanwhile, Underdog has another problem, that of being Race Fletcher, the urbane new professor on campus. His claim to fame is writing the bestselling book *Deconstruction Acres*, which theorises that country folk are more advanced in many ways than city folk. Ione and Race have become an item, heading to New York every weekend. Underdog begins his own quest to undermine Race, although he is more subtle than Judy is in handling her rival, Ione. When Underdog finds out that Race has a past (the specifics of which seem to be a stretch), he knows he's got the goods on *his* rival.

Even though this sounds like the synopsis of a Meg Ryan romantic comedy, it really isn't. With its drug use, bedhopping, erotic obsessions, and mild violence, *Deconstruction Acres* is too prickly to be mainstream, yet it is never anything other than good-natured. Try it if the unyielding extremism of novels such as *Hogg* [above] and *Motherfuckers* [below] leaves you cold.

III Publishing; $10

1997; softcover; 190 pp
1-886625-03-4

RESURRECTION 2027
by JG Eccarius

JG Eccarius is the author of the infamous underground novel *The Last Days of Christ the Vampire* [*Outposts* p 225]. The much-anticipated *Resurrection 2027* could be considered, if not a sequel, then at least a companion piece to its predecessor. Its plot centres on Ann, who was raised from the dead in 2013, after the Apocalypse occurred. For fourteen years she has been living in Zion (formerly the USA) and going to a strict Catholic school run by the Virgin Mary's accomplices, known as the Mothers. Ann went to remembrance classes so she could recall her first, pre-Armageddon life as a nurse. In 2027, when Ann is fourteen years old again, she is called upon to assist with the Resurrection, which occurs to only a few people at a time, instead of everyone at once.

The novel's other main character is Jake, one of the 50,000 or so people who were in Mary's good books and survived the Apocalypse. He is forced to work at the holy vineyards in Zion but is soon asked to assist in speeding up the Resurrection by helping the newly reborn children adjust to their reawakening.

But there's trouble in Paradise. Ann is just too curious about the past for her own good. Jake is dissatisfied and longs for escape from Zion. And the Mothers keep preaching that God is a woman, that Mother Mary must be worshipped above all, and that men are only good for menial tasks, because "their brains were not usually fit for mental or supervisory work." The resurrection process is pretty strange, too. Instead of people popping out of the ground, the Mothers and their assistants get DNA from corpses, reassemble it with the help of computers, and then grow the faithful in incubators. Is this really God's handiwork or just a menacing feminist dystopia? Ann, Jake, and other people are starting to wonder too, and that spells trouble for Mother Mary.

Resurrection 2027 is vastly entertaining, even suspenseful. It's also a wonderful piece of religious satire, definitely a worthy successor to *The Last Days of Christ the Vampire*.

Ill Publishing; $7
1995; paperback; 185 pp
0-9622937-7-6

WE SHOULD HAVE KILLED THE KING
by JG Eccarius

The first chapter of this book tells about the peasant revolt in England in 1381 and one of its leaders, the anarchist Jack Straw. The rest of the book follows the life of a modern day man named Jack Straw. Born in the US in the 1950s, he wanders around the country, working as a wage slave and meeting nonconformists. He becomes more and more radical until he eventually turns into an anarchist and environmental saboteur. Supposedly, the story is based on the author's friend, who really is named Jack Straw.

Ill Publishing; $5
1990; paperback; 191 pp
0-9622937-1-7

Anarchy meow! *Anarchist Farm*.

PERMEABLE PRESS

CHER WOLFE AND OTHER STORIES
by Mary Leary

As part of its effort to make the work of talented writers more accessible, Permeable Press has published this booklet containing six very short stories by Mary Leary. The dominant theme here seems to be people's failed efforts to overcome their loneliness and isolation, and Leary plays with several literary forms in the process. In "Go West, Young Woman" — a satire of lesbian romantic fiction — the narrator heads to San Francisco and immerses herself in the lesbian scene, only to be jilted. The wacky title character in the Kafkaesque "Tuna Man" thinks for some reason that smearing tuna all over his body will attract the opposite sex. "… [I]f women were anything like cats, he was in like Flint."

Only slightly less delusional is the narrator of the standout story, "Postal Buddy", who falls in love with a machine at the Post Office. The title story is in the form of a letter written entirely in bad French and "Southern black" to Cher Wolfe from "La Belle Tigre". In "E.M. Gives a BJ", which parodies hardcore porn, the pathetic Elephant Man (not the one that Michael Jackson bought, but a guy who literally has the head of an elephant) gives a blowjob to Johnny Mathis. "'Aaaaa've gaught too haaav yeeugh,' said the Elephant Man, kneeling slowly and with extreme difficulty. Johnny's hand moved to the zipper of his corduroy jeans."

> Permeable Press; $1.51
> 1994; staple-bound booklet; 12 pp
> illus; no ISBN

THE FINAL DREAM AND OTHER FICTIONS

by Daniel Pearlman

In these science fiction stories, the world hasn't changed radically, but just enough is different to create unusual situations that comment on universal human issues. In "The Defenders of the Golden Tower", an ageing Spanish millionaire has the chance to be among the first humans to colonise a new planet and make some serious money while doing it. Even though he's torn about going, he decides to, but finds that it's not so easy to get away from his old life. No matter where you go, there you are.

Rodriguez — the main character of "Another Brush with the Fuzz" — lives in a totalitarian society. He has tracking chips implanted in his body and, when a cop pulls him over, he meets an even worse fate — a D.A.B. belt. The cop explains, "For your information a D.A.B. belt is a dick-and-asshole belt. The black rubber cork goes up your ass. It stays there. The little wire muzzle here with the pee-hole in it clamps over your wang and shocks the shit out of you as soon as you stare to long at one of your black-eyed little Pepitas walking down the street." If Rodriguez tries to monkey around with the belt, the police will track him down and castrate him. He makes a desperation move and runs the cop down. He learns to his dismay, though, that authority never really dies.

A little bit more of a hopeful note is sounded in "The Ground Under Man", about a mortician in the twenty-first century. Unfortunately for him, burial is now considered a revolting, barbarous act. The accepted way of handling the dead is to have them "freeze-framed", so they are perfectly preserved. These mannequin-corpses are then positioned in the family's house in life-like positions. The protagonist considers this a creepy attempt to avoid dealing with the finality of death. When his wife dies, he arranges to have her buried, to the revulsion of her family, the community, and even the entire country. Her family moves to thwart his heinous act of burial, but he ends up having the last laugh.

In Pearlman's near-future stories, people are still struggling to be free, whether they're fighting the law or social mores. Sometimes they win, and sometimes they lose, but either way, it makes for an exciting read with crisp dialogue that rings true. The stories are accompanied by Jill Tyler's scratchboard illustrations.

> Permeable Press; $14.95
> 1995; softcover; 268 pp
> illus; 1-882633-05-9

SAVOY

THE GAS

by Charles Platt

A reprint of the underground classic first published by the infamous Essex House, which specialised in erotic science fiction, including some by well-known writers such as Charles Platt. The plot revolves around a secret gas that escapes from a germ warfare lab, causing everyone in Southern England to act out their most repressed impulses. Things quickly turn into an orgy of sex and violence. Everybody is screwing and sucking everybody else with no regard to gender, age, attractiveness, familial relations, religious vocation, or any other factors. As the story progresses, the action becomes even more extreme — bestiality, torture, snuffing, and cannibalism are the order of the day. The Gas smashes taboos that even most other transgressive sex fiction steers clear of. Consider it a vital addition to anyone's collection of "back room" literature.

> Savoy; $10.95
> 1970, 1980; softcover; 166 pp
> 0-86130-023-8

LORD HORROR

by David Britton

Unfortunately, Lord Horror has recently slipped out of print, but I will mention it anyway, because if you can manage to snag a copy, you should. Brilliant and belligerent, it is one of the great pieces of transgressive literature of the 1990s, but — for some reason — it does not appear to be very well-known. It tells the story of a parallel world in which the British Lord Horror (loosely based on the real-life Lord Haw Haw, who broadcast Nazi propaganda from Germany during W.W.II) and his minions Meng and Ecker search the world for Hitler, who has become a recluse.

Lord Horror has come under major fire (it was been banned and then unbanned in Britain) because of the anti-Semitism and racism it portrays. What confuses people is that the book does not condone these attitudes but portrays them in all their over-the-top ugliness and brutality. There are no sympathetic characters. Everyone in the book is pure evil, and the reader must deal with that. Actually, the novel makes pointed observations about many things, including hatred. For example, there is a character based on James Anderton, who was the Chief Constable of Manchester during the 1980s. The author used one of Anderton's venomous anti-gay speeches verbatim and simply replaced the word "homosexuals" with "Jews", showing that officially sponsored hatred is alive and well — it just has a new "acceptable" target.

> Savoy; £10.95; OUT OF PRINT
> 1990; hardcover; 192 pp
> 0-86130-072-6

A debauched classic from a well-known science fiction writer. *The Gas*.

MOTHERFUCKERS
The Auschwitz of Oz
by David Britton

This sequel to *Lord Horror* follows the exploits of Horror's henchmen, Meng and Ecker, who were created by Dr. Mengele during his concentration camp experiments. The basic plotline is that M&E are trying to find Horror, whose whereabouts are unknown, but this is basically just an excuse to let the boys ride roughshod over every sense of decency, good taste, and morality.

A long and impossibly vile chapter is devoted to Meng's "stage act", in which he regales an audience in Manchester with an unending litany of racist and anti-Semitic jokes, riddles, and one-liners. During the course of his inflammatory monologue, several people rush the stage, only to have Meng kill them without even breaking his train of thought. This, of course, is nothing new for the nihilistic, hedonistic crossdresser, who constantly snuffs people on a whim. The police and the other residents of Manchester warily tolerate Meng's homicidal disposition because, it is implied, his hate-filled stand-up comedy routines regularly pack the theatre, bringing lots of money to the local economy.

Several of the chapters go back in time to revisit Meng and Ecker's days in the concentration camps. It is in one of these chapters that David Britton gives an important clue concerning what he is trying to accomplish with the Lord Horror series of books and comix.

Auschwitz, thought Ecker, is a semaphore from the past that spelled the future.

Fifty years on, Horror had confided to Ecker, Auschwitz would be a recognisable brand name, a mythic character as well-known as Sherlock Holmes or Tarzan. A fortune awaited the author who could bring "Mr Auschwitz" to life. To recreate the persona of Auschwitz would be an ordained mission. Auschwitz, the holy end-all of life's futile pattern, slinking through the subconscious of humanity, the one archetypal riff common to all nightmares, fuelled on the anvil of Little Richard.

In a hundred years, Auschwitz would form its own genre and become the most successfully marketed product in the history of the world, a name as well-known globally as Coca-Cola, taking all media under its encompassing umbrella… Guilt would never stand in the way of commerce, assured Horror, his cobra eyes stealing the dark.

Several pop culture figures, including Elvis and Mickey Mouse, make surprise appearances. Meng runs into Mickey on the streets of Manchester, and the famous rodent explains that he and Minnie are taking a vacation because of all the problems occurring at Disneyland, including the invasion of insects. "'Beetles!' Mickey's face clouded. 'Thousands of them loose in Disneyland. Everywhere you look. And **Blatta orientalis**. Couldn't put a foot down without hearing a crunch.' The mouse shivered. 'Worse than fucking Auschwitz, you remember?' His shoes danced. 'Last Tuesday the smell of corpses got so bad I expected to see Mengele riding the Switchback Ride on Magic Mountain. Half of Euro-Disney looks like Auschwitz 1943 — extermination is no substitute for a good holiday. Mengele's moving closer every day.'"

Motherfuckers is a monumentally disturbing and offensive work. On the surface, it is so repugnant that it will probably never be popular even among fans of "alternative fiction", although it deserves to be. For the most part, it is powerfully written with many passages achieving a weird sort of poetic anti-beauty. It's not the easiest book to interpret, but to label it as hate literature is wrong. It uses some of the trappings of hate literature to make deep points about bigotry, violence, greed and hypocrisy, the simultaneous vapidity and power of popular culture, and, of course, the role of Auschwitz and the other concentration camps as symbols of human evil. I'm not always sure *exactly* what these points are, but I feel confident that they are there and that they're worth digging for.

Savoy; $29.95
1996; hardcover; 250 pp
0-86130-098-X

THE SAVOY BOOK
edited by David Britton & Michael Butterworth

This collection — originally published in 1978 — is a mix of cutting edge science fiction, erotic fiction, experimental fiction, and poetry, with some similarly wild artwork.

Legendary rock critic Lester Bangs contributes a piece

in which he interviews Jimi Hendrix from the Great Beyond. Jimi talks about how drugs affected his lyrics. "I started out sincere, but half the time I couldn't fuckin' think straight, so stuff I knew was sloppy-ass jive time mumbo-jumbo come tumblin' out, and people jump up like whores for a blow of coke: 'Oh wow, Jimi, far out…'"

Paul Buck's "The Kiss: Violation 22" is a short prose poem about sex. "Toward the end of the first kiss her cunt negates all comparison with her other openings. Desire is held over the anus. It is abandoned by careful language and changes which obliterate the provocation." I'm not exactly sure what it means, but it sure sounds purty.

In the poem "Howl Now" J. Jeff Jones takes a shot at the once-legendary San Francisco literary scene: "I saw the best minds of my generation destroyed by/success,/flatulent smug fashionable,/chauffeured through the neon avenues at sunset looking for where it's at/prettyfaced celebrities hungry for the latest admiration/connection".

The Savoy Book also contains an interview with Brian Aldiss, "Eggsucker" by Harlan Ellison (the prequel to "A Boy and His Dog"), "The Incalling" by M. John Harrison, minimalist fiction from Richard Kostelanetz, and illustrations by David Britton and Jim Leon.

Savoy; $10.95
1978; softcover; 144 pp
illus; 0-352-33001-5

WHITE WOLF PUBLISHING

BENDING THE LANDSCAPE
Fantasy
edited by Nicola Griffith & Stephen Pagel

In this first volume of the *Bending the Landscape* trilogy of anthologies, queer writers and mainstream fantasy writers offer up original, mainly non-erotic fantasy stories with gay and lesbian themes. Includes "Frost Painting", "Prince in the Dark Green Sea", "Cloudmaker", "The King's Folly", "There Are Things Which Are Hidden From the Eyes of the Everyday", "Young Lady Who Loved Caterpillars", and "In the House of the Man in the Moon". The future two volumes in the series will cover science fiction and horror.

White Wolf Publishing; $19.99
1997; hardcover; 362 pp
1-56504-836-9

DANTE'S DISCIPLES
edited by Peter Crowther & Edward E Kramer

Have you ever been told that you're going to burn in hell?

(Well, you are, because you're reading *Psychotropedia*! Sorry, I guess I should've warned you sooner.) Before you find out first-hand, you may want to read this anthology of 26 horror/dark fantasy stories about the Netherworld. Specifically, all of these original (i.e., not reprinted) stories deal with gateways that lead to the fiery Pit.

"Hell Is for Children" by Nancy Holder is about a computer virus that leads to cyberhades. Well, not actually. People who look at their screen when the virus kicks in just hallucinate that they're burning in the pits for a terrible sin — the vision can last for an hour or it can earn people a permanent spot in a psych ward. But the high school girl who created it is about to learn that hell hath no fury like a sister scorned.

In Harlan Ellison's story, "Chatting with Anubis", a palaeontologist and an archaeologist are called to investigate a gigantic structure that was unearthed by an earthquake in the Sahara desert. People are speculating that it is the Shrine of Ammon, also called the Temple of the Oracle, a mythical building that Alexander the Great is rumoured to have visited. It is actually a tomb guarded by the god Anubis, who tells the visiting scientists who he is guarding and why. This knowledge is the same "great secret" that triggered Alexander's life-ending marathon of drinking and debauchery.

Steve Rasnic Tem turns in a disturbing little number, "The Burdens". Do you ever feel like everyone depends on you? That your burdens are crushing you, squeezing the life out of you? For the story's protagonist this becomes more than just a metaphor.

Other stories include "Hell Is a Personal Place" by Brian Lumley, "Screams at the Gateway to Fame" by Ray Garton, the poem "Elegy for a Maestro" by Alexandra Elizabeth Honigsberg, and "The Mark 16 Hands on Assembly of Jesus Risen, Formerly Snake-o-rama" by Michael Bishop.

White Wolf Publishing; $14.99
1996; softcover; 422 pp
1-5604-907-1

EDGEWORKS
by Harlan Ellison

The *Edgeworks* series is a projected twenty-volume project that will reprint at least thirty-one of Harlan Ellison's books, spanning around forty years of prodigious output from this master of speculative fiction. Each volume kicks off with a new intro by Ellison, and many of the writings either contain updated commentary or have been returned to their original pristine state after being brutalised by shmuck editors. Expect to see two volumes per year, generally with two of Ellison's books in each volume.

Edgeworks, Volume 1: *Over the Edge* and *An Edge in My Voice*. The first part of the book is the short story collection *Over the Edge*, which has been out of print since its original publication in 1970. As with the entire projected series of *Edgeworks*, it has been significantly revamped and modified. Six of the original stories have been taken out (they will appear in future volumes), while four stories and two essays — none of which has ever appeared in a previous collection — have been added, leaving the number of pieces at twelve (plus new introductions by Ellison and Norman

Spinrad). The second part of this volume is a resurrection of *An Edge in My Voice*, a 1985 collection of essays Ellison wrote as columns for *Future Life* and *The LA Weekly*. New commentary has been injected into these essays from the early 1980s. [$21.99; 1996; 640 pp; illus; 1-56504-960-8]

Edgeworks, Volume 2: *Spider Kiss* and *Stalking the Nightmare*. First up is *Spider Kiss*, one of only three novels Ellison has ever written. It follows the musical career of Stag Preston, a wholesome guy from Louisville who must deal with the bitch-goddess known as success. Foremost rock critic Greil Marcus of *Rolling Stone* considers this the best rock and roll novel ever written. It is published here uncut, for the first time ever. The other half of the book is Ellison's 1982 short story collection, *Stalking the Nightmare*, which I'd rank as a second-level Ellisonian classic. It contains one of the man's absolute best stories, "Grail", an infinitely depressing commentary on the search for love and friendship. The "Scenes from the Real World" series of four essays is also top-notch, covering Ellison's short-lived stint as a writer for Disney, his witnessing of a murder, and being locked in a cell — as a thirteen-year-old runaway — with a completely wetbrained alcoholic going through withdrawal. [$21.99; 1996; 513 pp; 1-56504-961-6]

Edgeworks, Volume 3: *The Harlan Ellison Hornbook* and *Harlan Ellison's Movie*. Published in 1990, *The Harlan Ellison Hornbook* is a collection of over three dozen essays and rants, including "Getting Stiffed", "The Tyranny of the Weak, and Some Foreshadowing", "No Offence Intended, but Fuck Xmas!", "The Day I Died", "Troubling Thoughts About Godhood", "Why I Fantasise About Using an AK-47 on Teenagers", "The Death of My Mother, Serita R. Ellison", "Revealed at Last! What Killed the Dinosaurs! And You Don't Look So Terrific Yourself.", and "I Go to Bed Angry Every Night, and Wake Up Angrier the Next Morning". There are also several "Interim Memos" in which Ellison updates or gives background on his essays. The other part of this volume is the screenplay for a movie script Ellison wrote in 1972-3 for Twentieth Century Fox, who gave him creative *carte blanche*. The movie was never made. [$21.99; 1997; 591 pp; 1-56504-962-4]

Edgeworks, Volume 4: *Love Ain't Nothing But Sex Misspelled* and *The Beast That Shouted Love at the Heart of the World*. Here we have two of Ellison's best fiction anthologies together. The title of the first collection has to be one of the most cynically insightful observations ever made about sex and love, all the more amazing because it's only six words long. The anthology itself is a collection of non-science fiction stories that explore various forms of love, sometimes in roundabout ways. Unavailable since 1983, it also contains a previously uncollected story and an unproduced teleplay. The second anthology includes, not surprisingly, "The Beast That Shouted Love at the Heart of the World", my favourite Ellison story. Written in small pieces that jump locations and ignore chronological sequence, the story must be assembled like a jigsaw puzzle in your head. Also extremely noteworthy is the novella "A Boy and His Dog", a kickass postapocalyptic story that became a cult movie starring pre-*Miami Vice* Don Johnson. This film was the inspiration for the *Road Warrior*

Being in a rock band in the dismal future or being a university professor in the 1990s – which is weirder? *Burnt*.

movies, themselves leading to a string of imitators. [$21.99; 672 pp; 1997; 1-56504-963-2]

Borealis Legends (White Wolf Publishing); all hardcovers

MIDNIGHT BLUE
The Sonja Blue Collection
by Nancy A. Collins

This volume collects all three of Nancy Collins' streetwise, high octane vampire novels: *Sunglasses After Dark*, *In the Blood*, and — published for the first time anywhere — *Paint It Black*. They all star Sonja Blue, a beautiful woman who was turned into a bloodsucker when her old self — a young American heiress — was abducted and raped by a suave vampire in London. Now she prowls through the night with her mirrorshades and silver switchblade, killing her own kind in order to save humans from the fate she has been condemned to. Along the way she must deal with other "fringe races" that mix with humans (succubi, ogres, seraphim), violent humans (pimps, gang members), and the Other, the mysterious demon that shares her mind and body. The Other craves violence, and when it takes control of Sonja, it won't be satisfied until blood has been spilled.

The writing in *Midnight Blue* hums along with a swaggering confidence. It effortlessly mixes *noir* creepiness with Splatterpunk intensity. One of the subtly chilling moments occurs near the start of the book, when Claude, the night orderly at an insane asylum, makes his rounds, checking on a sinister patient (who turns out to be Sonja) locked in a bare room. He opens the observation plate on the door to see her crouched silently in the middle of the floor. "She turned her head in his direction. Claude's stomach tightened and there was a thundering in his ears. He felt as if he was barrelling down a steep hill in a car without breaks. Her eyes locked on him with a predator's guile. She inclined her chin a fraction of an inch, signalling her awareness of his presence. Claude felt himself respond in kind, like a puppet on a string, and then he was hurrying back down the corridor."

Later, we see an example of Collins' hard-assed violence in the scene where Sonja finds herself surrounded by a gang in the pool room of a sleazy bar. "Rafe lurched forward, wrapping his arms around her waist. He intended to slam her onto the pool table and fuck the bitch until she bled. Her knee pistoned up, smashing into his denimed crotch and rupturing his testicles; it was as if a napalm bomb had gone off in Rafe's jeans. He managed one high, thin scream before collapsing. The agony of his ruined cojones was so great he didn't even know she'd fractured his pelvis."

Midnight Blue is unquestionably one of a small number of essential works of modern vampire fiction.

White Wolf Publishers; $14.99
1995; softcover; 560 pp
1-56504-900-4

WORDCRAFT OF OREGON

BURNT
by Lance Olsen

The prose in Lance Olsen's post-cyberpunk novel *Tonguing the Zeitgeist* [*Outposts* p 215] snapped, crackled, and popped like a short-circuiting electric chair. His writing this time around, in the novel *Burnt*, displays a similar but lesser electricity. But if the writing isn't as high-voltage this time, there's good reason: instead of a dystopian rock'n'roll novel, this is the tale of a professor at a Southern university. Murph Porter, an avant-gardist in the English department, is teaching a lunkhead who happens to be the star quarterback of the school's football team. When it becomes clear that the jock isn't going to pass, Porter receives veiled and even unveiled threats, bribes, and other attempts at coercion. Just how far will the various parties involved (including Porter) go to take care of the situation? Pretty darn far, it turns out...

With verve and irony, Olsen describes the hypocrisy and hilarity of campus politics. His descriptions of the various professors are a gas: Chairman Richard Attley, "a kind of Ancient Mariner at the helm of our department, only there

were gale-force winds blowing against him, and Richard was facing backwards, and he had his eyes closed"; Brian Anders, "a hairy associate professor who had a degree in film from somewhere in California"; Donna Lowden, "our department's token black"; Charlie Bleistein, "our token deconstructionist"; Maurice Clifton, who "wore polyester three-piece suits and taught graduate seminars in major sixteenth-century French essayists"; Al Bodine, who "once threatened a fiction writing student of his in the middle of class by pulling out an oily blue .38 on him so the young man, given to writing story after story about sensitive melancholy young men, could experience what real fear and potential for loss felt like"; and Rhodry Draven, "the HP Lovecraft Professor of History... Without looking at us Rhodry raises his limp right wrist as though shooing away a bumble bee. I take this to be a greeting and wave back, calculating his salary."

Olsen also uses *Burnt* to comment on the vacuousness and unoriginality of pop culture. While walking across campus, he tells another prof about "my theory, which I stole from Jean Baudrillard, that says there is nothing original in our culture." The two of them pass by one of Porter's students, Poison, who is a member of the Goth subculture. When the other professor comments that she seems original, Porter replies: "Poison's a replica of a trendy type in Geldington, which is itself a replica of a trendy type in LA and New York, which is a replica of a trendy type in London, which is a replica of 1970s vampire movies, which are replicas of 1930s vampire movies, which are replicas of nineteenth-century vampire novels, which are replicas of various folktales that in fact have no origin."

Being in a rock band in the dismal future or being a university professor in the 1990s — which is weirder? In Olsen's hands, it's hard to tell.

Wordcraft of Oregon; $11.95
1996; softcover; 169 pp
1-877655-20-1

THE DIN OF CELESTIAL BIRDS
by Brian Evenson

"He did not believe that the brain was, as the traditional view held, a soft, gray folded organ. Rather, it was a series of black and white cords stretched tightly from one side of the skull to the other, held in place by delicate hooks of bone. Thought ran on these cords, either the black or the white. The black cords were evil, the white good." This strange idea belongs to President General Mensavi, one of many South American dictators, militarists, and rebels in this collection of seventeen magical realist stories. The protagonist of "One Thick Black Cord", Mensavi is a megalomaniac who usurps the presidency of an unnamed country and cheats death when rebels try to kill him.

Similarly, in "The Revolution", a group of rebels try to recreate the murdered leader of their country by transforming one of their number into him using plastic surgery and other means. "Through electroshock we razed Franco's tabula. With headphones, with electrodes, with rapidly blinking lights, with message cards, with hypodermic syringes, we engraved it with information that had belonged to

Verdugo. When he slept, faceless on the white table, cas-trated boys in a specially constructed loft above him whis-pered, 'You are Verdugo. You are Verdugo.'"

"A Difference in Ideology" is a more brutal version of Kafka's *The Trial*. "Administrator Saenz" is kidnapped, beaten, and systematically cut to pieces, but no one ever explains why, despite his protestations that they have the wrong man. In the title story, a suspected rebel encounters a strange birdcage in a stone shelter carved into the side of a cliff. He unwittingly unleashes a flock of spirit-birds that prey on people of European ancestry.

Other bleak stories include "The Death of the Old Man", "Amparo the Bastard", "Water and Angels", "Altmann in Bo-livia", and "The Killer".

Wordcraft of Oregon; $10.95
1997; softcover; 151 pp
1-877655-24-4

MISCELLANEOUS

THE AGONY OF LEWIS CARROLL
by Richard Wallace

The image of Lewis Carroll — pseudonymous author of *Alice's Adventures in Wonderland, Through the Looking Glass*, and other classic works of children's literature — that has been imprinted on history is that of an extremely shy, slightly weird, religious, celibate man who only felt comfort-able with the prepubescent girls who became his best friends. That image has taken some lumps in recent years. Morton Cohen's biography *Lewis Carroll* shows that Carroll's inter-est in girls had a sexual element to it, although he probably never acted on it. Karoline Leach will soon be publishing her book *In the Shadow of Sin*, forwarding her unique theory that Carroll — far from being a lifelong virgin — had an affair with Alice Liddell's mother, who was married to the dean of Christ Church in Oxford, where Carroll was a deacon. *Jack the Ripper: "Light-hearted Friend"* [reviewed in the Merry Mischief chapter] by Richard Wallace, astoundingly asserts — in all seriousness — that Carroll was Jack the Ripper. And in *The Agony of Lewis Carroll*, Wallace claims that Carroll was filled with a soul-consuming rage that was hidden in the text and illustrations of his books.

This rage came from many factors. Carroll was born to a remote father and a domineering mother who totally control-led their son, trying to force him into being the man his father wished he had been. During the many years that the weak, effeminate Carroll spent in notoriously violent English board-ing schools, he was constantly raped by the other students, becoming a virtual sex slave. "For it was during these years that the spirit of Charles Dodgson, the special and perfect child, with an already damaged and depleted self, filled with

The Agony of Lewis Carroll

Richard Wallace

Carroll's vorpal blade went snicker-snack and burbled as it came. *The Agony of Lewis Carroll.*

latent rage, died. But he would survive, finally resurrecting himself, but now fuelled with the venom of full-blown rage that would go unabated to his final death at age sixty-five." Wallace also believes that the grown Carroll had homosexual feelings, which only added to his frustration and anger.

Consumed by the need to release his feelings and re-late his experiences, but wanting to do so in a hidden rather than direct way, Carroll used his seemingly benign writings to vent his rage at his family, who actively and passively worked to destroy him during his formative years, and at a hypocritical society that, among other things, hated gays but looked the other way while he was sexually assaulted for years. He also used his works to hide erotic ideas, secretly exposing children to descriptions of sexual activities includ-ing homosexuality, masturbation, and bestiality. He did this through his books' symbolism and illustrations but mainly by creating anagrams. An anagram is achieved when the let-ters making up a word, sentence, or paragraph are rear-ranged to form new words, sentences, or paragraphs.

An example of an anagram is found in the opening verse of "Jabberwocky", the nonsense poem contained in *Through the Looking Glass*. There are many themes at work, one of them being a reflection of Carroll's masturbatory fantasies. When rearranged the first verse becomes:

Bet I beat my glands til,
With hand-sword I slay the evil gender.

A slimey theme; borrow gloves,
And masturbate the hog more!

Wallace later says that the masturbation theme can even be seen directly. "By re-reading the poem and substituting *penis* for *Jabberwock* (a Doublet *Jabbercock*?) we have the masturbatory fantasy of the boy attempting to control his compulsion. Rising from the 'tulgey wood' (pubic hair) in response to erotic thoughts/images, it 'burbled as it came.'"

The later work *Sylvie and Bruno* contains some key anagrams. In the preface, Carroll specifically mentions two sentences that appear in the book. In one sentence, a character says: "My ancestors were all famous for military genius," which is an anagram of, "I was a terror from all my incestuous family genes." In the book, the Lady Muriel responds: "It often runs in families, just as a love for pastry does," which converts to, "I stir for pederast unions as often as family love." The character who made the first statement is known as "His Adiposity, the Baron Doppelgeist", which can be rearranged to form, "O, I pity Dodgson, his path a rebel spite."

Even the title *Alice's Adventures in Wonderland* is an anagram: "Censure an evil and stained world."

Carroll himself lends some credence to Wallace's interpretations. In a letter Carroll wrote to one of his child friends, he claimed that *Alice* is about "malice". Other critics and biographers have picked up on the anger in Carroll's works, though none of them has taken the premise as far as this.

While some of the anagrams often seem to be a stretch, Wallace makes a compelling case. Whether or not you see Carroll's works as blasts of pure hatred and repressed sexuality, this book is absolutely fascinating.

Gemini Press; $13
1990; softcover; 301 pp
illus; 0-9627195-5-2

ATTACK GOD INSIDE
by Tricia Warren

Tricia Warren's poems and brief proses pieces display the anger and disillusionment that colours so many of the books from Henry Rollins' 2.12.61 Publications. Luckily, she has enough humour and hope — plus a knack for turning a phrase — to give her outpourings real depth.

Warren sometimes writes about specific incidents — being raped, being verbally harassed because she's white, being in bad relationships (luckily this is kept to a minimum) — and other times she writes about the general sadness of life. Her long poem about being raped, "Sickness", begins: "i'm getting rid of the old demons/to make room for the new ones". In a shorter poem called "And a Horse Killed Nietzsche" she writes: "being raped will tell you more/of what it is like to be a woman in this world/not high heels or make up/what did not kill me mister has made me insane".

"Living Arrangement Bitch #200,000,047" is a funny look at the emptiness of social interactions. "I'm bored with all these retarded expected reactions. When someone walks into a room i might as well pick a nice juicy booger and flick it at them while they try to catch it in their mouth. We could call this greetings. When some guy comes over and he hits me in the head with a baseball bat i can call that marriage. When my mother shoves 62 lollipops up her ass and sings hari krishna let's all call that christmas." More of Warren's humour comes out in "Self Portrait": "anyone who says the square peg/does not fit in the circular hole/has never seen a crazy bitch with a hammer".

Deep down, Warren seems to understand the pointlessness of angst-ridden teeth-nashing. The short poem "A Statement of Clarity Found in a Hunk of Bullshit" closes with these lines:

pain clichés drop dead
in the light of truth

suicide my friend
is feeling sorry for yourself

2.13.61 Publications; $11
1996; softcover; 159 pp
illus; 1-880985-33-0

BLASTER
The Blaster Al Ackerman Omnibus
by Al Ackerman

"Blaster" Al Ackerman is a regular in the world of zines. His bizarre tall tales have appeared in dozens of publications, most of which are defunct or known only to the heartiest litzine readers. Apparently, Blaster leads an unusual and precarious existence. "One jump ahead of the sheriff, the finance company and the straight jacket" is how he sums up his quasi-vagabond life.

These 50+ stories (and the accompanying 100 or so illustrations) revel in absurdity presented with a straight face. Try to imagine Salvador Dalí crossed with your crazy uncle who loves to tell stories, and you're on the right track. In "Confessions of an American Ling Master", the narrator constantly steals from libraries. But he's not after books. He sneaks up to the librarian's desk and steals those white return-mail postcards that publishers ask librarians to fill out, indicating how well a particular title is being received. Once he has absconded with this important object, he fills out the card in a proscribed manner. "That night after I returned to my lair, I ritualistically drank a glass of Mogen David wine and then donned my Ling hood and got down to work."

The title character of "Joe Damballa in Hell" is a young boy whose uncle is taking him to see President Franklin Roosevelt at a Catholic rest home. For reasons that we cannot know, FDR has agreed to pay seventy-five cents just to shake the boy's hand. "A short pause — hanging back — my hand clenched nervously behind me. 'Well?' the President shouted suddenly, as though he lacked much self-control. 'What are you — some kind of sis? Here!' He stuck his hand straight out at me. 'Be a man and shake! SHAKE!' he screamed again; 'Shake, you goofy little son of a bitch!'" Eventually, they shake hands, after which FDR makes a lewd comment. A bunch of nuns run out to bring the President under control. One nun smacks him several times with a big iron keyring, and they manage to get him back inside. "The boy is relieved but notices that dog hairs are growing from his palm."

Considering that Blaster has been getting published since 1978, it's high time that he has his own anthology. To read it is to enter a wonderfully warped parallel world where ventriloquists have their hands surgically made into dummies and suits constructed of 2976 vienna sausages are a way to attract women.

Feh! Press; $12.95
1994; softcover; 288 pp
illus; 0-945209-09-6

THE BOMB
The Classic Novel of Anarchist Violence
by Frank Harris

Frank Harris is best known for his epic, multi-volume erotic autobiography, *My Life and Loves*, but he also wrote *The Bomb*, which Aleister Crowley proclaimed was the best novel he'd ever read. It is told from the point of view of the unknown person who threw a bomb at the famous Haymarket riot, killing police who were getting ready to brutalise a gathering of labour protesters. It also deals with the show trial that sent five innocent anarchists to their deaths.

Feral House; $12.95
1909 (1996); softcover; 213 pp
illus; 0-922915-37-7

CAFFEINE MACHINE
by Mark Sperry

A collection of short writings by Mark Sperry, a pissed off guy in New York. The poems, reflections, rants, and travelogues all seethe with anger. "Life, is being sold a lemon, sight unseen, no test drive, no parking any time, limited mileage, and the keys are locked inside." "I live alone because the idea of dragging around the company of a nagging, pushy, whining, ball and chain makes me sick. A person who makes you do anything that you do not want to do is an opponent to be avoided or annihilated. Some people will compromise their every belief for a few acts of sex."

Dirty Rotten Press; $4
1989; softcover; 95 pp
illus; no ISBN

CHOCOLATE DREAMS AND DOLLARS
by Mohammed Mrabet

The latest of twelve books that American writer and composer Paul Bowles has translated and transcribed from the spoken stories of Mohammed Mrabet, a Moroccan fisherman and boxer. *Chocolate Creams and Dollars* is the loosely autobiographical tale of a Moroccan boy and the rich Englishman living in Arzila who hires him as a servant. The book is illustrated with found images, the covers of Moroccan 45 records from the 1970s, and photographs of life in Morocco by Philip Taaffe.

Inanout Press; $29.95
1992; hardcover; 186 pp
illus; 0-96225119-6-X

COFFEEHOUSE
Writings from the Web
edited by Levi Asher & Christian Crumlish

Correct me if I'm wrong, but I believe this is the first multi-author anthology of writings that were originally published on the Web. (And I'm positive it won't be the last.) These 46 stories, poems, and essays were first released either on the authors' personal Webpages or in Webzines that publish works by various people. They don't have a whole lot in common except perhaps an enthusiastic, energetic aura that might come from being part of a new publishing medium.

"Getting the Hang of Yin and Yang" by Gael Morlan is the overly didactic story of a middle-aged former punk rocker who has more or less settled into a life of conformity, complete with a bowling league team. "When it was her turn to host the after-game activities, they would, often as not, find her scrapbooks with the old press clippings and dig out her albums to study the covers, sometimes reading the lyrics aloud and thereby causing Violet to wince; their deadpan delivery of her soul's primal screams was an unintentional insult."

Walter Miller's "intervention", strewn with intentional typos and misspellings, is a darkly funny story told by a young man whose eccentric grandfather treats him badly. "Yes, my grandfather's threats and abbuse go on. One threat is to rip my colon out thru my annus down hard, then jerk it up quikly up and voer my head and then tye a knot on top as to encase me in my own pollish suasage. Another threat is to skin me allive with a boxcutter and roll me in breadcrums and leave me in a bad part of Los Angelles. He continnues to call me names and hit me. Favvorite names of late are 'CandyAss' and 'Panteywaist'. Also 'Star Trek Faggot.'"

The most overtly experimental pieces are found in the section entitled "The Center Cannot Hold". Christian Crumlish's "No Bird but an Invisible Thing" uses an unprecedented form of hypertext. "The first line of each paragraph is a hyperlink; when that line is clicked a page is retrieved that expands that paragraph and a few selected others into their full form, while the rest remain closed links. Thus the story can fold and unfold countless different ways, each time revealing different aspects of its meaning." Unfortunately, though, in book form it must be printed linearly. "Flux", a hodgepodge of snippets from four different writers, is the most avant garde piece in the book:

> There.is.a.risk.writers.take@listserv.prodigy.com,
> I.suppose@listserv.prodigy.com,
> in.exposing.their.wounds.to.the.air.known.as.an.audi
> ence.When.the.air.comes.back@listserv.prodigy.com,
> in.the.form.of.commentary —
> .which.I.admittedly.invite.and.hope.for —
> .sometimes.it.is.of.the.healing@listserv.prodigy.com

The section "A Thousand Words" contains graphic pieces that although predominantly visual, still have a narrative feel to them. "Very Short Stories" by Steve Seebol is a set of humorous digitally manipulated photos accompanied by a sentence or two or three. A picture of a dog with strange eyes has the following text under it: "After careful observation I have come to the conclusion that nothing on Earth is as slimy as the inside of a dog's mouth." The graphics in Mark Napier's "Negative Space" are his attempts to scan his entire apartment.

An interesting pattern is that a large number of these stories have very bold, attention-getting first lines. This might be due to the nature of the Web. You've literally got a few seconds to capture people's interest or they'll be clicking on to something else. Here are a few examples of intriguing opening lines:

☞ "There's something very sad, very melancholy, about not masturbating." ("Dry Popcorn" by Sudama Adam Rice)

☞ "When Richard Gillman was killed, he was driving north through Los Angeles on the Santa Monica-bound 110." ("The Damnation of Richard Gillman" by Greg Knauss)

☞ "Nigga couldn't fine no work." ("Nigga What Couldnt Fine No Work" by Scott W. Williams)

☞ "I'm sitting in the sleazy grimy Greyhound station waiting for the bus to New York, and I'm thinking: it was 'My Fair Lady' that screwed up Todd's mind." ("Apparition" by Levi Asher)

☞ "The first day after my stash ran out I realised I was in hell, even though I had decided to quit taking speed anyway." ("Jerry Was" by Jamie Fristrom)

☞ "It started when Frank's CD player tried to kill me on my way to work." ("Gravity" by Jason Snell)

Coffeehouse ends with two appendices. The first lists resources for good writing on the Web. It's a fairly long list, but it ignores literary e-zines devoted to erotica even though many of them, including Fish Net and Nerve, are of extremely high quality. (Further evidence of the ghettoisation of sexual writing, perhaps?) The other appendix suggests how to get your writings published on the Web. Strangely, the authors advise people that the best way is to submit their work to Webzines, which once again puts authors at the mercy of editors, a situation that the "everyone's a publisher" ethic of the Web is supposed to eliminate.

Although the appendices could've been stronger, the selections in *Coffeehouse* are consistently above average in terms of quality. Though not as always as perfectly crafted as they could be, they have a invigorating freshness and vitality about them.

Manning Publications; $24.95
1997; softcover; 319 pp
illus; 1-884777-38-4
WWW: www.coffeehousebook.com

CONFESSIONS OF A FLESH-EATER

by David Madsen

This is the story of Orlando Crispe, one of the greatest chefs in the world. A man so obsessed with the act of eating flesh that he, well, has to try *every* type of meat.

For Crispe, who is not one for modesty ("... I am a great artist. Indeed, I am an artist of international repute. I am a creator, a demiurge, the image of an aeon, and the primordial material out of which I give birth to the children of my ideation is food"), meat is his mistress. "It is the raw material of my creative genius. I chose it (or rather, *it* chose *me*) as a painter might choose to work in watercolours or oils, as a composer might choose to specialise in opera; it is a subtle and enigmatic thing, this marriage of man and element..." From the time he was an infant, Crispe had the taste for flesh. He tried to bite a chunk out of his mother's breast once when she was feeding him. As a boy, he picked up the mauled body of a bird in his backyard. "Then something very extraordinary happened: quite without warning, I was overwhelmed with the urge to suck its flesh."

After graduating from school, Crispe was apprenticed to a famous chef, who became his lover. But he wasn't the only one. In one of the most bizarre sex scenes you'll ever read, young Crispe gets it on with a flank of beef. "The impress of damp, ripe flesh, the solid interstratification of flesh and fat against my exposed genitals, was sensational... I kissed its fibres lingeringly, I licked it, gnawed at it with exquisite tenderness, as a young husband might lick and gnaw the stiffening nipples of his new bride."

Eventually, Crispe decides to sample the most forbidden meat of all — human flesh. I won't give away any more of this rich, decadent novel, except to say that several people end up inside Crispe and the patrons of his restaurant.

In its wild treatment of the intersection of food, sex, and the body, *Confessions* is rare. In its evocative use of language, it is well done. My compliments to the chef!

Dedalus Ltd; £7.99
1997; softcover; 223 pp
1-873982-47-X

COP KILLER

by Donald Gorgon

"Ripped from today's headlines", this tough as nails novel sides with its title character, Lloyd Baker. Corrupt cops pressure a drug dealer into giving them names of other dealers in London. The frightened ratfink gives them Baker's name, even though he's not in the drug scene. When the cops raid his pad, he's not there, but in the heat of the moment they waste his mother. The Inspector who pulled the trigger is more worried about himself than the old woman: "That fucking black bitch, Keith. My career will be fucked because of this. Fucking ruined..." The cops are suspended while an inquest is held. The killing is found to have been accidental, and the police are off the hook.

Over the following months, Lloyd's physical and mental health deteriorate. He finally decides to take revenge, not just against the Inspector, but against all the police. He begins a genocidal campaign that involves guns, knives, heavy concrete blocks, and car "accidents" and culminates in his bombing a police station. A reporter discovers his identity, and he grants her an interview. "While the rest of the world viewed him as a sick killer he saw himself as someone who was fighting a justified war against corrupt oppressors. 'There ain't no justice — just me!' he said repeatedly, and he really believed it. He was on a self-obsessed jihad against the evil

"I decided about 15 years ago that I could not wear a tie because to me it represented, in a crazy sort of way, the colonization of my body. It was a throwback to the days of lynching — of hanging by the neck — and in the agony of my imagination I took action. I became a tie quitter."
— Molefi Kete Asante
Afrocentric Culture Critic

"The ephemeral is an essential bridge to the immortal."
— Sir Peter Ustinov
Raconteur

A page from the Grim Reaper's notebook.
Death Writes.

that had shattered his life and he was taking no prisoners."

For some reason, the reporter doesn't turn Lloyd in. He goes on to kill the Inspector that shot his mother and, having done that, he retires from the cop killing business and lives happily ever after.

A book like *Cop Killer* would unleash a furore in the US. The title character is portrayed sympathetically. He kills a bunch of policeman, but — unlike what you would expect — there isn't a nice, safe law-and-order ending. He gets away with it and feels no remorse.

The X Press; £4.99
1994; paperback; 186 pp
1-874509-06-9

DEATH BY SUICIDAL MEANS
The Killing of Wardell Burge
by Walter Henderson

This novel is a fictionalised version of a real-life miscarriage of justice that occurred in North Carolina in 1965. An insane African American man named Walter Henderson was accused of terrorising people on a stretch of road that he said was "his" and holding a congregation hostage at a black church while he preached in the nude. Under North Carolina's outlawry proclamation, anyone can file an affidavit with a judge accusing a person of a felony and stating that that person escaped apprehension. Once that is done, the person is considered an "outlaw", even if no arrest warrant is ever issued. Once a person is an outlaw, any person — whether law enforcement or a private citizen — can try to catch him, and if he does not surrender, "any citizen may slay him without accusation of any crime."

In this particular case, a sheriff, deputy, district attorney, and SWAT team member set out to get Henderson. After trapping him on the second story of his house, they lobbed in tear gas, then set fire to the place with an incendiary device. Henderson was killed. After assembling an all-white panel — including Klan members — to officially determine the cause of death, it was ruled as "death by suicidal means

and was directly due to asphyxiation and burning and that no criminal act or default was involved." The official story was that Henderson set the fire himself rather than be captured.

The outlawry proclamation was ruled unconstitutional by the Supreme Court in 1976, but it still remains on the books as North Carolina General Statute 15-48. This book's appendices contain the Court's ruling — including the verbatim statute — and reprints of articles from several local papers about the incident.

Inheritance Press; $8.95
1994; hardcover; 227 pp
0-9638086-1-3

DEATH WRITES
A Curious Notebook
by Darlene Barry Quaife

Death Writes is a small square softcover penned by none other than the Grim Reaper. In a prefatory note to the main text, Darlene Quaife explains that she found *Death Writes* on a table at a coffeehouse. In its original form, it was a notebook for a gradeschooler in the year 1921. Apparently Death stumbled onto this "scribbler" during its travels and decided to add commentary, meditations, ramblings, doodles, and favourite quotes underneath the words carefully written by the notebook's original owner. Death muses on the human condition, particularly on our attitudes and fears concerning death, making for some unique observations.

Under the letter "A", Death writes: "Acquired a dog today, will call it Anubis. The ancient Egyptians had guts and knew how to store them. No gloom and doom for that bunch. Embalming rooms were called 'the house of vigor' (rigor mortis to vigor mortis) and black was the colour of rebirth. The pleasure of eternity depended on the dog god. Anubis took the human soul between his teeth, as gently as a retriever with a dead duck, and deposited it on a set of scales balanced by truth in the form of a feather."

Later, he is writing about Emily Dickinson. "I once quoted Emily to T.S. Eliot. I never forgave him for calling me a 'snickering footman.' I thought he could take a lesson in humour from Miss Dickinson, so I let him have it — 'We never know we go when we are going — /We jest and shut the door — / Fate — following — behind us bolts it — /And we accost no more — .' Eliot's J. Alfred Prufrock seems such a whiner with his 'I have seen the eternal Footman hold my coat, and snicker.'"

Death also hires a consultancy firm to analyse his image, looks at the euphemisms we use regarding death and dying, relates some telephone conversations from the early twentieth century, and examines ancient Chinese beliefs about reincarnation. The last nineteen pages of *Death Writes* are a scrapbook in which Death has pasted articles on strange ways people have died, superstitions in Newfoundland, a necrophilia joke, post-mortem practices, and quotes about death, such as Nietzsche's "The thought of suicide is a great consolation: by means of it one gets successfully through a bad night."

Arsenal Pulp Press; $11.95Can, $9.95US

1997; small softcover; 144 pp
heavily illus; 1-55152-038-9

DESIRE BY NUMBERS

by Nan Goldin & Klaus Kertess

Like all of the books published by Artspace, *Desire by Numbers* is a deft integration of prose and photography. In the short story by Klaus Kertess, a man is visiting a friend in the hospital. The first man (neither of them is named) tells his friend about his encounters with John, an American male prostitute. John is completely average in every way, yet the man is strongly attracted to him, perhaps — his friend suggests — because he is so generic and "safe". He also tells about his failed relationship with a man named Peter, who had sex with male teenage prostitutes across Asia. Peter eventually died of AIDS because of his adventures. The man's friend keeps interrupting the narrative to ask questions or make pointed observations. "You needed John only because you were scared to imagine something better. Peter may have ended up with Kaposi Sarcoma, but he imagined *Kama Sutra*. He was careless. His end is horrible, but your beginning is insipid."

Throughout the text, Nan Goldin's colour photographs of boy prostitutes from Southeast Asia offer a counterpoint to the somewhat romantic vision offered by the story. Seeing these kids stripping, dancing, and entangled with each other on the stages of sleazy clubs provides a reality check.

Artspace Books; $15
1994; hardcover; 44 pp
heavily illus; 0-9631095-3-7

A DIFFERENT BEAT
Writings by Women of the Beat
Generation

edited by Richard Peabody

Apparently, since this book and *Women of the Beat Generation* [below] were published within less than a year of each other, the idea of paying special attention to the women involved in the Beat movement is an idea whose time has come. Although both books have the same basic concept, they take different approaches, and they overlap to a surprisingly small degree.

A Different Beat is strictly an anthology of writings by the women directly involved in the movement, as well as fellow travellers. Twenty-seven writers are represented by poems, stories, and memoirs, some of which were published only in obscure journals or chapbooks of the day. A few have never been published at all until now.

Throughout the late 1950s and early 1960s, the Beats broke new ground by writing openly about drugs, sex, alienation, dissatisfaction, and desperate hope. Although the men in the movement received more recognition, this volume shows that the women were writing about the same themes in ways that are as powerful as those of their male counterparts.

As forerunners of Riot Grrrls and sex-positive feminists, many of the female Beats wrote honestly and explicitly about sex. One of the small number of poems written by Elise

Cowen, who committed suicide in 1962 at age 29, starts out: "I want a cunt of golden pleasure/purer than heroin/To honour you in". Lenore Kandel opens "Love-Lust Poem" like so: "I want to fuck you/I want to fuck you all the parts and places/I want you all of me".

You won't find a better poem railing against the ugly, soul-killing aspects of society than Kandel's "First They Slaughtered the Angels":

First they slaughtered the angels
tying their thin white legs with wire cords
and
opening their silky throats with icy knives
They died fluttering their wings like chickens
and their immortal blood wet the burning earth

An excerpt from *Nobody's Wife* — the unpublished memoirs of Jack Kerouac's second wife, Joan Haverty Kerouac — gives some insight into the legendary figure. After Joan became pregnant, Jack delivered an ultimatum: she could either have him or have the baby. "I laughed. 'You mean, which baby do I want? The husband or the one in here?' I patted my belly. Jack sputtered." Joan didn't get an abortion, and the result was Jan Kerouac, who wrote two books of her own, both of which are excerpted here. (Jack never accepted Jan as his, and they only saw each other twice before his death.)

Overall, this collection is superb, a must for Beat lovers and a treasure for any fan of trailblazing fiction.

High Risk Books (Serpent's Tail); $13.99
1997; softcover; 235 pp
1-85242-431-1

DYING FOR VERONICA

by Matthew Remski

Concept: A 23-year-old Catholic man writes this book to his sister, for whom he yearns sexually.

Approach: Highly experimental. Surrealistic. Sometimes absurdist. Creative typography. Beautiful language piled on top of itself until it becomes endlessly dense and lush.

Juxtapositions: Catholicism and incest; the sacred and the profane; sex and death.

Telling Quote: "I estimate that in eleven years of sad sexual awareness I have spunked over three thousand loads of jit through my clenched hand onto the wood and lino and dirt of this planet and I have called your name every time."

Telling Quote #2: "You will never be a footnote in my book, dear sister. I am the footnote. Look for me at the bottom of every page, fallen."

Typically Beautiful Quote: Retelling a dream in which Veronica, as a nine-year-old, sings in church: "You begin to sing with the voice of fine bone. There is a slowness in the way the words leave you, such that they become visible in the air, as though your body was enwrapped by a timeless arctic bent on recording your breathing. The words become vessels. Actual vessels in the air. Ceramics of nouns. Dishes and plates and chalices painted with the words you sing. They hang on invisible display hooks."

Choice Morsels: "making a rosary out of dried cranberries"; "your white panties with their oval auburn stain hanging from a branch like the skin of a collapsed fruit"; "her nylons swishing like fronds of palm leaves"; "this lonely bench smeared with guano and seeping out the ass-warmth of Sunday-walking widowers"; "Your ass was a white seaflower nudged by hormonal undercurrents."; "The room filled with the light you see when the purple curtains of your confessional cleave open like the dress of a whore mounting the steps of a gallows."; "The altar looks like a birthday cake for a corpse."; "He falls asleep with his hands running braille patterns over her vertebrae... He is reading this sentence over and over again as he falls into sleep, trying to make sense of the string of words."

Bottom Line: The author's mixture of (forbidden) sex, religion, and death is completely seamless. His gift for coruscating, blindingly brilliant language has me turning green with envy. *Dying for Veronica* is one of the best books in this chapter.

Insomniac Press; $18.99Can, $14.99US
1997; softcover; 211 pp
illus; 1-895837-40-5

HARD CORE LOGO
by Michael Turner

Using small bites of information, Michael Turner tells the story of Hard Core Logo, a once-great but now disbanded punk group who get together for a reunion tour. A hodgepodge of poetry, lyrics, diary entries, graffiti, contracts, answering machine messages, faxes, an interview, and photos manage to piece together a realistic look at life in the great rock'n'roll circus. Made into an independent film by Bruce McDonald.

Arsenal Pulp Press; $14.95, $16.95Can
1993, 1996; softcover; 197 pp
illus; 1-55152-033-8

LESS ROCK, MORE TALK CD

Over 70 minutes of spoken word performances from eleven diverse people, including Noam Chomsky ("Propaganda and Control of the Public Mind"), Jello Biafra ("Gotta Be Ready"), Penny Rimbaud from CRASS ("Falling"), Norman Nawrocki ("The World's Greatest Slavonic Lover"), Steve Pottinger ("Thailand"), Jerme Spew ("I Miss You Claire"), and Peter Plate ("Snitch Factory").

AK Press; $13.98
1997; CD; 71 min
1-873176-84-8

THE LETTERS OF WANDA TINASKY
edited by TR Factor

From 1983 to 1988, a series of letters to the editor appeared in two local newspapers in Mendocino County, California. Displaying rapier wit, a gift for language, and a wide range of knowledge, a person known as Wanda Tinasky wrote short missives that needled everyone from local poets and businesspeople to the powers-that-be, as well as commenting on just about everything under the sun. What makes this

Life in the great rock'n'roll circus.
Hard Core Logo.

newsworthy is that during this same time period, literary giant Thomas Pynchon was writing his novel *Vineland*, which is set in 1984 in Northern California — most assuredly the Mendocino area. It would only make sense that he actually lived in the area for a period of time in order to get the general atmosphere and the specific details down so perfectly. Suspicion has it that Pynchon and Tinasky are one and the same. Pynchonian scholars are divided on the issue, although the case is strong enough to make even the doubters study the situation. Steven Moore, himself a Pynch scholar, writes in his foreword: "Well, if it ain't Pynchon, it's someone who has him down cold: his inimitable literary style, his deep but lightly worn erudition, his countercultural roots, his leftist/populist politics, his brand of wit and humour, his encyclopaedic range of reference, his street smarts and raffish charm, his immersion in pop culture and sports, and his hatred of all agents of repression."

In her first letter, Tinasky touched off a tempest in a teapot, by telling the *Mendocino Commentary* that its last few issues "have been literally fabulous, except for the 'poetry,' which I think is a disservice to poets and to children." When that drew the ire of some folk, she continued the insults: "Leonard Cirino's 'poetry' really tore me up. 'Solemn, like a church' Now there's a figure of speech! 'Sublime light'... that really makes me feel like light is sublime, you know? 'The ash forest burns'... we got ash forest around here? But maybe that's too subtle for me. 'The dog barked. The horse and children ran. My brother called from the barn something about the hay.' I didn't make this up, I read it in your 'poetry' column. Your poetry editor wouldn't know a poem if it bit her in the ass in broad daylight."

Some other choice bits include: "I do not have my head up my ass; I know that people are being murdered so that I can get bananas three pounds for a dollar." "I spent the past few weeks keeping warm, with nothing much to do but watch TV, read the comics as our British cousins call them, scrub toilets, and pray for the salvation of all sentient beings down to the level of deputy sheriffs and liver flukes..." To the *Anderson Valley Advertiser*'s editor: "I suppose you have more important things on your mind... submarines sinking with 18 atomic bombs aboard (although there's nothing to worry about in that, as Dan Rather told me himself, & and he was in no mood to kid, having just been beaten up in a toilet)... prostate cancer... the 'summit meeting of Gorbachev & Reagan'... Jesus H. Christ... a guy with shit *on* his head & a guy with shit *in* his head..."

The letters ended in August 1988, until *Vineland* was published and the *AVA*'s editor commented that he believed Tinasky must have been Pynchon. Two more letters arrived from the mystery "woman", jokingly denying the connection.

This volume reproduces every letter from Tinasky, as well as letters that seem to be written by her but are signed in different names and, conversely, letters from pseudo-Tinaskys, who signed her name but were obviously impostors. There are also letters written by others during the time period who commented on Tinasky or otherwise contributed to the fun 'n' games. Each of Tinasky's letters is heavily annotated with explanations of all the local, historical, political, literary, and other allusions. Cute illustrations based on the letters are supplied by one Fred Sternkopf.

The Letters of Wanda Tinasky deserves a spot on every Pynchon fan's bookshelf because, at the very least, it's an intriguing footnote to the mythos (and a fun read), but it might actually be an official part of the canon, although we'll probably never know for sure. (The man himself refuses to comment, while his editor and his agent — who is also his wife — deny he's the author.)

vers libre press; $22
1996; oversized softcover; 233 pp
heavily illus; 0-9652881-0-2

LINELAND
Mortality and Mercy of the Internet's Pynchon-L@Waste.Org Discussion List
by Jules Siegel, Christine Wexler, *et al*

Independent publishers are discovering that the Internet contains a large amount of great, highly-publishable writing, although it is buried beneath tons of spam, porno JPEGs, and self-indulgent drivel. I'm sure that before too long — maybe even by the time you read this — the corporate publishers will have finally caught on and we'll be seeing lots of anthologies of Net writings, plus novels and nonfiction works originally published online. I doubt, however, any giant publishing house will have the nerve to publish something as unprecedented, esoteric, and altogether *different* as *Lineland*. Since this is a completely unique book, it might be a little difficult to explain and comprehend, but let me give it a shot.

First of all, you need to understand the concept of an email discussion list. Such a list — which can be on any topic in the world — is simply a way for a group of people to engage in a dialogue via email. There is one central email address for each discussion list. When you email a message to this address, it is duplicated and a copy is sent to each member of the list. This way, you can introduce a new line of thought (often referred to as a thread) and other members of the list can respond, or you can respond to something another member has written.

Secondly, it helps to know something about Thomas Pynchon. He is a notoriously reclusive writer whose complex novels inspire awe and devotion in everyone from academics and the literati to Laurie Anderson, Nirvana, Warren

THOMAS RUGGLES PYNCHON, JR.
AS HE MIGHT APPEAR IN 1997

Illustration from memory by Christine Wexler
Pencil on paper, 14 cm. by 21 cm.

Christine Wexler's drawing of what Thomas Pynchon might look like in 1997. *Lineland.*

Zevon, all kinds of nonconformists, and hordes of loyal fans. His books include *V.* [*Outposts* p 228], *The Crying of Lot 49*, *Gravity's Rainbow* (universally hailed as a modern masterpiece), *Vineland*, and *Mason & Dixon*. Since becoming famous in the late-1960s, this extremely private man has neither given an interview nor been photographed from the front.

OK, bearing that in mind, we now turn our attention to the email discussion list Pynchon-L, which, as you may guess, is devoted to the life and works of Thomas Pynchon. Freelance author Jules Siegel came across the list while searching for references to himself on the Net. Siegel, you see, had been a friend of Pynchon's when they were students at Cornell. Pynchon had an affair with Siegel's then-wife, Christine Wexler, which prompted Siegel to write the article "Who Is Thomas Pynchon... and Why Is He Taking Off With My Wife?" (*Playboy*, March 1977). This article had been posted, without permission, to the Website that archives the Pynchon-L list. When Siegel emailed the site's Webmaster about this, he was invited to join in the discussion list. Join in he did. Soon after making his presence known, Siegel was deluged with questions about Pynchon and their relationship with each other.

Not too much later, Wexler came to visit the daughter she had had with Siegel. When Siegel announced that his ex-wife was visiting and would answer questions about Pynchon, things cranked up another notch. She managed to dispel some myths about her ex-lover: "He doesn't carry toy animals around. He has a large collection of statues of pigs and piggy banks. He collects porcelain and clay pigs." She also said things that tend to contradict the common wisdom: "He's a conservative old-fashioned workaholic with good values, strict Anglo-Christian values. He just happens to be a conservative artist instead of a conservative investment banker." And occasionally she said some negative things, claiming that Pynchon made anti-Semitic comments and that he ridiculed her in *Gravity's Rainbow*.

From here, things go completely nuts. A huge "flame war" ensued, with people both attacking and defending Siegel and Wexler, with Siegel himself weighing in much of the time. Many of the list members accused Siegel of being egotistical, bitter, vengeful, or an outright fraud. Typical of the extremes to which the hostilities went is this message: "Siegel, you truly are a pompous, self-serving arse. It is good to have a whiff of narcissism on an otherwise thoughtful list. Do you have any claim to fame, or even listenability, other than having had Pynchon bonk your wife way back when?"

After engaging in numerous written confrontations and spending lots of mental energy and bandwidth simply defending himself, Siegel quit the list and compiled this book. Although made up mostly of messages from the mailing list, *Lineland* also contains private email exchanges, photographs of Wexler taken during the love-triangle period, previously unpublished drawings by Robert Crumb and Gilbert Shelton (both of whom Siegel knew), the "Who Is Thomas Pynchon…" article, and a drawing by Wexler of what Pynchon may look like now.

Although Pynchon fans will no doubt be interested in *Lineland*, it should be noted that this is not really a book about the famed author. It is actually about the Internet and the nature of this new form of communication. To a degree, it also grapples with ideas about privacy (many people felt Pynchon's secretiveness should be respected) and the images we have of our idols (one person comments that "many members of the list seemed thin-skinned and too protective of Thomas Pynchon as some kind of literary deity."). Even the publishing of *Lineland* itself poses some questions, since many of the participants were not asked for their permission to reprint their postings. Finally, it cannot be forgotten that this book is very much about Siegel himself. The introduction is actually his eight-and-a-half page autobiography, and the book closes with Siegel answering frequently asked questions… about himself.

Lineland is a completely original work. It can be interpreted on so many levels — an autobiography of Siegel; a partial, highly-unauthorised biography of Pynchon; a statement on love, relationships, privacy, fame, writing, and other topics; an investigation of a relatively new communications medium; an experimental form of literature — that, in a way, it almost becomes like a Pynchon novel. Kind of ironic, eh?

Intangible Assets Manufacturing; $11.95

1997; softcover; 182 pp

illus; 1-885876-04-1

MARK TWAIN'S BOOK FOR BAD BOYS AND GIRLS

by Mark Twain

If you have a bad impression of Mark Twain because you associate him with your worthless education, then cheer up, because ol' Samuel Langhorne Clemens is actually a dyed-in-the-wool subversive. If you ever get the chance, hunt down the out-of-print book *The Outrageous Mark Twain* (edited by Charles Neider, published by Doubleday, 1987), which contains his most scatological, sexual, and blasphemous writings, most of which are unavailable elsewhere because their publication was blocked for decades after his death.

But on to the business at hand. *Mark Twain's Book for Bad Boys and Girls* is a compendium of short pieces — ranging from one sentence quotes to eight-page excerpts — that offer wicked observations and advice about getting the most out of life as a child (but adults will also learn a thing or two). The contents are broken into chapters, based on themes like "Risky Business", "Nasty Tricks", "What Becomes of Good Children", "How to Get to Heaven", and "Reforming Sinners".

The chapter on "Advice to Young People" opens with the admonition, "Be respectful to your superiors, if you have any." That quote comes from a longer piece in the chapter, the hilarious speech "Advice to Youth", which is all the more funny because Twain actually delivered it to a teenage girls' club in 1882. Among the pearls of wisdom he passed on to these impressionable minds: "Always obey your parents, when they are present… Now as to the matter of lying. You want to be very careful about lying; otherwise you are nearly sure to get caught… An awkward, feeble, leaky lie is a thing which you ought to make it your unceasing study to avoid; such a lie as that has no more real permanence than an average truth."

In the chapter "Defying Authority", Twain recounts one of many episodes from his boyhood. He apprenticed in a print shop with an older boy, Wales McCormick, who was a troublemaker. One Saturday morning, they were printing a pamphlet containing a long religious sermon when they discovered that they had left out a couple of words. Not wanting to have to reprint all the subsequent pages, McCormick made room for the words by shortening Jesus's name to J.C. When they sent the new proofs to the preacher, he stormed in and told them to redo the whole thing with Jesus's full name, thus destroying their plans to go fishing. So this time, McCormick expanded the troublesome name — to "Jesus H. Christ". They printed the whole run that way.

One of literature's classic lessons in wiliness is presented in "Tom Sawyer Slaughters the Innocents". Told to paint a fence by his Aunt Polly, Tom figures out a way to get all the other kids to do it for him and pay him for the privilege. The chapter on "Stretching the Truth" offers the maxim: "Truth is the most valuable thing we have. Let us economise it."

Mark Twain's Book is rollicking, high-spirited fun, but you may not want to give it to your kids. Remember, boys and girls: "You ought never 'sass' old people — unless they 'sass' you first."

Contemporary Books; $12.95

1995; small hardcover; 179 pp

illus; 0-8092-3398-3

MEMORIES THAT SMELL LIKE GASOLINE

by David Wojnarowicz

The master of many media, the late David Wojnarowicz displays his writing talents here, buttressed by ink paintings and cartoonish ink drawings. The first of the four writings, "Into the Drift and Sway", is a breathless recounting of a man's sexual encounter with a truck driver. In the title story, the narrator is in a theatre lobby when he sees a man who raped him fifteen years ago during his stint as a teenage prostitute. "Doing Time in a Disposable Body" is another tale of a dangerous, violence-tinged encounter.

The longest piece is "Spiral", an insightful glimpse into the effects of AIDS. The reason it's so insightful is that Wojnarowicz had the disease, and so did a good friend that he talks about in "Spiral". His friend is in bad shape and sinking fast. "There is also the question of dementia, an overload of the virus's activity in his brain short-circuiting the essentials and causing his brain to atrophy so that he ends up pissing into the telephone." In one of the most revealing passages, Wojnarowicz tells what it felt like when he learned that he was HIV-positive. "When I found out I felt this abstract sensation, something like pulling off your skin and turning it inside out and then rearranging it so that when you pull it back on it feels like what it felt like before, only it isn't and only you know it."

The ten ink paintings portray nameless, faceless sex in Third Avenue movies houses. The ten captioned cartoons are scenes from Wojnarowicz's life — like being repeatedly "picked up" by men when he was ten — and his dreams. "He burst into my room naked and covered in Kaposi threw me on the bed: 'You would've thought I was sexy if you saw me before I got sick.' I kissed him then pushed him off and ran from the apartment. Woke up."

Artspace Books; $15
1992; hardcover; 61 pp
illus; 0-9631095-0-2

MINIMAL FICTIONS
by Richard Kostelanetz

Richard Kostelanetz is a highly experimental writer. This collection samples his forays into minimalism. And when I say "minimalism", I mean it. Each page contains one to twenty words. By using different typefaces and playing with the words' physical appearances, Kostelanetz tries to create "word-pieces whose ostensible content would be as slight as possible and yet suggestive."

The piece on page eleven has seven words forming the shape of a tombstone. The base is the word "**Rehabilitation.**" "**Perversions.**" runs up the left side, "**Depending.**" forms an arc across the top, and "**At heaven's gate.**" comes down the right side. Where the epitaph would be is the word "**Vacant.**", written larger than the others.

On page 74 the word "**Constipation.**" — with at least one space between each letter — runs down along the left side of the page. To the right of the second *n* is the word "Murmuring." written in a lighter type.

I really can't say what most of this means. Occasionally, it's easy to tell that a word has been manipulated to reflect its meaning. On page 78, the word "pulsations" is written so that every other letter is big and bold, making the word appear as though it's throbbing. On the same page is the word

The kickass Charles Burns cover, available only on the UK edition. *My Education.*

"Censorshi ."

By far the longest pieces is the erotic story "More or Less", which clocks in at fifteen pages. Here's how it's set up: there are 127 explicit vignettes separated by tiny repeating symbols (triangles, checkmarks, scissors, etc. — known as "dingbats" in computerese). The first vignette is one word — "Sex." Each vignette has one more word than the one before it, until the middle one reaches a maximum of 64 words. Then each vignette has one less word than the preceding one, until it's back to one word again. The first vignette with 62 words goes like this: "She paid me a dollar when I bent her lap around the edge of the mattress and fucked her from behind, while I returned the dollar when she sucked my cock; and she paid me ten dollars for lifting her off the floor with my cock still inside her, while I returned ten to her for licking me from head to toe."

Asylum Arts; $9.95
1994; softcover; 104 pp
1-878580-06-X

MY EDUCATION
A Book of Dreams
by William S. Burroughs

Dreams have always fascinated me. Those unrestricted romps through the subconscious can disturb, confuse, and delight like nothing in the waking world can. And no one could whip up strange dreams like Uncle Bill Burroughs. In the beginning of this collection of his dreams, he reflects upon, among other things, his lack of attachment to any place, group, or other earthly creation. "Perhaps my home is the dream city, more real than my so-called waking life precisely because it has no relation to waking life."

The hundreds of dreams, ranging from a sentence to several pages, are not categorised by theme or chronology. They are presented without any clue as to when they occurred. Burroughs asks, "Should I tidy up, put things in rational sequential order?" The answer is obviously no. Doing so would impose a false order on the chaos of dreams. Like a dream itself, this book is a disjointed, jarring experience.

One dream, in its entirety, reads: "Drafted into the Army. One hundred Secret Service men there." The following dream nicely includes many of Burroughs' motifs: cats, the government, famous friends, and drugs. "Under a blue blanket I find arrowhead fragments, a yellow cat, an old motorcycle. My knees and teeth need filling. Government off to collaborate on the book with Tim Leary. Playing dice for morphine tablets." In a longer dream, Burroughs meets aliens, who give him a pair of glasses. He's suddenly in an optometrist's store, and then back eating with the aliens in a Parisian restaurant.

Of course, just because this is a book of dreams, Burroughs sees no reason to stick to the theme. Interwoven with his nocturnal adventures are his thoughts on alien abduction, painting with the colour blue, and jerks (animal torturers, violent bigots, world leaders). He even offers a recipe for botulism.

The cover flap of *My Education* says that Burroughs got much of his imagery from his dreams. Indeed, this book at times reads like *Naked Lunch*'s cousin. The fragmentary scenes, jolting transitions, and characters that pop in and out seem straight out of a Burroughs novel.

If you can, you'll definitely want to get the UK edition of *My Education*, published by Picador (an imprint of Macmillan General Books/Cavaye Place/London SW10 9PG/UK). It features a show-stopping, candy-coloured cover by comix artist Charles Burns. It's a portrait of Burroughs in his characteristic three-piece suit and hat. Half of his face has mutated into a green, bumpy reptile-being, and he clenches a snub-nosed pistol in his left hand. Behind him a fire rages, as flaming meteors fall from the sky. The cover of the US edition, on the other hand, is monumentally boring. It's a collage of two of Burroughs' own paintings — a mottled brown surface and an orange window. The man could paint some pretty exciting pictures, but these two are way, way too subdued for the cover of such an unapologetically strange book. The American cover simply can't hold a candle to its British counterpart.

Viking (Penguin); $10.95
1995; hardcover; 193 pp
0140094547

NAUGHTY SHAKESPEARE
The Lascivious Lines, Offensive Oaths, and Politically Incorrect Notions of the Baddest Bard of All
by Michael Macrone

If you only know Shakespeare from your high school and possibly college classes, then you probably don't know Shakespeare very well. We were all taught the moments of supreme beauty and cultural importance in the Bard's works, but there's another aspect that's been so deeply buried that relatively few people even know of its existence. Namely, the subversiveness of Shakespeare's plays and poems — the sex, violence, suicide, vulgar language, racism, sexism, anti-Semitism, and anti-establishment attitudes of the most respected writer in the English language. *Naughty Shakespeare* offers an entertaining and thorough look at these "problem areas".

Several plays are so filled with gratuitous violence that they could be considered forerunners of slasher movies and Splatterpunk horror fiction. The most violent of the plays, the revenge tragedy *Titus Andronicus*, contains a human sacrifice, nine murders, four executions (including one by a torturous method), an act of cannibalism in which a mother unwittingly eats her two sons, and a double rape, after which the victim's tongue and hands are cut off. She survives the attack and spends most of the play walking around bloody and mutilated.

Shakespeare's plays spew generous amounts of insults and venom at the Turks, the French, the Italians, the Spanish, the Greeks, the Dutch, the Danes, the Germans, the Jews, and people of African descent. As the author points out, this inflammatory speech sometimes comes from villains, but it just as often comes from "good guys". In *The Merchant of Venice*, the Jewish Shylock is referred to as "misbeliever", "cut-throat dog", "faithless Jew", "the villain Jew", "the dog Jew", "harsh Jew", "inexecrable dog", and "this currish Jew". In *Titus Andronicus*, when the white Tamora gives birth to an illegitimate child fathered by a Moor, the nursemaid says the baby is "loathsome as a toad/Amongst the fair-fac'd breeders of our clime."

If you want sex, Shakespeare delivers. His plays are full of "horning", "mounting aloft", "playing on her back", and — if you can believe it — "making the beast with two backs" (said in *Othello*). However, most of the references to sex weren't so unequivocal. Will often used puns and double entendres to get across the real meaning of the dialogue. Some of this bawdy wordplay is lost on us today, but once you know it's there, you can appreciate the plays the way the original audiences did. For example, in *Much Ado About Nothing*, when Benedick says to his love that he will "die in thy lap", it helps to know that "die" also means to have an orgasm, and "lap" was another word for crotch.

Other examples, though, aren't too hard for us moderns to figure out. When referring to the randy and clumsy knight John Falstaff, the Hostess in *Henry IV, Part 2* says: "Alas the day, take heed of him! He stabbed me in mine own house, most beastly, in good faith. 'A cares not what mischief he does, if his weapon be out. He will foin [thrust] like any devil, he will spare neither man, woman, nor child." *The Taming of the Shrew* contains this exchange: "'Away, you three-inch fool!' cries Curtis. 'Am I but three inches?' retorts Grumio; 'Why, thy horn is a foot, and so long am I at the least.'" In *Romeo and Juliet*, Mercutio says, "the bawdy hand of the dial is now upon the prick of noon." In other cases, Shakespeare actually uses the word "dildos" and puns on "fuck" and "cunt", although he never directly spells out those two words. There are many, many more examples of salty language, but this should give you the basic idea.

Elsewhere in this enlightening book, the author examines the Bard's attitudes towards women, marriage, and adultery; use of the Lord's name in vain; naughty nuns and priests; references to homosexuality; and the censorship of Shakespeare's plays for political, religious, and sexual reasons. Besides being an excellent introduction to the subversive aspects of the literary canon, *Naughty Shakespeare* could encourage a student you know to take a greater interest in English class.

Andrews & McMeel; $16.95
1997; small hardcover; 221 pp
illus; 0-8362-2757-3

NEVER HIT THE GROUND
by Kirk Lake

A smooth, dark novel by spoken word/music artist Kirk Lake. A small-time London hustler tries to get rich quick — with the help of Loose Joints, a retired cat burglar — by ripping off his organised crime-connected boss, who owns a club called Hades. Meanwhile, two male-to-female transsexuals — Queen Anne Approximately and Absolutely Sweet Marie — have travelled to Amsterdam to star in a porn movie they hope will catapult them to celebrity.

Pulp Books (Pulp Faction); £10, $18
1997; softcover; 218 pp
1-901072-07-X

POSTMODERN AMERICAN FICTION
A Norton Anthology
edited by Paula Geyh, Fred G Leebron, Andrew Levy

I sure wish an anthology like this had been around when I was taking my English classes in college. Not that there's anything wrong with Chaucer, Shakespeare, Byron, Dickinson, Whitman, Faulkner, and the rest of the gang. They're actually much more subversive than most people give them credit for. But it's still not the same as seeing this collection — obviously aimed at college courses but perfect for individuals too — which is chock-full of the most daring, groundbreaking fiction, essays, graphics, and unclassifiable writings published in the second half of the twentieth century. The editors weren't afraid to include science fiction, comics, hypertext and other bastard genres that are usually excommunicated from literature by academics.

Here are a few of the selections you'll find:
- from *The Crying of Lot 49* by Thomas Pynchon
- from *Nova Express* by William Burroughs
- from *Trout Fishing in America* by Richard Brautigan
- from *Yellow Back Radio Broke-Down* by Ishmael Reed
- from *Breakfast of Champions* by Kurt Vonnegut
- "Living with Contradictions" by Lynne Tillman
- from *In Cold Blood* by Truman Capote
- from *The Armies of the Night* by Norman Mailer
- from *The Rainbow Stories* by William T. Vollmann
- *Krazy Kat* comic strips by Jay Cantor
- comics from Lynda Barry
- multimedia from *Stories from the Nerve Bible* by Laurie Anderson
- from *Tooth Imprints on a Corn Dog* by Mark Leyner
- "Shiloh" by Bobbie Ann Mason
- from *Wild at Heart* by Barry Gifford
- from *Maus* by Art Spiegelman
- from *Catch-22* by Joseph Heller
- from *The Turn of the Screw* by Joyce Carol Oates
- from *Great Expectations* by Kathy Acker
- from *Neveryona* by Samuel Delany
- "The Gernsback Contiuum" by William Gibson
- two stories by Ursula K. LeGuin
- from *White Noise* by Don DeLillo
- from *The Female Man* by Joanna Russ
- from *Snow Crash* by Neal Stephenson
- from *Generation X* by Douglas Copeland
- from *A Cyborg Manifesto* by Donna Haraway
- the postscript to *The Name of the Rose* by Umberto Eco
- "Postmodern Blackness" by bell hooks
- from *Simulacra and Simulation* by Jean Baudrillard

Pound for pound, you won't find a better survey of progressive post-war fiction anywhere. If you're interested in exploring the most important and influential writers of cutting-edge fiction, but you're feeling overwhelmed by all the choices, start here. The capsule biographies provided by the editors will give you leads for further reading, should you like a certain author's work.

WW Norton & Co; $24.95
1997; softcover; 695 pp
illus; 0-393-31698-X

POUNDING NAILS IN THE FLOOR
WITH MY FOREHEAD
by Eric Bogosian

Eric Bogosian is a successful dramatist/monologuist/stand-up comic hybrid whose solo shows have won Obie and Drama Desk Awards. In this book of monologues from his fifth solo show, Bogosian creates a number of characters who savagely lampoon America's psychopathology and portray the frustration of living in an alienated, media-saturated world.

"Molecules" is a monologue by an unhygienic homeless man on a subway train: "I am your worst nightmare! I got shit in my pants, I got fleas in my beard, I got so much syf-liss and gonorrhoea pouring outta my penis, you can turn it on and off like a faucet." It turns out that the man has a disease called fear, and everybody on the train will catch it eventually. "'Cause we all infected see? 'Cause we all on the same train. And nobody gets off this train."

In "Red" a motorcycle-ridin', chemical-partyin', unemployed Vietnam vet is talking about the good life to an unknown person who stopped by. "I know some people, they

Reality is just one option in *Pussycat Fever*.

make all this money, they waste it on expensive cars, expensive boats, houses. They waste it on their kids. Kids' college education. What's the point of making all this money if you're not going to enjoy it, if you're not going to use it to either get fucked-up or get fucked, you know what I mean?" Like so many of Bogosian's monologues, this guy may be loud and obnoxious but he does make some good points. Is he an asshole or is he on the right track? The situation is purposely ambiguous.

Other characters include an upper-middle class suburbanite who doesn't have much of a life, but at least he's concerned about all the bad stuff he sees on the evening news. A self-help guru helping people get in touch with their inner baby. A director shooting a porn film. A recovering male. An angry young man: "Blow me. Blow me Bill Clinton. Blow me Hillary Rodham Clinton. Blow me Al Gore. Blow me Tipper Gore." A doctor prescribing medication with a few side effects: "You may experience some temporary blindness. It's only temporary. You'll get up in the morning, you won't be able to see for a while... Also in the morning it's common to experience nausea, incontinence, vomiting... And I tell my patients taking this drug make sure to keep your meals small because you will be throwing up quite a bit."

Theatre Communications Group; $8.95

1994; softcover; 82 pp
1-55936-096-8

PUSSYCAT FEVER
by Kathy Acker

Pussycat Fever is a section from a larger work, *Pussy: King of the Pirates* by the late pomo literary terror, Kathy Acker. The sexually-charged story of an eight-year-old orphaned girl is told in a hallucinatory manner with scenes that slide and melt into each other like a dream. In fact, a lot of the action occurs within dreams. The only thing is, the parts that don't take place in a dream are just as bizarre as the ones that do. Illustrated by comix artist Diane DiMassa (of *Hothead Paisan*) and collage artist Freddie Baer.

AK Press; $7
1995; softcover; 75 pp
illus; 1-873176-63-5

THE RAGGA AND THE ROYAL
by Monica Grant

Leroy Massop is a wheeling and dealing Jamaican businessman in England. He organises raves, sells shoes, whatever he can do to rise above his humble beginnings. It's worked pretty well — by 29 he's driving around in a swank BMW and wearing Armani suits and expensive jewellery. Hoping to gain respect in the community and make some important contacts, Leroy opens a youth centre in the middle of the Westview Estate, a ghetto in Harlesden. In addition, he starts Groove FM, a radio station aimed at the young people in the area, but British law is set up to exclude young blacks from getting station licenses. But Leroy has an idea... when Princess Diana comes into the inner city Friday, he'll talk her into supporting the station, and the authorities will have to grant it a license.

When Di arrives, she meets Leroy:

"Nuff respect, Princess," he greeted her.

"I beg your pardon?" she said, not quite catching his words.

"I said 'nuff respect... big up yuhself, I like your style, you know — wicked!"

"Thank you," the Princess said with a warm smile.

The Princess, being upset and bored by her strained marriage, shows an interest in Leroy. She invites him to her country home for a party, where they dance and take a stroll together. One thing leads to another and they're about to get naked in Di's bedroom, but a disturbance at the party aborts the tryst. They try to meet on other occasions, but things never work out, partly because the Prince and the royal bodyguards are trying to stop this almost-consummated affair. They're upset enough that the Princess is philandering, but the fact that Leroy is black makes it 100 times worse in their eyes. Meanwhile, Leroy's steady girl, Patsy, is being dogged by another guy.

The Ragga and the Royal is a lot of fun. It's not the highest calibre of writing, but all of the slang makes it interesting. The book never refers to Diana by name, only as "the Prin-

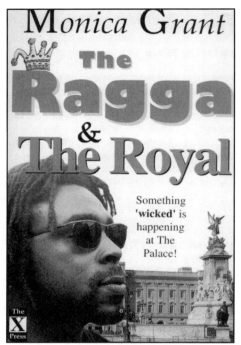

A novel of royal jungle fever that wimps out in the end.
The Ragga and the Royal.

cess", even though the details make it obvious exactly which princess the author has in mind. Not to mention the fact that X Press's catalogue specifically names Diana as a character.

The biggest disappointment was that Leroy and Di never got it on. What makes it even more frustrating is that the novel is set up as the cop-out cliché, "it was all just a dream". So why couldn't they have engaged in some royal jungle fever? I guess that would've been too controversial, even for the daring X Press.

> The X Press; $7.99, £5.99
> 1994; softcover; 205 pp
> 1-874509-08-5

RANDOM FACTOR
edited by Elaine Palmer

Pulp Faction of London is doing more than its fair share to keep fiction alive, vibrant, and risky. *Random Factor* is its fifth anthology, containing eighteen original pieces of fiction — "Palace of Nicotine", "insect.txt", "Marc Bolan Stole Your Giro", "Americancola²", "Cough Syrup", "Resenter", "A Question of What, Exactly?", and a chapter from Jeff Noon's newest novel, *Nymphomation*, which was only published in the UK — incorporated into a radical design. I wish all publishers put this much effort and imagination into the layout of their books.

> Pulp Faction; £7.50,
> 1997; softcover; 126 pp
> heavily illus; 1-899571-04-3

REALITY IS WHAT YOU CAN GET AWAY WITH
by Robert Anton Wilson

This book contains the script for a movie that could never be made. It is an epic montage of old film and documentary footage cemented together with new scenes and new dialogue. As historical figures, actors, fictional figures, and the narrator/author (Robert Anton Wilson) find themselves inhabiting the same universe, we are shown the hypocrisies, absurdities, and banalities of *fin de* millennium life. Includes lots of still shots (often humorously doctored) from classic movies.

> New Falcon Publications; $14.95
> 1992; softcover; 162 pp
> heavily illus; 1-56184-080-7

SALON
A Journal of Aesthetics

Salon is a thick, filling zine with plenty of thoughtful essays, reviews, comix, quotes, humour pieces, occasional poems, and even more stuff for you to sink your teeth into. There is no table of contents or index, and, for the most part, similar material is not grouped together. The whole thing is set up without any kind of rigid plan, enabling you to simply wander around, discovering the unexpected.

In issue 23, Anne Alexander contributes an intensely personal essay, "The Mind's Eye Never Closes", about several defining moments in her life that have been burned into her brain. The first one was seeing her best friend's parents holding each other while smiling and gazing into each other's eyes, something she had never seen her parents do. Another childhood memory involves the first time she used the word "nigger", when she was twelve or thirteen in a restaurant. "Two seats away on the right was a very old black man. He leaned forward a bit, to see past the person between us, and fixed me with a look that I will never forget. There was no anger or bitterness or any negative emotion in his face, only an expression of such pure and elemental sadness as I haven't seen again since that day."

Editor Pat Hartman writes in-depth book reviews, which often go beyond commenting on the book to become essays in their own right that use the books as a springboard. In her review of *Wisconsin Death Trip* — a collection of photographs recording life in a small Wisconsin town from 1885 to 1890 — she notes that the stories behind many of the photos prove that the idea of an innocent, non-violent America of the past is a myth. "A teenage girl sets fire to several buildings because her father whipped her. A mother chokes her illegitimate baby to death, another poisons herself and her ten-year-old daughter with arsenic…"

Tucked away at the bottom of page 22 is a comic on the "Perils of Genetic Engineering", which shows what might happen when science creates an argyle gargoyle — known as an argoyle. In a four-page comic adventure, the sociopathic dairy products known as Milk and Cheese go on a stand-up comedian-killing rampage.

Issue 25 has poetry as its theme. Hartman believes that the vast majority of poetry sucks but the one percent that is

History and pop culture in a blender.
Reality Is What You Can Get Away With.

great deserves to be lauded. Surprisingly, the number of poems in this issue is not all that high, and a lot of it is indeed very good. "Young Jack Kerouac" by Ralph Haselmann Jr. imagines what would happen in the famous Beat went on his road trip in the present day. He almost gets carjacked and then shoots heroin at the Viper Club. "Young Jack Kerouac went on the road today and visited a local jazz club, but it was just Kenny g playing all night. 'Jazz ain't what it used to be,' he sighed as he headed for the door and downtown towards Harlem."

Most of the writing in this issue is not poetry, though, but writing *about* poetry. The lives, works, and eccentricities of TS Eliot, Wanda Coleman, Kate Braverman, Arthur Rimbaud, Hart Crane, Alexander Pushkin, and others are examined. Hartman expresses her admiration of Andrei Codrescu, Leonard Cohen, Kenneth Patchen, and the poetry journal *Shocks*, while other contributors talk about what poetry means to them or look specifically at scientific poetry and Dylan Thomas's "Do Not Go Gentle into That Good Night".

Each limited-edition issue of *Salon* is individually numbered, and the inside back cover is signed by all of the contributors.

Salon/305 W Magnolia, Suite 386/Fort Collins CO 80521
Single issue: $5
Subscription (no specifics mentioned): $20

THE SIEGE OF GRESHAM
by Ray Murphy

A motley group of drinkers in Portland, Oregon, are deciding what to do now that the bar is closing for the night. The plan: Their ancestors conquered the land as they headed West, but since that's no longer possible, they head East to "conquer development". Specifically, they had to Gresham for an orgy of burning, hijacking, and violence.

AK Press; $10, £7
1997; softcover; 134 pp
1-873176-05-8

SOME OTHER FREQUENCY
Interviews with Innovative American

Authors
by Larry McCaffery

As a co-editor of the magazine *Fiction International* and editor of *Storming the Reality Studio: A Casebook of Cyberpunk and Postmodern Science Fiction* [*Outposts* p 215] and *Avant-Pop: Fiction for a Daydream Nation* [*Outposts* p 220], Larry McCaffery has been at the forefront of cutting-edge fiction. This volume, his fourth book of interviews, contains his discussions with fourteen experimental fiction writers. The three most well-known are Kathy Acker, William T. Vollmann, and Mark Leyner, but followers of pomo writing will probably be familiar with at least some of the others too: David Antin, Lydia Davis, Kenneth Gangemi, Marianne Hauser, Lyn Hejinian, Harold Jaffe, Robert Kelly, Richard Kostelanetz, Clarence Major, Derek Pell, and Gerald Vizenor.

Each interview is preceded by a background essay concerning the author in question, plus an amazingly thorough bibliography. Some common themes run throughout the interviews — the roles of fiction and of the author, the boundaries of fiction, the hows and whys of experimenting with narrative, the influence of other media on fiction, the mixing of genres, the concepts of the narrator, originality, appropriation, and more.

There are many fascinating moments. Kathy Acker — who is famous for directly appropriating pieces of other writers' works and for writing books with titles like *Great Expectations* and *Don Quixote* — says, "When I was in my teens I grew up with some of the Black Mountain poets who were always giving lectures to writers to the effect that, 'when you find your own voice, then you are a poet.' The problem was, I couldn't find my own voice. I didn't *have* a voice as far as I could tell. And yet I wanted very badly to write. So I began to do what I *had to* if I wanted to write: appropriate, imitate, and find whatever other ways I could to work with and improvise off of other texts... It's been that way ever since."

Asked about the unique "charge" from people like murderers and rapists, Harold Jaffe responds: "Certainly the criminal or outcast figure indirectly interrogates institutionalised normalcy. I can't say that I condone antisocial violence per se, but I tend to feel closer to the serial killer than to the authorities who apprehend him."

The interviews in *Some Other Frequency* are detailed, involved, and peppered with references to other avant garde writers, artists, and theorists, so readers with a serious interest in the vanguard of fiction will probably be the main ones who enjoy this book.

University of Pennsylvania Press; $19.95
1996; softcover; 333 pp
illus; 0-8122-1442-0

STICKMAN
John Trudell — Poems, Lyrics, Talks, a Conversation
edited by Paola Igliori

John Trudell was the spokesman and chairman on the radical American Indian Movement during the Native American occupation of Alcatraz Island (see *Alcatraz! Alcatraz!* in the No Compromises chapter). Ten years later, he burned a US flag during a Washington rally as a protest against the desecration of the US by "injustice and racism and classism". Less than twenty-four hours later, unknown persons torched his house, horribly killing Trudell's wife, their three children, and his mother-in-law. During the long dark period that followed, Trudell turned to writing poetry and songs (he has recorded several albums). *Stickman* collects his poetry, lyrics, lectures, and an interview.

Trudell rails against oppression, intolerance, war, greed, the abuse of the earth, and other wrongs. In "Voices Catching Up", he sings:

> Babylon falling down, falling down
> Society a broken promise
> economies war, citizen whores
> political pimps leaving us
> flat on our backs
> trading today, waiting
> for the promised land

He also writes of spirituality, honouring the earth and each other, and living in this vale of tears. Towards the end of the poem "Apology 6", he writes: "I feel as though someone/knocked me unconscious/when I entered this world/it's been a lifetime trying/to come to". During a talk at a Wordcraft Workshop, he expressed his anarchist beliefs: "We're **not** conquered. We're not defeated. **Only we can conquer ourselves...** Only we can defeat ourselves. No one else can do it. Our sovereignty — we are sovereign. All we must do is accept it. Ask no one for your sovereignty. No one can give it to you. We are sovereign because we entered into this reality as individuals. We brought it with us."

Stickman is impressively designed, with photos of Trudell and Native American artwork, creative typography, and pull quotes from Trudell and other Native Americans.

Inanout Press; $19.95
1994; softcover; 168 pp
illus; 0-9625119-8-6

"TOO MUCH LIGHT MAKES THE BABY GO BLIND"
30 Plays in 60 Minutes
by Greg Allen, et al.

The Neo-Futurists are a Chicago acting troupe who write and perform their own plays. What makes them unusual is that they perform 30 plays in an hour. They "believe that you can, in fact, write a two-minute play with just as much depth and humour and poignance as something that takes five acts, twenty characters, fifteen set changes, and two hours and ten minutes to complete. Perhaps — dare we say it? — we can achieve even more."

Everything about the performance of *Too Much Light* is out of the ordinary, including the treatment of the audience. "They paid a random admission ($1 times the roll of a single-sided die), were each slapped with an erroneous nametag by a Walkman-wearing host, and forced on stage and questioned about their lives by the ensemble." During the plays, audience members are allowed and even encouraged to yell out comments and come up on stage.

This book reprints 100 of the 1296 plays the group has created and performed under the title *Too Much Light Makes the Baby Go Blind*. These micro-plays incorporate Futurism, Dada, absurdism, performance art, and extreme satire. The quality varies as widely as you can imagine, from pointless and contrived attempts at avant gardism to brilliant and insightful takes on the human condition. In "Duelling Bigots" no words are spoken. The musical piece "Dueling Banjos" is played while two people hold up flash cards containing epithets like "Jap", "faghag", and "Nazi" as others walk by.

"Rape" pointedly demonstrates how sexual violence has become a watered-down metaphor. Four friends are sitting around talking about how they felt as though they had been raped when a co-worker rummaged through one of their desks, a friend had read another's personal mail, etc. Then the fourth cast member recites a graphic depiction of a brutal rape, bringing home the fact that no petty violation of privacy is like being raped.

"In Someone Told Me When You Wake Up in the Morning You Should Just Be Happy You're Alive", three cast members comment on petty, inane, and violent everyday situations. After each one has said something, the chorus sings a line from the theme song of *The Beverly Hillbillies*. "Traps" is simply a short monologue delivered by a woman who is afraid of a mouse she saw in her bathroom. When the group performs "Déjà Vu", the entire ensemble gets on the stage and repeats the previous play as specifically as possible, including any "audience interaction, fuck ups, or mis-cues."

Too Much Light will provide fertile material for any acting troupe that would like to try something a little stranger than *Romeo and Juliet*. Simply reading it is mildly entertaining, but I'd much rather see it performed, as long as they don't lure me on stage and command me to strip (which is what they do to audience members in "Manifest Destiny").

Chicago Plays; $8.95
1993; softcover; 126 pp
1-56850-031-9

TORNADO ALLEY
by William S. Burroughs

This book is a slim collection of six very short stories and one poem. The poem, "Thanksgiving Day, Nov. 28, 1986" (also known as "Thanksgiving Prayer"), is one of best things William Burroughs ever wrote. It takes a harsh look at America and is best when read aloud with as much sarcasm in your voice as you can muster: "thanks for a Continent to despoil and poison-/... thanks for the AMERICAN DREAM to vulgarise and falsify until the bare lies shine through-/... thanks for 'Kill a Queer for Christ' stickers-/... thanks for Prohibition and the War on Drugs-..."

The stories are actually more like fragments than fully-realised narratives with plot, characterisation, etc. "Jerry and the Stockbroker" opens with the line: "Jerry Ellisor, the retarded boy from next door, went on to harass timid WASPs from *New Yorker* cartoons, the type of person who doesn't want to get mixed up in things, a passer-by on the other side..." In "To Talk for Joe the Dead" a psychiatrist gets in a

"Thanks for a Continent to despoil and poison."
S. Clay Wilson art for *Tornado Alley.*

shoot-out with one of his patients in the consulting room. "Dead-End Reeking Street" is a grotesque story about a man whose body is inhabited by "something between a centipede and a plant, growing in his intestines, spreading its roots."

Tornado Alley contains two wicked drawings by the demon-ted comix artist S. Clay Wilson. It's not one of Burroughs' essential books, but it is enjoyable if you're already familiar with the man's work.

Cherry Valley Editions; $9
1989; softcover; 53 pp
illus; 0-916156-83-4

WALKING WOLF
A Weird Western
by Nancy A. Collins

A tale of cowboys and Indians… and werewolves. The narrator is named Walking Wolf, and for good reason. He was born in 1844 to white parents — including a werewolf dad — who were killed by other settlers. A Comanche brave named Eight Clouds found and raised Walking Wolf, who is now telling us the story of his younger days. "I don't recommend getting lynched. Even for folks such as myself, who are notoriously difficult to kill, being hung is hardly a picnic."

Mark V. Ziesing; $25
1995; hardcover; 181 pp
0-929480-42-2

WHO WROTE SHAKESPEARE?
by John Mitchell

The authorship of the works credited to William Shakespeare is one of the most intriguing and hotly-debated mysteries in the field of literature. Most scholars and professors, of course, don't think there *is* a mystery, pooh-poohing the idea that anyone other than the man known as Will Shakespeare is responsible. However, just the idea that so many towering, incomparable plays, sonnets, and other poems came from one mind is already enough to raise doubts. Add to that the generally accepted notion that good ol' Will was not exactly a worldly, well-educated man, and you have the recipe for all kinds of alternative theories.

Who Wrote Shakespeare? is the book on this subject that I have always been seeking. While there are a good number of books that question Shakespeare's authorship, they always have one particular candidate in mind, and the authors only present the evidence that supports their pet theory. John Mitchell, on the other hand, doesn't have an axe to grind. He has simply created an even-handed overview of the whole controversy, examining all the major contenders and the evidence and counter-evidence regarding each one.

To start things off, Mitchell begins with the literature in question. By examining the Shakespearean Works, we can see that the author was extraordinarily well-versed — to the point of being an expert — in a large number of demanding fields of knowledge. Various specialists in each field have affirmed that "Shakespeare" must have been initiated in the law, aristocratic living, philosophy, statesmanship, military matters, seamanship, Biblical scholarship, classical literature and languages, music, painting, sculpture, mathematics, astronomy, medicine, psychology, heraldry, folklore, Freemasonry, and many other areas. Quite a tall order for anyone. Furthermore, various scholars have estimated that Shakespeare's vocabulary is at least twice that of any other writer in the English language.

So who could have possibly had the experience, knowledge, and unparalleled talent to write such a body of work? The first candidate to be examined is none other than Will Shakespeare. "The known facts about Shakespeare's life, as the Heretics constantly exclaim, can be written down on one side of a sheet of notebook paper." Mitchell recounts these scanty facts, along with some tangential and conjectural events. He sums up by describing Shakespeare as "an ordinary, unpretentious, unacclaimed Stratford property-owner" whom no other literary figure of the time, except for Ben Jonson, ever claimed to have known.

Those who believe that someone else wrote the Works often accuse Shakespeare of being illiterate. As it turns out, this is not as far-fetched as it sounds. Shakespeare's parents were illiterate, as were his own two children (the younger one couldn't even sign her name). There is nothing to indicate that Will ever went to school, nor is there any indication of his literacy. "There is no scrap of evidence, no letters, notes, or drafts in his own hand, to prove that Shakespeare could use a pen. It is not known that he ever read or owned a book."

The alternate candidate who receives the most attention is Francis Bacon, who is often seen as the most likely suspect. Bacon was a philosopher, scientist, and statesman who lived during almost exactly the same period as Shakespeare. From a biographical standpoint, the aristocratic, educated genius of Bacon seems a more logical driving force behind the Works.

Mitchell recounts the pros and cons of the Baconian view, as always with a high degree of objectivity. Because Bacon was a statesman who developed and studied ciphers, it is thought that if he were the author, he would have hidden some sort of statement to that effect in the writings. Some people have spent their entire careers trying to find hidden codes in Shakespeare's Works. "The scale of their ambitions has ranged from the quest for anagrams and simple arrangements of letters, giving a version of the name Francis Bacon, to lengthy decipherings of entire Shakespeare plays, from which alternative texts have been extracted, with details of Bacon's secret life-story and his reasons for masquerading under the name of Shakespeare. For all practical purposes, the results of this vast, prolonged industry have been no more than zero." However, the author goes on to reveal some of the more tantalising examples that have been discovered.

Other candidates who are covered in detail are Edward de Vere, Earl of Oxford; William Stanley, Earl of Derby; Roger Manners, Earl of Rutland; Sir Walter Raleigh; and Christopher Marlowe, who is widely acknowledged by orthodox scholars as having collaborated with Shakespeare on at least some of the plays. There is also a section on Group theories, which maintain that Shakespeare was actually a group of writers.

In the end, the author offers some of his own thoughts and opinions concerning all that he has learned. He believes it is reasonable to say that Bacon wrote the poem *Venus and Adonis*, that de Vere wrote the Sonnets, and that other writers had a hand in individual plays. However, when all is said and done, there is no conclusive evidence for any candidate, including Shakespeare himself.

Thames and Hudson; $24.95
1996; hardcover; 272 pp
illus; 0-500-01700-X

WOMEN OF THE BEAT GENERATION
The Writers, Artists and Muses at the Heart of a Revolution
by Brenda Knight

While *A Different Beat* [above] is strictly an anthology of writings with capsule biographies of the contributors, *Women of the Beat Generation* aims to fully document the contributions of the women in and around the Beat movement. It does this by not only printing some of their works, but also through large biographical sections, photographs, and commentary from people who knew them.

The first section covers four forerunners of the Beats, including Scottish-born poet prodigy Helen Adam and Jane Bowles. "In terms of literature, Jane represents the transitional years of the forties and fifties, a modernist with roots firmly in the classic traditions of American literature. Her writ-

A chip off the old block: Jan Kerouac and her daddy-o (inset). *Women of the Beat Generation.*

ing is sharp and smart — close to the bone... She is at her best in describing the odd tensions between people, frustrated relationships, and human loneliness."

"The Muses" deals with five women who aren't known as much for their writing as for the roles they played in the lives of their Beat husbands: Joan Vollmer Adams Burroughs (common-law wife of William Burroughs), Carolyn Cassady (wife of Neal Cassady), Eileen Kaufman (wife of Bob Kaufman), and Jack Kerouac's two wives, Edie Parker Kerouac and Joan Haverty Kerouac. All of them except Joan Burroughs wrote memoirs, which are excerpted here. Joan is recalled in fragments from Herbert Hunke's autobiography and the William Burroughs bio *Literary Outlaw.*

The longest section looks at the female writers of the movement, fifteen in all. "At the age of twelve, Denise Levertov sent several of her poems to TS Eliot. Far from thinking her cheeky, the great poet wrote back two pages of 'excellent advice' and encouragement to continue writing based on what he deemed to be great promise." Lenore Kandel wrote one of the most controversial books to come out of the movement. "*The Love Book*, her most notorious collection of what she calls holy erotica, sent shockwaves throughout the Bay Area when it was published in 1965. After police raids on the Psychedelic Shop and City Lights bookstore in San Francisco, the chapbook was deemed pornographic and obscene. When challenged in court, Lenore defended it as a 'twenty-three-year search for an appropriate way to worship' and an attempt to 'express her belief that sexual acts between loving persons are religious acts.'"

The final, and shortest section, looks at two visual artists of the period — painter and multi-mediaist Jay DeFeo and painter Joan Brown, the primary founder of the California Figurative Art movement. Ted Jones and Ann Charters —

both of whom know many of the players in the Beat movement — contribute essays, and a detailed bibliography of all the writers rounds out the offerings.

Women of the Beat Generation covers 26 women — one less than *A Different Beat* — but only sixteen of them are the same. As far as the actual writing selections are concerned, there is surprisingly little overlap. In fact, there are only a handful of duplicates. This book tends to stay away from the more openly subversive material dealing with sex and drugs, while *A Different Beat* embraces it. If I could only get one book, it would probably be *Women of the Beat Generation*, because of the extensive background it provides, as well as the writings themselves. However, both books taken together go a very long way towards filling in the yawning chasms in available Beat literature.

Conari Press; $19.95

1996; hardcover; 370 pp

illus; 1-57324-061-3

4 DADA SUICIDES
translated by Terry Hale and others

This anthology presents work from four eccentric individuals who existed at the fringes of Dada. Centred in 1920s Paris, Dada was a nihilistic art movement whose attitudes were anti-government, anti-religion, anti-art… actually, anti-everything, including anti-Dada. Many of the Dadaists — full of grim humour — considered life to be a bad joke and dying by one's own hand to be a fitting end. Two of the men in this book committed suicide, and two simply disappeared. All of them were untamed rapscallions whose writings were just by-products of their wild lives (which were their true works of art).

Arthur Craven assumed the roles of poet, professor, boxer, dandy, forger, critic, sailor, draft dodger, prospector, thief, and more — "He was a tireless transverser of borders and resister of orders — a mongrel of nations with a vexatious urge to disarm. He took experience in the most extreme doses and sought life in the most extreme conditions he could find." He was last seen in Mexico in 1918 and speculation has run wild concerning his fate. Among the 47 pages of prose, poetry, and hybrids is "Hie!" — "I brazenly get drunk/

Even on bad smells./A complete mixture/Of elephant and angel;/Reader, under the moon I serenade/Your future misfortune…"

Jacques Rigaut was a dandy, gigolo, alcoholic, and heroin addict. He shot himself in the heart in 1929, and almost all of his work was published afterwards. Throughout his work, Rigaut's obsession with suicide and death bubbles up. In "Jacques Rigaut" he writes: "I cocked the hammer, I could feel the cold of the steel in my mouth… I pressed the trigger, the hammer clicked, but the shot didn't fire. I then laid the weapon on a small table, laughing a little nervously. Ten minutes later I was asleep. I think that I just made a rather important remark. What was it again? But of course! It goes without saying that I did not for an instant consider firing a second shot. The important thing was not whether I died or not but that I had taken the decision to die."

Julien Torma disappeared when he was thirty-one. Most of what he left behind are fragmentary thoughts about an impossibly wide selection of topics. "For my part, a creature interests me only when its reactions become totally alien to me. The leech isn't too bad, the starfish is quite an improvement. But slugs! Speak to me of slugs!" "The world is a tapestry whose reverse, variegated with hanging threads and whip-stitches, is the poem. When one has had a quick look BEHIND, one cannot prevent oneself having this in mind while looking at the right side." "The sacrilege that is truly sacrilegious is unselfconscious and ambiguous-like beauty. And it is more amusing."

Jacques Vaché was an editor and unpatriotic soldier who participated in a double suicide by overdosing on opium with an army buddy. His literary legacy consists of letters he wrote to André Breton and Théodore Fraenkel that were often illustrated with cartoonish drawings. These letters are the weakest part of the book, and are so boring I can't even find a good quote to use.

With the obvious exception of Vaché's letters, *4 Dada Suicides* preserves a worthwhile set of writings from some of the most intriguing eccentrics of their day.

Atlas (Serpent's Tail); £9.99, $17.99

1995; softcover; 269 pp

illus; 0-947757-74-0

GRAB BAG

HUMOUR

BARBIE UNBOUND
A Parody of the Barbie Obsession
by Sarah Strohmeyer

We all know that Barbie represents crass materialism, next-to-impossible beauty standards, and cynically-marketed careerism, but Sarah Strohmeyer is the latest in a string of satirists to make this expressly clear. Her book presents a line of Barbies that surely have the suits at Mattel seeing re—, er, pink.

Twenty-seven more realistic Barbies, represented by black and white photos and instructions for play, bring the plastic prima donna down to earth. They manage to mock Barbie's superficiality, while at the same poking fun at society's treatment of real women. The satire is as pointed as Barbie is bland.

In the first part of the book, Barbie takes on some real life roles that would undoubtedly leave her befuddled. There's Overweight Adolescent Outcast Barbie, Teenage Pregnant Barbie (Hormonally-Overcharged Ken denies responsibility: "'I was out driving in the Mustang with the guys,' he told everyone. 'Barbie who?'"), Grunge Barbie, Safe Sex Barbie, Barbie Boss from Hell, Pro-Life Barbie, Hot Flash Barbie, "P.C. Barbie Goes to the Co-op", "midge d. lang and Barbie DeGeneres: A Love Story", and Welfare Queen Barbie ("'Thank goodness for welfare,' she sighed as she poured herself another Coke and lit a Lucky. 'I couldn't work now anyway. Who'd look after my 13 Baby Sister Kellies?'").

In the second part, Barbie is cast in roles of historical import: Barbie D'Arc, Barbie Hearst ("Comes with rich parents, beret and nickname. AK-47 sold separately."), Barbie Clinton ("I don't make no cookies."), Anita Hill Barbie (you'll also need to buy a panel of white Kens and a Conservative African American Supreme Court Justice Ken), "It Rhymes with Bitch: Barbie at Salem", and Barbie Antoinette at the French Revolution. Occasionally, the humour goes from acid to pitch black. Barbie Braun is matched up with Führer Ken. "He was one anti-Semitic, angry murderous little Führer, but, hey, he was her anti-Semitic, angry, murderous little Führer." Barbie Plath is pictured sticking her head in an E-Z Bake Oven. Her poem "Barbby" (1962) reads: "Barbby I have to kill you/Except you are already dead—/Must think of something else instead/How 'bout this pencil in your head?"

Every once in a while, the humour is too obvious (PMS Barbie) or utterly inexplicable (the instructions for Barbie Curie), but this risky book proves that Barbie has come a long way, baby. Buy it immediately before it's forced off the market by Mattel.

New Victoria Publishers; $12.95

Overweight Outcast Adolescent Barbie.
Barbie Unbound.

1997; softcover; 120 pp
heavily illus; 0-934678-89-8

THE DEVIL'S DICTIONARIES
The Best of the Devil's Dictionary and
the American Heretic's Dictionary
by Ambrose Bierce & Chaz Bufe

In 1911 the American writer Ambrose "Bitter" Bierce — a rival and antagonist of Mark Twain — published *The Devil's Dictionary*, a collection of over 1000 cynical "definitions" that he had coined. Like so much of Bierce's other work, his dictionary skewered the hypocrisy and stupidity of the human race, along with serving up heaping doses of negativity and misanthropy.

In 1992 anarchist writer and publisher Chaz Bufe created his own thoroughly modern book of definitions, *The American Heretic's Dictionary* [*Outposts* p 16]. In this volume, Bufe has revised some of his definitions and added over 140, for a total of 450. He has also included around 200 entries from Bierce's dictionary, in order to create a single volume of cynicism that spans a century.

Here are some of Bierce's entries:

☞ "Abstainer, n. A weak person who yields to the temptation of denying himself a pleasure."

☞ "Birth, n. The first and direst of all disasters..."

☞ "Bride, n. A woman with a fine prospect of happiness behind her."

☞ "Christian, n... One who follows the teachings of Christ in so far as they are not inconsistent with a life of sin."

☞ "Destiny, n. A tyrant's authority for crime and a fool's excuse for failure."

☞ "Jealous, adj. Unduly concerned about the preservation of that which can be lost only if not worth keeping."

☞ "Philanthropist, n. A rich (and usually bald) old gentleman who has trained himself to grin while his conscience is picking his pocket."

☞ "Tariff, n. A scale of tax on imports, designed to protect the domestic producer against the greed of his consumer."

☞ "Year, n. A period of three hundred and sixty-five disappointments." (They didn't call him Bitter Bierce for nothing, you know.)

Here are a few of Bufe's definitions:

☞ "Accurate, adj. In accordance with one's opinions."

☞ "Desktop Publishing, n. A huge advance in communications technology, desktop publishing has put within the reach of nearly everyone the ability to produce hideous-looking printed materials…"

☞ "Folk Music, n. In the United States, a rudimentary variety of acoustic music played on $2,000 Martin guitars by down-home, folksy types from the backwoods of Boston, Manhattan, and San Francisco."

☞ "Long Term Relationship, n. An indication of mutual desperation. Put less delicately, a sure sign that both partners in a conjugal relationship feel certain that they are so unattractive that should they part, they would never, ever, get laid again…"

☞ "Objectivity, n. A journalistic term signifying gross servility to the powerful."

☞ "Political Dissident, n. A courageous, praiseworthy individual who challenges political and social evils in other countries. Political dissidents, of course, do not exist in the United States; instead, we are cursed with 'peaceniks,' 'eco-freaks,' 'pinkos,' 'commies,' 'eco-terrorists,' 'outside agitators,' 'tree huggers,' 'feminazis,' 'unpatriotic malcontents', and 'un-American crybabies.'"

☞ "Senator, n. A millionaire or, if newly elected, about to become one."

When this book first came out, I thought Bufe's pairing of his definitions with those of Bierce might be an act of hubris, but, after seeing them side by side, I think Bufe has created a worthy successor to *The Devil's Dictionary*. The stylised, often grotesquely distorted illustrations by JR Swanson complement the wicked wit displayed in this volume.

See Sharp Press; $9.95
1995; softcover; 144 pp
illus; 1-884365-06-X

HUNTING FOR LAWYERS
A Modest Proposal

by Marcus Meleton

It's no secret that lawyers are destroying America. People who just received word that a loved one has died in an accident get calls from lawyers. A man tossing his son in the air accidentally throws him into the blades of a ceiling fan. He sues the fan company and receives $60,000. An overweight guy with a bum ticker dies of a heart attack while starting his lawn mower. His family is awarded $1.7 million. Twenty million lawsuits are filed annually in the US — one for every ten adult Americans. What's going on here?

It's simple. There are too damn many lawyers. It's estimated that the US has 5% of the world's population but 70% of the world's lawyers! From 1970 to 1990 the number of lawyers almost tripled. This glut of ambulance-chasers has produced a shortage of sueable targets, so now anything and everything is lawsuit-bait. Lawyers are literally trying to keep themselves in business by creating new ways to sue your fellow human beings.

Marcus Meleton has the perfect solution. When an animal population becomes so large that it runs out of food, one method of dealing with the problem is to thin out the population. Same thing applies here. We simply declare hunting season on lawyers. It's the humane thing to do.

Hunting for Lawyers examines not only the reasons behind committing mass-murder of lawyers, it also looks at how this plan can be put into effect in a practical manner. First of all, the author doesn't want any vigilantism, so lawyer hunting must be legalised. To this end he provides model legislation called "Tough Love for Lawyers Act". He goes on to discuss licensing, general provisions, weapons and ammunition, camouflage, the different subspecies of lawyers, hunting methods (advanced methods include using a cellular phone-guided lawyer-seeking missile), and more. There are some ethical questions that must also be addressed. For example, "Is it ethical to hunt lawyers within 100 yards of BMW, Lexus, Mercedes, or Porsche dealerships? Or is it no more sporting than taking pot-shots at ducks resting on water?"

Filled with humorous cartoons, illustrations, and charts (and a bumper sticker), *Hunting for Lawyers* has the guts to call for a solution to a problem that affects every one of us (or will affect every one of us, sooner or later).

Sharkbait Press; $9.95
1995; softcover; 126 pp
heavily illus; 0-9635826-2-3

RADIO JIHAD

Judging from the many tapes that are circulating, prank phone calls are a difficult art form to master. *Radio Jihad* is definitely one of the funnier of these attempts. It consists of calls made to Christian radio shows and prayer lines. In one, an "old lady" is talking to the hosts when she yells at her husband to turn down the TV. A few moments later she shrieks, "Frank, is that a porn video? In the name of Jesus!…" and her voice trails off as she hangs up. During the next call, the prankster provokes an argument when he says that at his church they handle snakes because it's the "Word of God". When the hosts start snidely challenging him, he begins "speaking in tongues".

A supposed former bisexual swinger calls a prayer line

and begins talking about Annie Sprinkle, Jeff Stryker, and his favourite movie, *San Fernando Fudgepackers*. Some of the victims figure out what's going on, and they get steamed. One radio host rants that the prank calls they've been getting lately are "obviously coming from the homosexual community." He proclaims that the perpetrators "are a stench in the nostrils of God."

PolyEster Records and Books; $9.95Australian + $6 Airmail
1996, cassette tape

HISTORY

BLACK SLAVEOWNERS
Free Black Slave Masters in South Carolina, 1790-1860
by Larry Koger

It may seem beyond belief, but some slaveowners were themselves African Americans. Using a wealth of primary documents — wills, advertisements, the census — Larry Koger examines this apparent paradox. Although the number of black slaveholders (454 in 1890) was minimal compared to the number of whites, they still owned many slaves. "In Louisiana, Maryland, South Carolina, and Virginia, free blacks owned more than 10,000 slaves, according to the federal census of 1830."

There were many ways in which an African American could come to be a slaveholder. Some were former slaves who were freed because they saved a life, served valiantly in the military, etc. Others were freed because one of their parents was white. Many were second or third generation free blacks, so they never experienced slavery themselves.

It is true that some black slaveowners bought family members or friends in order to free them, but this doesn't apply to most cases. "To many black masters, slaves represented valued property being used to produce more wealth. These slaveowners, therefore, bought slaves as commercial assets"

Black Slaveowners is an eye-opener that proves once and for all that history is not predictable or neat and tidy, even though it was presented to us that way in school.

University of South Carolina Press; $14.95
1985; softcover; 286 pp
1-57003-037-5

COLUMBUS, KY AS THE NATION'S CAPITAL
Legend or Near Reality? — A Compilation of Accounts
by Allen Anthony

Examines the numerous legends that say the town of Columbus, Kentucky — located on the banks of the Missis-

sippi River — was almost chosen to be the nation's capital. These stories refuse to die out, and the author investigates whether or not they contain a kernel of truth.

River Microstudies; $12.95
1993; softcover; 160 pp
illus; 0-9625865-1-X

COOK & PEARY
The Polar Controversy, Resolved
by Robert M. Bryce

The question of which explorer reached the North Pole first — Frederick A. Cook or Robert E. Peary — created an ugly controversy in its day and remains one of history's greatest mysteries. Until now, that is. Relying almost exclusively on primary documents — many of which have never been published — Robert Bryce has created a mammoth, 1100-page tome that peels away the levels of controversy, exposes fallacies and hidden agendas, and finally reveals exactly what each explorer did and did not do.

Stackpole Books; $50
1997; hardcover; 1141 pp
illus; 0-8117-0317-7

LIES MY TEACHER TOLD ME
Everything Your American History Textbook Got Wrong
by James W. Loewen

It will hopefully come as no surprise that American history textbooks are to a large extent biased and misleading pieces of propaganda. In this book, James Loewen doesn't just talk in abstractions… he examines twelve popular American history textbooks (for junior high, high school, and college students) to see how they have played fast and loose with the truth.

This book has an overall leftist bias, but Loewen shows that textbooks whitewash anything that would make anybody — liberal or conservative — uncomfortable with US history. For example, only two books treat President Woodrow Wilson's racism in any depth. Five of the books mention it in passing, and the other five ignore it. "He was an outspoken white supremacist — his wife was even worse — who told 'darky' stories in cabinet meetings. His administration submitted a legislative programme intended to curtail the civil rights of African Americans, but Congress would not pass it. Unfazed, Wilson used his power as chief executive to segregate the federal government."

Conversely, textbooks also generally leave out the fact that Helen Keller became a radical socialist/communist after she found out the truth about disabilities. "Through research she learned that blindness was not distributed randomly throughout the population but was concentrated in the lower class. Men who were poor might be blinded in industrial accidents or by inadequate medical care; poor women who became prostitutes faced the additional danger of syphilitic blindness." She joined the Industrial Workers of the World and lavished praise on the new communist government in the Soviet Union.

A large part of the book focuses on the European take-over of America and subsequent relations with Native Americans, which is perhaps the most whitewashed subject of the textbooks. You can learn many fascinating facts here. When Columbus landed on Haiti, he demanded that the native people bring him the tons of gold he thought they were hiding. When they didn't bring enough, he had their hands chopped off. Anyone who attempted to resist in any way had his ears or nose cut off and was sent back to his village to serve as an example. "Spaniards hunted Indians for sport and murdered them for dog food." By 1555 — just 63 years after Columbus set up shop — there were no more native Haitians left. They had all either been massacred or sent to Spain and Portugal to be slaves. All of this is revealed in primary source material, such as letters written by Columbus and other members of his expedition.

Lies further blows the whistle on textbooks' treatments of violent abolitionist John Brown, Abraham Lincoln, the working class, the federal government, military interventionism, the Vietnam War, and the notion of progress. It also turns a critical eye on the images these textbooks use. Loewen says that when he asks people who were alive during the Vietnam War to recall the most powerful and important images from that war, they always talk about the South Vietnamese police chief shooting a suspected Viet Cong in the head, the little girl covered in napalm running down the road, the Buddhist monk burning himself to death in protest, and two others. Yet only one of the twelve textbooks reproduces a single one of these pictures (the execution shot). The next-to-the-last chapter discusses the dirty politics involved in creating an American history textbook.

Lies is highly recommended for those who would like a clearer picture of America's past and a look at how that past is being rewritten.

Touchstone Books (Simon & Schuster); $14.00
1995; softcover; 372 pp
illus; 0684818868

NAGASAKI JOURNEY
The Photographs of Yosuke Yamahata, August 10, 1945

by Yosuke Yamahata

On August 9, 1945, the US dropped a second atomic bomb on Japan, this one at Nagasaki. Less than twenty-four hours later, photographer Yosuke Yamahata, having been dispatched by the Japanese Army, was on the scene. He started taking pictures before dawn on the 10th and didn't stop until that night. He ended up with over 100 pictures, the most complete known photographic record of the destruction of Nagasaki or Hiroshima.

This book reproduces 70 of Yamahata's images, marking the first time in over 40 years this archive has been published. The photographs are beautifully printed as duotones from digitally restored negatives. They make for an unforgettable body of work.

There are almost no buildings in the pictures... just debris, debris, and more debris. The photo on page twelve shows the still-standing skeleton of a large building, perhaps a factory, with three smokestacks still intact. Mounds of wood

Complete decimation.
Nagasaki Journey.

and metal litter the rest of the frame. Page 49 contains one of the most haunting pictures. Accompanied by his mother, a little boy holding a rice ball stares solemnly at the camera. His face is blood-spattered, and his expression is an impenetrable mixture of about a dozen emotions, including sadness, shock, and numbness. There is a certain resignation in his features that you won't soon forget.

Picture after picture reveal a desolate landscape, filled with smoke from countless smouldering fires. One such scene also contains the head and neck of a dead horse jutting from underneath a wagon. Jun Higashi, a writer who accompanied Yamahata on his voyage, wrote this: "At one point I found myself walking on something soft and spongy. In the light of a crescent moon I realised I was standing on the corpse of a horse. There were what looked like coverless bomb shelters everywhere in front of me. As I tried to avoid one of the openings, using the light of the moon and the waning fires to see, some black creature rose suddenly from the hole and clung to my leg. I yelled in surprise, and a moan of 'Help me!' came from the creature — a bomb victim — holding my leg."

Other shots show bodies reduced to piles of charcoal. Perhaps the most horrifying picture (page 76) shows two little children, sprawled face up. In their blackened faces you can make out teeth and blank, staring eyes. Several photos are from an aid station. One shows a woman staring off into space as a dirty-faced baby nurses her left breast. Higashi writes, "Many of those treated suddenly stiffen and die, their bodies falling forward..."

This lavishly-produced book, printed in an oversized horizontal format, also contains an introduction by Robert Jay Lifton, three essays, a piece of fiction, a rare interview with Yamahata, technical notes, and a biography of Yamahata. He died aged forty-eight, not surprisingly, of cancer.

Pomegranate; $22.95

1995; oversized softcover; 128 pp

heavily illus; 0-87654-360-3

NOT SO!
Popular Myths About America from Columbus to Clinton
by Paul F. Boller Jr

History professor Paul Boller gleefully shreds 44 common misconceptions about US history. Most of these essays run roughshod over "common knowledge" notions most of us have. Some of the revelations are simply entertaining, while some are of great importance. Many people have a vested interest in believing these "facts", so their being dismantled may prove upsetting to liberals in some cases, and to conservatives in others.

The first essay addresses the notion we all learned in kindergarten — that Columbus was bucking the prevailing belief that the earth was flat. Wrong. "Most educated people in Columbus's day believed that the earth was round, not flat, and the problem Columbus faced in seeking support for his 'Enterprise of the Indies' centred on the size, not the shape, of the earth." Another essay says that before Columbus showed up, Native American society was not an idyllic, blissful utopia, but had its fair share of war, torture, and despotism.

People often say that the Vietnam War was the first war the US ever lost. It depends on your definition of losing, but it certainly appears as though America lost the War of 1812. "During the conflict, the United States sustained several major defeats at the hands of the British, experienced the humiliation of having British troops invade Washington, and, in the end, achieved none of the objectives for which it fought."

It's common to hear people griping that political campaigns are sleazy mudslinging campaigns and that no one respects the President anymore, unlike the way things were "in the good ol' days". Dirty campaigns and vicious attacks on the Prez are recent occurrences and show that our country is going down the tubes. Boller proves that this is so much malarkey. In one essay he demonstrates that Presidential elections used to be more vicious and nastier than they are today. "What respectable person today would think of announcing that one of the candidates for the highest office in the land was a 'carbuncled-faced old drunkard'? Or a 'mutton-headed cucumber'? Or a 'howling atheist'? Or a fool, drunkard, lecher, syphilitic, gorilla, crook, spy, thief, pickpocket, traitor, anarchist, revolutionary, madman, degenerate, murderer?"

In the essay on president-bashing, we learn that Clinton hasn't been subjected to any unprecedented name-calling. The public has always dissed Presidents mercilessly. "They called John Adams a fool and a criminal, Thomas Jefferson a coward and an atheist, Andrew Jackson a thief and a murderer, Martin Van Buren sly, selfish, and treacherous,... Grover Cleveland a wife-beater, William Howard Taft a Mr.

Malaprop, and Woodrow Wilson a syphilitic." To top it off, Washington, Lincoln, and FDR were treated much worse than that.

Elsewhere, we read that the Puritans didn't believe in religious freedom, the Continental Congress voted for independence from Britain on July 2, 1776, Washington didn't have wooden dentures, the Founders openly distrusted democracy, Thomas Paine wasn't an atheist, Uncle Tom was not a weak, submissive slave, Eleanor Roosevelt didn't have affairs, Senator McCarthy didn't uncover any communists in high places, the Pledge of Allegiance was written by a flaming socialist, Hillary Rodham Clinton is not the most assertive or influential First Lady in US history, and more.

History is a very squishy, subjective subject, and Boller's essays cannot be taken as gospel on the matters they address. He is at his weakest when he tries to pooh-pooh conspiracy theories. Yes, there is evidence that FDR didn't know about Pearl Harbor in advance and that Oswald did act alone, but to simply ignore the persuasive evidence to the contrary doesn't make sense. Boller refers to Gerald Posner's anti-JFK conspiracy book *Case Closed* as a "superb study" even though it has been shown to be deeply flawed, to the point of allegedly containing concocted quotes.

Still, *Not So!* presents many unarguable facts (e.g., the Pledge was written by a die-hard extreme leftist), and presents lots of food for thought about other cherished beliefs.

Oxford University Press; $10.95

1995; softcover; 278 pp

0-19-510972-4

SLAVERY AND THE FOUNDERS
Race and Liberty in the Age of Jefferson
by Paul Finkelman

In this book, Paul Finkelman — an historian who has published several books on slavery — shows the crucial role that pro-slavery thinking played in the formation of the US. During the Constitutional Convention, slavery was a heated topic of debate. But in the final analysis, "the slaveowners got substantially what they wanted: a Constitution that protected slavery." Besides examining how and why the Constitution condones slavery, Finkelman also looks at the effects of the Northwest Ordinance and the Fugitive Slave Law of 1793.

Two chapters focus specifically on the most influential of the Founders, Thomas Jefferson. The author feels that most historians have tried to whitewash Jefferson's support of slavery. During the time that Jefferson wrote the Declaration of Independence — including its famous lines about all men being created equal and having inalienable rights — he owned over 150 slaves. Many of his contemporaries released their slaves before and during the Revolution, but Jefferson never did. "To the contrary, as he accumulated more slaves he worked assiduously to increase the productivity and the property values of his labour force. Nor did he encourage his countrymen to liberate their slaves, even when they sought his blessing. Even at his death, Jefferson failed to fulfil the promise of his rhetoric. In his will he emancipated only five bondsmen, condemning some 200 others to the auction block."

Slavery and the Founders is an unforgiving look at the hypocrisy of the Founders of the US.

M.E. Sharpe; $21.95
1996; softcover; 230 pp
1-56324-591-4

100 YEARS OF LYNCHINGS
by Ralph Ginzburg

This just might be the most harrowing of all the books in *Psychotropedia*. It reprints newspaper accounts of lynchings and other extreme violence against African Americans from 1880 to 1961. There is no narration or background — only one brutal account after another, for 250 pages.

The first report comes from the *New York Truth Seeker*, April 17, 1880. Under the headline, "First Negro at West Point Knifed by Fellow Cadets", it reads: "James Webster Smith, the first coloured cadet in the history of West Point, was recently taken from his bed, gagged, bound, and severely beaten, and then his ears were slit. He says that he cannot identify his assailants. The other cadets claim that he did it himself."

If you think that lynchings were simple "string-'em-up" affairs, this book will give you a harsh dose of reality. Mobs weren't content to just kill their victims — they often tortured them mercilessly first. In 1904 on a Mississippi plantation, it was alleged that Luther Holbert — a black man — shot and killed a white plantation owner. Holbert and his wife fled, but were hunted by a mob, who killed two other African Americans during the chase because one of them looked like Holbert. The next day, they caught up with the Holberts.

Here is how an eyewitness described the scene in the Vocksburg (Mississippi) *Evening Post*, February 8, 1904: "When the two Negroes were captured, they were tied to trees and while the funeral pyres were being prepared, they were forced to hold out their hands while one finger at a time was chopped off. The fingers were distributed as souvenirs. The ears of the murderers were cut off. Holbert was beaten severely, his skull was fractured and one of his eyes, knocked out with a stick, hung by a shred from the socket.

"Some of the mob used a large corkscrew to bore into the flesh of the man and woman. It was applied to their arms, legs and body, then pulled out, the spirals tearing out big pieces of raw, quivering flesh every time it was withdrawn."

The atrocities continue non-stop, with headlines such as "Burned Alive", "Texans Lynch Wrong Negro", "Lynch Mob May Have Erred", "Negro Tortured to Death by Mob of 4,000", "Mob Lynches Negro Man, Flogs Three Negro Women", "Negro Youth Mutilated for Kissing White Girl", "Bumps into Girl; Is Lynched", "Lynch Leaders Declare Lynching Was 'Humane'", "Heart and Genitals Carved from Lynched Negro's Corpse", "Was Powerless to Aid Sister Who Was Raped and Lynched".

A few of the articles display frightening attitudes towards these types of killings. An editorial from the *Memphis Commercial-Appeal*, August 5, 1913, is headlined, "Lynch-ing Bad for Business". It says: "The killing of Negroes by white people in order to fatten an average ought to be stopped, and killing Negroes just because one is in bad humour ought also to be stopped." After talking about all the good work that blacks do, the writer concludes: "Commercially, then, he is a very valuable asset. It is not good business to kill them."

Black Classic Press; $14.95
1962, 1988; softcover; 270 pp
933121-18-0

MISCELLANEOUS

ALL THE SECRETS OF MAGIC REVEALED
The Tricks and Illusions of the World's Greatest Magicians
by Herbert L. Becker (The Great Kardeen)

Herbert Becker — known as the Great Kardeen — got into the *Guinness World Book of Records* for the fastest escape from a straight jacket (24 seconds). His other biggest claim to fame is that he served as Bozo the Clown's foil on the famous TV show. Now Becker is breaking the cardinal rule of magic by telling how a dozen magicians performed some of their most famous tricks.

One of Harry Houdini's legendary acts was to be lowered head-first into a telephone booth-like cell filled with water. Despite having his hands cuffed behind his back, he would always manage to escape. Becker lets the cat out of the bag… the handcuffs are props that release when the magician pushes a button on them, and the lid of the booth — which is securing the magician's feet — also has a release latch. Houdini would escape within a few seconds, but would wait two or three minutes to come staggering through the curtains around the booth.

Becker literally lets the cat out of the bag when he shows how Sigfried and Roy do their famous "tiger to assistant" trick. A cage on a wheeled base is rolled onstage. Inside the cage is an 800-pound Siberian tiger. The cage is covered with a large cloth, and panels attached to the base are raised to further cover the cage. Chains hanging from the ceiling are attached to the cage, which is lifted above the stage. The cloth is whisked away to reveal that the tiger is gone, just as the panels fall to reveal the magicians' assistant on the wheeled base. The first part of the trick — making the tiger disappear — occurs when the cloth is put over the cage. The back of the cage drops down to make a "drawbridge", and the feline slips out and through the stage curtains. The assistant is hiding in the false bottom of the wheeled base, and she comes out when the side panels are up. Tah-dah!

Becker also divulges the secrets of David Copperfield,

Surreptitious photo of Ruth Snyder getting fried in 1928. *Blood and Volts.*

Robert Houdin [sic], Howard Thurston, Harry Kellar, Houdini's brother Hardeen, Walter Gibson, Mark Wilson, Doug Henning, and the Amazing Kreskin, as well as his own tricks, such as the straightjacket escape. The main disappointment is the chapter on Copperfield. Despite Becker's promise to reveal the "big illusions" and the "great tricks", he doesn't tell how Copperfield made the Statue of Liberty or a jet plane disappear. Maddeningly, he mentions these feats in his intro to the chapter, but then goes on to reveal only such sleight-of-hand tricks as "the impossible knot" and "linking paperclips". Boo! Hiss!

Lifetime Books; $14.95
1994; softcover; 160 pp
illus; 0-8119-0822-4

BATTERED HUSBANDS
The Battle of the Sexes Is
Running Amuck
by Howard Gregory

In this book, Howard Gregory launches an all-out attack on feminism. "Empirical data shows that drugs, crime, poverty, teen-age pregnancy and practically everything that's wrong with the country is a result of the so-called Woman's Revolution. Why? The reason is so simple: It is a fact that the major cause of crime in the United States is broken families and it is also a fact that the Women's Movement is the primary cause of broken families — the dissolution of the American family." Divorce proceedings are initiated by women 70% to 91% of the time, according to various studies (including

one by Shere Hite, who came up with the 91% figure).

Gregory presents some ultra-politically-incorrect assertions. He quotes numerous studies and stats showing that husbands are just as often or more often victims of spousal abuse than wives. One study in a 1984 issue of *Justice Quarterly* even stated that: "Males are injured more often and more seriously than are female victims." Another nation-wide study showed that half of spousal murders committed by wives were premeditated, and one-third of the husband-killers had been previously arrested for violent crimes.

The way women and men are portrayed on TV and in the movies presents a problem for Gregory. Women are shown dominating their wimpy, indecisive men, who are constantly mumbling "Yes, dear," and trying to appease their wives/girlfriends. "Young girls are being brainwashed to believe the false values that are being ladled out on TV. Later when she's married with kids, she discovers that hubby won't conform and be a wimp like she's been taught to believe men should behave. A quick easy divorce is the only answer."

Two chapters look at cases of blatant inequality in the criminal justice system. Numerous women have received light sentences and even probation or acquittal for first degree murder. Women who statutorily rape underage boys often get off scot-free. In one case, a 19-year-old woman had sex with a 12-year-old boy and became pregnant. Under Wisconsin law, the boy's parents may become financially liable for the child.

While Gregory does bring up some facts and opinions that make good food for thought, sometimes he seems to be pointlessly reactionary. For example, he complains about the fact that there are female judges at boxing matches. In another chapter, he flatly states that "a father-headed family works, the mother-headed family doesn't."

And then there are the cartoons. Hundreds of them, taking up over 50% of the book. They are almost all of the "nagging pain-in-the-ass wife and put-upon henpecked husband" variety... *The Lockhorns, Herman, Beetle Bailey, Hagar the Horrible, Blondie*, etc. They were obviously added for humorous effect, but don't they convey the exact same message that Gregory rails at when it's depicted in TV and movies?

Battered Husbands may make you see red, or you may agree with it completely. Or you may think it makes some good points and some bad ones. No matter how you react to it, though, it is a bold statement supporting a much-hated position.

Howard Gregory Associates; $14.95
1991; oversized softcover; 126 pp
heavily illus; 0-9607086-7-7

BLOOD AND VOLTS
Edison, Tesla, and the Electric Chair
by Th. Metzger

A surprising history of how the electric chair was invented. Covers the history of electrocution as a method of killing, the original sociopolitical debates over using the Chair, and the corporate influences at work in deciding which type of current (AC or DC) would be used to fry the condemned.

Autonomedia; $12
1996; softcover; 191 pp
illus; 1-57027-060-0

BULLFIGHT
by Garry Marvin

Bullfight is a thorough, balanced examination and exploration of the modern Spanish bullfight. The author explains how the bullfight developed and evolved, its role in Spanish society, exactly what happens during a bullfight, how the bulls are bred, tested, and selected, the career aspects of being a matador, the psychological and sociological aspects of bullfights, and much more.

University of Illinois Press; $16.95
1988, 1994; softcover; 235 pp
illus; 0-252-06437-2

BUMPER STICKER WISDOM
America's Pulpit Above the Tailpipe
by Carol W. Gardner

I have to admit that when I first heard about this book, I didn't have high hopes. For some reason I was picturing a quickie book that just reprinted a bunch of bumpersticker phrases, one to a page, with no commentary. I was pleasantly surprised to see that *Bumper Sticker Wisdom* is at the other end of the spectrum — a coffee-table book that is imaginatively designed, expensively produced, and more in-depth than I ever would have guessed. Rather than just list phrases from bumperstickers, Carol Gardner chased down the people driving the vehicles and talked with them about their means of expression.

Each oversized page is devoted to one sticker, which is reproduced large as life. There is also a colour photograph of the sticker's owner, posing next to his or her vehicle. The following stats are given for each person: age, education, occupation, favourite pastime(s), favourite book, favourite movie, and pet peeve. They tell why they chose to display their stickers, and Gardner occasionally offers an interesting anecdote.

The messages on the stickers cover a wide range — serious and goofy, political and religious, cynical and optimistic. Quite a few of the stickers deal with sex and relationships. One 23-year-old guy with a blue sticker that reads, "Why Can't I Be Rich Instead of Well Hung!", says, "Girls drive by and give me a thumbs-up sign." Gardner comments, "He told me about not being rich, but I don't think he was comfortable commenting on the second half of the message." The one sticker that made me laugh out loud belongs to a Portland graphic designer: "My Son Knocked Up Your Honor Roll Student." His other sticker, which he also created, says, "My Kid Sold Drugs To Your Honor Roll Student."

Sometimes stickers with opposing messages are featured on facing pages. On one left-hand page is an elderly man displaying his "Rush Is Right!" sticker. Across from him, a young guy brandishes a sticker proclaiming, "Rush Is Reich". Elsewhere, a middle-aged man sports a sticker that says: "Keep the Queens Out of the Marines". The author

The matador kills the weakened bull.
Bullfight.

notes that the man's wife "doesn't like his bumper sticker and told me she won't ride in his car until he takes it off." He sure wouldn't get along well with the guy on the opposite page, whose sticker declares: "The Marines Are Looking For a Few Good Men... So Am I!" next to a pink triangle.

Some of the other stickers featured:

☞ "Question Internal Combustion", on a bicycle.
☞ "A Drunk Driver Killed My Daughter"
☞ "You Are on Indian Land"
☞ "I Know Jack Shit!"
☞ "Jelly Donuts — Not Nazis" ("... it is a Dada statement in that it means absolutely nothing and means a lot of things at the same time.")
☞ "My Goddess Gave Birth To Your God!"

Bumper Sticker Wisdom is an engaging book. If you've ever seen a sticker and wondered, "What kind of jerk would put that on their car?" or, "I bet that person's pretty cool," here's your chance to find out.

Beyond Words Publishing; $19.95
1995; oversized softcover; 174 pp
heavily illus; 1-885223-17-X

THE COCKFIGHT
A Casebook
edited by Alan Dundes

The existence of cockfighting forcefully reminds me that the human race is still a savage, sub-reptilian bunch of Cro-Magnons. At least with the other most popular blood sport — bullfighting — there's some sort of challenge. And there's always the possibility that a matador will hopefully get a taste of his own medicine. Cockfighting, though, consists of watching a couple of birds slice each other to shreds. That's a sport? But cockfighting definitely has an appeal. It's been around for over 2500 years and despite being outlawed right and left, it continues to flourish.

Still, despite its age, this gruesome and usually illegal activity is shrouded in mystery and secrecy. Thus, it is perfect outpostish material. Ultra-cool folklorist Alan Dundes, author of *Cracking Jokes* [*Outposts* p 234] and co-author of the "office folklore" series, has collected 18 essays, stories, and articles that represent the absolute pinnacle of "cockfighting scholarship".

The first two essays are from age-old observers, St. Au-

Balinese farmer with his fighting cock, 1956.
The Cockfight.

gustine and Yuan Hung-Tao of the Ming Dynasty, who wonder why cocks fight and why men are so attracted to the bloody spectacle. The next essay, "The Rules of Cockfighting", reveals that this is not a haphazard activity but, rather, it has a set of absolutely binding rules, which may vary in different locations and times.

Six selections present vivid, at times fictional, accounts of cockfights from all over the world — London, Tahiti, Southern California, Ireland, Mexico, and Puerto Rico. In the latter essay, an anthropologist describes a fight in which one bird is badly wounded. During a lull, in which both birds stop fighting, the owners rush in and each grabs his bird. "One takes the bloody head and neck of his pet into his mouth, and sucks the congealing blood, and then breathes new life into the sinking cock from his own lungs; the other resorts to a water bottle from which he fills his mouth and blows it on the head and neck, and under the wings of his bird until the closing eyes brighten from the refreshing spray." Incidentally, cockfighting is still legal in Puerto Rico. It is promoted by the government and is virtually the national male pastime.

The rest of the essays try to answer the whys of this bloodsport. "The Fraternity of Cockfighters" uses interviews with breeders, referees, and spectators to see how these people justify their participation and interest. Most often they accuse those who condemn cockfighting of hypocrisy, pointing to such "acceptable" barbarisms as lobster-cooking and boxing. They also excuse their interest by saying that the cocks were born to fight. It's genetically wired into them, and by slashing each other to ribbons they are achieving self-actualisation (hey, that's what this article says).

Anthropologist H. B. Kimberly Cook invaded the all-male

world of cockfighting in Venezuela for her study, in which she theorises: "Cockfighting is, in part, a ritualistic form of aggression which serves as a format or context in which culturally derived patterns of hostility can be expressed, negotiated, and temporarily resolved." Pushing, shoving, and fist-fighting at these events are tolerated and almost expected. The editor, in his essay, "Gallus and Phallus", attempts to "demonstrate that the cockfight is a homoerotic male battle with masturbatory nuances."

Through its use of extremely varied sources, *The Cockfight* sheds a unique light on this disturbing custom.

University of Wisconsin Press; $19.95
1994; softcover; 290 pp
illus; 0-299-14054

COSMIC TRIGGER, VOLUME III
My Life After Death
by Robert Anton Wilson

Robert Anton Wilson is a reality-hacking guerrilla ontologist who delights in blasting us out of the rigid "reality tunnels" we've let ourselves get locked into. This is the much-anticipated third volume of interconnected essays in the *Cosmic Trigger* series. "This book revels in mysteries, wallows in puzzles and ambiguities. We will, so to speak, peer at wiggling things that look like rattlesnakes from one side and look much more like the middle of next week from a different but equally plausible angle of view."

Wilson discusses one of the most successful Internet hoaxes, which happened to involve him. On February 22, 1994, someone posted an obituary for Wilson, claiming that it came from the *Los Angeles Times*. He only found out about it when friends started calling his house to see if he had indeed shuffled off this mortal coil. Like a modern-day Mark Twain, he was happy to report that rumours of his death were greatly exaggerated, but it got him thinking that maybe he had died and didn't even realise it. He refers to a line of reasoning Jonathan Swift once proposed that says "just because a man claims he hasn't died and may even believe it himself, this does not logically require us to credit his unsupported testimony." Later, Wilson's friend and writing partner Robert Shea died, but, ironically, some people didn't believe it, saying that it was another hoax.

"Painter Jailed for Committing Masterpieces" deals with a notorious art forger known as Elmyr. This mysterious man's paintings are so beautifully and perfectly rendered that many of the art world's greatest "experts" have declared them genuine works of the Masters. Not all of Elmyr's fakes have been uncovered, and the general consensus is that perhaps 2% of the paintings we attribute to the great artists are actually Elmyrs. Wilson speculates that perhaps 25% to 50% of the masterworks of the twentieth century (Elmyr's speciality) could have come from the hand of this faker. "Every time you walk through a museum and see a Picasso or a Matisse that you particularly like, you should stop and ask, 'Now did Picasso or Matisse do that, or did Elmyr do it?'" Later he muses that perhaps *Cosmic Trigger III* is a Robert Anton Wilson forgery. "Assuming some literary Elmyr perpetrated this, do you regard it as a 'good' forgery (containing very

Wilsonian prose) or a 'bad' forgery (a weak imitation of Wilsonian prose)?"

Through the rest of the book Wilson gleefully romps through conspiracy theories, the theory of evolution, *The Bell Curve*, Orson Welles' *Touch of Evil*, Timothy Leary, Carl Sagan, Philip K. Dick, and dozens of other topics, using them as springboards into wild trains of thought that help our minds run off the rigid tracks of reality.

New Falcon Publications; $14.95
1995; softcover; 247 pp
1-56184-112-9

EVERYTHING YOU KNOW IS WRONG

by Paul Kirchner

An endlessly readable book that trashes around 300 things that almost all of us unthinkingly accept as fact. For example, no "witches" were burned in Salem, Massachusetts. Of the twenty people convicted of being witches, nineteen were hanged and one was crushed. Also, abortion has not been illegal throughout most of US history. There were no anti-abortion laws until the 1820s, and it wasn't until the end of that century that abortion was generally outlawed. It's been estimated that for every six live births in the second half of the nineteenth century, there was one abortion.

Among the other "truths" that are deflated: the American Revolution was not just against the British (almost as many American colonists fought against the Revolution as for it); violent student protests in the US didn't start in the 1960s (one of the earliest occurred in 1818); Captain Kirk never said, "Beam Me Up, Scotty"; Chief Seattle never made his eloquent environmental speech (i.e., "How can you buy the sky?..."); diamonds are not the most valuable gemstone; one dog year does not equal seven human years; Einstein and Churchill were actually outstanding students; the word "gay" has been used to denote attraction to the same sex since the early 1900s, "and some linguists date it back to Elizabethan England"; John Kennedy was not the US's youngest President; human beings are not the only animals that kill for sport; Napoleon was not short; during Prohibition it was not illegal to drink alcohol (it was only illegal to "manufacture, sell or transport" it); and suicides are not most common during holidays.

General Publishing Group; $14.95
1995; oversized softcover; 192 pp
heavily illus; 1-881649-70-9

THE F WORD

edited by Jesse Sheidlower

Fuck yes! Finally, a whole fucking book devoted to the most useful word in the English motherfucking language. It's a noun, a verb, an adjective, an adverb, an interjection, and an infix (a word placed inside another word). What the fuck is this wondrous word? What do you think it is, fuckhead? "Fuck"? You're absofuckinglutely correct!

The F Word is an awe-inspiring compilation of "fuck", as it's been used in endless variations and permutations. Besides listing and giving the meaning of every way to use "fuck" or any other word or phrase with "fuck" in it, this book lists examples of how those words and phrases have been used in literature, popular fiction, men's magazines, the military, the general population, and, to a lesser extent, the Internet and pop culture. These examples are generally presented as a clause or a single sentence with the minimum bibliographical information necessary to identify its source. For instance, under "clusterfuck" is this gem: "**1977** *National Lampoon* (Aug.) 50: Well, they're usually pretty wrapped up in a cluster-fuck with the photo models." "BFD" (big fucking deal) contains this reference: "**1988** J. Brown & C. Coffey *Earth Girls Are Easy* (film): 'There's a UFO in my pool. A UFO.' 'BFD.'"

The word "fuck", all by itself, has over 20 meanings. As a noun it can mean an act of copulation, copulation itself, a sexual partner, a damn ("not worth a fuck"), anything whatsoever ("don't know fuck"), as a standard of comparison, ("It's raining like a fuck"), a bit of difference, semen (now used rarely), a despicable person, an evil turn of events. When used as a verb, it can mean to copulate, to harm ("I was, in short, fucked"), to botch, to cheat or victimise, to cease or abandon, or to toy or meddle ("Don't fuck with my mind!"), as well as being used in phrases implying brutalisation, as an interjection to express dismay, or as a curse or oath. In the adjectival sense, it means depicting copulation ("fuck films").

"Fuck", in its simplest form, is used in the phrases "flying fuck", "for fuck's sake", "fuck of" ("This is a fuck of a rain"), "holy fuck!", "the fuck" ("the fuck you do"), "fucked by the fickle finger of fate", "fuck 'em all but six", "fuck the dog", "get fucked", ad fucking infinitum.

The F Word also covers such indispensable members of the English language as "ass-fuck", "celebrity-fucker", "dumbfuck", "fan-fucking-tastic", "fist fuck", "FNG" ("fucking new guy"), "fuckable", "motherfucker", and "RTFM" ("read the fucking manual"). Naturally, the military acronym "SNAFU" ("situation normal all fucked up") is here, along with its numerous bastards — "FUBAR" ("fucked up beyond all recognition"), "FUBIS" ("fuck you, buddy, I'm shipping out"), and "JANFU"("joint Army-Navy fuck up"). The final category of words covered are the euphemisms for "fuck" and its relatives — "eff", "farg", "freaking", "frig", "futhermucker", "mofo", etc.

For years, I've wondered where the phrase "fucking-A" came from (it has several meanings, but it's generally an interjection expressing complete agreement). No regular dictionary, swear word dictionary, slang dictionary, or military slang dictionary I've checked has even mentioned it, never mind given an etymology. Finally, the answer is close at hand, or so I thought: "origin unknown; perhaps taken from a phrase such as 'you're fucking A-number-one right!'" A fucking lot that helps me!

Actually, the word "fuck" itself is of dubious origin. In his introductory essay, the editor discounts certain theories as too uncertain. He completely lays to rest the common fallacy that "fuck" started as an acronym for "For Unlawful Carnal Knowledge", or any other such phrase. So where the fuck does it come from? "'Fuck' is a word of Germanic origin. It is related to words in several other Germanic languages, such as Dutch, German, and Swedish, that have sexual meanings as well as meanings like 'to strike' or 'to thrust'." Despite the fact that it was developed much earlier, "scholars have yet to discover an example of "fuck" (or any of its Germanic relatives) before the fifteenth century."

The book's last section discusses the equivalents of "fuck" in other languages, including French, German, Spanish, Dutch, Hebrew, and Esperanto (just in case you want to cuss someone out in a universal language).

The F Word is unfuckingbelievable. What else can I say?

Random House; $12.95

1995; small softcover; 235 pp

0-679-76427-5

Young Kanzi using his keyboard to communicate. *Kanzi.*

GOLD!
The Way to Roadside Riches
by Tom Bishop

This slim booklet will get you on your way to prospectin' for gold. You can do it in your spare time with inexpensive supplies, or you can take a more serious approach using $5000+ worth of equipment. The author covers the tried and true method known as panning. You take your pan into a stream, fill it with a shovelful of gravel, and dip it into water. Scrape off an inch of the gravel with a piece of wood and shake the pan. Fill it again with water, scrape, and shake. You'll eventually get down to fine sand. You may have gotten a nugget, but if not, you'll have to do some more work to recover the gold flakes. Use a magnet to remove most of the magnetite. You can then put a small amount of mercury in the pan. "The mercury will roll around and pick up the gold without picking up anything else." Pretty nifty, eh?

If you want to get more involved, you can buy or make a rocker, sluice, Long Tom, or riffle. Diagrams are included. If you strike it big and hit a motherlode of the shiny stuff, there are several gold recovery machines that you can get. Should you want to cheat by using a new-fangled invention, the author describes several mineral detectors.

Knowing where to look is important, so you can refer to the maps of the best gold-bearing areas in a dozen Western states. Once you've found gold, you'll need to refer to the chapter on staking your claim. Finally, there's a glossary of terms and a listing of further reading material.

Johnson Books; $4.95

1971; staple-bound softcover; 51 pp

illus; 0-933472-31-5

GREASY GRIMY GOPHER GUTS
The Subversive Folklore of Childhood
by Josepha Sherman & TKF Weisskopf

Man oh man, does this book send me reeling back to my younger years. Folklorist Josepha Sherman and publisher TKF Weisskopf have recorded for posterity hundreds of those disgusting, forbidden rhymes that we sang to other kids on the playground but didn't dare tell our parents, as well as newer chants the whippersnappers nowadays are singing.

The authors offer a little commentary on the various themes running through subversive children's folklore and on some of the individual rhymes, but they keep it to a minimum. They abstain from sweeping theorisation and let the kids speak for themselves.

The first section, "Getting Down to Basics", shows that even if adults won't deal openly with topics like sex, death, illness, bodily functions, and other "gross stuff", kids definitely will. The book's title comes from perhaps the most widespread of the gross-out rhymes, presented in twenty different versions. The eleventh version is closest to the way I remember it: "Great green globs of greasy grimy gopher guts,/ Mutilated monkey meat, Chopped-up baby parakeet,/ French-fried eyeballs rolling down the dirty street,/And I forgot my spoon..." Then there are the famous adventures of Rosie (sometimes Miss Suzy, or, the way I learned it, the insatiable Lulu). "Rosie had a rooster,/Rosie had a duck./ She put them both together/To see if they could — " (The last line of each verse is a "dirty word" and is never sung). And who could ever forget that immortal paean to beans?: "Beans, beans, they're good for your heart,/The more you eat, the more you fart..."

In the section "Dealing with Authority", kids use rhymes to zap teachers, the church, politics, bullies, and other threats to their well-being. "Glory, glory hallelujah,/Teacher hit me with a ruler./I met her at the door/With a loaded .44,/And she ain't my teacher no more." A simple change of a word subverts a Christian children's song: "Jesus hates you this I know/ 'Cause the Bible tells me so."

The final section, "Advertising Follies", shows that kids can cast a jaded eye on corporate culture. Many rhymes parody commercial jingles, TV theme songs, rock songs, superheroes, etc. One such ditty slams a fast food joint: "McDonald's is your kind of place,/Hamburgers smashed in your face,/French fries up your nose,/Pickles between your toes..." A new genre of rhymes has cropped up in response to Barney the Dinosaur's media blitzkrieg. These anti-Barney songs are so numerous that they have earned their own chapter. Most of them parody the closing song, an innocuous bit of feel-good doggerel which starts out: "I love you, you love me..." One of the many satirical versions goes like this: "I hate you, you hate me,/Let's get together and kill Barney,/With a shotgun blast and Barney's on the floor./No more purple dinosaur."

Greasy Grimy Gopher Guts is a fun book that is also a near-definitive statement on an important but ignored area of folklore.

August House; $14.95
1995; softcover; 250 pp
0-87483-444-9

INTUITION
A Magazine for the Higher Potential of the Mind

Intuition is a magazine devoted to what are sometimes called "right brain" functions — particularly intuition and creativity. Although there is some theorising about these functions of the mind, the emphasis is on how people are harnessing them and how you can tap into them to a greater degree. Past articles have covered intuition and healing, intuition and science, creativity in the classroom, painting with light, harnessing your brainwaves, synchronicity, shamanism, the hidden history of creativity, emotional intelligence, writers who get ideas from their dreams, and intuition and the Internet. "I pondered whether there was some way in which, if we all had our own separate Web pages where we hyperlinked ourselves to every other Web page, we could become a kind of electronic universal mind, in which each of us was but a single neuron in a great landscape of synapses linking everything to everything else." (From the April 1996 issue.)

Intuition Magazine/PO Box 460773/San Francisco CA 94146-9806
Single issue: $6
Six issue sub (one year): $19.95. Can/Mex: $24.95. Elsewhere: $29.95

KANZI
The Ape at the Brink of the Human Mind

by Sue Savage-Rumbaugh & Roger Lewin

One of the world's foremost experts on ape communication tells of her research and adventures with Kanzi, a chimpanzee whose language and reasoning skills are so advanced that he's forced scientists to rethink ideas about intelligence and linguistics as they relate to primates, including ourselves. Through controlled experiments and day-to-day interaction, we see that Kanzi and the other apes being studied seem to truly think (e.g., plan ahead, make informed decisions), use symbolic language, co-operate with each other, use "human" gestures, and do other things that indicate sophisticated mental capacities.

John Wiley & Sons; $15.95
1994; softcover; 308 pp
illus; 0-471-15959-X

LEST WE FORGET WHITE HATE CRIMES
Howard Beach and Other Racial Atrocities

by Alphonso Pinkey

A harsh look at the rise of white violence against blacks during the 1980s, focusing specifically on several incidents: the twelve white teenagers in Queens who beat a black man and chased another one onto the highway where he was killed; a white serial killer who murdered four black men in

The Superstition Mountains, said to be home of the fabled Lost Dutchman Mine. *Lost Gold and Buried Treasure*.

Manhattan over an eight-hour period; Bernhard Goetz, who shot four black teenagers he believed were trying to rob him on a New York subway; and others.

Third World Press; $14.95
1994; softcover; 284 pp
0-88378-088-7

LET'S DEVELOP!
A Guide to Continuous Personal Growth

by Dr. Fred Newman

Dr. Fred Newman — author of *The Myth of Psychology* (see the Freedom chapter) — offers a radical new approach to helping yourself. Psychologists often say that development ends after early childhood, but Newman thinks that we can — and must — keep developing throughout our entire lives. This book is about changing your attitude toward life and learning to look at things differently. "The practical question, from the social therapeutic point of view, is not How much can I get from this? Nor is it What's the right thing to do? Rather, in any and all life situations, good and bad, early and late, big and little, I urge that the question be How do we develop from this? That, as I see it, is an emotionally healthy attitude in a sometimes very sick world."

Castillo International; $11.95
1994; softcover; 263 pp
0-9628621-6-9

LOST GOLD AND BURIED TREASURE
A Treasure Hunter's Guide to 250 Fortunes Waiting to Be Found

by Kevin D. Randle

In the United States alone, billions of dollars' worth of treasure remains undiscovered. If you'd like to get in on the action, this book will give you all the known facts to point the way. Seventeen hidden fortunes (five lost mines and a dozen buried treasures) are covered in detail. The other section of the book gives brief descriptions of hundreds of lost treasures, with at least two, and usually more, located in every state in the US.

M. Evans and Company; $19.95
1995; hardcover; 301 pp
illus; 0-87131-792-3

MATHEMATICAL SCANDALS

by Theoni Pappas

When you think about which branches of human endeavour have been filled with feuds, controversies, backstabbing, intrigue, and eccentric personalities, the first ones that might come to mind are art and literature. There's no end to the scandals, alliances, betrayals, drunkeness, and thievery that have surrounded artists and writers for hundreds of years. In the sciences, the most obviously heated area is probably psychology. Things got off to a rocky start when mentor Sigmund Freud and disciple Carl Jung had their acrimonious parting of ways, and things haven't calmed down a whole lot since then. So when you're trying to name tumultuous fields of study, mathematics is probably way, way down on the list. Just the mention of maths brings up images of boring, unyielding formulas being worked on by quiet, shy men in dark university offices. As this book will demonstrate, though, mathematics has been a hotbed of intrigue, arguments, and weird characters.

Twenty-one short chapters — each devoted to one subject — reveal the sordid, seamy side of the field: the gambling addiction of Ada Byron Lovelace (the world's first computer programmer and daughter of George Gordon, Lord Byron), the theft of L'Hospital's Rule from Bernoulli and Leibniz, the true origins of the Platonic Solids (hint: Plato didn't discover them), Kurt Gödel's rampant paranoia, Isaac Newton's mood swings and erratic behaviour, the destruction of Georg Cantor's career and mental health by a fellow mathematician, the brawl over who invented calculus, and the politically and religiously inspired murder of Hypatia, the first famous female mathematician.

Mathematician and computer theorist Alan Turing helped end World War II by playing an instrumental role in cracking the Germans' Enigma code. Proving that no good deed goes unpunished, Turing was later arrested for being gay and was forced for one year to take experimental drugs to "cure" him of his orientation. Turing's death a year later has been ruled a suicide, but there have been suggestions that he was taken out by the intelligence community.

In recent years, people have begun to question whether Albert Einstein is wholly responsible for the theories he is said to have developed. Some contend that Einstein's first wife, Mileva Maric — whom he met when they were both college students in Switzerland — either was an equal partner with Einstein or was the principal architect of the theory of relativity and other breakthroughs. Some of the tantalising evidence the author reveals comes from letters Einstein wrote to Maric when they were separated during college breaks. "His letters make reference to *our* work, *our* theories, *our* investigations. For example, in a letter to Maric in 1901 he writes: 'How happy and proud I shall be when together *we* shall conclude victoriously *our* work on relative motion.'"

Mathematical Scandals is written in a way that is easy for the layperson to digest. Besides relating mathematical skulduggery, it also manages to inject a healthy dose of orthodox knowledge, meaning that you'll learn not only that Hippasus was possibly killed by angry Pythagoreans but also

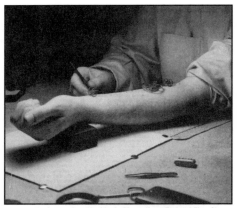

Professor Roy Heckler's Marvellous Trained Flea Circus takes a working lunch. *Shocked and Amazed!*

what he discovered that upset them so badly.

Wide World Publishing; $10.95
1997; softcover; 151 pp
heavily illus; 1-884550-10-X

MORBID CURIOSITY

Morbid Curiosity is a magazine — which, due to the large amount of text and scarcity of ads, seems more like a book — that covers "dark" subjects that hold a forbidden fascination. As of this writing, only the premiere issue is available (the second issue will be out by the time you read this). Most of the essays are first-person accounts of encounters with the hidden, the strange, and the macabre. Several authors recount their experiences with drugs, including mescaline, DMT, absinthe, and a potion called a Gargle Blaster (absinthe, ether, nitrous oxide, GHB, candy corn, two flavours of Schnapps, and an optional olive). Of the latter, Jasmine Sailing writes: "It literally does feel like your brain is getting bashed out at the moment you swallow it... Eventually I drifted into a zone and was happy with lying in a hammock in the middle of the room (more of the cold and floating surreality than absinthe alone gives you), watching people mill around. Or flap around, if they had just quaffed a Gargle Blaster — some of the funniest reactions were the people who bugged their eyes out and immediately began flapping around the room like headless chickens."

A lot of the adventures have to do with death... trips to the Dachau concentration camp, the Westgate death museum/gallery, a crematorium, and the San Francisco College of Mortuary Science; a history of erotic strangulation; an encounter with a ghost; confessions of a necrophile; and a look at the personifications of death.

Other pieces involve the Torture Museum in Amsterdam, fossils, firewalking, spontaneous shrines, and edible insects (with recipes). Contributors write about attending a Black Mass, viewing the aurora borealis, and helping to make extremely heavy SM movies.

I hope this magazine will have a long run. My morbid curiosity can never be completely satisfied, but a publication like this sure helps.

Automatism Press/PO Box 170277/San Francisco CA 94117
Email: AutomPress@aol.com
WWW: www.charnel.com/automatism
Single issue: $6 ppd. Can: $8 ppd. Elsewhere (Airmail): $9

OPUS MALEDICTORUM
A Book of Bad Words
edited by Reinhold Aman

Reinhold Aman is probably the only academic to devote his full-time studies to cuss words, blasphemies, insults, sex slang, slurs, and the other "black sheep" of language. He has been an independent scholar since 1974, when he left the ivory tower of academia because the prudes there don't think that *maledicta* (Latin for "bad words") are a proper area of inquiry, which is downright idiotic when you consider how widely such language is used and how many problems it triggers (from wars and nation-wide censorship to foul-mouthed kids getting beaten by their parents). Aman edits and publishes *Maledicta: The International Journal of Verbal Aggression*, the only publication of its kind, which is the source for the 49 articles found in *Opus Maledictorum*. (For some reason, many of these articles also appeared in Aman's 1993 book, *Talking Dirty* [*Outposts* p 237].)

In "Analysis of a Four-Letter Word", professor Margaret Fleming subjects the word "shit" to a fascinating etymological history. Now, you would really think that a word as old and as ubiquitous as this one would have rated reams of research. Whole books. Bachelor Degree programmes at major universities. But we must be content with this twelve-page article, which reveals, among other things: "The conjectural Indo-European root *skei-* had the basic meaning of 'to separate', and it has given us, in addition to "shit", such widely differing words as "science" (from the Latin *scire*, 'to know' — that is to 'separate' one thing from another), "shin" (from "shinbone", originally 'a piece cut off'), "sheaf", "scissors", and "schizophrenia", in all of which the notion of separation can be discerned."

"How to Hate Thy Neighbor" relays 23 pages of slurs based on race or nationality, often giving notes on usage and origin. "Dago" is derived from the first name "Diego"; "frog" is a shortened version of "frog-leg eater", "hebe/heeb" is a shortening of "Hebrew"; "spic" comes from the Latin pronunciation of "speak". A "honky" is "Any white person in black ghetto slang, but especially one espousing liberal causes, integration in particular. The implication may be that such people honk their horns a lot, i.e. make noise, but don't actually do much about what they profess to believe."

The other articles cover talking dirty in Spanish, sexual rhyming slang, Russian obscenity, graffiti on desks in college classrooms, pet names for genitals, Canadian sexual terms, Italian blasphemies, euphemisms for farting, offensive rock band names, Mozart's odd behaviour as Tourette's syndrome, and comedians' responses to hecklers. Whoever thought that linguistics could be this much fun?

Marlowe and Company; $14.95
1996; softcover; 364 pp
illus; 1-56924-836-2

Phallic procession at Tagata shrine in Japan.
The Strangest Human Sex, Ceremonies and Customs.

SHOCKED AND AMAZED!
On & Off the Midway
edited by James Taylor

This irregularly published, profusely-illustrated book series delves into the culture of side-shows, carnival midways, grind shows, and dime museums. The first two instalments are out of print, but the second two are still around. Volume 3 (1996) displays the Human Blockhead, Ripley's Strange Man, the Siamese twin Hilton Sisters, chastity belts, chimp wrestling, a history of torture, and more. Step right up to Volume 4 (1997) to see female sword swallowers, the Gorilla Girl, a murderous snake, the armless Kitty, and other wonders.

Atomic Books and Dolphin-Moon Press; $12.95 each
oversized softcovers; 104 pp each
heavily illus; no ISBNs

SKULLDUGGERY

This catalogue contains museum-quality replicas of bones, mostly prehistoric skulls. For example, you can get a large American lion skull for $299 and a truly wicked looking sabre tooth tiger skull for $213 (both skulls come with a display stand). If you'd like something that's not extinct (yet), check out the adult male grizzly bear skull and the adult female mountain lion skull. Should you want to turn your den into a scene from a Georgia O'Keeffe painting, get the impressive buffalo cranium. If your tastes run along more hominid lines, you can buy skulls of *Australopithecus afarenis*, Neanderthal, *Homo erectus*, *Homo sapiens*, and others. For the truly bizarre, try a human skull with an annular deformation or one that's been trephined (i.e., had a hole drilled in it while the original owner was still alive).

Skullduggery also carries replicas of Raptor claws, giant sloth claws, an eleven-inch Tyrannosaurus rex tooth, dinosaur eggs, a trilobite, a Triceratops skull, shark teeth, bronze replicas, some interesting jewellery, moulds for casting fossils, and more great Mesozoic stuff.

Skullduggery/624 South B St/Tustin CA 92680

WWW: www.skullduggery.com

Catalogue: free, but mention that you heard about them in *Psychotropedia*

SONIC TRANSFORM
Brain Hemisphere Harmonic Healing
by John Now & Michael Mantra

Sonic Transform is a tape designed to alter your consciousness and produce positive feelings without using subliminal messages of any kind. It sounds like waves crashing on the shore with synthesisers floating in the background. But this is not simplistic feel-good New Age music: "The artists mix Eastern and Western brain hemisphere synchronisation techniques to transform negative yin emotions to a more positive yang emotions [sic]." It is best used with headphones.

Tranquil Technology Music;

1991; cassette

THE STRANGEST HUMAN SEX, CEREMONIES AND CUSTOMS
by J. Talalaj & S. Talalaj

Part of *The Strangest* series from the Australian publisher Hill of Content, *The Strangest Human Sex, Ceremonies and Customs* is a potpourri of short (averaging a page) descriptions of the world's most bizarre sexual, religious, and other customs and beliefs. Seventy-five pages are devoted to sexual strangeness. The female native inhabitants of Micronesia, when having sex, would burn the arms of their men by igniting little patches of powdered breadfruit stump. Later, when cigarettes were introduced to the island, they used them to do the job. In the sixteenth century, the Topinamba men of Brazil would increase their endowments by getting poisonous snakes to bite their penises. "As a result the men were in pain for about half a year, but their penises became monstrously big and they were convinced that the suffering was worthwhile since the women were so delighted."

Among the bizarre gods and goddesses that have been worshipped is the nineteenth century Amanjaka, a Japanese tapeworm deity. It was believed that there were certain nights of the year during which this god could crawl into a person's body, discover all the sins that person committed, leave the body, and report the bad news to the celestial god. During these nights, people tried to avoid sleeping, so the worm wouldn't have a chance to ratfink on them.

One of the most unusual customs surrounding death was observed by the Hiji, who live in the mountains between Nigeria and Cameroon. When a person died, they would strip all the skin off the corpse before burying it. Other topics that are dealt with include genital sheaths, defloration rituals,

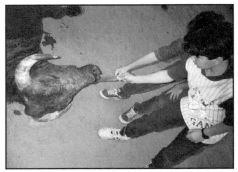

At the end of the bullfighting day.
Taurobolium.

Japan's vagina festival, compulsory prostitution, ritual intercourse, marriage to a tree, embryo marriage, self-flagellation, head shrinkers, burying people alive, infanticide, blood drinking, and crocodile blood brothers.

Something bugs me about this book. It's never blatant, but there's a subtle undercurrent of smarminess to the whole thing. Instead of being a wide-eyed look at some of the most extreme aspects of human behaviour, it feels like the authors are gawking and snickering. On top of that, the simplistic writing style — chock full of simple sentences — makes me feel like I'm reading a seventh-grade textbook.

Hill of Content; $16.95

1994; softcover; 193 pp

illus; 0-85572-247-9

TAUROBOLIUM
The Tijuana Bullfight Documentary
by Larry Wessel

Journey South of the Border with filmmaker Larry Wessel as he chronicles the bullfights of Tijuana, Mexico. Using no narration, this documentary lets you drink in the sights and sounds of three years' worth of bloody spectacles seamlessly woven together to look like one marathon bullfight.

Matadors parade around. A fight breaks out in the crowd. A Mexican band jams. Then in charges the bull. Even though his neck muscles have been jabbed, he's still fast, agile, and madder than hell. The matadors wave their capes as the bulls brush beside them, turn right around, and come back for another near miss. During this phase of the bullfight, it's apparent that there is an art to the "dance" occurring between the two adversaries. Of course, the best part is when the bull gets the upper horn, and the matador goes flying.

During the next phase, a picador comes out on a blindfolded horse and spears the bull's neck and back muscles, weakening it for the matadors. After the picador is done gouging the bull and the bull is done gouging the horse, the matadors do something different. They hold two decorated spikes, and when the bull charges them, they bury the spikes in the bull's back.

With the bull looking like a walking pincushion, it's back to cape-twirling, this time with a sword in the other hand. The matadors take a few jabs at the bull when it passes them. It's obvious that the bull is slowing down after all this torture, but then again, so are the matadors. This is when things get rough. One matador gets his pants half ripped off but continues to fight the bull with his butt hanging out. Two other matadors get thrashed so badly they have to be carried out of the ring. Call me a misanthrope if you will, but I was cheering like a sumbitch whenever a bull got a piece of matador.

By now, things are looking bad for the *toro*. It's bleeding from the mouth and keeps stumbling into the dirt. At last, a matador delivers the final thrust, and the bull shudders, pukes blood, and dies. The beast's ears are then cut off as mementoes.

The bull is dragged into another area to be butchered. Shots of the matadors strutting, signing autographs, and acting like bigshots are interspersed with gruesome footage of the bull being methodically drained, skinned, disembowelled, and cut into pieces. When it's all over, kids play in the ring, while the ring's workers drink and clown around.

Taurobolium captures the many contradictory facets of the bullfight. On one hand, it's a daring art form and a timeless contest between man and beast. On the other, it's a bunch of guys in tights torturing a confused, enraged animal to death. Either way, it makes for a powerful documentary.

Wesselmania; $25

1994; VHS videocassette; 108 min

THAT GUNK ON YOUR CAR
A Unique Guide to Insects of
North America
by Mark Hostetler, PhD

Driving through some areas of North America during certain parts of the year can leave you with a windshield filled with splotches that are the remains of head-on crashes with insects. Instead of thinking of these smooshed remains as a nuisance, think of them as an opportunity to learn more about nature. This book by zoologist Mark Hostetler will help you do just that.

Written basically for children (but enjoyable for everyone), *That Gunk on Your Car* contains a full-colour centre section with photorealistic illustrations of twenty-four blotches you're likely to see on your windshield, grille, or bumper. Each smear is identified (antlion, butterfly, dragonfly, firefly, mosquito, etc.), while a second illustration shows you what it looked like before you killed it. The bulk of the book is taken up by interesting facts about the crawly critters, as well as suggestions for keeping them in captivity. Did you know that dragonflies are known to attack hummingbirds? Or that two lovebugs will have sex (actually, the author uses *copulate*… "Daddy, what does that word mean?") for an average of two days and eight hours — and they live only three to five days?

Ten Speed Press; $9.95

1997; softcover; 133 pp

illus; 0-89815-961-X

ULTRAMEGALOPOLIS
This documentary from Larry Wessel is a stream-of-consciousness trip through that bastion of West

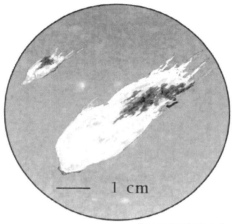

The remains of a horsefly.
That Gunk on your Car.

Coast weirdness, Los Angeles. There is no narration, just one scene after another showing dozens of the more unusual aspects of the City of Angels. Among the things you'll see:

- A party attended by body-modified punks, Marie Antoinette clones, leatherpeople, and normals.
- A tight facial shot of a man talking about his experiences in Youth Authority and federal prison.
- A welcome-home parade for Desert Storm troops.
- A woman doing some impressive drumming on found objects.
- A man with no legs or right arm dancing on the sidewalk. He does all kinds of "sexy" moves, like pelvic thrusts, while rap blares from his tape player.
- A sidewalk preacher wearing headphones and screaming the Word, punctuated by his own outbursts. "Those that have a pure heart, they will see God, wooooo! As He is, wooooo! He's a saving God, wooooo! Glory be, glory be, hallelujah!"
- A fundamentalist Christian sect of African Americans on a sidewalk, quoting the Bible to show that Jesus was black and that white and gay people are the scum of the earth.
- A male model and a female model imitating mannequins. Suddenly, they move and step out of the window.
- A black man and a white woman in a room. She's gets on her knees and starts using her mouth on his dick through his pants. He yells, "Don't be bitin' that shit, bitch!"
- A guy dressed as a cowboy onstage performing "speed country". He thrashes around while singing fast, indecipherable lyrics. The only word I could understand was the much-repeated "Cornhole!"
- A middle age guy doing a horrendous karaoke version of Joe Cocker's "You Are So Beautiful."

☞ A Michael Jackson imitator dancing around on Hollywood Blvd.

☞ Badly staged "pro" wrestling.

☞ A bullfight in which an unarmed "matador" goads a bull into charging him. It does, and it takes seven other matadors to restrain the bull long enough for the idiot to get off the bull's horns.

☞ Graffiti artists plying their craft.

☞ Hare Krishnas dancing and chanting.

Ultramegalopolis provides an entertaining look at LA, but it would have been much better if many of the scenes had been edited down. Some of them — like the guy who talks about his experiences in correctional institutions — drag on forever. Despite this weakness, I still enjoyed most of the film. If you live in La La Land, you may not want to see it, because you have to live it everyday. But for the rest of us, it provides a safe way to find out what we've (luckily) been missing.

Wesselmania; $25

1996; VHS videocassette; 155 min

THE WALLS CAME TUMBLING DOWN

by Robert Anton Wilson

In this film script for a movie that has yet to be made, RAW shows what happens when the reality one man stubbornly clings to is suddenly pulled out from under him. Michael Ellis, a Harvard professor of mathematical physics, is a militant materialist who refuses to acknowledge even the possibility that anything paranormal/supernatural might have even a grain of truth to it. His wife, also a mathematical physicist, is willing to at least consider the possibility, and Tree, a sexy student he's having an affair with, wholeheartedly believes in reincarnation, channelling, astrology, etc. Michael, though,

is adamantly close-minded. He belongs to an organisation of "debunkers". The scene in which he gives a talk is described: "*Scientists (all white, male and middle-aged) sit at a table in front. They wear armbands saying SSA, with the SS's represented by lightning bolts. A banner above the table explains the initials, saying SCIENTIFIC SKEPTICS ASSOCIATION.*"

It comes as an incredible shock, then, when an extreme toothache causes Michael to be under the influence of a codeine analogue and sodium Pentothal, triggering hallucinations (maybe), an out-of-body experience, an alien abduction, and visits to parallel universes. Of course, he eventually comes out of it, but in voice-over he declares: "I knew, in some way, that this was only the beginning, only the first crack in the fabric." With the help of his friend Simon the psychologist, Michael tries to figure out what's happening to him. Did he really experience an abduction and a previous life? Did he tap into the basic fabric of reality and become so overwhelmed that he interpreted it the only way he knew? Is someone trying to control his mind with technology?

Mixed into the equation are the radical theories of quantum physics, Michael's guilt about physicists' role in building the atom bomb, some sex scenes, and a creepy guy with a veiled agenda who gives Michael magic mushrooms. Having read some of Wilson's previous work, the resolution is not at all what I expected. Instead of an enigmatic ending that leaves the questions up in the air, there is a fairly clear statement given about what Michael experienced. Things get quite *X-File*-ish but, unlike that show, you aren't left hanging in the air.

New Falcon Publications; $14.95

1997; softcover; 174 pp

1-56184-091-2

Appendix A

General book catalogues

Getting some catalogues specialising in outpostish material is essential for getting hold of non-mainstream ideas. Below are several great catalogues that offer the widest possible variety of books, magazines, comix, videos, audio, T-shirts, etc. This is the only part of the book where I include material that was also in <u>Outposts</u>. Because these resources are so important, I figured they needed repeating.

AK Distribution
Around 3000 books, zines, comix, CDs, and videos covering anarchism, radical leftism, utopianism, labour issues, resistance, and revolution, with healthy doses of sex, drugs, rock and roll, conspiracies, Satanism, fiction, radical art, and more. AK carries every title in print from Autonomedia, Loompanics, Creation, Savoy, City Lights, Headpress/Critical Vision, RE/Search, V/Search, Juno Books, and other important alternative publishers. Lots of hard-to-find material from the UK. Also stocks cool T-shirts, bumpersticker, buttons, and other goodies.
AK Distribution/PO Box 40682/San Francisco CA 94140-0682
Email: akpress@akpress.org
WWW: www.akpress.org
US catalogue: free, but $1 for postage is greatly appreciated
AK Distribution/PO Box 12766/Edinburgh EH8 9YE/SCOTLAND
Email: ak@akedin.demon.co.uk
UK catalogue: free, but they do appreciate people from Britain/Europe sending a LARGE stamped self-addressed envelope or three International Reply Coupons. Americans wanting the UK catalogue should send $2 cash

Atomic Books
Atomic Books provides a well-rounded selection of material on all kinds of unusual topics — sex, drugs, conspiracies, privacy, revenge, body art, erotic and alternative fiction (e.g., Kathy Acker, JG Ballard, Katherine Dunn, etc.), fraud, crime, killers, death, cult films, pop culture, art, music (indie, goth, industrial, punk), "girlie stuff" (*Net Chick*, *Bust*, etc.), and general New Edge fringy-ness. They have an especially impressive selection of underground and adult comix and graphic novels, fetish magazines, and zines in all categories. Atomic's big catalogue not only lists all of their offerings and describes most of them, but it also contains many great articles by

well-known nonconformists.
Atomic Books/229 W Read St/Baltimore MD 21201
Email: atomicbk@atomicbooks.com
WWW: www.atomicbooks.com
Catalogue: $3 and 18+ age statement

Autonome Distribution/ Crescent Wrench Books
Autonome/Crescent offers somewhere in the neighbourhood of 650 books and pamphlets, plus zines, audiotapes, T-shirts, posters, and scads of buttons, stickers, and postcards. The material is mainly from anarchist and similarly radical anti-authoritarian positions. Topics include radical environmentalism, armed resistance, communal living, labour, anti-capitalism, anti-communism, psychedelics, anarchism (of course), and related topics. Most of the books in this catalogue would belong in the Freedom and No Compromises chapters of *Psychotropedia*.
Autonome Distribution/PO Box 30058/New Orleans LA 70190
Catalogue and an update: $2

Black Planet
Politically radical and subversive books. Covers the same basic territory as AK and Left Bank but not as extensive.
Black Planet/2 W Read St #140/Baltimore MD 21201
Email: blackplanet@aol.com
WWW: www.blackplanetdirect.com
Catalogue: $2

The Book Tree Catalogue
This catalogue offers an interesting mix of hundreds of books, videos, booklets, and stapled reports. It's hard to put my finger on exactly what the common denominator is. Obviously, all of the material is nonconformist, but it's not all-inclusive. Some of the subjects that are covered include the unexplained (crop circles, abductions, ancient astronauts), conspiracy (smart cards, New World Order, AIDS), freedom (BATF, tax protest), metaphysics (alchemy, reincarnation), religion (Paganism, Gnosticism, manipulation by organised religion), and a smattering of other topics. The conspiracy material covers what are typically considered "right wing concerns", yet the Book Tree also slags organised religion (especially Christianity), preferring a New Age slant to their spirituality (although they don't hesitate to poke fun at New Age-ism either).
Book Tree also sells buttons with messages like, "My God Can Beat Up Your God," and, "TV Made Me Do It!" and a few T-shirts, such as one that shows a picture of Gandhi and says, "Another Skinhead for Peace".
Totally unpredictable and very worth having.
The Book Tree/PO Box 724/Escondido CA 92033
WWW: www.thebooktree.com
Catalogue: $1

Essential Media
A newcomer to the field, with a twist. Essential Media has discount prices. Typically, they knock $1 off of merchandise around $10, $1 to $1.50 off stuff that's around $15, and $2 off items that list for around $20. Zines are typically 50¢ under retail. EM mainly carries books, including RE/Search and its progeny, Loompanics, William Burroughs, Robert Anton Wilson, SubGenius, anarchism, cocktail culture, sex, drugs, comix, body modification, conspiracies, fiction, and more. They also stock zines, videos (cult movies, music, and great documentaries), and CDs (ambient/dub/trip hop, punk, Sun Ra, The Residents). Currently approaching 1000 items and growing all the time.
Essential Media/PO Box 661245/Los Angeles CA 90066
Email: underground@essentialmedia.com
WWW: www.essentialmedia.com
Catalogue: $2US (worldwide)

Flatland Books
A smaller but quality selection of books, magazines, and pamphlets on conspiracies, UFOs, Wilhelm Reich, government bullyboys, Situationism, fiction, and more. [Be sure to checkout *Flatland* magazine in the Conspiracies chapter.]
Flatland/PO Box 2420/Fort Bragg CA 95437
Email: flatland@mcn.org
WWW: www.flatlandbooks.com
Catalogue: free

Last Gasp
Thick catalogue that is virtually definitive when it comes to alternative and erotic comix/graphix, music books, and SM/fetish magazines. Also contains lots of sex, drugs, fiction, magick, alternaculture, and interesting artefacts (T-shirts, trading cards, posters, etc.).
Last Gasp/777 Florida St/San Francisco CA 94110
Email: lastgasp@hooked.net
WWW: www.lastgasp.com
Catalogue: $2 and 18+ age statement

Left Bank Distribution
Close to 1000 books, pamphlets, and zines on anarchism, radical leftism, minority rights, plus Loompanics, Autonomedia, comix, and more.
Left Bank Distribution/1404 18th Ave/ Seattle WA 98122
Email: leftbank@leftbankbooks.com
WWW: www.leftbankbooks.com
Catalogue: free, but donations of $1 in cash or stamps are appreciated

Loompanics Unlimited
Over 1000 books, with a heavy emphasis on committing illegal and quasi-legal acts, along with self-sufficiency, self-defence, censorship, "heresy/weird ideas", sex, drugs, life extension, and much more. Also contains original articles on deviant topics. Manages to incorporate a sense of fun into the heavily subversive proceedings.

Loompanics Unlimited/PO Box 1197/Port Townsend WA 98368
WWW: www.loompanics.com
Catalogue: $5 or free with any purchase

Marginal Distribution

Based in Canada, Marginal does an incredible job bringing non-mainstream books to the people of the frozen North (and anyone else, for that matter). Stocks complete backlists and hot-off-the-presses releases from a large number of independent publishers. Currently they have over 2000 titles from 150 publishers, including some seriously obscure ones. Marginal mainly acts as a distributor to retailers, but they also handle individual mail order.
Marginal Distribution/277 George St North, Unit 103/Peterborough Ont K9J 3G9/CANADA
Email: marginal@ptbo.igs.net
WWW: ptbo.igs.net/~marginal
Catalogue: US/Can: $2. Elsewhere: $5

Newspeak KataZzzine

see review in the "Miscellaneous" section of the Conspiracies chapter.

PolyEster Records and Books

A spirited collection of books and zines on merry mischief, art, fiction, sex, drugs, weird movies, occult, conspiracies, body modification, and UFOs, plus comix, trading cards, and videos. Also has a huge selection of independent CDs. PolyEster is located in Australia, so those of you Down Under will want to immediately get a copy of their catalogue. Those of us in the US will get hammered by shipping charges, but they offer a bunch of titles I've never seen anywhere else, so it's worth a look for you hardcore book and CD buyers.
PolyEster Records and Books/Box 73/Fitzroy VIC 3065/AUSTRALIA
Email: fools@polyester.com.au
WWW: www.polyester.com.au/PolyEster/index.html
Catalogue: $3US concealed in an envelope

Quimby's Queer Store

A medley of cool and unusual books, zines, and comix on all sorts of topics.
Quimby's Queer Store/1328 N Damen Ave/Chicago IL 60622
1854 W North Ave/Chicago IL 60622
Catalogue: $3

See Hear

See Hear's strong points include zines, comix, and music books, although they carry a lot of other great material too. Expect a smattering of sex, drugs, wild art, alternaculture, Loompanics, Feral House, and some explosively subversive material.
See Hear Mail Order/59 East 7th Street/New York NY 10003
WWW: www.zinemart.com
Catalogue: $3. Non-US: $4

Appendix B

Publishers' ordering information

This information is provided because I hate reading about a good book — especially if it's put out by an independent publisher — and then not knowing how to get ahold of it. Although the majority of this information was checked just before going to press, my publisher and I make no guarantees concerning accuracy. There are approximately 550 publishers listed here, so some errors are bound to have snuck in. Also, ordering info can have an extremely short shelf life, so if possible, you may want to check with a publisher first, especially if you're ordering anything in mid-1999 or beyond. I have created a special page on my Website that will list updated information for these publishers: www.mindpollen.com/psy/pubs.htm. Please email me at pubs@mindpollen.com if you find anything in this section that is incorrect or outdated.

Voice and fax numbers are given for ordering only. Phone numbers are only given for publishers who accept credit card payment.

When ordering through the mail or via fax with a credit card, be sure to include number, expiration date, your name as it appears on the card, and authorised signature. Give some thought before ordering with a credit card over the fax. You never know exactly where the receiving fax is or who might see your number.

Shipping charges are for the United States and in US funds, unless otherwise noted. Many of the publishers have more shipping options than I've listed. Get in touch with them for details.

All payment must be made in the currency of the publisher's country and checks must be drawn on a bank in the publisher's country, unless otherwise noted.

Almost all publishers require that you pay sales tax when you order if that publisher is in your state. If they are out of your state, you generally don't have to pay tax. The exceptions are those publishers who have offices, distribution centres, etc. in different states. Citizens of each of those states must pay. Also, some publishers are

non-profit, so nobody has to pay sales tax. So, unless specifically noted, you need to include sales tax when ordering from a publisher in your state (unless, of course, you live in a state with no sales tax).

☞ ck: personal cheque
☞ mo: money order
☞ MC: Mastercard
☞ Disc: Discover
☞ Amex: American Express
☞ Ground: Ground Mail (also known as Surface Mail)
☞ Air: Airmail

A Distribution

84b Whitechapel High St/London E1/UK
available from Autonome Distribution [below]

Abbeville Press

488 Madison Avenue/New York NY 10022
Voice: 1-800-ARTBOOK
Fax: 212-644-5085
Email: abbeville@abbeville.com
WWW: www.abbeville.com

ABC-CLIO

PO Box 1911/Santa Barbara CA 93116-1911
Voice: 800-368-6868
Fax: 805-685-9685
Email: sales@abc-clio.com
UK email: oxford@abc-clio.com
WWW: www.abc-clio.com
Shipping: none. Canada: 8%.
Payment: cash, ck, mo, Visa, MC, Amex

Academic Research

7831 Woodmont Ave, Suite 341/Bethesda MD 20814
Shipping: none
Payment: ck, mo

Academy Chicago Publishers

363 W Erie St/Chicago IL 60610
Voice: 1-800-248-READ
Email: academy363@aol.com
WWW: www.academychicago.com
Shipping: Continental US: $4.50 for 1 or 2 books. Outside Continental US: $5 for 1 or 2 books
Payment: ck, mo, Visa, MC, Amex, Diner's Club

Adams Media Corporation

260 Center St/Holbrook MA 02343
Voice: 1-800-USA-JOBS (872-5627)
Fax: 617-767-0994
Email: bapub@aol.com
WWW: www.adamsmedia.com
Shipping: $4.50 for up to ten books.
Non-US: inquire first
Payment: ck, mo, Visa, MC, Amex

Added Dimensions Publishing

100 S Sunrise Way, Suite 484/Palm Springs CA 92263
Fax: 919-266-6366

WWW: www.male.com
Shipping: $2 first book, $1 each additional.
Non-US: $5 first book, $3 each additional
Payment: cash, ck, mo, Visa, MC

Addison-Wesley
Addison-Wesley Longman Publishing
Company
ATTN: Order Services/One Jacob Way/
Reading MA 01867
Voice: 1-800-358-4566
WWW: www.aw.com

Adventures Unlimited
303 Main St/Kempton IL 60946
Voice: 815-253-6390
Fax: 815-253-6300
Shipping: $2 first book, 50¢ each
additional. Canada: $3 first book, 75¢ each
additional. Elsewhere Surface: $5 first, $2
each additional. Elsewhere Air: $10 each
items
Payment: ck, mo, Visa, MC
Other: 10% discount for 3 or more books
Catalogue: free

Aegina Press
1905 Madison Ave/Huntington WV 25704

African American Images
1909 W 95th St/Chicago IL 60643
Voice: 1-800-552-1991
Fax: 312-445-9844
WWW: www.africanamericanimages.com
Shipping: $2.80 first book, $1.25 each
additional
Payment: ck, Visa, MC, Amex
Sales tax: none

AK Press
UK: PO Box 12766/Edinburgh EH8 9PE/
Scotland
Voice: 0131-555-5165
Fax: 0131-555-5215
Email: ak@akedin.demon.co.uk
US: PO Box 40682/San Francisco CA
94140-0682
Voice: 415-864-0892
Fax: 415-864-0893
Email: akpress@akpress.org
WWW: www.akpress.org
Shipping: $2.50 first item, 25¢ each
additional. Canada: $4 first item, 50¢ each
additional. Elsewhere: $4.50 first item, 50¢
each additional.
Payment: cash, ck, mo, international mo,
Visa, MC
Catalogue: see Appendix A
*You can become a "Friend of AK Press" for
$15 (or more) a month, for a minimum of
three months. Your money will go
completely toward publishing new books.
During your term as a Friend, you will
receive a copy of every book AK publishes
and get 10% off all orders.*

Alamo Square Press
PO Box 14543/San Francisco CA 94114
Shipping: $2 first book, 50¢ each additional
Payment: ck, mo

Allen & Unwin
PO Box 374/French Forest NSW 2086/
AUSTRALIA
Voice: 61-2-9452-6233
Fax: 61-2-9452-2644
Email: orders@allen-unwin.com.au
WWW: www.allen-unwin.com.au
Payment: Aus ck, mo, Visa, MC, Amex

Alsyon Publications
6922 Hollywood Blvd, Suite 1000/Los
Angeles CA 90028
WWW: www.alyson.com

Alternate Sources
PO Box 19591/55 Bloor St W/Toronto Ont
M4W 3T9/CANADA
Email: sales@alternate.com
WWW: www.alternate.com
Shipping: Canada: $5Cdn. US: $5. UK: £4.
Elsewhere: $8US
Payment: ck (Cdn, US, UK), mo,
international mo, Visa
*Alternate Sources is also available on CD-
ROM*

Amarillo Records
5714 Folsom Blvd, Suite 300/Sacramento
CA 95819-4608
Email: amarillo@earthlink.net
WWW: members.aol.com/starleigh7/
amarillo.html
Shipping: none. Can/Mex: $1.50 first CD,
50¢ each additional. Europe: $3.50, $1
Payment: cash (by registered mail), ck,
mo, international mo

America West Publishers
PO Box 2208/Carson City NV 89702
Voice: 1-800-729-4131
Fax: 406-585-0703
Shipping: $2.75 first title, 75¢ each
additional. Can/Mex: $4 first title, $1.50
each additional. Others: $6 first title, $1.75
each additional
Payment: ck, mo, Visa, MC, Disc

American Justice Federation
3850 S Emerson Ave/Indianapolis IN
46203
Voice: 1-800-749-9939
Fax: 317-780-5209
Email: lindat@snowhill.com
Shipping: $4 per item
Payment: ck, mo, Visa, MC, Amex, COD

American Institute for Mindfulness
PO Box 390309/Cambridge MA
02139-0004

Amnesty International
Attn: Publications Dept/322 8th Ave/New
York NY 10001
Voice: 212-807-8400
Fax: 212-627-1451
Email: pminges@igc.apc.org
WWW: www.amnesty.org
Shipping: $2 first book, 50¢ each
additional. Non-US: inquire first
Payment: cash, ck, mo, Visa, MC

Amok Books
1764 N Vermont Ave/Los Angeles CA
90027
Voice: 213-665-0956
Fax: 213-666-8105
Email: amok@primenet.com

Anchor Books
*division of Bantam Doubleday Dell
Publishing Group*

Andrews and McMeel
4520 Main St/Kansas City MO 64111-7701
Voice: 1-800-642-6480
Fax: 816-932-6559
Shipping: $2. Non-US Surface: $4.
Non-US Air: $9.50
Payment: ck, mo, Visa, MC

Anti-Slavery International
Thomas Clarkson House/The Stableyard/
Broomgrove Rd/London SW9 9TL/UK
Voice: +44 (0)171 924 9555
Fax: +44 (0)171 738 4110
Email: antislavery@gn.apc.org
WWW: www.charitynet.org/~asi/
Shipping: UK: £1; overseas: "at cost"
Payment: UK ck, international money
order, Visa, MC, Amex, Diners, Access,
CAF

Antique Collectors' Club
Market Street Industrial Park/Wappingers
Falls NY 12590
Voice: 1-800-252-5231
Fax: 914-297-0068
Email: info@antiquecc.com
WWW: www.antiquecc.com
Shipping: $3
Payment: ck, mo, Visa, MC, Amex

Anvil Press
c/o General Distribution Services
85 River Rock Dr #202/Buffalo NY 14207
Voice: 1-800-805-1083
Shipping: US/Can: $2.50 for 1-5 books.
Others: $3 for 1-3 books
Payment: cash, ck, mo

Aperture
20 E 23rd St/New York NY 10010
Voice: 1-800-929-2323
Fax: 212-598-4015
Shipping: $5 first book, $1.50 each
additional. Non-US: $8 first book, $2 each
additional
Payment: ck, mo, Visa, MC, Amex

Apex Press
*division of Coucil on International and
Public Affairs/777 United Nations Plaza,
Suite 3C/New York NY 10017*
Email: cipany@igc.apc.org
Payment: cash, ck, mo, Visa, MC, Amex
Sales tax: none

Arcade Publishing
141 5th Ave/New York NY 10010
order from Little, Brown and Company

Aries Rising Press
PO Box 29532/Los Angeles CA

90029-0532
Shipping: $2 for one book, $3 for two or more
Payment: ck, mo

Arsenal Pulp Press
103, 1014 Homer St/Vancouver BC V6B 2W9/CANADA
Voice: 1-888-600-7857
Fax: 604-669-8250
Email: arsenal@pinc.com
Shipping: $3US first book, $1.50US each additional (worldwide)
Payment: ck, mo, Visa, MC

Art Insights
PO Box 626/Litchfield CT 06759

Art Matrix
PO Box 880/Ithaca, NY 14851
Email: jes@lightlink.com
Shipping: 1-4 books: $5
Payment: ck, mo, Visa, MC, Amex, Disc

Artspace Books
123 S Park/San Francisco CA 94107
Shipping: $2.50 per book
Payment: ck, mo

Association for World Peace
PO Box 1214/Quincy IL 62306
Shipping: "Skull and Bones Conspiracy...": $1. *On New Economic Partnership*: $7
Payment: cash, ck, mo

Asylum Arts
5847 Sawmill Rd/Paradise CA 95969
Email: www.coyote-arts.org/valentine/asylum.html
Shipping: $1.50 first book, 25¢ each additional. Non-US: $3
Payment: cash, ck, mo

Atomic Books
1018 North Charles Street/Baltimore MD 21201
Voice: 1-800-778-6246 or 410-625-7955
Fax: 410-625-7945
Email: atomicbk@atomicbooks.com
WWW: www.atomicbooks.com
Shipping: $5 flat fee. Non-US Surface: $7.50 flat fee
Payment: cash, ck, mo, Visa, MC, Disc, Amex

Attack International
Box BM 6577/London WC1N 3XX/UK
available from AK Press and Autonome Distribution

August House Publishers
PO Box 3223/Little Rock AR 72203
Voice: 1-800-AUGUST-H (284-8784)
Fax: 501-372-5579
WWW: www.augusthouse.com
Shipping: $3.90. Non-US: $7.90
Payment: cash, ck, mo, Visa, MC, Disc, Amex

Aurum Press
25 Bedford Ave/London WC1B 3AT/UK
widely distributed in the US

Austen Press
620 Park Ave #119/Rochester NY 14607
Shipping: $1.50. Non-US: $3.50
Payment: ck

Automatism Press
PO Box 170277/San Francisco CA 94117-0277
Email: automatism@charnel.com
WWW: www.charnel.com/automatism
Shipping: $2 per copy. Non-US: $3 per copy
Payment: cash, ck, mo

Autonomedia
PO Box 568, Williamburgh Sta/Brooklyn NY 11211-0568
WWW: www.autonomedia.org
Shipping: $2 first book, $1 each additional. Non-US: US shipping plus 12% of book cost
Payment: ck, international mo
available through AK Press and other mail order operations

Autonome Distribution
Crescent Wrench Books/PO Box 30058/New Orleans LA 70190
Shipping: $3 first book, $1 each additional. Non-US Surface: $3 plus 15% of total order. Non-US Air: Surface rate plus $3 per book
Payment: ck, mo, international mo
Catalogue: see Appendix A

Avery Publishing Company
Order Dept/120 Old Broadway/Garden City Park NY 11040
Voice: 1-800-548-5757
Fax: 516-742-1892
Payment: ck, Visa, MC

Avon Books
1350 Avenue of the Americas/New York NY 10019
Voice: 1-800-223-0690
WWW: AvonBooks.com

Banned Books
PO Box 33280/Austin TX 78764

Bantam Doubleday Dell Publishing Group
1540 Broadway/New York NY 10036
WWW: www.bdd.com
Does not sell directly to consumers. Their books are widely available

Barricade Books
Barricade Books has ceased all operations after losing a libel suit brought by casino owner Steve Wynn.

Bay Press
115 W Denny Way/Seattle WA 98119
Voice: 206-284-5913
Fax: 206-284-1218
Shipping: $2.50 first book, 55¢ each additional. Non-US: $2.75 first book, $1 each additional
Payment: ck, mo, Visa, MC

Beacon Press
25 Beacon St/Boston MA 02108-2892
Voice: 617-742-2110 ext 596
Fax: 617-723-3097
WWW: www.beacon.org
Shipping: under $25: $3.95; $25.01 to $60: $5.25
Payment: ck, mo, Visa, MC

Bear & Company
PO Box 2860/Santa Fe NM 87504-2860
Voice: 1-800-932-3277
Fax: 505-989-8386
Shipping: $4.50 (free within New Mexico)
Payment: ck, mo, Visa, MC, Amex

Beef Eye
PO Box 20321/Seattle WA 98102
Shipping: $1 per item. Foreign Surface: add 10% of price. Foreign Air: add 40% of price
Payment: cash, ck, mo
Catalogue: free illustrated brochure available

Bend Press
3017 Kashiwa Street/Torrance CA 90505
Email: melbend@crl.com
Shipping: $1.55. Non-US: $3
Payment: ck, mo

Benedikt Taschen Verlag
Distributed through Random House

The Berkeley Publishing Group
200 Madison Ave/New York NY 10016

Berkshire House, Publishers
480 Pleasant Street, Suite 5/Lee MA 01238
Voice: 1-800-321-8526
Email: info@berkshirehouse.com
WWW: www.berkshirehouse.com
Shipping: $4
Payment: ck, Visa, MC, Amex

Beyond Words Publishing
4443 NE Airport Rd/Hillsboro OR 97214
Voice: 1-800-284-9673
Fax: 503-693-6888
Shipping: under $30: $4.95; $30-$49.99: $5.95. Non-US: inquire first
Payement: ck, Visa, MC, Amex

Bion Publishing
323 E Matilija #110-151/Ojai CA 93023
Voice: 1-800-805-8254 or 805-646-2865
Fax: 805-646-1506
Shipping: 1 or 2 books: $2.50. Non-US: inquire first
Payment: cash, ck, mo, Visa, MC

Bisexual Resource Center
BRC/PO Box 639/Cambridge MA 02140
WWW: www.norn.org/pub/other-orgs/brc
Email: brc@norn.org
Shipping: none
Payment: cash, ck, mo, international postal order

Black Books
PO Box 31155/San Francisco CA 94131
Voice: 415-431-0171
Fax: 415-431-0172
Email: BB@blackbooks.com
WWW: www.blackbooks.com
Shipping: US: $3 per book. Can/Mex: $5
per book. Others: $9 per book
Payment: cash, ck, mo, Visa, MC, Disc,
Amex [ck and mo payable to The Black
Book]
Catalogue: $1 (non-US: $2) and age
statement

Black Classic Press
PO Box 13414/Baltimore MD 21203-3414
Voice: 410-358-0980
Fax: 410-358-0987
Email: bcp@charm.net
WWW: www.blackclassic.com
Shipping: 1 book: $3; 2 books: $4
Payment: cash, ck, mo, Visa, MC, Amex
Sales tax: none

Black Crow Books
PO Box 414, Station E/Toronto ON M6H
4E3/CANADA
Email: blcr@web.net
WWW: www.web.net/~blcr
Shipping: none (anywhere in the world)
Payment: ck, mo

Black Flag
BM Hurricane/London WC1N 3XX/UK

Blackwattle Press
PO Box 142/Broadway NSW 2007/
AUSTRALIA
Voice/Fax: 612-9212-3047
Email: blackwattle@pinkboard.com.au
WWW: www.pinkboard.com.au/
~blackwattle
Shipping: Aus: none. Non-Aus Air: $5Aus
per book (maximum of $20Aus). Non-Aus
Surface: $2Aus per book (maximum of
$8Aus)
Payment: Aus ck, Aus mo, Visa, MC,
Bankcard

Blast Books
PO Box 51, Cooper Station/New York NY
10276
Shipping: $2.50 first book, $1 each
additional

Bloat
PO Box 254/Burbank CA 91503
Email: bloat@cinenet.net
Shipping: $2. Non-US: $3
Payment: cash, ck, mo

Blue Books
Publishing House/Trinity Place/Barnstaple
Devon EX32 9HJ/UK
Shipping: UK: included in price. Non-UK
Air: £2 per book
Payment: cash, UK ck, UK mo,
international money order

Blue Dolphin Publishing
PO Box 8/Nevada City CA 95959
Voice: 1-800-643-0765
Fax: 530-265-0787

Email: bdolphin@netshel.net
WWW: www.netshel.net/~bdolphin
Shipping: up to $10: $4; $10.01 to $20: $5.
Non-US: add $2 to US shipping
Payment: ck, Visa, MC

Blue Moon Books
61 4th Ave/New York NY 10003
Voice: 1-800-535-0007 or 212-505-6880
Fax: 212-673-1039
Email: bluoff@aol.com
WWW: www.bluemoonbooks.com
Shipping: $5 flat rate. Canada: $8 flat rate.
Others: $12 flat rate
Payment: ck, mo, Visa, MC

Blue Press
2633 Lincoln Blvd, Suite 256/Santa Monica
CA 90405
*also available through Loompanics
Unlimited [below]*

Blue Water Publishing
PO Box 726/Newberg OR 97132
Voice: 1-800-366-0264
Fax: 503-538-8485
Email: bcrissey@bluewaterp.com
WWW: www.bluewaterp.com
Shipping: up to $10.99: $3; $11-$15.99:
$3.50; $16-$25: $4; $25.01-$35: $5. Can/
Mex: US shipping + $1 per item. Others:
US shipping + $1.20
Payment: ck, mo, Visa, MC, Disc, Amex

Bonus Books
160 E Illinois/Chicago IL 60611
Voice: 1-800-225-3775
Fax: 312-467-0580
WWW: www.bonus-books.com/
bonuspage1.html
Shipping: $4 first book, $3 each additional
Payment: cash, ck, mo, Visa, MC, Amex

Book Sales Ltd
Newmarket Rd/Bury St Edmunds/Suffolk
IP33 34B/UK
Voice: 01284-702600
Fax: 01284-768301
Payment: cash, ck, mo, Visa, MC
*Available in the US from Music Sales
Corp/257 Park Avenue South, 20th Floor/
New York, NY 10010. Often available at
Tower Books and Records*

The Book Tree
PO Box 724/Escondido CA 92033
Voice: 1-800-700-TREE (8733)
Fax: 619-489-5222
Email: mary@cts.com
WWW: www.thebooktree.com
Shipping: up to $10: $3; $10 to $40: $4.50.
Non-US: add $5 to US shipping
Payment: cash, ck, mo, Visa, MC
Sales tax: none

Books in Focus
PO Box 77005/San Francisco CA 94107
Voice: 1-800-463-6285 or 510-297-4012
Email: bif@igc.apc.org
WWW: www.igc.apc.org/BooksinFocus
Shipping: US/Can: $3.50 per book.
Europe/Asia Ground: $5 per book. Europe/
Asia Air: $15 per book

Payment: ck, mo, Visa, MC, Amex, Disc

Borage Books
3762 W 11th Ave, Suite 188/Eugene OR
97402
Email: borage@efn.org
WWW: www.boragebooks.com
Shipping: $3.50. Non-US: $5
Payment: ck, mo
Sales tax: none

Borderland Sciences
PO Box 220/Bayside CA 95524
Voice: 707-825-7733
Fax 707-825-7779
Email: info@borderlands.com
WWW: www.borderlands.com
Shipping: $3 first book, $1 each additional.
Can/Mex: $4 first book, $1.50 each
additional. Elsewhere Surface: $6 first
book, $2 each additional
Payment: ck, mo, Visa, MC

Branden Publishing Company
17 Station St/Box 843 Brookline Village/
Boston MA 02147
Voice: 1-800-359-7031
WWW: www.branden.com
Shipping: $4 first book, $1 each additional
Payment: ck, mo, Visa, MC

Brandon Book Publishers
order from Irish Books and Media
1433 E Franklin Ave/Minneapolis MN
55404-2135
Voice: 1-800-229-3505 or 612-871-3505
Fax: 612-871-3358
Email: irishbook@aol.com
WWW: www.irishbook.com/ibm.htm
Shipping: $3.50 first book, 50¢ each
additional
Payment: cash, ck, mo, Visa, MC, Amex

Brassey's, Inc
PO Box 960/Herndon VA 22070
Voice: 1-800-775-2518
Fax: 703-661-1501
Email: brasseys@aol.com
WWW: www.brasseys.com
Shipping: $4 first book, $1 each additional
Payment: ck, mo, Visa, MC

Bridger House Publishers
PO Box 2208/Carson City NV 89702
Voice: 1-800-729-4131

Bridging the Gap Communications
1014 Sycamore Dr/Decatur GA 30030
Voice: 1-800-721-6990 or 404-373-0530
Fax: 404-373-0480
Shipping: 1 to 10 copies: $3.05 per book.
Non-US: inquire first
Payment: ck, mo, Visa, MC

Brooks/Cole Publishing Co
511 Forest Lodge Rd/Pacific Grove CA
93950-5098
Voice: 800-354-9706

WWW: www.thomson.com/brookscole/
default.html
Payment: ck, Visa, MC, Amex

Brotherhood of Life

110 Dartmouth SE/Albuquerque NM 87106
WWW: www.brotherhoodoflife.com
Shipping: 1 book: $4.25; 2 books: $5.25; 3
books: $5.50
Payment: ck, Visa, MC, Disc, Eurocard

C.K. Smith

PO Box 2422/Eugene OR 97402
Email: cksmith@rio.com
Shipping: none. Non-US: $3
Payment: cash, ck, mo
Send a signed 21+ age statement

Calder Press

PO Box 1386/Orem UT 84059-1386
or 1250 N 1750th/W Provo UT 84604
Voice: 801-374-1444
Fax: 801-375-1646
Shipping: $2 first book, $1 each additional.
Non-US: add $1 to US charges
Payment: cash, ck, mo, Visa, MC, Amex

Caliber Press

225 N Sheldon Rd/Plymouth MI
48170-1524
Voice: 1-888-22-COMIC
Fax: 734-451-9836
WWW: calibercomics.com
Shipping: under $10: $3; $10.01 to $25: $4.
Non-US: add $5 to US shipping costs
Payment: ck, mo, Visa, MC

Californians for Compassionate Use

1444 Market Street/San Francisco CA
94102
Email: cbc@marijuana.org
WWW: www.marijuana.org

Cambrian Publications

PO Box 112170/Campbell CA 95011-2170
Email: orders@cambrianpubs.com
WWW: www.cambrianpubs.com
Shipping: $2 first book, $1 each additional.
Elsewhere Surface: $5 first book, $3 each
additional. Elsewhere Air: $10 first book,
$6 each additional
Payment: ck, mo, Visa, MC

Cambridge University Press

Customer Service Department/110
Midland Avenue/Port Chester NY 10573
Voice: 1-800-872-7423
Fax: 914-937-4712
Email: information@cup.org;
orders@cup.org
WWW: www.cup.org
Shipping: $4 first book, $1 each additional.
Non-US Surface: £2.50 flat rate. Non-US
Air: £2.50 + £2.50 per book
Payment: Visa, MC, Barclaycard, Access,
Eurocard
UK address: The Edinburgh Building/
Cambridge CB2 1BR
UK WWW: www.cup.cam.ac.uk

Capt. Paul Watson

c/o Sea Shepherd Conservation Society/
PO Box 628/Venice CA 90294
WWW: www.seashepherd.org
Shipping: $2.50. Non-US: $4
Payment: cash, ck, mo (payable to Capt.
Paul Watson)

Carl Klang

PO Box 217/Colton OR 97017
WWW: www.klang.com
Shipping: none
Payment: cash, ck, mo (payable to C.P.A.)

Carmen Willcox

Paradise Farm/Westhall/Halesworth/
Suffolk/IP19 8RH/UK
Shipping: US: $2 per book
Payment: UK cash, UK ck, international
money order

The Carol Publishing Group

Order Dept/600 Madison Ave/New York
NY 10022

Cassell

c/o Books International/PO Box 605/
Herndon VA 20172-0605
Voice: 1-800-561-7704
Fax: 703-661-1501
Shipping: US/Can: $5 first book, $1 each
additional
Payment: ck, mo, Visa, MC
UK address: Wellington House/125 Strand/
London WC2R 0BB

Castillo International

The East Side Institute/500 Greenwich St
#202/New York NY 10013
Voice: 1-800-435-7453
Fax: 212-941-8340
WWW: www.maxracks.com/castillo/
bookstore.html
Shipping: $3 per book
Payment: ck, mo, MC, Visa, Amex, Disc

Catasonic Records

PO Box 2727, 1615 Wilcox Ave/Hollywood
CA 90078
WWW: www.catasonic.com

Catherine Steinmann

1185 Park Avenue #4H/New York NY
10128
Email: cath48@tuna.net
WWW: users.tuna.net/Cath48
Shipping: $5
Payment: ck
*Be sure to indicate if you would like
Steinmann to sign or inscribe the book to
you*

Cato Institute

1000 Massachusetts Ave NW/Washington
DC 20001
Voice: 1-800-767-1241
Fax: 202-842-3490
Email: cato@cato.org
WWW: www.cato.org
Shipping: none
Payment: cash, ck, mo, Visa, MC, Amex
Sales tax: none

Elizabeth Gips

PO Box 7305/Santa Cruz CA 95061
Email: changes@cruzio.com
WWW: www.changes.org
Shipping: $2. Non-US: $8
Payment: cash, ck, mo

Charles H. Kerr Publishing Company

PO Box 914/Chicago IL 60690
or 1740 W Greenleaf Ave/Chicago IL
60626
Email: beasley@mcs.com

The Charles Press, Publishers

PO Box 15715/Philadelphia PA 19103
Voice: 215-545-8933
Fax: 215-545-8937
WWW: rivendell.org/charlespress.html
Shipping: $3 first book, $1 each additional.
Non-US: $5.50 first book, $2 each
additional
Payment: ck, mo, Visa, MC

Cherry Valley Editions

PO Box 303/Cherry Valley NY 13320
Payment: cash, ck

Chicago Plays

2632 N Lincoln/Chicago IL 60614
Voice: 312-348-6757
Fax: 312-348-5561
Shipping: 1 book: $3; 2-5: $4
Payment: ck, mo, Visa, MC, Disc, Amex

Chronicle Books

Customer Service/275 5th St/San
Francisco CA 94103
Voice: 1-800-722-6657
Email: frontdesk@chronbooks.com
WWW: www.chronbooks.com
Shipping: 1-2 books: $3.50; 3-4: $4.50
Payment: ck, mo, Visa, MC, Amex
Sales tax: CA, DC, HI, IA, IL, KS, MA, MN,
NE, NM, WI
UK address: Hi Marketing/38 Carver Road/
London SE24 9LT/UK
UK Voice: 44-171-738-7751
UK Fax: 44-171-274-9160

Cinco Puntos Press

2709 Louisville/El Paso TX 79930
Voice: 1-800-566-9072
Shipping: $2.50 for one book, $3.50 for two
or more
Payment: cash, ck, mo, Visa, MC

Circlet Press, Inc.

1770 Massachusetts Avenue #278, Dept
P/Boston MA 02215
Email: circlet-info@circlet.com;
circlet-catalog@circlet.com [catalogue]
WWW: www.circlet.com
Shipping: $3 first book, $1 each additional.
Canada: $4 first book, $1 each additional.
Elsewhere Air: $6 first book, $2 each
additional
Payment: cash, ck, mo
Catalogue: 32¢ SASE.

Citadel

Carol Publishing Group/Order Dept/120

Enterprise/Seacus NJ 07094

Citizens for Honest Government
PO Box 220/Winchester CA 92596
Voice: 1-800-828-2290
WWW: www.chg.org
Shipping: $10 to $20: $3; $20 to $30: $4.50; $30 to $40: $6
Payment: ck, mo, Visa, MC, Amex, Disc
A new, updated version of The Clinton Chronicles video is available for $19.95. Be sure to order The New Clinton Chronicles.

City Lights Books
261 Columbus Ave/San Francisco CA 94133
Voice: 415-362-1041
Fax: 415-362-4921
WWW: www.citylights.com
Shipping: US/Can/Mex: up to $20: $5.50; $20 to $40: $7. Elsewhere: $5 per softcover; $9 per hardcover
Payment: ck, mo, Visa, MC, Amex
Catalogue: free

Cleis Press
PO Box 14684/Los Angeles CA 94114
Voice: 1-800-780-2279 or 415-575-4700
Fax: 415-575-4705
Email: cleis@aol.com
Shipping: 15% of order
Payment: ck, mo, Visa, MC

CodeX
PO Box 148/Hove, East Sussex BN3 3DQ/ UK
Email: otl@pavilion.co.uk [info]
Shipping: UK £1. Europe: £2. Others (including US): £3, $6US
Payment: US or UK cash, ck or mo in UK funds from UK bank (or Eurocheque with card number)

Columbia University Press
Attn: Order Dept/136 S Broadway/Irvington IL 10533
Voice: 1-800-944-8648 or 914-591-9111
Fax: 914-591-9201
WWW: www.cc.columbia.edu/cu/cup
Shipping: $4.50 flat rate
Payment: ck, mo, Visa, MC, Amex

Common Courage Press
PO Box 702/Monroe ME 04951
Voice: 1-800-497-3207 or 207 525-0900
Fax: 207-525-3068
Email: comcour1@agate.net
WWW: www.agate.net/~comcour
Payment: ck, mo, Visa, MC, Amex
Shipping: $3 first book, $1 each additional

Communities
138-W Twin Oaks Rd/Louisa VA 23093
Voice: 540-894-5798
Email: order@ic.org
WWW: www.ic.org
Shipping: included.
Payment: cash, ck, mo, Visa, MC, Disc
Sales tax: MO, OR, VA

The Complete Guide
PO Box 206/Ottawa IL 61350-0206
Shipping: $3.50. Non-US: $7.50
Payment: ck, mo, Visa, MC

Conari Press
1144 65th St, Suite B/Emeryville CA 94608
Voice: 1-800-685-9595
Email: conaripub@aol.com
WWW: www.conari.com
Payment: ck, mo, Visa, MC

The Constantine Report
current address not known
The two Constantine Reports reviewed are available from AK Press. The Florida/ Hollywood Mob Connection, the CIA and O.J. Simpson is reprinted in whole in Virtual Government [reviewed in the Conspiracies chapter].

Contemporary Books
3250 South Western Ave/Chicago IL 60608

The Continuum Publishing Co
370 Lexington Avenue/New York NY 10017
Voice: 1-800-937-5557
Fax: 615-793-3915
WWW: www.continuum-books.com
Shipping: $3 first book, $1 each additional
Payment: ck, Visa, MC, Amex

Cormorant Books
RR 1/Dunvegan ONT K0C IJ0/CANADA
Email: cormoran@glen-net.ca
order from General Distribution Services
85 River Rock Dr, Suite 202/Buffalo NY 14207
Voice: 1-800-805-1083
Fax: 1-416-445-5967

Country People Productions
2554 Lincoln Blvd, Box 456/Marina Del Rey CA 90291
Voice: 1-800-BURY-IRS
Fax: 310-396-7612
Shipping: $3
Payment: ck, Visa, MC
Also available: Nine videotapes featuring much more of the 150 hours of footage that was prepared for Death & Taxes. For details, write or check out www.taoslandandfilm.com/ Mini-series.html.

Craig Morey, Morey Studio
7253 Osceola Dr/Madeira OH 45243
Fax: 513-272-6202
Email: chm@moreystudio.com
WWW: www.moreystudio.com
Shipping: $3.50. Overseas: $8
Payment: ck, Visa, MC

Creation Books
83, Clerkenwell Road/London EC1R 5AR/ UK
Voice: 0171-430-9878
Fax: 0171-242-5527

Email: creation@pussycat.demon.co.uk
WWW: www.pussycat.demon.co.uk
Shipping: UK: 10% of price (maximum £5). US: 20% of price (maximum £10)
Payment: UK ck, Visa, MC
All Creation titles are available from AK Press [above]

Creatopia Productions
General Delivery/Lamy NM 87540

The Crossing Press
PO Box 1048/Freedom CA 95019-1048
Voice: 1-800-777-1048
Fax: 1-800-722-2749
Email: crossing@aol.com
WWW: www.crossingpress.com

Crown Publishers
a division of Random House

Da Capo Press
Plenum Publishing/Ordering Dept/233 Spring St/New York 10013

Daedalus Publishing Co
584 Castro St, Suite 518/San Francisco CA 94114
Voice: 415-626-1867
Email: daedalus@bannon.com
WWW: www.bannon.com/daedalus
Shipping: $4 first book, $1 each additional.
Canada: $5 first book, $1 each additional.
Europe: $12 first book, $5 each additional
Payment: ck, mo, Visa, MC, Amex

Dalkey Archive Press
ISU Campus Box 4241, Normal IL 61790-4241
Fax: 309-438-7422
Email: aweaser@ilstu.edu
WWW: www.cas.ilstu.edu/english/dalkey/ dalkey.html
Shipping: $3.50 first book, 75¢ each additional. Non-US: $4.50 first book, $1 each additional
Payment: cash, ck, mo, Visa, MC

D.A.P. [Distributed Arts Publishers]
636 Broadway 12th Flr/New York NY 10012
Voice: 1-800-338-BOOK
Fax: 212-673-2887
WWW: www.artbook.com
Shipping: $3.50. Non-US: inquire first
Payment: cash, ck, mo, Visa, MC

Dark Star
5 Caledonian Rd/London N1/UK
can be ordered from Autonome Distribution [above]

David Steinberg
PO Box 2992/Santa Cruz CA 95062
Email: eronat@aol.com
Shipping: $3.05
Payment: ck, mo (payable to David Steinberg)

The DBJ Projects
PO Box 14692/Ft. Lauderdale FL 33302-4692

Email: dbjay3@mindspring.com
WWW: www.sover.net/~dbjay3
Shipping: $4.50. Priority: $6.50. Non-US
Surface: $15.50. Non-US Air: $24.75
Payment: ck, mo, Visa, MC

Debcar Publishing
PO Box 030153/Ft Lauderdale FL 33303
Voice: 1-800-355-9590
Fax: 954-467-3882
Email: debcarpub@aol.com
WWW: www.smac.net/debcar/index.htm
Shipping: $3. Non-US: $6
Payment: cash, ck, mo if ordering by mail.
Visa, MC, Disc, Amex are only accepted
for phone orders

Dedalus Ltd.
Langford Lodge, St. Judith's Lane/Sawtry,
Cambs PE17 5XE/UK
*Widely available from retailers and
distributors in the US. Check with local
bookstores.*

Delectus Books
27 Old Gloucester St/London WC1 3XX/
UK
Shipping: UK: £1.30 per book. Europe: £2
per book. US: £5.35 per book
Payment: US ck, UK ck, Eurocheque,
postal mo, Visa, MC, Access, Eurocard
*Available in the US through AK Press
[above]*

Dell Publishing
*Part of the Bantam Doubleday Dell
Publishing Group [above]*

Demarais Studio
64 Lawn Park Ave/Trenton NJ 08648
Shipping: $3.05. Non-US: $4.05
Payment: ck, mo

Diamond Sword
PO Box 4428/Bozeman MT 59772
Shipping: none
Payment: ck, mo (payable to Randy
Young)

Diesel: A Bookstore
5433 College Ave/Attn: John Evans or
Allison Reid/Oakland CA 94618
Voice: 510-653-9965
Shipping: $4. Non-US: $10
Payment: ck, Visa, MC
*Sunbelt Stories will not be available again
until November 1998*

Dirty Rotten Press
PO Box 11/Rock Island TX 77470
Shipping: $1.50 per book. Non-US: $3 per
book
Payment: ck
Catalogue: SASE

**Dorrance Publishing
Company**
Attn: Book Order Dept/643 Smithfield St/
Pittsburgh PA 15222
Voice: 1-800-788-7654 or 412-288-4543 x
26
Fax: 412-288-1786
Email: dorrordr@usaor.net

WWW: www.usaor.net/dorrance
Shipping: $3.50 first book, $2 each
additional. Non-US: $5 first book, $3 each
additional
Payment: cash, ck, mo, Visa, MC, Disc,
Amex

Doubleday
*Part of the Bantam Doubleday Dell
Publishing Group [above]*

Dover Publications
31 E 2nd St/Mineola NY 11501
Shipping: $3 flat charge
Catalogs: free

Down There Press
938 Howard St, #101/San Francisco CA
94103
Voice: 1-800-289-8423 (1-800-BUY-VIBE)
Fax: 415-974-8989
Email: goodvibe@well.com
WWW: www.goodvibes.com
Shipping: Continental US: up to $20:
$4.50; $20.01 to $40: $5.95. AL/HI: add an
extra $1.25. Can/Mex: up to $20: $8.75;
$20.01 to $40: $10.75. Overseas: up to
$100: $20.
Payment: cash, ck, mo, Visa, MC, Disc,
Amex
*Credit cards cannot be used for orders by
mail*

Dr. Deborah Anapol
PO Box 4322/San Rafael CA 94913
Email: pad@well.com
WWW: www.lovewithoutlimits.com
Shipping: $4 first book, $2 each additional.
Non-US: $10 each
Payment: cash, ck, mo

Dragon's World Ltd
7 St. George's Square/London SW1V 2HX/
UK
Voice: 0171-630-9955
Fax: 0171-630-9921
Shipping: UK: £2. Non-UK: £3
Payment: ck or mo in sterling, Visa,
Access

**Drawn and Quarterly
Publications**
PO Box 48056/Montreal Quebec H2V 4S8/
CANADA
Voice/Fax: 514-279-2221
Email: dqdrawn@jonction.net
WWW: www.eggcite.com/quarterly
Shipping: US/Can: included. Elsewhere
Ground: included. Elsewhere Air: 50% of
cost
Payment: Can ck, US ck, mo, international
mo in US funds, Visa, MC, Amex

Dream Distributors
division of EcoFrontiers
32038 Caminito Quieto/Bonsall CA 92003
Shipping: $3

DS4A
c/o Box 8, Greenleaf Bookshop/82 Colston
St/Bristol Avon BS1 5BB/UK
Shipping: shipping to US included in prices
Payment: US or UK currency, UK ck, UK

mo, international mo
Also available through AK Press

Dufour Editions
PO Box 7/Chester Spings PA 19425-0007
Voice: 1-800-869-5677
Fax: 610-458-7103
Shipping: $3.50 per order
Payment: ck, mo, Visa, MC

Duke University Press
PO Box 90660/Durham NC 27708-0660
Voice: 919-668-5134
Fax: 919-688-2615
WWW: www.duke.edu/web/dupress
Shipping: $4 first book, 95¢ each
additional. Non-US: $5 first book, $2 each
additional
Payment: ck, mo, Visa, MC

Earthpulse Press
PO Box 201393/Anchorage AL 99520
Voice: 907-249-9111
Fax: 907-696-1277
Email: drnick@alaska.net
WWW: www.earthpulse.com
Shipping: $3 first book, $1 each additional.
Non-US: $6 first book, $3 each additional
Payment: cash, ck, mo, Visa, MC

The Einhorn Press
Box 500, Route 3/Parkersburg WV 26101
Shipping: $3.50 first book, $1 each
additional. Non-US: $7 first book, $2 each
additional
Payment: cash, ck, mo

Element Books
PO Box 830/Rockport MA 01966
WWW: www.penguin.co.uk/Penguin/
Browse/1_100_Title.html
WWW: www.eastwest.com/Element
Order through Penguin [below]

Elliott & Clark Publishing
PO Box 21038/Washington DC
20009-0538
Voice: 1-800-789-7733
Fax: 212-483-0355
Shipping: $3 for 1-2 books, $5 for 3 or
more. Non-US: inquire first
Payment: ck, mo, Visa, MC

**Elliot & James
Publishing**
116 Prospect St/Seattle WA 98109
Voice: 206-283-0638
Fax 206-283-0649
Shipping: $3. Non-US: $7
Payment: cash, ck, mo, Visa, MC

Elysium-Sunwest
814 Robinson Rd, Dept P/Topanga CA
90290
Voice: 1-800-350-2020
Fax: 310-455-2007
WWW: www.elysium-sunwest.com
Shipping: up to $25: $3.95; over $25:
$4.50. Non-US: inquire first
Payment: ck, mo, Visa, MC

Emery Dalton Books
1110 Camino del Mar, Suite C/DelMar CA

92014
order from: NBN/4720-A Boston Wy/
Lanham MD 20706
Voice: 1-800-462-6420

EMP, Inc

757 Front St/Cleveland OH 44017-1608
Voice: 1-800-209-3033
Fax: 216-234-0045
Shipping: $2.50 per book
Payment: cash, ck, mo, Visa, MC

Equinox Press

144 St. John's Place/Brooklyn NY 11217
Voice: 1-800-929-WELL or 718-636-1679
Fax: 718-636-0186
WWW: www.ralphmoss.com/catalog.html
Shipping: $4 for one book
Payment: ck, mo, Visa, MC, Amex

EROS Comix

PO Box 25070/Seattle WA 98115
Voice: 1-800-657-1100
Fax: 206-524-2104
WWW: www.eroscomix.com
Shipping: under $40: $4. Non-US: under
$40: $6.
Payment: ck, international mo, Visa, MC

Exhibit A Press

4657 Cajon Way/San Diego CA 92115
Email: jackieandbat@compuserve.com
WWW: exhibit.edgeglobal.com
Shipping: $2 per book. Non-US: $4 per
book
Payment: cash, ck, mo

Factor Press

PO Box 8888/Mobile AL 36689
Voice: 1-800-304-0077
Email: factorpress@zebra.net
Shipping: $3 first book, $1.50 each
additional. Mex/Can: $4 first book, $2 each
additional. Elsewhere: $6 first book, $3
each additional
Payment: ck, mo, Visa, MC

Facts on File

460 Park Ave S/New York NY 10016
Voice: 1-800-322-8755
WWW: www.factsonfile.com

Faiz Ansari

Box 37542-1520 Lonsdale Ave/North
Vancouver BC V7M-3L7/CANADA
Fax: 604-985-0732
Email: info@penis-enhancement.com
WWW: www.penis-enhancement.com
Shipping: Can: $3. US: $5US. Elsewhere:
$7
Payment: international mo (payable to Faiz
Ansari), Visa (online only)

Fantagraphics Books

7563 Lake City Way NE/Seattle WA 98115
Voice: 1-800-657-1100
Fax: 206-524-2104
Email: fbicomix@fantagraphics.com
WWW: www.fantagraphics.com
Shipping: under $40: $4. Non-US: under
$40: $6.
Payment: ck, mo, Visa, MC
Catalogue: free

FC2

Unit for Contemporary Literature/Illinois
State University/109 Fairchild Hall/Normal
IL 61790-4241
Voice: 1-800-621-2736 or 312-568-1550
Fax: 312-660-2235
Email: ckwhite@rs6000.cmp.ilstu.edu
WWW: www.litline.org/html/fc2.html
Shipping: none
Payment: cash, ck, mo
Sales tax: none
Can also be ordered through Northwestern
University Press [below]

Fearless Books

1678 Shattuck Ave #319/Berkeley CA
94709
Voice: 1-800-480-2776
Fax: 510-704-0972
Email: fearlessbook@aol.com
Shipping: none
Payment: ck, mo

Feh! Press

200 E 10th St #603/New York NY 10003
Shipping: none. Non-US: $2
Payment: cash, ck, mo

Femme Distribution

PO Box 268, Prince St Station/New York
NY 10012
Voice: 1-800-456-LOVE
Email: custserv@royalle.com
WWW: www.royalle.com
Shipping: 1 movie: $4.95, 2 movies: $6.25
Unable to ship to PO Boxes, APO or FPO
addresses

Feral House

2532 Lincoln Blvd #359/Venice CA 90291
Email: cult@feralhouse.com
WWW: www.feralhouse.com
Shipping: $3 first book, $1 each additional.
Canada: $3 first book, $1.50 each
additional. Elsewhere Surface: $4 first
book, $3 each additional. Elsewhere Air:
$10 first book, $8 each additional
Payment: ck, mo
Credit card users can order Feral House
publications from Atomic Books [above]

Firebrand Books

141 The Commons/Ithaca NY 14850
Voice: 1-800-663-1766
Shipping: $3 first book, 50¢ each
additional. Non-US: $4 first book, $1 each
additional.
Payment: cash, ck, mo, Visa, MC

Fireside

a division of Simon & Schuster

Fithian Press

PO Box 1525/Santa Barbara CA 93102
Voice: 1-800-662-8351
Fax: 805-962-8835
Shipping: $2.50 per order. Non-US: $5 per
order
Payment: cash, ck, mo, Visa, MC

Flashback Books

20 Sunnyside Ave, Suite A195/Mill Valley
CA 94941

Email: flashbks@nbn.com
Shipping: $3 worldwide
Payment: cash, ck, mo, Visa, MC, Disc
Sales tax: none

Four Walls Eight Windows

39 W 14th St, #503/New York NY 10011
Voice: 1-800-788-3123
Email: eightwind@aol.com
WWW: www.fourwallseightwindows.com
Shipping: $3.75 first book, 75¢ each
additional
Payment: ck, mo, Visa, MC

Fourth Estate

289 Westbourne Grove/London W11 2QA/
England
order from Tiptree Book Services Ltd
Cash Sales Dept/Tiptree/Colchester Essex
C05 OSR/UK
Voice: 1621-816362
Fax: 1621-819968
Shipping: non-UK Surface: £1.20. Non-UK
Air: £2.50
Payment: Visa, MC

Fox & Wilkes

938 Howard St #202/San Francisco CA
94103
Voice: 1-800-326-0996
Fax: 415-541-0597
Email: LFB@panix.com
Shipping: up to $25: $3.25; $25 to $50:
$4.50. Non-US Surface: $3 per book
Payment: ck, mo, Visa, MC, Disc

Frank Kowalik

c/o Universalistic Publishers/PO Box
70486/Oakland Park FL 33307-0486
Shipping: $3.55 first book, $1 each
additional
Payment: ck, mo (payable to Frank
Kowalik)

Frank Wallis

PO Box 641741/San Francisco CA 94109
Shipping: $3

Franklin Square Press

division of Harper's Magazine/666
Broadway/New York NY 10012

The Free Press

division of Simon & Schuster [below]

Free Soul

PO Box 1762/Sedona AZ 86339
WWW: www.freesoul.net
Shipping: none. Non-US: inquire first
Payment: cash, ck, mo
There is instructor training available for
those wanting to teach the methods in
Access Your Brain's Joy Center.

Free Spirit Publishing

400 1st Ave N, Suite 616/Minneapolis MN
55401
Voice: 1-800-735-7323 or 612-338-2068
WWW: www.freespirit.com
Shipping: $10.01 to $19.95: $4.25
Payment: ck, mo, Visa, MC, Amex, Disc

Freedom Press
available from AK Press [above] and Autonome Distribution [above]

Futuremed
PO Box 13837/Scottsdale AZ 85267
Voice: 1-800-800-8849
Fax: 1-602-998-1530
Email: selfheal@aol.com
Shipping: $4. Non-US: $10
Payment: cash, ck, mo, Visa, MC, Disc, Amex

Gallaudet University Press
800 Florida Ave NE/Washington DC 20002-3695
Voice: 1-800-451-1073 or 202-651-5488
Fax: 202-651-5489
WWW: www.gallaudet.edu/~gupress
Shipping: 10% of total or $3, whichever is greater. Non-US: 15% of total or $10, which ever is greater
Payment: ck, Visa, MC

Garrett County Press
PO Box 896/Madison WI 53701
Email: garrett@gcpress.com
WWW: www.gcpress.com
Shipping: Book Rate: included. First Class: $2. Non-US: $4
Payment: cash, ck

Garrett Publishing
384 S Military Trail/Deerfield Beach FL 33442
Voice: 1-800-333-2069 or 305-480-8543
Fax: 305-698-0057
WWW: www.garrettpub.com
Shipping: $4.50 per title
Payment: ck, mo, Visa, MC

Gates of Heck
954 Lexington Avenue, Suite 118/New York NY 10021
Voice: 800-213-8170 or 212-343-8878
Fax: 212-334-4042
Email: orders@heck.com; catalog@heck.com
WWW: www.heck.com
Shipping: US/Can: $5 per order; Elsewhere: $10
Payment: cash, ck, mo, Visa, MC, Amex

Gateways Books
PO Box 370-P/Nevada City CA 95959-0370
Voice: 1-800-869-0658 or 916-272-0180
Fax: 916-272-0184
Email: gateway@oro.net
WWW: www.slimeworld.org/gateways
Shipping: $3.50 first book, $1 each additional. Non-US: inquire first
Payment: cash, ck, mo, Visa, MC, Amex

The Gay Men's Press
PO Box 247/Swaffham PE37 8PA/UK
Email: Sales@gmppubs.co.uk
WWW: www.gmppubs.co.uk
Shipping: Surface: 10%. Air: 15%
Payment: UK ck, Eurocheque, Visa, MC, Amex

Gay Sunshine Press
PO Box 410690/San Francisco CA 94141

Gemini Press
33 Belmont Place/Melrose MA 02176-1713
Email: rdwallace@sprintmail.com
Shipping: $2 each
Payment: ck, mo

General Publishing Group
Fulfillment/2701 Ocean Park Blvd #140/Santa Monica CA 90405
Voice: 1-888-CALLGPG
Fax: 310-314-8080
Email: gpg140@aol.com
Payment: cash, ck, Visa, MC
Sales Tax: CA, IN, OH, TN, VA

Get Lost! Publishing
Box 18521/1001 WB/Amsterdam, The Netherlands
Voice: 1-800-BUY-HEMP
Fax: 3120-626-8192
Email: getlost@xs4all.nl
WWW: www.xs4all.nl/~getlost
The address above is for wholesale orders only. Individuals should order from the phone number, online from Amazon.com (www.amazon.com), or their local bookstore.

Glenbridge Publishing
6010 W Jewell Ave/Lakewood CO 80232
Voice: 1-800-986-4135 or 303-986-4135
Fax: 303-987-9037
Shipping: $3 first book, 50¢ each additional.
Payment: ck, mo, Visa, MC

Glenn Belverio/S.O. Productions
PO Box 20553/New York NY 10009
Email: orgsmadict@aol.com
Shipping: $3. Non-US: $6
Payment: mo only

Glittering Images
Via Ardengo Soffici 11/13, 50142 Florence/ITALY
Shipping: Non-Italy Surface: 15.000 lira flat rate. Non-Italy Air: 15.000 lira per book
USA Distributor: Spartacus-Centurion/PO Box 429, Dept. A/Orange CA 92666

Global City Press
Simon H. Rifkind Center for Humanities/City College of New York/138th St. and Convent/New York NY 10031
WWW: www.webdelsol.com/GlobalCity/toc.htm
Shipping: $2

Global Health Solutions
PO Box 3189/Falls Church VA 22043
Voice: 1-800-759-3999 or 703-848-2333
Fax: 703-848-2334
Shipping: $3. Non-US: inquire first
Payment: ck, mo, Visa, MC

Goldtree Press
1174 S Diamond Bar Blvd, Suite 631/Diamond Bar CA 91765

Email: goldtreepr@aol.com
Shipping: $1.50 first book, 75¢ each additional. Non-US Surface: $3 first book, $1 each additional. Non-US Air: 50% of order cost
Payment: cash, ck, mo
Also available from Amazon.com (www.amazon.com)

Good Taste Products
PO Box 267869/Chicago IL 60626
Shipping: $2.05

Goofy Foot Press
PO Box 69365/West Hollywood CA 90069-0365
Voice: 1-800-310-PLAY or 310-659-8430
Fax: 310-652-2995
Email: bigbang@well.com
Shipping: $4 first book, $1 each additional
Payment: cash, ck, mo, Visa, MC

Govardhan Hill Publishers
PO Box 1920/Alachua FL 32616-1920
Voice: 904-462-0466
Fax: 904-462-0463
Email: ghi@nerdc.ufl.edu
WWW: nersp.nerdc.ufl.edu/~ghi
Shipping: Book rate: $3. Priority: $4. Non-US Surface: $5.
Payment: cash, ck, mo

Graphis Press
141 Lexington Ave/New York NY 10016
WWW: www.graphis.com
Shipping: $5 per book
Payment: ck, Visa, MC, Amex

Green Fir Publishing
division of Sturgeon Engineering Co/598 Innovation Rd/Petrolia CA 95558
Shipping: $2.05. Non-US: $4
Payment: ck, mo

Greenery Press
3739 Balboa Ave #195/San Francisco CA 94121
Voice: 888-944-4434
Fax: 415-242-4409
Email: verdie@earthlink.net
WWW: www.bigrock.com/~greenery
Shipping: $3 first book, $1 each additional. Non-US: same; if you want faster delivery, contact for a quote
Payment: ck, mo, Visa, MC
Catalogue: SASE and age statement

Greenwood Publishing Group
88 Post Rd W, Box 5007/Westport CT 06881
Voice: 1-800-225-5800
Fax: 203-222-1502
WWW: www.greenwood.com
Shipping: $4 first book, $1 each additional.
Can: $5 first book, $1 each additional
Payment: ck, MC, Visa, Amex
Sales Tax: IL, CT, MA

Grey Matter
available from AK Press

Griffin Publishing
c/o Continuing Life Research
PO Box 11036/Boulder CO 80301

Grove/Atlantic
841 Broadway/New York NY 10003

Guides for Living
PO Box 1104/Longmont CO 80502-1104
Voice: 1-800-225-1860
Fax: 1-800-413-1781
Shipping: $6 per book. Non-US: inquire first
Payment: cash, ck, mo, Visa, MC
Sales tax: none
"Will accept purchase orders from qualified institutions."

The Guilford Press
Order Dept/72 Spring St/New York NY 10012
Voice: 1-800-365-7006
Fax: 212-966-6708
Email: info@guilford.com
WWW: www.guilford.com
Shipping: $3.50 first book, $1.50 each additional
Payment: ck, mo, Visa, MC, Amex

Gun Owners Foundation
8001 Forbes Place, Suite 102/Springfield VA 22151
Voice: 1-800-417-1486
Email: GOAMAIL@gunowners.org
WWW: www.gunowners.org

Hampton Roads Publishing Company
134 Burgess Lane/Charlottesville, VA 22902
Voice: 1-800-766-8009
Fax: 1-800-766-9042
Email: hrpc@hrpub.com
WWW: www.hrpub.com
Shipping: $3 first book, $1 each additional.
Non-US: $6 first book, $2 each additional
Payment: cash, ck, mo, visa, MC, Disc, Amex

Happy Capitalist Productions
119 W 23rd St, Room 407/New York NY 10011
Voice: 1-800-642-7796
Fax: 212-462-4050
Email: info@happycapitalist.com
WWW: www.happycapitalist.com
Shipping: $3
Payment: cash, ck, mo, Visa, MC, Amex, Disc

Harcourt Brace & Co Trade Division
Order Fulfillment/6277 Sea Harbor Dr/Orlando FL 32887-4300
Phone: 1-800-543-1918
Fax: 1-800-235-0256
WWW: www.harcourtbooks.com
Shipping: $1 first book, 50¢ each additional. Non-US: "not accepted (except Canada)"
Payment: ck, mo, Visa, MC, Amex
Sales tax: all states

Hardy Marks Publications
722 Columbus Ave/San Francisco CA 94133
Email: hmarks@pop.sirius.com
WWW: www.sirius.com/~hmarks
Shipping: US/Can: $5 first book, $1 each additional. UK/Europe: $10 per book. Asia/Aus/NZ: $15 per book
Payment: ck, mo

Harmony Concepts
PO Box 69976, Dept P/Los Angeles CA 90069
Voice: 818-766-1448
Fax: 818-766-9679
WWW: www.harmonyconcepts.com
Shipping: none. Non-US: none
Payment: cash, ck, mo, Visa, MC

HarperCollins Publishers
10 E 53rd St/New York NY 10022-5299
WWW: www.harpercollins.com

Headpress
40 Rossall Avenue/Radcliffe/Manchester/M26 1JD/UK
Shipping: $6
Payment: cash in registered letter, UK check
available in the US from AK Press [above] and Last Gasp [below]

Health Action Press
6439 Taggart Rd/Delaware OH 43015
Shipping: $1.50 first book, 50¢ each additional. Non-US: $2.50 first book, $1 each additional
Payment: cash, ck, mo

Health Communications
3201 SW 15th St/Deerfield Beach FL 33442

Health Freedom Resources
1533 Long St/Clearwater FL 34615
Voice: 1-800-393-7954 or 813-443-7711
Email: onlineshop@healthfree.com
WWW: www.healthfree.com
Shipping: $2
Payment: ck, mo, Visa, MC

H.E.M.P.
5632 Van Nuys Blvd, Suite 310/Van Nuys CA 91401
Shipping: $3 per book (worldwide)
Payment: ck, mo

Henry Holt and Company
115 W 18th St/New York NY 10011
WWW: www.henryholt.com

Herb Crawford
4741 W Camino Terra/Tucson, Arizona
[note: use of the full state name and absence of zip code are on purpose]
Email: halkire@rtd.com
Shipping: none (worldwide)
Payment: cash, ck, mo
Sales tax: none

Heyday Books
PO Box 9145/Berkeley CA 94709
Voice: 510-549-3564
Fax: 510-549-1889
Email: heyday@heydaybooks.com
WWW: www.heydaybooks.com
Shipping: $3. Non-US: $5
Payment: cash, ck, mo, Visa, MC

Hill of Content Publishing
order from: Seven Hills Distributors
49 Central Ave/Cincinnati OH 45202
Voice: 513-381-3881

The Hobo Press
1044 Linden Ave/Deerfield IL 60015
Shipping: $1 first book, $1.24 for 2-4 copies
Payment: cash, ck

Holt Associates, Inc.
2269 Massacheussetts Ave/Cambridge MA 02140
Voice: 617-864-3100
Fax: 617-864-9235
Email: holtgws@erols.com
WWW: www.holtgws.com
Shipping: Continental US: $3.90. AK/HI/Can: $3. Elsewhere: 40% of total
Payment: cash, ck, mo, Visa, MC

Horus House Press
PO Box 55185/Madison WI 53705
Voice/Fax: 608-537-2383
Shipping: $2 per book. Non-US: $4 per book.
Payment: ck, mo, Visa, MC

Houghton Mifflin Company
Attn: Order Dept./222 Berkeley St/Boston MA 02116-3764
WWW: www.hmco.com

Howard Gregory Associates
640 The Village, Suite 209/Redondo Beach CA 90277
Shipping: $2. Non-US: inquire first
Payment: ck

Hudson Hills Press
230 5th Ave, Suite 1308/New York NY 10001-7704

Humanities Press International
165 First Avenue/Atlantic Highlands NJ 07716
Voice: 732-872-1441
Fax: 732-872-0717
Email: hpmarketing@humanitiespress.com
WWW: www.humanitiespress.com
Shipping: $4 first book, 75¢ each additional. Non-US Ground: same as US
Payment: ck, mo, Visa, MC
Must ship to a street address

Hunter House, Inc.
PO Box 2914/Alameda CA 94501-0914

Voice: 1-800-266-5592
Fax: 510-865-4295
Email: info@hunterhouse.com
WWW: www.hunterhouse.com
Shipping: $2.50 first book, 75¢ each additional. Non-US: $6 first book, $3 each additional
Payment: ck, mo, Visa, MC, Disc

Huntington House Publishers
PO Box 53788/Lafayette LA 70505

Hyperion
114 Fifth Ave/New York NY 10011

Hysteria Publications
PO Box 38581/Bridgeport CT 06605
Voice: 800-784-5244 or 203-333-9399
Fax: 203-367-7188
Email: laugh@hysteriabooks.com
WWW: www.hysteriabooks.com
Shipping: $3 first book, 50¢ each additional
Payment: ck, mo, Visa, MC, Amex

III Publishing
PO Box 1581/Gualala CA 95445
Email: 71321.3177@compuserve.com
WWW: ourworld.compuserve.com/homepages/iiipub
Shipping: $2 per order. Non-US: $2 per title
Payment: cash, ck, mo
Sales tax: "None. Sales tax on books, magazines, and newspapers is prohibited by the First Amendment of the Constitution."

IllumiNet Press
PO Box 2808/Lilburn GA 30226
Voice: 1-800-680-INET (4638)
Fax: 770-279-8007
Email: info@illuminet.com; orders@illuminet.com
WWW: www.illuminet.com
Shipping: $2 first book, $1 each additional. Canada: $3 first book, 75¢ each additional. Others: $5 first book, $2 each additional
Payment: ck, mo, Visa, MC
Catalogue: free

Inanout Press
431 E 6th St/New York NY 10014
Shipping: $4 first book, $1 each additional
Payment: ck

Independent History and Research
PO Box 849/Coeur d'Alene ID 83816
WWW: www.hoffman-info.com
Shipping: $2.50 first book, 75¢ each additional. Non-US: $5
Payment: cash, ck, mo

INDEX Publishing Group
3368 Governor Dr, Suite 273/San Diego CA 92122
Voice: 1-800-546-6707
Fax: 619-281-0547
Email: ipgbooks@indexbooks.com
WWW: www.electriciti.com/~ipgbooks
Shipping: $4.75 first book, $2.50 each additional. Non-US: inquire first

Payment: cash, ck, mo, Visa, MC, Amex

Inheritance Press
207 E Rosemary St/Chapel Hill NC 27514
Shipping: $2.50. Non-US: $5.50
Payment: ck, mo

Inner Light Publications
PO Box 753/New Brunswick NJ 08903
Shipping: $4 flat fee
Payment: ck, mo, Visa, MC, Disc

Inner Traditions International
PO Box 388/One Park St/Rochester VT 05767
Voice: 1-800-2-GO-TO-IT (246-8648)
Fax: 802-767-3726
Email: orders@gotoit.com; info@gotoit.com
WWW: www.gotoit.com
Shipping: $3 first book, $1 each additional. Non-US: $4 first book, $2 each additional
Payment: cash, ck, mo, Visa, MC

Insignia Publishing
1429 G St NW, Suite 535-300/Washington DC 20005
Voice: 1-800-606-BOOK [2665]
Fax: 301-540-3795
Email: InsigniaPC@aol.com
WWW: www.insigniaUSA.com
Shipping: $5 first book, $1 each additional
Payment: ck, mo, Visa, MC, Amex, Disc

Insomniac Press
378 Delaware Avenue/Toronto ON M6H 2T8/CANADA
Email: insomnia@pathcom.com
WWW: www.insomniacpress.com

Intangible Assets Manufacturing
828 Ormond Ave/Drexel Hill PA 19026-2604
Voice: 610-853-4406
Fax: 610-853-3733
Email: info@iam.com
WWW: www.iam.com
Shipping: Book rate: $2; Priority: $5. Non-US Ground: $3. Non-US Air: $6
Payment: cash, ck, mo, Visa, MC

Intelligence Incorporated
2228 S El Camino Real/San Mateo CA 94403

The International Patriarchy
c/o R.J. Daniel/537 Jones St #9295/San Francisco CA 94102
Payment: mo only

inter-relations
Attn: Frank Moore/PO Box 11445/Berkeley CA 94712
Email: fmoore@lanminds.com
WWW: www.eroplay.com
Shipping: included. Non-US: $2.50
Payment: cash, ck

Island Records
400 Lafayette St/New York NY 10003
Voice: 1-800-622-1387
Fax: 212-995-7892
WWW: www.island.co.uk

Ivan R. Dee
1332 N Halsted St/Chicago IL 60622
Voice: 1-800-634-0226
Fax: 312-787-6269
WWW: www.ivanrdee.com
Shipping: $3.50 first book, 50¢ each additional
Payment: ck, mo, Visa, MC, Amex

James E. Bare, DC
8005 Marble Ave NE/Albuquerque NM 87110
Voice: 505-268-4272
Fax: 505-268-4064
Email: rifetech@rt66.com
WWW: www.rt66.com/~rifetech/
Shipping: $5. Non-US Air: $10
Payment: cash, ck, mo, Visa, MC
Sales tax: none
If you buy the book and the video at the same time, you only pay shipping charges for the book (ie, $5 or $10).

Jenkins Publishing
Email: jcjenkins@jenkinspublishing.com
WWW: www.jenkinspublishing.com
order from: Chelsea Green Publishing/PO Box 428/White River Jct VT 05001
Voice: 1-800-639-4099
WWW: www.madriver.com/ymorrow/chelsea.htm
Shipping: $4. Canada: $5
Payment: ck, mo, Visa, MC, Amex, Disc
in UK: Greenbooks/Foxhole, Dartington/Totnes Devon TQ9 6EB
WWW: www.greenbooks.co.uk
Payment: ck, postal order, Visa, MC, Access
Shipping: £1.50

Jewish Radical Education Project
1 Union Square W, Room 302/New York NY 10003
Email: jeyrep@aol.com
WWW: www.jeyrep.org
Shipping: $1.50 per book
Payment: ck

Jews for the Preservation of Firearms Ownership
2874 S Wentworth Ave, Dept RK/Milwaukee WI 53207
Voice: 414-769-0760
Fax: 414-483-8435
WWW: www.jpfo.org
Shipping: none. Non-US: contact first
Payment: cash, ck, mo, Visa, MC, Amex

John Brown Publishing
The New Boathouse/Crabtree Lane/Fulham, London SW6 6LU/UK
WWW: www.forteantimes.co.uk/merchandise/books.html
Shipping: none (worldwide)
Payment: UK ck, international mo, Visa,

MC, Amex, Access

John Wiley & Sons
Distribution Center/1 Wiley Drive/Somerset
NJ 08875-1272
Voice: 1-800-225-5945
Fax: 732-302-2300
Email: bookinfo@wiley.com
WWW: www.wiley.com
Shipping: $2.50
Payment: ck, mo, Visa, MC, Amex, Disc

Johnson Books
1880 S 57th Court/Boulder CO 80301
Voice: 303-443-9766
Fax: 303-443-1679
Shipping: $3.50. Non-US: inquire first
Payment: cash, ck, mo, Visa, MC

Jolly Roger Press
PO Box 295/Berkeley CA 94701

Jonathan Ott Books/
Natural Products Co
PO Box 1251/Occidental CA 95465
Shipping: $3 each book. Non-US: $5 each
book
Payment: cash, ck, mo

J.R. Schwartz
Box 1810/Boise ID 83701-1810
WWW: www.hookersex.com
Shipping: included. Non-US: $2
Payment: cash, ck, mo

Juno Books
180 Varick St, 10th Floor/New York NY
10014
Voice: 1-800-758-5238 or 212-807-7300
Fax: 212-807-7355
Email: junobook@interport.net
WWW: www.junobooks.com
Shipping: $4 first book, $1 each additional.
Non-US: $10 first book, $3 each additional
Payment: cash, ck, mo, Visa, MC

Kensington Publishing
Corporation
Attention: Order Dept/850 Third Avenue/
New York NY 10022
Voice: 1-888-345-BOOK
WWW: www.kensingtonbooks.com
Shipping: $2 + 50¢ per book. Non-US $3 +
$1.50 per book
Payment: ck, mo, Visa, MC

Knopf
Division of Random House [below]

Kodansha America
114 Fifth Ave/New York NY 10011
Voice: 1-800-788-8262
Fax: 201-933-2316
WWW: www.kodansha.co.jp
Shipping: $3.50 for one book, $4.25 for 2.
Payment: ck, mo, Visa, MC, Amex

Korinsha Press
East of Aburanokoji/Motoseiganji St/
Kamigyo/Kyoto 602/JAPAN
Voice: 011-075-441-6793
To order a signed copy of Linea *directly
from the artist, see Craig Morey [above]*

Krieger Publishing
Company
PO Box 9542/Melbourne FL 32902
Vocie: 407-724-9542
Fax: 407-951-3671
Email: info@krieger-pub.com
WWW: www.web4u.com/krieger-publishing
Shipping: $3 for one copy
Payment: ck, mo, Visa, MC, Disc

Larry Townsend
PO Box 302/Beverly Hills CA 90213
Voice: 213-463-2333
Fax: 213-655-7314
WWW: www.larrytownsend.com
Shipping: $2.25 per book (maximum of
$9.50). Europe/UK/South America: $4.95
per book. Australia/Asia/Africa: $6.50 per
book
Payment: cash, ck, mo, Visa, MC
Catalogue: $2 and age statement

Larry Wessel
PO Box 1611/Manhattan Beach CA
90267-1611
Shipping: none. Non-US: inquire first
Payment: ck, mo
Catalogue: SASE

Last Gasp
777 Florida St/San Francisco CA 94110
Voice: 1-800-848-4277 or 415-824-6636
Fax: 415-824-1836
Email: lastgasp@hooked.net
WWW: www.lastgasp.com
Shipping: US: up to $19.99: $3; $20 to
$99.99: $6. Non-US Surface: $1 to $100:
$7. Europe Air: $1 to $100: $30. Others
Air: $40. Non-US Surface: $7
Payment: ck, mo, Visa, MC, Amex, Disc
Sales tax: none

Last Rights Publications
The Right to Die Society of Canada
PO Box 39018/Victoria BC V8V 4X8/
CANADA
Email: rights@rights.org
WWW: www.rights.org/deathnet
Shipping: none
Payment: ck, mo, international mo
*You must send a signed age statement
(21+) to order any of these publications. In
the US, you can order from C.K. Smith
[above]*

Laugh Lines Press
PO Box 259/Bala Cynwyd PA 19004
Voice: 1-800-356-9315
Email: rozwarren@aol.com
Shipping: $1 per book. Non-US: $3 per
book
Payment: cash, ck, mo
*Credit cards may be used only for phone
orders*

Left Bank Books
1404 18th Ave/Seattle WA 98122
Voice/Fax: 206-322-2868
Email: leftbank@leftbankbooks.com
WWW: www.leftbankbooks.com
Shipping: $2 first book, 35¢ each
additional. Non-US Surface: $3.50 first
book, 75¢ each additional

Payment: cash, ck, mo, Visa, MC

Lexington Books
imprint of Paramount Publishing/866 3rd
Ave/New York NY 10022

Leyland Publications
PO Box 410690/San Francisco CA 94141

Liberty Library
300 Independence Ave SE/Washington DC
20003
Voice: 1-800-522-6292
Payment: cash, ck, mo, Visa, MC

Lifeservices
PO Box 4314A/Boca Raton FL 33429
Shipping: $2. Overseas: $5
Payment: cash, ck, mo

Lifetime Books
2131 Hollywood Blvd/Hollywood FL 33020
Voice: 1-800-771-3355
Fax: 305-925-5244
WWW: www.lifetimebooks.com
Shipping: $3.95. Non-US: $7.95
Payment: ck, mo, Visa, MC

Lisa Brosig
PO Box 18228/Chicago IL 60618
Shipping: none
Payment: cash, ck, mo

Little, Brown and
Company
Order Dept/1271 Avenue of the Americas/
New York NY 10020
WWW: www.littlebrown.com

Llewellyn Publications
PO Box 64383/St Paul MN 55164
Voice: 1-800-843-6666
Fax: 612-291-1908
WWW: www.llewellyn.com
Shipping: under $15: $4; over $15: $5.
Non-US Surface: add $1 to US rates.
Non-US Air: add retail price of the book
Payment: ck, mo, Visa, MC

Loompanics Unlimited
PO Box 1197/Port Townsend WA 98368
Voice: 1-800-380-2230 or 360-385-2230
Fax: 360-385-7785
Email: loompanx@olympus.net
WWW: www.loompanics.com
Shipping: up to $20: $4.95; $20.01-$35:
$5.95; $35.01-$45: $6.95. Non-US: add
12% of order to US rates
Payment: ck, mo, Visa, MC
Catalogue: see Appendix A

Lowell House
2020 Avenue of the Stars, Suite 300/Los
Angeles CA 90067
Voice: 310-552-7555, ext 10
Fax: 310-552-7573
Shipping: $3 + 75¢ per book
Payment: cash, ck, Visa, MC, Amex, Disc

Lowry House Publishers
PO Box 1014/Eugene OR 97440-1014
Voice: 503-686-2315
Fax: same

Shipping: $2 for one book; $3 for two; $3.50 for three
Payment: cash, ck, mo, Visa, MC

Lund Humphries
Park House/1 Russell Gardens/London NW11 9NN/UK
available in the US from Antique Collectors' Club [above]

Lysias Press
PO Box 192171/San Francisco CA 94119
Also can be ordered from Index Publishing Group [above]

M. Evans and Company
216 E 49th St/New York NY 10017
Email: mevans@sprynet.com
Shipping: $3 per book
Payment: ck, mo

M.E. Sharpe
80 Business Park Dr/Armonk NY 10504
Voice: 1-800-541-6563
Fax: 914-273-2106
WWW: www.mesharpe.com
Shipping: US/Can: $3.50 first book, $1.50 each additional. Elsewhere Surface: $5 first book, $3 each additional

Mainstreet Media
PO Box 364/Irvine CA 92650
Email: Nathancal@aol.com
Shipping: none
Payment: ck

Maisonneuve Press
PO Box 2980/Washington DC 20013-2980
Voice: 301-277-7505
Fax: 301-277-2467
Shipping: $2 first book, 50¢ each additional. Non-US Surface: $4 for one book. Non-US Air: $7 for one book
Payment: cash, ck, mo, Visa, MC

Manning Publications
3 Lewis St/Greenwich CT 06830
Voice: 1-800-247-6553
Fax: 419-281-6883
Email: orders@manning.com
WWW: www.browsebooks.com
Shipping: $3 first book, $1 each additional. Can/Mex: $9 first book, $5 each additional. UK/Europe: $10 first book, $5 each additional. Asia/Pacific Rim: $12
Payment: ck, mo, Visa, MC, Amex

Mark I. Chester
PO Box 422501/San Francisco CA 94142
Email: mchester@best.com
WWW: www.best.com/~mchester/
Shipping: $5. Non-US: $15
Payment: cash, ck, mo
Diary of a Thought Criminal is also available in hardcover ($50) and leatherbound ($350) editions

Mark V. Ziesing
PO Box 76/Shingletown CA 96088
Voice: 916-474-1580
Fax: same
Email: ziesing@bigchair.com
WWW: www.bigchair.com/ziesing

Shipping: up to $30: $3.75. $30-$100: $5.
Payment: cash, ck, mo, Visa, MC

Marlowe and Company
632 Broadway, 7th Flr/New York NY 10012

Martin Park Communications
S22, C35/Gabriola BC V0R 1X0/CANADA
Email: brownjay@island.net
WWW: www.island.net/~brownjay/index.html
Shipping: included
Payment: ck, mo (made out to Heide Brown)

Masquerade Books
Masquerade Direct/801 2nd Ave/New York NY 10017

McFarland & Company
PO Box 611/Jefferson NC 28640
Voice: 1-800-253-2187
Fax: 910-246-5018
WWW: www.mcfarlandpub.com
Shipping: $4 first book, 75¢ each additional. Non-US: $6 first book, $1.50 each additional
Payment: cash, ck, mo, Visa, MC, Amex

M.Ed Marketing
PO Box 28550/San Diego CA 92127
Voice: 1-800-551-5328
Fax: 619-676-0433
Email: medmktg@cts.com
Shipping: $5 first item, $1 each additional. Non-US: $12
Payment: cash, ck, mo, Visa, MC, Amex, Disc

MediPress
1717 Lincoln Way #108/Coeur d'Alene ID 83814
Voice: 800-456-1723
Shipping: $3.50

Mercury House
785 Market St, Suite 1500/San Francisco CA 94103
Voice: 415-974-0729
Fax: 415-974-0832
WWW: www.mercuryhouse.com
Shipping: $3 first book, 50¢ each additional; Non-US: inquire first
Payment: ck, mo, Visa, MC

Merit, Inc.
PO Box 694/Louisville KY 40201
Shipping: $5. Non-US: $10
Payment: cash, ck, mo

The Message Company
4 Camino Azul/Santa Fe NM 87505
Voice: 505-474-0998
Fax: 505-471-2584
Shipping: Continental US: $2 per order. AL/HI/Can: $2 + 10%. Elsewhere: $2 + 25%. For Air, add another $8 per book
Payment: ck, mo, Visa, MC, Amex, Disc

Mho & Mho Works
PO Box 33135/San Diego CA 92163
Email: poo@cts.com

WWW: www.ralphmag.org/mho.html
Shipping: $1.50 first book, $1 each additional (worldwide)
Payment: cash, ck, mo

Mike Hunt Publications
PO Box 226/Bensenville IL 60106
Shipping: $2. Non-US: $3
Payment: cash, ck, mo

The Mindreach Publishing Company
3419 Virginia Beach Blvd #D37/Virginia Beach VA 23452
Voice: 1-800-430-3956
Shipping: $2.50 each book
Payment: cash, ck, mo, Visa, MC, Disc, Amex

MIT Press
Five Cambridge Center/Cambridge MA 02142
Voice: 1-800-356-0343
Fax: 617-625-6660
Email: books@mit.edu; mitpress-orders@mit.edu
WWW: www-mitpress.mit.edu
Shipping: $3.50 first book, 75¢ each additional. Non-US: $3.50 each book
Payment: ck, mo, Visa, MC, Amex
Sales tax: none

Miwok Press
PO Box 1582/Novato CA 94948
Voice: 1-800-488-0550
Shipping: $2.45
Payment: ck, mo, Visa, MC

Moniker Media
PO Box 1640/Kaneohe HI 96744
Email: vwoodhull@aol.com
WWW: www.tricky.com/woodhull
Shipping: 4th class: free. 1st class: $2 per book. Non-US: $5 per book
Payment: cash, ck, mo

Monthly Review Foundation
122 W 27th St/New York NY 10001
Voice: 212-691-2555
Fax: 212-727-3676
Shipping: $3 first book, 50¢ each additional
Payment: cash, ck, mo, Visa, MC

Morningstar Books
PO Box 4032/San Rafael CA 94913-4032
Voice: 1-800-842-8338
Fax: 415-479-1320
WWW: www.bookzone.com/bookzone/indexed/10000332.html
Shipping: $2. Non-US: $6
Payment: ck, mo, Visa, MC, Disc

Morpheus International
9250 Wilshire Blvd, Suite LL15/Beverly Hills CA 90212
Voice: 310-859-2557
Fax: 310-859-7455
Email: curator@morpheusint.com
WWW: www.morpheusint.com
Shipping: $4 first book, $2 each additional. Non-US Surface: same as US
Payment: ck, mo, Visa, MC

Mouth
61 Brighton St/Rochester NY 14607
Shipping: $5
Payment: ck, mo, Visa, MC, Amex, Disc
Write for a free sampler of Mouth, *the militant disability rights zine*

Mystic Rose Books
PO Box 1036/Fairfield CT 06432
Fax: 203-371-4843
Email: mystrose@palace.com
WWW: palace.com/rose/mystic2.htm
Shipping: $3.50. Can/Mex: $5. Elsewhere: $12
Payment: ck, Visa, MC, Disc

NAMBLA
PO Box 174, Midtown Station/New York NY 10018
Email: arnoldschoen@juno.com
WWW: www.nambla.org
Publications can also be ordered from the boylove booksellers Ariel's Pages/PO Box 2487/New York NY 10185. Add $1.55 each for shipping. Or — if you'd rather keep your name off the FBI blacklists — See Hear *(listed in Appendix A) is the only general-purpose alternative bookseller I know of that has the nerve to carry NAMBLA's publications*

NBM
185 Madison Ave, Suite 1504/New York NY 10016
Voice: 1-800-886-1223
Fax: 212-545-1227
WWW: www.nbmpub.com
Shipping: $3 first book, $1 each additional ($6 max.). Non-US Surface: $4 first book, $1 each additional. Non-US Air: $10 first book, $5 each additional
Payment: ck, mo, Visa, MC

Negativmailorderland
1920 Monument Blvd MF-1/Concord CA 94520
Email: jake@negativland.com
WWW: www.negativland.com
Shipping: included. Canada: $2. Elsewhere: $4
Payment: cash, ck, mo, international mo (payable to Neagativland)

New Atlantean Press
PO Box 9638-R/Santa Fe NM 87504
Voice: 505-983-1856
Email: global@new-atlantean.com
WWW: www.new-atlantean.com
Shipping: 7% of order ($3.50 minimum). Non-US Surface: 9% of order (minimum $3.50).
Payment: cash, ck, mo, Visa, MC, Amex
Catalogue: free

New Falcon Publications
1739 E Broadway Rd, Suite 1-277/Tempe AZ 85282
Email: info@newfalcon.com
WWW: www.newfalcon.com
Shipping: $2 first book, $1 each additional (add an additional $2 for each hardcover book). Non-US: $4 first book, $2 each

additional (add an additional $3 for each hardcover book)
Payment: cash, ck, mo, international mo

New Harbinger Publications
5674 Shattuck Ave/Oakland CA 94609
Voice: 1-800-748-6273
Fax: 510-652-5472
Email: nhhelp@newharbinger.com
WWW: www.newharbinger.com
Shipping: $4 first book, $1 each additional. Canada: $3.80 first book, $2 each additional. Overseas: $10 first book, $1.25 each additional
Payment: ck, mo, Visa, MC

The New Press
Distributed by W.W. Norton & Co

NewSage Press
PO Box 607/Troutdale OR 97060
Voice: 503-695-2211
Fax: 503-695-5406
WWW: www.teleport.com/~newsage
Shipping: $2.50 first book, $1 each additional
Payment: ck, mo, Visa, MC

New Society Publishers
PO Box 189/1680 Peterson Rd/Gabriola Island, BC V0R 1X0/CANADA
Voice: 1-800-567-6772
Fax: 1-800-567-7311
Email: nsp@island.net
WWW: www.newsociety.com
Shipping: $3.50 first book, $1 each additional. Non-US: $5 first book, $1.50 each additional
Payment: Visa, MC, Amex

New Victoria Publishers
PO Box 27/Norwich VT 05055
Voice/Fax: 1-800-326-5297
Email: newvic@aol.com
WWW: www.opendoor.com/NewVic/
Shipping: $2 first book, 25¢ each additional
Payment: cash, ck, mo, Visa, MC

New York University Press
Order Dept/70 Washington Square S/New York NY 10012
Voice: 1-800-996-NYUP (6987)
Fax: 212-995-3833
WWW: www.nyupress.nyu.edu
Shipping: $3.50 first book, $1 each additional. Non-US Surface: $5 first, $3.50 each additional. Non-US Air: $10 first book, $5 each additional
Payment: cash, ck, mo, Visa, MC

Noble Press
213 W Institute Pl, Suite 508/Chicago IL 60610
Voice: 1-800-486-7737
Fax: 312-642-7682
Shipping: $2.50
Payment: ck

North Atlantic Books
1456 Fourth Street/Berkeley CA 94710
Voice: 1-800-337-2665

Fax: 510-559-8279
WWW: www.northatlanticbooks.com
Shipping: $2.50 first book, $1 each additional
Payment: ck, international mo, Visa, MC

North Ridge Books
818 N Via Alhambra/Laguna Hills CA 92653
Email: NRBooks@aol.com
Shipping: $3. Non-US: $8
Payment: cash, ck

Northeastern University Press
c/o CUP Services/Box 6525/Ithaca NY 14851
Voice: 607-277-2211
Fax: 800-688-2877
Email: webmaster@www.neu.edu
WWW: www.neu.edu/nupress
Shipping: $3.50 first book, 75¢ each additional. Non-US: $4 first book, $1 each additional
Payment: ck, Visa, MC, Amex

Northwestern University Press
Chicago Distribution Center/11030 S. Langley/Chicago IL 60628
Voice: 1-800-621-2736 or 312-568-1550
Fax: 312-660-2235
Email: nupress@nwu.edu
WWW: nupress.nwu.edu
Shipping: $3.50 first book, 75¢ each additional. Non-US: $4.50 first book, $1 each additional
Payment: cash, ck, mo, Visa, MC
Sales tax: none

Norton
See W.W. Norton & Co

NutriVoice
PO Box 946/Oak Park IL 60303
Shipping: $1.40 for one book; $2.30 for 2 to 5.
Payment: ck

Ocean Press
PO Box 834/Hoboken NJ 07030
Voice: 201-617-7247
Fax: 201-864-6434
Cuba: Calle 21 #406/Vedado, Havana
Australia: PO Box 3279/Melbourne, Victoria 3001

Odonian Press
Odonian Press has merged with Common Courage Press, so all of their books should be ordered through Common Courage [above]

The Olive Press
PO Box 99/Los Olivos CA 93441
Shipping: $3. Non-US: $5
Payment: ck, mo

One 8 Publishing
PO Box 2075/Forks WA 98331
Voice: 1-800-504-1818
Shipping: none
Payment: cash, ck, mo, Visa, MC

Open Court Publishing
Order Dept/PO Box 599/Peru IL 61354
Voice: 1-800-435-6850
Fax:1-800-417-5091
Shipping: $3 first book, $1 each additional ($10 maximum). Non-US: $5 first book, $1 each additional
Payment: ck, mo, Visa, MC, Amex
Sales tax: CA, IL, WA

Open Magazine Pamphlet Series
PO Box 2726/Westfield NJ 07091
Email: openmag@intac.com
Shipping: $1 flat rate. Non-US: $2 flat rate
Payment: cash, ck, mo, Amex traveler's cheques

O'Reilly & Associates
101 Morris St/Sebastopol CA 95472-9902
Voice: 1-800-998-9938
Fax: 707-829-0104
Email: nuts@ora.com; order@ora.com
WWW: www.ora.com
Shipping: up to $49.99: $4.50
Payment: ck, mo, Visa, MC, Disc, Amex
Sales tax: CA, MA, MO, TX, MI

Open Media
PO Box 2726/Westfield NJ 07091
Email: openmag@intac.com
Shipping: $1 per order. Non-US: $2 per order
Payment: cash, ck, mo

Orbis Books
PO Box 302/Maryknoll NY 10545-0302
Voice: 1-800-258-5838
Fax: 914-945-0670
Email: orbmarketg@aol.com
WWW: www.maryknoll.org/orbis/mklorbhp.htm
Shipping: 1-2 books: $3.50; 3 or more: $4
Payment: ck, mo, Visa, MC
Sales tax: CA, NY

Orchises Press
PO Box 20602/Alexandria VA 22320-1602
Email: rlathbur@osf1.gmu.edu
WWW: mason.gmu.edu/~rlathbur
Shipping: one book: $1.24; two books: $1.74; three: $2.24. Non-US: $1.56
Payments: cash, ck, mo

Natural Energy Works
PO Box 1148/Ashland OR 97520
Voice/Fax: 541-552-0118
Email: demeo@mind.net
WWW: id.mind.net/community/orgonelab/index.htm
Shipping: US/Can: $4 first item, 50¢ each additional. Elsewhere Surface: $7 first item, $4 each additional. Elsewhere Air: multiply Surface rate by 2.5.
Payment: ck, mo, international mo, Visa, MC

Oryx Press
4041 N Central Ave, Suite 700/Phoenix AZ 85012
Voice: 1-800-279-6799 or 602-265-2651
Fax: 602-265-6250
Email: info@oryxpress.com
WWW: www.oryxpress.com
Shipping: 10% of price
Payment: cash, ck, mo, Visa, MC, Amex
Sales Tax: AZ, Canada

The Overlook Press
2568 Route 212/Woodstock NY 12498
Voice: 914-679-6838
Fax: 914-679-8571
WWW: www.overlookpress.com
Shipping: $3.50 first book, $1.25 each additional
Payment: ck, mo, Visa, MC
Also distributed through Penguin

Oxford University Press
Order Dept/2001 Evansa Rd/Cary NC 27513
Voice: 1-800-451-7556
Fax: 1-919-677-1303
WWW: www.oup-usa.org
Shipping: $3.50 first book, $1 each additional
Payment: ck, Visa, MC, Amex

Ozark Mountain Publishers
PO Box 754/Huntsville AR 72740
Voice: 1-800-935-0045
Fax: 501-738-2348
Email: ozarkmt@ix.netcom.com
Shipping: $2 first book, $1 each additional (Nostradamus set: $3). Non-US: $3 first book, $2 each additional (Nostradamus set: $6)
Payment: cash, ck, mo, Visa, MC

PakDonald Publishing
6663 SW Beaverton-Hillsdale Hwy, Suite 175/Portland OR 97225
Voice: 1-800-755-0206
Fax: 503-224-9823
Shipping: $3
Payment: ck

Paladin Press
PO Box 1307/Boulder CO 80306
Voice: 1-800-392-2400
Fax: 303-442-8741
WWW: www.paladin-press.com
Shipping: $5 flat fee. Non-US Surface: $6 or 5% of total, whichever is greater.
Payment: ck, mo, Visa, MC, Disc
Catalogue: free

Panda Ink
2389 NW Military Hwy, Suite 572/San Antonio TX 78231
Email: Strike_knows_X@msn.com
WWW: www.lycaeum.org/~strike
Shipping: none. Can/Mex: $4. Elsewhere Surface: $2. Elsewhere Air: $8
Payment: cash, mo

Panic Button Priest
PO Box 217, Old Chelsea Station/New York NY 10113
Email: bobzark@escape.com
WWW: www.escape.com/~bobzark
Payment: cash, ck, mo

Panther Press
1032 Irving #514J/San Francisco CA 94122
Shipping: $2 per book. Overseas: $5 per book
Payment: ck, mo
Other: Credit card users can order from F.S. Book Company, 1-800-635-8883
On News Years Eve 1996, DM Turner — the author of both books published by Panther Press — passed away, apparently having drowned while using ketamine in a bathtub. Panther Press appears to be defunct, leading me to believe that Turner was the one who ran it. Remaining copies of his books should be snatched up wherever you can find them, including FS Book Company, Loompanics, AK, Mind Books, and elsewhere.

Paradox Press
division of DC Comics/1700 Broadway/New York NY 10019
Voice: 1-800-887-6789
WWW: www.dccomics.com/paradox

Paragon House Publishers
2700 University Ave W, Suite 200/St Paul MN 55114-1016
Voice: 612-644-3087
Fax: 612-644-0997
Email: paragon@paragonhouse.com
WWW: www.paragonhouse.com
Shipping: $3.50. Non-US: "actual cost of shipping"
Payment: ck, mo, Visa, MC

Paranoia
PO Box 1041/Providence RI 02901
Shipping: $2.50 per book

Parapsychology Foundation, Inc.
228 E 71st St/New York NY 10021
WWW: www.parapsychology.org
Shipping: $1 per book. Non-US $2 per book
Payment: ck, mo

Passion Press
PO Box 277/Newark CA 94560
Voice: 1-800-724-3283
Fax: 650-328-3604
Email: info@passionpress.com
WWW: www.passionpress.com
Shipping: 1 or 2 tapes: $3; 3 or more tapes: $5. Overseas: add $10
Payment: ck, Visa, MC

Pathfinder Press
410 West St/New York NY 10014
Voice: 212-741-0690
Fax: 212-727-0150
gopher://gopher.std.com/11/Book%20Sellers/Pathfinder%20Press
Shipping: $3 first title, 50¢ each additional
Payment: ck, mo, Visa, MC

PATNWO
PO Box 8712/Phoenix AZ 85066
Alternate: c/o Aid & Abet Police Newsletter/PO Box 8787/Phoenix AZ 85066
WWW: www.police-against-nwo.com

Shipping: $1.50 for one or two books.
Non-US: $1.95 for one or two books
Payment: cash, Postal money order
If you order two to six copies of Operation Vampire Killer 2000, *the price drops to $4.25 each*

PAUK
153 Tomkinson Rd/Nuneaton Warks CV10 8DP/UK
Shipping: £6 for one book. UK: £2. Europe: £4
Payment: cash, ck, mo

Peachtree Publishers
494 Armour Circle NE/Atlanta GA30324-4088
Voice: 1-800-241-0113

Peanut Butter Publishing
1101 Alaskan Way, Suite 301/Seattle WA 98101-2982
Phone: 206-748-0345
Fax: 206-748-0343
Email: pnutpub@aol.com
WWW: www.pbpublishing.com
Shipping: $3 first book; $5 for two
Payment: ck, mo, Visa, MC

PEC Publishing
28 W Henderson Rd/Columbus OH 43214-2628
Voice: 614-261-9343
Fax: 614-261-8280
Email: oralcaress@aol.com
WWW: oralcaress.com
Shipping: $3.75 first book, $2.50 each additional. Non-US: $5 first book, $3.75 each additional
Payment: ck, mo, Visa, MC

Pelican Publishing Company
PO Box 3110/Gretna LA 70054
Voice: 1-888-5-PELICAN
Fax: 504-368-1195
Email: sales@pelicanpub.com
WWW: www.pelicanpub.com
Payment: ck, Visa, MC

Pendulum Plus Press
141 Indian Trail/Jasper GA 30143
Voice: 1-800-842-8338
Fax: 810-987-3562
WWW: www.bookzone.com/pendulum
Shipping: $1.05
Payment: ck, mo, Visa, MC

Penguin
Order Dept/375 Hudson St/New York NY 10014
Voice: 1-800-253-6476
WWW: www.penguinputnam.com
Shipping: $2 per order
Payment: ck, mo, international mo, Visa, MC

Penguin Books (NZ) Ltd
Private Bag 102902, North Shore Mail Centre/Auckland/NEW ZEALAND
Voice/Fax: 64-9-4154702
For more information, you can email Jim Sprott at sprott@iconz.co.nz

Permanent Press
4170 Noyac Rd/Sag Harbor NY 11963
Voice/Fax: 516-725-1101
Email: info@thepermanentpress.com
WWW: www.thepermanentpress.com
Shipping: $4 first book, 50¢ each additional
Payment: ck, mo, Visa, MC
Sales tax: none

Permeable Press
WWW: www.cambrianpubs.com/permeable/permeable.html
Permeable Press has merged with Cambrian Publications [above]. All orders should go to Cambrian.

Phaidon Press
Regent's Wharf/All Saints St/London N1 9PA/UK
Distributed in the US by Chronicle Books [above]

Photographic Gallery of Fine Art Books
PO Box 370175/San Diego CA 92137
Voice: 619-221-0340
Fax: 619-223-5744
Shipping: 1 or 2 books: $4
Payment: cash, ck, mo, Visa, MC
Many of the images from Winged Victory *are online at www.canceranswers.org/gallery/myers.htm*

Pink Flamingo Publications
PO Box 632-K/Richland MI 49083
Voice: 616-629-0051
Email: information@pinklamingo.com; orders@pinkflamingo.com
WWW: www.pinkflamingo.com
Shipping: $3 per order. Canada: $5 per order. Elsewhere: $5 first book, $2 each additional
Payment: cash, ck, mo, Visa, MC
Catalogue: $1

Planet Press
PO Box 4544/Tubac AZ 85646
Shipping: $3.50. Non-US: $5.50
Payment: cash, ck, mo
Sales tax: AZ, CA
If you want to buy Hot Planet, *the author/publisher urges you to request that a local bookstore special order it from Ingram Book Company*

Playful Pleasure Press
PO Box 8733/Atlanta GA 30306
Email: rlibby@mindspring.com
WWW: drrogerlibby.com
Shipping: $3.05. Canada: $4.55.
Elsewhere: $6.05
Payment: cash, ck, mo

Plenum Publishing
233 Spring St/New York NY 10013-1578
Voice: 212-620-8047
WWW: www.plenum.com
Shipping: $3.50 first book, $1.50 each additional. Non-US: add 8% of order
Payment: ck, Visa, MC, Amex, Diner's Club
Sales tax: NJ, NY

PolyEster Records and Books
Box 73/Fitzroy VIC 3065/AUSTRALIA
Fax: +61 3 9419 5154
Email: weirdshit@polyester.com.au
WWW: www.polyester.com.au/PolyEster/index.html
Shipping: Aus: $5 first item, $2 each additional. Elsewhere: $10Aus first item, $3Aus each additional
Payment: Visa, MC, Bankcard
Catalogue: see Appendix A

Pomegranate Artbooks
PO Box 6099/Ronhert Park CA 94927
Voice: 1-800-227-1428
Email: info@pompub.com
WWW: www.pomegranate.com

Positive Attitudes, Publishers
87344 Prince Ln/Eugene OR 97402
Shipping: $1.50
Payment: cash, ck, mo

powerHouse Books
powerHouse Cultural Entertainment, Inc/180 Varick Street, Suite 1302/New York NY 10014-4606
Voice: 212-604-9074
Fax: 212-366-5247
Email: orders@powerhousebooks.com
WWW: www.powerhousebooks.com
Shipping: $3 first book, $1.50 each additional
Payment: ck, mo, Visa, MC

Press Gang Publishers
#101-225 E 17th Ave/Vancouver BC V5V 1A6/CANADA
Email: pgangpub@portal.ca
WWW: www.pressgang.bc.ca
Shipping: $4 first book, $1 each additional
Catalogue: free

Pressure Drop Press
PO Box 460754/San Francisco CA 94146
Shipping: none. Non-US: $1
Payment: cash, ck, mo
Catalogue: two 32¢ stamps

Prima Publishing
3875 Atherton Rd/Rockein CA 95765
Voice: 1-800-632-8676
Fax: 916-632-4405
Email: sales@primapub.com
WWW: www.primapublishing.com
Shipping: up to $14.99: $3; $15 to $29.99: $4; $30 to $40.99: $6
Payment: cash, ck, mo, Visa, MC

Princeton University Press
California-Princeton Fulfillment Services, Inc/1445 Lower Ferry Road/Ewing NJ 08618
Voice: 1-800-777-4726 or 609-883-1759
Fax: 1-800-999-1958 or 609-883-7413
Email: orders@cpfs.pupress.princeton.edu
WWW: pup.princeton.edu
Shipping: US/Can: $3.75 first book, 75¢ each additional. Elsewhere: $4.50 first 2 books, $1 each additional

Payment: ck, mo (payable to California-Princeton Fulfillment Services), Visa, MC
Sales Tax: CA, NJ

Prism Press
2 South St/Bridport Dorset DT6 3NQ/UK
Distributed in the US by Avery Publishing Group

Prometheus Books
59 John Glenn Dr/Amherst NY 14228
Voice: 1-800-421-0351 or 716-691-0133
Fax: 716-691-0137
Email: pbooks6205@aol.com
WWW: www.prometheusbooks.com
Shipping: $4.45 first book, $1 each additional
Payment: ck, mo, Visa, MC

ProMotion Publishing
3368 F Governor Dr, Suite 144/San Diego, California Republic/Postal Zone 92122
Voice: 1-800-231-1776
Email: promopub@worldnet.att.net
WWW: www.promotionpub.com
Payment: ck, Visa, MC, Disc

The Public Domain Software Library
Winscombe House, Beacon Rd/Crowborough, East Sussex TN6 1UL/UK
Voice: 01892-663298
Fax: 01892-667473
Shipping: US: £2. Europe: none
Payment: Sterling ck, Visa, MC

Pulp Faction
Pulp Books Direct/PO Box 12171/London N19 3HB/UK
WWW: www.pulpfact.demon.co.uk
Shipping: UK/Europe: included.
Elsewhere: £1.50 per book
Payment: UK ck, international mo

PVS Publications
1223 Wilshire Blvd, Suite 651/Santa Monica CA 90403
Voice: 310-393-8596
Email: macgruder@aol.com
Shipping: US/Canada: $3; Europe/Asia: $11
Payment: cash, ck, mo, Visa, MC, Disc, Amex
"Book is unavailable in bookstores."

Quicksilver Press
10 E 87th St/New York NY 10128
Voice: 1-800-423-6722 or 212-874-6526
Fax: 212-876-6278
Email: lydia.bronte@prodigy.com
Shipping: $3 first book, $2 each additional
Payment: cash, ck, mo, Visa, MC, Disc

Quick American Archives
An imprint of Quick Trading Company

Quick American Publishing
An imprint of Quick Trading Company

Quick Trading Company
PO Box 429477/San Francisco CA 94142-9477

Voice: 1-800-428-7825 ext 102
Fax: 510-533-4911
Email: webmaster@quicktrading.com
WWW: www.quicktrading.com
Shipping: $5 to street address, $7 to a PO Box. Canada & South America Air: $10 first book, $3 each additional ($23 max). Elsewhere Air: $10 first book, $8 each additional ($42 max)
Payment: ck, mo, Visa, MC

R. René
31 Burgess Place/Passaic NJ 07055
Shipping: none. Non-US Air: $6
Payment: cash, ck, mo

Rainbow Books
PO Box 430/Highland City FL 33846-0430
Voice: 1-888-613-BOOK
Fax: 941-648-4420
Email: NAIP@aol.com
Shipping: $3. Western Europe: $6.95. Pacific Rim: $8.95
Payment: ck, mo, Visa, MC, Amex, Disc

Random House
Mail Sales Department, Dept. #05001/House Distribution Center/400 Hahn Road/Westminster, Maryland 21157
Voice: 1-800-793-2665 or 410-848-1900
Fax: 1-800-659-2436 or 410-386-7049 (Attn: Dept #05001)
WWW: www.randomhouse.com
Payment: ck or mo by mail. Visa, MC, Amex by phone/fax only

Raven Entertainment
PO Box 2130/Germantown MD 20875-2130
Voice: 301-515-RAVN (7286)
Fax: 301-515-4128
Email: ravent@erols.com
WWW: www.raventertainment.com
Shipping: none. Non-US Surface: $5 first book, $2 each additional. Non-US Air: $10 first book, $4 each additional
Payment: ck, mo, Visa, MC

Rawhide Western Publishing
PO Box 327/Safford AZ 85548
Voice: 1-800-428-5956
Shipping: $2 flat fee
Payment: ck, mo, Visa, MC
Rawhide offers discounts for ordering more than one book

Real Comet Press
1463 E Republican St #126/Seattle WA 98112

Red Crane Books
2008-B Rosina St/Santa Fe NM 87505
Voice: 1-800-922-3392
Fax: 505-989-7476
Email: publish@redcrane.com
WWW: www.redcrane.com
Shipping: $4 first book, 75¢ each additional. Non-US: $12
Payment: cash, ck, mo, Visa, MC

Rescue Press
8048 Midcrown #11/San Antonio TX 78218

Shipping: $3.05
Payment: cash, ck, mo

Reverse Speech Enterprises
PO Box 1037/Bonsall CA 92003-1037
Voice: 1-800-669-5789 or 760-732-3097
Fax: 760-732-0229
Email: revspeech@reversespeech.com
WWW: www.reversespeech.com
Shipping: $5
Payment: cash, ck, mo, Visa, MC
You can call 1-900-USA-4300 ($2.99/minute) to hear reversals

REW Video
1404 Arnold Ave/San Jose CA 95110
Voice/Fax: 1-800-528-1942 or 408-451-9310
Email: rewvideo@tongass.batnet.com
Shipping: $5 per order
Payment: mo, Visa, MC, Amex
Catalogue: $1 and age statement

River Microstudies
PO Box 259/Fort Davis TX 79734
Voice: 915-426-3570
Fax: 915-426-3844

Road Kill Press
3727 W Magnolia Blvd #705/Burbank CA 91510
Shipping: $2
Payment: cash, ck, mo

Ronin Publishing
PO Box 522/Berkeley CA 94701
Voice: 1-800-858-2665 or 510-548-2124
Fax: 510-548-7326
Email: RoninPub@aol.com
WWW: www.roninpub.com
Shipping: $3 + $1 per book. Non-US Surface: $3 per book. All of the following prices are for Air: Canada: $3 + $2 per book. Europe: $3 + $7 per book. Asia/Pacific: $3 + $10 per book.
Payment: cash, ck, mo, Visa, MC
Catalogue: free

Rosetta
P.O. Box 4611/Berkeley CA 94704-0611
Shipping: included

Routledge
WWW: www.routledge.com
US orders from:
thomson.com/7625 Empire Drive/Florence KY 41042
Voice: 800-634-7064
Fax: 800-248-4724
Email: fastline@kdc.com
Non-US orders from:
thomson.com/Cheriton House/North Way/SP10 5BE/England
Voice: 44-1264-342926
Fax: 44-1264-343005
Email: orders@routledge.com

Roxan Books
1126 S Federal Highway, Suite 252/Ft Lauderdale FL 33316
Voice: 1-800-205-8254
Fax: 612-933-9664

Shipping: $2.75. Non-US: $5.75
Payment: cash, ck, mo, Visa, MC, Disc, Amex

Rude Shape Productions
511 6th Avenue, #325/New York, NY 10011
Email: purehades@aol.com
WWW: www.horrornet.com/
funeralparty.htm
Shipping: $3
Include an over 21 age statement

Sage-Femme!
3457 N University, Suite 120/Peoria IL 61604-1322
Shipping: $3 first book, $1 each additional. Non-US: $5 first book, $1 each additional
Payment: ck, mo
Sales tax: MI

Salem Press
580 Sylvan Ave/Englewood Cliffs NJ 07632
Voice: 1-800-221-1592
Fax: 201-871-8668
Email: salem@ix.netcom.com
Shipping: $2 per volume
Payment: ck, mo, Visa, MC

Samuel Weiser
PO Box 612/York Beach ME 03910-0612

Sand River Press
1319 14th St/Los Osos CA 93402
Email: bigowerk@concentric.net

Savoy
Order from AK Press [above]

Scholarly Resources
104 Greenhill Ave/Wilmington DE 19805-1897
Voice: 1-800-772-8937 or 302-654-7713
Fax: 302-654-3871
Email: scholres@ssnet.com
Shipping: none
Payment: ck, mo, Visa, MC
Sales tax: none

ScienTerra Book Service
PO Box 1180/32352 Preussisch Oldendorf/GERMANY
Fax: 49/5742 930455
Email: 101557.3036@compuserve.com
WWW: ourworld.compuserve.com/
homepages/ScienTerra/homepage.htm
Available in the UK from D.H. Books/PO Box 176, East Grinstead/Sussex RH19 4FU (leshii@globalnet.co.uk) and in the USA from Art Matrix [above].
All books available in English and German

Second Chance Press
An imprint of Permanent Press [above]

Secret
BP 1400/1000 Brussels 1/BELGIUM
Voice: 32-2-223-09-14
Fax: 32-2-223-10-09
Email: secretmag@glo.be
Shipping: $20US
Payment: cash, Visa, MC, Amex

Secret Garden Publishing
5631 West Placita del Risco/Tucson AZ 85745
Phone: 1-888-845-8400
Fax: call for fax number
WWW: secretgardenpublishing.com

See Sharp Press
PO Box 1731/Tucson AZ 85702-1731
Voice: 1-800-533-0301
Email: seesharp@earthlink.net
WWW: home.earthlink.net/~seesharp
Shipping: $2.50 flat rate. Non-US Surface: $2.50 flat rate. Non-US Air: $5 + 10% of order
Payment: ck, mo, Visa, MC

Serpent's Tail
180 Varick St/New York NY 10014
Voice: 212-741-8500
Fax: 212-741-0424
Email: Info@serpentstail.com
WWW: www.serpentstail.com

Seven Stories Press
632 Broadway, 7th Flr/New York NY 10012
Fax: 212-995-0720
Email: sales@sevenstories.com
WWW: www.sevenstories.com
Shipping: $3.50 first book, 50¢ each additional
Payment: ck, mo, Visa, MC, Amex

Shade Tree Press
5647 Shaddelee Lane West/Fort Myers FL 33919

Shake Books
449 12th St/Brooklyn NY 11215
Shipping: $2 first book, $1 each additional. Non-US Air: $6 each
Payment: cash, ck, mo

Shapolsky Publishers
136 W 22nd St/New York NY 10011
Voice: 212-633-2023
Fax: 212-633-2123
Email: info@spibooks.com;
sales@spibooks.com
WWW: www.spibooks.com
Shipping: Continental US: $3.50 first book, 50¢ each additional. AL/HI/Can: add an extra $6. Elsewhere: add an extra $9
Payment: ck, mo, Visa, MC

Sharkbait Press
939 W 19th St, Suite E1/Costa Mesa CA 92627
Voice: 1-800-507-2665
Shipping: $3.05 flat fee. Non-US: $5.05 flat fee
Payment: ck, mo, Visa, MC, Amex (credit cards are only accepted at the 800 number)
Sales tax: none

Sierra Club Books
Mail Order Division/85 2nd St/San Francisco CA 94105
Voice: 1-800-935-1056
Fax: 415-977-5793
Email: online.store@sierraclub.org

WWW: www.sierraclub.com/books
Shipping: $4. Non-US Air: $15
Payment: ck, mo, Visa, MC

Silent Records
340 Bryant St, 3rd Floor East/San Francisco CA 94107
Voice: 415-957-1320
Fax: 415-957-0779
Email: mailorder@silent.org
WWW: www.silent.org
Shipping: $2 first CD, 50¢ each additional. Can/Mex/South America: $2 first CD, 75¢ each additional. Europe: $3 first CD, $1.25 each additional. Elsewhere: $4 first CD, $2 each additional.
Payment: ck, mo, Visa, MC
Cannot ship to PO Boxes in the US

Simon & Schuster
The Information SuperLibrary
c/o Macmillan Publishing USA/Attn: Order Processing/201 West 103rd St/Indianapolis IN 46290
Voice: 800-716-0044
Fax: 317-228-4304
Email: orders@superlibrary.com;
info@superlibrary.com
WWW: www.simonandschuster.com
Shipping: up to $29.99: $3.65; $30.00 to $59.99: $5.95
Payment: mo, Visa, MC, Amex

Sinbins, Inc.
3706 N Ocean Blvd, Suite 250/Ft Lauderdale FL 33308
Voice: 1-800-848-1722
Fax: 954-564-4183
Email: ed@redlightguide.com
WWW: www.redlightguide.com
Shipping: $3. Non-US: $6
Payment: cash, ck, mo, Visa, MC, Amex

Sisters of the Heart
PO Box 94534/Las Vegas NV 89193
Voice: 1-888-535-LOVE [5683] or 702-227-4466
Fax: 702-889-3275
Email: brothelbible@bigfoot.com
WWW: www.brothelbible.com
Shipping: $3.95. Non-US: $9.95
Payment: ck, mo, Visa, MC, Disc, Amex
The cover of The Brothel Bible is available as a t-shirt ($12.95) and as a poster ($6.95)

Sky Books
PO Box 769/Westbury NY 11590
Shipping: $3. Non-US: $5
Payment: mo

Slave Labor Graphics
979 S Bascom Ave/San Jose CA 95128
Voice: 1-800-866-8929
Fax: 408-279-0451
Email: danslave@aol.com
WWW: www.slavelabor.com
Shipping: $1.75 for one comic, 25¢ each additional. Canada: $2.25 first comic, 25¢ each additional. Elsewhere: $3.50 first comic, 50¢ each additional
Payment: ck, mo, Visa, MC

Smart Publications
PO Box 4667/Petaluma CA 94955
Voice: 1-800-976-2783
Fax: 707-763-3944
Email: info@smart-publications.com
WWW: www.smart-publications.com
Shipping: $3.95 first book, $1 each additional
Payment: ck, mo, Visa, MC

Soma Graphics
PO Box 19820, Dept O2/Sacramento CA 95819-0820

Sophie Cossette
PO Box 41/Place du Parc/Montreal, Quebec H2W 2M9/CANADA
Shipping: included in price

The Sourcebook Project
PO Box 107/Glen Arm MD 21057
WWW: www.knowledge.co.uk/xxx/cat/sourcebook
Shipping: $1.50; free if order is over $30. Non-US: $2 per book
Payment: ck, mo (payable to William Corliss)
"Canadian dollars and pounds sterling are accepted at prevailing exchange rates."

South End Press
116 Saint Botolph St/Boston MA 02115
Voice: 1-800-533-8478
Email: south.end.press@lbbs.org
WWW: www.lbbs.org/sep/sep.htm
Shipping: $3 first book, 75¢ each additional
Payment: ck, mo, Visa, MC

Southern Illinois University Press
Box 1774, Dept of Art and Design/Edwardsville IL 62026

Special Aviation Publications
Route 1, Box 730/China Spring TX 76633
Shipping: $3.50 (worldwide)
Payment: ck, mo

Spectre Press
404 Center Street/PO Box 5112/N Muskegon MI 49445-5112
Voice: 616-766-5076
Email: spectre@spectre-press.com
WWW: www.spectre-press.com
Shipping: $2. Non-US: $5
Payment: cash, ck, mo, Visa, MC, Amex, Disc

St. Martin's Press
175 Fifth Ave/New York NY 10010
Voice: 1-800-221-7945
Email: inquiries@stmartins.com
WWW: www.stmartins.com
Payment: ck, mo, Visa, MC

Stackpole Books
5067 Ritter Rd/Mechanicsburg PA 17055
Voice: 1-800-732-3669
Fax: 717-796-0412
Email: sales@stackpolebooks.com
WWW: www.stackpolebooks.com
Shipping: $4 first book, $1 each additional.

Non-US: "actual shipping"
Payment: cash, ck, mo, Visa, MC, Amex

StarChief Press
PO Box 7515/Spokane WA 99207
Voice: 509-487-6067
Fax: 509-838-0311
Email: scp@pobox.com
WWW: www.ior.com/~randc
Shipping: included. Non-US: contact
Payment: ck, mo, Visa, MC

State University of New York Press
c/o CUP Services/PO Box 6525/Ithaca NY 14851
Voice: 1-800-666-2211 or 607-277-2211
Fax: 1-800-688-2877 or 607-277-6292
Email: orderbook@cupserv.org
WWW: www.sunypress.edu
Shipping: US/Can: $3.50 first book, 75¢ each additional. Elsewhere: $4 first book, $1 each additional
Payment: ck, mo, Visa, MC, Amex, Disc

Steerforth Press
PO Box 70/South Royalton VT 05068
Voice: 1-800-639-7140
Fax: 802-763-2818
Email: info@steerforth.com
WWW: www.steerforth.com
Shipping: $3 first book, $1 each additional
Payment: ck, mo, Visa, MC

Sterling Publishing Company
387 Park Ave S/New York NY 10016-8810
Voice: 1-800-848-1186 or 212-532-7160
Shipping: $3 first book, 75¢ each additional. Non-US: $5 first book, $1 each additional
Payment: ck, mo, Visa, MC, Amex

Still Steaming Press
PO Box 8005 #306/Boulder CO 80306
Shipping: $2. Non-US: $3
Payment: ck, mo
"So hot, our shit's still steaming..."

Stoddart Publishing
30 Lesmill Road/North York ON M3B 2T6/CANADA
Voice: 1-800-387-0141 or 1-800-387-0172 or 416-445-3333 ext 616
Fax: 416-445-5967
Email: operator@gpaix.genpub.com
WWW: www.genpub.com/stoddart2

Stone Bridge Press
PO Box 8208/Berkeley CA 94707
Voice: 1-800-947-7271
Fax: 510-524-8711
Email: sbp@stonebridge.com
WWW: www.stonebridge.com
Shipping: Book rate: $2 first book, 50¢ each additional. First class: $3.50 first book, 75¢ each additional. Non-US: inquire
Payment: cash, ck, mo, Visa, MC, Disc
Catalogue: free

Sub Rosa Records
PO Box 808/1000 Brussels/BELGIUM
Available from AK Press

Sunset Research Group
608 N West #236/Wichita KS 67203
Shipping: included. Non-US: 25% of order
Payment: cash, ck, mo

Synthesis Books
PO Box 610341/Birmingham AL 35261
Shipping: $2. Non-US: $5
Payment: cash, ck, mo, Visa, MC

Syracuse University Press
Order Dept/1600 Jamesville Ave/Syracuse NY 13244-5160

Takarajima Books
95 Horatio St, Suite 7S/New York NY 10014
order from National Book Network
4270 Boston Way/Lanham MD 20706
Voice: 1-800-462-6420
Fax: 301-459-2118
Shipping: $3 first book, 75¢ each additional
Payment: ck, mo, Visa, MC

Talonbooks
General Distribution Services/85 Rock River Dr #202/Buffalo NY 14207-2170
Voice: 1-800-805-1083
Email: talon@pinc.com [info]
Shipping: $3
Payment: ck, mo, Visa, MC
Canada: GDS/30 Lesmill Rd/Don Mills Ont M3B 2T6/CANADA

Temple University Press
University Services/1601 N Broad St, Room 305/Philadelphia PA 19122
Voice: 1-800-447-1656
Fax: 215-204-4719
Email: tempress@astro.ocis.temple.edu
WWW: www.temple.edu/tempress
Shipping: $4 first book, 75¢ each additional (worldwide)
Payment: ck, mo, Visa, MC

Ten Speed Press
PO Box 7123/Berkeley CA 94707
Voice: 1-800-841-2665
Fax: 510-559-1629
Email: order@tenspeed.com
Shipping: $3.50 first book, 50¢ each additional
Payment: ck, mo, Visa, MC, Amex

Tetrahedron, Inc.
20 Drumlin Rd/Rockport MA 01966
Voice: 1-800-336-9266
Fax: 508-546-9226
WWW: www.tetrahedron.org/publish.htm
Shipping: $4.50. Non-US: $9.50
Payment: ck, mo, Visa, MC, Amex

Thames and Hudson
500 Fifth Ave/New York NY 10110
WWW: www.wwnorton.com/thames/welcome.htm
Distributed by WW Norton and Company [below]

Thaneros Press
PO Box 773/Lone Pine CA 93545
Email: myron@well.com

Shipping: $3 per book. Non-US Surface: $3 per book. Non-US Air: $9 per book.
Payment: cash, ck, mo

Theatre Communication Group, Inc.
Order Dept/355 Lexington Ave, 4th Flr/
New York NY 10017-0217
Voice: 212-697-5230
Shipping: $3 first book, $1 each additional.
Non-US: add $7 to total
Payment: cash, ck, mo, Visa, MC, Amex

Third World Press
7822 S Dobson Avenue/Chicago IL 60619
WWW: www.thirdworldpress.com

Thunderbolt Publishing
BCM Thunderbolt/London WC1N 3XX/UK
Shipping: UK: none. Non-UK: £2 per order
Payment: cash, ck

Thunder's Mouth Press
632 Broadway, 7th Floor/New York NY
10012
WWW: www.marlowepub.com

Times Change Press
Box 1380/Ojai CA 93024-1380
Publishers Services/PO Box 2510/Novato
CA 94948
Voice: 1-800-488-8595
Shipping: $1.50 first book, 75¢ each
additional ("minimum total $5"). Non-US:
Add 30% and round to the nearest dollar.
Payment: ck, mo, Visa, MC

Timothy Patrick Butler
PO Box 642712/San Francisco CA 94164
Email: info@weirdart.com
WWW: www.weirdart.com
Shipping: $2. Non-US: $4
Payment: cash, ck, mo (payable to
Timothy Patrick Butler)

Tom Davis Books
PO Box 1107/Aptos CA 95001-1107
Voice: 408-475-8341
Email: davibook@tdbooks.com
Shipping: $3 first book, 75¢ each
additional. Non-US: $3.50 first book, $1.25
each additional
Payment: cash, ck, mo, Visa, MC, Amex,
Disc

Tom of Finland Company
PO Box 26716, Dept RK2/Los Angeles CA
90026
Voice: 1-800-334-6526
Fax: 213-666-2105
Email: tomfinland@earthlink.net
WWW: www.gayweb.com/413/tom.html
Shipping: $5 first book, $1 each additional.
Non-US: $5 first book, $4 each additional
Payment: cash, ck, mo, Visa, MC
Catalogue: $10 (credited towards first
order)

Tony Ryan
C/- Grove P.O., Grove/Tasmania 7109/
AUSTRALIA
Email: Tony.Ryan@utas.edu.au
WWW: www.imalchemy.com/Tony.Ryan

Shipping: included (worldwide)
Payment: cash, ck, mo
*Ryan plans to start accepting Visa and
MasterCard soon.*

Tranquil Technology Music
PO Box 20463/Oakland CA 94620
Shipping: $1 per item. Non-US: $2 per item
Payment: ck, mo, international mo

Transaction Publishers
390 Campus Drive/Somerset NJ 08073
Voice: 1-888-999-6778 or 908-445-2280
ext 235
Fax: 908-445-2280
WWW: www.transactionpub.com
Shipping: $4.25 first book, $1 each
additional. Non-US Surface: $5.50 first
book, $1.25 each additional. Non-US Air:
$10 per book
Payment: mo, Visa, MC, Amex, Disc
Sales tax: "Where state law requires."

Transform Press
PO Box 13675/Berkeley CA 94712
Voice: 510-934-2675
Fax: 510-934-5999
Shipping: Book rate: $4 first book, $1 each
additional. First Class: $6 first book, $2
each additional. Non-US Surface: $8 first
book, $2 each additional. Canada Air: $9.
Europe Air: $22. Pacific Rim Air: $29.
Payment: cash, ck, mo, Visa, MC, Amex

TriX Publishing
2255B Queen St E #249/Toronto Ontario
M4E 1G3/CANADA
Email: publisher@trixnet.com
WWW: www.trixnet.com
Shipping: Can: $5.00Can. US: $5.50US.
Elsewhere: $9US
Payment: certified ck, international mo

Trom Publishing
5013 N Stevens St/Spokane WA 99205
Voice: 1-800-350-6469
Shipping: $1.75. Non-US: $2.50
Payment: cash, ck, mo

Truth Seeker Publications
PO Box 28550/San Diego CA 92198
Voice: 1-800-551-5328
Fax: 619-676-0433
Email: marysz@home.com
WWW: www.banned-books.com
Shipping: $5 first book, $1 each additional.
Non-US: add an extra $1.50 to US
shipping cost
Payment: ck, mo, Visa, MC, Disc, Amex

Tuppy Owens
PO Box 4ZB/London W1A 4ZB/UK
Voice: 0171-460-0044
Fax: 0171-493-4479
WWW: www.sfc.org.uk/orders/default.htm
Shipping: included in prices
Payment: cash, US ck, UK ck, mo, Visa,
MC, Amex
Available in the US through AK Press

TVT Records
23 E 4th St/New York NY 10003
Voice: 1-888-4TVT-CDS
Fax: 212-979-6489
Email: orders@tvtrecords.com
WWW: www.tvtrecords.com

Ulysses Press
PO Box 3440/Berkeley CA 94703-3440
Voice: 1-800-377-2542 or 510-601-8301
Fax: 510-601-8307
Email: ulypress@aol.com
Shipping: Book rate: free. Priority Mail: $3
first book, $1 each additional. Non-US: $3
first book, $1 each additional
Payment: ck, mo, Visa, MC

Universe Books
*Available from Autonome Distribution
[above]*

University of Arizona Press
1230 N Park Ave, Suite 102/Tucson AZ
85719-4140
Voice: 1-800-426-3797 or 520-626-4218
Fax: 520-621-8899
Email: uapress@uapress.arizona.edu
WWW: www.uapress.arizona.edu
Shipping: $3 first book, $1 each additional.
Non-US Surface: $5 first book, $2 each
additional
Payment: ck, mo, Visa, MC

University of California Press
Order Dept/2120 Berkeley Way/Berkeley
CA 94720
Voice: 800-822-6657
Fax: 800-999-1958
Email:
UCPRESS.COMMENTS@ucop.edu
WWW: www-ucpress.berkeley.edu
Shipping: US/Can: 1 or 2 books: $3.75,
75¢ each additional. Elsewhere: 1 or 2
books: $4.50, $1 each additional
Sales Tax: CA, NJ
UK Voice: 011-44-1243-779777
UK Fax: 011-44-1243-842167

University of Chicago Press
Direct Mail Department/5801 S Ellis
Avenue/Chicago IL 60637
Voice: 1-800-621-2736
Fax: 773-702-9756
Email: marketing@press.uchicago.edu
WWW: www.press.uchicago.edu
Shipping: $3.50 first book, 75¢ each
additional. Non-US: $4.50 first book, $1
each additional
Payment: ck, mo, Visa, MC
UK address: c/o John Wiley & Sons Ltd
Distribution Centre
1 Oldlands Way/Bognor Regis, West
Sussex PO22 9SA/UK

University of Georgia Press
330 Research Dr/Athens GA 30602
Voice: 1-800-BOOK-USA or 706-369-6130
Fax: 706-369-6131
Payment: ck, mo, Visa, MC

University of Illinois Press
Order Dept/1325 S Oak St/Champaign IL 61820-6903
Voice: 1-800-545-4703 or 410-516-6927
Email: uipress@uillinois.edu
WWW: www.press.uillinois.edu
Shipping: $4 first book, 75¢ each additional
Payment: ck, Visa, MC

University of Manitoba Press
WWW: www.umanitoba.ca/news/publications/uofmpress/UMPressIndex.html
Order from University of Toronto Press

University of Minnesota Press
c/o Chicago Distribution Center/11030 South Langley Avenue/Chicago IL 60628
WWW: www.upress.umn.edu
Shipping: $3.50 first book, 75¢ each additional. Non-US: $4.50 first book, $1 each additional
Payment: ck (payable to Chicago Distribution Center), Visa, MC

University of Nevada Press
Mail Stop 166/Reno NV 89557-0076
Voice: 702-784-6573
Fax: 702-784-6200
Shipping: $4.50 first book, 50¢ each additional. Non-US: $5 first book, $1 each additional
Payment: cash, ck, mo, Visa, MC, Disc
Sales tax: none

The University of North Carolina Press
PO Box 2288/Chapel Hill NC 27515-2288
Voice: 800-848-6224 or 919-966-3561
Fax: 800-272-6817
Email: uncpress@unc.edu
WWW: sunsite.unc.edu/uncpress
Shipping: none. Non-US: $4 first book, $1 each additional
Payment: ck, mo, Visa, MC

University of Oklahoma Press
4100 28th Avenue NW/Norman OK 73069-8218
Voice: 1-800-627-7377
Fax: 1-800-735-0476
WWW: www.ou.edu/oupress
Shipping: $3 first book, 50¢ each additional. Non-US: $4 first book, $1 each additional
Payment: cash, ck, mo, Visa, MC, Amex

University of Pennsylvania Press
PO Box 4836, Hampden Station/Baltimore Maryland 21211
Voice: 1-800-445-9880
Fax: 410-516-6998
WWW: www.upenn.edu/pennpress
Orders from the UK and Europe:
Academic and University Publishers Group
One Gower St/London WC1E 6HA/

ENGLAND
Voice: 0171-580-3994
Fax: 0171-580-3995

University of South Carolina Press
718 Devine St/Columbia SC 29208
Voice: 1-800-768-2500
Fax: 1-800-868-0740
WWW: www.sc.edu/uscpress
Shipping: $4 first book, 50¢ each additional. Non-US: $6 first book, $1 each additional
Payment: cash, ck, mo, Visa, MC, Disc

University of Toronto Press
5201 Dufferin St/Downsview ONT M3H 5T8/CANADA
Voice: 1-800-667-0892
Fax: 1-800-665-8810
Email: utpbooks@utpress.utoronto.ca
WWW: www.utpress.utoronto.ca
Payment: ck, mo, Visa, MC, Amex

University of Wisconsin Press
2537 Daniels Street/Madison WI 53718-6772
Voice: 800-829-9559 or 608-224-3900
Fax: 800-473-8310 or 608-224-3907
Email: uwiscpress@macc.wisc.edu
WWW: www.wisc.edu/wisconsinpress
Shipping: $3 first book, 50¢ each additional. Non-US Surface Mail: $3.50 first book, $1 each additional
Payment: ck, mo, Visa, MC

The University Press of Kentucky
Order Dept/663 S Limestone/Lexington KY 40508-4008
Voice: 1-800-839-6855
Fax: 606-323-4981
Email: abwebs0@pop.uky.edu
WWW: www.uky.edu/UniversityPress
Shipping: $3.50 first book, 75¢ each additional. $4 first book, $1 each additional
Payment: ck, mo, Visa, MC, Amex, Disc

University Press of Mississippi
3825 Ridgewood Rd/Jackson MS 39211
Voice: 1-800-737-7788 or 601-982-6205
Fax: 1-601-982-6217
Email: press@ihl.state.ms.us
Shipping: $4 first book, 75¢ each additional. Canada: $5 first book, $1.25 each additional. Elsewhere: $5.50 first book, $2 each additional
Payment: ck, mo, Visa, MC, Disc, Amex

USA Publications
PO Box 66734/Los Angeles CA 90066
Email: info@usapublications.com
WWW: www.usapublications.com
Shipping: $5. Non-US: $10
Payment: cash, ck, mo

Valley of the Sun Publishing
The Sutphen Corporation/PO Box 38/Malibu CA 90265

Voice: 1-800-421-6603
Fax: 310-457-1478
Email: valleyinfo@pathgate.com
WWW: www.pathgate.com/Valley/Home.htm
Shipping: up to $25: $3.25. Canada: up to $25: $10.75
Payment: ck, mo, Visa, MC, Amex

Veritas Press
GPO Box 1653/Bundaberg QLD 4670/AUSTRALIA
Shipping: Australia: none. Others: $10Aus
Payment: cash, ck, mo

vers libre press
PO Box 2911/Portland OR 97208-2911
Email: tinasky@aol.com
WWW: members.aol.com/tinasky
Shipping: $3 each. Canada: $4.87. Mexico: $6.80. UK/Europe: $11.40. Pacific Rim: $15.55. Asia/Africa: $14.08
Payment: ck, mo
"Orders from Outisde the U.S. please remit in U.S. money orders."

Verso
Email: versoinc@aol.com
WWW: www.verso-nlr.com
US: order from W.W. Norton [below]
UK: Blackwell Publishers/108 Cowley Road/Oxford Ox4 1JF

Viking
A division of Penguin [above]

Vintage
A division of Random House [above]

Visible Ink Press
645 Griswold Ave #835/Detroit MI 98226
Voice: 1-800-776-6265
Fax: 313-961-6812
WWW: http://www.thomson.com/vip.html
Shipping: $1.75 first book, $1.50 each additional. Non-US: orders from outside the US will be referred to the agent for that country.
Payment: ck, mo, Visa, MC, Disc, Amex

V/Search Publications
20 Romolo #B/San Francisco CA 94133
Voice: 415-362-1465
Fax: 415-362-0742
WWW: www.vsearchmedia.com
Shipping: $4 first book, $1 each additional. Non-US Surface: $6 first book, $2 each additional. Non-US Air: $15 first book, $12 each additional
Payment: cash, ck, mo, Visa, MC

Water Row Press
PO Box 438/Sudbury MA 01776
Voice: 508-485-8515
Fax: 508-229-0885
Email: waterrow@aol.com
WWW: www.waterrowbooks.com
Shipping: $4 per order. Non-US: $7.50 per order
Payment: cash, ck, mo, Visa, MC
"Satisfaction guaranteed or money back."
Water Row also has a free catalogue of new and out-of-print books by Beat authors

and original t-shirts featuring the Beatsters.

Watershed Books
1300 Glendale Rd/Marietta OH 45750
Voice: 1-800-484-1624 + Code Number 7036
Fax: 614-373-0253
Payment: cash, ck, mo, Visa, MC

Wayne State University Press
The Leonard N Simons Bldg/4809 Woodward Ave/Detroit MI 48201-1309
Voice: 1-800-WSU-READ [978-7323]
Fax: 313-577-6131
WWW: www.libraries.wayne.edu/wsupress
Shipping: $3 first book, $1 each additional.
Non-US: $4 first book, $2 each additional
Payment: ck, mo, Visa, MC

We the People
c/o 17011 Beach Blvd #900/Huntington Beach California/Postal Code 92647
Voice: 714-375-6631
Fax: 714-375-6699
Shipping: $3
Payment: cash, ck, mo, Visa, MC, Disc, Amex

Wesselmania
See Larry Wessel

Westview Press
5500 Central Ave/Boulder CO 80301
WWW: www.hcacademic.com/westview.htm
Shipping: US/Can: $3 first book, 75¢ each additional
Payment: ck, Visa, MC, Amex

Wexford Press
"Copies sould be ordered through gay retail bookstores", such as A Different Light 8853 Santa Monica Blvd/West Hollywood CA 90069
Voice: 1-800-343-4002
WWW: www.adlbooks.com

White Devil Records
PO Box 85811/Seattle WA 98105
Email: WDevilInc@aol.com
WWW: www.sni.net/central/manson
Also available through AK Press

White Pine Press
10 Village Square, Suite 28/Fredonia NY 14063
Voice: 716-672-5743
Fax: 716-672-4724
Email: wpine@netsync.net
WWW: www.netsync.net/users/wpine
Shipping: Book rate: $3. First class: $4. Non-US $6
Payment: ck, mo, Visa, MC

White Wolf Publishing
780 Park North Blvd, Suite 100/Clarkston GA 30021
Voice: 1-800-454-WOLF
Fax: 404-292-9664
Email: Wolfmail@white-wolf.com
WWW: www.white-wolf.com
Shipping: 1-5 books: $4. Non-US FedEx

Mail: 1-3 books: $20
Payment: cash, ck, mo, Visa, MC, Disc

Wide World Publishing
PO Box 476/San Courlos CA 94070
Voice: 650-593-2839
Fax: 650-595-0802
Email: wwp61@aol.com
Shipping: $4.95. Non-US: $9
Payment: cash, ck, mo, Visa, MC

The Wildcat Collection
16 Preston St/Brighton BN1 2HN/ENGLAND
Shipping: included
Voice: 1273-323758
Payment: cash, Visa, MC

Wild Flower Press
An imprint of Blue Water Publishing

William Morrow & Company
Order Dept/1350 Avenue of the Americas/New York NY 10019
WWW: www.williammorrow.com

Wingbow Press
a division of Bookpeople/7900 Edgewater Dr/Oakland CA 94621
Shipping: $2.50. Non-US: $4
Payment: ck, MC

Winning Publications
2372 Leibel Street/White Bear Lake MN 55110
Voice: 1-800-34-NO-TAX or 1-800-346-6829
Email: www.taxhelponline.com/request.htm
Shipping: $2 per book
Payment: mo, Visa, MC, Disc

Winston-Derek Publishers
PO Box 90883/Nashville TN 37203
Voice: 1-800-826-1888
Fax: 615-329-4824
Payment: cash, ck, mo, Visa, MC, Amex

Winter Publishing
PO Box 80667/Dartmouth MA 02748
WWW: www.winterpublishing.com/ls
Shipping: $3. Canada: $7. Elsewhere: $10
Payment: cash, mo, Visa, MC, Amex, Disc

Wordcraft of Oregon
PO Box 3235/La Grande OR 97850
Email address: wordcraft@oregontrail.net
Shipping: none. Non-US: $2 first book, 75¢ each additional
Payment: cash, ck, mo
Books are also available through Permeable Press [above] and, in the UK, the BBR Catalogue: www.syspace.co.uk/bbr/catalogue.html

W.W. Norton & Co
Order Department/Keystone Industrial Park/Scranton PA 18512
Voice: 1-800-233-4830
Fax: 1-800-458-6515
Email: webmaster@wwnorton.com

WWW: www.wwnorton.com
Shipping: none
Payment: ck, mo, Visa, MC, Amex
Sales Tax: CA, NY, PA, VT, IL

The X Press
55 Broadway Market/London E8 4PH/UK
Payment: UK ck, international money order

Yale University Press
Order Department/PO Box 209040/New Haven CT 06520-9040
Voice: 1-800-987-7323
Fax: 1-800-777-9253
WWW: www.yale.edu/yup
UK address: 23 Pond St/Hampstead, London NW3 2PN/UK
UK Voice: 44-171-431-4422
UK Fax: 44-171-431-3755

Zanja Press
PO Box 11813/Berkeley CA 94701
Shipping: $3 first book, $1.25 each additional. Non-US: $5 first book, $2 each additional
Payment: cash, ck, mo
510/597-0474

Ziggurat
PO Box 25193/Rochester NY 14625
Shipping: none

Zinks International Career Guidance
PO Box 790/Richland MI 49083
Shipping: $2 flat fee. Non-US: 30%
Payment: cash, ck, mo

Zoland Books
384 Huron Ave/Cambridge MA 02138
Voice: 617-864-6252
Email: zolandbks@aol.com
Shipping: $2.50 first book, $1 each additional
Payment: cash, ck, mo, Visa, MC

2.13.61 Publications
PO Box 1910/Los Angeles CA 90078
Voice: 1-800-992-1361
Email: two1361@aol.com
WWW: www.two1361.com
Shipping: $3.50 first book, $1 each additional
Payment: ck, mo, Visa, MC, Amex
UK address: 2.13.61 Limited/6 Shaftesbury Centre/85 Barlby Road/London W10 6BN/ENGLAND
UK Email: two1361uk@aol.com
UK WWW: www.two1361.com/ordering.europe.html

Index

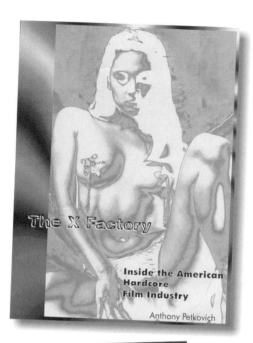

The X Factory

Inside the American Hardcore Film Industry

Anthony Petkovich

SEX MURDER ART

The films of Jörg Buttgereit

David Kerekes

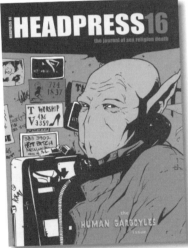

HEADPRESS16

the journal of sex religion death

HUMAN GARGOYLES

headpress 17

into the psyche

INTENSE DEVICE

A Journey through Lust, Murder & the Fires of Hell

IMPERIAL PERVERTS | MASS MURDER

Simon Whitechapel